APULEIUS MADAURENSIS

GRONINGEN COMMENTARIES ON APULEIUS

APULEIUS MADAURENSIS
METAMORPHOSES

Book X
Text, Introduction and Commentary

M. ZIMMERMAN

EGBERT FORSTEN, GRONINGEN 2000

ISBN 90 6980 128 0

This book meets the requirements of ISO 9706:1994
Information and documentation
Paper for documents-requirements for permanence

© Egbert Forsten Publishing, Groningen 2000

All rights reserved. No part of this publication may be reproduced, stored in a retrieval system, or transmitted, in any form or by any means, electronic, mechanical, photocopying, recording, or otherwise, without the prior written permission of the publisher.

This book was printed with financial support from the Netherlands Organisation for Scientific Research (N.W.O.)

CONTENTS

Preface	5
Introduction	7
Note to the text	35
Text Liber X	36
Commentary	51
Appendix I Apuleius' *'Phaedra'*	417
Appendix II The *spurcum additamentum* to *Met.* 10,21	433
Appendix III Generic shifts in the two inner tales of this book, and the function of these tales	440
Bibliography	445
Index Rerum	466
Index Verborum	471
Index Locorum	475

PREFACE

This book has been with me for many years. When I was preparing GCA 1995 (book IX) for publication, I optimistically referred in that volume to this commentary on book X as 'GCA 1996'. It has become: 'GCA 2000'. While apologizing for the confusion this may have caused, I do not regret the delay. During all those years each of the various activities and obligations which kept me from regular and steady work on this book have contributed to the end result. Although this is the first volume of GCA which has been written by one author only, it is still very much the product of my work with the GCA group on other sections of Apuleius' Metamorphoses. Therefore my thanks go in the first place to the members of that group for the intense and fruitful discussions we shared.

Organizing the Groningen Colloquia on the Novel and editing the GCN volumes that issued from those meetings has on the one hand of course affected the tempo of preparation of this book, but that work and the inspiring communications with so many colleagues from all over the world have on the other hand enriched and deepened my appreciation of Apuleius' intriguing novel and its place on the literary and cultural map of the Roman empire in the second century A.D.

The English version of this commentary was prepared by Dr. Corrie W. Ooms Beck. It is hard to express in words what her careful reading and weighing words, and the continuous dialogue between the two of us have meant for me. Prof. Philippa Goold was so kind to read through the entire translation and not only corrected the English where necessary. She also commented on the content of many of my lemmas with a keen eye for argumentation and structure. Even at those occasions where I had to decide not to take over her criticism and suggestions, they always have incited me to express my own stand with more precision. I am deeply grateful for her generous cooperation.

Thanks are due again to the Netherlands Organization for Scientific Research, NWO, for financial help with the publication. I also want to thank the staff of the University Library of Groningen for their indispensable support, and the Buma Bibliotheek at Leeuwarden for their long-term loans.

I realize that both the Introduction and the commentary proper on the 35 chapters of book X have become rather voluminous, but this has been unavoidable, since there has been much to explore in this part of Apuleius' novel, which in the overall studies of the *Metamorphoses* up to now has received less attention than other books. While studying it, I became more and more convinced that book X is an important part of the novel, being, as it were, the 'threshold' between books I-IX and the 'Isis book'. Still, a commentary like this is never complete, and often I have had to restrict myself in order not to overburden the lemmas. No doubt other commentators would have placed different accents: this commentary is very much the result of its author's idiosyncratic curiosities. However, while writing it I have always kept in mind what different users of this kind of work would want to find in it. I can only hope that this volume will be a worthy addition to the series of Groningen Commentaries on Apuleius of which more volumes are about to appear in the forthcoming years.

Maaike Zimmerman, August 2000

INTRODUCTION

1.1-6	Content and structure of the book
2.1-6	Book 10 as a part of the *Metamorphoses*
3.1-5	Narratological analysis and interpretation
4.1-2	The text
5	The translation
6	Notes on grammar and style
7	Organization of the bibliography

1 Content and structure of the book

1.1 Summary of the content

The soldier who made his appearance at the end of the previous book takes Lucius the ass on a journey to a provincial town, where he is left behind at the house of a *decurio* (1); this is followed by the story of the amorous stepmother, which is presented as a drama that took place there during that period (2-12).[1] The thread of the framing tale is resumed with the ass being sold to two slaves, brothers, who are employed as cooks by a wealthy man. Every night, when his two proprietors are at the baths, the ass feasts on the leftover food they have taken home. When the brothers notice that food is disappearing they first suspect each other, but then discover through a trick that it is their ass who is stealing the food. The hilarity caused by this comes to the attention of the cooks' wealthy master, who lets the ass demonstrate his ability at a dinner party, to the delight of all present. The ass is now purchased by the cooks' wealthy master and entrusted to a trainer, who teaches him human tricks. Soon the fame of the performing ass and his owner spreads (13-17). The ass's new owner, Thiasus, is introduced in more detail: he is an official from Corinth, temporarily in Thessaly to buy wild animals for a *munus* in honour of the assumption of his duties as *duumuir quinquennalis*; with an impressive retinue Thiasus undertakes the journey to Corinth, preferring the ass as his steed to the comfortable carriages (18). The ass's trainer makes much money on the side by showing the prodigious animal to curious spectators. A distinguished *matrona* falls in love with the ass and pays his keeper a sum of money to be allowed to spend a night with the ass (19). A detailed description is given of this first encounter, during which it soon becomes clear that Lucius can completely satisfy the *matrona*'s desires; this tryst is followed by several others (20-21). Thiasus, having been informed of his ass's amorous accomplishments, decides that the high point of the show to be held in the theatre of Corinth is to be the copulation of the ass with a condemned murderess (22). This is followed by the account of the crimes and the conviction of this woman

---

[1] For a summary of this story see Appendix III.

(23-28).[2] Full of fear and revulsion the ass awaits the day of the *munus*. When the time has come, he is taken to the entrance of the theatre, from where he can witness the introductory shows: a Pyrrhus dance is described (29). This is followed by the elaborate description of a sensuous pantomime expressing the Judgement of Paris (30-33). The narrator interrupts this description with a diatribe against the corruptness of justice, starting with the mythical bribing of Paris by Venus, and culminating in historical times with the conviction of Socrates by the Athenian court. He promises to resume the story (33). The actress representing Venus performs a dance of victory and the stage set disappears (34). During the preparations for the Pasiphaë pantomime, in which he is to copulate publicly with the murderess, Lucius – terrified that both he and the woman will eventually be slaughtered by wild beasts – sees an opportunity to flee. He runs to the beach of Cenchreae, where he falls asleep (35).

1.2 Framing tale, inner tales, *ecphrasis*

1.2.1 Relation of framing tale to inner tales and *ecphrasis*

The progress of the framing tale is contained in ch. 1; chs. 13 - 22; a few lines of ch. 29; and chs. 34 (the larger part) - 35.

Chs. 2-12 and 23-28 are two inner tales: the story of the lovesick stepmother and the story of the Murderess of Five respectively. Chapters 29 (the larger part) through 34 (the first part) contain the *ecphrasis*[3] of the Pyrrhus dance and the Paris pantomime.

Thus, of the 35 chapters, roughly 14 are devoted to the continuation of the main narrative, which is 2/5 of the entire book. Almost half of the book is devoted to two inner tales (17 chapters in total). Consequently, in the space given to telling stories, book 10 matches the previous books[4] and contrasts with book 11, which contains no inner tales at all.[5] The *ecphrasis* (more than 5 chapters), too, is an interruption of the main story.

In relation to the framing tale, each of the three additions forms a digression which is detached from the main action, but the intensity with which narrator and protagonist of the framing tale are involved in these digressions increases: the first story takes place in the environment of the ass; the second story contains the previous history of the murderess with whom the ass is to make love in the theatre; the ballets described in the *ecphrasis* are the first and second parts of the spectacle of which the ass

---

2   For a summary of this story see Appendix III.
3   In ancient rhetorical works *ecphrasis* is a wider concept than in modern literary theory: not only works of art can be the subject matter of an *ecphrasis*, but also persons, objects, situations, landscapes, seasons, festivals. See Bartsch 1989,10 f. and n. 10; *DNP* 3,942-947 s.v. 'Ekphrasis' [Reitz].
4   Winkler 1985,26 f. calculates that 60 % of the entire text of the *Metamorphoses* is devoted to the activity of narrators and audience. See also 2.4.7 of this Introduction.
5   One other book in the *Met.* has no inner tales: book 3. Schlam 1992,31 regards the episode of the Risus festival in that book as a 'self-contained tale', but it is part of the main story.

himself, with the murderess, will form the third part.

1.2.2 Embedding of the inner tales

This book contains no embedded tales fitting together like 'Chinese boxes', as is the case in e.g. book 9,14-30. From the beginning to the end of book 10 there is only one narrator: Lucius, the narrator/protagonist of the framing tale, is also the narrator of the embedded tales.[6] In neither story is he an actor.

The first story takes place in the present of the framing tale; it contains an account of events that recently happened in the immediate environment of the ass, and so have come to his attention. Those events have no influence on the progress of the framing tale; they rather delay it. Immediately after the conclusion of this story, the framing tale is resumed. A transitional passage marks the contrast between the fortunate ending of the tribulations of the father in the story and the everlasting vicissitudes of the life of the narrator/protagonist.[7]

The second story is embedded in the framing tale as the previous history of a convicted criminal, the woman with whom the ass is later to perform in the arena of Corinth in pantomime of Pasiphaë. The story relates how this woman, because of a series of gruesome family murders, came to be condemned *ad bestias*. Although the narrator is not an actor in this tale, it becomes clear even before he tells the story that his fate is closely connected with that of the murderess; during the story the narrator reminds his audience of this fact.[8] Although the story is presented as additional information for the reader, its insertion has a delaying effect at a moment of great suspense because the decision to make the ass copulate in the theatre with a *uilis aliqua ad bestias addicta* has already been taken.[9]

1.2.3 Embedding of the *ecphrasis*

The narrator reports that in anticipation of his own performance he has been tethered immediately outside the theatre and is able, via an open gate, to enjoy the preliminary shows: a Pyrrhus dance and a pantomime enacting the Judgement of Paris. During this elaborate description the framing tale is completely forgotten. After the disappearance of the decor of the pantomime the framing tale continues abruptly without a concluding commentary.[10] The narrator did interrupt the description in ch. 33 with an indignant diatribe about corruption, in connection with the bribing of Paris by Venus, expressed on the stage.

---

6   In the first inner story, however, the narrator yields twice to a sub-narrator (ch. 8 f. and 11); see the note on *res* ch. 8 (243,16).
7   See the note on *talibus fatorum fluctibus uolutabar* ch. 13 (246,1 f.).
8   Ch. 24 (255,20 f.) *et ilico haec eadem uxor eius, quae nunc bestiis propter haec ipsa fuerat addicta*.
9   Ch. 23 (254,16 f.).
10 Ch. 34 (265,7) *Ecce miles ...*

From the point of view of narrative technique this detailed *ecphrasis* forms an significant delay: at a moment of great suspense in the framing tale, the tempo of the story is brought to a full stop.

1.3 Beginning and ending of the book

The beginning of this book is carefully marked: it coincides with the breaking of a new day,[11] and the ass gets a new owner, namely the soldier.

The end, too, is carefully marked: night falls[12] and the ass goes to sleep in the last sentence (ch. 35: 266,7 f.). Books 1, 2, and 4 also conclude with the hero falling asleep; this is an epic convention, which might be regarded as a contribution to the association (effected also in other ways) of Lucius' wanderings with those of Odysseus.[13] See *GCA* 1985, Introd. 1 f., with references, on the division of the *Metamorphoses* into books, which is due to Apuleius himself.[14]

1.4 Travel and structure

The book begins with a short journey (1). Its circumstances reflect the improved situation of Lucius the ass: the journey takes place on even ground, is not long, and ends with a stay in relatively comfortable lodgings.[15] The book contains another journey, that to Corinth, which occurs at the exact middle of the book (18). Not only is this journey itself described in detail, but in the surrounding text there are some points relating to form and content that make this journey a notable marker. For example, the geographical indications, which have been extremely vague up to ch. 18, now become remarkably precise (see below, 1.5). The beginning of ch. 18 is striking because the narrator unexpectedly addresses his readers directly. Moreover, the wealthy gentleman, who was already introduced in ch. 13 and has been playing an increasingly important part in the story, is at last named: Thiasus.[16] The proper name in itself forms a 'hinge' in the story: the name's evocation of banqueting and high spirits refers back to an earlier stage in the story (chs. 15-16: the ass as symposiast), but its Dionysian associations become stronger from now on.[17] Schlam 1992,29 f. (also 1968,33 f.), who divides the *Met.* into four sections, summarizes *Met.* 8,15-10,31 as section 3: 'On the road'. The journey in 10,18 is so strongly marked a transition that one could argue in favour of the beginning of a new, fourth section

---

11 Ch. 1 (236,10) *die sequenti*; see the introductory remarks to ch. 1.
12 For an outline of the days and nights in this book, see 1.6.1 below.
13 On the epic as a narrative model for the ancient novel, see Fusillo 1988,20 f.; for a comparison of the *Odyssey* with Apuleius' *Met.*, see Schlam 1992,19 f., ibid. 61, 68 f., with references. The fact that it is the tenth book, immediately before the re-metamorphosis, that has an epic closing suggests that the *diuina prouidentia* of Isis, who delivers Lucius from his ass's skin, can be compared to the protection of Athena, who makes Odysseus finally go home (cf. also Schlam l.c.,123 f.). See comm. on ch. 35.
14 The division of the separate books into chapters is by Hildebrand (1842).
15 See the introductory remarks to ch. 1.
16 This is the only proper name in book 10. On the absence of proper names in this book, which gives a 'less individual, more generic quality' to the characters, see Finkelpearl 1998,157 f.
17 See the note on *Thiasus* ch. 18 (250,17).

here. Since Schlam rightly considers travel an important structuring principle of the *Met.*, it is surprising that he does not give attention to this journey to Corinth.

1.5 Geography

Up to ch. 18 the geography in book 10 is as vague as in books 8 and 9.[18] In ch. 18 this changes. First, it becomes clear that the anonymous little town that formed the background for the events up to now is situated in Thessaly;[19] secondly, Corinth is mentioned here (on this geographical transformation in relation to the *Onos*, see below, 2.3). Thiasus is an official from Corinth, and takes the ass home with him; the rest of the book is set in Corinth. In ch. 35 the ass flees to Cenchreae, a port of Corinth, and ch. 35 (265,30) even mentions accurately that it is a gallop of 6 miles for the ass. We see therefore that in the course of book 10 fantasy landscapes are giving way to the real world that Penwill 1990,13 f. identifies in the eleventh book.

1.6 Time: narrated time, narrative time, and tempo

A distinction will be made between 'narrated time' and 'narrative time': 'narrated time' is the time that the events in the story took according to the narrator; 'narrative time' is the time taken by the presentation of the events, which is best measured in the number of pages (or lines) of text. The narrative tempo may be determined by the fluctuating relation between narrated time and narrative time.[20]

1.6.1 Narrated time in the framing tale

The text of book 10 contains only a few hints as to the number of days and nights in this book: ch. 1 (236,10): *die sequenti*; ch. 20 (252,14 f.) *nocturnas tenebras*; ch. 22 (254,9 f.) *iamque ... nocte transacta*; ch. 29 (260,13) *dies ecce ... aderat*; ch. 35 (266,7 f.) *nam et ... ultimam diei metam curriculum solis deflexerat*. Nowhere in the book is the beginning of a new day described in detail.[21] One could argue that day never really dawns in book 10. This gives an extra dimension to the breaking of the (important) new day in 11,7. See for this also the note on *at intus ... inalbabant* ch. 20 (252,14-15). The book ends with a striking description of nightfall.

However, something can be said in general about the time period of the events narrated in this book. First, the events are delineated by two indications of the season:

---

18 The robber stories of book 4 contain names of towns, although they are often hard to reconcile with the fantasy landscape in which e.g. bears can be caught around Plataeae; see *GCA* 1977,91 on 4,11 (83,4-6) and 109 on 4,13 (85,5-8). After the story of Amor and Psyche (4,28-6,24) place names are entirely absent; see *GCA* 1985,2.
19 Ch. 1 (236,22) *ad quandam ciuitatulam peruenimus*; ch. 18 (250,25) *tunc Thessaliam etiam accesserat*.
20 On tempo in the *Met.* in general, see Van der Paardt in *AAGA* 1978,84 f.; 93 n. 81 for the theoretic literature on the aspect of time in narrative texts.
21 See the note on ch. 35 (266,7-8) *nam et ultimam diei metam curriculum solis deflexerat*.

in 9,32 (227,4 f.) autumn is over and winter has begun;[22] in 10,29 (260,7 f.) spring has come. Therefore the events of book 10 must take place in a period of about 3 months. This period may be roughly divided as follows:

Ch. 1: one day's journey with the soldier.
Chs. 2-12: the stay with the *decurio*, where the ass indirectly witnesses the dramatic events concerning the stepmother. The narrator mentions that these occurred a few days after he had been stabled there.[23] There are no indications as to the passage of time in that story, but the period from the younger brother's apparent death (5) until the end of the trial (12) must have taken a few days (for narrated time and narrative time in this story, see 1.6.3).
Chs 13-17: the ass's stay with the cooks. This must take at least a few weeks since the ass has the opportunity to stuff himself daily 'for a long time',[24] and that he eventually has begun to look fat and glossy.[25]
Also ch. 17: the ass's training, and especially the spreading of his fame, suggest the passing of several weeks.
Chs. 18-19: the journey from Thessaly to Corinth must, in view of the distance, take more than one day, even when part of the journey is made by sea.[26]
Chs. 19-21: a night spent with the Corinthian *matrona* is preceded by an unspecified period during which the ass is daily shown to the public, and is followed by more nightly assignations.[27]
The organization of the theatre festival (ch. 23: 254,16 f.), the prospect of which fills Lucius with anxiety (ch. 29: 260,2 f.), will have lasted more than one day (for narrated time and narrative time in the story of 23-28, see 1.6.3 and 1.6.4).
Chs. 30-35, finally, describe the events of one day (including the performances in the theatre).[28]

The indications of time in this book are as vague and indefinite as in the previous books from book 7 onward.[29] What is interesting here is the strongly varying narrative tempo.

1.6.2 Tempo in the framing tale

A period of about 3 months is narrated in 30 pages of Teubner text. Compared to the

---

22 *Sed ecce siderum ordinatis ambagibus per numeros dierum ac mensuum remeans annus post mustulentas autumni delicias ad hibernas Capricorni pruinas deflexerat* (followed by a complaint about the cold suffered by Lucius the ass during that winter).
23 Ch. 2 (237,1) *post dies plusculos*.
24 Ch. 14 (246,25) *diu*.
25 Ch. 15 (248,7 f.).
26 Ch. 19 (251,11) *partim terrestri, partim maritimo itinere*.
27 Cf. ch. 22 (254,11): *condicto pari noctis futurae pretio*. On one of the following nights the ass's *magister* reveals to his *dominus* the intercourse of the ass and the *matrona* (ch. 23: 254,14 f.).
28 Based on 11,5 (270,6 f.) we can give an exact date to this day, at the end of which the ass falls asleep after his flight from the theatre. It is March 4, the day before the the ritual opening of the sailing season in the Isis cult, the *Ploiaphesia*. On calendar and calendar motifs in the *Met.*, see Witte 1997.
29 See Van der Paardt in *AAGA* 1978,85 f.; *GCA* 1981,3 and *GCA* 1985,2; *GCA* 1995,5 f.

tempo of *Met.* 1,2-3,28 (70 pages for 10 days) the narrative tempo is therefore relatively high. Within the book, however, one gets the impression of a calm tempo: on the one hand, an (indefinite) longer period is given an apparently unhurried treatment because a single detail, illustrative of the whole period, is treated at length.[30] On the other hand, there are are long sections of 'scene'[31] and fragments of dialogues rendered in direct discourse; in these passages, because narrative time and narrated time are equal, the tempo is very low.

Ch. 1 describes one day in 1 page: how the ass is loaded up by the soldier is described in detail.
On the tempo of the inner tale in chs. 2-12, see 1.6.4.
Ch. 13: a period of several days is summarized in 1 page: still, a calm tempo prevails because most of the page is devoted to a decription of the delicacies set before the ass.
Ch. 14: beginning with the dialogue between the two brothers, which is rendered in direct discourse, narrated time and narrative time coincide: hence a low tempo. This continues in chs. 14-16: the evening during which the ass is caught in the act and made to participate in a symposium is described in a 'scene' of about 2 pages' length; in this section there are several passages of direct discourse.
Ch. 17: a longer period is summarized in 1 page, but again the tempo is masked by 'stagnierendes-verweilendes Erzählen' (see above and n. 30), i.e. a detailed description of one action illustrative of that period: the training of the ass.
Ch. 18: the narrated time comes to a halt: Thiasus is introduced to the reader.
The journey in chs. 18-19 lasts a few days (1 page), but here again, as in ch. 13 and ch. 17, there is a relatively high tempo and yet a calm narrative style, describing how Thiasus prefers (and decks out) the ass as his mount.
Ch. 19: less than half a page (251,11-19) to summarize a few days; then about 4 pages for the introduction to, and the description of, one night with the *matrona*. On the inner tale of chs. 23-28, see 1.6.3.
The last 6 pages are devoted to the description of the ballets in the theatre (one day); the last lines describe the ass's escape and his falling asleep that same evening.

Summing up, one may say that the framing tale continuously uses a relaxed narrative tempo. The two inner tales show a much stronger variation in tempo.

1.6.3 Narrated time in the inner tales

Chs. 2-12: the orienting introduction summarizes several years (ch. 2: 237,6-9). Not much can be said about the duration of the events described in the rest of ch. 2 (the *nouerca*'s falling in love, inner struggle, and becoming ill). The beginning of ch. 3 supposes that a long time has passed.[32] Ch. 3 itself describes a conversation in the

---

30 An example of what Lämmert [8]1983,84 calls 'stagnierend-verweilendes Erzählen' as a possible form of 'iterativ-durative Raffung'.
31 For 'scene' and 'summary' in narrative texts, see Hägg 1971,87 f., with references.
32 Ch. 3 (238,4 f.) *diutinum rupit silentium*.

bedroom. Ch. 4 suggests the passing of several days. From ch. 5 onward the narrated time of this story runs parallel to that of the framing tale, which was discussed above (1.6.1).

The narrated time of the second inner story (chs. 23-28) does not run parallel to that of the framing tale: it is the story of the crimes that lead to the conviction of the woman with whom the ass is to perform in the theatre; all these events have taken place before the events of the framing tale. Here, too, the narrated time of the orientating introduction (ch. 23: 254-255,5) covers many years, from the girl's birth until the time she reaches marriageable age. Chs. 24-28: the murders are committed at intervals, so this period until the conviction lasts some days or weeks.

So, while the framing tale takes place within a period of 3 months, the inner tales cover a much longer time. Both start with a summary of many years; then, the dramas unfold in periods (that cannot be precisely measured) of some days to a few weeks at most.

1.6.4 Tempo in the inner tales

Chs. 2-12: the dramatic nature of the story –the peripeteias and moments of suspense – are reflected in a strongly varying tempo. After the situation has been sketched in a few lines that summarize many years (see 1.6.3), the tempo comes to a complete standstill as the symptoms of love-sickness are described. In ch. 3 the tempo is quite low: the analysis of the stepmother's inner scruples is followed by her declaration of love in direct discourse (narrated time = narrative time). The following two pages of text (chs. 4 and 5), however, have a high tempo: events of many days succeed each other at high speed; this is accompanied by a remarkable number of terms indicating 'suddenness' or 'haste'.[33] At the beginning of ch. 6, the description of the father's pitiful appearance in the forum takes up half a page of 'scene'. The next half page, on the other hand, is characterized by a feverish speed.[34] The beginning of the court session is 'scene', and the entire session and its dénouement take up the last 4 pages of the story: in two long speeches by the doctor, rendered in direct discourse, the narrated time equals the narrative time. The constantly low tempo of the second part of the story – in which the reader is unexpectedly proven wrong in his anticipation of the ending – receives extra emphasis because of its difference in tempo from the first part.

Chs. 23-28: about 1 page (254,23-255,17) contains the background information for this story; approximately 17 years are summarized. A transitional passage of 8 lines (255,17-25) describes the fatal reversal in the family in a still relatively high tempo. The tempo becomes increasingly lower; the murder of the girl takes up almost an entire page. The poisoning of the girl's brother, and the poisoning and death of the doctor at the same time, are described in a low tempo in almost 2 pages. In these, ch.

---

33 See the note on *repentino* ch. 4 (239,1).
34 See the note on *ilico* ch. 7 (241,23).

25 (256,28-258,7) is 'scene', where at a high point of suspense (ch. 26: 257,5-14) the tempo is lowest because of the murderess's reasoning, rendered in direct discourse. At the beginning of ch. 27 (258,8-11) a period of a few days is summarized in high tempo, after which, in the remaining almost 2 pages of the story, the two simultaneous murders of the doctor's wife and the woman's own daughter are told in increasingly low tempo, resulting in the 'scene' of the death of the doctor's wife. Finally, the judicial investigation, which is held *confestim* (ch. 28: 259,20), and the verdict are summed up in one sentence of 6 lines, which in a high tempo brings the time of the story back to the present of the framing tale.

The variations of tempo in this story enhance its horrors: the narrator always uses a low tempo for the murders and dying scenes, and a somewhat higher tempo for the events in between.

2 Book 10 as a part of the *Metamorphoses*

2.1 Boek 10 as an independent entity

It is suggested above that book 10 has a clearly marked beginning, a 'hinge' exactly in the middle (see 1.4), and an impressive ending (see 1.3). The two inner stories are linked to each other by many elements (see Appendix III). Prominent in the entire book is the theme of the often vague dividing line between human and animal, the question of what makes a person human (see 2.4.3-2.4.3.2), which is an appropriate theme for the last book before the re-metamorphosis. In addition, book 10 has rightly received the title 'Liber de Spectaculis' from some scholars. Finally, it can be argued that in book 10 the Latin *Met.* leaves the intertext of the *Onos* for good (see 2.3).

Dowden 1993,107 concludes at the end of his impressive analysis of book 8 of the *Met.* that this book 'has a distictive and coherent identity. And we have seen through the identification of themes and intertexts how Book 8 makes a connected, continuing and intense contribution to the sense of the whole work. It has a satisfying structure, a clear beginning, a thematically relevant end. But much of its coherence lies in its dialogue with other areas of the novel.' The following sections will show that the last sentence of this citation from Dowden applies equally well to book 10.

2.2 The problem of the unity of the *Metamorphoses*

At the end of book 10 the reader, along with the narrator, finds himself on the brink of fundamental changes both in the protagonist's existence and in the kind of pleasure the reader was promised in the Prologue (1,1: 2,3-4 *lector intende, laetaberis*). As Sandy 1999,96 remarks, 'Book 11 literally comes out of the blue (sea), as the goddess Isis rises from it in response to Lucius's anguished prayer'. The problem of the role of book 11 in the whole of the *Metamorphoses* and the connected problem of the unity of Apuleius' novel continue to challenge those who study this work to attempt new approaches. This is not the place for extensive discussion of this matter; useful surveys are Harrison 1996,508 f.; 511-515; Shumate 1997,1-14; Harrison

1999,XXXII-XXXVIII.[35] Both this introduction and the commentary highlight the important position of book 10 within this problematic entirety. Our anchor and guideline is the text itself. In a series of articles Nimis[36] shows that critical assertions about the ancient novel are usually based on what he calls the novel's 'poetics'; such an approach '... sees a text as a totality to be apprehended as such, so its linear unfolding is a progressive "revelation" of a predetermined meaning, as if language is a neutral instrument that an author can choose to use to communicate ideas and feelings that are independent of language.' Against this, Nimis poses a 'prosaics' approach: 'Prosaics ... sees the unfolding of a text as a *managerial* process that deploys various heterogeneous elements into a fabric with multiple and contradictory effect, and it notes how an author negotiates this heterogeneity, manages it, articulates it, operates within it, without seeking to reduce it to a spurious unity.'[37] Such an approach is productive and liberating for the writing of a line-by-line commentary: the commentator can indicate contradictions without explaining them away, and point out digressions, 'hinges', and 'thresholds of decision' (see n. 37). On the other hand, a 'prosaics' approach does not release the researcher from the obligation to signal convergences and connecting elements in the narrative as an entirety. Apuleius' competence as a literator is no longer disputed; as he wrote his long nove, he was working toward an ending he may not have had clearly in mind when he began but which took shape in the process of writing; however, it is not inconceivable that previously drafted parts of the novel were revised at a later stage. Certain themes important to the author, with which he toyed as he wrote, acquired a motivating function within the entire work as it neared completion.[38] The great advantage of a 'prosaics' approach is that it becomes possible to describe these centripetal elements as a continuous and gradually developing process, not as preconceived 'blocks' with an inflexible, absolutely consistent meaning.

Sections 2.4.1 - 2.4.8 discuss important themes that are found throughout the *Met.* and figure, or even culminate in book 10; sections 2.5.1-2.5.4 deal with mirroring; 2.6 treats the connection between the inner stories of this book and those of previous

---

35 None of these surveys mentions Finkelpearl 1998, which appeared too recently to be included in them. This book focuses on the function of literary allusions in the *Met.* and proposes 'one theory of Apuleian allusion – that it represents an experimentation with various genres in an attempt to find the novel's place and begins to represent a struggle as the book progresses, a struggle that is resolved in Book 11' (Finkelpearl 1998,35). Finkelpearl's final chapter discusses book 11 as 'Escape and a New Voice'.

36 Nimis 1994,387 f.

37 Nimis 1998,401; he bases his concept of 'prosaics' on W. Godzich and J. Kittay, *The Emergence of Prose: An Essay in Prosaics*, Minneapolis 1987, quoted in Nimis 1994,400 f.: 'This is where an approach that would be more characteristic of what we have taken to call prosaics may be called for. Trained as we are to perceive texts as totalities, we seek to apprehend their structure and, in the description of that structure, to assert our mastery over the text. Prosaics seeks instead to espouse the movement of the text as it manages the economy of its discourses, to establish where the thresholds of decision arise, what the decisions are, and what their motivations and determinations as well as their consequences have been. In other words, we must learn to follow the processive threading of the text' (Godzich-Kittay 1987,48).

38 See Nimis 1998,221, referring to the theme of 'unequal' forms of eros in Achilles Tatius' novel: 'The accumulation of repetitions produced by what Margaret Doody (1996,93) calls "thematic pressure" is a good example of the way a main idea takes form in the actual telling of the story. Rather than progressively unveiling a pre-existing idea, the author seems to be "working out" his conception ... by creating a series of "first drafts".'

books. But first I will deal with the 'threshold of decision' (see n. 37) which is crossed at the end of book 10: here the *fabula Graecanica* that the narrator promised in the Prologue (1,1: 2,3) is left behind.

2.3 Book 10 and the relation between *Onos* and *Metamorphoses*.

It is unnecessary to review the literary-historical-genetic question of the *Metamorphoses*. Nowadays there is a virtual consensus among scholars that both the Pseudo-Lucianic Λούκιος ἢ "Ονος[39] and Apuleius' Latin novel *Metamorphoses* go back to a Greek Vorlage, which has not survived but is described by Photius. Photius (*Bibl.* 129) calls it the Μεταμορφώσεις by an author otherwise unknown to us, Lucius of Patrae, and compares the *Onos* (which he ascribes to Lucian) with the longer work.[40] Similarly, the question whether the tales and digressions embedded in Apuleius' work appeared in the lost Greek Vorlage – and, if so, whether all or only some of them did – will not be discussed here.[41] The *Onos*, however, has survived and it can be seen that the first 10 books of the *Met.* follow the course of events in the *Onos*, with entire passages fragments of Latin matching the corresponding passages in the *Onos* word for word.[42] It is instructive for the interpretation of the *Met.* to examine the specific intertextuality between the *Onos* as architext and the *Met.* as phenotext[43]. Apuleius' book 10 has an important place in that relationship: besides passages that match the *Onos* verbatim, it contains important transformations in regard to that architext; and at the end of this book so drastic a transformation takes place that from then on the *Met.* can no longer be regarded as a phenotext of the *Onos*.

The two inner tales and the *ecphrasis* can be regarded as transformations in the form of additions.[44] The *Onos* relates only the main action, so within this specific intertextual relationship we can regard all additions in the form of inner stories and digressions in the *Met.* as transformations, and book 10 is no exception in relation to the preceding books. Neither are those transformations to be regarded as particular to book 10 in which the author of the *Met.* enriches or deepens particular details, or adds a dimension of irony, or sometimes puts information from the *Onos* in a different order.[45] A drastic transformation, however, can be identified at the exact

---

39 From now on referred to as '*Onos*'.
40 For a survey of the literature until 1971, see Schlam 1971,291 f. For the literature after 1971, see Mason 1994, 1998 (a revision of his article in *AAGA* 1978,1 f.), and 1999; Steinmetz 1982,239 f.; Kussl 1990,379 f.
41 Lesky 1941,43 f. (= 1966,549 f.); Schlam 1971,291 f.; Mason 1998,222 f.; Scobie in *AAGA* 1978,43 f.; Holzberg 1984,163 f.
42 See the synoptic edition of Van Thiel 1972.
43 See Holzberg 1989,549 f. (= Anhang to the new Tusculum-edition of the *Met.*); Mason 1998,223 f. For the terminology see Claes 1988,50 f.; 'phenotext' is used as early as Kristeva 1969.
44 See Claes 1988,55 f. for a typology of forms of transformation in intertextuality, parallel to the transformations used in the Transformational Generative Grammar: addition, deletion, substitution, repetition.
45 These types of changes in the Latin *Met.* in relation to the *Onos* are discussed by Junghanns 1932. For such transformations in book 10, see e.g. the commentary on *illi uero* ch. 14 (247,6); *tandem ... mollius mihi renidentis Fortunae contemplatus faciem* ch. 16 (248,27 f.); *quadruplum ... pretium* ch. 17 (249,24). See Mason 1994,1679 f. ('Apuleius' Use of the Greek Original').

middle of the book, where in the *Met.* the journey to Corinth and the arrival there are described: in the *Onos* the new owner of the ass comes from Thessaloniki and takes him there, and the re-metamorphosis takes place in the theatre of that city. The importance of this geographical transformation is demonstrated by Mason 1971: first, through this change the circle of Lucius' wanderings is closed;[46] and second, Corinth was chosen especially because of the associations this city would call up in contemporaneous readers. Mason demonstrates that Corinth traditionally represented a kind of 'Vanity Fair', known for its loose morals and perversities, the cruelty of its gladiatorial games, and its greed for money; this is the special setting the author chooses for the main character's last adventures before his 'salvation' through the mercy of Isis.[47] This brings us to the last and most fundamental transformation of the *Met.* as compared to the *Onos*: in ch. 35 the ass flees from the Corinthian theatre, still before his re-metamorphosis. In the *Onos* the re-metamorphosis takes place in the theatre of Thessaloniki because Λούκιος gets the opportunity to eat roses. The *Onos* after that ends in a piquant burlesque atmosphere. After the flight from the Corinthean theatre, the *Met.* can no longer be regarded as a phenotext of the *Onos*. On the beach of Cenchreae, where the ass has fallen asleep after his escape, an epiphany of Isis takes place; this takes us into the eleventh book, which deals with the successive initiations of Lucius, re-metamorphosed through the mercy of Isis, into the cult of Isis and Osiris. Tatum 1969,49 rightly states that not the beginning of book 11 but the end of book 10 is the point where *Met.* and *Onos* diverge permanently.[48] As has been shown above, this transformation has already been prepared for by the earlier, geographical transformation; at the end of the book it is expressed on a narrative level in the form of an escape (see 2.4.8).

2.4 Themes in the *Metamorphoses* and their incorporation in book 10

Instructive for the interpretation of the *Met.* is the interconnected network of themes that pervade the framing tale and the embedded tales. Riefstahl 1938,73 f. already pointed out the 'Motiventsprechungen', typical of the *Met.*, in which, however, he saw primarily a 'baroque tendency'. Although in some cases certain motifs are repeated and played with exclusively in order to amuse, various studies have shown

---

46 See Veyne 1965.241 f.: in *Met.*1,22 (20,12) and 2,12 (35,1) it turns out that Lucius comes from Corinth. 'Loukios' of the *Onos* comes from Patrae.
47 That Corinth was also known for the Isis shrine in the harbour of Cenchreae, where during a procession Lucius is indeed delivered from his ass's skin by Isis, is of secundary importance according to Mason l.c. 160 f. (with a discussion of the relevant references). But see Gwyn Griffiths in the introduction to his commentary on book 11 about 'The setting in Cenchreae' (14-20), with extensive references.
48 This concept of the 'diverging' of the two texts is based on the text of the *Met.* transmitted to us and ending with the eleventh book, which contains no passage for which parallels can be found in the *Onos*. From physical evidence in some of the most important manuscripts of the *Met.*, Pecere 1987 concluded that part of the original text may have been lost at the end of book 11; this could be a final line, a few lines, a folio, or more. Van Mal-Maeder 1997b drew from this the conclusion that originally the *Met.* may have consisted of 12 books, with the *Met.* returning to the burlesque ending of the *Onos* in book 12. Such a solution to the interpretative problems of book 11 (which are by many scholars regarded as formidable) is a solution not to the *Met.* as it exists but to a phantom text; in any case, the present introduction and commentary seek to show that in the tenth book the far-reaching transformations in respect to the *Onos* lead up to the *Met.*'s definitive departure from the *Onos*.

that certain recurring motifs, as they cumulate in the framing tale and/or the embedded tales, develop that 'thematic pressure' that Doody 1996,93 regards as a unifying element for 'all novels, old and new'.[49] Many of the themes that were present in earlier books recur in book 10, sometimes 'alla rovescia', sometimes in a culminating form.

2.4.1 *Fortuna*

The importance of *Fortuna* as a unifying theme in the *Met.* has long been recognized.[50] The use of the theme in book 10 illustrates with great intensity the unpredictability and capriciousness of this power in human life, and emphasizes the contrast with Isis/Fortuna's *prouidentia* in book 11. *Fortuna*[51] plays contrasting roles in the two inner tales. In the first story, two references to *Fortuna* form a kind of framework for the ultimately happy ending of this story.[52] In the second story it is the *feralis nutus Fortunae* which causes the fatal reversal in what was till then a favourable course of events.[53] In the part of the framing tale between these two stories, the narrator mentions twice that *Fortuna* is finally well-disposed toward him.[54] This view is relativized by the two stories, which, as if in counterpoint on either side, show contrasting roles of *Fortuna*. Another remarkable point is that, while in the first inner story of the *Met.* the first personified mention of *Fortuna* is as it were the announcement of her role in the *Met.*,[55] the last mention of this personification is found in the last inner story of the *Met.* (see note 53). This is also the very last mention of *Fortuna* before the re-metamorphosis, which is described as a victory over *Fortuna*.[56] The observation by Winkler 1985,148 that for the linear reader the only function of the 'Fortuna statements' in the *Met.* is 'to connect episodes, to mark the narrator's control of his units by reminding us of his presence at the points of transition' is an underestimation of what stands out even to the linear reader as a recurring contrapuntal motif.

---

49 See Schlam 1971,294 f. for references up to 1968. Smith 1968, Introduction, XXI f. discusses the motifs of 'forced entry', 'death and resurrection', and 'dangerous wild animals'. See also Heath 1982,57 f.; James 1988,113 f. discusses the theme of C/*cupido* in the *Met.* Important thematic research can be found in Schlam 1992, chs. 4, 5, 6, 7, 9, and 10; Dowden 1993; Panayotakis 1997b.
50 For a survey of the extensive literature on this topic, see *GCA* 1981,92; Kajanto 1981,551 f.; Schlam 1992,58 f., with notes. On the personification, see the note on on *haud ullo tempore tam beniuolam Fortunam expertus* ch. 13 (246,14 f.).
51 On the personification, see the note on *haud ullo tempore tam beniuolam Fortunam expertus* ch. 13 (246,14 f.).
52 Ch. 5 (239,28 f.) *forte fortuna puer ille iunior ... uini poculum, in quo uenenum latebat inclusum, ... continuo perduxit haustu*; ch. 12 (245,26 f.) *et illius ... senis ... fortuna prouidentiae diuinae condignum accepit exitum.*
53 Ch. 24 (255,17 f.) *sed haec bene atque optime ... disposita feralem Fortunae nutum latere non potuerunt.*
54 Ch. 13 (246,14 f.) *haud ullo tempore tam beniuolam Fortunam expertus*; ch. 16 (248,27 f.) *tandem ex aliqua parte mollius mihi renidentis Fortunae contemplatus faciem.*
55 1,7 (6,13) *fruatur diutius tropaeo Fortuna, quod fixit ipsa.*
56 11,12 (275,19 f.) *quod tot ac tantis exanclatis laboribus, tot emensis periculis deae maximae prouidentia adluctantem mihi saeuissime Fortunam superarem.*

2.4.2 *Spectacula (curiositas)*

Schlam 1968,90 f.[57] remarks that although the word *curiositas* is not found in book 10, the concept is prominent: Lucius to an increasing extent becomes the object of the *curiositas* of others.[58] Now others spy on him through a crack in the door (ch. 15: 248,14 f.) while in 3,21 (68,1 f.) it was Lucius who spied on the witch Pamphile through a crack; his fateful curiosity led immediately afterwards to his metamorphosis (3,24). Here in book 10, after the cooks have spied on him, the ass increasingly becomes a public spectacle for the townspeople to gape at. One of these curious sensation-seekers is eventually the *matrona*, who keeps coming to marvel at him and so conceives a passion for him. This leads to a *nouum spectaculum* (ch. 23: 254,14) for Thiasus (who is always keen on novelties) and to the plan of making the ass's copulation with the condemned murderess a *spectaculum* for a crowd of thousands in the theatre. In this respect book 10 forms a remarkable phase in the reversal, observed by Slater 1998,46, between the first book and the eleventh: 'Once master of the gaze, whether viewing Fotis' beauty or Pamphile's magic rites, he ends as the object of the gaze, both of the statue of Isis behind him and of the crowds in front of him.'

From the beginning of the *Met.* a recurring motif is the pursuit of *spectacula* and its dangers;[59] Schlam 1968,93 f. and 1992,54 f. rightly includes this in his treatment of *curiositas*. The pursuit of *spectacula* is one of the main themes of the tenth book, which Fick 1990,223 calls the 'Liber de Spectaculis' of the *Met.* Not only does this book culminate in a detailed description of a theatre performance, but associations with theatre are found throughout the book.[60] Another reason for calling book 10 a 'Liber de Spectaculis' is its constant occupation with the contrast between appearance and reality.[61]

Although the emphasis in this book is on Lucius as the object of *curiositas*, he is still curious himself, and, just as earlier in the *Met.* his curiosity made it possible for the narrator to present the reader with a good story,[62] so now it leads to a splendid

---

57 In a detailed study of *curiositas* in the *Met.*, where all relevant literature is listed. See also Schlam 1992,48 f.

58 A reversal in respect to the previous books: it is Lucius' *curiositas* for magic that leads to his metamorphosis; in the last part of book 9 it is Lucius the ass who by his *curiositas* causes the ruin of the *hortulanus*: 9,42 (235,23 f.) *curiosus alioquin et inquieti procacitate praeditus asinus*; see *GCA* 1995,349 f. ad loc.

59 See Shumate 1996,205 f. for a thematic connection in this respect between Apuleius' *Met.* and Augustine's *Confessions*. See the note on *prospiciens ... delectatur exumie*, ch. 16 (248,23 f.).

60 Ch. 2 (237,12 f.) mentions *soccus* and *coturnus*. The episode of the cooks contains many references to a comic situation; see e.g. on *opiparas cenas* ch. 13 (246,16); see May 1998. The 'human ass' is called a *spectaculum* in ch. 16 (248,30). When the ass's groom informs his master of the trysts of the *matrona* and the ass, he *totam detegit scaenam* (ch. 23: 254,15 f.); in the preceding sentence (ch. 23: 254,15 f.) he is looking forward to preparing his master a *nouum spectaculum*.

61 See the note on *me phaleris aureis ... exornatum* ch. 18 (251,5 f.), and cf. the numerous expressions which underline the illusionary quality of the 'Judgement of Paris' pantomime from *mons ligneus* (ch. 30: 261,3) onward. See also Holzberg 1984,171 f., and 175 f.

62 Cf. e.g. 9,14, where as an illustration of the advantages of his animal body (the long ears satisfy his *ingenita curiositas* in 9,13: 212,24) the narrator promises the readers a wonderful story, which indeed follows. Cf. 9,23 (220,27 f.), where the *pistor*'s wife is *noscendae rei cupiens* (*GCA* 1995,208 ad loc.: 'clearly a circumlocution for *curiosa*'). Her curiosity provides the reader with the story about the adultery of the fuller's wife.

description.[63] Thus the narrator of the *Met.* constantly makes the reader, too, guilty of curiosity.[64] This changes at the end of book 10: Lucius refuses to cooperate any longer in the theatre performance and flees. One might also say that the narrator disappoints those readers who, like the audience in the theatre, are eagerly awaiting (the description of) the promised Pasiphaë pantomime. Did not the readers, along with the audience, share the inquisitiveness of the *curiosulus uentus*, which in ch. 31 (262,1 f.) lifted the gown of the seductive dancer? In book 11 the narrator will explicitly tell his readers: 'Much as you would like to hear this, I am not allowed to tell you': 11,23 (285,7 f.) *quaeras fortis satis anxie, studiose lector, quid deinde dictum, quid factum; dicerem, si dicere liceret, cognosceres, si liceret audire. Sed parem noxam contraherent et aures et linguae illae temerariae curiositatis.* At the end of book 10 the readers are as *anxii* as the theatre audience to learn *quid deinde factum* but are told *deinde facta* that are entirely different from what they expect at that point. Throughout the *Met. curiositas* is presented as a bad quality, not a good one;[65] book 10 focuses on its morbid aspects, such as sensationalism, and at the end of the book, the *curiositas*, both of the characters and the readers, is foiled by the ass's flight from the theatre (see also 2.4.8).

2.4.3 The human being within the ass

From the metamorphosis (3,24) onward, the narrator repeatedly emphasizes that although Lucius has the body of an ass and is an ordinary ass in the eyes of other actors in the story, he nevertheless remains human inside. The theme of 'the human being within the ass', which in different ways plays a part in the *Met.* in general and in book 10 in particular, is discussed below.

2.4.3.1 Human and animal food[66]

Lucius the human being has never been able to get used to the animal food he is given as an ass. In the earlier books this has been described in various ways, sometimes by using the opposition of raw vs. cooked, as e.g. 4,22 (91,15 f.) *ego uero, numquam alias hordeo crudo cibatus, cum minutatim et diutina coquitatione iurulentum semper esserim.*[67] This expresses the contrast between animal and human, nature and culture, through one of the most famous structuralistic dichotomies.[68] In combination with that it is often emphasized that, although Lucius the ass keeps his taste for human food, he also has the voracity of an animal.[69] Another contrast is suggested shortly after the metamorphosis: although the robbers eat human food

---

63 Ch. 29 (260,18 f.) *curiosos oculos patente porta spectaculi prospectu gratissimo reficiens.*
64 This already begins in the prologue: 1,1 (1,6) *ut mireris.*
65 See Penwill 1975,66 f.; Walsh 1981,25; Skulsky 1981,91 f.; Schlam 1992,48 and n. 3; Hijmans in GCA 1995,372 f.
66 Only the aspects relevant to the introduction to book 10 are listed here. For a more complete discussion see Heath 1982,57 f. and the chapter 'Animal and Human' in Schlam 1992 (99 f.). See also Dowden 1993,104 f.
67 This is the reading adopted by GCA 1977,168 and discussed there, 212 f.
68 Cf. Lévi-Strauss 1964.
69 See the note on *adfatim saginabar* ch. 13 (246,22).

(roasted or cooked meat with baked bread), they devour it with the voracity of animals: 4,8 (80,12 f.) *estur ac potatur incondite, pulmentis aceruatim, panibus aggeratim ... ac iam cetera semiferis Lapithis cenantibus Centaurisque similia.* This passage raises, at least implicitly, the question whether humans and animals can be distinguished from each other by what they eat; the question is raised again in book 10, where Lucius' consuption of human food before his re-metamorphosis has often been seen as an important step in his re-humanization.[70] From the very beginning of the description of the tidbits presented to the ass as a 'gift from the gods' (ch. 13: 246,22 *oblatis ... diuinitus dapibus*) there is a strong emphasis on the 'cuit' aspect of the human food and also on the decadence of the dishes .[71] This also creates a contrast with the poor *hortulanus*, the first to treat the ass as a friend and a companion and to serve him the same food as himself, which, however, was poor and uncooked: 9,32 (227,15 f.) *namque et mihi et ipsi domino cena par ac similis, oppido tamen tenuis aderat, lactucae ueteres et insuaues.* In addition, the ass's animal voracity is once more ironically emphasized.[72]

2.4.3.2 The human being within the ass / the animal within the human being

In this book, human form and human behaviour on the one hand and bestiality and inhuman behaviour on the other begin to intermingle in a complicated way.[73] The two cooks receive the ass as a *contubernalis* in their little house. They are pictured sympathetically, and their touchingly described brotherly love[74] makes them the only truly humane characters in this book: they cannot bear the thought that either of them would deceive the other – an action they call *ne humanum quidem*.[75] Immediately after the episode of the cooks the ass is accepted by people as their *conuiua*, but at the same time the animal pleasures of these people are highlighted:[76] soon after the sumptuous dinners we meet the *matrona* with her perverted desires and then the inhuman murderess. In the nightly trysts of the ass and the *matrona*, human being and animal literally merge and the *matrona* shows more animal traits than the ass.[77] In the inner story of the Murderess of Five the main character becomes an animal already with her first murder.[78] Therefore Lucius is justified in anxiously asking himself (ch. 34: 265,17 f.) whether the wild animals in the arena of Corinth will be able to distinguish between him, the human being within the ass, and her, the animal within a human body. The surprising statement made shortly before, that the ass eagerly eats the grass at the entrance of the theatre, is significant, too, because it is

---

70 See e.g. Schlam 1992,103.
71 Ch. 13 (246,9 f.); see the notes ad loc.
72 See above, n. 69.
73 For a survey throughout the novel of the vocabulary of wild animals transferred to human beings, see Shumate 1996,91 f. and 107 f.
74 See the note on *suspicio non exilis fratrum pupugit animos* ch. 14 (247,3 f.).
75 Ch. 14 (247,11); see the note there.
76 See the note on *ad explorandam mansuetudinem* ch. 16 (249,6 f.).
77 Not only does the narrator pay extra attention to his animal shape (ch. 22: 253,12-20; see notes there), but he also ascribes an animal drive to the *matrona*. See the note on ch. 22 (254,5) *nisu rabido*.
78 Ch. 24 (256,9) *efferata*; see the note there.

here for the first time in his existence as an ass, that he enjoys animal food.[79]

2.4.4 The danger of being killed by animals

Smith 1968, Introd. XXIV points out this theme which permeates the entire *Met.* and also plays a part in book 10, when Lucius is in danger of being mauled in the arena by the wild animals.[80] In 4,19 (89,9 f.) Thrasyleon, disguised as a bear, is killed by dogs; 8,17 (190,11 f.) travelers are attacked by fierce dogs; 9,36 (230,19 f.) the evil neighbour sets savage dogs on his adversary's three sons, the youngest of whom is torn apart and devoured.[81] In the Isis procession (11,7-8) the gentleness of Isis' rule over all nature is expressed by tamed animals participating in the pageant (11,8: 272,15 f.: a bear dressed in women's clothes.)

2.4.5 Apparent death and rebirth

In ch. 5 of book 10 the younger brother falls down 'dead' after drinking the cup of poison intended for his stepbrother. He is buried, but in ch. 11 a physician reveals that the cup contained a sleeping potion, not poison. The boy is taken from the grave as he is waking from a coma, and his awakening is described in terms of a rebirth.[82] Throughout the *Met.* we repeatedly encounter cases of rebirth, from either apparent or real death.[83] The theme of apparent death and rebirth finally culminates in Lucius' rebirth thanks to Isis (11,16: 278,12 f. *renatus quodam modo*) and the initiation, which is described as a 'journey through Proserpina's realm' (11,23: 285,14 f.).

2.4.6 *Salus*

The occurrences of terms like *salus, salubre, salutaris* throughout the *Met.* illustrate how a repeated motif gradually develops 'thematic pressure' as the book proceeds (see 2.2 and n. 38). Here, as in the previous books, notions like *salus, salubre, salutaris* (in their concrete meanings of 'preservation of life', 'beneficial, healthy' respectively) occur frequently, and sometimes acquire extra weight.[84] In light of the new connotation acquired by *salus* in the eleventh book, they are significant; the narrator's remark that he flees from the theatre *de salute ipsa sollicitus* (ch. 35: 265,22 f.) forms a distinct 'hinge' to the new connotation of *salus* in the Isis book.

---

79 Ch. 29 (260,16 f.) *pabulum ... libens adfectabam*; see Heath 1982,65 and Schlam 1992,103.
80 Other passages in book 10 also mention the fear to become the prey of wild animals: ch. 17 (250,8 f.); ch. 22 (253,20 f.).
81 See also Schlam 1992,104 f.; Dowden 1993,104 f. on 'Man, beast, brigands' in book 8.
82 See the note on *remeabit ad diem lucidam* ch. 11 (245,8). On the association of this young man with Hippolytus/Virbius, see App. I,6B.
83 1,17 (15,12 f.) Socrates, presumed dead by Aristomenes, 'arises'; 2,29 (48,26 f.) a dead man is temporarily brought back to life by an Egyptian priest; 3,9 (59 3 f.) Lucius, who already imagined himself to be 'in the realm of Proserpina and Orcus', returns to life; 6,21 (144,9 f.) Psyche is overcome by an *infernus somnus ac uere Stygius*, from which Amor wakes her (ibid. 144,13 f.).
84 See the note on *salus unica* ch. 3 (238,21); *saluti* ch. 4 (239,5); *saluti* ch. 11 (244,30), with references.

2.4.7 *Narrare*

Winkler 1985,26 f. calls the activities of narrators and listeners, i.e. the semantics and hermeneutics of the act of narrating, 'arguably the single most coherent subject of the novel'. This is true in particular for the first inner story of book 10, where the assessment of the truth value of someone else's story is undoubtedly one of the themes.[85] But generally speaking, book 10 is similar to the other books of the *Met.* in that a continuous dialogue is suggested between the narrator and his audience, in which the narrator – with his comments, his evaluations, and his remarks about his activity as narrator – takes up a position between the narrated event(s) and the reader, thus claiming attention for the problems connected with the interpretation of a narrative text. The reader is constantly challenged to increase his own interpretative activities and to adopt an independent attitude toward the narrator, since the narrator repeatedly makes it clear that his evaluations and preliminary announcements, his assessment of the situations presented, only reflect the individual vision of a *persona* who is closely involved in the events, often prejudiced, and certainly not infallible in his judgement.

On the one hand, an oral situation is suggested in the *Met.* from the Prologue onward: *at ego tibi ... uarias fabulas conseram auresque tuas beniuolas lepido susurro permulceam* (1,1: 1,1 f.). But on the other hand the author cleverly manipulates the situation that this is a written text, which the reader can reread if necessary. This not only enables the reader to catch the narrator at inaccuracies or errors but also to recognize connections that went unnoticed at first and were not pointed out by the narrator. Apuleius shows elsewhere that he is aware of this aspect of a written text and its consequences for the interaction between author and reader: *sic enim ferme adsolet apud prudentes uiros esse in operibus elaboratis iudicatio restrictior, in rebus subitariis uenia prolixior. scripta enim pensiculatis et examinatis, repentina autem noscitis simul et ignoscitis, nec iniuria ...* (Frg. <*Florida*> 105 Beaujeu). Behind the fictive narrrator, who talks on in a seemingly spontaneous way, hides the author who carefully weighs his words and expects the reader to do the same.

2.4.8 Escape

'Narrow escape' is an element that frequently occurs in the *Onos* as well: the unsuccessful escape of the ass and Charite (*Met.* 6,27 f.) has a parallel in *Onos* 23; their successful escape (*Met.* 7,12) in *Onos* 26; and the ass's escape from imminent castration (*Met.* 7,25) has one in *Onos* 34. In addition, the ass's escape from being butchered by a cook (*Met.* 9,1) is found in *Onos* 40, and the escape from the weapons with which the apparently rabid ass is about to be killed (*Met.* 9,2 f.) is found in *Onos* 41; here the version in the *Met.* is considerably elaborated (see Schmidt in *GCA* 1995,356 f.). But the culmination of the theme of escape is found at the end of book

---

[85] See the note on *perspiciens ... uerberonem ... causificantem* ch. 9 (243,23 f.). Winkler's (1985,76 f.) explanation of the inner story in that sense is acute but too limited. That more is involved than just 'a systematic comparison of events and how they were known' may become clear from the commentary and Appendices I and III.

10: the escape from the theatre (ch. 35). This escape, which has such far-reaching consequences for the story of the *Met.*, has no parallel in the *Onos*: this is, in fact, the point at which the *Met.* 'escapes' from the template of the *Onos* and takes its own course (see 2.3). In 'Die Flucht des Erzählers',[86] Hofmann shows in a careful discussion, supported by a narratological analysis, that the ass's escape from the Corinthian theatre is at the same time the narrator's escape, and a turning point at the level of both *histoire* and *récit*. Thus a recurring motif in the *Met.* acquires through its culminating treatment a 'thematic pressure' that this element lacks in the *Onos* (see also above, 2.4.6 *salus*).

2.5 Cases of mirroring

Various episodes or passages in this book mirror episodes from other books of the *Met.*, thus reinforcing the coherence of the entire work.[87]

2.5.1 The Risus festival and book 10

The ass's performance (averted at the last moment) in the theatre of Corinth recalls in many respects Lucius' 'performance' (fully executed) in the theatre of Hypata during the Risus festival (3,2-12). Both performances take place in the theatre. At the Risus festival Lucius undergoes a humiliating experience as the unwitting object of ridicule; in Corinth the ass knows exactly what is in store for him and refuses to become the centre of attention in this way. Habinek 1990,49 f. discusses these two festivals in connection with the third festival in the *Met.*, i.e. the Isis procession (11,8 f.), where Lucius is again the centre of attention because of his re-metamorphosis. Habinek discusses the three festivals in terms of 'rites de passage' and formulates the contrast between Hypata and Cenchreae thus: '... whereas in Hypata he (sc. Lucius) was transformed from insider to outsider, from welcome guest to out-of-town dupe, in Cenchreae he makes the reverse transition'. Lucius' performance in the theatre of Corinth does not take place; one might say that it is replaced by the *spectaculum* in Cenchreae, which is the true mirroring of the Risus festival.[88]

The Risus festival is mirrored differently in book 10. In chs. 15-16 the abundant laughter about the ass is repeatedly emphasized, often with verbal reminiscences of the Risus festival. This creates a mirroring contrast: in the Risus festival Lucius was an unwitting actor in a joke which he experienced as extremely humiliating, so that he refused all further cooperation once he understood the joke;[89] in chs. 15-16 he shows himself a willing and cooperative comic actor, which provides him with a position as *parasitus* in the company of Thiasus. His cooperation leads directly to the

---

86 Hofmann 1993a,111-141.
87 As Nimis suggested (in personal communication) to me, these cases of mirroring may be seen as interventions by the author into the meaning of the story: not signposts indicating the coherence of the work, but predications of coherence made along the way. See on Nimis' 'prosaics' approach above (2.2).
88 See also Schlam 1992,53 f. and 55: 'The projected ultimate spectacle (i.e. that in Corinth) is replaced with the revelation of Isis.'
89 3,11-12 (60,17 f.); see James 1987,89 f.

plans for his performance in the theatre.[90]

2.5.2 Two love scenes

The scene in which the sexual intercourse of the *matrona* and the ass is described (chs. 20-23) can be seen as a mirroring of the elaborately described foreplay and intercourse between Fotis and Lucius in 2,15-17[91] and 3,19-20. Compare also Lucius' declaration of passion to Fotis 3,19 (66,16 f.), in which he emphasizes that she is 'holding' him (*teneas*), to the *matrona*'s words *teneo te ... teneo* in 10,22 (253,21 f.). The complete self-abandon both women demand from Lucius can also be seen as a contrasting mirroring of the complete abandon with which Lucius surrenders himself to Isis in the eleventh book.[92] It has been remarked that in his sexual intercourse with the *matrona* Lucius the ass shows a more human attitude (his fear of hurting her in ch. 22: 253,12 f.) than Lucius the man did with Fotis.[93] This view is based on the idea that in the first ten books of the *Met.* the main character is going through a positive development via his ordeals. But the narrative text itself does not support this: Lucius the ass's fear of hurting the *matrona* is based on his fear of punishment.[94]

2.5.3 The *ecphrasis*

The *ecphrasis* in chs. 29-34, in particular the description of the pantomime of 'The Judgement of Paris', is structurally opposed to another *ecphrasis* in the *Met.*, the description of the statues of Diana and Actaeon. This is found at the beginning of the second book (2,4: 27,3 f.), while the *ecphrasis* of the ballet performances occurs at the end of the second book from the end. The Diana-Actaeon *ecphrasis* has an anticipatory function (which Lucius himself does not understand); the Paris pantomime retrospectively holds up a mirror to Lucius (who does not understand this either), showing his own choice of Fotis as a seductive 'Venus'. The description of Venus dancing with her retinue of *Cupidines*, (ch. 32: 263,1-19), seductively swaying her hips, also recalls Fotis through verbal analogy.[95]

The diatribe on the corruption of justice in ch. 33, provoked by Venus bribing Paris, reminds the reader of the deliberate suppression of the element of bribery in Venus' monologue in 4,30 (98,13-15), where she uses her selection by Paris as an argument for her persecution of Psyche.[96]

---

[90] See the note on *quid bonum rideret familia* ch. 16 (248,22).
[91] See also Schlam 1992,72 f., who mentions the following points: Fotis sips the wine, together with Lucius, and the *matrona* rubs the ass down with the same perfume with which she anoints herself; both women have taken measures to remove the slaves for the sake of privacy. As a contrast Schlam mentions that the *matrona* 'uses' the ass while Lucius thinks that he 'uses' Fotis to get closer to the magic. See also the note on *cenati* ch. 20 (252,3).
[92] See Gwyn Griffiths in *AAGA* 1978,156 f.
[93] Journoud 1965,35; Nethercut 1968,110 f.; idem 1969,125.
[94] See the note on *ei parcens* ch. 22 (254,4).
[95] See more extensively the commentary on ch. 32, and Zimmerman-de Graaf 1993,150 f.
[96] See van Mal-Zimmerman 1998,98 f.

2.5.4 Other cases of mirroring

Ch. 33 (264,14 f.) reverently mentions Socrates and recalls his conviction. The Socrates in the story of 1,5-19, however, is a kind of anti-Socrates, who became the victim of a *Venus vulgaria*[97] and is found in a wretched condition in Thessaly – the country to which the historical Socrates had refused to flee to escape the death penalty (Plato, *Crito* 53D).

In ch. 16 f. Thiasus is consistently depicted as a *sititor nouitatis*, a term which Lucius used to described himself (1,2: 3,4). Thus, a mirror is held up to Lucius (which, by the way, the narrator does not signal).[98]

The exuberant attention paid to food and gastronomy in book 10 is in contrast with the emphasis on *abstinentia* in the eleventh book.

In ch. 29 a spring description is given, but some traditional elements of spring descriptions are conspicuously lacking (birds; the return of the seafaring season; see notes in ch. 29). The 'completion' of this spring description is to be found in book 11 (11,7).

2.6 Connections between the inner tales in book 10 and those in other books

Although the two inner stories of book 10 can be connected with each other in many aspects (see App. III), in a different aspect they can also be connected with the last inner story of book 9, about the destruction of the three brothers and their father (9,35-38). All these three tales deal with a disaster that strikes an entire family; only in the second of them is the disaster eventually averted. The long inner story of 9,14-31, too, ended with the ruin of the *pistor*'s entire *familia*, and indeed disasters ruining a house are thematic in the *Met.* from the beginning of book 8 onward.[99] The sudden reversals from prosperity to ruin that often go hand in hand with this theme connect these disasters with the theme of *fortuna* (see 2.4.1).

3. Narratological analysis and interpretation

A narratological study of the *Met.* is as yet unwritten. Winkler 1985, who gave his book *Auctor & Actor* the subtitle of *A Narratological Reading of Apuleius's The Golden Ass*, offers both more and less than a narratological study: more, in that a large and important part of *Auctor & Actor* (*Part III, Conjectures*) is devoted to a discussion of the *Met.*'s intertextual and interdiscursive relation with the cultural-historical and literary tradition(s) of the period in which this work was written; less, in that *Auctor & Actor* offers no consistent narratological analysis of the entire work,

---

97 See Van der Paardt in *AAGA* 1978,82 and n. 59 (with references), and 84 and n. 77; Fick 1991,143 f.
98 See the note on *nouitate ... laetus* ch. 16 (248,30).
99 See the note on *domus cladem* ch. 4 (239,8 f.).

based on a coherent theory. Winkler uses the basic narrative situation in the *Met.* (see 3.2 below) and the form of the frame narrative as a starting-point for a discussion of a number of salient passages, in which this basic situation has meaningful consequences for the reading of the work. The fragmentary and eclectic narratological observations have been made subordinate to the interpretation of Apuleius' *Met.* as an aporetic text, an 'open-ended problem text that the reader must supplement' (Winkler 1985,241).

A philological-interpretative commentary on book 10 of the *Met.* is not the place for a thorough narratological study of the work, but it is necessary and meaningful to include a narratological analysis because, as has been discussed before (see 2.4.7), the act of narrating in the *Met.* has been thematized (see 2.2.7). In this commentary, however, a narratological analysis is not a goal but a means, through which certain phenomena that take place at the level of narrative technique can be pointed out in the text, named, and interpreted. Technical terms are used as little as possible, and only when they are useful in signaling changes in the narrative situation.

To avoid terminological confusion, this commentary consistently uses the typology developed by Lintvelt 1981 (^{2}1989). This is discussed extensively in *GCA* 1995,7-12 and will not be repeated here. A short discussion of the terminology used in the commentary will suffice.

3.1 Concrete author - concrete reader

The concrete author, the actual creator of the literary work, addresses a literary message to the concrete reader, the 'recipient'. Concrete author and concrete reader are historical and biographical persons, who are not part of the literary work but lead an autonomous life in the real world. Whereas the concrete author Apuleius was one person, fixed at the historical moment of his literary creation the *Metamorphoses*, the concrete readers of the work vary in the course of time; this often entails quite diverse receptions of the same work. In the commentary, the concrete author is mentioned whenever it is relevant to point out other works of Apuleius, which for example give an insight into certain philosophical views expressed by the author in his other works. For the interpretation of this specific work of the author it is sometimes also important to point out movements, political backgrounds, or educational systems which, on the ground of biographical information about the author, may have exerted an influence on his thinking that may be reflected in certain aspects of this one work.

In a commentary on the *Met.*, the concrete reader is brought to notice in various ways. First, the writer of a commentary is her/himself a concrete, present-day reader, who in the reception of the text is influenced by contemporary views and cultural background. At the same time, there is a continous reaction to receptions of this work by other concrete readers both in the past and in the present; these receptions are absorbed in their turn. But secondly, in a commentary on a work as distant in time as the *Met.*, attention must be paid to the concrete readers of the time of its origin. In fact, almost all exegetic notes to the text are to be understood as attempts to clarify the way in which the concrete contemporary readers of the *Met.* probably understood the text. The attention paid to realia in the commentary should also be seen in that light: in creating the fictive world of his novel the author bases himself on, and employs, a reference frame that to the contemporary concrete reader was his everyday, historical reality, but which a reader of many centuries later must investigate by various means.[100]

3.2 Abstract author - abstract reader

The abstract author is the literary projection that the concrete author produces of himself while writing his literary work. In that way, the abstract author represents the deep meaning of the literary work, and the abstract reader is the ideal understander, pre-supposed by the entire work, of that deep meaning. Abstract author and abstract reader are part of the literary work, but are never directly represented in it, neither is there a real linguistic communication between the two of them. For a clarifying application of the concept 'abstract author', see the note on ch. 35 (265,26) *meis cogitationibus liberum tribuebatur arbitrium*.

In many passages irony is achieved because of a marked divergence between the ideology of the abstract author and the opinions expressed by certain characters in the work, among them the fictive narrator. It is therefore important for the interpretation to distinguish between fictive narrator and abstract author. For example, notes on ch. 18 show that the abstract author subtly nuances the fictive narrator's naive enthusiasm about his luxurious surroundings.

The distinction between concrete author and abstract author is also important because the concrete author creates, along with his literary work, a kind of superior version of himself. At an ideological level, important divergences may exist between the ideology of the abstract author and that of the concrete author as he displays it in his extra-literary life. For example, from the description of the trial in book 10 and from other passages in the book emerges a pessimistic view of the abstract author as to the fairness of judicial procedure. This may, but need not, be the concrete author's view. The same applies to e.g. the opinions about the inevitability of fate which are found in numerous passages in the *Met*. Other works by the concrete author Apuleius lead us to conclude that he, a *philosophus platonicus*, had different ideas on the subject.

---

[100] This leads us to the examination of Apuleius' 'authorial readership'. This is the name given by Rabinowitz 1986,117 f. to the audience (reading or listening) that the concrete author had in mind when he created the text. Cf. Prince 1973,180 f. on the 'lecteur virtuel'. Although an author never knows who will read his book, still when making decisions and choices for his text he forms an image of the values, knowledge, and conventional outlook of his potential readers, and appeals to these. Hijmans 1986,350 f., for instance, examines the possible associations a concrete contemporary reader might make while reading the passage in *Met.* 8,7, where Charite reveres her deceased husband as the divinity Liber (Dionysus), and what its consequences are for the interpretation of this passage by us, concrete readers of today.

3.3 Fictive narrator - fictive narratee

The fictive narrator imparts the 'narrated world' to the fictive narratee. Between these two a dialectic relationship develops. The requisite function of the fictive narrator is to tell the story. This function is always combined with the function of control and direction: he controls the structure of the text, he quotes (in indirect or direct discourse) the actors' words, and may even convey their intonations by means of 'stage directions'. These roles cannot be reversed.

Besides these requisite functions the fictive narrator can exert optional functions: he can make interpreting, evaluating, and commenting statements. As has been remarked in 2.4.7 above, the narrator of the *Met.* uses these optional functions in abundance. This gives extra importance to the passages in which the narrator abstains from comment and only registers what the actors do and say. Here the reader is challenged to evaluate and interpret for himself.

The reader can indirectly form an image of the fictive narratee (the audience of the fictive narrator) through the remarks directed by the narrator to that audience.[101]

3.4 Actors

The actors play the part of 'dramatis personae' in the action of the novel. In Lintvelt's opinion, an actor can never fulfill the functions of narrating and control. The dichotomy between narrator and actor is permanent: even when a story is told in the first person, one has to distinguish between 'I' the narrator (with his function of direction and control) and 'I' the actor.

3.5 The basic narrative form and the narrative type in the *Met.*

Like Genette, Lintvelt[102] distinguishes two basic forms of narrative on the basis of the dichotomy narrator-actor, namely the heterodiegetic and the homodiegetic narrative form. In a heterodiegetic narrative the narrator does not play a part in the action of the narrative. In a homodiegetic narrative the narrator is himself an actor (protagonist or co-actor) in the narrative. It is evident that the main action of the *Met.*, at any rate, is narrated in the homodiegetic form: the narrator tells a story in which he plays a part himself.

Within the homodiegetic narrative form, Lintvelt distinguishes two types of narration:[103] the actorial type of narration, in which the centre of orientation for the reader lies in the character as an actor (the 'experiencing I', 'je-narré'), or the auctorial type of narration, in which the centre of orientation for the reader lies in the character as a narrator (the 'narrating I', 'je-narrant'). Because the reader understands

---

101 For examples see the note on *dii boni* ch. 2 (238,1) and *dii boni* ch. 20 (252,50).
102 Lintvelt 1981,34 f.
103 Lintvelt 1981,79 f.

that the main action of the *Met.* must be the retrospective story of a narrator who relates a past event in which he was an actor/ protagonist, he will expect a homodiegetic-auctorial narrator. However, when telling his story, the narrator of the *Met.* has almost constantly the attitude of an actorial narrator, i.e. the centre of orientation lies almost always in the narrator as an actor, an 'experiencing I'.[104] This appears from the following characteristics, typical of the homodiegetic-actorial narrator: the narrator has no deeper insight into the events than he did when he was an actor in the story. Although the narrator can give flashbacks, he cannot anticipate an event with any certainty. The position from which he presents the story is the same as the one he has as an actor: he cannot be omnipresent. He cannot use hindsight in his comments on current events; only his reactions as an actor at the moment itself can be told. The advantages of this homodiegetic-actorial type of narration for the reader are fully exploited in the *Met.*: the narrator allows the reader to join in the events with all their suspense and surprising peripeteias; like the narrator the reader does not know beforehand how a situation will turn out or whether another actor is lying or telling the truth; this leads to all kinds of misunderstandings, which the reader shares with the narrator/protagonist. The narrative situation (someone writing about a past event in which he was an actor/protagonist) remains the same, however; thus, an intruding into the narration of the *auctor* remains a possibility which, theoretically, the interpreting reader must continuously be aware of.[105] This double role of the narrator is sometimes used for a humorous effect: an often-cited example is 6,25 (147,4 f.), where the narrator, having reached the end of the long inner story of Amor and Psyche, sighs that at the time it saddened him, the ass, not to have pen and notebook to take down such a fine story. But in other passages the switching between – or the overlapping of – auctorial and actorial narrative situation is less clear-cut, and its consequences for the interpretation can be recognized only through re-reading.[106] The sudden switch in ch. 33, where the auctorial narrator temporarily takes the place of the actorial narrator, and its consequences for the interpretation, has been discussed elsewhere.[107]

The narrative situation is complicated even further by the numerous embedded tales in the *Met.*, where either the chief narrator, or subnarrators (sometimes to the third degree), each with an idiosyncratic narrative status, recount tales (which may or may not relate to the framing tale) sometimes in a heterodiegetic, sometimes in a homodiegetic form (auctorial or actorial respectively). As has been discussed in 1.2.2, the manner in which the digressions are embedded in book 10 is relatively simple.

---

104 This has often been noticed before: Smith 1968, Introd. XVII refers to a 'running commentary' of the narrator, to be distinguished from a 'retrospective commentary' on the *Metamorphoses*. See also Van der Paardt in *AAGA* 1978,76 f.; Dowden 1982,419 f. In this connection Winkler 1985,140 f. discusses 'The suppression of the *Auctor*-narrator'.

105 This already becomes evident in all those passages where the narrator *as a narrator*, i.e. in an auctorial way, refers to his narrative action via metanarrative remarks. In those passages the concrete reader is reminded, via the fictive narrator's remarks to his fictive narratee, of the direction and structuring activity of the *auctor*. Cf. e.g. the introductory note on ch. 2 (237,1-3).

106 Cf. Winkler 1985,135 f., 'The duplicities of *auctor/actor*'. Lintvelt 1981,185 f. cites Lotman 1973,410: 'Le texte artistique n'est pas seulement la réalisation de normes structurelles, mais aussi leur transgression'.

107 See the note on ch. 33 (264,1-7); Zimmerman-de Graaf 1993,154 f.

The commentary, however, in various notes on chs. 2-12, points out important shifts in the narrative form of that inner story,[108] which surprise the reader by their unexpectedness, with the result that the reader's reaction to this inner story can, in a sense, be seen as a metaphor of the reader's reaction to the entire *Met.*[109]

A remarkable interruption of the homodiegetic-actorial form of narrative can be observed in ch. 15 (248,10 f.) *sed iste corporis mei decor pudori peperit grande dedecus*. As already noted (3.5), the homodiegetic-actorial narrator can give flashbacks but cannot anticipate an event with any certainty; this makes the anticipating remark here all the more remarkable. Somewhat comparable is 9,39 (232,28 f.) *nec innoxius ei saltem regressus euenit* (see *GCA* 1995,324 ad loc.). The switch from an actorial to an auctorial narrative form in an anticipatory remark demands special attention on the reader's part: in both of these passages an immediately following *nam* gives what at first sight seems a plausible explanation of the anticipatory remark. Both anticipatory remarks, however, are phrased in such a way that their full strength becomes evident only much later in the story. The words *nec innoxius ... euenit* in 9,39 will eventually (9,42: 236,4 f.) turn out to mean that the *hortulanus* will probably be condemned to death. In the passage of book 10 discussed here, the *grande dedecus* seems at first sight to be the fact that the ass is caught in the act of stealing. Later in the story, however, the *matrona*'s infatuation (ch. 19: 251,20 f.) and the resulting plans for the ass's copulation with the *uilis aliqua* (ch. 23: 254,19 f.) turn out to be the much farther-reaching point of this anticipatory phrase. The rarely occurring anticipatory remarks in the *Met.* thus enhance the surprise effect for the reader: the strength of the anticipation increases as the story develops, but the reader must discover this on his own because the narrator does not come back to his first explanation, which turns out to be not really incorrect but certainly incomplete. These and similar procedures in the *Met.* lead to a certain reading attitude in which the reader is trained to suspend an opinion because time and again s/he finds as s/he reads on that an opinion which s/he has formed needs to be revised. In this way they contribute to the 'Verunsicherung', which Sallmann 1988,99 calls a 'Produktionsästhetisches Prinzip' in the *Met.*

4 The text

4.1 The constitution of the Latin text printed in this commentary

The text printed here is based on the final Teubner edition of Helm 1955 (reprint of Helm 1931), with his page and line numbers. Helm's basis for the constitution of the text was the Laurentianus 68,2 (= F) and its copy, Laurentianus 29,2 (= φ); the latter often provides the correct reading of F. The investigations of the manuscripts by Robertson and ²Giarratano have always been taken into consideration in establishing the reading text. These two editors were the first to point out the importance of the

---

108 See the note on *exanimis terrae procumbit* ch. 5 (240,5); on *res* ch. 8 (243,16).
109 See the note on ch. 11 (245,1) *dedi uenenum, sed somniferum*.

group 'Class I'.[110] Pecere 1987 demonstrates that this group of manuscripts represents a tradition independent from F, but deriving from the same ancestor as F. A new text edition of the *Metamorphoses*, with a complete collation of the manuscripts of Class I, is justified; however, this commentary does not aim at a new critical text edition. All disputed passages have been scrutinized anew; departures from Helm's text are discussed in the commentary, and are listed at the beginning of the commentary.

4.2 Spelling

The principles formulated in *GCA* 1985,10 are followed here: 'spelling variations in F may possibly represent less than rigid standards on the part of the author. Our practice has been to follow F also in this respect, if there is evidence that for a given word the ancient spelling was inconsistent ... The list of words whose spelling differs within the Apuleian tradition is rather long. See e.g. Oldfather's Index on *Carthago/Karthago; Diofanes/Diophanes; dirrumpo/dirumpo; faetor/fetor; penna/pinna; reccino/recino*. It should be emphasized, however, that in retaining the variation we do not pretend to reconstruct Apuleius' spelling habits, but merely indicate that the available evidence does not allow us to assume consistency on his part.' Cf. in this book e.g. the note on *sobolis* ch. 5 (240,29); also, on the other hand, the note on *arc[h]anis* ch. 24 (255,11), where there is no ancient evidence to support F's variant.

5 The translation

The translation given after every section is not an artistic translation but a working translation. Although a smoothly running translation is sought, the first objective is always to follow the Latin text as closely as possible and to intervene as little as possible in the order of the constituents of the sentence as it is found in the Latin text.

6 Notes on grammar and style

Morphological and syntactical peculiarities of the Latin of Apuleius' *Met.* are discussed as to their synchronic and diachronic aspects. The emphasis is on innovations, those that make themselves felt in the semantics and syntax of the Latin of late antiquity, especially patristic Latin. Therefore many references are made to the material consulted in the *Thesaurus Linguae Latinae (ThLL)*. The lemmas of the *ThLL* are referred to according to column and line numbers. Besides, searches have been conducted regularly in electronic files (PHI, Cetedoc Library of Christian Latin Texts, and in the last stage of the writing of this commentary the Bibliotheca Teubneriana Latina); this has not been mentioned explicitly in the commentary.

---

110 Robertson 1924,27-41; idem in Vallette-Robertson Tome I, 1940, XLVII f. The siglum a*, which is sometimes mentioned in the commentary, is borrowed from Robertson, who uses it to indicate the agreement between certain members of Class I. See also Giarratano-Frassinetti 1960,XVII f.; XLVII f.

Much attention has been paid to questions relating to the use of tenses and word order. Especially in these problems, the traditional grammars' normative approach is usually not very helpful for gaining a true insight: a deviation from what is regarded as the 'classical' usage is often described as a deviation from the supposed norm, or explained as an attempt at variation. Here, use has been made of contemporary insights into linguistic theory and analysis.

Stylistic and rhetorical notes are also part of this commentary. Here we often see a fluid transition to the interpretative commentary, in view of the close connection between form and content.

7 Organization of the bibliography

Part IV of the bibliography continues the bibliographies of Apuleian Studies in the previous volumes of *GCA*. However, at the request of a number of users of *GCA*, part III of this bibliography contains a complete list of the references used in this commentary on book 10. This means that Apuleian Studies up to 1995 (those to which the commentary refers) can be found in part III of the general bibliography, and Apuleian Studies from 1995 onward in part IV.

NOTE TO THE TEXT

I have followed Helm's text, as printed in his latest Teubner-edition (1931, reprinted with Addenda and Corrigenda 1955). However, I have used capitals at the beginning of new sentences, and added paragraph numbers throughout. In the following places I have chosen a different reading. Changes of punctuation are not listed here, but are argued in the commentary, where necessary. The same applies for cases where I have chosen a capital for personifications.

	This text	Helm's text
236,16	*galeam <gerebam>* Helm 1955	*galeam* F
236,17	*longe* prae*lucens* Helm 1955	*longius relucens*
237,9	*superg<r>esserat* Colvius	*supercesserat* Dousa
238,6	*in eo[s] ipso, s<cilice>t* Colvius	*in eo si p[s]osset* Rohde
238,9	*uxoris patris matrisque* F	*uxori[s] patri matri[s]que* Lipsius
240,21	*tamen <tam>* Van der Vliet	*tam[en]*
242,10	*promptissimum* F	*potissimum*
242,21	*neclexisse* F, Helm 1955	*nec secus ille*
242,22	*eximia enim* F, Helm 1955	*eximia ac nimis* Leo
242,24	*perferente* F	*proferente*
245,9	*si ue<re> ... si* Hildebrand	*sine ... si<n>e*
246,12	*praedestinarant* F	*prae[de]stinarant*
248,3-4	*pastus* a*	*partes* ς
249,21	*per<h>ausi*	*perduxi*
249,21	*Et clamor*	*Clamor*
249,26	*magna ... diligentia* F	*magna<m> ...diligentia<m>*
251,1	*praedarum* F	*[p]raedarum*
251,27 f.	*nequaquam <curans an ei quicquam> posset ...*	*nequaquam <sollicitus, quidnam> posset...*
252,10	*modicis* F	*medic<at>is*
252,18	*balsamo* F	*balsam<in>o*
253,11	*ungento flagrantissimo* F	*ung<u>ento fraglantissimo*
254,1	*passarem* F	*passerem*
254,6	*adpliciore* F	*adplici<ti>ore*
254,19	*acquiritur* F	*anquiritur*
255,2	*nata[m] puella[m]* Pricaeus	*<cum uideret> natam puellam*
256,27	*illa* F	*ipsa*
256,28	*quo compecto* Stewech	*quo confecto* F
257,3	*Proserpinae sacra Saluti* F	*Proserpinae sacra [Saluti]*
257,12	*offendet* F	*offendit* Van der Vliet
258,19	*consentit* F	*consensit*
260,1	*confarraturus* F	*confarr<e>aturus*
261,8	*Paridis, Frygii pastoris* F	*[Paridis] Frygii pastoris*
261,13-14	*cognatione* F	*con<gluti>natione*
262,4	*<de>liniaret* Vulcanius	*liciniaret* F
262,7-8	*<sui comitabantur>* Oudendorp	*<sui sequebantur>*
265,6	*decepit* F	*recepit* ς
266,8	*uespernae* F	*uesper<ti>nae* ς

35

TEXT
LIBER X

1 ¹Die sequenti meus quidem dominus hortulanus quid egerit nescio, me tamen miles ille, qui propter eximiam impotentiam pulcherrime uapularat, ab illo praesepio nullo equidem contradicente diductum abducit atque a suo contubernio - hoc enim mihi uidebatur - sarcinis propriis onustum et prorsus exornatum armatumque militariter producit ad uiam. ²Nam et galeam <gerebam> nitore praemicantem et scutum cetera longe *prae*lucens, sed etiam lanceam longissimo hastili conspicuam, quae scilicet non disciplinae tunc quidem causa, sed propter terrendos miseros uiatores in summo atque edito sarcinarum cumulo ad instar exercitus sedulo composuerat. ³Confecta campestri nec adeo difficili uia ad quandam ciuitatulam peruenimus nec in stabulo, sed in domo cuiusdam decurionis deuertimus. ⁴Statimque me commendato cuidam seruulo ipse ad propositum suum, qui mille armatorum ducatum sustinebat, sollicite proficiscitur. 236 H

2 ¹Post dies plusculos ibidem dissignatum scelestum ac nefarium facinus memini, sed ut uos etiam legatis, ad librum profero. ²Dominus aedium habebat iuuenem filium probe litteratum atque ob id consequenter pietate, modestia praecipuum, quem tibi quoque prouenisse cuperes uel talem. ³Huius matre multo ante defuncta rursum matrimonium sibi reparauerat ductaque alia filium procreauerat alium, qui adaeque iam duodecimum annum aetatis superg<r>esserat. ⁴Sed nouerca forma magis quam moribus in domo mariti praepollens, seu naturaliter impudica seu fato ad extremum impulsa flagitium, oculos ad priuignum adiecit. ⁵Iam ergo, lector optime, scito te tragoediam, non fabulam legere et a socco ad coturnum ascendere. ⁶Sed mulier illa, quandiu primis elementis Cupido paruulus nutriebatur, imbecillis adhuc eius uiribus facile ruborem tenuem deprimens silentio resistebat. ⁷At ubi completis igne uaesano totis praecordiis immodice bacchatus Amor exaestuabat, saeuienti deo iam succubuit, et languore simulato uulnus animi mentitur in corporis ualetudine. ⁸Iam cetera salutis uultusque detrimenta et aegris et amantibus examussim conuenire nemo qui nesciat: pallor[e] deformis, marcentes oculi, lassa genua, quies turbida et suspiritus cruciatus tarditate uehementior. Crederes et illam fluctuare tantum uaporibus febrium, nisi quod et flebat. ⁹Heu medicorum ignarae mentes, quid uenae pulsus, quid coloris intemperantia, quid fatigatus anhelitus et utrimquesecus iactatae crebriter laterum mutuae uicissitudines? ¹⁰Dii boni, quam facilis licet non artifici medico, cuiius tamen docto Veneriae cupidinis comprehensio, cum uideas aliquem sine corporis calore flagrantem. 237 H

238 H

3 ¹Ergo igitur inpatientia furoris altius agitata diutinum rupit silentium et ad se uocari praecipit filium — quod nomen in eo[s] ipso, s<cilic>e*t* ne

ruboris admoneretur, libenter eraderet. ²Nec adulescens aegrae parentis moratus imperium, senili tristitie striatam gerens frontem, cubiculum petit, uxoris patris matrisque fratris utcumque debitum sistens obsequium. ³Sed illa cruciabili silentio diutissime fatigata et ut in quodam uado dubitationis haerens omne uerbum, quod praesenti sermoni putabat aptissimum, rursum improbans nutante etiam nunc pudore, unde potissimum caperet exordium, decunctatur. ⁴At iuuenis nihil etiam tunc sequius suspicatus summisso uultu rogat ultro praesentis causas aegritudinis. ⁵Tunc illa nancta solitudinis damnosam occasionem prorumpit in audaciam et ubertim adlacrimans laciniaque contegens faciem uoce trepida sic eum breuiter adfatur: ⁶'Causa omnis et origo praesentis doloris et etiam medela ipsa et salus unica mihi tute ipse es. ⁷Isti enim tui oculi per meos oculos ad intima delapsi praecordia meis medullis acerrimum commouent incendium. ⁸Ergo miserere tua causa pereuntis nec te religio patris omnino deterreat, cui moriturum prorsus seruabis uxorem. ⁹Habes solitudinis plenam fiduciam, habes capax necessarii facinoris otium. Nam quod nemo nouit, paene non fit.'

4 ¹Repentino malo perturbatus adolescens, quanquam tale facinus protinus   239 H
exhorruisset, non tamen negationis intempestiua seueritate putauit exasperandum, sed cautae promissionis dilatione leniendum. ²Ergo prolixe pollice[re]tur et, bonum caperet animum refectionique se ac saluti redderet, impendio suadet, donec patris aliqua profectione liberum uoluptati concederetur spatium, statimque se refert a noxio conspectu nouercae. ³Et tam magnam domus cladem ratus indigere consilio pleniore ad quendam compertae grauitatis educatorem senem protinus refert. Ne<c> quicquam diutina deliberatione tam salubre uisum quam fuga celeri procellam Fortunae saeuientis euadere. ⁴Sed impatiens uel exiguae dilationis mulier ficta qualibet causa confestim marito miris persuadet artibus ad longissime dissitas festinare uillulas. ⁵Quo facto maturatae spei uaesania praeceps promissae libidinis flagitat uadimonium. Sed iuuenis, modo istud modo aliud causae faciens, execrabilem frustratur eius conspectum, quoad illa, nuntiorum uarietate pollicitationem sibi denegatam manifesto perspiciens, mobilitate lubrica nefarium amorem ad longe deterius transtulisset odium. ⁶Et adsumpto statim nequissimo et ad omne facinus emancipato quodam dotali seruulo perfidiae suae consilia communicat; nec quicquam melius uidetur quam uita miserum priuare iuuenem. Ergo missus continuo furcifer uenenum praesentarium comparat idque uino diligenter dilutum insontis priuigni praeparat exitio.

5 ¹Ac dum de oblationis opportunitate secum noxii deliberant homines, forte fortuna puer ille iunior, proprius pessimae feminae filius, post   240 H
matutinum laborem studiorum domum se recipiens, prandio iam capto sitiens repertum uini poculum, in quo uenenum latebat inclusum, nescius fraudis occultae continuo perduxit <h>austu. ²Atque ubi fratri suo paratam mortem ebibit, exanimis terrae procumbit, il[l]icoque repentina pueri pernicie paedagogus commotus ululabili clamore matrem

totamque ciet familiam. Iamque cognito casu noxiae potionis uarie quisque praesentium auctores insimulabant extremi facinoris. ³Sed dira illa femina et malitiae nouercalis exemplar unicum non acerba filii morte, non parricidii conscientia, non infortunio domus, non luctu mariti uel aerumna funeris commota cladem familiae <in> uindictae compendium traxit, missoque protinus cursore, qui uianti marito domus expugnationem nuntiaret, ac mox eodem ocius ab itinere regresso personata nimia temeritate insimulat priuigni ueneno filium suum interceptum. ⁴Et hoc quidem non adeo mentiebatur, quod iam destinatam iuueni mortem praeuenisset puer, sed fratrem iuniorem fingebat ideo priuigni scelere peremptum, quod eius prob<r>osae libidini, qua se comprimere temptauerat, noluisse<t> succumbere. ⁵Nec tamen <tam> inmanibus contenta mendacis addebat sibi quoque ob detectum flagitium eundem illum gladium comminari. Tunc infelix duplici filiorum morte percussus magnis aerumnarum procellis aestuat. ⁶Nam et iuniorem incoram sui funerari uidebat et alterum ob incestum parricidiumque capitis scilicet damnatum iri certo sciebat. Ad hoc uxoris dilectae nimium mentitis lamentationibus ad extremum subolis imp<el>lebatur odium.

6 ¹Vixdum pompae funebres et sepultura filii fuerant explicatae, et statim 241 H ab ipso eius rogo senex infelix, ora sua recentibus adhuc rigans lacrimis trahensque cinere sordentem canitiem, foro se festinus immittit. ²Atque ibi tum fletu, tum precibus genua etiam decurionum contingens nescius fraudium pessimae mulieris in exitium reliqui filii plenis operabatur affectibus: illum incestum paterno thalamo, illum parricidam fraterno exitio et in comminata nouercae caede sicarium. ³Tanta denique miseratione tantaque indignatione curiam, sed et plebem maerens inflammauerat, ut remoto iudicandi taedio et accusationis manifestis probationibus et responsionis meditatis ambagibus cuncti conclamarint lapidibus obrutum publicum malum publice uindicari. ⁴Magistratus interim metu periculi proprii, ne de paruis indignationis elementis ad exitium disciplinae ciuitatisque seditio procederet, partim decuriones deprecari, partim populares compescere, ut rite et more maiorum iudicio reddito et utrimquesecus allegationibus examinatis ciuiliter sententia promeretur nec ad instar barbaricae feritatis uel tyrannicae impotentiae damnaretur aliquis inauditus et in pace placida tam dirum saeculo proderetur exemplum.

7 ¹Placuit salubre consilium et ilico iussus praeco pronuntiat, patres in curiam conuenirent. Quibus protinus dignitatis iure consueta loca residentibus rursum praeconis uocatu primus accusator incedit. ²Tunc demum clamatus inducitur etiam reus, et exemplo legis Atticae Martiique iudicii causae patronis denuntiat praeco neque principia dicere 242 H neque miserationem commouere. ³Haec ad istum modum gesta compluribus mutuo sermocinantibus cognoui. ⁴Quibus autem uerbis accusator urserit, quibus rebus diluerit reus ac prorsus orationes altercationesque neque ipse absens apud praesepium scire neque ad uos, quae ignoraui, possum enuntiare, sed quae plane comperi, ad istas litteras proferam.

⁵Simul enim finita est dicentium contentio, ueritatem criminum fidemque probationibus certis instrui nec suspicionibus tantam coniecturam permitti placuit ⁶atque illum promptissimum seruum, qui solus haec ita gesta esse scire diceretur, sisti modis omnibus oportere. ⁷Nec tantillum cruciarius ille uel fortuna tam magni iudicii uel confertae conspectu curiae uel certe noxia conscientia sua deterritus, quae ipse finxerat, quasi uera adseuerare atque adserere incipit: ⁸quod se uocasset indignatus fastidio nouercae iuuenis, quod, ulciscens iniuriam, filii eius mandauerit necem, quod promisisset grande silentii praemium, ⁹quod recusanti mortem sit comminatus, quod uenenum sua manu temperatum dandum fratri reddiderit, quod ad criminis probationem reseruatum poculum neclexisse suspicatus sua postremum manu porrexerit puero. ¹⁰Haec — eximia enim ad ueritatis imaginem — uerberone illo simula<ta> cum trepidatione perferente finitum est iudicium.

8 ¹Nec quisquam decurionum tam aequus remanserat iuueni, quin eum 243 H
euidenter noxae compertum insui culleo pronuntiaret. ²Cum iam sententiae pares, cunctorum stilis ad unum sermonem congruentibus, ex more perpetuo in urnam aeream deberent coici, quo semel conditis calculis, iam cum rei fortuna transacto, nihil postea commutari licebat, sed mancipabatur potestas capitis in manum carnificis, unus e curia senior prae ceteris compertae fidi atque auctoritatis praecipuae medicus orificium urnae manu contegens, ne quis mitteret calculum temere, haec ad ordinem pertulit: ³'Quod aetatis sum, uobis adprobatum me uixisse gaudeo, nec patiar falsis criminibus petito reo manifestum homicidium perpetrari nec uos, qui iure iurando adstricti iudicatis, inductos seruuli mendacio peierare. ⁴Ipse non possum calcata numinum religione conscientiam meam fallens perperam pronuntiare. Ergo, ut res est, de me cognoscite.

9 ¹Furcifer iste, uenenum praesentarium comparare sollicitus centumque aureos solidos offerens pretium, me non olim conuenerat, quod aegroto cuidam dicebat necessarium, qui morbi inextricabilis ueterno uehementer implicitus uitae se cruciatui subtrahere gestiret. ²At ego, perspiciens malum istum uerberonem blaterantem atque inconcinne causificantem certusque aliquod moliri flagitium, dedi quidem potionem, dedi; ³sed futurae quaestioni praecauens non statim pretium, quod offerebatur, accepi, sed "ne forte aliquis", inquam, "istorum, quos offers, aureorum nequam uel adulter repperiatur, in hoc ipso sacculo conditos eos anulo tuo praenota, donec altera die nummulario praesente comprobentur". ⁴Sic inductus signauit pecuniam, quam exinde, ut iste repraesentatus est 244 H
iudicio, iussi de meis aliquem curriculo taberna promptam adferre et en ecce perlatam coram exibeo. ⁵Videat et suum sigillum recognoscat. Nam quem ad modum eius ueneni frater insimulari potest, quod iste comparauerit?'

10 ¹Ingens exinde uerberonem corripit trepidatio et in uicem humani coloris succedit pallor infernus perque uniuersa membra frigidus sudor emanabat: ²tunc pedes incertis alternationibus commouere, modo hanc, modo

illam capitis partem scalpere et ore semiclauso balbuttiens nescio quas afannas effutire, ut eum nemo prorsus a culpa uacuum merito crederet. Sed reualescente rursus astutia constantissime negare et accersere mendacii non desinit medicum. ³Qui praeter iudicii religionem cum fidem suam coram lacerari uideret, multiplicato studio uerberonem illum contendit redarguere, donec iussu magistratuum ministeria publica contrectatis nequissimi serui manibus anulum ferreum deprehensum cum signo sacculi conferunt, quae comparatio praecedentem roborauit suspicionem. ⁴Nec rota uel eculeus more Graecorum tormentis eius apparata iam deerant, sed offirmatus mira praesumptione nullis uerberibus ac ne ipso quidem succumbit igni.

11 ¹Tum medicus: 'Non patiar', inquit, 'hercules, non patiar uel contra fas de innocente isto iuuene supplicium uos sumere uel hunc ludificato nostro iudicio poenam noxii facinoris euadere'. Dabo enim rei praesentis euidens argumentum. ²Nam cum uenenum peremptorium comparare pessimus iste gestiret nec meae sectae crederem conuenire causas ulli praebere mortis nec exitio, sed saluti hominum medicinam quaesitam esse didicissem, uerens, ne, si daturum me negassem, intempestiua repulsa uiam sceleri subministrarem et ab alio quopiam exitiabilem mercatus hic potionem uel postremum gladio uel quouis telo nefas inchoatum perficeret, dedi uenenum, sed somniferum, mandragoram 245 H illum grauedinis compertae famosum et morti simillimi soporis efficacem. ³Nec mirum desperatissimum istum latronem certum extremae poenae, quae more maiorum in eum competit, cruciatus istos ut leuiores facile tolerare. Sed si uere puer meis temperatam manibus sumpsit potionem, uiuit et quiescit et dormit et protinus marcido sopore discusso remeabit ad diem lucidam. Quod si ue‹re› peremptus est, si morte praeuentus est, quaeratis licet causas mortis eius alias.'

12 ¹Ad istum modum seniore adorante placuit, et itur confestim magna cum festinatione ad illud sepulchrum, quo corpus pueri depositum iacebat. Nemo de curia, de optimatibus nemo ac ne de ipso quidem populo quisquam, qui non illuc curiose confluxerit. ²Ecce pater, suis ipse manibus coperculo capuli remoto, commodum discusso mortifero sopore surgentem postliminio mortis deprehendit filium eumque complexus artissime, uerbis impar praesenti gaudio, producit ad populum. ³Atque ut erat adhuc feralibus amiculis instrictus atque obditus deportatur ad iudicium puer. ⁴Iamque liquido serui nequissimi atque mulieris nequioris patefactis sceleribus procedit in medium nuda Veritas et nouercae quidem perpetuum indicitur exilium, seruus uero patibulo suffigitur et omnium consensu bono medico sinuntur aurei, opportuni somni pretium. ⁵Et illius quidem senis famosa atque fab‹ul›osa fortuna prouidentiae diuinae condignum accepit exitum, qui momento modico, immo puncto exiguo, post orbitatis periculum adulescentium duorum pater repente factus est.

13 ¹At ego tunc temporis talibus fatorum fluctibus uolutabar. ²Miles ille, 246 H qui me nullo uendente comparauerat et sine pretio suum fecerat, tribuni

sui praecepto debitum sustinens obsequium, litteras ad magnum scriptas principem Romam uersus perlaturus, uicinis me quibusdam duobus seruis fratribus undecim denariis uendidit. His erat diues admodum dominus. ³At illorum alter pistor dulciarius, qui panes et mellita concinnabat edulia, alter cocus, qui sapidissimis intrimentis sucuum pulmenta condita uapore mollibat. ⁴Unico illi contubernio communem uitam sustinebant meque ad uasa illa compluria gestanda praedestinarant, quae domini regiones plusculas pererrantis uariis usibus erant necessaria. ⁵Adsciscor itaque inter duos illos fratres tertius contubernalis, haud ullo tempore tam beniuolam Fortunam expertus. ⁶Nam uespera post opiparas cenas earumque splendidissimos apparatus multas numero partes in cellulam suam mei solebant reportare domini: ille porcorum, pullorum, piscium et cuiusce modi pulmentorum largissimas reliquias, hic panes, crustula, *l*ucunculos, hamos, lacertulos et plura scitamenta mellita. ⁷Qui cum se refecturi clausa cellula balneas petissent, oblatis ego diuinitus dapibus adfatim saginabar. Nec enim tam stultus eram tamque uere asinus, ut dulcissimis illis relictis cibis cenarem asperrimum faenum.

14 ¹Et diu quidem pulcherrime mihi furatrinae procedebat artificium, quippe adhuc timide et satis parce subripienti de tam multis pauciora nec illis fraudes ullas in asino suspicantibus. ²At ubi fiducia latendi 247 H pleniore capta partes opimas quasque deuorabam et iucundiora eligens abligurribam dulcia, suspicio non exilis fratrum pupugit animos et quanquam de me nihil etiam tum tale crederent, tamen cotidiani damni studiose uestigabant reum. ³Illi uero postremo etiam mutuo sese rapinae turpissimae criminabantur, iamque curam diligentiorem et acriorem custodelam et dinumerationem adhibebant partium. Tandem denique rupta uerecundia sic alter alterum compellat: ⁴'A*t* istud iam neque aequum ac ne humanum quidem cotidie *te* partes electiores surripere atque iis diuenditis peculium latenter augere, de reliquis aequam uindicare diuisionem. ⁵Si tibi denique societas ista displicet, possumus omnia quidem cetera fratres manere, ab isto tamen nexu communionis discedere. Nam uideo in immensum damni procedentem querelam nutrire nobis immanem discordiam.' ⁶Subicit alius: 'Laudo istam tuam mehercules et ipse constantiam, quod cotidie furatis clanculo partibus praeuenisti querimoniam, quam diutissime sustinens tacitus ingemescebam, ne uiderer rapinae sordidae meum fratrem arguere. ⁷Sed bene, quod utrimquesecus sermone prolato iacturae <re>medium quaeritur, ne silentio procedens simul[a]tas Eteocleas nobis contentiones pariat.'

15 ¹His et similibus altercati conuiciis deierantur utrique nullam se prorsus fraudem, nullam denique subreptionem factitasse, sed plane debere 248 H cunctis artibus communis dispendii latronem inquiri; ²nam neque asinum, qui solus interesset, talibus cibis adfici posse et tamen cotidie past*u*s electiles conparere nusquam nec utique cellulam suam tam immanes inuolare muscas, ut olim Harpyiae fuere, quae diripiebant Fineias dapes.

³Interea liberalibus cenis inescatus et humanis adfatim cibis saginatus

corpus obesa pinguitie compleueram, corium aruina suculenta molliueram, pilum liberali nitore nutrieram. ⁴Sed iste corporis mei decor pudori peperit grande dedecus. Insolita namque tergoris uastitate commoti, faenum prorsus intactum cotidie remanere cernentes, iam totos ad me dirigunt animos. ⁵Et hora consueta uelut balneas petituri clausis ex more foribus per quandam modicam cauernam rimantur me passim expositis epulis inhaerentem. Nec ulla cura iam damni sui habita mirati monstruosas asini delicias risu maximo dirumpuntur uocatoque uno et altero ac dein pluribus conseruis demonstrant infandam memoratu hebetis iumenti gulam. ⁶Tantus denique ac tam liberalis cachinnus cunctos inuaserat, ut ad aures quoque praetereun[c]tis perueniret domini.

16 ¹Sciscitatus denique, quid bonum rideret familia, cognito quod res erat, ipse quoque per idem prospiciens foramen delectatur exumie; ac dehinc risu ipse quoque latissimo adusque intestinorum dolorem redactus, iam patefacto cubiculo proxime consistens coram arbitratur. ²Nam et ego tandem ex aliqua parte mollius mihi renidentis Fortunae contemplatus facie<m>, gaudio praesentium fiduciam mihi subministrante, nec tantillum commotus securus esitabam, ³quoad nouitate spectaculi laetus dominus aedium duci me iussit, immo uero suis etiam ipse manibus ad   249 H
triclinium perduxit mensaque posita omne genus edulium solidorum et inlibata fercula iussit adponi. ⁴At ego quanquam iam *be*llule suffarcinatus, gratiosum commendatioremque me tamen ei facere cupiens esurienter exibitas escas adpetebam. ⁵Nam et, quid potissimum abhorreret asino, excogitantes scrupulose, ad explorandam mansuetudinem id offerebant mihi, carnes lasere infectas, altilia pipere inspersa, pisces exotico iure perfusos. ⁶Interim conuiuium summo risu personabat. Quidam denique praesens scurrula: 'Date', inquit, 'sodali huic quippiam meri.' ⁷Quod dictum dominus secutus: 'Non adeo', respondit, 'absurde iocatus es, furcifer; ualde enim fieri potest, ut contubernalis noster poculum quoque mulsi libenter adpetat.' ⁸Et 'heus', ait, 'puer, lautum diligenter ecce illum aureum cantharum mulso contempera et offer pa<ra>sito meo; simul, quod ei praebiberim, commoneto.'

⁹Ingens exin oborta est epulonum expectatio. Nec ulla tamen ego ratione conterritus, otiose ac satis genialiter contorta in modum linguae postrema labia grandissimum illum calicem uno haustu per<h>ausi. Et clamor exurgit consona uoce cunctorum salute me prosequentium.

17 ¹Magno denique delibutus gaudio dominus, uocatis seruis suis, emptoribus meis, iubet quadruplum restitui pretium meque cuidam acceptissimo liberto suo et satis peculiato magna praefatus diligentia tradidit. ²Qui me satis humane satisque comiter nutriebat et, quo se patrono commendatiorem faceret, studiosissime uoluptates eius per meas argutias instruebat. ³Et primum me quidem mensam accumbere suffixo cubito, dein adluctari et etiam saltare sublatis primoribus pedibus perdocuit, ⁴quo<d>que   250 H
esset adprime mirabile, uerbis nutum commodare, ut quod nollem relato, quod uellem deiecto capite monstrarem, sitiensque pocillatore[m] respecto, ciliis alterna coniuens, bibere flagitarem. ⁵Atque haec omnia

perfacile oboediebam, quae nullo etiam monstrante scilicet facerem. Sed
uerebar, ne, si forte sine magistro humano ritu ederem pleraque, rati
scaeuum praesagium portendere[m] uelut monstrum ostentumque me
obtruncatum uulturiis opimum pabulum redderent. ⁶Iamque rumor
publice crebruerat, quo conspectum atque famigerabilem meis miris
artibus effeceram dominum: 'hic est, qui sodalem conuiuamque possidet
asinum luctantem, asinum saltantem, asinum uoces humanas intellegentem, sensum nutibus exprimentem.'

18 ¹Sed prius est, ut uobis, quod initio facere debueram, uel nunc saltem
referam, quis iste uel unde fuerit: Thiasus – hoc enim nomine meus
nuncupabatur dominus – oriundus patria Corintho, quod caput est totius
Achaiae prouinciae, ut eius prosapia atque dignitas postulabat, gradatim
permensis honoribus quinquennali magistratui fuerat destinatus et ut
splendori capessendorum responderet fascium, munus gladiatorium
triduani spectaculi pollicitus latius munificentiam suam porrigebat.
²Denique gloriae publicae studio tunc Thessaliam etiam accesserat
nobilissimas feras et famosos inde gladiatores comparaturus, iamque ex
arbitrio dispositis coemptisque omnibus domuitionem parabat. ³Spretis
luculentis illis suis uehiculis ac posthabitis decoris praedarum carpentis, 251 H
quae partim contecta, partim reuelata frustra nouissimis trahebantur
consequiis, equis etiam Thessalicis et aliis iumentis Gallicanis, quibus
generosa suboles perhibet pretiosam dignitatem, ⁴me phaleris aureis et
fucatis ephippiis et purpureis tapetis et frenis argenteis et pictilibus
balteis et tintinnabulis perargutis exornatum ipse residens amantissime
nonnumquam comissimis adfatur sermonibus atque inter alia pleraque
summe se delectari profitebatur, quod haberet in me simul et conuiuam
et uectorem.

19 ¹At ubi partim terrestri, partim maritimo itinere confecto Corinthum
accessimus, magnae ciuium turbae confluebant, ut mihi uidebatur, non
tantum Thiasi dantes honori quam mei conspectus cupientes. Nam tanta
etiam ibidem de me fama peruaserat, ut non mediocri quaestui praeposito illi meo fuerim. ² Qui cum multos uideret nimio fauore lusus meos
spectare gestientes, obserata fore atque singulis eorum sorsus admi<s>sis, stipes acceptans non paruas summulas diurnas corradere
consuerat. ³Fuit in illo conuenticulo matrona quaedam pollens et opulens. Quae more ceterorum uisum meum mercata ac dehinc multiformibus ludicris delectata per admirationem adsiduam paulatim in
admirabilem mei cupidinem incidit; nec ullam uaesanae libidini medelam capiens ad instar asinariae P[h]asiphaae complexus meos ardenter
expectabat. ⁴Grandi denique praemio cum altore meo depecta est noctis
unius concubitum; at ille nequaquam <curans an ei quicquam> posset 252 H
de me suaue prouenire, lucro suo tantum contentus, adnuit.

20 ¹Iam denique cenati e triclinio domini decesseramus et iam dudum
praestolantem cubiculo meo matronam offendimus. Dii boni, qualis ille
quanque praeclarus apparatus! ²Quattuor eunuchi confestim puluillis
compluribus uentose tumentibus pluma delicata terrestrem nobis cubi-

43

tum praestruunt, sed et stragula ueste auro ac murice Tyrio depicta probe consternunt ac desuper breuibus admodum, sed satis copiosis puluillis, aliis nimis modicis, quis maxillas et ceruices delicatae mulieres suffulcire consuerunt, superstruunt. ³Nec dominae uoluptates diutina sua praesentia morati, clausis cubiculi foribus facessunt. At intus cerei praeclara micantes luce nocturnas nobis tenebras inalbabant.

21 ¹Tunc ipsa cuncto prorsus spoliata tegmine, taenia quoque, qua decoras deuinxerat papillas, lumen propter adsistens, de stagneo uasculo multo sese perungit oleo balsamo meque indidem largissime perfricat, sed multo tanta impensius cura etiam nares perfundit meas. ²Tunc exosculata pressule, non qualia in lupanari solent basiola iactari uel meretricium poscinummia uel aduentorum nega<n>tinummia, sed pura atque sincera instruit et blandissimos adfatus: ³'Amo' et 'Cupio' et 'Te solum diligo' et 'Sine te iam uiuere nequeo' et cetera, quis mulieres et alios inducunt et suas testantur adfectationes, capistroque me prehensum more, quo didiceram, reclinat facile, ⁴quippe cum nil noui nihilque difficile facturus mihi uiderer, praesertim post tantum temporis tam formonsae mulieris cupientis amplexus obiturus; nam et uino pulcherrimo atque copioso memet madefeceram · et ungento flagrantissimo prolubium libidinis suscitaram. 253 H

22 ¹Sed angebar plane non exili metu reputans, quem ad modum tantis tamque magnis cruribus possem delicatam matronam inscendere uel tam lucida tamque tenera et lacte ac melle confecta membra duris ungulis complecti labiasque modicas ambroseo rore purpurantes tam amplo ore tamque enormi et saxeis dentibus deformi[s] sauiari, nouissime quo pacto, quanquam ex unguiculis perpruriscens, mulier tam uastum genitale susciperet: ²Heu me, qui dirrupta nobili femina bestiis obiectus munus instructurus sim mei domini! Molles interdum uoculas et adsidua sauia et dulces gannitus commorsicantibus oculis iterabat illa, et in summa: ³'Teneo te', inquit, 'teneo, meum palumbulum, meum passarem' et cum dicto uanas fuisse cogitationes meas ineptumque monstrat metum. Artissime namque complexa totum me prorsus, sed totum recepit. ⁴Illa uero quotiens ei parcens nates recellebam, accedens totiens nisu rabido et spinam prehendens meam adpliciore nexu inhaerebat, ut hercules etiam deesse mihi aliquid ad supplendam eius libidinem crederem nec Minotauri matrem frustra delectatam putarem adultero mugiente. ⁵Iamque operosa et peruigili nocte transacta, uitata luci[u]s conscientia facessit mulier condicto pari noctis futurae pretio. 254 H

23 ¹Nec grauate magister meus uoluptates ex eius arbitrio largiebatur partim mercedes amplissimas acceptando, partim nouum spectaculum domino praeparando. Incunctanter ei denique libidinis nostrae totam detegit scaenam. At ille liberto magnifice munerato destinat me spectaculo publico. ²Et quoniam neque egregia illa uxor mea propter dignitatem neque prorsus ulla alia inueniri p<o>tuerat grandi praemio, uilis acquiritur aliqua sententia praesidis bestiis addicta, quae mecum incoram publicam populi caueam frequentaret. Eius poenae talem cognoue-

ram fabulam.

³Maritum habuit, cuius pater peregre proficiscens mandauit uxori suae, matri eiusdem iuuenis - quod enim sarcina praegnationis oneratam eam relinquebat - ut, si sexus sequioris edidisset fetum, protinus quod esset editum necaretur. ⁴At illa per abs[tin]entia<m> mariti nata[m] puella[m] insita matribus pietate praeuenta desciuit ab obsequio mariti eamque prodidit uicinis alumnandam, regressoque iam marito natam necatamque nuntiauit. ⁵Sed ubi flos aetatis nuptialem uirgini diem flagitabat nec ignaro marito dotare filiam pro natalibus quibat, quod solum potuit, filio suo tacitum secretum aperuit. Nam et oppido uerebatur, ne quo casu, caloris iuuenalis impetu lapsus, nescius nesciam sororem incurreret. ⁶Sed pietatis spectatae iuuenis et matris obsequium et sororis officium religiose dispensat et arc[h]anis domus uenerabilis silentii custodiae traditis, plebeiam facie tenus praetendens humanitatem, sic necessarium sanguinis sui munus adgreditur, ut desolatam uicinam puellam parentumque praesidio uiduatam domus suae tutela receptaret ac mox artissimo multumque sibi dilecto contubernali, largitus de proprio dotem, liberalissime traderet.

255 H

24 ¹Sed haec bene atque optime plenaque cum sanctimonia disposita feralem Fortunae nutum latere non potuerunt, cuius instinctu domum iuuenis protinus se direxit saeua Riualitas. ²Et ilico haec eadem uxor eius, quae nunc bestiis propter haec ipsa fuerat addicta, coepit puellam uelut aemulam tori succubamque primo suspicari, dehinc detestari, dehinc crudelissimis laqueis mortis insidiari. Tale denique comminiscitur facinus.

³Anulo mariti surrepto rus profecta mittit quendam seruulum sibi quidem fidelem, sed de ipsa Fide[m] pessime merentem, qui puellae nuntiaret, quod eam iuuenis profectus ad uillulam uocaret ad sese, addito, ut sola et sine ullo comite quam maturissime perueniret. ⁴Et ne qua forte nasceretur ueniendi cunctatio, tradit anulum marito subtractum, qui monstratus fidem uerbis adstipularetur. At illa mandatu fratris obsequens - hoc enim nomen sola sciebat - respecto etiam signo eius, quod offerebatur, nauiter, ut praeceptum fuerat, incomitata festinat. ⁵Sed ubi fraudis extremae lapsa decipulo laqueos insidiarum accessit tunc illa uxor egregia sororem mariti libidinosae furiae stimulis efferata primum quidem nudam flagris ultime uerberat, dehinc, quod res erat, clamantem quo<d>que frustra paelicatus indignatione bulliret fratrisque nomen saepius iterantem uelut mentitam atque cuncta fingentem titione candenti inter media femina detruso crudelissime necauit.

256 H

25 ¹Tunc acerbae mortis exciti nuntiis frater et maritus accurrunt uariisque lamentationibus defletam puellam tradunt sepulturae. Nec iuuenis sororis suae mortem tam miseram et quae minime par erat inlatam aequo tolerare quiuit animo, sed medullitus dolore commotus acerrimaeque bili<s> noxio furore perfusus exin flagrantissimis febribus ardebat, ut ipsi quoque iam medela uideretur esse necessaria. ²Sed uxor, quae iam pridem nomen uxoris cum fide perdiderat, medicum conuenit quendam

45

notae perfidiae, qui iam multarum palmarum spectatus proeliis magna dexterae suae tropaea numerabat, eique protinus quinquaginta promittit sestertia, ut ille quidem momentarium uenenum uenderet, illa autem emeret mortem mariti sui. ³Quo com*pec*to simulatur necessaria praecor- 257 H diis leniendis bilique subtrahendae illa praenobilis potio, quam sacram doctiores nominant, sed in eius uice<m> subditur alia Proserpinae sacra Saluti. Iamque praesente familia et nonnullis amicis et adfinibus aegroto medicus poculum probe temperatum manu sua porrigebat.

26 ¹Sed audax illa mulier, ut simul et conscium sceleris amoliretur et quam desponderat pecuniam lucraretur, coram detento calice: 'Non prius', inquit, 'medicorum optime, non prius carissimo mihi marito trades istam potionem quam de ea bonam partem hauseris ipse. ²Unde enim scio, an noxium in ea lateat uenenum? Quae res utique te tam prudentem tamque doctum uirum nequaquam offendit, si religiosa uxor circa salutem mariti sollicita necessariam adfero pietatem.' ³Qua mira desperatione truculentae feminae repente perturbatus medicus excussusque toto consilio et ob angustiam temporis spatio cogitandi priuatus, antequam trepidatione aliqua uel cunctatione ipsa daret malae conscientiae suspicionem, indidem de po[r]tione gustauit ampliter. ⁴Quam fidem secutus adulescens etiam, sumpto calice, quod offerebatur hausit. Ad istum modum praesenti transacto negotio medicus quam celerrime domum remeabat, salutifera potione pestem praecedentis ueneni festinans extinguere. ⁵Nec eum obstinatione sacrilega, qua semel coeperat, truculenta mulier ungue latius a se discedere passa est – 'priusquam', inquit, 'digesta potione medicinae prou*e*ntus appareat' -, sed aegre precibus et obtestationibus eius multum ac diu fatigata tandem abire concessit. ⁶Interdum perniciem 258 H caecam totis uisceribus furentem medullae penitus adtraxerant, multum denique saucius et grauedine somnulenta iam demersus domum peruadit aegerrime. ⁷Vixque enarratis cunctis ad uxorem mandato, saltem promissum mercedem mortis geminatae deposceret, sic elisus uiolenter spectatissimus medicus effundit spiritum.

27 ¹Nec ille tamen iuuenis diutius uitam tenuerat, sed inter fictas mentitasque lacrimas uxoris pari casu mortis fuerat extinctus. Iamque eo sepulto, paucis interiectis diebus, quis feralia mortuis litantur obsequia, uxor medici pretium geminae mortis petens aderat. ²Sed mulier usquequaque sui similis, fidei supprimens faciem, praetendens imaginem, blandicule respondit et omnia prolixe adcumulateque pollicetur et statutum praemium sine mora se redditturam constituit, modo pauxillum de ea potione largiri sibi uellet a*d* incepti negotii persecutione<m>. ³Quid pluribus? Laqueis fraudium pessimarum uxor inducta medici facile consentit et, quo se gratiorem locupleti feminae faceret, properiter domo petita<m> totam prorsus ueneni pyxidem mulieri tradidit. Quae grandem scelerum nancta materiam longe lateque cruentas suas manus porrigit.

28 ¹Habebat filiam paruulam de marito, quem nuper necauerat. Huic infantulae quod leges necessariam patris successionem deferrent, sustinebat aegerrime inhiansque toto filiae patrimonio imminebat et capiti.

²Ergo certa defunctorum liberorum matres sceleratas hereditates excipere, talem parentem praebuit, qualem exhibuerat uxorem, prandioque commento pro tempore et uxorem medici simul et suam filiam ueneno eodem percutit. ³Sed paruulae quidem tenuem spiritum et delicata ac tenera praecordia conficit protinus uirus infestum, at uxor medici, dum noxiis ambagibus pulmones eius pererrat tempestas detestabilis potionis, primum suspicata, quod res erat, mox urgente spiritu iam certo certior contendit ad ipsam praesidis domum magnoque fidem eius protestata clamore et populo concitato tumultu, utpote tam immania detectura flagitia, efficit, statim sibi simul et domus et aures praesidis patefierent. ⁴Iamque ab ipso exordio crudelissimae mulieris cunctis atrocitatibus diligenter expositis, repente mentis nubilo turbine correpta semihiantes adhuc compressit labias et, attritu dentium longo stridore reddito, ante ipsos praesidis pedes exanimis corruit. ₅Nec ille, uir alioquin exercitus, tam multiforme facinus exc*etrae* uenenatae dilatione languida passus marcescere confestim cubiculariis mulieris adtractis ui tormentorum ueritatem eruit atque illa<m>, minus quidem quam merebatur, sed quod dignus cruciatus alius excogitari non poterat, certe bestiis obiciendam pronuntiauit.

29 ¹Talis mulieris publicitus matrimonium confarraturus ingentique angore 260 H oppido suspensus expectabam diem muneris, saepius quidem mortem mihimet[u] uolens consciscere, priusquam scelerosae mulieris contagio macularer uel infamia publici spectaculi depudescerem. Sed priuatus humana manu, priuatus digitis, ungula rutunda atque mutila gladium stringere nequaquam poteram. ²Plane tenui specula solabar clades ultimas, quod ue*r* in ipso ortu iam gemmulis floridis cuncta depingeret et iam purpureo nitore prata uestiret et commodum dirrupto spineo tegmine spirantes cinnameos odores promicarent rosae, quae me priori meo Lucio redderent.

³Dies ecce muneri destinatus aderat: ad conseptum caueae prosequente populo pompatico fauore deducor. Ac dum ludicris scaenicorum choreis primitiae spectaculi dedicantur, tantisper ante portam constitutus pabulum laetissimi graminis, quod in ipso germinabat aditu, libens adfectabam, subinde curiosos oculos patente porta spectaculi prospectu gratissimo reficiens. ⁴Nam puelli puellaeque uirenti florentes aetatula, forma conspicui, ueste nitidi, incessu gestuosi, Graecanica<m> saltaturi pyrricam dispositis ordinationibus decoros ambitus inerrabant nunc in orbe<m> rotatum flexuosi, nunc in obliquam seriem conexi et in quadratum patorem cuneati et in cateruae discidium separati. ⁵At ubi discursus reciproci multinod*as* ambages tubae terminalis cantus expli- 261 H cuit, au*la*eo subducto et complicitis siparis scaena disponitur.

30 ¹Erat mons ligneus, ad instar incliti montis illius, quem uates Homerus Idaeum cecinit, sublimi[s] instructus fabrica, consitus uirectis et uiuis arboribus, summo cacumine, de manibus fabri fonte manante, fluuialis aquas eliquans. ²Capellae pauculae tondebant herbulas et in modum Paridis Frygii pastoris, barbaricis amiculis umeris def<l>uentibus,

pulchre indusiatus adulescens, aurea tiara contecto capite, pecuarium simulabat magisterium. ³Adest luculentus puer nudus, nisi quod ephebica chlamida sinistrum tegebat umerum, ⁴flauis crinibus usquequaque conspicuus, et inter comas eius aureae pinnulae cognatione simili sociatae prominebant; quem caduceum et uirgula Mercurium indicabant.⁵Is saltatorie procurrens malumque bracteis inauratum dextra gerens <ei>, qui Paris uidebatur, porrigit, quid mandaret Iuppiter, nutu significans et protinus gradum scitule referens e conspectu facessit. ⁶Insequitur puella uultu honesta in deae Iunonis speciem similis: nam et caput stringebat diadema candida, ferebat et sceptrum. ⁷Inrupit alia, quam putares Mineruam, caput contecta fulgenti galea, et oleaginea corona tegebatur ipsa galea, clypeum attollens et hastam quatiens et qualis illa, cum pugnat.

31 ¹Super has introcessit alia, uisendo decore praepollens, gratia coloris ambrosei designans Venerem, qualis fuit Venus, cum fuit uirgo, nudo et intecto corpore perfectam formonsitatem professa, nisi quod tenui pallio bombycino inumbrabat spectabilem pubem. ²Quam quidem laciniam   262 H
curiosulus uentus satis amanter nunc lasciuiens reflabat, ut dimota pateret flos aetatulae, nunc luxurians aspirabat, ut adhaerens pressule membrorum uoluptatem grafice <de>li[ci]niaret. Ipse autem color deae diuersus in speciem, corpus candidum, quod caelo demeat, amictus caerulus, quod mari remeat. ³Iam singulas uirgines, quae deae putabantur, <sui comitabantur> comites, Iunonem quidem Castor et Pollux, quorum capita cassides ouatae stellarum apicibus insignes contegebant, sed et isti Castores erant scaenici pueri. ⁴Haec puella uarios modulos Iastia concinente tibia procedens quieta et inadfectata gesticulatione nutibus honestis pastori pollicetur, si sibi praemium decoris addixisset, et sese regnum totius Asiae tributuram. ⁵At illam, quam cultus armorum Mineruam fecerat, duo pueri muniebant, proeliaris deae comites armigeri, Terror et Metus, nudis insultantes gladiis. At pone tergum tibicen <D>orium canebat bellicosum et permiscens bombis grauibus *tinni*tus acutos in modum tubae saltationis agilis uigorem suscitabat. ⁶Haec inquieto capite et oculis in aspectu[m] minacibus citato et intorto genere gesticulationis alacer demonstrabat Paridi, si sibi formae uictoriam tradidisset, fortem tropaeisque bellorum inclitum suis adminiculis futurum.

32 ¹Venus ecce cum magno fauore caueae in ipso meditullio scaenae,   263 H
circumfuso populo laetissimorum paruulorum, dulce subridens constitit amoene: illos teretes et lacteos puellos diceres tu Cupidines ueros de caelo uel mari commodum inuolasse; nam et pinnulis et sagittulis et habitu cetero formae praeclare congruebant et uelut nuptialis epulas obiturae dominae coruscis praelucebant facibus. ²Et influunt innuptarum puellarum decorae suboles, hinc Gratiae gratissimae, inde Horae pulcherrimae, quae iaculis floris serti et soluti deam suam propitiantes scitissimum construxerant chorum, dominae uoluptatum ueris coma blandientes. Iam tibiae multiforabiles cantus Lydios dulciter consonant.

³Quibus spectatorum pectora suaue mulcentibus, longe suauior Venus placide commoueri cunctantique lente uestigio et leniter fluctuante spi[n]nula[s] et sensim adnutante capite coepit incedere mollique tibiarum sono delicatis respondere gestibus et nunc mite coniuentibus, nunc acre comminantibus gestire pupulis et nonnumquam saltare solis oculis. ⁴Haec ut primum ante iudicis conspectum facta est, nisu brachiorum polliceri uidebatur, si fuisset deabus ceteris antelata, daturam se nuptam Paridi forma praecipuam suique consimilem. Tunc animo uolenti Frygius iuuenis malum, quod tenebat, aureum uelut uictoriae calculum puellae tradidit.

33 ¹Quid ergo miramini, uilissima capita, immo forensia pecora, immo uero 264 H togati uulturii, si toti nunc iudices sententias suas pretio nundinantur, cum rerum exordio inter deos et homines agitatum iudicium corruperit gratia et originalem sententiam magni Iouis consiliis electus iudex rusticanus et opilio lucro libidinis uendiderit cum totius etiam sui stirpis exitio? ²Sic hercules et aliud sequens iudicium inter inclitos Achiuorum duces celebratum, uel cum falsis insimulationibus eruditione doctrinaque praepollens Palamedes proditionis damnatur, uirtute Martia praepotenti praefertur *Ulixes* modicus Aiaci maximo. Quale autem et illud iudicium apud legiferos Athenienses catos illos et omni<s> scientiae magistros? ³Nonne diuinae prudentiae senex, quem sapientia praetulit cunctis mortalibus deus Delphicus, fraude et inuidia nequissimae factionis circumuentus uelut corruptor adulescentiae, quam frenis cohercebat, herbae pestilentis suco noxio peremptus est relinquens ciuibus ignominiae perpetuae maculam, cum nunc etiam egregii philosophi sectam ei<u>s sanctissimam praeoptent et summo beatitudinis studio iurent in ipsius nomen! ⁴Sed nequis indignationis meae reprehendat impetum secum sic reputans: 'Ecce nunc patiemur philosophantem nobis asinum?', rursus, unde decessi, reuertar ad fabulam.

34 ¹Postquam finitum est illud Paridis iudicium, Iuno quidem cum Minerua tristes et iratis similes e scaena redeunt, indignationem repulsae gestibus professae, Venus uero gaudens et hilaris laetitiam suam saltando toto cum choro professa est. ²Tunc de summo montis cacumine per quandam 265 H latentem fistulam in excelsum prorumpit uino crocus diluta sparsimque defluens pascentis circa capellas odoro perpluit imbre, donec in meliorem maculatae speciem canitiem propriam luteo colore mutarent. Iamque tota suaue fraglante cauea montem illum ligneum terrae uorago decepit.

³Ecce quidam miles per mediam plateam dirigit cursum petiturus iam populo postulante illam de publico carcere mulierem, quam dixi propter multiforme scelus bestis esse damnatam meisque praeclaris nuptiis destinatam. ⁴Et iam torus genialis scilicet noster futurus accuratissime disternebatur lectus Indica testudine perlucidus, plumea congerie tumidus, ueste serica floridus. ⁵At ego praeter pudorem obeundi publice concubitus, praeter contagium scelestae pollutaeque feminae, metu etiam mortis maxime cruciabar sic ipse mecum reputans, quod in amplexu

Venerio scilicet nobis cohaerentibus, quaecumque ad exitium mulieris bestia fuisset immissa, non adeo uel prudentia sollers uel artificio docta uel abstinentia frugi posset prouenire, ut adiacentem lateri meo laceraret mulierem, mihi uero quasi indemnato et innoxio parceret.

35 ¹Ergo igitur non de pudore iam, sed de salute ipsa sollicitus, dum magister meus lectulo probe coaptando destrictus inseruit et, tota familia partim ministerio uenationis occupata, partim uoluptario spectaculo adtonita, ²meis cogitationibus liberum tribuebatur arbitrium nec magnopere quisquam custodiendum tam mansuetum putabat asinum, paulatim furtiuum pedem proferens po<r>tam, quae proxima est, potitus ³iam cursu me celerrimo proripio sexque totis passuum milibus perniciter confectis Cenchreas peruado, quod oppidum audit quidem nobilissimae 266 H coloniae Corinthiensium, adluitur autem Aegaeo et Saronico mari. Inibi portus etiam tutissimum nauium receptaculum magno frequentatur populo. ⁴Vitatis ergo turbulis et electo secreto litore prope ipsas fluctuum aspergines in quodam mollissimo harenae gremio lassum corpus porrectus refoueo. ⁵Nam et ultimam diei metam curriculum solis deflexerat et uespernae me quieti traditum dulcis somnus oppresserat.

CHAPTER I

The soldier takes the ass along on a journey as his own pack animal.

The episode of the *hortulanus* is concluded and the ass, with the soldier as his new owner, is heading for new adventures.

Book 10, like books 2, 3, 7, 8, and 11, begins with a new day (*die sequenti*). For the careful book divisions of the *Met.* see Junghanns 1932,126, n. 13; *GCA* 1995,33 on 9,1 (202.21-25); ibid. 355 on 9,42 (236,7-8).

That ch. 1 is partly transitional in function appears from references to the latest events in the preceding book (the *hortulanus* is mentioned 1. 10; cf. also 1. 11 f. *miles ille, qui ... uapularat*). On the other hand, the short journey described here makes it clear that the chapter also begins a new phase in the story and that certain details in the description of the journey may symbolize future changes in Lucius' existence. See below, on *onustum et prorsum exornatum*; *campestri nec adeo difficili uia*; *nec in stabulo, sed in domo cuiusdam decurionis*; see also Introd. **1.4**.

In the first chapters of books 2, 3, 7, and 8 we find, as we do here, references to events in previous books interwoven with the announcement of new events and circumstances (for book 8 see *GCA* 1985, Introd. 1). The first chapter of book 7 contains references that reach beyond the most recent events, as if to remind the reader briefly of the events in the main narrative previous to the long embedded tale of 4,28 - 6,24. Reader — or should we rather say listener? This recapitulation at the beginning of a new book may indicate that the story was read aloud to an audience, book by book, on successive occasions. On this possibility see Wesseling 1988,71 with references; Reardon 1991,72 and n. 47. See, however, the introductory note on ch. 2 (237,1-3).

The *ciuitatula*, which the soldier reaches with the ass at the end of this chapter, will form the background for the events related in chs. 2-12.

236,10-16 Die sequenti meus quidem dominus hortulanus quid egerit nescio, me tamen miles ille, qui propter eximiam impotentiam pulcherrime uapularat, ab illo praesepio nullo equidem contradicente diductum abducit atque a suo contubernio - hoc enim mihi uidebatur - sarcinis propriis onustum et prorsum exornatum armatumque militariter producit ad uiam: How my master, the gardener, fared the next day, I don't know; as for me, that soldier (the one who had paid for his outstanding violence by a very fine beating) took me from the manger there and led me away with no one at all objecting; from his own quarters — for that is what they seemed to me — he led me, loaded with his personal baggage, fully equipped and kitted out like a soldier, on to the main road.

Die sequenti: on the indication of time in this book see Introd. **1.6.1**.

meus quidem hortulanus quid egerit nescio: cf. *Onos* 46,1: τῇ δὲ ὑστεραίᾳ τί μὲν ἔπαθεν ὁ κηπουρὸς ὁ ἐμὸς δεσπότης, οὐκ οἶδα. After this point we find no parallel to the *Onos* in the *Met.* until ch. 13 (246,1 f.), where the ass is sold by the soldier; in the *Onos* this episode occurs in ch. 46, immediately after the words cited above. On the

51

specific intertextual relationship between *Onos* and *Met.*, and on its importance for the interpretation of this book, see Introd. **2.3**.

Heine in *AAGA* 1978,28 gives a survey of the many minor characters in the *Met.* who, having appeared briefly on the stage, quietly make their exit with no clue about their further fate; see *GCA* 1985,10 (Introd. 5.2) on 'narrative economy'; ibid. 197 on 8,23 (194,28-195,2); *GCA* 1995,346 on 9,41 (235,18) *nec quisquam ... asinus* ('onocentrism') with further examples; ibid. 102 on 9,10 (210,8-10) and 223 on 9,25 (221,1-3); see also on ch. 13 (246,2 f.) *miles ille*. In contrast to the examples mentioned above, the exit of the *hortulanus* is accompanied by the comment *meus quidem dominus ... nescio*, which, because of 9,42 (236,4 f.) *miserum hortulanum poenas scilicet capite pensurum in publicum deducunt carcere*, acquires a grim undertone. So our passage provides a sort of 'in memoriam' for the *miser hortulanus* after all, before he disappears from the story.

quid egerit nescio: in 9,42 (236,4 f., cited in the previous note) the narrator has already made it quite clear what would probably (*scilicet*) happen to the *hortulanus*. The words *meus quidem dominus ... nescio* in our passage accompany a change in the object of observation, a shift in the camera's focus: the immediately following words *me tamen* etc. indicate that the camera is 'zooming in' again on the 'I', Lucius.

tamen: in combination with *quidem* below, it is here comparable to the Greek μέν ...δὲ ...; these particles are, indeed, found in the corresponding passage of the *Onos*. *Tamen* should therefore not be taken in a purely adversative sense here; cf. *GCA* 1985,166 on 8,18 (191,18). Löfstedt 1911,27 f. points out the originally deictic function of *tamen* and gives examples from Plautus.

miles ille, qui propter eximiam impotentiam pulcherrime uapularat: a reference to the end of Book 9 (see the introductory remarks to this chapter). We have here a further characterization of the soldier, who receives more and more traits of the '*miles gloriosus*'; see *GCA* 1995,322 on 9,39. See also below, on *uapularat*; *sarcinis propriis onustum*; *scutum ... longe praelucens*; *propter terrendos miseros uiatores*, and *sollicite profiscitur*. In the next chapter, when the narrator introduces the stepmother story (237,12 f.), and warns the *lector optimus* that there will be an ascension from the *soccus* to the *coturnus*, he refers, perhaps, not only forward to the tragic context of the story that is beginning (see note there), but also backward to the comic associations in the episode of the soldier.

Once the narrative has been securely anchored in the past by *qui ... uapularat*, the story continues in historic presents (*abducit, producit ...* through to *proficiscitur*); see Pinkster 1990,224 f. (*nescio* in l. 11 is not a historic present; it refers to the time of narration).

eximiam impotentiam: an ironical juxtaposition; see Bernhard 1927,240. *Eximius* always refers to good qualities; *ThLL* s.v. 1494,6 f. mentions only two exceptions: Apul. *Met.* 2,10 (33,3) *cruciatum uoluptatis eximiae,* and our passage. Readers of Apuleius' time must have been familiar with funerary inscriptions (many for soldiers, but also for civilians) containing phrases like *ob* (or *propter*) *eximiam beneuolentiam* (or *probitatem*) *eius*. (Cf. the numerous references to *CIL* in *ThLL* 1493,51 f., e.g. VI,32415 *eximiam eius erga se beniuolentiam*; VIII,23219 *ob eximiam ... condis<ipu>latus affectionem*). For such a reader, the phrase *propter eximiam impotentiam* may have had the comic force of an ἀπροσδόκητον.

impotentiam: here, of course, not 'impotence', but 'lack of control', as elsewhere in Apuleius, who uses the word in contexts of tyranny and abuse of power; cf. ch. 6 (241,21); *Apol.* 18,3 (sc. *paupertas*) *neminem umquam superbia inflauit, neminem impotentia deprauauit, neminem tyrannide efferauit*; *Pl.* 2,24 (256) and 28 (262). Both the noun and the adjective (*impotens*) may be ambiguous (for the adjective see Svennung 1935,574 and n. 4 with literature). The noun is so used here: the soldier is *impotens* (uncontrolled) in his arrogance and misuse of power, but has been beaten up and rendered *impotens* (weak) by the *hortulanus* (9,40: 233,25 f.). Cf. Serv. ad Verg. 1,502 *sunt enim multa quae pro locis intelleguntur, ut 'inpotens' et 'satis' et 'minus' et 'nihil potens' significat.*

pulcherrime: here used ironically. *OLD* s.v. *pulchre* 2c gives, in addition to our passage, only examples from Plautus, e.g. *Mil.* 404 *si ad erum haec res prius praeuenit, peribis pulchre*. See Maurach 1988,108 on Pl. *Poen.* 457; Hofmann *LU* 71.

uapularat: a continuing evocation of comedy (see previous note); the verb is always translated 'take a beating'. Its original meaning is probably 'scream with pain, (call "*uae*")'. Its use in Latin comedy is then comparable to the use of οἰμώζω in Aristophanes (e.g. *Vesp.* 1033). See Callebat 1968,38 f. with references.

ab illo praesepio: for *praesepium* = 'manger, rack' see *GCA* 1981,170 on 7,14 (164,14-18). The text does not make it clear where this manger was located; we may assume that the soldiers had taken the ass to their barracks and there tied him to a manger along with the other pack animals. The *Onos* (45,8) mentions in addition that the magistrates turned the ass over to the soldiers. The *Met.*, however, does not have this; it would be inconsistent with the (unfavourable) characterization of the soldier, which is much more elaborate than that of the *Onos* (cf. *GCA* 1995,325 on 9,39; 233,1 *superbo atque adroganti sermone*); see above, on *qui ... uapularat*; here, on his own authority, he appoints himself the ass's new owner.

nullo equidem contradicente: cf. ch. 13 (246,2 f.) *miles ille, qui me ... sine pretio suum fecerat* (see comm. ad loc.). The ass's career has reached an all-time low: nobody thinks he is worth paying money for any more and nobody protests when the soldier takes him away. In other passages where he changes owner, the narrator as experiencing I always shows a great interest in the price he fetches (8,25: 197,9 f., see *GCA* 1985,220 ad loc.; 9,10: 210,13 f.; 9,31: 226,24 f.; ch. 13: 246,6 and ch. 17: 249,24; see there, on *quadruplum ... pretium*). The indignant insertion *nullo equidem contradicente* fits in with the characterization of the narrator: the abstract author (see Introd. **3.2**) often achieves an ironical effect by depicting the main narrator as somewhat of a smart-aleck, who, even in the shape of an ass, retains a high opinion of himself, although the actors around him see him only as an ordinary ass and treat him as such.

equidem: in his works other than the *Met.* Apuleius adheres strictly to the 'classical' use, where *equidem* is used with the first person only. The use of *equidem* as the equivalent of *quidem*, as it is found here and also elsewhere in the *Met.*, is frequent in comedy. See Van der Paardt 1971,192 f. on 3,27 (72,5) with references; Solodow 1978,19 f. discusses the etymology and use of *equidem*; ibid. 24 f. on the use in Apuleius, with references.

diductum abducit ... producit: sound-play has undoubtedly been a factor in the choice of these three compounds of *ducere*. But this does not seem to be a case of empty 'Klangspielerei' (contra Bernhard 1927,237 f.). Each compound adds an essential element to the information (see the following notes). A similar succession occurs also in 6,25 (147,12-16), with *producunt, perducunt,* and *reducunt*; see *GCA* 1981,29 ad loc.

diductum: this is the reading in F, retained by all modern editors, against *deductum* in φ (see Helm Praef. *Fl.* XLIV on the interchange of *e* and *i*). Oudendorp ad loc. (followed by Hildebrand) prefers *deductum*, with the argument that the *praesepium* of domestic animals was always situated in an elevated location. *ThLL* s.v. *deduco* 271,24 also reads *deductum* in this passage. In 6,27 (149,7), where F and φ have *diducere*, all editors, following ς, change this to *deducere* (see *GCA* 1981,43 ad loc.). In our passage, however, *diductum* can be retained in the meaning of 'remove' (*ThLL* s.v. *diduco* 1017,23 f.); cf. Vallette 'me détacha de ma mangeoire'.

diductum abducit: the participle is not pleonastic (contra Von Geisau 1912,34 and Bernhard 1927,46 f.). Rather, we have here an example of precise phrasing: two different aspects of one action are described in sequence. See *GCA* 1995,205 on 9,23 (220,12-19) *suppositum abscondit*, with further examples.

hoc enim mihi uidebatur: the parenthesis has a double function. On the one hand, the narrator directly addresses his fictive audience: in his function of narrator, he 'steps out of the story' for a moment (see Callebat 1968,108 and 462 f.). On the other hand, this insertion confirms his limited perspective as a homodiegetical actorial narrator (see Introd. **3.5**).

sarcinis propriis onustum: with *propriis* the narrator refers back to the moment the ass was commandeered by the soldier, who then claimed that the ass was needed to transport the luggage of the *praeses* (9,39: 233,10 f.; see *GCA* 1995,327 f. ad loc.). This detail continues the characterization of the soldier, who now cynically takes advantage of the catastrophic consequences of that requisitioning.

sarcinis propriis onustum et prorsum exornatum armatumque militariter: chiasmus and variation. *Onustum* is modified by the preceding *sarcinis propriis*, while *et prorsum exornatum* is followed by the specification *armatumque militariter*.

onustum et prorsum exornatum: this is the last passage in the *Met.* where *onustus* is used to describe Lucius as a beast of burden. (For a survey of all the different loads Lucius has had to carry during his life as an ass, see on *me ... residens* ch. 18: 251,5 f.) The qualification *et prorsum exornatum* is added here for the first time; *exornatum* (without *onustum*) is used again in ch. 18 (251,7), where Thiasus has the ass magnificently decked out as his personal mount; after his return to human form Lucius is called *exornatus* for the last time, after his first initiation (11,24: 286,6). Thus, the addition *et prorsum exornatum* in our passage is meaningful because it indicates to the re-reader that an improvement in Lucius' life is imminent. See also below, on *campestri nec adeo difficili uia*.

prorsum: this is the older form, particularly often attested in Plautus (Callebat 1968,537 f. and LHSz 2,222). The form *prorsus* is much more frequent in the *Met.* (see Van der Paardt 1971,32 on 3,2: 53,6). Possibly *prorsum* has been chosen here because of the Plautine register in this whole passage (see above on *pulcherrime*; *uapularat*; below on *scutum longius relucens*); moreover, the form in *-um* adds to the series of homoioteleuta: *onustum ... prorsum exornatum armatum*.

armatumque militariter: this is the only occurrence of the adverb *militariter* in Apuleius; it is attested in Livy (e.g. 4,41,1 *oratio ... militariter grauis*; 27,3,2 *tecta militariter ... aedificare*); after that in Tacitus (*Hist.* 2,80,2; cf. Heubner ad loc.). *ThLL* s.v. *militariter* 956,73 f. notes all occurrences of this rather rare adverb, whose shade of meaning must be inferred from the context in each instance, as is evident from the passages cited above. *ThLL* ibid. compares with our passage [Aur.Vict.] *Orig.* 13,1 *militariter instructos* (opp. *sudibus armati*). In our passage the phrase must mean something like 'armed in truly soldierly fashion'. This long and phonically varied adverb reflects the cumbersome and complex nature of the ass's load.

236,16-21 Nam et galeam <gerebam> nitore praemicantem et scutum cetera long*e prae*lucens, sed etiam lanceam longissimo hastili conspicuam, quae scilicet non disciplinae tunc quidem causa, sed propter terrendos miseros uiatores in summo atque edito sarcinarum cumulo ad instar exercitus sedulo composuerat: For I carried both a helmet, flashing with splendour, and a shield, which shone its light far and wide on everything else, but also a lance, conspicuous for its extremely long shaft: objects which (this time obviously not because it was an order but because of scaring the wretched travellers) he had carefully arranged high on top of the already heaped-up pile of baggage — it looked like an army.

Nam et galeam <gerebam> nitore praemicantem et scutum cetera longe praelucens: F and φ have *nam et galeam nitore praemicantem et scutum cetera longiore lucens*. This reading offers three problems: a. the main clause before the relative clause with *quae* lacks a finite verb of which *galeam, scutum,* and *lanceam* must be the objects; b. *longiorem* cannot modify the neuter *scutum*; c. *cetera* seems not to have a function in the sentence.

Ad a and c: In Oudendorp's opinion the missing verb had to be found in *cetera*, a word difficult to explain, and therefore seen as a corruption. Instead of *cetera* he proposed *ceperam* or *gerebam*. The latter has been adopted by most editors. Frassinetti alone prints *dederat* (also in the place of *cetera*); he prefers the third person singular of a pluperfect here (Frassinetti 1960,130). Augello defends *gerebam*, pointing out the narrator's self-ironizing description of the ass, burdened by all kinds of armament. Indeed, an imperfect fits well in this explanatory clause introduced by *nam* (for this kind of imperfect see Pinkster 1990,238). The reading proposed by Leo, *iniecerat* for *cetera* (honored by Robertson in his app. crit. with 'fort. recte'), is for the reasons mentioned above less attractive than Oudendorp's *gerebam*.

There is another possibility, however, which has been included in this text. That is to follow Helm 1931,300 in not replacing *cetera* with a finite verb but adding *<gerebam>* after *galeam*, where it could have been omitted through haplography. This has the great advantage that *cetera* can be retained (it is hard to explain how *gerebam* could be corrupted to *cetera*, which is much harder to understand). Augello defends Helm's proposal, which is printed in the edition of Helm-Krenkel. Augello, referring to other passages in the *Met.*, takes *cetera* as an adverbial accusative. But then it would mean 'for the rest', 'in all other respects' (cf. e.g. ch. 14: 247,15; see *ThLL* s.v. *ceterus* 973,38 f.), which does not make sense here. It is better to take *cetera* as the object of *praelucens* (see below), with *praelucere* meaning 'to make (something else) visible through its own light or radiance'; cf. Helm-Krenkel 'der alles Übrige weit überstrahlte'. This fits well in the context, too, because the narrator makes it clear that this armour is meant in particular to frighten off other people, even at a distance.

Ad b.: most editors follow the emendation of Elmenhorst, who changes *longiore lucens* to *longius relucens*. With Augello 1977,206 f. (but without borrowing his argumentation; see above) Helm's reading *longe praelucens*, proposed in his Addenda et Corrigenda in the edition of 1931, and printed in the edition of Helm-Krenkel, is here followed. The process of corruption would presumably have been *longe prelucens*; in *prelucens* the downstroke of the *p* disappeared, which led to *orelucens*, The 'correction' of *longe orelucens* to *longiore lucens* would then be almost inevitable.

nam: the explanatory sentence, which starts innocently enough as an explanation of *militariter*, ends in an unmistakenly hostile characterization of the soldier (see the following notes). It also offers a comic description of the ass walking along the road, loaded with military equipment '*ad instar exercitus*'.

praemicantem: this verb is first attested in Apuleius in the *Met.* and is found, in addition to our passage, in 5,20 (118,15); 11,1 (266,12); and 11,10 (274,3). After Apuleius it occurs in Minuc. 5,9; Prud. *Peri.* 1,84; and metaphorically Cass. *Hist. eccl.* 2,1,9 (sc. *in concilio*) *ministrorum ... dei alii sapientiae sermone fulgebant, alii continentia uitae ... coruscabant ...; erant ... alii ... animi robore praemicantes* (*ThLL* s.v. *praemico* 702,5 f.).

scutum ... longe praelucens: cf. the *miles gloriosus*, Pl. *Mil.* 1 f.: *Curate ut splendor meo sit clupeo clarior / quam solis radii esse olim, quom sudumst solent / ut, ubi usus ueniat, contra conserta manu / praestringat oculorum aciem in acie hostibus*, cited by Apul. *Soc.* 11 (145).

disciplinae: 'sensu militari' (*ThLL* s.v. *disciplina* 1324,73 f.), meaning 'order', 'regulation'.

propter terrendos miseros uiatores: this completes the picture of the Roman soldier begun in 9,39 (see *GCA* 1995,322; ibid. 325 f. on 233,4-6); in the provinces Roman soldiers were a privileged class, whose presence was feared by the common people (see Millar 1981,67 f. [= Millar 1999,255 f.] with references). This particular soldier, coward as he is, makes use of his status symbols to defend himself on the way. The *hortulanus* was, of course, a *uiator miser* when he met the soldier (9,39), but managed to knock him out (9,40). The soldier now takes elaborate pains to ensure that this does not happen again. He has lost his *spatha* in the fight (see *GCA* 1995,341 on 9,41: 234,27 f. *ob amissam spatham*), which explains its absence from the list of weapons here.

propter: *propter* with the accusative of the gerundive is first attested in Var. *Gramm. frg.* 237,23 Goetz-Scholl (265,99 Funaioli); in prose from Livy onward *propter* more and more often replaces *ob* in this construction (see LHSz 2,246).

miseros uiatores: *uiatores* often are outlawed, in antiquity in general and in the *Met.* in particular (see Schmidt 1979,173 f. with references). This is emphasized by *miseros*. At the same time, the unfavourable characterization of the soldier is continued: he is made to look cowardly and foolish, because it is not *latrones*, for example, that he wishes to deter, but *miseros uiatores*.

in summo atque edito sarcinarum cumulo: see Vogel 1973,40 and 58-60 on the amazing quantity of luggage asses are often seen carrying in Greece (and the Middle East); the sight of a walking pile of baggage, showing nothing of the ass but his head and four thin legs, must have been familiar also to Apuleius and his contemporaries.

ad instar exercitus: the *uiatores*, seeing the flash of the weapons from afar, are intended to get the impression that an entire army is approaching, only the vanguard of which is visible. Here the ass is an 'army'; in 8,28 (200,8 f.) he is *et horreum simul et templum* (see *GCA* 1985,252 ad loc.); in 9,4 (205,17-19) he is a *circumforaneum mendicabulum* (see *GCA* 1995,57 ad loc.).

ad instar: this adverbial phrase (the 'classical' form is *instar* without *ad*), formed by analogy with *ad exemplar* and derived from the *sermo cotidianus*, is attested in literary prose from the second century A.D. onward. See Callebat 1968,137 f. with examples from Apuleius and his contemporaries; cf. 2,21 (42,11 f.) *ad instar oratorum conformat articulum*. See also *GCA* 1981,105 f. on 7,4 (157,2-11).

sedulo: 'carefully'. See *GCA* 1981,85 on 7,1 (154,21-155,4), with references, on the meaning and (uncertain) etymology of this adverb, which is found in Latin prose of all periods (see Van der Paardt 1971,41 on 3,3: 54,5).

236,21-24 Confecta campestri nec adeo difficili uia ad quandam ciuitatulam peruenimus nec in stabulo, sed in domo cuiusdam decurionis deuertimus: Having completed our journey, which went across level ground and therefore was not so difficult, we arrived at a small country town and put up not at an inn, but at the house of a councillor.

Confecta ... uia ... peruenimus: it is unnecessary to adopt Leo's proposal <*et*> *confecta*: the ablative absolute marks the transition to the next scene. This syntactic pattern, which is quite frequent in historians (see Chaussery-Laprée 1969,65 f.), is found several times in the *Met.* (cf. 8,22: 193,19-20 with *GCA* 1985,186 ad loc.). After the narrator has described the ass's military equipment with a certain self-irony (see the previous notes), he now affects the tone of someone describing a military operation.

campestri nec adeo difficili uia: descriptions of journeys made by the ass, burdened with more or less heavy loads, have repeatedly shown a correlation between the I-narrator's complaints (or lack thereof) about the condition of the road and his perception of the circumstances surrounding the journey. See *GCA* 1995,93 on 9,9 (209,2-4); ibid. 94 on 209,6-9 and 105 on 9,10 (210,15-17). The information in our passage that the road was level and easy anticipates an imminent improvement in the principal narrator's existence; see above, on *onustum et prorsum exornatum*.

ad quandam ciuitatulam: the geographical descriptions are still as vague in this section of the book as in the previous books (see Introd. **1.5**). From ch. 18 onward, however, these descriptions become extremely precise (see s.v. *Corintho* 250,19). From ch. 18 (250,25 *tunc Thessaliam etiam accesserat*) we may conclude that this small town, the scene of the action of chapters 2-17, is situated in Thessaly.

ciuitatula as the diminutive of *ciuitas* = 'town' is first attested in this passage. It occurs however in Sen. *Apoc.* 9,4, in the meaning of 'citizenship in a small town'. *ThLL* s.v. *ciuitatula* 1240,32 f. notes Gloss. V,316,49 *oppidum: castellum uel ciuitatula*, and passages in Hieronymus, Isidorus, and Cassiodorus.

nec in stabulo, sed in domo cuiusdam decurionis: definitely an improvement in the circumstances of the ass, who only in 9,32 (227,8) expressed his disgust at his *intecto ... stabulo*; see also on *contubernalis* ch. 13 (246,14). The statement that the ass is stabled in the house of a *decurio* - where people are living in relative comfort - contributes to the general impression that his living conditions are improving considerably (see the introductory remark to this chapter and on *quod caput est totius Achaiae prouincia* ch. 18: 250,19 f.). That so-called 'respectable' accommodations do not always mean actually improved circumstances has already become clear from 8,30 f. (201,19 f.), where the ass, with the priests, stayed in the house of a *uir principalis*, but soon found himself in mortal danger (8,31: 201,26 f.). Something similar happens at the end of this book: the ass comes into the house of the Corinthian Thiasus, a ranking official (ch. 17), but has to fear for his life when Thiasus wishes him to perform in the arena with the condemned murderess (ch. 23: 254,15 f.).

stabulo: in the sense of *caupona, diuersorium* as in 1,4 (4,15); see Molt 1938,47 and Scobie 1975,89 ad loc. See *RAC* 14, 602-626 s.v. 'Herberge' [Hiltbrunner]. *Stabulum*, as 'pars pro toto', is a standard expression for a lodging house that provides stabling for riding and pack animals (see Kleberg 1957,18 f.).

in domo ... deuertimus: cf. Prisc. in *GL* 3,323 *illi* καταγομαι και καταλύω και ὁρμίζομαι *et ad locum et in loco ponunt. similiter nostri 'deuerto domi' et 'domum'*. See also *GCA* 1977,22 f. on 4,1 (74,10-11) *apud ... senes deuertimus*; *GCA* 1995,58 on 9,4 (205,19-25).

in domo cuiusdam decurionis: probably the soldier belongs to the retinue of the provincial governor, the *legatus Augusti pro praetore* (the *praeses* mentioned in 9,39: 233,10-14; see *GCA* 1995,327 ad loc.). In this capacity he has the right to stay at the house of local *decuriones*, who were obliged to provide these lodgings (cf. Millar 1981,68 [= Millar 1999,256]). On this duty to provide *hospitium* see Jones [4]1971,141 f.; on the Roman governor's duty to tour his province to hear court cases see Sherwin-White [3]1985,640 on Plin. *Ep.* 10,58,1.

decurionis: a member of the local βουλή. This council, which formed the actual government in the provincial towns of the Roman empire, consisted of the *decuriones*, whose number varied according to the size of the town. To be appointed *decurio* a citizen had to meet certain criteria of property, age, status, and reputation. In the provincial towns of the Roman empire the office of *decurio*, originally a position of honour, became an inevitable *munus* of the affluent; see Neesen 1981,203 f. See also *GCA* 1995,158 on 9,17 (215,10-11); *DNP* 3,356-358 s.v. *Decurio, decuriones* [1] [Gizewski].

The fact that the ass is stabled with a *decurio* enables him to overhear the story which is about to follow, since the criminal case mentioned in that story is conducted before the town council (see below, on *patres in curiam conuenirent* ch. 7: 241,24), of which the *decurio* is a member.

236,24-26 Statimque me commendato cuidam seruulo ipse ad propositum suum, qui mille armatorum ducatum sustinebat, sollicite proficiscitur: And, entrusting me at once to the care of a slave-boy, he himself set out punctually to his superior, who was charged with command of a thousand armed men.

seruulo: *GCA* 1985,190 on 8,22 (194,12-18) suggests a possibly derogatory use of the diminutive *seruulus*. If the diminutive in our passage reflects the soldier's opinion, it may have a similar connotation here. See also on *seruuli* ch. 8 (243,14).

praepositum: see *OLD* s.v. *praepositus* 'a person placed in charge'. For *praepositus* in a military sense, referring to the commander of a specific contingent (often of auxiliaries, but sometimes also of a special task force), see *RE* Suppl. 8,548,59 - 553,13 s.v. *praepositus* [Enβlin]. From the addition *qui mille armatorum ducatum sustinebat* it appears that the commander in question is a *praefectus cohortis*, also called a *praepositus cohortis* (Enβlin ibid. cites many examples of these phrases from inscriptions). In ch. 19 (251,16) *praepositus* is used of the (civilian) freedman who is entrusted with the ass's care. On this non-military use of *praepositus* see Enβlin ibid. 540,11 f. and *ThLL* s.v. *praepositus* 776,57.

In ch. 13 (246,3) this *praepositus* is referred to as the soldier's *tribunus*. See Millar 1981,67 n. 17 (= Millar 1999,255 n. 27).

ducatum: for this military term see *GCA* 1981,138 on 7,9 (160,16-18).

sollicite profiscitur: the soldier behaves in a manner consistent with his entire characterization. Arrogant toward the 'common man' (cf. 9,39: 233,1 *superbo atque adroganti sermone* with *GCA* 1995,325 ad loc.), he punctiliously obeys orders from a superior. Cf. on *debitum sustinens obsequium* ch. 13 (246,3 f.).

CHAPTER II

A new tale is introduced: in this story, a woman is infatuated with her own stepson.

237,1-3 Post dies plusculos ibidem dissignatum scelestum ac nefarium facinus memini, sed ut uos etiam legatis, ad librum profero: I remember a crime that was revealed in that very place several days later, a criminal and nefarious offence; but in order that you too may read it, I will put it on record.

As always, a short metanarrative phrase (on this term, used as in Gülich 1976,224-256; see *GCA* 1995,12) introduces the subsequent tale. For a comparable introduction see e.g. 8,22 (193,21-22) with *GCA* 1985,187 ad loc. The metanarrative phrase in our passage is noteworthy in that it emphasizes the written character of the narrative (*ut uos ... legatis*; *ad librum*; *lector optime*): other introductions to embedded tales in the *Met.* do not have this emphasis; cf. e.g. 9,14 (213,6 f.) *fabulam ... ad aures uestras adferre decreui* (cf. also 8,22: 193,21). Crismani 1997,125 considers phrases like this one, as well as 1,1 (2,4) *lector intende, laetaberis* and 9,30 (225,10) *lector scrupulosus* as arguments against oral diffusion of the ancient novels. She also compares Chariton 8,1 where, likewise, a reader is addressed; see also comm. on ch. 11 (245,1) *dedi uenenum ...*, on the need to re-read.

Post dies plusculos ibidem: the newly introduced embedded tale is at once given boundaries of space and time (Gülich 1976,242 f.: 'Gliederungsmerkmale'). On the indication of time in this book see Introd. **1.6.1**.

plusculos: this diminutive adjective is found in Apuleius in the *Met.* only (13 times); it is attested in comedy; in Cicero, both in his letters and in his orations; and in Columella, Plinius Maior, Fronto, and Gellius (see Van der Paardt 1971,130 and 159; *GCA* 1981,85 on 7,1: 154,21-155,4).

ibidem: the small Thessalian town (see on *ad quandam ciuitatulam* ch. 1: 236,22) is emphatically mentioned here as the scene of the action of the next tale. Soon it will become clear to the reader that this tale is a version of the Phaedra-Hippolytus tragedy, in which the leading parts are played not by mythical figures, but by the inhabitants of a small country town. The narrator offers this story as an event which took place in the town where he was stabled at the *decurio*'s and which, as an ear-witness, he can guarantee as 'true'. What is more, the *decurio* must have been a member of the town council which acts as jury in the lawsuit (see on ch. 7: 241,24 f. *patres in curiam conuenirent*; cf. on *haec et istum modum gesta cognoui* ch. 7: 242,1 f.; on the office of *decurio* see on *decurionis* ch. 1: 236,23).

dissignatum: 'brought to light, revealed'. All modern translations translate *dissignatum* here as *designatum,* i.e. 'schemed' or 'perpetrated'; Carlesi alone translates correctly: 'Mi ricordi che dopo alcuni giorni si scoprì in quel posto ...'. Neither *OLD* nor *LS* give *dissigno* a lemma of its own: the verb is mentioned s.v. *designo* as a variant; it appears, indeed, that in different manuscripts of the same texts *designo* and *dissigno* are frequently interchanged (*ThLL* s.v. *designo* 719,80 f.). Interested as Apuleius is in etymology (see e.g. *GCA* 1995,95 on 9,9: 209,9-14 and for further examples ibid. Index Rerum; also the Index Rerum of this volume s.v. 'etymology'), he cannot but have sensed and exploited the difference between the verbs: he uses *designo* twice in the *Met.*, 6,7 (133,11) and 10,31 (261,26). The verb *dissigno* means 'break the seal of something', hence 'bring to light, make known what was hidden' (*ThLL* s.v. *dissigno*, 1469,61 f.); *designo* means 'mark (with a seal), indicate', and then 'mark, assign, plan, perpetrate' (*OLD* s.v. *designo* 1-7).

The meaning 'revealed, brought to light' fits well in the context of this passage; in the other passage in the *Met.* where the ms. tradition has *dissigno*, the meaning 'reveal (divulge secrets)' would also fit the context (*GCA* 1985,246 f. ad 8,28: 199,12 give a different interpretation). Cf. Wilkins 1958,123 on Hor. *Ep.* 1,5,16 f., where the best mss. read *quid non ebrietas dissignat* (Porph. ad loc. remarks *dissignat: aperit*; the passage continues with *operta recludit*).

scelestum ac nefarium facinus: differently from other inner tales, the narrator announces this inner tale not as a *fabula* but as a *facinus*. Cf. 8,22 (193,21 f.) *inibi coeptum facinus ... narrare cupio*; see Murgatroyd 1997,132 f. on this opening. Cf. below, *tragoediam, non fabulam*. Actually, the following story contains several *facinora*, which the narrator here summarizes in one phrase. Similarly, the *facinus* announced in 8,22 encompasses three crimes (Schlam 1992,76). See Summers 1967,133 f. with nn. 1 and 2 for *facinus* in the *Met.*

The adjectives *scelestum* and *nefarium* indicate that *facinus* is to be taken in the sense of 'crime' (see on *necessarii facinoris* ch. 3: 238,27 f.). There is, perhaps, a difference in connotation between the two adjectives: *scelestus* 'violating human laws'; *nefarius* 'violating religious laws'. Cf. 2,27 (47,15 f.), equally in a context of adultery and poisoning, *extremum facinus in nefariam scelestamque ... feminam ... uindicate*.

By the use of these two adjectives, in combination with the absence of a designation like *fabula*, the tone for the following tale is already being set in the metanarrative introduction: this story will clearly not be light reading. See Gülich 1976,242 f. on the 'rezeptionssteuernde' signals which can be distinguished in the introductions to narrative texts. Our tale is in its opening abundantly supplied with such signals (see below). All these, however, prepare the reader for only one part, one aspect of the story, so that at the conclusion of the tale he still has to decide how to evaluate and interpret the whole (see the introductory note on ch. 12: 245,26-29).

memini, sed ut uos etiam legatis, ad librum profero: this is an example of 'Exordialtopik': knowledge creates the obligation to inform (see *GCA* 1985,30 on 8,1: 177,1-4). On *legatis* and *librum* see the introductory note to this section.

There is a remarkable difference between the narrator's attitude here and in other places of the first ten books of the *Met.*, and his attitude in book 11 (where inner tales are absent), represented for instance by 11,23 (285,17 f.) *ecce tibi rettuli, quae, quamuis audita, ignores tamen necesse est*. See Teuber 1993,225 'Mit dieser Paradoxie kommt nicht nur der Karneval, sondern Sprache und Erzählkunst überhaupt an ihr Ende.'

memini ... profero: the present tenses, referring to the time of narration, mark off this introductory clause from the tale itself, which is opened by *habebat* (l. 3). This imperfect, which is the tense characteristic of the 'orientation phase', opens the actual tale.

ad librum profero: cf. ch. 7 (242,7) *ad istas litteras proferam*. The combination of *profero* with *ad librum* (and with *ad istas litteras*) is surprising: *proferre ad* is otherwise attested exclusively with people, in the sense 'to present or submit something to someone', or in a juridical context 'to produce in evidence' to the judge or jury. Possibly in view of this problem *ThLL* s.v. *ad* 551,50 f. groups our passage (ib. 551,55) with examples of *ad* 'used instrumentally'. Callebat 1968,211 rightly disagrees with this; he explains the combination by analogy with the increasing use of *ad* + accusative with 'verbes de déclaration'. He also points out examples of *proferre ad* in legal language; finally he mentions the use of *in medium, in lucem,* etc. *proferre.*

Possibly there is a contamination of *ad uos in hoc libro profero* and *in medium profero.* The surprising phrase *ad librum*, where one would have expected *ad uos*, accentuates what is written, the book, as the medium. In this way, the concrete author (see Introd. **3.1**) addresses his public and asks its attention for his literary creation. Moreover, this happens just when he is about to present his own version of a theme that has been treated in literature in many different ways (see also on *unicum* ch. 5: 240,10). Undoubtedly *profero* has that connotation as well: cf. Pl. *Amph.* 118 *ueterem atque antiquam rem nouam ad uos proferam* and Hor. *Ars* 129 f. *rectius Iliacum carmen deducis in actus / quam si proferres ignota indictaque primus* (see *OLD* s.v. *profero* 6a and cf. Brink on *proferres* in his comm. on Hor. *Ars* ad loc.).

237,3-6 Dominus aedium habebat iuuenem filium probe litteratum atque ob id consequenter pietate, modestia praecipuum, quem tibi quoque prouenisse cuperes uel talem: A home-owner had a son, who had received an excellent literary education and so as a consequence was a paragon of obedience and modesty: you, too, would wish to have him or someone like him as your son.

Here the actual story begins. It opens with an orientational phase (for the division of narrative texts into 'orientation, complication, and solution' see Gülich 1976,250 f. with literature), which continues to *supergresserat* (l. 9); the 'orientating' tenses are imperfects and pluperfects, which serve to provide background information.

Dominus aedium: there is no indication in the text that the subsequent drama took place in the family of the *decurio* of ch. 1 (236,23), as is suggested by many translations (e.g. Vallette 'Le maître de la maison avait un fils ... '); it is better, therefore, to translate neutrally as do e.g. Brandt-Ehlers: 'Ein Hausbesitzer hatte einen jungen Sohn.'

iuuenem filium probe litteratum atque ob id consequenter pietate, modestia praecipuum: the narrator stresses the causal connection between the young man's education and virtue. This highly coloured characterization of the young man makes him a sort of counterpoint to Hippolytus (whose part he is to play in the forthcoming tragedy: see below, on *iam ergo ... ascendere*. See also App. I,6B).

The connection between a good education and virtue is a topos in Greek novels and in biographies (see Braun 1934,34 f.). A fine example is Chariton 2,4,1 Διονύσιος δὲ ἐτέτρωτο μέν, τὸ δὲ τραῦμα περιστέλλειν ἐπειρᾶτο, οἷα δὴ πεπαιδευμένος ἀνὴρ καὶ ἐξαιρέτως ἀρετῆς ἀντιποιούμενος. Cf. *Menandri sententiae* 50 Jäkel Ἅπαντας ἡ παίδευσις ἡμέρους τελεῖ; Ov. *Pont.* 2,9,47 f. *adde quod ingenuas didicisse fideliter artes / emollit mores nec sinit esse feros*; Tabula Cebetis 33,3 γράμματα ... καὶ τῶν ἄλλων μαθημάτων ἃ καὶ Πλάτων φησὶ ὡσανεὶ χαλινοῦ τινος δύναμιν ἔχειν τοῖς νέοις. It appears from many passages in both the *Florida* and the *Apology* that Apuleius himself was convinced of the connection between literary training and high moral standing. Cf. e.g. *Fl.* 17,4 *Ad hoc ita semper ab ineunte aeuo bonas artes sedulo colui, eamque existimationem morum ac studiorum cum in prouincia nostra tum etiam Romae penes amicos tuos quaesisse me tute ipse locupletissimus testis es.* The high degree of erudition which the author continuously displays in the *Apology* is meant to serve as sufficient evidence that he cannot possibly be guilty of the crimes he has been charged with. Cf. also *Apol.* 28,7 f., which contains the same idea, but now put in the negative: *priuignum meum, ...* (referring to Pudens) *curae meae eruptum, postquam frater eius Pontianus et natu maior et moribus melior diem suum obiit, atque ita in me ac matrem suam nefarie efferatum, non mea culpa, desertis liberalibus studiis ac repudiata omni disciplina, scelestis accusationis huius rudimentis patruo Aemiliano potius quam fratri Pontiano similem futurum.* See Hijmans 1987,466 on the importance of erudition in the work of Apuleius, *philosophus platonicus.*

On the level of the fictive narrator it is relevant that Lucius, too, can be characterized as *probe litteratus* (cf. *Met.* 3,4-6: 55,6-57,2: Lucius' defense, where he gives evidence of a sound rhetorical education; in 11,15: 277,7 f. the priest mentions Lucius' *doctrina,* which, however, has been of no avail to him).

The idea that the study of literature teaches virtue, because poets and historiographers describe examples of upright behaviour, is traditional (see Marrou [4]1958,234 f.; 304 f.; cf. Ar. *Ran.* 1026 f.). Plato, too, admits that certain poetry can be educative (cf. *Apol.* 28c-d; *Leg.* 660a-661d); see also Florus *Verg. orator an poeta* 187,1-19 Rossbach. But, according to moralists like Epictetus (e.g. *Diatr.* 1,4,25-26 and 2,22,32-35) and Plutarch, poets and historiographers can also educate young people by showing them the disastrous consequences of evildoing. In this vision all literature is suitable for moral education, provided that it is presented to the young in an appropriate manner. This we find extensively illustrated in e.g. Plut. *Quomodo adulescens* (e.g. *Mor.* 28d-e; cf. also 19e). Plutarch also puts this idea into practice, as in the introduction to the lives of Demetrios and Antonius (*Dem.* 1,4-7). Since the fictive narrator of the *Met.* has presented himself as a relative of Plutarch (cf. *Met.* 1,2: 2,6 and 2,3: 26,12 f.), the qualification *probe litteratus* may also have this typically 'Plutarchian' connotation (Walsh 1981 points out other examples in the *Met.* of Plutarch's influence; see on *magistratus* ch. 6: 241,15). Through this notable phrase the reader is invited, as it were, to reflect on the value of literature in moral education - and this in the introduction to a version of the notoriously immoral Phaedra-Hippolytus tale (Aeschylus, in Ar. *Ran.* 1043, mentions Phaedra as one of Euripides' detestable creations; cf. also ibid. 1052 f.).

probe: this adverb, borrowed from the colloquial language and comedy, is frequent in the *Met.*; see Van der Paardt 1971,62. With an adjective the adverb often has a 'valeur superlative'; see Callebat 1968,537). In our passage there is still another possibility: not only does the adverb lend a superlative value to *litteratus* ('very learned'), it also indicates that the young man has been instructed in literature 'properly' (see the previous note).

litteratus: *ThLL* s.v. *litteratus* 1532,68 f. notes 'cf. Gloss. γεγραμματισμένος, γραμματικός'. In the passages mentioned by *ThLL* under this heading ('respicitur eruditio: a.: de hominibus ... adj.'), the adjective is often translatable as 'lettered'. For other meanings of *litteratus* in the *Met.* see 3,17 (65,5) with Van der Paardt 1971,132; 9,12 (212,6) with *GCA* 1995,122 f.

atque ob id consequenter: from Cicero and especially Sallust onward *atque ob id* is used as a conjunction, the relative complexity of which has been weakened to the point of becoming formulaic. Apuleius appears to put new life into this 'formula' (see Callebat 1968,419 f.), reinforcing it by *consequenter*, to heavily underscore the causal connection of 'right' moral education and character of the young man. Valpy rightly opposes the view that we have a case of pleonasm here ('διακριτικῶς positum'). The expressions are, indeed, not synonymous: *atque ob id*: 'so, therefore'; *consequenter*: 'as a consequence (of what he had learned)'.

pietate, modestia: thus F and φ. The *Met.* has only a few certain examples of such asyndeton, collected by Bernhard 1927,56. Oudendorp preferred *pietate modestiaque*; all modern editions, however, retain F (Robertson in his app. crit. praises Scriverus' proposal *pietate <et> modestia* with 'fortasse recte'). After the wordiness of *atque ob id consequenter* the absence of a conjunction is surprising and strikes one as highly stylized. Perhaps this effect is intentional, since the description of a well-educated young man is involved; moreover, he is introduced in two phrases of equal length: *iuuenem filium probe litteratum* (12) and *pietate modestia praecipuum* (12) - whose symmetry is even supported by rhyme.

We are given in a nutshell those good qualities of the young man that will be functional in the forthcoming story: *pietas* (he refuses to commit adultery with his father's wife) and *modestia* (he allows rational consideration to prevail over an instinctive, harsh rejection of his stepmother's propositions; see, however, on *non tamen ... exasperandum, sed ... leniendum* ch. 4: 239,2 f. and the following notes).

pietate: here in the sense of 'sense of duty, parental love, filial love', as in e.g. 8,7 (181,23); 10,23 (255,2); 10,26 (257,14). For its more general meaning 'pity' see *GCA* 1981,43 on 6,27 (149,8-10).

The *probe litteratus* young man, (and also the lettered reader) knows, of course, the textbook examples of *pietas* in literature (cf. V. Max. 5,4-6), above all Aeneas: Plin. *Nat.* 7,121-122; Hyg. *Fab.* 254,4. The emphasis on this quality of the young man, together with the Aenean associations evoked by the word, gives a deeper meaning to the addition *quem tibi quoque prouenisse cuperes uel talem* (cf. Verg. *A*. 3,480 *o felix nati pietate*, Helenus to Anchises); its irony is recognized by the re-reader, who knows that the father will believe the *nouerca*'s accusation without a thought and will even want his virtuous son to be condemned to death (ch. 5: 240,25 f.).

modestia: = σωφροσύνη, 'prudence'. In Apul. *Pl.* 2,6 (229) *modestia* (*abstinentia, continentia*) is, as a third virtue, linked to that part of the soul where *cupidines* and *desideria* (in the sense of 'passions'; see Beaujeu 290, n. 2 ad loc.) reside. *Modestia* is achieved by subjecting one's lower instincts to *ratio*, as the young man does in ch. 4 (239,1 f.). In 6,31 (153,4) one of the robbers cynically prides himself on his *modestia*, when he advises his comrades to kill Charite and the ass not rashly, in a fit of rage, but deliberately, by slow torture; he then proceeds to describe the process in great detail.

quem tibi ... prouenisse cuperes uel talem: cf. Pl. *Mos.* 120 f. *primumdum parentes fabri liberum sunt. /i fundamentum supstruont liberorum; / extollunt, parant sedulo in firmitatem, / et ut in usum boni et in speciem / poplo sint sibique, hau materiae reparcunt, / nec sumptus ibi sumptui esse ducunt ... / nituntur ut alii sibi esse illorum similis expetant.* Cf. also Dio Cassius 69,20,3 (Hadrian in praise of the dead Commodus) καὶ διὰ τοῦτο πρότερον μὲν τὸν Λούκιον ἐξ ἁπάντων ἐξελεξάμην, οἷον οὐδ' ἂν εὔξασθαι παῖδα ἠδυνήθην ἐμαυτῷ γενέσθαι.

cuperes: see *GCA* 1977,69 on 4,8 (80,8) *arbitrarere*; LHSz 2,419 'In diesen und ähnlichen Fallen schwebt noch ein unbestimmtes Subjekt vor, d.h. die 2. Pers. ist auf eine Reihe von Personen anwendbar.' But, especially because of the emphatic *tibi quoque*, the phrase here apostrophizes the reader (cf. de Jong 1989,54 f. on similar 'signs of the you' in Homer's

Iliad). It involves him/her in the events and suggests that the following could happen to anyone who had such a son.

237,6-9 Huius matre multo ante defuncta rursum matrimonium sibi reparauerat ductaque alia filium procreauerat alium, qui adaeque iam duodecimum annum aetatis superg<r>esserat: After the death of this boy's mother, a long time ago, he had renewed his married state once again and, after marrying another wife, had produced another son, who also by now had passed the age of twelve.

rursum ... reparauerat: the redundant use of *rursum* has an alliterative effect, as on several other occasions in the *Met.*; see e.g. *GCA* 1981,158 on 7,11 (163,1-3). The pleonastic use of *rursum* is frequent also in comedy (see Van der Paardt 1971,98 f. on 3,12: 61,12 f. *qui ... rursum reuerterim*). Cf. also *GCA* 1985,37 on 8,2 (177,15-19) *deorsus delapsum.*

matrimonium sibi reparauerat: this combination is attested here only (*ThLL* s.v. *matrimonium* 477,48 f.). More usual is *matrimonium iterare* or *matrimonium repetere*. Neither does the *ThLL* material s.v. *reparo* give any parallels for this combination, which can be interpreted in various ways according to various connotations of *reparare*. It can mean 'revive, renew' (*OLD* s.v. *reparo* 4), so that our phrase is comparable to e.g. Sen. *Ag*. 183 f. *Veneri uacat / reparatque amores* (see Tarrant ad loc., with parallels). Quint. *Inst*. 10,1,75 *intermissam historias scribendi industriam noua laude reparauit*. But *reparare* can also have more 'practical' meanings: 'recover something lost' (see *OLD* ibid. 1) and 'repair' (*OLD* ibid. 3). In the latter case, *matrimonium sibi reparauerat*, combined with the subsequent *ductaque alia filium procreauerat alium*, characterizes the *dominus aedium* as extremely practical: after the death of his first wife he 'restores the married state for himself', and his second wife is the instrument with which he produces another son.

From ch. 5 (240,23 f.) *tunc infelix ... percussus magnis aerumnarum procellis aestuat* onward, the *dominus aedium* is depicted as a wretched old man; at the very end of the story (ch. 12: 245,26 f.), however, a miraculously happy conclusion awaits him. Thus, as far as the *dominus aedium* is concerned, this tale illustrates Fortuna's fickleness, inscrutable to human beings, which is one of the main themes of the *Met*. (see Introd. **2.4.1**). Cf. also below, on *forma magis quam moribus*.

By remarrying when he has already a son from his first marriage, the *dominus aedium* acts counter to the warnings about stepmothers which are found in Greek literature as early as Plato, and only become stronger in Roman literature. Cf. e.g. Ov. *Ep*. 12,187 f. (Medea to Jason) *communis respice natos; / saeuiet in partus dira nouerca meos*. See Watson 1995,5 f. with literature. Sen. *Con*. 4,6 deals with a case of a father who has a son from a first marriage, and after remarrying gets another son; both boys are being brought up in the countryside. When they return, and are very much alike, the second wife wants to know which of the two is her own son; the father refuses to tell her: *dum alterius uis esse mater, utriusque es nouerca*. See below, on the *nouerca* in *declamationes*.

adaeque: 'equally, likewise'. We have to infer from *multo ante* that the first son had already passed the age of twelve. *Adaeque* is attested in Plautus, but always in negative clauses; after that it is not found until in Fronto, Apuleius, and later authors. In Apuleius it occurs for the first time in positive sentences (*ThLL* s.v. *adaeque* 560,44 f.). In translating 'qui venait d'atteindre l'âge de douze ans', Vallette follows a proposal by Kronenberg, who wants to read *adaeque* in the sense of *eo ipso tempore*; see, however, *GCA* 1985,273 on 8,31 (201,26-202,3).

superg<r>esserat: F and φ have *supergesserat*. The verb *supergerere* is attested only twice: once in Col. 11,3,6 and once in *Met.* 9,40 (234,18; see *GCA* 1995,338). If one were to read *supergesserat* here, the phrase would mean 'had already heaped the twelfth year on his lifetime'. In that case one could read *aetati* instead of the mss. reading *aetatis* (the *s* explained by dittography with *supergesserat*). Most modern editions follow Dousa's *supercesserat*; Augello 1977,207 calls this 'un emendamento prossimo alla certezza'; the interchange of *c* and *g* is, indeed, frequent in F (see Helm, Praef. *Fl.* XLV).

Since, however, *supercedere* is attested nowhere else, *supergresserat*, the reading proposed by Colvius, is preferable for the following reasons. a) *supergredi* is sometimes used in the sense 'pass a certain age'; e.g. Sen *Suas.* 6,6 *sexaginta supergressus es* and Sol. 30 *quadragesimum annum supergreditur.* b) An active form of the deponent *supergredi* should not present any problem, according to Flobert 1975,308. c) There are other examples of F's scribe omitting *r* after *g*; cf. 8,16 (189,18-19), where F and φ have *adgessionibus*, ς *adgressionibus*.

Robertson and Hanson follow the reading of ς, *supergressus erat* (thus also Van Thiel). This, too, is paleographically defensible: *supergress; erat* became *supergresserat*. *Supergresserat*, however, is the lectio difficilior.

237,9-12 Sed nouerca forma magis quam moribus in domo mariti praepollens, seu naturaliter impudica seu fato ad extremum impulsa flagitium, oculos ad priuignum adiecit: Well — the stepmother, who, more on account of her looks than of her character, ruled the roost in her husband's house, cast — whether because she was shameless by nature or because fate drove her to the ultimate outrage — a covetous eye on her stepson.

Sed ... adiecit: this is the beginning of the part of the story that is described as a 'complication' (see above, on 237,3-6); therefore *sed* indicates a transition here, not an antithesis (cf. e.g. 8,15: 188,11 with *GCA* 1985,142 ad loc.). The use of the perfect tense *adiecit*, after the series of pluperfects in the preceding sentence, also indicates that after some introductory information ('orientation') a new part of the story begins here.

nouerca: with this single word the narrator calls up a world of associations with evil, cruel women who deal in poisons and spells. Cf. 9,31 (226,16): not until the very end of the story about the *pistor*'s wicked wife it is mentioned, almost in passing, that she is a *nouerca* — which rounds off her characterization as a thoroughly evil woman.

Throughout world literature we meet the wicked stepmother (cf. the evil queen in Snow White; see Watson 1995,258 f.); examples in ancient literature are Hera and Ino. The malice of stepmothers is proverbial; cf. the old Dutch proverb (Harrebomée 1856, 2,3060) 'Die ene stiefmoeder heeft, mag rouwen zo lang hij leeft' ('He who has a stepmother will rue it as long as he lives'). A few examples from Otto 1890,245 f. s.v. *nouerca*: Verg. *Ecl.* 3,33 *iniusta nouerca*; *G.* 2,128 *pocula si quando saeuae infecere nouercae*. See also Bömer on Ov. *Met.* 1,147 *lurida terribiles miscent aconita nouercae;* cf. Courtney on Juv. 6,627. For the *nouerca* as 'stock character' in *declamationes*, see App. I, 5.4. Cf. e.g. Quint. *Decl.* 327,3 *ea quae tres priuignos habuit. expecto ex his aliquid nouercalibus factis. uenenum parauit? insidiata est liberis tuis? uel (quod leuissimum est) expugnare animum tuum uoluit?* Cf. Hier. *Ep.* 54,15 *quodsi de priori uxore habens subolem te domum introduxerit, etiamsi clementissima fueris, omnes comoediae et mimographi et communes rhetorum loci in nouercam saeuissimam declamabunt*; see Zinsmaier 1993,139 f. on [Quint.] *Decl.* 6,10 (120,21 f. Håkanson) *si perseuerat esse filii sui nouerca*, with references. Otto also mentions Greek examples, e.g. the proverb ἄλλοτε μητρυιὴ πέλει ἡμέρη, ἄλλοτε μήτηρ, as in Hes. *Op.* 825; see West ad loc. with references and parallels. An example of how firmly the image of the wicked stepmother is established in Latin, is the fact that in military jargon an extremely difficult piece of country is called *nouerca* (Hyg. *Mun. Castr.* § 57 Lange); Watson 1995,4 and n. 12. Gray-Fow 1988 collects a wealth of passages from Latin literature and investigates whether certain stepmother-figures in Roman history added to the stereotype of the 'wicked stepmother'.

forma magis quam moribus in domo mariti praepollens: the verb *praepollere* can mean 'excel' (see *ThLL* s.v. *praepolleo* 767,21 f.); in that case the ablatives *forma* and *moribus* indicate in what respect the woman did or did not excel (for this use *ThLL* cites our passage, 10,31: 261,25, and 10,33: 264,9-10 as the first occurrences): she was the most beautiful person in the house, but not the most honourable. In addition, *praepollere* can mean 'have the upper hand, dominate' (see *ThLL* ibid. 766,69 f.); in that case the ablatives indicate by what means power is exerted: the woman exploited her beauty to achieve power, but it was not her character that had earned her that authority. Both meanings play a part here, as we will see in the continuation of this note.

The description of this woman, as an evil person who dominates her household, evokes associations with a similar stock character in the mime (see Wiemken 1972,140). For the connections of this tale with the mime see App. I,5.3 and below, on *iam ergo, ... ascendere*. In many tales in which a stepmother occurs, she is depicted as both beautiful and tyrannical (cf. Ino and the wicked queen in 'Snow White').

forma magis quam moribus: it is probably a universal phenomenon that some correlation is expected between personal appearance and moral character. In the second century A.D. there was an especially great interest in physiognomic theories (Evans 1969,11 f.), and Apuleius, too, gives evidence of that in many passages of his work (Evans 1969,72 f.; Opeku 1979,470 f.; Mason 1984,307 f.). But physiognomic thinking existed long before the theories about it (Evans 1969,6 f.). In Latin literature there are many passages where the pair *forma* (*uultus, facies*, etc.) / *mores* (*animus, mens*, etc.) is linked, e.g. in historiography, when a main character is described. Cf. Suet. *Tit.* 3,1 *in puero statim corporis animique dotes explenduerunt* and ibid. *Dom.* 18,2 (Domitian about himself to the senate) *usque adhoc certe et animum meum probastis et uultum*. Also [Spart.] *Hist. Aug.* Ael. 5,1 *fuit hic uitae laetissimae, eruditus in litteris, Hadriano, ut maleuoli loquuntur, acceptior forma quam moribus*. The combination is frequent in poetry; cf. Bömer on Ov. *Met.* 7,696; cf. Ov. *Ep.* 16,290 *lis est cum forma magna pudicitiae* (see Evans 1969,71 on the attention paid to the correspondence between *forma, facies* on the one hand and *animus, mens* on the other hand in Ovid's works). Also Juv. 10,297 f. *rara est adeo concordia formae / atque pudicitiae* and Mart. 8,54 (53) *formonsissima quae fuere uel sunt / sed uilissima quae fuere uel sunt, / o, quam te fieri, Catulla, uellem, / formonsam minus aut magis pudicam!*

Ideally, a beautiful appearance reflects a noble character. For Apuleius cf. *Apol.* 4,9 *itemque multos philosophos ab ore honestissimos memoriae prodi, qui gratiam corporis morum honestamentis ornauerint*. Rhetorical schooling also paid attention to physiognomy (Quint. *Inst.* 3,7,12; Plin. *Pan.* 4,7). In the *Met.* the narrator, too, makes the connection: *nam et forma scitula et moribus ludicra* (2,6: 30,5).

This also adds, again, to the characterization of the father: in choosing his second wife he has apparently been guided only by her physical beauty (cf. Ov. *Rem.* 713 *nec solam faciem, mores quoque confer et artem*) and now allows her to dominate the house (*praepollens in domo mariti*). In this first part of the tale not one phrase characterizes the father directly; indirectly, however, his character is described in a great many ways; see e.g. above, on *matrimonium sibi reparauerat*. Nowhere in the story is he pictured in a truly positive way, so that the final sentence of the tale, which mentions his *famosa atque fabulosa fortuna*, has a surprising effect and seems to be an implicit illustration of the unpredictable way in which blind Fortuna distributes her favours (see Introd. **2.4.1**).

forma ... praepollens: cf. 6,22 (145,17 f.) *in terris puella praepollet pulcritudine*; ch. 31 (261,25) *uisendo decore praepollens.*

seu naturaliter impudica seu fato ad extremum impulsa flagitium: this phrase is not necessarily a contradiction of the views which the narrator has expressed up to now throughout the nine books of the *Met.*: he is convinced that one cannot escape one's personal *fatum*. Cf. e.g. 1,20 (18,23) *utcumque fata decreuerint, ita cuncta mortalibus prouenire.* We repeatedly encounter this conviction, which, interestingly, is either voiced with some resignation and emotional distance (as in the example above and in e.g. 4,21: 90,18; 4,33: 101,14; 5,22: 119,20), or expressed in emotional outbursts — which always relate to the the narrator's own ordeals; see e.g. 9,1 (203,12 f.) with *GCA* 1995,38 f. ad loc., where *diuinae prouidentiae fatalis dispositio* can be equated with *fatum* (εἱμαρμένη).

In reference to this passage, Fry 1984,163 f. erroneously speaks of a 'brèche dans un déterminisme qui était apparu jusqu' à présent sans faille': the word *impulsa* is the key to understanding this passage: either the woman was naturally shameless and therefore a willing tool of her *fatum*, or she was driven, willy-nilly, to an *extremum flagitium* because this was her *fatum*. It may be observed that the narrator is not a '*philosophus platonicus*': such a person would know that *omnia quae naturaliter et propterea recte feruntur prouidentiae custodia gubernantur nec ullius mali causa deo poterit adscribi* and *nec sane omnia referenda esse ad uim fati ... , sed esse aliquid in nobis et in fortuna esse non nihil* (Apul. *Pl.* 1,12 205-206; see Beaujeu 1973,272 f. ad loc. and Hijmans 1987,446 f.).

Though the narrator suggests to his fictitious audience that it had better not rack its brain about the question implied in *seu ... seu*, the words in themselves have the effect of making the reader aware of this matter by suggesting an important difference between the various literary treatments of the Phaedra story, which show a strong discrepancy in their way of treating the Phaedra character (see App. I,2 with references). If so interpreted, the narrator's comment forms, again, a 'rezeptionssteuernd' signal (see on *scelestum ac nefarium facinus* above).

Seu fato possibly refers to the words generally ascribed to Phaedra in Sophocles' *Phaedra*, Frg. 680 Radt νόσους δ'ἀνάγκη τὰς θεηλάτους φέρειν. In Euripides' *Hipp. Steph.*, too, Phaedra's infatuation has been aroused by Aphrodite. One may also think of Ov. *Ep.* 4,53, where Phaedra, referring to Pasiphaë, calls her perverted passion *generis fatum* (cf. also Sen. *Phaed.* 113).

oculos ad priuignum adiecit: a *nouerca*'s eyes bode no good for the person towards whom they are turned: Hor. *Epod.* 5,9 *quid ut nouerca me intueris* (Sen. *Con.* 4,6 *nouercalibus oculis*). Cf. also on *noxio conspectu nouercae* ch. 4 (239,8).

For the expression *oculos adicere ad aliquem* in the sense of 'cast a covetous glance on someone', cf. Pl. *As.* 769 *ad eorum ne quem oculos adiciat suos*; *ThLL* s.v. *adicio*

666,52-56 quotes several passages in Cicero where the expression occurs in the sense 'turn one's eyes desirously to'. It is possible that the expression is here a reference, which a contemporaneous reader would recognize, to Greek short stories in circulation at the time, based on the 'Potiphar's wife' motif (see Appendix I,5). Another version of the expression is known from Genesis 39 καὶ ἐπέβαλεν ἡ γύνη ... τοὺς ὀφθαλμοὺς ἐπὶ Ιοσὴφ (in the Vulgate *iecit domina oculos suos in Joseph*). Cf. also Heliod. 7,2,2 and 7,8,6. In Greek the expression is also common in contexts that have no connection with the 'Potiphar's wife' motif, e.g. *Onos* 4,6 μοῖχος γάρ ἐστι δεινὴ καὶ μάχλος καὶ πᾶσι τοῖς νέοις ἐπιβάλλει τὸν ὀφθαλμόν (cf. *Met.* 2,5: 29,5 f. *nam simul quemque conspexerit ... iuuenem ... ilico in eum et oculum et animum detorquet*; Ach. Tat. 4,2,1).

adiecit: for the perfect tense see above, on *sed ... adiecit*.

237,12-14 I am ergo, lector optime, scito te tragoediam, non fabulam legere et a socco ad coturnum ascendere: Know now therefore, most worthy reader, that you are reading a tragedy, not an amusing story, and that you are rising to a higher level, exchanging the low slipper of comedy for the high boot of tragedy.

Having just begun the 'complication' section (see above, on *sed*), the narrator again interrupts the story with the most urgent instructions to the fictive reader about how to receive the story. There is, however, a discrepancy between these 'instructions' at the level of the fictive narrator and narratee on the one hand, and, on the other, the 'rezeptionssteuernde' signal sent here by the abstract author to the abstract reader (see Introd. **3.2**).

Already from *sed ... adiecit* (above) onward it is clear to any lettered reader that he must watch for references to the Phaedra-Hippolytus tragedy. One important difference between the *iuuenis* and the Hippolytus of tragedy has already become evident to the *lector optimus*, however: through the characterization *probe litteratus ... pietate, modestia praecipuus* the young man has almost become the antithesis of the impetuous Hippolytus, devoted to Artemis, who in Eur. *Hipp. Steph.* 79 f. proudly joins those ὅσοις διδακτὸν μηδέν, ἀλλ' ἐν τῇ φύσει / τὸ σωφρονεῖν εἴληχεν, and who in Sen. *Phaed.* 483 f., with its glorification of the 'vie sauvage', certainly does not represent the ideal of a *iuuenis probe litteratus*. The *iuuenis* seems more akin to the virtuous Joseph in the Potiphar-novella of Philo and Josephus (see App. I,4): there Joseph, with his elaborately rendered speeches, is a true *iuuenis litteratus*; moreover, Josephus (*AJ* 2,39) mentions that Potiphar παιδείαν ... τὴν ἐλευθέριον ἐπαίδευε him. On the characterization of the *iuuenis* see also App. I,6B.

The person playing opposite the *iuuenis* in this story, the *nouerca*, has certainly shown, and will show in the immediate future, characteristics in common with the various Phaedra-characters; but in the course of the narrative she evolves into a type that corresponds with *nouercae* from the *declamationes*, the mime, and the novel (see App. I,6C and App. III).

lector optime: this is ambiguous. At first sight it is just a polite formula ('my dear reader'), but it can also be read as an exhortation to the reader addressed here to apply himself to a *lectio optima* of this story; in other words, not merely to enjoy it but to read it accurately. See the introductory note to *dii boni* below.

scito: see *GCA* 1985,205 ad 8,24 (195,25) *scitote* on the form of this imperative and on the function of imperatives of this type, addressed to the reader.

fabulam: this word is hard to translate because of its wide range of meanings (see *GCA* 1981,56 and Mason in *AAGA* 1978,7; Fick-Michel 1991,31 f.), including the meaning 'tragedy'. In its position here, contrasted with *tragoedia*, it is perhaps best rendered 'amusing story', or, in the light of *a socco*, 'comic plot'.

a socco ad coturnum ascendere: the words *soccus* and *coturnus* are traditionally used to indicate comedy and tragedy respectively (see Brink on Hor. *Ars* 80); this may include the contents and subject matter of tragedy or comedy (e.g. Juv. 15,29), and style (e.g. Verg. *Ecl.* 8,10; Hor. *Carm.* 2,1,12; Quint. *Inst.* 10,1,68). Cf. Apul. *Fl.* 16,7 (on the comedies of Philemon) *ioca non infra soccum, seria non usque ad coturnum.*

Blümner proposed to read *coturnum <me> ascendere;* he was of the opinion that the *lector optimus* could hardly be said to rise from *soccus* to *coturnus*. His conjecture, though not adopted by any of the modern editors, has a heuristic value: the narrator does not say that he himself is rising from *soccus* to *coturnus*; he assumes that the (naive) fictive reader, whom he is addressing, will do so as soon as he reads about an 'infatuated stepmother'. Through these words of the fictive narrator, directed at the fictive reader, the abstract reader (see Introd. **3.2**) gets a clue how to receive the text that comes next (see on *lector optime* above).

There is a possible reference to Juv. 6,634 f. *fingimus haec altum satura sumente coturnum / scilicet, et finem egressi legemque priorum / grande Sophocleo carmen bacchamur hiatu / montibus ignotum Rutulis caeloque Latino, / nos utinam uani. sed clamat Pontia 'feci'*. Juvenal means here that the crimes of women in tragedy do not belong exclusively to fiction: they are found in real life as well (cf. ibid. 655 f. *occurrent multae tibi Belides atque Eriphylae / mane, Clytaemestram nullus non uicus habebit*). The reminiscence of Juvenal in our passage would give it a deeper meaning: perverted stepmothers are found not only in tragedy and mythology but also in the everyday, small-town 'reality' of our story.

a socco: one is so easily inclined to read the phrase *a socco ad coturnum ascendere* exclusively as a 'misleading' reference to the tragic nature of the story introduced here, that it is easy to overlook the fact that *a socco* obviously refers back to the comedy in the description of the '*miles gloriosus*' in the preceding episode. See on *miles ille, qui ... uapularat* ch. 1 (236,11 f.).

237,14-16 Sed mulier illa, quandiu primis elementis Cupido paruulus nutriebatur, imbecillis adhuc eius uiribus facile ruborem tenuem deprimens silentio resistebat: Well then, as long as the infant Cupid was in the earliest stage of nurture, that woman could easily resist his powers, which were weak as yet, by silently suppressing her faint glow.

Sed: after a metanarrative remark (*iam ergo ... ascendere*; for the term 'metanarrative' see above, on 237,1-3), *sed* again (see above, on *sed ... adiecit*) marks a transition and resumes the 'complication' part of the tale.

mulier illa: she is not called *nouerca* now: here we have a general description of a woman in the clutches of an illicit passion. The individual notes will show that we have a 'collage' of the different tragic Phaedra figures here; that the description of the woman's pangs of love contains references to Vergil's *A.* 4 (Dido), Alexandrian poetry, and Roman elegy; and that there are unmistakable references to the Antiochos-Stratonice tale (see

App. I,5,3). On symptoms of love in the Greek novel and the Greek Anthology, see Maehler 1990,1 f.

In these first passages of the story, the woman's suffering is described with a certain sympathy; but we have already been warned that she has sisters in other literary genres: see above, on *nouerca*; *forma magis quam moribus ... praepollens*, and *oculos ... adiecit*.

quandiu: thus F; both Helm, Robertson, and Hanson adopt *quamdiu* from ς. According to the principle that F is the basis of the textual edition and that accordingly F's spelling must be adhered to wherever and whenever possible (see *GCA* 1985, Introd. 10), *quandiu* is retained here: in the pronunciation, nasal *m* before the occlusive *d* had already become *n* (cf. *eumdem/eundem*), even though the official spelling remained *quamdiu*. The spelling *quandiu* is attested in e.g. *CIL* 6,10231 (see Sommer 1914,236 f.).

primis elementis ... nutriebatur: this can be interpreted in different ways. Given an infant Cupid, the phrase must surely be taken at first sight as being concerned with his feeding, and we have the picture of baby Cupid still being fed the blandest of baby food; but *primis elementis nutriebatur* could be translated 'was being nurtured in the first rudiments (of a child's education)', and, looking ahead to the description of *Amor* as a blazing fire, the phrase could be interpreted as 'was being fed with its first fuel' (see *OLD* s.v. *elementum* 4: 'beginnings, germs, seeds', also of a fire). *Nutrire* is also used metaphorically of 'nursing' passion; cf. e.g. Ov. *Ars* 3,579; Prop. 1,12,5, and Ov. *Met.* 1,496 with Bömer ad loc.; see also *GCA* 1985,37 on 8,2 (177,17) *nutriens amorem*. Moreover, we have to wonder who is the agent of *nutriebatur*. If it is the woman, we may infer that she resisted her feelings only half-heartedly. Cf. Sen. *Phaed.* 134 f. (the *nutrix* to Phaedra:) *qui blandiendo dulce nutriuit malum / sero recusat ferre quod subiit iugum*. See also below, on *ruborem*.

Cupido paruulus: this evokes the image of the baby god which was a creation of Hellenistic literature and visual art (cf. Dar.-Sagl. s.v. Cupido 1595 and 1600 f.). In the next sentence he becomes the formidable god Amor about whom Tib. 1,8,7 f. says: *deus crudelis urit, / quos uidet inuitos succubuisse sibi*. Cf. Naev. *com.* fr. 55 Ribbeck *edepol, Cupido, cum tam pausillus sis, nimis multum uales*. See Fliedner 1974,69 f., and 78. In ch. 32 (263,2 f.) the dancer who impersonates Venus is surrounded by sweet little Cupids; see note there.

ruborem: thus F and φ; this is rightly retained by all modern editors, against conjectures like *ardorem* (Lennep) or *feruorem* (Seyffert). Wiman defends *ruborem* but agrees with the scholars mentioned above that the next sentence here requires a word like 'heat' or 'glow'; he shows that *rubor* can certainly have that association, e.g. Hor. *Carm.* 3,13,7 and *S.* 2,5,39.

The translation 'glow' has been chosen because of the next sentence, which refers to love as a fire. Another connotation of *rubor* is also relevant here: 'that which causes one to blush or feel ashamed' (*OLD* s.v. *rubor* 3). Cf. also e.g. Helm-Krenkel 'die keimende schamvolle Neigung" and Scazzoso 'un colpa ancor lieve'; cf. Lateiner 1998,178: 'flickering sense of shame'. Other translators opt for *rubor* = 'blush'.

silentio resistebat: cf. Eur. *Hipp. Steph.* 393 f. ἠρξάμην μὲν οὖν / ἐκ τοῦδε, σιγᾶν τήνδε καὶ κρύπτειν νόσον; having failed in spite of increasingly frantic attempts, she is determined to take her own life. This thought cannot be found in Apuleius' Phaedra figure. Seneca's Phaedra is doubtful in this respect; see Appendix 1,4 and on ch. 4 (239,24) *uita miserum priuare iuuenem*.

237,17-20 At ubi completis igne uaesano totis praecordiis immodice bacchatus

Amor exaestuabat, saeuienti deo iam succubuit, et languore simulato uulnus animi mentitur in corporis ualetudine: But when her entire inner self was filled with an insane fire and Amor, in a frenzy of excitement, blazed forth beyond control, she eventually succumbed to the god's violence and, feigning an infirmity, concealed her heart's wound in physical illness.

This description resembles in many respects the description of Thrasyllus' frenzied passion for Charite in *Met.* 8,2 (178,6-8), where, however, the traditional metaphorical use of *amor = ignis, flamma* is more consistently adhered to. See *GCA* 1985,40 ad loc. (*amburat*) and cf. Ov. *Met.* 3,372 with Bömer ad loc. (see also the following notes). The mingling of the metaphor of love as fire with the image of Amor as a formidable and merciless god makes this passage virtually untranslatable. This mixing of images is already visible in the preceding sentence; see there, on *primis elementis ... nutriebatur* and on *ruborem*. In the present sentence the logical subject is the woman, but in the introductory clause *ubi ... exaestuabat* it is Amor, dancing madly around the fire, on whom the narrator's (and through him the reader's) eyes are focused; subsequently the narrator calls our attention back to the woman, who experiences Amor as a *deus saeuiens* to whom she eventually submits.

Cf. Sen. *Phaed.* 184 f.: (Phaedra) *quid ratio possit? uicit ac regnat furor, / potensque tota mente dominatur deus*, to which the nurse answers (195 f.): *deum esse amorem turpis et uitio furens / finxit libido, quoque liberior foret / titulum furori numinis falsi addidit* and (202 f.) *uana ista demens animus asciuit sibi / Venerisque numen finxit atque arcus dei.*

Finkelpearl 1998,162 f. and n. 27 refers to Vergil's description of Dido in *A.* 4,2 *uulnus alit uenis et caeco carpitur igni* and 66 *est mollis flamma medullas / interea et tacitum uiuit sub pectore uulnus*. Seneca, too, has drawn his inspiration for his Phaedra from the description of Dido, as Fantham 1975,4-5 shows. As early as Verg. *A.* 6,442 f. Dido is found among those *quos durus amor crudeli tabe peredit*. In our case the literary associations include more than just Seneca's Phaedra and Vergil's treatment of Dido's grief, as will appear from the notes below.

ubi ... exaestuabat: the construction of temporal *ubi* and *ut* with an imperfect indicative is rare, but Callebat 1968,348 gives examples from Plautus onward, including prose authors like Livy and Caesar, which show that this construction can be used to indicate that the situation described in the dependent clause extended over a long period of time in the past. See KSt 2,2,361.

completis igne uaesano totis praecordiis: the *rubor tenuis* (l. 16) has grown into a blazing fire that completely possesses her, the result of *nutriebatur* (see on *primis elementis ... nutriebatur* above) or of *deprimens* (l. 16): it is a topos that *tectus amor* often becomes more ardent, in the same way that a *tectus ignis* flares up all the higher. Cf. Ov. *Met.* 4,64 *quoque magis tegitur, tectus magis aestuat ignis* with Bömer ad loc.

igne uaesano: a comparable combination is found in Catul. 100,7 *cum uesana meas torreret flamma medullas* (Kroll ad loc. assumes enallage here, but the combination *uesana fames* is attested more than once. Cf. Sen. *Phaed.* 361 *flammis ... insanis*).

igne: i.e. *amore*; Crawley [2]1927,1,237 f.: 'There is an universal connection, seen in all languages, between love and heat.' This quotation is to be found at the end of Pease's extensive note on Verg. *A.* 4,2 (sc. Dido) *caeco carpitur igni.* For the topos 'love as fire' in the Greek novel and the Anthology, see Maehler 1990,4 f. The universal character of this topos makes it less necessary to assume in this passage a direct reference to Seneca (and through him to Vergil): of course the literary reader is supposed to be aware not only of the fire-topos but also of the passages in question in Seneca and Vergil; however, all through this description of the woman's tormented love, a much broader reference to literary models can be found (see App. I,6 and 7).

uaesano: for the spelling *uae/uesanus* see *GCA* 1995,45 on 9,2 (204,6).

bacchatus: Finkelpearl 1998,163 notes the corresponding 'cluster of images' in Verg. *A.* 4,300 f. *saeuit inops animi totamque incensa per urbem / bacchatur.* Apuleius, however, transfers all Vergil's descriptions of Dido to Amor: *saeuit*: *saeuienti deo*; *inops animi*: *igne uaesano*; *bacchatur* (sc. Dido): *bacchatus* (sc. Amor); Dido is *incensa*, whereas here Amor is himself represented as a blazing fire. In our passage *bacchari* cannot mean 'to act like a Bacchante' (cf. *GCA* 1985,71 on 8,6: 181,3-7), but is used 'latiore sensu' in the sense of *furere* (*uoluptate, gaudio*, etc.). See *ThLL* s.v. *bacchor* 1663,36 f. (ibid. 1663,59 f. *amore*; also 1663,64 f. our passage); cf. e.g. Hor. *Carm.* 2,7,26 f. *non ego sanius / bacchabor Edonis: recepto / dulce mihi furere est amico.* In this instance there is a similarity of language, but to the opposite effect: Dido is running about in despair, but Amor is beside himself with excitement and joy.

exaestuabat: see *GCA* 1985,40 on 8,2 (178,7 f.) *exaestuans.*

saeuienti deo iam succubuit: there is no reason to change the word order of F to *saeuienti iam deo succubuit*, as proposed by Pricaeus, defended by Oudendorp ad loc., and mentioned in Robertson's app. crit. with 'fort. recte'. The reason for this proposal was, possibly, the thought that *saeuienti iam deo* would give a nice parallel with *imbecillis adhuc eius uiribus* (above). In its position as transmitted *iam* underlines the perfect tense *succubuit*: after the imperfects in this sentence, which describe the woman struggling with her passion and being gradually overpowered, this perfect states a fact that is important for the development of the story: 'in the end she admitted defeat.'

This phrase reminds us of the oracular description of *Amor* in 4,33 (100,24 101,2) as a *saeuum ... malum, / quod ... cuncta fatigat / flammaque et ferro singula debilitat.* On *saeuus* as a 'stock epithet of love or Cupid' see Kenney on 4,33 (100,24) with examples. See also Fliedner 1974,69 f.

succubuit ... mentitur: on the variation of perfect and historical present see on ch. 3 (238,5) *rupit ... praecipit.*

et languore simulato ... ualetudine: the woman is still depicted here as feigning illness, which brings her very near to the type of evil, deceitful woman whom we have met before in the *Met.* (the *pistor*'s wife 9,14: 213,10 f.), and who belongs in the original version of the Potiphar-tale (see Braun 1934,50 f.; Trenkner 1958,65 and n. 5; also App. I). In e.g. Euripides' *Hipp. Steph.* Phaedra actually is ill with love, and that impression prevails in the immediately following section of our story. In the Antiochus-Stratonice story (see App. I, 5,3) the illness of the love-stricken Antiochus is also not feigned (see below, on *uulnus ... mentitur*, and *heu medicorum*).

uulnus animi mentitur in corporis ualetudine: thus F and φ, adopted by Helm, Giarratano, and Terzaghi. Robertson proposes *[in] corporis ualetudine<m>* (Leo's conjecture); Giarratano-Frassinetti *in corporis ualetudine<m>* (Bernhardy). Blümner proposes *uertitur* instead of *mentitur*, and, of course, *ualetudinem*. These conjectures are obviously based on two problems:

a) *mentiri* must mean 'hide' here. This is a rare use of the verb, which is, however, attested on several occasions: see *ThLL* s.v. *mentior* 779,17 f. with e.g. Pl. *Poen* 152 *quid nunc tibi uis? cur ego apud te mentiar? amo*; Maurach 1975,168 ad loc. '*mentiri* i.q. *celare*: Ob es sich um einen wieder aufgetauchten umgangssprachlichen Usus handelte (for *ThLL* gives also examples from Stat. and Manil.) oder um ein gewollt wiederbelebtes verbum priscum kann kaum entschieden werden.' b) The construction *mentiri* (i.q. *celare*) *aliquid in aliqua re* is unique. But Ruiz de Elvira 1954,106 f. argues that the use of *in* + ablative with instrumental force expanded greatly in later Latin. Callebat 1968,226 follows him; so does Augello 1977,207 f., retaining the reading of F.

uulnus animi - corporis ualetudine: chiasmus.

uulnus ... mentitur: unlike Dido, who, according to general interpretation, is not yet aware herself of her *tacitum ... uulnus* (Verg. *A.* 4,67; see Pease ad loc. and on 4,2 *caeco ... igni*), this *nouerca* is aware of her 'wound' but hides it by means of lies. See also *GCA* 1995,228 f. on 9,26 (222,18-21) *taciti uulneris* (discussing the literary background for *uulnus* as 'wound of love'; see also Maehler 1990,4). *Mentitur* reminds us for the first time of a story which gives a kind of inverted version of the Potiphar-tale, namely the Antiochus-Stratonice story (see App. I,5.3). A striking resemblance to our passage is offered by the following phrase in a version of the Antiochus-Stratonice story transmitted by Aristaenetus (*Ep.* 1,13) σώματος μὲν ἀφανῆ πλαττόμενος ἀλγηδόνα, ψυχῆς δὲ τοῖς ἀληθείας αἰτιώμενος νόσον. Later our *nouerca* uses a feigned illness to lure her stepson into her bedroom (ch. 3: 238,4 f.), following the behaviour of Potiphar's wife. So, although the reference to the Antiochus-Stratonice tale may have briefly raised expectations for an equally happy end in our story, these hopes are disappointed from 238,4 f. onward. Of course, a happy ending has been ruled out from the beginning by the story's designation as a *scelestum ac nefarium facinus* (237,1 f.).

237,20-25 I am cetera salutis uultusque detrimenta et aegris et amantibus examussim conuenire nemo qui nesciat: pallor <in or>e deformis, marcentes oculi, lassa genua, quies turbida et suspiritus cruciatus tarditate uehementior. Crederes et illam fluctuare tantum uaporibus febrium, nisi quod et flebat: That, in general, detrimental influences on health and appearance of both invalids and lovers correspond exactly, everybody knows: unsightly facial pallor, lack-lustre eyes, shaking knees, disturbed sleep, and painful sighing, all the more violent because of its slowness. You might have thought that she, too, was shaking only with the fiery attacks of fever, if she were not also weeping.

The narrative is interrupted here; for the nature and function of this interruption for commentary, see below, on *dii boni*.

Love as illness: this conception, widespread in folklore (Thompson T 24 and T 24.1) and very old (see Amundsen 1974,332 with literature in notes), is known to us from the earliest Greek poetry onward, especially Sappho (Frg. 2,14 f. D: 31 L.-P.); as a literary topos it has acquired a rich and fascinating history in ancient Greek and Roman literature (much information can be found in Pease on Verg. *A.* 4,65 f. and Pöschl 1964 s.v. 'Krankheit'; Geisler 1969, p. 57 f. in his introduction to Ov. *Rem.* 1-396 'Liebe als Krankheit'). See Lateiner 1998,187, and n. 51, with references, on the '*nosos*-love syndrom in Greek novels. Sappho's famous poem, in which she lists the symptoms she observes in herself, remains in all later manifestations of the motif the model which was varied and elaborated upon, cf. Catul. 51,9 f. That this poem was indeed a 'textbook example' appears from e.g. [Longinus] *De subl.* 10,2 and Plut. *Dem.* 38,4 (on Antiochus' symptoms of being in love) ἐγένετο τὰ τῆς Σαπφοῦς ἐκεῖνα περὶ αὐτὸν πάντα. The same poem was also often used as a basis for the exercise in paraphrasing poetry into prose (Stark 1957,325 f., especially 334 f.).

Euripides used the motif of lovesickness in his *Hipp. Steph.*; afterwards it had a regular, though not always justified, place in later versions of the Phaedra story (see e.g. Zwierlein 1987,18 f. with literature). In the catalogue of symptoms there are several intertextual allusions to the Antiochus-Stratonice story (see App. I,6D, and above on *uulnus ... mentitur*).

salutis uultusque detrimenta: here at once begins the professional terminology that characterizes the entire following list, reminding the reader what the school-exercises have done to Sappho's famous poem (see the preceding note): *ThLL* s.v. *detrimentum* 837,10 f. remarks that this word occurs almost exclusively in prose (see also Axelson 1945,59). This passage is, in fact, a sort of detached, scientific prose, which achieves an ironical and comical effect (see also the following notes and Fiorencis/Gianotti 1990,88).

Elsewhere (e.g. *Mun.* 19 (332), *Met.* 11,1: 266,19 f.) Apuleius uses *detrimentum* in the meaning given by *ThLL* 837,14 f.: i.q. *comminutio* (cf. e.g. 6,6: 132,19). In this passage, too, the original meaning is present: *comminutio* refers to someone's wasting away because of 'lovesickness'; see Norden on Verg. *A.* 6,442 *quos durus amor crudeli tabe peredit* and Maehler 1990,5. A further meaning is also appropriate (*ThLL* 839,17): *detrimentum* i.q. *corruptio, deprauatio, in deterius mutatio, peremptio*; cf. e.g. Col. 12,26,1 (about *mustum*) *ita diutius nihil durabit et nihil detrimenti fiet*. It is unnecessary to follow *ThLL* 839,24 f. and assume a special meaning ('fere i.q. *foedatio*') for our passage and one passage in Cels. *dig.* 8,1,9. For our passage that is actually incorrect, because *foedatio* could be substituted for *detrimenta* in conjunction with the objective genitive *uultus*, but not with *salutis*.

examussim: 'precisely'. See *GCA* 1977,138 on 4,18 (88,7-10) for this Plautine word.

nemo qui nesciat: this phrase is the fictive narrator's irony at the expense of characters in the story (the stepson as well as the doctors) who, as the continuation of the story shows, obviously fail to recognize the situation. See also below, on *dii boni*.

pallor deformis: F and φ have *pallore deformis*; with Helm, Frassinetti, Terzaghi, Hanson (see also Augello 1977,208), the emendation of ς: *pallor[e] deformis* has been adopted. It has the virtue of matching the other items in the catalogue, which all consist of adjective (or participle) + noun or vice versa. It does not, however, account for the ablative in F and φ. Other conjectures are based on an attempt to retain the ablative *pallore* in F: Giarratano has *pallore deformis <facies>*, probably following Van der Vliet *<facies> pallore deformis*. Rohde: *uultus pallore deformis*.

pallor: the enumeration of the symptoms of love opens with the tradional *pallor amantium* (cf. Hor. *Carm.* 3,10,14); see Pichon s.v. *pallor* and Murgatroyd on Tib. 1,8,51 f.; see also Bömer on Ov. *Met.* 9,535 f. Psyche's *nimius pallor* in *Met.* 5,25 (123,3) is one of the signs that lead Pan to conclude that she is suffering from lovesickness. See Kenney ad loc.; Lateiner 1998,166 discusses examples in ancient novels for *pallor*, 'an inverse blush' as an indication of lovesickness, with many references in notes.

deformis: this addition to *pallor* probably indicates a sickly paleness (cf. *pallor nimius* mentioned in the preceding note), since a pale complexion in itself was an ideal of female beauty. The adjective *deformis* often has an 'active' meaning, as Monteil 1974,65 f. shows, with examples. The phrase may then be translated 'a paleness which disfigures the face'. Cf. 8,8 (183,8-10) *pallore deformem ... faciem*, and see *GCA* 1985,90 ad loc., and ibid. 201 ad 8,23 (195,14-17) *dolore deformem* on the frequent occurrence of *deformitas* in descriptions in Apuleius.

marcentes oculi: Finkelpearl 1998,164 assumes with Erbse 1950,113 a reference to Sen. *Phaed*. 379-80 *et qui ferebant signa Phoebeae facis / oculi nihil gentile nec patrium micant* (see Zintzen 1960,44 for Euripides' *Hipp. Steph.* as Seneca's model in this passage). There is, however, no direct verbal resemblance (but see the following note *lassa genua* for a possible connection with the corresponding passage in Seneca), and the symptom described here is also found in Sappho (fr. 2 D = 31 L-P,11 ὀππάτεσσι δ'οὐδεν ὄρημμ'). Cf. also e.g. AR 3,962 f. ὄμματα δ'αὔτως / ἤχλυσαν. Plut. *Dem*. 38,4 lists it with ὄψεων ἀπόλειψις under 'τὰ τῆς Σαπφοῦς ἐκεῖνα περὶ αὐτὸν πάντα', and we also find it in Lucianus *Syr. D.* 17: ὀφθαλμοί τε ἀσθενέες. The latter two citations occur in the context of a version of the Antiochus-Stratonice story (see the introductory note above, on *iam cetera salutis*).

Apuleius' phrase *marcentes oculi* is original, probably suggested by expressions in which *marceo* is used for the fading of stars or lamplight getting dim (*ThLL* s.v. *marceo* 373,6 f.). In the *Met*. it also occurs in 4,24 (93,21). After Apuleius the combination occurs in Fulg. *Myth*. 1, praef. p. 13,21 Helm (*marcentia ... lumina*) and Ambr. *Psalm*. 118; Ps. Ambr. *Serm*. 19,22. See Kenney on 5,25 (123,2 f. 'the language of the eyes') with literature.

lassa genua: after an enumeration of *uultus detrimenta* we now get *detrimenta salutis*. The list of symptoms is chiastically arranged in relation to the phrase *salutis uultusque detrimenta*.

Finkelpearl 1998,164 calls Apuleius' *lassa genua* a 'sly, allusive pun on Phaedra's *lassae genae*' (Sen. *Phaed*. 364), correcting, as it were Seneca's phrase *lassae genae / lucem recusant*, which, in turn, is suggested by Eur. *Hipp. Steph.* 178 (see Zintzen 1960,42). Grimal ad loc. refers to Enn. and Prop. for *genae* 'au sens d'yeux, ou peut-être de paupières' (cf. also *Culex* 185). The 'correction' of Seneca's passage is perhaps carried even further: *Phaed*. 364 begins *erumpit oculis ignis*, which is contradicted by *lassae genae* (see the previous note); Apuleius, by writing *lassa genua*, corrects the inconsistency between *erumpit oculis ignis* and *lassae genae*.

The phrase *lassa genua* expresses the same idea as Sen. *Phaed*. 367 *soluto labitur ... gradu* and 377 *populatur artus cura, iam gressus tremunt*, passages for which Zintzen (l.c.) indicates no direct parallels in Eur. Cf. Apul. *Met*. 5,25 (123,2 f.) *isto titubante et saepius uacillante uestigio*; AR 3,964 f. (referring to Medea) γούνατα δ'οὔτ' ὀπίσω οὔτε προπάροιθεν ἀεῖραι / ἔσθενεν. *Hist.Apoll*. 18 (Kortekaas 1984,316,15 f.) *cum non posset puella ulla ratione uulnus amoris tollerare, in multa infirmitate membra prostrauit fluxa, et cepit iacere imbecillis in thoro*.

For the use of *lassus* (= *fessus*) in the *Met*. see *GCA* 1985,172 on 8,19 (192,8-14).

quies turbida: a pointed oxymoron summarizes a topos which, from Hellenistic love poetry onward, has its fixed place in the 'catalogue of love symptoms'; see Murgatroyd on Tib. 1,8,64. A graffito found on the Palatine (*CEL* 943 B.) formulates this universal motif thus: *[Vis] nulla est animi, non somnus claudit ocellos / noctes [atque] dies aestuat omnis amor*. See Harrison 1997,66 on a possible witty contamination of two passages from Verg. A. 4 (5 and 351 f.) in the description of this lovesick woman.

et suspiritus cruciatus tarditate uehementior: the previously enumerated symptoms counted 5 or 6 syllables each, and thus gave a staccato-effect. The list ends with a phrase of 18 syllables, the many long vowels illustrating the content.

The Latin admits of different grammatical explanations. This translation has opted for the view of *ThLL* s.v. *cruciatus* 1219,72, where *suspiritus* is taken as an attributive genitive with the nominative *cruciatus* (see *ThLL* 1219,52 f. for other examples). *Vehementior* then modifies *cruciatus*. Other translations regard *uehementior* as a qualification of a nominative *suspiritus*, and *cruciatus* as a genitive with *tarditate*; so e.g. Helm-Krenkel 'Und mit der Länge der Qual immer mehr zunehmendes Seufzen' (likewise Vallette). This is quite possible: the *ThLL* material for *tarditas* gives parallels where *tarditas* can implicitly mean 'long duration': Suet. *Ves.* 12 *fatigatus tarditate et taedio pompae* (the slowness, and therefore also the long duration of the procession); Col. 3,9,5 *temporis tarditas*; Plin. *Nat.* 10,170; Cael Aurel. *Chron.* 2,13,165 *tarditate temporis aucta uirtute* (see Vietmeier 1937,19.59 *tarditas* = χρονιότης).

So: pain while sighing, all the more violent because of the slow tempo (of the sighs). Thus the last phrase sounds like a medical diagnosis, and the context, too, indicates to the reader that s/he should supply in her/his thoughts something like 'and the physicians consulted were unable to identify the disease from which the woman was suffering'. Cf. *Hist.Apoll.* 18 (Kortekaas 1984,316,22 f.) *Rex ... sollicitus adhibet medicos. Qui uenientes medici temptantes uenas tangunt singulas corporis partes, nec omnino inueniunt egritudinis causas* (unlike the astute doctor in the Antiochus-Stratonice story; see App. I,5.3 and 6D).

suspiritus: occurs 5 times in the *Met.* (see also *GCA* 1985,141 on 8,15: 188,7-8) and once in *Apol.* 85,3 *suspiritus numeras*, used, as here, of the deep sighs of someone in love. Cf. 5,25 (123,3 f.) *assiduo suspiritu* with Kenney ad loc. Apuleius clearly prefers the rarer word *suspiritus* to the more common *suspirium*, which is not attested in his works. *Suspirium*, on the other hand, occurs quite often in elegy as a *signum amoris*, and is also very frequent in Ovid. See e.g. Ov. *Met.* 9,537 with Bömer ad loc. Cf. also *suspirare in* + ablative: 'be madly in love with' (*OLD* s.v. *suspiro* 1b: Hor. *Carm.* 3,7,10; Catul. 64,98; Ov. *Fast.* 1,417).

cruciatus: cf. *cruciabilem suspiritum ducens* in *Met.* 1,7 (6.22). *ThLL* s.v. *cruciatus* 1219,1 f. mentions for *cruciatus* 'de tormentis amoris' only Apul. *Met.* 2,10 (33,3) and 9,18 (216,16; see *GCA* 1995,169 ad loc.).

illam fluctuare tantum uaporibus febrium: see Finkelpearl 1998,165 f. on the allusions to Sen. and Verg. and their functions. The narrator tells us that the woman would seem to be shivering from fever alone, if it were not for her tears. However, the choice of *fluctuare* for 'shiver' is very unusual. It is likely that Apuleius has chosen it because of its frequent use to describe emotional turmoil (see Pease on Verg. A. 4,532 and *GCA* 1977,28 on 4,2: 75,9); nautical metaphors occur abundantly both in Greek and Latin literature (see Svennung 1945,80 f. with n. 72-75). Apuleius uses *fluctuare* similarly in 5,23 (121,9), where Psyche, after beholding Amor, *saucia mente fluctuat*: in her case the mental turmoil may be understood to produce the physical trembling which causes her to spill oil from the lamp. Trembling is, of course, one of the standard symptoms of love: Sappho *Fr.* 2D = 31 L-P,13 f. τρόμος δὲ / παῖσαν ἄγρει; Theocr. 2,85 f.

Similarly, *uapor* can be explained in two ways: one meaning, as Finkelpearl l.c. remarks (confirmed by the *ThLL* material), is 'ardour' or 'excited state of mind', which is a typical

Senecan use of the word; it can also be used in a concrete sense, e.g. with *febrium* 'the heat of fever'. *ThLL* s.v. *febris* 410,35 f. gives passages for *ardores febrium* and *feruores febrium*, but only our passage for *uapores febrium*. It is therefore probable that Apuleius indeed alludes to a Senecan use of *uapor*.

nisi quod: 'apart from the fact that ... '; see on ch. 30 (261,11) *nisi quod*.

237,25-238,1 Heu medicorum ignarae mentes, quid uenae pulsus, quid coloris intemperantia, quid fatigatus anhelitus et utrimquesecus iactatae crebriter laterum mutuae uicissitudines?: Alas for the perception of the doctors, who do not know what to make of the throbbing of the veins, of the changes in color, of the laborious breathing and the constant tossing and turning, over and over again, from one side to the other!

Heu medicorum ignarae mentes, quid ... : this is generally recognized (see e.g. Walsh 1970,54 f.; Westerbrink in *AAGA* 1978,71) as a parody of Verg. *A*. 4,65 f. *heu, uatum ignarae mentes! quid uota furentem / quid delubra iuuant.* This is a typical instance of the ancient rhetorical figure of parody: a famous verse is quoted, with one element changed, without any ridiculising intention as implied in our modern notion of parody. Cf. Lelièvre 1931,71 f.; Lazzarini 1986,132, who quotes Quint. *Inst.* 6,3,97 and Hermog. *Meth.* 305; she discusses our passage ibid. 145; see also Harrison 1997,66.

Vergil's poetic representation of a woman consumed by love has been an example for many after him, and in Seneca's Phaedra, too, one can recognize characteristics of Vergil's Dido (Fantham 1975). By replacing *uatum* with *medicorum*, the totally different contexts are contrasted with each other: Dido, who through sacrifices asks the gods to sanction her love for Aeneas, versus the *nouerca*, who just has been said to feign illness. Another effect is that the very prosaic list of love symptoms is briefly interrupted and contrasted with what was generally regarded as the culmination of poetic art: Vergil's verse describing a woman tormented by love.

At the same time, *medicorum* suggests that the bed is surrounded by physicians, and that image is perpetuated in the following passage. Thus, the character of the doctor has been quietly introduced; but he will turn out to play an entirely different part from what one would expect from the allusions to the Antiochus-Stratonice story (see above on *uulnus ... mentitur*; also App. III).

quid uenae pulsus, quid coloris intemperantia, quid fatigatus anhelitus et utrimquesecus iactatae crebriter laterum mutuae uicissitudines: the anaphora, imitated from Vergil, has been extended here to an anaphoric tricolon with first 4, then 8, and again 8 syllables, followed by a laborious phrase which disturbs the rhythm of the whole; see the note ad loc.

quid: *OLD* s.v. *quis* 12 gives examples of elliptic (rhetorical) question, introduced by a (repeated) *quid* ('What do you say about ... ? What of ... ?'), with the noun sometimes (as here) in the nominative, sometimes in the accusative. Cf. Verg. *A*. 7,365 f. *quid tua sancta fides? quid cura antiqua tuorum / et ... data dextera Turno?* See LHSz 2,424 f.

uenae pulsus: in the Antiochus-Stratonice story (see above on *uulnus ... mentitur*) the wise physician makes his diagnosis mainly by feeling the patient's pulse or heartbeat. Cf. Lucian. *Syr. D.* 17 χειρὶ μὲν τῇ δεξιῇ εἶχε τοῦ νεηνίσκου τὴν καρδίην; V. Max. 5,7, ext. 1 *intrante enim Stratonice et rursus abeunte, bracchium adulescentis dissimulanter adprehendendo, modo uegetiore modo languidiore pulsu uenarum comperit cuius morbi aeger esset*; Aristaenet. *Ep.* 1,13. Galen 18,2 p. 40 K. comments on this kind of scene that there is no specific pulse rate typical of cases of lovesickness, but that an increased pulse rate can be an indication of inner turmoil. See also Perkins 1995,155 f. on Galen's discussion of diagnoses based on an irregular pulse.

coloris intemperantia: this phenomenon, too, is described in the versions of the Antiochus-Stratonice story mentioned in the preceding note. E.g. V. Max. l.c. *ad introitum Stratonices rubore perfundi ... eaque egrediente pallescere*; Lucian. *Syr. D.* 17 τήν τε χροιὴν ἠλλάξατο. It is obvious that this second recital of symptoms refers directly to the Antiochus-Stratonice story. The first series mentioned only *pallor deformis*, the traditional *pallor amantium* (237,22; see note there).

et utrimquesecus iactatae crebriter laterum mutuae uicissitudines: cf. Sen. *Phaed.* 366 *artusque uarie iactat incertus dolor*; Heliod. 7,9,3 (referring to the amorous Arsake) παννύχιος γοῦν ἔκειτο πυκνὰ μὲν πρὸς ἑκατέραν πλευρὰν τὸ σῶμα διαστρέφουσα. Cf. Homer *Il.* 24,3 f., where Achilles turns restlessly from side to side, kept from sleep by the thought of Patroclus. Apuleius' longwinded and roundabout description of the woman tossing and turning on her bed makes fun of the physicians, who, unable to make a diagnosis, hide behind a long-winded and roundabout catalogue of symptoms.

utrimquesecus: see on ch. 14 (247,23).

iactatae crebriter: for the use of the intensive *iactare* in the *Met.* see *GCA* 1981,225 f. on 7,22 (170,25-171,2).

238,1-4 Dii boni, quam facilis licet non artifici medico, cuiuis tamen docto Veneriae cupidinis comprehensio, cum uideas aliquem sine corporis calore flagrantem: Good gods, how simple is the recognition of love's passion, if not for a medical practitioner, then certainly for any educated person, when you see someone all in a flame without the body being overheated!

With a final exclamation the narrator concludes the commentating interruption of the actual narrative, which started with '*iam cetera*' (237,20 f.). All through this section he has addressed the reader and appealed to her/his erudition by means of numerous allusions to various literary models (see the preceding notes). By now he has created a kind of alliance between the *docti* among the audience and himself, as being superior to the actors in the story, who still do not understand what is going on (see the following notes). For the abstract reader (see Introd. **3.2**) this final sentence functions as a 'rezeptionssteuernd' signal (see above, on *scelestum ac nefarium facinus* 237,1 f.) in the private conversation between the fictive parties: if one receives this story in the manner of the *doctus*, i.e. with an open eye/ear for the intertextual references, one will understand — better than any actor in the story itself — what this story is about.

Dii boni: the exclamation seems to suggest the greatest amazement at such a lack of understanding on the part of the doctors. See *GCA* 1995,120 on 9,12 (212,2-5) for other examples in the *Met.* Cf. also Ter. *Eu.* 225 f. *di boni, quid hoc morbist? adeon homines inmutarier / ex amore*. Callebat 1968,176 remarks that this expression is borrowed from the *sermo familiaris*, the informal colloquial language used in educated circles, as often reflected in Cicero's letters. Thus, from the very beginning of this sentence, the narrator creates a kind of solidarity with the *docti* in his audience (see on *docto* below).

artifici medico: see *GCA* 1985,275 on 8,31 (202,13-17) *aduenam ... asinum* on the combination of two nouns, one of which modifies the other. But *artifex* is also quite often used as an adjective in the sense of 'skilled, expert' (*ThLL* s.v. *artifex* 701,83 f.), which makes good sense in our passage.

docto: the Latin is more ambiguous than can be conveyed in a translation. The genitive *Veneriae cupidinis* can be taken with *docto* (e.g. Brandt-Ehlers 'für jeden der sich in der Liebesleidenschaft auskennt'; Augello 'Basta avere un piccolina d'esperienza de cose amorose'; thus also Vallette). But if this genitive is taken with *comprehensio* (as by e.g. Helm-Krenkel 'wie leicht ist ... das Erfassen der Liebesleidenschaft'), *docto* has to stand by itself in the sense of 'any educated man' (Hanson); for everyone with a literary education is familiar, through literature, with the examples of the 'catalogue of symptoms of love'. The narrator, who undoubtedly regards himself as *doctus*, jokes, along with the *docti* in his audience, at the stupidity of the actors in the story. Possibly this is also a brief allusion to the *iuuenis probe litteratus*, who, on the ground of this descriptive phrase, can also be considered as *doctus* but has no idea yet what is going on, and for whom his *nouerca*'s disclosure (described in the following chapter) will come as a bolt from the blue (see there, on *nihil etiam tunc ... suspicatus*).

cum uideas: see on the first position of the verb in the subordinate sentence comm. on ch. 32 (263,21) *si fuisset*.

flagrantem: on the spelling of *flagrare* see *GCA* 1977,210 f.

CHAPTER III

The woman attempts to seduce her stepson.

238,4-7 Ergo igitur inpatientia furoris altius agitata diutinum rupit silentium et ad se uocari praecipit filium — quod nomen in eo[s] ipso, s<cilic>et ne ruboris admoneretur, libenter eraderet: Well then, deeply tormented by her inability to cope with her madness, she broke her long silence and gave orders to summon her son to her — a name she in his case in particular would have gladly erased, undoubtedly so as not to be reminded of her shame.

Ergo igitur: this combination is quite frequent in the *Met.*; see Van der Paardt 1971,144 with references. Recent research (Kroon 1995) shows, however, that these connectors cannot be regarded as synonyms, and have different functions in discourse. It is therefore incorrect to label this combination as 'pleonastic'. See also Hofmann, *LU* 97 and Sonnenschein on Pl. *Mos.* 848. The combination is found before Apuleius in Pl. *Mos.* 848 and *Trin.* 756 only ; after that it occurs only in Apul. *Met.*, 17 times. Apuleius clearly has a special preference for this Plautine turn of phrase, which he finds suitable for connecting certain parts of his narrative. In this combination, *igitur* has a function in the macro-structure of the text: it introduces a new stage in the narrative, i.e. marks the beginning of a new 'paragraph'; *ergo* introduces a conclusion which the addressed person could have drawn himself from information received before, but which is nevertheless made explicit (see also Kroon 1998,48 f.). Making such a 'logical' consequence explicit is, in a narrative text like ours, a technical device to resume the thread of the story. In our passage *ergo* appeals to the reader's understanding (from earlier information in the text, and also from the evidence of other texts) that such a desperate passion cannot long be kept a secret; *igitur* introduces a new phase (Kroon 1998,46).

furoris: the description of intense passion in terms of 'madness, frenzy' occurs frequently in poetry, and is not uncommon in prose (cf. Cic. *Clu.* 6,15); see Svennung 1945,126 on this metaphor in Catullus and on his Greek models. See also Kiessling-Heinze on Hor. *S.* 2,3,325 *mille puellarum, puerorum mille furores*. Cf. Verg. *A.* 4,101 *ardet amans Dido traxitque per ossa furorem*; Bömer on Ov. *Met.* 3,350 gives many examples of *furor* in the sense of *amor, libido*. Finkelpearl 1998,167 f. points out the many passages in Verg. *A.* 4 describing Dido's love as *furor*, and supposes it was exactly Dido's *furor* that made her so interesting to Seneca in the creation of his Phaedra, who is equally tormented by love. However, see on *igne* ch. 2 (237,17). *Furor* and related notions appear throughout the *Met.*; see *GCA* 1985,44 on 8,3 (178,19-20); Shumate 1996,110 f. and n. 10; Puccini 1998.

altius: in our passage the comparative adverb may very well refer to the worsening condition of the stepmother. *GCA* 1985,142 on 8,15 (188,10) *altius miserantes* are not quite correct in referring to a 'weakened meaning' of the comparative (see also 9,29: 224,22 f. *altius commota* with *GCA* 1995,250 ad loc.); Furneaux on Tac. *Ann.* 1,32,7 discusses the metaphorical use of *alte/ -ius*.

agitata: = *uexata*; *OLD* s.v. *agito* 8b gives examples from Plautus onward, e.g. Hor.

Ep. 1,18,98 *num te semper inops agitet uexetque cupido.* In the *Met.* it is found in 5,21 (119,9) and 5,27 (124,12). Callebat 1968,390 notes that in the *Met.* this verb always retains its quality as a frequentativum/intensivum.

rupit ... et ... praecipit: this shift from perfect to historical present in one sentence, two parts of which are connected by *et* or another coordinator, occurs very frequently in narrative parts of the *Met.*; 'Streben nach Mannigfaltigkeit' (Bernhard 1927,153) is not a sufficient explanation for this phenomenon. LHSz 2,307 and 815 mention that this 'regellose Wechsel' becomes more common in later Latin from Petronius onward (see Löfstedt 1918,103 f.). Callebat 1968,429 f. sees a difference in nuance between the perfect (used for 'faits simplement envisagés pour eux-mêmes') and the historical present (used for 'faits brusquement fixés dans le temps, rapprochés du lecteur et dramatisés').

Looking not only at this one isolated sentence, but seeing it in its larger context, we notice that the perfect tense *rupit* in this episode occurs at the point where, after a long, general reflection (237,20-238,4), the actual story is resumed; from the historical present *praecipit* onward, the events of this following episode are narrated in historical presents until the direct discourse (238,20 f.). Thus, the perfect *rupit* marks the beginning of a new episode ('its normal function', according to Pinkster 1983,310; see also Pinkster in *AAGA* 2,1998,107 f.). Cf. in this story e.g. ch. 2 (237,18) *succubuit (et ... mentitur)*; ch. 4 (239,3) *putauit (pollicetur ... suadet ...)*; ch. 5 (240,4) *perduxit (procumbit ... ciet ...)*; ch. 5 (240,13) *traxit (insimulat)*; ch. 7 (241,23) *placuit (pronuntiat ... incedit ...)*; ch. 10 (244,7) *corripit (succedit ... emanabat ...*; see note ad loc.); ch. 12 (245,11) *placuit (et itur ...*; see also on *confluxerit* ch. 12: 245,15).

rupit silentium: solemn language. The combination *rumpere silentium* or *silentia* is first found in prose in Curt. 9,2,30 (Alexander in a speech to his soldiers) *date hoc precibus meis et tandem obstinatum silentium rumpite*; otherwise only in poetry, from Lucr. 4,583 onward. In the passages from poetry collected by Bömer on Ov. *Met.* 1,208, the context is practically always in an elevated style; in most cases it is a divinity who breaks the silence (e.g. Juno in Verg. *A.* 10,63 f. and V. Fl. 3,509). Even where this is not the case (e.g. Hor. *Epod.* 5,85; Ov. *Met.* 1,384), the context suggests that the *silentium* is an awe-struck silence, imposed by higher powers. Up to now the *nouerca* has concealed her true feelings; with her decision to speak out she breaks a taboo.

quod nomen in eo ... libenter eraderet: cf. Sen. *Phaed.* 609 f. *matris superbum est nomen et nimium potens: / nostros humilius nomen affectus decet; / me uel sororem, Hippolyte, uel famulam uoca.* The reluctance to use a word that indicates kinship with the beloved is already found in very old stories about incestuous love (Tschiedel 1969,11); especially Ovid in his *Met.* uses this motif frequently in the stories about incestuous desire; cf. Ov. *Met.* 9,528 f. *scripta 'soror' fuerat; uisum est delere sororem / uerbaque correptis incidere talia ceris* (*eraderet* in our passage evokes the image of someone wiping out a word on a wax tablet). In Ovid's Byblis-story the words *soror* and *frater* are found throughout the passage as a kind of 'Leitworte' (see Bömer on *Met.* 9,456; the same is true for the word *pater* in the Myrrha-story in Ov. *Met.* 10,298 f.; see also Zwierlein 1987,67 with note 135). In Ov. *Ep.* 4,129 f. and 138 Phaedra tries to convince Hippolytus that the *nomen cognatum* should not deter him. See below, on *uxoris patris ....* Finkelpearl 1998,173 f. connects the obsession with family relationships (often gone awry) in this book with the author's own feelings about his 'family relationship' to his literary predecessors.

in eo ipso scilicet ne ruboris admoneretur: this is Colvius' conjecture (supported by

Oudendorp) for F and φ's reading *in eos ipsos sed ne ruboris admoneretur*. In Colvius' proposal, Rohde found *ipso* 'überflüssig' and *scilicet* 'müssig'. His ingenious conjecture *in eo, si posset, ne ruboris admoneretur* is adopted by all modern editors. However, Colvius' solution is attractive: a) paleographically: an abbreviation of *scilicet* could have led to *in eo ipso s et ne* ...; a later scribe altered that to *in eo ipsos sed ne* ...; and eventually a scribe changed *eo* to *eos* to agree with *ipsos*. Cf. Apul. *Fl.* 18,29, where the mss. have *sed*; there, too, Colvius' proposal *scilicet* has been adopted by the editors (the edition of Bernardus Philomathes 1522 ['Junt. 2'] *scilicet* had there already adopted *scilicet*). b) rather than 'müssig', *scilicet* is quite appropriate here. It calls the reader's attention to the fact that the narrator gives a subjective judgment about the *nouerca*'s motives. See Van der Paardt in *AAGA* 1978,79 for more examples where in uncertain textual situations in the *Met.* the emendation *scilicet* has been favoured. The function of this *scilicet* is not to maintain the narrator's perspective (see Van der Paardt in *AAGA* 1978,77; Dowden 1982,422 f.): after all, in this part of the story we have an heterodiegetic auctorial narrator (see Introd. **3.5**; for a changed narrative situation see on *exanimis terrae procumbit* ch. 5: 240,5). With remarks like these he avails himself of the 'fonction évaluative', which is characteristic of this type of narrator. The use of *scilicet* here corresponds exactly with the use of 'sans doute' (analyzed by Lintvelt 1981,63 f. and 66 as 'discours modal') in a passage of Duras's 'Moderato Cantabile'.

Rohde's (paleographically clever) conjecture is itself open to the objection that *si posset* could be regarded as 'müssig'.

ruboris: 'sense of shame'; see on *ruborem* ch. 2 (237,16).

238,7-10 Nec adulescens aegrae parentis moratus imperium, senili tristitie striatam gerens frontem, cubiculum petit, uxoris patris matrisque fratris utcumque debitum sistens obsequium: The young man carried out his ailing mother's order without delay and, his forehead furrowed with an old man's gravity, went to her bedroom, rendering the obedience due in all circumstances to his father's wife, his brother's mother.

The young man goes to his stepmother's bedroom, but now the situation is presented entirely from his point of view: *aegrae parentis imperium*. He cannot but obey an order given by his father's wife. The effect of this manner of presentation is dramatic irony (see the following notes).

Both Wiemken 1972,139 f. and Steinmetz 1982,367 f. see Apuleius' story as the equivalent (in narrative form) of a mime (see App. I,5.4; cf. Andreassi 1997,1 and n. 4), and both have the actual play begin in this chapter (they see the preceding events as the 'prologue'). Our passage can, in this view, be the 'epische Umgestaltung' of a monologue by the young man, addressed to the public; the mention of his furrowed brow would then be a reference to the actor's performance in character.

senili tristitie striatam gerens frontem: cf. Sen *Phaed.* 453 (the nurse to Hippolytus) *frons decet tristis senem* and 915 f. (Theseus to Hippolytus) *ubi uultus ille ... morumque senium triste*; 798 f. (the chorus about Hippolytus) *quam grata est facies torua uiriliter / et pondus ueteris triste supercili!*

This description of the *iuuenis*, who arranges his face in the appropriate expression, is consistent with his highly praised *pietas* (ch. 2: 237,4 f.). But we have an example of dramatic irony: both the alerted fictive reader (cf. ch. 2: 237,12 f.) and the abstract reader (see Introd. **3.2**) can appreciate here the reference to the grim expression on the face of the chaste Hippolytus, devoted to Artemis (see the Seneca-passages cited above). The young man himself is not yet aware of this resemblance and naturally assumes a serious expression when summoned to the bedside of his ailing stepmother. *Probe litteratus* (ch. 2: 237,4) though he is, he has not yet grasped the fact that he is an actor in a version of the 'Hippolytus'. That will dawn on him only after his stepmother's confession (see also on *non tamen ... exasperandum, sed ... leniendum* ch. 4: 239,2 f.).

senili tristitie: old age is often associated with dejection. Cf. Verg. *G.* 3,66 f. *optima quaeque dies miseris mortalibus aeui / prima fugit; subeunt morbi tristisque senectus,* and *A.* 6,275. The noun *senium*, originally 'old age, decay' acquires the meaning 'melancholy' (cf. Hor. *Ep.* 1,18,47; Pers. 1,26; see Kißel ad loc.). Nevertheless, here the translation 'graveness' has been chosen: *tristitia* (*tristities*) can also mean 'serious dignity', without sadness; thus e.g. Gel. 14,4,2 *reuerendae cuiusdam tristitiae dignitate* (see *OLD* s.v. *tristitia* 3).

striatam gerens frontem: cf. Sen. *Phaed.* 431 f. (Hippolytus to the nurse) *quid huc seniles fessa moliris gradus, / o fida nutrix, turbidam frontem gerens / et maesto uultu?* According to *ThLL* s.v. *gero* 1933,45 f., *gero* in our passage might be taken as *prae se ferre, ostendere*; ibid. 1932,47 f. it is noted along with Mart. 3,93,4 (cited in the following note) and Lact. *Inst.* 4,27,3 *signatam frontem gerere*. It is indeed possible that in our passage the verb has a connotation of *prae se ferre, ostendere*, implying a certain doubt as to sincerity; cf. Juv. 2,8 *frontis nulla fides* with Courtney ad loc. (see *GCA* 1995,237 on 9,27: 223,18-21 *serena fronte*).

striatam frontem: the combination is attested elsewhere only in Pacuv. *incert. sed.* 20. The comparison of a lined face to a ploughed field is not unusual, e.g. Ov. *Met.* 3,276 and cf. Apul. *Apol.* 16,7 *relicto aratro mirarere tot in facie tua sulcos rugarum*. *Striae* can also be used for the pleats in a garment; Vitr. 4,1,7 *truncoque toto strias uti stolarum rugas matronali more demiserunt*. A wrinkled face, too, is sometimes compared to a pleated garment, e.g. Mart. 3,93,4 *rugosiorem cum geras stola frontem*. So, even though the combination *frons striata* is only attested in Pacuvius and here, the imagery underlying it is common.

cubiculum petit: neither in Seneca nor in Euripides' *Hipp. Steph.* does a proposition by Phaedra to Hippolytus take place in Phaedra's bedroom. It is possible that it did take place there in Euripides' first *Hippolytus (Hipp. Kal.)*, no longer extant (see App. I,2), and that this feature here in Apuleius' story (and therefore in the mime possibly represented here) gives a glimpse of Euripides' lost first *Hippolytus*. Zwierlein 1987,65 f. also supposes a conversation in the bedroom in Sophocles' *Phaedra*, known from only a few fragments (from Frg. 678 Radt he concludes that the proposition must have taken place off stage). At any rate, when in the Potiphar story Joseph is summoned by Potiphar's wife, who is shamming illness, he comes to her bedroom (see App. I,1 and 5).

uxoris patris matrisque fratris utcumque debitum sistens obsequium: prompted by *pietas* (see ch. 2: 237,4), he shows obedience to this woman, who is, moreover, *praepollens in domo mariti* (see above, on *nouerca* ch. 2: 237,9).

The cumulation of genitives in F and φ has troubled some critics, and Lipsius' emendation *uxori[s] patris matri[s]que fratris*, supported by Oudendorp, is adopted by all subsequent editors except Hildebrand and Eyssenhardt. Hildebrand regards *uxoris patris* and *matris fratris* as modifying *cubiculum* and notes the dramatic irony: 'has vero multiplices pro matre notiones eam ob causam cumulavit Apuleius, ut indicaret iuvenem in cubiculum matris decedentem tale quid suspicatum non fuisse, quia illa mulier non solum erat patris uxor sed fratris quoque sui mater, hinc eo magis venerabilis ac pia mente colenda' (for dramatic irony see also above on *senili ... frontem*). The text of F can be retained; moreover, it is unlikely that *uxori patris matrique fratris* (Lipsius' proposed text) would have been corrupted to a string of genitives (see also LHSz 2,65 on 'Häufung der Genitive', avoided by careful stylists). Unlike Hildebrand, this translation takes the genitives *uxoris* and *matris* as objective genitives with *obsequium*, a very common construction according to *ThLL* s.v. *obsequium* 181,10 f. (cf. also ch. 23: 255,3 *obsequio mariti*). Lipsius' emendation may have been based not only on a stylistic objection but also on the need for a dative with *debitum*. However, *ThLL* s.v. *debitus* 103,51-104,82 gives numerous examples where a dative is absent, e.g. Cic. *Tusc.* 3,64 *haec omnia recta, uera, debita putantes faciunt in dolore*; Sen. *Phaed.* 631 *pietate caros debita fratres colam*; Plin. *Ep.* 10,102 *diem, quo in te tutela generis humani felicissima successione translata est, debita religione celebrauimus*.

There is a comparable play with terms of kinship in the Myrrha story in Ov. *Met.* 10,346 f. *et, quot confundas et iura et nomina, sentis? / tune eris et matris paelex et adultera patris? / tune soror nati genetrixque uocabere fratris?* See Bömer ad loc.

utcumque: frequently used as an indefinite adverb (= *utique*) in the *Met.*; this usage occurs from Livy onward and is quite common in late Latin (see *GCA* 1985,273 on 8,31: 202,3-8).

sistens obsequium: *ThLL* s.v. *obsequium* gives no examples of this combination, nor does it mention our passage (see also on *sustinens obsequium* ch. 13: 246,4). *OLD* s.v. *sisto* 2b explains the combination in our passage by analogy with the legal term *uadimonium sistere* (see *GCA* 1977,137 on 4,18: 88,5-7). A 'corruption' of this legal term for 'to comply with a summons to present oneself in court at the appointed time' is certainly acceptable in this passage, and fits in well with the image of the well-behaved young man, who acts correctly on the summons to appear — not in the courtroom but in his stepmother's bedroom. Cf. ch. 4 (239,16) *promissae libidinis flagitat uadimonium*, with note ad loc.

The *obsequium* to which the boy feels committed is of an entirely different nature from the *obsequium* that the infatuated stepmother would wish from him: in elegy, *obsequium* is the standard attitude of the lover; cf. e.g. Tib. 1,4,39 f. *tu, puero, quodcumque tuo temptare libebit, / cedas: obsequio plurima uincit amor* with Murgatroyd ad loc.; see Danesi Marioni 1996,146 and n. 5, with references.

238,10-14 Sed illa cruciabili silentio diutissime fatigata et ut in quodam uado dubitationis haerens omne uerbum, quod praesenti sermoni putabat aptissimum, rursum improbans nutante etiam nunc pudore, unde potissimum caperet exordium, decunctatur: The woman, who had been worn down by the torment of silence for a very long time, ran aground on the shoal of doubt, as it were: each statement that she thought most appropriate for the present conversation she rejected again the next moment, for while even now her sense of shame still wavered, she kept hesitating how best to begin.

Sed illa: the narrator alternately focuses on the *nouerca*, on the *iuuenis* (*nec adulescens* ...), in our passage on the *nouerca* (*sed illa*...), on the *iuuenis* again (*at iuuenis* ...), and finally on the *nouerca* again (*tunc illa* ...). By this means he calls the attention of his readers to the entirely different ways in which the situation is seen by the besotted *nouerca* on the one hand and by the unsuspecting *iuuenis* on the other, thus making the most of his opportunities in creating dramatic irony.

cruciabili silentio diutissime fatigata: Apuleius gives the speechlessness of the love-struck woman (a topos: see below on *omne uerbum ... rursum improbans*) a psychological colouring: she has suffered so long from keeping silent about her feelings that, now that she finally has a chance to express them, she is speechless.

cruciabili: with the active meaning of *qui cruciatum affert*, which it always has in the *Met*. On this adjective, attested from the 2nd century A.D. onward, see *GCA* 1981,222 f. on 7,21 (170,14-18).

diutissime: formally to be taken as an adverb with *fatigata*, but also to be connected with *silentio*, especially because of the preceding *diutinum silentium*. Thus Vallette: 'harassée par la torture d'un long silence'.

ut in quodam uado dubitationis haerens: a favourite metaphor in elegy and epigram: the irresolution of the person in love is compared with the vicissitudes to which a ship at sea is exposed; see Nisbet-Hubbard on Hor. *Carm*. 1,5,16 on 'the sea of love'; Murgatroyd 1982,102 on Ov. *Ars* 1,437 f. *cera uadum temptet, rasis infusa tabellis, / cera tuae primum conscia mentis eat. / blanditias ferat illa tuas imitataque amantum / uerba, nec exiguas, quisquis es, adde preces*. Camps on Prop. 2,14,29 f. *nunc ad te, mea lux, ueniatne ad litora nauis / seruata, an mediis sidat onusta uadis* compares *AP* 12,167,3-4 (Meleager) ἀλλά μ' ἐς ὅρμον / δέξαι, τὸν ναύτην Κύπριδος ἐν πελάγει.

ut: 'as it were'; this introduces the metaphor described above. Von Geisau 1916,280 regards *ut ... haerens* as a grecism: 'zur Bezeichnung eines (scheinbaren) Grundes' (cf. ὡς + participle). This explanation is unnecessary, and several of the examples given by him are unconvincing.

uado: for ships at sea, a *uadum* is a dangerous place where they may get stuck. Cic. *Cael*. 21,51, too, uses the word metaphorically: *sed quoniam emersisse iam e uadis et scopulos praeteruecta uidetur esse oratio mea, perfacilis miho reliquus cursus ostenditur*. Austin ad loc. compares the opposite meaning of *uadum*: 'ford', i.e. a safe shallow place to cross a river. This is the meaning in which it is used, again in a metaphorical sense, particularly in comedy, e.g. Pl. *Aul*. 803 *haec propemodum iam esse in uado salutis res uidetur*; Ter. *An*. 845 *omni' res est iam in uado* (cf. Donatus ad loc. '*in uado' in securitate: nam ut in profundo periculum est, ita in uado securitas*).

haerens: different connotations of *haerere* play a part here: first, *OLD* s.v. *haereo* 8a 'to be unable to move, be held up, stick' (e.g. a ship running aground); cf. Tac. *Hist*. 4,27 *nauem ... cum per uada haesisset*; Curt. 9,9,19 *classis ... in uado haerebat*. For another connotation see *OLD* ibid. 9 'to be at a loss, be stuck or in difficulties', i.e. to be in an impasse; cf. Ov. *Pont*. 2,3,87 *inter confessum dubie dubieque negantem / haerebam*; Sil. 6,570 *dubius responsi nuntius haesit*; in the *Met*. cf. 3,9 (59,4 f.) *subito in contrariam faciem obstupefactus haesi nec possum nouae illius imaginis rationem idoneis uerbis expedire*; cf. also 11,14 (276,17 f.). The verb is also found in two passages contextually very close to this passage: Ov. *Ep*. 4,7 f. (Phaedra) *ter tecum conata loqui ter inutilis haesit / lingua, ter in primo restitit ore sonus* and V.Fl. 7,431 f. *illa tremens, ut supplicis aspicit ora / conticuisse uiri iamque et sua uerba reposci / nec quibus incipiat demens uidet, ordine nec quo / quoue tenus, prima cupiens effundere uoce / omnia, sed nec prima pudor dat uerba timenti / haeret*; cf. AR 3,652 f. ἤτοι ὅτ' ἰθύσειεν ἔρυκέ μιν ἔνδοθεν αἰδώς,

/ αἰδοῖ δ'ἐργομένην θρασὺς ἵμερος ὀτρύνεσκεν, / τρὶς μὲν ἐπειρήθη, τρὶς δ'ἔσχετο. It is possible that both Vergil (A. 4,76 *incipit effari mediaque in uoce resistit*) and Ovid (*Ep.* 4,7; see above) had this passage of Apollonius Rhodius in mind. But the locus communis of the speechlessness which overcomes a person in love goes eventually back to Sappho Fr. 2 D (= 31 L-P),7 f. ὡς γὰρ ἔς σ'ἴδω βρόχε', ὥς με φώναι- / σ' οὐδ' ἓν ἔτ' εἴκει. Fr. 149 D (= 137 L-P) θέλω τί τ'εἴπην, ἀλλά με κωλύει / αἴδως ... αἰ δ'ἦχες ἔσλων ἵμερον ἢ κάλων / καὶ μή τί τ' εἴπην γλῶσσ' ἐκύκα κάκον, / αἴδως κέν σε οὐκ ἦχεν ὄππα τ' / ἀλλ' ἔλεγες περὶ τὼ δικαίω. Seneca's Phaedra is also overcome with this speechlessness: *Phaed.* 602 *sed ora coeptis transitum uerbis negant* (see also ibid. 606 and 637).

omne uerbum, quod praesenti sermoni putabat aptissimum, rursum improbans: cf. the passages cited in the previous note and Ov. *Met.* 9,523 f. (Byblis tries to declare herself to Caunus in a letter) *incipit et dubitat, scribit damnatque tabellas, / et notat et delet, mutat culpatque probatque / inque uicem sumptas ponit positasque resumit.*

nutante etiam nunc pudore: this is another subjective explication (especially coloured by *etiam nunc*) by the narrator, who in this passage avails himself abundantly of the 'fonction évaluative', typical of the heterodiegetic auctorial narrator (see the note on *in eo ipso scilicet ne ... admoneretur*).

It is possible that here, too (see above, on *cubiculum petit*), the 'mime represented in narrative form' shows a feature of Euripides' *Hipp. Kal.*, for this last vestige of shame is found both in Ov. *Ep.* 4,9 *qua licet et sequitur, pudor est miscendus amori* and Sen. *Phaed.* 592 f., where Phaedra puts the same thought (expressed here by *etiam nunc*) into the following words (594 f.): *magna pars sceleris mei / olim peracta est; serus est nobis pudor.*

nutante: with *OLD* s.v. *nuto* 6 the verb has here been translated by 'waver, be undecided'; 'to remain in doubt'. Of course, the notion 'to be about to be conquered' (ibid. 2a 'to incline from the vertical, sink, nod, esp. from drowsiness or weakness') plays along as well here. Cf. Ov. *Met.* 1,717 *nutantem* (sc. *Argum*) *uulnerat ense*; V.Fl. 8,88 f. *nutat ... coactum / iam caput* (the drugged dragon).

unde ... caperet ..., decunctatur: as quite commonly (see Ernout-Thomas 408 f.), a historic tense of the subjunctive depends on a historic present. Callebat 1968,360 f. supposes that this is more common in the *sermo cotidianus* than in literary Latin and gives examples from the *Met.* See also LHSz 2,551 and *GCA* 1995,286 on 9,34 (228,18-20).

decunctatur: this compound is not attested before Apuleius; in the *Met.* it occurs also at 7,24 (172,8). See *GCA* 1981,240 ad loc.

238,14-16 At iuuenis nihil etiam tunc sequius suspicatus summisso uultu rogat ultro praesentis causas aegritudinis: But the young man, still not suspecting anything amiss, with downcast eyes asked, unprompted, the causes of her present illness.

nihil etiam tunc ... suspicatus: again, the narrator avails himself of his 'fonction évaluative' (see above, on *nutante...pudore*; cf. also on ch. 14: 247,4 *etiam tum*); he addresses his audience directly. By means of the literary allusions in the preceding narrative, he has already alerted the reader to the situation (well-known in literature) of the young man (see above, on *senili tristitie ... frontem*). The reader, together with the narrator, knows more than the actor does, and up to ch. 7 (242,1 f.; see there, on *haec ad istum modum gesta ... cognoui*) this knowledge will be the source for the reader of ambiguities and dramatic irony. For a similar situation see *GCA* 1995,208 f. on *et sic, ignarus* ... (9,23: 220,29-221,2).

sequius suspicatus summisso: alliteration, combined with a continuation of the *u*-sounds which are already heard in the previous sentence.

sequius: this comparative of *secus* literally means 'otherwise than expected' (thus e.g. 9,29: 225,5); E-M 608 f. s.v. *secus*[2] A1a points to the use 'par litote' of *secus* in the meaning of *male*, e.g. in *secus accidere*, cf. Pl. *Cas.* 377 f. The comparative *sequius*, too, is often used euphemistically in the sense of 'badly' (see *OLD* s.v. *secus*), as it is here; also e.g. *Met.* 8,11 (185,23-24), where, however, *GCA* 1985,112 suggest that Apuleius uses *sequius* and *setius* interchangeably. But an examination of all occurrences in Apuleius of *setius* and *sequius* (through Oldfather s.v. [*secius* &] *sequius* & *setius*), shows that Apuleius invariably uses *setius* in the sense of *minus* (see E-M 621) and *sequius* in the sense of 'otherwise than expected' or 'badly'.

summisso uultu: again, possibly a reference to the performance of the actor in mime (see the introductory note on 238,7-10); *submittere uultum* as a sign of respect also in Sen. *Nat.* 7,30,1 *ad sacrificium accessuri uultum submittimus*. Cf. 9,40 (233,26) *summissus* with *GCA* 1995,332 ad loc.

rogat ... causas: by inquiring of his own accord (*ultro*) after the causes of his stepmother's illness, the young man unintentionally puts an end to her hesitation and silence and even prompts her in her groping for *unde potissimum caperet exordium*. See below, on *causa*.

238,16-19 Tunc illa nancta solitudinis damnosam occasionem prorumpit in audaciam et ubertim adlacrimans laciniaque contegens faciem uoce trepida sic eum breuiter adfatur: Then, having obtained the disastrous opportunity of being alone with him, she flung herself headlong into audacity; shedding copious tears she covered her face with her garment and in an agitated tone briefly addressed him as follows:

Tunc illa ... adfatur: only at this point it is certain that the *nouerca* will personally confess her love to her stepson. In this she follows the lead of the Phaedra of Euripides' first *Hippolytus* (*Hipp. Kal.*), and Seneca's Phaedra, as well as the women from the Potiphar novellas, and definitely deviates now from the Phaedra of Euripides' *Hipp. Steph.* (see App. I,2 and 6C on this important distinction). Until now it has been uncertain whether she will declare herself, and that uncertainty was elaborated upon in the previous passage. But now it is the young man himself, who has unknowingly removed the last inhibitions in the woman (see above, on *rogat ... causas*). On a literary level, therefore, the *lector optimus* can detect an important peripeteia in the narrative with the *iuuenis* acting as a catalyst; see App. I. This will be the case to an even greater degree in the next chapter; see also App. III.

nancta solitudinis damnosam occasionem: creating the opportunity of being alone with the beloved is a familiar motif in Hellenistic erotic literature (Braun 1934,49). This μόνωσις motif was apparently also present in Euripides' *Hipp. Kal.* (see App. I,2): it is present in all the related passages in the Greek novel (Zintzen 1960,70) as well as in Sen. *Phaed.* 599 f. and in Josephus' version of the Potiphar story (see App. I,5.1), Jos. *AJ* 2,45 θηρωμένη μόνωσιν καὶ σχολὴν (cf. also *otium*, l. 28 below). The motif, therefore, was already part of the Potiphar novella before Euripides.

solitudinis occasionem: this combination is elsewhere attested only in Tac. *Ann.* 15,50,7, in the context of a conspiracy against Nero's life. Our passage may be an allusion to it; certainly our *iuuenis*, like Nero, is in great danger, and an attempt will be made on his life later in the story (ch. 4: 239,18 f.). *Solitudinis* is an explicative genitive with *occasionem*; cf. 8,2 (177,19-20) *nanctus denique praesentiae suae tempestiuam occasionem*.

Zeno Ver. 1,1,2 (1,4,2 M) had probably this passage of Apuleius in mind when he wrote: *denique in solitudine, quae a moechantibus uocatur occasio, se tamquam arbitrium timet omneque secretum plus quam publicum reueretur*.

damnosam: again an evaluating comment by the narrator (see above, on *in eo ipso, scilicet ne ... admoneretur*).

prorumpit in audaciam: *prorumpere* can be used for sudden, unexpected outbursts; cf. 6,17 (141,11 f.) *turris prorumpit in uocem subitam*; see also 9,24 (221,6) *prorumpit in adulterum quempiam* with *GCA* 1995,212 ad loc. See Callebat 1968,227 f. for consecutive/final *in* in similar expressions, and cf. Tac. *Hist.* 2,73 *ipse exercitusque ... saeuitia libidine raptu in externos mores proruperant* with Heubner ad loc.

ubertim: always in a context of extravagant grief; the adverb occurs 4 times in the *Met.*: 3,1 (52,11 f.) *ubertim flebam*; 5,5 (107,7); 8,19 (192,11); cf. also e.g. Catul. 66,17. Apuleius shows in the *Met.* a preference for adverbs in *-tim* (some are neologisms, some are archaic, others are attested in Ciceronian Latin); in this he fits in with a tendency observed by Gellius 12,15,1 in Sisenna's work: *cum lectitaremus historiam Sisennae adsidue huiuscemodi figurae aduerbia in oratione eius animaduertimus, cuius modi sunt haec: 'cursim, properatim, celatim, uellicatim, saltuatim'*. Reitzenstein 1912,57 (= Reitzenstein in Binder-Merkelbach 1968,131 f.) adds further examples from Sisenna, and assumes that Apuleius is making a conscious stylistic connection with the *satura* and the *Milesiaca*. See also Callebat 1968,477 f. and Maurach 1988,59 on Pl. *Poen.* 96 *efflictim* with references; Van der Paardt 1971,33 f. on 3,2 (53,9) *angulatim*.

adlacrimans: an unmistakable reference to Verg. *A.* 10,628 *et Iuno allacrimans* ..., where Juno tries to mollify Jupiter. Before our passage, the verb is attested in the Vergil passage only; after Apuleius only in Chiron (*Mulomed.*) 269; see *ThLL* s.v. *adlacrimo* 1659,73 f.

On shedding tears in order to arouse the pity of the beloved, cf. *Anth. Lat.* 1, 279,3 f. (Riese) = 273,3 f. Sh.-B.: *inmensum locutura nefas, metus unicus urget, / ne speret iuuenis lacrimas finxisse nouercam*; Ov. *Ep.* 4,175 f. *addimus his precibus lacrimas quoque, uerba precantis / perlegis et lacrimas finge uidere meas*. The effect of tears is extensively examined in Ach. Tat. 6,7,4 ἔστι μὲν γὰρ φύσει δάκρυον ἐπαγωγότατον ἐλέου τοῖς ὁρῶσι· τὸ δὲ τῶν γυναικῶν μᾶλλον, ὅσῳ θαλερώτερον τοσούτῳ καὶ γοητότερον.

laciniaque contegens faciem: an action, frequent both in Greek and Latin literature, of someone who is about to say something he/she is ashamed of; e.g. Ov. *Met.* 10,420 (Byblis) *conataque saepe fateri / saepe tenet uocem pudibundaque uestibus ora / texit et ... dixit*; Ov. *Fast.* 2,819 f. (Lucretia). An example famous in antiquity was Pl. *Phaedr.* 237a, where Socrates ironically covers his head before giving his first speech on love. That this passage was indeed famous appears from e.g. Gel. 19,9,9 (the rhetor Antonius Julianus is challenged to refute the assertion that the early Roman poets were unable to write naughty love poetry) *permitte mihi, quaeso, operire pallio caput, quod in quadam parum pudica oratione Socraten fecisse aiunt*; cf. Apul. *Met.* 1,6 (6,7 f.) for a humorous reference to Socrates' famous gesture. On the one hand, then, we have a Platonic reference; on the other hand it is possible to see a contrasting reference to Eur. *Hipp. Kal.*: it is generally assumed that the play received its name from Hippolytus covering his head in shame, as he listened to Phaedra's declaration of love (see App. I,2). Roisman 1999,407 f., with references, argues that it is unlikely that Hippolytus veiled his head, because in all instances of the gesture the person veils his/her head as a response to a shameful act of his own. In Eur. *Hipp. Steph.* it is Phaedra herself who says, 243 f.: μαῖα, πάλιν μου κρύψον κεφαλήν· / αἰδούμεθα γὰρ τὰ λελεγμένα μοι. / κρύπτε. The gesture of our *nouerca*, then, could also be considered as a final reminiscence of Phaedra, at a point in our tale from where the *nouerca* is going to drift ever farther away from that tragic model.

uoce trepida: cf. Sen. *Phaed.* 593 *intrepida constent uerba*. The combination *uox trepida* occurs also in Stat. *Theb.* 6,468 *trepidaque timet se uoce fateri*. The adjective *trepidus* can be used both psychologically ('fearful') and physically ('quivering, trembling'; *OLD* s.v. *trepidus* 4); see Collectanea Schrijnen 1939,122. This combined physical/psychological use of the adjective occurs also in e.g. Verg. *A.* 12,901 *manu ... trepida* and ibid. 4,672 *trepido ... cursu*; it is very frequent in Statius (see Dewar on Stat. *Theb.* 9,35 *trepidas ... aures*).

breuiter: the *nouerca*'s speech is, indeed, short, and she speaks in notably short sentences, each of them consisting of two lines or less of Teubner text. Possibly this suggests a contrast with the long monologues of the Phaedra characters in the tragedies and in Ov. *Ep.* 4. In the novelistic versions of the Potiphar's-wife motif (see App. I,5) the amorous women, like our *nouerca*, do not waste words in their first attempt at seduction.

238,20-21 'Causa omnis et origo praesentis doloris et etiam medela ipsa et salus unica mihi tute ipse es': 'The entire cause and source of my present suffering, and also the cure itself and my one and only salvation, is you yourself.'

These words and their subsequent explanation embody the proverb whose Greek form is ὁ τρώσας ἰάσεται. Otto 1890,23 f. s.v. *amor* 3 mentions, among other Latin examples, Publil. Syr. 31 *amoris uulnus idem sanat, qui facit*. Cf. Ov. *Rem.* 44 *una manus uobis uulnus opemque feret*. See also Nachträge Otto 1968,52 and 132.

Causa: the woman's first word echoes the *iuuenis*' question (*rogat ... causas*). Donnini 1981,152 compares Sen. *Phaed.* 645 f., where the name of *Theseus*, spoken by Hippolytus, is echoed by Phaedra as she begins to confess her love for him.

For calling a person '*causa*' cf. also 3,13 (61,24 f.), where Fotis calls herself the *causa* of Lucius' *molestia*. See also next note.

origo: used metonymically; see *OLD* s.v. *origo* 3a 'that from which something (material or immaterial) is derived, an origin, source'. Cf. e.g. Ov. *Met.* 1,186 *ex una pendebat origine bellum*; Quint. *Inst.* 8,4,22 *faciem illam* (sc. *Helenae*) *ex qua tot lacrimarum origo fluxisset*; Juv. 14,226 *mentis causa malae tamen est et origo penes te*; *ThLL* s.v. *origo* 984,33 f. mentions e.g. Liv. 28,27,11 *causa atque origo omnis furoris penes auctores est, uos contagione insanistis*. The combination *causa et origo* is frequent.

In our passage a person is the *origo* of something: *ThLL* ibid. 986,65 f. gives examples in which 'rerum origo esse dicuntur animantes' from Ovid onward, both for gods (Ov. *Met.* 1,79; Apul. *Apol.* 64,7; *Met.* 4,30: 98,8) and for other 'animantes' (Ov. *Met.* 5,262 f. *est Pegasus huius origo / fontis*; Plin. *Ep.* 4,9,3 *Theophanes fax ... accusationis et origo*). In Apul. *Met.* 3,13 (61,24 f., cited above in the note on *causa*), Van der Paardt 1971,104 defends and adopts Walter's conjecture *origo* (instead of *causa*).

Origo occurs also as a technical term in medical texts, e.g. Cels. 1 *Proem*. 16 *eum ... recte curaturum, quem prima origo causae non fefellerit* (see further *ThLL* s.v. *origo* 984,43 f.). See next note for the medical connotations in the first part of this sentence.

doloris: 'suffering'. The first part of the *nouerca*'s sentence has not yet made it unambiguously clear to the young man what exactly is the trouble; although *dolor* is quite customary in love poetry for 'pangs of love', it is also the normal word for physical pain. The nouns *causa*, *origo* (see previous note), *medela* (see below), and *salus* (see the following note) are all common terms in medical texts. Not until the young man hears the words '*tute ipse es*', does it dawn on him what kind of illness is meant here.

et etiam: thus F and φ, Helm, Giarratano-Frassinetti, Hanson; Robertson adopts Oudendorp's proposal *sed etiam*. Augello 1977,208 defends F's *et etiam* and compares ch. 17 (250,1); see Callebat 1968,329 on *etiam* in the *Met*.

medela: no doubt we are to understand that the young man first takes this word in a purely medical sense (see above, on *doloris*, and cf. *ThLL* s.v. *medela* 517,64 f.). See also Apul. *Apol*. 51,4 *quibuscumque caducis a dextero morbus occipiat, eorum esse difficiliorem medelam* and *Met*. 10,25 (256,21). Callebat 1968,133 remarks that this word is first attested in the 2nd century A.D., in a great number of authors (he gives examples); according to him, the word, is borrowed from the *sermo cotidianus*. E-M 392 s.v. *medeor* sees in *medela* an archaic word (cf. *loquela*, *tutela*, etc.), which in Ciceronian Latin had been superseded by *remedium*, but apparently was revived in the 2nd century A.D. by archaists; see Marache 1957,249 and n. 3. Apuleius seems to be the first to use *medela* of persons (according to *ThLL* s.v. *medela* 519,9 f.); after him we find this use in Aus. 11,15,4 Green *medella nostri, Nepotiane, pectoris*; Ps. Fulg. *Aet*. 13, p. 172,23 *salutis remedium ... , mortis medelam* (sc. *de Christo*); P. Nol. *Carm*. 18,257; Fort. *Carm*. 3,6,16.

salus unica: cf. Corn. Sev. *poet*. 13,12 *unica sollicitis quondam tutela salusque* (sc. Cicero). See *OLD* s.v. *salus* 6b: '(of persons): saviour'; e.g. Cic. *Ver*. 5,129 *me suam salutem appellans, te suum carnificem nominans*; in Ov. *Ep*. 4,1 f. (*quam nisi tu dederis ..., caritura est ipsa, salutem / mittit Amazonio Cressa puella uiro*) and Ov. *Met*. 9,530 f. (*quam, nisi tu dederis, non est habitura salutem / hanc tibi mittit amans*) there is a pun on the *salutem* formula - what is (a formal allusion to) the addressee's good health is also the salvation of the writer. In Plautus *salus* is often used as a term of endearment, e.g. *Cist*. 644 *o salute mea salus salubrior*; *Poen*. 366 *meus ocellus, meum labellum, mea salus, meum sauium*. The dramatic irony of this passage is enhanced for the re-reader by the extra weight given to the word *salus* by its use in book 11 (see Introd. **2.4.3**).

tute ipse es: the bolt from the blue for the unsuspecting young man, who has had no reason to expect other than a medical cause, comes at the very end of this first sentence. Three harsh plosives *t-t-p* and two sibilants enhance the effect.

That the young man is both cause and cure, is repeated four times: *causa omnis*; *medela ipse*; *salus unica*; *tute ipse*.

238,21-23 'Isti enim tui oculi per meos oculos ad intima delapsi praecordia meis medullis acerrimum commouent incendium' : 'For those eyes of yours, which, by way of my eyes, have sunk deep into my heart, are kindling a most violent fire in my marrow.'

First of all the woman explains why she considers her stepson the *causa* of her *dolor*. The idea that love enters through the eyes is a topos in Greek novels (see Rohde [4]1960,158 f. and n. 2). Cf. e.g. Ach. Tat. 1,4,4 ὡς δὲ εἶδον, εὐθὺς ἀπολώλειν· κάλλος γὰρ ὀξύτερον τιτρώσκει βέλους καὶ διὰ τῶν ὀφθαλμῶν εἰς τὴν ψυχὴν καταρρεῖ· ὀφθαλμὸς γὰρ ὁδὸς ἐρωτικῷ τραύματι, with Vilborg ad loc. Probably, this image ultimately goes back to Plato, *Phaedr.* 251b. On the influence of Plato's *Phaedrus* on authors of the 2nd century A.D., see Trapp 1990,141 f.; on the often-borrowed image of the 'creation of love by the outflow of beauty ... via the eyes' in the *Phaedr.*, see ibid. 155 f., with references.

In this *enim*-sentence the woman discloses the second connotation of her previous sentence (see the notes there), which the young man can no longer fail to recognize. From now on the young man cannot possibly avoid the true meaning of his stepmother's words, even if some of them could still be taken as medical terms (*praecordia, medulla*). The woman, on her part, uses all the commonplaces from literature (see the following notes), knowing that he is sufficiently *probe litteratus* to understand her.

Isti enim tui oculi per meos oculos: the parallelism in the phrasing, with polyptoton, gives emphasis; *isti tui* suggests a pointing gesture as the words are spoken; this supports the notion that this is a narrative representation of a mime performance. See the introductory note on 238,7-10 above.

ad intima delapsi praecordia: here, too, it is possible to picture a gesture by the woman (see previous note).

delapsi: the use of *delabor* for the penetrating of the body by a weapon appears to be original with Apuleius (see *OLD* s.v. *delabor* 1b; see also Finkelpearl 1998,171 and n. 53); he has it three times in the *Met.*: 1,18 (16,9), 2,16 (38,10 f.: Cupid's arrow), and here.

Cf. Anacreon 26,4 f. (West 1984, p. 20) οὐχ᾽ ἵππος ὤλεσέν με, / οὐ πεζός, οὐχὶ νῆες, / στρατὸς δὲ καινὸς ἄλλος / ἀπ᾽ ὀμμάτων με βάλλων.

medullis: for *medullae* as the seat of emotions, especially love, see Pease on Verg. *A.* 4,66 *est mollis flamma medullas* with references and examples; see also Lazzarini 1985,145; see especially the thorough study by Rosenmeyer 1999. The image, in one form or the other, can be found in all versions of the Phaedra story (see App. I); cf. Eur. *Hipp. Steph.* 253 f. χρῆν γὰρ μετρίας εἰς ἀλλήλους / φιλίας θνητοὺς ἀνακίρνασθαι· / καὶ μὴ πρὸς ἄκρον μυελὸν ψυχῆς; Ov. *Ep.* 4,15 *ut nostras auido fouet igne medullas*; Sen. *Phaed.* 282 *sed uorat tectas penitus medullas*. Finkelpearl 1998,170 f. concentrates on the Latin sources.

commouent: the present tense has full force: the torment is still continuing.

incendium: see on *igne* ch. 2 (237,17).

238,23-25 'Ergo miserere tua causa pereuntis nec te religio patris omnino deterreat, cui moriturum prorsus seruabis uxorem': 'Therefore have pity on her, who is perishing because of you, and don't be deterred by your respect for your father, whose wife, doomed to die, you will actually save from death.'

The woman now begins her plea, and expands the second part of her opening sentence: you are my *medela* and my *salus*.

miserere: cf. Ov. *Ep.* 4,161 f. *miserere priorum / et mihi si non uis parcere, parce meis. / ... flecte, ferox, animos.* In Sen. *Phaed. miserere* is heard three times, as a sort of refrain: 623 *miserere uiduae*; 636 *miserere, taciti mentis exaudi preces*; 671 *miserere amantis.* Zintzen 1960,75, who cites similar passages in Heliodorus and Achilles Tatius, sees this as an element from Eur. *Hipp. Kal.* (see App. I,2). This speech of the *nouerca* contains many parallels with Ov. *Met.* 9,530 f. (Byblis' letter to Caunis), including (561) *miserere fatentis amorem.* Cf. also Apul. *Met.* 2,16 (38,7), Lucius to Fotis: *miserere ... et subueni maturius.* Invoking the beloved's pity was a standard element in Hellenistic erotic literature (as reflected in e.g. the citations from Ovid and *Anth. Lat.* 1,279,3 f. Riese = 273,3 f. Sh.-B., cited above, s.v. *adlacrimans*; cf. Parth. 5,2 and 11,3; Aristaenet. 2,13 and 2,18); via Euripides it probably became a fixed part of the Phaedra-Hippolytus story, too (as it did in Josephus' version of the story of Potiphar's wife, Jos. *AJ* 2,45 f.; see App. I,5,1).

pereuntis: *perire* (*deperire*) sc. *amore* is already found in Plautus, e.g. *Poen.* 96 *earum hic adulescens alteram efflictim perit*; see Maurach 1975,148 f. and 1988,59 ad loc. with references; Fordyce on Catul. 45,5; also Verg. *Ecl.* 8,41 and 10,10. In Apuleius' *Met.* cf. 2,10 (33,16 f.) *pereo, inquam, iam dudum perii* (Lucius to Fotis).

religio patris: *religio* is used here in the sense of 'awe, respect', of which *OLD* s.v. *religio* 7a gives examples. Cicero uses the word often in this sense, e.g. *Rosc.* 24,66 *magnam uim, magnam necessitatem, magnam possidet religionem paternus maternusque sanguis.* See also *GCA* 1985,269 on 8,30 (201,19) *religiosus.* With this word the *nouerca* refers to the young man's much-praised *pietas* (ch. 2: 237,4), and in the subsequent clause *cui ... seruabis uxorem* even tries to convince him that by meeting her wish he will carry out an act of *pietas* toward his father.

cui morituram prorsus seruabis uxorem: this ingenious argument is not found in Ov. *Ep.* 4, although Phaedra does suggest ibid. 139 f. that open expressions of affection between her and Hippolytus could be interpreted as laudable by the outside world. An argument like the one put forward here by the *nouerca* would not surprise us from Ovid's Phaedra in Ov. *Ep.* 4 (see Finkelpearl 1998,172 f.).

morituram: she refers to herself as being at death's door, but that has more to do with persuasion tactics à la Byblis (Ov. *Met.* 9,606 *et, si reicerer, potui moritura uideri*) than with the sincere wish to die expressed by both Euripides' Phaedra (Eur. *Hipp. Steph.* 400 f.) and Seneca's Phaedra 669 f. *certa descendi ad preces: / finem hic dolori faciet aut uitae dies* (Phaedra's desire for suicide in Seneca has been explained as a pretext to make the nurse change her mind; see Zwierlein 1987,12 f. with references). In our passage the *nouerca* uses *moritura* to blackmail her literate stepson, who surely knows the tragedies too, by suggesting that she will end up like Phaedra if he does not yield. Later (ch. 4: 239,18 f.) it will appear that, once rejected, she does not wish to take her own life, but that of her 'Hippolytus' instead. For the increasing distance between this *nouerca* and the tragic Phaedra see also on *non ... non ... commota* ch. 5 (240,10 f.), and App. I,6C.

Possibly the *nouerca* also refers her literate stepson to Dido, who in Verg. *A.* 4,308 and 604 calls herself *moritura*, and receives that 'epithet' also in 415 and 519 (Finkelpearl 1998,172 regards the Vergilian reminiscence as primary here).

prorsus: in the context this can emphasize both the preceding *morituram* and the following *seruabis*; in the translation a choice is inevitable. For a comparable case see 7,5 (158,10) *totamque prorsus deuastaui Macedoniam* with *GCA* 1981,115 ad loc.

238,25-26 'Illius enim recognoscens imaginem in tua facie merito te diligo': 'Since I recognize his image in your features I naturally love you.'

imaginem: 'likeness'; see *ThLL* s.v. *imago* 411,9 f. for examples from Pl. *Men.* 1063 *tuast imago, tam consimilest quam potest* onward. Cf. Verg. *A.* 4,84 f. *aut gremio* (sc. Dido) *Ascanium, genitoris imagine capta, / detinet.*
  In the *Hipp. Kal.*, too (see App. I,2), Phaedra may have compared Hippolytus with the young Theseus. Zintzen 1960,77 concludes this from the fact that this motif occurs in all versions that, according to him, depend on the *Hipp. Kal.*: Ov. *Ep.* 4,63 f.; Sen. *Phaed.* 646 f.; also Heliod. 1,10,2 where Knemon says about Demainete ἣ δὲ ἐπειδὴ τὸ πρῶτον εἶδεν, ἐκτὸς ἑαυτῆς γίνεται, καὶ οὐδὲ ἐσοφίστευεν ἔτι τὸν ἔρωτα, ἀλλ' ἀπὸ γυμνῆς τῆς ἐπιθυμίας προσέτρεχε, καὶ περιβαλοῦσα "ὁ νέος ˙ Ἱππόλυτος, ὁ Θησεὺς ὁ ἐμὸς" ἔλεγε. Racine, *Phèdre*, acte 2. scène 5 'Que dis-je ? il n'est point mort, puisqu'il respire en vous; / Toujours devant mes yeux je crois voir mon époux.'
  merito: 'naturally'; see for this slightly weakened meaning of *merito* ('fere i.q. *consequenter, ... ut consentaneum est*') *ThLL* s.v. *merito* 824,68 f., and cf. Apul. *Met.* 2,21 (43,7). With this addition Apuleius' *nouerca* not only explains but craftily seeks to justify her passion. Again the literary predecessors (see previous note) are alluded to, but also 'out-bidded'.

238,27-28 'Habes solitudinis plenam fiduciam, habes capax necessarii facinoris otium. Nam quod nemo nouit, paene non fit': 'You have now the full security offered by solitude, you have now ample leisure to do what is necessary. For what nobody knows about has almost not happened.'

Habes ... habes: the anaphora gives a compelling quality to these last words of the *nouerca* (therefore in the translation 'now' is added for emphasis).
  solitudinis fiduciam: the translation opts for *solitudinis* as a subjective genitive with *fiduciam*; thus, the woman calls up the image of *solitudo* as the ally of both. Formally it is also possible to take *solitudinis* as an objective genitive with *fiduciam*: 'you have the certainty that we are alone.' *OLD* s.v. *fiducia* 3b gives examples of *fiducia* with an objective genitive: 'a confident expectation of ...'; cf. Caes. *Civ.* 3,96,1 *uictoriae fiduciam*; Sen. *Ep.* 74,4 (sc. *procella*) *in ipsa sereni fiducia solet emergere.*
  capax: *ThLL* s.v. *capax* 303,64 f. gives, before this passage, only three examples where *capax*, in the sense of 'qui capere potest res incorporales', is used to describe 'incorporalia: actiones, tempora, notiones': Sen. *Her.O.* 1419 *pro capax scelerum dies!* and *Ep.* 58,13, and [Quint.] *Decl.* 11,6 (226,1 Håkanson) *nihil est tam capax malignitatium ... quam bellum.* See Callebat 1968,187 on *capax* with abstracts, frequent in Christian authors.
  necessarii facinoris: both words are ambiguous: *necessarius* is 'necessary' or 'connected by close ties of relationship'; *facinus* is 'deed' or 'crime'. hence the phrase may mean 'the necessary deed' (obviously what the woman intends the *iuuenis* to understand; Floridus explains the phrase as 'facinus meae saluti necessarium'), but it is typical of Apuleius to choose these precise words because their other meaning is an apt description of the situation that is developing - 'an incestuous crime', or, in the words of Beroaldus, 'facinus quod cum persona necessaria sive necessitudinis vinculo copulata committitur'.
  Nam quod nemo nouit, paene non fit: this resembles a proverb, partly because of the alliteration and the remarkable ending with two monosyllables. Kirchhoff 1903,31 points

out the trochaic metre and the rhyme *nouit* and *non fit*. Like many proverbs this one is quite amoral: the Stoics in particular fulminate against it, e.g. Sen. *Dial.* 3 (*Ira* 1),14 *innocentem quisque se dicit respiciens testem, non conscientiam*. Valpy cites ἕως ἂν ἐλεγχῶμεν, οἰόμεθα λανθάνειν καὶ διὰ τοῦτο μηδὲ ἡμαρτηκέναι δοκεῖν as a statement of Epictetus, who indeed expresses such ideas in his works, though this exact sentence is not found there.

The *nouerca* shows an attitude opposite to Phaedra's in Euripides' *Hipp. Steph.* 413 f. μισῶ δὲ καὶ τὰς σώφρονας μὲν ἐν λόγοις, / λάθρᾳ δὲ τόλμας οὐ καλὰς κεκτημένας. In Sen. *Phaed.* 159 f. the nurse remonstrates with Phaedra as follows: *sed, ut secundus numinum abscondat fauor / coitus nefandos utque contingat stupro / negata magnis sceleribus semper fides, / quid poena praesens, conscius mentis pauor / animusque culpa plenus et semet timens? / scelus aliqua tutum, nulla securum tulit.* See Grimal ad loc. for parallels in other works of Seneca.

paene: Helm mentions in his app. crit. ad loc. that it seems as if F first had *paene*, which was changed to *penitus* by the same hand. Zeno Ver. 1,47 p. 121,6 f. (= 2,25 M) *paene pro infecto habetur quod non diffamatur* is an argument in favour of F. Moreover, φ and a* (belonging to Robertson's Class I; see Introd. **4.1**) also have *paene*. The scribe of F may have changed *paene* to *penitus* for the same reason that persuaded Petschenig to maintain *penitus*: according to him, the *nouerca*, who is anxious at all costs to persuade her stepson, is better served by *penitus* ('absolutely') than by *paene* ('almost').

CHAPTER IV

The *iuuenis* reacts cautiously. The stepmother's love turns to hatred.

239,1-4 Repentino malo perturbatus adolescens, quanquam tale facinus protinus exhorruisset, non tamen negationis intempestiua seueritate putauit exasperandum, sed cautae promissionis dilatione leniendum: The young man was deeply disturbed by this sudden calamity; although he at once recoiled from such a deed, he thought nevertheless that he should not aggravate the matter by a tactlessly stern refusal but, instead, should soothe it by means of the delay provided by a cautious promise.

Repentino malo perturbatus: the same phrase is found in 9,20 (218,1 f.); cf. Sen. *Ep.* 74,5 *omnium animos mala ... repentina sollicitant*. In the *Met.*, confusion as a result of sudden occurrences often leads to *inopia consilii* (9,20: 218,2; 10,26: 257,15 f.); this *iuuenis*, however, reacts calmly and deliberately, since he is *modestia praecipuus* (ch. 2: 237,4 f.). On the implications of this unusual reaction see below, on *non tamen ... exasperandum, sed leniendum*.

Repentino: according to Heine 1962,177 f., the motif of 'Eile' is a phenomenon that pervades the entire *Met.*; the speed with which the events develop is emphasized also verbally: *repentino* l. 1; *protinus* l. 2; *statim* l. 7; *protinus* l. 10; *fuga celeri* l. 12; *impatiens uel exiguae dilationis* l. 13; *confestim* l. 14; *festinare* l. 15; *uaesania praeceps* l. 16; *statim* l. 21; *continuo* l. 25; *uenenum praesentarium* l. 25; in ch. 5 *ilicoque* 240,5 f.; *repentina ... pernicie* 240,6; *protinus* 240,14; *ocius* 240,15. See also Junghanns 1932,52, Anm. 74; Dowden 1993,102.

facinus ... exhorruisset: *exhorrescere* can mean both '*uehementer timere*' (see ThLL s.v. *exhorresco* 1440,54 f.) and 'vi pressiore de aversatione et abominatione: *detestari, abicere, auersari, repudiare* sim.' (see ThLL ibid. 1440,83 f. with examples from V.Fl. onward). In this passage the latter meaning is appropriate: the young man, *pietate ... praecipuus* (ch. 2: 237,4 f.), will feel not so much fear as a moral aversion to his stepmother's proposition. Cf. V.Fl. 7,278 (Hippodamia) *patrios exhorruit axes*; Suet. *Aug.* 53,1 *domini appellationem ut maledictum et obprobrium semper exhorruit*. See also the passages in V.Max. given by Sobrino 1978,711 s.v. *exhorresco*, e.g. 3,1,2 (1,154,45 Briscoe) *et propositum* (sc. *Catonis*) *exhorruit*; Sobrino translates the perfect tense of *exhorresco* as 'tener repugnancia (de)'.

non tamen ... exasperandum, sed ... leniendum: after his stepmother's confession the young man finally understands that he is the Hippolytus in a Phaedra tragedy (see on *senili tristitie ... frontem* ch. 3: 238,8 and *nihil etiam tunc ... suspicatus* ibid. 238,14 f.). At this point we see a distinct difference between his reaction and that of Hippolytus (in both Euripides and Seneca; see the introductory note on *iam ergo...* in ch. 2: 237,12-14). Whether Hippolytus learns of Phaedra's love from the nurse (Eur. *Hipp.Steph.*) or from Phaedra herself (Sen. *Phaed.* and probably Eur. *Hipp.Kal.*; see App. I,2), his reaction is violent and instinctive (Eur. *Hipp.Steph.* 601 f.; Sen. *Phaed.* 671 f.); this is in keeping with his character, for his devotion to Artemis results in absolute chastity and an aversion to the female sex. The *iuuenis* of this story is *probe litteratus atque ob id consequenter pietate, modestia praecipuus* (ch. 2: 237,4 f.). His reaction to the *nouerca*'s declaration of love is violent shock (*perturbatus*) and repulsion (*exhorruit*), but it is short-lived, unlike the intuitive abhorrence that characterized Hippolytus and caused his death. This young man is educated enough to see the parallel with Phaedra, and on the basis of his book knowledge he deliberately acts differently from Hippolytus, whose reaction he calls an *intempestiua seueritas*. See App. I,6B and App. III on Apuleius' play with intertextuality in this story and its function in Book 10.

Assuming that we have here a rendition of a mime (see on ch. 3: 238,7-10, introductory note), it is conceivable that we should imagine the *iuuenis* at this point also referring to the Hippolytus story in an 'aside'; but that remains, of course, quite hypothetical. His cautious, rational reaction gives evidence of his *modestia* (see on *modestia* ch. 2: 237,4 f.), while his *pietas* (see ibid. on *pietate* 237,4) can be seen in *tale facinus protinus exhorruisset*.

Because of the disastrous outcome of the young man's conduct as it appears from the continuation of the story, some irony can be detected on the level of the abstract author (see Introd. **3.2**), who had the fictive narrator speak in laudatory tones of the young man's qualities (ch. 2: 237,5 f. *quem tibi quoque ... uel talem*; see also below, on *perfidiae suae*). Possibly this same irony can be found in the verbose phrase *probe litteratus atque ob id consequenter* (ch. 2: 237,4): *modestia* and *pietas* acquired from books turn out to be insufficient. Tappi 1985,190 proposes a 'Freudian' explanation of Apuleius' characterization of this *iuuenis*, by linking it to the characterization Apuleius in his *Apology* gives of Pontianus: our *iuuenis* is comparable to Pudentilla's 'titubante figlio', namely Pontianus, the dutiful and well-educated son, who in *Apol.* 96,7 is held up as an example to his brother and ibid. 98,9 is called a *disertus iuuenis*, but who is shown (*Apol.* 72 f.; 77 f., and 94) to be easily influenced and unstable.

intempestiua seueritate: *intempestiuus* = ἄκαιρος. In combination with *seueritas* it also occurs in Liv. 29,37,9 *intempestiua iactatione seueritatis* and Tac. *Ann.* 13,13,3 *quin et fatebatur intempestiuam seueritatem*.

putauit: after the confession of love in direct discourse, a new episode in the story is signalled by a finite verb in the perfect tense; the subsequent events are described by finite verbs in the historical present. See on *rupit ... et ... praecipit* (ch. 3: 238,5).

exasperandum ... leniendum: a slight ellipsis of the pronoun *id*, which can easily be supplied from the context (sc. *malum*), is not uncommon in the *Met.*; see Callebat 1968,450 f.

Ever since Colvius editors maintain the neuter forms, as in F; ς have *exasperandam ... leniendam* (sc. *illam*). Oudendorp defended the feminine endings because *exasperare* is used mostly of living beings; this is indeed true for its meaning *acerbare, irritare, ad iram incitare* (see *ThLL* s.v. *exaspero* 1187,46 f.); cf. *Met.* 8,25 (197,8) and 9,29 (224,23). But that meaning is derived from the first meaning of the verb, which is used of objects: 'make rough, hard' (*ThLL* ibid. 1186,14-1187,45); cf. e.g. 1,10 (10,4) *montis exasperati*. It can also be used of the sharpening of a sword (5,20: 118,12 f. *nouaculam ... exasperatam*; see *ThLL* ibid. 1187,25 f.). In our passage, with *malum*, it may be interpreted as 'make an illness worse' (*ThLL* ibid. 1186,61 f.), also because of the fact that it is used in contrast with *leniendum*: the scene takes place at the *nouerca*'s sickbed.

cautae promissionis dilatione leniendum: the motif of 'soothing by means of making promises; asking for a postponement' is frequent in the Greek novel. Braun 1934,42 f. gives examples, such as Heliod. 7,21,4 εἰ δὲ εὖ ποιῶν ἄτοπον δοκιμάζεις τὸ αἰτούμενον, ἀλλὰ σύ γε πλάττου τὸ συγκατατίθεσθαι, καὶ τρέφων ἐπαγγελίαις τῆς βαρβάρου τὴν ὄρεξιν, ὑπερθέσεσιν ὑπότεμνε τὸ πρὸς ὀξύ τι καθ' ἡμῶν βουλεύσασθαι, ἐφηδύνων ἐλπίδι, καὶ καταμαλάττων ὑποσχέσει τοῦ θυμοῦ τὸ φλεγμαῖνον. Cf. also Heliod. 1,26,2 f.; 7,26,17 f. Anthia uses the same tactics (e.g. Xen. *Eph.* 2,13). The prototype for this motif is, of course, Penelope. In our case, however, it turns out that the young man is mistaken about this line of action: his *nouerca* is *impatiens uel exiguae dilationis* (below).

239,4-8 Ergo prolixe pollice[re]tur et, bonum caperet animum refectionique se ac saluti redderet, impendio suadet, donec patris aliqua profectione liberum uoluptati concederetur spatium, statimque se refert a noxio conspectu nouercae: So he made promises lavishly and at length and strongly advised her to take heart and apply herself to the recovery of her health, until some journey of his father would give an open field for the fulfilment of desire; and at once he made off, out of the dangerous sight of his stepmother.

prolixe pollicetur: the same combination is also found in ch. 27 (258,14 f.); cf. also Cic. *Fam.* 7,5,1 *neque mehercule minus ei prolixe de tua uoluntate promisi*. *Prolixe* refers to the content of promise(s) (*OLD* s.v. *prolixe* 3a). It is also often found with verbs of speaking in the sense of 'at length, in detail' (see *OLD* ibid. 2); this connotation, too, applies here, since the young man is *probe litteratus* (ch. 2: 237,3 f.). For another use of *prolixe* see *GCA* 1981,169 on 7,14 (164,14-18).

pollicetur: this is φ's emendation of *polliceretur* in F (which may be due to anticipation of the following subjunctives).

bonum caperet animum ... se ... redderet, ... suadet: see *GCA* 1981,104 f. on 7,4 (157,2-11) for *suadere* with a subjunctive without *ut*. For the imperfect subjunctive with the historical present *suadet* in the main clause, see above, on *unde ... caperet ..., decunctatur* (ch. 3: 238,13 f.).

bonum caperet animum: *OLD* s.v. *capio* 16 'to entertain (a feeling etc.), adopt (an attitude)' cites passages from Pl. *Trin.* 650 *cape sis uirtutem animo* onward. For the exhortation *bono animo es* see *GCA* 1981,161 on 7,12 (163,8-11).

refectioni se ac saluti redderet: in a subtle way the young man seems to correct his *nouerca* with this hendiadys: she having called him her *salus unica* (ch. 3: 238,21; see note), he points out to her that her *salus* is to be found in physical recovery. On *refectio* see *GCA* 1985,170 on 8,19 (192,3-6).

impendio: cf. 2,18 (39,17) *impendio excusarem*. The use of this ablative with verbs, in the sense of *ualde*, is attested before Apuleius only in Laev. frg. 9, ap. Gel. 19,7,10 (in a discussion on interesting language in Laevius) *item 'fiere' inquit, 'inpendio infit', id est 'fieri inpense incipit'*. *ThLL* s.v. *impendium* 544,47 f. may be right in suggesting that a comparative form may have been omitted from the Laevius quotation. In that case the use with verbs is first attested in Apuleius, namely in the two passages in the *Met.* and four times in his other works: *Apol.* 3,9; 15,5; *Fl.* 18,33; *Soc.* 20,166. After Apuleius also e.g. Amm. 26,6,7 *impendio maerens*; 31,14,6 *impendio ... formidanda*; Symm., Aug.; cf. also *CIL* XI 5265 (4th cent. A.D.) 22 *impendio posceretis* and 77 f. *impendio postulastis*. As a reinforcement of comparatives, *impendio* (in the sense of *multo*) is attested in Pl. (*Aul.* 18), Ter., and once Cic. *Att.* 10,4,9; after that not until Gellius (e.g. 11,18,4), but not in Apuleius. (*ThLL* ibid. 544,39 f.).

donec patris aliqua profectione ... concederetur spatium: the young man's verbosity (*prolixe*) will be his undoing: as the continuation of the story will show, the woman takes his words literally.

patris aliqua profectione: the young man is quite familiar with literary tales of adultery: the husband's absence is one of the requirements. Theseus, too, is absent in all versions of the Phaedra-Hippolytus story (Zintzen 1960,11 f.), and comes home only when the tragedy has been set in motion.

liberum uoluptati ... spatium: *spatium* should be understood here in a broad sense: 'room, opportunity', as in 7,27 (174,26 f.) *nec tamen tantillum saltem gratulationi meae quietiue spatium datum*. See *OLD* s.v. *spatium* 5 and 10.

uoluptati concederetur: the young man couches his promise in vague, general terms (cf. *cautae promissionis* above) and makes no allusion to himself in connection with the prospect of *uoluptas*. Cf. the much more direct promise made by Fotis to Lucius in 2,10 (33,19 f.) *nec uoluptas nostra differetur ulterius, sed prima face cubiculum tuum adero*. For the theme of *uoluptas* in the *Met*. see Schlam in *AAGA* 1978,95 f.; Gwyn Griffiths ibid. 155 f., and passim (see index *AAGA* s,v, *uoluptas*; Krabbe 1990,110 with references).

statimque: see above, on *repentino*.

noxio conspectu nouercae: the ambiguity of the Latin is impossible to convey in translation. Both *conspectu nouercae* and *noxio conspectu* are ambiguous in meaning. *Nouercae* may be subjective or objective genitive with *conspectu*. If it is subjective (like e.g. the genitive *dominae* in 6,9: 134,19 f. *Psychen ... iterum dominae conspectui reddunt*), the implication is that the *nouerca*'s gaze, focused on the *iuuenis*, is harmful to him (cf. on ch. 2: 237,11 f. *oculos ad priuignum adiecit*, and e.g. Plin. *Nat*. 11,142 *noxii uisus* for 'the evil eye'). If the genitive is objective, 'the sight of the *nouerca*' (thus *deae* in 11,19: 280,22 *ad deae gratissimum mihi refero conspectum*), a decision must be made about *noxio*: does it mean 'guilty, delinquent' (*OLD* s.v. *noxius* 1) or 'harmful, injurious, noxious' etc. (*OLD* s.v. 2; see Thome 1993,90 f. on the two meanings of *noxius*; also ibid. 212 f.)? If 'harmful', it is clear that the harm is done to the *iuuenis* (cf. Graves' rendition 'even the sight of her made him feel ill'); if 'guilty', who feels the guilt? The *nouerca*, according to Butler's translation: 'he departed from the guilty presence of his stepmother'. Or the young man feels guilty by the very sight (or proximity, cf. *ThLL* s.v. *conspectus* 492,76 f.) of his *nouerca*; cf. Ov. *Tr.* 2,103 *cur aliquid uidi? cur noxia lumina feci ?*

At any rate, from now on he takes good care to keep out of her way; see below, *execrabilem frustratur eius conspectum*.

239,8-10 Et iam magnam domus cladem ratus indigere consilio pleniore ad quendam compertae grauitatis educatorem senem protinus refert: And because he thought that such a tremendous family crisis required especially extensive deliberation, he put the matter immediately to an old schoolmaster, whose high standards were known to him.

Et iam: this emendation by Pricaeus has been adopted by all modern editors. F has *et*, followed by a rasura of 4 letters, the last of which seems to be an *a*, according to Helm and Robertson in the app. crit. ad loc. φ has *etiā*, over which a different hand has written *et iā*. Van der Vliet reads *et iam*, which, also in connection with the situation in φ, is certainly worth considering. *Et iam magnam ... cladem ratus indigere consilio pleniore* is easy to understand: 'thought that this family crisis, which was already great now (i.e. even before real damage had been done), required extensive deliberation'.

tam magnam = *tantam*; see *GCA* 1977,65 on 4,7 (79,17-20).

domus cladem: the young man regards the *nouerca*'s infatuation as a *domus clades* and knows, through his study of literature, that the Phaedra tragedy, in both Euripides and Seneca, ends in a *clades* for the house of Theseus. His reaction of hurrying to his old *educator* to discuss the matter has an anticlimactic effect (see also above, on *non tamen ... exasperandum, sed ... leniendum*). Besides, it appears from the continuation of the story that his tactics of evasion will eventually lead to a (near-) disaster for the house all the same (ch. 5: 240,13-14 *cladem familiae ... domus expugnationem*).

Disasters striking entire households are thematic in the later books of the *Met.*: 8,1 (176,18 f.) *domus totius infortunio*, i.e. the *domus* of Charite and Tlepolemus; the same event is mentioned again 8,15 (188,9 f.); 9,31 (226,14) *domus infortunium* (the downfall of the *pistor*'s house); 9,35 (229,10 f.) *magnas et postremas domino illi fundorum clades* (the rich *dominus* and his three sons); the same disaster is referred to 9,39 (232,24 f.) *dilapsae domus fortunam*. It is true that the disaster threatening the household of our story is averted at the last moment (though not because of the caution of this *iuuenis*), but the murderous woman in the next tale in this book (chs. 23-28) is the ruination of not one but two families. Adultery (or attempts at adultery), rapacity, and jealousy play their parts in these cases of downfall, but above all the stories illustrate the power of *Fortuna* (see Introd. **2.4.1** and **2.6**). Kautzky 1989 examines *Met.* 9,33-38, 10,2-12, and 10,23-28 as 'Drei Familientragödien'.

ad quendam educatorem senem refert: the young man lacks the inner strength to act independently: he seeks the authority of an *educator*. The fact that the *educator* (who could, after all, have acted as a witness for the defence in the trial conducted later) plays no part at all in the rest of the story (see on *finitum est iudicium*, ch. 7: 242,24) reinforces the impression that this addition has been made solely for the sake of characterizing the young man (see above, on *non tamen ... exasperandum, sed ... leniendum*). Moreover, the polarity between the honourable *iuuenis* and his shameless *nouerca* is emphasized by the difference in their advisers; see below, on *nec quicquam ... iuuenem*.

grauitatis: the young man asks the *educator* for advice because he is acquainted with his *grauitas*, which he sees as an admirable quality; cf. *OLD* s.v. *grauitas* 5b 'strictness of life or morals, austerity' or 6b 'seriousness of approach, earnestness'. It appears from what follows that the *grauitas* of the *educator* can also be understood in a less positive sense, namely (*OLD* ibid. 2b) 'dullness, sluggishness'; cf. Cic. *Luc.* 52 *si ... in sensibus ipsius est aliqua forte grauitas aut tarditas*; see Hiltbrunner 1958,72 and n. 27, with references, on the uses of *grauitas*; Hiltbrunner 1954,203 f. on *grauitas uitae*, often especially connected with old age; cf. Cic. *Ver.* 2,1,66 *homo, qui et summa grauitate et iam id aetatis et parens esset*; Verg. A. 1,151 f. *tum, pietate grauem ac meritis si forte uirum quem / conspexere ... / ille regit dictis animos et pectora mulcet*. Below, the *diutina deliberatio* under the guidance of the old man has the effect that speedy flight (*fuga celeri*) is no longer possible.

educatorem senem: here as often elsewhere *senex* has full adjectival value (see LHSz 2,157 f. on the fluid boundaries between an attributive adjective and a noun in apposition, with many examples). In the case of *senex* it is better not to speak of a noun becoming an adjective, because *senex* is actually an adjective: cf. the comparative *senior*, and e.g. Cic *Sen.* 4,10 *nemo ... est tam senex qui ...* .

educatorem: this is not the term for a particular official, although Tacitus uses the word in the *Annales* as an equivalent of παιδαγωγός (see Furneaux on *Ann.* 15,62,2). We need not visualize the boy's offical tutor here, because the noun is modified by *quendam*; instead, we should think of one of the older people in his environment, who has been involved with his education in one way or another. See Summers 1967,96 f., who translates 2,3 (26,17) *inter tuos educatores* as 'one of those who took part in rearing you' (Byrrhena speaking about herself to Lucius).

protinus: see above, on *repentino*.

239,10-12 Ne<c> quicquam diutina deliberatione tam salubre uisum quam fuga celeri procellam Fortunae saeuientis euadere: And as a result of a lengthy deliberation nothing seemed to them as beneficial as escaping the storm of Fortune's rage by a hasty flight.

Nec quicquam ... euadere: see below, on *nec quicquam ... iuuenem*.

Nec quicquam: F and φ had *ne quicquam*; in both the *c* has been added by a later hand.

diutina deliberatione ... fuga celeri: see above, on *grauitatis*, and see also next note. Alliteration and chiasmus emphasize the irony in the description of how the *iuuenis* and the *educator* let the right moment for a speedy flight go by because of their long-winded deliberations. This passage reminds us of the popular 'scholasticus' jokes. The *Philogelos*, whose transmitted text is of the 4th or 5th century A.D. but contains much older material, has a great deal of jokes about the scholasticus. Winkler 1985,160 states that the essence of these jokes is 'to strike a perfect balance between acuity and fatuousness' and (ibid. 161) 'self-defeating cleverness'. Compare our deliberating 'scholastici' with e.g. *Philogelos* 3, in which 'scholasticus' writes a letter to his father from Athens: 'I hope you will have to stand trial for a capital crime, so that I can show you how good a rhetor I am!' See Winkler 1985,160 f. on the 'scholasticus' jokes as a comparandum for the *Met.*, and for the connections between *Philogelos* and mime. See also Bremmer 1997,17 f.

diutina deliberatione: instead of acting promptly, the two devote an extensive *deliberatio* to the matter and, as perhaps we are invited to understand, turn it into a rhetorical exercise in the *genus deliberatiuum*. Eventually they reach the theoretical conclusion *fuga celeri ... euadere*; a less well-formulated but really rapid flight should have been undertaken right away, without lengthy deliberations. Moreover, it appears from the continuation of the story that the *iuuenis* does not put the theory of the hasty flight into practice (see also below, on *nec quicquam ... iuuenem*). In 7,10 (161,21 f.) the consequence of a *diutina deliberatio* is a *mora consilii*.

procellam Fortunae: the combination is first found here; for *procella* in the sense of 'violent attack, disturbance' see *GCA* 1985,164 f. on 8,18 (191,9-11) *canum ... procella*.

A 'precursor' of the expression *procella Fortunae* might be seen in Verg. *A.* 7,594 *'frangimur heu fatis' inquit, 'ferimurque procella!'* A comparable passage in the *Met.* is 11,15 (277,5 f.) *magnisque Fortunae tempestatibus et maximis actus procellis* and cf. *uitae procellis* 11,25 (286,25; see also 11,5: 270,8 f. with Harrauer 1973,35 f. ad loc.). The same metaphor occurs in Arn. 2,45 *sub procellis agerent tempestatibusque cotidie fortunae* and 2,76. A striking similarity with our passage is found in Amm. 14,1,1 *fortunae saeuientis procellae*.

Fortunae saeuientis: cf. Sal. *Cat.* 10,1 *saeuire fortuna ac miscere omnia coepit*; Hor.

S. 2,2,126 *saeuiat atque nouos moueat Fortuna tumultus* (cf. *Met.* 11,15: 277,12 f.); Sen. *Ben.* 5,3,2 *quisquis ... saeuientis fortunae ui ... oppressus non submittit animum*. For *saeuissima* as one of the epithets of *Fortuna* in the *Met.*, see *GCA* 1985,204 on 8,24 (195,21).

The editions diverge in this passage as to the spelling *fortuna* or *Fortuna*. Here, with Giarratano-Frassinetti, Terzaghi, Scazzoso, and Helm-Krenkel, the capital has been chosen for the sake of the greatest possible consistency in this difficult matter (see on this in detail below, on *haud ullo tempore tam beniuolam Fortunam expertus*, ch. 13: 246,14 f.): in 11,15 (277,5 f.) all editors spell *Fortunae tempestatibus*.

euadere: elsewhere in the *Met.* (e.g. 9,1: 203,12-15) the narrator stresses the fact that such an escape is impossible — except with the help of *prouidentia* (11,15: 277,25 f.) or the *salutaris dextera* of Isis (11,25: 286,25 f.).

239,12-15 Sed impatiens uel exiguae dilationis mulier ficta qualibet causa confestim marito miris persuadet artibus ad longissime dissitas festinare uillulas: The woman, however, could not bear even the slightest delay, and by concocting some reason or other with marvellous craftiness, she immediately persuaded her husband to hurry at once to their most distant farms in the country.

Sed impatiens uel exiguae dilationis mulier: cf. Sen. *Phaed.* 583 *sed Phaedra praeceps graditur, impatiens morae* (cf. also *praeceps* below). In her impatience, Phaedra spoils the nurse's plan, and after that the tragedy moves fast to its close; in her impatience our *nouerca* counters the dilatory tactics of the *iuuenis* (by sending her husband away). The *lector optimus* (ch. 2: 237,12-14; see note ad loc.), alerted by the reminiscence of Sen. *Phaed.*, will now be sure that the story will move fast to its conclusion, but his further expectation, i.e. that the *iuuenis*, like Hippolytus, will die, is destined to come to nothing (see also App. III).

impatiens uel exiguae dilationis: a variant of Apuleius on the usual *impatiens morae* (*ThLL* s.v. *impatiens* 524,56 f.), as in e.g. Sen. *Oed.* 99 f. *saxa ... impatiens morae / reuulsit unguis* and, among others, Luc. 6,424. Cf. Aug. *Conf.* 6,15 *at ego infelix ... dilationis impatiens, tanquam post biennium accepturus eam quam petebam, quia non amator coniugii sed libidinis seruus eram, procuraui aliam, non utique coniugem ...*. *ThLL* ibid. notes *impatiens dilationis* in Ambr. *In psalm.* 118 and *Serm.* 22,39.

dilationis: this echoes *dilatione* above, and thus underscores the futility of the plan outlined there by the *iuuenis* (see above, on *non tamen ... exasperandum, sed ... leniendum*).

confestim: see above, on *repentino*.

miris artibus: *miris* is a comment of the narrator, whose 'fonction évaluative' and 'fonction émotive' overlap here (see Lintvelt 1981,65 f.; Introd. **3.3**). In *miris* one can detect disapproval of the *nouerca*'s tricks, but also grudging admiration on the part of the narrator: throughout the *Met.* the narrator is characterized as fond of *mira*, and from the prologue (1,1: 1,6 *ut mireris*) onward he has imagined a reader who shares this preference with him. See also on *mira praesumptione* ch. 10 (244,22) and *mirati monstruosas asini delicias* ch. 15 (248,17); *GCA* 1985,100 on 8,9 (184,11-13) *astuque miro*.

persuadet ... festinare: the use of *(per)suadere* with the infinitive became more common from the Augustan period onward (see Callebat 1968,306 f. with references); von Geisau 1916,270 gives examples from as early as Cicero.

dissitas: in the sense of *situ disiunctas*. According to *ThLL* s.v. 2 *dissitus* 1493,18

101

f. Apuleius is the first to use the word in this meaning (also 9,15: 214,19, and *Fl.* 2,6). On the origin and occurrence of homonyms see *GCA* 1981,236 on 7,23 (171,20-172,2). Here the assonance with *longissime* may have motivated the choice. See also Ferrari 1968,133 f. on Apul. *Fl.* 2,6 *neque longule dissita neque proxume adsita*.

uillulas: we have here a prosperous family, which possesses distant estates; see also on *cursore* ch. 5 (240,14) and *centumque aureos solidos*, ch. 9 (243,19). Elster 1992,148 remarks that this *dominus aedium*, with his possession of outlying estates, is more like a Roman senator than a distinguished inhabitant of a Greek provincial town.

In the *Met.* there are 5 occurrences each of *uilla*, and of *uillula*; Callebat 1968,56 thinks that in none of these passages does the diminutive still have a true diminutive quality. In our passage, it cannot be determined whether the diminutive has its original value, as it definitely does in 7,19 (168,26-169,3); see *GCA* 1981,207 ad loc. and ibid. n. 1). Portalupi 1974,118 sees in the diminutive here an expression of the inadequateness, the futility of the pretext (see also De Biasi 1990,12 f. and n. 37). It could be argued that the narrator uses the diminutive to emphasize *miris artibus*: it is a marvel that the woman manages to convince her husband that he must leave immediately for those small (unimportant) rural estates. Keeping in mind, moreover, that the *dominus aedium* is the Theseus of this Phaedra story, it is possible to detect here a humorous, downgrading tendency: while the disastrous events between Phaedra and Hippolytus were taking place, Theseus was, as the *docti* among the readers would recognize immediately, away on a heroic expedition to Hades (thus in Seneca's *Phaedra* and probably also in Sophocles' *Phaedra*, cf. Frg. 686, 687, and 687a Radt; Ov. *Ep.* 4 also connects Theseus' absence with this journey). Our 'Theseus' is sent away by his wife to their *uillulas*.

239,15-16 Quo facto maturatae spei uaesania praeceps promissae libidinis flagitat uadimonium: Now that she saw her hope close to fulfillment by having brought this about, she became mad, she could not be stopped any more, and she demanded the redemption of the promise of lust.

Quo facto: 'by having brought this about': probably the *festinatio mariti* is meant. Thus also Carlesi: 'Ottenuto ciò'.

maturatae spei: now it turns out that in his clumsiness the young man himself has raised her hopes (*bonum caperet animum* above; see also above, on *dilationis*). For the transitive use of *maturare* with an inanimate object, *ThLL* s.v. *maturo* ('i.q. *ad statum opportunum perducere*, interdum potius i.q. *ad effectum perducere*') 496,23 f. gives as the first passage V.Max. 8,2,2 (2,508,27 f. Briscoe) *quod spem praedae suae morte non maturasset* (see also Sobrino 1978,1230 s.v. *maturo*); then our passage and Serv. *A*. 10,254 *propinques augurium: ... prosperes, matures, propitium facias*. If we adhere to the basic meaning of *maturare*, the translation could be 'the madness of her ripened hope' (Hanson).

spei: the motif of hope is a topos in Hellenistic love poetry; see e.g. Tib. 2,6,19-28 with Smith ad loc.; Ov. *Rem.* 685 f. *desinimus tarde, quia nos speramus amari. / dum sibi quisque placet, credula turba sumus*; *Met.* 1,491 f. (sc. Phoebus) *quodque cupit sperat, suaque illum oracula fallunt*, and 496 *uritur et sterilem sperando nutrit amorem*; *Fast.* 2,766 and *Ep.* 20,16. Cf. also the passage in Heliodorus cited above, on *cautae promissionis dilatione*.

praeceps: this evokes again Sen. *Phaed.* 583 (see above, on *sed impatiens uel exiguae dilationis mulier).*

promissae libidinis flagitat uadimonium: this word order is quite typical of the *Met.*: the finite verb in the next to last position, and the last word usually a noun whose modifier is placed before the verb (see Bernhard 1927,17). Möbitz 1924,122 f. sees in the frequent occurrence of this pattern (which, for that matter, occurs throughout Latin literature but especially to avoid hiatus or to achieve a correct clausula) a phenomenon typical of the novel (it is also quite frequent in Petronius). For another example, this time in a dependent clause, see below *ad longe deterius transtulisset odium*.

The legal term *uadimonium* stands for the guarantee (made by a surety) that one will appear before the judge at an appointed time; noncompliance with *uadimonium* is punishable (see Summers 1967,149 f.). The fact that the narrator connects the legal term with an amorous tryst (cf. 9,22: 219,20 f. with *GCA* 1995,195 ad loc. and on *sistens obsequium*, ch. 3: 238,10) has on the one hand a humorous effect, as is achieved at several occasions in the *Met.* by the inappropriate use of legal language (see e.g. 7,25: 173,2-3 with *GCA* 1981,248; Keulen 1997); on the other hand, the term *uadimonium* suggests that because of the *iuuenis'* clumsy promises the woman, strictly speaking, is 'in the right'; it hints at the inevitable consequences of his *promissio*, which therefore was far from *cauta* (239,3). See also above, on *maturatae spei* and below, on *perfidiae suae*.

239,17-21 **Sed iuuenis, modo istud modo aliud causae faciens, execrabilem frustratur eius conspectum, quoad illa, nuntiorum uarietate pollicitationem sibi denegatam manifesto perspiciens, mobilitate lubrica nefarium amorem ad longe deterius transtulisset odium**: The young man, however, kept stalling the accursed tête-à-tête by fabricating now this excuse, now another; eventually she perceived clearly from his ever-varying messages that she was being denied the fulfillment of the promise, and in treacherous fickleness she turned her outrageous love to a far worse hatred.

modo istud, modo aliud causae faciens: cf. above, the *iuuenis'* idea that he can find a remedy by *cauta promissio*; see also Appendix I,6B.

execrabilem eius conspectum: *execrabilem* from the point of view of the *iuuenis*. As a matter of fact, the Latin contains here the same ambiguity as observed in the note *noxio conspectu nouercae* above. There is an active and a passive side to *execrabilis*. For its active aspect see *ThLL* 1834,33 f. s.v. *exsecrabilis* (*execr.*): i.q. exsecrationem adferens, syn. *dirus, perniciosus*, etc.; e.g. Plin. *Nat.* 2,138 *fulmina saeua maxime et execrabilia*; ibid. 9,155 *pestiferum animal araneus ... aculeo noxius, sed nullum ... execrabilius quam radius super caudam eminens trygonis*. For its passive aspect see *ThLL* ibid. 1834,44 f.: i.q. *exsecratione dignus, abominabilis* sim.; e.g. Acc. *trag.* 270 R (*Diom.* 539 Dangel) *tyranni saeuom ingenium atque exsecrabile*; Liv. 27,17,11 *transfugae nomen execrabile ... sociis ... esse*. See also on *uenerabilis*, ch. 23 (255,11).

frustratur: like *uadimonium* above, *frustrari* sounds quasi-legal: in a legal context it is used of procrastinating legal action in the hope of preventing it, e.g. Gaius *Dig.* 50,16,233 '*si caluitur': et moretur et frustretur*; Macer *Dig.* 49,5,4 *qui ideo causam agere frustratur* (see *ThLL* s.v. *frustro* 1437,55 f. and 1438,79 f.). Cf. also Apul. *Fl.* 18,22 *coepit nolle quod pepigerat, sed callide nectendis moris frustrari magistrum diutuleque nec agere uelle nec reddere*.

This episode in the tale, so entirely different from the one critical clash between the main characters in the tragedies, resembles the situation suggested in e.g. the Potiphar novella (see App. I,5.1) in Philo, *Jos.* 41: ᾽Επεὶ δὲ ζωπυροῦσα καὶ ἀναφλέγουσα τὴν ἔκνομον ἐπιθυμίαν ἀεὶ μὲν ἀπεπειρᾶτο, ἀεὶ δ᾽ ἀπετύγχανε... Steinmetz 1982,369 recasts our episode as the second scene of the second act of the mime that he (following Wiemken 1972) sees paraphrased here by Apuleius (see App. I,5.4).

quoad ... transtulisset: KSt 2,2,381 cite this passage as one of the very rare occurrences of a pluperfect subjunctive with *quoad* where there is no question of the thought of another person being reflected ('oblique Nebensatz', ibid. 2,2,199 f.). This is also found (in a dependent clause with *donec*) in Liv. 5,17,5 *nunquam desitum interim turbari comitia interpellantibus tribunis plebis donec conuenisset* ... It is possible that the pluperfect in our passage expresses the notion that the young man was still thinking up excuses while the *nouerca* had already turned her love to hatred.

See *GCA* 1985,103 on 8.9 (184,17-185,4) on the use of the subjunctive with *quoad*, also in those instances where no final nuance can be discerned (found from Livy onward, according to KSt 2,2,380 f.).

mobilitate lubrica: since it is clear that *mobilitas* has here the negative meaning 'inconstancy, fickleness' given by *OLD* s.v. *mobilitas* 4, the translation opts for the negative aspect of *lubricus* ('treacherous'; see *OLD* s.v. *lubricus* 4 and 5), as well. One has to bear in mind that the adjective is also used for 'slippery' snakes (see Thome 1993,204 f. on the 'snakey' associations of *lubricus*). In a positive sense the adjective occurs e.g. 2,17 (39,6 f.) *lubricisque gestibus mobilem spinam quatiens*.

nefarium amorem ad longe deterius transtulisset odium: here we have an illustration of the universal wisdom that spurned love turns to hatred, and that this hatred is then formidable indeed. Cf. Congreve 3,8 'Heav'n has no rage like love to hatred turn'd, / Nor Hell a fury like a woman scorn'd'. Similarly, Dido's love turns to hatred eventually; see Lyne 1989,26 f. Cf. also Circe's words to Picus, who spurned her love (Ov. *Met.* 14,384; see Bömer ad loc.): *laesaque quid faciat, quid amans, quid femina, disces*; Plut. *Cat.Min.* 37,3 ὅτι κινδυνεύει τὸ λίαν φιλεῖν, ὥς φησι Θεόφραστος, αἴτιον τοῦ μισεῖν γίνεσθαι πολλάκις. In Heliod. 7,20,4 Arsake's old nurse warns Theagenes, speaking from her experience of life: αἱ χρησταὶ ... καὶ φιλόνεοι γυναῖκες ἀμείλικτοι γίνονται καὶ βαρυμήνιδες ἀποτυγχάνουσαι καὶ τοὺς ὑπερόπτας ὡς ὑβριστὰς εἰκότως ἀμύνονται. Ibid. 5 εὐλαβήθητι καὶ μῆνιν ἐρωτικὴν φυλάξαι καὶ τὸ ἐκ τῆς ὑπεροψίας νεμεσητόν.

Love turning to hatred is also a standard element in tales based on the Potiphar's wife-motif (see App. I); then it is the motive which, combined with the fear that her attempt at adultery will be discovered, drives the scorned woman to utter the false accusation; thus already in Hom. *Il.* 6,160 f. (the Bellerophon story). Cf. Ov. *Met.* 15,500 f. *me Pasiphaeia quondam / temptatum frustra patrium temerare cubile, / quod uoluit, uoluisse, infelix, crimine uerso / (indiciine metu magis offensane repulsae?) / damnauit*; Sen. *Phaed.* 824 *quid sinat inausum feminae praeceps furor*? Zintzen 1960,88 f. demonstrates that in his second Hippolytus (*Hipp. Steph.*) Euripides toned down Phaedra's hatred in order to make her more sympathetic. In the first Hippolytus (*Hipp.Kal.*) the hatred of the scorned Phaedra was probably much stronger; this appears from the passages in Greek literature (after Euripides) that were possibly borrowed from the *Hipp.Kal.* (see App. I,4). E.g. Parth. 14,2 (Antheus) ὡς δὲ ἐκεῖνος ἀπεωθεῖτο, ποτὲ μὲν φάσκων ὀρρωδεῖν μὴ κατάδηλος γένοιτο, ποτὲ δὲ Δία Ξένιον καὶ κοινὴν τράπεζαν προϊσχόμενος ἡ Κλεόβοια κακῶς φερομένη ἐν νῷ εἶχε τείσασθαι αὐτόν, ἀνηλεῆ τε καὶ ὑπέραυχον ἀποκαλουμένη. Cf. Xen. *Ephes.* 2,5,5 ἡ Μαντὼ ἐν ὀργῇ ἀκατασχέτῳ γίνεται καὶ ἀναμίξασα πάντα, φθόνον, ζηλοτυπίαν, λύπην, φόβον, ἐνενόει ὅπως τιμωρήσαιτο τὸν ὑπερηφανοῦντα. The motif is also present in Jos. *AJ* 2,54 and Heliod. 1,10 and 8,6 (see Braun 1934,90 f.). In literature Phaedra remained a typical example of spurned love having turned to formidable hatred; see e.g. Juv. 10,328 f., where the words (which sound like a *sententia*) *mulier saeuissima tunc est / cum stimulos odio pudor admouet* are associated with Phaedra and Stheneboia (see also Courtney ad loc.).

ad longe deterius odium: hatred originating from love is especially vehement (see above), but a stepmother's hatred is even more disastrous; cf. Tac. *Ann.* 12,2,1, who uses *nouercalia odia* as a term that needs no further explanation. See on *nouerca* ch. 2 (237,9); Watson 1995,17 f.

239,21-24 Et adsumpto statim nequissimo et ad omne facinus emancipato quodam dotali seruulo perfidiae suae consilia communicat; nec quicquam melius uidetur quam uita miserum priuare iuuenem: Immediately she recruited a slave, who had been part of her parents' household, a villain of the worst kind, who was available for every criminal deed, and imparted to him the plans sprung from her perfidious mind; and nothing seemed better to them than to take the wretched young man's life.

Here the cunning slave, a stock type from comedy, novella, and mime, enters the story as the *nouerca*'s henchman; his entry is symptomatic of the change of generic context (see App. I,6C and App. III).

nequissimo: for this term of abuse, frequent in the *Met.*, see GCA 1985,98 on 8,9 (184,5-9). The adjective is here the narrator's comment; in the *nouerca*'s opinion the slave is undoubtedly quite valuable, which is why she takes him into her confidence. The slave is called *nequissimus* again ch. 10 (244,18; see note there). See also below, on *furcifer*.

ad omne facinus emancipato: Norden 1912,133 tries to explain the expression from the legal use of *emancipare*, but Summers 1967,23 (referring to e.g. Gaius 1,132) disagrees: in legal terminology *emancipare* refers to the release of a child from the *potestas* of the *pater familias*, which does not give a satisfactory sense here; he concludes that the legal term has been used incorrectly here. Thus also Elster 1992,135. It is simpler to explain *emancipatus* from the reflexive verb *se emancipare*, which lies outside the legal domain. Cf. *ThLL* s.v. *emancipare* 445,20 f. 'c. notione sui ipsius in potestatem alterius tradendi, ita ut alteri plane subiectus sis, i.q. quasi mancipium se alteri dedere, subdere sim.', e.g. Pl. *Bac.* 92 *mulier, tibi me emancupo: tuos sum, tibi dedo operam*; for the participle cf. e.g. Cic. *Sen.* 11,38 *senectus honesta est, ... si ius suum retinet, si nemini emancipata est* and Hor. *Epod.* 9,12 *Romanus ... emancipatus feminae* (sc. Cleopatra). *ThLL* ibid. also gives passages in Seneca and mentions our passage at 445,33 f. This is the only passage where the verb is construed not with a dative but with *ad* + accusative; cf. for the modal use of *ad* 8,25 (196,17) *ad usus omnes quietum* with GCA 1985,212 ad loc., with references.

dotali seruulo: *dotalis* means 'belonging to the dowry (*dos*)'. A *seruus dotalis*, therefore, was a slave from the woman's parental home, who was given to her at her marriage. We do not know enough about the stipulations regarding such a *seruus dotalis* (*Cod.Just.* 7,8,7;

Buckland 1908,583 f.; Summers 1967,317 f.). At any rate it is to be expected that such a slave maintained a strong tie with the woman with whom he came; cf. Pl. *As.* 85 f. *dotalem seruom Sauream uxor tua / adduxit, quoi plus in manu sit quam tibi.* Ussing ad loc. refers to Sen. *Con.* 7,6 (21),1 and 3, and to Claud. *In. Eutr.* 1,104. In the passage in Gel. 17,6,10 (also mentioned by Ussing) Gellius seems to explain the term *seruus recepticius*, used by Cato, in the sense of *seruus dotalis* (although he does not use this adjective): '*seruum recepticium' hoc est proprium seruum suum, quem cum pecunia reliqua receperat neque dederat doti, sed retinuerat; non enim seruo mariti imperare hoc* (i.e. to reclaim her money from her husband) *mulierem fas erat, sed proprio suo.*

On the possibly denigrating use of the diminutive *seruulus*, see on *seruulo* ch. 1 (236,24).

perfidiae suae: in view of the abundance of evaluating expressions (*nequissimo* and *miserum*), the narrator leaves his readers in no doubt as to which side has his sympathy. The black-and-white view of this fictive narrator is, however, weakened by the abstract author (see Introd. **3.2**) because of the subtle signals of criticism of the *iuuenis*' behaviour that can be found in the text; see notes above, on *non tamen ... exasperandum, sed ... leniendum*; *maturatae spei*, and *promissae libidinis ... uadimonium*.

communicat: we have to understand *cum eo*, if *adsumpto ... seruulo* is ablative absolute; it is, however, also possible to take these words as dative with *communicat*. In Ciceronian Latin the normal construction with *communicare* is *aliquid cum aliquo*, and the construction *aliquid alicui* is possible under certain conditions only (see Krebs-Schmalz 1,306 f. s.v. *communicare*). But the construction with the dative is not uncommon in later Latin (see Krebs-Schmalz ibid. and Hoppe 1903,27).

nec quicquam melius uidetur quam ... iuuenem: there is a distinct parallelism in the description of the young man, who puts the matter before a wise old *educator*, and that of the *nouerca*, who makes a criminal slave, who is entirely devoted to her, her partner in crime. The decision process of both parties is expressed by *nec quicquam ... uisum* and *nec quicquam ... uidetur*. The parallelism in the description places the two main characters in a sharp contrast to each other, and underlines the differences: the latter couple has no need of a *diutina deliberatio*, and the content of their decision sounds dangerously concrete in comparison with the high-minded but impractical philosophising in *fuga celeri procellam Fortunae saeuientis euadere* (see also above, on *diutina deliberatione*).

uita miserum priuare iuuenem: Hippolytus dies eventually (by a curse of Theseus), and in the tragedies known to us Phaedra has, to a greater or lesser degree, vengeful plans toward him, but there is no indication anywhere that she wants to take his life. This *nouerca*, with her murderous intent, acts according to the literary tradition of the 'wicked stepmother'; see on *nouerca* ch. 2 (237,9) and on *non ... non ... commota*, ch. 5 (240,10 f.); Watson 1995,13 f. and 22 f. with references. Cf. Juv. 6,628 *priuignum occidere fas est*; see Courtney ad loc. with references. On the figure of the murderous stepmother in the *declamationes* see Opelt 1965,201 f. with examples from Sen. *Con.* 6; Watson 1995,92 f. Cf. the continuation of the passage from Hier. *Ep.* 54,15, cited on *nouerca* (ch. 2: 237,9): *si priuignus languerit et condoluerit caput, infamaberis ut uenefica. si non dederis cibos, crudelis, si dederis, malefica diceris.*

miserum: by using this adjective the narrator again shows his own sympathy; see above, on *perfidiae suae*. The adjective will certainly not have occurred in the discussion of the plan by the *nouerca* and her slave.

239,24-26 Ergo missus continuo furcifer uenenum praesentarium co mparat idque uino diligenter dilutum insontis priuigni praeparat exitio: And so the gallows-bird was at once sent out, bought a fast-working poison and, having carefully diluted it in wine, prepared it for the death of the innocent stepson.

continuo: not only by the words *continuo* and *praesentarium* is the speed of action emphasized (see above, on *repentino*): it is also evident from the very condensed manner in which this one short sentence sums up a series of actions, each of which must have taken some time.

furcifer: an invective which is typically used of slaves, and goes back to a punishment often inflicted on them for a slight offence; see Opelt 1965,59 n. 6. Cf. Don. Ter. *An.* 618 *oh tibi ego ut credam, furcifer?: furciferi dicebantur, qui ob leue delictum cogebantur a dominis ignominiae magis quam supplicii causa circa uicinias furcam in collo ferre subligatis ad eam manibus et praedicare peccatum suum.* This term of abuse, quite common in comedy, is used not only by masters to their slaves, but also by slaves among themselves. In speeches of Cicero, it is used especially in an 'argumentum ad hominem', to insinuate that the person in question is of lowly origin; see Opelt 1965,212 and cf. also Sen. *Con.* 7,6,15 and other passages in the *declamationes* mentioned by Opelt 1965,203. Apuleius uses this invective only three times, all in this book. Twice it refers to this slave (here and ch. 9: 243,18); once it is used by Thiasus, good-naturedly, addressing a *scurrula* in his company (ch. 16: 249,13). This shows that the word *furcifer* need not imply a serious accusation (see also the citation from Donatus); it may have been chosen here for that very reason, to suggest that this slave is no more than the executor of the real criminal's plans. See also on *serui nequissimi atque mulieris nequioris* ch. 12 (245,21 f.).

uenenum praesentarium comparat: by buying the poison with which the stepson is to be killed, the slave is liable to punishment according to the *lex Cornelia de sicariis et ueneficiis* (Summers 1967,318 f. and n. 3; see ibid. 74 f.; Elster 1992,138 f.); see on *nouercae quidem perpetuum indicitur exilium, seruus uero patibulo suffigitur* ch. 12 (245,23 f.).

Later (ch. 11: 245,1; see also on *res* ch. 8: 243,16), the doctor to whom this slave had turned will reveal that he did not provide him with a deadly poison but a sleeping draught. Before the doctor's disclosures, which come as a surprise to the reader as well as the participants, the narrator will admit that he is not omniscient but dependent on what he heard in the stable (ch. 7: 242,1 f.). But in the present passage the linear reader has still the impression of having to do with a heterodiegetic-auctorial narrator (see Introd. **3.5**) and believes himself, together with that type of narrator, to be omnipresent and omniscient. On the changing narrative situation see on *exanimis terrae procumbit* ch. 5 (240,5).

uenenum praesentarium: on *praesentarius* 'fast-working' see on *praesentarium* ch. 9 (243,18).

The plotting of her stepson's murder has already indicated that this *nouerca* is no longer acting like Phaedra; her choice of poison as her murder weapon places her in a long literary tradition of poison-mixing stepmothers; cf. Verg. *G.* 2,128 f. *pocula si quando saeuae infecere nouercae, / miscueruntque herbas et non innoxia uerba* (= 3,283) and Ov. *Met.* 1,147 *lurida terribiles miscent aconita nouercae* (with Bömer ad loc.) and *Ep.* 6,127 f. That this tradition is also widely represented in the mime and the *declamationes* is demonstrated by the passage from Hier. *Ep.* 54,15 f. cited above, on *uita miserum priuare miserum*.

diligenter dilutum: alliteration and assonance (the sound of the mixing of the poisonous draught drop by drop into the wine ?).

insontis priuigni: cf. Sen. *Phaed.* 825 *nefanda iuueni crimina insonti apparat*. This possible reference to Seneca emphasizes the difference between Phaedra and our *nouerca* (see above, on *uenenum praesentarium*): Phaedra prepares to utter a false accusation against the *iuuenis*, our *nouerca* intends to poison him. In [Quint.] *Decl.* 1,1 and 2, in the trial of a murder case in which a stepmother and stepson oppose each other, the stepson is repeatedly called *innocentissimus* (see e.g. Håkanson 1,9; 21,8; 23,26). According to Watson 1995,9 f., the invariable innocence of stepchildren is a corollary of the wickedness of stepmothers.

insontis: for the biased fictive narrator this is an established fact. The abstract reader (see Introd. **3.2**), however, is entitled to some reserve as to this qualification; see above, on *perfidiae suae*. By his half-hearted behaviour this young man has proved that he cannot be a 'Hippolytus', and this has had a catalytic effect on his stepmother's 'Metamorphosis': in this chapter she has changed from a tragic, love-struck 'Phaedra' to a typical *nouerca* of the novella, mime, and the *declamationes* (see App. I,6C and App. III).

CHAPTER V

By accident, the *nouerca*'s own son drinks the poison intended for the stepson; the *nouerca* accuses her stepson.

239,27-240,4 Ac dum de oblationis opportunitate secum noxii deliberant homines, forte fortuna puer ille iunior, proprius pessimae feminae filius, post matutinum laborem studiorum domum se recipiens, prandio iam capto sitiens repertum uini poculum, in quo uenenum latebat inclusum, nescius fraudis occultae continuo perduxit <h>austu: And while these malicious people were still discussing their chance of administering the poison, a whim of fate intervened: the younger boy, the dreadful woman's own son, came home after a morning's hard work at his studies; once he had eaten his lunch, he was thirsty, and found the cup of wine in which lurked the poison. Unaware of the hidden danger, he drained the cup in one long draught.

secum = *inter se*. The use of *secum* with *deliberare* and verbs of a similar meaning is apparently confined to Apuleius' *Met*. See *GCA* 1981,68 on 6,31 (152,19-20).

noxii ... homines: *noxii* means 'criminal' (*OLD* s.v *noxius* 1a; see *GCA* 1981,227 f. on 7,12: 171,4-8) but also 'malicious': these people are as venomous as the poison they have prepared. Cf. below, *noxia potio* (also ch. 26: 257,11 and ch. 33: 264,17 f.) and e.g. Plin. *Nat*. 22,99 *noxii ... fungi*; Curt. 9,10,13 *insalubrium ciborum noxii suci*. Because they are plotting a murder, they are also *noxii* in the legal sense of the word (Summers 1967,80 and 319). See Thome 1993,90 f. and 212 f., with extensive references, for a summary of the development of the connotations of *noxius* (from *damnosus* to *sons* and then in a moral sense: *malignus, scelestus*); ibid. 229 f. on Apuleius' use of the word.

forte fortuna puer ... continuo perduxit haustu: the motif of poison accidentally taken by the wrong victim is common in folklore: see Thompson K527 (poison accidentally swallowed by an animal; cf. Eur. *Ion* 1196 f.); N332.1-7; cf. Lucian *Dial. Mort*. 7; Heliod. 8,7,7. Winkler 1985,235 points to a parallel to our story in Plut. *Mor*. 401e-f (one of the novella-like anecdotes in *De Pythiae oraculis*). In most stories the mistake leads to justice in the form of the detection or death of the criminal. Here, however, the accidental poisoning of the younger brother leads to further complications in the story; compare the complex 'detective'-stories that we meet in the show trials of the *declamationes*. Steinmetz 1982 (170 f. and 189 f.) gives examples and (192 n. 78a) points out the similarities in subject matter between the *declamationes* and the mime (see App. I,5.5 and App. III).

Later we will see that the *uenenum* was a strong sleeping draught (on the narrative situation in this connection, see below, on *nescius fraudis occultae*). For the motif of a sleeping potion instead of poison, see on ch. 11 (245,1 f.) *dedi uenenum, sed somniferum*.

Slowly but surely, this carefully wrought sentence is moving toward a climax: *forte fortuna* prepares the reader for a remarkable event; then new bits of information are added one by one until *continuo perducit haustu*. The reader sees everything happen as if before his eyes (see Elsom 1989,141 f. on the 'cinematic qualities' of the text of the *Met*.). In this dramatic presentation of events, even a linear reader will hardly fail to notice that the manner in which the story is told is becoming much more direct: it has the character of an eyewitness report. This also entails a change in the status of the fictive narrator and the degree of his insight and general understanding; see below, on *exanimis terrae procumbit*. Steinmetz 1982,369 (with Wiemken 1972) describes this episode as a scene from a mime (see App. I,5.4), and we can, indeed, imagine ourselves as the audience of a scene performed by silent players.

Most translators take *forte fortuna* closely with *domum se recipiens*. However, *forte fortuna* rather modifies the rest of the sentence. Therefore the translation here follows the solution of Hanson: 'While the evil pair were deliberating ..., the chance of fortune intervened. The younger boy, ...'.

A well-wrought presentation enhances the effect of this sentence, in which a reversal in the story, a new complication is described:
Ac dum de oblationis opportunitate secum noxii deliberant homines (26 syllables)
forte fortuna puer ille iunior (12): fort- ... fort- ...
proprius pessimae feminae filius (12): alliteration; see also note ad loc.
post matutinum laborem studiorum domum se recipiens (19): the ending -*um* occurs 3 times.
prandio iam capto sitiens (9): rhyming -*iens* with previous kolon.
repertum uini poculum in quo uenenum latebat inclusum (19): the ending -*um* occurs 4 times.
nescius fraudis occultae (8)
continuo perduxit haustu (9).

forte fortuna: colloquial Latin abounded in etymologising assonances like this. This expression, frequent in comedy (e.g. Pl. *Mil.* 287), is also attested elsewhere, e.g. Cic. *Div.* 2,18 and Gel. 1,3,30. Don. ad Ter. *Phorm.* 841 connects it with the Italic deity *Fors Fortuna* (later equated with Greek Τύχη), who from times immemorial had a sanctuary on the Forum Boarium (see Kajanto 1981,503 f., with references): *aliud Fortuna est, aliud Fors Fortuna ... nam 'Fors Fortuna' est, cuius diem festum colunt, qui sine arte aliqua uiuunt; huius aedes trans Tiberim est*. See Tromaras ad Ter. *Eu.* 134 *forte fortuna*, with references.

Here we see the beginning of an important turn in the story: the planned murder fails. The words *forte fortuna* at the beginning, together with the explicit attribution of the happy ending to *fortuna* (ch. 12: 245,26 f.), form a kind of framework for this second part of the story, where Fortuna and her unpredictable ways are made responsible for the outcome. See Introd. **2.4.1**.

puer ille iunior: *ille* in the sense of 'whom I mentioned before' (ch. 2: 237,7 f.). From now on, the elder brother (the stepson) no longer plays an active role in the story. See App. I,4 and 6B.

proprius pessimae feminae filius: double alliteration, rhyming word-endings in chiasmus, and four successive cretic words.

pessimae feminae: here the *nouerca* receives, for the first time in the story, a clearly pejorative adjective. First described in rather moderate terms (*forma magis quam moribus in domo mariti praepollens* and *seu naturaliter impudica seu fato ... impulsa* ch. 2: 237,9 f.), she has been depicted since then primarily as the tormented victim of an illicit passion. Earlier notes (e.g. *nouerca* ch. 2: 237,9; *mulier* ibid. 237,14; *uita miserum priuare iuuenem* ch. 4: 239,24, and *insontis priuigni* ibid. 26) pointed out her development from a tragic 'Phaedra' into the cliché of the malicious stepmother. This development seems now complete: below she will be called *dira illa femina et malitiae nouercalis exemplar unicum* (see note there). With the adjective *pessima* the narrator treats her as an equal to the *pistor*'s crafty wife (9,14: 213,10 f. *pessimam et ante cunctas mulieres longe deterrimam*; surprisingly enough, that woman is suddenly called *nouerca*, too: 9,31: 226,16; see *GCA* 1995,267 ad loc.).

post matutinum laborem studiorum: the boy receives the same proper education as his elder stepbrother did (*probe litteratus* ch. 2: 237,4); cf. Sen. *Dial.* 1 (*Prov.*), 2,5 *illi* (i.e. the fathers) *excitari iubent liberos ad studia obeunda mature*.

laborem studiorum: cf. Apul. *Pl.* 1,2 (184) *et pubescentis primitias labore atque amore studendi inbutas refert*. For the combination of the two words cf. Plin. *Nat.* 34,166 and Quint. *Inst.* 1,12,8 *Illud quidem minime uerendum est, ne laborem studiorum pueri difficilius tolerent*. The statement serves here to explain why the boy is so thirsty that he drinks the wine in one gulp. *Apol.* 4,10 sums up the long-term effects of *labor litteratus* (including 'dehydration') with witty exaggeration: *continuatio etiam litterati laboris omnem gratiam corpore deterget, habitudinem tenuat, sucum exsorbet, colorem obliterat, uigorem debilitat*.

domum se recipiens: this happened, as was customary in well-to-do families, under the escort of a *paedagogus* (see below, on *paedagogus*).

prandio iam capto sitiens: *prandium*: 'lunch'. At the end of the morning a meal was taken which was somewhat more substantial than the light breakfast (*ientaculum*) eaten early in the morning. The *prandium* consisted of fish, eggs, and vegetables, and was served with wine and water (see *DNP* s.v. 'Mahlzeiten' 706 [Gutsfeld]).

uenenum: at this moment it will not yet have occurred to the linear reader to take this in any other meaning but 'poison'; see above, on *uenenum praesentarium comparat*, ch. 4: 239,25; for the ambiguities in the text see below, on *exanimis terrae procumbit*. For the play with the term *uenenum* in this story see the following note, and on *dedi uenenum, sed somniferum* ch. 11: 245,1.

nescius fraudis occultae: as the previous *in quo uenenum latebat inclusum*, this phrase emphasizes the boy's ignorance: again, the narrator and the readers know more than this actor. But later it will become clear to the reader that the narrator's omniscience, which is still implied here, no longer prevails and that the poison is only a sleeping potion. See the references in the previous note.

The younger brother is *nescius fraudis occultae*; the father is *nescius fraudium* (ch. 6: 241,6). This emphasis on the ill-fated naivety of both son and father calls our attention to the *nouerca*'s deception (begun in ch. 2: 237,19 *mentitur* and culminating in this chapter at 240,16-23; see there, on *insimulat*). The clever physician, who uses his head and therefore sees through people's deceit, will be the first to be able to break the chain of lies.

fraudis occultae: *fraus* can mean 'detriment, danger, etc.' (see *OLD* s.v. *fraus* 1), but also 'fraud, deception, stratagem, etc.' (see *OLD* ibid. 5); cf. *fraus abdita* 5,14 (114,15); in connection with poison also e.g. Sil. 1,219 *nudo sine fraudibus* (i.e. not coated with poison) *ensi*. Comparable in the *Met.* is 6,20 (143,23 f.) *offulae sequentis fraude caninis latratibus obseratis*. In Livy the combination *fraus occulta* is found in the sense of 'hidden ambush', e.g. 10,34,6 *auidum inuadendi deserta moenia militem detinet, ne quam occultam in fraudem incautus rueret*; in the meaning of 'a snake in the grass' in 3,18,6 *si edoceri se sissent, quae fraus ab tribunis occulta in lege ferretur* (also 3,25,4); in 24,38,3 it has the meaning of 'underhanded fighting methods' (as opposed to 'an open fight'), which is the meaning in Luc. 10,345 f. *nec parat occultae caedem committere fraudi / inuictumque ducem detecto Marte lacessit*. On *fraus* in the *Met.* see also on *fraudes ... in asino* ch. 14 (246,27).

continuo perduxit haustu: cf., also in the context of poison, Mart. 3,22,4 *summa uenenum potione perduxti*. See *ThLL* s.v. *perduco* 1289,48 f. for other occurrences of the verb in the sense of 'drink up'. Cf. below, on ch. 16 (249,21) *illum calicem uno haustu perhausi*.

Merkelbach 1962,83 remarks: 'In einer bestimmten Weihe wurde dem Mysten ein solcher Schlaftrunk gereicht, den er in einem Zug leeren musste, um dann wie tot niederzusinken', but does not give any examples. On his interpretation of this story see App. I,6B.

perduxit: the perfect tense marks a new episode; the series of events within this episode are from now on indicated by historical presents (see on *rupit ... praecipit* ch. 3: 238,5).

continuo ... haustu: the phrase evokes the irrevocability of the fateful event: the thirsty boy gulps down the potion without pausing to taste it, and so does not give himself time to notice a strange flavour. *ThLL* s.v. *haustus* gives no other examples of this combination. Cf. ch. 16: 249,21 *uno haustu*. The topos of drinking 'ad fundum' occurs also in the Charition mime, 55, and in Eur. *Cyclops* 417 f. and 570 f. There, as here and in ch. 16 (249,21), it bodes no good for the drinker.

haustu: F has *austu*, φ *haustu*. *ThLL* s.v. *haustus* 2574,58 f.: aspiratur in titulis ... in cod. antiquissimis. See *ThLL*. s.v. *haurio* 2566,83 f.

240,4-7 Atque ubi fratri suo paratam mortem ebibit, exanimis terrae procumbit, il[l]icoque repentina pueri pernicie paedagogus commotus ululabili clamore matrem totamque ciet familiam: And when he had drained the death prepared for his brother, he fell to the ground unconscious, and at once the boy's attendant, horrified by the sudden disaster that had struck the boy, with howling cries called his mother and the whole household to the scene.

Atque: F has *Qui*, written, however, by a different hand in an erasure; φ and a* (part of the mss. of Class I; see Introd. **4.1** with footnote) have *atque*.

fratri suo paratam mortem ebibit: the wording of this whole passage is such that the re-reader, on reflection, can establish that there is no unambiguous, explicit statement that death actually occurs. Here it only says that he drunk the death 'prepared' for his brother. See below, on *exanimis terrae procumbit*.

mortem ebibit: 'when he had drunk ... death' (cf. e.g. Carlesi 'ma appena ebbe così bevuto la morte preparata per suo fratello ...'; thus also Vallette). Some translators 'explain', cf. e.g. Helm-Krenkel 'Todestrank'. *ThLL* s.v. *mors* 1504,71 f. collects the passages where *mors* is used 'pro causa mortis'; in all these passages a translator must make a choice between a literal translation of the expression (which is equally daring and expressive in Latin) and a more 'explicative' translation (see also Billotta 1975,67). Cf. e.g. Sen. *Con.* 7,3,8 (a father catches his son in the act of mixing poison; the son throws it away, claiming that he had wanted to commit suicide) *mortem, inquit* (sc. the father bringing charges against his son), *meam effudit* (cited as a cleverly formulated *sententia* in the style of the mime-writer Publilius Syrus; see Winterbottom ad loc.); cf. Luc. 9,616 f. *'pocula morte carent': dixit, dubiumque uenenum / hausit*; [Quint] *Decl.* 13,5 (270.15 f. Håkanson) *sparsit omnibus floribus mortem* (the praefatio has *flores suos ueneno sparsit*). Cf. ch.

25 (256,26 f.) *ut ille quidem momentarium uenenum uenderet, illa autem emeret mortem mariti sui.*

As the boy 'drinks death' in our passage, so Dido 'drinks love' (at the banquet with Aeneas and his men) in Verg. A. 1,749 *longumque bibebat amorem* (see Lyne 1989,29 f.).

exanimis terrae procumbit: thus far, the story has been presented by a heterodiegetic narrator (see Introd. **3.5** and on *in eo ipso scilicet ne ... admoneretur* ch. 3: 238,6 f.): he told a story in retrospect, was not an actor in it himself, and was omniscient and omnipresent. In this way he was able to tell what was going on in the *nouerca*'s bedroom (ch. 3: 238,8 f.) and what the various actors were thinking or feeling. The linear reader assumes that he participates in the omniscience of this narrator and that he will continue to do so; in this he is once more confirmed by *nescius fraudis occultae* above (see note there). Meanwhile, however, the narrative situation has changed drastically. The linear reader has not been informed of this explicitly; at most he may have noticed that the presentation of the events has become more direct and dramatic from the opening of this chapter onward (see above, on *forte fortuna puer ... haustu*): in the continuation of this story the fictive narrator receives an actorial status, i.e. he becomes one of the spectators: his insight into events has now the same limitations as that of the fictive audience. Consequently, the reader (who is in the hands of this fictive narrator) now also ceases to be omniscient and omnipresent. Apuleius uses here a narrative technique (shown by Effe 1975,148 to have been first introduced into the Greek novel by Achilles Tatius) which considerably enhances the elements of surprise and suspension. Especially in passages where the motif of apparent death plays a role (see Effe l.c. 149), the element of surprise for the reader is intensified by this technique, which Effe calls 'personale Erzählweise' (a term used by Stanzel; see e.g. Stanzel [8]1976,17). Apuleius enhances the effect of this narrative style even more: in a single story he first gives the reader, through an indisputably omniscient narrator (see above), a sense of superiority due to omniscience; then he gradually changes the status of his narrator. Not until ch. 7 (242,1 f.) is the reader made aware of the narrative situation: that the reader is depending for his information on a narrator who has everything from hearsay, 'from people who had been present'; see note there. From now on the author can have his fictive narrator use all kinds of expressions which the linear reader will not – but the re-reader will – take as ambiguous. The linear reader will therefore think, as will the fictive actors present here (e.g. the *paedagogus*), that the boy falls down dead. Only in retrospect, with the knowledge of the entire story, will one be able to recognize that *exanimis* is used here as a kind of key word, exactly because, in addition to 'dead', it can also mean 'unconscious'. On the need to re-read this story, see on *dedi uenenum, sed somniferum* ch. 11 (245,1).

exanimis: for the meaning 'unconscious' cf. e.g. Sil. 15,398 *exanimem* (sc. *Crispinum*) *sonipes ad signa reuexit* and in the *Met*. 4,26 (95,14) *exanimem saeuo pauore* (see ThLL s.v. *exanimis* 1173,80 f. for other examples). For *exanimis* in the sense of 'dead' cf. e.g. Verg. A. 5,481 *exanimis ... procumbit humi bos*; in the *Met*. e.g. 9,30 (226,5 f.) *uident e quodam tigillo constrictum iamque exanimem pendere dominum*.

terrae: the dative with verbs of motion is found in poetry as early as Ennius; its expansion, especially in Augustan poets, is to be attributed to Greek influences, according to KSt 2,1,320. This construction is rare in Ciceronian prose, but occurs frequently in later prose.

ilicoque: Giarratano, Robertson, and Hanson follow ς and write *ilicoque*. Helm retains F's *-ll-*; this is the only passage where F uses this spelling, and the variant seems to reflect uncertainty about the spelling at the time of F's origin rather than uncertainty on the author's part. Cf. E-M 309 s.v. *ilico*; *ThLL* s.v. *ilico* 330,11 f. 'scribitur *ill-* hic illic in codd. recc.'.

repentina ... pernicie: see on *repentino* ch. 4 (239,1) for the repeated emphasis on fast, sudden events in this episode.

pueri pernicie paedagagus: alliteration.

pernicie: again a word that the re-reader will interpret differently from the linear reader (see above, on *exanimis terrae procumbit*). See *OLD* s.v. *pernicies* 1: 'physical destruction, fatal injury'; b. 'ruin, undoing'. In many passages in the *Met.* where *pernicies* occurs, it can only be deduced from the context whether it means actual 'death' or merely 'ruin, disaster' without a fatal outcome. Cf. e.g. 7,22 (170,20 f.) *animos pastorum in meam perniciem atrociter suscitauit*; 9,30 (225,15 f.) *cuncta, quae in perniciem pistoris mei gesta sunt, cognoui*.

paedagogus: in Greece he was a house slave, who was entrusted with the boys' education, accompanied them to and from school, and was responsible for their behaviour. The Romans became acquainted with this type of *paedagogus* through the comedies of Plautus (e.g. *Bac.* 441 f.). In Hellenistic Rome the prestige of the *paedagogus* grew gradually, and it became an important profession also practiced by freedmen. See *RE* s.v. 'Paidagogus' 2375,17 f. [Schuppe].

ululabili: this adjective is first attested in Apuleius' *Met.*; see *GCA* 1977,41 on 4,3 (76,14-17) with references; on the expansion of formations in *-bilis* in late Latin see Bajoni 1994,1800 and n. 71, with references. In all three places where *ululabilis* is used, the *ululabilis plangor* (4,3), and *ululabilis uox* (5,7: 108,13, and here) indicate bewailing of a person presumed - but not actually - dead.

familiam: the phrase *matrem totamque familiam* shows that *familia* is used here in what Summers 1967,95 calls the 'narrowest sense' of the four meanings distinguished by him. It refers here to all *serui* and also to the people *in loco seruorum* employed in a household.

240,7-9 Iamque cognito casu noxiae potionis uarie quisque praesentium auctores insimulabant extremi facinoris: And when it was found out that a noxious potion was involved, every one of those present were soon voicing their suspicions in various ways as to the perpetrators of the nefarious crime.

Iamque ... insimulabant: the imperfect is descriptive; moreover, in combination with *iamque* (see on '*iam* de préparation', Chaussery-Laprée 1969,479 f.), it prepares for a sudden reversal in the story. Usually such a clause is followed by a *cum inversum*. Here, however, that function is performed by a new main clause, introduced by *sed*: by means of her own accusations, the *nouerca* puts a stop to all the imputations the members of the household are bringing forward. Cf. also 7,24 (172,10-14) *iamque ... recidebat. et ecce ... proserpit ursa* with *GCA* 1981,242 ad loc.

The description of the bystanders' reaction is true to life: each thinks he knows who the culprit is, and voices his opinion. If we imagine this to be the rendition of a mime (see the introductory remark to ch. 3: 238,7-10), then this passage could be a scene in which the entire troupe can give a comic performance. See Bonaria 1965,4 and n. 1, with references, on how big a company of mime-actors might be.

uarie: a case of narrative economy: the various allegations expressed by those present,

which are of no consequence for the development of the story, are summed up in *uarie*.

quisque ... insimulabant: for the plural verb cf. 4,10 (82,14-15) *unus quisque ... territus ... decurrunt anxii* with *GCA* 1977,85 ad loc.

insimulabant: cf. *insimulat* below. The use of *insimulo* in these two passages shows a difference in gradation. The people of the *familia* 'voice suspicion' (*ThLL* s.v. *insimulo* 1911,64 f. 'i.q. (simulando) *proferre, suspicari* sim.'); the *nouerca* 'accuses, brings charges' (*ThLL* ibid. 1911,76 f. '(simulando) *accusare, criminari* sim.'). The repetition of the same verb, used first for the suspicions expressed by the *familia*, then for the *nouerca*'s (false) accusation of the stepson, emphasizes her power: she is *in domo mariti praepollens* (ch. 2: 237,10).

extremi facinoris: cf. 4,20 (90,6) *extremum flagitium* with *GCA* 1977,155 ad loc. Van der Paardt 1971,56 f. on 3,5 (56,2) *extremos latrones*, gives examples for *extremus* in the sense of *nefarius*, a frequent meaning in the *Met*. Here, however, one should also bear in mind the connotation 'fatal', which *extremus* often has; cf. *ThLL* s.v. *exter* 2003,46 f., citing among other examples Cic. *Off.* 2,29 *iam extrema scelera metuentes*; cf. also Caes. *Civ.* 2,7,1 *ad extremum uitae periculum*.

240,9-17 Sed dira illa femina et malitiae nouercalis exemplar unicum non acerba filii morte, non parricidii conscientia, non infortunio domus, non luctu mariti uel aerumna funeris commota cladem familiae <in> uindictae compendium traxit, missoque protinus cursore, qui uianti marito domus expugnationem nuntiaret, ac mox eodem ocius ab itinere regresso personata nimia temeritate insimulat priuigni ueneno filium suum interceptum: But that abominable woman, that singular example of stepmotherly malice, not moved by the grievous death of her son, not by having the murder of a relative on her conscience, not by the misfortune that her house had suffered, not by the grief to her husband or the distress of a funeral, took the devastation of the family as an advantage to be exploited for her revenge: at once she despatched a messenger to bring word to her husband on his travels about the calamity that had struck his family; and presently, when he had hurried home from his journey, she made the accusation, playing her role with too much impudence, that her son's life had been cut short by her stepson's poison.

Sed: used here instead of a '*cum inversum*'; see above, on *iamque ... insimulabant*.

dira illa femina et malitiae nouercalis examplar unicum: this characterization of the woman is entirely in the style of the mime and the *declamationes* (see App. I,5.5 and App. III). At this point one would no longer think of comparing her with the tragic figure of Phaedra, had not the fictive audience (see Introd. **3.3**) been advised *iam ergo, lector optime, scito te tragoediam, non fabulam legere et a socco ad coturnum ascendere* (ch. 2: 237,12 f.; see note there). For the abstract reader (see Introd. **3.2**) this 'deceptive' introduction remains an incentive to reflect on the different literary genres through which the main characters of this story are wandering (see App. I,6 and App. III) and observe how much tragedy (in particular that of Euripides) has contributed to the stereotype of the malicious woman or wicked stepmother encountered here. This was recognized even in antiquity, as appears from a statement of Nicostratus (a sophist of the 2nd century A.D.), cited by Stob. *Ecl.* 4,23 (598,12 f. H.) λεκτέον δὲ οὕτως εἰδότα ὡς οὐδεμία μηχανὴ κρατῆσαι τῶν γυναικῶν, κἀκεῖνο ὥς εἰσι πάντων τέχνας τε ἐξευρεῖν καὶ πλέξαι σοφώταται·

εἰ δὲ ἀπιστεῖς, ἀναγίγνωσκε τὰς τραγῳδίας, ὁπόσα ἐποίησαν ἢ ἐβουλεύσαντο γυναῖκες ἐπιθυμίᾳ ξένων ἀφροδισίων. The schools of rhetoric will have played their part in turning Euripides' tragic heroines into rigid stereotypes. See also the next note.

dira illa femina: cf. Sen. *Phaed*. 559 f. *sed dux malorum femina. haec scelerum artifex / obsedit animos*; ibid. 563 f. *sileantur aliae! sola coniunx Aegei / Medea, reddet feminas, dirum genus!* Particularly Euripides' Medea became an example of the wronged woman who is capable of the most gruesome deeds in her vindictiveness; cf. Eur. *Med*. 263 f. γυνὴ γὰρ τἄλλα μὲν φόβου πλέα / κακή τ'ες ἀλκὴν καὶ σίδηρον εἰσορᾶν·/ ὅταν δ'ἐς εὐνὴν ἠδικημένη κυρῇ, / οὐκ ἔστιν ἄλλη φρὴν μιαιφονωτέρα. Like Medea, the *nouerca* is able to see the death of her own child (the recently poisoned boy was her *proprius ... filius*) as a means to avenge herself, as the rest of this sentence shows. Below the father is described as *infelix duplici filiorum morte percussus*, which makes him comparable to Jason.

dira: Shumate 1996,114 f. sees *dira* here as one of the references to the Furies, who play a role at different stages in the *Met.*: (116) 'Although the Furies begin their career in the *Metamorphoses* doing their narrow inherited duty, they ultimately are made to preside over violence that is gratuitous and irrational ... In this expansion of the Furies' province Apuleius is drawing here, as he often does, on Vergil'.

malitiae nouercalis: the combination *malitia nouercalis* is not found earlier; the first attestation of the adjective is Sen. *Con*. 4,6 (modifying *oculi*); other examples are Tac. *Ann*. 1,33,5 (*stimuli*); 12,2,1 (*odia*); [Quint.] *Decl*. 2,7 (Håkanson 26,18 f.; *nomen*) and Quint. *Decl*. 327,3: *facta*).

exemplar unicum: referring to people, the noun *exemplar* occurs also e.g. Cic. *Caec*. 28 *senator ... ornamentum iudiciorum, exemplar antiquae religionis*; Sen. *Cl*. 1,1,6 *nec, quod te imitari uelit, exemplar extra te quaerit*. In a negative sense, as here, it is found in Tac. *Ann*. 6,32,7 (sc. Vitellius) *exemplar apud posteros adulatorii dedecoris habetur*. The combination *exemplar unicum* is not attested before Apuleius (but cf. e.g. Liv. 1,21,2 *cum ipsi se homines in regis uelut unici exempli mores formarent*), but does occur after him, e.g. as a vocative in Hier. *Dan. Prol*. 1. 32 *Marcella, unicum Romanae sanctitatis exemplar unicum*; Cass. *Inst. Praef*. 7 *beatissime papa, unicum religionis et humilitatis exemplar*.

unicum: its meaning is here both 'having no match, singular, unique' (*OLD* s.v. *unicus* 2) and 'occurring only once' (as very often in the *Met*.: see *GCA* 1981,129 on 7,7: 159,17-21). In this phrase we hear, behind the narrator, the concrete author (see Introd. **3.1**), who calls the attention of his audience to the uniqueness of his literary creation: 'even though evil stepmothers appear in many forms in literature, *this* woman is my once-in-a-lifetime creation'; see on *ad librum profero* ch. 2 (237,2 f.).

non ... non ... non ... non ... commota: the asyndetic anaphora of *non* introducing the limbs of the tetracolon suggests that it is the narrator who is truly *commotus* as he describes the cold impassivity of the *non commota nouerca*.

The asyndeton is interrupted by the fourth colon, which contains the conjunction *uel*. Cf. e.g. 9,32 (227,2 f.) *dum fodiens, dum irrigans ceteroque incuruus labore* with *GCA* 1995,273 ad loc.

Partly because of the accumulation of facts — contained in a pathetic anaphora — that leave this woman unmoved, the comparison with the tragic figure of Phaedra forces itself upon us again: in Eur. *Hipp. Steph.*, from 669 onward, Phaedra is greatly agitated after discovering that the nurse has disclosed her love to Hippolytus, and commits suicide. In Seneca's tragedy Phaedra, seeing the dead Hippolytus, confesses her guilt in an emotional monologue (1159 f.) and takes her own life. See also on *uita miserum priuare iuuenem* ch. 4 (239,24).

Each colon illustrates another negative quality. *Non acerba filii morte*: she lacks a mother's love; *non parricidii conscientia*: she has no fear of the law; *non infortunio domus*: she feels no responsibility for her family; *non luctu mariti uel aerumna funeris*: she is wanting in affection for her husband and in compassion in general.

acerba filii morte: the first meaning of *acerbus* is 'sour, bitter' (thus Helm-Krenkel: 'den schmerzlichen Tod'). Because unripe fruits are sour, *acerbus* can also mean 'unripe' (*OLD* s.v. *acerbus* 2). In the expression *acerba mors* there is often a connotation of 'unripe' when it refers to the death of a young person: an untimely, premature death; thus Vallette: 'la mort prématurée'. Cf. also ch. 25 (256,15), and see *GCA* 1981,261 on 7,27 (175,1-5).

parricidii: in a legal-technical sense this woman is punishable under the *Lex Pompeia de parricidiis* (Summers 1967,320 f. with references; Elster 1991,147 f.). See also on *parricidam* ch. 6 (241,8); on the punishment of *parricidium* see on *insui culleo* ch. 8 (243,2).

As a 'minor theme', *parricidium* occurs in the *Met.* no less than 9 times; Cooper 1980,438 discusses this as an example of 'anti-epic' in the *Met.*: 'in his mind Apuleius compared many of the world's most heinous acts of aggression with the prototype of masculine action as portrayed in epic and myth'.

infortunio domus: also in 8,1 (176,18-20); see *GCA* 1985,28 ad loc. See also on *domus cladem* ch. 4 (239,8 f.). Molt 1938,55 on 1,6 (6,1) states that with this use of *in-fortunium* Apuleius resumes the archaic meaning of the word. See *GCA* 1977,201 on 4,27 (95,16-18) with references.

luctu mariti uel aerumna funeris: eager to make his rhetorical enumeration even more impressive, the narrator anticipates emotions which are yet to come but which, as he presumes already here, will equally fail to *commouere* this evil woman: at this moment, the husband is still ignorant of the facts. When his *luctus* and the *aerumnarum procellae* that assail him are described and he makes his griefstricken appearance (ch. 6: 241,1 f.), there is, in the turn the story is then taking, no room for the *nouerca*'s reaction.

aerumna: according to Quint. *Inst.* 8,3,26 this is an archaic word; Apuleius uses it frequently in the *Met.*, especially when the narrator indicates his hardships as an ass. See e.g. 7,2 (155,17-156,1) with *GCA* 1981,90 f. ad loc., and ibid. 78 on 6,32 (153,23-27).

cladem familiae <in> uindictae compendium traxit: Bährens argues against inserting *ad* or *in* in the reading of F, pointing to the widespread use of the accusative of direction without preposition, even when it leads (as here) to a double accusative; however, the examples he gives are primarily with compound verbs. Augello 1977,208 f. follows Bährens, and Terzaghi and Giarratano also retain F. All other editors adopt Modius's conjecture, defended by Oudendorp, reading *<in>* before *uindictae*. *OLD* s.v. *traho* 20b 'to assign, ascribe (to a meaning), take (in a particular way)' mentions passages from *Rhet. Her.* onward for this use of *traho* with *in* or *ad*; see e.g. Tac. *Ann.* 1,62,3 *Tiberio ... cuncta Germanici in deterius trahenti* with Koestermann ad loc. In our passage one can also think of the examples given by *OLD* ibid. 21 (also from *Rhet. Her.* onward) for *traho aliquid ad/in aliquam rem* 'to apply to the needs or purposes of', e.g. Ov. *Met.* 8,244 f. *spinas in pisce notatas / traxit in exemplum*; Tac. *Ann.* 15,67,1 *dissimilitudinem morum ad defensionem trahens*. In none of the examples given by *OLD* (under 20b and 21) is the preposition absent in this metaphorical use of *trahere*. Therefore it seems reasonable to follow Helm, Frassinetti, and Robertson in assuming *<in>* before *uindictae*; paleographically, the omission of *in* before *uindictae* is quite possible. Blümner proposes the conjecture *<a> clade familiae ... traxit* (honored by Robertson with 'fort. recte'). Paleographically this makes perfectly good sense (haplography of *a* after *commota*). The sentence should then be rendered as follows: 'she derived from the devastation of her family an advantage for her revenge' (cf. *OLD* s.v. *traho* 12 *aliquid ab aliqua re*). But then it is difficult to explain the accusative *cladem* in the mss. See Jacquinod 1992,81 f. on other cases of double accusative in the *Met.*, mistakenly emended by editors; he discusses our place at length ibid. 90 f., and, although admitting that it is difficult to explain the double accusative here, in the end pleads for retaining it, since we do not know enough about the usage of the 'langue familiaire' in this respect.

compendium uindictae: with e.g. Oudendorp and Hildebrand, some of the translators take this as 'a shortcut (*OLD* s.v. *compendium* 3) to revenge'. E.g. Helm-Krenkel 'benutzte das Leid der Familie, um auf kürzerem Wege ihre Rache zu erreichen'. An objection against this is that the context shows that the woman seizes the opportunity of her son's death with both hands to accuse her stepson of murdering his own brother, as well as trying to seduce her: this does not make her revenge faster, but it does make it worse. That is to say, that she uses the death of her son as a point to her advantage in her act of revenge, and *compendium* should be taken as 'gain, profit' (*OLD* ibid. 1). Thus e.g. Vallette 'ne voulut voir dans cette catastrophe domestique que le profit qu'en tirerait sa vengeance'. An explicative genitive with *compendium* in this sense is not unusual; cf. e.g. Man. 4,19 *damna et compendia rerum*; Gel. 2,27,5 *quaestu atque compendio gloriarum*; and in the *Met.* e.g. 4,25 (94,12) *compendio tuae redemptionis* and 9,29 (225,6 f.) *praemii destinatum compendium*.

uindictae: vengeance is the only motive for this woman. In the Phaedra-characters known to us, the false accusation of Hippolytus is motivated by a mixture of resentment and fear of discovery (cf. Ov. *Met.* 15,503 *indiciine metu magis, offensane repulsae?*), to which Euripides in his *Hipp. Steph.* adds Phaedra's wish to teach Hippolytus to σωφρονεῖν (730 f.). See Zintzen 1960,88 f.

traxit ... insimulat: on the change in tense from the perfect to the historical present see on *rupit ... et ... praecipit* ch. 3 (238,5).

cursore: a *cursor* (Var. *L.* 8,15) is a specially trained slave or freedman, used both in private and in public service as a kind of mail carrier (Gloss. δρομεύς, ταχυδρόμος). Another, more customary term for *cursor* is *tabellarius* (see *RE* s.v. 'Tabellarius' 1844,60 f. [Schroff]). Since these men were specially trained, not every private person could afford a *cursor* of his own (it may be one of the exaggerated signs of Trimalchio's exorbitant wealth that Encolpius and company see in Trimalchio's house a *grex cursorum* being coached by a trainer; Petr. 29,7). That the family of this story is affluent has been noted earlier; see on *uillulas* ch. 4 (239,15).

uianti: a verb *uiare* is not attested before Apuleius (*LS* mistakenly quotes Quint. *Inst.* 8,6,33 *'uio' pro 'eo' infelicius fictum*; this wrong quotation is apparently taken over from Krebs-Schmalz 2,734). Apuleius uses it three times, always as a participle (see *GCA* 1981,40 on 6,26: 148,24-149,2). He uses the verb to indicate the notion of 'being on one's way, *in uia*' (see also Callebat 1968,143 f. on Apuleius' care in choosing between different verbs meaning 'travel'). After Apuleius other forms of the verb are found as well, e.g.

Amm. 20,9,1 *legati intenti ad uiandum*; Prud. *Symm.* 2,772 f. *iter ... uiandi / multifidum.*

domus expugnationem: in Chariton 1,5,1 the narrator compares the grief for Callirhoe's supposed death with the grief for the capture of a city: καὶ πανταχόθεν ὁ θρῆνος ἠκούετο, καὶ τὸ πρᾶγμα ἐῴκει πόλεως ἁλώσει. In Latin no exact parallel for the combination *domus expugnatio* can be found. *ThLL* s.v. *expugnatio* 1806,69 f. mentions our passage as the first for this metaphorical use of *expugnatio* and compares Itala *prov.* 1,27 (= [Cypr.] *Singul. Cler.* 1, p. 174,20) *cum aduenerit uobis pressura et expugnatio* (πολιορκία, Vulg. *angustia*). The image behind it, however, is known in literature; cf. Ov. *Tr.* 1,3,25 f. *si licet exemplis in paruo grandibus uti / haec facies Troiae, cum caperetur, erat*; Prop. 4,8,55 f. *fulminat illa oculis, et quantum femina saeuit, / spectaclum capta nec minus urbe fuit.* Cf. also Tac. *Ann.* 1,41,1 and 13,25,2; an expression like *excidium domus* (Tac. *Hist.* 3,67,1) comes close. Cf. also the use of *expugnare* in e.g. Hor. *Carm.* 3,15,9 (sc. *puella*) *expugnat iuuenum domos*. For other examples see *ThLL* s.v. *expugno* 1808,35 f., which lists both the literal use of *expugnare domos, uillas*, etc., and the metaphorical use.

mox ... ocius: see on *repentino* ch. 4 (239,1) on the haste in this episode.

ocius: this comparative with positive meaning is often found in exhortations, especially in Plautus, and also in its only other occurrence in the *Met.*: 8,5 (179,20-24); see *GCA* 1985,58 ad loc. Here *ocius* may be an echo of the woman's instructions to the *cursor*.

personata nimia temeritate: cf. 8,9 (184,12, about Charite) *astuque miro personata* (see *GCA* 1985,100 ad loc.). Whereas in that passage the narrator shows his admiration for Charite's cleverly played role, here he gives evidence of disapproval in *nimia temeritate*. Here we have another of the many cases in the *Met.* where people are 'wearing a mask' (see Hijmans in *GCA* 1995,387 with n. 9). It is possible to read a suggestion in *personata nimia temeritate* that the *nouerca*, in her *nimia temeritas*, has changed from her 'Phaedra role' to the role of the malicious woman in the mime, the *declamationes*, and the novel (see App. III).

What the narrator means by *personata nimia temeritate* may perhaps be gleaned from the behaviour of other literary versions of the 'Potiphar's wife' figure, e.g. Xen. *Ephes.* 2,5,6 (where Manto, having been rejected, wants to accuse Habrokomes) ἡ Μαντὼ ... καὶ σπαράξασα τὰς κόμας καὶ περιρρηξαμένη τὴν ἐσθῆτα, ὑπαντήσασα τῷ πατρὶ ... ἔφη ...; Sen. *Phaed.* 826 f. (the chorus describes how Phaedra prepares herself for the false accusation) *en scelera! quaerit crine lacerato fidem, / decus omne turbat capitis, umectat genas: / instruitur omni fraude feminea dolus*. See Zintzen 1960,91 f. with more examples.

nimia: here to be taken literally: 'with too great an impudence', i.e. overacting her Phaedra-role, acting like an evil stepmother in the mime. Oudendorp, Hildebrand, and Valpy comment at length upon the (un)acceptability of a manuscript variation which, remarkably enough, offers *personata mima temeritate*.

Other passages in the *Met.* often have *nimius* in the sense of *magnus*; thus ch. 19 (251,16 f.). Cf. 11,1 (266,12) *candore nimio* with Harrauer 1973,1 ad loc.; also *GCA* 1981,99 on 7,3 (156,11-15).

insimulat: see above, on *insimulabant*. From now on we find a crescendo of expressions for the *nouerca*'s deceit: *insimulat, mentiebatur, fingebat, inmanibus ... mendacis, mentitis lamentationibus*.

priuigni ueneno filium suum interceptum: this is ambiguous (as the narrator will explain below: *et hoc quidem non adeo mentiebatur*). For the father and the other actors who are not part of the plot, however, there is only one interpretation of these words.

interceptum: (prematurely) snatched from life. When used to mean 'kill', the verb always retains its original sense as well. Cf. Tac. *Ann.* 2,71,3 *scelere Pisonis et Plancinae interceptus* with Furneaux ad loc. Like *acerba mors* (see above, on *acerba ... morte*), *interceptus* refers to an untimely (and violent) death; cf. *CIL* 10,1784 *sorori ... acerba morte interceptae*.

240,17-21 Et hoc quidem non adeo mentiebatur, quod iam destinatam iuueni mortem praeuenisset puer, sed fratrem iuniorem fingebat ideo priuigni scelere peremptum, quod eius prob<r>osae libidini, qua se comprimere temptauerat, noluisse<t> succumbere: And it was not even so much this she was lying about, because the boy had prevented the death that had already been intended for the young man, but she pretended that the younger brother had been killed criminally by her stepson because she had been unwilling to succumb to his shameful lust, by which he had attempted to violate her.

Combined with the extra complication in the story (the attempt at poisoning, the drinking of the poison by the wrong person, and the false accusation of murder), we find here a motif that is indissolubly connected with all versions of the 'Potiphar's wife' story (see App. I), namely, the *crimen uersum*, summarized in Ov. *Met.* 15,500 as follows: *me Pasiphaeia quondam / temptatum frustra patrium temerare cubile, / quod uoluit, uoluisse infelix crimine uerso / .... damnauit*; see also Bömer ad loc. Briefly summarized we find this motif in *PLM* 4,434 (Baehrens) *incestum si promiseris petii; / si negaueris, tu petisti*.

    mentiebatur, ... fingebat: the imperfects explain the content of *insimulabat* above. Cf. also *addebat* below, and see on *adfatur ... profitebatur* ch. 18 (251,8 f.).
    mortem praeuenisset: for the transitive use of *praeuenire* cf. 8,25 (197,9-14) *praeuenit cogitatum meum* with *GCA* 1985,219 ad loc.
    probrosae: this is ς's emendation of *probosae* in F. Compare the common confusion in mss. between *probum* and *probrum*.
    comprimere: 'rape', an expressive synonym for *uiolare* (Gloss. 2,111,46 *compremit* βιάζεται παρθένον), attested from Plautus (e.g. *Aul.* 30) onward; cf. also Liv. 1,4,2; Prop. 2,26,48; Tac. *Ann.* 5,9,3 (6,4,3). It is frequent in Hyg. *Astr.* and *Fab.*
    temptauerat: the relative clause *qua ... temptauerat* explains *libidini*; in such relative clauses it is not unusual for the indicative to be retained in indirect discourse (LHSz 2,548; KSt 2,2,542 f.).
    noluisset succumbere: F had *noluisse succumbere*, and a different hand changed *succumbere* to *succumberet*. φ had originally *noluisse succumbere*, and a different hand changed *noluisse* to *noluisset*.

240,12-23 Nec tamen <tam> inmanibus contenta mendacis addebat sibi quoque ob detectum flagitium eundem illum gladium comminari: But not satisfied with such monstrous lies, she added that on top of that he was threatening to kill her with his sword for exposing his shameful act.

    Nec tamen <tam>: F and φ have *tamen*. Following ς, most editors read *tam* here (it is very well possible that an original *tam* became *tamen* in the mss.). At any rate, *tam* should be taken with *immanibus ... mendacis*. In that case Van der Vliet's conjecture *tamen <tam>* is to be preferred; paleographically it is explicable as haplography of *tamen tam*. The combination *nec tamen* is quite frequent in the *Met.*, often introducing a culminating phase in the narrative. Two examples among many are 7,18 (167,22) and 8,31 (202,8).

mendacis: thus F; a different hand changed this to *mendaciis*. But cf. e.g. 8,28 (199,15), where F has *taenis* and ς *taeniis*, and see *GCA* 1985,247 ad loc. with examples and references.

ob detectum flagitium: in view of the present infinitive *comminari* (the threat is ongoing) and of the fact that the woman only now discloses (*detegit*) the young man's alleged *flagitium*, the phrase *ob detectum flagitium* must mean here *si detegeret flagitium* (the reason for Van der Vliet's proposal *ob detrectatum flagitium*). The woman suggests that the young man has told her: 'If you betray this, I will kill you with my sword.' But cf. e.g. Vallette 'pour ce qu'elle avait dénoncé ce scandale'.

eundem illum: for the use in the *Met.* of *idem ille* for 'someone or something mentioned recently', see *GCA* 1995,213 on 9,24 (221,8).

gladium: a direct object with *comminari* indicates the content of the threat. This is the common construction with *comminari*, which occurs very frequently in the *Met.* (e.g. 3,16; 64,1 f.; 9,20: 218,1). *Gladius* in the sense of 'death by the sword' is also found in legal texts, e.g. Ulp. *dig.* 28,3,6,6 *damnatus ... ad gladium*; Paul. *Sent.* 5,17,2 *ad gladium dantur*. Most translators, however, translate this passage as if it had an instrumental ablative *gladio*; and indeed Oudendorp proposed this as a conjecture here.

The explicit mention of a sword may be a reference to Seneca's *Phaedra*, where Hippolytus' sword plays an important role in the false accusation: after Phaedra's proposition Hippolytus intends to kill himself with his sword, but he drops it and flees. The nurse then uses the sword as 'proof' that Hippolytus wanted to overpower Phaedra at the point of the sword (Sen. *Phaed.* 720 f.). Our 'Phaedra' needs no nurse to suggest that.

240,23-25 Tunc infelix duplici filiorum morte percussus magnis aerumnarum procellis aestuat: Then, stricken by the twofold death of his sons, the unhappy man was shaken by violent gusts of distress.

The father believes his wife's lies at once — this is the set pattern in all the versions of the 'Potiphar's wife' tale (see App. I,6A), and the same pattern is also displayed by Theseus in the tragedies of Euripides and Seneca. Theseus has been blamed for his credulity throughout literature and became in later ethics something like a standard example: cf. Plut. *Rom.* 32,2 Θησέα δὲ πρὸς τὸν υἱόν, ἃ πάμπαν ὀλίγοι τῶν ὄντων διαπεφεύγασιν, ἔρως καὶ ζηλοτυπία καὶ διαβολαὶ γυναικὸς ἔσφηλαν. See Bömer on Ov. *Met.* 15,498 for more examples, to which can be added Lucian. *Cal.* 26. See also on *Vixdum ... et statim ab ipso rogo ... immittit* ch. 6 (241,1 f.). In our passage the father's credulity is also an example of the *Met.*'s theme of credulity as a source of 'false opinion' (see Shumate 1996,96 f.).

infelix: before this word, Van der Vliet inserts *<pater>*, Brakman proposes *<senex>*, and according to his app. crit., Robertson too seems to be in favour of a similar addition. However, the context clearly shows that *infelix* refers to the father, cf. the following *duplici filiorum morte percussus*.

duplici filiorum morte percussus: this is explained in the next sentence (*nam et ...*).

We are reminded of Jason, who was struck by a similar misfortune (on the man's wife as a second Medea, see above, on *dira illa femina*). This father, however, will get his sons back at the end of the story (ch. 12: 245,28 f.).

filiorum morte percussus: this in contrast to his wife, who was *non ... filii morte ... commota*. In the description of the father's emotions we find several words echoed from the description of his wife's impassivity; other examples are: *aerumna* vs. *aerumnarum* here; *funeris* vs. *funerari* here; *nimia temeritate* vs. *uxoris dilectae nimium*.

magnis aerumnarum procellis aestuat: cf. Catul. 64,62 *magnis curarum fluctuat undis*, a phrase frequently imitated by Vergil (*A.* 4,532; 8,19; 12,486). See on *procellam Fortunae* ch. 4 (239,12).

aerumnarum: see above, on *aerumna*.

240,25-27 Nam et iuniorem incoram sui funerari uidebat et alterum ob incestum parricidiumque capitis scilicet damnatum iri certo sciebat: For he both saw his younger son being buried before his eyes and knew for certain that his other son would undoubtedly be condemned to death because of incest and the murder of a close relative.

incoram sui ... uidebat et ... scilicet ... certo sciebat: the father sees the first event, the funeral of his younger son, actually happening before his eyes. The second event, mentioned in *alterum ... scilicet ... certo sciebat*, is such a certainty to him that he is already mourning the deaths of both sons; see the note on *scilicet* below. There is another important difference between the two events: for the first death the father is not to blame, but in the second death he is going to play an active part (ch. 6: 241,1 f.).

incoram sui: the construction of *incoram* with a genitive, by analogy with ἀντί, occurs only in Apuleius. See also *GCA* 1981,222 on 7,21 (170,10-14) and KSt 2,1,511.

funerari uidebat: the words have been chosen carefully: the father saw, indeed, his younger son being buried, but the text does not say that he has verified the fact that the boy was really dead. Such subtleties, which escape the linear reader, are only noted at a second reading (see above, on *exanimis terrae procumbit*).

funerari: *funerare* in the meaning of 'bring to the grave' is rather rare (in Apuleius' works it is only attested here). *ThLL* s.v. *funero* 1583,21 f. gives all its occurrences, the earliest of which are Sen. *Con.* 8,4 and an inscription from the first century B.C. (9390 Dessau). It is frequent in V. Max., e.g. 4,4,2 *nisi a populo conlatis in capita sextantibus funeratus esset*.

ob incestum parricidiumque capitis ... damnatum iri: Killing a close relative was a capital offence (see Summers 1967,76 f., and above, on *parricidii*). But a stepson's intercourse with his stepmother was, according to Roman law, not *incestum* but *adulterium*; see Summers 1967,320 with references; Elster 1991,147 f.

240,27-29 Ad hoc uxoris dilectae nimium mentitis lamentationibus ad extremum subolis imp<el>lebatur odium: In addition to that, he was driven by the feigned lamentations of his over beloved wife to an extreme hatred of his offspring.

Ad hoc ... odium: only with this observation is it fully made clear why the father *magnis aerumnarum procellis aestuat*. Cf. Theseus in Sen. *Phaed.* 1114 f. (after Hippolytus has been killed) *o nimium potens, / quanto parentes sanguinis uinclo tenes, / natura, quam te colimus inuiti quoque. / occidere uolui noxium, amissum fleo* (this is elaborated in the following verses).

uxoris dilectae nimium: *nimium* is an addition by the narrator, who avails himself of his 'fonction évaluative' (see on *nutante etiam nunc pudore* ch. 3: 238,13). Cf. also Jos. *AJ* 2,58 Πετρεφὴς δὲ μήτε δακρυούσῃ τῇ γυναικὶ μήθ' οἷς ἔλεγε καὶ εἶδεν ἀπιστεῖν ἔχων τῷ τε πρὸς αὐτὴν ἔρωτι πλέον νέμων, ἐπὶ μὲν τὴν τῆς ἀληθείας ἐξέτασιν οὐκ ἐτρέπετο. The phrase *uxoris dilectae nimium* may also be seen as a reference to a familiar theme in *controversiae*: an elderly man who was remarried to a young wife was imagined to be particularly susceptible to her blandishments; cf. Sen. *Con.* 2,2,4 (Papirius Fabianus) *uir, dum nimis amat uxorem, paene causa periculi fuit; uxor, dum nimis amat uirum, paene causa luctus fuit ... <di> seruate totam domum amore mutuo laborantem*; [Quint.] *Decl.* 6,1 (111,14 f. Håkanson) *sed mihi hoc quoque querendum est, quod me et uxor nimium dilexit et filius*; 2,14 (32,22 f. Håkanson) *notum hoc, iudices, ac uulgare facinus est, quod plerumque contra liberos amantur uxores, et sequentium matrimoniorum non aliunde quam de damno pietatis affectus est. genus infirmissimae seruitutis est senex maritus, et uxoriae caritatis ardorem flagrantius frigidis concipimus adfectibus.* See Noy 1991,350 f., with further references.

extremum ... odium: the connotation 'deadly' can again be detected in *extremum* (see above, on *extremi facinoris*, and cf. ch. 6: 241,6 f. *in exitium reliqui filii ... operabatur*).

subolis: in F the same hand has changed the original *sobolis* to *subolis*; in φ the original *subolis* has been changed to *sobolis*. F shows uncertainty about the spelling in other occurrences of the word as well; *OLD* s.v. *suboles* shows that *soboles* is a common spelling variant.

impellebatur: this is the emendation by ς of *implebatur* in F. The phrase *ad ... odium* would be difficult to understand if the verb which it qualifies did not express a motion of some sort. Cf. also 2,27 (47,21 f.); 8,3 (178,17); 9,29 (225,4) for the same use of *impellere*.

CHAPTER VI

The father indicts his elder son; the magistrates prevent an imminent lynching by insisting on regular legal procedures.

241,1-4 Vixdum pompae funebres et sepultura filii fuerant explicatae, et statim ab ipso eius rogo senex infelix, ora sua recentibus adhuc rigans lacrimis trahensque cinere sordentem canitiem, foro se festinus immittit: Scarcely had the funeral procession and the burial of his son been completed when straight from his son's grave the unhappy old man, still moistening his face with fresh tears and pulling out his ash-strewn grey hair, took himself to the agora in great haste.

Vixdum ... et statim ab ipso rogo ... foro se festinus immittit: the emphasis on the father's precipitate action invites comparison with Theseus in the Phaedra-Hippolytus story (see App. I,6A). Cf. Eur. *Hipp. Steph.* 1320 f. (Artemis to Theseus) σὺ δ' ἐν τ'ἐκείνῳ κἄν ἐμοὶ φαίνῃ κακός, / ὃς οὔτε πίστιν οὔτε μάντεων ὄπα / ἔμεινας, οὐκ ἤλεγξας, οὐ χρόνῳ μακρῷ / σκέψιν παρέσχες, ἀλλὰ θᾶσσον ἤ σ'ἐχρῆν / ἀρὰς ἐθῆκας παιδὶ καὶ κατέκτανες.

Continuing the comparison between this father and Theseus, we may observe the following: Theseus punishes Hippolytus immediately, on the basis of the promise made to him by Poseidon (Eur. *Hipp. Steph.* 885 f.; Sen. *Phaed.* 941 f.); Hippolytus is killed by a monster sent by Poseidon. The father in our story depends on the local magistrates, whom he humbly entreats to punish his son. Our 'Hippolytus' is then confronted, as it were, with two no less deadly 'monsters'. The first is the people, acting collectively, who want to stone him to death. This monster is replaced by the magistrates with a regular lawsuit, which, however, will turn out to be an equally deadly monster for the young man; see below, on *accusationis ... ambagibus*. The good physician will, in the nick of time, save the young man from the lethal clutches of this 'monster' (just before he appears there is mention of the hands of the *carnifex* already stretched out toward the *iuuenis*, ch. 8: 243,6 f.). See also on *unus ... pertulit* ch. 8 (243,7 f.) and *non patiar ... hercules, non patiar* ch. 11 (244,24 f.).

Vixdum ... et ... se ... immittit: the paratactic construction after temporal adverbs (frequent in the *Met.*, e.g. 1,11: 10,21; 3,1: 52,6 f.; see Van der Paardt 1971,23; 8,18: 191,9 f.; see *GCA* 1985,164) is often found in Latin: first in poetry, later also in prose, especially in historians. Von Geisau 1916,285 regards this as a Graecism (ἅμα ... καί), but LHSz 2,481 f. assume a development by analogy with expressions like *eodem tempore ... et, simul ... et*; see also Callebat 1968,436.

Vixdum: this temporal adverb, a reinforced *uix*, is found in Apuleius only here, but is quite commonly used in Latin from Cicero onward (see *OLD* s.v. *uixdum*). See Dziatzko-Hauler [4]1967,159 on Ter. *Ph.* 594 *uixdum dimidium dixeram, intellexerat*.

sepultura: see on *tradunt sepulturae*, ch. 25 (256,16 f.).

pompae funebres: for the plural cf. [Quint.] *Decl.* 5,19 (102,23 f. Håkanson) *quid sibi uelit ille funebrium longus ordo pomparum*. The singular *pompa funebris* occurs in Tac. *Hist.* 3,67,2 describing a sad procession, *uelut in funebrem pompam*; later, the funeral of the younger son in our passage will also turn out to have been a sham funeral (ch. 12:

245,11 f.). More common are expressions like *feralis pompa* (e.g. *Met.* 8,6: 181,12) or *pompa funeris* (e.g. Ov. *Fast.* 6,663), but *pompa* is most commonly used alone.

For funeral practices in the *Met.* see *GCA* 1985,278 f. From Fest. 506,16 f. L. it can be concluded that not everyone could afford a *pompa funebris*: *uespae et uespillones dicuntur qui funerandis corporibus officium gerunt ... quia uespertino tempore eos efferunt qui funebri pompa duci propter inopiam nequeunt*. On the affluence of the family involved here, see on *uillulas* ch. 4 (239,15).

fuerant explicatae = *erant explicatae*, a 'verschobenes Plusquamperfectum' (LHSz 2,320 f.). Occurrences of this form become much more frequent in the period when Apuleius was active. On its occurrences in the *Met.* see *GCA* 1995,219 on 9,25 (221,21) with references.

rogo: both from *sepultura* and from what follows (ch. 12: 245,11 f.) it appears that *rogus* is used here in the sense of 'grave'. In the *Met.* words like *bustum* and *rogus* elsewhere refer to a funeral pyre, not a grave (see *GCA* 1985,278 f. with references). Fiorencis-Gianotti 1990,96, n. 68 point out the use of *rogus* in the sense of 'grave' (e.g. Prop. 4,11,8) but also suggest the possibility of an inconsistency (with ch. 12: 245,11 f.) resulting from the different sources which may lie at the base of this story. They also consider it possible that *rogo* provides a touch of 'black humour' here, logic having been sacrificed in the process.

senex infelix: this is the first time that the *dominus aedium* (ch. 2: 237,3) is called a *senex*. The son of his second marriage is already over twelve years old (ch. 2: 237,8 f.), so he is probably getting on in years. The reason for calling him *senex* in this passage is probably to add to the pitiful aspect of his situation; see also on *canitiem* below.

ora sua ... rigans lacrimis: cf. Verg. *A.* 6,699 *sic memorans, largo fletu simul ora rigabat*; ibid. 9,251 *et uultum lacrimis atque ora rigabat*. Bömer on Ov. *Met.* 11,419 gives passages in Ovid and speaks of 'epische Diktion': *rigare* referring to tears is not attested in other Latin poetry (on the epic colouring of this entire passage see below, on *canitiem*). In the *Met.* the only other occurrence is 6,2 (130,4 f.) *Psyche pedes eius* (sc. of Ceres) *aduoluta et uberi fletu rigans deae uestigia*.

trahensque ... canitiem: cf. 7,27 (175,1 f.) *mater pueri, mortem deplorans acerbam filii ... manibus trahens cinerosam canitiem*, where *GCA* 1981,261 argue that *trahens* must mean 'tearing loose', since in Greek and Roman antiquity the hair was loosened, not torn out, as an expression of grief. This is true of women, for whom loosened hair was indeed one of the customary signs of grieving (see *RE* s.v. 'Trauerkleidung', esp. 2231,16 f. 'Raufen der Haare' [Herzog-Hauer]). In our passage, however, since the grieving person is a man, 'pulling out' is appropriate; cf. (in a comparable situation) 2,27 (47,11 f.) *canitiem reuellens senex*.

cinere sordentem: as a sign of mourning one sprinkled ashes on one's head; for the background of this ancient custom see the article in *RE* mentioned in the previous note, and *GCA* 1981,262 on 7,27 (175,1-5).

The description of the grieving father, who runs to the *forum* and accuses his son before the people, shows a strong similarity with Heliod. 1,13,1, where Knemon's father charges his son (similarly deluded by Knemon's stepmother Demainete) with attempted adultery with his stepmother and attempted murder of his father: Ἅμα δὲ τῇ ἕῳ λαβὼν οὕτως ὡς εἶχον δεσμῶν ἐπὶ τὸν δῆμον ἦγε, καὶ τῆς κεφαλῆς κόνιν καταχεάμενος ... Following this, the father begins his charge against his son with a detailed description of the careful education he gave Knemon; this reminds us of the description of our *iuuenis filius probe litteratus atque ob id consequenter pietate, modestia praecipuus* in ch. 2 (237,3 f.). On the connections between the story in Heliod. 1,9 f. and our story, see App. I,5.2.

canitiem: abstractum pro concreto (see Maurach ²1989,79 f. and ibid. 80 on *canities*); see also *GCA* 1981,261 on 7,27 (175,1-5). Cf. Catul. 64,224; Verg. *A*. 12,611 *canitiem immundo perfusam puluere turpans*; also ibid. 10,844. This entire passage has an epic coloration; see above, on *ora sua ... rigans ... lacrimis* and below, on *se festinus immittit*.

As remarked in *GCA* 1981,261, the hair of mourning people is always described as grey, no matter what their age; here, however, the person in question is described specifically as a *senex infelix*, which makes the total image even more pathetic and helps to motivate the people's rage described immediately afterwards.

foro se ... immittit: in all its occurrences in the *Met.*, *se immittere* is construed with the dative (instead of the usual *se immittere in*): 2,29 (48,24) with De Jonge 1941,111; 7,24 (172,19); 9,1 (202,27-203,3), and here. Cf. also Verg. *A*. 6,262 *antro se immisit aperto* and Ov. *Met.* 3,599 and 4,357 (mediopassive *immitti* with a dative).

se festinus immittit: the adjective *festinus* is used predicatively in Verg. *A*. 9,488 f. *quam* (sc. *uestem*) *noctes festina diesque / urgebam* and in epic poetry after Vergil, e.g. frequently in Statius; e.g. *Theb.* 4,806 f. *medium subit illa per agmen / non humili festina modo*. See *GCA* 1977,123 on 4,15 (86,15-18) with references; Pinkster 1990,149 f. on the predicative use of adjectives.

From early times Latin used certain adjectives predicatively, and the number of adjectives so used increased under the influence of poetry. In the case of e.g. *festinus* the explanation 'adjectivum pro adverbio' is inadequate, nor is it correct to speak of a deliberate choice by the author for the sake of 'greater liveliness' (thus e.g. Callebat 1968,411 f.). The cognate adverb is *festinanter*, attested from Cicero onward and then frequently found in prose (adverbs like *festinate, festino*, and *festine* are very late developments; see Krebs-Schmalz 1,588). In Apuleius' works *festinanter* is found only twice: *Met.* 5,7 (108,9) in a passage where *festinae* (sc. *sorores*) may have been avoided for euphonic reasons, and 5,23 (121,8) within an ablative absolute construction where neither a form of *festinus* nor a participle would be possible. Elsewhere he always uses the adjective or the present participle predicatively. It seems therefore that this is the 'normal' usage in Apuleius.

241,4-9 Atque ibi tum fletu, tum precibus genua etiam decurionum contingens nescius fraudium pessimae mulieris in exitium reliqui filii plenis operabatur affectibus: illum incestum paterno thalamo, illum parricidam fraterno exitio et in comminata nouercae caede sicarium: And there, not only with weeping but also with pleas, and even touching the councillors' knees, unaware of the wicked woman's schemes, he strove for the death of his remaining son, giving free rein to his emotions: 'that incestuous violator of his father's bedroom, that parricide with his brother's death on his conscience, that assassin who threatened his stepmother with death!'.

tum fletu, tum precibus genua etiam decurionum contingens: varying constructions (two ablatives of means, followed by a participial construction) and 'Wachsende Glieder' (3, 4, and 14 syllables respectively) illustrate the increasing pressure that the father exerts on the councillors.

genua ... contingens: for this classic gesture to invoke pity, see *GCA* 1985,172 on 8,19 (192,8-14) with references, and *GCA* 1995,332 on 9,40 (233,25 f.). The gesture occurs frequently in the *Met.*; therefore, the verbal similarity to 2,28 (48,10 f.) cannot be used as an argument that at a later time Apuleius inserted elements from our story into Telyphron's tale (as argued by Hammer 1925,75, n. 1, cited and endorsed by Van Thiel 1971,2,78 n. 64; on closer scrutiny, most of the other parallels adduced by Hammer lack cogency).

decurionum: see on *decurionis* ch. 1 (236,23).

nescius fraudium pessimae mulieris: see on ch. 5 (240,3) *nescius fraudis*. This addition emphasizes the narrator's and reader's superior insight into the full facts (but on the narrative situation in this story see on *exanimis terrae procumbit* ch. 5: 240,5) and thus enhances the dramatic force of the tale.

pessimae mulieris: see on *pessimae feminae* ch. 5 (239,28 f.).

in exitium ... operabatur: *operari*, i.q. '*occupatum esse, alicui vel alicui rei operam dare, studere*', is either used absolutely or construed with a dative; in the *Met.* e.g. 3,3 (54,15 f.; see Van der Paardt 1971,44 ad loc.) and 9,5 (206,5). *ThLL* s.v. *operor* 694,14 f. mentions our passage as the first for *operari in* + accusative (the accusative indicating the intended effect); after Apuleius this construction is attested in Tertullian (*Apol.* 33,2 *plus ego illi operor in salutem*) and other Christian authors (cf. also Sulp. Vict. *Rhet.* 32, p. 331 *in perniciem inimicorum*).

plenis ... affectibus: on the one hand, *affectibus* means 'eagerness, zeal' (*OLD* s.v. *affectus*[1] 6; thus Stat. *Silv.* 5, pr. 1 *omnibus affectibus prosequenda sunt bona exempla* and e.g. Apul. *Pl.* 2,21 (251) *philosophiam esse mortis affectum*. On the other hand, the phrase expresses the fact that the father is truly very emotional, as has been described in ch. 5 (240,23 f.). The inner torment caused by the need for revenge and the distress at the loss of another son (see on *ad hoc ... odium* ch. 5: 240,27 f.) is succinctly summarized by *plenis affectibus*: *affectus* is often used especially for the love of parents for their children, or affection in other family relations (see *OLD* s.v. *affectus*[1] 7).

illum incestum ... sicarium: observe the careful composition (with 'wachsende Glieder'): the first two cola are completely parallel, with anaphora; the second colon is longer than the first by a few syllables (11 and 13 respectively). In the third colon of 15 syllables the construction is varied, and the word order is chiastic in relation to the other cola: the invective, *sicarium*, is now at the end of the phrase, and the reason why he can be called a *sicarius* comes first.

incestum ... parricidam ... sicarium: cf. *ob incestum parricidiumque ... certo sciebat* ch. 5 (240,26 f.). In his zeal (cf. *in exitium reliqui filii ... operabatur*), the father adds a third accusation to the two accusations already mentioned, which in themselves would have been sufficient for the death penalty. The lawsuit described immediate afterwards and the punishment (ch. 8: 242,24 f.) will concentrate entirely upon the charge of *parricidum*.

incestum paterno thalamo: the parallelism with *parricidam fraterno exitio* is somewhat at the expense of clarity: the dative *paterno thalamo* explains what the young man has allegedly committed incest against. Cf. Sil. 15,448 f. *et incestum Catilina Nealcen / germanae thalamo obtruncat*.

incestum: sexual relations with relatives, no matter how far removed, were surrounded with taboo; they were considered *nefas* (cf. also *nefarium amorem* ch. 4: 239,20) and accordingly were punished in early Roman history as a religious crime, by death (*RE* 1246-47 s.v. *incestus* [Klingmüller]). During the Republic, *incestum* (from *in* + *castum*) originally referred to a sacral capital crime, namely the violation of the cultic vow of chastity of a Vestal virgin; even after its transference, which can no longer be clearly traced, from the cultic to the profane, sacral terms like *nefas* and *scelus* are still used to describe *incestum* (Mette-Dittmann 1991,46). Consequently, the father begins his series of accusations quite effectively with a term that will evoke a sacral shudder and violent moral indignation in the audience.

In recent literature the opinion prevails that, from the marriage legislation of Augustus onward, incest was also legally punishable in Rome under the *lex Julia de adulteriis*. See the extensive discussion, with the relevant citations from legal texts and references to secondary literature, in Mette-Dittmann 1991,42 f. (see also Treggiari 1991,281 with references); all unions between parties who were legally incapable of marrying each other on the ground of kinship (step-relationships included) were regarded as incest (see also Rousselle 1983,103 f.; Robinson 1995,54 f.).

paterno: the adjective replaces a possessive genitive *patris*. On the increasing frequency of this usage in Latin, see *GCA* 1981,175 on 7,14 (165,4-7) *greges equinos*, with references.

thalamo: here, as often elsewhere, the meaning 'marriage' (*OLD* s.v. *thalamus* 2b) cannot be separated from the concrete meaning 'conjugal bedroom' (*OLD* ibid. 2a); see Bömer on Ov. *Met.* 6,148 and cf. the Silius passage cited above s.v. *incestum paterno thalamo*.

parricidam: there is dramatic irony in the fact that the father uses this term, which, as the reader knows, actually describes his own wife; see on *parricidii* ch. 5 (240,11). In our passage the word is used in the correct legal sense; see *GCA* 1985,93 on 8,8 (183,16-18) on the use of *parricida/parricidium* in a broader sense, quite common in Apuleius.

fraterno exitio: the adjective replaces a subjective genitive (see on *paterno* above); *fraternus* (instead of *fratris* or *fratrum*) is often used in literature especially in the context of fratricide. Cf. e.g. Cic. *Clu.* 11,31 *tametsi in ipso fraterno parricidio nullum scelus praetermissum uidetur*; Hor. *Epod.* 7,17 f. *acerba fata Romanos agunt / scelusque fraternae necis*; *S.* 2,5,16; Luc. 1,95 *fraterno primi maduerunt sanguine muri*.

exitio: for the father, and also for the linear reader, this noun means unambiguously 'death'. Only when the brother rises from the grave alive, will it be possible, at the second reading, to take *exitium* in the meaning characterized by *ThLL* s.v. *exitium* 1530,18 as 'laxius', namely *miseriae, infortunium, damnum*. Cf. e.g. in the *Met.* 8,12 (186,11); 9,15 (214,14; see *GCA* 1995,148 ad loc.). On the many ambiguous expressions in this tale, see on *exanimis terrae procumbit* ch. 5 (240,5).

in ... caede: *in* with the ablative 'marquant une notion de relation' (see Callebat 1968,225). Cf. 9,14 (213,17 f.) *in rapinis turpibus auara, in sumptibus foedis profusa* with *GCA* 1995,138 with references. See also on ch. 31 (262,20) *oculis in aspectu minacibus*.

comminata novercae caede sicarium: note the alliteration of *c*, and *nouercae caede*.

comminata ... caede: the perfect participle of *comminari* has a passive meaning, as in 6,26 (148,9-10); see *GCA* 1981,35 ad loc., with references.

sicarium: see Summers 1967,74 f. on the *Lex Cornelia de sicariis et ueneficiis*. The meaning of the word is discussed in *GCA* 1985,117 on 8,11 (186,5-8). To have allegedly threatened the *nouerca* with a sword is indeed sufficient for the boy to be prosecuted as a *sicarius* (see also Elster 1991,147). Cf. e.g. Paul. *Sent.* 5,23,1-2 *Lex Cornelia poenam ... infligit ei qui hominem occiderit eiusue rei causa furtiue faciendi cum telo fuerit*.

241,9-14 Tanta denique miseratione tantaque indignatione curiam, sed et plebem maerens inflammauerat, ut remoto iudicandi taedio et accusationis manifestis probationibus et responsionis meditatis ambagibus cuncti

conclamarint lapidibus obrutum publicum malum publice uindicari:
Finally, the grieving man had evoked so much pity and so much indignation in the councillors, but also in the people, that all to a man cried that the nuisance of a legal action, namely the production of conclusive evidence by the prosecution and the crafty ways of beating about the bush by the defence, should be dropped: he should be stoned to death, this public evil, in public he should be punished.

Tanta ... miseratione tantaque indignatione curiam, sed et plebem maerens inflammauerat: the people, seeing a *senex infelix maerens* who displays all the appropriate characteristics and gestures, react with honest rage. The *curia*, seeing an accuser who skillfully reinforces his accusation with all the means at his disposal to invoke *affectus*, reacts by organizing the official session of the court. *Miseratio* and *indignatio* are rhetorical technical terms (see Zundel 1989 s.v. *miseratio* and *indignatio*). In the following, the reaction of the *plebs* is described first.

denique: here marks the transition from a descriptive passage to the resumption of the narrative. See Van der Paardt 1971,42 f. and cf. e.g. 8,28 (199,9) with *GCA* 1985,245 ad loc.

curiam: the usual Latin term (in provincial towns as well as in Rome) both for the senate itself and for the building in which it convened (= βουλευτήριον). In the *Met.* the term occurs only in this story; it refers sometimes to the members themselves (as here and e.g. *unus e curia* ch. 8: 243,7; see also on ch. 12: 245,13), sometimes to the assembly hall (ch. 7: 241,24). This passage suggests that on any day at least some of the councillors meet in session; in the next chapter the entire senate is called to the *curia* for the trial.

sed et plebem: without preceding *non modum, sed etiam* is attested from Cicero onward (mainly in his correspondence); *sed et* without preceding *non modum* is post-classical (LHSz 2,518 f.).

Apparently a large part of the *plebs*, too, was able to hear the old man's accusations: one can picture them following the *senex* into the *curia*, their curiosity aroused by the appearance of the mourning gentleman on the agora, where many people were always about during the day; cf. e.g. Plut. *Praecepta reip. ger.* 2 (*Mor.* 798c) Ὥσπερ γὰρ οἷς οὐδέν ἐστιν οἴκοι χρηστὸν ἐν ἀγορᾷ διατρίβουσι, κἂν μὴ δέωνται, τὸν πλεῖστον χρόνον. Millar 1981,69 (= Millar 1999,257 f.) mentions as 'one of the most vivid impressions left by the novel' (i.e. the *Met.*) the fact that 'the cities were run by a network of local aristocratic families, whose doings, public and private, were the subject of intense observer participation'.

inflammauerat, ut ... conclamarint: Callebat 1968,362 explains the striking use of the tenses by assuming that *inflammauerat* has the value of a perfect tense here. However, this passage should be regarded as the 'setting' for what follows: the old man's demeanour had finally impressed both people and councillors to such a degree that they crie out for 'stoning'. The magistrates have to act on this: *magistratus interim ...* According to this explanation, *inflammauerat* retains the value of the pluperfect, and the perfect subjunctive expresses the result as the 'fait accompli' with which the magistrates see themselves confronted. A comparable passage is 4,21 (90,19-22) *tanto ... terrore tantaque formidine coetum illum turbauerat, ut ... nemo quisquam fuerit ausus ... contingere*.

remoto ... taedio ... ambagibus: reflects what the *plebs* exclaimed; in free indirect discourse, the narrator's text and the actor's text are mixed here. See Bal [3]1985,138.

remoto ... taedio et ... probationibus et ... ambagibus: the singular *remoto* also qualifies the plurals *probationibus* and *ambagibus*. KSt 2,1,45 f.: 'Steht das Prädikat mit rhetorischem Nachdruck vor sämtliche Subjekten, so schließt es sich meistens an das zunächst stehende Subjekt an' and (46) 'Regelmäßig so beim Partizip (besonders im abl. abs.)'. Cf. Liv. 30,12,22 *misso Syphace et captiuis*.

iudicandi taedio: *taedium* should be taken here as 'offensive quality, ... nuisance' (*OLD* s.v. *taedium* 3). Comparable is Quint. *Inst.* 11,2,41 *taedium illud et scripta et lecta saepius reuoluendi et quasi eundem cibum remandendi*.

iudicandi: *iudicare* used absolutely, meaning 'to litigate, take legal action' is not mentioned by *OLD* in a separate lemma. Some of the passages mentioned for the absolute use in *ThLL* s.v. *iudico* 618,44 f. ('absolute') come close, e.g. Cic. *Inv.* 1,49,92 *equites Romanos cupidos iudicandi*.

accusationis manifestis probationibus et responsionis meditatis ambagibus: this explains what the man in the street meant by *taedium iudicandi*. Ironically, the continuation of the story will show that the *manifestae probationes* in this case are furnished by the defence only (as the bag of money ch. 9: 244,2 f. and the son rising from the grave ch. 12: 245,15 f.), and that it is the accusers who should be blamed for *meditatae ambages* (e.g. the convoluted story of lies told by the slave ch. 7: 242,15 f.). The irony becomes even stronger on reflection that it is not the official court but a single honest man, the doctor, who will prevent an innocent person from suffering the punishment demanded by the emotional *plebs*. From this story emerges, again, an abstract author (see Introd. **3.2**) with a pessimistic opinion of the court as the seat of justice. See above, on *uixdum ... et statim ... foro se festinus immittit* and below, on *barbaricae feritatis ... impotentiae*. Compare the fierce stab at corrupt judges ch. 33 (264,1 f.), which interrupts the description of the pantomime of the Judgement of Paris. Ebel 1970,174 calls the trial following here 'a model of fairness' (the only one in the *Met*.), but fails to recognize the irony signaled above.

responsionis meditatis ambagibus: this rendition of the common man's opinion of the lawyer's trade may betray some self-irony on the level of the concrete author (see Introd. **3.1**), who also wrote the *Apology*, a brilliant example of *ambages meditatae* in court. At a second reading of the *Met*. one can also detect irony at the level of the fictive narrator, who will later prosper as a lawyer (11,28: 290,2).

ambagibus: 'circumlocution, verbosity', but here, as often, with the connotation of 'obscurity' (referring to oracles e.g. Verg. *A*. 6,99) and also 'fraudulence, tortuous scheme', as e.g. 9,15 (214,15); see *GCA* 1995,148 ad loc.

cuncti conclamarint lapidibus obrutum publicum malum publice uindicari: alliteration and assonance (many *a*'s, *u*'s and *i*'s, and *la- ma- la- li- ma- lu- -li*) seem to illustrate the people's shouts.

conclamarint ... malum ... uindicare: Apuleius seems to be the first to use an accusative and infinitive construction after *conclamare* to express a demand; after him Ruf. *Hist.* 3,7 *auctorem uitae a semet uniuersa gens conclamauit* (ἱκέτευσεν) *auferri*. In the other examples given by *ThLL* s.v. *conclamo* the content of the accusative and infinitive construction is a statement, not a command; thus e.g. Cic. *Inv.* 2,5,15 *copo ... conclamat hominem esse occisum*. With *conclamare*, an accusative and infinitive with a gerund(ive) is occasionally found (e.g. Verg. *A*. 2,232 f. *ducendum ad sedes simulacrum orandaque diuae / numina conclamant*), but the usual construction is a subjunctive with or without *ut*. See LHSz 2,355 f. Callebat 1968,305 explains this as a borrowing from colloquial language that had become established in poetry and literary prose before Apuleius. Comparable is *denuntiare* with the accusative and infinitive in Tacitus, e.g. *Ann.* 11,37,3 (cf. Apul. *Met.* 9,41: 235,7 f.). See also *GCA* 1995,143 on 9,15 (213,24 f.) *nam et ... subiungi ... nouicium clamabat asinum*.

lapidibus obrutum publicum malum publice uindicari: the word order is notable: the participle *obrutum* precedes the accusative *malum* (of the accusative and infinitive construction *malum ... uindicari*) with which it is construed. Not only alliteration and assonance (see above) but also the word order suggests a mob shouting furious slogans, the first of which is: 'stone him!' Fehling 1974,75 (see below) points out the combination of shouting and stoning often found in the sources; e.g. Greek sources often quote the cry 'βάλλε βάλλε'.

According to most scholars, stoning is a primitive ritual act with a sacral meaning, a punishment carried out by the community, of which each member, by throwing a stone, not only expelled (or killed) the criminal but also contributed to the ritual cleansing of the community. See *RE* s.v. 'Steinigung' [Latte] with many references. Fehling 1974,59 f. gives an ethological explanation of stoning, with an extensive list of references and an index of passages. Pease 1907,11 f. suggests that stoning as a primitive punishment for incest lies behind Soph. *O.C.* 431 f., where Oedipus on the day of the discovery of his offence vainly wishes to die by stoning; Pease then compares our passage.

In the story of Knemon in Heliod. 1,13,4 the people also insist on stoning as a reaction to the father's behaviour (see also above, on *cinere sordentem*): ἀνεβόησαν ἅπαντες καὶ οὐδὲ ἀπολογίας μου μετεῖναι κρίναντες οἱ μὲν λίθοις βάλλειν οἱ δὲ τῷ δημίῳ παραδιδόναι καὶ ὠθεῖσθαι εἰς τὸ βάραθρον ἐδοκίμαζον. Cf. also *Met.* 1,10 (9,12 f.) with Scobie 1975,101 ad loc., and 2,27 (47,22 f.) with the people's response to the accusations which an old man addresses to the wife of his murdered grandson: *conclamant ignem, requirunt saxa.*

publicum malum publice uindicari: the polyptoton *publicum ... publice* has the effect of a slogan, repeated again and again by the mob. See also the previous notes on sound effect in this passage.

publicum malum: at Claudius' wedding the people feared a *malum publicum*: Tac. *Ann.* 12,5,2 *quin et incestum ac, si sperneretur, ne in malum publicum erumperet, metuebatur*. Here, in this possible reference to the Tacitus passage, *publicum malum* has been given a new twist and now refers to the person himself. For *malum* 'de personis rebusque personatis' *ThLL* s.v. *malus, -a, -um* 229,16 f. mentions chiefly passages in poetry from Plautus (e.g. *Mos.* 191 *quod malum uorsatur meae domi illud?*; *Rud.* 453) onward. Also Luc. 10,34 *terrarum fatale malum fulmenque* (sc. Alexander). It is frequent in Seneca's tragedies, e.g. *Med.* 362 and *Phaed.* 697. In the *Met.* it is found 4,33 (100,24) in oracle verses; see Kenney ad loc.

241,15-23 Magistratus interim metu periculi proprii, ne de paruis indignationis elementis ad exitium disciplinae ciuitatisque seditio procederet, partim decuriones deprecari, partim populares compescere, ut rite et more maiorum iudicio reddito et utrimquesecus allegationibus examinatis ciuiliter sententia promeretur nec ad instar barbaricae feritatis uel tyrannicae impotentiae damnaretur aliquis inauditus et in pace placida tam dirum saeculo proderetur exemplum: The authorities, meanwhile, went into action: for fear of danger to themselves, lest from the first small seeds of indignation an uprising start which would mean the end of law and order in the town, some appealed to the councillors, others calmed the people, pleading that, in accordance with the rules and the ancestral traditon, a trial should be granted and that a verdict should be pronounced in a civilized way when the allegations from both sides had been examined; it would not do, in the manner of uncivilized barbarians or high-handed tyrants, to condemn a man unheard and that in a time of peace so dreadful a precedent be passed on to the future.

Fehling 1974,74 (with examples) sees the many cases in literature where, as in our passage, the stoning never goes beyond the intention, as a support for his ethological explanation of stoning as an emotional release.

Magistratus: the higher offices in Greek provincial towns of the Roman empire were open only to the members of prominent, wealthy families. See Jones [4]1971,179 f. on class differences in the Greek towns (which had intensified under Roman rule), and 174 f. on the magistrates. It is one of these local dignitaries, Menemachos, whom Plutarch addresses in his *Praecepta reipublicae gerendae* (*Mor.* 798a-825f); the balance of power supposed there can be taken as a guide to the situation in Greek provincial towns of Apuleius' time (see Carrière 1984,33 f.), since only about fifty years separate Plutarch's *Praecepta* and the *Met.*

The 'realistic' backdrop to this tale is probably both sufficiently exact and sufficiently general to agree with the picture that the reading public (Romans, according to Dowden 1994,419) had of the situation in these Greek towns (cf. also Millar 1981,71 = Millar 1999,261, and see on *patres in curiam conuenirent* ch. 7: 241,24). A few readers would have gained this information first-hand, but most could picture it from literature, e.g. from Dio Chrysostomus, Plutarch, and Aelius Aristides. It is therefore impossible to draw from this suggestion of realism the far-reaching conclusions proposed by Colin 1965,335 f., who assumes that Apuleius, while travelling through Thessaly, interested as he was in legal matters, recorded certain aspects of the local administration of justice that caught his attention, and later used these in his *Met.*; on the basis of this assumption, Colin (336 f.) claims that this fictional text may be used as a source of information even on the status of Thessalian towns of that time (see also Elster 1991,154).

interim: because of the popular fury mentioned above, the magistrates do not have much time. The historical infinitives *deprecari ... compescere* suggest a frenetic activity (see below).

metu periculi proprii: the magistrates' fear comes from the fact that magistrates' power depended on the sovereign authority of Rome, which would intervene in the event of troubles such as civil disturbances (see Carrière 1984,39 f. with notes) and thus undermine the magistrates' powers and/or remove them from office. Plutarch gives in *Praecepta reip. ger.* 18 f. (*Mor.* 814c-815a) some examples of such intervention. The fact that the danger to themselves is mentioned as the first motive for their actions has the effect that the high-principled arguments mentioned next sound somewhat hollow.

proprii: for possibly legal connotations in this use of *proprius* see Callebat 1968,292 (with references). However, *proprius* can also have the obvious meaning that the magistrates are most interested in the risks to themselves, rather than in the danger to the young man of being stoned to death without a trial.

ne ... seditio procederet: the danger of riots in these provincial towns was not imaginery:

though many of them were very poor, the free citizens still convened in the assembly, which had to approve all decisions of the βουλή and the magistrates (see Jones [4]1974,177 f.), even if this became more and more a formality. On disturbances see e.g. Plut. *Praec. reip. ger.* 19 (*Mor.* 815d), and also e.g. the improvised assembly against Paul in Ephesus (*Acts* 19,29 f.). Plutarch indicates in his *Praecepta* that it was still worthwhile in his time to convince the assembly through eloquence (or through generous gifts to the community). See also Veyne 1976, esp. 298-327.

de paruis indignationis elementis ad exitium disciplinae ciuitatisque: Plut. *Praec. reip. ger.* 32 (*Mor.* 824f-825a) cautions against this danger in comparable terms: after describing how a small, private fire develops into a large city fire, he continues: ἀλλὰ πολλάκις ἐκ πραγμάτων καὶ προσκρουμάτων ἰδίων εἰς δημόσιον αἱ διαφοραὶ προελθοῦσαι συνετάραξαν ἅπασαν τὴν πόλιν (this notion is already found in Plato *Rep.* 5,12 (465a) and 8,10 (556e), and Arist. *Pol.* 5,3,1 f.(1303b,17). Clearly the magistrates are well versed in the philosophers' political works, but their motive for intervention (*metu periculi proprii*) is a long way from the ethical ideals which e.g. Plutarch wants to teach Menemachos in his *Praecepta*. Apuleius himself wrote a *De re publica*, from whose single transmitted quotation, *qui celocem regere nequit, onerariam petit* (Fulg. *Serm.* 44, p. 122 f. Helm), it appears at least that Apuleius reflected on the role of rulers.

exitium disciplinae ciuitatisque: cf. Cic. *Div.* 1,20 (= *Cons.* Fr. 3,51) *legum exitium*; Sen. *Dial.* 6, (*Cons. Marc.*) 17,5 *erit Dionysius illic tyrannus, libertatis, iustitiae, legum exitium*.

disciplinae ciuitatisque: cf. *disciplinae publicae* 3,8 (57,28) with Van der Paardt 1971,72 ad loc.

decuriones deprecari, ... populares compescere: the different verbs illustrate the power relations: both *decuriones* (see on *decurionis* ch. 1: 236,23) and magistrates belonged to the class of the *curiales*, which was primarily defined by property (see Jones [4]1971,179 f. on the origin of this class in Greek provincial towns and the eligibility of its members to the higher offices). The *decuriones*, united in the senate (βουλή), are approached with respect (*deprecari*) by the magistrates. *Compescere* reveals the same, somewhat patronizing attitude as that advised by Plutarch in several passages of the *Praec. reip. ger.* 3-4 (*Mor.* 799c f.; 800c-e); the people as a hard-to-tame animal: ibid. 28 (*Mor.* 821a-b); 29 (821f).

The nominalized plural *populares* is here, parallel to *decuriones*, to be understood in its political meaning (the opposite of the *nobilitas* or the *optimates*), as in e.g. Cic. *Sest.* 45,96; Nep. *Phoc.* 3,1 *populares Polyperchonti fauebant, optimates cum Cassandro sentiebant* (more examples in *OLD* s.v. *popularis*[2] 3a and b), although we should not think of an organized 'people's party'; possibly *populares* refers here to certain leaders of the *plebs*.

deprecari, compescere: Callebat 1968,426 f. (with references) discusses the literary character of the use of the historical infinitive in the *Met*. See Pinkster 1990,241 f. (with references) on the historical infinitive in narrative texts, instead of an imperfect; Rosén 1995,539 f. on tempus-aspect-discourse status of the historical infinitive. In ch. 10 (244,9 f.) three historical infinitives follow the imperfect *emanabat* (see note there). The examples collected by Callebat show that the historical infinitive in the *Met*. occurs practically always in a series (see for an extreme accumulation 8,7: 181,14 f. with *GCA* 1985,75 ad loc.); the infinitives usually describe a series of actions overlapping in time, or a series of hasty reactions to a dramatic event. By using historical infinitives instead of conjugated verbs the narrator creates an effect of agitation and urgency (Maurach [2]1989,39 f.). Here, too, the narrator suggests with the infinitives that the magistrates act in a great hurry.

ut ... promeretur nec ... damnaretur ... et ... proderetur exemplum: the *ut*-clause is used zeugmatically with both *decuriones deprecari* and *populares compescere*. *Ut* + subjunctive is the classical construction with *deprecari* in the sense of 'beg that ...' (for this and other constructions with *deprecari* in the *Met.*, see Van der Paardt 1971,177 on 3,24: 70,5 f. with references); *ut* + subjunctive with *compescere* is attested nowhere else. It is evident, however, that the dependent clause introduced by *ut* is a rendition in free indirect discourse of the arguments used by the magistrates in 'reining in' the *populares*. For *compescere* in a context of 'to calm with well-chosen words' cf. e.g. Tac. *Ann.* 1,42,4 *diuus Iulius seditionem exercitus uerbo uno compescuit*; Apul. *Soc.* 17,158 *desideraturque uir ... qui .... Pelidae ferociam conpescat*.

more maiorum: this is explained by the following *iudicio reddito*. Everyone's right to a fair trial is part of the set of norms and values summarized as *mos maiorum*: the venerable ancestral tradition (an extensive treatment of this concept, with many references, is given by Minyard 1985,5 f. and n. 3). By appealing to the *mos maiorum*, the magistrates hope to avert the threat of anarchy. An absence of *mos maiorum* is equated with an absence of fair trial; thus also Cic. *Vat.* 34 (*scias ...*) *in foro, luce, inspectante populo Romano quaestionem, magistratus, morem maiorum, leges, iudices, reum, poenam esse sublatam*; *Clu.* 2,5 *denique illa definitio iudiciorum aequorum quae nobis a maioribus tradita est retineatur*. Contemporary Roman readers (see Dowden 1994,419 f. on the Roman readership of the *Met.*) would undoubtedly smile at the absurdity of the idea that the local dignitaries of a small Greek town would appeal to an old-fashioned Roman notion like *mos maiorum* (see also Elster 1991,148). The term is not found elsewhere in Apuleius' works, except for one other occurrence also in book 10, ch. 11 (245,4 f.).

iudicio reddito: for *iudicium reddere* = 'to grant a trial' (*OLD* s.v. *reddo* 14b) cf. Ter. *Ph.* 404 *iudicium de eadem causa iterum ut reddant tibi*; Tac. *Ann.* 1,72,4 *consultante ... praetore, an iudicia maiestatis redderentur* with Furneaux ad loc. *Iudicio reddito* said by the magistrates seems to be a reaction to the exclamation of the excited people above: *remoto iudicandi taedio*: the *iudicium*, which *more maiorum* is the young man's right, must be 'returned' to him after the people wanted to take it from him.

utrimquesecus: see on *utrimquesecus* ch. 14 (247,23).

allegationibus: *adlegatio* can be found in Cicero, e.g. *Ver.* 2,1,44, meaning 'intermediaries, a delegation, sent to protect someone's interests'. In our passage it has the meaning described by *ThLL* s.v. *allegatio* 1662,56 f. as 'rerum (apud iudices plerumque) prolatarum'. Before our passage, *ThLL* mentions here only passages from the *Digesta*, e.g. Ulp. *Dig.* 48,5,2,5 *an lenocinii allegatio repellat maritum ab accusatione*; ibid. 48,18,1,26 *transmittenda allegatio dicentium ... se oneratos*, and one passage in Gel. 13,21,19 (where the word *adlegatus* is discussed). After Apuleius, *allegatio* in the sense of 'res prolatae' is frequently found also in non-legal texts, e.g. Tert. *Nat.* 2,7 *quotiens misera uel turpia ... deorum exprobramus, allegatione poeticae licentiae ut fabulosa defenditis*. Cf. in connection with our passsage Firm. *Math.* 1,3,7 *examinatis partium allegationibus*.

ciuiliter: though this is often a technical legal term meaning 'according to civil law' (cf. *OLD* s.v. *ciuiliter* 2 with passages from the *Dig.*), it is here used in a less technical sense, combining the meanings 'as between citizens, in a civil sphere' (*OLD* 1), in contrast with *tyrannica impotentia*, and 'in a manner suited to citizens' (*OLD* 3), in contrast to *barbarica feritas*.

nec ... et ... = *nec ... nec ...* . This usage, in the *Met.* only here and 9,5 (206,14-16), becomes more common in later Latin; see Callebat 1968,99 with references.

ad instar: see on ch. 1 (236,21).

barbaricae feritatis uel tyrannicae impotentiae: in carefully chosen words the magistrates appeal to the people's deeply rooted self-respect: first, the national awareness of not being 'barbarians', and second, pride in belonging to the nation that expelled the tyrants and from that time on had a profound distrust of anything that smacked of tyranny. This as far as the interpretation at the actors' level is concerned. At the level of the interaction between abstract actor and abstract reader (see Introd. **3.2**) this is a reference to the high-handed action of the autocrat Theseus in an era long before the achievements of civilization. Now, in the 'realistic' present of a Greek provincial town, the young man's fate will differ from that of Hippolytus long ago. Note, however, the irony at this level: one consequence of these 'achievements' of civilization is that the innocent young man comes within a hair's breadth of dying a gruesome death (see above, on *accusationis ... ambagibus*).

tyrannicae impotentiae: on the connection between *impotentia* and tyranny see on *impotentiam* ch. 1 (236,12).

inauditus: the meaning 'his case not having been heard' occurs first in Tacitus, who always couples it with *indefensus*; see Furneaux on *Ann.* 2,77,5. Possibly the phrase *inauditus et indefensus* was a fixed legal expression; see Bennett on Tac. *Dial.* 16,5.

in pace placida: cf. Plut. *Praec. reip. ger.* 32 (*Mor.* 824c) πέφευγε γὰρ ἐξ ἡμῶν καὶ ἠφάνισται πᾶς μὲν Ἕλλην πᾶς δὲ βάρβαρος πόλεμος. It is quite natural for the magistrates, who have close ties with the Roman rulers, to point to the peace now reigning in Greece. Not only panegyric literature but also official inscriptions, lauding individual emperors, contain numerous allusions to the *pax romana*, the 'official theme' since the personification of Pax Romana on the Ara Pacis.

pace placida: this alliterative phrase (cf. Cic. *Tusc.* 5,16,48 *placidissimam pacem*) is also found in Verg. *A.* 1,249 and 8,325; in the latter passage it is also connected with legislation following a period of barbarism, cf. 319 f. *uenit Saturnus Olympo ...*; (321 f.) *is genus indocile ac dispersum montibus altis / composuit legesque dedit*; (324 f.) *aurea quae perhibent, illo sub rege fuere / saecula; sic placida populos in pace regebat.* Cf. also Verg. *A.* 7,45 f. *urbes / ... longa placidas in pace regebat.* Ov. *Am.* 2,6,25 f. uses the phrase humorously: *non tu* (sc. *psittace*) *fera bella mouebas; / garrulus et placidae pacis amator eras.*

tam dirum saeculo proderetur exemplum: cf. Juv. 15,31 f. *accipe nostro / dira / quod exemplum feritas produxerit aeuo*. According to Opelt 1965,167, *dirus* is also frequent in contexts describing a hated monarch (cf. *tyrannica impotentiae* in this same sentence).

dirum exemplum: this could equally well refer to that consequence of 'civilized' jurisdiction, the *poena cullei* (ch. 8: 243,1 f.) almost inflicted on the innocent young man. On this irony in the story see above, on *accusationis ... ambagibus*.

exemplum: 'precedent' seems the most suitable translation; see *ThLL* s.v. *exemplum* 1338,9 f. for an extensive description of the use of *exemplum* in this sense, and e.g. Quint. *Inst.* 5,2,1 *rebus, quae aliquando ex paribus causis sunt iudicatae, quae exempla rectius dicuntur.* Besides, *exemplum* has the meaning 'extremely severe punishment' (*ThLL* ibid. 1341,46 f.), e.g. Gel. 7,14,4 *ueteres ... 'exempla' pro maximis grauissimisque poenis dicebant.*

CHAPTER VII

The trial. The stepmother's slave gives false evidence.

With the trial, described in the following chapters, the story introduces a motif which is frequent in the Greek novel and the mime (see Wiemken 1972,166 f. on the mime having borrowed this motif from the New Comedy; Mignogna 1996,240 and n. 30). The fictitious trials in the *declamationes* play a role in the background as well (see App. I,5.5).

241,23-24 Placuit salubre consilium et ilico iussus praeco pronuntiat, patres in curiam conuenirent: This beneficial advice met with approval, and the herald, who had been given this order, immediately proclaimed that the councillors should convene in the council chamber.

Placuit ... et ... praeco pronuntiat: the second clause, in parataxis, expresses the result of the first clause. This usage, frequent in the *Met.*, is undoubtedly borrowed from colloquial language but occurs also in literary Latin of all periods (see LHSz 2,482 f.; Callebat 1968,438 f.). For the alternation of perfect and historical present, see on *rupit ... et ... praecipit* ch. 3 (238,5).

Placuit salubre consilium: the verb comes first in the sentence; but since this sentence has only two constituents, predicate and subject, one can say either that the predicate comes first, or that the subject comes last. As to the first position of the verb, it may be noted that *placet/placuit* in the sense of '(this idea, proposal) met with approval' occurs four times in the *Met.*: 5,11 (111,21); 8,11 (185,23); 8,31 (202,18); and here. In three of these four passages the verb is in first position; in the fourth (8,31) it seems to have been 'displaced' to the second position because in this very emotional utterance (the ass is in mortal danger) the dative *nequissimo uerberoni* is placed first for emphasis (*nequissimo uerberoni sua placuit salus de mea morte*). The first position of *placet/placuit*, which clearly prevails in the *Met.*, may reflect the colloquial usage of *placet* in the sense of 'OK!', 'Good idea!', which is frequent in Plautus and Terence. There, quite naturally, this verb always occurs in the first position of a new sentence (combined with a change of speaker) as a reaction to another's remark or suggestion. Cf. e.g. Pl. *Rud.* 880 and 1137; *St.* 47; *Mil.* 869; Ter. *Ad.* 910 f. *A.: transduce et matrem et familiam omnem ad nos. B.: Placet, / pater lepidissime*.

salubre consilium: see GCA 1977,142 on 4,19 (88,26 f.) on this combination, common from Cicero onward. In our passage, unlike the other three *Met.* passages mentioned in the previous note, *placuit* has no dative, so that one may wonder whose opinion it is that this *consilium* is *salubre*. It is certainly *salubre* to the magistrates (who were afraid of risking their hides: *metu periculi proprii* ch. 6: 241,15) and to their peers, the *decuriones*. Their arguments have evidently also convinced and calmed the *populares* (ch. 6: 241,18 f.). For the young man, who is to stand trial, the direct danger of lynching (ch. 6: 241,13 f.) has indeed been averted, but the impending trial cannot be regarded as *salubre* to him: he will escape the death sentence by only a hair's breadth. His *salus* will ultimately be due to the wise physician (see Introd. **2.4.6** on the theme of *salus*).

ilico: there is no concrete indication of time in this passage (see Introd. **1.6.4**). It is difficult to imagine that all the events narrated here could take place on a single day. *Ilico* and also *protinus* in the next sentence only reflect the town councillors' great hurry in at all costs trying to prevent the popular rebellion. This haste is also expressed by the historical infinitives *deprecari ... compescere* ch. 6 (241,17 f.); see note ad loc.

praeco pronuntiat, patres: alliteration.

praeco: 'court official'. The public herald had an important function in Roman criminal law; see Dar.-Sagl. s.v. *praeco* and Summers 1967,136; in Greek tribunals the κῆρυξ had a similar function. Although the next sentence mentions the Areopagus, this *praeco* (who has a subordinate position) should not be confused with the Greek κῆρυξ τῆς ἐξ Ἀρείου πάγου βουλῆς, who especially in Roman times was an important state official, ranking immediately after the ἄρχων ἐπώνυμος and the στρατηγὸς ἐπὶ τὰ ὅπλα. See *RE* s.v. 'Keryx' [Oehler]; *DNP* 6,450 s.v. 'Keryx' [Beck].

pronuntiat, patres ... conuenirent: see on *bonum caperet animum ... suadet* ch. 4 (239,5 f.).

patres in curiam conuenirent: the *decuriones* of the provincial town constitute the senate of that town (see on *decurionis* ch. 1: 236,23) and as such can be called *patres*, especially since they are being convened for a trial in their official function of town councillors. Cf. e.g. Liv. 23,12,8, where the Carthaginian senate is also called *patres*.

A local court, consisting of the members of the senate of an anonymous small town in Thessaly (see on *ad quandam ciuitatulam* ch. 1: 236,22), is about to administer justice autonomously in a capital crime. Millar 1981,70 f. (= Millar 1999,260) sees here a contradiction with the fact that only the Roman governor of a province had the authority to pronounce the death sentence in a criminal case (but see ibid. n. 43 with references). Only towns that had acquired freedom according to a special *lex* were allowed to *uti suis legibus* (Abbott-Johnson 1926,43; 131 f.). Colin 1965,333 f. and 337 f. adduces this passage in the *Met.* to support his opinion that the towns of Thessaly had the official status of 'free towns' (for the objections against this see on *magistratus* ch. 6: 241,15). With Millar l.c. 71 (= Millar 1999,261) it can be argued that 'what the novel represents is Apuleius' assumptions as to how local justice worked in the Greek provincial cities, irrespective of their formal status, when the governor was not there'. Our passage emphasizes the fact that popular indignation demands quick action from the local rulers. The question whether the events represented here would strike contemporary readers as pure fiction is answered by Millar with the remark that the reality of local government of provincial towns was probably just as confusing and inconsistent as fiction. Nevertheless, the description of this trial contains a number of elements that made it clear to the contemporary reader that the trial as described here could never have been conducted that way in reality, and therefore should be regarded as pure fiction (legal archaisms like the punishment for *parricidium*: see below in this chapter, on *neque principia dicere neque ... commouere* and on *insui culleo* ch. 8: 243,2; *rota uel eculeus more Graecorum ... apparata* ch. 10: 244,21 f.; *perpetuum ... exilium* ch. 12: 245,23 f.; see Summers 1967,322 f.; on the blending of Greek and Roman procedures see Elster 1991,148 f.). See also below, on *haec ... cognoui*; *dicentium contentio*; *finitum est iudicium*.

curiam: here means βουλευτήριον; see on *curiam* ch. 6 (241,10).

241,24-26 Quibus protinus dignitatis iure consueta loca residentibus rursum praeconis uocatu primus accusator incedit: They took at once the accustomed seats to which they were entitled by their rank; then, again at the herald's summons, the accuser came forward first.

Quibus ... residentibus: in this and the following sentences the preliminary procedures of the trial are described methodically and in great detail. This makes for a contrast with the tumultuous scene in the previous chapter, where the grieving father appeared in the *agora* and stormed into the *curia*. It also illustrates *rite* (ch. 6: 241,18) in the magistrates' plea for an orderly *iudicium*.

protinus: see above, on *ilico*.

dignitatis iure consueta loca: the *patres* take their seats on the council. They owe their membership in that council to their *dignitas* as *decuriones* (see on *decurionis* ch. 1: 236,23). This somewhat laborious sentence (see on *quibus ... residentibus* above) possibly suggests that there was also an order of rank within the council, which was reflected in the seats. For *dignitas* in the sense of 'dignitas ex munerum ordinumque auctoritate accepta, inde fere i.q. *gradus*', numerous examples (in Cicero, among others) are given by *ThLL* s.v. *dignitas* 1137,63 f. For the combination *ius dignitatis* cf. Vell. 2,43,4 *reuocati ad ius dignitatis proscriptorum liberi*; cf. also Vell. 2,28,4 *ut ... senatorum filii et onera ordinis sustinerent et iura perderent*. See *OLD* s.v. *ius* 10a 'What one is entitled to ..., one's right, due, prerogative'.

consueta loca residentibus: for the transitive use of *residere* (already found in Cicero) see *GCA* 1985,162 on 8,17 (190,28-191,2) with references.

241,26-242,1 Tunc demum clamatus inducitur etiam reus, et exemplo legis Atticae Martiique iudicii causae patronis denuntiat praeco neque principia dicere neque miserationem commouere: Then, at last, the accused too was called up and brought in, and, after the example of the Athenian law and the court of Mars, the herald announced to the defenders that they were not to give introductory statements nor to arouse pity.

Tunc demum: 'Then at last ...': with these words the reader is invited, as it were, to share the eager expectations of the fictional audience, which, sensation-loving as it is, is looking forward to the accused's appearance. *Tunc* is more colloquial than *tum* and is more frequent in the *Met.*; see Van der Paardt 1971,65 f. on 3,7 (57,5).

clamatus: the name of the defendant was called aloud. This use of *clamare* 'call by name' (see *OLD* s.v. *clamo* 6) is, according to *ThLL* s.v. *clamo* 1253,31 f., mainly poetic; cf. e.g. Verg. *Ecl.* 6,43 f. *Hylan nautae quo fonte relictum / clamassent, ut litus 'Hyla, Hyla' omne sonaret*; Stat. *Silv.* 1,2,199 *clamatus Hylas*; Prop. 2,19,6 *nec tibi clamatae somnus amarus erit*. For *clamare* 'call up to appear in court' *ThLL* s.v. *clamo* 1253,56 gives in addition to our passage only *Cod. Just.* 7,40,3,3 (a. 531) *qui obnoxium suum in iudicium clamauerit*.

inducitur ... reus: cf. 3,7 (57,14) *reus capitis inducor*; on this legal use of *inducere* see Van der Paardt 1971,68 ad loc. with references.

exemplo legis Atticae Martiique iudicii: this refers to the court of the Areopagus, which had jurisdiction over cases of homicide. The pompousness of the magistrates in this little town seems somewhat comical: they want to follow the rules of the venerable Areopagus to the letter. The phrase may also remind the reader of the famous mythological trial conducted by the Areopagus concerning Orestes' parricide. It is also possible to see in this an allusion to the archaizing tendency which was in fashion among the Greeks during the period from the end of the first century until the beginning of the third century A.D. Bowie 1970 points out that this tendency affected not only language and literature, but also other areas of cultural activities. Within this movement, admiration for the past went hand in hand with admiration for Athens, and many literary men diligently studied the antiquities of Attica. Telephus of Pergamum wrote, among other works, 'On Athenian courts of law' and 'On Athenian laws and customs' (see Bowie l.c. 29 and notes).

legis Atticae Martiique iudicii: -que is explicative. Adjectives derived from proper names always come after the noun in Ciceronian Latin, but in Apuleius and other later authors they are often placed before the noun (Bernhard 1927,21 f. with examples also from other authors). In our passage the position of the adjective results in a chiasmus.

Martii iudicii: 'Mars' court' is the court of the Areopagus, which had jurisdiction over deliberate homicide; cf. Juv. 9,101 *curia Martis Athenis*. On the possible connection in the *Met*. of Mars with 'what is morally despised', see Cooper 1980,448 f. Cooper's notion that this mention of 'Martian justice' is a reference to the doubtful 'justice' of this trial is supported by other elements in this episode, as is shown in many of the notes.

denuntiat ... neque ... dicere neque ... commouere: for *denuntiare* with the infinitive (from Tacitus onward) see *GCA* 1995,344 on 9,41 (235,6-9).

praeco neque: the correct separation of the words is found in φ. F has *praeconēque*; the 'Nasalstrich' has been added by a different hand.

neque principia dicere neque miserationem commouere: this prohibition is often mentioned as typical of the Areopagus; cf. Quint. *Inst*. 6,1,7; Poll. *On*. 8,117 "Αρειος πάγος· ἐδίκαζε δὲ φόνου καὶ τραύματος ἐκ προνοίας, καὶ πυρκαϊᾶς, καὶ φαρμάκων ...· προοιμιάζεσθαι δὲ οὐκ ἐξῆν, οὐδ' οἰκτίζεσθαι. Quint. *Inst*. 4,1,14 and 27-29 says that the epilogue is the appropriate place to appeal to the sentiments, but that in the *exordium*, too, *parcius et modestius praetemptanda sit iudicis misericordia*.

This prohibition has put the defense at a disadvantage from the very beginning; the father, as the accuser, had an opportunity to play upon the feelings of the *curia* before a trial was even mentioned: ch. 6 (241,7) *plenis operabatur affectibus* and (241,9-10) *tanta ... miseratione ... curiam ... maerens inflammauerat* (see comm. ad loc.).

principia dicere: cf. Quint. *Inst*. 4,1,1 for *principium* in the sense of *exordium*; Gel. 9,15,9 *incipit statim ... in eandem hanc controuersiam principia nescio quae dicere*.

miserationem commouere: on this combination see *GCA* 1995,187 on 9,21 (218,26).

242,1-3 Haec ad istum modum gesta compluribus mutuo sermocinantibus cognoui: That this happened in this way I learned from several people who talked about it with each other.

The narrator finds it necessary to emphasize that he heard from several people who were discussing it that 'it happened that way'; this is a sign for us that the preliminary procedures of the trial described above appeared improbable also to contemporary readers (see above, on *patres in curiam conuenirent*). Even to these readers it will have been obvious that this 'Beglaubigungsformel' reinforces, rather than weakens, the fantastic and absurd character of the description. Compare Lucian's playing with the historiographical 'Autopsieanspruch' in *VH* 1,2-4; see Merkle 1989,56 f. with references; Maeder 1991,25 f.

This is the first time since ch. 2 (237,1 f.) *memini ... profero*) that the narrator speaks in the first person (*cognoui*, and see below) about his activity as a narrator: he tells his fictive audience how he received his information. In doing so, he also points out the complicated narrative situation to the concrete reader (see Introd. **3.1**): the orientation centre for our insight into what has been told is, so it appears now, a narrator who depends for his information on what he, an ass in the stable, could deduce from the conversations of actorial narrators; they were present at the events, not as actor-protagonists but as actor-witnesses (see Lintvelt 1981,79 f.). So the reader is now prepared for the possibility that any information necessary for a deeper insight into the events may initially be withheld. From now on we may expect to be taken by surprise by any new turn of events. This element of surprise will be the greatest charm of the subsequent second half of the story - there is no longer room for the dramatic irony that was so frequent in the first part (see e.g. on *uxoris patris ... obsequium* ch. 3: 238,9 f.; *sed illa* ibid.: 238,10; *parricidam* ch. 6: 241,8). On re-reading the story it will become apparent that the narrative situation (not acknowledged by the narrator until now), along with the resulting limited perception of the reader, had already taken effect from ch. 4 (239,24 f.) onward: see on *uenenum praesentarium comparat* ch. 4 (239,25) and on *exanimis terrae procumbit* ch. 5 (240,5). The change was gradual: from ch. 4 (239,24 f.) the narrative type evolved from auctorial to actorial, but the orientation center for the reader was still that of actor-protagonists: together with the *nouerca* and her slave, the reader knew that the wine had been poisoned and that the accusations uttered by the *nouerca* were false. From here on, however, the reader's insight has become restricted to that of actor-witnesses, as the narrator explicitly admits here (see also on *haec ad ordinem pertulit* ch. 8: 243,10 and *perspiciens ... uerberonem blaterantem ... inconcinne causificantem* ch. 9: 243,23 f.). The result of this is that the narrator transfers, as it were, the account of the subsequent trial scene to people who were there in person. This enables him to present a most dramatic eyewitness report, in which one dénouement follows the other, while at the same time leaving the illusion of his own limited perspective intact.

The surprising announcement about the narrator's status comes exactly in the middle of the story, dividing it into two parts.

compluribus mutuo sermonicantibus: the fact that the narrator did not get his information from one person, but through conversations carried on by several people with each other, is intended to enhance the 'credibility' even more; see the beginning of the previous note. On the narrator's posing as an historian in this passage, see the following notes.

242,3-7 Quibus autem uerbis accusator urserit, quibus rebus diluerit reus ac prorsus orationes altercationesque neque ipse absens apud praesepium scire neque ad uos, quae ignoraui, possum enuntiare, sed quae plane comperi, ad istas litteras proferam: But in what words the prosecutor pressed his case, and with what facts the defendant refuted the accusation, in short, the speeches and debates, I myself, absent as I was at the manger, can neither know, nor report to you what I was not aware of; but what I clearly learned I will commit to this document.

According to Sandy in *AAGA* 1978,126, one cannot fail to note that in these words Apuleius 'burlesques the explanations of such historians as Thucydides of their painstaking methods of gathering information and fabricating suitable speeches.' See also on *neque ipse absens ... sed quae plane comperi ...* immediately below, and on *haec ad ordinem pertulit* ch.

8 (243,10). See the extensive dicussion of this passage by Graverini 1997,266 f.

accusator urserit ... diluerit reus: chiasmus.

urserit: in F the *u* was changed to *o* by a different hand (at least, according to Robertson; Helm says: 'al. vel ead. m.'). φ has *urserit*.

In φ a later hand has inserted *reum* before *urserit*. In F there seems to be some extra space before *urserit*, and the first hand noted in the margin '.d.' (see Helm, Praef. *Fl*. XXXIV). This was a note of the scribe to himself that something was not quite in order here, that a word was possibly missing. Van der Vliet adopts φ's reading <*reum*> *urserit*. But Hildebrand defends F's reading *urserit* without an explicit object, and all modern editors follow him. The symmetry of the phrase, the typically Apuleian 'concinnitas', would be lost by any addition. As the object of both *urserit* and *diluerit* a word like *crimen* can be supplied. Castiglioni indeed proposes <*crimen*> before *urserit*, and Giarratano honors this suggestion with 'fort. recte'. Castiglioni argues that, although *urgere* is frequently found without an explicit object, *diluere* must have such an object. But cf. Cic. *Clu*. 2,6 *cum ego una quaque de re dicam et diluam*; Liv. 29,18,20 *coram ipse audiat, ipse diluat*.

prorsus: 'in a word', summing up after an enumeration of points (*OLD* s.v. *prorsus* 4b). This use of *prorsus* is attested first in Sallust (*OLD*, and the *ThLL* material; see also Vretska 1976,265 on Sal. *Cat*. 15,5). In the *Met*. it is exceptional (and is not mentioned by Callebat 1968,537 f.). Here it may give a 'Sallustian touch' to a passage in which the narrator poses as an historian (see comm. at the beginning of this section, and the next note).

orationes altercationesque: in a trial, the *orationes*, held without interruptions (*orationes continuae, perpetuae*), were followed by the *altercationes* (this is the only occurrence of the word in Apuleius), an exchange of questions and answers during which the speakers were permitted to interrupt each other. See Zundel 1989 s.v. *altercatio*.

neque ipse ... scire neque ad uos ... enuntiare, sed quae plane comperi: not only is the entire atmosphere of this passage Thucydidean (see the comm. at the beginning of this section and cf. e.g. Thuc. 1,22), but also the precision and parallelism in the expression *neque ... neque ...* evokes the style of Thucydides. In that context the addition *absens apud praesepium* has an ironical effect: the 'historian', painstakingly collecting data, turns out to be an ass, tied to a manger (thus also Graverini 1997,268).

ignoraui: whereas the present *possum* and the future *proferam* relate to the moment of narration, the perfects *ignoraui* and *comperi* refer to the time at which the narrator did or did not receive his information.

ad uos ... enuntiare: for *ad* with the accusative instead of the customary dative with *enuntiare*, see Callebat 1968,211. In both passages mentioned by him, *enuntiare* has the sense 'divulge, disclose (secrets)' (see *OLD* s.v. *enuntio* 1). Here, where the narrator emphasizes the impossibility of rendering a speech word for word, *enuntiare* has the meaning (*OLD* ibid. 2) 'to express ... in words, ... in definite terms'.

quae ... comperi: as Graverini 1997,267, n. 59 shows with references, *comperire* is a technical term referring to the activity of the historian.

ad istas litteras proferam: cf. ch. 2 (237,2 f.) *ad librum profero* with comm. ad loc.

ad istas litteras: 'in this document (that you, reader, now have in front of you)'. Callebat 1968,272 signals the frequent use of *iste* in dialogues in the *Met*., '... où il constitue une adresse à l'interlocuteur et un moyen de suggérer un geste ou d'intéresser plus intimement à l'énoncé la personne à qui l'on parle'. This is exactly the force of *istas* here, with which the narrator refers to the book in the hands of the reader, thus suggesting that he is in dialogue with that reader. Cf. also *enim* in the next sentence, with comm.

242,7-12 Simul enim finita est dicentium contentio, ueritatem criminum fidemque probationibus certis instrui nec suspicionibus tantam coniecturam permitti placuit atque illum promptissimum seruum, qui solus haec ita gesta esse scire diceretur, sisti modis omnibus oportere: As soon as the speakers' dispute was over, it was decided that the truth and reliability of the accusations must be established by sure proof, and that such a serious decision must not be based on suspicions: that most obliging slave, who was said to be the only who knew that it had happened like that, should by all means be produced in court.

Simul: for *simul* as a conjunction see Callebat 1968,432 f.; LHSz 2,638.

enim: Brandt-Ehlers, Vallette, Carlesi, and Hanson do not translate *enim*; cf. Helm-Krenkel 'Sobald nämlich'; Scazzoso 'Quando dunque'. The speaker uses *enim* here to suggest some knowledge or experience that he has in common with his audience (for this function see on *enim* ch. 3: 238,21). The particle is one means by which it is suggested that the reader is addressed directly in this passage (see Kroon 1995,179; see also on *ad istas litteras* above). It seems better to leave *enim* untranslated here; a translation like 'therefore' would suggest a causal connection.

dicentium contentio: mention was made earlier of an *accusator* (241,26 and 242,3) and of *causae patronis* (241,28), but in 242,4 above we have *diluerit reus*. Consequently, it is impossible to establish whether the accused defended himself or had managed to engage a lawyer. But, in view of the unreal atmosphere of the description of this trial, these are not the questions one should ask about the text. In a few evocative terms a trial is described here that is more like a Kafkaesque nightmare than an eyewitness report. The tenor of this part of the story is merely that an innocent person is in danger of being condemned to death. See also on *accusationis ... ambagibus* ch. 6 (241,12 f.); thus also Graverini 1997,268 and n. 64. See on the danger of being falsely accused as a theme pervading the *Met.* comm. on ch. 33 (264,7-12).

ueritatem criminum ... instrui: in the *dicentium contentio* the prosecutor has apparently had more success in his attempt to *urgere <crimen>* than the defence to *diluere <crimen>*, because there is no mention of attempting to furnish evidence of the defendant's innocence (see previous note).

probationibus certis: in ch. 6 (241,12 f.) the excited *plebs* demanded that the *manifestae probationes* to be adduced by the accusers be withheld. In the note ad loc. it has already been remarked that the accusers are unable to furnish *manifestae probationes*, but that the physician, who appoints himself as the defence, will be able to. See also on *illum seruum, qui ... diceretur* below.

nec suspicionibus tantam coniecturam permitti: Quint. *Inst.* 3,6,30 remarks on the etymology of *coniectura: coniectura dicta est a coniectu, id est derectione quadam rationis ad ueritatem;* see further ibid. 3,6,1-103 on *coniectura* in a technical-rhetorical sense, and 7,2,1-57 on rules concerning the use of *coniectura* in murder cases, among others. In this technical meaning *coniectura* means an opinion that comes as close to the truth as possible, on the basis of reasoning that includes all possible data. It is clear, therefore, that a *coniectura* based on mere *suspiciones* is weak indeed.

tantam coniecturam = *tantae rei coniecturam.*

illum ... seruum, qui solus ... diceretur: the reader understands at once that this refers to the *seruulus dotalis* of ch. 4 (239,22 f.; see comm. ad loc.), who will stand by his mistress, the *nouerca*, through thick and thin. But the narrator voices the *patres*' point of view in this sentence, which in its entirety depends on *placuit* (sc. *patribus*) and reflects the content of their deliberations in free indirect discourse. Apparently the *patres* have learned from the accuser that there is 'a slave who is the only one who knows how it happened': *illum seruum* 'that slave they were talking about'. While the *patres* expect *probationes certae* from this slave, the reader knows that his will be false testimony, disastrous for the young man. The narrator refrains from making any comment on the judges' misunderstanding (known to the reader and, in fact, also to the narrator) concerning *illum ... seruum, qui solus ... diceretur*; the reader is bound to feel some doubt about the possibility of a fair trial. On the pessimistic opinion expressed in the *Met.* of the court as the seat of justice, see on *accusationis manifestis probationibus et responsionis meditatis ambagibus* ch. 6 (241,12 f.).

promptissimum: the original reading of F, and also the reading of φ. *Potissimum*, a correction by the second corrector of F (after φ had been copied; see Lütjohann 1873,447), is adopted here by all editors (e.g. Hanson: 'in particular'). The reading *promptissimum*, however, which is strongly represented in the mss.(of the mss. of Class I, on which see Introd. **4.1**, group a* also give *prompt-*), is defensible: that slave is only too willing to bear (false) witness. It also renders the phrase *sisti modis omnibus* easier to understand: willing as the slave may be, it is necessary to find 'all possible ways' (*modis omnibus*) to enable him to bear witness, since a slave was not permitted to testify against his master. See Mommsen, *Röm. Str.* 414 with references, also on the ways in which this law was circumvented.

sisti: 'to be produced in court'; see *OLD* s.v. *sisto* 2a on this legal use of *sistere*.

modis omnibus: see on *promptissimum* above.

242,12-15 Nec tantillum cruciarius ille uel fortuna tam magni iudicii uel confertae conspectu curiae uel certe noxia conscientia sua deterritus, quae ipse finxerat, quasi uera adseuerare atque adserere incipit: And that gallows-bird, not in the least unnerved by what was at stake in this important trial, or by the sight of the packed council chamber, or at least by his own guilty conscience, started to affirm and assert as the truth what he had made up himself.

tantillum: the adverb, probably borrowed from comedy (see Callebat 1968,520), may in colloquial language have been accompanied by a gesture (Van der Paardt 1971,61). Here it suggests the liveliness of the conversations about the events in the *curia*, overheard by the ass.

cruciarius: occurs in the *Met.* only here. As an invective ('*cruce dignus*') it is not attested earlier; *ThLL* s.v. *cruciarius* 1218,24 f. gives only our passage and Amm. 29,2,9 *quae cruciarius ille conflauit*; cf. also Isid. *Or.* 10,49 *cruciarius eo quod sit cruce dignus*; meaning 'someone who is crucified' it occurs e.g. Sen. *Con.* 7,6,2 and passim; Petr. 112,5 *unius cruciarii parentes ... detraxere nocte pendentem*. For the re-reader this remarkable invective foreshadows the ultimate fate of this slave (ch. 12: 245,24).

uel fortuna tam magni iudicii uel confertae conspectu curiae uel certe noxia conscientia sua: an an-isocolic tricolon (11, 10, and 13 syllables; see Bernhard 1927,71). The last and longest colon differs from the two other, similar, cola in content as well: it contains a consideration of a moral nature. It receives special emphasis by *uel certe* ('or at least'): this implies not so much a rejection of the alternatives introduced by *uel ..., uel*, as an extra emphasis on the alternative introduced by *uel certe*. See *GCA* 1985,251 on 8,28 (200,1); also *GCA* 1995,251 f. on 9,29 (224,28).

fortuna ... iudicii: cf. Quint. *Inst.* 10,1,16 *nec fortuna modo iudicii, sed etiam ipsorum qui orant periculo adficimur*; Quint. *Decl.* 371,5 '*at enim dubia est iudicii fortuna.' sed nobis non timenda*.

confertae conspectu curiae: alliteration. As in the phrase *noxio conspectu nouercae* (ch. 4: 239,8; see note ad loc.) the genitive (here *curiae*) may be either subjective or objective ('the fact that the crowded *curia* was watching him' or 'the sight of the crowded *curia*'). The objective genitive is more likely, as we may assume that the people overheard by the ass talking about the trial (see above on *tantillum*) were indeed awe-struck at the sight of the crowded council chamber.

noxia conscientia: the combination is not attested before Apuleius (*ThLL* s.v. *conscientia* 365,69), who uses it twice in the *Met*.: here and 7,27 (175,12 f.) *est enim congruens pessimis conatibus contra noxiam conscientiam sperare securitatem*. Cf. e.g. Sal. *Fragm.* II,87 D (5d,2, p. 168 Kurfess) *conscientia noxarum* (also Amm. 15,8,2; 16,12,61; 21,15,4); Liv. 45,26,6 *conscientia ... noxae*; cf. also Ov. *Met.* 10,351 *noxia corda* with Bömer ad loc. *Conscientia* by itself can mean both 'clear conscience' and 'guilty conscience': cf. Quint. *Inst.* 5,11,41 with the proverbial *conscientia mille testes*; for 'guilty conscience' e.g. Cic. *Off.* 3,21,85 *hunc tu quas conscientiae labes in animo censes habuisse?*; in Apuleius e.g. *Met.* 7,11 (162,30); 8,12 (187,2). See Thome 1993,373 f. for a thorough research on the development of *conscientia* to 'guilty conscience', a meaning occasionally attested before Cicero, but fully developed in his works.

conscientia sua: although the addition *sua* seems unnecessary (LHSz 2,178 f.), it subtly emphasizes the difference from the two motives for *deterritus* mentioned earlier: those were based on external factors, while *conscientia sua* implies an internal factor.

quae ipse finxerat, quasi uera adseuerare atque adserere incipit: Pricaeus sensed an echo here of Sen. *Phaed.* 1193 f. *quod ipsa demens pectore insano hauseram, / mentita finxi*. We should keep in mind, however, that the story has by now evolved far from the Phaedra tragedy and become part of the intertextual entourage of the *declamatio* and mime (see on *sed dira illa femina ... exemplar unicum* ch. 5: 240,9 f.). The verbal echo is not cogent enough; a more striking parallel can be found in [Quint.] *Decl.* 7,6 (Håkanson 143,9) *non uacat adserere quae finxeris*; see below, on *ueneni* ch. 9 (244.5). In this phase of the story the *nouerca* hardly plays any further role, and from now on the emphasis is on the word of the wise physician opposed to that of the lying slave, a typical theme in the *declamatio* and mime (see also on *forte fortuna ... haustu* ch. 5: 239,28 f. and on *potionem* ch. 9: 243,25).

adseuerare atque adserere: see Bernhard 1927,164 f. with examples of 'Synonymik koordinierter begriffe' in Apuleius. This rhetorical device is as old as Latin literary prose itself and probably has its origin in cultic language and archaic law texts; see von Albrecht ²1983 s.v. 'Synonymhäufung' and 'archaïsche Doppelung', with references. The examples in Bernhard show that Apuleius employs this device readily and with great linguistic ingenuity, 'so daß sie eines der wesentlichsten, den Stil des Autors charakterisierenden Momente darstellt'. The wordplay is functional here: the duplication *adseuerare et adserere* illustrates a liar's superabundance of words, necessary to cover his lies.

adserere: because of the play on words (see the preceding note), *adserere* is used in a rather rare meaning: *ThLL* s.v. *assero* 865,36 f. gives some examples before Apuleius of *assero* i.q. *affirmare, confirmare, ... probando affirmare* sive *defendere*, but shows that in all these passages the reading in the mss. is disputed. *ThLL* ibid. 865,44: 'usitatissima est significatio inde ab Apul.'.

Possibly there is an etymological play with *serere* 'string together', for immediately hereafter the slave's story of lies is rendered in a series of *quod ...* sentences. On Apuleius' fondness of etymologizing see *GCA* 1985,67 and n. 1 on 8,6 (180,19-23 *et frontem adseuerat*), with references; see also Schlam 1992,138 n. 29; *GCA* 1995, Index Rerum s.v. 'etymology'.

242,15-22 ... **quod se uocasset indignatus fastidio nouercae iuuenis, quod, ulciscens iniuriam, filii eius mandauerit necem, quod promisisset grande silentii praemium, quod recusanti mortem sit comminatus, quod uenenum sua manu temperatum dandum fratri reddiderit, quod ad criminis probationem reseruatum poculum neclexisse suspicatus sua postremum manu porrexerit puero**: ... that the young man, indignant at his stepmother's rejection, had summoned him; that, wishing to avenge the insult, he entrusted him with the murder of her son; that he had promised him an ample reward for his silence; that when he refused, he threatened him with death; that he gave him a poison, mixed with his own hand, to administer to his brother; that he, suspecting him of having neglected (his instructions) and of keeping the cup as evidence of the crime, finally offered it to the boy with his own hand.

quod...: the six-fold anaphora of *quod* emphasizes each successive point of the slave's evidence, a string of lies that is reported in indirect discourse. In marked contrast, the speeches of the wise physician will be rendered in direct discourse (ch. 8-9: 243,11 f. and ch. 11: 244,24 f. below). See also on *haec ad ordinem pertulit* ch. 8 (243,10).

uocasset ... mandauerit ... promisisset ... sit comminatus ... reddiderit ... porrexerit: Callebat 1968,362 ascribes the alternation of perfect subjunctive with pluperfect subjunctive to 'recherche de variatio'. That 'variatio', however, is combined with a most careful use of tenses: naturally, the slave had been summoned (*uocasset*) before the order was given, just as the promise of a reward (*promisisset*) must have preceded the refusal and the subsequent threats.

indignatus fastidio: there are numerous constructions possible with *indignor* to express the cause of the indignation (*ThLL* s.v. *indignor* 1184,3-1186,5). Among these, the dative is a rather late development: attested first Ulp. *Dig.* 48,5,2,3 *quique contaminationi non indignatur* (see also Krebs-Schmalz 1,724 f. s.v. *indignari*; after this passage in Ulpian, *ThLL* ibid. 1184,21 f. gives Apul. *Met.* 9,39 (233,5) and our passage; next Tert. *Pudic.* 7,8; Cypr. *Ad Fort. praef.* 5, and others. In 9,29 (225,5 f.) the dative *numinibus* with *indignata* refers not to the cause but to the object of the indignation. *OLD* s.v. *indignor* 2d takes these two uses of the dative together; *ThLL* 1185,35 f. has a separate lemma for the dative 'in quam (sc. personam) ira vertitur'.

ulciscens: possibly with final nuance; see *GCA* 1985,100 on 8,9 (184,10) *obtundens*.

quod promisisset: for the first position of the verb in a subordinate clause see on ch.

32 (263,21) *si fuisset.*

grandem praemium: see on ch. 27 (258,21 f.) *grandem ... materiam.*

recusanti mortem sit comminatus: *recusanti* (sc. *sibi*) functions as a noun. This ellipsis of the dative of a personal pronoun is common, even in Cicero; see Bernhard 1927,160,d; Callebat 1968,452.

neclexisse: thus F, retained by Giarratano, Terzaghi, and Frassinetti (and Hanson, who prints *neglexisse*); thus also Helm in the Addenda et Corrigenda (in the reprint of Helm 1931, i.e. Helm 1955,300, in which he retracts *nec secus ille*, his own conjecture, still printed in his text). Augello 1977,209 also defends *neclexisse*. The suggested changes are motivated by the absence of an accusative subject for the infinitive of which *poculum* is the object. Wiman proposes the ingenious conjecture *'index esse'* for *neclexisse*, with *poculum* as the subject of the infinitive. Robertson prints a conjecture of his own, *neclexisse <se>*, paleographically quite acceptable, but unnecessary. F's text, without *se*, is understandable: *reseruatum poculum* is the object of *porrexerit* and also the object of *neclexisse* (the subject of the infinitive, the slave, is to be supplied). Thus, *poculum ... neclexisse* can be translated as 'to have ignored the orders concerning the *poculum*' For this somewhat elliptic use of *neglegere* cf. e.g. Ter. *Ph.* 54 *amo te et non neclexisse habeo gratiam* with Dziatsko-Hauler ad loc.; Juv. 9,92 *neglegit atque alium bipedem sibi quaerit asellum* (here *neglegit* is to be understood as 'he ignores my complaint').

242,22-24 Haec — eximia enim ad ueritatis imaginem — uerberone illo simula<ta> cum trepidatione perferente finitum est iudicium: This — an excellent story, surely, to create an impression of truth — was told by that scoundrel with pretended trepidation, and so the trial was brought to an end.

Haec eximia enim ad ueritatis imaginem: thus F. Numerous scholars have busied themselves with this phrase, finding difficulties in the expression *eximius ad*, and in the word *enim*. Castiglioni proposes *eximia enim <et> ad*, which is adopted by Giarratano, Terzaghi, and Frassinetti, and defended by Augello 1977,209. Lütjohann proposes *eximie enim ad*, followed by Helm 1931. Leo's conjecture *eximie nimis ad* is adopted by Robertson. Helm 1955 prints Leo's conjecture, with a correction of his own: *eximie <ac> nimis ad*, but in his Addenda et corrigenda p. 300 proposes to retain F's reading. Novak's proposal to read *eximie* and omit *enim* is followed by Van Thiel and Hanson: *haec eximie ad*. Koch offers the ingenious conjecture *examussim ad* (cf. on *examussim* ch. 2: 237,21). Blümner offers *eximie mentita* (defended by Shumate 1996,100,n. 5). Van der Vliet's conjecture *eximie enim imaginem <simulata>* is connected with his reading *sine ulla tum* for F's *simulatum* later in this sentence.

The transmitted text can be retained. *Eximia*, an adjective qualifying *haec*, must be taken with *ad ueritatis imaginem*; this use of *eximius ad* with the accusative, meaning 'most suitable for', is indeed attested once, according to ThLL s.v. *eximius* 1492,61 f.: Mela 1,65 *hominum genus ... ad belli pacisque munia eximium*. F's reading must be taken as a parenthesis, as in Helm-Krenkel (also Helm 1955,300): 'Als der Schurke dies — es erweckte ja ausnehmend den Anschein der Wahrheit — mit erheucheltem Zittern vorbrachte'.

enim: often used in a parenthesis (KSt 2,2,122 f.); see on *enim* above. In this parenthesis, too, the speaker uses *enim* to appeal to the addressed person's experience: 'that's the way it always goes: when someone tells a story which has the appearance of truth, he can pull the wool even over the judges' eyes, and no one will bother to check his statements.' On this pessimistic view see above, on *illum seruum, qui ... diceretur.*

uerberone: for this invective see *GCA* 1985,277 on 8,31 (202,18-10) and Opelt 1965,59 n.4.

simulata cum trepidatione: this is Oudendorp's generally accepted emendation for F *simulatum trepidatione*, which was changed by ς to *simulata trepidatione*. Van der Vliet points to ch. 10 (244,7), where the slave is seized by an *ingens trepidatio*, and therefore reads in this passage *sine ulla tum trepidatione*. This ingenious and paleographically plausible conjecture is adopted by Hanson. Still, Oudendorp's emendation is preferable: *sine ulla tum trepidatione* would be somewhat redundant after *nec tantillum ... deterritus*; moreover, this entire sentence emphasizes the slave's skillful play-acting, and his cleverly simulated fear fits in well with that (after all, he is supposedly betraying a dangerous murderer). Cf. Verg. A. 2,107 *prosequitur pauitans, et ficto pectore fatur* (sc. Sinon), where Servius remarks: *pavitans] quasi pavitans. pavitans hoc est simulans se pavere. et non tam propter mortem ... sed ut videretur cum timore civium suorum consilia vel secreta patefacere.* Finkelpearl 1998,82-101 discusses many other instances of Sinon as an important paradigm of trickery in the *Met.* Cf. also Serv. A. 11,406 f. *vel cum se pavidum contra mea iurgia fingit / artificis scelus: nam sceleratorum est simulare formidinem.*

perferente: thus F. It is unnecessary to read *proferente*, as Helm does, followed by Robertson and Hanson. Helm refers to the not infrequent interchange of the compendia for *per* and *pro* (see also Helm, Praef. *Fl.* XLVI f.). Augello 1977,209 defends the reading of F and shows that the *Met.* often has *perfero* in the sense of 'riferire', e.g. 7,4 (156,23).

finitum est iudicium: 'the case was declare closed, counsel for defence being given no opportunity to call the evidence of the schoolmaster in whom the stepson had confided, or of the slave who had been present when the child had picked up the cup and drunk it'; thus Graves [4]1954,245. His free supplement to the Latin text touches the sore spot and raises the inevitable reaction of any *lector scrupulosus*: 'Why do we hear nothing more about the old *educator* (ch. 4: 239,9 f.) to whom the young man presented his problem at an early stage and who could have proved his innocence, or about the *paedagogus* (ch. 5: 240,6) who was present when the younger son drained the cup of poison?' Graves supplies an answer: the defence did not get the opportunity to call these two witnesses. But that is another thing the narrator does not tell us; these two possible witnesses for the defence simply do not exist any more. We can only conclude that when the story definitively left the generic context of tragedy and 'changed over' to the world of the mime, novel, and *declamationes*, certain characters also left the scene (see also App. I,6C. and App. III). The *educator* and the *paedagogus* were typical wearers of the *cothurnus* and do not belong to the world of *planipedes* who are now on stage. As has been noted earlier, there are many elements in the description of this trial that contribute to a highly unreal atmosphere (see above, on *patres in curiam conuenirent*); this is one of these elements. On the priority of dramatic effect over dramaturgic logic in this story, see App. I.5.4.

CHAPTER VIII

An old physician prevents the death sentence.

242,24-243,2 Nec quisquam decurionum tam aequus remanserat iuueni, quin eum euidenter noxae compertum insui culleo pronuntiaret: And not one of the councillors had remained so favourable toward the young man that he would not sentence him, having been found clearly guilty of wrongdoing, to be 'sewn into the sack'.

Nec quisquam ... tam aequus remanserat ..., quin ...: the positive notion that 'all the *decuriones* wanted to condemn the young man' is changed to the negative, thus slowing down the action and increasing the suspense. This will make it all the clearer that there is only one among them who remains *aequus* toward the young man: the physician who below is referred to as *unus e curia*.

decurionum: these are the councillors, who in ch. 7 (241,24) are called *patres*; see note there; for the office of *decurio* see on *decurionis* ch. 1 (236,23).

aequus: referring to persons, this adjective has the more general sense of 'favourable, kindly' (*OLD* s.v. *aequus* 7a), with dative; when used of actions, laws, etc., *aequus* means 'fair, just, reasonable' (*OLD* s.v. 6a), and can equally be used of persons in the sense of 'fair-minded, impartial' (*OLD* s.v. 6c). The latter meaning certainly plays a part here: the injustice of this so-called fair trial is hinted at in many passages (see on *illum ... seruum, qui solus ... diceretur* ch. 7: 242,10 f.). The classification in *OLD* is preferable to that in *ThLL* s.v. *aequus* 1034,41 f., where the passages with *aequus* referring to persons are taken together under the heading 'i.q. *propitius, benignus, tranquillus, iustus*'.

remanserat: for the use of the pluperfect to indicate the setting or the background for subsequent events, see on *inflammauerat, ut ... conclamarint*, ch. 6 (241,11 f.).

eum ... insui ... pronuntiaret: *OLD* s.v. *pronuntio* 3a 'to pronounce (a judicial or sim. decision, a verdict or sentence)' gives many examples for this legal meaning; see also Van der Paardt 1971,26 f. on 3,1 (52,14 f.) *iudex ... qui me ... innocentem pronuntiare poterit*, with references. When it means 'pronounce a sentence', *pronuntiare* belongs to the category of verbs of command, like *imperare*, normally governing *ut* + subjunctive. Here, however, *pronuntiare* governs an accusative and infinitive, like *iubere*; see also 6,31 (152,21-24) with *GCA* 1981,69; 11,19 (281,6-7) with Gwyn Griffiths 272; LHSz 2,355. Cf. on ch. 6 (241,13 f.) *conclamarint ... publicum malum ... uindicari*.

noxae compertum: *compertus* with the genitive of the offence, in the sense of *conuictus*, is attested first Var. frg. Prisc. in *G.L.* 2,384,6 *Vestales incesti conpertae* (*ThLL* s.v. *comperio* 2055,16 f.). See also e.g. Tac. *Ann.* 1,3,4 (= 4,11,2) *nullius ... flagitii compertum*; Furneaux ad loc. quotes instances from Livy.

noxae: *noxa* is used here in the wider sense of 'injurious behaviour, wrongdoing' (*OLD* s.v. *noxa* 1). Cf. an expression like *noxa capitalis* in Liv. 3,55,5; on the technical and non-technical meaning of *nox(i)a* see Mommsen *Röm. Strafr.*, 8 f., with notes and references. Summers' interpretation of *noxa* here (1967,326), 'damage done by a slave or *filiusfamilias* to the person or property of a third party, damage for which the owner or *paterfamilias* was held to be liable', appears to be too specific.

insui culleo: this is a concise description of the notorious Roman punishment for *parricidium*, dating from the 3rd or early 2nd century BC (see Robinson 1995,47 f., with references); cf. Mod. *Dig.* 48,9,9 *poena parricidii more maiorum haec instituta est, ut parricida uirgis sanguineis uerberatus deinde culleo insuatur cum cane, gallo gallinaceo et uipera et simia: deinde in mare profundum culleus iactatur*. For an extensive discussion of this crime and its punishment see Cic. *S.Rosc.* 22,62-26,73, where, as in our passage (and often elsewhere), no animals are mentioned. According to *RE* s.v. *culleus* 1747,11 f. [Hitzig], the *poena cullei* was abolished by the *Lex Pompeia*, but the punishment lived on 'im Hausgericht'; see also Lassen 1992,150 f. According to Summers 1967,167 f. the punishment remained in force until Hadrian replaced it by throwing the criminal to the wild animals, except when parents or grandparents had been murdered by their own (grand)children; in those cases he prescribed the *poena cullei* but only *si mare proximum sit*. The text cited above, *Dig.* 48,9,9, continues with *hoc ita, si mare proximum sit; alioquin bestiis obicitur secundum diui Hadriani constitutionem*; [Dosith.] *Hadr. Sent.* 16. See Hitzig l.c. for further references, and Courtney on Juv. 8,213 f.; Winterbottom, index to Sen. *Con.* s.v. 'sack'; Robinson 1995,47 f.

It is improbable that this jury-court of councillors of a Greek provincial town would wish to enforce the *poena cullei*, and mention of this archaic Roman punishment contributes to the unreal, fantastic atmosphere of this trial; see on *patres in curiam conuenirent* ch. 7 (241,24); see also Elster 1991,147.

243,2-10 Cum iam sententiae pares, cunctorum stilis ad unum sermonem congruentibus, ex more perpetuo in urnam aeream deberent coici, quo semel conditis calculis, iam cum rei fortuna transacto, nihil postea commutari licebat, sed mancipabatur potestas capitis in manum carnificis, unus e curia senior prae ceteris compertae fidi atque auctoritatis praecipuae medicus orificium urnae manu contegens, ne quis mitteret calculum temere, haec ad ordinem pertulit: It was now the moment when the verdicts — identical because the pens of all the men agreed on the same formula — had by time-honoured tradition to be thrown into a bronze urn: once they were stored there, the defendant's fate was sealed; nothing after that was allowed to be changed, and authority over his life passed to the executioner. Then an older councillor, a physician, who was known above the rest for his trustworthiness and had exceptional authority, covered the mouth of the urn with his hand so that no one could put in his token rashly, and gave the following speech to the council:

This long sentence, which describes the setting in of a possible peripeteia in the fate of the innocent young man, is carefully structured: the unanimity of the votes is established in cola of 8 and 16 syllables; the next colon, of 19 syllables, reminds the reader that the votes are destined to be deposited in the urn; then the disastrous irrevocability of that act is described in three short cola (9, 10, and 9 syllables), and a long one (*sed ... carnificis*: 19 syllables). After this long subordinate clause (*cum ... carnificis*: a total of 90 syllables), which builds up to a powerful climax, we finally reach the main clause *unus e curia ... medicus ... pertulit* (63 syllables in cola of 9, 9, 14, 12, 11, and 8 syllables). The long opening subordinate clause enhances the suspense. The peripeteia from mortal danger to possible salvation is graphically contained in the image of the bronze urn: it seems as if the voting tablets will disappear into it irrevocably, but the hand of the physician, covering the opening, prevents that.

sententiae ... in urnam ... coici: the synecdoche, though entirely understandable, is quite daring: *sententiae*, as the subject of *in urnam deberent coici*, indicates the tablets on which the *sententiae* are written. Cf. Ov. *Met.* 15,47 f. *candidaque Herculeo sententia numine facta / soluit Alemoniden*, where, too, *sententia* is almost identical to *calculus*; cf. also Quint. *Decl.* 263,12 *posteaquam dinumeratae sunt populi sententiae*.

sententiae pares: the meaning 'identical votes' required here, is unusual in legal terminology, where the phrase always means 'equally divided votes'. *ThLL* s.v. *par* 267,10 f. 'in re iudiciaria de sententiis contrariis eodem numero prolatis' gives examples, e.g. Sen. *Con.* 1,5,3 *reum alter iudex damnat, alter absoluit; inter pares sententias mitior uincat*; Sen. *Ep.* 81,26 *reus sententiis paribus absoluitur*; Hermog. *Dig.* 40,1,24 *si dissonantes pares iudicium existant sententiae*. However, *OLD* s.v *par* 5c quotes several passages where *par*, used of words or opinions, means 'similar, to the same effect'; note especially Ov. *Fast.* 3,319 *dixerat haec Faunus, par est sententia Pici*. See also the next note. As the translation indicates, *pares* is here not attributive but predicative, and belongs closely with the explanatory ablative absolute that follows it; thus Brandt-Ehlers: 'Schon sollten die Stimmzettel — sie lauteten gleich, denn alle hatten denselben Wortlaut geschrieben — ...'.

cunctorum stilis ad unum sermonem congruentibus: this phrase explains the unusual meaning of *sententiae pares* (see the preceding note). *Stilus* is used ambiguously here, in a manner typical of Apuleius' own *stilus*. On the one hand it is abstract, as in e.g. Sen. *Cl.* 1,14,1 *non accedit* (sc. *pater*) *ad decretorium stilum* (i.e. the writing down of his decision to disinherit his son); Stat. *Silv.* 3 pr. *audaciam stili nostri*; Plin. *Ep.* 1,8,8 *munificentiae rationem ... stilo prosequi*; 7,9,7 *pugnacem hunc et quasi bellatorium stilum* (see further *OLD* s.v. *stilus* 4); on the other hand the phrase evokes the concrete image of pens all pointing the same way (because they are writing the same word; see the next note). It is unnecessary to follow LS (s.v. *stilus* II B 3), who give a special meaning for the word in this passage: 'a decision, verdict, opinion'.

sermonem: 'formula'; see *GCA* 1995,219 on 9.25 (221,20) *solito sermone*. Although in this story the trial is set in a small Thessalian town, the word *sermo* will suggest to the Roman readership of the *Met.* (as supposed by Dowden 1994,431 f.) the formula customary in Roman criminal cases (see also below, on *nihil postea commutari licebat*). There was a choice between three formulas: *absoluo, condemno*, or *non liquet*; for a conviction a majority of votes was needed (see Mommsen, *Röm. Strafr.* 444 f.); in the present trial, the identical votes presumably all bear the formula '*condemno*'.

ex more perpetuo: the phrase accentuates the solemn and irrevocable aspect of the situation. It also recalls the magistrates' words *more maiorum* (ch. 6: 241,18). Though the magistrates then used the phrase to argue for a fair trial for the young man, rather than summary stoning, it is now clear that, ironically, the trial is likely to result in the innocent young man's conviction through the operation of *mos perpetuus* (see also on *accusationis ... ambagibus* ch. 6: 241,12 f.).

in urnam aeream ... coici: the bronze urn for the voting tablets occurs also in the Edicts of Cyrene IV (ed. Visscher 1940,21 f.; see ibid. on 'Formation et fonctionnement du jury').

calculis: here another kind of voting is evoked than the one suggested above, where there is mention of *stili*, writing verdicts. The *calculus* is a white or black voting pebble, with which one voted for acquittal (white) or conviction (black); see *GCA* 1981,70 ad 6,31 (152,24-153,1). The *calculus* recurs below in this same sentence (*ne quis mitteret calculum temere*). Although Bömer ad Ov. *Met.* 15,44 suggests that *calculus* is used commonly for 'ψῆφοι', in fact that line is the first attested place for this use (*ThLL* s.v. *calculus* 141,77 f.). Indeed, the poet there apparently feels that he has to explain the use of the word. The passage is worth quoting in full, since there, as here, the *calculi* are mentioned in the context of a miraculous reversal (effectuated by Hercules) in the trial of an innocent young man: Ov. *Met.* 15,41 f. *mos erat antiquus niueis atrisque lapillis, / his damnare reos, illis absoluere culpam. / tunc quoque sic lata est sententia tristis; et omnis / calculus immitem demittitur ater in urnam. / quae simul effudit numerandos uersa lapillos, omnibus e nigro color est mutatus in album, candidaque Herculeo sententia numine facta / soluit Alemoniden.*

Cf. ch. 32 (263,24), where the golden apple handed over to Venus by Paris, is called (*uelut*) *uictoriae calculum*.

cum rei fortuna transacto: metaphorical use of a business term; see *GCA* 1985,80 f. on 8,7 (181,25-182,1) *iam cum luce transegerat*.

transacto: the nominal part of this absolute ablative is to be found in *cum rei fortuna*; see LHSz 2,141 f. and KSt 2,1,777 f. on the increasing frequency, especially from Livy onward, of a perfect passive participle used as an absolute ablative without a noun. See *OLD* s.v. *transigo* 3c for the impersonal use of the verb, with *cum* or *de*. The impersonal passive is also found e.g. Tac. *Ger.* 19,3 *tantum uirgines nubunt et cum spe uotoque uxoris semel transigitur*; see Lund ad loc.

nihil postea commutari licebat: a rule bearing on criminal trials brought by Roman senate and consuls is applied in this trial before a municipal council in a Greek provincial town. Cf. *Dig.* 49,2,1,2 *sciendum est appellari a senatu non posse principem, idque oratione diui Hadriani effectum*. The trial described here, with its mixture of Greek and Roman procedures and many legal anachronisms, must have contained some recognizable elements for the contemporary (Roman) reading public; on the other hand, it must have seemed like a fantasy-trial to these readers; see above, on *insui culleo*. In addition, the emphasis on the impossibility of appeal has in this passage the function of creating an atmosphere of irrevocability, just before the reversal.

licebat: 'it was allowed, possible'. *Licet* in a non-moral sense occurs also 7,3 (156,7 f.); see *GCA* 1981,96 f. ad loc.

mancipabatur ...in manum carnificis: strictly speaking, the addition *in manum* is unnecessary in view of the etymology of *mancipo*, but it makes the entire phrase more descriptive and sinister. *Mancipare* is used here in the sense of *tradere* (*ThLL* s.v. *mancipo* 258,71 f.). The usual construction is *mancipare aliquem (aliquid) alicui (rei)*, which makes the addition *in manum* here the more remarkable; see *ThLL* ibid. 259,11 f. See also Van der Paardt 1971,148 on 3,19 (67,2) about the frequent metaphorical use of *mancipare* in Apuleius. From the *ThLL* article on *mancipo* it appears that the considerably extended use of the verb as attested in Apuleius becomes frequent in Christian authors. See also *GCA* 1995,141 on 9,14 (213,19-23) *corpus manciparat*; Schmidt 1990.

unus ... pertulit: the doctor who has appeared so suddenly will give the story a most surprising turn, which will eventually lead to what the narrator calls a *prouidentiae diuinae condignum ... exitum* (ch. 12: 245,27). He makes truth come to light and thus fulfills the role of Artemis in Eur. *Hipp.Steph.* 1283 f. On this 'deus ex machina' see Appendix I,6D.

unus e curia senior ... medicus: even without the qualifications *prae ceteris ... praecipuae*, three reasons are given why the councillors should respect this man: he is one of them (*unus e curia*), *senior* (see note), and *medicus* (see note).

senior prae ceteris compertae fidi atque auctoritatis praecipuae medicus: the two qualifying phrases are enclosed by the adjective *senior* and the noun *medicus*; note also the chiasmus *compertae fidi / auctoritatis praecipuae*. Immediately at his first appearance, this *senior medicus* is carefully introduced as a prominent man, moving in the higher circles of this society. *Prae ceteris* can be seen as a reminiscence of Hom. *Il.* 11,514 ἰητρὸς γὰρ ἀνὴρ πολλῶν ἀντάξιος ἄλλων. This verse is cited by Plutarch in *De tuend.san.* 1 (*Mor.* 122c). During the Second Sophistic movement physicians could achieve great prestige (e.g. Galen; see Bowersock 1969, ch. 5), as is shown by the existence of the official title ἰατροσοφιστής for those who gave public lectures on medical subjects (Bowersock op. cit.,66 f. with references).

Therefore, as Amundsen 1974,324 n. 20 remarks, Walsh 1970,172 is mistaken when, in his discussion of this story, he refers to this physician as 'an old apothecary'; see also on *medicus* below (In his translation of 1994 Walsh has 'physician').

senior: this adjective in itself connotes *auctoritas*; cf Cic. *Sen.* 60 *apex est autem senectutis auctoritas*. See Powell 1988,24 f. on the tradition of moralistic philosophical works on old age before and after Cicero.

prae ceteris: on the comparative use of *prae*, and on the revival of the archaic expression *prae ceteris* in the literary language of the second century A.D., see Callebat 1968,209. The expression occurs five times in the *Met.*, e.g. 8,21 (192,28-193,5); see *GCA* 1985,179 ad loc. See also above, on *senior prae ceteris ... medicus*.

compertae fidi: this respectable physician comes from a world wide apart from the one discussed below in the latter part of the note on *medicus*. Cf. the addition *fidi* to *medici* in 1,18 (16,13 f.); for a character opposite to this doctor see the *medicum ... notae perfidiae* ch. 25 (256,23 f.); see also on *fides* ch. 10 (244,15), and Appendix III. Konstan 1994,132 f. regards this doctor as a polar opposite to the old *educator* of ch. 4, who has since disappeared from the story.

It appears from e.g. *Apol.* 40,1 f. that Apuleius himself was interested in medical matters but realized how vague the dividing line was between the physician as an expert on medicines and the physician as an expert on poisons.

fidi: this was the original reading in F, changed by a later hand to *fidej*. *Fidi* as the genitive of *fides* is attested in *CIL* 2, 5042,3 (Neue-Wagener 1,574 f.). Gel. 9,14 gives many examples of a genitive in *-i* of nouns like *fames, acies, luxuries*, etc.

medicus: the introduction of a physician entails an expectation of *salus* (see on *salubre consilium* ch. 7: 241,23), not only for the innocent young man but also for this 'sick' society, where even justice is about to fail. The comparison of a city as a sick person, who needs a doctor, is a topos; cf. e.g. Plut. *Praecepta reip.ger.* 19 (*Mor.* 815b-c) Οἱ μὲν γὰρ ἰατροί, τῶν νοσημάτων ὅσα μὴ δύνανται παντάπασιν ἀνελεῖν, ἔξω τρέπουσιν εἰς τὴν ἐπιφάνειαν τοῦ σώματος· ὁ δὲ πολιτικός, ἂν μὴ δύνηται τὴν πόλιν ἀπράγμονα παντελῶς διαφυλάττειν, ἐν αὐτῇ γε πειράσεται τὸ ταρασσόμενον αὐτῆς καὶ στασιάζον ἀποκρύπτων ἰᾶσθαι καὶ διοικεῖν, ὡς ἂν ἥκιστα τῶν ἐκτὸς ἰατρῶν καὶ φαρμάκων δέοιτο. See Carrière 192 ad loc., with references. (For a psycho-analytical interpretation of the appearance of a physician here, see von Franz 1970,133 f. [= von Franz 1992,168 f.]).

From this and the previous notes (e.g. *senior prae ceteris ... medicus*) it has become clear that this physician does not belong in the intertextual world of 'doctors as unpunished killers' characteristic of the mime and *declamatio* (on this notion see Kudlien 1970,98 f. and Amundsen 1974,320 f., both with numerous literary references). The attempts of the *nouerca* and her slave, who themselves have all the features of stock characters of *declamatio* and mime (see on *uita miserum priuare iuuenem* ch. 4: 239,24), to avail themselves of this physician as a provider of poison will turn out to be a great mistake: this physician refuses explicitly to play that part (ch. 11: 244,28 f.; see comm. there). The failure of the *nouerca*'s murderous plans can therefore be attributed to a literary 'mésalliance'; see Appendix III. The murderess of the other inner story does not make the same mistake: she selects a *medicum ... notae perfidae* (ch. 25: 256,22 f.). See also on *centumque aureos solidos* ch. 9 (243,19).

orificium: it appears from *ThLL* s.v. *orificium* 976,70 f. that this word is attested first in Apuleius, who uses it of 'openings' of various objects (four times: 2,15: 37,16; 9,40: 234,18; 11,11: 275,10, and here). According to *ThLL*, this meaning is next found in Victorin. Poetov. *fabr. mundi* 8 (on Zach. 4,2) *lucerna cum septem orificiis*. Meaning 'mouth of an animal' *orificium* is attested in veterinary texts, e.g. Veg. *Mulom.* 2,87,1 (*ThLL* ibid. 977,7 f.).

ne ... temere: the *senior* acts with the wisdom of old people, often contrasted with the *temeritas* of the young. Cf. Cic. *Sen.* 20 *temeritas est uidelicet florentis aetatis, prudentia senescentis* with Powell 1988,147 ad loc., with references.

haec ad ordinem pertulit: although as recently as ch. 7 (242,3 f.) the narrator has told us that he was not present at the trial and therefore cannot report the speeches word for word, he now reports a speech by the old physician in direct discourse, and will do so again in ch. 11 (244,24 f.). For the attentive reader, therefore, the narrative that follows is a reversal not only as to content, but also as to form: since ch. 7 (242,1; see there, on *haec ... cognoui*) the narrative situation has again changed, and from now on it is possible to point to many elements in the narrative method that are characteristic of a homodiegetic auctorial narrator (see Introd. **3.5**). He is now reporting on the event as if he had been present in the audience as an actor-witness. See also above, on *quod...* ch. 7 (242,15), and on *perspiciens ... uerberonem blaterantem ... inconcinne causificantem* ch. 9 (243,23 f.).

ordinem: *ordo* (sc. *decurionum*) is used in this sense also e.g. Tac. *Ann.* 13,48,1; see Furneaux ad loc., and *OLD* s.v. *ordo* 4c for other examples.

243,11-14 'Quod aetatis sum, uobis adprobatum me uixisse gaudeo, nec patiar falsis criminibus petito reo manifestum homicidium perpetrari nec uos, qui iure iurando adstricti iudicatis, inductos seruuli mendacio peierare': 'Up to this old age of mine, I am pleased to have lived in a way approved by you, and therefore I will not permit a manifest murder to be perpetrated because the defendant is the victim of false accusations, nor will I permit you, who pass judgment under oath, to perjure yourselves, misled by the lies of a mere slave.'

Quod aetatis sum = *id, quod aetatis sum*; this should be regarded as an internal accusative with *uixisse*. *Adprobatum* then qualifies that accusative. Cf. e.g. Liv. 25,6,23 *quidquid postea uiximus, id omne destinatum ignominiae est.* For the partitive genitive see Callebat 1968,191.

uobis adprobatum me uixisse gaudeo: this is the very reason why the *senior* enjoys such *auctoritas* now; cf. Cic. *Sen.* 62 *non cani nec rugae repente auctoritatem arripere possunt, sed honeste acta superior aetas fructus capit auctoritatis extremos*, with Powell 233 f. ad loc.

uobis adprobatum: see *OLD* s.v. *approbo* 2 for *approbare* with a dative: 'to render acceptable ... (to), win approval (in the eyes of ...)'.

uixisse: this is Beroaldus' generally accepted emendation for *dixisse* in F.

nec patiar: a logical connection between the first part of the statement (*quod aetatis sum ... gaudeo*) and this second part is suggested by *nec*: 'you approve of my conduct in life, so that gives me the authority to keep you from ...'. Cf. Brandt-Ehlers 'und so werde ich nicht dulden'. The physician's characterization by the narrator as a man *auctoritatis praecipuae* is illustrated by his direct discourse. Compare his repetition of *non patiar* in ch. 11 (244,24) below (see note there).

patiar ... homicidium perpetrari ... uos ... peierare: *pati* with the accusative and infinitive construction also in 3,22 (68,23 f.). See Van der Paardt 1971,166 ad loc. on the various constructions with *patior*.

falsis criminibus petito reo: for the passive use of *petere* with an instrumental ablative cf. 4,13 (84,13) *orbitatis duplici plaga petiti* with *GCA* 1977,101.

petito reo: the correct word separation for *petitor eo* in F (and φ) was made by the second corrector in F (see Lütjohann 1873,447).

manifestum homicidium: this is contrasted with *falsis criminibus* (the physician is an accomplished speaker): 'by condemning an innocent defendant to death, you yourselves are committing a manifest murder, while the murder of which *he* is accused is based on false accusations and therefore is not manifest. See on *accusationis manifestis probationibus et ... ambagibus* ch. 6 (241,12 f.).

iure iurando adstricti: *OLD* s.v. *astringo* 8 (w. abl.): 'to place under obligation or restraint, bind (by laws, promises, etc.)' cites e.g. Cic. *Off.* 1,13,40 *astrictos iure iurando*.

Iure Iurando. *RE* 10,1257 s.v. *iusiurandum*, 3a 'Der Richtereid' [Steinwenter]: 'Sowohl der Richter im Privat-, wie der *iudex* im Strafprozesse mußten schon in ziemlich früher Zeit schwören, daß sie ihr Amt nach besten Wissen und Gewissen ausüben und das Urteil nicht nach Gunst oder Mißgunst fällen wollen'. See also Mommsen, *Röm.Strafr.* 395 and n. 2; cf. Sen. *Con.* 9,2,11 *damnaturi iurant nihil se gratiae, nihil precibus dare*.

inductos seruuli mendacio: *inducere* is often found in the *Met.* with the connotation of deceit; see *GCA* 1985,133 on 8,14 (187,19-24) and cf. 9,21 (219,10) with *GCA* 1995,191 ad loc. *ThLL* s.v. *induco* 1242,68 f. ('i.q. *pellicere, seducere* ..., sc. in errorem vel in scelus') gives examples from Cicero onward (see also on ch. 9: 243,30 *sic inductus*). The authoritative physician apparently does not need to mince his words: he lectures his fellow councillors on their carelessness in severe tones. A slave's evidence was always considered to be of little value; see Mommsen, *Röm.Strafr.* 412 f. and 439, and cf. Mod. *Dig.* 22,5,7 *serui responsio tunc credendum est, cum alia probatio ad eruendam ueritatem non est.*

seruuli: the diminutive is undoubtedly derogatory here (see the preceding note). See on *seruulo* ch. 1 (236,24); also *GCA* 1985,190 on 8,22 (194,12-18), with references.

peierare: Cic. *Off.* 3,29,108 explains: *non enim falsum iurare periurare est, sed quod 'ex animi tui sententia' iuraris, sicut uerbis concipitur more nostro, id non facere periurium est*. This explanation accords with the physician's following words.

243,14-17 'Ipse non possum calcata numinum religione conscientiam meam fallens perperam pronuntiare. Ergo, ut res est, de me cognoscite': 'I myself cannot trample the reverence for the gods underfoot, deceive my own conscience, and pronounce a wrong verdict. Learn therefore from me what the fact of the matter is.'

calcata ... religione: a frequent metaphor (see *OLD* s.v. *calco* 7b; Neuenschwander 1913,20), in other languages as well as Latin.

numinum religione: by swearing an oath (*iure iurando adstricti*) the members of the jury entered into an agreement with the gods (see on *iudicii religionem ... fidem suam* ch. 10: 244,15). Deliberate perjury (*peierare*) was always a transgression against the gods to whom one had sworn the oath. Cf. Cic. *Off*. 3,29,104 *est enim ius iurandum affirmatio religiosa: quod autem affirmate et quasi deo teste promiseris, id tenendum est*.

conscientiam meam: 'my conscience' (*OLD* s.v. *conscientia* 3a), but also 'my knowledge of the truth' (*OLD* s.v. 2b 'private knowledge'); the speaker then proceeds to share his knowledge of the truth with his audience: *ergo, ut res est ... cognoscite*.

perperam: this adverb means 1. 'wrongly, incorrectly' in the sense of 'against the rules (of orthography, pronunciation, etc.)'; also (1a) 'wrongly, by mistake'; 2. 'wrongly, wrongfully', in the sense of 'unjustly, unlawfully'; thus e.g. Cic. *Caec*. 71 *cum sciens perperam iudicarit*. Before Apuleius, the combination *perperam pronuntiare* is attested usually in meaning 1; thus e.g. Plin. *Ep*. 3,5,12 *cum lector quaedam perperam pronuntiasset*. In meaning 1a it is found in Suet. *Dom*. 10,4 *quod ... perperam praeco non consulem ... sed imperatorem pronuntiasset*. Apuleius here uses the phrase with *perperam* in the sense of 'unjustly' (2). Thus also Ulp. *Dig*. 8,5,8,4 *siquidem is optinuerit, qui seruitutem sibi defendit, non debet ei seruitus cedi, siue recte pronuntiatum est, quia habet, siue perperam, quia ...* . See *ThLL* s.v. *perperam* 1622,56 f. for this use of *perperam*, as the opposite of *recte*, in juridical contexts. Of course, the moral sense of *perperam* plays along in the words of the physician (see *GCA* 1985,79 on 8,7 (181,17-24).

pronuntiare: 'pronounce a verdict'; see above, on *eum ... insui ... pronuntiaret*.

ergo: Kroon 1989,241: 'ergo-units are meta-comments on what the speaker wants the hearer to do with previously supplied information'. The physician has indeed made it clear that the accusations are false, and that he knows they are false. Therefore he now invites his audience to learn the truth from him.

ut res est: the indicative emphasizes the truth of the promised information; Callebat 1968,290 and 356 f. discusses this type of phrase in the *Met*.

res: 'the actual facts', a frequent use of *res*, also in the *Met*.; cf. e.g. 4,9 (81,130) *res ipsa ... fidem sermoni ... dabit* with *GCA* 1977,77.

Now the narrator temporarily gives the floor to a sub-narrator, so that another inner tale is embedded in the inner tale. This inner tale is told by a homodiegetic auctorial narrator (see Introd. **3.5**): the physician relates an event in which he played a part as a character, namely when the poison was purchased by the slave. This event had already been mentioned in the framing tale (ch. 4: 239,25); there the impression was created that the story was told by a heterodiegetic auctorial narrator, giving the reader the idea that he, along with the narrator, was omniscient and omnipresent (see on *uenenum praesentarium comparat* ch. 4: 239,25).

Through this new presentation of the event the reader is forced to readjust his view: it appears that there was some important information that only now comes to light via a sub-narrator. This effect of surprise has been made possible by the changes in the narrative situation from the beginning of the story onward (see above, on *haec ad ordinem pertulit*). By allowing his narrator to observe the events from many different angles (see Lintvelt 1981,81 on 'polyscopical presentation'), thus 'directing' the manner in which the information is offered —— sometimes after being temporarily withheld —— , the concrete author offers his concrete readers a story full of unexpected turns. See on *potionem* ch. 9 (243,25).

CHAPTER IX

Surprising disclosures by the physician.

243,18-22 'Furcifer iste, uenenum praesentarium comparare sollicitus centumque aureos solidos offerens pretium, me non olim conuenerat, quod aegroto cuidam dicebat necessarium, qui morbi inextricabilis ueterno uehementer implicitus uitae se cruciatui subtrahere gestiret': 'The gallows-bird over there had come to me not long ago, anxious to buy a fast-working poison, and offering a hundred solid gold pieces as payment; he said that the poison was needed for a sick man who had a very bad case of lethargy, caused by an incurable disease, and eagerly wished to release himself from the torture of life.'

Furcifer iste, uenenum praesentarium comparare sollicitus: there is a striking similarity in vocabulary between this passage and ch. 4 (239,25) *furcifer uenenum praesentarium comparat*. This reminds the reader that it is the same event that is again mentioned here, this time by a sub-narrator who was an actor in the event (though in the earlier account the *furcifer comparat* the poison from an unnamed source). See on *res* ch. 8 (243,16).

Furcifer: see on *furcifer* ch. 4 (239,25).

praesentarium: the adjective occurs in comedy meaning 'present, immediate' (cf. Pl. *Poen.* 793; thus also Apul. *Met.* 2,25: 45,23) or, referring to money, 'cash' (cf. Pl. *Mos.* 913; *Poen.* 705 with Maurach 1975,271 = 1988,125); in the sense of 'taking effect immediately' it is used in Gel. 7,4,1 *uenenum ... non praesentarium, sed eiusmodi, quod mortem in diem proferret*, followed by our passage. Before Gellius this meaning is commonly expressed by *praesentaneus*, e.g. Sen. *Ep.* 95,25 *boletos ... nihil occulti operis iudicas facere, etiam si praesentanei non fuerunt?*; Plin. *Nat.* 20,9; ibid. 24,2 *praesentaneo ueneno*; [Quint.] *Decl.* 17,11 (Håkanson 342,4 f. *uirus praesentaneum*). Cf. below, ch. 25 (256,27) *momentarium uenenum* for 'a poison with instantaneous effect'.

RAC 10,1209 f. s.v. 'Gift' [Barb] gives an extensive survey of the knowledge and use of poison in antiquity, with references; see also *DNP* 4,1065 f. s.v. 'Gifte' [Touwaide].

comparare sollicitus: in the sense of 'very much interested, eager', and construed with the infinitive, *sollicitus* is found e.g. Sen. *Phaed.* 976 f. (*cur ... abes,) non sollicitus / prodesse bonis, nocuisse malis?*, and Sil. 7,442 *tempora sollicitus litis seruasse, Cupido*. This is the only example in the *Met.* of *sollicitus* with the infinitive; for other constructions with *sollicitus* see *GCA* 1995,88 on 9,8 (208,16); see Callebat 1968,316 f. on the use of the infinitive with adjectives in the *Met.*

centumque aureos solidos: one *aureus* is 25 *denarii* (D.C. 55,12,4; Lucian. *Pseudolog.* 30; the drachma had been equalized to the *denarius*). So a sum of 2500 *denarii* is involved here, which equals *HS* 10.000 (in ch. 25: 256,26 a *medicus* is offered *HS* 50.000 for poison). Of course this extremely high price should be taken, within this fictional frame, as 'a vast amount of money'; in connection with these high prices for poison, Duncan Jones [2]1982,251 points out that in these sums allowance has been made for bribe money, but he remarks: 'Apuleius's commodity prices no doubt had a point for contemporaries, who would have been readily aware of the author's deliberate exaggerations and minimisations' (see also

GCA 1985,220 on prices in the *Met.*).

The high price is not only a further indication of the wealth of the woman who commissioned the purchase (see on *uillulas* ch. 4: 239,15); it illustrates also the misunderstanding of the prospective murderers, who approach this physician as the type of the avaricious doctor, widespread in literature, whose dubious services can be bought at a price (see on *medicus* ch. 8: 243,8-9 above). See Kudlien 1970,97 f. (especially 102) on the literary type of the physician as an 'unpunished killer', often linked with that of the greedy physician; this literary motif reflects a persistent prejudice against physicians among the public. Cf. Plin. *Nat.* 29,2-22 passim (e.g. ibid. 20 *quid enim uenenorum fertilius aut unde plures testamentorum insidiae*?). The unreliable, avaricious physician is a well-known character in comedy, epigram, and satire (extensively discussed by Brecht 1930,45 f.; cf. e.g. Lucill. in *AP* 11,257; Agathas in *AP* 11,382; Mart. 6,53), but he is also a type in the oldest forms of the mime known to us (Reich 1903,1,58; 469). In Quint. *Decl.* 321, where the brother of a deceased person and a *medicus* accuse each other of murder by poisoning, the brother suggests that the physician has acted from greed since he would inherit from the deceased. This character is also found in the Greek novel: in Xen. *Ephes.* 3,5,5 f. Anthia takes advantage of the doctor's greed in order to get what she wants; cf. also Ach. Tat. 4,4,8 οἶδεν οὖν τὴν θεραπείαν ὁ ἐλέφας καὶ προῖκα οὐκ ἀνοίγει τὸ στόμα, ἀλλ' ἔστιν ἰατρὸς ἀλαζὼν καὶ τὸν μισθὸν πρῶτος αἰτεῖ.

In collections of anecdotes the physician is described the same way, cf. *Philogelos* 139 'A Sidonian doctor received a legacy of 1000 drachmas in the will of a man who had been his patient. He turned up at the funeral and complained about the smallness of his bequest. Later, when he had been called to treat the dead man's son who had fallen ill in his turn, the doctor said, "Leave me 5000 drachmas in your will, and I'll cure you the way I cured your father"' (transl. Baldwin 1983; see also his note p. 87). Kudlien 1970,101 f. shows with examples how, from the Hippocratic oath onward, both Greek and Roman medical authors challenge and defend themselves against this low opinion of physicians held by the public. See Horstmanshoff 1992,51 f., with references, on the 'bad press' the physician had in the Greek and Roman literature of the Roman Empire.

Lucian varies with two types of doctor figure: the greedy physician is absent in his work, but we do find both the charlatan and a type similar to the doctor in our story: the physician as the mouthpiece of common sense, 'qui incarne la mesure dans une société en délire' (Bompaire 1958,214; see also ibid. n. 2 and Anderson 1976,43 and 173 f.).

aureos solidos: 'solid gold pieces'; cf. 9,18 (216,23-26) *solidos aureos*, where Myrmex yields to the sight of the *aurei solidi*. In our story, however, the physician stresses the fact that he does not accept the offered money. Eventually he will receive it anyway, as a reward for saving the lives of both sons (see on *bono medico sinuntur aurei* ch. 12: 245,25). In both of these passages the adjective *solidus* enhances the temptation presented by the coins: in 9,18 it makes Myrmex's weakness easier to understand, and here it renders the physician's self-control more impressive. The adjective has no special monetary meaning: the *aureus* was always of solid gold, though its weight was gradually reduced; see *RE* s.v. *aureus* 2547 [Kubitschek]. *ThLL* s.v. *aureus* 1490,42 f. mistakenly interprets *aureos* in 9,18 as an adjective (our passage is not mentioned); the noun would then be *solidos*, but the *solidus* as a light gold coin was not introduced until about 312 A.D. by Constantine. See *RE* s.v. *solidus* 920 f. [Regling], where the adjective and its use in these passages in Apuleius are also discussed. For the *aureus* as a means of payment of large sums see

RAC 9 s.v. 'Geld' [Bogaert], especially 832 f. The subject is also discussed in great detail in *RE* s.v. 'Münzwesen', 481 f. [Regling], on *aureus*.

offerens pretium: on the attention paid in the *Met.* to sales transactions, see on *sine pretio suum fecerat* ch. 13 (246,3). Offering the *pretium* on the spot is an important element in the sales transaction known as *emptio uenditio*. See Summers 1967,88 on 1,24 f.

non olim: 'only recently'. As a phrase 'in fig. litot.' this is first attested in Apuleius' *Met.*: here and 11,15 (277,27); after that in Tert. *Mart.* 4,5 and later Christian authors (*ThLL* s.v. *olim* 563,23 f.). Since the statement that the slave went out to buy poison there have been no concrete references to the passage of time, only a continuous suggestion of a very rapid sequence of events (ch. 5: 239,27 f.: there is not even time for the murderers to give the prepared potion to their victim, for the wrong person is already drinking it; after the accident the father comes home *mox ... ocius*; see further on *uixdum ... et statim ...* ch. 6: 241,1 f., and *ilico* ch. 7: 241,23).

aegroto cuidam: see Van Mal - Maeder 1994,216 f. for a discussion of instances in the *Met.*, where *quidam* intensifies an adjective.

qui morbi inextricabilis ueterno uehementer implicitus uitae se cruciatui subtrahere gestiret: the context shows clearly that the physician is not shocked or indignant at the request to help a terminally ill person commit suicide, but that he becomes suspicious because of the inconsistency of the slave's story. For a physician to be asked, in more or less guarded terms, to help end an incurably ill person's life was something that happened in real life and was generally accepted. See Van Hooff 1990,122 f., 157 f., and 184 f., with an extensive bibliography 283 f. It is, however, his observation of the slave *blaterantem atque inconcinne causificantem* that arouses the doctor's suspicion and causes him to consider the possibility of murder. The physician renders the slave's words in free indirect discourse, which enables the reader to conclude that they make no sense. Indeed, not only is the illness described in very vague terms (see the next note); it is also most improbable that someone suffering from *ueternus* is at the same time lucid enough to utter the express wish (which is clearly indicated by *gestiret*) to 'release himself from the torture of life' (see the next note on *ueternus* as a syndrome).

morbi inextricabilis ueterno implicitus: this probably suggests a comatose condition resulting from a serious disease, which is (deliberately) described in vague terms as a *morbus inextricabilis*. In any case it is a condition of unconsciousness, which will make it impossible for someone to actively '*gestire*' to end his suffering (see the preceding note). Most translators solve the problem of the cryptic phrase by translating *ueternus* as 'long duration' or, as Hanson does, 'slow decay'. However, no occurrences can be found of *ueternus* in that sense. Literally the phrase means 'enveloped in the *ueternus* of a *morbus inextricabilis*' (inversely Amm. 16,12,66 *morbo ueterni consumptus est* 'he is consumed by the disease *ueternus*'). Scazzoso's literal translation 'colpito ... dal languore di una inesplicabile malattia' is to be preferred. There are many descriptions of *ueternus* as a syndrome, 'a morbid state of torpor or lassitude' (*OLD* s.v. *ueternus* 1), especially in old people (but not only old people; cf. Gel. 4,19,1; Apul. *Fl.* 17,8 *desuetudo omnibus pigritiam, pigritia ueternum parit*; Vallette ibid. 'engourdissement'); e.g. Pl. *Men.* 891 *num eum ueternus aut aqua intercus tenet?*, where Jones translates *ueternus* as 'coma'. Plin. *Nat.* (e.g. 20,24; 25; 43; 138 et al.) mentions certain herbs as medicine for *ueternosi* or, as these patients are also called, *lethargici*.

inextricabilis: the adjective means both 'insoluble' (*OLD* s.v. 1c) and 'that one cannot escape or get free from' (*OLD* 1b; also said of an illness, e.g. Plin. *Nat.* 20,232 *semen (lapathi) stomachi inextricabilia uitia sanat*). Although both connotations apply here, only one of them can be retained in the translation. Because of *implicitus* 'entangled in', a translation like 'incurable' (i.e. 'that one cannot get rid of') may be preferable, and this is what practically all translators opt for, e.g. Helm-Krenkel 'unheilbare Krankheit'. Scazzoso, however, has 'una inesplicabile malattia'; he is probably the only one who has made an attempt to have his translation reflect the slave *inconcinne causificantem* (see the two previous notes).

implicitus: 'enmeshed, enveloped'; see *GCA* 1977,37 on 4,3 (76,3-5). Frequently in a context of illness, e.g. Lucr. 6,1232; Nepos *Cim.* 3,4; *Ages.* 8,6; Plin. *Ep.* 7,27,3; see Weissenborn-Müller on Liv. 23,34,11 for instances in Livy.

uitae se cruciatui subtrahere: this phrase could be added to those in the list of 'suicidal vocabulary' given by Van Hooff 1990,246 f. In the *Met.* also 8,9 (184,8) *aerumnabili uitae sese subtrahere*. In a context of suicide, *subtrahere* is found e.g. Liv. 8,39,14 *ipse morte uoluntaria ignominiae se ac supplicio subtraxit*; Quint. *Inst.* 7,4,39 *qui mori uult ut se legum actionibus subtrahat*; Sen. *Dial.* 6 (*Cons.M.*),26,2; Plin. *Ep.* 2,11,9.

uitae cruciatui: the combination *cruciatus uitae* can be traced back to Enn. *scen.* 48 (cited by Cic. *de orat.* 3,218) *terribilem minatur uitae cruciatum et necem*. ThLL s.v. *cruciatus* 1219,67 f. mentions in addition to the Ennius passage only Porph. ad Hor. *S.* 1,1,78 *pulcher et grauis sensus recusantis diuitias, quae cruciatum uitae domino adferant*.

For *cruciare* in the context of prolonging a patient's life unnecessarily cf. Plin. *Ep.* 2,20,8 (Regulus, keen on an inheritance from the rich Velleius Blaesus, who is terminally ill, reproaches the doctors) *quousque miserum cruciatis? quid inuidetis bona morte cui dare uitam non potestis?*.

243,22-25 'At ego, perspiciens malum istum uerberonem blaterantem atque inconcinne causificantem certusque aliquod moliri flagitium, dedi quidem potionem, dedi; ...': 'But I perceived that the evil scoundrel was just babbling away and that his reasoning made no sense, and I was convinced that he was planning some kind of criminal act. True, I gave him a potion, oh yes I did; ...'

At ego: in contrast with *furcifer iste* above. In this way the speaker introduces with some self-confidence his own shrewd reaction to the slave's babbling; see the next note, and on *At ego* ch. 13 (246,1).

perspiciens ... uerberonem blaterantem ... inconcinne causificantem: the reader of the *Met.* at this moment in the story could treat the remarks made by the main narrator the same way as this physician treats the remarks made by the slave. Although the narrator mentioned explicitly (ch. 7: 242,3 f.) that — and why — he is unable to render the speeches verbatim, that is nevertheless what he does here (see on *haec ad ordinem pertulit* ch. 8: 243,10). Thus the reader finds the main narrator *blaterantem atque inconcinne causificantem*, too; this is a role which the main narrator of the *Met.* imposes on his audience on several occasions and which, as Winkler 1985,79, in his discussion of our passage, remarks, resembles the reader's role in the modern detective story (cf. 9,30: 225,10 f. *sed forsitan lector scrupulosus* with *GCA* 1995,257 f. ad loc.; see also on *sic inductus* below).

uerberonem: see on *uerberone* ch. 7 (242,23).

blaterantem: for *blaterare* 'blather' and its use in Apuleius and other authors, see *GCA* 1977,179 on 4,24 (93,4-5) and *GCA* 1995,103 on 9,10 (210,8-10).

Through this vocabulary the physician illustrates that he is not impressed, and that he perceives (*perspiciens*) his visitor's exaggerated and convoluted choice of words (cf. above, on *morbi inextricabilis ueterno, uitae ... cruciatui*) at once as *blaterare*.

inconcinne causificantem: the c-c-c-c alliteration calls attention to this unusual expression for 'devising *causae* that are contradictory to each other'. In the slave's words described above one can, as is suggested in the notes there, detect the *inconcinnitas* of his reasoning, but one can also imagine that the doctor is summarizing a longer conversation, in which he asked the slave for some more details about the 'patient'.

inconcinne: the adverb *concinne* occurs frequently, but this is the first attestation of *inconcinne*, according to ThLL s.v. *inconcinne* 998,81 f.; it is later found in Aug. *Doct.Chr.* 2,16,26, and as a grammatical term in Priscian *G.L* 3,111,14 f. *si incongrua sit* (sc. *ratio contextus*), *soloecismum faciet, quasi elementis orationis inconcinne coeuntibus*. The form *inconcinniter* is attested only Gel. 10,17,2 *causam ... uertit ... in eam rem, quam tum agebat, non inconcinniter* (ThLL s.v. *inconcinniter* 999,3 f.).

OLD s.v. *inconcinne* translates the adverb in our passage as 'inelegantly, clumsily'. However, *inconcinne* is not an aesthetic judgement on the literary quality of the slave's speech; it refers to the incoherent, incongruous (cf. the grammatical term in Priscian) *causae*. On the etymology of *concinnare* see on *concinnabat* ch. 13 (246,8). Monteil 1964,182 f. gives for *concinne* in the meaning 'logically' among other examples Cic. *ND* 2,69 *concinneque, ut multa, Timaeus, qui cum in historia dixisset, qua nocte natus Alexander esset, eadem Dianae Ephesiae templum deflagrauisse, adiunxit minime id esse mirandum, quod Diana, cum in partu Olympiadis adesse uoluisset, afuisset domo*.

causificantem: the verb is attested only Pl. *Aul.* 755 f. *haud causificor quin eam / ego habeam potissimum* and here (see ThLL s.v. *caus(s)ificor* 704,54 f.); Callebat 1968,514 points out the accumulation of words from comedy in this passage: *uerbero, blaterare, causificari*.

aliquod moliri flagitium: *eum* is to be supplied. On this mild form of ellipsis in the *Met.*, see on *exasperandum ... leniendum* ch. 4 (239,3 f.).

aliquod flagitium: a euphemism, for it is clear to everybody that it stands for 'murder'.

dedi ... dedi: by repeating these words the physician emphasizes the fact that he has given, not sold, the *potio*. In addition, the epanalepsis will arouse the interest of his audience even more, so that they will prick up their ears to hear further details. In view of his previous words they had expected to hear *non dedi*, rather than *dedi*. Epanalepsis occurs frequently in the *Met.* in lively direct discourse, reflecting, as Callebat 1968,105 remarks, a spontaneous dialogue, in which the speaker, perhaps with an accompanying gesture (Hofmann *LU* 58 f.), emphasizes a phrase in a natural manner. See also Bernhard 1927,232 f. with examples, and cf. e.g. 3,16 (63,23-24) *audiui ... audiui* with Van der Paardt 1971,122 f. ad loc. Elsewhere in direct discourse, too, the physician makes the impression of a fierce and emphatic speaker: cf. ch. 11 (244,24 f.) *non patiar ... non patiar ...* with comm.

potionem: 'vox media': only in ch. 11 (245,1) the physician will reveal that this *potio* was a *uenenum soporiferum*. Although *uenenum* in itself is a 'vox media' too (Rayment 1959,50 f.), in the context of this story it has been used so often in malam partem, without any addition, that it is immediately understood as 'poison' (cf. ch. 4: 239,25; ch. 5: 240,3; 240,16; ch. 7: 242,19; ch. 9: 243,18). See also *GCA* 1985,114 f. on 8,11 (185,28-186,5). The speaker opts for the even more neutral *potio*, which can refer both to a medicinal draught (*OLD* s.v. *potio*[1] 3a) and a harmful potion (*OLD* 3b). Quint. *Decl.* 321 (see above, on *centumque aureos solidos*) repeatedly uses *potio* and *uenenum* as our passage does, e.g. 321,28 *potionem dedisti aut remedii aut ueneni: si remedii dedisses, uiueret. non id apparet. ergo uenenum dedisti*. On reminiscences of *declamationes* in this part of the story, see on *quae ipse finxerat ... incipit* ch. 7 (242,14 f.).

In this phase of the story *potionem* will still be understood as 'poison' both by the fictive audience and the linear reader, but the re-reader will appreciate the ambiguity: this *potio* has been a life-saving, not a lethal, drug for two people, as will be shown later. This first part of the physician's disclosures is already surprising because, thanks to his version of the slave's purchase of the poison, the reader gets an entirely new insight into what happened during that transaction (see above, on *furcifer iste ... sollicitus*). Although the most surprising disclosure by this sub-narrator is still to come (ch. 11: 244,28 f.), the reader will realize even now that this speaker is an actor who knows and perceives more than the narrator who was speaking until ch. 8 (243,10; see there, on *haec ad ordinem pertulit*, and see on *meis temperatam manibus ... potionem* ch. 11: 245,6 f.).

243,25-30 '... sed futurae quaestioni praecauens non statim pretium, quod offerebatur, accepi, sed "ne forte aliquis", inquam, "istorum, quos offers, aureorum nequam uel adulter repperiatur, in hoc ipso sacculo conditos eos anulo tuo praenota, donec altera die nummulario praesente comprobentur" ': '... but on my guard for a future investigation I did not immediately accept the sum of money that was being offered, but said: "Lest perhaps, among those gold coins that you are offering, a false or debased one is found, you must put them away in this pouch right here and mark them with your signet ring until they can be certified as genuine tomorrow in the presence of a money-changer."'

futurae quaestioni praecauens: the physician expects an investigation because he suspects that a murder is being planned (see on *aliquod flagitium* above). He knows the law and is aware that he, as the seller of the deadly poison, would be punishable under the *Lex Cornelia de ueneficiis*, as quoted Cic. *Clu.* 54,148 (sc. *uenenum*) *quicumque fecerit uendiderit emerit habuerit dederit ... deque eius capite quaerito*; Marc. *Dig.* 48,8,1,1. 1,3 pr. (Mommsen, *Röm.Strafr.* 636).

praecauens: here with a dative. For the many different constructions with *praecaueo* 'per totam Latinitatem', see *ThLL* s.v. 396,5 f.; at 397,7 f. it appears that its use with the dative is attested first in Apuleius; see also *Met.* 7,16 (166,11-15) with *GCA* 1981,188 ad loc. *ThLL* quotes after Apul. e.g. Tert. *Mon.* 9,10 *(Christus) ei soli causae permittens repudium, si forte praeuenerit* (sc. *adulterium), cui praecauetur*; and P. Nol. *Carm.* 31,408 *procurare bonis praeque cauere malis*.

non statim ... pretium accepi: this means that the transaction had not yet been concluded (see on *sine pretio suum fecerat* ch. 13: 246,3).

aliquis: on the increasing frequency (in Latin and in the *Met.*) of the use of *aliquis* in negative sentences, see *GCA* 1985,113 on 8,11 (185,23-24).

nequam uel adulter: these adjectives have different connotations: *nequam* 'worthless', i.e. not made of gold at all; *adulter* 'adulterated, debased', i.e. mixed with a less valuable metal. See the following notes.

nequam: when it refers to people (frequently *nequissimus*) it always has a moral connotation: 'depraved, inferior'. When describing objects, it has no moral colouring, e.g. Pl. *As.* 178

piscis ... nequam est nisi recens; *Cas*. 9 f. (also referrring to gold coins) *nunc nouae ... comoediae / multo sunt nequiores quam nummi noui*; Var. *Men*. 241 *in bona segete nullum est spicum nequam*. See *OLD* s.v. *nequam* 1.

adulter: for the meaning 'non genuinus, falsatus' cf. Ov. *Ars* 3,643 *nomine cum doceat, quid agamus, adultera clauis* (a pun on the two meanings of the adjective: *adultera clauis* is a 'false key', but also 'the key that opens the door to adultery'); Man. 2,22 *arbusta uagis essent quod adultera pomis*; Plin. *Nat*. 33,114 *id* (sc. *minii genus*) *esse adulterum*; 34,113 *siue sinceram siue adulteram*. (sc. *aeruginem*). Our passage is the first referring to money; comparable is Hier. *Ep*. 119,11,2 *nummus adulter*; *C.Th*. 9,22,1 *figuratum solidum adultera imitatione*.

sacculo: here a true diminutive (cf. *GCA* 1985,252 on 8,28: 200,1-9 on *sacculus* = *saccus*). *Sacculus* 'a small bag, pouch, purse' is a common term from Lucil. 1155 Marx onward (Callebat 1968,33); cf. e.g. Catul. 13,8 *plenus sacculus est aranearum*; Juv. 11,27; 14,138; Mart. 5,39,7; 11,3,6 *quid prodest? nescit sacculus ista meus*. Cf. Scaev. *Dig*. 18,3,8 *sacculum cum pecunia signatorum signis obsignauit*.

anulo tuo: it appears from ch. 10 (244,19) that this is an iron signet ring of the type slaves were allowed to wear. See *RE* s.v. 'Ringe' [Ganschinietz], esp. 827 f., on the important function of signet rings in Roman society. Cf. Plin. *Nat*. 33,23 on slaves who do their utmost to conceal the fact that their signet ring is made of iron; see also Petr. 32,3 with Smith 1975,69 ad loc.

In the other inner tale too (chs. 23-28), a signet ring plays a role. There it is used by the jealous wife to lure the girl to her death (see ch. 24: 255,26 and 256,2 f.); here the physician puts it to use to save people's lives. See Appendix III for other parallel or contrasting motifs in the two inner tales.

praenota: the compound is not attested before Apuleius, who uses it sometimes 'vi praeverbii fere evanida' (*ThLL* s.v. *praenoto* 737,7 f. cites several passages in Apuleius, followed by examples in Christian authors; cf. also *Met*. 6,25: 147,4-6 with *GCA* 1981,26 ad loc.). In our passage, however, the prefix has 'local' significance: 'praenotatur id, cui quid anteponitur, quod nota afficitur', according to *ThLL* 735,62, which gives our passage as an example for this meaning, followed by P. Nol. *Ep*. 32,12 *omne cubiculum* (sc. *basilicae*) *binis per liminum frontes uersibus praenotatur*. The compound with temporal *prae-* is attested from Tert. *Ieiun*. 2 onward, and then very frequently in Christian authors (*ThLL* 736,53 f.).

donec ... comprobentur: *donec* with a subjunctive has a final connotation here. For this use in Latin (especially from Tacitus onward) in general and in Apuleius in particular, see *GCA* 1981,273 on 7,28 (176,7-11), with references.

nummulario: the physician acts in a perfectly correct manner: in transactions involving a great amount of money and therefore requiring payment in silver or gold coinage, it was customary to have the coins tested by an *argentarius* or *nummularius*. If this expert was not immediately available, the purse of money was sealed (as it is here) to submit the money for testing later on; cf. Scaev. *Dig*. 18,3,8 (quoted above, on *sacculo*); African. *Dig*. 46,3,39 *si soluturus pecuniam tibi, iussu tuo signatam eam apud nummularium, quoad probaretur, deposuerim* (see Norden 1912,168 f.). The term *nummularius* is first attested from the first century A.D., referring to the 'money changer' who was called *argentarius* in Ciceronian Latin. See *RE* s.v. *nummularius* [Herzog]; *GCA* 1977,78 on 4,9 (81,16-19), *nummularius*, with further references.

243,30-244,3 'Sic inductus signauit pecuniam, quam exinde, ut iste repraesentatus est iudicio, iussi de meis aliquem curriculo taberna promptam adferre et en ecce perlatam coram exibeo': 'So he was talked into sealing the money; and as soon as he was brought before the court I ordered one of my people to fetch it from my surgery and bring it here, at the double, and look! it has been brought, and I am showing it for all to see.'

Sic inductus: compare *inductus seruuli mendacio* ch. 8 (243,14), also in the speech of this physician, and see the note ad loc. on *inducere* 'mislead'. The speaker himself takes pride in not being easily misled by the words of someone else. See above, on *perspiciens ... uerberonem blaterantem ... inconcinne causificantem*, on the reader's role, typical for the *Met.*, in weighing the doctor's words. A reader of the *Met.*, too, must be careful not to let himself become 'inductus' by the words of the main narrator.

exinde, ut iste repraesentatus est: the *lector scrupulosus*, who may have been wondering why the physician made his appearance so late, now receives an answer to that question: the physician recognized the slave only at the moment he was brought in to testify, and then he had to send for the evidence.

exinde ut: in the sense of *ubi primum* it is attested first in Apuleius (*ThLL* s.v. *exinde* 1509,7 f.) *Apol.* 3,10; 24,9; 98,1; and *Met.* 2,13 (36,8); cf. *exinde cum* in 1,24 (22,15). After Apuleius it is found in Porph. ad Hor. *Ep.* 1,19,3 (see Callebat 1968,534). In earlier (sc. than Apuleius) Latin *exinde ut* means 'according as'; e.g. Pl. *Mos.* 227 *ut famast homini, exin solet pecuniam inuenire* (see Sonnenschein ad loc. and Maurach 1975,280 and 1988,128 on Pl. *Poen.* 754); Var. *R.* 1,20,4 *in qua re alii asellis, alii uaccis ac mulis utuntur, exinde ut pabuli facultas est*.

curriculo: an allusion to the stock type of comedy, the *seruus currens*; cf. Ter. *Eun.* 36, with Tromaras ad loc. The adverbial ablative *curriculo* (cf. Greek δρόμῳ) is frequent in comedy (Duckworth on Pl. *Epid.* 14). After that, according to *ThLL* s.v. *curriculum* 1506,32 f., it is not found until Gel. 17,8,8; Apul. *Apol.* 63,4 (in a context quite comparable to this: *iussi curriculo iret aliquis et ex hospitio meo Mercuriolum afferret*); *Fl.* 2,1,1, and here.

taberna: in general 'place of business'; here the doctor's 'surgery'; cf. Cic. *Clu.* 63,178 *instructam ... et ... medicinae exercendae causa tabernam dedit*. See Jackson 1988,65 f., with notes, on *tabernae medicinae* excavated at Pompeii and other places.

For the separative ablative without a preposition (*taberna promptam*) see *GCA* 1985,27 on 8,1 (176,15-18).

en ecce: this combination occurs 4 times in the *Met.* (see *GCA* 1985,224 on 8,26: 197,14-17); outside the *Met.* it is rare. To this combination applies what *GCA* 1985,139 remarks on *en* (on 8,14: 188,4): 'not only in colloquial language, but also in fierce and pathetic passages'. Here and in 11,15 (277,24, in the priest's address) the element of pathos seems to prevail, as in the passages where this combination occurs in other authors, e.g. Sen. *Oed.* 1004 and *Phoen.* 42; [Quint.] *Decl.* 11,9 (Håkanson 229,4). With these words the physician asks the audience in solemn tones to give their undivided attention to an important piece of evidence, which he expects to be highly effective.

exibeo: thus F and φ; a different hand added a *h* in φ. But the spelling in F can be retained since the form without *h* is attested quite often, e.g. in inscriptions (cf. *ThLL* s.v. *exhibeo* 1416,12 f. 'saepe sine aspiratione scribitur' with many examples). Cf. also *Met.*

6,24 (146,13) and 11,13 (275,30); also *Apol.* 44,2 and 46,4, where originally the non-aspirated form is given in the manuscripts.

For *exhibeo* used in a legal context, in the sense of producing a person or evidence in court, see *ThLL* s.v. 1419,60-1420,35. Cf. e.g. Ulp. *Dig.* 43,29,1 and 43,29,3,8 *exhibere est in publicum producere et uidendi, tangendique hominis facultatem praebere; proprie autem exhibere est extra secretum habere.*

244,3-6 'Videat et suum sigillum recognoscat. Nam quem ad modum eius ueneni frater insimulari potest, quod iste comparauerit?': 'Let him see it and recognize his own seal. For how can the brother be blamed for the poison which that fellow bought?'

Videat ... recognoscat: the two hortatory subjunctives make the physician's words quite formal. Cf. *Apol.* 69,6 (where the speaker also presents a letter that incriminates his adversary) *legat, sua sibi uoce suisque uerbis sese reuincat.*

nam: the particle explains the preceding command. See Kroon 1989,234 f. for the function of *nam* as a 'connective particle, marking a supporting text unit'; also Kroon 1995,146 f.

ueneni: as a genitive of the crime with *insimulari* it cannot but be understood as *ueneficii*; as the antecedent of *quod iste comparauerit* it has the concrete meaning 'poison'. The physician ends his argument with an extremely pithy, but therefore somewhat elliptical, rhetorical question. In the *declamationes* many examples can be found of this kind of short, often elliptically phrased, rhetorical questions, which suggests that there is an intertextual reference here; the more so because obscure and complicated poisoning cases are quite frequent in the *declamationes* (e.g. Quint. *Decl.* 246; 268; 306; 307; 321; 327; 335; 350; 377; 380; 381). Cf. e.g. [Quint.] *Decl.* 17,11 (Håkanson 342,8 f.): a son, accused by his father of trying to poison him, maintains that he prepared the poison to commit suicide; after showing that it would have been impossible for him to administer this poison to his father, he asks: *rogo cui paraui uenenum quod dare non possum nisi mihi?.*

Thus this story, introduced as a *tragoediam, non fabulam* (see on ch. 2: 237,12-14), has ended up, step by step, entirely in the sphere of the *declamationes*, as we have already seen a few times during this trial (see on *quae ipse finxerat ... incipit* ch. 7: 242,14 f.). See also Appendix I and III on the generic shifts in this story.

quod ... comparauerit: the exclamatory main clause *quem ad modum ... insimulari potest* supposes a future situation (after assessment of the new evidence) in which it will be impossible to charge the innocent young man of poisoning; this may explain the use of the futurum exactum in the subordinate relative clause (see LHSz 2,323 f. on the futurum exactum in subordinate clauses).

CHAPTER X

The slave reacts in a suspicious way but persists in his earlier evidence.

244,7-13 Ingens exinde uerberonem corripit trepidatio et in uicem humani coloris succedit pallor infernus perque uniuersa membra frigidus sudor emanabat: tunc pedes incertis alternationibus commouere, modo hanc, modo illam capitis partem scalpere et ore semiclauso balbuttiens nescio quas a*f*annas effutire, ut eum nemo prorsus a culpa uacuum merito crederet: Thereupon an immense panic seized the scoundrel, a pallor like that of a shade of the underworld replaced his normal, human colour, and over his entire body he broke out in a cold sweat: in addition he kept shifting from one foot to the other, scratched now this side of his head, now the other, and stammering with his mouth half shut he poured out random excuses, so that, with good reason, absolutely no one believed him to be clear of guilt.

In this description, the physical symptoms of the slave's panic have many points in common with the symptoms of lovesickness described by Sappho *fr.* 31 L.-P. Apuleius could find the description of a panic-stricken reaction similar to Sappho's symptoms of love as early as Lucr. 3,152 f. *uerum ubi uementi magis est commota metu mens, / consentire animam totam per membra uidemus / sudoresque ita palloremque exsistere toto / corpore et infringi linguam uocemque aboriri, / caligare oculos, sonere auris, succidere artus, / denique concidere ex animi terrore uidemus / saepe homines* (Cavallini 1978,91 f.). Apuleius' description, however, differs from those by Sappho (and Catullus 51) and Lucretius, in that it restricts itself to the registration of external appearances.

Ingens ... trepidatio: the hyperbaton results in the *uerbero* being literally entangled in *ingens ... trepidatio*. The first word in the sentence, *ingens*, forms the effective opening of the eloquent description of the slave's panicky reaction. One might expect that the dénouement is close now; but it will take more than the suspicious reaction of the slave to bring it about.

On the hyperbolical use of *ingens* in poetry see Maurach [2]1989,34, with references; Skutsch on Enn. *Ann.* 205 *ingentibus signis* points out the great frequency of this adjective in Vergils *Aeneid*. In Vergil *ingens* is often used with abstract nouns (as it is here and e.g. 9,34: 229,5 *ingenti pauore*); e.g. *A.* 1,208 *curisque ingentibus aeger*. In prose, Sallust appears to have a preference for this adjective, and he too uses it often with abstract nouns; see e.g. *Cat.* 7,6 *gloriam ingentem* with Vrɘtska 178 ad loc. See also Löfstedt 1936,72 on the development of the more powerful and emphatic *ingens*, which displaces *magnus* more and more in colloquial language, but eventually is ousted by *grandis*, which survives in the Romance languages. This development has not taken place in Apuleius' works, as appears from Oldfather: 21 occurrences of *ingens*, 26 of *grandis*, more than 100 of *magnus*. The use of *ingens* here may therefore be considered a poetic hyperbole.

exinde: 'thereupon'. Even though the temporal aspect prevails, an 'admixture of the causal sense' can be observed (*GCA* 1981,32 on 6,26: 147,22-24.

uerberonem: see on *uerberone* ch. 7 (242,23).

corripit ... effutire: note the variations in verbal forms: two historical presents, one imperfect, then three historical infinitives. See *GCA* 1985,258 on 8,29 (200,12-22) s.v. *efferantur* for the frequent variation of present and imperfect in the *Met*. Bernhard 1927,152 f. gives more examples but considers it merely a 'Streben nach Mannigfaltigkeit'. Callebat 1968,427 f., on the other hand, places this phenomenon in a wider context of narrative texts in general and also sees differences in nuance. His comment on 5,7 (108,9 f.) applies here as well: the historical present indicates a quick succession of events, the imperfect gives a description of the situation (see also Kenney ad loc.). The description is continued here with a series of historical infinitives: *commouere ... scalpere ... effutire*. As has been remarked before, series of infinitives in the *Met*. occur usually in a context with imperfects; see on *deprecari ... compescere* ch. 6 (241,17 f.).

in uicem: 'in place of' (see *GCA* 1977,49 on 4,4: 77,19-22), but also with the connotation 'by turns, alternately' (*OLD* s.v. *inuicem* 2) because turning alternately red and pale is often mentioned as a typical sign of a guilty conscience (see on *pedes ... effutire* below).

pallor infernus: the slave is 'scared to death'. The psychosomatic symptom of turning pale with fear is here joined with the topical paleness of the shades in the underworld; thus also e.g. Verg. *A*. 4,644 *pallida morte futura*, where Austin ad loc. refers to Luc. 7,129 f. *multorum pallor in ore / mortis uenturae faciesque simillima fato*. *Pallor, pallens*, and *pallidus* are constant epithets in the description of shades in the underworld, e.g. Verg. *A*. 8,244 f. *regna ... pallida*; cf. Luc. 1,456 and 5,627 f. *non caeli nox illa fuit: latet obsitus aer / infernae pallore domus nimbisque grauatus*. Cf. in the *Met*. the description of the shade of Tlepolemus, who appears to Charite *pallore deformem attollens faciem* (8,8: 183,8-10; see *GCA* 1985,90 ad loc.). For extensive references see Pease on Verg. *A*. 4,26. Cf. *exsangui formidine* 9,23 (220,14) with *GCA* 1995,204; add Guastella 1985,70 f., a richly documented discussion of the 'fisiologia della paura'.

For *pallor* as a sign of a guilty conscience see e.g. Hor. *Epod*. 7,14 f. *an culpa? responsum date! / tacent, et albus ora pallor inficit*, where the scholiast remarks: *uelut qui conscientiam peccati monstraret*; Prud. *Psych*. 702 f. *pallor in ore / conscius audacis facti, dat signa reatus* (see on *pedes ... effutire* below).

infernus: 'like that of the underworld'. The adjective *Stygius* is used in the same way, e.g. Sil. 6,146 *lucus iners iuxta Stygium pallentibus umbris* (*Stygium* here as an adverbial accusative); cf. 6,21 (144,9) *infernus somnus ac uere Stygius*. *OLD* s.v. *infernus* 2b mentions Apul. *Met*. 6,21 and this passage as the first for the meaning 'like that of the underworld, deathlike'. *ThLL* s.v. *infernus* 1372,11 f. 'de iis qui (quae) cum Orco comparantur', 'velut infernus' gives passages from Ov. *Met*. 11,506 *inferno de gurgite*; but Bömer ad loc. argues that it actually refers to the river Styx, so that *infernus* has the literal meaning there. Many other passages before Apuleius that are mentioned by *ThLL* also lack persuasiveness for 'velut infernus'. In Sen. *Oed*. 48 f. *obtexit arces caelitum ... inferna facies* and *Ag*. 494 *inferna nox* we can see the image of *nox* or darkness rising from the underworld; in Tac. *Ger*. 43,4 *nouum ac uelut infernum aspectum* the addition *uelut* shows that the metaphor is still regarded as daring. After Apuleius the adjective is found e.g. in Claud. *In Eutrop*. 20,231 *turpis et infernas tenebris obscurior alas*.

perque uniuersa membra frigidus sudor emanabat: cf. Verg. *A*. 3,175 *tum gelidus toto manabat corpore sudor*, for which Macr. 6,1,50 cites Enn. *Ann*. 418 V. (417 Sk.) *tunc timido manat ex omni corpore sudor*; cf. also Sen. *Tro*. 487 *sudor per artus frigidus totos cadit.* The combination *sudor frigidus* is attested first Verg. *G.* 3,501, then Ov. *Met.* 5,632 *occupat obsessos sudor mihi frigidus artus*; Bömer ad loc. gives many parallels.

The description of the mendacious slave's panicky reaction, which so far has been highly stylized with an epic colouring (see also the previous notes), seems comically absurd against the subsequent series of signs of a guilty conscience, which are of an entirely different nature (see on *incertis alternationibus* and *modo hanc, modo illam capitis partem scalpere* below).

tunc: 'and besides, and furthermore...'. For this transitional function of *tunc* see *GCA* 1995,139 on 9,14 (213,19-23), with references.

pedes ... effutire: with *trepidatio* and *pallor* these are the traditional signs of a guilty conscience; cf. *Rhet. Her.* 2,5,8 *quaeritur, quae signa nocentis et innocentis consequi soleant. Accusator dicet, si poterit, aduersarium ... erubuisse, expalluisse, titubasse, inconsequenter locutum esse, concidisse, pollicitum esse aliquid; quae signa conscientiae sint*; Cic. *Clu.* 19,54 *timor eius* (sc. Oppianici), *perturbatio, suspensus incertusque uultus, crebra coloris mutatio, quae erant antea suspiciosa, haec aperta et manifesta faciebant.* Also [Quint.] *Decl.* 17,5 (Håkanson 336,7 f.) *non tamquam deprehensus obstipui, facinus me tacente non pallor, non est confessa trepidatio.* See also on *pallor* above.

If this passage is an allusion to mime (see on ch. 3: 238,7-10), then in the description from *tunc* onward we can see one actor play his part of 'slave with a guilty conscience' true to life.

incertis alternationibus: 'with uncertain, alternating movements'. Fest. p. 6,27 L. *alternatio per uices successio.* According to *ThLL* s.v. *alternatio* 1752,43 f. this noun is first attested here and three times in Apul. *Ascl.* (27, 30 and 31); then Arn. 7,28; Aug. e.g. *Civ.* 12,18; and a few passages in Macrobius. As a legal term in the sense of 'alternative, use of an alternative' it is found Ulp. *Dig.* 47,10,7,4 and 13,4,2,3; Maur. 483 (*G.L.* 6,340) uses it in the meaning 'ambivalence'. Billotta 1975,59 remarks about this description that the slave's confusion, as he shifts from foot to foot, is reflected in the vocabulary, which shifts between neologisms (*alternatio, afanna*) and archaisms (*effutire*); the *alternatio*, therefore, is to be found in the verbal sphere as well. *Effutire*, however, cannot be regarded as an archaism: even though it is attested from Varro onward, it also occurs in Cicero, Lucretius, and Horace (see below). On the other hand, one could point out an *alternatio* between registers, on which see next note.

modo hanc, modo illam capitis partem scalpere: on the various literary registers in this description see on *perque uniuersa membra ... sudor emanabat* above. Whereas for the first symptoms of fear (*ingens ... trepidatio; pallor infernus; frigidus sudor*) parallels were found only in lyric, epic, tragic, and other poetry, the expression *caput scalpere* brings us in the atmosphere of comedy and satire (see also *GCA* 1985,198 f. on 8,23: 195,7-11). Scratching one's head is not so much a sign of feeling guilty as of being in an awkward predicament. Sittl 1890,48 gives as the only parallel for this Apuleius passage Johann. Chrysost. *Homil.* 17 *in Eu. Iohann.* 4 πάντες κάτω νεύουσι καὶ κνῶνται καὶ χασμῶνται; but cf. e.g. Timocl. frg. 19,5 (p. 769 Kassel-Austin; *CGFP* 222[b]) κνώμενος τὸ κρανίον and Her. *Mimiamb.* 4,51 τὸ βρέγμα ... κνήσῃ. For *digito uno caput scalpere* as a sensuous, effeminate gesture cf. e.g. Juv. 9,133 with Courtney ad loc. The expression also brings us close to the Milesiaka: cf. Sisenna Frg. 6 (297,13 Peter) *quid nunc ostium scalpis, quid tergiuersaris nec bene nauiter is?*. See Fick-Michel 1991,44 f. on expressions from the Milesiaka in the *Met*.

ore semiclauso: *OLD* s.v. *semiclausus* gives in addition to this passage only Maur. 92 f. (*G.L.* 6,328 on the *consona muta*) *illis sonus obscurior impeditiorque / utcumque tamen promitur ore semicluso, / uocalibus atque est minor auctiorque mutis.* The *ThLL* material gives this Apuleius passage as the first one; in addition to the passage in Maur. it occurs two more times in grammarians: Mar. Vict. in *G.L.* 6,32,29 and 33,2 *ore semicluso.* Possibly Apuleius knew this adjective from grammatical works and was the first to use it in literary prose. Next, the *ThLL* material gives Amm. 18,6,11 *intra semiclausam posticam exposito puero*; Veg. *Mulom.* 4,6,3 *oculi semiclausi sunt*; Cael. Aurel. *Acut.* 2,3,18 *semiclauso ore*; Polyc. *tunc Polycarpus ore semicluso et qui non suo sed alieno sermone loqueretur ... ait.* In an inscription from Gallia of the 2nd century A.D. (*CIL* 12,103), *semiclusus* is used in the meaning 'half-enclosed': *siluane sacra semicluso fraxino / et huius alti summe custos hortuli*.

balbutiens: 'stammering' (cf. Non. p. 80,13 M. = p. 112,11 f. L.) *balbuttire est cum quadam linguae haesitatione et confusione trepidare*), but also 'muttering indistinctly'; cf. Cic. *Div.* 1,5 *Epicurum balbutientem de natura deorum*; Sid. 4,12,4 *quamquam esset trepidus et sternax, et prae reatu balbutiret ore*; *HA* 27 (*RA* 334,9 f. Kortekaas) *puella ... leni et balbutienti sermone ait*: ... On the spelling *-tt-* or *-t-* see *GCA* 1985,134 on 8,14 (187,19-24).

afannas effutire: alliteration. Billotta 1975,59 speaks of an onomatopoeic effect: *balbutiens*, onomatopoeic in itself, is phonetically illustrated by *afannas effutire*.

afannas: thus ς, for *asannas* in F and φ. The word is attested in Apuleius only, here and *Met.* 9,10 (210,8), on which the emendation by ς of our passage is based. See *GCA* 1995,103, with references, for the various etymological explanations of the word, whose meaning 'nonsensical prevarications' can be deduced from the context in both passages. *LS* use the spelling *afanniae*, which is based on a manuscript variant definitively rejected by Hildebrand (on *Met.* 9,10).

effutire: in the *Met.* only here; further in *Fl.* 3,8 (about Marsyas) *quaedam deliramenta barbare effutiuit;* *Apol.* 3,6 (on the accusers) *sueta ab imperitis mercennaria loquacitate effutierunt.* Var. *L.* 7,5,93 *euax uerbum nihil significat, sed effutitum naturaliter est;* Ter. *Ph.* 745 f. *perperam olim dixi* (sc. *nomen*) *ne uos forte inprudentes foris / effutiretis.* See Brink on Hor. *Ars* 231 *effutire leuis indigna tragoedia uersus*: '*effutire*, from *futis*, "watering can", is "to pour out, spout, babble"'; ps. Acro *proprie ... est "inepte loqui"'*. Thus also E-M s.v. *fundo* 261 and Walde-Hofmann s.v. *effutio* 394. *ThLL* s.v. *effutio* 229,80 f. mentions passages from comedy, then Cicero and Lucretius.

prorsus: reinforces *nemo*; see Callebat 1968,538 for the frequent use of this adverb in the *Met*.

a culpa uacuum: cf. Sal. *Cat.* 14,4 *quod si quis etiam a culpa uacuos in amicitiam eius inciderat*, with Vretska 254 on the different constructions with *uacuus* 'free from...'.

244,13-15 Sed reualescente rursus astutia constantissime negare et accersere mendacii non desinit medicum: But his craftiness revived again and with the greatest persistence he kept denying and accusing the doctor of lies.

reualescente ... astutia: *OLD* s.v. *reualesco* 1b '(of consciousness) to revive, (sim. of qualities)' gives only this passage and 8,8 (183,5) *reualescente paulatim spiritu*; the use of *reualescere* with a quality like *astutia* seems to be an Apuleian extension of the use of this verb. In the first occurrence where it does not apply to persons (= 'regain one's strength') it has the meaning 'regain validity': Tac. *Hist.* 2,54,1 *ut diplomata Othonis, quae neglegebantur, ... reualescerent*; Heubner ad loc. discusses the occurrence of *reualescere* and concludes: 'Tacitus hat das Wort also mit besonderer Freiheit verwendet'. It appears from the *ThLL* material that this passage in Apuleius is the first to use the verb of a mental quality. In Christian authors the use in a spiritual sense is frequently found beside the literal use (see Schmidt 1990 on the use of moral metaphors in Apuleius and Christian authors). E.g. Cypr. *Ep.* 55,17 *est in illis quod paenitentia sequente reualescat ad fidem*; Zacch. *Cons.* 2,17 (p. 87,30 Morin) *reualescentibus uitiis*.

reualescente rursus: strictly speaking, *rursus* is pleonastic; for the redundant use (also frequent in comedy) of *rursus* in the *Met.*, see Van der Paardt 1971,98 f. on 3,12 (61,12 f.) *rursum ... reuerterim*, with references.

constantissime: here, in a description of the *uerbero*, who keeps persisting in his lies, it is certainly not meant favourably but rather in malam partem: 'most stubbornly'. Cf. Hor. *S.* 2,7,6 *pars hominum uitiis gaudet constanter* (possibly meant ironically: 'it is better to be *constanter* bad than irresolute and fickle'). See on *constantia* in malam partem *GCA* 1995,231 f. on 9,26 (223,3), and see below, on *constantiam* ch. 14 (247,20). See also on *mira praesumptione* below.

accersere mendacii: for the genitive of the crime with this verb cf. Sal. *Jug.* 32,1 *quos pecuniae captae arcessebat*, with Koestermann ad loc. In addition to the literal meaning 'summon before a court', *accersere* is also used, in a broader sense, to mean 'accuse of'; for the first meaning cf. e.g. Tac. *Ann.* 4,29,1 *cum primores ciuitatis ... tumultus hostilis et turbandae rei publicae accerserentur*; for the broader sense cf. Gel. 19,14,8 (quoting Nigidius Figulus) *Graecos non tantae inscitiae arcesso*.

desinit: after the descriptive imperfects and historical infinitives this historical present resumes the course of events; with *sed* a new phase in the story has begun: after his initial stammering the slave now evidently utters clear negations and accusations.

244,15-20. Qui praeter iudicii religionem cum fidem suam coram lacerari uideret, multiplicato studio uerberonem illum contendit redarguere, donec iussu magistratuum ministeria publica contrectatis nequissimi serui manibus anulum ferreum deprehensum cum signo sacculi conferunt. quae comparatio praecedentem roborauit suspicionem: When the doctor saw that, in addition to the sanctity of the court, his own credibility was torn to shreds before his very eyes, he strove with redoubled effort to prove the scoundrel wrong until at last the officers of the court, on orders of the magistrates, grabbed and inspected the depraved slave's hands, found the iron signet ring and held it next to the seal on the pouch; and this comparison reinforced the suspicion that had risen earlier.

iudicii religionem ... fidem suam: *suam* has been taken only with *fidem* in the translation, while *iudicii religionem* has been taken as 'sanctity, sacred rules of the court', i.e. the observance of, and the awe for, the oath taken by judges and witnesses (see the following note). From the very beginning, the physician has set himself up as a defender of that *iudicii religio* (see on *numinum religione* ch. 8: 243,15). The false testimony of the slave and the possibility that the judges will believe it are contrary to the *iudicii religio*; but now that the slave openly accuses him of lying, his personal credibility (see on *fidem* below) is injured, and that makes him redouble his efforts. Thus e.g. Brandt-Ehlers: 'Als der sah, wie außer der Achtung vor dem Gerichtshof auch seine eigene Glaubwürdigkeit öffentlich heruntergerissen wurde'; Scazzoso: 'Questi allora vedendo che oltre all'autorità dell'assemblea veniva attaccata la sua onoratezza'; thus also Helm-Krenkel and Hanson. Other translators take *iudicii religionem* as the personal oath that the physician has sworn as a judge (and so do not take *suam* expressly with *fidem*), e.g. Vallette: 'se voyant publiquement diffamé et dans sa conscience de juge et dans sa honnêteté privée'; Carlesi: 'il quale, a parte i suoi scrupoli di giudice, vedendo anche attaccare ... il suo onore'.

iudicii religionem: cf. Quint. *Decl.* 331,10 *non potest omnino ita circumscribi religio et seueritas iudicii ut non poenam det pars ultralibet.*

Religio may here be understood as 'the sum of sacral rules applying to the *iudicium*'. On the development of the idea *religio* see *RE* s.v. *religio* 565,39 f. [Kobbert]; for our interpretation of this idea, see esp. 567,14-53 with examples; in addition it is possible to include in this phrase also the power of *religio* resulting from the above (*iudicii* is then an objective genitive): 'awe for the *iudicium* which is surrounded with sacral rules'. For this more subjective idea of *religio*, complementary to the first, objective meaning, see the same article in *RE* 572,21 f.: 'Die *religio* in ihrem ursprünglichsten Wesen ist demnach bei den Römern eine außerhalb des Menschen wirkende Macht, ein Tabu, das gewissen Zeiten, Orten und Dingen anhaftet, wodurch, des eigenen Willens sozusagen beraubt, der Mensch in seinem Tun behindert, gefesselt, gebunden wird'. After this, Kobbert provides many illustrative quotations.

fidem: cf. ch. 8 (243,8 f.), where this physician is described as *senior prae ceteris compertae fidi ... medicus*; one can understand that he will make an extra effort to prevent a mendacious slave from ruining the *fides* he has acquired during his long life (see the note ad loc.). Here *fides* is passive in meaning, which is by far the more frequent use: 'La confiance que j'obtiens', 'le crédit'; see Freyburger 1986,41 f., with references. In this sense (*ThLL* s.v. *fides* 672,13-55; 673,50-675,9; 685,41 f.: 'auctoritas, bona fama, probabilitas') it often occurs with a possessive pronoun. Cf. e.g. Pl. *Ps.* 631 *uae tibi! Tu inuentu's uero meam qui furcilles fidem*; Cic. *Caec.* 51 *fides mea custodem repudiat.*

coram: Helm-Krenkel and Brandt-Ehlers: 'öffentlich', Vallette: 'publiquement'; for this use of the adverb see *OLD* s.v. *coram* 2b. In this passage it can also mean 'in his own ... presence, before his own ... eyes' (according to *OLD* ibid. 2a 'often with verbs of perceiving'); see e.g. 3,19 (66,14), where Van der Paardt 1971,146 defends *coram* as an adverb ('face to face') with *magiae cognoscendae*, and 8,29 (200,30) with *GCA* 1985,261 ad loc.

lacerari: this is the only passage in Apuleius' works where *lacerare* is used in a metaphorical sense (in the *Met.* the verb is frequently found in a literal sense; in his other works the verb does not occur). *OLD* s.v. *lacero* 5 gives many examples of *lacerare* meaning 'to attack with abuse or accusations, lash; to tear to shreds (reputations and sim.)', e.g. Cic. *Phil.* 11,5 *cum uerborum contumeliis optimum uirum incesto ore lacerasset*; Ov. *Pont.* 4,16,1 *inuide, quid laceras Nasonis carmina rapti?* See also on *calcata ... religione* ch. 8 (243,15) for this practically universal type of imagery.

contendit ... conferunt ... roborauit: after the series of historical presents from *desinit* onward, which reflect the various acts following one another, comes the perfect *roborauit*, which sums up the result of the preceding acts and concludes a phase of the story. For the perfect as an 'episode-marker' see on *rupit ... praecipit* ch. 3 (238,5).

ministeria publica: abstractum pro concreto; cf. *publicis ministeriis* 9,41 (235,16 f.) with *GCA* 1995,345 ad loc., with references.

contrectatis ... manibus: *contrectare*: 'to touch repeatedly, handle, finger' (*OLD* s.v. *contrecto*[1]). Brandt-Ehlers, Helm-Krenkel, Vallette and others translate 'grasp', but one should rather say 'examined'; cf. *ThLL* s.v. *contrecto* 774,45 f. 'i.q. perscrutari' for our passage and Suet. *Cl.* 35,2; this meaning follows naturally from the use of *contrecto* in a medical context: 'feel, palpate'; cf. e.g. Sen. *Dial.* 2 (*Const.*) 13,2 *nec obscena ...* (*medicus*) *contrectare ... dedignatur*, thus passim in Celsius. For another use of the verb, in an erotic context, see *GCA* 1985,78 on 8,7 (181,17-24).

nequissimi serui: the invective reflects the narrator's own opinion of this slave, but also the contempt for a 'most inferior slave' on the part of the actors, i.e. the officers of the court who examine his hands (probably far from gently) to find the iron ring. For the invective see on *nequissimo* ch. 4 (239,21). This slave is called *seruus nequissimus* also ch. 12 (245,21); see note there.

anulum ferreum: for iron signet rings for slaves see on *anulo tuo* ch. 9 (243,29).

roborauit suspicionem: for the figurative use of *roborare* see *OLD* s.v. *roboro* 2, citing Cic. *Off.* 1,31,112 *Catoni, cum ... tribuisset natura grauitatem, eamque ipse perpetua constantia roborauisset*; cf. also Apul. *Met.* 5,9 (110,10 f.) *adfectione roborata*; *Pl.* 2,15 (241) *indulgentia cupidines roboratae*.

244,20-23: Nec rota uel eculeus more Graecorum tormentis eius apparata iam deerant, sed offirmatus mira praesumptione nullis uerberibus ac ne ipso quidem succumbit igni: And now neither the wheel nor the horse, set up for his torture according to the Greek custom, were absent any longer; but he had braced himself and persisted in his version in a remarkable way, and did not break down under the lashes nor even the fire.

rota uel eculeus more Graecorum ... apparata: strictly spoken, only the *rota* is a typically Greek (and by the Romans regarded as Greek) instrument of torture. See on this Van der Paardt 1971,76 on 3,9 (58,11 f.) *nec mora, cum ritu Graeciensi ignis et rota, cum omne flagrorum genus inferuntur*. The *eculeus*, on the other hand, is the typically Roman counterpart of the Greek 'wheel'. See *RAC* 8,112 f. s.v. 'Folterwerkzeuge' [Vergote], and on the *eculeus* especially ibid. 120 f., with a drawing of a reconstruction of this instrument on p. 121; *DNP* 4,584 f. s.v. 'Folter' [Schiemann]. The *eculeus* (literally 'small horse') was a wooden structure on which the person to be tortured was tied down and 'stretched' and, as with the Greek wheel, a fire of live coals (cf. *igni* below) was laid under it.

The words *rota uel eculeus* must have made it clear to Apuleius' contemporary readers that he was not trying to describe a realistic trial; see on *patres in curiam conuenirent* ch. 7 (241,24).

First the slave has given evidence without torture; now that the case has reached a stalemate, torture is applied. Greek jurisdiction made a strict distinction between βάσανος (i.e. torture of slave-witnesses), and μαρτυρία; rhetoricians also classified evidence obtained under torture in a separate group of ἄτεχνοι πίστεις. Moreover, in Greek jurisdiction torture always took place outside the court; to put the instruments of torture ready (*apparare*) during the trial is therefore not *more Graecorum* but typically Roman. Under Roman law slaves could not testify at all except under torture; on the different rules in Greek and

Roman jurisdiction for obtaining testimony under torture and the value attached to it, see *RAC* 8,101 f., s.v. 'Folter' [Thür], with references.

tormentis eius apparata: *tormentis* is a final dative with *apparata*. With *apparare* the goal is usually expressed by constructions like *ad* with an accusative, (e.g. Pl. *Capt.* 860 f. *iube / uasa tibi pura apparari ad rem diuinam cito*; Cic. *Mil.* 10,28 *qui iter illud ad caedem faciendum apparasset*), or a dative: Sil. 13,418 (Scipio) *apparat occulto monstrata piacula coepto*. See LHSz 2,98 on the final dative, which occurs in a few old set formulas (*receptui canere*, *alimento serere*, *remedio adhibere* etc.), and further in 'Militär-, Bauern-, Fachsprache'; the nouns expressing the goal are usually singular abstracts, but according to LHSz l.c. 'läßt die Fachsprache ... gelegentlich den Pluralis zu'. See Önnerfors 1956,70 f. with examples from Plin. *Nat.*, e.g. 33,1 *alibi diuitiis foditur ... alibi deliciis ... alibi temeritati*.

tormentis: *tormentum*, or the plural *tormenta*, is used both concretely for 'instrument(s) of torture' and, as here, for 'torture'. Cf. Plin. *Ep.* 1,12,5 *cum ... cruciatus et ... tormenta pateretur*; cf. also Quint. *Inst.* 5,4,1.

offirmatus: *offirmare* means in the first place 'to make firm, strengthen', then (*OLD* s.v. *offirmo* 2a '(refl., also intr.) to make up one's mind not to yield'; cf. Sen. *Ep.* 98,7 *ad tolerandum omne obfirmata mens*; see also *GCA* 1981,270 f. on 7,28 (176,1-7).

mira praesumptione: *GCA* 1985,248 f. on 8,28 (199,14-18) discusses the five passages where *praesumptio* occurs in the *Met.* and concludes (after consultation of the *ThLL* material) that *praesumptio* stands for 'a (preconceived) incorrect opinion, to which one sticks stubbornly'; this also applies here, even if this is not an 'opinion' but the slave's version of the event. Within the fiction of this story this phrase is naturally meant negatively: it refers to flagrant lies and false testimony. Yet the qualification *mira* achieves a positive connotation when seen within the frame of the entire work, which in the prologue (1,1: 1,6) makes the promise *ut mireris* to the reader. See on *miris ... artibus* ch. 4 (239,14); on *nec mirum* ch. 11 (245,3); and on *conspectum ... miris artibus* ch. 17 (250,12). In 9,15 (213,24) *miro ... odio* a similar ambivalence in the qualification *miro* is found: it refers there to the appalling hatred of the *pistor*'s wife for the ass, but also to a hatred so *mirum* that the ass's curiosity is roused, which for the reader results in a story (see *GCA* 1995,142 ad loc.). In our passage, too, the story is made extra suspenseful by the *mira praesumptio* with which the slave sticks to his point.

nullis uerberibus ac ne ipso quidem succumbit igni: for the description of resistance against torture writers probably could draw from rhetorical exempla collections; cf. V. Max. 6,8,1 (a slave of Antonius is tortured in court) *promissi fidem mira patientia praestitit: plurimis etenim laceratus uerberibus eculeoque impositus, candentibus etiam lamminis ustus, omnem uim accusationis custodita rei salute subuertit*; Sen. *Ben.* 3,19,3 (a slave resists torture) *nullis cruciatibus uictum*; Tac. *Ann.* 15,57,1 *at illam* (sc. Epicharin) *non uerbera, non ignes ... peruicere*.

uerberibus: the punishment of whipping seems to point to a specifically Greek custom (see on 'Folter' in *RAC* cited above on *rota uel eculeus ... apparata*); cf. Ar. *Pax* 452 ἐπὶ τοῦ τροχοῦ γ'ἕλκοιτο μαστιγούμενος.

igni: live coals were placed under both the Greek *rota* and the Roman *eculeus* to scorch the victim; see above, on *rota uel eculeus ... apparata*.

CHAPTER XI

The *medicus* makes an astonishing disclosure.

244,24-27 Tum medicus: 'Non patiar', inquit, 'hercules, non patiar uel contra fas de innocente isto iuuene supplicium uos sumere uel hunc ludificato nostro iudicio poenam noxii facinoris euadere': Then the physician said: 'I will not permit, by Hercules, I will not permit you to carry out the death sentence on that innocent young man unlawfully, nor will I permit this man here to scoff at our jurisdiction and to evade the punishment for his heinous crime.'

This second speech of the physician shows in its structure a strong parallelism with his first (ch. 8: 243,11-14). Kautzky 1989,159 demonstrates this as follows:

first speech		second speech
nec patiar (243,12)	the physician voices his protest	*non patiar ...* *non patiar* (244,24 f.)
nec ... nec (243,12 f.)	in two respects	*uel ... uel* (244,25 f.)
falsis criminibus ... homicidum perpetrari (243,12 f.)	worry no. 1: judicial murder	*contra fas... supplicium uos sumere* (244,25 f.)
uos, qui iure iurando adstricti iudicatis, ... peierare (243,13 f.)	worry no. 2: respect for the law will be lost	*hunc ludificato nostro iudicio poenam ... euadere* (244,26 f.)

Both speeches show a brief transition (*ergo ut res est de me cognoscite* ch. 8: 243,16 f. and *dabo enim rei praesentis euidens argumentum* 244,27 f. respectively) from the rhetorically swollen introduction to the more narrative part.

    Non patiar ... uos sumere: see on *nec patiar ... homicidum perpetrari ... uos ... peierare* ch. 8: 243,12 f.
    Non patiar, ... hercules, non patiar: on the epanalepsis see on *dedi ... dedi* ch. 9 (243,25, also spoken by the physician). When this repetition involves a finite verb, as it does there and in our passage, the combination of epanalepsis with first position of that verb enhances the emphasis of the statement. The physician's emphatic style and his repetition of *non patiar* are consistent with his general characterization from the moment he was introduced (ch. 8: 243,8 f.). Characteristic in this connection are his own first words (ch. 8: 243,11 f.) *Quod aetatis sum, uobis adprobatum me uixisse gaudeo*; after this introduction he similarly continues with *nec patiar* (ch. 8: 243,12), a phrase which almost becomes his 'stock expression'.
    The repeated *non patiar*, which the author has the physician say just before a surprising

turn in this story, underlines the key function of this actor. By himself, he opposes with all his might the course the story threatens to take; he succeeds by adding a new element to the tragic motif of the innocently condemned Hippolytus, which has already been combined with the intertexteme of the 'murderous stepmother', which was common in the schools of rhetoric (see App. I,5.5; for the term 'intertexteme' see the note there). The new element is the motif of the 'sleeping draught instead of poison' (see on *dedi uenenum, sed somniferum* below) and the motif often combined with it, that of 'apparent death' (see on *remeabit ad diem lucidam* below): both are intertextemes from the mime and the novel.

hercules: in Apuleius' work this interjection occurs only in the *Met.*; the expression belongs to the *sermo familiaris*: see Van der Paardt 1971,48 f. on 3,4 (55,3) with references. In an unpublished study J. Seubers examines the use of this interjection in the *Met.* and points out its frequent occurrences in the context of 'fight against injustice' (for other connotations see *GCA* 1995,155 on 9,16: 215,4); in addition to our passage cf. 7,26 (174,6); 9,14 (213,12); 9,37 (231,13); 10,33 (264,7). Seubers gives no further details of this phenomenon. In this context one may be reminded of the belief, widespread in antiquity, in Hercules as a helper in the fight against evil, and a victor over evil. This belief also underlies epithets like ᾽Αλεξίκακος, ῎Αλεξις, ᾽Απαλλαξίκακος, Καλλίνικος, Παραστάτης. See Farnell 1921,147 f. ('The functions of Heracles').

uel contra fas ... sumere, uel hunc ... euadere: in ch. 8 (243,12 f.) the physician announced that he would resist the condemnation of the innocent young man. Now (in *uel hunc ... euadere*) he explicitly adds that he will not allow the slave to go unpunished; a psychologically interesting feature, since in the intermediate part the slave has also damaged the doctor's personal *fides*: ch. 10 (244,15 f.) *cum fidem suam coram lacerari uideret*; see also on *ludificato nostro iudicio* below.

contra fas: the *medicus* said earlier (ch. 8: 243,13 f.) that to condemn the young man on the basis of the slave's lies is, in his opinion, *peierare*, i.e. *contra fas*. *Fas* is used here meaning '(as opp. to civil law ...) that which is in accordance with natural law' (*OLD* s.v. *fas* 3b); cf. e.g. Cic. *Mil.* 43 *nihil ... quod aut per naturam fas esset aut per leges liceret*; Tac. *Hist.* 1,44,1 *Pisonis ... caede laetari ius fasque credebat*. See Vretska on Sal. *Cat.* 15,1 *contra ius fasque*: '*ius*: das privatrechtlich erlaubte Verhalten (Kaser, Privatrecht 1,26); *fas*: die Erlaubtheit eines Verhaltens gegenüber den Göttern (Kaser l.c. 29)'. See Berger 1953,527.

de ... isto iuuene ... hunc: the pronouns *isto* and *hunc*, referring to the defendant and the witness respectively, suggest gestures of the speaker.

ludificato nostro iudicio: with these words the physician appeals to the honour of his fellow *decuriones*, and with the addition *nostro* (in contrast to the preceding *uos sumere*) he suggests that this is no longer a matter of a false witness against an innocent defendant, but of a threatening encroachment on the legal system. See also on *desperatissimum istum latronem* below.

A little later in this chapter, after the surprising new disclosure (see on *dedi uenenum* below), the readers could accuse the doctor himself (and the narrator behind the doctor) of '*ludificato nostro iudicio*' in a wider sense. See Shumate 1996,48 f. on other examples of 'playing games with our system of judgment' in the *Met.*

ludificato: this is the only occurrence of the verb in Apuleius' works. It is usually a deponent verb in Ciceronian Latin (see Koestermann on Sal. *Jug.* 36,2); *ludificare* is an archaism, attested in the passive in Plautus, e.g. *Bac.* 642 *ut ludificatust!*; Lucr. 1,939

(= 4,14) *ut puerorum aetas inprouida ludificetur*; then our passage; Tert. *An.* 17,14; Avian. *Fab.* 16,18, etc.; it is attested in the active 12 times in Plautus, only once in Cicero (*Quinct.* 54), and twice in Sallustius (*Jug.* 36,2 and 50,4). See Flobert 1975,86, 297, and 356.

poenam noxii facinoris: the adjective *noxius* qualifies *facinus* but seems also to explain *poenam*; the combination must mean something like 'the punishment for the (criminal) act of which he is guilty (*noxius*)'. Cf. 8,28 (199,10-13) *poenas noxii facinoris ... exposcere*, with *GCA* 1985,247 ad loc. See Thome 1993,220 f. and n. 571 on the 'Verbindung von Tatbestand und persönlicher Schuld' in *noxium facinus*.

244,27-28 'Dabo enim rei praesentis euidens argumentum': 'Therefore I will produce conclusive proof on the basis of the actual situation.'

Dabo enim ...: *dabo* is placed first in the sentence, as is often the case in an explanation or interpretation of a previous statement. See KSt 2,2,600 for examples of explicative or interpretative sentences with the main verb in the first place; e.g. Caes. *Gal.* 1,14,5 *consuesse enim deos immortales*; Col. 11,3,20 *habet enim ... spicas*. In addition, the striking position of the main verbs in this entire passage adds to the emotional charge of these introductory sentences of the physician, who, provoked to the utmost, is determined to bring out his last trump card. Cf. also 2,30 (49,18 f.) *rursus altius ingemescens: 'dabo' inquit, 'dabo uobis intemeratae ueritatis documenta'*.

enim: Kroon 1989,54 discusses the strongly assertive force of *enim*-sentences, and shows that '*enim*-units' often contain polemical statements, which certainly is the case here. The *enim*-sentence is used to support the preceding statement (especially its veracity), which may be less acceptable or obvious.

rei praesentis euidens argumentum: since the Latin is open to several explanations here, the translations differ: Brandt-Ehlers: 'für diesen Fall den schlagenden Beweis'; thus also e.g., Helm-Krenkel: 'einen untrüglichen Beweis in der vorliegende Sache' (for *res praesens* in the sense of 'the case in question', see *OLD* s.v. *praesens* 11b and c); Vallette, however, takes *res* in the sense of 'the real facts' (see e.g. on *res* ch. 8: 243,16) and translates: 'de la réalité des faits une preuve incontestable'; thus also Hanson 'plain proof of the real facts' (for a similar objective genitive with *argumentum* see *OLD* s.v. *argumentum* 1b). A third possibility is to take the phrase as 'a conclusive proof on the basis of the actual situation': the physician will ask the *decuriones* to go to the grave and see if the boy is indeed only apparently dead. Thus the speaker promises to supply his audience with evidence they can verify themselves on the spot. For a genitive with *argumentum*, expressing the 'source of evidence', see *OLD* s.v. *argumentum* 1a.

244,28-245,3 'Nam cum uenenum peremptorium comparare pessimus iste gestiret nec meae sectae crederem conuenire causas ulli praebere mortis nec exitio, sed saluti hominum medicinam quaesitam esse didicissem, uerens, ne, si daturum me negassem, intempestiua repulsa uiam sceleri subministrarem et ab alio quopiam exitiabilem mercatus hic potionem uel postremum gladio uel quouis telo nefas inchoatum perficeret, dedi uenenum, sed somniferum, mandragoram illum grauedinis compertae famosum et morti simillimi soporis efficacem': 'For when that evil man insisted on buying a deadly poison, I thought it was not in keeping with my professional code to provide someone with the means of death, for I had learned that medical science was invented not for people's ruination but for their well-being. So I gave him a drug, fearing that, if I refused to give it, I would by an untimely refusal pave the way for a crime: that by buying a deadly potion from someone else, or eventually with a sword or some other weapon, he would carry out the crime toward which he had already taken the first step. But the drug I gave him was a sleeping draught, the mandragora, famous for its comatose effect, which causes a sleep very similar to death.'

cum ... comparare ... iste gestiret nec ... crederem, ... sed ... didicissem, uerens, ne ... perficeret, dedi ...: the audience (and the linear reader with them) have to wait a long time for the surprising announcement *dedi uenenum* to which the physician is leading up with a complex series of subordinate clauses. He starts with *cum*, which is first used temporally (*cum ... gestiret*), then causally (*nec ... crederem, sed ... didicissem*). The sentence is continued with *uerens, ne ... subministrarem et ... perficeret*; within this construction a conditional clause (*si ... negassem*) and a participle construction (*mercatus*) have been inserted. On the one hand this creates an impression of spontaneity: the speaker seems to organize his thoughts while speaking; on the other hand it achieves an effect which is undoubtedly intentional: increased suspense (because the main clause *dedi uenenum ...* has been postponed) and surprise in that final important statement.

uenenum peremptorium: the addition of the adjective is not redundant, for the physician uses *uenenum* (correctly) as a vox media, as appears from *dedi uenenum, sed somniferum*; cf. e.g. Gaius, *Dig.* 50,16,236 *qui 'uenenum' dicit, adicere debet, utrum malum an bonum: nam et medicamenta uenena sunt*. See Rayment 1959,50 f. on the use of *uenenum* in rhetorical *declamationes*. See also on *potionem* ch. 9 (243,25).

peremptorium: the adjective (derived form *perimo* 'kill') is first attested in the second century A.D., in Gaius and Apuleius (who uses it only here). *ThLL* s.v. *peremptorius* 1317,34 f. traces its literal meaning ('deadly, fatal, mortal') from this passage in Apuleius through Tert. *An.* 25,5 (sc. *instrumentum medicorum aeneum*) ἐμβρυοσφάκτην *appellant ... utique uiuentis infantis peremptorium* to later Christian authors, who expand its use in a spiritual sense ('mortal sin'). The second, metaphorical, meaning ('final, decisive') is first found in Gaius, and is common in legal texts. Because Apuleius and Gaius are more or less contemporaries, it is possible that Apuleius should not be credited with the first occurrence of the literal meaning, but that he borrowed the adjective from legal terminology. In that case, the physician is using a euphemistic paraphrase.

Note the alliteration in *peremptorium comparare pessimus*.

gestiret: it is difficult (but unnecessary) to decide here between the meanings of *gestire* distinguished by McKibben 1951,170 n. 8: on the one hand 'intend', on the other 'itch, burn, strongly desire' (see *GCA* 1985,259 on 8,29: 200,22-26). Later, McKibben softens the distinction: 'the basic notion, purpose, is the same'. This holds also for our passage: the slave intends to buy poison but is also very keen to get it; cf. *comparare sollicitus* ch. 9 (243,18 f.). See also Van der Paardt 1971,107 on 3,14 (62,10).

nec meae sectae crederem conuenire ... sed ... didicissem: what the physician formulates here as his personal view of his profession is one of the most famous medical aphorisms: '*primum non nocere*' (cf. Hippocrates *Epid.* 1,11 ὠφελεῖν ἢ μὴ βλάπτειν; see Kudlien 1970,91 f., with references). In the Hippocratic Oath it is phrased as follows: διαιτήμασί τε χρήσομαι ἐπ' ὠφελείῃ καμνόντων κατὰ δύναμιν καὶ κρίσιν ἐμήν, ἐπὶ δηλήσει δὲ καὶ ἀδικίῃ εἴρξειν. οὐ δώσω δὲ οὐδὲ φάρμακον οὐδενὶ αἰτηθεὶς θανάσιμον, οὐδὲ ὑφηγήσομαι συμβουλίην τοιήνδε. Cf. also Larg. *Epistula dedicatoria* (i.e. the preface, in which he dedicates his pharmaceutical handbook to C. Julius Callistus), p. 2,26 Sconocchia *scientia enim sanandi, non nocendi est medicina*; and 2,14 f. *quia medicina ... omnibus implorantibus auxilia sua succursuram se pollicetur nullique umquam nocituram profitetur*. See also Deichgräber 1950,856 f. on this *'professio medici'*.

meae sectae: *secta* is here, especially in view of the following *sed ... didicissem*, to be understood as the 'professional code' of physicians; cf. Larg. in his above-mentioned *praef.* 10 (4,7 Sconocchia) (on the increasing number of incompetent doctors) *disciplinae ac sectae obseruatio perit*; Sen. *Ep.* 95,9: *alia est Hippocratis secta, alia Asclepiadis*; Plin. *Nat.* 26,11. But the pronoun *meae* makes it clear that the word should also be understood in the wider sense of 'my course of behaviour, my guiding principles'; cf. Luc. 2,380 f. *hi mores, haec duri immota Catonis / secta fuit, seruare modum finemque tenere*; in Apuleius e.g. *Met.* 6,31 (153,3-7) *nec sectae collegii nec mansuetudini singulorum ... congruit pati uos ultra modum delictique saeuire terminum*; *Pl.* 2,22 (251) *(boni omnes) potestate ipsa, qua mores eorum sectaeque conueniunt, amici sunt habendi*; ibid. 2,8 (231) *rhetoricae duae sunt apud eum partes, quarum una est disciplina contemplatrix bonorum, iusti tenax, apta et conueniens cum secta eius qui politicus uult uideri*. See also *GCA* 1977,136 f. on 4,18 (88,3-5) and *GCA* 1995,115 on 9,12 (211,23-24), where (apart from a possible play on other meanings) the meaning 'my line of conduct up to now' fits very well. Cf. also 9,27 (224,1) *ex secta prudentium* with *GCA* 1995,242 ad loc.

causas ulli praebere mortis: here the phrase is concrete, meaning the physical causes of death, the 'means of death'. At the end of his speech, the doctor will use the same phrase in an abstract sense, the 'reasons for his death'; see the note there.

saluti: Tatum 1969,83 with n. 155, and 85 with n. 158, is right in arguing that *salus* is a key word in the *Met.*, in view of the special connotation it acquires in the Isis-book, e.g. 11,21 (283,5 f. three times); see Gwyn Griffiths ad loc. and idem in *AAGA* 1978,153 f. and 156. Christian authors, too, frequently use the double meaning of *salus*, (a) in a physical sense: 'recovery' or, as in the salutation in letters, 'health', and (b) in a religious sense: 'salvation'; cf. Smolak 1973,52 s.v. *aeternam ... salutem* and ibid. 59 f., s.v. *salutifer*. Tatum also points out the role played by *salus* in the transition from the tenth to the eleventh book, where, for example, a re-reader can no longer understand ch. 35 (265,22 f.) *de salute ipsa sollicitus* at only one level. It seems that some passages in this Phaedra-story, too, are about the different (and in the light of 11,21 only partly correct) opinions of *salus* held by different people. See Introd. **2.4.6**, and e.g. on *salus unica* ch. 3 (238,21); *refectionique se ac saluti redderet* ch. 4 (239,5 f.), and *salubre consilium* ch. 7 (241,23). Here, where the physician is speaking, it is obviously meant in a physical sense. Cf. e.g. Var. *L.* 5,8 *quod ... in salute nostra ... facit cum aegrotamus medicus*; Larg. 84 *qui pollicentur salutis custodiam ... se facturos*; see *OLD* s.v. *salus* 2.

intempestiua: literally 'at the wrong time', hence 'rash, premature', but also 'tactless, ill-advised'; see on *intempestiua seueritate* ch. 4 (239,2 f.).

uiam sceleri subministrarem: 'that I would pave the way for a crime', in other words: 'if I refused, I would no longer be able to prevent a crime, just because I had washed my hands of it'. Cf. Sen. *Her.O.* 877 *sceleribus feci uiam* (said by Deianira, meaning that by killing Hercules she has deprived humanity of the combatant of crime).

ab alio quopiam exitiabilem mercatus hic potionem: the physician has no illusions about the ethics of his colleagues; indeed, in the other inner tale of this book we will encounter another *medicus*, who has no scruples about selling deadly poison (ch. 25: 256,23 f. *medicum ... quendam notae perfidiae*). The surprising turn in this story is partly caused by the misunderstanding of the *nouerca* and her slave, who find themselves confronted with the 'wrong' type of physician (i.e. a physician from a different generic context than that of the *declamatio* and the mime, to which they belong themselves). See on *medicus* ch. 8 (243,8 f.).

exitiabilem ... potionem: 'a deadly potion'. The adjective turns the 'neutral' *potio* into *uenenum* (see on *potionem* ch. 9: 243,25, and on *meis temperatam manibus ... potionem* below). For *exitiabilis* see *GCA* 1977,83 on 4,10 (82,9-10).

dedi uenenum, sed somniferum: on this dénouement at the end of this long sentence, see the first note on this section. A phrase of four words offers the audience in the courtroom (and the reader) a double surprise: *dedi uenenum — sed somniferum*. A correct use of the term *uenenum* (see on *uenenum peremptorium* above) is effectively applied here: throughout the story, *uenenum* (with or without a qualifying adjective) has been associated directly with 'poison' (ch. 5: 239,25; 240,3 and 16; ch. 7: 242,19; ch. 9: 243,18; 244,5 and in this chapter: 244,28). In a concise way, the addition *sed somniferum* now reduces *uenenum* to the status of a vox media, and compels the fictive audience and the linear reader to readjust their views on what has happened. The effect of surprise on the reader of this story is as strong as it must have been on the audience watching the 'Mime of the Poisoner' (Ox. Pap. 413, line 186; see Wiemken 1972,89, and ibid. 100 f. and 235, n. 153): until the 'poisoned' master of the house awakes, the audience takes it for granted that he, as well as Aesopus and Apollonia, has died from poison (on this motif in the mime, see below). But there is also an important difference between the use of this motif in the mime and its literary adaptation by Apuleius: unlike the audience of the mime, the reader of the *Met.* will, at this point, have a need (which s/he can satisfy) to go back and re-read the story, since s/he feels somewhat 'taken in'. Then it appears that in all crucial passages the vocabulary has been such that nowhere was information given that, strictly speaking, was inconsistent with this surprising dénouement (see on ch. 5 *fratri suo paratam mortem*: 240,4 f.; *exanimis terrae procumbit*: 240,5; *funerari uidebat* 240,26; ch. 9 *potionem*: 243,25). Those passages have only led the reader, along with the actors, toward an interpretation that now turns out to be incorrect. One could argue that the reader of the *Met.*, in the limited framework of this one inner tale, has the same experience as s/he feels after completing all eleven books, when, after reading the Isis-book, one also feels a need to re-read the story in order to find out whether, as a *lector scrupulosus,* one might have been able to anticipate the Isis-dénouement. See Penwill 1990,4 f., who discusses the *repentina mutatio* in the Risus Festival in similar terms, and places this in the wider context of the Isis-dénouement in the *Met.* See also Shumate 1996,43 f. on 'questions of epistemology lying at the heart of the *Metamorphoses*'.

The motif of the interchange of deadly poison and sleeping potion (for its occurrence in folklore see Thompson K 518,4 en T 37,0,1) is also present in other novels: Jambl. *Babyl.* 4 (Photius *Bibl.* 94,74B) and 7 (Photius *Bibl.* 94,75A); Xen. *Ephes.* 3,5,11, where the physician Eudoxos exchanges the deadly poison requested by Anthia for a sleeping potion: θανάσιμον οὐχὶ φάρμακον, ὑπνωτικὸν δέ. See Crismani 1993,184, with references, on this motif in the Greek novels. Wiemken 1972,167 argues that the novel has borrowed this motif (like other motifs) from the mime. The Mime of the Poisoner is not the only place where it is found: cf. also Laber. *mustum somniculosum* (*Mim.* 86, Ribbeck *CRF*

2 p. 356). It possibly plays a role also in the mime mentioned by Plut. *De soll.anim.* 19 (*Mor.* 973e f.), where he saw a clever dog acting out, true to life, all the stages of losing and regaining consciousness. Andreassi 1997,4 f., who discusses this motif in connection with the Oxyrrhynchus mime and Apuleius, refutes Wiemken's thesis that Apuleius borrowed the motif directly from the mime: 'the Oxyrrhynchus mime could be one more variation on a *topos* deeply rooted in everyday life as well as in literature'.

mandragoram illum ... efficacem: all editors adopt here the reading transmitted in φ and a*: this was also the original reading in F before a different hand erased the 'Nasalstrich' over the last *a* of *mandragora*, turned the original *illū* into *illu'*, and changed the original *efficacē* to *efficax* (Lütjohann 1873,448 mentions this as one of the examples where φ reflects the original reading of F, copied before the second hand was active in F).

mandragoram: the mandrake, of which root, leaves, and berries are all strongly poisonous. See the comprehensive article 'Mandragoras' in *RE* [Steier]; on its narcotic effects known in antiquity see ibid. 1030,68 f. Physicians used it as an anaesthetic. Diosc. 5,71 gives precise prescriptions for its dosage; and cf. Diosc. 4,75,3 χρώμενοι ... καὶ ἐφ' ὧν βούλονται ἀναισθησίαν τεμνομένων ἢ καιομένων ποιῆσαι; Plin. *Nat.* 25,150 *bibitur ... ante sectiones punctionesque, ne sentiantur*; [Apul.] *Herb.* 131 *si aliqui aliquod membrum fuerit emutilandum, comburendum, uel serrandum, bibat cum uino unciam mediam et tantum dormiet quousque abscindatur membrum aliquo sine dolore et sensu*. People were aware of the danger of an overdose (Thphr. *C.P.* 6,4,5); a caution about using it as an anaesthetic appears from e.g. Cels. 5,25 *quibus uti, nisi nimia necessitas urget, alienum est*. The narcotic effect of mandrake seems to be almost proverbial in Pl. *R.* 6,488C μανδραγόρᾳ ἢ μέθῃ ... ξυμποδίσαντας, or Demosthenes 10,6 μανδραγόραν πεπωκόσιν ... ἐοίκαμεν. Cf. also the expression ἐκ μανδραγόρου, ὑπὸ μανδραγόρᾳ καθεύδειν for 'sleep very deeply', e.g. Lucian. *Dem.Enc.* 36, *Tim.* 2 (Zenobius does not mention it as a proverb).

However, the mandrake's root and leaves are mentioned as a cooling and soothing medication for sores, eye infections, etc. (Plin. *Nat.* 25,149; 26,121). In view of these beneficial medical properties, it would not be suspicious for a physician to have it available in his pharmacopoeia. By adding *meis temperatum manibus* the physician implies that he knows the right dosage and that this potion cannot have caused the boy's death: 'but if the boy turns out to be dead anyway, that cannot be blamed on my potion, so you will have to look elsewhere for the cause of death'. Merkelbach 1962,85, n. 3 suggests the possibility of an allegorical interpretation of the mandrake in connection with Osiris, but admits himself: 'Beweisbar ist dies alles nicht'. See App. I,6B.

Bocciolini 1986,165 f. discusses how the mandrake-motif of ancient literature, including its treatment here by Apuleius, is used in e.g. the novella *Mandragola* by Machiavelli.

illum ... famosum: on this use of *ille* ('that well-known ...') in the *Met.*, see Callebat 1968,276 f. *ThLL* s.v. *famosus* 257,70 f. has many examples of *famosus* combined with *ille*.

grauedinis compertae famosum: 'famous for its proven stupefying effect'. *ThLL* s.v. *famosus* 258,72 f. has this passage as the only example of a genitive ('indicatur causa') with this adjective; the common construction is with the causal ablative. It is probably better to explain the genitive *grauedinis compertae* as expressing the area to which the adjective *famosum* applies. For the genitive with adjectives 'um den Bereich auszudrücken, für den das Adjektiv gilt', see KSt 2,1,443 f. The examples given there show that genitives of this type often have an almost causal force, as here, but that it is difficult to classify them into different categories. Von Geisau 1916,248 f. sees the use of this genitive in Apuleius as poetic: under the influence of Greek it becomes much more frequent in Latin from the Augustan poets onward. Cf. Verg. *A.* 11,416 *fortunatusque laborum*; Prop. 1,16,2 *ianua ... nota pudicitiae*, with Postgate ad loc.; Sil. 13,821 *inclita leti*; in Apul. e.g. *Met.* 3,16 (64,7) *maleficae disciplinae perinfames*, with Van der Paardt 1971,126 ad loc.; 8,2 (177,14 f.) *morum ... inprobatus*, with *GCA* 1985,35 f. ad loc.

grauedinis: cf. Plin. *Nat.* 25,149 *sic quoque noxiae uires* (sc. *mandragorae*) *grauedinem adferunt*. In addition to this passage, the word occurs once in the *Met.*: in the other inner tale the doctor has been forced to drink his own deadly poison; as he is dying, he is described as *grauedine somnulenta iam demersus* (ch. 26: 258,3). *Grauedo* is a medical term for 'head cold', also 'sluggishness, stupor' in general; cf. Plin. *Nat.* 21,130 *grauedines capitis inpositis ... discutiunt (uiolae)*; Cels. 4,5,2 *haec* (sc. *grauedo*) *nares claudit, uocem obtundit, tussim siccam mouet*; Larg. 52; Apul. *Fl.* 17,6 *nares grauedine oppletae*.

morti simillimi soporis: cf. Verg. *A.* 6,522 (on the sleep of Deiphobus) *dulcis et alta quies placidaeque simillima morti*, which line itself was inspired by Hom. *Od.* 13,79 f.; see Graverini 1998,139 on other allusions to the Deiphobus episode in the *Met.* Of course, the topos of 'deathlike sleep' is rather common, both in Greek and Latin. Besides a possible allusion to the image of Sleep as the brother of Death, established from Homer (*Il.* 14,231) onward, in the context here this is also an explicit reference to a well-known effect of *mandragora*, cf. Fron. *Str.* 2,5,12: Hannibal has drugged the rebellious Maharbal and his men with wine mixed with *mandragora*: *in modum defunctorum strati iacerent*. For the theme of 'death-like sleep' in the *Met.*, see on *remeabit ad diem lucidam* below.

soporis efficacem: the genitive with *efficax* is attested first in this passage, but Sen. *Dial.* 1 (*Ira* 1),3,7 has already *inefficax* with a genitive: *uerborum inefficax*. After this, *ThLL* s.v. *efficax* 161,25 f. mentions Aus. 308,4 (XIII,217 Peiper = Green XXVI,217) *is ... rei gerendae efficax* (but it is pointed out that this may be a dative, as is usual with *efficax*); further e.g. Ambr. *Abr.* 2,8,52 *sermo noster efficax operationis*; Boeth. *Cons.* 5,2,12 *efficax optatorum ... potestas*, etc. Von Geisau 1916,248 sees here both a Greek influence (cf. e.g. ποιητικός with a genitive in Pl. *Def.* 411D and Arist. *Top.* 137[a] 4) and an analogy with Latin *efficiens* + objective genitive, e.g. Cic. *Off.* 3,33,116 *efficiens ... uoluptatis*; *Tim.* 51 *efficientes pulcherrimarum rerum*). See LHSz 2,80 on the extension of the genitive with verbal adjectives on *-ax* in postclassical Latin.

For *efficax* as a medical term meaning 'effective' see *ThLL* ibid. 161,4 f. In non-medical terminology, *efficax* occurs frequently with that meaning, usually with a dative, but also with *ad* + accusative, or with an infinitive. Cf. e.g. Liv. 1,9,16 *quae maxime ad muliebre ingenium efficaces preces sunt*; Hor. *Carm.* 4,12,19 f. *spes donare nouas largus amaraque / curarum eluere efficax*.

245,3-6 'Nec mirum desperatissimum istum latronem certum extremae poenae, quae more maiorum in eum competit, cruciatus istos ut leuiores facile tolerare': 'No wonder that this outrageous criminal, knowing the ultimate penalty that applies by tradition to his case, easily endured his present tortures as being less hard to bear.'

Nec mirum: unlike his audience, the physician is not impressed by the *mira praesumptio* (ch. 10: 244,22; see note) with which the slave braced himself during his torture: he gives a rationalizing explanation for it here.

desperatissimum istum latronem: by his choice of invectives the speaker manages to reinforce his earlier suggestion that this is a case of encroachment threatening the legal system (see above, on *ludificato nostro iudicio* 244,26): both the adjective *desperatus* and the term of abuse *latro* are invectives typically used in political speeches in which the speaker depicts his adversaries as subversive. See Opelt 1965,162: '*desperatus* ist derjenige, von dem man nichts mehr erhofft, der schon Aufgegebene ... In der politischen Terminologie sind die *desperati* jene Bürger, von denen der Staat nichts mehr zu hoffen hat' (see further ibid. Index s.v. *desperatus*); ibid. 132 f.: 'Die häufigste Bezeichnung des politischen Gegners als Störers der staatlichen Ordnung, illegal Handelnden, Revolutionärs und Anarchisten — auf dem Boden der Gewalt, nicht des Rechts, stehend — ist die Rechtsmetapher *latro*' (see further ibid. Index s.v. *latro*). In 9,38 (232,6) the narrator calls the rapacious neighbour a *furiosus latro*; earlier (9,36: 230,18 f.) he is described as *suspendium sese et totis illis et ipsis legibus mandare proclamans*. The physician's invectives here are therefore of a different order from those he used earlier for the same person (ch. 9: 243,18 *furcifer*; 243,23 *uerberonem*). In Apul. *Pl.* 2,18 (245) extremely wicked people are compared with patients who have been 'given up' by the doctors: *desperata corpora*. Coming from a physician, *desperatissimus* is therefore a quite weighty term.

certum extremae poenae: for *certus* with a genitive see GCA 1995,168 on 9,18 (216,12 f.) *certusque fragilitatis humanae fidei*. See also KSt 2,1,437 f.

extremae poenae: from ch. 12 (245,24) it becomes clear that this means 'crucifixion'. See note there.

in eum competit: *competere* is found in the *Met.* only here. With a dative, in the sense of 'to suit, to be in accordance with' e.g. *Apol.* 10,6 *negat id genus uersus Platonico philosopho competere*; *Soc.* 3,123. In the sense of 'to be relevant for ...' e.g. *Apol.* 30,4; 36,8; *Fl.* 16,7. As a legal term, 'to apply to', similarly with *in* + accusative, it is found in Quint. *Inst.* 3,6,11 *ut actionem competere in equitem Romanum neget*; with *contra* + acc. in Ulp. *Dig.* 17,1,29,5 *repetitio contra eum competit*, cf. ibid. 21,2,51,3 *cum ... plenior aduersus heredem uel heredi competat obligatio*. See OLD s.v. *competo* 7.

245,6-8 'Sed si uere puer meis temperatam manibus sumpsit potionem, uiuit et quiescit et dormit et protinus marcido sopore discusso remeabit ad diem lucidam': 'But if the boy really has taken the potion mixed by my hands, then he is alive, he is resting, he is sleeping, and soon he will shake off the sluggishness of sleep and return to the light of day.'

meis temperatam manibus sumpsit potionem: as *uenenum*, having had the connotation of 'poison' throughout the story, regained in 245,1 above the status of a vox media through the addition of *sed somniferum*, so does *potionem* by the addition of *meis temperatam manibus* (for the importance of this phrase see on *mandragoram* above); cf. earlier in this chapter *ab alio quopiam exitiabilem mercatus ... potionem*. It is only now that the fictive audience, along with the reader, knows that *potionem* in ch. 9 (243,25) did not mean 'poison'.

uiuit et quiescit et dormit et protinus marcido sopore discusso remeabit ad diem lucidam: the speaker enhances the powerful effect of his important announcement by means of polysyndeton and a striking colometry: three short commata (of 2, 4, and 3 syllables respectively) are followed by a concluding colon of 23 syllables. Cf. e.g. 9,16 (215,1-4), where in the *anus*' praise of Philesitherus the same procedure is used to persuade the *pistor*'s wife (see *GCA* 1995,154 ad loc.; Bernhard 1927,78 f.).

marcido sopore: the sleep, which renders someone *marcidus*, is itself called *marcidus*. Cf. Stat. *Silv.* 1,6,33 *illi marcida uina largiuntur*, and see *ThLL* s.v. *marcidus* 376,27 f. ('i.q ... segnitiam prodens uel efficiens'), where the Statius passage could be added. Cf. expressions like *exsangui formidine* (9,23: 220,14; see *GCA* 1995,204 ad loc.).

discusso: because a physician is speaking here, *discutere* may be used as a medical term for dispelling or curing an illness (*ThLL* s.v. *discutio*, 1373,44 f.). However, the use of *discutere* for shaking off sleep, intoxication, or tiredness is quite general (*ThLL* ibid. 1374,31 f.); cf. also 8,13 (187,5 f.) *crapulam cum somno discutit*, with *GCA* 1985,128; 11,1 (266,23) *discussa pigra quiete*; Prop. 3,10,13 *pura somnum tibi discute lympha*.

remeabit ad diem lucidam: at first sight the phrase can be read as an elevated expression for 'he will wake up' (cf. Sen. *Oed.* 219 *caelo lucidus curret dies*; *Phaed.* 571 *Tethys lucidum attollet diem*; Apul. *Met.* 11,22: 284,2, on the breaking of day, *necdum satis luce lucida*). But the words also suggest 'he will return to the land of the living'. In 11,23 (285,15) *remeaui* stands for 'I returned from the underworld'; cf. moreover Stat. *Theb.* 4,480 f. *nec simplex manibus esto / in lucem remeare modus*; Sen. *Phaed.* 946 *non cernat ultra lucidum Hippolytus diem*. The young man's sleep is, after all, *morti simillimus*, and he has already been buried (ch. 6: 241,1 f.). On the association of this younger brother, 'rising from the dead', with Hippolytus/Virbius, see App.I,4, and ibid. 6B. Smith 1968, Intr. XXIII f., and n. 1 points out the theme of 'death-like sleep' in the *Met*.: 'a theme which has been treated on various levels — the macabre, the ludicrous, and the metaphorical — is finally given its most meaningful form, as Lucius experiences the "death and resurrection" which accompany religious initiation' (11,23: 285,14 f.) Cf. the *infernus somnus ac uere Stygius*, by which Psyche is overcome 6,21 (144,9 f.), and from which Amor awakens her (see Kenney 1990a,193 f.; Dowden in *AAGA* 2,1998,12 f.). Once, an 'apparent death' is followed by an actual death in the *Met*.: in 7,12 (163,16 f.) the robbers are lying in a stupor, drugged by the wine to which Tlepolemus has added a soporific; this is described in terms of apparent death: *cuncti ... uino sepulti iacebant, omnes parati morti* (see *GCA* 1981 App. II on the reading *parati*); later, still unconscious, they will be killed (7,13: 164,6 f.).

The 'apparent death' theme in the *Met.* is one of the elements tying the entire work together, culminating in the rebirth of Lucius in the Isis-book (see also Fiorencis-Gianotti 1990,71 f., discussed in App.I,7). This motif is also found in other novels in antiquity; see Sandy 1994,1515 f. and n. 7. Bowersock concludes the richly documented chapter 'Resurrection' (Bowersock 1994,99-119) with the question (p. 119) 'whether ... we would be justified in explaining the extraordinary growth in fictional writing, and its characteristic and concomitant fascination with resurrection, as some kind of reflection of the remarkable stories that were coming out of Palestina precisely in the middle of the first century A.D.'

The 'apparent death' theme may also be connected with an inherent fear in the human psyche of being buried alive (see Thompson N694 on the occurrence of this theme in folklore). Apart from the novel, we encounter the theme also in stories, apocryphal or not, about famous physicians. The best-known story in this connection is the story about Asclepiades of Prusa, a physician in Rome in the first century A.D., who happened to meet a funeral procession and discovered that the person believed to be dead was still alive. This tale is found in Celsus (2,6,15), twice in Plinius (*Nat.* 7,37,124 and 26,8,15), and also in Apul. *Fl.* 19.

diem lucidam: see GCA 1977,22 on 4,1 (74,9-10) about *dies*, which in the *Met.* is used 37 times as a masculine, 24 times as a feminine. Fraenkel 1964,57 f. and 58, n. 1 discusses the increasing use of *dies* as a feminine in Apuleius, having examined (27 f.) the rules governing the choice between feminine and masculine forms in Republican authors. The use of *dies* as a feminine noun clearly increased in colloquial language (Fraenkel ibid. 51 gives examples from Petronius). But an author like Ammianus, who learned Latin in school, is much more reserved in his use of *dies* as a feminine and keeps to the rule formulated by Servius on Verg. A. 2,324: '*dies*' *autem si feminino genere ponatur, tempus significat ... si masculino, ipsum diem* (see Fraenkel, ibid. 58 f.).

245,8-10 'Quod si ue<re> peremptus est, si morte praeuentus est, quaeratis licet causas mortis eius alias': 'But if he really has been killed, if he has been overtaken by death, then you should look for the causes of his death elsewhere.'

Quod si uere peremptus est si morte praeuentus est: in the place of *si uere*, F and φ have *siue*; if one retains this first *siue* of F, one has to adopt the second *si<ue>* from ς (note that, by a printing error, Helm 1931 and 1955 have *sine* twice in the text). Thus all modern editors, except Robertson, who reads with Oudendorp *[siue peremptus est] si morte praeuentus est*; this reading is mentioned by Hanson in his footnote ad loc. with 'perhaps rightly'. The consideration leading to the removal of *siue peremptus est* is (in addition to the problem that F has no second *siue*) that it is somewhat redundant and that *siue peremptus est* can be regarded as a gloss on *si morte praeuentus est*. Augello 1977,210, however, defends the reading in F (albeit with the second *si<ue>*) because there certainly is a slight difference in nuance between the two expressions: the first part of the statement can be seen as a reference to a violent death, whereas the second part can be explained more neutrally: in what was intended to be a deep coma, death has nevertheless occurred by some cause or other (see the following note). In addition, Augello rightly points out the physician's general 'verbositas', which he traces back to the 'tradizioni del medico borioso' in comedy (he provides relevant references). The physician's speech does indeed contain other verbose passages (ch. 8: 243,12 f. *nec patiar ... peierare*; ch. 9: 243,23 f. *blaterantem atque inconcinne causificantem*; 243,25 *dedi ... dedi*; above, in this chapter 244,24 f. *non patiar ... non patiar ...*; 244,29 f. *nec meae sectae ... didicissem*; 245,7 *uiuit et ... dormit*). In the reading adopted by all modern editors (except Robertson), one has to assume that the scribe of F wrote *si* instead of *siue* in the second member of the phrase. In the bilingual edition of Helm-Krenkel, which reads *si[ue] peremptus est si<ue> morte praeuentus es*, the critical apparatus mentions that the second *siue* is found in A. This is the most important manuscript of Class I; see Introd. **4.1**.

The text printed here follows a proposal by Hildebrand (also read by Van der Vliet), who points out that ς read *si uere* instead of the first *si*. It may be that this was the reading of F's exemplar, but that F's scribe, misreading the abbreviation of *uere*, interpreted *si ue(re)* as *siue*.

morte praeuentus: 'overtaken by death', in other words, death came upon him suddenly. So in this phrase there is no reference, as with *peremptus est*, to foul play, but to a fatal accident. Cf. Ov. *Tr.* 5,4,31 f. *tempus ... / quod non praeuentum morte fuisse dolet*; Plin. *Ep.* 9,1,3 *sed iam paratam editionem morte praeuentam*; Suet. *Tit.* 10,1 *inter haec morte praeuentus est*. See also GCA 1995,335 on 9,40 (234,6-8).

quaeratis licet: for the verb in the first place of the main clause after a dependent clause, see on *possumus* ch. 14 (247,15).

quaeratis ... causas mortis eius alias: by repeating *causas mortis* the physician refers emphatically to his earlier assurance above (244,30) that *he* does not regard *alicui causas mortis praebere* in accordance with his professional code, and that he therefore bears no responsibility, should the boy, against all expectations, be found dead.

This remark of the physician, placed at the very end of his speech, throws some light on his reason for waiting so long to make this disclosure: if the boy is found dead, the doctor himself will run the risk of being accused of *ueneficium*. Cf. Paul. *Sent.* 5,23,1-2 *Lex Cornelia poenam deportationis infligit et qui ... et qui uenenum hominis necandi causa habuerit uendiderit parauerit ... mortisue causam praestiterit* (see Summers 1967,73 f., with references). His emphasis on his medical-ethical considerations (see above in this chapter: 244,29 f.) can then be seen as a precautionary measure against possible legal consequences of his actions. From the point of view of narrative strategy, this surprising disclosure of the physician is of course a masterstroke in enhancing the suspense of the story, but some logical motivation has been provided as well. Münstermann 1995,118 f. explains the physician's late disclosure by the idea that Apuleius has deliberately brought this doctor on stage as an Asklepios figure, who as a 'deus ex machina' creates a truly dramatic peripeteia. The 'loose ends' in his behaviour, obvious to every reader (cf. Konstan 1994,132), induce the reader, according to Münstermann, to see in this figure the 'besonnener Mann', who follows his 'daimonion' and so acquires a god-like quality (cf. Apul. *Soc.* 20,167).

CHAPTER XII

The boy, who was believed to be dead, is taken from the grave alive; the true culprits are punished.

245,11-13 Ad istum modum seniore adorante placuit, et itur confestim magna cum festinatione ad illud sepulchrum, quo corpus pueri depositum iacebat: Such were the words of the old man, which met with approval; they hurried in great haste to the tomb where the boy's body lay at rest.

Ad istum modum seniore adorante placuit, et itur: In his app. cr. Robertson reports Van der Vliet's proposal *<experiri> placuit* with 'fortasse recte'; however, he himself prefers *<explorare>*, which Hansen also favours. Brakman proposes *<periclitari> placuit*. Oudendorp defends the reading of F, assuming a Graecism: 'ablativum cum participio ponens pro nominativo. Quasi legeretur: Quando sic adorabat senior, placuit'. Hildebrand, however, is not convinced by the Latin parallels given by Oudendorp, and defends F's reading as follows: 'placuit igitur absolute est dictum, et ad dicta factaque referendum senis medici, quae modo exposuerat.'

It is possible to take *ad istum modum* ἀπὸ κοινοῦ with *seniore adorante* and with *placuit* (i.e., *ad istum modum placuit* = *sic placuit*; cf. e.g. 2,24: 44,15 *sic placito consurrexit*; Hor. *Epod*. 16,23 *sic placet? an* ...). Moreover, *et itur* ..., which follows paratactically, can be taken as the equivalent of *(ut) iretur* (see on *placuit* ... *et* ... *praeco pronuntiat* ch. 7: 241,23 f.), so that the context answers the question what the content is of the decision reported in *placuit*.

Ad istum modum: see GCA 1985,127 on 8,13 (187,3) for the frequency in the *Met*. of this and similar expressions at the beginning of a new pericope.

placuit ... *itur*: for the change in tenses, see on *rupit* ... *praecipit* ch. 3 (238,5).

adorante: *adorare* in the sense of 'address' is an archaism; see ThLL s.v. *adoro* 819,3 f. and Van der Paardt 1971,40 on 3,3 (54,2) with references. There and in 2,29 (49,9) the verb is construed transitively, in both passages with the accusative *populum*. That it also can stand without an object, as it does here, appears from Paul. *Fest*. 17,26 L. *adorare apud antiquos significabat agere*.

itur: cf. Verg. *A*. 6,177 f. *haud mora, festinant flentes aramque sepulcri / congerere arboribus caeloque educere certant. / itur in antiquam siluam*; cf. 4,35 (102,16-17) *itur ad constitutum scopulum*, where Kenney ad loc. points to the Vergilian echo. This echo is certainly present here, too. There is a contrast with the Vergilian passage: there the Trojans are preparing a funeral pyre to give Misenus who has been found dead a proper funeral; here people are going to the grave of a person who has already been buried, but they will find him alive.

The impersonal or 'subjectless' passive is used here to focus on the action itself, and its qualification *confestim magna cum festinatione*; besides, it soon appears that it would be difficult to specify the subject because a large and heterogeneous group goes to the tomb en masse (*nemo de curia* ... *qui non* ... *confluxerit*). See Pinkster 1992,175 (also 169 f. on 'implicit Agents' with the impersonal passive). Thus, just as *placuit* lacks a dative specifying who approved of the doctor's proposal (though the context makes it plain that it is the councillors in the *curia*), so *itur* lacks specific agents. One might expect the 'implicit Agents' of *itur* to be identical with the approvers of the proposal, but, as noted above, the agents of *itur* are specified in the next sentence as a much wider group.

confestim magna cum festinatione: Apuleius is undoubtedly aware of the etymological connection between these two expressions (on his fondness for etymologising see on *adserere* ch. 7: 242,15, with references), each of which, however, has its own function here: *confestim* expresses the immediate reaction to the decision, while *magna cum festinatione* qualifies *itur*.

ad illud sepulchrum, quo: for *quo* meaning *ubi*, see *GCA* 1977,61 f. on 4,6 (79,11), with references.

depositum: a well-chosen word, now that both actors and readers have learned that the boy is probably only comatose. On the one hand, *deponere* can mean 'lay down' (cf. Verg. *A.* 7,107 f. *Aeneas primique duces ... / corpora sub ramis deponunt arboris altae*; see *OLD* s.v. *depono* 1b); on the other hand it can mean 'secure, put in a safe place' (cf. Hor. *S.* 1,1,42 f. *argenti pondus et auri / defossa ... deponere terra*; see *OLD* ibid. 6a); in addition, there is a play on the legal meaning of 'put into custody, entrust to a third party (in this case, to the grave)'; cf. Afric. *Dig.* 13,7,31 *cum depositus uel commodatus seruus furtum faciat*; Gaius *Dig.* 10,2,5 (*OLD* ibid. 7; cf. also Summers 1967,328 f. on this passage: 'an extremely clever legal metaphor'; *RE* s.v. *depositum*, 233 f. [Leonhard]).

ThLL s.v. *depono* 583,26 gives our passage as the first for the meaning 'i.q. *sepelire*', but the first passage where *deponere* means *sepelire* exclusively (which does not apply to our passage, as explained above) is Cypr. *Ep.* 67,6,2 *filios ... apud profana sepulcra depositos et alienigenis consepultos*. Paul. *Dig.* 11,7,40 does not yet regard *deponere* and *sepelire* as synonyms by any means: *si quis ... eo animo corpus intulerit, quod cogitaret ... magis temporis gratia deponere, quam quod ibi sepeliret mortuum*. The expression *deponere cinerem* for interring someone's ashes is already attested in a funeral inscription dated to the time of Catullus: *CIL* 1,1214,14 f.: *in tumulo cinerem nostri corporis ... parcae deposierunt*; in Christian funerary inscriptions *deponere corpus* is found, e.g. *CIL* 10,1230 *sub hoc ... deponen<s> marmore corpus*. See also *RAC* 12,555 s.v. 'Grabinschrift' [Pietri-Engemann] on the term *depositus* on funeral inscriptions. In *Fl.* 19,3 Apuleius describes as *prope deposito* a man whose burial is about to take place, but who will soon turn out to be still alive: *certe quidem iacenti homini ac prope deposito fatum attulit* (sc. Asclepiaden).

245,13-15 Nemo de curia, de optimatibus nemo ac ne de ipso quidem populo quisquam, qui non illuc curiose confluxerit: There was no one from the *curia*, no one from the notables, and not even anyone from the common people, who did not flock together there, full of curiosity.

Nemo de curia, de optimatibus nemo ac ne de ipso ... populo quisquam: the second and third members of this tricolon are placed chiastically in respect to the first member; the first and second cola are marked by asyndeton; moreover, the three cola are formed according to the 'Gesetz der wachsenden Glieder': 6, 8, and 12 syllables respectively.

de curia, de optimatibus ... de ... populo: only *decuriones* (i.e. *optimates*) could be members of the *curia* as 'city council' (see on *decurionis* ch. 1: 236,23); here, therefore, *curia* must be understood as the 'assembly', or even the 'assembly hall' where the lawsuit took place (see on *curiam* ch. 6: 241,10); so the enumeration *curia ... optimatibus ... populo* does not reflect a hierarchical order. The phrase *de optimatibus ... ... curiose confluxerit* illustrates one of the recurring themes in the *Met.*, namely the pursuit of *spectacula* (see Introd. **2.4.2**): as far as *curiositas* is concerned, there is no difference between *optimates* and *populus*; everyone hurrries to the place where there is something unusual to be seen. Cf. ch. 19 (251,12 f.) *magnae ciuium turbae confluebant* (i.e. to see the ass performing tricks).

For this use of *de* cf. 4,19 (89,7-9) *nec ... quisquam de tanta copia* with GCA 1977,147 ad loc., with references. Elsewhere Apuleius uses the partitive genitive, e.g. ch. 8 (242,25) *nec quisquam decurionum*.

curia ... curiose: a play on words. Both meanings of *curiose* (1. 'diligenter'; 2. 'with curiosity') play a part here: the crowd follows the doctor's advice 'diligenter', but naturally they also flock to the grave 'full of curiosity'. See GCA 1995,36 on 9,1 (203,5-9); ibid. 373 and n. 52 (Appendix III *Curiositas* [Hijmans]).

confluxerit: the use of the tenses in this chapter full of dramatic events is quite varied, but this variation is functional from a narrative point of view. In l. 11 a perfect tense *placuit* marks the end of the previous episode and the beginning of a new one after a long section of direct discourse; *itur* is a historical present, which in this whole passage is the 'temps de base' for the description of the consecutive events (for the notion 'temps de base' see on *rupit ... praecipit* ch. 3: 238,5); the perfect *confluxerit* indicates the result of *itur* and is the starting point for the narration of what happens afterwards, namely the historical presents *deprehendit, producit, deportatur, procedit, indicitur, suffigitur,* and *sinuntur*; finally, the story is concluded with the perfect tenses *accepit* and *factus est*.

245,15-19 Ecce pater, suis ipse manibus coperculo capuli remoto, commodum discusso mortifero sopore surgentem postliminio mortis deprehendit filium eumque complexus artissime, uerbis impar praesenti gaudio, producit ad populum: And look, the father with his own hands took the lid off the coffin and found his son just at the moment when he had shaken off his deadly sleep and was lifting up, returning from death; he embraced him most fervently and, unable to speak because of the joy of the moment, he brought him forth for the people to see.

Ecce: the previous sentence described how a huge crowd gathered around the grave; *ecce* now invites the reader to imagine himself a spectator at the grave and a participant in the emotional event. In the *Met. ecce* often marks a dramatic reversal (as here and e.g. 6,25: 147,6; see GCA 1981,27 ad loc.); in other passages it is used, as in comedy, to mark the entry of a new person (cf. 9,22: 220,5 with GCA 1995,200 ad loc.). Whatever the circumstances, the function of *ecce* is the same: to involve the reader closely in the story. See the indices of GCA 1977, 1981 and 1985 s.v. *ecce*, and Van der Paardt 1971,87 on 3,11 (60,1) with further references; to these can be added that *ecce* is frequently so used by Vergil in the *Aeneid* (Heinze 1915,374). Cf. Servius on *A.* 4,152 (*ecce ferae, saxi dejectae uertice, caprae*): *et bene hac particula utitur; facit enim nos ita intentos ut quae dicuntur putemus uidere*.

coperculo capuli: c-p-c-l-c-p-l. Reading aloud, one can 'hear' the creaking sound of the coffin being opened.

coperculo: 'lid', not exclusively of a coffin; in 6,21 (144,9) it is the lid of the *pyxis* opened by Psyche. Cf. also Plin. *Nat.* 23,109 *in olla noua, coperculo inlito*.

capuli: meaning 'hilt, sword-handle', *capulus* is common throughout Latinity (see *OLD* s.v. *capulus* 1). For the meaning 'coffin' (as here and 4,18: 87,29; see *GCA* 1977,135 ad loc.), *ThLL* s.v. *capulus* 383,82 f. gives some passages from comedy (e.g. Pl. *As.* 892), Lucilius 61, Var. *Men.* 222 (see Cèbe 1983,1053 ad loc.); then Lucr. 2,1174 (cf. Bailey ad loc.), and then Apuleius. After Apuleius it occurs in Tert. *Res.* 32 (about Jonah:) *triduum concoquendae carni uiscera ceti suffecissent quam capulum, quam sepulcrum.* It is interesting to see how an archaic word, preserved by Apuleius (who either borrowed it as an archaism from Lucretius, or found it himself in the comic poets) is given new life by Tertullian. In *Res.* 7 he uses it metaphorically of the body as a prison: *deus ... animae suae umbram (animam humanam) ... uilissimo alicui commiserit capulo.*

commodum: 'a little while ago; only just'. Apuleius uses the adverb 25 times in the *Met.*, 3 times in the *Fl.*, not at all in the *Apol.* Callebat 1968,435, n. 190 concludes from the frequent occurrences of *commodum* in Plautus and Cicero's letters (it is less frequent in his orations) that it was common in colloquial language, and that Apuleius therefore found it appropriate to an informal narrative style; see also *GCA* 1977,69 on 4,8 (80,6-8).

discusso mortifero sopore: cf. ch. 11 (245,8) *marcido sopore discusso* and the note there. The words which the physician used to predict that the boy would be found waking up from a coma are here repeated almost exactly, with chiasmus. This repetition gives to the description of the awakening the implication 'Sure enough, the doctor spoke the truth!'

mortifero sopore: in ch. 12 (245,2 f.) the *medicus* mentioned a *morti simillimus sopor*, and later on (245,8) a *marcidus sopor*; in his case the term *mortifer* would have been ill-chosen because of its potential legal risk. In our passage, where the narrator wants to convey the dramatic nature of this moment to his audience, *mortifer* is effective and accurate: this sleep could certainly have been lethal for the boy who had been buried alive, and might also have been *mortifer* for his stepbrother. Later, when the happy outcome of the story is revealed, the narrator uses the term *opportunus somnus*.

postliminio mortis: on the 'resurrection' theme see on ch. 11 (245,8) *remeabit ad diem lucidam. Postliminium* is a legal term for the resumption of civic rights, held in suspension during exile, capture, etc. on one's return ... (*OLD* s.v. 1). As Bowersock 1994,109 notes, Apuleius, in transferring the legal term to the restoration of the dead to life, 'equates death with the servility of a captive and life with the restoration of full citizen right.' See also Gianotti 1986,27 and n. 46.

Elsewhere in the *Met.* Apuleius also uses the ablative *postliminio*, meaning *rursus, retro*, e.g. 1,25 (23,3 f.) *postliminio me in forum cupidinis reducens*; 3,25 (71,2): *postliminio redibis*; 5,7 (108,23), and 9,21 (219,11). But in three passages we find it combined with a genitive: here and 2,28 (48,7) *postliminio mortis*; 4,25 (94,10 f.) *postliminio pressae quietis* (see *GCA* 1977,189 ad loc. with much information about the legal background of *postliminio*, with references, but with no explanation of this genitive). The *ThLL* material offers no instances before Apuleius of a genitive with *postliminio*. It is possible that in these passages Apuleius plays with the etymology of the word and construes, as it were, a genitive with *limen*: 'back, across the threshold of death or (in 4,25) deep sleep'. Cf. Justin. *Inst.* 1,12,5 *dictum est autem postliminium a limine et post, ut eum, qui ab hostibus captus in fines nostros postea peruenit, postliminio reuersum recte dicimus. nam limina sicut in domibus finem quendam faciunt, sic et imperii finem limen esse ueteres uoluerunt ... ab eo postliminium dictum, quia eodem limine reuertebatur, quo amissus erat.*

A genitive with *postliminium* occurs in Tert. *An.* 35,6 (Elias who will return) ... *mundo reddendus, de quo est translatus, non ex postliminio uitae* (i.e. not to return to life), *sed ex supplemento prophetiae*; see Waszink ad loc. for other instances; cf. also Zeno Ver. 1,1,5 *mortuorum in postliminium uitae animas reductas inspira*.

245,19-21 Atque ut erat adhuc feralibus amiculis instrictus atque obditus deportatur ad iudicium puer: And as he was, still swathed and entangled in his burial clothes, the boy was carried to the courthouse.

feralibus amiculis instrictus atque obditus: it was the custom to bury the dead in a beautiful shroud, and besides, to prevent the mouth from falling open, linen or woollen bands were bound around forehead, cheeks, and chin. See *RE* s.v. 'Bestattung' 334,33 f. [Mau], and *RAC* s.v. 'Bestattung' 202 f. [Stommel]. Cf. Lucian. *Luct.* 11.

instrictus: *instringere* i.q. (*arte*) *ligare, amicire, implicare* is rare: *ThLL* s.v. *instringo* 2007,10 f. mentions only [Quint.] *Decl.* 5,16 (Håkanson 102,2 f.) (*corpus*) *iacet inter uincula, quibus instrinxerat ... pirata captiuum.* ThLL regards the reading *instrictam* of M' in Ov. *Met.* 11,167 as 'vix recte'; cf. also Bömer ad loc. After Apuleius it is found, used metaphorically, in Aug. *in epist. Ioh.* 5,2 *fortiter instrinxit apostolus (quaestionem uix solubilem proponendo)*. See also *GCA* 1985,189 on 8,22 (194,5-7) *instricta*.

obditus: cf. *OLD* s.v. *obdo* 3: 'To restrain by tying; to hamper, encumber'. There is no reason to adopt Helm's proposal *obsitus* in his app. crit. (referring to 3,8: 57,20, which, however, is not about a dead person but an old woman in mourning clothes). *Obditus* makes good sense: the boy is dressed in a shroud which impedes his movements (consequently, he is being carried: *deportatur*); it may also refer to the bands around his face (see above, on *feralibus amiculis ... obditus*) that prevent him from speaking.

deportatur ... puer: the passive construction sustains the image of a crowd acting collectively (see above, on *itur*). It also shifts the 'spotlight' gradually from the father (the passage started with *ecce pater*) to the son. See also the following note on the structure of this passage.

puer: Bernhard 1927,19 speaks of 'gedankliche Betonung' of the subject *puer* which is placed at the end of the sentence, and collects the passages in the *Met.* where the subject is placed in that position. These, indeed, include cases where that position gives the subject strong emphasis, e.g. 7,24 (172,13-14) *et ecce de proximo specu ... proserpit ursa* with *GCA* 1981,242 ad loc.; 9,19 (217,6 f.) *formidinem mortis uicit aurum* with *GCA* 1995,176 ad loc. Rather than the somewhat vague notion 'emphasis', it might be better to say that in these examples the key word of the sentence comes at the end, as the climax.

It is worth noting that the position of *puer* in the last sentence means that the whole pericope (lines 15-21) is enclosed by the two main characters - the father (l. 15 *ecce pater*) and the son he believed to be dead.

245,21-25 Iamque liquido serui nequissimi atque mulieris nequioris patefactis sceleribus procedit in medium nuda Veritas et nouercae quidem perpetuum indicitur exilium, seruus uero patibulo suffigitur et omnium consensu bono medico sinuntur aurei, opportuni somni pretium: And now that the crimes of the wicked slave and his even worse mistress had been clearly brought to light, naked Truth came out into the open. The stepmother was condemned to perpetual exile, while the slave was crucified, and by unanimous consent the good doctor was granted the gold pieces, a reward for the opportune sleeping draught.

Iamque: in its initial position, *iam* affects the entire sentence and thus accentuates the inevitability of the events now rapidly succeeding each other: the true culprits exposed, the entire truth brought to light, the villains brought to justice, and the good doctor rewarded. See Chausserie-Laprée 1969,497 f. on 'Iam d'ouverture' in dramatic narration in historiographers.

serui nequissimi atque mulieris nequioris: *nequissimus* has already been used to describe the slave at his first introduction (ch. 4: 239,21 with note), and again ch. 10 (244,18). As the type of the murderous stepmother, the *nouerca* has twice been called *pessima* (ch. 5: 239,28, see note; ch. 6: 241,6) and also *dira* (ch. 5: 240,9). Now she is described as even more evil than the *nequissimus seruus*. This may be just the narrator's subjective opinion, but it could also be a reflection of the judges' opinion after the revelation of the crimes.

procedit ... nuda Veritas: cf. Lucian. *Cal.* 5 τὴν 'Αλήθειαν προσιοῦσαν. In 8,7 (181,14-17), all editors print *Veritatem* with a capital (cf. *GCA* 1985,76 ad loc.). Here, too, *Veritas* is personified (*procedit in medium*), a point which editors (printing here *ueritas*) may have overlooked, possibly because 'the naked truth' is a common metaphor in many modern languages. (For a similar editorial problem see on *haud ullo tempore tam beniuolam Fortunam expertus* ch. 13: 246,15). For the personification cf. also Hor. *Carm.* 1,24,6 f. *cui Pudor et Iustitiae soror, / incorrupta Fides, nudaque Veritas*, with Nisbet-Hubbard ad loc., with references. Apuleius may well be alluding to the Horace passage, since the appearance of *nuda Veritas* is immediately followed by the punishments which are the result of the operations of *Iustitia*.

Like the Greek 'Αλήθεια, the Roman *Veritas* is not a cultic personification. According to Nilsson *Gr.Rel.* ²1955,748, the personified 'Αλήθεια is a creation of Pindar (Frg. 205 = 83 Puech: ὤνασσ' 'Αλάθεια; *O.* 10,3 f.: θυγάτηρ / 'Αλάθεια Διός); under the influence of rhetoric (prosopopoeia), it is further developed by (comic) poets and philosophers. Consequently, there is no extensive iconography for *Veritas*. The nudity of *Veritas* in Horace and Apuleius, and after him Aug. *Ep.* 242,5, is to be interpreted not iconographically but ethically; it can be understood through statements such as Soph. frg. 301 Radt πρὸς ταῦτα κρύπτε μηδέν· ὡς ὁ πάνθ' ὁρῶν / καὶ πάντ' ἀκούων πάντ' ἀναπτύσσει χρόνος and Men. *Sent.* 33,13 Jaekel ἄγει δὲ πρὸς φῶς τὴν ἀλήθειαν χρόνος. In descriptions of the few illustrations of Aletheia in antiquity she is said to be wearing a white garment, e.g. Philostr. *Imag.* 1,27,3 Schönberger 'Αλήθεια λευχειμονοῦσα. Botticelli is the first to depict Truth as a nude female figure; see *LIMC* s.v. *Aletheia*, 486 f. [Settis]; *RE* s.v. 'Personifikationen', 1042,64 f. [Stößl]. For a survey of personifications in the *Met.* see *GCA* 1977,110 f. on 4,14 (85,8-10). See also on *Riualitas*, ch. 24 (255,20).

nouercae ... suffigitur: the *Lex Cornelia de sicariis et ueneficiis* was still valid, though slightly modified (Summers 1967,73 f.), during the Empire. The relevant provisions of the law are given in Paul. *Sent.* 5,23, 1-2: *Lex Cornelia poenam deportationis infligit ei qui hominem occiderit eiusue rei causa furtiue faciendi cum telo fuerit, et qui uenenum hominis necandi causa habuerit uendiderit parauerit, falsum testimonium dixerit, quo quis periret, mortisue causam praestiterit. Ob quae omnia facinora in honestiores poena capitis uindicari placuit, humiliores uero in crucem tolluntur aut bestiis obiciuntur. Homicida est qui aliquo genere tali hominem occidit mortisue causam praestitit*. Whether the poisoning was successful or not (as here), has no effect on the penalty; see Mommsen, *Röm.Strafr.* 627 f. with nn. 1 and 2. The status of the criminal, however, makes a difference to the penalty: distressing as it may seem to us, the *seruus*, because he is *humilior*, automatically receives a severer penalty than the *mulier nequior*, because she is (socially) *honestior* (see Summers 1967,76 f. and Elster 1991,147 f.).

perpetuum ... exilium: in the 'Phaedra' novella in Heliodorus it is the innocently convicted Knemon who is condemned to exile (Heliod. 1,14,1). *Perpetuum exilium* is the most severe form of exile, namely *deportatio*. It was always for life, and to a specific place; it implied loss of citizenship and property *in toto* (*Dig.* 48,22,6; 48,22,15, and ibid. 7 on the difference between *relegatio* and *deportatio*). From Tiberius onward it became more and more the standard punishment for *honestiores* and displaced the milder forms of exile (*RE* s.v. *Exilium*, 1684,60 f. and s.v. *Deportatio*, 231,34 f. [Kleinfeller]; see also Grasmück 1978,129). For the combination *exilium perpetuum* ThLL s.v. *exilium* 1490,35 f. gives several passages from legal codices but also e.g. V.Max. 5,6,3; Quint. *Inst.* 7,4,43 *cum perpetuo an quinquennali sit exilio multandus, in controuersiam uenerit.* Cf. Quint. *Decl.* 244,2 *si in perpetuum exilium missus essem, forsitan ...* .

Again it can be noted that the rules applied in this trial in a small Greek town are typically Roman: we would almost forget that this *nouerca* is being banished from a town in Thessaly, not from Rome (see on *patres in curiam conuenirent* ch. 7: 241,24).

bono medico sinuntur aurei: these are the *centumque aureos solidos* (ch. 9: 243,19) that the slave paid for the supposed poison. The physician had the coins sealed (ch. 9: 244,1), and later brought to court (244,3) as evidence. That the doctor now receives this very large sum of money for his services is on the one hand regular Roman practice; on the other hand, there is an obvious moral to be drawn from this instance of an honest physician (cf. ch. 8: 243,8) so handsomely rewarded.

bono medico: cf. *serui nequissimi ... mulieris nequioris*. The adjectives, chiastically placed, emphasize this (at first sight) most satisfactory case of poetic justice, where evil is punished and virtue rewarded: 'just rewards' for all. But also the father, who almost had his innocent son condemned to death, fares very well in the end, as we can read immediately below. Then the question arises for the interpreting reader whether that 'reward' is truly deserved (see on the father figure in this tale on *matrimonium sibi reparauerat* ch. 2: 237,7). Throughout the story there are returning signals that we should read the father's vicissitudes above all as an illustration of the fickleness of *Fortuna*, who *semper suas opes ad malos et indignos conferat* (7,2: 155,22 f.; see *GCA* 1981,91 f. ad loc.); see also on *magnis aerumnarum procellis aestuat* ch. 5 (240,24 f.). The virtuous *iuuenis* who was almost condemned to death is not mentioned at all again.

opportuni somni: the sleep that came at the right moment; cf. *Fl.* 15,27 *opportuni silentii*. ThLL s.v. *opportunus* 777,40 f. gives more examples of this meaning; cf. the frequent phrase *mors opportuna*, e.g. Liv. 6,1,7 *cui iudicio cum mors adeo opportuna, ut uoluntariam magna pars crederet, subtraxit.* Moreover, in medical terms the sleeping potion was an *opportunum remedium*; see the examples given by *ThLL* ibid. 778,23 f. for 'de cibis, remediis, sim. salutaribus'.

F has *opportu sonji*, in which the superscribed *n* seems to be written by the first hand, the *i* by another hand; originally it read *sōī*, which was changed to *sonji* by a different hand; φ has *oportunus omni*. In this passage, where φ shows an incorrect word separation in addition to *oportunus* instead of *oportuni*, and where in F many different hands have obscured the situation, a clearer reading is offered by the mss. indicated as a* (part of Class I; see Introd. **4.1**): a* have here *opportuni sompni*.

245,26-29 Et illius quidem senis famosa atque fab<ul>osa fortuna prouidentiae diuinae condignum accepit exitum, qui momento modico, immo puncto exiguo, post orbitatis periculum adulescentium duorum pater repente factus est: And the much talked-of and dramatic fortune of that old man received an ending worthy of divine providence: in a short time, nay in one tiny moment, he suddenly became, after the threat of childlessness, the father of two young men.

The story is not evaluated as a whole, but concludes with a coda (on evaluation and coda as constitutive elements of narrative texts see Gülich 1976,252 f., with references), in which the ending of the story — at least for the *senex* (*illius quidem senis*) — is described in terms reminiscent of the themes of many comedies: *qui momento modico ... adulescentium duorum pater ... factus est* (see also on *fabulosa* below). This ending however, with its unmistakable allusions to the themes of comedy, forms a problem for the reader, in whom the narrator earlier has awakened very specific expectations — not once, but twice (see on *scelestum ac nefarium facinus* ch. 2: 237,1 f. and the introductory remarks to 237,12-14). The absence of an evaluation afterwards, or at least a reference to the expectations that were awakened at the beginning and now have come to nothing, results in a 'Leerstelle': it is up to the reader to supply an overall interpretation and a reviewed evaluation (for the absence of an 'ideal' reader in the text, see Schuerewegen 1987,247 f.).

illius quidem senis ... fortuna: *fortuna*: 'what happens to someone; one's fate, fortunes' (*OLD* s.v. *fortuna* 8). Cf. in the *Met.*, also with a genitive, 4,5 (78,8 f.) *miseri commilitonis fortunam cogitans*; 7,2 (155,17 f.) *ueteris fortunae et illius beati Lucii praesentisque aerumnae ... facta comparatione*; with a possessive pronoun e.g. 2,15 (37,5 f.) *ferat suam Diophanes ille fortunam*; cf. 11,18 (280,8 f.) *Fama uolucris ... meamque ... fortunam memorabilem narrauerat passim*. In this meaning we also find the plural *fortunae* in the *Met.*, e.g. 3,1 (52,19 f.) *fortunas meas heiulabam*; 8,23 (195,13 f.) *in meas fortunas ridiculos construebat iocos* (see *GCA* 1985,200 ad loc.); 9,13 (213,5 f.) *uariisque fortunis exercitatum*. On the father's *fortuna* and its function in this story, see above, on *bono medico* and on *forte fortuna* ch. 5 (239,28), and Introd. **2.4.1**. *Quidem* (not translated) makes it clear that this sentence should be regarded as connected with the next one, which starts with *At ego tunc temporis* ... (246,1), and that the lucky *fortuna* of the old man is contrasted by the narrator with his own uncertain fate of that time: *fatorum fluctibus uolutabar* (246,1 f.). As we know, the *Met.*'s division into capita was not made by the author himself but by Hildebrand; although a new 'chapter' in the main story is about to begin here and Hildebrand is right, therefore, in starting with a new caput number, we should note that the author has made a special effort to create a smooth transition from inner story to main story by means of *illius quidem senis ... at ego...* .

famosa ... fabulosa fortuna: alliteration.

famosa: 'which everyone spoke about; the *fama* of which spread everywhere'. Cf. 5,31 (128,3 f.) *nec enim uos utique domus meae famosa fabula et ... filii mei facta latuerunt*.

fabulosa: 'about which stories are told'; for the first appearance of this use of the adjective see Hor. *Carm.* 1,22,7 f. *fabulosus ... Hydaspes*, with Nisbet-Hubbard ad loc., who regard this a coinage of Horace's own (on the lines of μυθῶδες). The continuation of the sentence shows how this could be made into a *fabula* about the *senex*, who *momento modico ... post orbitatis periculum adulescentium duorum pater repente factus est* (a typical comic plot; cf. e.g. Hegio at the end of Plautus' *Captiui*); see also on *fabulam* ch. 2 (237,13).

Apart from this passage, *fabulosus* occurs once more in the *Met.*, meaning 'resembling an invented tale, incredible' (*OLD* s.v. *fabulosus* 2), in 1,20 (18,18): *nihil ... hac fabula fabulosius*. Cf. also [Apul.] *Ascl.* 12 (296) *sed aliis incredibile, aliis fabulosum, aliis forsitan uideatur esse deridendum*.

The emendation *fabulosa* for *fabosa* (in F and φ) was made by a different hand in the margin of F, before the transcription by φ (Lütjohann 1873,447).

prouidentiae diuinae condignum ... exitum: the notion of *prouidentia* is not associated with Isis until book 11, e.g. 11,15 (277,20); cf. Gwyn Griffiths 1975,253 ad loc. In the first ten books, the narrator or other persons in the story use the term (*diuina/caelestis*) *prouidentia* in case of good luck, whereas in the case of bad luck they speak of *fortuna*. There are a few passages where the use of *diuina/caelestis/deum prouidentia* seems to illustrate that an event can be considered as *diuina* (etc.) *prouidentia* for one person, but bad luck for another. This is the case in e.g. 8,31 (202,12), where the cook's wife regards the presence of the ass (who can be butchered in order to disguise the theft of a haunch of venison) as a case of *deum prouidentia*, while for the ass this is one of the many cases in which *Fortuna* commits an assault on his life (cf. 9,1: 203,12 f.; see *GCA* 1995,38 f. ad loc.). Inversely, in 9,27 (223,7 f.) Lucius regards the opportunity to expose the hidden lover as having been sent by *caelestis prouidentia*, but the exposed lover and the *pistor*'s wife will experience this as an extreme case of 'bad luck' (see *GCA* 1995, App. VI,388 [Hijmans]). This is probably the 'irony' in the use of *prouidentia* referred to by Heine 1962,138: this kind of passage may lead the reader of the entire *Met.* to wonder what exactly the implication is of Isis' *prouidentia*, which the narrator exalts so much in the eleventh book, and whether the *prouidentia* in our passage might not be an equally subjective experience. See F. Jones 1995,17 f. on the relationship between Providence and Chance in the *Met.*, with a discussion of relevant passages. For *prouidentia* in Apuleius' philosophical works, see Hijmans 1987,444 f.

prouidentiae ... condignum: *condignus* with a dative is also found 7,14 (164,18-21): see *GCA* 1981,170 f. ad loc. on this adjective, borrowed from comedy, and on its construction. Marache 1957,112 points out the popularity of this word, which was re-discovered in the second century A.D.

accepit exitum: *accipere finem* meaning 'come to an end, conclude', is attested from Mela 1,108 onward. The combination *accipere exitum* is found in *Cod. Just.* 3,31,12,1a *non debet iudicium differri, sed exitum suum accipere*. For *exitus* in connection with someone's *fortuna* cf. also Apul. *Mun.* 19,333 (*ciuilis ratio*) ... *receptrixque sit naturarum ad diuersa tendentium fortunarumque per uarias fines exitusque pergentium*.

qui: far removed from its antecedent *senis*. See Bernhard 1927,29 f. for other examples in the *Met*. Bernhard mentions 'rhetorische Gründe', which applies here: *illius senis* has been placed first because of the contrast with *at ego* (ch. 13: 246,1; see above, on *illius quidem ... fortuna*); the relative clause *qui ... factus est* explains the preceding *fortuna ... prouidentiae diuinae condignum accepit exitum*. For a similar case cf. 7,25 (173,12 f.) *te nos tractamus inciuiliter, qui nostrum asinum furatus abducis?* See also LHSz 2,692, with references.

momento modico, immo puncto exiguo: cf. Plin. *Pan.* 56,2 *quod momentum, quod immo temporis punctum ...* . The short time span within which an entire reversal of someone's *fortuna* can occur is frequently emphasized in the *Met.*, e.g. 3,9 (59,2); 7,6 (158,16) with *GCA* 1981,117 ad loc.; see also 9,39 (232,24) with *GCA* 1995,322.

puncto: sc. *temporis*. *OLD* s.v. *punctum* 5 gives examples of the omission of *temporis*. The image of *punctum temporis* (= στιγμή χρόνου) can be explained by the fact that the ancient theories of time regard στιγμή as a point between past and future.

post orbitatis periculum: cf. ch. 5 (240,24-27) *infelix duplici filiorum morte percussus ... nam et ... certo sciebat*, with comm. ad loc.

adulescentium duorum pater ... factus est: cf. ch. 5 (240,24) *duplici filiorum morte percussus*. The wording of this phrase (another possibility would have been: he got his two sons back) suggests, again, a (re)birth of the sons. On this recurring theme in the *Met.* see on ch. 11 (245,8) *remeabit ad diem lucidam*, and Introd. **2.4.5**.

The narrator concentrates entirely on the experiences of the father and ignores those of the two sons: at the beginning of this chapter the *puer*, snatched from the grave, was briefly shown to the people as 'silent evidence'; the *iuuenis*, almost condemned to death and now acquitted, is not mentioned at all. Now that the great reversal has taken place, the story is quickly concluded, and the people who played a role in it are forgotten. The transition to the next episode in the main story is achieved by a contemplation of the reversal in the *fortuna* of a single actor. The disappearance of actors who play a temporary role in the *Met.* is often a question of 'narrative economy', as *GCA* 1985,10 remark. See also on *meus quidem hortulanus ... nescio* ch. 1 (236,10 f.).

adulescentium duorum: it is unusual, in Apuleius and in Latin in general, for the numeral to follow the noun (see Bernhard 1927,24). The special position draws attention to the numeral: one moment the father was still threatened with childlessness, the next he was a father of not one but two sons.

pater repente factus est: similarly, the comedy 'Mandragola' by Machiavelli ends with a sudden, unexpected paternity; see Bocciolini 1986 (cited on *mandragoram* ch. 11: 245,1 f.), 169,n. 53.

CHAPTER XIII

The ass enters the service of a confectioner and a cook.

246,1-2 At ego tunc temporis talibus fatorum fluctibus uolutabar: As for me at that moment, this is how I was being tossed on the waves of fortune.

At ego: Pinkster 1987,369 f. examines the pragmatic motivation for the use of subject pronouns in Petronius' narrative prose; the systematic application of the pragmatic notions of Topic and Focus leads to the conclusion that Petronius' use of subject pronouns differs much less from classical usage (the examples are from Cicero) than is usually assumed. The same is true of Apuleius' usage: in our passage *ego* has a focal function; it forms a contrast with *illius quidem senis ... fortuna* (ch. 12: 245,26; see note there). Besides, *at ego* indicates here the return to the framing tale (Bernhard 1927,266 f.).

tunc temporis: this combination is first attested in Apuleius' *Met.*, here and 3,4 (55,2); see Van der Paardt 1971,48 ad loc. Cf. Justin. 3,6,6 *paruae tunc temporis ... uires Atheniensibus erant*; ibid. e.g. 1,4,4; 8,3,7. LHSz 2,57 assume that it is a later 'Hinzubildung' by analogy with expressions like *id temporis* (e.g. Cic. *S.Rosc.* 97 *ut ... id temporis Roma proficisceretur*). *Tunc temporis*, possibly already a set formula in the *sermo cotidianus* of the 2nd century A.D. (see Callebat 1968,191), is also found in charters from the 11th century onward; it is used by witnesses to indicate that they were present as subscribers when the document was drawn up (see Du Cange s.v. *tunc temporis*).

talibus fatorum fluctibus uolutabar: although the old man's trials in the recently concluded inner story are (happily) over, the narrator's own situation at this time (*tunc temporis*) is still unstable (*fatorum fluctibus uolutabar*); see above on *At ego*. This contrast is reinforced by the imperfect *uolutabar* (versus the perfect in ch. 12: 245,27 *accepit exitum*)

In comparison with other transitional formulas in the *Met.* where a complaint about *Fortuna* accompanies a new turn in the narrative, this transitional formula sounds relatively neutral; cf. *talibus aerumnis edomitum nouis Fortuna saeua tradidit cruciatibus* (7,16: 166,3 f.). Cf. also 7,2 (155,17-156,1) with *GCA* 1981,91 f.; 7,17 (167,4 f.); 7,25 (173,4 f.); 8,24 (195,21 f.) with *GCA* 1985,203 f. Nevertheless, the remark in our passage is also a complaint about the ass's ever-changing fate, and can therefore be regarded as a subtle advance qualification of the seemingly positive remark *haud ullo tempore tam beniuolam Fortunam expertus* (below; see note there). See *GCA* 1995,269 on 9,31 (226,22-24) on the fact that a reference to *fortuna* frequently accompanies a transition to the ass's next sojourn.

In the *Met.* as well as in the *Apology*, the use of *fatum* and *fata* reflects 'common parlance' (see Hijmans 1987,446 and n. 214) rather than the strict terminology of a defined philosophical theory. In other passages *fatum* is practically identical with *fortuna* (e.g. 9,38: 232,4 *iniquitate fati*; see *GCA* 1995,317 ad loc.). In other passages *fatum* suggests inevitability; cf. 1,20 (18,23), *utcumque fata decreuerint, ita cuncta mortalibus prouenire* (sc. *arbitror*), and the discussion on ch. 2 (237,10 f.) *seu naturaliter ... seu fato ad extremum impulsa flagitium*. See also *GCA* 1977,37 on 4,3 (76,3 f.) *talibus fatis implicitus*, and 161 on 4,21 (90,18). In our passage, as in the passages just mentioned, *fatorum* expresses the notion of an inevitable course of events which propel one along irresistably (see also below on *qui me nullo uendente ... fecerat*). In addition, there is a contrast with the end of the recently concluded inner story; the ass's story has still not come to an end, and he is still being tossed *fatorum fluctibus*. So now, about halfway through the next to last book of the *Met.*, we can detect the first intimation of a longing for the end; in 11,1 (266,20 f.) this is expressed in the words: *fato scilicet iam meis tot tantisque cladibus satiato*. The image evoked in this passage of a wind-tossed ship at sea (see the following notes) calls up by association the desire to reach port safely: at the end of this book, the main character escapes to *Cenchreae, portus ... tutissimum nauium receptaculum* (ch. 35: 266,3 f.); cf. also 11,15 (277,5 f.) *magnisque Fortunae tempestatibus et ... procellis ad portum Quietis ... tandem, Luci, uenisti*. See also below on *fatorum fluctibus*.

talibus: this points ahead to the next sentence, where the transfer to new owners, and by consequence the encounter with new adventures, illustrate *fatorum fluctibus uolutari*.

fatorum fluctibus: the metaphorical use of *fluctus* ('aestus, tempestates, perturbationes vitae, sim.'; see *ThLL* s.v. *fluctus* 947,54 f.) is attested from Accius, *trag.* 608 R (= 403 Dangel) *quam turbam, quantos belli fluctus concites*, onward, and is found in Latin of all periods. In many of the passages mentioned by *ThLL* ibid., the image of the *fluctus* (*uitae, rei publicae, fortunae* etc.) is explicitly or implicitly connected with the escape from it (e.g. to a 'safe haven'. Cf. Cic. *Sest.* 73 *spe reliquae tranquillitatis praesentis fluctus tempestatemque fugisse*; Lucr. 5,11 f. (*deus ille. ..) fluctibus et tantis uitam tantisque tenebris / in tam tranquillo et tam clara luce locauit*; Sen. *Dial.* 10 (*Brev.*),18,1 *in tranquilliorem portum ... recede, cogita, quot fluctus subieris, quot tempestates ... sustinueris*. For the combination *fatorum fluctibus* no examples are given by *ThLL* ibid. before our passage; however, cf. Catul. 68,13 *merser fortunae fluctibus*; Sen. *Con.* 1,1,10 *(diuitias) huc atque illuc incertae fortunae fluctus appellet*.

uolutabar: passive voice, imperfect tense, and intensive value of this verb contribute to the image of being incessantly and unresistingly rolled over and over. See *OLD* s.v. *uoluto* 2: 'to impel with an undulating or turbulent movement, cause to roll'; cf. Sen. *Nat.* 4a,2,6 *inter rapidam insaniam Nili et reciprocos fluctus uolutati* (sc. *nautae*). The verb occurs once elsewhere in the *Met.*, at 9,5 (206,20) in an erotic context; see *GCA* 1995,68 ad loc.

246,2-6 Miles ille, qui me nullo uendente comparauerat et sine pretio suum fecerat, tribuni sui praecepto debitum sustinens obsequium, litteras ad magnum scriptas principem Romam uersus perlaturus, uicinis me quibusdam duobus seruis fratribus undecim denariis uendidit: Since the soldier who had acquired me with nobody selling me, and who had taken possession of me without paying a purchase price, had to uphold the obligatory obedience to an order from his tribune, he was to take to Rome a letter written to the great emperor; he sold me for eleven denarii to two slaves in the neighbourhood who were brothers.

After the inner story (chs. 2-12), which is absent in the *Onos*, the narrative from here to ch. 23 (254,23 f.) runs practically parallel to *Onos* chs. 46-52 (see Introd. **2.3**). Whole passages of the *Met.* here seem to offer verbatim translation of the *Onos*; when the two versions differ, the discrepancies are all the more obvious; see the next note, and below, on *haud ullo tempore ... expertus*; *adfatim saginabar*; ch. 14 (247,6) on *illi uero* and *postremo*;

in ch. 16 on *tandem ... mollius mihi renidentis Fortunae ... faciem* (248,27 f.); in ch. 17 on *quadruplum ... pretium* (249,24); in ch. 17 on *quo se patrono commendatiorem faceret* (249,27 f.). See also the remarks on ch. 18 (250,16-17) *sed prius est, ut ... unde fuerit*.

Miles ille, qui ... comparauerat et ... suum fecerat: after the long inner story (chs. 2-12) the main narrative is resumed with a short summary of the events immediately preceding it (ch. 1: 236,10-26). On this procedure see the introductory remarks on ch. 1. In the *Onos* such a summary is not needed because there is no inner story; accordingly, all the remarks that expand and deepen the characterization of the soldier are absent in the *Onos*, which has (46,1): ... ὁ δὲ στρατιώτης πωλήσειν με ἔγνω, καὶ πιπράσκει με πέντε καὶ εἴκοσιν ᾿Αττικῶν.

Miles ille: the soldier, who has played an important role as actor in the main narrative from 9,39 (232,30 f.) onward, makes a final appearance before he disappears from the story once and for all. His final exit is given a good reason: he is leaving for Rome. For minor actors entering and leaving the stage in the *Met.*, see on *meus ... dominus hortulanus ... nescio* ch. 1 (236,10 f.). On the characterization of this soldier see *GCA* 1995,325 on 9,39 (233,4 f.) *familiarem ... insolentiam*. See further on *miles ille, qui ... uapularat* ch. 1 (236,11 f.) and also below, on *debitum sustinens obsequium*.

qui me nullo uendente comparauerat et sine pretio suum fecerat: the cola *me ... comparauerat* and *et ... fecerat* have a practically equal number of syllables: 12 and 11 respectively. This emphasizes the tautology of the phrases: evidently it rankles with the narrator that the soldier misappropriated him, the ass. See on *nullo ... contradicente* ch. 1 (236,12 f.).

In a single sentence we are reminded how the ass passed from the hands of the *hortulanus* into those of the soldier, and learn further that he is sold again to the two brothers. This emphasizes the change of masters (see Heine in *AAGA* 1978,27 and n. 33 on the similarity in this respect between the main character of the *Met.* and the picaro). The entire sentence is therefore a good illustration of *fatorum fluctibus uolutari* (above).

sine pretio suum fecerat: whereas the literal meaning of *sine pretio* is 'without (paying) a price', the phrase can almost be translated as 'without an official sale having taken place', since a sales transaction was official only after the *pretium* had been paid. The soldier has therefore obtained the ass illegally as well as highhandedly. Norden 1912,167 f. points out that Apuleius is often remarkably precise in mentioning the payment of the *pretium*, even when it is obvious from the context that a sale is taking place; cf. e.g. 9,6 (206,26 f.) *istud ... quinque denariis cuidam uenditaui, et adest, ut dato pretio secum rem suam ferat*. In ch. 9 (243,25 f.) the physician says that, though he took money offered for supplying poison, no offical sale took place: *sed ... non statim pretium ... accepi*. Cf. also 9,14 (213,9 f.) *pistor ille, qui me pretio suum fecerat* (see *GCA* 1995,135 ad loc. on *suum facere*): *qui me pretio suum fecerat* emphasizes the *pistor*'s honesty, whereas in our passage *et me sine pretio suum fecerat* is a last dig at the soldier, who has been consistently depicted as disagreeable (see the references mentioned above on *miles ille*). For the use of *suum facere* in a context of illegality, cf. Ov. *Fast.* 2,689 f. *ceperat hic* (sc. *Tarquinius*) *alias, alias euerterat urbes,/ et Gabios turpi fecerat arte suos*.

tribuni sui: this person, the soldier's immediate superior, was referred to in ch. 1 (236,25 f.) as *praepositum suum, qui mille armatorum ducatum sustinebat*; see the note there on *praepositus*.

debitum sustinens obsequium: since his first arrogant appearance in 9,39 (233,1 f.), the soldier's subordinate position has often been mentioned. In 9,41 he is terrified of being punished; see *GCA* 1995,340 f. on *iniuriam*, 234,23). See also the previous note, and on *sollicite proficiscitur* ch. 1 (236,26). In his characterization of the soldier, Apuleius' obvious allusion to the *miles gloriosus* of comedy (see on *miles ille, qui ... uapularat* ch. 1: 236,11 f.) may have been intended to play on the hostility prevalent in the provinces towards the Roman military. Their arrogance towards the local people must have created bad feeling; this appears also from non-literary sources; see Millar 1981,67 f. (= Millar 1999,255).

sustinens obsequium: cf. ch. 3: (238,10) *sistens obsequium*, with note; Apuleius often uses a verb with *obsequium* as its direct object to express the meaning 'obey'. They are, in addition to those already mentioned, 3,12 (61,3) *obsequium commodare* (see Van der Paardt 1971,96 ad loc.); 6,12 (137,3 f.) *obsequium ... functura*; 6,20 (144,3 f.) *festinans obsequium terminare*; 10,3 (238,10) *sistens obsequium*; 11,9 (273,1 f.) *commonstrarent obsequium*; 11,28 (289,28 f.) *obsequium diuinum frequentabam*. The use of a phrase with *obsequium* may here have occurred to Apuleius because *obsequium* quite commonly means a soldier's compliance with orders: see *ThLL* s.v. *obsequium* 182,63 f.

litteras ad magnum scriptas principem Romam uersus perlaturus: this is a case of free indirect discourse: in this remark one can almost hear the soldier self-importantly explain to the two brothers why he is selling the ass.

With *magnum ... principem* (the same combination occurs 7,7: 159,23 f. *tantum potest nutus etiam magni principis*) the soldier seeks to enhance the importance of his mission. His phrase is not the usual one, since *magnus* seems not to have become a *cognomen* except in the case of Pompey. It is attested three times in poetry: Hor. *Carm.* 1,12,50 f. *magni / Caesaris* (see Nisbet-Hubbard ad loc.); *Eleg. Maec.* 6 *magnum magni Caesaris illud opus*; Mart. 9,61,19 *o dilecta deis, o magni Caesaris arbor*). Cf. also Plin. *Pan.* 60,6 *magnus princeps* (again 88,2); 88,5 *an satius fuit Felicem uocare? ... satius Magnum? cui plus inuidiae quam pulchritudinis inest*: the Romans probably associated the epithet *magnus* especially with Pompey. After Apuleius the combination is found in Amm. 22,8,1 *occasione magni principis*. *ThLL* s.v. *magnus*, 143,17 f. lists some inscriptions in which *optimus maximus* occurs with *princeps* or *imperator*.

Observe once again how subtly and cleverly this *miles gloriosus* is depicted here: in the phrase *tribuni ... obsequium* the narrator informs us that the soldier is bound to do what his superior tells him to do, and in the next phrase *litteras ... perlaturus* he shows us the soldier's pomposity toward the two *serui fratres*.

Romam: the name of the capital is found only here in the first ten books of the *Met*. On the one hand, the name has to support the soldier's 'distant' journey (and therefore his disappearance from the story); on the other, it characterizes the soldier again as an arrogant representative of the foreign oppressors (see above on *debitum sustinens obsequium*). See Methy 1983,37 f. on the role of Rome as the imperial capital in the works of Fronto and Apuleius.

In the eleventh book Rome becomes more important as the place where Lucius is to go for further initiations (11,26: 287,21 *Romam*; 287,25 *sacrosanctam ... ciuitatem*; 11,29: 290,24 *Romae*) and where he is now practising as a lawyer. See also Millar 1981,66 (= Millar 1999,253 f.) on the signals in the *Met.* that place the 'World of the Golden Ass' in the larger context of the Roman empire.

seruis fratribus: the adjectival use of *seruus* is already found in Cic. *Ver.* 2,3,91 *seruos homines*; it is frequent in Livy (KSt 2,1,232 f.). See also *GCA* 1985,225 on *hominem seruulum*

8,26 (197,20), with references.

Slaves were able to acquire property such as a domestic animal or even an 'under-slave'; they could buy this with their *peculium* (Norden 1912,72 f.; *Dig.* 15,1,6); in ch. 14 (247,13) one of these slaves refers to this *peculium* himself. From the following (ch. 17: 249,23 f.) it appears that they are also capable of conducting business transactions with their *dominus*. See *RE* s.v. 'Peculium' 13 f. [Von Uxkull]; especially ibid. 16,1-26.

undecim denariis uendidit: in the parallel passage of the *Onos* (46,1) the soldier sells the ass for 25 drachmae, a normal price for an ass according to *RE* s.v. 'Esel' 644 [Olck]. The Greek *drachma* has the same value as the *denarius* (see on *centumque aureos solidos* ch. 9: 243,19). For the soldier, who had acquired the ass without paying a penny (*sine pretio suum fecerat*), the low price of 11 *denarii* is pure profit. On the various prices of the ass in the *Met.* and in this book, see on *quadruplum ... pretium* ch. 17 (249,24).

246,7-10 His erat diues admodum dominus. At illorum alter pistor dulciarius, qui panes et mellita concinnabat edulia, alter cocus, qui sapidissimis intrimentis sucuum pulmenta condita uapore mollibat: They had a very rich master. Now, one of the two was a confectioner, who was skilled in preparing rolls and honeycakes; the other was a cook, who knew how to make meat dishes seasoned in sauces prepared with the most savoury ingredients, by braising them in steam until tender.

His erat diues admodum dominus: from ch. 15 (248,21) onward this *dominus* will play an important role in the story, but it is not until ch. 18 (250,16 f.) that he is elaborately introduced by the narrator to the reader with the apology *quod initio facere debueram*. An extensive description of the *dominus* would certainly have been awkward here from the point of view of narrative strategy (see on *quod initio ... debueram* ch. 18: 250,16), whereas the introduction of the two cooks and particularly the reference to their culinary skills are important for the development of the story. However, in what follows now, the *dominus* is already being subtly and implicitly characterized: through the elaborate description of the special skills of these two slaves their wealthy *dominus* is indirectly represented as decadent (see also below on *intrimentis sucuum ... condita*; *uapore mollibat*; *uasa illa compluria ... necessaria*, and *opiparas cenas ... apparatus*). Cf. Liv. 39,6,8-9 (in the context of tendencies to *luxuria* transmitted from Asia) *epulae quoque ipsae et cura et sumptu maiore apparari coeptae. tum coquus, uilissimum antiquis mancipium et aestimatione et usu, in pretio esse et, quod ministerium fuerat, ars haberi coepta*. Another contribution to the characterization of the *dominus* is his behaviour when he discovers the ass's preference for human food (ch. 16; see the notes there). By the time the narrator informs the reader *quis iste uel unde fuerit* (ch. 18: 250,17), and mentions his name, Thiasus, the reader has already received enough clues to be aware of at least some of the connotations of this significant name. See on *Thiasus* ch. 18 (250,17 f.).

Schlam 1968,50 f. and 1970,477 f. sees in the juxtaposition of these two cooks and the good doctor in the preceding tale a reference to Plato, *Gorg.* 464b f. (paraphrased in Apul. *Pl.* 2,9,232 f.), where medical and culinary arts are contrasted. Anderson 1982,157 n. 45 objects that our passage, in its turn, is followed by a story with a bad doctor (chs. 23-28), which 'would ... turn Platonic values upside down'. But the actions of the doctor in that second story can be understood as the 'bad' use of medicine, which is morally repugnant also to Platonists; accordingly, that physician pays with his life.

At illorum alter pistor ... mollibat: the extensive description of the culinary skills of the ass's new owners, at the very beginning of this new episode, creates a hedonistic atmosphere, which will characterize the rest of this book (with the exception of the story of the *uilis aliqua* in chs. 23-28).

No less than three times (here, l. 18 f., and ch. 16: 249,7 f.), the narrator elaborates on tasty human food in this episode, revealing a thorough knowledge of cookery. From the beginning of the *Met.*, food has been a recurrent motif (Schlam 1968,111 f. was the first to point out the importance of this motif, on the one hand often combined with the motif of sex, on the other hand contrasting with the motif of *abstinentia* in the eleventh book; see also Schlam 1992,99-112); after Lucius' metamorphosis, the motif occurred especially in the form of the inability of the ass to get used to animal food (see Introd. **2.4.3.1**). From now onward, the preference of the ass for human food will become a motivating factor in the continuation of the main story; it may be noted that this happens immediately before the Isis-book, where *abstinentia* becomes so important.

pistor dulciarius: cf. Mart. 14,222 *pistor dulciarius: mille tibi dulces operum manus ista figuras / extruet: huic uni parca laborat apis*, the only passage before Apuleius which *ThLL* (s.v. *dulciarius* 2187,3 f.) lists for the adjective; after Apuleius *ThLL* mentions Firm. *Math.* 8,11,3; cf. also Aug. *Man.* 2,6,41 *de ... coquis et dulciariis ministris*. As a noun, *dulciarius* (= *pistor*) is attested from Porph. ad Hor. *S.* 2,4,47. *Dulcia* is the general term for various sweet dishes that were eaten both separately and as a part of an elaborate dinner (André 1961,213 f.).

mellita ... edulia: *mellitus* is to be taken literally here: 'containing honey, honeyed' (*OLD* s.v. *mellitus* 1). Cf. 8,22 (194,18 f.) *mellitum corporis nidorem* (referring to the honey-smeared body of the punished *adulter*). In the *Met.* the adjective also occurs in its metaphorical meaning, as an endearment; e.g. 5,6 (108,3) *mi mellite*. See Van der Paardt 1971,167 on *mea mellitula* 3,22 (68,26).

edulia: the neuter plural of the adjective *edulis* used as a noun is first attested in Afran. *Com.* 259, and occurs frequently after that (see *ThLL* s.v. *edulis* 124,28 f.). Callebat 1968,27 classifies the use of the word in the *Met.* as 'vocabulaire de la vie courante'.

concinnabat: like *mollibat* below, this imperfect expresses the professional skill of this slave: 'he knew how to ...'. For the occurrence and use of *concinnare* in the *Met.*, see *GCA* 1981,214 f. on 7,20 (169,24). The two passages in the *Met.* where the verb occurs in its concrete meaning 'prepare' (referring to food both here and 7,11: 162,19 f.; see also *GCA* 1981,154 ad loc.) show that *concinnare* (the etymology of which is uncertain; see E-M 136 s.v. *concinno*) is not just a synonym of *parare*. It is to be understood to mean 'skillfully compose a beautiful entity from different parts', and therefore is used here quite aptly to describe a baker who creates beautifully shaped confections from different ingredients (cf. below *crustula* etc.). According to Monteil 1964,171 this use is archaic; before our passage it is found only in Cato *R.* 106,2.

cocus: see above, on *his erat ... dominus*.

sapidissimis intrimentis sucuum pulmenta condita uapore mollibat: cf. the advice of the cook's wife in 8,31 (202,15 f.) to her husband to cook the haunch of the ass in a savoury stew: *femusque eius ... accuratius in protrimentis sapidissime percoctum adpone domino*. See André 1961,1499, with references, on the Roman custom of stewing, rather than roasting, all meat, and ibid. 222 on the great importance of highly seasoned sauces in the preparation of all food in Roman cooking.

sapidissimis: see *GCA* 1985,276 on 8,31 (202,13-17) for the adjective *sapidus*, which is attested first in Apuleius.

intrimentis sucuum ... condita: 'seasoned or flavoured (see *OLD* s.v. *condio* 1) with a savoury liquid, which is stirred into it'. The noun *intrimentum* is not attested earlier, and occurs after Apuleius only in Zeno Ver. 1,24 *diuersis epulis intrimentorum lenocinio saporis de summa certantibus* (*ThLL* s.v. *intrimentum* 51,36 f.). As is often the case, the choice of an unusual word has been triggered by the wish to achieve a sound-effect (*intrimentis ... pulmenta*; for our passage see Facchini Tosi 1986,127). Hiltbrunner 1958,160 f. discusses both passages in detail, explaining them in the light of a recipe from Chiron *Mulom.* 199: meat is cooked until very tender, then *conditur eodem modo, ut pulmentum sub tritura: similiter ut cocus condire solet liquamine optimo et mero et oleo et piperis, quod satis fuerit*. Hiltbrunner concludes that *intrimenta sucuum* can be identified as a form of *liquamen*, a well-known ingredient in Roman cooking (André 1962,198). *Intrimentum* is therefore 'what is stirred in'; *sucuum* is an explicative genitive with *intrimenta*. In Hiltbrunner's words: 'in ein Gericht werden würzige Säfte eingerührt'.

sucuum: for *sucus* as a noun of the 4th declension, see *GCA* 1995,277 on 9,32 (227,18). For *sucus* as 'the juice of a thing (as determining its flavour)', see *OLD* s.v. *sucus* 1c. Cf. Lucr. 3,226 f. *multa minutaque semina sucos / efficiunt et odorem*; Hor. *S.* 2,8,28 (*conchylia*) *dissimilem noto celantia sucum*.

This intricate phrase with its accumulation of unusual terms suggesting complex culinary procedures makes it clear that this cook has to make culinary tours de force to tempt the discerning palate of his *dominus*. Cf. Mart. 14,220 *non satis est ars sola coco: seruire palatum / nolo: cocus domini debet habere gulam*.

pulmenta: 'meat (or fish) cut into small pieces, stew meat', hence 'stew'; see *GCA* 1977,68 on 4,7 (79,24-80,2).

uapore mollibat: a meaningful reminiscence of Lucr. 5,1102 *cibum coquere ac flammae mollire uapore* (see also Bömer on Ov. *Met.* 15,78 f.), which occurs in the context of the development of civilization, and is shortly followed (1117 f.) by the demoralizing influence of increasing prosperity of the people. The fact that in our passage the expression *uapore mollire* is combined with the preparation of complicated sauces (see above, on *intrimentis ... condita*) strenghtens the association of decadence which the contekst of Lucretius' line evokes.

mollibat: for the imperfect in -*ibam* in verbs of the 4th conjugation, see *GCA* 1977,59 on 4,6 (79,1) *scaturribat*, with references, and KSt 1,1,724,3.

246,10-13 Unico illi contubernio communem uitam sustinebant meque ad uasa illa compluria gestanda praedestinarant, quae domini regiones plusculas pererrantis uariis usibus erant necessaria: Together, sharing one single lodging, they earned a joint living, and they had designated me to carry those quantities of equipment that were necessary for the various needs of their master as he travelled from one region to the other.

Unico ... contubernio communem uitam: choice and position of the words emphasize the brothers' close companionship; their mutual attachment is also expressed in their dialogue later in the story (ch. 14: 247,11 f.). See on ch. 14 (247,3 f.) *suspicio non exilis fratrum pupugit animos*.

Unico ... contubernio: This can be understood in a concrete sense: they lived together in the same quarters (see *OLD* s.v. *contubernium* 4; the noun occurs twice in the *Met.* meaning 'soldiers' tent': 9,41: 234,25 and 10,1: 236,13 f.). But it can also be understood as 'in a unique companionship or fellowship' (see *OLD* ibid. 2): in the *Met.* e.g. 4,26 (94,24 f.): *indiuiduo contubernio* (the same combination also Apul. *Apol.* 53,10; 72,3 *arto ... contubernio intime iunctus*); 11,19 (281,3 f.) *contuberniisque sacerdotum indiuiduus et numinis magni cultor inseparabilis*; cf. also 9,13 (212,11) *meo iumentario contubernio* with *GCA* 1995,125 ad loc.

Unico: not only, in a concrete sense, 'only one, single', but also 'unique, singular'; hence the author uses the adjective to refer to his 'unique' creation of this fraternal couple. On the use of *unicus* in de *Met.*, see on *unicum* ch. 5 (240,10).

communem uitam sustinebant: the phrase combines the notions 'they led a joint life' and 'they kept each other alive'. *Vita communis* is found e.g. Cic. *Off.* 1,17,58 *quam ob rem necessaria praesidia uitae debentur iis maxime, quos ante dixi, uita autem uictusque communis ... in amicitiis*. Cf. also Cic. *Div.* 1,50 with Pease ad loc. For *sustinere* 'to support with food, resources or sim.', see *OLD* s.v. *sustineo* 3b; the combination *uitam sustinere* occurs in a verse by Maecenas quoted by Sen. *Ep.* 101,10 *uita dum superest, bene est./ hanc mihi, uel acuta / si sedeam cruce, sustine*.

meque ad uasa illa ... gestanda praedestinarant, quae domini regiones plusculas pererrantis uariis usibus erant necessaria: For the re-reader, this is dramatic irony: the brothers do not yet know that in ch. 18 (250,28 f.) the ass will be elected the carrier of the travelling *dominus* himself. To them, he is a beast of burden useful only to carry domestic utensils. On this and other examples of dramatic irony in the *Met.*, see Rosati 1997,107 f.

uasa illa compluria ... necessaria: once again (see above, on *diues admodum dominus*) we see an indirect characterization of the *dominus*, who likes his comforts even while travelling (cf. the long baggage train described in ch. 18: 250,28 f., with the notes there).

praedestinarant: Thus F and φ; ς emended to *prae[de]stinarant*, adopted by Helm, Robertson, and other modern editors, who refer to 4,15 (86,17); see *GCA* 1977,123 ad loc. There the emendation is necessary: the context clearly demands the meaning 'to buy', and *praedestinare* is not attested in that meaning. In our passage, however, the reading of the mss. need not be changed: a verb meaning 'designate in advance' is appropriate to the context, and that is the regular meaning of *praedestinare*. The main difficulty about retaining F's reading is that the verb is not otherwise attested either so early or in secular literature, unless *praedestinantis* is correct at Liv. 45,40,8 (*destinantis* Novak; *ThLL* is dubious; LS give the Livy reference without comment; *OLD* has no entry of the verb). Hanson prints F's reading in both passages, but expresses doubt in the app. crit. in both cases. At any rate, if *praedestinarant* is retained here, it must be translated 'they had designated'; emendation to *praestinarant* requires 'they had bought'. Scazzoso and Augello, however, read *praestinarant*, but translate 'mi avevano destinato a portare'.

domini regiones plusculas pererrantis: only in ch. 18 (250,19 f.) will we learn the reason for the *dominus*' journey. Here the narrator confines himself to giving information from the limited point of view of the two slaves, to whom it is important only that (not why) their master is on a journey and that therefore a beast of burden would be useful.

246,13-15 Adsciscor itaque inter duos illos fratres tertius contubernalis, haud ullo tempore tam beniuolam Fortunam expertus: And so I was admitted into the company of the two brothers as a third house-mate — never had I experienced Fortuna so benevolent.

Adsciscor: the narrator uses a formal term for a very important change in his life as an ass (see *GCA* 1981,108 f. on 7,5: 157,18-20, *adscisci*). The finite verb, placed first in the sentence, gives no surprising new information but marks a change in point of view: the passive form indicates that after the introduction of the two brothers, the 'I' has become central again ('promotion of the patient': see Pinkster 1992,161 f., with references). This sentence informs us how this 'I' experiences the event that has just been mentioned; the experience is restated with rising emphasis: that he is now the *contubernalis* of the two brothers is important, but *haud ... expertus* is the climax of the sentence, explained in the next sentence with *Nam...* . A passage like this illustrates how the order of the constituents in a sentence can often be explained by extending one's examination to the elements both preceding and following the sentence; see Pinkster 1990,243 f. 'Beyond the sentence'.

contubernalis: 'one who shares the same room or tent', but always with the connotation of 'one who shares life's ups and downs'; see *GCA* 1995,210 on 9,24 (221,3). Since the low point of *iumentario contubernio* in 9,13 (212,11), the ass is doing increasingly better as far as his shelters are concerned. This upward trend continues to 11,19 (281,1 f.), where, after his re-metamorphosis, Lucius is living in *contubernium* with the Isis-priests; see also *GCA* 1995,125 on 9,13 (212,11). The stay with the *hortulanus* in 9,32 (226,26 f., particularly 227,9-16) shows, though the word *contubernium* is not mentioned, the beginnning of the trend: the *hortulanus* shares his (frugal) livelihood entirely with the ass. See also on *nec in stabulo sed in domo cuiusdam decurionis* ch. 1 (236,23).

haud ... expertus: this participle construction following the main verb contains the most important information of the sentence. Bernhard 1927,43 f. collects examples in the *Met.* of such participle constructions, and regards them primarily as characteristic of a somewhat 'unfinished' and 'unpolished' narrative style: an afterthought is tagged on at the end of the sentence. But he, too, acknowledges (ibid. 45) that the idea expressed in the participle construction often represents a 'sehr wesentliche Gedanke'. As has been explained above (on *adsciscor*), the composition of the consecutive parts of the sentence is pragmatically motivated. For the development of Latin participle constructions placed after the predicate, especially in historiography and epic, see Schlicher 1933,294 f.

haud ullo tempore tam beniuolam Fortunam expertus: compared to the *Onos*, the *Met.* here shows a stronger emphasis on the fickleness of *Fortuna*. The *Onos* has one (positive) remark on Τύχη in its version of this episode (see on *tandem ... mollius mihi renidentis Fortunae contemplatus faciem* ch. 16: 248,27 f.); the *Met.* has three: above, *talibus fatorum fluctibus uolutabar* (see note there), the present passage, and ch. 16 (248,27 f.). Here the narrator gives expression to a pervasive and often noted theme of the *Met.*, the theme of *Fortuna*'s capriciousness, which in the eleventh book is contrasted with the enduring blessings of Isis for all who entrust themselves to her. The remarks here and ch. 16 (248,27 f.) about a finally well-disposed *Fortuna* does not alter her fickleness. See the extensive note in *GCA* 1981,91 f. on 7,2 (155,17-156,1) and the note on *mollius mihi renidentis ... Fortunae faciem* ch. 16 (248,27 f.). So soon after an enthusiastic description of delicious food, and with more to come in the next sentence, the words *beniuola Fortuna* would surely evoke the image of the horn of plenty, abundantly represented in iconography as an attribute of *Fortuna*.

Helm prints *fortunam* with a lower-case initial. Helm-Krenkel print a capital initial but combine it with a translation that does not personify: 'und zu keiner Zeit habe ich ein so angenehmes Los getroffen'. But cf. Brandt-Ehlers (who print *Fortunam*): 'und habe zu keiner Zeit Fortuna so gnädig angetroffen'. This is not the only passage where editors and translators differ on whether or not to regard *F/fortuna* as personified (see also above on *Fortunae saeuientis* ch. 4: 239,12). This issue, which is a problem for all editors of ancient texts, is discussed by Greene in his thoughtful article 'Personifications' (with references) in *OCD*. See also on *procedit ... nuda Veritas* ch. 12 (245,22 f.) and on *Riualitas* ch. 24 (255,20). Schlam 1992,141 f. discusses in detail the use of *fortuna* and the problem of personification in the *Met*. Using the classification in *ThLL* s.v. *fortuna* 1176-77, he examines the 68 occurrences of the word in the *Met.*, 36 of which he regards as common nouns, and 31 as personifications. He also notes that Helm 1970 (= Helm-Krenkel) regards more instances of *Fortuna* as personifications than does Helm 1931. Unfortunately, he has not categorized our passage. Here the personification *Fortuna* is supported by *beniuolam*, since the adjective is used almost exclusively of persons and deities (*ThLL* s.v. *beneuolus* 1897,43 f.; ibid. 1898,5 our passage is mentioned, with *Fortunam*). When the adjective qualifies 'res incorporeae' (*ThLL* ibid. 1898,9 f.), it often occurs in the phrase *beniuolus animus* and with other notions linked with persons, like *officium* (Cic. *Inv.* 2,53,161), *studium* (V.Max. 6,8,7) etc. Cf. also *Met*. 1,1 (1,2) *auresque tuas beniuolas* and 6,1 (129,17 f.) *beniuolam misericordiam*.

See *ThLL* s.v. *experior* 1675,54 f. for many examples of *experiri* with humans or divinities as its direct object. Cf. e.g. Prop. 3,15,29 f. *durum Zethum et lacrimis Amphiona mollem / experta est* (sc. Antiopa); Sen. *Ben.* 1,1,4 *multos experimur ingratos, plures facinus*; of deities: Ov. *Tr.* 3,2,27 *di, quos experior nimium constanter iniquos*; Juv. 13,102 f. *exorabile numen / fortasse experiar*.

246,15-21 Nam uespera post opiparas cenas earumque splendidissimos apparatus multas numero partes in cellulam suam mei solebant reportare domini: ille porcorum, pullorum, piscium et cuiusce modi pulmentorum largissimas reliquias, hic panes, crustula, lucunculos, hamos, lacertulos et plura scitamenta mellita: For in the evening, after the sumptuous dinners, for which everything had been prepared most splendidly, my masters used to take a great number of portions back to their little apartment: one the vast amounts of leftovers of pork, chicken, fish, and all kinds of meat dishes, the other rolls, tartlets, fritters, croissants, cookies, and many honey-sweet delicacies.

uespera: 'every evening', as in 5,17 (116,22) *accolae plurimi uiderunt eum uespera redeuntem e pastu*; cf. Plin. *Nat.* 32,36 *haec singula et matutina et uespera dantur, dein post aliquot dies bina uespera*. For this ablative of time, used by Apuleius in addition to the adverb *uesperi*, see *GCA* 1977,139 on 4,18 (88,10-13).

opiparas cenas earumque splendidissimos apparatus: the addition of *earumque splendidissimos apparatus* underlines the elaborateness of these *opiparae cenae*, and the slaves' daily efforts. It appears from the context (*solebant reportare*) that these plentiful meals were a daily event; so this phrase adds to the indirect characterization of the *dominus* (see above, on *his erat diues admodum dominus*). The opulence is emphasized by several expressions in this sentence: *opiparas, splendidissimos apparatus, multas numero partes, largissimas reliquias*. Cf. also the extensive enumeration of dishes, each list ending with a suggestion that this is only part of the menu: *porcorum* ..., concluded with *et cuiusce modi pulmentorum*, and *panes* ..., concluded with *et plura scitamenta mellita*.

opiparas cenas: in other passages Apuleius uses *opiparis* (third declension) to avoid rhyme of the endings of noun and adjective; see *GCA* 1981,152 on 7,11 (162,15). As an adjective of the third declension it is attested first in Apuleius (the next examples listed by *ThLL* s.v. *opiparus* 729,19 f. are Ambr. *Hex.* 6,2,5 and Mutian. 25,3). In our passage, the choice of the second declension may have been inspired by a wish to follow the usage of comedy: according to *ThLL* ibid. 729,30 f., the passages in Apuleius are the first where *opiparus* is attested after Plautus. After Apuleius it is found in Porph. ad Hor. *C.* 1,37,2-4 *saliares cenas ...: opiparas et copiosas*; Arn. 7,25; Ps. Ambr. *Paen.* 34, p.997[b] *opiparas cenas et copiosarum dapum uberem affluentiam*.

Opiparus is one of several words and phrases from comedy which combine to evoke a comic atmosphere in the episode of the cooks. Using other examples from the *Met.*, Callebat 1964,355 f. points out Apuleius' use of comic language, which goes beyond the mere application of archaisms. See also below, on *porcorum, pullorum, piscium ... pulmentorum; scitamenta*; ch. 14 (247,25) *Eteocleas ... contentiones*, and on
ch. 15 (248,4) *electiles*. See May 1998 for an elaborate interpretation of the reminiscences of comedy in this episode. She notes (148) that also the *diues dominus* is a character of comedy.

earumque: this reading in F is rightly adopted by most editors. Kroll's ingenious conjecture *escarumque* is printed by Giarratano only; Augello 1977,210 praises it but leaves F unchanged.

multas numero partes: a similar redundant expression is found e.g. 4,7 (79,15 f.) *tot numero iuuenum*. See *GCA* 1977,64 ad loc., with references.

porcorum, pullorum, piscium ... pulmentorum: this alliterative enumeration of dishes is seen by Weinreich 1930,363 f. as related to many similar lists in Greek and Latin literature, particularly in comedy; according to Weinreich, this playing with letters goes back to a playful use of 'Buchstabenmystik', found in the colloquial usage of all languages. Weinreich gives many examples, e.g. Alexis Fr. 12 κορίαννον ... κύμινον, κάππαριν ... σφάκον, σίραιον, σέσελι, πήγανον, πράσον. Plautus, too, has such alliterative lists, e.g. *As.* 865 f. *ait sese ire ad Archidemum, Chaeream, Chaerestratum / Cliniam, Chremem, Cratinum, Diniam, Demosthenem*. Cf. Fraenkel 1922,275 n. 1, who regards this not as 'Buchstabenmystik' but rather as a parody on the exhaustive comprehensiveness typical of some scientific alphabetized enumerations.

cuiusce modi = *cuiuscumque modi*; see *GCA* 1985,159 on 8,17 (190,10-19), with references.

largissimas reliquias: see above, on *opiparas cenas ... apparatus*.

crustula, lucunculos ... lacertulos: the sound pattern is strongly determined by this sequence of diminutives, which also has a semantic effect: it expresses Lucius' intense pleasure in the delicacies offered to him for the first time in his existence as an ass. See Abate 1978,81 and n. 26; Facchini Tosi 1986,123.

crustula: usually a collective noun for various kinds of small, sweet pastries (see Hauri-Karrer 1972,30 f., with references). It cannot be determined whether the pastries listed after *crustula* are different kinds of *crustula*; see Hauri-Karrer (who has incorporated all the Thesaurus material, both published and unpublished) 1972,33. See also Petersmann on Pl. *St.* 691 *olea, entriptillo, lupillo comminuto, crustulo*.

lucunculos: F had *Iucunculos*; Scaliger's emendation *luc...* is adopted by all editors.

ThLL s.v. *lucuntulus* 1750,44 follows Lindsay in *ALL* 1900,332, who argues that *lucuntulus* is the correct form (see also Augello 1977,10 f.). Kronenberg (in Helm Praef. *Fl.* XLIV) also wants to read *lucuntulos* here; he is followed by Giarratano. Helm, Robertson, Terzaghi, Giarratano-Frassinetti, and Hanson are right in retaining *lucunculos*: the spelling transmitted in F is attested elsewhere, e.g. Tert. *Spect.* 27,4 *de lucunculo uenenato*; Ital. *Ex.* 16,31; *Num.* 11,8. *Lucunculus* is sufficiently attested as a variant of *lucuntulus* (cf. e.g. Afran. *com. frg.* 162, p. 185 Ribbeck *mittat fratris filio lucunculos*; Stat. *Silv.* 1,6,17, and the Greek form λούκουντλοι transmitted in Athen. 14,647D; see Hauri-Karrer 1972,100 f.). The word is presumably related to a Greek form *γλυκοῦς (see Hauri-Karrer l.c. 101, with references). In the few passages where *lucuns*, *lucuntulus* or *lucunculus* is found, it usually refers to an especially sweet pastry.

hamos: as a name for a pastry, *hamus* is attested only here. Since the word means 'hook' or 'hook-shaped object', we can assume that it refers to a crescent-shaped pastry (see Hauri-Karrer 1972,71). Another meaning of *hamus* is 'fishhook' (*OLD* s.v. *hamus* 2). Because the word is used only here to indicate a kind of cookie or tart, it is tempting to assume that Apuleius is playing with the meaning 'fishhook', which is often used in a figurative sense in other passages as well, e.g. Pl. *Cur.* 431 *meus hic est, hamum uorat*; *Truc.* 42; Plin. *Pan.* 43,5 *Caesarum munera illitos cibis hamos*; for more examples see *ThLL* s.v. *hamus* 2523,30 f. The ass, gobbling up these dainties, is 'hooked' (by Thiasus, ultimately, with dire consequences). Our ass experiences here the same as what is expressed by the 'I' in one of the fragments from an unknown Greek novel in the period of the Second Sophistic: ἠσπαλιεύθην ὡς οὐκ οἶδ' εἴ τις ἰχθῦς ὑπὸ τοῦ δελέατος τῆς ἡδονῆς καὶ ἐνείχετό μοι τὸ ἄγκιστρον (see Alpers 1995,31 and n. 40; ibid. 51). See also below on *escas* ch. 16 (249,5).

lacertulos: Colvius's proposal *laterculos* is mentioned by Robertson in his app. crit. with 'fortasse recte'; Hanson adopts it in the text. Other editors retain the spelling of F, already defended by Oudendorp and Hildebrand. Colvius's proposal is based on Pl. *Poen.* 325, which has *laterculos* in a list of dainty dishes. Oudendorp rightly argues that the Plautus passage (the only passage where *laterculus* is attested as a term for a delicacy — 'little tile' — with possibly Cato *Agr.* 109 as a second example; see *ThLL* s.v. *laterculus* 1001,73 f.) is not a sufficient argument to reject *lacertulus*, which is strongly represented in the mss. In this, Oudendorp follows Beroaldus, who assumes that the word refers to cookies shaped like *lacertae* (lizards) or *lacerti/lacertae*, a kind of fish (mackerel); see *OLD* s.v. *lacerta* 1 and 2. Oudendorp opts for the meaning 'cookies shaped like fish', and suggests that the baker may have attached these ingeniously to the previously mentioned *hami*. To Hildebrand, this is pushing things too far, but otherwise he follows Oudendorp/Beroaldus. *ThLL* s.v. *lacertulus* 829,44 f., quotes only this passage for the word, and refers to the Italian word for lizard, 'lucertola' (M-L 4822). Hauri-Karrer 1972,63 ignores the reading *lacertulos* here, and discusses the passage in Plautus (see above) and our passage together s.v. *laterculus*.

scitamenta: 'delicacies', derived from the adjective *scitus* 'refined, sophisticated' (Perrot 1961,198 f.). Like e.g. *condimenta*, *salsamenta*, it is found only in the plural, referring to a group of related objects (see Perrot 1961, 261 en 263). As a culinary term (see above on *intrimentis sucuum ... condita*) it is attested Pl. *Men.* 209 *aliquid scitamentorum de foro opsonarier*; then in Gel. 18,8,1 in a figurative sense, for 'refined stylistic procedures'; in a culinary sense again here in Apuleius, and also Macr. 7,14,1. In our passage, it is one of the many comedy-signals (see above, on *opiparas cenas*).

mellita: see above, on *mellita ... edulia*.

246,21-22 Qui cum se refecturi clausa cellula balneas petissent, oblatis ego diuinitus dapibus adfatim saginabar: And when they had gone to the baths to refresh themselves, I for my part gorged myself abundantly on the meal dished up for me by divine providence.

se refecturi: Apuleius frequently uses the future participle with a final meaning. This use developed from Livy onward, also in poetry; see *GCA* 1985,46 on *indagaturus* 8,4 (178,21-24), with references.

clausa cellula balneas petissent: once the brothers suspect him of being the thief, they trap him in the following way (ch. 15: 248,13 f.): *et hora consueta uelut balneas petituri clausis ex more foribus per quandam modicam cauernam rimantur me*. The situation described here is possible only when one pictures the ass (with his crib) actually stabled in the *cellula* of the slave brothers, with consequently free access to the food put out there.

ego: the pronoun is emphatically placed in opposition to *qui*: *they* go to the baths, *I* go to my meal (see above, on *At ego* at the beginning of this chapter).

oblatis ... diuinitus dapibus: a comical paradox: the leftovers from a dinner, taken home by two slaves to their modest dwelling, are referred to in grandiloquent terms as a 'meal provided by divine intervention'. As a matter of fact, the narrator presents the entire situation in which the ass now finds himself, as a benevolent gesture of *Fortuna* (see above, on *haud ullo tempore ... expertus*); see also the next note.

adfatim saginabar: a less than reverent reaction to a meal that has been 'offered by divine providence': the primary meaning of *saginare* is 'to fatten', referring to animals (*OLD* s.v. *sagino* 1); when the verb refers to people (*OLD* ibid. 2), its connotation is always 'gorge, stuff oneself (like an animal)'. See *GCA* 1977,26 on 4,1 (75,1-2) *et quamuis crudis holeribus, adfatim tamen uentrem sagino*. As in that passage, the wording here emphasizes the animal aspect of Lucius, the ass; in that light, the narrator's subsequent statement that he was not *tam ... uere asinus*, sounds ironical; see the note there. This irony is absent in the *Onos*; however, Lucius's inability to get used to animal food (present in both the *Onos* and the *Met.*; see *GCA* 1981,171 on 7,14: 164,19 f. *non canem sed asinum*) is emphasized in the *Onos*: (46,7) κἀγὼ τοῖς παρακειμένοις κριθιδίοις μακρὰ χαίρειν λέγων ταῖς τέχναις καὶ τοῖς κέρδεσιν τῶν δεσποτῶν ἐδίδουν ἐμαυτόν.

adfatim: 'in abundance'; on the etymology and form of the adverb, see *GCA* 1977, cited in the preceding note.

246,23-24 Nec enim tam stultus eram tamque uere asinus, ut dulcissimis illis relictis cibis cenarem asperrimum faenum: For I was not so stupid and so much of a real ass that I would leave that marvellously delicious food and eat horribly scratchy hay.

For the irony in this remark, see above, on *adfatim saginabar*. From 3,26 (71,6 f.) onward the narrator has repeatedly pointed out the contrast between his animal shape and his human mind: *ego uero quamquam perfectus asinus et pro Lucio iumentum sensum tamen retinebam humanum*. See *GCA* 1977,2; cf. also 4,2 (75,13) *non usquequaque ferina praecordia* with

GCA 1977,30 ad loc.; 9,11 (211,9) *nec tamen sagacitatis ac prudentiae ... oblitus* with *GCA* 1995,111 ad loc. From now on, this contrast will play a complicated role: his human nature makes it easy for Lucius to please his new masters, e.g. by eating exotic dishes (ch. 16: 249,5 f.), drinking wine (ch. 16: 249,19 f.), and learning tricks (ch. 17: 250,6 f.); this makes his life increasingly comfortable. On the other hand, the human mind inside the ass is more and more disgusted by the bestial pleasures that the people around him try to force on him; hence his apprehension (which subsequently turns out to be unfounded) about hurting the amorous *matrona* (ch. 21: 253,12 f.) during the sexual intercourse craved by her (see on *rabido* ch. 22: 254,5). When his aversion from indulging the prurience of those around him is greatest, he truly enjoys, for the first time in his life as an ass, eating animal food: ch. 29 (260,16 f.) *pabulum laetissimi graminis ... libens adfectabam.* See also above on *At illorum alter pistor ... mollibat,* and Introd. **2.4.3.1** and **2.4.3.2**.

stultus ... tamque uere asinus: on the one hand, this alludes to the ass's stupidity, which was proverbial in antiquity as well (see *RAC* s.v. 'Esel', 577 [Opelt]). But it also refers to the distaste a true ass would have felt for these seasoned dishes: a real ass would undoubtedly have preferred *asperrimum faenum*. Cf. ch. 16 (249,5 f.), where the people, in order to test the ass's *mansuetudo*, offer him exotically seasoned dishes, devising *quid potissimum abhorreret asino*.

uere asinus: the adverb shows that *asinus* is used here as an adjective. See Bernhard 1927,105 for other examples, and *GCA* 1995,201 on 9,22 (220,3-8) *puer admodum*.

dulcissimis ... asperrimum: the superlatives underline the contrast (which is obvious also to Lucius) between the dainty dishes and the fodder, and emphasize the stupidity of preferring the latter to the former. In ch. 29 (260,16 f.), however, the superlative *laetissimi* qualifies the animal fodder eaten by Lucius with so much relish (see the introductory note to this pericope).

CHAPTER XIV

The two brothers notice that food is disappearing and begin to suspect each other of theft.

246,25-247,1 Et diu quidem pulcherrime mihi furatrinae procedebat artificium, quippe adhuc timide et satis parce subripienti de tam multis pauciora nec illis fraudes ullas in asino suspicantibus: And for a long time the stealing trick went off wonderfully well for me, because thus far I was timidly and quite sparingly pilfering just a few bites from these large quantities, and they did not suspect any fraudulent practices in an ass.

Et diu quidem: since the ass is becoming visibly fat and sleek (ch. 15: 248,7-10), the indefinite *diu* in this passage must refer to a period of more than just a few days. On the passage of time in this book, see Introd. **1.6.1**.

pulcherrime mihi ... procedebat artificium: *procedere* with an adverb, meaning 'to succeed, make (good or bad) progress', is frequent in Plautus, e.g. *Am.* 463 *bene prospere hoc hodie operis processit mihi*. For *pulchre procedere* cf. Ter. *Ad.* 130 *processisti hodie pulchre*; Cic. *Phil.* 13,40 *ei pulcherrime priora processerint*. According to Monteil 1964,84 the original meaning of *pulcher* ('blessed by the gods') can still be sensed in the combination of *pulchre* with verbs meaning 'succeed'.

furatrinae ... artificium: the narrator looks back with pride on this 'clever trick' of Lucius. But the word *furatrina* itself is also an *artificium* of the concrete author (see Introd. **3.1**): the word, which is not attested before Apuleius, occurs three times in the *Met.*: 6,13 (138,1); 8,3 (178,15; see *GCA* 1985,43 ad loc.), and here. In all of these three occurrences we have an unusual 'stealthy act', for which, accordingly, an unusual word has been created (cf. also Billotta 1975,56 f.): in 6,13 *furatrina* refers to Psyche's theft of the golden wool (she succeeds only through a trick suggested by the speaking reed); in 8,3 the word indicates a *furatrina coniugalis* never committed by the chaste Charite; and here it refers to the unique occurrence of an ass pilfering human food.

Apuleius uses *artificium* here for 'cunning device' (*OLD* s.v. *artificium* 4) also in e.g. *Apol.* 4,8 *Zenonem illum ..., qui primus omnium ... artificio ambifariam dissoluerit*; ibid. 61,6. For *artificium* referring to verbal skill cf. e.g. Cic. *de Orat.* 2,56 *Thucydides omnis dicendi artificio ... facile uicit*; Sal. *Jug.* 85,31 *illis artificio opus est, ut turpia facta oratione tegant*; Apul. *Fl.* 18,21 *artificia dicentium*. *Artificium* occurs only once more in the *Met.*, also in book 10: ch. 34 (265,19) (sc. *bestia*) *artificio docta* '(the wild animal), skillfully trained'; cf. *OLD* ibid. 1: 'skill as exhibited in an art, craft, etc.'.

On the reversal of the theft motif in our passage, see May 1998,138 f. In comedy it is the cooks who are clever thieves (May gives examples and references); here it is their servant, the ass, who is stealing from the cooks, who are themselves scrupulously honest.

adhuc timide et satis parce ... pauciora: the ass's initial modesty, which is emphasized here, seems to be inconsistent with *adfatim saginabar* above (ch. 13: 246,22). But that passage was meant to be ironical (see the note ad loc.); moreover, *de tam multis pauciora* can still amount to quite a lot of food (see also the next note).

satis parce: for *satis* as 'Apuleius' favourite intensifier', see Kenney 1990,123 on

4,30 (98,20); *GCA* 1985,208 on 8,24 (196,5-7). The combination *satis parce* is a mild oxymoron; see also the preceding note.

nec illis fraudes ullas in asino suspicantibus: the narrator has often pointed out that Lucius' animal shape has not only disadvantages but also advantages, which Lucius does not hesitate to turn to good account. Cf. e.g. 9,13 (212,23 f.) *nec ullum uspiam cruciabilis uitae solacium aderat, nisi quod ingenita mihi curiositate recreabar, dum praesentiam meam parui facientes libere, quae uolunt, omnes et agunt et loquuntur* with *GCA* 1995,130 ad loc. The fact that no one would expect an ass to steal human food or, in a more general sense, to commit *fraudes*, is used as an opportunity by the ass to do just that. On the programmatic and specialized theme of this book, 'the human being within the ass', see Introd. **2.4.3** and **2.4.3.2**.

fraudes ... in asino: expressions with *fraus* and *fraudes* tend to occur in the *Met.* in connection with specific persons: three times with the sisters of Psyche (see S. Panayotakis 1996); twice with Thrasyllus; once in connection with the *pistor*'s wife; twice in connection with the *nouerca*; twice in connection with the *uilis aliqua*; and finally once in ch. 33 (264,15) in connection with those who condemned Socrates. Thus, to commit *fraus* is regarded in the *Met.* as typically human behaviour. Cf. also 4,5 (78,9 f.), where Lucius, having only recently become an ass, decides to *dolis abiectis et fraudibus asinum me bonae frugi dominis exhibere*: there, too, it is suggested that to commit *fraudes* is a human trait not befitting an ass. The ass, who in book 10 will be treated more and more like a human being by his masters, is ingesting here not only his first human food since a long time, but also the human capacity for committing *fraus*.

In view of the preceding *furatrina*, *fraus* comes close to the stricter meaning *furtum*. See *ThLL* s.v. *fraus* 1270,67 f.: 'de damno pecuniae qua quis privatur dolo malo rebus ementitis, hinc accedit ad notionem furti, peculatus', which omits our passage but does mention Publil. *Frg.* 7 *fraus est accipere, quod non possis reddere*; Cic. *Phil.* 12,12 *num fraude poterit carere peculatus?*. The Horace passages given by *ThLL* are less persuasive (see Kiessling-Heinze on Hor. *Carm.* 4,9,37). It is only in Christian authors that the use of *fraus* in the narrow sense of *furtum* is unambiguously attested, e.g. Tert. *Idol.* 1,3 *fraudis condicio ..., si quis alienum rapiat*; see Turcan on Tert. *Spect.* 2,10. Again we see how the moral narrowing of a more general notion is clearly attested first in Apuleius, and in Christian authors afterwards; see e.g. *GCA* 1995,238 on 9,27 (223,22-27) *agresti morum squalore*, and ibid. 251 on 9,29 (224,26) *maleficiis*. See also Schmidt 1990.

247,1-5 At ubi fiducia latendi pleniore capta partes opimas quasque deuorabam et iucundiora eligens abligurribam dulcia, suspicio non exilis fratrum pupugit animos et quanquam de me nihil etiam tum tale crederent, tamen cotidiani damni studiose uestigabant reum: But when I had gained more confidence that I would not be caught, and kept wolfing down all the richest morsels, selecting the especially delicious sweets to gobble up, a not unfounded suspicion stabbed the brothers to their hearts; and although at the time they did not believe anything like that of me, yet they carefully examined who should be blamed for the daily damage.

ubi ... deuorabam ... abligurribam: for *ubi* with the imperfect see above on Ch. 2 (237,17 f.) *ubi ... exaestuabat*.

partes opimas quasque ... iucundiora eligens: rather than becoming greedier, the ass is becoming more fastidious.

opimas quasque: Helm in his app. crit. ad loc. opts for *optimas*; Robertson mentions this proposal with 'fortasse recte'. One would indeed expect a superlative before *quasque*. However, *opimus* is to be regarded as an adjective with the value of a superlative; LHSz 2,170 give examples from Lucretius onward of similar adjectives in the positive with *quisque* (e.g. Lucr. 5,1415 *pristina quaeque*; Liv. 1,7,5 *eximium quemque*; Tac. Ann. 6,27,3 *egregium quemque*; in the plural ibid. 14,31,1 *praecipui quique*). F's *opimas* is rightly retained by all editors.

deuorabam ... abligurribam: in addition to the meaning 'to eat (up)', both verbs have the connotation 'squander'; see *OLD* s.v. *deuoro* 3: 'to swallow up, use up (money, property, etc.)'. For *abligurrire* cf. Apul. *Apol.* 59,7 *patrimonium omne iam pridem abligurriuit*. In its first attested occurrence it has that meaning (see *ThLL* s.v. *abligurrio* 106,18 f.): Ter. *Eu.* 235 *patria qui abligurrierat bona*; cf. Sid. *Ep.* 9,6,2 *quantum de bonusculis auitis paternisque sumptuositas domesticae Charybdis abligurrisset*. Thus, the description of the feasting ass suggests also that he is consuming the nest egg of the two slaves; see below on *peculium latenter augere ... diuisionem* (cf. also *damni*, twice in this ch.).

abligurribam: on the imperfect in *-ibam* see on *mollibat* ch. 13 (246,10).

suspicio non exilis fratrum pupugit animos: the examples in *OLD* s.v. *pungo* 4 show that *pungere* in the sense of 'vex, disturb' always expresses a severe torment: for the brothers to suspect someone, and each other at that, is like being stabbed in the heart (see also below on *postremo*). This harmonizes with their early characterization as decent fellows (see above on *unico ... contubernio communem uitam* ch. 13: 246,10 f.). This characterization is continued in the dialogue that follows; Junghanns 1932,114: 'Hübsch ist die brüderliche Mäßigung auf beiden Seiten (Seelenhaltung!) gezeichnet' (see also below on *peculium latenter augere ... diuisionem*).

suspicio non exilis: for the same litotes see on ch. 22 (253,12) *non exili metu*.

pupugit: with the perfect tense a new phase in the story begins (see on ch. 3: 238,5 *rupit ... et ... praecipit*). The tenses in chs. 14-16 reflect the relaxed atmosphere of this passage, which is also expressed by a rather low narrative tempo (see Introd. **1.6** and **1,6,2**). From the previous perfect *uendidit* (ch. 13: 246,6) onward, which also marked the beginning of a new phase and was continued by the historical present *adsciscor*, Lucius' new situation has been described by imperfects and pluperfects. From *et diu ... procedebat* a series of imperfects has provided a frame for the important fact of the following episode, namely *suspicio ... pupugit fratrum animos*. With the historical present *dirigunt* (ch. 15: 248,13) this episode picks up speed again with a rapid succession of historical presents *rimantur* (ch. 15: 248,15), *dirumpuntur* (248,17), *demonstrant* (248,18 f.), *delectatur* (ch. 16: 248,24), and *arbitratur* (248,26). The episode of the ass being caught in the act is concluded with *quoad ... iussit ... perduxit ...iussit* (ch. 16: 248,30-249,2).

quanquam ... crederent: the subjunctive with *quanquam* is common in the *Met.*; cf. *GCA* 1985,43 on 8,3 (178,9-15), with references.

quanquam: Hanson is the only one of the modern editors who 'normalizes' and reads *quamquam*. In F *quamquam* and *quanquam* occur about equally often (see Oldfather s.v. *quamquam & quanquam*). See on *quandiu* ch. 2 (237,14).

etiam tum: 'even then' (when I was stealing food more and more brazenly). The narrator lets the readers share in his surprise and amusement at the brothers' gullibility. Comparable is ch. 3 (238,14 f.) *nihil etiam tunc ... suspicatus*; see the note there. On *etiam tunc* and *etiam tum* in the *Met.* see *GCA* 1981,135 on 7,8 (160,4-6).

uestigabant: on the frequency of this verb in Apuleius' time and in Ciceronian Latin, see *GCA* 1981,109 on 7,5 (157,18-20).

247,6-8 Illi uero postremo etiam mutuo sese rapinae turpissimae criminabantur, iamque curam diligentiorem et acriorem custodelam et dinumerationem adhibebant partium: But at last they even accused each other back and forth of a most disgraceful theft and now began to exercise caution more diligently, keep a sharper look-out, and count the portions one by one.

Illi uero: the proposals of Van der Vliet and Leo, *immo uero* and *taciti uero* respectively, draw our attention to the possibility that a sentence from the *Onos* (46,10, cited in the next note) has been incorporated here a little too soon. Hence Robertson in his app. crit. ad loc.: 'vid. Apul. orationibus insertis praecedentia indiligenter retinuisse'. But Apuleius, who characterizes the two brothers in more detail than the *Onos* does (see above on *suspicio ... pupugit animos*), has placed enough signals in the context to enable the reader to take the imperfect *criminabantur* as conative. See the following note, and on *dinumerationem ... partium*.

postremo: the brothers, who used to share and share alike (*communem uitam sustinebant* ch. 13: 246,10 f.), can only after long hesitation bring themselves to suspect each other (see the previous note). Once the mutual suspicion has taken hold, they still have to conquer their diffidence before accusing each other directly: *tandem denique rupta uerecundia*. The next passage depicts with much sympathy and humor their mutual attachment and willingness to trust each other again. Compare to this the succinct statement in the *Onos* (46,9 f.) καὶ ἐπειδὴ ᾔσθοντο ἤδη τῆς ζημίας, τὰ μὲν πρῶτα ἄμφω ὕποπτον ἐς ἀλλήλους ἔβλεπον καὶ κλέπτην ὁ ἕτερος τὸν ἕτερον καὶ ἅρπαγα τῶν κοινῶν καὶ ἀναίσχυντον ἔλεγον, καὶ ἦσαν ἀκριβεῖς λοιπὸν ἄμφω καὶ τῶν μερίδων ἀριθμὸς ἐγίνετο.

rapinae turpissimae: the adjective reflects the thoughts of the brothers, to whom robbing each other is an abominable form of theft (see the previous note). Cf. below, *ne uiderer rapinae sordidae meum fratrem arguere*. When they catch the real thief (ch. 15: 248,16 f.), they regard the whole event as a good joke, and the notion of *rapina turpissima* is forgotten.

Strictly spoken, the homodiegetic narrator (see Introd. **3.5**) cannot know the brothers' thoughts; but the subsequent dialogue, which the narrator could theoretically have overheard at the time, makes it clear that the brothers regard stealing from each other as *turpissimum*.

criminabantur: in the *Met.* this verb always occurs in the context of a false incrimination (*GCA* 1981,231 ad 7,23: 171,9-12 discusses the passages in question). Here, too, at least the reader (with the narrator) knows that the mutual accusations are unfounded.

dinumerationem ... partium: in the *Onos* (cited above s.v. *postremo*) the cooks do not start counting until after they have accused each other. In the *Met.* it fits in with their more detailed characterization that they keep up their vigilance until they can bring themselves to entertain the idea that one of them is robbing the other.

247,8-10 Tandem denique rupta uerecundia sic alter alterum compellat: At last one of them finally cut short his embarrassment and rebuked the other as follows:

Tandem denique rupta uerecundia: the combination *tandem denique* occurs three times in the *Met.*: 2,15 (37,4 f.); 3,22 (68,21; see Van der Paardt 1971,166 ad loc.); and here. All three passages refer to a mental process, a self-conquest, which, it is implied, requires much effort and time. Consequently, the combination should not be regarded as an empty pleonasm in any of these passages. See also on *postremo* above.

uerecundia: the second speaker in the following dialogue makes clear what this *uerecundia* consists of; see below on *quam diutissime sustinens tacitus ingemescebam*. Cf. also above, on *suspicio non exilis ... animos*.

compellat: 'calls him names'. Apuleius uses *compellare* six times in the *Met.* (not in his other works): 4,7 (79,16); 8,5 (179,19); 9,9 (209,13); 9,28 (224,16); 9,38 (231,29; and here. In all these passages *compellare* is used 'i.q. *iniuriose alloqui, conuiciari, increpare*'; *ThLL* s.v. 1 *compello* 2028,78 f. notes for this meaning only Pl. *Mos.* 616; Cic. *Red. Sen.* 12 (32) and *Phil.* 3,17; Hor. *S.* 2,3,297 (see Palmer ad loc.); Fron. p. 232,18 N., and the passages in Apuleius. It appears that in his use of the verb Apuleius selected this specific, possibly colloquial, meaning.

247,11-14 'A*t* istud iam neque aequum ac ne humanum quidem cotidie *te* partes electiores surripere atque iis diuenditis peculium latenter augere, de reliquis aequam uindicare diuisionem': 'But that is not fair and not even civilized any more, that you are sneaking the tastier morsels every day and, by selling them left and right, secretly adding to your nest egg, and then claiming a fair share of what is left over.'

At: the generally accepted emendation by ς for *Ad* in F. On this interchange in the manuscripts, see *GCA* 1985,166 on 8,18 (191,11-15), with examples.

ne humanum quidem: unwittingly, the slave hits the nail on the head. By *ne humanum quidem* he means 'not morally worthy of humanity, unkind, inconsiderate' (see *OLD* s.v. *humanus* 6 and cf. e.g. Pl. *Mos.* 814 *esse existumo humani ingeni*; Ter. *Hec.* 552 f. *nonne ea dissimulare nos / magis humanumst?*; Apul. *Apol.* 84,7 *hocine uerum fuit, ... hoc non dico pium, sed saltem humanum*). He does not know that it is, indeed, not a human being but an ass who is pilfering the food. The ironical play with *humanum* becomes more complex when one considers that it is his very *sensus humanus* (cf. *GCA* 1977,167 on 4,22: 91,13-15) that makes the ass steal human food: he has never become used to eating *faenum*. On the other hand, however, he shows himself to be not *humanum* (in the sense meant by the slave) in stealing the savings of these hard-working brothers, whose *tertius contubernalis* (ch. 13: 246,14) he has become. See also above on *fraudes ... in asino*.

te: Elmenhorst's generally accepted emendation for *ac* in F. See Helm Praef. *Fl.* XLI (with examples) on the not infrequent interchange of *ac* and *te* in F. This kind of mistake leads to the conclusion that F, itself a Beneventine manuscript, has been copied from another Beneventine manuscript.

peculium latenter augere ... diuisionem: in ch. 13 (246,10 f.) it was explicitly mentioned that these brothers *communem uitam sustinebant* (see the note there); in 246,15 f. it was mentioned that they took the leftovers of their master's sumptuous meals to their *cellula*. Now it turns out that they sold the leftovers and shared the profit equally (cf. also below, *societas ista*; *nexu communionis*). Apparently the brothers agreed to save as much *peculium* as possible to buy their freedom (cf. also Vallette's note on this passage). Therefore each must be cut to the quick (*suspicio non exilis ... pupugit animos*) by the suspicion that the other is stealthily trying to collect more *peculium* than he. However, it appears from their dialogue that both would prefer this to be done openly if it would prevent a quarrel between them (cf. below, *immanem discordiam*; *Eteocleas contentiones*). On the importance of the unqualifiedly sympathetic characterization of the ass's temporary owners, see Introd. **2.4.3.2**.

peculium: see on *seruis fratribus* ch. 13 (246,6), and the previous note.

de reliquis ... uindicare diuisionem: asyndetically, the narrator heaps the second reproach on the first.

247,14-16: 'Si tibi denique societas ista displicet, possumus omnia quidem cetera fratres manere, ab isto tamen nexu communionis discedere': 'But if you are dissatisfied with that partnership, we can stay brothers in all other respects, but disengage ourselves from that relationship in which we share everything.'

Even in their quarrel the brothers use parallel lines of argument: after his first outburst of reproach the first speaker gives a pleasanter turn to the rest of his words, concluding with a magnificent sentence that expresses his worry about this fraternal discord. Likewise, the other brother begins with a stern rebuke and a sneering *laudo*, but his words, too, end in concern about brotherly love.

societas ista ... isto ... nexu: most translators translate as if the text had *nostra ... nostro*. However, the demonstratives may suggest a vague gesture by the speaker: he points at their shared *cellula*, and by implication at their form of *contubernium*.

societas: the first of a series of legalistic terms (cf. above, *uindicare*; here: *nexu*; below, *damnum*; *querimonia*); in comedy, too, cooks are often characterized by their use of grand terms (see also on ch. 15: 247,27 *subreptionem*; for another example of the cooks' pretentious language, see below, on *Eteocleas ... contentiones*; May 1998,139 f.). Summers 1969,331 f. discusses, with texts and references, *societas* as a recognized institution of Roman law.

possumus: the initial position of the verb in a main clause directly following a dependent clause is relatively rare in Latin (see Bernhard 1927,13 f. with references; KSt 2,2,601, Anm.5). Bernhard remarks that this occurs most frequently after temporal dependent clauses introduced by *cum* or *ubi*. It is noteworthy that the examples from the *Met.* given by Bernhard for the initial position of the verb after conditional clauses are always in direct discourse, as we have here. It is possible that this word order reflects a trait of spoken Latin. For a comparable passage cf. 6,29 (151,9-11) *quodsi uere Iupiter mugiuit in bouem, potest in asino meo latere aliqui uel uultus hominis uel facies deorum*; 6,8 (133,18 f.; Mercurius speaks) *si quis ... demonstrare poterit ..., conueniat ...*; 7,23 (171,20) *nisi uobis suadeo ..., possum ...* with *GCA* 1981,235 ad loc.; cf. ch. 11 (245,8 f.) *quod si ..., quaeratis licet ...*

omnia ... cetera fratres manere: the neuter plural of *ceterus*, used adverbially, is attested from Ennius onward; cf. also Pl. *Mil.* 927 *quiescas cetera?* See LHSz 2,789. Von Geisau 1916,89 (88 f.) gives more examples for neuter adjectives used by Apuleius as adverbs and remarks that this use, which should be regarded as genuinely archaic Latin, becomes more common in poetry, probably under the influence of the Greek cognate accusative.

fratres manere: see above on *suspicio non exilis ... animos* about brotherly love; this

215

notion is elaborated in the next statement and taken up by the brother in his answer.

ab isto ... nexu communionis discedere: OLD s.v. *discedo* 6 gives examples of *discedere ab* in the abstract sense 'to cease from, to give up', etc. Cf. in Apul. *Mun.* 38 (374) *(Necessitas) ... eorum qui a sacra lege discesserint uindex futura.* In *Apol.* 58,10 *potest nec in testimonio dando discedere longius a culina* we find a play on the concrete and abstract meanings of the verb.

247,16-18: 'Nam uideo in immensum damni procedentem querelam nutrire nobis immanem discordiam': 'For I see that the outrage, swelling to an immense degree, about the damage, is fostering a monstrous discord between us.'

Nam uideo: with *nam*, the brother justifies the proposal (which undoubtedly seems radical to him) to break up the partnership (see on *nam* ch. 13: 246,15). *Video* is then placed first for pragmatic reasons: it contains the justification of the proposal made in the previous sentence: '(I make you this drastic proposal) because I see with my own eyes that ...'.

in immensum ... procedentem querelam ... immanem discordiam: the speaker uses hyperbolic expressions to justify his proposal, which he himself feels to be outrageous. Eager not to disturb their fraternal love, he resorts to high-flown style and represents *querelam*, the subject of *nutrire nobis ... discordiam*, as an external force to which they are about to fall victim. In his answer, his brother takes up this formal manner of speaking (see below, on *Eteocleas ... contentiones*). The effect of the brothers' parallel discourse is to suggest that they are of the same mind even when quarreling (see above on *suspicio non exilis ... animos*, and on *de reliquis ... uindicare diuisionem*).

in immensum ... procedentem: cf. 4,29 (97,10) *sic immensum procedit in dies opinio*; Col. 5,3,9 *ne in infinitum procedat disputatio nostra*. In the translation, *in immensum* has been taken in an absolute sense: 'to an immense degree', 'enormously'; cf. e.g Cic. *N.D.* 3,52 *hoc ... in immensum serpet*; Ov. *Am.* 3,12,41 *exit in immensum ... licentia uatum* (see Nummlnen 1938,176 f. for a discussion). The genitive *damni* is taken with *querela* (see the next note). Thus also e.g. Helm-Krenkel: 'die ins Unendliche fortschreitende Klage über den Verlust'. Others take *damni* with *immensum* (thus also *ThLL* s.v. *immensus* 453,63), e.g. Hanson: 'For I see this complaint causing us enormous loss'. The speaker's train of thought, however, is that the *querela* is assuming such immense proportions that it is growing into an *immanis discordia*, which is exactly what he wishes to prevent.

damni ... querelam: for the genitive cf. e.g. Cic. *Pis.* 1 *iamne sentis quae sit hominum querela frontis tuae?* The noun *querela* in the sense 'reason to complain' (here translated 'outrage') is also found in the *Met.* in 2,3 (26,21 f.) *absit ... ut ... hospitem sine ulla querela deseram*; see also *GCA* 1981,214 on 7,20 (169,20-24) *querelas*.

nutrire ... discordiam: *nutrire* is used to mean 'nursing' emotions within oneself (see on *primis elementis ... nutriebatur* ch. 2: 237,14 f.), and also for 'fostering' emotions of others, as here (cf. Tac. *Hist.* 3,53,3 *simultates, quas ... Mucianus callide ... nutriebat*). See *OLD* s.v. *nutrio* 4.

247,19-23 Subicit alius: 'Laudo istam tuam mehercules et ipse constantiam, quod cotidie furatis clanculo partibus praeuenisti querimoniam, quam diutissime sustinens tacitus ingemescebam, ne uiderer rapinae sordidae meum fratrem arguere': The other interposed: 'By Hercules, I must say I like your nerve! First you secretly steal some of the food every day, and then you get ahead of me with the complaint that I have been keeping to myself for ages, groaning in silence so that I wouldn't seem to be accusing my own brother of a mean theft.'

Subicit: asyndeton and initial position of the verb work together to suggest a quick reaction (or possibly even an interruption; cf. *OLD* s.v. *subicio* 9) by one brother to the words of the other. This is customary in the representation of lively dialogues, not only in Apuleius but also in other authors; thus also e.g. V. Fl. 2,659 *subicit Aesonides: 'utinam'*. Cf. also *GCA* 1977,76 on 4,9 (81,6-8).

Laudo: ironically: 'my compliments on ...'. Hanson: 'I really congratulate you...'.

istam tuam ... constantiam: the derogatory *istam tuam* (see *GCA* 1981,65 on 6,30: 152,7-10) supports the irony of *laudo* (see the previous note).

mehercules: this interjection, which is not frequent in the *Met.*, expresses emotion; see *GCA* 1977,175 f. on 4,23 (92,14-20), with references.

et ipse: with these words the speaker parries his brother's reproach. Most translators omit *et ipse*, but cf. Vallette: 'c'est à moi d'admirer ton aplomb'; Brandt-Ehlers: 'Du hast Nerven, das muß ich bei Gott auch selber anerkennen'.

constantiam: sustains the irony (see above on *laudo*). For *constantia* used in malam partem, see on *constantissime* ch. 10 (244,14).

clanculo: attested first in Apuleius (see Van der Paardt 1971,74 f. on 3,8: 58,8); then frequently in Ammianus, Tertullian, and St. Augustine. Plautus (e.g. *Am.* 523) and Terence (e.g. *Eun.* 589) use *clanculum* (not so Apuleius, who always uses *clanculo* and once *clam* in *Apol.* 77,7).

praeuenisti querimoniam: see on *mortem praeuenisset* ch. 5 (240,18).

quam diutissime sustinens tacitus ingemescebam: this is explained by *ne uiderer ... arguere*, which is the substance of *uerecundia* above; see the note there.

rapinae sordidae: cf. above, on *rapinae turpissimae*.

meum fratrem: the possessive pronoun, which is strictly speaking unnecessary here, has an affective connotation: 'to accuse my own flesh and blood!' For a comparable case cf. ch. 25 (256,28) *mariti sui*.

247,23-25 'Sed bene, quod utrimquesecus sermone prolato iacturae <re>medium quaeritur, ne silentio procedens simul[a]tas Eteocleas nobis contentiones pariat': 'But it is a good thing, now that we have brought the subject up on both sides, that a remedy for our loss is being sought, lest a feud grow silently and produce Eteoclean conflicts between us.'

bene quod: cf. 6,8 (134,6) *sed bene, quod meas ... manus incidisti* with Kenney 1990,201 ad loc. See also Callebat 1968,86 and 115: the expression is frequent in Cicero, and very frequent in Tertullian (see Waszink 1947,42).

utrimquesecus: before Apuleius it is attested only in Cato *Agr.* 21,3; Lucil. 584; and Lucr. 4,939. Apuleius has it five times (see *GCA* 1995,347 on 9,42: 235,20 for the passages). After Apuleius, the *ThLL* material lists *Itin. Alex.* 34 *utrimquesecus pellium pagmenta usum ratium integrauerat sibi pecorique*; Amm. 21,12,9; 29,1,4; Capel. 5,464 and 6,709. The *ThLL* material does not mention Lucr. 4,939, possibly because the editors print *utrimque secus* there. It is more consistent to treat *utrimquesecus* as one word, like other compounds with *-secus* (see Cupaiuolo 1967,119).

iacturae remedium quaeritur: it is typical of the mutual affection between the brothers that the speaker is at once ready to believe that the loss is caused by something else, and suggests that they find a solution together (see above on *suspicio non exilis ... animos*).

iacturae remedium: this is Beroaldus' emendation of *iacturae medium* in F and φ (haplography of *-rae re-*), which has been adopted by all editors.

ne silentio procedens simultas Eteocleas nobis contentiones pariat: all editors have adopted this emendation by ς of the version transmitted in F and φ *ne silentio procedens simulatas eteocleas nobis contentionibus pariat*. Oudendorp proposed *ne silentio procedens simulata Eteocleas nobis contentiones lis pariat*. Hildebrand rejects this arguing that the meaning of *simulata ... lis* is unclear; in any case one would rather expect *dissimulata lis*. F's three errors in one sentence suggest that the scribe, having misunderstood the mythological parallel, lost his bearings for a moment.

silentio procedens simultas: cf. above, *procedentem querelam*, and see the previous notes on *de reliquis ... uindicare diuisionem* and *fratres manere* on the parallel argument of these two brothers.

Eteocleas ... contentiones: the adjective *Eteocleas* is more grandiose than a genitive. Cf. Verg. A. 2,542 f. *corpus .../ Hectoreum*, with Austin ad loc.; Nisbet-Hubbard on Hor. Carm. 1,4,17 *domus exilis Plutonia*, with references; in the *Met.* cf. 2,14 (36,12) *Ulixeam peregrinationem*, and 10,15 (248,6) *Fineias dapes*.

References to mythology are frequent in the *Met*. For various interpretations of the function of these references, see *GCA* 1985,153 f. on 8,16 (189,20-26). In Petr. 80,3, Giton uses the same image to quell the quarrel between Ascyltos and Encolpius (see C. Panayotakis 1995,112 and n. 4, with references). Although the Petronius passage suggests that this may be a proverbial expression, in our passage it is undoubtedly one of the frequent reminiscences of comedy we have met here (cf. also *Fineias dapes* ch. 15: 248,6): both in Greek and in Roman comedy, cooks often use high-flown mythological parallels. On this see Handley 1965,299 f. on Men. *Dysk.* 946-53, and May 1998,143 f. Cf. Pl. *Ps.* 834 *(coquus:) haec ad Neptuni pecudes condimenta sunt*; ibid. 868 f. *(coquus:) quia sorbitione faciam ego hodie te mea, / item ut Medea Peliam concoxit senem / quem medicamento et suis uenenis dicitur / fecisse rursus ex sene adulescentulum*. In comedy, slaves in general — not only cooks — often display mythological expertise, e.g. Chrysalus in Pl. *Ba*. 915 f. For the many reminiscences of comedy in this passage, see on *opiparas cenas* ch. 13 (246,16).

contentiones pariat: see *GCA* 1981,221 on 7,21 (170,8-10) *crimina pariet* for this use of *parere*. Cf. ch. 15 (248,10 f.) *iste corporis decor ... peperit grande dedecus*; *OLD* s.v. *pario* 6 gives many examples of the metaphorical use of *pario*.

CHAPTER XV

The ass is caught in the act of gorging himself.

247,26-248,2 His et similibus altercati conuiciis deierantur utrique nullam se prorsus fraudem, nullam denique subreptionem factitasse, sed plane debere cunctis artibus communis dispendii latronem inquiri;...: Having conducted their argument with these and similar reproaches, they both swore that they had committed absolutely no fraud, in short no pilferage at all, but that clearly by all means that thief must be sought who was the cause of their common loss.

His et similibus ... conuiciis: cf. 4,24 (93,4-5) *his et his similibus blateratis* with *GCA* 1977,179 ad loc. The preceding dialogue shows that these *conuicia* consist of good-natured scolding with an undertone of mutual devotion; see on ch. 14 (247,3 f.) *suspicio non exilis ... animos*.

altercati conuiciis: *altercati* is specified by the ablative; cf. 9,33 (228,4 f.) *iis poculis mutuis altercantibus* with *GCA* 1995,282 ad loc. on the use of *altercari/altercare* in the *Met. OLD* s.v. *altercor* 2 gives for 'to exchange conversation' (without animosity, cf. *OLD* ibid. 1) only passages in the *Met.*; *ThLL* s.v. *altercor* 1751,15 f. notes under 'laxiore sensu i.q. *colloquendi*' in the first place four passages in the *Met.*: 5,16 (115,18); 6,26 (148,3); 9,3 (204,19) and 9,33 (228,5); cf also 2,3 (26,25). After Apuleius *ThLL* notes Porph. ad Hor. *S.* 2,3,187 *dialogicon fecit. introduxit enim quendam altercantem cum Agamemnon<e>*, and also two passages in the Vulgate: *Eccl.* 9,13 *non alterceris cum illa* (sc. *muliere aliena*) *in uino*; *Ep. Iudae* 9. As the rest of the sentence shows, the two brothers are once again in heartfelt agreement. The first real *conuicium* is used by them not for each other but for the thief: *latronem*.

deierantur: the deponent is attested only here; elsewhere in the *Met.* Apuleius always has *deierare* (see Oldfather s.v. *deiero*). For that reason Oudendorp wants to read *deierant* here; Hildebrand defended the transmitted form. All editors retain *deierantur*, the reading in F. Flobert 1975,212 compares *iurare/iuratus sum* and points out semantically related verbs like *exsecrari, polliceri*, etc. He explains *deierantur* as an archaism or a pseudo-archaism.

nullam ... nullam: the anaphora illustrates the solemn oath they both swear.

prorsus: reinforces *nullam*. See Callebat 1968,537 f. on the use of *prorsus* in the *Met.*; cf. also *GCA* 1981,115 on 7,5 (158,9-10).

subreptionem: of course, the brothers mean 'theft', forming *subreptio* from *subripere*. In legal language, however, the term *subreptio* is always derived from *subrepere* and is to be understood as 'break-in, burglary'; cf. Heumann-Seckel s.v. *subreptio*. This passage is the first in which the form *subreptio* is attested as a formation from *subripere*. In their solemn vow the cooks are a little off the mark in their use of a highly technical legal term. After our passage, the *ThLL* material mentions for *subreptio* 'theft' Non. p. 310 on Verg. *G.* 4,346 *furtum est occulta subreptio* and a few passages in Christian authors; cf. also Blaise s.v. *subreptio* II.

factitasse: the verb has iterative value here (contra Callebat 1968,141): the daily food-pilfering has been going on for a long time. *ThLL* s.v. *factito* 139,4 f. shows no support for the assumption that the frequentative value of the verb has been lost. Cf. also Gel. 9,6,3, who mentions *factito* in his list of frequentatives (in that case, *factitauerant* in *Met.* 9,9: 209,17 should also be regarded as an iterative; see *GCA* 1995,98 ad loc.).

sed plane debere ... inquiri: this phrase is somewhat zeugmatically construed with *deierantur*. See on the increasing frequency of indirect discourse in the second half of the *Met. GCA* 1985,149 on 8,15 (189,4-12).

plane: here 'emphasizing the correctness of a statement' (*OLD* s.v. *plane* 2). In this meaning, *plane* is frequently found in 'contextes de style familier'; so also in Cicero (Callebat 1968,536 f.; Hofmann *LU* 73). Cf. in the *Met.* e.g. 7,26 (174,19) *plane ... libet*; 10,22 (253,12) *angebar plane*; see also on ch. 29 (260,7 f.) *plane tenui specula solabar*.

communis dispendii latronem: *communis dispendii* is a genitivus criminis with *latronem*: 'the scoundrel who was the cause of their common loss'; cf. e.g. Helm-Krenkel 'dem Räuber ..., der ihnen gemeinsam Schaden zufüge'. Such a genitive is common with *reus*; therefore, *latronem* must imply *reum*. Cf. ch. 14 (247,5) *cotidiani damni studiose uestigabant reum*. This uncommon use of a genitivus criminis with *latronem* suggests that, again, the cooks just miss the mark in their attempt at using high-flown legal language (see above on *subreptionem*, and on *Eteocleas ... contentiones* ch. 14: 247,25).

248,2-6 ...**nam neque asinum, qui solus interesset, talibus cibis adfici posse et tamen cotidie pastus electiles conparere nusquam nec utique cellulam suam tam immanes inuolare muscas, ut olim Harpyiae fuere, quae diripiebant Fineias dapes**: For neither could the ass, who was the only one present, relish this kind of food — and yet each day the choicest food was nowhere to be found — nor certainly did flies fly into their little room so monstrous as long ago were the Harpies, who used to plunder Phineus' meals.

nam ... posse ... conparere ... inuolare: the brothers mention two 'explanations', both equally absurd in their eyes, but with the former they have unknowingly hit the nail on the head. This is an example of what Rosati 1997,114 calls 'il caso limite' of dramatic irony: a character thinks he is making an ironical statement, but because of it he becomes the object of dramatic irony himself. See Rosati 113 f. for more examples. See also on *ualde ... fieri potest ut ... adpetat* ch. 16 (249,13 f.).

adfici: Beyte proposed to read *adlici*. Hildebrand is much in favour of Beyte's proposal but gives as a possible parallel for *adfici* meaning *delectari* Plin. *Ep.* 3,1,9 *sunt in usu et Corinthia, quibus delectatur nec afficitur*; in that passage, *afficitur* is explained by *ThLL* s.v. *afficio* 1209,40 f. as 'ardet nimis'. Cf. also Tac. *Ger.* 5,2-3 *nec tamen adfirmauerim nullam Germaniae uenam argentum aurumue gignere: quis enim scrutatus est? possessione et usu haud perinde afficiuntur. est uidere apud illos argentea uasa, legatis et principibus eorum muneri data, non in alia uilitate quam quae humo finguntur*.

pastus: ever since Oudendorp decreed that '*pastus* hinc alienum est', editors have adopted his reading *partis* (Hanson follows ς: *partes*). In F the original *pastis* has been changed by a different hand to *pa~tes*; φ has *pastis*. Robertson mentions that a* (a sub-group of Class I; see Introd. **4.1**) has *pastus*. Since, therefore, *-st-* is strongly represented in the manuscripts, the reading *pastus* of a* should not be brushed aside. If Apuleius wrote *pastus*, he was perhaps alluding to Lucr. 6,1127 *hominum pastus pecudumque cibatus*, the first attested passage in which *pastus* is used of human food (after Lucretius, *ThLL* s.v. 2 *pastus*

649,9 f. gives Tert. *Paen.* 9,4; Ambr. *Off.* 1,28,132; Prud. *Cath.* 7,70). In using this remarkable phrase, Lucretius may have wished to suggest that disease and decay, when they occur in nature, do not distinguish between human and animal food. If so, Apuleius in referring to Lucretius' remarkable line is playing on the dichotomy between animal and human food which is prominent in this context: like Lucretius, he transfers *pastus*, which is used especially of animal food, to human food. Below we see a similar play: the paradox of the ass, who like a true animal (cf. *inescatus, saginatus,* with the notes ad loc.) eats *humanis ... cibis*. See also on *adfatim saginabar* ch. 13 (246,22).

electiles: except here, it is attested only Pl. *Mos.* 730 f. *uino et uictu, piscatu probo electili / uitam colitis*. See on *opiparas cenas* ch. 13 (246,16), about the function of comic usage in this episode.

conparere nusquam: cf. 7,2 (155,6) *nec exinde usquam compareret* with GCA 1981,87 ad loc.; Pl. *Aul.* 629 *qui modo nusquam comparebas, nunc quom compares peris*.

nec utique = *nec omnino*; Callebat 1968,97 gives examples in the *Met.* and states that this is the only passage where this turn of phrase is not used in a lively dialogue. In our passage, however, the lively dialogue of the cooks is rendered in indirect discourse (cf. above, on *sed plane debere*, and the next note).

tam immanes muscas, ut olim Harpyiae fuere: not only is the exaggeration in itself comical, but this second mythological comparison also portrays the cooks as related to their colleagues in comedy: see on *Eteocleas ... contentiones* ch. 14 (247,25).

diripiebant Fineias dapes: again the cooks use grandiose language (the adjective *Fineias* is grander than a genitive; cf. on *Eteocleas ... contentiones* ch. 13: 247,25) and a high-flown mythological comparison (see the previous note). There are, moreover, verbal reminiscences of Verg. *A.* 3,212 f.: the Trojans, having reached the Strophads, encounter the *Harpyiae* (212); cf. ibid. *Phineia ... domus* and 227 *diripiuntque dapes*. Possibly there is also an implicit allusion to Phineus' blindness: these cooks are blind to the fact that the ass does not touch his own food and yet becomes fatter and sleeker (their eyes are not opened until below, after which it does not take them long to catch the thief).

248,7-10 Interea liberalibus cenis inescatus et humanis adfatim cibis saginatus corpus obesa pinguitie compleueram, corium aruina suculenta mollilueram, pilum liberali nitore nutriueram: Meanwhile, gorged with the lavish dinners and amply stuffed with human food, I had filled out my body with a plump layer of fat, I had got a smooth skin from the succulent lard, and developed a fine gloss on my coat.

The sentence which describes how the ass has become a 'feast for the eye' has been carefully construed so as to become, itself, a 'feast for the ear':
Interea liberalibus cenis inescatus (15)
et humanis adfatim cibis saginatus (13): these two cola show syntactic parallellism and rhyme. They are followed by an asyndetic isocolic tricolon (see Bernhard 1927,67):
corpus obesa pinguitie compleueram (13)
corium aruina suculenta mollilueram (14)
pilum liberali nitore nutriueram (13): the syntactic parallel of these three cola has been taken to the extreme, which makes especially the far-fetched last colon difficult to translate (literally: 'I had nourished my coat with a fine gloss'). For a similar procedure, see ch.

221

21 (253,10 f.) with note. The cola are ranged asyndetically, and the rhyming verbal forms at the end of each colon are metrically identical.

liberalibus cenis inescatus: 'stuffed with lavish meals'. *Liberalis* has the meaning given in *OLD* s.v. *liberalis* 6: 'done or provided on a generous scale, ample, liberal, lavish'. However, *liberalis* can also be understood in the first meaning: 'of or relating to free men', i.e. 'gentlemanly' (*OLD* ibid. 2), which gives the phrase the value of an ironic oxymoron: *inescare* is especially used of fattening animals. See *GCA* 1981,172 on 7,14 (164,18-21), signaling a similar ironical use of *inescatos*. Cf. on *adfatim saginabar* ch. 13 (246,22); also *humanis ... cibis saginatus* below.

liberalibus: for the possible connotations of this adjective see the previous note. The adjective *liberalis* occurs eight times in the *Met*, three times in this chapter: here, *liberali nitore*, and *liberalis cachinnus* below. It functions here almost as a catchword for the elation and high spirits evoked in this and the following chapter, in which the master of the house enters the story for the first time. One should keep in mind that *liberalis* also means 'of or belonging to *Liber*', as in the *ludi liberales*; cf. Naev. *com*. 113 *libera lingua loquemur ludis liberalibus*. See C. Panayotakis 1995,76 and n. 59 on puns on *Liber* in comedy and mime. Laughter, Γέλως, was characteristic of the Dionysian thiasus (see Münstermann 1995,82 with references.). A Dionysian atmosphere is evoked here before we learn the name of the *dominus aedium*, which turns out to be Thiasus (ch. 18: 250,17 f.; see the note there).

humanis adfatim cibis saginatus: another ironic oxymoron: *adfatim ... saginatus* suggests an animal feeding on *humanis cibis* (see above on *liberalibus cenis inescatus*; also on *adfatim saginabar* ch. 13: 246,22).

corpus ... compleueram, corium ... molliueram, pilum ... nutriueram: for the composition of the cola see the note at the beginning of this pericope. The first colon takes a close look at the ass's body as a whole; the next two cola, at his skin and coat respectively.

obesa: for this adjective in the *Met*. and elsewhere see *GCA* 1985,53 on 8,4 (179,5-11) with references.

pinguitie: *pinguities* is attested here for the first time. The *ThLL* material notes once *pinguitia* (Arn. 7,20) and a few times *pinguities* in later medical authors, Vindic. *Med*, and Cael. Aur.

corium: used particularly of the skin of animals (cf. *GCA* 1985,53 on 8,4: 179,5-11). The fact that the ass has a *corium* rather than a human skin is emphasized by the narrator from the beginning: 3,24 (70,11) *cutis tenella duratur in corium*. From that moment onward the stick is used lavishly on his *corium*: in 3,29 (73,18 f.) the robbers no longer understand his ass's sounds when he tries to invoke the emperor: *aspernati latrones clamorem absonum meum, caedentes hinc inde miserum corium*. After that, *corium* is repeatedly associated with a beating taken by the ass: 7,11 (163,3, see *GCA* 1981,158 ad loc.); 7,15 (165,20, see *GCA* 1981,181 ad loc.); 7,17 (167,13). In other passages his *corium* is often mentioned in the context of the theme 'a human in animal skin', e.g. 6,26 (148,16 f.), where Lucius considers an attempt at escape and reasons thus: *nam et illa ... praeclara magia tua uultum laboresque tibi tantum asini, uerum corium non asini crassum, sed hirudinis tenue membranulum circumdedit* (see *GCA* 1981,37 ad loc.); also 8,25 (196,18 f.) *ut in asini corio modestum hominem inhabitare credas*. Finally, in 11,6 (270,16 f.), Isis announces Lucius' re-metamorphosis: *pessimae mihique detestabilis ... beluae istius corio te protinus exue*. Although in our passage Lucius is not yet allowed to remove his ass's skin, there is a noticeable change from the period when he received beatings on his *corium*: *corium ... molliueram* is one of the first signals of the ass's 're-humanification' which is thematic in this book (see on ch. 16: 249,9 *conuiuium summo risu personabat*; Introd. **2.4.3.2**).

When we compare this lush description of the fat, sleek Lucius with the description of his *iumentarium contubernium* 9,13 (212,11 f.), it becomes even clearer how much better the ass's circumstances are now. Cf. e.g. 9,13 (212,19 f.) *totumque corium ueterno atque scabiosa macie exasperati*; the narrator concludes his description of the exhausted, emaciated animals *talis familiae funestum mihi ... metuens exemplum ... maerebam* (9,13: 212,20 f.).

suculenta: with *aruina* the adjective must mean something like 'juicy'; see also Van Mal-Maeder 1998,85 on 2,2 (26,6) *suculenta gracilitas*. The adjective is attested first in the *Met*. After that, the *ThLL* material gives e.g. Non. 69 *adipatum ueteres honeste pro pingui et suculento et opimo posuerunt*; Hier. *Ep*. 52,11,4 *suculento ualidoque sum corpore*; Sid. *Ep*. 1,2,3 *colli non obesi sed suculenti*. In Prud. *Ham*. 57 praef. it is used metaphorically: *furores suculenti*.

aruina: 'fat, lard'; cf. Verg. *A*. 7,626 f. *pars leuis clipeos et spicula lucida tergent / aruina pingui*. Suet *Fr*. 170, p. 272 Re. *aruina pingue durum, quod est inter cutem et uiscus, alii aruinae nomine laridum dicunt*.

liberali nitore: see above, on *liberalibus*. Here the adjective means 'worthy of a free man in personal appearance, fine, noble' (*OLD* s.v. *liberalis* 3).

nitore: often used of the sheen on the hide of a healthy animal (*OLD* s.v. *nitor*[2] 3b and s.v. *niteo* 4). Phaed. 3,7,2 f. *cani perpasto macie confectus lupus / forte occucurrit ... 'unde sic, quaeso, nites?'*.

248,10-11 Sed iste corporis mei decor pudori peperit grande dedecus: But that grace of my body caused a great disgrace for my honour.

For this anticipation, unusual for the narrator of the *Met*., see Introd. **3.5**.

Sed ... peperit: the pluperfects *interea ... compleueram ... molliueram ... nutriueram* formed the background against which new events are now beginning to stand out. The perfect *peperit* is different from the narrative perfects in the next chapter: *iussit* (ch. 16: 248,31), *perduxit* (249,1), and *iussit* (249,2) that conclude the episode beginning here, the events in the episode from *dirigunt animos* (l. 13) onward having been narrated in historical presents. *Peperit* is part of a retrospective comment of the narrator (see Pinkster in *AAGA* 2,1998,107 f. on such "authorial" perfects, which in a narrative text are used for author comments outside the story line.

grande dedecus: cf. Hor. *S*. 2,2,95 f. *grandes rhombi patinaeque / grande ferunt una cum damno dedecus ... et frustra mortis cupidum, cum deerit egenti / as, laquei pretium*. Lucius, too, lacks the means to commit suicide when he wants to, in order to escape the *dedecus* of the theatre performance (to which the anticipation here ultimately refers, as is explained in Introd. **3.5**): ch. 29 (260,3 f.); see the note there. For the use of *grandis* see on ch. 27 (258,21 f.) *grandem ... materiam*.

248,11-13 Insolita namque tergoris uastitate commoti, faenum prorsus intactum cotidie remanere cernentes, iam totos ad me dirigunt animos:

The unusual breadth of my back surprised them since they saw that my oats remained entirely untouched every day, and so now they fixed their full attention on me.

namque: occurs in the *Met.* in both first and second position in the sentence; see *GCA* 1977,142 on 4,19 (88,27-28) with references.

tergoris uastitate: an amusing detail: the brothers bought the ass as a pack animal (ch. 13: 246,11 f.); his essential part is therefore his back, as far as they are concerned. The ass's prosperous appearance (above) is wasted on them. *Vastitas* is used hyperbolically here; cf. Sen. *Ep.* 82.24 (the African snake that wreaked havoc on Regulus' army) *cum ingens magnitudo pro uastitate corporis solida ferrum et quicquid humanae torserant manus reiceret*.

commoti: without warning the two brothers have again become the subject. See below on *ad me dirigunt animos*.

faenum ... intactum: cf. ch. 13 (246,23 f.) *nec enim tam stultus eram tamque uere asinus, ut ... cenarem asperrimum faenum*. The ass's cleverness, in which the narrator took such pride, now becomes his downfall.

remanere: Giarratano-Frassinetti print *remmanere*, following a proposal by Schober 1904,47, who wished to make *remmanere cernentes* as metrically equivalent to *uastitate commoti*. Augello 1977,212 rightly rejects such an intervention: Apuleius' prose rhythms elsewhere are not so rigid as to suggest that he would wish here to change the pronunciation of the word.

ad me dirigunt animos: Robertson in his app. crit. ad loc. mentions Rohde's proposal to read above *commoti <mei>* (sc. *domini*); it is, indeed, curious that there is no specification of the changed subject. Robertson prefers *<mei>* after *me*. Brakman proposes *faenum <fratres>*, which could have been omitted after *prorsus*. In the narrative flow, however, the two brothers have been the main characters since ch. 14 (247,1); the context makes it obvious that they are the subject of *dirigunt animos*; all modern editors rightly follow F without addition. The change in subject has already been prepared for by the nominative plural participle *commoti*.

248,13-19 Et hora consueta uelut balneas petituri clausis ex more foribus per quandam modicam cauernam rimantur me passim expositis epulis inhaerentem. Nec ulla cura iam damni sui habita mirati monstruosas asini delicias risu maximo dirumpuntur uocatoque uno et altero ac dein pluribus conseruis demonstrant infandam memoratu hebetis iumenti gulam: And at the usual time, as if they were on their way to the baths, they locked the doors as was their custom, peeked through a crack, and saw me utterly absorbed in the delicacies displayed all over the place; they were no longer concerned at all about their own loss and, surprised at the bizarre preferences of their ass, they exploded with laughter, called one and the other and then even more fellow-slaves, and showed them the refined taste, indescribable beyond words, of a dumb pack-animal.

hora consueta: Plin. *Ep.* 3,1,8 *ubi hora balnei nuntiata est (est autem hieme nona, aestate octaua)*.

per ... cauernam rimantur: *rimari* must mean here 'to watch through a *rima*'. *OLD* s.v. *rimor* gives this passage as the only example of this meaning. It is typical of Apuleius to give words an unusual, etymological meaning; see *GCA* 1985,66 on 8,6 (180,17-19) *definito* and see in this book the note on *adserere* ch. 7 (242,15). Originally, *rimari* is an agricultural term: 'to make *rimae* in the soil'; cf. e.g. Verg. *G.* 3,534 *rastris terram rimantur*. From that it takes on the metaphorical meaning 'scrutinize, explore' (cf. e.g. 2,26: 46,10) or 'search for, investigate' (cf. 3,27: 72,17). This use of *rimari* is, according to Dahlmann 1979,13 f., on line 9 of the probably Apuleian poem in Gel. 19,11, typical for Apuleius.

Before his metamorphosis, Lucius himself looked through a *rima* as he watched the witch Pamphile change herself into an owl (3,21: 68,3). Now it is he who is being watched, as he was in 9,3 (204,23 f.), when the *cinaedi* peered through a *rima* to see whether the ass was infected with rabies. Whereas later in the ninth book the ass himself is continuously the curious observer, from now on he becomes more and more the object of private and public curiosity; see below on *mirati ... delicias*.

Nec ulla cura iam damni sui habita: a load has been taken off the brothers' shoulders. The entire former chapter emphasized that their main concern was not the loss in itself but the notion that one was robbing the other; see on *suspicio non exilis ... animos* ch. 14 (247,3 f.).

mirati monstruosas asini delicias: throughout the *Met.* the desire for *mira*, characteristic of the time in which the work was created, plays an important part (see on *miris ... artibus* ch. 4: 239,14). *Monstruosas ... delicias* expresses clearly what the reason is for the present wonder: the unnatural, paradoxical image of an ass feasting on human food (on *monstruosus* see *GCA* 1981,225 on 7,22: 170,22-24; cf. also the note on ch. 17: 250,7 f. *sed uerebar, ne ... redderent*). Before his metamorphosis (2,1: 24,18 f.) the narrator described himself as *anxius alioquin et nimis cupidus cognoscendi quae rara miraque sunt*. From this passage onward Lucius becomes more and more a *mirum* himself, which people come to gawk at (Schlam 1992,53; Hijmans in *GCA* 1995,362 f.). Cf. the expectation among those present, when they try to find out if the ass also wants to drink wine ch. 16 (249,18 f.), and the way in which the ass's fame spreads like wildfire, making his master famous ch. 17 (250,11 f.; see there, on *conspectum ... miris artibus*). Also ch. 19 (251,11 f.), where people show up in droves when the famed, miraculous ass arrives in Corinth. See Scobie 1969,43 f. on the revival of paradoxography during the time of Hadrian and his successors as an obvious concession to the public interest at that time, and on paradoxography as one of the important antecedents for Apuleius' *Met.*; cf. Winkler 1985,270. On *spectacula* as a theme in the *Met.* and in this book, see Introd. **2.4.2**.

delicias: here 'i.q. *mollities, luxuria*' (*ThLL* s.v. *delicia* 447,8 f.). Cf. e.g. Mart. 12,15,4 f. *stupet superbi / regis delicias grauesque lusus*; the heading of Gel. 3,5: *deliciarum uitium*. See *GCA* 1981,180 on 7,15 (165,15-17). For the connotation 'luxurious preferences, hobbies', present here, cf. Var. *Men.* 85 *domini delicias*, with Cèbe 382 f. ad loc., with parallels.

risu maximo dirumpuntur: cf. 3,2 (53,6) *risu dirumperetur*; 3,7 (57,10 f.) *risu ... diffluebant ... Milonem risu maximo dissolutum*. In these passages Lucius was a laughing stock, even before his metamorphosis; what frightened him then was the fact that he did not understand why the people laughed. Now he is well aware of the reason for the irrepressible laughter, which calls up an atmosphere of carefree merriment that is rare in the *Met.* Cf. also 9,12 (211,23) *risum* with *GCA* 1995,115 f. ad loc. On the mirroring of the Risus-festival see Introd. **2.5.1**; see Krabbe 1989,162 f. on *risus* and *cachinnus*, and on the 'metamorphosis of laughter' in de *Met.*

See Van der Paardt 1971,32 on 3,2 (cited above) on the possible imitation of Afran. *Fr.* 127 *ego misera risu clandestina rumpier*; on this metaphor see also Otto 1890,303 s.v. *rumpere* and ibid. 301 s.v. *risus*. See also on *delibutus gaudio* ch. 17 (249,23).

infandam memoratu: the phrase is an explanation of *demonstrant*. They are so overcome by laughter that they are incapable of speech – they can only point.

hebetis iumenti gulam: *gulam* must be understood here as 'refined taste', as e.g. Plin. *Nat.* 9,66 *proceres gulae* and Mart. 6,11,6 *non minus ingenua est et mihi ... gula*. Then the contradiction which the phrase must convey becomes clear: 'such a dumb animal, and yet such a refined taste!' Thus the phrase expresses the same as *monstruosas asini delicias*.

248,20-22 Tantus denique ac tam liberalis cachinnus cunctos inuaserat, ut ad aures quoque praetereun[c]tis perueniret domini: Such a loud and unrestrained roar of laughter eventually overcame the whole group that it also reached the ears of their master, who was passing by.

liberalis cachinnus: unrestrained, hearty laughter (see above on *risu ... dirumpuntur*): the slaves no longer make an effort to laugh discreetly. Their master, who from his introduction onward is depicted as a true bon vivant, is obviously not especially strict: he reacts to the boisterous laughter of his slaves not with anger but with interest.

Teuber 1993,230 f. explains the difference between the light-hearted mirth at the pilfering ass and the disapproving tone in the description of a youthful lapse (filching plums) in Aug. *Conf.* 2,3-9 as a difference between the *Met.* as a 'karnevalesker Text' and the *Confessiones* as an 'entkarnevalisierter Text'.

liberalis: here 'abundant' (*ThLL* s.v. 1293,73 f.). There is another connotation present here that is connected with a frequent meaning of the adverb *libere*, namely 'freely, openly', cf. e.g. Pl. *Cas.* 872 f. *audacius licet / quae uelis libere proloqui* (*OLD* s.v. *libere* 3a gives other examples). See above, on *liberalibus*.

cachinnus cunctos inuaserat: cf. Capel. 8,809 *talia adhuc canente Satura, uetitus ille ac durissime castigatus denuo me risus inuasit*. *Inuadere* ('attack') is frequently used of emotions etc. which 'overpower' someone; *ThLL* s.v. *inuado* 111,36 f. notes not only examples of illness and emotions in the strict sense but also passages with e.g. *horror* or *somnus* as the subject of transitive *inuado* (cf. 4,18: 88,3 f. *tempore, quo somnus obuius impetu primo corda mortalium ualidius inuadit*). In view of this frequent use of *inuadere* we may assume that a personification of *cachinnus* (thus Neuenschwander 1904,19) is no longer felt. On the laughter in this episode, see on *delibutus gaudio* ch. 17 (249,23).

inuaserat: the pluperfect indicates that this is the background for new events.

praetereuntis perueniret domini: on this word order see on *promissae libidinis flagitat uadimonium* ch. 4 (239,16).

praetereuntis: F has *praeter cunctis*; in φ this has been corrected by the first hand. See Helm, Praef. *Fl.* XLIV, with examples, for the frequent confusion of *c* and *e* in F.

CHAPTER XVI

The ass as symposiast.

248,22-26 Sciscitatus denique, quid bonum rideret familia, cognito quod res erat, ipse quoque per idem prospiciens foramen delectatur exumie; ac dehinc risu ipse quoque latissimo adusque intestinorum dolorem redactus, iam patefacto cubiculo proxime consistens coram arbitratur: So he asked why in the world his people were laughing so; and when he had learned what the matter was, he in his turn looked through the same crack to his intense delight; he, too, had to roar with laughter until his stomach hurt; and once the door of the room was opened, he positioned himself close by and openly inspected the situation.

Sciscitatus ... familia: from his first appearance this gentleman is characterized as a good-humoured master, who is always game for a good joke (see below on *quid bonum rideret familia*).

sciscitatus ... cognito: Bernhard 1927,42 f. gives examples in the *Met.* of the collocation (frequent in the historians) of a participle in agreement with the subject and an ablative absolute. See also LHSz 2,385.

denique: here, as often in the *Met.*, in the sense of *ergo*; see GCA 1977,54 on 4,5 (78,13-14) with references.

quid bonum rideret familia: GCA 1977,188 on 4,25 (94,9-11 *quid malum fleret*), regard *malum* there and *bonum* here as interjections, as if the punctuation were: '*quid, bonum, rideret familia*'; cf. Hanson: 'what in heaven's name the servants were laughing at'. Likewise, Georges s.v. *bonus* takes our passage 'Als Ausruf, etwa "du meine Güte!"'. ThLL s.v. *bonus* 2093,67 also groups our passage under *bonus* = *felix, prosper*. So we have here a somewhat elliptic interjection (for e.g. *bonum sit*), for which there are no parallels. A different interpretation is found in Helm-Krenkel: 'Er fragt denn schliesslich was das Gesinde Schönes zu lachen habe' (thus also Vallette and Brandt-Ehlers). Cf. Pl. *Rud.* 415: *hem, quid hoc bonist?*, where, according to Sonnenschein ad loc., *boni* has become equivalent to *noui*.

This phrase introduces a characteristic of the master of the house, which is important for the continuation of the story: his appetite for ever-changing, novel kinds of entertainment; (see below, on *nouitate spectaculi laetus*). At the moment Lucius still regards this quality as a smile of *Fortuna* (see below) and, like the servants, is eager to please this master (249,3 f.; ch. 17: 249,28 f. *uoluptates eius* - sc. *domini* - *per meas argutias instruebat*; ch. 23: 254,14 *nouum spectaculum domino praeparando*), but eventually this same characteristic will have awkward consequences for Lucius. See also below on *parasito meo* 249,16 f.

cognito quod res erat = *re cognita*. On the ablative absolute where the noun is replaced by a dependent clause, see GCA 1985,49 on 8,4 (179,1) *mandato ... inuaderent*; cf. also 7,4 (157,2 f.) *cognitoque quosdam ... oppetisse* with GCA 1981,104 ad loc. with references.

quod res erat: for this turn of phrase, frequent in the *Met.*, see GCA 1995,220 on 9,25 (221,22). Cf. also ch. 24 (256,10) *quod res erat, clamantem*.

per idem prospiciens foramen: see on *per ... cauernam rimantur* ch. 15 (248,14 f.).

prospiciens ... delectatur exumie: here begins an episode in which the ass, who readily and frequently observed others (cf. 9,12: 212,1 f.; 9,15: 214,6 f.; 9,42: 235,25 f.; and 2,5: 28,11, cited in the following note), becomes himself a *spectaculum*. See also the passages cited on *quid bonum rideret familia* above, and ch. 19 (251,11 f.). See Introd. **2.4.2** on *spectacula* as a recurrent theme in the *Met*.

Because of the atmosphere of innocent amusement throughout this episode, the linear reader is not yet aware that the seeds are now being sown of the repugnant *spectaculum* for which the ass will be prepared from ch. 23 (254,16) on. It is not by any means anticipated in this episode: the narrator tells the story from the point of view of the experiencing I, and as such does not get ahead of the events (for an exception, however, see on *sed ... dedecus* ch. 15: 248,10 f.).

delectatur exumie: cf. 2,5 (28,11) *dum haec identidem rimabundus eximie delector*; V. Max. 7,4,2 *re eximie delectatus*; Gel. 11,13,4 *cursus ... hic et sonus ... sententiae eximie nos et unice delectabat*. For the word-order see comm. on ch. 32 (263,3) *constitit amoene*.

exumie: as at 8,30 (201,20), F has *exumie*, φ *eximie*, which has been adopted by all modern editors. It is better here to adhere to the spelling of F, on the principle laid down in *GCA* 1985,269 ad loc. (see Introd. **4.2**).; see also *ThLL* s.v. *eximius* 1491,60 f.

risu latissimo = *risu amplissimo*; for the metaphorical use of *latus* cf. Apul. *Fl*. 15,17 *latis pecuniis*. *ThLL* s.v. 1 *latus* 1022,8 f. gives other examples for *latus* 'de variis actionibus, condicionibus, sim.', from *Rhet. Her*. 2.21,33 *latiorem locum defendendi* onward. The combination *risus latissimus* is attested only here. In 6,9 (134,11) Kenney 1990,201 follows Robertson in adopting the reading of ς *latissimum cachinnum* for F's *laetissimum cachinnum*. Cf. Greek πλατὺ γελάσαι, καταγελᾶν, in e.g. Philostr. *VA* 7,39; *VS* 1,202,2. On the laughter in this episode see on *risu maximo dirumpuntur* ch. 15 (248,17), and on *delibutus gaudio* ch. 17 (249,23).

adusque intestinorum dolorem redactus: a similar expression is found 3,10 (59,13), where, before his metamorphosis, Lucius attends the Risus festival and makes the people there double up with stomach pains caused by laughter. He experiences this as a bitter humiliation and refuses to contribute further to the Risus festival (James 1987,89 f.; see also below on *gaudio praesentium fiduciam mihi subministrante*). There are a few other passages in the *Met*. where the ass is laughed at: 8,24 (195,20 f.); 9,12 (211,23 f.; see *GCA* 1995,115 ad loc.); and 9,42 (236,6; see *GCA* 1995,353 ad loc.). In none of these passages does the narrator mention how he feels about this laughter at his expense. Here, however, he regards it as a smile of *Fortuna*, which gives him *fiducia*; in 249,3 f. he even tries to make the people laugh again, and succeeds: 249,9 *conuiuium summo risu personabat*. Our passage, as far as its interpretation by the narrator is concerned, is therefore diametrically opposed to 3,12 (61,10 f.) *at ego uitans oculos omnium et, quem ipse fabricaueram risum obuiorum declinans*. There, Lucius would perhaps have done better to oblige the god *Risus* (James 1987,89 f.). Here, because of the laughter felt by Lucius as a smile of *Fortuna* and because of his eagerness to please the master of the house, Lucius becomes for a while that master's pampered darling (ch. 18: 250,28-251,10). However, eventually this results in a dire situation (see above on *quid bonum rideret familia*).

patefacto cubiculo: this addition (not discussed by Seelinger 1986,364 f.) symbolizes an atmosphere of liberation after the earlier references to closed doors (ch. 15: 248,14 *clausis ... foribus*) and to look through a crack into a locked room (ch. 15: 248,23 f.), but the 'liberation' is short-lived (ch. 19: 251,17 *obserata fore*). The nights of love with the *matrona* also take place *clausis ... foribus* (ch. 20: 252,13); shortly before the performance in the theatre there is again a reference to an open door: *patente porta* (ch. 29: 260,18); this could be taken as an announcement of an eventually self-chosen liberation: ch. 35 (265,28 f.) *paulatim furtiuum pedem proferens portam ... potitus iam cursu me celerrimo proripio* (see also Seelinger 1986,365). In 9,2 and 3 the ass, suspected of having rabies, is locked up *clausis obseratisque super me foribus* (9,2: 204,10 f.); later, when his tameness has been proven, we read *foribus patefactis plenius* (9,3: 204,25).

arbitratur: see GCA 1995,118 on 9,12 (212,1) on Apuleius' use of *arbitrari* in the archaic meaning *spectare*. See also Zurli 1987,217 f. In our passage the Plautine meaning of *arbitrari* ('essere testimonio clandestino'), demonstrated by Zurli for other passages in the *Met.*, does not apply.

248,27-249,2 Nam et ego tandem ex aliqua parte mollius mihi renidentis Fortunae contemplatus facie<m>, gaudio praesentium fiduciam mihi subministrante, nec tantillum commotus securus esitabam, quoad nouitate spectaculi laetus dominus aedium duci me iussit, immo uero suis etiam ipse manibus ad triclinium perduxit mensaque posita omne genus edulium solidorum et inlibata fercula iussit adponi: For now that I saw that Fortuna's face was, at last, smiling at me in a somewhat milder way, and since the high spirits of those present boosted my self-confidence, I kept on eating, carefree and not in the least perturbed, until the master of the house, delighted with the novelty of the spectacle, ordered me to be led – or rather, took me with his own hands – to the dining room, and after a table had been placed there, ordered all kinds of complete dishes and untouched plates to be served.

tandem ... mollius mihi renidentis Fortunae contemplatus faciem: a personification is assumed (hence the capital *F*), following Helm-Krenkel, Brandt-Ehlers, and Hanson. On the problem of *Fortuna* or *fortuna* see on *haud ullo tempore tam beniuolam Fortunam expertus* ch. 13 (246,14 f.).

The corresponding passage in the *Onos* also describes τύχη smiling, but only after the ass has been taken to the dining room and seated at the table laden with food (47,8): κἀγὼ τὴν τύχην ὁρῶν ἤδη ἁπαλόν μοι προσμειδιῶσαν... The transferral of this remark to an earlier point in the *Met.* makes its effect quite different: the narrator of the *Met.* experiences the laughter at himself as the smile of *Fortuna*. This encourages the reader to compare this reaction of Lucius with his reaction in other passages where he is ridiculed (see above on *adusque intestinorum dolorem redactus*). In the *Onos*, on the other hand, the narrator says that the ass reacts to the laughter with deep embarrassment (47,6): κἀγὼ σφόδρα ἠχθόμην ἐπὶ τοῦ δεσπότου κλέπτης ἅμα καὶ λίχνος ἑαλωκώς. There, the remark about the smiling τύχη is a reaction to the delicious food he is being served at the master's table. Thus, the seemingly inconsequential transferral of a short sentence in the Vorlage has significant effect on the interpretation of the whole. See Junghanns 1932,116, n. 178 on the carefulness with which the author of the *Met.* undertakes these 'Translokationen' in relation to his Vorlage; see also on *me phaleris aureis ... exornatum* ch. 18 (251,5 f.).

mollius mihi renidentis Fortunae ... faciem: cf. 7,20 (169,8) *sed in rebus scaeuis adfulsit Fortunae nutus hilarior*. There, the notion of a kindly smiling *Fortuna* is at once toned down by *nescio an futuris periculis me reseruans* (see GCA 1981,210 ad loc.); here, the added *ex aliqua parte* also implies some reserve on the part of the narrator. Moreover, *renidere* 'smile, beam at', has remarkably often a connotation of insincerity (which is not always made explicit). This is the case in the *Met.* in all passages where the verb occurs meaning 'smile radiantly' (*OLD* s.v. *renideo* 3): 2,13 (35,12); 3,12 (60,21 f.); 6,16 (140,13, see also Kenney 1990,211 ad loc.). A notion of artificial, insincere smiling certainly also applies to Catul. 39,1 f. *Egnatius, quod candidos habet dentes, / renidet usquequaque*: in that poem, the recurring *renidet* works up to 39,15 f *tamen renidere usquequaque te nollem / nam risu inepto res ineptior nulla est*. Cf. also Tac. *Ann*. 4,60,3 with Furneaux ad loc.; Sen. *Phaed*. 277 f. *iste lasciuus puer* (sc. Cupido) *et renidens / tela quam certo moderatur arcu!* See also Den Boeft (et alii, edd.) on Amm. 22,9,10 *renidens*.

gaudio praesentium fiduciam mihi subministrante: in 3,10 (59,12 f.), the episode of the Risus festival, *gaudium* of the onlookers is also mentioned, but there it does not boost Lucius' confidence – to the contrary, he is in a panic for a long time (*trepidus*: 3,10: 59,22). For the comparison with the Risus festival see above on *adusque intestinorum dolorem redactus*. Both our passage and the Risus passage suggest a theatre performance; cf. 3,10 (59,12 f.) with Van der Paardt 1971,83 ad loc. and here *nouitate spectaculi*. See also below on 249,4 *commendatioremque me ... ei facere cupiens*; play-acted inability ch. 17 (250,6 f.); *scaenam* ch. 23 (254,15 f.). Unwittingly, Lucius has been an *actor* in the Risus festival (3,11: 60,11); when he realizes that, he refuses any further cooperation as *actor*. Here he is an over-eager *actor*, unaware of the gruesome *spectacula* in which, thanks to his 'talent', he will eventually have to perform. See also the previous notes and Introd. **2.5.1**; see Shumate 1996,225 on the theme of thwarted expectations in the *Met*.

tantillum: this colloquial-sounding adverb (see on *tantillum* ch. 7: 242,12) may suggest the onlookers' amused remarks about the ass who, cool as a cucumber, continues eating.

esitabam: the verb has undoubtedly frequentative force here. Cf. Gel. 9,6,3 *ab eo, quod est 'edo' et 'ungo'... 'esito' et 'unctito', quae sunt eorum frequentatiua*. See Scobie 1975,118 on 1,19 (17,7 f.) and cf. *GCA* 1981,263 on 7,27 (175,5-9). *Esitare* often means 'be accustomed to eat, have as one's usual nourishment'; cf. e.g. Plin. *Nat*. 31,89 *salem cum pane esitasse eos* (sc. *ueteros*) *prouerbio apparet*; Gel. 11,7,3; 4,11,1 *Pythagoram philosophum non esitauisse ex animalibus*. Thus also in the *Met*. 9,36 (230,19 f.) *canes ... adsuetos abiecta per agros essitare cadauera*; see *GCA* 1995,304 ad loc.

nouitate spectaculi laetus dominus: for this *dominus*'s liking for *spectacula*, see the earlier note *quid bonum rideret familia*; for the theatrical connotations in this passage, see above on *gaudio praesentium fiduciam mihi subministrante*.

nouitate ... laetus: a case of mirroring: even if the narrator does not expressly make the connection, the reader is probably supposed to think back to 1,2 (3,4), where the narrator labeled himself a *sititor ... nouitatis*. In this *dominus* he meets another *sititor nouitatis*, whose thirst for novelties will assume grotesque and (for the ass at least) disagreeable forms; as for Lucius, his own thirst for *nouitas* has already caused him much trouble. On the theme of 'thirst for novelty' as a connecting element between Apuleius' *Met*. and Augustines *Confessions*, see Shumate 1996,243 f.

dominus aedium duci me iussit: all objections against the transmitted text, and the arguments to change that text, become invalid when the next part of the sentence, namely *immo uero suis etiam ipse manibus ad triclinium perduxit*, is taken into consideration. The objection that *duci* lacks an adjunct of direction led Beyte to conjecture <*intus*> *aedium* (cf. 8,29: 200,26-201,1 with *GCA* 1985,260 ad loc.), adopted by Helm-Krenkel, and endorsed by, among others, Kronenberg and Damsté. Castiglioni proposed <*ad*>*duci*; Helm <*in*>*duci*. But it is also possible to take *ad triclinium* both with *duci* and with *perduxit* (249,1), regarding *immo uero ... manibus* as an insertion. This is Armini's reasoning; cf. also Augello 1977,212 f. The argument (of e.g. Kronenberg and Damsté) that *dominus aedium* 'moleste abundet', because he was simply called *dominus* before, becomes invalid when one recognizes that *dominus aedium* sustains the effect the narrator is striving for with the addition of *immo uero suis manibus ... perduxit*: 'I was escorted by the master of the house himself!' This is only the first in a series of statements by the naive fictive narrator (see Introd. **3.3**), who repeatedly emphasizes how much he is favoured and shown preferential treatment by Thiasus. In what follows, however, the abstract author (see Introd. **3.2**) is gradually working up to a more critical attitude towards this wealthy, socially prominent *dominus*, whom the fictive narrator boasts about. See on this notion the comm. on *quinquennali magistratui* ch. 18 (250,21), which also discusses the difference from the *Onos*, where this kind of irony is absent. The passage in the *Onos* (47,7) comparable to our passage has καὶ ... κελεύει με εἴσω ἄγεσθαι εἰς τὸ ἐκείνου συμπόσιον.

edulium solidorum et inlibata fercula: from a pilferer of leftovers the ass now becomes an honoured guest at a symposium: it is emphasized that the ass is no longer helping himself to the *reliquiae* (cf. ch. 13: 246,19) but that he is served a dinner prepared especially for him. At this point it is still merely amusing that the *dominus*'s appetite for diversion is boundless and that money is no object where his entertainment is concerned. The linear reader has to discover on her/his own that this characteristic of Thiasus is gradually taking on a morbid aspect. The naive fictive narrator does not anticipate later events (see above on *prospiciens ... delectatur exumie*), nor does he, in retrospect, revise his opinion about this wealthy *dominus*, who treats him as a favourite (see above on *dominus aedium duci me iussit*).

edulium: see on *edulia* ch. 13 (246,8).

solidorum: *solidus* here meaning 'in its entirety, complete'. Cf. Verg. *A.* 6,253 *et solida imponit taurorum uiscera flammis*. Plin. *Nat.* 8,210 *solidum aprum Romanorum primus in epulis adposuit P. Seruilius*.

inlibata fercula: *inlibata* underlines Lucius' new status (see above on *edulium solidorum et inlibata fercula*). The original meaning of *fercula* is 'the dishes on which the food was carried in'; hence 'the courses of a meal' (*ThLL* s.v. *ferculum* 490,24 f.). In that meaning the word is often found in a context of opulent dinners with many courses, sometimes with a critical undertone. E.g. Hor. *S.* 2,6,104; V. Max. 9,1,1 *qua* (sc. *tempestate*) *non Oratae mensae uarietate ferculorum abundarent*; Juv. 1,94 f. *quis fercula septem /... cenauit auus?* The fact that this *dominus* serves *inlibata fercula* to an ass contributes to his overall characterization as an extravagant millionaire; see on *his erat diues admodum dominus* ch. 13 (246,7) and on *ex arbitrio dispositis* ch. 18 (250,27); cf. also below, on *aureum cantharum*.

249,3-5: At ego quanquam iam *bellule* suffarcinatus, gratiosum commendatioremque me tamen ei facere cupiens esurienter exibitas escas adpetebam: And although I was already pretty stuffed, I fell hungrily on the food laid out before me because I wished to please him and to ingratiate myself with him even more.

quanquam ... suffarcinatus: the use of *quamquam, etsi, quamuis* with participle or adjective is found occasionally in Ciceronian Latin, and becomes increasingly frequent after that (KSt 2,2,444 f.; Von Geisau 1916,279).

quanquam: on the spelling see on *quanquam* ch. 14 (247,4).

bellule: F has *uellule*; φ has *bellule*; this is the case also in the two other passages in the *Met.* where the adverb occurs (5,31: 128,12 and 11,30: 291,6). On the frequent confusion of *b* and *u* in F, see Helm Praef. *Fl.* XLVI. The adjective is found in Plautus (*ThLL* s.v. *bellulus* 1822,24 f.), e.g. *Mil.* 988 f. *edepol haec .../ bellulast. ThLL* ibid. 1822,27 gives for the adverb *bellule* only Pl. *Bac.* 1068 (where, however, it is Leo's conjecture for mss. *ueluti*; cf. Pl. *Fr. inc.* Goetz-Scholl 151,79); *Fest.* 36,4 (p. 32 L.); and the three passages in Apul. *Met.* Monteil 1964,226 f. discusses the nuances in meaning of *bellus* and *belle*, and our passage ibid. 228.

suffarcinatus: like *bellule* (see the previous note), this word from comedy is not attested again before Apuleius (see *GCA* 1995,83 on 9,8: 208,4-7). This passsage shows a remarkable cluster of expressions borrowed from comedy, obviously well-suited to the ridiculous story of an ass who enjoys human food and drink. The episode of the gourmet ass may owe something to the well-known anecdote about the death of the comic poet Philemon (whom Apuleius greatly admired: *Fl.* 16): V. Max. 9,12, ext. 6 *Philemonem autem uis risus inmoderati abstulit. Paratas ei ficus atque in conspectu positas asello consumente puerum ut illum abigeret inclamauit. Qui cum iam comestis omnibus superuenisset, 'Quoniam', inquit, 'tam tardus fuisti, da nunc merum asello'. Ac protinus urbanitatem dicti crebro anhelitu cachinnorum prosecutus, senile guttur salebris spiritus grauauit.* The same story is told by Lucian. *Macr.* 25, and, about Chrysippus, by Diog. Laërt. 7,185 = *SVF* 2,2. It must, however, be noted that in *Fl.* 16 Apuleius gives a different account of Philemon's death, which suits its context in the *Fl.*

gratiosum commendatioremque: on such juxtapositions of positive and comparative, see KSt 2,2,476 A. 20, who cite our passage as well as examples from early Republican authors (e.g. Cato *R.* 6,4 *crassus ... aut nebulosior*) and passages from post-Augustan authors (e.g. Suet. *Nero* 51,1 *oculis caesis et hebetioribus*). LHSz 2,168 f. point out the original meaning of the comparative as the expression not of an absolutely higher degree but of a relatively high degree, which in early colloquial language could lead to positive and comparative being used together. In comic verse this usage was sometimes applied metri causa; cf. e.g. Pl. *Rud.* 1301 *rutilum, atque tenuius fit.* Sonnenschein ad loc. explains: 'the comparative meaning attaches to both adjectives', which is true also for our passage. LHSz see no reason to assume Greek influence (contra von Geisau 1912,30).

commendatioremque me ... ei facere cupiens: cf. ch. 17 (249,27 f., the man appointed as the ass's groom) *quo se patrono commendatiorem faceret, studiosissime uoluptates eius per meas argutias instruebat.* Lucius already knows that this *dominus* is someone whom people are anxious to please by meeting his needs for amusement (see above on *quid bonum rideret familia,* and on *ex arbitrio dispositis* ch. 18: 250,27). Remarkably enough. Lucius begins his career with this new master by doing something that repels him (i.e. eating while he is already full; see below on *parasito meo*), and will end it by refusing to comply with his master's wish that he should do something that positively disgusts him (chs. 34-35).

esurienter exibitas escas adpetebam: someone who reads this aloud has to open his mouth remarkably often for the repeated *e*'s and *a*'s; thus, the sound seems to illustrate the content of the phrase.

esurienter: for this adverb *ThLL* s.v. *es(s)urio* 867,64 f. gives only this passage and Zeno Ver. 1,24 (*caeleste prandium*) *esurienter accipite*. See comm. on ch. 23 (254,14-15) *incunctanter*.

exibitas escas: *exhibere* is also used of serving food in 6,24 (146,13). On the spelling *exibitas* see on *exibeo* ch. 9 (244,3).

escas: *esca* or *escae* is used of human and animal food. Another meaning, however, is 'bait', so that Lucius eagerly swallows the bait here. For the double meaning cf. also Pl. *Mil.* 581 *numquam hercle ex ista nassa ego hodie escam petam*. See on *hamos* ch. 13 (246,20).

249,5-8 Nam et, quid potissimum abhorreret asino, excogitantes scrupulose, ad explorandam mansuetudinem id offerebant mihi, carnes lasere infectas, altilia pipere inspersa, pisces exotico iure perfusos: For they also minutely thought out what would be most repugnant to an ass, and to test my tameness they offered me just that: meat dishes seasoned with *laser*, poultry sprinkled with pepper, and fish swimming in an exotic sauce.

quid ... abhorreret asino: *abhorrere*, in all sense, is normally construed with *a* + ablative. Sometimes, as here, the preposition is omitted. Cf. Curt. 6,2,5 *inconditum et abhorrens peregrinis auribus carmen*, where the verb means 'be uncongenial or repugnant (to), jar (on)' (*OLD* s.v. 4), as it does in our passage.

ad explorandam mansuetudinem: in all passages in the *Met.* where *mansuetudo* (or *mansuetus*) occurs (usually in connection with the ass), it is used by people who themselves demonstrate a certain degree of animality in their behaviour. Cf. the prospective buyer of the ass (one of the debauched priests of the Dea Syria) 8,24 (196,15 f.) *de mansuetudine ... mea percontatur anxie*; 9,3 (204,25 f.) *an iam sim mansuetus, periclitantur*; 10,35 (265,26 f.: the people preparing a bestial show) *nec ... quisquam custodiendum tam mansuetum putabat asinum*; 9,39 (233,15 f.) the *hortulanus* asks the soldier *ciuilius atque mansuetius uersari commilitonem*, but shortly afterwards (9,40: 233,28 f.) he behaves like a fierce animal himself (see *GCA* 1995,333 ad loc.). Cf. also 7,23 (171,18) some peasants want to make the ass *mansuetus* by castrating him. 6,31 (153,3 f.) one of the robbers first refers to his own and his comrades' *mansuetudo*, then proposes a gruesome punishment for the ass and Charite. In this way, the abstract author (see Introd. **3.2**) of the *Met.* suggests that in terms of *mansuetudo* there is a very thin dividing line between a human being and an animal (cf. ch. 33: 264,1 f., where judges are addressed as *forensia pecora, immo uero togati uulturii*; see also below on *conuiuium summo risu personabat*). Thus, the terms *mansuetudo, mansuetus* etc. in the *Met.* illustrate a passage from Apul. *Soc.* 3 (125 f.) *in qua praecipuum animal homines sumus, quamquam plerique se incuria uerae disciplinae ita omnibus erroribus ac piacularibus deprauauerint, sceleribus inbuerint et prope exesa mansuetudine generis sui inmane efferarint, ut possit uideri nullum animal in terris homine postremius*. See Beaujeu 212 f., nn. 1-4 ad loc.; Schlam 1992,104 f.; see also Introd. **2.4.3.2**.

carnes lasere infectas, altilia pipere inspersas, pisces exotico iure perfusos: an asyndetic tricolon (see Bernhard 1927,67), in which each colon is two syllables longer than the last. The servants think out *scrupulose* which dishes should be offered to the ass; equally *scrupulose* the author has composed the prose to be relished by the reader.

carnes lasere infectas: meat in itself is unsuitable food for an ass, but this meat is even seasoned with *laser*. The juice of sylphium (= *laserpicium*) was used in many Roman dishes to tenderise the meat (André 1961,207 f. with references). Cf. Aelian. *Var. Hist.* 12,37 ἐπεκούρει δὲ αὐτοῖς τὸ σίλφιον πολὺ ὂν ὥστε τὰς σάρκας συνεκπέττειν. It had a tart flavour, and was used in very small quantities (it is probably the same as asafoetida, used in Indian cooking). *Carnes lasere infectas* suggests an excessive use of the *laser*, which would make the taste overpowering (and to an ass even more disgusting). Pl. *Ps.* 816, too, exaggerates: *eo laserpitii libram pondo diluont*. For *laserpicium*, a plant originating from Cyrene, see Sonnenschein on Pl. *Rud.* 630 with many references.

altilia pipere inspersa: poultry is no food for an ass, let alone sprinkled with pepper. *Piper* (André 1961,209) came into use in the Roman cuisine relatively late, but then occurs in a great many recipes. Plin. *Nat.* 12,29 expresses his surprise at people's preference for *piper* in their food: *quis ille primus experiri cibis uoluit aut cui in appetenda auiditate esurire non fuit satis? utrumque siluestre gentibus suis est et tamen pondere emitur ut aurum uel argentum.*

pisces exotico iure perfusos: once again food that in itself is totally inappropriate for an ass receives an unusual seasoning to boot.

exotico: *exoticus* (ἐξωτικός): 'foreign', cf. Pl. *Men.* 236 *Graeciam ... exoticam* (= *Magnam Graeciam*); Apul. *Met.* 1,1 (1,13 f.) *exotici ... sermonis*. Thus, *exoticum ius* must mean a sauce prepared with foreign ingredients and therefore 'strange-tasting'. What comes from foreign countries is also expensive; this connotation of *exoticus* may also play a part in this context with its emphasis on the exaggerated luxury of this household (cf. below, the golden cup). Cf. Pl. *Mos.* 42 *non omnes possunt olere unguenta exotica.*

249,8-9 Interim conuiuium summo risu personabat: In the meantime, the company at the table filled the air with boisterous laughter.

conuiuium summo risu personabat: in Hanson's translation, 'the banquet-hall resounded with uproarious laughter' (thus also e.g. Helm-Krenkel), *conuiuium* has the meaning of 'banquet-hall', which is also possible for the Greek συμπόσιον (see *LSJ* s.v. III); cf. the corresponding passage in the *Onos* (47,8) τὸ δὲ συμπόσιον ἐκλονεῖτο τῷ γέλωτι. *OLD* s.v. *conuiuium* gives only the meanings 'dinner-party' and 'the people at a dinner-party': cf. 2,20 (41,21 f.) *inter haec conuiuium totum in licentiosos cachinnos effunditur*; Ov. *Am.* 3,1,17 *nequitiam uinosa tuam conuiuia narrant*. In *ThLL* s.v. *conuiuium* 885,71 f. some parallels can be found for *conuiuium* meaning 'dining room, banquet hall', e.g. Tac. *Ann.* 15,37,2 *in stagno Agrippae fabricatus est ratem cui superpositum conuiuium nauium aliarum tractu moueretur*; Plin. *Nat.* 19,19 *ardentesque in focis conuiuiorum ex eo uidimus mappas*. Cf. also Mart. 7,97,11 f. *te conuiuia, te forum sonabit, / aedes, compita, porticus, tabernae* (grouped by *ThLL* ibid. 885,61 f. not with *conuiuium* 'i.q. *triclinium, conclave*' but with *conuiuium* 'i.q. *convivae, sodales*'). So in our passage, too, *conuiuium* may refer to the dining room; however, this is not necessary since *personare* is commonly found with people (or animals) as its subject, with the ablative of the sound they make (*OLD* s.v. *persono* 1; see also 9,33: 228,7 with *GCA* 1995,282 ad loc.). Thus Brandt-Ehlers: 'erhob die Gesellschaft ein mächtig schallendes Gelächter'. Vallette adopts a middle course with 'la table retentissait de vastes éclats de rire'. On the laughter in this episode see above on *delibutus gaudio*.

Now that Lucius has made the company laugh, he is unreservedly accepted: the other guests call him *sodalis* and *contubernalis*, and drink his health when, like a good symposiast, he has drained *otiose et satis genialiter* the cup offered to him. In this boisterous atmosphere of eating and drinking (soon to be followed by sexual pleasures: ch. 19: 251,20 f.) Lucius makes a pseudo-return of the ass to the human world (see also on *corium* ch. 15: 248,9). The dividing line between animal and human becomes increasingly vague in this and the following chapters (cf. above on *ad explorandam mansuetudinem*), culminating in the *matrona* copulating with the ass (the main character rightly fears ch. 34 : 265,16 f. that the wild animals in the arena will make no distinction between the woman they are about to tear to pieces and the 'ass' who is lying with her; see also Introd. **2.4.3.2**). Shumate 1996,117: 'Apuleius constructs an inverted parallel of movement in which the degeneration and feralization of human beings unfolds alongside the graduation of the ass (back) into humanity.'

There is a contrast here with the real re-metamorphosis of Lucius in book 11, where as a *contubernalis* (11,19: 281,1 f.) of the Isis priests he will subject himself to a regimen of fasting and abstinence (on the eleventh book as a book of *abstinentia*, see Heath 1983,66 f. with references.).

249,9-11 Quidam denique praesens scurrula: 'Date', inquit, 'sodali huic quippiam meri.': Finally some joker who was present said: 'Give our friend here some unmixed wine'.

scurrula: the *ThLL* material gives for this diminutive of *scurra* only this passage and Arn. 6,21. A *scurra* was a professional joker, who earned his keep by making witty remarks at the dinner parties of rich hosts; see Ferguson on Juv. 4,31; Damon 1997,109 f. To amuse his host, the *scurrula* echoes Philemon's suggestion about the ass (quoted above on *suffarcinatus*) - a suggestion that the *dominus* will now comply with.

'Date', inquit: on the low tempo in this episode see Introd. **1.6.2**. The frequent passages of dialogue (beginning at ch. 14: 247,11 f.) contribute to the comic atmosphere, manifested also in the vocabulary. See also above on *suffarcinatus*.

sodali: this emphasizes the fact that the *dominus* and his company, having convinced themselves of the ass's *mansuetudo*, regard him now as 'one of the club'; cf. *contubernalis noster, parasito meo*. See also above, on *conuiuium summo risu personabat*; ch. 17: *sodalem conuiuamque* (250,12); *simul et conuiuam et uectorem* ch. 18 (251,10).

quippiam meri: Callebat 1968,190 points out the artificality of this combination of the partitive genitive with the archaic *quippiam*. See also LHSz 2,52 and 196. It is possible, of course, that the *scurrula* affects a mincing pronunciation for his absurd joke.

meri: the anecdote in V. Max. (cited above on *suffarcinatus*) also has *merum*, and both Diog. Laërt. 7,15 and Lucian. *Macr.* 25 (telling the same anecdote) have ἄκρατον. For an ass to drink unmixed wine is an extra absurdity. The *dominus* orders no *merum* for the ass, but *mulsum*, a sweet honey-wine, probably because that is what the company are drinking as an aperitif (see below, on *mulsi*).

249,12-15 Quod dictum dominus secutus: 'Non adeo', respondit, 'absurde iocatus es, furcifer; ualde enim fieri potest, ut contubernalis noster poculum quoque mulsi libenter adpetat.': The master, supporting this remark, answered: 'Your joke, you scoundrel, is not that absurd; for it is very likely that our companion eagerly craves a cup of mead as well.'

Quod dictum ... secutus: cf. *OLD* s.v. *sequor* 13 'to support, back (a proposal in the senate etc.)'. See Bernhard 1926,50 about this expression in the *Met.*
furcifer: the *dominus* addresses his *scurrula* with good-humoured invective (see on *furcifer* ch. 4: 239,25). This is consistent with his characterization; see above on *sciscitatus ... familia*.
ualde ... fieri potest, ut ... adpetat: this remark is meant as an absurd possibility, but the *dominus* unwittingly hits the nail on the head: the man inside the ass would undoubtedly very much like some wine.
ualde ... fieri potest: the adverb *ualde* is attested only three times in Apuleius' works: *Soc.* 21,168; *Met.* 9,17 (215,19); and here. It is used here and 9,17 as a 'sentence adverbial' (see Pinkster 1990,32 f.); *OLD* s.v. *ualde* 2a gives examples of this usage from Cicero onward, especially in letters, e.g. *Att.* 2,5,3 *ualde ... exspecto tuas litteras*.
mulsi: *mulsum* is wine sweetened with honey (οἰνόμελι). It was usually drunk at the beginning of a banquet.
libenter adpetat: cf. Phaed. 5,4,5 *libenter istum prorsus adpeterem cibum*. This may be deliberate wordplay by the *dominus* (see also below, on *contempera*): for the ass's preferences, regarded as unnatural by the company, he uses a verb that often means (*OLD* s.v. *appeto* 3) 'to have a natural desire for, seek instinctively'. Cf. also the combination *naturalis appetitio*, with which e.g. Cic. *Fin.* 4,14,39 translates the Greek noun ὁρμή.

249,15-17 Et 'heus', ait, 'puer, lautum diligenter ecce illum aureum cantharum mulso contempera et offer pa<ra>sito meo; simul, quod ei praebiberim, commoneto': And he said: 'You there, boy! Look, that gold cup there, wash it carefully, fill it with mead, and offer it to my sponger; at the same time, remind him that I already took the first sip in drinking his health'.

heus: colloquial; cf. 7,22 (170,25) *et 'Heus tu, puer', ait*, with *GCA* 1981,225 with references.
lautum diligenter ... aureum cantharum: to make the practical joke complete, the *dominus* exaggerates the rules of etiquette that must be observed in offering the ass wine; cf. also the following *simul ... commoneto*.
cantharum: this word, borrowed from Greek, for a large drinking vessel, is found regularly in Plautus (*GCA* 1981,162 on 7,12: 163,14-16); see also *GCA* 1995,97 on 9.9 (209,14-20), where an *aureus cantharus*, part of the serving set of a cultic meal, has been stolen by the priests of the Dea Syria. In our passage we may have an association, often evoked by the word *cantharus*, with the cult of Dionysus; see Nisbet-Hubbard on Hor. *Carm.* 1,20,2. For the Dionysian associations in this passage, see on *liberalibus* ch. 15 (248,7), and below on *genialiter*. The *cantharus* was a very large vessel; so the host's ownership of a golden one is illustrative of his extravagance. Moreover, the cup's size makes it even more amazing to the guests that the ass downs it in one draught; cf. *grandissimum illum calicem*.
contempera ... offer ... commoneto: imperatives of the present and the future in one sentence; see LHSz 2,340 f. Callebat 1968,503 gives examples of this variation in the

Met., calling it a 'procédé cher aux comiques'. See also KSt 2,1,197 f.

contempera: first attested here in literary prose. It is a technical term e.g. Apic. 4,2,33 *adicies sorba, in se contemperabis, frangis oua VIII. ThLL* s.v. *contempero* 646,34 f. gives for the use of this verb in the sense *commiscere* many passages in veterinary works. The verb is therefore probably used humorously here for mixing *mulsum* for an ass. After Apuleius we find *contemperare* in Christian authors (e.g. Mamert. *St.an.* 1,14; Aug. *Trin.* 11,2,3 (*corpori*) *anima suo quodam miro modo contemperatur*). From St. Augustine onward the verb is frequently used in a metaphorical sense (*ThLL* ibid. 646,43 f.).

offer: thus φ; F had *offers* but the *s* has been erased. F has *profers* in 1,23 (21,21); *aufers* 2,6 (30,1); *defer surnula* (*defers urnula*) 6,13 (138,12 f.). At 5,2 (104,24) the mss. have *cubiculo te refer*. Paratore in his edition of *Cupid and Psyche* 1948,33 f. on 5,2 discusses all these places extensively, and pleads for acceptance of the imperative form in -*s* in all these cases; cf. also Augello 1977,37 ad 1,23 (21,21). *ThLL* s.v. *offero* 499,39 f. accepts *offers* in our passage, and notes several parallels from the *Itala*, as well as Iuvenc. 1,740 for this form. For a future text edition of the *Met.* our place will have to be reconsidered, since F originally had *offers*. A (the most important ms. of Class I; see Introd. **4.1**), has *offeres*.

parasito meo: at first sight, the host's reference to the ass as *parasito meo* is a good-humoured joke: he alludes to the ass's enormous appetite, a characteristic of the *parasitus*; cf. Ter. *Hau.* 38 *edax parasitus*; Hor. *Ep.* 2,1,173; Gel. 3,3,5 *parasitus ... esuriens*. Damon 1997,27 f. and n. 16. notes in our passage an inversion of the use of animal metaphors for parasites (references from Greek and Latin literature are given): here an ass is called *parasitus*. To the re-reader of the *Met.* the joke also acquires a sinister aspect: another characteristic of the *parasitus* was that he must please the host in all respects, however degrading; see *RE* s.v. 'Parasitus', 1397,30 f. [Hug]; cf. Pl. *Men.* 162 *id enim quod tu uis, id aio atque id nego*; see the extensive note of Petersmann ad Pl. *St.* 228 *adsentatiunculas*. Lucius, too, will later be expected by the *dominus* to cooperate in a degrading spectacle (ch. 23: 254,16 f.; see Damon 1997,187 f. on the *parasitus* as gigolo). See also above on *commendatiorem ... me ... ei facere cupiens*.

quod ei praebiberim, commoneto: see Callebat 1968,339 with examples of *quod*-clauses instead of the accusative and infinitive with verba declarandi.

praebiberim: for the use of *praebibere* meaning *propinare*, *ThLL* s.v. *praebibo* 391,29 f. gives in addition to our passage only Cic. *Tusc.* 1,40,96; there it is used with the object *uenenum* in an anecdote, repeated by Cicero from Xenophon *HG* 2,3,56, about Theramenes, who takes poison in prison and drinks a (fatal) toast to Critias. In other passages *praebibere* means 'to begin with a drink of'. This passage in Apuleius is the only occurrence where *praebibere* is used without an accusative object (*ThLL* ibid. 391,29).

249,18-22 Ingens exin oborta est epulonum expectatio. Nec ulla tamen ego ratione conterritus, otiose ac satis genialiter contorta in modum linguae postrema labia grandissimum illum calicem uno haustu per<h>ausi. Et clamor exurgit consona uoce cunctorum salute me prosequentium: At this, an immense feeling of intense expectation arose among the diners. But I was not in any way taken aback, and calmly and most genially, with my lower lip curved into a kind of tongue, I drained that gigantic chalice in one draught. And a shout arose from them all, and they toasted my health with one voice.

Ingens ... expectatio: about the hyperbolic use of *ingens* see on *ingens ... trepidatio* ch. 10 (244,7).

satis genialiter: for the use of *satis* see on *satis parce* ch. 14 (246,26).

genialiter: cf. Ov. *Met.* 11,95 *hospitis aduentu festum genialiter egit*, where Bömer remarks ad loc.: 'genialiter: fere i.q. liberaliter, voluptuose', referring to his note on Ov. *Met.* 10,95, where he discusses the adjective *genialis* in connection with *genio indulgere*. The adverb *genialiter* is attested only three times, namely in the Ovid passage cited above, our passage, and *carm. epigr.* 1106,3 *accumbentem sculpi genialiter arte*. If we assume that *genialiter* is a reference to the Ovid passage (where Midas hospitably entertains Silenus), we may conclude that *genialiter* contributes to the Dionysian atmosphere of this episode pointed out above (ch. 15: 248,7 s.v. *liberalibus*; see also above, on *cantharum*), and that *satis genialiter ... perhausi* suggests that by now Lucius has come entirely under the influence of this Dionysian atmosphere (Bömer in the note mentioned above makes a clear connection between *genialis* and Bacchus; cf. e.g. Ov. *Met.* 4,14, where Bacchus is called *genialis consitor uuae*). For Thiasus as Silenus see on *me ... residens* ch. 18 (251,5 f.).

contorta in modum linguae postrema labia: being an ass, Lucius cannot pick up the cup to bring it to his mouth; instead, he makes a kind of funnel with his lower lip – as he would with his tongue (*in modum linguae*) if he did not have a thick ass's tongue – through which he sucks up the wine from the cup. From the very beginning of his existence as an ass, Lucius has managed to make use of the mobility of his lower lip; cf. 3,25 (70,21 f.) and his attempt at speaking 7,3 (156,14 f.); in both passages, as here, the ass uses his lower lip in an attempt to do something human. This is the way the scene described here should be visualized, if a realistic representation is needed at all. Shackleton Bailey 1988,175, troubled by this passage, wants to read *lagunae* instead of *linguae*; Hanson reads *ligulae*, following a conjecture by Blümner, which Robertson mentions in his app. crit. ad loc. with 'fortasse recte'. All other editors accept the transmitted reading.

uno haustu perhausi: F has *perauxi*; φ has *pausi* (with the *h* written over it by a second hand); A has *perhausi*. This is sufficient reason to read *perhausi*, which yields good sense ('I drained it completely') as an unusual expression for an unusual event: an ass who, with his lower lip curved, empties a gigantic wine cup. *ThLL* s.v. *haurio* 2567,44 f. points out the possibility of confusion between *(h)ausi* and *auxi* in the codices, so that *perauxi* may well have taken the place of *per(h)ausi* (see *ThLL* ibid. 2566,82 f. on the occurrence of non-aspirated forms of *haurio*) in F. Oudendorp defends *perhausi*, pointing to the figura etymologica *haustu perhausi*. *ThLL* s.v. *perhaurio* 1438,39 f. mentions our passage, and *Aetna* 421; further a few passages in Christian authors, e.g. Tert. *Nat.* 1,15. Blaise s.v. *perhaurio* remarks that the verb is found in Plautus, namely Pl. *Mil.* 34, where one ms. reads *perhaurienda* (the variant *peraudienda* is preferred in the editions) in the metaphorical sense 'to absorb entirely'. Georges s.v. *perhaurio* accepts the verb both in the Plautus passage and here in Apuleius; *LS* s.v. *perhaurio* also mention these two passages. *OLD* s.v. *perhaurio* cites only *Aetna* 421.

Most editors read *perduxi* (the conjecture of a 'vir doctus', which is mentioned but not adopted by Oudendorp), referring to ch. 5 (240,4) *continuo perduxit haustu*. *Perducere* in the sense of 'to empty one's glass' is rare, but attested elsewhere; *ThLL* s.v. *perduco* 1289,48 f. gives, apart from our ch. 5 (see above) Scrib. Larg. 135; Mart. 3,22,4 *summa uenenum potione perduxti*, and a few later examples. However, the confusion of *d* and *a*, which would produce *perduxi*, does not occur elsewhere in F (Helm, Praef. *Fl.* XLIII).

Et clamor: according to Robertson, this was the reading in F; a later hand erased *et* and changed *clamor* to *Clamor*. Except for Helm, all editors print *Et clamor*...

clamor exurgit ... salute me prosequentium: during a banquet, when someone drained a large cup to the bottom, it was customary to wish him good health; cf. D.C. 72,18,2 "Επιεν ... οἶνον ... ἀμυστί· ἐφ' ᾧ καὶ ὁ δῆμος καὶ ἡμεῖς παραχρῆμα πάντες τοῦτο δὴ τὸ ἐν τοῖς συμποσίοις εἰωθὸς λέγεσθαι ἐξεβοήσαμεν, 'Ζήσειας'.

consona uoce: cf. Ov. *Met.* 13,610 f. *consonus ... plangor* and see Bömer ad loc. The combination *consona uox* is first attested Sil. 5,198 f. *lacus hinc, hinc arma simulque / consona uox urget* (Sil. 17,443 *uox consona linguae*). Apuleius has a preference for this poetic phrase in the *Met.*: 3,2 (53,12); 4,16 (87,5); 11,13 (276,15); cf. also *ore consono* 2,1 (24,21) and 4,34 (102,7); *consone clamitarent* 1,10 (9,22). After Apuleius *consona uoce* or *uoce consona* is frequent in Christian authors; e.g. Aug. *Serm.* 20, ed.: SL 41, line 3 *uoce consona ... diximus*; Hier. *comm. Is.* 16,57,17 *populum Iudaeorum, qui consona uoce clamauit ... crucifige, crucifige talem*.

CHAPTER XVII

Effortlessly the ass learns human tricks, thus bringing fame to his master.

249,22-26 Magno denique delibutus gaudio dominus, uocatis seruis suis, emptoribus meis, iubet quadruplum restitui pretium meque cuidam acceptissimo liberto suo et satis peculiato magna praefatus diligentia tradidit: Brimming over with great joy, the master of the house eventually sent for his slaves, the ones who had bought me, and gave orders to reimburse them fourfold what they had paid; me he entrusted to a favourite freedman who was very comfortably off, prefacing the transaction with a careful lecture.

delibutus gaudio: cf. 3,10 (59,14) *laetitia delibuti* with Van der Paardt 1971,83 on this metaphor from athletics, which has been borrowed from Terence; cf. also 7,13 (163,23) *gaudio delibuti* with GCA 1981,164 ad loc.; 11,7 (280,2-3) *gaudio delibuti populares* (at the *Ploiaphesia*); see Gw. Griffiths ad loc.

From ch. 15 onward, this episode has repeatedly and in ever-varying phrases indicated great hilarity at the sight of the ass eating human food and drinking wine: ch. 15 (248,17) *risu maximo dirumpuntur*; (248,20) *tam liberalis cachinnus cunctos inuaserat*; ch. 16 (248,24 f.) *risu ... latissimo adusque intestinorum dolorem redactus*; (248,28) *gaudio praesentium*; (248,30) *nouitate spectaculi laetus*; (249,9) *conuiuium summo risu personabat*. The recurrent laughter underlines the atmosphere of mirth in the episode from ch. 13 onward. But in addition there are unmistakable references to the Risus festival (3,1-12), which go unnoticed by the naive actorial narrator (see Introd. **3.5**) but can be spotted by the interpreting reader. Thus, the laughter acquires an additional dimension but at the same time loses some of the lightheartedness it suggests at first sight; see on *adusque intestinorum dolorem redactus* ch. 16 (248,25). Lucius resigns himself here to his role of buffoon, which will earn him the dubious favours of Thiasus; see on *parasito meo* (ch. 16: 249,16 f.); Introd. **2.5.1**.

seruis suis, emptoribus meis: for the ability of slaves to acquire and sell property of their own, see ch. 13 (246,5 f.), and ibid. on *seruis fratribus*.

iubet ... tradidit: the historical present *iubet* is in line with the preceding *exurgit*, thus reflecting a sequence of events; the perfect *tradidit* concludes this episode. See Pinkster 1983,312 with references. For a discussion of the use of tenses in this episode see on *pupugit* ch. 14 (247,3).

quadruplum ... pretium: the slaves paid eleven *denarii* for the ass (ch. 13: 246,6); now they receive a price of forty-four *denarii*. As has often been observed (see Introd. **2.3**), we see here an exaggeration in relation to the *Onos*, where the price was only doubled (48,1). Whereas in the previous book the amounts paid for the ass become smaller and smaller (see GCA 1995,4), the values mentioned in this book are extreme: in ch. 1 (236,10 f.) the ass fetches nothing at all (see comm. there, on *nullo equidem contradicente*); in ch. 13 (246,6) the two brothers buy the ass for a pittance, namely eleven *denarii* (see comm. there, on *undecim denariis uendidit*); here the ass fetches forty-four *denarii*, the highest price ever paid for him. The narrator in the *Met.* mentions the prices paid for the ass at the various transactions much more emphatically than the narrator of the *Onos* does; moreover, in the *Met.* those prices are much more extreme, i.e. either extremely high or extremely low; cf. also Duncan-Jones ²1982,248 f. After the absolute low of the price in the transition from book 9 to book 10, the upward trend of the prices in this book suggests an improvement in Lucius' situation. Adams 1995,106 n. 10 remarks that the price suggested here (176 sesterces) is still low; he compares evidence for prices of a common donkey on Egyptian papyri of the second century A.D., where the average price is 250 sesterces. However, the prices mentioned each time add to the characterization of the buyers and sellers: the soldier gets the ass for nothing (see above), i.e. nobody at that moment 'cares twopence' for the ass, including the soldier himself, as it appears. So, for a trifle he passes the ass on to the two brothers (see the beginning of this note) when he wants to get rid of him. To Thiasus, who pays *quadruplum pretium*, the ass seemingly is worth a lot. But here the high price emphasizes the life of luxury and outward appearances that characterizes Thiasus (for another example see on *me phaleris aureis ... exornatum* ch. 18: 251,5 f.). The *quadruplum pretium* paid by Thiasus, the luxury with which he surrounds the ass, and his kind words (see ch. 18: 251,7 f. with the note on *simul et conuiuam et uectorem*) contrast with the ease with which, for the sake of some brief amusement in the theatre, he will yield the ass to the wild animals in the arena. Compare to this the *hortulanus*, who could barely afford the amount of approximately eighteen *denarii* (9,31: 226,22-26) and fought tooth and nail to defend his precious possession – to such a degree that it eventually led to his own downfall.

acceptissimo liberto suo et satis peculiato magnam praefatus diligentiam: this phrase emphasizes the care with which the ass's new *dominus* both selects a groom for his newly-purchased ass and instructs him on the special treatment he desires for this exceptional animal. This mollycoddling of the ass will be stressed even more in the next chapter (see also the previous note).

satis peculiato: for the use of *satis* in the *Met.* see on *satis parce* ch. 14 (246,26).

peculiatus: 'provided with *peculium*' (see on *seruis fratribus* ch. 13: 246,6). The term is found in legal works, e.g. Ulp. *Dig.* 19,13,4 *si ita peculiatus esset* (sc. *seruus*); see Heumann-Seckel s.v. In this phase of the story the *dominus* is characterized merely as a gay blade, who likes to spend his wealth on vulgar pleasures; only later will his taste for obscenities be revealed (ch. 23: 254,12 f.). Yet it is relevant to acknowledge already here the obscene connotation of the passive participle *peculiatus*. Via the original meaning of *peculium* ('private property, i.e. one's share of the herd') this word often acquires the meaning 'penis' in Plautus (see Adams ²1987,43 f.). Similarly, *peculiare* 'to provide someone generously with *peculium*' can become a metaphor for 'anal punishment', as in e.g. Pl. *Per.* 192 *aliqui te peculiabo*; see Woytek 1982,231 ad loc. Thus, *satis peculiatus* 'reasonably well off' can also have the connotations 'often peculiated' by his master' or 'endowed with a large penis'. In the latter meaning the participle occurs e.g. *Priap.* 52,6 f. *accedent duo, qui latus tuentur, / pulcre pensilibus peculiati*. When we remember the ass's large penis (mentioned several times; see the introductory remarks to ch. 22: 253,12-20), we may conclude that as a groom this *libertus satis peculiatus* is a good match for the ass.

magna praefatus diligentia: thus F and φ. The ablative *magna ... diligentia* is difficult but not impossible. One possibility is that it is an elliptical expression to which something has to be added, e.g. *(magna diligentia) seruandum, curandum me* (as Pricaeus proposed). Another is that *magna diligentia* is an ablative of manner modifying *praefatus*, used absolutely in the sense 'speak/write by way of preface (this is proposed by Oudendorp, who nevertheless opts for the accusative proposed by Groslot). Cf. in the *Met.* 3,20 (67,10) *ut initio praefata sum.* See *ThLL* s.v. *praefor* 651,16 f. for examples of *praefari* 'absolute vel accedente adv., abl. modi', where, however, we see mostly adverbs with *praefari*; the only example of an ablativus of manner is Stat. *Theb.* 6,137 (Eurydice) *longis praefata ululatibus infit.* For our passage *ThLL* ibid. 650,68 assumes the accusative, as proposed by Groslot and followed by all editors. Helm, Praef. *Fl.* XLVII, gives many examples of the omission of a Nasalstrich in F; cf. also the expression *praefari ueniam* (in the *Met.* e.g. 1,1: 1,13 *praefamur ueniam*). However, the reading of F and φ can be retained, as has been explained above; it yields an interesting parallel with 7,15 (165,7-9), where the ass is also transferred *magna cum praefatione* (see *GCA* 1981,176 ad loc.). The *praefatio* in that passage, however, does not prevent the ass from being cruelly mistreated. The *libertus* in our passage, to whom the ass is handed over with many words of introduction, will from ch. 19 onward use the ass for his own profit by hiring him out as a kind of gigolo; this in turn will lead to the plans for the ass's performance in the arena.

249,26-29 Qui me satis humane satisque comiter nutriebat et, quo se patrono commendatiorem faceret, studiosissime uoluptates eius per meas argutias instruebat: And this man looked after me very humanely and very kindly, and in order to secure his patron's favour he most diligently organized his amusement by means of my clever tricks.

me satis humane satisque comiter nutriebat: irony. The actorial narrator, Lucius the ass, judges the behaviour of the man who takes care of him, the ass, as *satis humane*. The irony becomes more profound when, reading on, one realizes that even though the ass's new caretakers are the first to give him humane treatment during all his existence as an ass, this humaneness is no more than outward appearance. See on *conuiuium summo risu personabat* ch. 16 (249,9).

satis ... satisque: for this use of *satis* see on *satis parce* ch. 14 (246,26).

quo se patrono commendatiorem faceret. cf. ch. 16 (249,4) *commendatiorem ... me ... ei facere cupiens* and the note there. Although there is a strong superficial similarity between the *Met.* and the *Onos* at this point, subtle differences appear at every turn, which result above all in a more elaborate characterization of the main characters in the episode in the *Met.*; see e.g. on *illi uero* ch. 14 (247,6). This is true also for this passage: in the *Onos* it is the rich gentleman himself who orders the freedman to teach the ass tricks for his amusement (48,1 καὶ εἶπεν κατηχεῖν ὅσα ποιῶν μάλιστα ψυχαγωγεῖν αὐτὸν δυναίμην). In the *Met.*, on the other hand, the wealthy *dominus* is characterized in great detail as a spoiled pleasure-seeker who has surrounded himself with parasites and flatterers, who of their own accord do everything they can to please him. On the master's significant name in the *Met.*, Thiasus (called Μενεκλῆς in the *Onos*), see on *Thiasus* ch. 18 (250,17 f.).

uoluptates ... instruebat: cf. 4,13 (84,18 f.) *publicas uoluptates instruebat*. For the wider use of *instruere* 'i.q. *struendo parare* aut *comparare*', see *ThLL* s.v. *instruo* 2015,55 f.

uoluptates eius per meas argutias: the possessives, placed close to each other in this chiastic phrase, put *uoluptates* and *argutias* in contrast to each other: like everything else in this household, *argutia* serves only to enhance the *uoluptates* of the *dominus*. The re-reader of the *Met.* sees here a foreshadowing of the extreme demand that will be made on the ass later in this episode to satisfy the *dominus*' desire for *uoluptates*. See Smith 1968,97 f. on the connotations of *argutia* in the *Met*.

249,29-250,6 Et primum me quidem mensam accumbere suffixo cubito, dein adluctari et etiam saltare sublatis primoribus pedibus perdocuit, quo<d>que esset adprime mirabile, uerbis nutum commodare, ut quod nollem relato, quod uellem deiecto capite monstrarem, sitiensque pocillatore[m] respecto, ciliis alterna coniuens, bibere flagitarem: And first he taught me to recline at the table, leaning on my elbow, then he taught me to wrestle and even to dance with my forelegs raised and, to be especially extraordinary, to match gestures to words, so that I showed what I did not want by raising my head, and what I did want by lowering it, and when I was thirsty, asked for a drink by looking at the cupbearer and blinking my eyelids alternately.

Callebat 1968,466 gives this sentence as one of the examples of how in the *Met*. casualness and skill are often perfectly combined in 'phrases lentes'. Indeed, the very long sentence is carefully constructed: for the reader (reading aloud) it produces a tableau which unfolds steadily in a well-organized sequence of short statements. One might say that the structure of the sentence illustrates how the groom, over a long period, applies himself patiently and conscientiously to the task of training the ass:

Et primum me quidem mensam accumbere
                              suffixo cubito
dein adluctari
et etiam saltare
sublatis primoribus pedibus
                           perdocuit
quodque esset adprime mirabile
uerbis nutum commodare
ut quod nollem relato
quod uellem deiecto   *capite monstrarem*
sitiensque
pocillatore respecto
ciliis alterna coniuens
                       bibere flagitarem

See also the notes below that deal with the sound effects of this passage.

    primum ... quidem: corresponding with *dein* (250,1); for this use of '*quidem solum*' (i.e. without a following adversative), see Solodow 1978,67 f.

    mensam accumbere: for the accusative without a preposition with *accumbere*, see GCA 1985,93 on 8,8 (183,16) *mensam accumbas*.

    adluctari: attested only in Apuleius (*ThLL* s.v. *adlucto[r]* 1697,59 f.), twice, both times in the *Met*.: here and (in a metaphorical sense) in 11,12 (275,21) *adluctantem mihi ... Fortunam*. See Callebat in *AAGA* 1978,173 f. on the many compound verbs created by Apuleius. Facchini Tosi 1986,146 f. suggests that in this passage, which is rich in sound effects, *adluctari* was created to achieve assonance with *accumbere ... adluctari*: the prefix has no semantic value here, and the end of the chapter, which aims at other sound effects (see below), has the simple verb with exactly the same meaning.

saltare: this is the first expression which suggests that the wealthy *dominus*' taking the ass into his house and pampering him is comparable to the way in which prominent wealthy people, including emperors such as Verus (see Jones 1986,69 f.; Zucchelli 1995,318), would entertain famous pantomime-stars at their homes and appear in public with them (see also below on *conspectum atque famigerabilem meis miris artibus effeceram dominum*, and on *sensum nutibus exprimentem*). See e.g. Plin. *Ep.* 7,24,4; Lucian. *merc. cond.* 28; Juv. 6,63 f. All these passages are discussed by Kokolakis 1959,16 f. Accordingly, it is not long before a *matrona* falls in love with this Lucius/ass/*saltator* (ch. 19: 251,20 f.); this suggestion is present in the *Onos* as well. Kokolakis 18 points this out but asserts (incorrectly) that Apuleius has deliberately eliminated this suggestion in the *Met*. Because Kokolakis compares the two texts too much on the basis of isolated text fragments, he fails to notice the subtle transpositions made by Apuleius in regard to the *Onos* (for similar transpositions see on *tandem ... mollius mihi renidentis Fortunae contemplatus faciem* ch. 16: 248,27 f.). The image suggested, of the ass as a famous pantomime dancer, will come to an ironic climax when plans are made for his performance in the theatre with the condemned murderess: ch. 29 (260,14) *prosequente populo pompatico fauore deducor*.

primoribus pedibus perdocuit: alliteration.

quodque esset adprime mirabile: an ironical aside from the narrator to the reader: both know that it is not *mirabile* that Lucius can do these things. The subjunctive *esset* expresses the end the trainer wants to achieve through his efforts. Cf. also Vallette: 'et, prodige entre tous fait pour étonner,...'

quodque: the correction was made already by the second hand in F for *quoque*. It is one of the examples given by Lütjohann 1873,447 for corrections by the second hand in F that offer a better reading than φ does.

adprime: see *GCA* 1995,135 on 9,14 (213,10) for this archaic adverb, 're-discovered' by authors like Gellius and Apuleius.

commodare: F and φ have *commodarē*; the scribe of F made several incorrect Nasalstriche in this part of the story, e.g. *pocillatorē*, *portenderē* (see the notes there). The errors can be explained from nearby forms like *monstrarem*, *flagitarem*, *facerem* and *ederem*.

relato ... deiecto capite: cf. Greek ἐπινεύειν, κατανεύειν and ἀνανεύειν. See Sittl 1890,82 f. and 92 f. for these gestures of refusal/denial and assent, which are still universal in the Mediterranean. See also Van Mal-Maeder 1998,80 on 2,2 (26,1), where *deiecto capite* is a conjecture by Colvius for *reiecto capite* in F.

pocillatore: both in F and in φ the Nasalstrich was removed by a more recent hand (see above, on *commodare*). The noun *pocillator* is attested only in Apuleius' *Met.*: here, 6,15 (139,13 f.) and 6,24 (146,17, referring to Ganymede as *pocillator Iouis*). Kenney 1990,210 remarks that the word also occurs in glosses and the Thesaurus material refers to e.g. *Thes.Gloss.Emend.* II,407,40 (πιγκέρνης), II,381,4 (οἰνοχόος). The word is derived from the diminutive *pocillum* (e.g. Var. *Men.* 116; Liv. 10,42,7; see also Bigorra 1983,824) or from a verb **pocillare* (thus Funck, *ALL* 4,1887,85). Facchini Tosi 1986,132 f. examines Apuleius' works for examples of neologisms formed with -*tor*, a very productive suffix in Latin of all periods, which in Apuleius is often motivated by the aim for sound effects. Here it reinforces the assonance of -*to*- in the series *relato ... deiecto ... pocillatore respecto*.

alterna coniuens: cf. Plin. *Nat.* 11,138 *supercilia homini et pariter et alterna mobilia*. On the neuter plural accusative used as an adverb, see on *omnia ... cetera fratres manere* ch. 14 (247,15).

coniuens: this is the emendation, already in φ, of the original *conibens* in F. On the confusion of *b* and *u* in F see Helm, Praef. *Fl.* XLVI.

bibere flagitarem: on the infinitive with verbs meaning 'demand' see KSt 2,1,675 f. (examples ibid. 681 f.; especially frequent in poetry, this construction is also found in prose from Livy onward). For this use in Apuleius, Callebat 1968,308 f. assumes an influence of the *sermo cotidianus*. Graverini 1997,250 n. 11 points out that this construction with the infinitive also occurs in more formal prose (Sallust) and advocates restraint in assuming that it is colloquial in origin.

250,6-11 Atque haec omnia perfacile oboediebam, quae nullo etiam monstrante scilicet facerem. Sed uerebar, ne, si forte sine magistro humano ritu ederem pleraque, rati scaeuum praesagium portendere[m] uelut monstrum ostentumque me obtruncatum uulturiis opimum pabulum redderent: With the greatest of ease I complied with all this, which, even without anyone showing me the way, I would do as a matter of course. But I was afraid that, if I were to do most of it like a human being without an instructor, people would regard me as an unlucky portent, cut me to pieces as an unnatural monster, and give me to the vultures as a rich morsel.

Atque haec ... facerem: this aside of the narrator to his audience, neatly inserted between the description of the trainer working himself to the bone (see on *quodque esset adprime mirabile* above) and that of people in awe of marvels, ridicules both parties. Thus the narrator, together with the reader (see below, on *scilicet*), adopts a superior attitude towards the actors in his story. With *sed uerebar ne...* he explains why he played along at the time.

haec omnia ... oboediebam: although in the Latin of the Antonine period there are possible parallels for *oboedire* with an accusative of the direct object (see *GCA* 1985,82 f. on 8,7: 182,5-10 *oboediens*), it seems more plausible to regard *haec omnia* as an internal accusative. See *OLD* s.v. *oboedio* 2b; also KSt 2,1,279 f.

scilicet: here certainly not in the 'perspective-preserving' sense that is so frequent in the *Met.* For this term see Dowden 1982,422, who, however (n. 22), incorrectly ranges *scilicet* in this passage under 'speculation to preserve perspective'. *Scilicet* is used here in the quite common meaning of 'naturally, as you know', a usage that Dowden 424 describes as typical of Petronius and atypical of Apuleius (he gives only one example from the *Met.*, namely 5,17: 116,16; see also Kenney 1990,162 ad loc.). In our passage *scilicet* emphasizes the suggestion, mentioned above, of a mutual understanding between narrator and reader, who together know more than the actors do.

Sed uerebar, ne ... redderent: anyone unfamiliar with the true nature of this ass would regard an ass who without any training displays all kinds of human behaviour, and understands human language, as an *ostentum*, an unnatural creature, and, as such, a bad omen (see on *mirati monstruosas asini delicias* ch. 15: 248,17). See *GCA* 1995,282, with references, on 9,33 (228,5) *ostentum*. The interest in *omina* and *ostenta* in the *Met.* is seen by many as a personal trait of the concrete author Apuleius (see *GCA* 1995, l.c. with references). Cf. *Onos* 48,6: καὶ οἱ μὲν ἐθαύμαζον τὸ πρᾶγμα ὡς παράδοξον ἀγνοοῦντες ἄνθρωπον ἐν τῷ ὄνῳ κείμενον. On the interest in *mira* and *paradoxa* in the time the *Met.* was written, see e.g. Scobie 1969,46 f.; Winkler 1985,270.

si ... ederem pleraque, rati scaeuum praesagium portendere uelut monstrum ... me ... redderent: this is the punctuation according to Rohde; F's original reading *pleraque* (ϛ *plerique*) is retained by all editors from Hildebrand onward. With the comma after *pleraque* (Helm places it before), it provides an object for *ederem* (= *peragerem*, cf. *OLD* s.v. *edo*², 5). This punctuation is also adopted by Robertson and Hanson. Another problem is that F has *portenderē*. Helm reads *portendere*, the reading in φ; *portendere* is then the verb in the accusative and infinitive *pleraque ... praesagium portendere*. With Rohde's punctuation, *pleraque* cannot be the the subject of *portendere*; consequently, Rohde proposed *portendi, e re*. Van der Vliet proposed *portendere <rem>*; Brakman, *rati <sc. id> scaeuum praesagium portendere*. All these proposals were made to provide a subject for the accusative and infinitive *scaeuum praesagium portendere*. But the absence of a pronominal accusative like *me* is no prohibitive objection: it can be supplied from the immediately following *me ... redderent*. For these light cases of ellipsis in the *Met.* see on *exasperandum ... leniendum* ch. 4 (239,3 f.); cf. also ch. 9 (243,24 f.) *certus ... aliquod moliri flagitium* (sc. *eum*). Shackleton Bailey 1988,176 proposes *haec ederem pluraque* (*<haec>* Salmasius): 'But for the reason he gives, the donkey could have performed other human actions besides those in which he had been instructed'. This intervention is unnecessary; it is sufficient to adopt the punctuation proposed by Rohde and to read *portendere* with φ.

me obtruncatum uulturiis ... pabulum redderent: cf. *GCA* 1981,32 on 6,26 (147,24-148,2) *uulturiis ... pabulum* with parallels. On the fear of being mauled by wild animals that pervades the *Met.*, see Introd. **2.4.4**.

opimum pabulum: the addition *opimum* is a somewhat wry reference to the ass's well-fed condition (cf. ch. 15: 248,7 f.): as a *monstrum ostentumque*, his dead body (*obtruncatum*) would have been thrown to the vultures, which alone would profit from his healthy condition.

pabulum: F had *pauulum*, but this was changed by a second hand to *pabulum*, which is also found in φ. See above on *coniuens*.

250,11-15 Iamque rumor publice crebruerat, quo conspectum atque famigerabilem meis miris artibus effeceram dominum: 'hic est, qui sodalem conuiuamque possidet asinum luctantem, asinum saltantem, asinum uoces humanas intellegentem, sensum nutibus exprimentem': And the rumour had already spread among the public, by which I had made my master distinguished and famous by my wondrous skills: 'This is that man who has as a friend and table companion an ass that can wrestle, an ass that can dance, an ass that understands human speech and expresses his meaning by nodding his head.'

publice crebruerat: here the narrator revels in the public attention; the adverb *publice* will be uttered with disgust in ch. 34 (265,14; see note there); see Van Mal - Maeder 1995 on similar cases of the subjectivity of the narrator in the *Met.*

conspectum atque famigerabilem meis miris artibus effeceram dominum: characterization of the *dominus*, who relies on the *artes* of others to gain prestige and uses his wealth to buy fame; see on *gloriae publicae studio ... nobilissimas feras et famosos ... gladiatores comparaturus* ch. 18 (250,25 f.). See also above on *uoluptates eius per meas argutias* (249,28 f.) and *saltare* (250,1).

conspectum ... miris artibus: flocking together to gape at anything *mirum* is a constant characteristic of the people inhabiting the world of the *Met.*; see on *miris ... artibus* ch. 4 (239,14); Introd. **2.4.2**.

conspectum atque famigerabilem: as is often the case in the *Met.*, the second adjective indicates the effect of the first one; see Bernhard 1927,166 with more examples.

conspectum: 'attracting attention, ... distinguished' (*OLD* s.v. *conspectus* I,2). *ThLL* s.v. 1. *conspicio* 497,19 f. gives examples of *conspectus* = *conspicuus* from Plautus onward, but also e.g. Verg. *G.* 3,17 *uictor ego et Tyrio conspectus in ostro*. Cf. Liv. 45,7,3 *fama conspectum eum efficiebat*; see Bömer on Ov. *Met.* 4,19 *conspiceris*. Apuleius uses *conspectus* for this meaning only here; elsewhere he uses *conspicuus*.

famigerabilem: the word is discussed by Varro (*L.* 6,7,55), but after that it is not found before Apuleius; see *GCA* 1995,62 on 9,5 (206,2).

'*hic est, qui ... exprimentem*': Hanson rightly places this section in quotation marks (thus also Brandt-Ehlers): it reports in direct discourse what the people who see the *dominus* say about him – in other words, his *fama* (cf. *famigerabilis* above).

qui sodalem ... possidet asinum luctantem, asinum saltantem, asinum uoces humanas intelligentem, sensum nutibus exprimentem: Helm, followed by modern editors, so punctuates in his edition of the text of F. Hildebrand has *qui sodalem conuiuamque possidet asinum, luctantem asinum, saltantem asinum*; Leo proposes *qui sodalem conuiuamque possidet <asinum,> asinum luctantem, asinum*. Van der Vliet proposed *luctantem asinum, saltantam asinum, <asinum> uoces ... intelligentem*. Helm's punctation leaves nothing to be desired and gives a triple anaphora of *asinum*, suggesting people gossiping and *fama* buzzing about the miraculous ass, in a fine colometry with the four phrases rhyming:

 asinum luctantem (6)
 asinum saltantem (6)
 asinum uoces humanas intelligentem (3 + 10)
 sensum nutibus exprimentem (9)

The ass's tricks are listed in the same order as they were 'learned' (249,29-250,6); *mensam accumbere*, the first trick, is found now in *sodalem conuiuamque*.

sodalem conuiuamque: it is repeatedly emphasized that the *dominus* regards and treats the ass as his *sodalis* and *conuiua*. See on *sodali* ch. 16 (249,10), and on *simul et conuiuam et uectorem* ch. 18 (251,10). This contrasts sharply with the casualness with which he later abandons his *sodalis* to the wild animals in the arena; see above on *quadruplum ... pretium* (249,24).

sensum nutibus exprimentem: *exprimere sensum* often means 'to express an opinion verbally', e.g. Cic. *Sest.* 119 *si intimos sensus ciuitatis expressero* (see *ThLL* s.v. *exprimo* 1793,80 f.). *ThLL* 1794,67 gives our passage as the first use of *sensum exprimere* to mean 'express ... in a non-verbal way'. But cf. e.g. Cic. *de Orat.* 3,220 *gestus, non hic uerba exprimens scaenicus, sed uniuersam rem ... significatione declarans*; *Brut.* 141 *gestus erat non uerba exprimens, sed cum sententiis congruens*; Quint. *Inst.* 11,3,77. All these examples of *exprimere* (not combined with *sensum/-s*) used of feelings are listed in *ThLL* ibid. 1790,74 f.; all of them occur in a context of acting. Thus we have here another suggestion of the ass as a favourite *histrio* or *pantomimus* (see above on *saltare*; see also on *nimio fauore ... gestientes* ch. 19: 251,16 f.).

CHAPTER XVIII

The journey to Corinth.

250,16-17 Sed prius est, ut uobis, quod initio facere debueram, uel nunc saltem referam, quis iste uel unde fuerit: But first I must do what I should have done at the beginning: tell you now, at least, who he was and where he came from.

The narrator interrupts the account of his experiences at the house of the wealthy *dominus* with a metanarrative phrase (see on ch. 2: 237,1-3) addressed to the readers (*uobis*). The preceding sentence *iamque ... crebruerat ... effeceram* was still describing the setting in which new events in the story will take place. The pause in the narration caused by this unexpected interruption marks an important moment in the progress of the *Met*. in its relation with the Vorlage (see on *miles ille ... uendidit* ch. 13: 246,2 f.): the ass's last journey will take him not to Thessaloniki (as in *Onos* 49) but to Corinth. For the importance of this difference from the *Onos*, see Introd. **2.3**. Since the preceding narrative was practically parallel to that in the *Onos*, with entire passages seeming to be word-for-word translations from the Greek, the deviations from the architext (see for this term Introd. **2.3**) will be more obvious to the reader who studies the texts in relation to each other. See also below on *quod initio facere debueram*.

prius est, ut ... referam: the expression *est ut...* has gradually extended to phrases such as *proximum est, ut ..., tertium est, ut ..., reliquum est, ut ..., extremum est, ut ...*; as transitional formulas, these are already frequent in Cicero, especially in the letters, which suggests a development of the *sermo cotidianus*. The expressions *ante est, ut ...* and *prius est, ut ...* are attested later (LHSz 2,644 f.). *OLD* s.v. *prior* 7a gives as the first occurrence Gaius *Inst*. 2,100 *prius est, ut de his (hereditatibus) dispiciamus* (see Norderblad 1932,96 f.). Cf. Arn. 1,12 *quare habere si locum uestras uultis querimonias, homines, prius est ut doceatis, unde uel qui sitis*. See also Löfstedt 1917,71.

quod initio facere debueram, uel nunc saltem referam: the statement is presented as a sort of afterthought, but the reader of the *Met*. has learned by now to mistrust any suggestion that such an afterthought might be unimportant; to the contrary, it is likely to contain a thought or information that deserves special attention or is especially surprising. For examples in the *Met*. see Harrauer-Römer 1985,361 n. 31 and Winkler 1985,112 on *Met*. 2,22 (43,23 f.). Here we can be certain that it is not by chance, as the narrator suggests, that information about the name and origin of the *dominus* is given only now; it is carefully timed from the point of view of narrative strategy. See the remarks at the beginning of this pericope and on *Thiasus* below.

debueram: from the point of view of the speaker, the pluperfect in this inserted relative clause is logical: 'what I ought to have mentioned before I came to this point in my story'. See KSt 2,1,139 f. on this use of the pluperfect, often in coordinate clauses, with many examples from Plautus and Terence onward. Cf. also e.g. Cic. *Caec*. 15 *cum esset, ut dicere institueram, constituta auctio Romae*. The phrase *ut dixeram ante* is common (see also LHSz 2,320 f.).

uel nunc saltem: 'at least now'; for *uel* meaning 'at least' cf. in the *Met*. e.g. *uel illic* 6,14 (138,16); *OLD* s.v. *uel* 6.

The narrator pretends to address a reader who is waiting impatiently for the information *quis iste uel unde fuerit*, and pretends now to satisfy his curiosity. In fact, the reader is manipulated by the strategy of the narrator (who in his turn is manipulated by the author), who determines what information he will give and in what order, and also what he will hold back (see Introd. **3.5**).

quis ... uel unde: the Homeric-sounding question (cf. e.g. Hom. *Od.* 1,170 τίς πόθεν εἰς ἀνδρῶν;) emphasizes again the tardiness of this information; this type of question is 'a normal reaction to an encounter with a stranger' (Austin on Verg. *A.* 2,74). See Keulen 2000,310 f. on the reverse order of these questions at 1,5 (5,1-2) *ut prius noritis, cuiatis sim, qui sim*.

uel: for *uel, aut, -ue* as a connective between questions, see Austin on Verg. *A.* 2,75 and 150, with references.

250,17-24 Thiasus – hoc enim nomine meus nuncupabatur dominus – oriundus patria Corintho, quod caput est totius Achaiae prouinciae, ut eius prosapia atque dignitas postulabat, gradatim permensis honoribus quinquennali magistratui fuerat destinatus et ut splendori capessendorum responderet fascium, munus gladiatorium triduani spectaculi pollicitus latius munificentiam suam porrigebat: Thiasus – for this was the name by which my master was addressed – came originally from Corinth, the capital of the entire province of Achaia, and, as the dignity of his birth required, had moved up through the offices in due order. Now he had been appointed *duumvir quinquennalis* and to reflect the splendour of the office he was about to assume, he had promised a three-day gladiator show, wanting to display his munificence in an especially grand manner.

Thiasus: as here, the *dominus* in the *Onos* is not named until this point in the story, but there he is called Μενεκλῆς. This name, meaning 'standing firm in fame' or 'retaining one's fame' would have been quite appropriate for our wealthy high official from Corinth, but in fact Apuleius calls him Thiasus, a name of very different connotations. The name has a double function here (already described in broad outline by Hijmans in *AAGA* 1978,112). The noun *thiasus* (= Greek θίασος) has two meanings in Latin: 1. 'orgiastic dance in honour of Bacchus'; see e.g. Verg. *Ecl.* 5,30 with Coleman 161 ad loc. (the group of those taking part in such a dance is also called a *thiasus*); 2. 'a *collegium* devoted to the cult of Bacchus' (see *OLD* s.v. *thiasus* 1 and 2). The Dionysian associations of the name will play an important part in what follows; see below on *me ... residens* 251,5-7. The name will emphasize the Dionysian, orgiastic atmosphere in the following episode (see also Schlam in *AAGA* 1978,103). For a possible Dionysian association observed earlier in this book, see on *liberalibus* ch. 15 (248,7); see also below on *praedarum carpentis*, and on *me ... residens*. However, the Greek θίασος has still another meaning: 'feast, banquet' (*LSJ* s.v. III); with that meaning the name Thiasus refers to what has happened earlier; in the reader it evokes an 'Aha Erlebnis' in view of the convivial parties at the house of the *dominus* that were described in preceding chapters.

In Roman inscriptions from the Augustan period through the second century A.D., the name *Thiasus* occurs rather frequently as the name of freedmen (originally Greek slaves):

see Solin 1971. For the inscriptions see Solin 1982,II,1038 f. and III,1350.

hoc enim nomine meus nuncupabatur dominus: Vallette: 'Thiasus - tel était le nom de mon maître -'; Hanson: 'Thiasus was my master's name'; Brandt-Ehlers: 'diesen Namen trug mein Herr'. A more precise translation of *hoc enim nomine ... nuncupabatur* is offered here: it reflects a frequent phenomenon in the *Met.*, the attitude of the narrator, who always explains how he obtained his information. Here he reports: 'for by that name my master was addressed (sc. I could hear them calling him that)'. Cf. 8,25 (197,9-14) *Philebo; hoc enim nomine censebatur iam meus dominus* with *GCA* 1985,221 ad loc. See Van der Paardt in *AAGA* 1978,76 f. and Dowden 1982,419 f.

Corintho: see Introd. **2.3** for the importance of this geographical transformation in relation to the *Onos*. In Apuleius' time Corinth was a prosperous city; like Athens, it received many favours from Hadrian, and many buildings were erected also by Herodes Atticus in the second century A.D. Famous sophists often met in Corinth (for an extensive discussion see Wiseman 1979,508 f.).

quod caput est totius Achaiae prouinciae: this information (see Wiseman l.c. 438 f.), was probably not needed by the contemporary reader of the *Met*. The reason for the insertion is to be found in the fact that it puts extra emphasis on Thiasus' importance: he is a high official, not of some small provincial town but of the capital of Achaia. The narrator mentions with a certain naive pride that he was engaged by – and became the favourite of – such a distinguished gentleman. The low social status and the poverty of the masters he served as an ass often caused the narrator to bemoan the discrepancy between his present life and his former existence as the well-bred and well-to-do young man Lucius. From the beginning of this book the ass can be observed steadily climbing the social ladder, from the time he was stabled in the house of a *decurio*; see on *nec in stabulo, sed in domo ... decurionis* ch. 1 (236,23). There it was only a *decurio cuiusdam ciuitatulae*; now the ass has risen to the position of table companion and personal mount of a high official of the provincial capital. But at the same time this book repeatedly and unmistakably emphasizes to the interpreting reader the gap between appearance and reality, between high social rank and innate refinement. See below on *prosapia* and *quinquennali magistratui*; and in ch. 16 on *dominus aedium duci me iussit* (248,30 f.); *conuiuium summo risu personabat* (249,9); Introd. **3.2**.

prosapia: an archaizing term, which was already regarded as old-fashioned in Cicero's time; cf. Cic. *Tim.* 11,39 *Iouem atque Iunonem, reliquos ... et eorum, ut utamur ueteri uerbo, prosapiam*. Quintilian (*Inst.* 1,6,40 and 8,3,26) disapproves of the use of it as being too old-fashioned. It is attested once in Sallust (*Jug.* 85,10). Apuleius uses it often (see also Callebat 1964,348 and Scobie 1975,73 on *Met.* 1,1: 1,9). *Prosapia* lives on in the writings of Christian authors (Courcelle 1976,192 f.). With Apuleius, the word has a somewhat solemn ring ('venerable lineage'), sometimes used ironically. Thus e.g. 9,35 (229,16 f.), where the greedy neighbour is called '*potens et diues ... et prosapiae maiorum gloria male utens*'; cf. *Soc.* 23,174, where *prosapia* is listed among a man's external characteristics that ought not to influence one's judgement of him. Seen in this light, *prosapia* is yet another element in Thiasus' description suggesting that the naive narrator is mistaken in being so much impressed by the high status of this man (see the previous note). See Mason 1983,135 f. on the discrepancy between social and moral status as a theme in the *Met.*: the main character, Lucius, is characterized as a young man from the upper class, but in

11,15 (277,7 f.) Isis' priest points out to him that *nec tibi natales ac ne dignitas quidem ... profuit.*

gradatim permensis honoribus: Wiseman 1979,499 f. gives information on the *cursus honorum* in Corinth. *Gradatim* in connection with the *cursus honorum* occurs also e.g. Cic. *Red.Pop.* 5 *honores, quos eramus gradatim singulos adsecuti.*

permensis: passive also at 8,18 (191,18-22; see *GCA* 1985,167 ad loc. with references).

quinquennali magistratui: the translation of Brandt-Ehlers 'Nun war er auf fünf Jahre in die leitende Behörde eingesetzt worden' is not quite right: the *duouiri iure dicundo* were chosen every year, but once in five years they had the title of *duumuiri quinquennales* (= στρατηγοὶ πενταετηρικοί) and besides their normal legal and executive powers had the authority to hold the *census* and appoint new members of the βουλή (Wiseman 1979,498). Thus, *duumuir quenquennalis* was the summit of the Corinthian *cursus honorum*.

The *Onos* says about Μενεκλῆς only that he is σφόδρα πλούσιος (46,1); the narrator of the *Met.* repeatedly emphasizes Thiasus' high status. See above on *quod caput est totius Achaiae prouinciae* and on *prosapia*.

ut splendori capessendorum responderet fascium, munus gladiatorum triduani spectaculi pollicitus: a striking illustration of the institution of 'benefactorship' (the 'benefactor' is the Greek εὐεργέτης; see Veyne 1976 on 'l'évergétisme'). This system, well known from inscriptions, of benefits for the community and reciprocal honours for the benefactor was typical of the power of dignitaries in the cities of the Roman empire. For the πρῶτοι this meant that they spent money liberally for the community, while the citizens recognized their benefactors by conferring honours on them. The πρῶτοι – in this period a rather exclusive class of rich people – not only constituted the government of the city as senators, but also had an obligation to fulfill public needs at their own expense: they organized public banquets, paid for the construction of public buildings, handed out money, sold oil, wine, and grain at low prices, and entertained the people with games. In return, the people showed their gratitude by conferring high offices to them, decreeing to erect statues to them and to give them public acclamations, etc. See Veyne 1976, especially 298-327. See also below on *latius munificentiam suam porrigebat.*

triduani spectaculi: 'consisting of a show of three days'. *Triduanus* is first attested here; Callebat 1968,139 groups it with a series of terms that are encountered first in Apuleius but were probably common in daily life. See also Löfstedt 1911,68 on this and other (often very old) adjectival formations in *-anus*, e.g. *decimanus* (already from Lucil. 502 onward).

latius munificentiam suam porrigebat: *munificentia* is expected from Thiasus (see above on *ut splendori ... pollicitus*), but he wants to display his generosity 'in an extra-expansive way' (*latius*). That is illustrated by the following *denique ... Thessaliam etiam accesserat ... comparaturus*; his motive is given as *gloriae publicae studio*. It is such exaggerated generosity inspired by the wrong motives that Plutarch warns the young politician Menemachos against in his *Praecepta reipublicae gerendae*, e.g. in 29-30 (*Mor.* 821f-822c), concluding with χρηστὰς δὲ καὶ σώφρονας ἀεὶ ποιοῦ τῶν ἀναλωμάτων ὑποθέσεις ... ἢ τὸ γοῦν ἡδὺ καὶ κεχαρισμένον ἄνευ βλάβης καὶ ὕβρεως προσούσης (cf. also ibid. 5: *Mor.* 802d with Carrière 1984,165 f., n. 2 ad loc.). Thiasus is undoubtedly the antithesis of Plutarch's ideal politician. For Plutarch's ideas incorporated in the *Met.*, see on *magistratus* ch. 6 (241,15) with references.

munificentiam ... porrigebat: here *porrigere* means *extendere* (cf. also 4,29: 97,12 *fama porrecta*), but contains also its metaphorical meaning (*OLD* s.v. *porrigo*[1] 6c). The metaphorical use is infrequent before Apuleius: it is attested mostly in Cicero, e.g. *Ver.* 5,153 *cui ciui supplicanti non illa dextera ... fidem porrexit?* (see also Leeman-Pinkster on Cic. *de Orat.* 1,184). Possibly Cicero took up an archaic use of the verb: Andr. *trag.* 20 f. *da mihi hasce opes, / quas peto, quas preco, porrige opitula!*, Hor. *Carm.* 2,16,31 f. *et mihi forsan tibi quod negarit, / porriget hora*. In Christian authors the metaphorical use becomes quite frequent: cf. e.g. Tert. *Pud.* 17 *adiecisset enim et haec, si talibus ueniam porrigere consuesset uel porrigi omnino uoluisset*. See Melin 1946,114 f. Curiously, Blaise s.v. *porrigo* ignores this use.

munificentiam: 'generosity, liberality', but also in a more special sense 'generosity in organizing public shows (*munera*)'; see *ThLL* s.v. *munificentia* 1651,43 f. with examples from V. Max. 2,4,7 *athletarum certamen a M. Scauri tractum est munificentia*; Suet. *Jul.* 10,1 *uenationes ... ludosque et cum collega et separatim edidit, quo factum est, ut* (sc. *collega quereretur*) *... suam Caesarisque munificentiam unius Caesaris dici*.

250,24-28 Denique gloriae publicae studio tunc Thessaliam etiam accesserat nobilissimas feras et famosos inde gladiatores comparaturus, iamque ex arbitrio dispositis coemptisque omnibus domuitionem parabat: And so, in his pursuit of public favour, he had finally also come to Thessaly to get hold of the finest wild animals and renowned gladiators there; and now that he had arranged and bought up everything according to his wishes, he was preparing his homeward journey.

Denique: as often in the *Met.*, it introduces here a climax or rather an exaggeration of what has been mentioned before. See Van der Paardt 1971,42 f.

gloriae ... studio ... nobilissimas feras et famosos ... gladiatores comparaturus: The only way Thiasus can acquire the fame he craves is by buying someone else's qualities. See on *conspectum ... effeceram dominum* ch. 17 (250,12 f.).

gloriae publicae studio: Greek φιλοτιμία, which Plut. *Praecepta reip.ger.* often mentions (e.g. 27: *Mor.* 819f-820c) as an undesirable trait in a politician (see above on *latius munificentiam suam porrigebat*). *Gloria* has on the one hand an abstract sense ('good reputation'); on the other hand it suggests the many concrete tributes that supposedly await Thiasus (see above on *ut splendori capessendorum responderet fascium, munus ... pollicitus*), like statues, inscriptions, etc. (cf. *GCA* 1977,160 ad 4,21: 90,18 *gloriam sibi reseruauit* on the notion of *gloria* in the *Met.* and elsewhere, with references).

nobilissimas feras: *nobilis* here not only 'of good breed' (*OLD* s.v. *nobilis* 5e) but also 'renowned': the wild animals from Thessaly are famous and will make Thiasus famous too. Cf. 4,13, where a Thessalian with the significant name of Demochares prepares a splendid *munus gladiatorum* to entertain the people of Plataeae.

famosos ... gladiatores comparaturus: how a *munerarius* acquired gladiators, is described by Robert 1940,283 f. with epigraphical sources.

comparaturus: 'in order to buy'; in poetry, and in prose from Livy onward, this final use of the future participle becomes increasingly frequent in Latin, probably under the influence of Greek. Apuleius uses it often; see *GCA* 1985,46 on 8,4 (178,22) *indagaturus* with references.

ex arbitrio dispositis: 'arranged according to his wishes'; cf. Sen. *Dial.* 11 (*Cons.P.*),6,4 *non licet tibi ... ex tuo arbitrio diem disponere* and in the *Met.* e.g. 4,17 (87,18 f.) *ut ex arbitrio nostro caueam locaremus*. Thiasus is consistently characterized as the sybaritic millionaire who does as he pleases and expects others to indulge his whims. Lucius will experience this to his regret; see on *parasito meo* ch. 16 (249,16).

domuitionem: see Kenney 1990,136 on 4,35 (102,20) for this archaic word, re-discovered by Apuleius. Before Apuleius, *ThLL* s.v. *domu(m)itio* 1948,57 f. gives only passages from tragedy (Pac. *trag.* 173; Accius; Lucil. 607 is also from a tragedy, as is *Rhet. Her.* 3,21,34); cf. *Dictys* 1,20 (Ulixes) *domuitionem confirmans magnum*. See Callebat 1964,346 f. on the original way in which Apuleius manipulates the archaizing tendencies of his time (cf. also above on *prosapia*).

250,28-251,10 Spretis luculentis illis suis uehiculis ac posthabitis decoris praedarum carpentis, quae partim contecta, partim reuelata frustra nouissimis trahebantur consequiis, equis etiam Thessalicis et aliis iumentis Gallicanis, quibus generosa suboles perhibet pretiosam dignitatem, me phaleris aureis et fucatis ephippiis et purpureis tapetis et frenis argenteis et pictilibus balteis et tintinnabulis perargutis exornatum ipse residens amantissime nonnumquam comissimis adfatur sermonibus atque inter alia pleraque summe se delectari profitebatur, quod haberet in me simul et conuiuam et uectorem: He rejected those splendid wagons of his, and passed over the fine carriages drawn by wild animals, wich followed - some closed, some open - without purpose at the end of the procession, and also the Thessalian horses and other beasts of burden from Gaul, on which noble pedigree confers a high value; instead, he had me decked out with gold head ornaments, dyed caparisons, purple blankets, silver bit, embroidered bands, and clear-tinkling bells, and chose to ride on my back, often speaking to me most affectionately in terms of endearment, and among much else he declared that he was simply delighted to have me as at once a companion and a mount.

The long sentence, composed of an abundance of elaborate phrases, illustrates the rich caravan, composed of many ornate elements, with which the millionaire sets out on his journey. The overwhelming sound-play (see notes below) elicited from Eicke 1956,44 n. 1 the exclamation: 'Welch virtuose Wortspielerei und - grandiose Geschmacklosigkeit!'

luculentis: *ThLL* s.v. *luculentus* 1748,67 f. notes the passages where the adjective has a special association with wealth, e.g. Pl. *Cist.* 559 f. *te reduco ... ad ... diuitias, / ubi tu locere in luculentam familiam*; *Rud.* 1320 *diuitias ... habuisti luculentas*; Cic. *Phil.* 12,19 *qui ex naufragio luculenti patrimoni ad haec Antoniana saxa proiectus est*. The connotation of wealth is also present in our passage. To attribute a 'hermeneutic' function to the use of *luculentus* in the *Met.* and regard it as 'a *signum* pointing to Isis' (Krabbe 1989,131 f.) seems far-fetched.

illis suis: Callebat 1968,279 f. (contra Wolterstorff 1917,222, who sees these combinations as proof of *ille* as almost a definite article) points out that each word retains its own function: the possessive reflects the affective relation between the possessor and the object, and the demonstrative accentuates either the familiarity with that object or its special quality. Here, *illis* enhances the laudatory quality of *decoris*; cf. e.g. 9,19 (217,2) *decora illa monetae lumina* with *GCA* 1995,175 ad loc. Thus the narrator emphasizes the statement, 'he preferred me to those splendid wagons he already had'.

praedarum carpentis: thus F and φ; Oudendorp defends the ms. reading, explaining the phrase as meaning 'wagons drawn by wild animals (*praedae*)'. Although Oudendorp regards this use of *praedae* as quite common, exact parallels are hard to find, and *ThLL* s.v. *praeda* gives no meaning 'i.q. *fera*' or the like. Some passages come close, e.g. Sol. 53,19 *uenatibus indulgent nec plebeias agunt praedas, quippe cum tigrides aut elephanti tantum requirantur*, but this use of *praedae* always refers to hunted or captured wild animals. It is possible to read *praedarum* in this sense here too: in Thessaly, Thiasus has collected wild animals to be used as *praedae* in a planned *uenatio*, and has them harnessed to chariots during the homeward journey (for this exotic image see below). A genitive of animals pulling a chariot is also found e.g. Cic. *Rep.* 3,14 *illo Pacuuiano 'inuehens alitum anguium curru'*; Verg. *G.* 4,388 f. (Proteus) *aequor / et iuncto bipedum curru metitur equorum* (cf. *Ciris* 395); Ov. *Met.* 5,360 f. *exierat curruque atrorum uectus equorum / ambibat*; Suet. *Cl.* 11,2 *currum elephantorum* (for more examples see *ThLL* s.v. *currus* 1522,43 f.).

Even if *praedarum carpentis* is a *lectio difficilis*, Modius' solution, followed by others, is not satisfactory either. Modius proposed *[p]raedarum carpentis*, which, however, creates a new problem: a *raeda* is a four-wheeled carriage, a *carpentum* is a closed two-wheeled carriage. Yet all modern editors adopt Modius' proposal, and the translators skip over the problem. The explanation proposed by *ThLL* s.v. *carpentum* 490,60 f. is also unconvincing: it tries to defend *raedarum carpentis* by reading *carpenta* in this passage 'metonymice de iumentis'. But the following *quae partim contecta, partim reuelata ... trahebantur* makes it clear that carriages, not animals, are referred to.

Retaining the reading of the manuscripts has two consequences, both of which are acceptable in the context. First, it makes the pageant even more exotic and impressive, so that the preference for the ass as a mount becomes more conspicuous (which, as has been shown above, is clearly the intention of this sentence). Secondly, the phrase adds to the Dionysian associations of the episode (see also above, on *Thiasus*), since in visual arts and in poetry wild animals are pictured pulling Dionysus' carriage: panthers (see *RE* s.v. 'Panther', 752,2 f. [Jereb] with references); lions; especially lynx (cf. Prop. 3,17,8 *lyncibus ad caelum uecta Ariadna tuis*; Fedeli 1985,521 ad loc. gives many parallels); tigers (Ov. *Ars* 1,549 f. *iam deus in curru, quem summum texerat uuis, / tigribus adiunctis aurea lora dabat*). Thiasus, who prefers to ride on the ass rather than on the *praedarum carpenta*, is thus associated with Dionysus' entourage, in which frequently Silenus is pictured sitting on an ass; cf. Ov. *Ars* 1,541 f. *ecce, Mimallonides, sparsis in terga capillis, / ecce, leues Satyri, praeuia turba dei / ebrius, ecce, senex pando Silenus asello / uix sedet et pressas continet arte iubas*. See also *RE* s.v. 'Esel' 669-75 [Olck], and *RAC* s.v. 'Esel' 573 f. [Opelt] for associations of the ass with Dionysus and his company. The ass is also found often in depictions of Dionysus on his way to a symposium; cf. *LIMC* 3,1,457-459; ibid. 384-403 and 565.

nouissimis consequiis: 'the very last part following behind'. *ThLL* s.v. *consequius* 404,9-12 gives only one other passage, also in the *Met.*: 5,24 (121,21); see Kenney 1990,173 ad loc., who, unlike *ThLL*, assumes a neuter plural noun *consequia* there (which in our passage is undisputed).

equis ... Thessalicis: 'fine (and expensive) horses': horses from Thessaly had an excellent reputation. Cf. Var. *R.* 2,7,6 *nobiles ... in Graecia Thessalici equi*. See the extensive note of Jebb on Soph. *El.* 703 f. κἀκεῖνος (sc. Orestes) ἐν τούτοισι Θεσσαλὰς ἔχων ἵππους.

et aliis iumentis: *alius* here means 'further', 'as well' (cf. Greek ἄλλος). See LHSz

2,208 with examples and literature; KSt 2,1,651, Anm. 16 (cf. e.g. Liv. 4,41,8 *plaustra iumentaque alia* with Weissenborn-Müller ad loc.: 'und andere Transportmittel, nämlich Lasttiere').

iumentis Gallicanis, quibus generosa suboles perhibet pretiosam dignitatem: this probably means that these Gallic *iumenta* were valuable because they were crossbred from excellent horses and asses; *iumenta* here means not horses but *mulae*. Col. 6,36 f. makes it clear how carefully the parents had to be selected to produce valuable *mulae*. On the costliness of mules see Adams 1995,107 f., with documentation. Evidence that Gallic *mulae* were unusually expensive may exist in the mention of ἡμίονοι Γαλατικαί in Plut. *Mor.* (*De Cup.Div.*) 524a in the enumeration of costly objects on which the rich lavish money (Klaerr 1974,173 n. 3 ad loc. takes Γαλατικός in this phrase as 'from Galatia', but cf. *LSJ* s.v. Γαλάται). Claud. *Carm. Min.* 18 is a laudatory poem *De Mulabus Gallicis*.

generosa suboles: 'noble pedigree'; for *generosus* 'of good stock, breeding, etc.; choice, superior', see *OLD* s.v. *generosus* 3a. In Plin. *Nat.* 7,31 *suboles* means also 'breeding': *maribus interemptis praeter quam subolis causa*.

pretiosam dignitatem: no parallels can be found for this combination. *Dignitas* is used in the sense of 'exceptional quality' (*OLD* s.v. *dignitas* 2a); referring to animals it is also found e.g. Var. *R.* 1,21,1 *canes potius cum dignitate ... paucos habendum quam multos*. In that case, *pretiosa dignitas* means 'excellence that makes valuable'. In technical literature, *pretiosus* is often used in connection with the breeding of pedigree horses, mules, etc. The *ThLL* material gives numerous examples of this, e.g. Col. 6,37,9-10 *sed, si iam est equa ueneris patiens, confestim abacto uiliore, pretioso mari subigitur*; ibid. 7,2,3-4 *nunc Gallicae pretiosiores habentur*. At any rate, everything in this description contributes to emphasize the flamboyance of the wealthy Thiasus, who can afford the best of everything.

me ... residens: Lucius concludes his career as beast of burden by carrying a figure who is clearly to be associated with Silenus (see above on *praedarum carpentis*). When employed by the robbers, he was loaded up with booty (3,28: 73,3 f.; 4,4: 77,8; 4,5: 78,5); the evil *puer* made him carry loads of wood (7,17: 167,6; 7,17-18: 167,16 f.) and even burning hemp (7,19-20: 168,26 f.); the *pistor* gave him grain to carry (9,10: 210,13 f.); in the service of the market gardener he transported vegetables (9,32: 226,29 f.); for the soldier he carried weaponry (10,1: 236,11 f.); and the cooks wanted to use him for carrying the dinner service of their travelling *dominus* (10,13: 246,11 f.). In addition he acted as a mount for Charite as she was fleeing (unsuccessfully 6,27: 149,20 f.; 6,29: 151,5 f.; successfully 7,12: 163,19 f.; 7,13: 163,25 f.); he carried a *uiator* (7,25: 172,22 f.), and also fleeing women, children, pet animals, and household goods of the *familia* of the deceased Charite (8,15: 188,11 f.). The priests of the Dea Syria used him to carry the image of the goddess (8,27: 198,16 f.; 8,28: 200,6 f.; 8,30: 201,15 f.; 9,4: 205,18 f.) and the golden drinking cup hidden in the image (9,10: 209,20 f.); and he carried the market gardener (9,33: 227,26 f.; 9,39: 232,25 f.; 9,40: 234,8 f.). Thus, the description of the various burdens carried by Lucius the ass is a constant element in the story. Looking at these as a whole, however, one cannot detect a distinct line of symbolism, except that the ass's burden is always congruous with his environment of that moment. Neither is it possible to speak, with Shumate 1996,209, n. 3, of an ever-increasing burden. The ass's most difficult time is in the service of the vicious *puer*; after that he is given many loads of a different nature, which sometimes give him cause to complain, sometimes not. However, it can be argued that carrying loads in general concretizes, over and over again and in ever-varying ways,

Lucius' 'suppression' during his existence as an ass.

GCA 1985,239 f. (see also ibid. App. IV) point out the important contrast between the ass as the carrier of the image of the Dea Syria while in the service of the *cinaedi* and Lucius as the *pastophorus* of Isis (11,30: 291,15 f.). In this antithesis between the Dea Syria and Isis, our passage – in which Lucius carries a character who evokes unmistakable associations with Dionysus – functions as an intriguing transition. It is up to the interpreting reader to make this kind of connection, since the narrator himself gives no hints: in our passage, he emphasizes especially the ass's pride in being the 'chosen one' and the fact that he is magnificently decked out.

me phaleris aureis ... exornatum: in the *Onos* too the ass is beautifully decorated (48,8): καὶ σκεύη μοι ἦν πολυτελῆ, καὶ στρώματα πορφυρᾶ ἐπιβάλλομαι, καὶ χαλινοὺς εἰσεδεχόμην ἀργύρῳ καὶ χρυσῷ πεποικιλμένους, καὶ κώδωνες ἐξήπτοντό μου μέλος μουσικώτατον ἐκφωνοῦντες, but the decoration is described not in connection with the journey but in a passage corresponding with ch. 17 (250,11) in this book. See on *tandem ... mollius mihi renidentis Fortunae contemplatus faciem* ch. 16 (248,27 f.) for the importance of such differences from the *Onos*. Here the transposition has the effect that the embellished ass becomes part of Thiasus' travelling procession, which is described as impressive and ostentatious in itself; the adorning of the ass becomes part of his being chosen, which the narrator has emphasized so strongly in this passage of the *Met*. 'An solchen Translokationen zeigt sich wieder: Apul. nimmt keineswegs Satz für Satz der Vorlage her, ... (sondern) er wählt von seinem Stoff sorgsam und mit sicherem Überblick aus, was seinen im Vergleich zu denen des Vorlagendichters viel differenzierteren und feineren Anschauungen über die Möglichkeiten heftiger und tiefer Wirkung auf den Leser in jedem Augenblick am besten entspricht' (Junghanns 1932,116, n. 178).

Interestingly, at the beginning of this same book the narrator describes the ass as *exornatus*, with military equipment; see on *onustum et prorsum exornatum* ch. 1 (236,15).

Ostensibly the ass is doing very well here. But, as has been remarked before, in the Thiasus episode a discrepancy between appearance and reality is subtly thematized (see e.g. above on *quod caput est totius Achaiae prouinciae*, 250,19 f.). In this context cf. Apul. *Soc*. 23,172 f. *neque enim in emendis equis phaleras consideramus et baltei polimina inspicimus et ornatissimae ceruicis diuitias contemplamur, si ex auro et argento et gemmis monilia uariegata dependent, si plena artis ornamenta capiti et collo circumiacent, si frena caelata, si ephippia fucata, si cingula aurata sunt. Sed istis omnibus exuuiis amolitis equum ipsum nudum et solum corpus eius et animum contemplamur ... similiter igitur et in hominibus contemplandis noli illa aliena aestimare, sed ipsum hominem penitus considera*. The interrelation between that passage and ours is reinforced by several words and phrases that occur in Apuleius' works only in these two passages (see below, on *fucatis ephippiis* and *balteis*).

We are also reminded of a promise (which never came true) of Charite, who in 6,28 (150,9 f.), during the unsuccessful flight of the girl and the ass, promised to decorate him with gold and gems.

phaleris aureis et ... et ... et ... et ... et tintinnabulis perargutis: the various decorations, all ending in *-is*, are polysyndetically strung together. Moreover, the first five cola have practically the same number of syllables each: 6, 7, 7, 6, 7; the last colon *tintinnabulis perargutis*, with 9 syllables, is longest. Polysyndeton, rhyme, and colometry phonically illustrate the exaggerated attention paid to the decoration of the ass.

phaleris: a decoration on a horse's headstall, consisting of a kind of necklace with metal (here gold!) crescents. It is a special decoration, as appears from e.g. Verg. A. 5,310 *primus equum phaleris insignem uictor habeto* and Plin. *Nat.* 37,194 *ut equis regum in oriente frontalia ac pro phaleris pensilia facerent*. On the luxury of *phalera(e)* as ornaments for horses, and on the *ephippia* as a sign of oriental luxuriousness see the extensive note by Cèbe on Var. *Men.* 97 *ubi illa phalera gemmea atque ephippia / et arma margariticandicantia*. In 3,1 (52,6) the horses of the sun chariot wear *punicantibus phaleris*; see Van der Paardt 1981,23 ad loc. This first detail sets the tone for the description of the ass splendidly decked out like a royal horse, and shows *aemulatio* in relation to the Vorlage (in the corresponding description in the *Onos*, cited above, this detail is absent).

fucatis ephippiis: *ephippium* (ἐφίππιον) literally: 'something that is put on a horse', hence 'saddle'. In Var. *Men* 97 (quoted in the previous note), *ephippia*, like *phalerae*, are a sign of oriental luxury; Xen. *Cyr.* 8,8,19 tells that the Persians placed more blankets on their horses than on their beds; cf. Chariton 6,4,2, where the horse of the Persian king is magnificently decked out (to impress Callirhoe).

In Apuleius *ephippium* occurs only here and in the *Soc.* passage mentioned above, as does *fucatus* 'dyed with artifial colours'; thus e.g. Plin. *Nat.* 35,198 *fucatus* (sc. *color*) ... *deprehenditur nigrescitque et funditur sulpure*. Another meaning of *fucatus* is 'not genuine, faked, sham, counterfeit' (*OLD* s.v. 2). The adjective reinforces the theme of 'Schein und Wesen' which pervades this entire passage (see above on *quod caput est totius Achaiae prouinciae*, 250,19 f.); cf. e.g. Cic. *Amic.* 95 *secerni ... blandus amicus a uero ... tam potest ... quam omnia fucata et simulata a sinceris atque ueris* and the flattering words below (see below, on *amantissime ... uectorem*).

pictilibus balteis: 'colourfully embroidered bands'. *Pictilis* is attested only here. The adjective in *-ilis* is an alternate form of the more common *pictus*, which originally meant 'embroidered', later 'painted'. Leumann 1917,54 discusses *pictilis* and compares for a similar formation the alternates *textilis* and *textus* (e.g. Lucr. 2,35 *textilibus ... in picturis*); consequently, he regards *pictilis* as 'recht alt'.

balteis: used only here and in the above-mentioned passage in Apul. *Soc.* in the sense of 'horse collar, chest bands'. Traina 1981,135 f., with references, shows that this use by Apuleius is to be regarded as a neologism. He also shows that Beroaldus' explanation for *balteus* in our passage (*cingula, quasi bullata dicta, quibus etiam equi exornantur in pectoralibus*) has been so influential that in archeology *balteus* has become the common term for a horse's bronze breast plate.

tintinnabulis: a wonderfully onomatopoeic word, attested already in early Latin (Pl. *Ps.* 332; *Trin.* 1004; Lucil. 510). After that Petr. 47,8; Juv. 6,441; Suet. *Aug.* 91,2; see Eichenbeer 1986,158. A nice parallel to our passage is *Phaed.* 2,7,1 f. *muli grauati sarcinis ibant duo; / unus ferebat fiscos cum pecunia, / alter tumentes multo saccos hordeo. / ille onere diues celsa ceruice eminet / clarumque collo iactat tintinnabulum* (of course, it is the mule with the riches which is robbed and killed by robbers).

perargutis: 'clear-ringing'. Apuleius is the first to use the adjective in this meaning (also *Fl.* 13,2 for the swallow's chirp). In Cic. *Brut.* 167 it means 'sharp, quick-witted': *Afranius poeta, homo perargutus*. These are the only three attested occurrences.

amantissime ... comissimis adfatur sermonibus ..., quod habetur in me simul et conuiuam et uectorem: Adams 1995,106 f. provides several examples of people in antiquity, treating their horses as human beings, but remarks that this seems not to have been the case with donkeys. All the more remarkable is our passage. To the re-reader of the *Met.* this description of Thiasus' words, flattering but probably insincere, is significant: as long as it suits him, he treats the ass as a *conuiua* (see on *sodali* ch. 16: 249,10), but when the whim strikes him to have his ass perform in the arena, where he will undoubtedly be mauled by the animals, then the *conuiua* will become no more than just an animal, a *uector*.

adfatur ... profitebatur: the change from historical present to imperfect is functional (contra Bernhard 1927,153, who regards this as a 'Streben nach Mannigfaltigkeit'): the sentence *atque inter alia pleraque summe se delectari profitebatur quod haberet in me simul et conuiuam et uectorem* gives one specific example of the more general statement *amantissime nonnumquam comissimis adfatur sermonibus*. Cf. e.g. Sal. *Hist.* Frg. 5c, p. 169 Kurfess *tumultum faciunt neque se arma ... credituros firmabant*. See also Callebat 1968,427 f.

quod habetur: see on the first position of the verb in the subordinate clause the comm. on ch. 32 (263,21) *si fuisset*.

CHAPTER XIX

Lucius progresses from public attraction to gigolo. The amorous *matrona*.

251,11-14 At ubi partim terrestri, partim maritimo itinere confecto Corinthum accessimus, magnae ciuium turbae confluebant, ut mihi uidebatur, non tantum Thiasi dantes honori quam mei conspectus cupientes: Now when, having made a journey partly by land, partly by sea, we arrived in Corinth, big crowds of townspeople flocked together, as it seemed to me not because they set such great store by a tribute to Thiasus as because they wished to see me.

partim terrestri, partim maritimo itinere: the fact that a journey from Thessaly to Corinth includes the passage of the Gulf of Corinth is carefully mentioned: apparently, the geographical transformation in relation to the *Onos* (which situates the following episode in Thessaloniki) must not escape the reader's notice; see next note.

Corinthum accessimus: from 1,22 (20,12) and 2,12 (35,1 f.) it can be inferred (though the narrator never says so directly) that Lucius came from Corinth (see Veyne 1965,243 f.). This allusion to Corinth as Lucius' *patria* (1,22: 20,12) was already a difference from the *Onos* (Λούκιος was from Patrae; thus, the substitution of Corinth here for Thessaloniki in the *Onos* has been carefully prepared; see Introd. **2.3**). In this way Apuleius has closed the circle of his main character's wanderings. Thus Fick-Michel 1991,340 f.; Veyne 248 f. takes this as a reference to Apuleius's own spiritual odyssey, i.e. that the author means to indicate that he himself was 'reborn' in Corinth through initiation into the cult of Isis.

We might expect the narrator to note that he (Lucius, the ass) was now returning to his town. That he does not do so has been observed by many (see e.g. Veyne 1965,245 and 249; van Thiel 1971,16, n. 47; Fick-Michel 1991,150 f. even uses it as a counterargument against Corinth as Lucius' *patria*). Perhaps we should conclude that, along with his human shape, Lucius has also lost his 'proof of identity', like parentage, place of birth, name. After all, shortly before his metamorphosis he was so fascinated by Fotis and her magic that he assured her: *nec larem requiro nec domuitionem paro et nocte ista nihil antepono* (3,19: 67,3 f.). Penwill 1990,12 f. discusses the important theme of 'loss of home' in the books before the metamorphosis and points out that the devotion to Isis in the eleventh book also causes a certain renunciation of the ties with home. There is no mention of any tie with a *patria* in the eleventh book: after a brief visit to his *patrium larem* (11,26: 287,18 f.) Lucius settles in Rome, and in 11,27 (289,7 f.) he is *Madaurensis*!

magnae ... turbae confluebant ... mei conspectus cupientes: crowds flocking together to see something unusual are thematic in the *Met.* But these repeated gatherings of people give us, perhaps, a glimpse of the contemporaneous reality of the period during which the *Met.* was created; for the theme of sensationalism in the *Met.* and especially in book 10, see Introd. **2.4.2**, and see on *conspectum ... miris artibus* ch. 17 (250,12). Cf. 4,16 (87,2-3): *multi numero mirabundi bestiam confluebant*; 4,29 (97,12 f.) *iam multi mortalium longis itineribus atque altissimis maris meatibus ... confluebant* (to see Psyche; see Kenney 1990,119 ad loc.); 8,6 (181,7 f.) *confluunt ciuium maestae cateruae ... ciuitas cuncta uacuatur studio uisionis* with GCA 1985,71 ad loc.; 11,23 (285,3 f.) *tum ecce confluunt undique* *turbae*. See also this comm. on ch. 12 (245,13 f.).

Shumate 1996,221 f. seems to be engaged in 'hineininterpretieren' (from St. Augustine's *Confessions*) when she calls these frequent gatherings of curious crowds 'symbols of malaise'. The text of the *Met.* does not support her remark that these gatherings 'are presented as being rooted in boredom' (222, n. 16).

non tantum Thiasi dantes honori: thus F and φ. Following Helm and Giarratano-Frassinetti, the reading of F is retained; it was already defended by Oudendorp ('not because they attached such great importance to the tribute to Thiasus but because they...'). Cf. Sen. *Cl.* 1,15,5 *principes multa debent etiam famae dare*; for other examples (similarly with a dative) see *OLD* s.v. *do* 16a. Augello 1977,213 prefers the reading *Thiasi studentes honori* proposed by Robertson (who compares 9,41: 235,10 *saluti ... studens eius*); Hanson follows Robertson.

In the corresponding passage of the *Onos*, (49,2 and 50) the narrator elaborates much more on the sensation created by the ass's arrival in Thessaloniki than does the narrator of the *Met.* (see Junghanns 1932,117 n. 184). But the complacency observed above, coupled with a somewhat patronizing attitude toward Thiasus, is absent in the *Onos*. On these differences see Introd. **2.3**.

mei conspectus cupientes: this desire to see the ass will, for one person in the crowd, become a desire for the ass as a sex object; cf. below *mei cupidinem*. On *cupiens* with a genitive (as early as Ennius and as late as Claudianus) see *GCA* 1995,208 on 9,23 (220,27 f.) with references. For the use of the possessive pronoun instead of an objective genitive, see KSt 2,1,599, A.5. With *conspectus* e.g. Ter. *Hec.* 788 *scio pol eis fore meum conspectum inuisum*; Cic. *Planc.* 2 *uester, iudices, conspectus ... recreat mentem meam*. Compare *uisum meum* below.

251,14-16 Nam tanta etiam ibidem de me fama peruaserat, ut non mediocri quaestui praeposito illi meo fuerim: For so far had the talk about me spread even there that I was a considerable source of profit to the man in charge of me.

ibidem ... peruaserat: Kaibel proposed *ibi[dem] ... peruaserat*; it may indeed be a case of dittography with *de me*. The reading in F can be retained, however: ch. 17 (250,11-15) told in detail how the ass and his owner became famous in the small Thessalian town where they were at the time; *ibidem* emphasizes that the fame had spread not only there but also in Corinth.. For *ibidem* in the sense of 'there, in that very place' see *ThLL* s.v. *ibidem* 156,53 f. ('de pleonasmo'). Cf. the common combination *hic ibidem*; e.g. Cic. *S.Rosc.* 13 *hic ibidem ante oculos uestros* (in the *Met.* e.g. 1,22: 20,13; 7,2: 155,10).

non mediocri quaestui: on the frequent use of litotes in the *Met.* see *GCA* 1981,35 on 6,26 (148,9) s.v. *nec ... mediocris* with references. There is another instance of litotes in this chapter, also in connection with the profit the ass makes for his boss; see below, on *non paruas summulas*.

praeposito illi meo: the freedman to whom Thiasus entrusted the ass (ch. 17: 249,25 f.). For *praepositus* see on *praepositum* ch. 1 (236,25).

illi meo: see on *illis suis* ch. 18 (250,28); here, too, *illi* should not be taken as 'almost an article' but as referring to a person mentioned earlier.

251,16-19 Qui cum multos uideret nimio fauore lusus meos spectare gestientes, obserata fore atque singulis eorum sorsus admi<s>sis, stipes acceptans non paruas summulas diurnas corradere consuerat: When he saw that many people in excessive enthusiasm were eager to see my tricks, he bolted the door and let them in separately, one by one. Pocketing the admission fees, he got used to raking in a tidy little sum each day.

nimio fauore lusus meos spectare gestientes: the similarity to the cult of pantomime stars is obvious here. Those darlings of the public often became the protégés (and lovers) of well-born ladies; the same is about to happen to Lucius (see ch. 17 on *saltare*: 250,1 and on *sensum nutibus exprimentem*: 250,15).

nimio: here translated 'excessive'; for *nimius = magnus* see on *nimia* ch. 5 (240,16).

gestientes: for the connotations of *gestire* see on *gestiret* ch. 11 (244,29) with references.

obserata fore: for the theme of open and closed doors in the *Met.* and in this book, see on *patefacto cubiculo* ch. 16 (248,26).

stipes acceptans: *acceptare* has its full frequentative value, just as in e.g. Pl. *Ps.* 626 f. *mihi ..., qui res rationesque eri / Ballionis curo, argentum accepto, et quoi debet dato*, where it is, moreover, combined with a frequentative *datare*. Cf. Quint. *Inst.* 12,7,9 *cum ... Zenon, Cleanthes, Chrysippus mercedes a discipulis acceptauerint*; see also Heumann-Seckel s.v. *acceptare = saepius dare*, with examples in legal texts.

non paruas summulas: in this juxtaposition of a diminutive and an attribute meaning the opposite, Bernhard 1927,137 sees proof of a weakening of the diminutive value; Van der Paardt 1971,161 on 3,21 (68,11) *fortes pinnulae* agrees, giving further references. Abate 1982,52 f. regards this and other similar phrases as 'consciously created for stylistic effect'. This applies to our passage too: the juxtaposition has the effect of an ironical litotes. In addition, the diminutive *summulas* has a hypocoristic connotation here; this often occurs in expressions of profit: 'a tidy little sum'. See *GCA* 1985,254 on 8,29 (200,12) *largioris quaesticuli*.

Summula is first attested Sen. *Ep.* 77,8 *minutas itaque summulas distribuit flentibus seruis*. Then, with a somewhat cynical connotation, Juv. 7,174 f. *summula ne pereat qua uilis tessera uenit / frumenti*. In the *ThLL* material follow two passages in Apuleius' *Met.*, ours and 11,28 (289,20) *sufficientem conrasi summulam*. In these two passages the diminutive has, in addition to the hypocoristic connotation, an ironic effect: in both cases the profit is actually very large. It also sounds ironical (about the enormous wealth of the church) in Prud. *Peri.* 2,132 (cited from 125 onward) *unum sed orans flagito / indutiarum paululum / quo fungar efficacius / promissionis munere, / dum tota digestim mihi / Christi supellex scribitur: / nam calculanda primitus / tum subnotanda est summula*.

corradere: literally 'rake together'; Var. *L.* 5,31,136 *homo in pratis per fenisecia eo* (sc. *rastello*) *festucas corradit*. Lucr. 1,401 uses it metaphorically for 'assembling' evidence (cf. also ibid. 6,304 and 444). In comedy it is used for scraping together money, as it is in the *Met*. See *GCA* 1981,136 on 7,8 (160,6-10) and *GCA* 1985,252 on 8,28 (200,6 *conradentes*).

251,20-21: Fuit in illo conuenticulo matrona quaedam pollens et opulens: Now, there was in this company a married lady, influential and wealthy.

Fuit in illo conuenticulo matrona quaedam: this marks the beginning of a new episode in more than one respect: *fuit* is the first perfect since *perdocuit* in ch. 17 (250,2; there is only one other perfect, in the dependent clause *ubi ... accessimus*, above). The intervening material has been dominated by descriptive imperfects and explicative, background-creating pluperfects: in the next to last sentence, for example, *nam ... peruaserat* explained the descriptive *turbae confluebant* which preceded it; the section was concluded by *corradere consuerat*, which formed the setting for this new episode, that begins with *Fuit ... matrona*. For the perfect as 'episode-marker', see on *rupit ... et ... praecipit* ch. 3 (238,5). See Risselada 1997,106 f. on this function of *fuit* in Liv. 39,9,6 *huic consuetudo ... cum Aebutio fuit*, another passage in which imperfects and pluperfects dominate. See also Kroon-Rose 1996. The use of introductory *fuit* is already to be found in Plautus, e.g. *Men.* 17 *mercator quidam fuit Syracusis senex*; ibidem 32 *Epidamniensis quidam ibi mercator fuit*; see on the afterlife of this way of starting a tale in French romance De Felice 1957,7 and n. 2; see also Weinrich ²1971,136 f.

The initial position of *fuit* is significant. For more examples of similar story openings see *GCA* 1981,119 on 7,6 (158,19-21) *fuit quidam*; for an enumeration of these passages in the *Met.* see *GCA* 1985,32 on 8,1 (177,5 f.) *erat in proxima ciuitate iuuenis*. Kortekaas 1984,110 and 241 (n. 604), on *Hist. Apoll.* RB 1,1 *fuit quidam rex*, gives parallels from Greek literature; KSt 2,2,601 A.4 explain that whenever an episode, i.e. a new element, begins with a finite verb in initial position, the general and indefinite character of that verb serves to prepare the audience for the new element that is about to be introduced; they give examples from Greek and Latin authors. Jones 1991,91, with Siewierska 1988,94, explains the word order in these introductory phrases as a function of the 'given>new hierarchy', in which new information is shifted to the 'right-hand side' of the sentence unit, thus 'avoiding a sort of hiatus in the reader's/listener's processing of the information sequence while he deals with new content before a frame has been established for it.' That this is, indeed, an audience/reader-friendly introduction of something entirely new was already observed by KSt, but, strictly speaking, in such a sentence everything is new: Pinkster 1990,183 f. mentions 'brand-new sentences' and remarks that in such 'presentative sentences', in which everything is new, no explanation can be made on the basis of the pragmatic functions Topic and Focus, more research is needed. In the sentence *Fuit in illo conuenticulo matrona*, the words *illo conuenticulo* (which also come relatively early in the sentence) serve as a connecting element, i.e. an element of 'given' (Topic); this is enhanced by the anaphora *illo*. See Risselada 1997,114 f. on the importance of word order in the 'dosage' of new information.

At any rate, our sentence *Fuit ... matrona* marks a new episode; the word order is common for the opening of a fairytale, a story, or the introduction of something new. Much more notable, therefore, as far as word order is concerned, is a beginning like the one of the story of the 'Widow of Ephesus', Petr. 111,1 *Matrona quaedam ... erat*.

conuenticulo: found only here in Apuleius. The word is rare in pre-Christian Latin; before our passage, *ThLL* s.v. *conuenticulum* 844,28 f. gives only a few places, e.g. Cic. *Dom.* 74: *plebi quoque urbanae maiores nostri conuenticula et quasi concilia quaedam esse uoluerunt*; *Sest.* 91: *tum conuenticula hominum, quae postea ciuitates nominatae sunt*; also Tac. *Ann.* 14,15,2. After Apuleius *conventiculum* is attested three times in Amm.: 15,5,30 *Siluanum ... ad conuenticulum ritus Christiani tendentem ... trucidarant*; 27,3,13; 28,4,29. The somewhat condescending connotation with which Cicero already uses the word (cf. also Ammianus) is appropriated by the Church Fathers, who often use it deprecatingly of gatherings of non-Christians (*ThLL* 844,32 f. 'saepe cum contemptu dictum, apud ecclesiasticos praecipue de haereticis'); cf. e.g. Aug. *Quaest. evang.* 1,38 *unumquodque enim scisma et unaquaque heresis aut locum suum habet in orbe terrarum partem aliquam tenens, aut occultis atque obscuris conuenticulis curiositatem hominum decipit*. It is possible that in our passage it is also meant in a somewhat derogatory way, thus emphasizing the presence of the well-born lady in this group.

Conuenticulum occurs once in Tacitus (*Ann.* 14,15,2) in the meaning of 'meeting place' (in that meaning it is not found again until Arn. 4,36). The context of the Tacitus passage is interesting for the use of the word in our passage: it is about Nero's lowly amusements, e.g. the games he organized under the name of *Iuvenalia*, where all sorts of people, but especially many distinguished ladies and gentlemen, engaged in acting: *quin et feminae inlustres deformia meditari; exstructaque ... conuenticula et cauponae et posita ueno inritamenta luxui*. Our passage, too, deals with a lady of rank who *deformia meditatur*. In the next sentence, *multiformibus ludicris* reinforces the idea of the ass as a celebrated *histrio*; see also above on *nimio fauore lusus meos spectare gestientes*.

matrona ... pollens et opulens: in the *Onos* (50,4) it is a γυνὴ ξένη οὐ μέτρια κεκτημένη who falls in love with the ass. Here we have a (similarly well-to-do) *matrona*: a married, free-born woman (see *RE* s.v. *matrona* 2300,139 f. [Schroff]). Although the connotations of virtue and gentility of the word *matrona* are secondary, they are frequently found in literature: cf. e.g. Pl. *Cist.* 25 *ubi istas uideas summo genere gnatas, summatis matronas*; cf. Austin on Cic. *Cael.* 13,32 *petulanter facimus, si matrem familias secus quam matronarum sanctitas postulat nominamus*. See also *GCA* 1981,169 on 7,14 (164,14-18). Our lady is called *matrona* again in chs. 20 (252,4) and 22 (253,14: *delicatam matronam*); cf. also ch. 23 (253,20) *nobili femina*; ch. 23 (254,17 f.) *egregia illa uxor mea propter dignitatem* ... with comm. ad loc.

It is significant that it is a prominent and respected resident of Corinth who is about to enter into a perverted love affair with the ass: those few words evoke an image of the social environment into which Lucius has been introduced. For contemporary readers they will have confirmed the associations that the name of Corinth evoked anyway: the town had a reputation as a morass of vice or, as Mason 1971,165 puts it, 'an ancient Vanity Fair'. Mason 160 f. gives for these associations of Corinth many examples from literature. In the proverbially rich city of Corinth (cf. Strabo 8,6,20 about Corinth's traditional epithet ἀφνειός) Lucius immediately gets acquainted with the loose morals of high society. Through casual remarks of the fictive narrator, the abstract author (see Introd. **3.2**) also emphasizes the outward appearances kept up in this world: the trysts of the lady and the ass take place secretly, in the dead of night; cf. ch. 22 (254,10 f.) *uitata lucis conscientia facessit mulier condicto pari noctis futurae pretio*. When the equally well-born Thiasus plans to exhibit his ass's amatory activities, it goes without saying that the *egregia ... uxor* must stay out of this *propter dignitatem* (ch. 23: 254,17 f.; see the notes there). On the increasing discrepancy between appearance and reality in this book, see ch. 18 on *prosapia* (250,20) and *me phaleris aureis ... exornatum* (251,5 f.).

pollens et opulens: the *Met.* is preeminently a text to be 'heard': here, the jingle of the paronomasia resounds in the surrounding text, emphasizing to the attentive listener those concepts that play an important part in this entire episode. For a similar effect see e.g. *GCA* 1985,73 on 8,6 (181,11-13) *inuita remansit in uita* with references; Kenney 1990,159 on 5,15 (115,7) *mellita ... mollita*.

251,21-26 Quae more ceterorum uisum meum mercata ac dehinc multiformibus ludicris delectata per admirationem adsiduam paulatim in admirabilem mei cupidinem incidit; nec ullam uaesanae libidini medelam capiens ad instar asinariae P[h]asiphaae complexus meos ardenter expectabat: Like the others, she paid to see me and subsequently delighted in my various tricks and, repeatedly coming to marvel at me, she gradually fell into an astonishing desire for me; and seeking no cure for her frenzied lust she ardently longed, like an ass-Pasiphaë, for my embraces.

uisum meum: see above on *mei conspectus*.

multiformibus ludicris: like the adjective *ludicer*, the noun *ludicrum* ('joke, game') is often used in a theatrical context (*OLD* s.v. *ludi(cer?) -cra, -crum* 2 and s.v. *ludicrum* 2). Here it refers to the various tricks that the ass learned in ch. 17 (249,28 f.), but also suggests the theatre performance of a favourite *histrio* (see above on *nimio fauore lusus meos spectare gestientes*). Cf. ch. 29 (260,15) *ludicris scaenicorum choreis*.

per admirationem adsiduam in admirabilem mei cupidinem incidit: the repetition *admirationem ... admirabilem* catches the attention: because she constantly watches, with utter amazement (*per admirationem adsiduam*), the *mirum* of the performing ass, the woman herself develops feelings that in their turn cause another *mirum*, something paradoxical: *admirabilem ... cupidinem*. From *OLD* s.v. *admirabilis* 1 and 2 it becomes clear that *admirabilis* (found only here in the *Met.*) has positive connotations only secondarily; in the first instance it means 'astonishing, paradoxical, unheard-of'. Cf. Apul. *Apol.* 81,2 *uersutiam tam insidiosam, tam admirabili scelere conflatam negabis te umquam cognouisse*.

in ... cupidinem incidit: for *incidere in* + accusative and transitive *incidere* in the *Met.*, see *GCA* 1995,194 on 9,22 (219,15-18). *OLD* s.v. *incido* 5 gives examples of *incidere in* meaning 'to pass (esp. suddenly...) into specified circumstances, usu. unpleasant...', and 5c meaning '(to pass) into an emotional state'. Cf. e.g. Cic. *Off.* 1,10,32 *in maximos luctus incidit*; Sen. *Con.* exc. 3,5 *in amorem filiae istius incidi*.

nec ullam ... medelam capiens: to her, the only *medela* for her disease is the gratification of her desires; cf. the proverbial ὁ τρώσας ἰάσεται, discussed in the comm. on ch. 3 (238,20-21).

uaesanae libidini: the qualification *uaesanae* in itself does not refer to the fact that the object of her desire is an animal; it indicates the vehemence of her feelings. Cf. 5,27 (124,11 f.) *uesaniae libidinis ... stimulis agitata* (Psyche's sister). The lovesick *nouerca*, too, is *uaesania praeceps* in ch. 4 (239,16). Passion described in terms of insanity is also found e.g. Catul. 7,10; ibid. 100,7 *cum uesana meas torreret flamma medullas*. See Puccini 1998 on insane love in the *Met.*

medelam: see on *medela* ch. 3 (238,21).

ad instar asinariae Pasiphaae: Pasiphaë is mentioned in the *Onos*, too (51,11), in connection with the woman in love with the ass. But in the *Met.* she is mentioned twice: here and ch. 22 (254,8) *Minotauri matrem*. The author of the *Met.* makes a wider and, as appears from many notes in the commentaries on the preceding books, more subtle use of mythological comparisons than does the author of the *Onos*. See e.g. *GCA* 1985,153 on 8,16 (189,20-26) with references. J. Seubers, in an unpublished doctoral thesis, has examined the mythological comparisons in the *Met.* with their varying degrees of profundity. In connection with Pasiphaë she remarks that by mentioning Pasiphaë twice Apuleius makes the *matrona* the center of the comparison, whereas in the *Onos* (51,11) the ass himself is compared to the bull (τοῦ τῆς Πασιφάης μοιχοῦ). Seubers points out that the comparison with Pasiphaë turns this *matrona* into one of the many 'mythological witches' in the *Met.*, so that the comparison is one of the elements that connect book 10 to the rest of the *Met*. Because Pasiphaë is the mother of Phaedra, the present episode is also connected with chs. 2-12, in which, as we have seen, a 'Phaedra' is a prominent figure. A further connection will later emerge with chs. 23-28, in which a 'Medea' is the murderess: Medea's father Aietes and Pasiphaë are both children of Helios.

asinariae Pasiphaae: brachylogy: the adjective *asinariae* takes the place of a much longer description. Cf. 3,27 (72,1) *auxilio rosario*, with Van der Paardt 1971,191 ad loc., who gives many examples in the *Met*. Cf. also 6,19 (142,21) *polentacium damnum* with Kenney 1990,215 ad loc.

complexus meos ardenter expectabat: except for this passage and the corresponding passage in the *Onos*, the only stories in ancient literature that mention sexual acts between humans and animals are mythological: e.g. Pasiphaë, whom our narrator mentions; Semiramis and a horse, in Plin. *Nat.* 8,64; Leda and the swan. Juv. 6,332-334 is often mentioned as a possible proof of such perversities in the Rome of his time: *hic si / quaeritur et desunt homines, mora nulla per ipsam, / quo minus imposito clunem summittat asello*. But this may be rhetorical hyperbole, to illustrate how oversexed are the women he describes. Possibly he plays on the double meaning of *asellus*, not only 'little ass' but also 'a sexually very active man' (cf. Juv. 9,92 *bipedem ... asellum* with Courtney ad loc.; Petr. 24,7). Commentators on the Juvenal passage refer only to our passage in Apuleius and to the *Onos*. This makes it all the more remarkable that there are illustrations on lamps, described by Bruneau 1965,349 f., of a woman coupling with an ass (not a horse: Bruneau 352 f.). All these illustrations date from the second and third centuries A.D. According to Bruneau, this may indicate a theme in literature or subliterature that was popular just at that time (cf. *RE* s.v. 'Mimos',1758 [Wüst]). This may be reflected in the occurrence of this story in the *Onos* and in Apuleius, and probably also in the Greek *Metamorphoses* of 'Lucius of Patrae' (see Introd. **2.3** and App. II).

expectabat: thus F and φ, rightly retained by all modern editors. Löfstedt 1908,94 f. explains *expectare* as 'longingly look forward to' (see also *OLD* s.v. *ex(s)pecto* 3). Cf. Liv. 28,27,9 *fama mortis meae non accepta solum, sed etiam exspectata est* with Drakenborch ad loc. For amorous longing cf. e.g. Ter. *Eu.* 193 f. *dies noctisque me ames, me desideres / me somnies, me expectes, de me cogites* and Pl. *Truc.* 675 *tuam expecto osculentiam*. There is therefore no reason to adopt Beroaldus' proposal *expetebat*.

251,26-252,2 Grandi denique praemio cum altore meo depecta est noctis unius concubitum; at ille nequaquam <curans an ei quicquam> posset de me suaue prouenire, lucro suo tantum contentus, adnuit: Eventually, for a high price, she bargained with my keeper for one night's assignation; and he, not caring at all whether anything pleasant could happen to her through me but only content with his own profit, assented.

altore: found only here in the *Met*. The earliest passage mentioned by *ThLL* s.v. *altor* 1770,31 f. is Sal. *Hist.* Frg. 3,14 *(Cretenses) uetustatem ... altores Iouis celebrauisse*. Then the word occurs mostly in poetry (see Koestermann on Tac. *Ann.* 6,37,4) and is (as in

Sallust) an elevated term for a guardian; cf. e.g. Ov. *Met.* 11,101, where Silenus is called the *altor* of Bacchus. Cic. *N.D.* 2,86 also uses it in a solemn context: *omnium ... rerum ... seminator et sator et parens, ut ita dicam, atque educator et altor est mundus.* Apuleius is the first to use it for the keeper of an animal (*ThLL* 1770,41 f.). After that, P. Nol. *Carm.* 24,865 (animals as nourishers of animals): *mixti (aues senes) pullis ... altoribus.* In our passage, the elevated word *altor* is used ironically of the *praepositus*, who has no qualms about lending the ass to the lady for a night provided he can make a good profit on it.

depecta est: Apuleius uses the verb twice: here and *Apol.* 75,7 (in the unflattering characterization of Herennius Rufinus) *anulos aureos et omnia insignia dignitatis abicit, cum creditoribus depaciscitur.* Cf. Ulp. *Dig.* 3,6,3,2: *depectus autem dicitur turpiter pactus.* Cf. also the noun *depector* Apul. *Apol.* 74,6 (again about Her. Rufinus) *omnium litium depector, omnium falsorum commentator.* Thus, the verb may have the connotation of a shady deal, as it does in some passages of Cicero, e.g. *S. Rosc.* 110 and ibid. 115. See also *ThLL* s.v. *depectio* 562,75 f., which notes that lawyers always use the word 'de pactione turpi'.

concubitum: Apuleius may have Verg. *Ecl.* 6,49 f. in mind: after mentioning Pasiphaë's love for the bull, the poet says that Proteus' daughters, who had been changed into cows, did *not* fall in love with a bull (*at non tam turpis pecudum tamen ulla secuta / concubitus*; see also Thomas ad loc. on *concubitus*). Apuleius uses various terms for 'intercourse' in the *Met.* (see Callebat 1968,53). One of these is *concubitus*, which is found, in addition to our passage, three other times. Three times it is used of an animal sexual act: our passage; 5,18 (117,8 f., in which Psyche's sisters mention her union with the mysterious husband, whom they suggust is a serpent) *periculosi concubitus et uenenati serpentis amplexus*; in ch. 34 (265,14) the word refers to the copulation which is to take place in the theater between the ass and the murderess. The fourth passage concerns a furtive act of humans: in 8,10 (185,14) Thrasyllus eagerly agrees *de furtiuo concubitu*.

Although the agreement about the nightly tryst of the *matrona* and the ass is couched in terms of disapproval, and the emphasis is on unscrupulousness of the ass's *altor*, the description of the night itself (chs. 21-22) is full of tenderness.

at ille nequaquam curans an ei quicquam posset de me suaue prouenire: F and φ have *at ille nequaquam posset de me suaue prouenire* (over the first *a* of *nequaquam* F has an erasure of a Nasalstrich; in A (the most important ms. of Class I; see Introd. **4.1**) there is a lacuna at this point, which, according to Robertson's app.cr., can be filled in with about twelve words. F's reading is not intelligible Latin. Looking for a solution, Oudendorp consulted the text of the *Onos*, which at this point is very close to the text of the *Met.* (*Onos* 50,4-5): καί ποτε γυνὴ ξένη οὐ μέτρια κεκτημένη, τὴν ὄψιν ἱκανή, παρελθοῦσα ἔσω ἰδεῖν ἐμὲ ἀριστῶντα εἰς ἔρωτά μου θερμὸν ἐμπίπτει, τοῦτο μὲν τὸ κάλλος ἰδοῦσα τοῦ ὄνου, τοῦτο δὲ τῷ παραδόξῳ τῶν ἐμῶν ἐπιτηδευμάτων εἰς ἐπιθυμίαν συνουσίας προελθοῦσα. καὶ διαλέγεται πρὸς τὸν ἐπιστάτην τὸν ἐμὸν καὶ μισθὸν αὐτῷ ἁδρὸν ὑπέσχετο, εἰ συγχωρήσειεν αὐτῇ σὺν ἐμοὶ τὴν νύκτα ἀναπαύσασθαι. κἀκεῖνος οὐδὲν φροντίσας, εἴτε ἀνύσει τι ἐκείνη ἐξ ἐμοῦ εἴτε καὶ μή, λαμβάνει τὸν μισθόν. Oudendorp proposed *nequaquam <curans> posset<ne> de me suaue prouenire*. Hildebrand, taking the erased Nasalstrich in F into consideration, prefers *at ille nequam quum posset de me suaue promerere*, which, however, loses the idea present in the *Onos*. All other conjectures are based on the tenor of the sentence in the *Onos*. Augello 1977,213, who discusses the readings found in the modern editions, prefers the solution of Helm IV (Helm-Krenkel) *nequaquam <sollicitus quid> posset de me suaue prouenire*. Helm 1931 has *<sollicitus quidnam>*; Giarratano adopts Lütjohann's proposal *nequaquam <sollicitus, si quo modo illa> posset*; Robertson (followed by Frassinetti and Hanson) has *nequaquam <anxius ecquid>*, rejected by Augello because *ecquid* occurs only once in the works of Apuleius (*Apol.* 48,3). An attractive conjecture (not mentioned by Augello) is Novák's *nequaquam <curans an>*, which is here expanded to *nequaquam <curans an ei quicquam> posset de me suaue prouenire*, in an attempt to explain the omission: it is possible that the scribe's eyes jumped from *nequaquam* to the last part of *quicquam* ('saut du même au même').

For *curare* with an indirect question ('to care whether...') cf. *OLD* s.v. *curo* 8d. *Curare* often occurs in negative phrases: 'not care about something'. For *prouenire* with a dative cf. e.g. *Met.* 1,9 (8,23 f.) *ut illi quoque simile ... proueniret*; 9,1 (203,12 f.) *nihil Fortuna rennuente licet homini nato dexterum prouenire*, where *nihil ... dexterum* is comparable to *quicquam ... suaue* here.

contentus: thus φ, and also U,E, and S (members of 'Class I'; see Introd. **4.1**); in F a second hand has changed *contentus* to *consensus*.

CHAPTER XX

Preparations for the encounter of the *matrona* and the ass.

252,3-5 Iam denique cenati e triclinio domini decesseramus et iam dudum praestolantem cubiculo meo matronam offendimus: We had already had dinner and left my master's dining room; in my bedroom we found the *matrona*, who had been waiting there for a long time.

cenati: dining may be regarded as the first preparation of the ass for his night of passion. Cf. the proverbial *sine Cerere et Libero friget Venus* (Ter. *Eu.* 732); see Otto 1890,366. The wine, too, will be mentioned later in this episode: ch. 21 (253,10 f.). The close connection between food, wine, and sex repeatedly emerges in the *Met.* and is a commonplace also outside the *Met.*; see Boldrini 1989,121 f. (with reference to Petronius' tale of the Widow of Ephesus). Lucius' first assignation with Fotis, which is mirrored in many respects by the episode of the Corinthian *matrona* (see Introd. **2.5.2**), begins with a lavish dinner where the wine flows freely (2,15 f.: 37,10 f.; see Van Mal-Maeder 1998,234 f. ad loc.).

e triclinio domini decesseramus: a casual illustration of the status of *conuiua* which the ass has acquired in Thiasus' household; cf. ch. 17 (250,13 f.) *qui sodalem conuiuamque possidet asinum*; ch. 18 (251,9 f.) *quod haberet in me ... conuiuam*.

iam dudum praestolantem ... matronam: on the use of *matrona* for this lady see on ch. 19 (251,20) *matrona*. The strenght of the *matrona*' desire for the ass and appetite for lovemaking becomes apparent from various details in this episode. Cf. ch. 19 (251,25 f.) *complexus meos ardenter expectabat*; ch. 21 (253,9 f.) *mulieris cupientis amplexus obiturus*; see also ch. 22 (254,4 f.) The desire is all on the *matrona*'s part: the narrator is still apparently trying to prove that the accusations of the evil *puer* in 7,21, that the ass was trying to assault passing women, were unfounded. See GCA 1981,223; see also this comm. on *inscendere* ch. 22 (253,14).

praestolantem cubiculo meo: *praestolari* is also found with an ablative of place in 5,4 (106,2 f.) *statim uoces cubiculo praestolatae nouam nuptam interfectae uirginitatis curant*. On *praestolari* or *praestolare* in the *Met.*, see Van der Paardt 1971,45 ad 3,3 (54,23 f.).

cubiculo meo: another detail suggesting the ass's treatment as a human (cf. also above *e triclinio domini decesseramus*): he has a *cubiculum* of his own. Cf. 9,2 (204,15 f.), where he gratefully makes use of an unexpected opportunity: *super constratum lectum abiectus, post multum equidem temporis somnum humanum quieui*.

252,5-6 Dii boni, qualis ille quanque praeclarus apparatus!: Good gods, what a splendid spread was made there!

Dii boni: with these words the narrator expresses the surprise of Lucius/*actor* at the moment he enters the bedroom. This actorial narrative style, typical of large parts of the *Met.* (see Introd. **3.5**), directly involves the reader in the event, especially with an exclamation like *dii boni!* Through this exclamation, common in the casual daily speech of cultured people (see on *dii boni* ch. 2: 238,1), the fictive narrator characterizes not only himself as a well-bred person (ironically, just as an obscene episode is being introduced) but also his audience as well-bred, but nevertheless interested in racy stories. It is this same fictive audience that will be disappointed at the end of book 10, when the theatre performance of the ass's copulation with the criminal woman does not take place (see Introd. **2.4.2** end).

quanque: thus F. The spelling in φ, *quamque*, has not been adopted here, according to the principle of *GCA* (see on *quandiu* ch. 2: 237,14). In pronunciation the *m* had undoubtedly been assimilated with the following velar, as appears from the frequently attested *utrunque* and *utcunque*. See Sommer 1914,236 f. and cf. *GCA* 1981,128 on *nanque* and *namque* in F.

252,6-12 Quattuor eunuchi confestim puluillis compluribus uentose tumentibus pluma delicata terrestrem nobis cubitum praestruunt, sed et stragula ueste auro ac murice Tyrio depicta probe consternunt ac desuper breuibus admodum, sed satis copiosis puluillis, aliis nimis modicis, quis maxillas et ceruices delicatae mulieres suffulcire consuerunt, superstruunt: Four eunuchs at once prepared a bed for us on the floor with a number of pillows airily filled with fine down and they also neatly spread cloths embroidered with gold and Tyrian purple, and these they covered with a top layer of rather small but fairly many cushions and other quite small ones that refined ladies use to support their cheeks and necks.

Quattuor eunuchi: the *Onos* (51,2) describes the preparation of the bed with passive verbs; the next sentence there mentions only τῆς γυναικὸς θεράποντες. The four eunuchs of the *Met.* intensify the atmosphere of wealth and luxury which is emphatically being created in this episode and which draws the interpreting reader's attention to the contrast between the luxury and refinement of Corinth's 'high society' on the one hand and their perverted pleasures on the other. Having eunuchs is associated with the decadence of Oriental monarchs; cf. e.g. Cic. *Orat.* 232 *neque ... aurum et argentum, quo nostros ueteres Marcellos ... multi eunuchi e Syria ... uicerunt*; Liv. 9,17,16. In Petr. 27,3 two *spadones* are mentioned as a notable element in Trimalchio's household; Smith ad loc. suspects they are mentioned to emphasize Trimalchio's 'claim to regal magnificence'. The ban on castration, repeatedly issued from Domitian onward, remained ineffective (see Mommsen, *Röm.Strafr.* 637; Mayor on Juv. 10,307).

uentose: 'airy' (i.e. filled with down). *OLD* s.v. *uentose* translates 'with the appearance of being inflated'. The adverb is first attested in this passage; after Apuleius it occurs in Fulg. *Myth.* 3,9 *quod tibia uentose ... sonet*; Aug. *Ep.* 112,3 *adsurge in illum, qui non uentose alleuat conuersos ad se*; Aug. *C. Iul.* 5,13,49 *campo ... uerborum, ubi uentose atque inaniter curreres*; Prud. *Apoth.* 411 *pulsus abi, uentose liquor, Christus iubet, exi*. In those last three passages *uentose* is used metaphorically meaning 'vainly, hollowly'. The metaphorical use of the adjective *uentosus* (literally: 'windy, puffed up') is common in Latin of all periods; see *OLD* s.v. *uentosus* 5 and 6.

pluma: the use of down is also associated with luxury. Cf. Lucil. 252 *pluma atque amphitapoe et si aliud quid deliciarum*; Sen. *Dial.* 1 (*Prov.*),3,9: *tam uigilabit* (sc. Maecenas) *in pluma quam ille in cruce*; Juv. 10,360 f. (about the ideal of the steady and frugal human being) *cupiat nihil, et potiores / Herculis aerumnas credat saeuosque labores / et uenere et cenis et pluma Sardanapalli*. In our passage, too, we see an interconnection between sumptuous food, sex, and Oriental luxury. Cf. also Courtney on Juv. 6,88.

At the preparation of the equally luxurious 'wedding bed' of the ass and the murderess in the Corinthian theatre (ch. 34: 265,11 f.), the bed is among others *plumea congerie tumidus*; see notes there.

delicata: the adjective functions as a catchword in this passage; cf. below, *delicatae mulieres* and ch. 22 (253,14) *delicatam matronam*. Its repeated use emphasizes the absurdity of the desire of this woman, the epitome of refinement, for the ass, the coarseness of whose body will be emphasized in ch. 22. The adjective also has erotic connotations; see *GCA* 1981,48 on 6,28 (149,22-26) with references.

terrestrem ... cubitum: 'a bed on the ground'. The combination, attested nowhere else, is possibly the translation of a term in the Greek Vorlage; cf. *Onos* 51,2 χαμεύνιον. Elsewhere Apuleius uses *terrestris* to translate another Greek word: *Pl.* 1,11 (204): *terrenum atque terrestre - sic enim* πεζόν *et* χερσαῖον *censui nuncupanda ... terrestria uero, quae alit ac sustinet tellus*. For an unusual kind of bed the author has created an unusual expression; see also the following note.

cubitum: here used in the sense of *cubile*, which is rare; more common is *cubitus* in the meaning of 'the state of sleeping, the act of lying down' (cf. e.g. 3,13: 61,21). The only real parallel is Plin. *Nat.* 24,59 *matronae Thesmophoriis Atheniensum castitatem custodientes his foliis cubitus sibi sternunt*. In addition to Pliny, *ThLL* s.v. 2. *cubitus* cites Cato *Agr.* 5,5 *primus cubitu surgat, postremus cubitum eat*, where, however, *cubitus* could also mean 'sleeping'.

praestruunt: in Apuleius' works this verb is found only here, and in an unusual, literal meaning at that: 'to construct beforehand, i.e. as a foundation'. The usual meaning of *praestruo* is 'to extend in front as a protection, obstruction' or figuratively 'to contrive beforehand' (see *OLD* s.v. *praestruo* 1 t/m 3). The reading of ς is *praesternunt*, and Leo proposed *construunt*. It is typical of Apuleius, however, to use a compound in its literal meaning; cf. e.g. his use of *adfirmatum* 7,22 (171,2; see *GCA* 1981,226 f. ad loc.). Moreover, a parallel for this use of *praestruere* is offered by Col. 1,5,9 *quippe ab imo praestructa ualenter resistent contra ea, quae postmodum superposita incumbant*. Because of this parallel, the use of *praestruunt* in our passage acquires a comical tone: the bed needs a strong foundation indeed to withstand the love-play of the dainty lady and the huge ass (his size is described in great detail in ch. 22).

stragula ueste: a common term for an underblanket (see *GCA* 1977,95 on 4,12: 83,14-19).

auro ac murice Tyrio depicta: for a rug that is spread under, not over, the bed-linen, this decoration seems extravagantly luxurious.

murice Tyrio: murex is the shellfish from which the purple dye was made. Again, this suggests Oriental splendour; cf. Verg. *A.* 4,261 f. (Mercury, sent by Jupiter to Carthage to remind Aeneas of his mission, finds Aeneas taken in by Dido's expensive gifts) *atque illi stellatus iaspide fulua / ensis erat Tyrioque ardebat murice laena / demissa ex umeris, diues quae munera Dido / fecerat*. See Austin ad loc.: 'the whole picture is dazzling - and oriental.'

desuper ... superstruunt: Bernhard 1927,177 gives other examples in which an adverb 'überflüssig zum Verbum steht'. Here, the redundant expression emphasizes the elaborateness of the bed made up for the unusual assignation. See the next note, and below on *superstruunt*.

breuibus admodum, sed satis copiosis puluillis, aliis nimis modicis: thus F and φ.

Because of its redundancy, *nimis modicis* has been suspected as a gloss on *breuibus admodum*; Van der Vliet deletes *nimis modicis*, followed by Van Thiel. Helm has *nimis medic<at>is* ('highly perfumed') and compares Mart. 14,207,1 *sume Cytheriaco medicatum nectare ceston*. Robertson prints F's reading, but mentions Van der Vliet's proposal with 'fortasse recte' (so too Hanson). Colvius wanted to change *aliis* to *ac iis*; Pricaeus proposed *illis* instead of *aliis*. Armini defends F, saying that *breuibus* here means *paucis*, and compares 1,19 (17,14) *breuitas ipsa commeantium*. Augello 1977,213 f. also defends F, arguing that it is in keeping with the overexaggerated scene (see the previous notes) of the eunuchs making the bed that, on top of the many rather small cushions (*breuibus admodum, sed satis copiosis*), an extra layer of tiny cushions (*nimis modicis*) is added. Giarratano, Robertson, Terzaghi, Frassinetti, and Hanson all keep the manuscript reading. If Augello's reasoning is followed, a comma should be placed before *aliis*.

    breuibus admodum - satis copiosis: chiasmus. See Bernhard 1927,30 on adverbs following the adjective they qualify.

    superstruunt: cf. *praestruunt* above: the impression of an elaborately built-up bed, like a towering structure, is emphasized by the two compounds of *struere*. Cf. Fron. *Str.* 3,9,8: *naues ... contabulauit superstruxitque eis turres*.

    quis maxillas et ceruices delicatae mulieres suffulcire consuerunt: this addition, too, reinforces the absurdity of the situation in which this frail, dainty lady, who needs extra pillows to support her cheeks and neck, is about to have the huge ass on top of her.

    quis = *quibus*; see comm. on ch. 27 (258,11) *quis*.

    delicatae mulieres: see above on *delicata*.

252,12-13: Nec dominae uoluptates diutina sua praesentia morati, clausis cubiculi foribus facessunt: And not delaying their mistress's pleasures by their prolonged presence, they closed the doors of the bedroom and withdrew.

At the beginning of the love scene with Fotis (2,15: 37,11 f.) it is also mentioned that the slaves have been removed to ensure privacy: *nam et pueris extra limen, credo ut arbitrio nocturni gannitus ablegarentur, humi quam procul distratum fuerat* (see Introd. **2.5.2** on the mirroring of these two love scenes).

    clausis ... foribus: on the symbolism of closed and open doors in this book and in the *Met.*, see on *patefacto cubiculo* ch. 16 (248,26).

    cubiculi foribus: Scobie 1975,103 f. on 1,11 (10,17) *adducta fore*, who examines the use of *foris* and *fores* in the *Met.*, shows that Apuleius consistently uses the singular to refer to the 'monothuros' of modest houses, and the plural for the double doors of grander houses.

    facessunt: meaning *recedere, abire*, this verb is an archaism, frequently used by Apuleius in the *Met.*; see Van der Paardt 1971,55 f. on 3,5 (55,25). Sometimes it is used with an ablative of separation (with or without a preposition; see *GCA* 1977,149 on 4,20: 89,12), but also, as here, absolutely, e.g. 2,15 (44,23). The only time Tacitus uses the verb, it is also absolute: *Ann.* 16,34,2 *flentes ... qui aderant facessere ... hortatur*.

252,14-15 At intus cerei praeclara micantes luce nocturnas nobis tenebras inalbabant: Inside, the wax candles, glowing with a radiant light, brightened the darkness of night for us.

The only mention of light in this book refers to artificial light, which 'whitens' the darkness of night. In the whole book no mention is made of daylight or sunrise (see Introd. **1.6.1**). As often in the *Met.*, artifical light is associated with eroticism; cf. 2,11 (34,6 f.), where Lucius urges Fotis that during the night they will spend together *oleo lucerna ... abundet*. On this association of artificial light and eroticism, see De Smet 1987,33 f. (also on the *lucerna* in the story of Amor and Psyche), who unfortunately does not discuss our passage. See also Kenney 1990,168 on 5,22 (121,13 f.) on the 'traditional role as confidant and voyeur' of the *lucerna*.

Many scholars have commented upon the antithesis in the *Met.* between witches, who know how to make light shine during the night, and Isis as the true source of light (see De Smet l.c.,35 f. with references; Schlam 1968,80 f. and 116 f.; Krabbe 1989,131 f. discusses the many facets of light in the *Met.*); in this connection they discuss the significant names Fotis and (possibly) Lucius. Our passage is the culminating phase of the false light versus Isis' gentle, true light for the initiated. Cf. e.g. 11,15 (277,19-20) *Fortunae, ... uidentis, quae suae lucis splendore ceteros etiam deos illuminat*. In 11,23 (285,15 f.) Lucius sees an entirely different light from that which he sees here, but there, too, it is in the dark of night: *nocte media uidi solem candido coruscantem lumine*. See below, on *praeclara ... luce*.

cerei: the use of wax candles or tapers is discussed in *GCA* 1977,146 on 4,19 (89,6-7) with references. The use of this expensive form of lighting (see *GCA* ibid.) points, again, at the luxury so strongly emphasized in this passage.

praeclara ... luce: in all the other passages in the *Met.* where *praeclarus* occurs, it is used in the most frequent meaning (*OLD* s.v. *praeclarus* 2 en 3) 'splendid, outstanding, glorious' (often with irony, cf. *GCA* 1977,33 on 4,2: 75,18-20); in its concrete meaning 'brilliant' it is found here only. This is the first passage given by *ThLL* s.v. *praeclarus* 489,68 f. in connection with the brilliance of *artificial* light. Describing the light of celestial bodies the adjective occurs in Cicero, e.g. *Arat.* Frg. 2,2 *praeclara insignia caeli*; *N.D.* 2,107 *praeclara species* (sc. *Draconis*). Cf. Lucr. 2,1032 *solis praeclara luce nitorem*. If there is a conscious allusion to this Lucretius passage it would make an ironic contrast between the radiant light of the sun and the artificial light in the darkness of this night of passion. See the introductory remarks to this pericope.

inalbabant: the transitive verb *inalbare* is attested for the first time in Apuleius in the *Met.*, here and 9,24 (221,13, where it used for the 'whitening' action of sulphur on laundry). In a figurative sense (i.q. *mundare*) it is frequently used by Christian authors, e.g. Cypr. *Ad Quir.* 1.24 (in a quotation from Jesaia) *si fuerint peccata uestra ut phoeniceum, ut niuem exalbabo; et si fuerint quasi coccum, ut lanam inalbabo*. See *ThLL* s.v. *inalbo* 816,28 f. For *inalbare/inalbere* see also *GCA* 1981,80 f. on 7,1 (154,5) *inalbebat*.

CHAPTER XXI

Foreplay: the charming *matrona*'s protestations of love have the intended effect.

252,15-20 Tunc ipsa cuncto prorsus spoliata tegmine, taenia quoque, qua decoras deuinxerat papillas, lumen propter adsistens, de stagneo uasculo multo sese perungit oleo balsamo meque indidem largissime perfricat, sed multo tanta impensius cura etiam nares perfundit meas: Then, after she had removed all the clothes that covered her, also the band with which she had bound her charming breasts, she stood close to the light and rubbed herself with balsam-oil from a tin jar, and very profusely rubbed me too from the same jar and with even more care moistened my nostrils extra-generously.

cuncto prorsus spoliata tegmine: *prorsus* emphasizes both *cuncto* and *spoliata*, which is not unusual; see on *prorsus* ch. 3 (238,25).

spoliata tegmine: the expression suggests that the woman renders herself defenseless against the ass: she 'adopts a vulnerable attitude'. *Spoliata* has to be taken as a middle voice, which is rather unusual: generally, *spoliare* is something that others do, and in an antagonistic or prosecutorial situation at that. This also applies to a situation where the verb is used of the removal of clothes, as it is here; cf. Liv. 2,55,5: *consules spoliari hominem et uirgas expediri iubent*; Call. *Dig.* 48,20,2 *non ut quis in carcerem ductus est, spoliari eum oportet, sed post condemnationem*. Used as a middle, also with the connotation of 'making oneself defenseless', in V. Max. 2,7,8 *scissa ueste spoliatoque corpore lictorum se uerberibus lacerandum praebuit*.

tegmine: 'covering'. In 4,31 (99,21) it is used for a silken veil as a protection against the sun: *ille serico tegmine flagrantiae solis obsistit inimici*. The use of *tegmen* meaning 'clothing' is mainly poetic (Bömer on Ov. *Met.* 3,108).

Whereas the oblique forms of this noun are always contracted, the nominative is usually *tegimen* or *tegumen*. Cf. 9,32 (227,10 f.) *stramen aliquod uel ... tegimen* (about the poor *hortulanus*, who had no roof over his head for himself or the ass). See also Williams on Verg. *A.* 3,594.

taenia ... qua decoras deuinxerat papillas: the description directs the reader's attention to the lady's *decoras papillas* rather than to the garment she takes off. *Taenia* is an unusual word for *strophium* or *fasciae mamillares* (see *RE* s.v. 'Strophium' 378,44-380,27 [Bieber]; *GCA* 1981,269 on 7,28: 176,1-7 s.v. *fasciam*, with references. See also KlP. s.v. *Fasciae* 4, 517,39 f.). *OLD* s.v. *taenia* 1c gives only our passage for *taenia* meaning 'breast-band'. *LSJ* s.v. ταινία I ('breastband for young girls') mentions, among other passages, Anacreont. 22,13.

Stephens-Winkler 1995,356 point out the similarity between Lollianos *Phoinikaka* B.1 verso 24-25 and our passage. But the similarity goes no further than the one word ταινία since the context in Lollianus is entirely different: the corpse of a young girl is stripped of her clothes, including the ταινία; see also Sandy 1994,1516 n. 7.

lumen propter adsistens: anastrophe of prepositions is found in the *Met.* only in the case of *propter*. *GCA* 1985,28 f. on 8,1 (176,18-20) list all occurrences (except for this one) and refutes Bernhard 1927,28, who regards *propter* as an adverb in all these cases. Anastrophe, especially of di- and trisyllabic prepositions, is found with increasing frequency in poetry from Lucretius onward, and in prose from Tacitus onward (KSt 2,1,586 f.).

stagneo: from *stagnum* 'tin', an alloy of lead and silver. Cf. Plin. *Nat.* 34,159: *plumbi nigri origo duplex est: aut enim sua prouenit uena nec quicquam aliud ex sese parit aut cum argento nascitur mixtisque uenis conflatur. huius qui primus fuit in fornacibus liquor, stagnum appellatur; qui secundus, argentum*. Elsewhere Pliny uses the term *plumbum album* for pure tin, while by *stagneum* he seems to mean the so-called 'Werkblei'; however, in *Nat.* 34,160 *stagnum* must mean 'tin': *stagnum inlitum uasis aereis saporem fecit gratiorem ac compescit uirus aeruginis*. On this problem see Bluemner 1912,4,81 f., and Anm. 6 with references. Cf. also Plin. *Nat.* 29,35 *tum in stagnea pyxide conditur* (sc. *oesypum*). Pl. Frg. inc. 134 (in *Fest.* s.v. *narica*) *muriaticam autem uideo in uasis stagneis*. See also Forbes 1964,135 f.

In the *Onos* (51,4) the woman takes the perfumed ointment ἔκ τινος ἀλαβάστρου; the fact that our author has opted for a *stagneum uasculum* possibly adds another element to the fairy-tale atmosphere of Oriental luxury: tin was mined especially in Britain (Cornwall) but was transported and traded by the Phoenicians. For commercial reasons they kept the metal's sources a secret for a long time: Strabo 3,5,11 tells an anecdote about a Roman captain who followed a Phoenician ship in order to find the source of the tin; through a ruse of the Phoenicians he was shipwrecked.

uasculo: 'jar'; cf. 6,13 (138,13), where Psyche is given a *uasculum* to fetch water. See Callebat 1968,35, with references, for this word from the *sermo cotidianus*. Cf. 2,7 (30,20) *cibarium uasculum* and see Van Mal-Maeder 1998,153 on the erotic connotation of *uasculum* in that passage.

perungit ... perfricat ... perfundit: the repetition of *per-* underlines the carefulness with which the *matrona* performs the preliminaries to their lovemaking.

oleo balsamo: thus F, whose text is adopted here, following Giarratano and Terzaghi. *Balsamum*, the name of the perfume itself, can easily be used in apposition to the general term *oleum*, as Kronenberg already remarked in defense of F's text. Cf. e.g. 5,28 (125,8 f.) *auis ... gauia*; *Fl.* 12,1 *psittacus auis*.

All other editors adopt Cornelissen's conjecture *balsam<in>o*. *Balsaminus* is attested only in Plin. *Nat.* 23,92. Augello 1977,214 defends the conjecture of Cornelissen, pointing out Apuleius' preference for adjectives in *-inus*. ThLL s.v. *balsameus* 1709,71 and s.v. *balsamum* 1710,24 f. suggests *balsam<e>o* in our passage.

Balsamum was not only a widely-used medicine (Plin. *Nat.* 23,92 mentions many applications) but also a much-prized perfume: Plin. *Nat.* 12,111 *sed omnibus odoribus praefertur balsamum*. Cf. 6,11 (136,5 f.) *sed initio noctis e conuiuio nuptiali uino madens et fraglans balsama Venus remeat*. See Kenney 1990,204 on the use of perfume at weddings, and cf. 6,24 (146,19 f., at the wedding of Amor and Psyche) *Gratiae spargebant balsama*. It is possible that our passage suggests a wedding night: in ch. 23 (254,17 f.) the narrator refers to this *matrona* as *illa uxor mea*. In 11,9 (273,4 f.), where during the Isis procession women sprinkle the streets with balsam and other perfumes, the words *geniali balsamo* are used; although Gwyn Griffiths 1975,183 ad loc. interprets *geniali* differently there, he mentions its meaning 'of or connected with marriage' (*OLD* s.v. *genialis* 2). See Adams 1982,159 f. on the description of purely sexual liaisons in terms of marriage.

indidem: GCA 1981,270 on 7,28 (176,1-7) points out the instrumental use of *indidem* and interprets *indidem* thus in our passage. But that is unnecessary: *indidem* refers to *de stagneo uasculo* and means 'from the ... same source or supply...' (*OLD* s.v. *indidem* 2). Cf. ch. 26 (257,19) *indidem de potione gustauit ampliter*.

sed multo tanta impensius cura etiam nares perfundit meas: F's reading is defended by Kronenberg, retained by Helm, Giarratano, and Terzaghi; *tanta* modifies *cura*. Robertson, Frassinetti, and van Thiel Leo's proposal to delete *cura* as a gloss (see, however, on *impensius* below). In this case we have a Plautine idiom (*multo tanta* + comparative; see Petersmann ad Pl. *St.* 339 *multo tanta plus*), found 7,15 (165,12-15); see *GCA* 1981,178 f. ad loc. Augello 1977,214 f. also deletes *cura*: to him, the vulgar word *cura* ('parola indugiosa e ordinaria') is incongruous with *perfundit*, which he feels to be 'strepitoso'. These are subjective arguments.

Hanson follows a conjecture of Wiman: (*meque indidem largissime perfricat*), *sed multo tanta impensius; tura etiam nares perfundit meas*.

impensius: the first meaning of *impense* is 'immoderately, excessively', but an additional, later meaning is 'lavishly', first attested Pers. 6,68 f. *impensius ungue,/ ungue, puer, caules*. See Harvey 1981 ad loc. and Kißel 1990,849, n. 265 with references. If we take *impensius* as 'more generously' in our passage, there is no tautology with *multo tanta ... cura* (see the previous note). It is, then, a subtle hint that the smelly ass needs much more perfume than the lady.

In the margin of φ and in a few other manuscripts are found some lines with an indication that they are to be inserted after *meas*; this passage is generally referred to as the *Spurcum Additamentum*. See App. II.

252,20-253,6 Tunc exosculata pressule, non qualia in lupanari solent basiola iactari uel meretricium poscinummia uel aduentorum nega<n>tinummia, sed pura atque sincera instruit et blandissimos adfatus: 'Amo' et 'Cupio' et 'Te solum diligo' et 'Sine te iam uiuere nequeo' et cetera, quis mulieres et alios inducunt et suas testantur adfectationes,...: Then she kissed me ardently yet gently, not such kisses as are usually given in a brothel, the prostitutes' kisses-at-a-price or their customers' kisses-with-a-hand-on-the-purse – no, she bestowed pure, sincere kisses and the most flattering words on me: 'I am in love with you', and 'I want you', and 'I love you alone', and 'I can no longer live without you', and the other phrases that women use both to lead others on and also to express their own desires, ...

pressule: this adverb is found only in Apuleius' *Met.*: 4,31 (99,12; see Kenney 1990,126 ad loc.), here, and ch. 31 (262,3), where a soft breeze, *adhaerens pressule*, delineates the contours of a dancer's body by blowing her silk garment against it. In *Fl.* 9,22 Apuleius formed the diminutive adjective *pressula* meaning 'somewhat flattened' to tone in with a series of diminutives in *-ul-* (Ferrari 1968,120). Here it seems best to follow *OLD* s.v. *pressule* and take the adverb to mean 'with gentle pressure'. Mart. 6,34,1 mentions *basia ... pressa*, which in view of the context must mean 'many kisses, one after the other': *basia da nobis, Diadumine, pressa. 'quot' inquis? / oceani fluctus me numerare iubes / et maris Aegaei sparsas per litore conchas / et quae Cecropio monte uagantur apes*.

basiola: before Apuleius, this noun is only found in Petr. 85,6 *aggressus simulantem aliquot basiolis inuasi*. ThLL s.v. *basiolum* 1773,68-72 points out *Not.Tir.* 88,64 *basium basiolum* and an inscription on a *gemma* (Leblant nr. 158) *sana me basiolis*.

Abate 1978,76 f. discusses the accumulation of hypocoristic diminutives in this passage: *papillas*; *uasculo*; *pressule*; *basiola*; in ch. 22: *unguiculis* (253,19); *uoculas* (253,22); *palumbulum* (254,1). The love scene between Fotis and Lucius in 2,17 f. also contains many diminutives of this kind (on the connection between these two scenes, see Introd. **2.5.2**).

meretricum poscinummia uel aduentorum negantinummia: this is the only passage in which either *poscinummia* or *negantinummia* is found. The mention of kisses exchanged in a *lupanar* inspired the author to create these Plautine-sounding compounds. This type of formation, in which the first part contains a verbal notion and the second part is governed by that notion, is influenced by the Greek language, according to Friedrich Skutsch 1914,154. What *poscinummia* must mean is quite clear: the verb *poscere* is frequently found in the context of *meretrices*. Cf. Gel. 1,8,3 on the *meretrix* Laïs, who had many admirers: *neque admittebatur nisi qui dabat quod poposcerat*; Catul. 41,1 f.: *Ameana puella defututa / tota milia me decem poposcit*. Cf. Ov. *Am*. 1,10,11 on the negative effect on the lover's feelings when his beloved turns out to have business interests at heart: *cur sim mutatus, quaeris? quia munera poscis*; Juv. 6,125 *excepit blanda intrantes atque aera poposcit* (see Courtney ad loc.). The adjective *negantinummia*, created for the sake of parallelism, is less obvious: it is possible that the clients by their way of kissing avoid seeming too much in love, lest it cost them more money; another possibility is the translation 'calculating kisses', by which a customer does his best to make the *meretrix* forget to ask for money. See also Facchini Tosi 1962,151 f. with references.

Bernhard 1927,138 f. fully shares Norden's opinion (1915,602) about the 'tyrannische Selbstgefälligkeit' with which Apuleius revels in neologisms, especially in the *Met*. Callebat 1964,357 explains Apuleius' linguistic creativity from the author's familiarity with the comic authors, especially Plautus (who also shows great spontaneity in his vocabulary). Marache 1957,271 f. notes the same trait in Fronto and even more in Gellius, both of whom created many neologisms in spite of Fronto's theoretical objections against them: 'Leur rupture avec la langue classique, absolument fixée et définie dans tous les termes, les aurait remis en contact avec les forces vives du latin naissant.' In this respect Apuleius enthusiastically continues a tendency of his time. See also Kenney 1990 (Introd. *Cupid and Psyche*),29.

negantinummia: Lipsius' emendation of *negatinummia* in F is generally accepted.

pura atque sincera: 'pure and sincere', i.e. without ulterior motives (in contrast with the calculating kisses of the prostitute and her customer; see above).

Both adjectives are carefully chosen to express the narrator's sense of the *matrona*'s purity. Except for 8,29 (201,3) and 9,8 (208,6; see *GCA* 1995,83 ad loc.), where the superlative of the adjective is used ironically of the appalling priests of the *Dea Syria*, *purus* and its adverb do not occur in the *Met*. until book 11, in connection with Isis (11,10: 273,19 f. *linteae uestis candore puro luminosi*; 11,16: 278,17-21 *nauem ... purissime purificatam*; 11,21: 283,18 *purissimae religionis secreta*; 11,23: 284,25-27 *me ... purissime circumrorans abluit*). See *GCA* 1985,289 with n. 11 on the terminology (which is meaningful in the *Met*.) surrounding *(im)purus*.

There may be a deliberate allusion to Catul. 78a,1 f. *sed nunc id doleo, quod purae pura puellae / sauia conminxit spurca saliua tua*, where the poet apparently is indignant at a foul lover who kisses a 'pura puella', and develops a contrast by *p*-alliteration for the girl and *s*-alliteration for the lover who does not deserve her. In the next chapter our narrator will develop the grotesque contrast between this dainty *matrona* and the ass's body.

Sincera also deserves attention: it is hapax legomenon in the *Met.* The adjective is used once in the *Apology* for the purity of the Platonic idea of Beauty: *Apol.* 12,5 *eius pulchritudinis, quam prius ueram et sinceram inter deos uidere.* In *Pl.* 1,15 (213) the combination *purus atque sincerus* is used in a concrete sense: 'free from harmful substances' (the liver); *Pl.* 2,3 (224) has *neque sinceras ... uirtutes* (i.e. mixed with improper elements). In *Mun.* 3 (295) and 8 (306), *sincerus* is used of clear light and pure air respectively.

The emphasis on the purity of the *matrona*'s feelings, which is absent in the corresponding passage in the *Onos*, induces many interpreters to see the unexpected tenderness of this love scene as 'a crucial step in his (sc. Lucius') progress to Isis' (see Shumate 1996,126 with references in nn. 15 and 16). See, however, the notes below on our narrator's naiveté, with a more ironic interpretation of this entire passage.

adfatus: a poetic noun, not found in prose before Fronto (*Ep. ad Ant. Imp.* 1,2,1: 87,9 vdH. 1988) *uestro conspectu et adfatu*, and [Quint.] *Decl.* (15,9; Håkanson 312,12). *ThLL* s.v. *affatus* 1174,33 f. mentions as its first occcurrence Verg. *A.* 4,283 f. *quo nunc reginam ambire furentem / audeat adfatu?*; after that, Sen. *Med.* 187, some passages in V.Fl., and numerous passages in Stat. *Theb.* Apuleius uses it only in the *Met.*: in addition to our passage also 3,5 (55,22 f.); 3,10 (59,23); 4,11 (82,26); 4,33 (101,5); and 5,4 (106,12).

Amo ... Cupio ... Te solum diligo ... Sine te iam uiuere nequeo: the woman's utterances form a sequence with an increasing number of syllables (2,3,6,10).

There is irony at the level of the abstract author (see Introd. **3.2**): the naive narrator describes the woman's kisses as *pura atque sincera*, but immediately afterwards he quotes, in direct discourse, some truly banal formulas used by the woman (see the following notes).

Te solum diligo: here is a woman who really *diligit bestiam*; cf. 5,21 (119,15: Psyche's dilemma) *in eodem corpore odit bestiam, diligit maritum.* The use of *diligere* rather than *amare* is significant and adds to the remarkable tenderness of the scene: *diligere* is used of love of 'a spiritual, non-physical quality'; thus Quinn, with references, on Catul. 72,3 f. *dilexi tum te non tantum ut uulgus amicam, / sed pater ut gnatos diligit et generos.*

Sine te iam uiuere nequeo: a traditional assurance given by lovers. In the Greek novel this motif can be found in many variations, e.g. Xen. *Eph.* 1,11,3-6; Ach. Tat. 3,10 and 17; Heliod. 5,24; Longus 2,39,1. In love poetry, too, such protestations of devotion are often mentioned in retrospect by the deceived lover, when they have been found to be empty. Catul. 45 plays with this motif (see Quinn's commentary on this poem). See also Ov. *Am.* 3,11a,31 f. *desine blanditias et uerba, potentia quondam, / perdere - non ego sum stultus, ut ante fui!* Cf. also Ter. *Ad.* 332 *qui sine hac iurabat se unum numquam uicturum diem!* (thus Sostrata, disappointed in her lover). Cf. Petr. 127,4 (Circe about Encolpius' love for Giton) *sine quo non potes uiuere.*

quis ... inducunt: on 'verbal stimulation' in lovemaking see Kay 1985,279 on Mart. 11,104,11 *nec motu dignaris opus nec uoce iuuare*; cf. Ov. *Ars* 3,795 f. *nec blandae uoces iucundaque murmura cessent, / nec taceant mediis improba uerba iocis.*

quis: see on *quis* (= *quibus*) ch. 27 (258,11).

inducunt: *GCA* 1985,133 on 8,14 (187,19-24) discuss the connotation of deceit which is often found in *inducere* in the *Met.*, and include our passage (see also comm. on ch. 8: 243,14 *inductos seruuli mendacio*). Here the situation is ambiguous: the narrator, from his point of view as 'experiencing I' (see Introd. **3.5**), delights in the *matrona*'s sincere love (cf. *pura atque sincera* above, with notes) and takes *inducunt* neutrally as 'bring into a (specific) state of mind, stimulate'; cf. also the following *et suas testantur adfectationes* and e.g. 3,26 (71,19) *agnitione ac miseratione quadam inductum*. Central in this passage is the naiveté of the ass, who allows himself to be completely taken in by the lady, assuming that her sweet words and gestures are signs of sincere love, whereas the reader (and especially the re-reader) sees through *sine te iam uiuere nequeo* etc. as empty words and takes *inducere* in its meaning 'lead on'. In the *Onos* the ironization of the naive narrator is absent: (51,5) εἶτά με καὶ ἐφίλησεν καὶ οἷα πρὸς αὑτῆς ἐρώμενον καὶ ἄνθρωπον διελέγετο.

adfectationes: this is the only occurrence of *adfectatio* in Apuleius' works. This word, too, can be ambiguous (see the previous note): it can mean 'striving, aspiration', but also (in rhetoric) 'straining after effect, affectation'. See Zundel 1989 s.v. *affectatio* for Quintilian's use of this term.

253,6-10 ...capistroque me prehensum more, quo didiceram, reclinat facile, quippe cum nil noui nihilque difficile facturus mihi uiderer, praesertim post tantum temporis tam formonsae mulieris cupientis amplexus obiturus;:
... and she took me by my halter and made me lie down in the way I had learned, easily, because I felt I was going to do nothing new and nothing difficult, especially because after so much time I was about to devote myself to the eager embraces of so lovely a woman.

capistroque me prehensum: the last reference to the *capistrum*. The word occurred a few times in the previous books, where it concretized the ass's subjection to his temporary owners and his being at the mercy of their whims. Here, too, the phrase clarifies the relationship. Cf. the first mention of the *capistrum*: Charite tugs at the *capistrum* of the ass, to have him change direction, thus thwarting their flight: 6,29 (151,14 f.) *me adrepto capistro dirigere dextrorsum magnopere gestiebat*; in 7,18 (168,5 f.) the ass's tormentor (the evil *puer*) maltreats him when he slips and falls: *cum deberet egregius agaso manum porrigere, capistro suspendere, cauda subleuare ... nullum quidem defesso mihi ferebat auxilium*; in 7,25 (173,8 f.) the *pastores* reclaim the ass from the *uiator* who had found him: *statimque me cognitum capistro prehensum attrahere gestiunt*; in 9,4 (205,13 f.) the ass submits to being handled by the *cinaedi* in order to show he is not suffering from rabies: *et plausus manum et aurium flexus et ductum capistri et quiduis aliud periclitantium placide patiebar*.

capistro: see *GCA* 1981,250 on 7,25 (173,6-9) for the etymology of this noun, which is probably connected with *capere*.

more, quo didiceram: if taken with *reclinat*, this phrase refers to the training of the ass described in ch. 17; cf. 249,29 f.: *et primum me quidem mensam accumbere ... perdocuit*. It is also possible, however, to take it with *capistroque me prehensum*, in which case the narrator refers with some bitterness to the occasions when he was taken by the halter.

nil noui nihilque difficile: the partitive genitive of third-declension adjectives is very rare; the partitive genitive of nominalized adjectives like *bonum, malum, nouum*, on the other hand, is attested from Plautus onward. See Löfstedt [2]1942,110 f. and LHSz 2,57 f. with references.

post tantum temporis tam formonsae mulieris cupientis amplexus obiturus: with these words the narrator himself reminds his audience of the love scenes between Lucius and Fotis before the metamorphosis, which are mirrored by this love scene (see Introd. **2.5.2**).

The momentary delight and rapture are still carefully maintained throughout the chapter; the grotesque aspects of the situation and the ass's worries about his coarse body are not yet mentioned (ch. 22). Nevertheless, the references to Lucius' earlier assignations, enjoyed while he still had a man's body, are already drawing the reader's attention to the difference between the two situations.

formonsae: for the orthography of this adjective and its occurrences in the *Met.*, see GCA 1977,203 on 4,27 (95,24-25) with references. See also Coleman (in the Introduction to his commentary on Verg. *Ecl.*) 39, and Kenney 1990,117 on 4,28 (96,24).

formonsae mulieris cupientis amplexus: if *cupientis* is taken as an accusative (see the translation) with *amplexus*, both nouns are qualified by an adjective. Thus Vallette: 'les avides embrassements d'une si belle femme', and Hanson: 'the passionate embraces of a very beautiful woman'. A comparable phrase is found in 9,16 (215,1) *tuas uolentes amplexus*. Other translators take both qualifications with *mulieris*.

amplexus ... obiturus: the combination *obire amplexus* is attested in Apuleius only (*ThLL* s.v. *amplexus* 1998,34). See also 9,24 (221,6 f.) *furtiuos amplexus obiret* with GCA 1995,212 ad loc.; cf. ch. 34 (265,14) *obeundi ... concubitus*.

253,10-12 ... nam et uino pulcherrimo atque copioso memet madefeceram et ungento flagrantissimo prolubium libidinis suscitaram: For not only had I drenched myself in an abundance of excellent wine, but through the extremely fragrant ointment I had also aroused my appetite for lust.

The parallelism of the two parts of this sentence, *nam et uino ... memet madefeceram* (20 syllables) and *et unguento ... prolubium ... suscitaram* (21 syllables), suggests a great personal effort on the ass's part to get into the right mood; actually, the *matrona* had taken the initiative in using sweet-scented ointments to arouse desire. As has been noted on several occasions, parallelism and rhyme (*madefeceram - suscitaram*) are achieved at the expense of intelligibility; see comm. on ch. 15 (248,8-10).

Within the parallel sentences, polysyndeton and climax are present, along with rhyme: *et uino pulcherrimo ... et ungento flagrantissimo*. The superlative *flagrantissimo* is attested here for the first time; see Facchini Tosi 1962, 111 f. with references.

uino ... memet madefeceram: in the love scene with Fotis, too, Lucius reaches a state of physical excitement by drinking an abundance of wine: 2,16 (38,2 f.) *sequens et tertium inter nos uicissim et frequens alternat poculum, cum ego iam uino madens nec animo tantum, uerum etiam corpore ipso pronus ad libidinem ... inquam...* See also on *cenati* ch. 20 (252,3).

uino pulcherrimo atque copioso: at the table of Thiasus (see on *e triclinio domini decesseramus* ch. 20: 252,3). One of the ass's tricks was *sitiensque pocillatore respecto, ciliis alterna coniuens, bibere flagitarem* (ch. 17: 250,5 f.).

pulcherrimo: the man within the ass knows how to appreciate good wine. *Pulcher* is often used of food of superior quality; see Monteil 1964,87. Cf. e.g. Plin. *Nat.* 14,92 *uinum pulchrum*; Cato *Agr.* 104,2 *acetum acerrimum et pulcherrimum erit*; Hor. *S.* 1,5,89 *panis longe pulcherrimus*.

memet madefeceram: alliteration.

madefeceram: Ovid was the first to use *madefacere* in the sense of *potum reddere*, *inebriare* (see *ThLL* s.v. *madefacio* 31,62 f.) in *Ars* 3,765 *turpe iacens mulier multo madefacta Lyaeo*. Columella (10,309) imitated Ovid with the variation *multo madefactus Iaccho*. In addition to Ov. and Col., *ThLL* ibid. mentions only our passage; Amm. 15,3,7 *poculis amplioribus madefacti*; and Greg. Tur. *Franc.* 9,6. A dubious case is Sil. 12,18 *molli luxu madefacta meroque*: here, *madefacere* may be used metaphorically in the more frequent meaning of (*umore*) *emollire, dissoluere, digerere*.

ungento: thus F and φ. In φ, a manus recentissima added *u*, which Helm adopts in his text, as do Brandt-Ehlers and Hanson. Other editors rightly retain *ungento*, which is accepted by Helm and others in 4,27 (95,22); see *GCA* 1977,202 ad loc.

flagrantissimo: thus F and φ. Helm (followed by Hanson) 'corrects' here with Van der Vliet, reading *fraglantissimo*. *GCA* 1977,210 f., with references, discuss *flagrare, fraglare* = *ardere* and *flagrare, fraglare* = *olere* in the mss. of Apuleius and other authors, and accept the variants of F in the orthography of both verbs.

prolubium libidinis: sound-play.

prolubium: this noun, meaning 'tendency to..., liking for...', is found in Apuleius' works only here. It occurs in Ter. *Ad.* 985 in an imitation of Caecil. (*com.* 91) *quod prolubium? quae istaec subitast largitas?*, where it means *promptus animus ad largiendum*, as Donatus ad loc. remarks (for this passage in Terence and for the confusion in the mss. between *proluuium* and *prolubium*, see Carilli 1980,55 f., who defends *prolubium*). See Marache 1957,128 f. on *prolubium* in Gellius, who uses the word (which is found in comic authors but also in Acc. *trag.* 106) more than once. Cf. e.g. Gel. 4,11,10 *Empedoclen ... a rei ueneriae prolubio uoluisse homines deducere*; 16,19,13 *immanes nauitas* (sc. the crew of Arion's ship) *prolubium tamen audiendi subit*.

CHAPTER XXII

A night of passion.

253,12-20 Sed angebar plane non exili metu reputans, quem ad modum tantis tamque magnis cruribus possem delicatam matronam inscendere uel tam lucida tamque tenera et lacte ac melle confecta membra duris ungulis complecti labiasque modicas ambroseo rore purpurantes tam amplo ore tamque enormi et saxeis dentibus deformi[s] sauiari, nouissime quo pacto, quanquam ex unguiculis perpruriscens, mulier tam uastum genitale susciperet: But I felt quite anxious, reflecting with great fear how, with so many and such huge legs, I would be able to mount the delicate lady, or embrace her body of milk and honey, so translucent and so tender, with my hard hooves, and kiss her dainty lips, gleaming red and ambrosia-bedewed, with such a large mouth, so enormous and misshapen because of its rock-like teeth; and finally, how the woman, even if she was titillated from top to toe, could receive such a formidable penis.

With much humor, the author of the *Met.* expands upon the incongruous bodies of the unusual couple. For the first time since the metamorphosis (3,24) the ass's external appearance is described in great detail, but here the description is concentrated upon the elements of the ass's body that are relevant to the embraces with the *matrona* and thus enhances the grotesque contrast between the dainty lady and the coarse ass. The description culminates in the enormous phallus, typical of the ass, which is now (though only briefly) a cause for concern. In 3,24 (70,16 f.) the description of the metamorphosis ended with the same physical part, but there it was regarded by the narrator as the only advantage of his ass's body: *nec ullum miserae reformationis uideo solacium, nisi quod mihi iam nequeunti tenere Fotidem natura crescebat* (see also below, on *teneo*). In the description of the re-metamorphosis in 11,13 (276,4 f.) this physical part is not referred to, although everything else is mentioned that decreases in size when the ass becomes a man again: in that context of *abstinentia* and chastity the priapic aspect of the ass is no longer of interest. On the ass as the animal of Priapus, see the Bömer 1957,46 f. on Ov. *Fast.* 2.

After Loukios' re-metamorphosis in the *Onos*, the loss of his large ass's member (56,6 ἐκεῖνό ... τὸ μέγα τοῦ ὄνου σύμβολον) plays a crucial role in the wealthy lady's rejection of him after he regains his human body; it is remarkable therefore that in this passage the narrator of the *Onos* fails to mention this aspect of the ass as a cause for worry: *Onos* (51,7) has only καὶ σφόδρα ἠπόρουν ὅπως ἀναβήσομαι τὴν ἄνθρωπον. This is followed by the remark (absent in the *Met.*) that Loukios, since becoming an ass, has not mated even with female asses; after that, the fear is expressed (as in *Met.*, below) that he will be punished if the woman is injured by their coupling.

On the basis of this passage, Scobie 1978,219 f. discusses the 'faithful and elegant' translation by López de Cortegana (1525): 'Perhaps because Cortegana had been too faithful to his original, his translation was put on the Index Expurg., published at Seville in 1559'.

Sed angebar: the so-called 'gedeckte Anfangsstellung' of the finite verb (a term borrowed by Bernhard 1927,11 f. from Kroll 1918) is functionally just as noticeable as an 'open' Anfangsstellung (see Panhuis 1982,148, who refers to KSt 2,601): as a 'real sentence constituent', *angebar* is in fact placed first in the sentence, the preceding *sed* merely emphasizing its contrastive function. *Angebar* makes a strong contrast with the previous passage, which was filled with ecstasy and delight; now we are suddenly aware of a distressing anxiety.

plane: see on *plane* ch. 15 (248,1).

non exili metu: cf. ch. 14 (247,3) *suspicio non exilis*. On litotes in the *Met.* see on *non mediocri quaestui* ch. 19 (251,15).

tantis ... cruribus - delicatam matronam (inscendere) ... tam lucida ... membra - duris ungulis (complecti): a chiastic formation: the ass's legs – the delicate *matrona* with her tender *membra* – the ass's hard hooves. Thus, the ass's coarse limbs embrace the *matrona* also in the word formation.

tantis tamque magnis cruribus: *tantis* is used here in the sense of *tot* (see Callebat 1968,289 with references) and *tam magnis* stands for *tantis*. GCA 1977,65 on 4,7 (79,17-20), with references, discuss this passage and remark that, while many translators miss the point, Vallette translates correctly 'avec tant et de si grand jambes'. See also Hanson: 'with so many and such large legs'. A comic hyperbole for our quadriped's limbs.

tam magnus is colloquial; cf. Mart. 11,60,9 *exorare, dei, si uos tam magna liceret* with Kay 1985,203 ad loc., with references.

tamque: this passage has *tam* six times, with the adjectives qualifying alternately the delicate lady and the coarse ass. To the reader (reading aloud) this repeated *tam* keeps 'hammering away' at the huge differences between the two partners.

delicatam: see on *delicata* ch. 20 (252,7).

matronam: see comm. on ch. 19 (251,20) *matrona*.

inscendere: in the sexual sense 'mount, cover' the verb is used only here and 7,21 (170,13 f.); see ThLL s.v. *inscendo* 1839,14 f. Thus it is one of several reminiscences of the passage (7,21) where the ass's tormentor, the evil *puer*, accuses him of attempts to rape passers-by. Many of the insinuations made by the *puer* are repeated in our passage. In the earlier passage the narrator emphasized that those insinuations were blatant lies; in our passage the narrator underlines the strong initial reserve on the part of the ass and the very active role played by the *matrona* (see also on *iam dudum praestolantem ... matronam* ch. 20: 252,4). Other recurring terms from 7,21 are *angebar* (cf. 169,26 *angit*, where the *puer* expresses his anxiety about the ass's alleged amorous assaults on passers-by, whereas here it is the ass himself who is anxious; these are the two only occurrences of *ango* in the *Met.*); *tenera* (170,2 *tener*); *sauiari* (170,7 *sauii*); *ungulis* (170,16 *ungulis*); below, *dirrupta* (170,17 *dirupta*).

lacte et melle confecta: an interesting expression: the lady's *membra* are not *lactea* or *mellita* but 'genuinely' consisting of milk and honey. One might have expected *uelut* or *ut* here. Cf. Enn. *Ann.* 10,352 *erubuit ceu lacte et purpura mixta*. *Lacteus* is already used of skin by Vergil (e.g. *A.* 8,660). Cf. in the *Met.* 3,14 (62,13 f., Lucius to Fotis) *tuam plumeam lacteamque ... cutem* with Van der Paardt 1971,108 ad loc.; 5,22 (120,15) *ceruices lacteas* with Kenney 1990,169 f. ad loc.

In the sense of *fieri, componi*, the verb *confici* is usually construed with *e(x)* plus ablative, but ThLL s.v. *conficio* 200,23 f. mentions also passages with the ablative without *e(x)*, e.g. Cic. *Tusc.* 1,42 *corpora nostra terreno principiorum genere confecta*; Lucr. 4,291 *aeribus binis ... res confit utraque*.

labiasque modicas ambroseo rore purpurantes / tam amplo ore tamque enormi et saxeis dentibus deformi: for someone reading aloud, the contrast in appearance is matched by a contrast in sound: the early words can be read in a smooth flow, the line ends in sounds that repeat themselves (*ambroseo rore pur-purantes*), and the prevailing consonants are labials. The second part of the sentence moves along more jerkily because of the number of dentals, the repetition of *tam*, and the hiatus in *amplo ore*.

labias ... ambroseo rore purpurantes: exalted and poetic language makes the contrast between the ass and the *matrona* as strong as possible: here she almost becomes a divinity (see Lieberg 1962 on the deification of the beloved in Latin literature; see also Lyne 1980,308, n. 20 on this topos in love poetry). Apuleius is the first to use the adjective *ambroseus* in prose. See (also for the spelling *-eus* instead of *-ius*) GCA 1985,101 on 8,9 (184,14-17). There Charite refers to the *ambroseum corpus* of her deceased husband; it becomes quite clear from the context that she reveres him as a deity. Elsewhere in the *Met.*, the adjective *ambroseus* and the noun *ambrosia* are used only of divine beings: 5,22 (120,14), see Vallette's note ad loc.; 6,23 (146,10), see Kenney 1990,223 ad loc.; 11,4 (269,9: Isis). In ch. 31 (261,25 f.) the adjective is used to describe the dancer acting the part of Venus: *gratia coloris ambrosei designans Venerem*. From this last passage it becomes clear that *color ambroseus* does not refer to something red but, instead, to a 'divine complexion' (Vallette: 'l'immortel éclat de son teint'). Our passage, therefore, does not mean that the woman's lips were red from *ambrosia* (see also below on *purpurantes*). Of the qualities of this food (or drink; cf. the discussion in Athen. 2,8) of the gods, its sweetness in particular was stereotypical, in addition to its ability to confer immortality. Cf. e.g. Catul. 99,2 *suauiolum dulci dulcius ambrosia*.

purpurantes: as a qualification of the lips it probably means 'red', but also 'gleaming, shining'. Cf. *EV* s.v. *purpureus* [Masselli]; see also Edgeworth 1979 with references.

The intransitive *purpurare* is also found Col. 10,101 *quae pallit humi, quae frondens purpurat auro, ponatur uiola*; there, too, *purpurare* means in the first place 'shine, glow'. Apuleius uses this rare, poetic verb once more in the *Met.* but in a transitive sense: 6,24 (146,19) *Horae rosis et ceteris floribus purpurabant omnia*.

saxeis dentibus: here, *saxeus* refers in particular to the size of the (ass's) teeth: 'as big as boulders'. Cf. *B.Afr.* 47,1 *nimbus cum saxea grandine subito est exortus*, where *saxeus* clearly refers to the magnitude of the hailstones. This hyperbolical expression is found again at the re-metamorphosis: 11,13 (276,10 f.) *dentes saxei redeunt ad humanam minutiem*. In Ovid's *Met.*, *saxeus* belongs to the typical 'Termini der Metamorphosensprache' (Bömer ad Ov. *Met.* 4,557). In 'De verliefde Ezel', Couperus has Charmides say in his description of his metamorphosis: '... en mijn tanden vierkantten zich tot mozaiekstenen zo groot...'. Elsewhere in the *Met.*, *saxeus* means 'made of stone' (4,24: 93,14 f. *saxeo carcere*), 'hard as stone' (6,12: 137,11), or 'full of rocks, stony' (7,17: 167,9).

nouissime: 'finally', used for the last item in an enumeration. Apuleius uses it only here, and at *Soc.* 24 (177). On this adverb from colloquial language, see Callebat 1968,176 with examples from Cicero's letters onward.

quanquam ... perpruriscens: for *quamquam*, *quamuis* with a participle see on *quanquam ... suffarcinatus* ch. 16 (249,3); for the spelling *quanquam* see on *quanquam* ch. 14 (247,4).

ex unguiculis perpruriscens: an unmistakable reference to Pl. *St.* 760 f. (the only other attested passage for *perpruriscere*): *cantionem aliquam occupito cinaedicam,/ ubi perpruriscamus usque ex unguiculis*. See Petersmann ad loc. and cf. Otto 1890,355 f. for the expression 'to one's fingertips', i.e 'all over'. Cf. Petr. 102,13 *a capillis usque ad ungues*. The allusion to Plautus adds two more points of contrast between the *matrona* and the ass: her *unguiculis* are opposed to his *duris ungulis*; and while she is *perpruriscens*, he is mainly diffident (see above on *inscendere*).

tam uastum genitale: for this conspicuous characteristic of the ass, see the introductory remark to this chapter.

genitale: opposed to the *matrona*'s lustfulness, suggested by *ex unguiculis perpruriscens*, is the ass's bashfulness: the narrator uses a polite word for his large penis. On *genitale*, which is found from Celsus onward and especially frequently in Pliny in the *Nat.*, see Adams 1982,59 f. with references, who calls the use of the word here 'a polite euphemism'. The plural *genitalia*, referring to the *testiculi*, is used 7,23 (171,12); see *GCA* 1981,232 ad loc.

253,20-21 Heu me, qui dirrupta nobili femina bestiis obiectus munus instructurus sim mei domini: Woe is me, when I have broken this well-born woman apart, I will be thrown to the beasts and thus be part of the show offered by my master.

Heu me, qui ... instructurus sim: the thoughts of Lucius the *actor* are represented by the narrator in direct discourse. This homodiegetic-actorial narrative enhances the suspense for the linear reader (see Introd. **3.5**). For the re-reader, who knows that the ass will indeed have to perform in Thiasus' *munus* but that this will be a consequence of his most satisfactory lovemaking with the *matrona*, this is a case of dramatic irony.

qui dirrupta: the emendation by ς for *quid irrupta* in F (φ has *quid dirrupta*).

dirrupta: on the spelling with *-rr-*, also attested elsewhere, see *GCA* 1985,200 (with references) on 8.23 (195,12-14). The fear expressed here, that the ass will *dirumpere* the woman, is also mentioned (as a narrowly averted mishap) in the *puer*'s false accusations about the ass: 7,21 (170,16 f.) *misera illa compauita atque dirupta* (referring to a woman who, according to the *puer*, had been assaulted by the ass). On the connections between the two passages, see above on *inscendere*. Adams 1982,150 f. discusses the various sexual meanings of *dirumpere*. Pl. *Cas.* 326 has *diruptam* as a metaphorical equivalent of *fututam*: *ego edepol illam mediam dirruptam uelim* (Adams compares Priap. 54,2 *qui medium uult te scindere*). Here (and 7,21) Apuleius uses *dirrupta* literally to describe a putative physical effect of *fututio*.

253,21-254,3 Molles interdum uoculas et adsidua sauia et dulces gannitus commorsicantibus oculis iterabat illa, et in summa: 'Teneo te', inquit, 'teneo, meum palumbulum, meum passarem' et cum dicto uanas fuisse cogitationes meas ineptumque monstrat metum: Meanwhile, she redoubled her tender words and continuous kisses and gentle cries with gazes that touched me to the quick – in short, she said: 'I've got you, I've got you, my little dove, my sparrow', and as she spoke she demonstrated that my worries had been unfounded and my fear foolish.

Molles ... uoculas: cf. Ov. *Am.* 1,12,22 *molliaque ad dominam uerba ferenda dedi* (i.e. to the writing tablet). Another example of *uoculas* in an erotic context are the *delicatas uoculas* which the ass tries to whinny to Charite in 6,28 (149,25 f.); see *GCA* 1981,48 ad loc. See also on *quis...inducunt* ch. 21 (253,5).

uoculas: here, and in the passage cited above, the plural of the diminutive has the value of 'sweet, coaxing words', as in e.g. Gel. 17,20,6 *non ad uocularum eius amoenitatem nec ad uerborum uenustates deuorsitandum (est)*. Elsewhere Apuleius uses the singular, meaning 'small, squeaky voice', as in 4,7 (79,23; see *GCA* 1977,67 ad loc.); in this sense, *uocula* is attested first in Titin. *com.* 172 *feminina fabulare succrotilla uocula*. After that, the *ThLL* material gives occurrences in Cicero for both meanings. Cf. e.g. Cic. *Att.* 2,23,1 *recreandae uoculae causa* and *Fam.* 2,16,2 *incurrit haec nostra laurus non solum in oculos, sed iam etiam in uoculas maleuolorum*.

dulces gannitus: *gannitus* is used in an erotic context also at 2,15 (37,11 f.). Apuleius is the first to use *gannitus* and *gannire* for (inarticulate) human sounds. *ThLL* s.v. *gannitus* 1692,42 f. remarks that in this use *gannitus* corresponds with *garritus*. See Van der Paardt 1971,152 on 3,20 (67,12) and *GCA* 1977,24 on 4,1 (74,13-15) with references; see Van Mal - Maeder 1998,237 on 2,15 (37,11 f.), who cites in this connection *Anth. Lat.* 712,15 (Riese), a poem attributed to Apuleius (see also Mattiacci 1985,270).

commorsicantibus oculis: *commorsicare* is attested in Apuleius only, here and 7,16 (166,21; see *GCA* 1981,190 ad loc.) In the latter passage it is used when the ass is really bitten, by a horse. But cf. 2,10 (33,7: Fotis looking at Lucius) *morsicantibus oculis*. Likewise, *morsicare* is attested nowhere except *Fest.* 60,12 L. Cf. also 7,21 (170,7-8, where the *puer* accuses the ass falsely; see above on *inscendere*) *nam imaginem etiam sauii mentiendo ore improbo compulsat ac morsicat* with *GCA* 1981,220 ad loc. The translation 'with looks that touched me to the quick' is inspired by Beroaldus' interpretation of 2,10 (33,7; see above): 'Significantissimo vocabulo vim venustorum oculorum expressit, qui illices sunt veneris et potentissimum amoris incitamentum, quorum fulgor et amabilis intuitus quodam quasi morsu vitalia populatur et morsicatim medullas depascitur'. See Krautter 1971,110 f. about more of these sensitive comments by Beroaldus. Compare with this Oudendorp's interpretation (reacting to Beroaldus) of the same phrase in 2,10: 'malim ego intellegere oculos mobiles, identidem se aperientes claudentesque, oris manducantis instar'.

in summa: 'to make a long story short'. With an extremely pragmatic adverbial phrase (hapax legomenon in Apuleius) the narrator summarizes the woman's extensive efforts to get the ass in the right mood. See Nordeblad 1932,90 about this expression from colloquial language (e.g. Gaius 1,47 *in summa sciendum est*), which is frequent in Cicero's letters, Pliny the Younger, Quintilian, and in the pseudo-Quintilian *Declamationes*.

Teneo te ..., teneo: the repetition gives the woman's words an affective connotation. See LHSz 2,809 f. on the development of this colloquial turn of speech into a rhetorical figure.

Teneo: here unmistakably erotic in connotation; cf. Tib. 2,6,52 *quisue meam teneat, quot teneatue modis* (see Adams 1982,181 f. for words meaning 'holding, embracing' used as euphemisms for *coitus*). Cf. also Mart. 11,40,1 f. *formosam Glyceran amat Lupercus / et solus tenet imperatque solus*. In the *Met.* 5,13 (114,3: Psyche to her unknown lover) *teneo te, meum lumen*. But the repetition of *teneo te...* by the *matrona* also expresses that she has the ass in her power, thus reminding the reader of the other love affair in the *Met.*: in 3,19 (66,16-67,3) Lucius confesses to Fotis that she has him completely in her power: *semper alioquin spretorem matronalium amplexuum sic ... in seruilem modum addictum atque mancipatum teneas uolentem* (see Introd. **2.5.2**). For *teneo* 'in the meaning of *uinculis amoris obstrictum sibi tenere*', see Van der Paardt 1971,117 on 3,15 (63,14) *teneor*, with references.

We see here a reversal in relation to 3,24 (70,16 f.), cited at the beginning of this chapter: there the recently transformed ass regrets that he is no longer able to *tenere* Fotis; here, against Lucius' expectations, the Corinthian *matrona* is perfectly able to *tenere* him with his huge sexual organ.

meum palumbulum, meum passarem: these pet names used by the woman have a comical effect after the narrator's detailed description of the ass's huge, coarse body. But love makes blind, as ironically illustrated by Lucr. 4,1155-1169.

palumbulum: this diminutive is attested in Apuleius only, here and 8,26 (197,26; see *GCA* 1985,228 ad loc.). There, the priests of the Dea Syria call themselves the *palumbuli* of their leader, referring to their sexual relation with him. Apparently Apuleius wished to create a special pet name for the two bizarre erotic situations. Abate 1978,29 f. discusses the frequency of new diminutives in the *Met*. See the next note for the *salacitas* of doves mentioned in Plin. *Nat*. 10,104 f.

passarem: all editors adopt *passerem*, the correction by a later hand in F. But the original reading in F (and also in φ) may go back to a variant spelling already current in Apuleius' time (see *GCA* 1985,144 on 8,15: 188,15 f.) and accordingly is retained here.

In 8,15 *passares* are among the pet animals taken along by Charite's *familia* on its flight. See *GCA* 1985,228, with references, for the possible meaning of *passer* (probably a small songbird) and for the Roman custom of keeping such birds as pets (for children). Cf. the famous poem by Catullus (2) on Lesbia's *passer*. In 6,6 (132,23 f.) *passeres* accompany the chariot of Venus: *currum deae prosequentes gannitu constrepenti lasciuiunt passeres*; see Kenney 1990,197 ad loc., with references, about the notorious lasciviousness of sparrows. But other songbirds were also called *passeres* (see *OLD* s.v. *passer* 1). In calling the ass *meum passarem*, the amorous *matrona* undoubtedly refers also to the salaciousness of the *passer*, thus encouraging the ass to *lasciuire*. See also Opelt 1965,121 and n. 27 with references. Cf. Plin. *Nat*. 10,107, where the *salacitas* of *passeres* is equated with that of *columbae* and *turtures* discussed in his previous chapters.

As a pet name, *passer* is found e.g. Pl. *Cas*. 138: *meu' pullus passer, mea columba, mi lepos*. A lively debate continues among scholars about the possible obscene connotation of *passer* (= *mentula*) because of Catul. 2,2 f. and Mart. 1,7,3; 11,6,16. Adams 1982,32 f. challenges this view and gives the relevant references. In an extensive note, Kay 1985,75 f. on Mart. 11,6,16 *donabo tibi passerem Catulli* argues in favour of the ambiguity of *passerem* in that passage.

cum dicto: 'suiting the action to the word'. As she is saying *teneo te...*, she shows that she can truly hold him, as the next sentence shows.

254,3-4 Artissime namque complexa totum me prorsus, sed totum recepit: For she clung to me very tightly and received me entirely, but fully and entirely.

complexa totum me ... recepit: cf. *Onos* 51,9 περιβάλλεται με καὶ ἄρασα εἴσω ὅλον παρεδέξατο.

totum me ... recepit: as if penetrated by a weapon, cf. e.g. Cic. *S. Rosc*. 33 *quod non totum telum corpore recepisset*. See *OLD* s.v. *recipio* 4b for additional examples.

Many have associated the expression here with a fragment of Sisenna (*Mil*. 10) *eum penitus utero suo recepit*. But Mason in *AAGA* 1978,7 (= Mason 1998,228) questions the parallel and wonders whether *utero recipere* in the Sisenna fragment might not refer rather to conception.

totum me prorsus, sed totum: see *GCA* 1981,162 on 7,12 (163,16-17), with references, for this affirmative function of *sed* (KSt 2,2,76 f.; LHSz 2,487). See also Van der Paardt 1981,102 on *sed* in 11,27 (289,8), with references.

254,4-9 Illa uero quotiens ei parcens nates recellebam, accedens totiens nisu rabido et spinam prehendens meam adpliciore nexu inhaerebat, ut hercules etiam deesse mihi aliquid ad supplendam eius libidinem crederem nec Minotauri matrem frustra delectatam putarem adultero mugiente: Indeed, each time that, in order to spare her, I drew back my buttocks, she came toward me with a frenzied thrust and, grasping my back, clung to me with an even tighter clasp so that I – so help me Hercules – actually began to believe that I was somehow insufficient to fulfill her desires, and thought that it was not for nothing that the Minotaur's mother had been attracted to her mooing lover.

quotiens ... recellebam: see *GCA* 1985,143 on 8,15 (188,12 f.), with references, for the indicative in iterative dependent clauses in Apuleius. For the development of the iterative subjunctive in general, see LHSz 2,547; with *quotiens*, see ibid. 606 with references.

quotiens ... totiens: the correlation, found only here in the *Met.*, illustrates in an expressive manner the rhythmical movements during intercourse.

ei parcens: 'to spare her'. As the narrator mentioned earlier (253,20 f.), the ass's caution is inspired by his fear of being thrown to the wild animals, should the *matrona* succumb to his *tam uastum genitale* (253,19). This considerate attitude of the ass toward the woman has sometimes been interpreted as a positive development in Lucius' character since the love scene with Fotis. The text gives no distinct clue for this (see Introd. **2.5.2**); but in setting the ass's thoughtfulness against the *rabido nisu* of the *matrona* it subtly raises the question which of the two is actually more like an animal; see below on *rabido*.

recellebam: cf. 7,24 (172,15 f.) *totum corporis pondus ... recello*; for this rare verb see *GCA* 1981,243 ad loc. with references.

rabido: thus φ; F had originally *rauido*, changed to *rapido* by a different hand. On the frequent confusion of *b* and *u* in F, see Helm, Praef. *Fl.* XLVI. The words *rabido nisu* may remind one of the passages where *rabidus* or *rabies* connote a raging sexual appetite (see *OLD* s.v. *rabidus* 3 and s.v. *rabies* 2b); thus e.g. Prop. 3,19,10 *rabidae stimulos frangere nequitiae*. But more important is here the association with wild animals, which is the original meaning of *rabidus*; cf. e.g. Stat. *Theb.* 7,530 *rabidi ... leones*; Verg. *G.* 2,151 *rabidae tigres*. Meaningful for our passage is Ov. *Ars* 3,501 f. *pertinet ad faciem rabidos compescere mores: / candida pax homines, trux decet ira feras*. Thus, the contrast between the ass's caution and the woman's *rabidus nisus* raises the question (programmatic in this book) of 'human(e) beasts' and 'bestial humans'; see Introd. **2.4.3.2**).

adpliciore: thus F (φ has *appliciore*). Helm, Giarratano, Robertson, Terzaghi, and Hanson read with Oudendorp *adplic<it>iore*. Colvius and Hildebrand defend *adpliciore*; Van der Vliet, too, retains F. Armini borrowed the arguments already used by Colvius and Hildebrand: the comparative *adplicior* may be based on a positive **adplex, -plicis*, cf. *supplex, -plicis*. ThLL s.v. *applicus* (or *applex*), 299,49 f. explains the adjective as 'ad *applicare* retro formatum'.

287

hercules: the forceful interjection may refer here to Hercules' sexual feats, well-known in literature and iconography; cf. e.g. his thirteenth labour; see *GCA* 1995,155, with references, on 9,16 (215,4); see also on *hercules* ch. 11 (244,24).

deesse mihi aliquid: precisely what is supposed to be lacking is discreetly left unspecified by the use of *aliquid*.

ad supplendam eius libidinem: *supplere* is ambiguous here. In a concrete sense it means 'fill up', as in e.g. Cato *Agr.* 69,1 *amurca impleto (dolia) dies VII, facito ut amurcam cotidie suppleas*; Col. 12,10 *quae* (sc. *cepa*) *cum ius combiberit, simili mixtura uas suppleatur*. With *libidinem eius* as its object it is used here also in the abstract sense: 'fulfill, satisfy'; cf. e.g. Gel. 3,16,21: *an ... infans ex utero uiuus editus et statim mortuus ius trium liberorum suppleuisset*.

Minotauri matrem ... delectatam putarem ... mugiente: a striking repetition of the letter *m*, a letter that 'moos like a cow (bull)', as Quint. *Inst.* 12,10,31 remarks: *pleraque nos illa quasi mugiente littera cludimus 'm'*.

Minotauri matrem: again the *matrona* is compared to Pasiphaë; see on *ad instar asinariae Pasiphaae* ch. 19 (251,24 f.).

adultero mugiente: a comical paradox: Pasiphaë's *adulter* moos loudly, whereas human *adulteri* do their best not to be heard; cf. Charite's repetition of *tacitus* when she promises the would-be *adulter*, Thrasyllus, a rendezvous (8,10: 185,10 and 18). Cf. Tib. 1,2,33 f. *reseret modo Delia postes / et uocet ad digiti me taciturna sonum*. Lovers always whisper; see Hor. *Carm.* 1,9,19 *lenes ... sub noctem susurri* with Nisbet-Hubbard ad loc.

254,9-11 Iamque operosa et peruigili nocte transacta, uitata luci[u]s conscientia facessit mulier condicto pari noctis futurae pretio: After a laborious and sleepless night the woman, avoiding the tell-tale light of day, left after agreeing upon a price for a similar night in the future.

operosa: terms like *opus* are often used euphemistically for the man's part in lovemaking; cf. Kay 1985,203 on Mart. 11,60,7 f. *at Chione non sentit opus nec uocibus ullis / adiuuat*. See also Adams 1982,157.

peruigili nocte: before Apuleius, the adjective, attested first in Ovid and quite frequent thereafter, is always active in meaning: 'awake or sleepless all night long'; cf. e.g. Ov. *Am.* 1,6,44 *peruigil in mediae sidera noctis eras*. Apuleius is the first to use *peruigil* to modify *nox* with passive meaning: 'a wakeful, sleepless night' (here and 2,11: 34,6). After Apuleius *peruigil nox* becomes fairly common (see Souter and Blaise s.v. *peruigil*). See also *GCA* 1995,49 on 9,3 (204,18) *peruigiles excubias*.

lucis conscientia: elsewhere, *conscientia* is attested only with a subjective genitive of persons; *ThLL* s.v. *conscientia* 364,49 notes our passage as unusual, which suggests that there is a certain personification of *lux*. Cf. 5,26 (123,23) *conscio lumine*; thus also Minuc. 9,7.

facessit: see on *facessunt* ch. 20 (252,13).

condicto ... noctis ... pretio: a transaction as in a brothel is suggested here, with the ass's groom as the brothel keeper and Lucius as his employee. Cf. the passage in the *Apology*, where the house of Herennius Rufus is depicted as a brothel: *Apol.* 75,1 *domus eius tota lenonia*; 75,3 *cum ipso* (sc. Herennius) *... de uxoris noctibus paciscuntur*; and *Apol.* 97,3 about Rufinus, Pontianus' calculating father-in-law, *magno quidem pretio noctium computarat* (i.e. nights that Pontianus spent with his daughter). Cf. also Minuc. 25,11 *conducuntur stupra, tractantur lenocinia*. Macr. 2,2,11 *ubi dimidium talentum unius pretium noctis audiuit*. Cf. Ov. *Am.* 1,8,67 *quia pulcher erit, poscet sine munere noctem*.

CHAPTER XXIII

Thiasus prepares a *spectaculum* in which the ass is to perform a love scene with a condemned woman. The beginning of her history.

254,12-14 Nec grauate magister meus uoluptates ex eius arbitrio largiebatur partim mercedes amplissimas acceptando, partim nouum spectaculum domino praeparando: And without compunction my trainer lavished the pleasures of love on her according to her preference, on the one hand accepting handsome fees and on the other preparing a new spectacle for his master.

Nec grauate: resumes the point made in ch. 19 (251,27-252,2; see the note there). The adverb is attested only here in Apuleius' works. The same litotes occurs also Cic. *de Orat.* 1,208 *cum uobis ... non grauate respondero*; *Balb.* 36 *benigne, non grauate*.

magister meus ... ex eius arbitrio ... spectaculum domino praeparando: the emphasis on hierarchical relations characterizes the ass's powerlessness, even though he is now living in the lap of luxury. He must obey his *magister*, and the *magister* in his turn is subordinate to the *matrona* and the *dominus*, Thiasus, who is fond of *spectacula*. It is therefore incorrect to change *meus* to *meas*, as Van der Vliet proposes. The sentence emphasizes again (see also the previous chapter) that the *uoluptates* are not those of the ass: he is only the instrument which the *magister* uses to provide the lady with *uoluptates*.

magister meus: the same expression is used for the ass's groom in ch. 35 (265,23); see note there on the associations of *magister*.

uoluptates ... largiebatur: 'was generous with *uoluptates*'. The unusual expression sounds somewhat bitter coming from the narrating I (see the previous note). The imperfect indicates that the *magister* provides repeated favours.

uoluptates ex eius arbitrio: 'the pleasures of love according to her choice'; the phrase underlines the bizarre nature (also in the eyes of the *magister*; see on ch. 19: 251,27-252,1) of the *matrona*'s wishes. For *ex arbitrio* see on ch. 18 (250,27).

partim mercedes ... acceptando, partim ... spectaculum ... praeparando: the modal ablative of the gerund (see LHSz 2,380; KSt 2,1,752 f. on the gradually increasing frequency of this use; Väänänen [3]1981,150) can have an accusative of the object, as is the case here. Cf. Hor. *Ars* 343 f. *omne tulit punctum qui miscuit utile dulci, / lectorem delectando pariterque monendo*; see Aalto 1949,69 for more examples. Here, as in the Horace citation, the modal function (indicating a 'concomitant circumstance') has a final connotation: the ablatives reflect the *magister*'s motivation for *non grauate ... largiri*. Cf. Vallette: 'il voyait là le moyen tout à la fois de faire de beaux gains et de préparer à son maître un spectacle inédit'. Augello: 'sia per i grossi guadagni che si beccava, sia perché così...'. See Aalto 1949,76 f. for (late) examples of a final ablative of the gerund.

nouum spectaculum domino praeparando: for Thiasus as a *sitior nouitatis* see on ch. 16 (248,30) *nouitate ... laetus*.

254,14-16 Incunctanter ei denique libidinis nostrae totam detegit scaenam: Without hesitation he therefore revealed to him the full tableau of our sexual activity.

Callebat 1968,443 treats this short sentence as an example of 'brièveté narrative (phrase courte imprimant un mouvement vif à l'énoncé et dégageant avec clarté les éléments de la narration)'. This short sentence and the next (16-17) report a development of great importance for the ass.

Incunctanter: the adverb is not attested before Ulpian and Apuleius; see *GCA* 1977,69 on 4,8 (80,7). The formation of new adverbs in *-ter* (from participles or adjectives) reaches its culmination in the second century A.D. (Callebat 1994,1617 and n. 7). Cf. *esurienter* in ch. 16 (249,4).

denique: here in the sense of *ergo*; see *GCA* 1985,44 on 8,3 (178,19). The narrator draws a logical conclusion from the previous sentence. Van der Paardt 1971,42 with references discusses the various functions of *denique* in the *Met.*

libidinis ... scaenam: in *OLD* s.v. *scaena* 5c, all the examples of *scaena* meaning 'tableau' are from Apuleius' *Met.*; cf. e.g. 8,29 (201,1-3) *iamiamque uicinos undique percientes turpissimam scaenam patefaciunt*. See *GCA* 1985,112 on 8,11 (185,23) for a discussion of the various meanings of *scaena* in the *Met.* For book 10 as the pre-eminent *liber de spectaculis* of the *Met.*, see Introd. **2.1** and **2.4.2**.

libidinis nostrae: *libido* is used here for the (lustful) deed itself. *OLD* s.v. *libido* 3b gives examples of this use in the plural; *ThLL* s.v. *libido* 1333,68 f. has also examples in the singular, e.g. Sen. *Ep.* 77,6 *cogito, quamdiu iam idem facias: cibus, somnus, libido*; Cels. *praef.* 70 *praecipiunt ... ut uitetur frigus, aestus, satietas, labor, libido*.

254,16-17 At ille liberto magnifice munerato destinat me spectaculo publico:
He gave his freedman a princely reward and designated me for a public show.

For this short sentence see the introductory note to the previous pericope. This particular *libertus* had shown before that he knew his master inside out (see on ch. 17: 249,25 f.). This short sentence exactly reflects the motivation of the *libertus* as explained in the gerund constructions above.

liberto magnifice munerato destinat me spectaculo publico: not only the end rhyme (*munerato ... publico*) resulting from the somewhat contrived word order (*destinat* placed at the beginning of the main clause) but also the equal number of syllables (11 + 11) and the soft consonants that predominate in the first colon versus the hard *st* - *t* - *sp* - *ct* - *p* - *c* - sequence in the second colon emphasize the contrast observed by the narrating I in Thiasus' treatment of the *libertus* and of the ass. This contrast is one of promotion versus degradation: performing in a *spectaculum publicum* was a shameful occupation for a free person. Now the re-reader can appreciate the scope of the anticipatory words *sed iste corporis mei decor pudori peperit grande dedecus* (ch. 15: 248,10 f.; see the note there). The following story about the multiple misdeeds of the woman who will be Lucius' partner in this scene adds to his disgrace. See also the following note.

magnifice: the adverb is used only here in Apuleius' works. The adjective occurs only four times, always in highly laudatory terms: 'magnificent, splendid' (*Apol.* 40,7; *Fl.* 9,24; in the *Met.* once: 11,11: 275,2 *magnificae religionis*; *Pl.* 1,3,186). In our passage the adverb emphasizes again the contrast signaled in the previous note.

publicum: a significant Leitwort in the next episode, where the public nature of the event takes Lucius to a low point in his existence as an ass (it also occurs below in this chapter; cf. also, enclosing the story about the murderess, ch. 29: 260,1 *publicitus*; 260,5 *publici spectaculi*; in ch. 34: 265,8 f. the criminal woman is taken *de publico carcere*, and the ass feels shame at the prospect *obeundi publice concubitus*). See also the note on *publice* ch. 17 (250,11).

254,17-21 Et quoniam neque egregia illa uxor mea propter dignitatem neque prorsus ulla alia inueniri p<o>tuerat grandi praemio, uilis acquiritur aliqua sententia praesidis bestiis addicta, quae mecum incoram publicam populi caueam frequentaret: And since, because of her rank, neither that outstanding spouse of mine nor any other woman could be found at a high price, a cheap woman sentenced by the governor to be thrown to the beasts was acquired; together, she and I were publicly to ... draw a massive audience to the theatre.

Here the plan is devised to have the ass and the condemned woman perform a Pasiphaë mime. On this kind of performances, where in a public show a literary tradition is converted to a 'real event', see Coleman 1990 ('Fatal Charades'); Bartsch 1994,50-62; Mignogna 1997,231 f. with notes; C. Panayotakis 1997,319 with references.

egregia illa uxor mea propter dignitatem: for the irony of *uxor egregia*, see on ch. 24 (256,8); *GCA* 1995,203 on 9,23 (220,12) *tunc uxor egregia* with additional examples in the *Met*. In our passage the narrator triples the irony: a second irony is *uxor mea* for the Corinthian *matrona* who secretly commits adultery with an ass; in this context *propter dignitatem* is the third irony.

For the narrator there is no difference between this Corinthian *matrona* and the condemned woman with whom he will have to perform in the theatre. In the next chapter (256,8) he calls the latter, equally ironically, *illa uxor egregia*.

neque uxor mea propter dignitatem neque ... ulla alia inueniri potuerat: after *propter dignitatem*, Van der Vliet added <*adhiberi poterat*>. Brakman proposed *uxor mea* <*parata erat*>, arguing that *parata erat* could have been dropped before a compendium of *propter*. Their reasoning is probably that one can hardly say of the *matrona* that she cannot be found. But any addition to the reading of F causes the extra irony to be lost: now that a public performance is planned, the *matrona* is nowhere to be found, not even *grandi praemio*.

p<o>tuerat: F had *ptuerat*, emended in φ. The reading of ς is *poterat*.

grandi praemio, uilis ... aliqua: a contrasting juxtaposition. First, Thiasus offers a large reward to find a woman willing to cooperate; only when he does not succeed he contents himself with *uilis aliqua*. It is certainly meaningful that this episode is set in Corinth. See Mason 1971,160 f., with references, on the fame of this town as a pool of αἰσχροκέρδεια; on this passage see Mason 164: 'the Corinthians had tried to find a volunteer, *grandi praemio*; they failed, but only Corinthians, one suspects, would have thought of trying'. The qualification *uilis* is in the first place in contrast with *grandi praemio*: the condemned woman is cheap (*OLD* s.v. *uilis*), but since she is also contemptible (*OLD* 3) there is also a contrast with the Corinthian *matrona* (*egregia uxor*), who could not perform in the theatre *propter dignitatem*. Another meaning of *uilis* is 'of inferior rank' (*OLD* 5a). In view of her punishment (*bestiis addicta*) she probably belongs to the lower classes (*OLD* 5b; see Elster 1991,140 f. on the legal background of this verdict). She is not poor (cf. ch. 27: 258,19, where she is referred to as *locuples*).

grandi praemio: see comm. on *grandem ... materiam* ch. 27 (258,21 f.).

acquiritur: the original reading in F, printed by Robertson, Giarratano-Frassinetti, and Hanson; Helm prints *anquiritur* (which he considers the original reading in F - incorrectly, according to Robertson). In F the original *acquiritur* was changed by a different hand to *anquiritur*; in φ a different hand wrote an *n* over the *c* of *acquiritur*; a* (a sub-group of the mss. Class I; see Introd. **4.1**) has *acquiritur*. There is no need to search for (*anquirere*) the *uilis aliqua*: she is already in prison, so she is simply procured. Apuleius uses *acquirere* a few times in the *Apol.* (e.g. 23,4; 85,7; cf. also *Pl.* 2,9,233); in Apuleius' works *anquirere* is used once (*Apol.* 48,9), with a dependent question.

See Millar 1981,68 f. (= Millar 1999,257 f., and n. 35) on 'one of the most curious features of the judicial system of the Empire ... that local office-holders ... could buy condemned prisoners from the state and have them eaten by wild beasts for the delectation of large crowds'.

praesidis: the governor of the province of Achaia had his seat in the capital, Corinth. This *praeses* will play a part at the end of the inner story (ch. 28: 259,17 f.) that now follows; his being mentioned here supports the close connection between the following embedded tale and the main narrative (see below on *eius poenae...*). For the title *praeses* see GCA 1995,327 on 9,39 (233,10-14) with references.

bestiis addicta: on this punishment prescribed by the *lex Cornelia de sicariis et ueneficis*, see Elster 1991,141 with references. At the end of the story about this 'Murderess of Five' her punishment is described as *minus ... quam merebatur* (ch. 28: 259,21 f.; see the note there).

quae mecum incoram publicam populi caueam frequentaret: thus F and φ, retained here, with Helm and Giarratano-Frassinetti. In the translation I opt for an ἀπροσδόκητον indicated by an ellipsis. Whereas the reader expects: '... who was publicly to perform the sexual act with me', the narrator says: '... who was publicly to ... draw an audience to the theatre with me'. Not only has this solution the advantage of retaining F, but it is also an indirect characterization of the narrator, Lucius, who is too modest to say outright that he is to copulate with this *uilis aliqua* (see the note below, on *populi caueam frequentaret*). Moreover, this anticipates exactly what is about to happen: the ass and the *uilis aliqua* do indeed cause the theatre to fill up with an audience eager for a bestial show, but the show will not take place (see ch. 35).

Numerous solutions have been offered for the difficult reading in the manuscripts. The conjectures are based on the problems of the text in F, which are here represented by a) and b).

a) Apuleius uses *incoram* a few times in the *Met.* as a preposition with the genitive (e.g. 7,21: 170,13 *incoram omnium*; see GCA 1981,222 ad loc. for additional examples). If *incoram* is taken as a preposition also in this passage, solutions are sought to connect it with a genitive. One possibility (a1) is to connect it with the genitive *populi*; thus Roaldus, who proposed *mecum incoram populi publicam caueam frequentaret*. His solution is followed by ThLL s.v. *incoram* 1023,64 f., Helm-Krenkel, and Augello 1977,216. Another possibility (a2) is to delete *publicam* as a gloss: thus Becker, Hildebrand ad loc., Giarratano, and Scazzoso. A third possibility (a3) is to add <*omnium*> after *incoram*, proposed by Castiglioni 1938,560. Armini's (1928,321) defense of *incoram* as a preposition governing the accusative *publicam ... caueam* is connected with his proposal (to be discussed below) for the interpretation of *mecum ... frequentaret*. *Incoram* with an accusative is nowhere attested (see Wackernagel, *Synt.* 2,162; LHSz 2,259; Callebat 1968,240 f.); a few Christian authors have *coram* with the accusative (*ThLL* s.v. *coram* 947,23 f.). It is possible, however, to take *incoram* here as an adverb, as in 9,42 (235,28); see *GCA* 1995,351 ad loc.

b) There is no verb here that states that the woman has to copulate with the ass. Wasse (in Oudendorp) thought an addition unnecessary because *mecum ... frequentaret* could mean *mecum ... coiret*. Armini l.c. took up this idea: *frequentare* could be taken elliptically as *<nuptias> frequentare*, and so be a euphemism for *coire*. Cf. Aur. Vict. *Caes.* 4,11 *et sane in id progressa mulier* (sc. Messalina) *erat, ut animi ac pellicum gratia marito Ostiam profecto Romae nuptias cum altero frequentaret*. But, as Oudendorp already remarked: 'aliud est frequentare, aliud frequentare mecum incoram'. Oudendorp proposed *quae mecum <coitura> incoram, publicam populi caueam frequentaret*. In that case, *frequentaret = frequentem (plenam spectatoribus) redderet*, a common meaning (*OLD* s.v. *frequento* 1 groups our passage under this heading). Hildebrand proposed *<cubitura> incoram* (e.g. Pl. *Am.* 112 *meu' pater ... cum illa cubat*; Catul. 78,4; and in the *Met.*: 9,28: 224,7 *ipse cum puero cubans*, with *GCA* 1995,244 ad loc.). *ThLL* s.v. *incoram* 1023,66: 'an mecum incoram cubitans populi?'.

Wiman 1927,73 f. regards *publicam* as a corruption of *publicans*, in the meaning of *<se> publicans*, and gives examples of *se publicare* meaning *se prostituere*. For the reflexive use of transitive verbs see LHSz 2,295 f. Wiman, too, interprets *populi caueam frequentare* as 'to fill the theatre with people'; cf. d'Anna's translation of our passage, quoted below.

Worth mentioning is Robertson's conjecture *quae mecum incoram publica<ns pudicitia>m*. Paleographically this is plausible ('saut du même au même'), and the parallel he adduces from Tac. *Ger.* 19,1, *publicatae enim pudicitiae nulla uenia*, fits in well with the context: in that passage, Tacitus idealizes the chastity of Germanic women (certainly hinting at the morals of Rome in his time); our passage is in a context of extreme moral corruption in Corinth. Robertson is followed by Brandt-Ehlers and Hanson, and is the basis of the translation of e.g. Augello [3]1980 and Walsh 1994. Fortasse recte.

publicam ... caueam: here, *cauea* refers to the auditorium (*OLD* s.v. *cauea* 4); *publicam* is, strictly spoken, redundant. The redundancy is functional: the narrating I repeatedly emphasizes his disgust at the public aspect of his humiliation; see above on *spectaculo publico*.

For archeological information about the theatre at Corinth, see on ch. 29 (260,13 f.) *conseptum caueae*.

populi caueam frequentaret: cf. Gel. 2,15,3 *ad prolem populi frequentandam praemiis atque inuitamentis usus fuit*. Oudendorp (see above in the note on the textual problem in this passage) already suggested that *frequentare* is used here meaning 'to fill with people'. See *ThLL* s.v. *frequento* 1308,38 f. with many examples. None of the well-known translations has opted for this; but cf. D'Anna 1995 'essa avrebbe dovuto attirare, insieme con me, una gran quantità di gente'.

254,21-22 Eius poenae talem cognoueram fabulam: About her conviction I had heard the following story:

This is the most concise metanarrative announcement of an imbedded tale in the entire

Met. The narrator gives no indication of how he expects his tale to be received, such as is usually found in the introductions to embedded tales in the *Met.* (see e.g. 9,14: 213,6-8 with *GCA* 1995,133 f. ad loc.; Fick-Michel 1991,147 f.). The restraint of the announcement – which is easily missed – has the effect that the story stands out from the framing tale less prominently than previous inner tales. This story has, indeed, a very close and sinister connection with the framing tale: the main character of the inner tale will be playing opposite the ass in the planned show and the reader is clearly meant to keep this aspect in mind. See the note above on *praesidis* and on ch. 24 (255,20 f.) *haec eadem uxor eius, quae nunc bestiis ... fuerat addicta*.

For the structure of this last inner story and its function in the *Met.*, see App. III.

poenae ... fabulam: see *ThLL* s.v. *fabula* 32,59 f. for different constructions that denote 'fabularum argumenta'. Of the construction with a genitive, as we have here, examples are cited from Ovid onward, e.g. Ov. *Met.* 8,123 *generis ... fabula* (the first example in *ThLL*, Ov. *Ars* 3,326, is incorrect: the genitive *Arionae ... lyrae* goes with *uoci* in 325). In Apuleius, e.g. *Met.* 5,31 (128,3 f.) *domus meae famosa fabula*; there *fabula* unmistakably means 'rumores vulgi et malevolorum sermo' (*ThLL* ibid. 25,41 f.; cf. also 11,20: 282,5 *cognitis ... fabulis meis*). In view of the remarks in the previous note we can state that *fabula* has the same connotation here, even though it is followed by an inner story that can be regarded as a *narratio*. Fick-Michel 1991,149 paraphrases 'les crimes de la condamnée, retracés d'après la rumeur publique'.

talem: demonstrative pronouns (*talem ... fabulam* here, *talis mulieris* in ch. 29: 260,1) frame the embedded tale. Cf. 9,25 (221,9) *talium* with *GCA* 1995,224 ad loc.

254,23-255,1 Maritum habuit, cuius pater peregre proficiscens mandauit uxori suae, matri eiusdem iuuenis - quod enim sarcina praegnationis oneratam eam relinquebat - ut, si sexus sequioris edidisset fetum, protinus quod esset editum necaretur: She had a husband, whose father, when he left on a journey abroad, ordered his wife, the mother of the young man in question – because, 'in fact', he left her encumbered with the burden of a pregnancy – that, if she bore a child of the weaker sex, then what was born should immediately be killed.

Maritum ... cuius pater ... uxori suae, matri eiusdem iuuenis ... fetum: in his introduction, the narrator made no promise to his audience of any aesthetic pleasure (see above on *eius poenae ...*). Neither does the first sentence of his story, as it clumsily conveys necessary information, make concessions to aesthetic considerations; rather, it forces the reader to pay close attention. The history of the main character's *poena* begins some generations earlier; the awkward description of the family relations may be taken as an illustration of how her neighbours talk about this woman (see above on *poenae ... fabulam*). In addition, this introductory sentence in several respects evokes the complicated and terse explanations with which the *declamationes* often begin. As in the *declamationes*, all characters in this tale as well as in the tale of chs. 2-12 are nameless. On the intertextual relations of the inner stories of this book with the *declamationes*, see Append. I,5.5 and App. III. See also the interesting discussion by Finkelpearl 1998,157 f. on the absence of names in the whole of book 10 (apart from Thiasus): (158) 'When characters are not named, the stories in which they appear seem more generic, less individual'.

Maritum habuit: the subject, *uilis aliqua*, is not mentioned; it must be supplied from the previous sentence. This, too, emphasizes the strong connection of this inner tale with the framing tale. Contrast e.g. the beginning of the previous inner tale: ch. 2 (237,3) *dominus aedium habebat iuuenem filium...*

habuit: the perfect is to be regarded as 'auctorial', a statement by the narrator that is still outside the story line; see Kroon 1998,44 and 57 f. on the authorial perfect as an 'exposition-tense', quoting (at p. 44) Liv. 30,26,10 *duo sacerdotia habuit*; Pinkster in *AAGA* 2,1998,107. Only the re-reader will recognize a different nuance in the perfect: the husband has been murdered, so the *uilis aliqua* does not have a husband in the 'now' in which the ass hears her story. *Habuit*, therefore, could almost be translated with 'once she had a husband (but not now)'. Cf. Pl. *Rud.* 1321 *habuisse et nil habere*; Cic. *Tusc.* 1,36,87 *triste enim est nomen ipsum carendi, quia subicitur haec uis: habuit, non habet, desiderat, requirit, indiget*. See KSt 2,1,125 for further examples of this special use of the so-called present perfect; Menge [14]1965, par. 318, Anm. 2.

pater peregre proficiscens: alliteration.

peregre proficiscens: for the frequent combination *peregre proficisci* see ThLL s.v. *peregre* 1299,67 f. with examples from Pl. *Most.* 976 onward. The combination is especially frequent in the *declamationes*; thus e.g. Quint. *Decl.* 306 (199,6 f. Ritter = Sh. B. 178,1), which has a thematic correspondence with the point of departure of this story in Apuleius: *maritus peregre proficiscens praecepit uxori, ut partum exponeret*. Cf. also [Quint.] *Decl.* 5 (84,19 Håkanson) and 16 (318,9 Håkanson). See Appendix III for the intertextual relation of our story with the *declamationes*.

The adverb *peregre* is hapax legomenon in Apuleius. Meaning 'to foreign parts' it is frequent in comedy (e.g. Pl. *Cist.* 579); cf. Hor. *S.* 1,6,102, and in legal texts (Heumann-Seckel s.v. *peregre*); this last may account for its frequent occurrences in the *declamationes*.

mandauit ... ut ... fetum ... necaretur: the *paterfamilias* could exercise absolute authority over his *familia*, even in matters of life and death. See Lacey 1986,121-44 with references; Boswell 1988,58 f. with examples and references; Wiedemann 1989,36 f. on the attitude towards infanticide in Greek and Roman writers.

quod enim = *quia enim*, which is frequent in comedy (see Callebat 1968,534 f.). Kroon 1995,176 observes that 'all 27 instances of the combination *quia enim* ("because of course") in Plautus and Terence ... occur ... as an answer to a "why-question"'. Here, too, the narrator answers a supposed question 'why?' from his audience: in this combination, *enim* has a 'truth-emphasizing character' (Kroon 1989,236).

sarcina praegnationis oneratam: *sarcina* for *onus uteri* is attested, in addition to our passage and 1,9 (9,6), only in Ov. *Met.* 6,224 (see Bömer ad loc.) and Phaedr. 3,15,6 (where it is used of sheep). *Praegnatio* for 'pregnancy' is, before Apuleius (five times in the *Met.*: 1,9: 9,6 f. - *sarcina praegnationis* - and again 9,7 f.; 5,16: 116,3; 5,18: 117,2; and here,[1] only attested in Var. *R.* 2,1,18, where it is used of the gestation of animals. After that, ThLL s.v. *praegnatio* 662,73 f. gives passages in Ser. Samm. (615) and in Christian authors from [Ambr.] *trin.* 12 onward. *Onerata* for 'impregnated' is unusual, too; ThLL s.v. *onero* 631,60 f. gives only our passage for *onerare* used of a human fetus; see ThLL ibid. for *onerare* used of e.g. trees laden with fruit (e.g. Ov. *Met.* 7,281 and passages in Columella).

---

1 Cf. *Ascl.* 41, in a prayer to the *deus summus exsuperantissimus*: *o uitae uera uita, o naturarum omnium fecunda praegnatio*.

The expression in its entirety is therefore unusual and seems to emphasize the heavy responsibility heaped by the *maritus* on his pregnant wife.

ut ... sexus sequioris ... fetum ... necaretur: this was often the fate of girls; see e.g. Posidippus, *Frg.* 11 υἱὸν τρέφει πᾶς κἂν πένης τις ὢν τύχῃ, θυγατέρα δ' ἐκτίθησι κἂν ᾖ πλούσιος. Kaser I² 1971,60 f.; 65; 342. For the striking parallels with Ter. *Hau.* 626 f., see below on *natam necatamque nuntiauit* (255,4). Cf. also the story of Iphis in Ov. *Met.* 9,666 f.; ibid. 675 f. (Ligdus to his pregnant wife) *quae uoueam, duo sunt: minimo ut releuere dolore, / utque marem parias. onerosior altera sors est, / et uires fortuna negat: quod abominor, ergo, / edita forte tuo fuerit si femina partu, / (inuitus mando: pietas, ignosce!), necetur!* Arnaldi 1959 regards Ovid's story of Iphis, with Isis playing a beneficent part, as a kind of prototype for Apuleius' entire novel. See also Orders 1971,102.

Bömer on Ov. *Met.* 9,679 *necetur*, with references, discusses the exposure of infants both in real life and in mythology and literature. In practice, exposure amounted to killing (although Boswell 1988,42 f. argues against an over-simplified equation of abandonment and infanticide). When the Christians are accused of secretly practising this custom, Justin. Martyr *Apol.* 27 refutes these accusations with a precise description of the practice, concluding with καὶ τὰ φανερῶς ὑμῖν πραττόμενα καὶ τιμώμενα ὡς ἀνατετραμμένου καὶ οὐ παρόντος φωτὸς θείου ἡμῖν προσγράφετε. If the author can represent his adversaries' dreadful practices as 'daily routine', his representations are probably based on the reality in the second century A.D. See Pomeroy 1975,165 on (male and female) infanticide in Rome. See Kudlien 1989,25 f., with references, on the exposure of infants as 'a theme between fiction and real life in the ancient novel'.

sexus sequioris ... fetum, ... quod esset editum: the long-winded abstract language suggests that even before the birth the father avoids visualizing his female offspring as an actual child: *fetus* is almost exclusively used of animal young; when used of human beings, it is usually of the unborn fetus (thus e.g. 1,9: 9,7). See *ThLL* s.v. *fetus* 637,5 f.; Murgatroyd's remarks about *fetus* at Tib. 2,5,91 *et fetus matrona dabit*; cf. the distinction between animal and human offspring in Papin. *Dig.* 33,7,3 *augmenta fetuum et partuum*. Especially in poetry, *fetus* can also be used of people, but meaning 'descendants, posterity' (i.q. 'proles': *ThLL* 637,41 f.).

sexus sequioris: *sequior* is an adjectival back-formation from the adverb *secus* (comp. *sequius*), first attested in Apuleius; see *GCA* 1981,134 (with literature) on 7,8 (159,26-160,3), where the same expression is found and various interpretations are discussed. The phrase reflects the generally accepted view of women as the 'weaker sex' in a concrete sense, which is, however, often countered by philosophers with the notion that women, in spite of their lesser physical strength, have the same potential for ἀρετή as men: e.g. Pl. *Meno* 73a-b; Xen *Symp.* 2,9: δῆλον ... ὅτι ἡ γυναικεία φύσις οὐδὲν χείρων τῆς τοῦ ἀνδρὸς οὖσα τυγχάνει, γνώμης δὲ καὶ ἰσχύος δεῖται. See Stadter 1965,3 f. (in the Introduction of his Analysis of Plutarch's *Mulierum Virtutes*).

255,1-4 At illa per abs[tin]entia<m> mariti nata[m] puella[m] insita matribus pietate praeuenta desciuit ab obsequio mariti eamque prodidit uicinis alumnandam, regressoque iam marito natam necatamque nuntiauit: But during her husband's absence, impeded by the love of children innate in mothers, she abandoned the submissiveness towards her husband and when a girl was born she gave it to neighbours to bring up, and when her husband returned she reported that a girl had been born and killed.

per absentiam mariti: Beroaldus' emendation of F's *pro abstinentia* (φ has *pro abstinentiam*) is accepted by all editors. See Helm, Praef. *Fl.* XLVI on the frequent confusion of abbreviations of *per* and *pro*. *Abstinentia* is a good example of 'monastic corruption' (see Ogilvie 1971,32 f.; Reynolds-Wilson ³1991,231).

mariti ... mariti ... marito: in spite of the fact that the *maritus* is mentioned three times, the point of the sentence is that his orders are disobeyed!

nata puella: Pricaeus's proposal, printed also by Robertson, Brandt-Ehlers, Giarratano-Frassinetti, and Hanson. F and φ have *natam puellam*. The accusative, impossible to construe in this sentence, may have been caused by the close proximity of *mariti nata puella* and *marito natam necatamque*.

An objection against the reading chosen here is the somewhat obscure asyndetic accumulation of forms ending in -*a*. Kronenberg defends F, comparing *Apol.* 60,4 *testimonio Crassi, cuius oboluisse faecem uidebant, nec ipsi ausi sunt perlegere nec quicquam eo niti*. Kronenberg assumes that Apuleius meant to write *natam puellam, desciscens ab obsequio mariti, prodidit* but, having come halfway, wrote *ab obsequio mariti desciuit* as an independent paratactical phrase, and then added *eamque* to provide *prodidit* with an object. Augello 1977,216 f. argues for Kronenberg's opinion, and Giarratano and Terzaghi also retain F. It remains to be seen, however, whether in this relatively short sentence an anacoluthon of this kind can be ascribed to a careful stylist like Apuleius.[2]

Oudendorp proposed *nacta puellam*. Other proposals provide a verb to govern the transmitted accusative: Hildebrand <*necare*> *natam puellam ... praeuenta*; Helm <*cum uideret*> *natam puellam*; Van der Vliet *natam puellam* <*perimere*> *...praeuenta*; Brakman *puellam* <*necare*> *... praeuenta*. Hildebrand's proposal is attractive: *necare* before *natam* could have been overlooked by the scribe. This gives a fine structure to the whole sentence: the woman, *necare natam puellam ... praeuenta*, disobeys her husband (*ab obsequio ... desciuit ... eamque ... prodidit*), and gives her husband (chiastically in respect to the description of what she did not have the heart to do) the false report: *natam necatamque*.

insita matribus pietate praeuenta: this woman contrasts with the main character of this story (her daughter-in-law), the murderess who poisons even her own young daughter (ch. 28: 259,2 f.).

In Ter. *Hau*. 626 f. Sostrata confesses to Chremes that she gave the daughter she had to dispose of to a *Corinthia anus*, who was to abandon it. Chremes shows understanding for the *animus maternus* (ibid. 637) that moved her.

pietate praeuenta: for *praeuentus* with the ablative meaning 'impeded, hampered by', see *GCA* 1995,335 on 9,40 (234,6-8), and comm. on ch. 11 (245,9) *morte praeuentus*.

eam ... prodidit ... alumnandam: *prodo* means 'give up, abandon'; cf. Ter. *Hec*. 671 f. *an non alemus, Pamphile? / prodemus quaeso potius?* No parallel is attested for a predicative gerundive after *prodere*, but the analogy with similar constructions after *dare, tradere* is obvious; see LHSz 2,371 f. on the verbs (whose number increases in late Latin) that

---

2 Bernhard 1927,94 prefers emendation in all the cases of anacoluthon in Apuleius. See also *GCA* 1977,45 on 4,3 (76,25-77,6) about cases of anacoluthon in the *Met.*; in 3,18 (65,22 f.) Van der Paardt 1971,140 f. defends the manuscript reading resulting in an anacoluthon.

allow this construction.

alumnandam: for *alumnor* (deponent)/*alumno*, see *GCA* 1985,159 on 8,17 (190,10-19) with references. The verb is first attested in Apuleius' *Met.*, where it occurs four times: twice in the context of training dogs (to attack people); in 6,23 (145,26), where Jupiter tells how he has 'brought up' Amor with his own hands; and here. The contexts in which the verb occurs in the *Met.* do not suggest an entirely positive connotation of the verb (the 'upbringing' Jupiter claims to have given Amor acquires an ironical connotation in the passages of 'Amor and Psyche' where Jupiter is presented as far from averse to amorous adventures, e.g. 6,22). Seen in that light, our passage may suggest that the little daughter will possibly be 'educated' to be a prostitute. The mother's fear, mentioned below, that her son will unknowingly bed his own sister, supports that suggestion. See the note there.

natam necatamque nuntiauit: alliteration. The juxtaposition of *natam* and *necatam* and the ellipsis of *eam ... esse* lend the phrase a cynical directness.

The situation depicted so far shows parallels with the situation described by Chremes in Ter. *Haut.* 634 f.: *nam iam primum, si meum / imperium exsequi uoluisses, interemptam oportuit, / non simulare mortem uerbis, reapse spem uitae dare*. See also above on *insita matribus pietate praeuenta*, and the final remark on this chapter.

255,4-7 Sed ubi flos aetatis nuptialem uirgini diem flagitabat nec ignaro marito dotare filiam pro natalibus quibat, quod solum potuit, filio suo tacitum secretum aperuit: But when the bloom of her years required a wedding day for the girl, and the mother could not, without her husband's knowledge, provide her daughter with a dowry in keeping with her parentage, she did the only thing she could: she disclosed the undivulged secret to her son.

Sed ubi ... flagitabat nec ... quibat: many years have gone by between the events mentioned in the two previous sentences and the situation described here. From this point onward the narrative tempo slows down (see Introd. **1.6** and **1.6.3**); the flowery description of the girl reaching marriageable age suggests at once a calmer narrative style. For *ubi* with the imperfect indicative, see on ch. 2 (237,17 f.) *ubi ... exaestuabat*.

flos aetatis: this phrase is frequent especially in poetry and often connotes 'source of sexual attraction' besides 'youthful beauty'; e.g. Lucr. 4,1105 f. *membris collatis flore fruuntur / aetatis* (see also on ch. 31: 262,2 f. *flos aetatulae*). It does so here, as the next sentence shows.

pro natalibus: for the plural *natales*, used from the post-Augustan period onward as a noun meaning 'origin', see e.g. 3,15 (63,7) with Van der Paardt 1971,114 f. with references. Cf. e.g. Sen. *Ben.* 3,32,1 *tenebrasque natalium suorum ... discuteret*; Plin. *Nat.* 18,37 *L. Tarius Rufus infima natalium humilitate*.

quibat: from the passages cited by Neue-Wagener 3,624 it appears that this form of the imperfect is archaic (e.g. Pl. *Trin.* 657 *non quibam*) and in post-classical Latin should be regarded as an archaism.

tacitum secretum: Apuleius prefers to give secrets extra weight by adding a redundant adjective like *tacitus* or *arcanus*. Bernhard 1927,175 collects examples. See e.g. 8,8 (182,19 f.) *tacita pectoris sui secreta* with *GCA* 1985,87 ad loc.; 6,2 (130,8) *per tacita secreta cistarum*.

255,7-9 Nam et oppido uerebatur, ne quo casu, caloris iuuenalis impetu lapsus, nescius nesciam sororem incurreret: For she was also very much afraid that by accident, thrown off balance by an impulse of youthful passion, he would unwittingly approach his equally unwitting sister.

Nam et ... uerebatur: this sentence explains why, of all people, she takes her son into her confidence. *Et ... uerebatur* indicates that this is a second worry, in addition to the worry (marrying off her daughter), mentioned in the previous sentence.
oppido: see *GCA* 1985,187 on 8,22 (193,21) with further references.
ne ... incurreret: Justin Martyr mentions this very danger in his discussion of the practice (which he denounces) of abandoning children (see above on 254,24 f.): Just. Martyr *Apol.* 1,27,3 καὶ τῶν τούτοις χρωμένων τις πρὸς τῇ ἀθέῳ καὶ ἀσεβεῖ καὶ ἀκρατεῖ μίξει, εἰ τύχοι, τέκνῳ ἢ συγγενεῖ ἢ ἀδελφῷ μίγνυται; cf. also Clem. Al. *Paed.* 3,3. Like so many abandoned children, the girl has possibly been 'educated' to become a prostitute (see above on *alumnandam*; Boswell 1988,112 f. with references).
caloris iuuenalis impetu lapsus: cf. Verg. *A*. 8,390 *intrauit calor et labefacta per ossa cucurrit*.
calor iuuenalis: this combination is also found Quint. *Inst*. 2,15,28, in a non-erotic sense, for 'youthful enthusiasm'. *Calor* for 'love's fire' is poetic (*ThLL* s.v. *calor* 182,25 f. gives examples from Propertius onward). See the previous note and Fedeli on Prop. 3,8,9. In the *Met*. also 5,13 (113,23); cf. 6,23 (145,26 f., Jupiter about Amor) *cuius primae iuuentutis caloratos impetus ... cohercendos existimaui*.
nescius nesciam: on the figure of polyptoton, frequent in the *Met.*, see *GCA* 1981,113 on 7,5 (158,3-7) *uolentem uolentes*, with examples and references. In our passage, the polyptoton denotes precisely the two characters who will be the innocent victims in the following story. On 'unwitting' victims, see the note on ch. 5 (240,3 f.) *nescius fraudis*.
incurreret: *ThLL* s.v. *incurro* 1089,3 f. gives our passage as the first in which the verb is used in an erotic sense; next, [Prob.] on Verg. *G*. 1,20. Cf. also 7,21 (169,26-170,4), where *GCA* 1981,218 compare Juv. 6,331 *seruis incurritur* (sc. *a femina impudica*). In [Probus] and Juvenal, *incurrere* has a clearly aggressive ring; in our passage the aggressiveness is weakened by the context (*quo casu ... caloris iuuenalis impetu lapsus ... nescius*). The young man, who is depicted in the next sentence also as very conscientious, is excused in advance.

255,9-17 Sed pietatis spectatae iuuenis et matris obsequium et sororis officium religiose dispensat et arc[h]anis domus uenerabilis silentii custodiae tradi*tis*, plebeiam facie tenus praetendens humanitatem, sic necessarium sanguinis sui munus adgreditur, ut desolatam uicinam puellam parentumque praesidio uiduatam domus suae tutela receptaret ac mox artissimo multumque sibi dilecto contubernali, largitus de proprio dotem, liberalissime traderet: But the young man, who was noted for his conscientiousness, scrupulously discharged both his deference toward his mother and his duty toward his sister; he placed the family secrets in the custody of a respectful silence and, while on the face of it he could use common human kindness as a pretext, he so put himself to the necessary task required by his blood relationship that he took the neighbour's girl, who was all alone and bereft of parental protection, into the safety of his own house and subsequently married her very well to a very close friend who was especially dear to him, paying a handsome dowry out of his own purse.

Sed: the young man's action entirely dispels the mother's worries expressed in the previous sentence. In addition, *sed* counters a possible expectation of the reader, who has been expecting a comedy: in it the *iuuenis* would be the *adulescens amans*, who gets into trouble through his irresponsible behaviour and must then be rescued by a *seruus callidus*. See Konstan 1983,153 f. (on Strabax in Pl. *Truc.*); Hunter 1985,97 f.; Slater 1985, Index s.v. 'stock characters', *adulescens*.

pietatis spectatae iuuenis ... obsequium ... officium ... religiose: many keywords remind the reader of the previous inner tale, which also started with a *iuuenis ... pietate praecipuus* (ch. 2: 237,3 f.) who showed *matris ... obsequium* (ch. 3: 238,9 f.) and whose stepmother tried to lead him away from *religio* (ch. 3: 238,24 f.). These signals connect the two stories (see also App. III) and prepare the observant reader for another *clades domus* (see on ch. 4: 239,8 f. *domus cladem*).

et matris obsequium et sororis officium: the parallelism between the cola, with anaphora of *et* and rhyming endings, underscores the young man's conscientious behaviour. *Matris obsequium* is elaborated in *arcanis ... traditis*, the phrase *plebeiam ... humanitatem* takes us from his oath of secrecy (*matris obsequium*) to his fraternal duty, and the rest of the sentence illustrates the *sororis officium*. This very combination, however, – the concealment of the true family circumstances and the fulfilment of his duty as a brother – will lead to his wife's fatal jealousy.

dispensat ... adgreditur: the historical presents, appearing here for the first time, set the story in motion. The alternation of narrative perfects and historical presents gives the story a lively rhythm, which will be discussed in the notes.

dispensat: ThLL s.v. *dispenso* 1403,37 f. groups our passage under 'i.q. administrare ... gubernare ... ministrare', and adds 'sensu latiore'. However, the verb is used here in its original sense: the young man carefully weighs two divergent matters: *matris obsequium* (he must keep the secret) and *sororis officium* (at the same time, he must fulfill his brotherly duty).

et: used explicatively: 'and that ...', 'namely'.

arcanis ... traditis: *traditis* is Oudendorp's emendation of *tradidit* in F and φ.

arcanis domus: cf. Tac. *Ann.* 1,6,6 *ne arcana domus ... uulgarentur*.

arc[h]anis: the emendation by ς is generally adopted. The spelling of this word in F is inconsistent (see Oldfather s.v. *arcanus* and *archanus*), but the spelling with *-h-* is not attested even in inscriptions.

uenerabilis silentii: 'respectful silence'. For the active meaning of *uenerabilis* see also 11,23 (285,1) *uenerabili continentia*. Leumann 1917,95 f., with many examples, explains the active use of many adjectives in *-lis* from an originally instrumental meaning. He illustrates (121 f.) the difference between 'instrumental' and 'active' by e.g. V.Max. 2,4,4 *uenerabilibus erga deos uerbis* (instrumental) and ibid. 1,1,15 *quanto nostrae ciuitatis senatus uenerabilior in deos* (active).

plebeiam humanitatem: the adjective *plebeius* is found in Apuleius only here. ThLL s.v. *humanitas* 3079,63 f. explains our phrase as 'i.e. humanitatem in puellam pauperam'. Better: 'the *humanitas* that ordinary people display toward each other'; cf. Sen. *Ben.* 7,17,1 *duo sunt beneficia: unum, quod dare nisi sapiens sapienti non potest, hoc est absolutum et uerum beneficium; alterum uulgare, plebeium, cuius inter nos imperitos commercium est.*

humanitatem: ThLL s.v. *humanitas* 3079,1 f. gives examples of the noun meaning 'comitas, benignitas, clementia, φιλανθρωπία', which increases especially during the Empire. Gel. 13,17,1 *qui uerba Latina fecerunt quique his probe usi sunt, 'humanitatem' non id esse uoluerunt quod uolgus existimat quodque a Graecis* φιλανθρωπία *dicitur et significat dexteritatem quandam beniuolentiamque erga omnis homines promiscam, sed 'humanitatem' appellauerunt id propemodum quod Graeci* παιδείαν *uocant, nos eruditionem institutionemque in bonas artes dicimus*. From Cicero onward *humanitas* occurs frequently in the sense of 'goodness toward a fellow human being'; e.g. Cic. *Off.* 1,20. In the *Met.* e.g. 3,7 (57,6) *humanitate commotos, misericordia fletuum adfectos*. See also Blaise s.v. *humanitas* 4 for many examples in Christian Latin.

praetendens: the verb is attested only twice in Apuleius, here and ch. 27 (258,13 f.). Here it is used meaning 'to put forward as a ... reason (for something else': *OLD* s.v. *praetendo* 4a) but, unusually, in a positive sense; in ch. 27 it is used meaning 'to offer or show deceptively, make a pretence of' (*OLD* ibid. 5).

necessarium sanguinis sui munus: *necessarium ... munus* here means both 'necessary task' and 'duty of a relative' (for a similar ambiguous use of *necessarius* see on ch. 3: 238,27 *necessariii facinoris*).

adgreditur ut ... receptaret ... traderet: for the imperfect subjunctive after a main clause with a historical present, see on ch. 3 (238,13 f.) *unde ... caperet ... decunctatur*.

desolatam uicinam puellam parentumque praesidio uiduatam: the sonorous (homoioteleuton of *-am*, alliteration of *p*, repetition of *ui-*, and a heroic clausula) description of the girl's wretched situation underlines the brother's good deed.

desolatam: 'left'; cf. Tac. *Ann.* 16,30,3 (similarly combined with *uiduata*) *contra filia ... nuper marito ... pulso uiduata desolataque*. For this use ('i.q. *solum relinquere*'), ThLL s.v. *desolo* 734,3 f. gives as the first occurrence Verg. *A.* 11,870 f. *disiectique duces desolatique manipli / tuta petunt*. In Apuleius: *Fl.* 17,15 *Orpheus exsilio desolatus*; *Met.* 2,25 (45,13).

tutela: the brother's house cannot protect the girl from the murderous woman who lives there. As sometimes is the case in the *Met.*, *tutela* is a only a momentary, deceptive protection. See e.g. 4,13 (85,5-8), where the most careful protection cannot preserve Demochares' precious animals from the catastrophe described in 4,14. Cf. also 9,18 (216,9) and *GCA* 1995,34 on 9,1 (202,27). See Tatum 1969,85 f. and n. 160, with examples, on the deeper meaning that words regularly occurring in books 1 to 10 of the *Met.*, like *salus* and *tutela*, acquire in the Isis-context of book 11 (see also Introd. **2.4.6**).

artissimo ... contubernali: see *GCA* 1995,205 on 9,23 (220,18) *contubernalis artissimi*.

multum ... dilecto: see LHSz 2,163 for *multum* and other intensifying adverbs that are characteristic of lively colloquial language. *OLD* s.v. *multum*² gives many examples in Plautus; cf. also Hor. *S.* 2,3,147 with Palmer ad loc.; Hor. *Carm.* 1,25,5 with Nisbet-Hubbard ad loc. This use of *multum* survives in e.g. the Italian 'molto bene' (Väänänen 1981,118 f.).

sibi dilecto: the dative with *dilectus* is primarily poetical; e.g. Verg. *A.* 5,569 *puer dilectus Iulo*; Ov. *Met.* 10,152 f. *pueros .../ dilectos Superis*; in prose e.g. Tac. *Ann.* 15,63,3 *ne sibi unice dilectam ad iniurias relinqueret*; Apul. *Fl.* 15,11 *Polycrati tyranno dilectus*. ThLL s.v. *diligo* 1184,70 f. describes the participle in such passages (including ours) as 'p.p.p. pro adjectivo, i.q. *carus, amatus, gratus*'. See LHSz 2,91 f. for the dative with this type of adjective ('Bestimmungsdativ im engeren Anschluß an den zugehörigen Verbalbegriff').

largitus ... dotem: Norden 1912,96 Anm. 6 sees it as a Greek custom for a brother to be under obligation to pay a *dos*. This brother, however, who tells no one that the girl is his sister, is apparently performing a regular *officium* of the well-to-do, i.e. paying a *dos* on behalf of friends. Cf. Apul. *Apol.* 23,3 *nam et amicorum plerisque opem tuli et magistris plurimis gratiam rettuli, quorundam etiam filias dote auxi* (see Crook 1986,68 f. with examples).

de proprio: 'from his own purse'. According to the *ThLL* material this expression is attested in legal texts (Heumann-Seckel s.v. *proprius*), and occurs frequently in inscriptions (also in the form *ex/de proprio suo*); e.g. *CIL* 5,8744 *Fl. Dassiolus ueteranus ... arcam siui de proprio conparauit, siue filius suus Variosus*; ibid. 8775. Cf. *SHA* (Iul. Capit.) 3 (*Anton. Pius*),4,9 *congiarium militibus populo de proprio dedit*; 20 (*Gordiani tres*),4,6; (Flav. Vopiscus Syrac.) 27 (*Tacitus*),10,5.

liberalissime traderet: the long, carefully composed sentence concludes with a series of three cretics (Schober 1904,17). The superlative of the adverb is attested only here in Apuleius' works. Besides the meaning already indicated by *largitus de proprio dotem* ('generously...; unstintingly': *OLD* s.v. *liberaliter* 2), it may well connote 'in a manner worthy of a free person' (*OLD* ibid. 1). Apparently, the brother selects a worthy partner for his sister.

The initial situation presented here is an ingredient in the plots of several comedies by Plautus and Terence. It lends itself to comic complications and dénouements (scenes of recognition). The reader who recognizes the comic situation, and bases certain generic expectations on it, will find it the more remarkable that from ch. 24 onward the story moves rapidly farther and farther away from its 'comic' start. See App. III.

CHAPTER XXIV

False suspicions lead to misplaced jealousy; a gruesome murder ensues.

255,17-20 **Sed haec bene atque optime plenaque cum sanctimonia disposita feralem Fortunae nutum latere non potuerunt, cuius instinctu domum iuuenis protinus se direxit saeua Riualitas**: But these arrangements, made rightly and most properly and in full accordance with religious principle, could not be shielded from the fatal whims of Fortuna; at her instigation, cruel Jealousy made her way at once to the young man's house.

In this story, the part played by *Fortuna* and *Riualitas* combined forms a contrast with the part of Τύχη in New Comedy, who makes everything come right in the end. See App. III.

Fortuna's fatal intervention, with which she undoes well-intentioned human actions, not only contrasts with Τύχη's activities in New Comedy but also recalls passages in Euripides' tragedies, e.g. Eur. *Ion* 1512 f. ὦ μεταβαλοῦσα μυρίους ἤδη βροτῶν / καὶ δυστυχῆσαι καὖθις αὖ πρᾶξαι καλῶς, / Τύχη... In the Greek novels, especially in Chariton, Τύχη repeatedly causes reversals in the main characters' fates; see Alperowitz 1992,77 f. with references. Very close to our passage is e.g. Chariton 2,8,3-4 κατεστρατηγήθη δ'ὑπὸ τῆς Τύχης, πρὸς ἣν μόνην οὐδὲν ἰσχύει λογισμὸς ἀνθρώπου ... ἐπεβούλευσεν ἡ Τύχη τῇ σωφροσύνῃ τῆς γυναικός. Jealousy is one of the motivations characteristic of Τύχη (see Alperowitz 1992,82 f. with references); in the same way, *Riualitas* is here an 'accomplice' of *Fortuna*.

bene atque optime plenaque cum sanctimonia: a climactically structured tricolon puts strong emphasis on the excellence of the precautions taken by the good brother. This underscores the fact that nothing can withstand Fortuna's whims.

Bernhard 1927,151 f. gives further examples in the *Met.* of the combination of adverb and prepositional phrase; as pointed out above, the fullness of expression has a clear function in the context. Thus also e.g. 4,22 (91,12-13) *adfatim et sine ulla mensura*; see GCA 1977,167 ad loc.; see also below in this chapter (255 29 f.) on *sola et sine ullo comite*.

bene atque optime: this combination of positive and superlative of the adverb is attested nowhere else; however, cf. 8,9 (184,17 f.) *boni ... et optimi consules, si...* with GCA 1985,102 ad loc.; 6,17 (141,10 f.) *recte atque pulcherrime*. Cf. Cic. *ND* 3,27,68 (in a quotation from Accius) *recte et uerissume*. Since phrases of this kind are frequently found in inscriptions, Bernhard 1927,167 f. assumes that they were common in colloquial language. Callebat 1968,401 f. giving other examples in the *Met.*, and pointing to the use of this kind of expressions in stylized rhetorical writers like Arnobius, discusses these not as colloquialisms, but as conscious artistic choices.

In our passage, *bene atque optime* is to be understood in a moral sense: *recte, probe, honeste*; ThLL s.v. *bonus (bene)* 2118,21 f. compares the expression here with καλῶς κἀγαθῶς.

sanctimonia: this noun is hapax legomenon in Apuleius. It is first attested in *Rhet.*

Her. 4,33 *non illae te nuptiales tibiae eius matrimonii commonebant? nam hic omnis sanctimonia nuptiarum uno signo tibiarum intellegitur*; cf. e.g. Cic. *Quinct.* 93 *non habere* (sc. *se*) *domum clausam pudori et sanctimoniae.*

feralem Fortunae nutum latere non potuerunt: there is no reason to assume for *nutus* here the meaning 'eyes, glance' (contra *GCA* 1977,93 f. on 4,22: 83,9-10 and *GCA* 1981,49 on 6,28: 150,1-3). Even in a passage like 2,30 (50,13 f.) *directis digitis et detortis nutibus praesentium denotor*, which is often cited in support of this 'weakened' meaning, *detortis nutibus* should be interpreted not as 'rolling their eyes' (thus De Jonge ad loc.), but as 'twisting their heads round to nod at me' (Hanson). See the criticism of Dowden 1969,69 on *GCA* 1977,93 f. Most translators understand *nutus Fortunae* to mean 'das Walten des Schicksals' (Helm-Krenkel) or 'the nod of Fortune' (Hanson) or even 'the whims of Fortune' (Scazzoso: 'al malaugurato capriccio della sorte'). Cf. Verg. *A.* 7,591 f. *uerum ubi nulla datur caecum exsuperare potestas / consilium et saeuae nutu Iunonis eunt res*; Sen. *Dial.* 2 (*Const.*),5,7 *at quae dissipata et direpta ferebantur, non iudicabat sua, sed aduenticia et nutum fortunae sequentia.* Cf. in the *Met.* 4,12 (83,9-10) *Fortunae nutum*; 6,16 (140,11 f.) *nec tamen nutum deae saeuientis ... expiare potuit*; 11,25 (287,1 f.) *tuo nutu spirant flamina, nutriunt nubila.*

latere: in this context 'be safe', as e.g. Cic. *Mur.* 22 *urbanae res ... latent in tutela ac praesidio bellicae uirtutis.* Another possibility is 'shelter', e.g. from a storm: Verg. *A.* 10,803 f. *si quando grandine nimbi / praecipitant, omnis campis diffugit arator/ omnis et agricola, et tuta latet arce uiator.* On the 'storms of fortune' see comm. on ch. 4 (239,12).

feralem: as often in the *Met.*, this adjective points ahead to a fatal, deadly outcome; see *GCA* 1985,112 on 8,11 (185,23). Thome 1993,187 n. 12 discusses the uncertain etymology of *feralis*, which is always used in connection with death and the underworld, and then often meaning 'unheil-, todbringend'. Indeed, Fortuna's 'nod' will cause no less than five deaths in this tale.

protinus: the first hint of the speed with which *Fortuna* will put the fatal events into motion. See on *ilico* in the next sentence.

saeua Riualitas: for this and other personifications, see *GCA* 1977,110 f. on 4,14 (85,8-10) with references. In this context, the more specific *Riualitas* is aptly chosen rather than *Inuidia*, which is much more frequently personified. The first attestation of the noun is possibly a personification as well: Publ. Syr. 6-7 R. *regnat non regitur, qui nihil nisi quod uult facit / Riualitatem non amat Victoria*, followed by Cic. *Tusc.* 4,26,56; then Char. *Gramm.* p.435,9 B. and our passage.

Vergil himself formulates the possibility of an emotion being 'deified' in *A.* 9,184 f. *dine hunc ardorem mentibus addunt, / Euryale, an sua cuique deus fit dira cupido?* See *EV* 4,37 f. s.v. 'personificazione' [Pöschl], with references. On poetic personification see also Maurach [2]1989,45 with references.

The two personifications in this sentence, *Fortuna* and *Riualitas*, herald the murderess's series of crimes inevitably set in motion by evil powers. The epithet *saeua*, now used for *Riualitas*, makes her even more an 'extension' of *Fortuna*, who is often named *saeua* in the *Met.* (e.g. 5,5: 106,16; 8,24: 195,21); see also on ch. 4 (239,12) *fortunae saeuientis.*

One is reminded of Chariton 1,2,5, where one of the rejected suitors of Callirhoe announces: ἐφοπλιῶ γὰρ αὐτῷ (sc. against Chaereas) Ζηλοτυπίαν.

255,20-24 Et ilico haec eadem uxor eius, quae nunc bestiis propter haec ipsa fuerat addicta, coepit puellam uelut aemulam tori succubamque primo suspicari, dehinc detestari, dehinc crudelissimis laqueis mortis insidiari: And at once this same wife of his who now had been condemned to the beasts because of these facts, began first to suspect the girl as a rival in her marriage and as a concubine, then to detest her, and then to lie in wait for her with the most cruel, deadly snares.

This part of the story shows similarities with Xen. *Eph.* 5,5, where Polydios' wife maltreats Anthia as her husband's supposed mistress. See Trenkner 1958,93 f. for parallels in novellas.

ilico ... primo ... dehinc ... dehinc: the woman's (presumably gradual) change from suspicion to murderous intent is quickly summarized. The use of *ilico* at the beginning of the sentence, together with the staccato effect of *primo ... dehinc ... dehinc*, confirms the suggestion already made in the previous sentence by *protinus* (see note there) that the destruction wreaked by *Fortuna* will be swift.

haec eadem ..., quae nunc bestiis ... fuerat addicta: the pattern described by Hijmans in *AAGA* 1978,114 f. (proper names are never used in stories that the narrator tells auctorially, i.e. stories that Lucius hears from others) leads here to 'rather involved phrasing', as Hijmans puts it (121, n. 39). Despite the involved phrasing the renewed mention of the *uxor* is a signal that the sententious preface is ended and that the actual story of *uilis ... aliqua ... bestiis addicta* (ch. 23: 254,19 f.) is now beginning. With no less than six pronouns in one sentence, this renewed introduction of the woman who is the subject of this story is as clumsy as her first introduction (see on ch. 23: 254,23 f. *maritum ... cuius pater ... fetum*).

The repetition of *bestiis ... addicta* picks up the thread of ch. 23 (254,19 f.).

haec eadem: the combination *hic idem*, though attested in the *Met.* only here, is common from comedy onward (Callebat 1968,269 with references; also frequent in inscriptions; LHSz 2,188). The use of *eadem* suggests that we are to hear something more about this woman, but the first information given here is merely a close paraphrase (*quae ... fuerat addicta*) of what we learned earlier (ch. 23; *uilis aliqua ... bestiis addicta*). A proper name here would have made things much easier (see the previous note); cf. Juv. 6,112 *hic Sergius idem...*

nunc: refers to the 'now' of the framing tale: this is the woman with whom the ass is to perform in the theatre. From the embedded tales that start halfway through book 9 (the story of the *pistor*; the story of the *pater familias* and his sons) we see the *fabulae* and the 'reality' of Lucius the ass becoming increasingly entwined: the tale of the stepmother happened while he was right on the spot (see ch. 2: 237,1 f. and ch. 7: 242,1 f.; see also Introd. 1.2.1). The main character of this last *fabula* in the *Met.* is expected to enter into close physical relationship with Lucius the ass: she will step out of the *fabula* into the 'reality' of the framing tale. It is from this increasingly oppressive narrative situation that the ass flees at the end of the book. See also Hofmann 1993a,133 f. In book 11 there are no more embedded tales to be found.

propter haec ipsa: *haec* could be taken as pointing ahead to the events to come, i.e. the murders committed by the woman. It is also possible, however, to read *haec ipsa* as a reference to what happened immediately before, i.e. *Fortuna*'s fatal intervention in a development that up to then had been favourable. In that case, the criminal woman eventually becomes a victim of *Fortuna* too, just like Lucius until he manages to struggle out of *Fortuna*'s grasp (11,15: 277,24 f. *en ecce pristinis aerumnis absolutus Isidis magnae prouidentia gaudens Lucius de sua Fortuna triumphat*).

fuerat addicta: for the 'verschobene plusquamperfectum', see on ch. 6 (241,1 f.) *fuerant explicatae* with references.

addicta: see on ch. 23 (254,20) *bestiis addicta*. In that passage *addicta* could still be regarded as the extension of a legal term. But here *addicere* is used in the non-legal meaning 'to condemn, doom'. Cf. Hor. *Epod*. 17,11 f. *addictum feris / alitibus atque canibus ... Hectorem*.

aemulam tori succubamque: cf. 5,28 (126,7 f.) *Psychen ... meae formae succubam, mei nominis aemulam*. In the Psyche passage, *succuba* seems to be simply a synonym of *aemula* 'rival', but in our passage *aemulam ... succubam* may represent a progression from 'rival' to 'supplanter', just as the verbs *suspicari ... detestari ... insidiari* represent a progression in the woman's reaction to her supposed rival. Bernhard 1927,166 gives other examples in the *Met.* of a common prosaic expression next to an almost synonymous uncommon expression.

In both passages the meaning of *succuba* is 'a woman who supplants another'; cf. Hyg. *Astr.* 2,1 *cui* (sc. *Iunoni*) *Callisto succubuerit ut paelex*. The rare *succuba* is not attested before Apuleius. After Apuleius it is found only in Prud. *Peri.* 10,192 (for a male 'mistress') and Greg. Tur. *Hist. Franc.* 1,25. For the possible connection of *succuba* with an erotic use of *succumbere* (e.g. Catul. 111,3; Petr. 126,10; Mart. 14,201,1), see Montero Cartella 1973,177 f.

See Shumate 1996,93 f. on 'mistaken beliefs' leading to fatal chain reactions in the later books of the *Met.*

tori: metonymically for 'marriage', as occasionally elsewhere in the *Met.*; see *GCA* 1985,189 on 8,22 (194,7-12). Before Apuleius this usage is almost exclusively poetic.

primo suspicari, dehinc detestari, dehinc crudelissimis laqueis mortis insidiari: in this tricolon, the first two cola have an equal number of syllables (6), and the third colon is almost three times as long (17) as either of the first two. The three cola are connected by final rhyme; the last two cola by the repetition of *dehinc*. These stylistic devices, in addition to the topheaviness of the third colon, suggest a mercilessly and climactically progressing chain reaction. See also above on *ilico ... primo ... dehinc ...dehinc*. The elaborate parallelism results in some unusual constructions; see the following note and on *insidiari* below.

puellam ... suspicari: when construed with an accusative of the object, *suspicari* usually means 'assume' (so also in the *Met.*, e.g. 8,11: 185,23 f. *nec sequius aliquid suspicatus*; 9,5: 206,6 *nihil ... tale suspicans*; cf. also ch. 3: 238,14 f.). For the sake of parallelism, the accusative of the object is used here with *suspicari* in the sense 'suspect', a much rarer construction. See KSt 2,1,263; cf. e.g. Hor. *C.* 2,4,22 *fuge* (sc. *eum*) *suspicari*, with Nisbet-Hubbard ad loc. There, too, *suspicari* occurs in the context of sexual jealousy.

laqueis mortis: cf. Hor. *C.*3,24,8 *non mortis laqueis expedies caput*. That verse, too, occurs in the context of inexorable fate (*dira Necessitas*, ib. 6), against which there is no protection. As a kind of catchword, *laqueus* is found three times in connection with our murderess: here; below (256,7); and ch. 27 (258,18). See Shumate 1996,238 on *laquei* and *insidiae* as recurring motifs in the first ten books of the *Met.*

insidiari: although ThLL s.v. *insidior* 1895,4 f. gives our passage as an example of the intransitive use of the verb, it is more probable that *puellam*, the object of *suspicari* and *detestari*, is also the object of *insidiari*. For the transitive use *ThLL* ibid. 1896,63 f. gives only a few examples from *Vulg.* and *Itala*, e.g. *Itala, deut.* 19,11 *si fuerit homo odiens proximum et insidiatur eum*.

255,24-25 Tale denique comminiscitur facinus: Therefore she devised the following outrage.

The same transitional formula occurs in 7,19 (168,26) *Denique tale facinus in me comminiscitur*; see *GCA* 1981,207 ad loc.

comminiscitur: from *Sed haec* (255,17) onward, the narrator has been displaying his opinion about the pernicious role of Fortuna and Rivalitas. With its main verbs in the perfect (*potuerunt ... direxit ... coepit*), that part can be designated 'expositio' in the pattern outlined by Kroon-Rose 1996,75: 'On the one hand the *expositio* contains all kinds of evaluative comments of the author/narrator on the reported events... On the other hand one might also assign to the *expositio* those parts of a text in which events are narrated that are essentially part of a narrated world, but somehow fall outside the chronological order of the gradually developing, actual story' (see Kroon-Rose 1996,76 f. and n. 13). Now the main storyline is resumed with the historical present *comminiscitur*.

255,26-256,1 Anulo mariti surrepto rus profecta mittit quendam seruulum sibi quidem fidelem, sed de ipsa Fide[m] pessime merentem, qui puellae nuntiaret, quod eam iuuenis profectus ad uillulam uocaret ad sese, addito, ut sola et sine ullo comite quam maturissime perueniret: Having secretly taken her husband's ring, she left for the country and sent a wretched slave who was, indeed, loyal to her but did Loyalty herself a very ill service; he was to report to the girl that the young man had gone to his little farm and summoned her to him, with the added stipulation that she should come as quickly as possible, alone, without any companion

The following story contains remarkably many motifs that occurred also in the first story (ch. 2-12), often in contrast with their function here. See below on *anulo*; *seruulum*; *ad uillulam uocaret*; *medicum ... quendam notae perfidiae* (ch. 25: 256,23-24), and *momentarium uenenum* (ch. 25: 256,27). See also App. III.

Anulo: on the signet ring as an element typical of comedy, where it is often a sign of recognition, see App. III. Here, in contrast with comedy, this sign of recognition becomes an instrument of deceit in the woman's murderous plans (see below on 256,1-3).
In the previous embedded tale a signet ring also played a part: there it was used by the good physician to unmask the deceit of the stepmother's slave (ch. 9: 243,29; 244,4 and ch. 10: 244,19).

rus profecta: F has *profecto*. The emendation is by Beroaldus.
The woman lures the girl to a desolate place in the country, a place pre-eminently suited to commit a crime. See De Biasi 1990,12 f. on the functions of the frequent 'remote places' in the *Met*. Cf. also *sola et sine ullo comite* below.

mittit ... qui ... nuntiaret: on the imperfect subjunctive in the subordinate clause with the historical present in the main clause, see comm. on ch. 3 (238,13 f.) *unde ... caperet, decunctatur.*

seruulum: in view of the following description, the diminutive may have a denigrating nuance. Callebat 1968,508 opts for a 'truly diminutive value' in this passage. However, at other places Callebat sees in the use of the diminutive a deliberate evocation of a comic atmosphere (*seruulus* is frequent in comedy). That might in a way apply here as well: this devoted slave, running errands for his mistress, evokes such characters in comedy. His occurrence here is at a point where the tale, which started on a comic theme, will move into a quite different direction (see the concluding note to the previous chapter).

The wicked women in both tales of this book have a devoted slave as their helper (cf. ch. 4: 239,21 f.; ch. 7: 242,10 f.). These slaves are the opposites of Myrmex, who acts in the context of a light-hearted story of adultery in 9,17-21; cf. 9,17 (215,23 f.) *seruulum suum Myrmecem fidelitate praecipuum cognitum.*

sibi quidem fidelem, sed de ipsa Fide pessime merentem: the description of the slave, which involves a kind of pun on *fidelem* and *Fide*, characterizes his mistress as well. Cf. Cic. *Clu.* 176 *seruum ... nimium domino fidelem.*

Fide[m]: de emendation is by ç. On the personification of *Fides* see *RAC* 818 [Becker]; cf. also 3,26 (71,21 f.) *Fidei secreta numina*, with Van der Paardt 1971,189. On the personifications in the *Met.* see on ch. 12 (245,22 f.) *procedit ... nuda Veritas*, with references.

nuntiaret, quod...: this is the only instance in Apuleius of *nuntiare* followed by a *quod*-clause rather than by the accusative and infinitive. Callebat 1968,337 f. gives other examples of Apuleius' use of *quod*-clauses after verbs of saying; see ibid. 339 for other examples in late-classical and Christian authors (e.g. Hier. *Matt.* 2,12,46). Billotta 1975,512, with n. 35 remarks that Apuleius with this use in fact revives constructions which can be found in e.g. Plautus; cf. Pl. *Asin.* 52 f. *equidem scio iam filius quod amet meus / istanc meretricem.*

ad uillulam uocaret: in the other tale, the *nouerca* sends her husband to *dissitas ... uillulas* (ch. 4: 239,15) so that she is free to commit adultery in his absence. On the diminutive see the note there.

addito, ut ... perueniret: the deceit is phrased in solemn language (cf. also *sola et sine ullo comite* and *fidem uerbis adstipularetur*). *OLD* s.v. *addo* 14 gives for *addere ut* the definition 'to add (to a law) as a special stipulation, proviso, etc. ...'; thus e.g. Cic. *Phil.* 8,25 *addit praeterea ut, quos ipse ... dederit agros, teneant ei quibus dati sint.* See *ThLL* s.v. *addo* 590,24 f. For the ablative absolute cf. Plin. *Nat.* 15,62 *similiter* (sc. *praecipiunt*) *deligi* (sc. *poma*) *... ante perfectam maturitatem, addito ut luna infra terram sit.*

For the ablative absolute in which the noun has been replaced by a dependent clause, see on *cognito quod res erat* ch. 16 (248,23).

sola et sine ullo comite: the adjective with a synonymous prepositional phrase, especially frequent with *sine*, occurs from time to time in pre-classical Latin, but is especially frequent in solemn poetry and post-classical prose. Cf. Lucr. 5,841 *muta sine ore ..., sine uoltu caeca*; also in a context of murder Sen. *Con.* 10,1,15 *Euctemon ..., cum patrem suum narrasset solum sine comite oppressum et occisum, dixit....* See LHSz 2,788 and 795. See also below on *incomitata.*

maturissime: according to Char. *gramm.* 1,114,14-15 this is the correct form: (sc. *inuenimus*) *etiam 'maturrime' aduerbialiter, cum debeat 'maturissime'.* Both forms are found in Latin of all periods.

256,1-3 Et ne qua forte nasceretur ueniendi cunctatio, tradit anulum marito subtractum, qui monstratus fidem uerbis adstipularetur: And for fear that some delay in her coming might chance to occur, she gave him the ring that she had stolen from her husband, to lend his words extra credibility when it was shown.

ueniendi cunctatio: for the genitive of the gerund with *cunctatio*, *ThLL* s.v. *cunctatio* 1391,52 f. gives, in addition to our passage, only Liv. 5,41,7; 21,56,4; Val. Max. 8,1 *amb.* 2.

anulum: see above on 255,26 *anulo*.

subtractum: *subtrahere* here means 'to remove (an object) so as to deprive someone of the use or enjoyment of it; to appropriate' (*OLD* s.v. *subtraho* 2); by stealing the ring the woman not only deprives her husband of its use, but also makes improper use of it for her own purposes. The verb is used also in 4,18 (88,10-13) *ianitorem ipsum gladio conficit clauique subtracta fores ianuae repandit* (*GCA* 1977,138 ad loc. interprets *sub-* as 'from under'). Cf. Gaius *Inst.* 3,200 *si debitor rem, quam creditori pignori dedit, subtraxerit*. See Heumann-Seckel s.v. *subtraho* for more examples in legal texts.

fidem uerbis adstipularetur: *adstipulari* is a legal term meaning 'to join in a stipulation or covenant'; Heumann-Seckel s.v. *adstipulor*; see also Flobert 1975,126; *ThLL* s.v. *adstipulor* (*astipulor*) 952,11 f.; cf. Gaius *Inst.* 3,112 *ille* (sc. *adstipulator*) *sic adstipulari potest: idem fide tua promittis?* In its broader sense, the verb is also used in Liv. 39,5,3 *adstipularique irato consuli* (*ThLL* 952,17 f.: 'i.q. *adsentiri, comprobare*').

Transitive *adstipulari* is not attested before our passage (Callebat 1968,179 points out the common transitive use of the simple verb *stipulari*); *ThLL* s.v. 952,24 f. notes e.g. Iul. Val. 1,20 *ueredicentiae isti testis accedo nec labores uestras, quos praetenditis, non adstipulor*; Symm. *Ep.* 1,94 *si ... Palladium spectatum bonis omnibus facundia adstipuler*. Our passage is also first to use a thing, rather than a person, as the subject of *adstipulari* (*ThLL* s.v. 952,38 f.); after Apuleius e.g. Ambr. *Hex.* 3,2,7 *adstipulantem nobis lectionis seriem testificamur*.

The dative *uerbis* in our passage is the same dativus commodi as in the Livy passage cited above; cf. also e.g. Ael. Gall. *gram.* 5 *qui alteri adstipulatus est*.

256,4-6 At illa mandatu fratris obsequens - hoc enim nomen sola sciebat - respecto etiam signo eius, quod offerebatur, nauiter, ut praeceptum fuerat, incomitata festinat: The girl, complying with the instructions of her brother – for this appellation was known to her alone – and having also checked his seal, which was shown to her, readily hurried off, unaccompanied as she had been instructed.

At illa: as often in the *Met.*, *at* marks the transition of the focus to a different actor.

mandatu: this is the only passage where *mandatu* is attested as a dative (*ThLL* s.v. 261,3 f.); see LHSz 1,271.

hoc enim ... sciebat: Callebat 1968,108, pointing out its occurrence in historians and poets like Vergil, rightly refutes the notion that parenthesis occurs only in unaffected spoken language (Bernhard 1927,91), a notion based on the supposedly improvised character of parenthesis. In the *Met.*, parentheses are often part of a conscious narrative technique, by which the narrator directly addresses his audience for a moment (see comm. on ch. 1: 236,14 *hoc enim mihi uidebatur* and ch. 18: 250,18 *hoc enim nomine*...). In our passage, the parenthesis contributes to a complex dramatic irony: the girl walks into a trap because she believes the false *mandatum* – but the murderess and the slave, and also the narrator and his audience, know better; on the other hand, the girl knows more than the other actors about the identity of the *iuuenis*. The narrator in his omniscience is superior to all the actors and uses the parenthesis to allow his readers to enjoy the dramatic irony.

Of the examples of parenthesis collected by Bernhard 1927,92, the passages in 1,13; 4,30; 10,18; 10,24; 5,26; 5,28 are about someone's *nomen*. Many tales in the *Met.* involve the theme of people's true or false identity.

sola sciebat: of the actors in this episode, the girl is indeed the only one who knows that the *iuuenis* is her brother. But her mother and the *iuuenis* himself know it, too. Now the *uenerabile silentium* in which the *iuuenis* kept this secret (ch. 23: 255,11 f.), turns out to be a fatal error.

nauiter: see *GCA* 1981,46 on 6,27 (149,20-22) on this adverb, which is often found in the *Met.*; on its form see ibid. 153 on 7,11 (162,16-18).

ut praeceptum fuerat: for the 'verschobene Plusquamperfectum' see on ch. 6 (241,1 f.) *fuerant explicatae*.

incomitata: cf. Dido's nightmare in Verg. *A.* 4,466 f. *semperque relinqui / sola sibi, semper longam incomitata uidetur / ire uiam*, with Austin ad loc.; cf. also Ceres desolately wandering around looking for Persephone in Ov. *Fast.* 4,513 f. *'mater' ait uirgo... 'quid facis in solis incomitata locis?'*. In addition to desolation, this adjective may also suggest death: see *ThLL* s.v. *incomitatus* 984,7 f.; e.g. *Epiced. Drusi* 298 *cur sine me, cur sic incomitatus abis?* Cf. in the *Met.* 8,1 (177,1) *incomitata Manis adiuit*; see Graverini 1997,253 with more references in n. 21.

256,7-14 Sed ubi fraudis extremae lapsa decipulo laqueos insidiarum accessit tunc illa uxor egregia sororem mariti libidinosae furiae stimulis efferata primum quidem nudam flagris ultime uerberat, dehinc, quod res erat, clamantem quo<d>que frustra paelicatus indignatione bulliret fratrisque nomen saepius iterantem uelut mentitam atque cuncta fingentem titione candenti inter media femina detruso crudelissime necauit: But when, misled by the deceit of criminal lies, she walked into the snares of the ambush, then that outstanding wife, made wild by the spurs of unbridled fury, first gave her husband's sister, all naked, a thrashing with a whip almost to death, and then, as the girl shouted what the facts were, and that she was boiling with rage about adultery for nothing, and as she repeated the word 'brother' again and again, the woman killed her in the most cruel fashion, as if she were a liar who was making it all up, by thrusting a blazing firebrand right between her thighs.

fraudis extremae lapsa decipulo: *decipulo* has been taken here as a causal ablative with *lapsa*. For *labi* meaning *errare, peccare*, see *ThLL* s.v. *labor* 1,784,34 f., where our passage is noted; for the combination with a causal ablative cf. e.g. Sal. *Jug.* 104,4 *errasse regem et Iugurthae scelere lapsum*. This creates a contrast with the 'wrong step' from which the mother tries to preserve her children earlier in the story: ch. 23 (255,8 f.) *ne ... caloris iuuenalis impetu lapsus, nescius nesciam sororem incurreret*. Now her daughter commits a truly fatal blunder. Therefore there is no tautology with the following *laqueos ... accessit*. Most translators render *lapsa decipulo* as 'walked into the trap' (*decipulo* is then dative for *in decipulum*), so that the same idea is repeated; thus e.g. Brandt-Ehlers 'Als sie aber der unerhörten Tücke in die Falle gegangen war und schon in den Schlingen des Anschlags steckte'. When Apuleius uses the rare noun *decipulum* (three times; see GCA 1985,57 on 8,5: 179,14-19) it occurs in a context of 'misleading words'; cf. *Fl.* 18,21 *Igitur Euathlus postquam cuncta illa exorabula iudicantium et decipula aduersantium et artificia dicentium uersutus alioqui et ingeniatus ad astutiam facile perdidicit*.

fraudis extremae: an explicative genitive with *decipulo*. For *extremus* = *nefarius*, see on ch. 5 (240,9) *extremi facinoris*.

laqueos ... accessit: for *accedere* with an accusative see GCA 1981,32 on 6,26 (147,22-24).

laqueos insidiarum: see above on 255,24 *laqueis mortis*.

illa uxor egregia: the irony (see on ch. 23: 254,17 *egregia illa uxor*) is made even more bitter by *sororem mariti ... uerberat ... necauit*). After this, there is no more lighthearted irony, and the woman is described as *uxor, quae iam pridem nomen uxoris cum fide perdiderat* (ch. 25: 256,22 f.). Cf. e.g. 2,29 (49,12), where the woman who has poisoned her husband is also called *uxor egregia*. Graverini 1998,128 plausibly argues that the ironical phrase *uxor egregia*, frequently found in the *Met.*, is an allusion to Verg. *A.* 6,523, where the treacherous Helen is not mentioned by name but is referred to as *egregia ... coniunx*.

libidinosae furiae stimulis efferata: the metonymical use of *furia* in the singular is rare and late. *ThLL* s.v. *furia* 1616,73 f. ('i.q. *nimietas affectuum*, sc. *ira, rabies...*') gives as its first occurrence Apul. *Met.* 6,12 (137,16), then our passage; next e.g. *Itala deut.* 11,17 *furia irascitur dominus*; Comm. *instr.* 2,22,7; *Anth.* 294,5 *cur in horrendam furiam recedis?* The metonymical use here does not alter the fact that in the phrase *libidinosae furiae stimulis efferata* there is certainly a suggestion of the Furies (on the theme of the Furies in the *Met.*, see Shumate 1996,115 f. and 1996b,110 f.).

In connection with our passage, Shumate speaks of 'fury of lust ... not one of vengeance'; cf. also Walsh 1994 'lustful fury'. However, the adjective has here no sexual connotation at all, and is used in its first meaning 'self-willed, arbitrary, capricious' (*OLD* s.v. *libidinosus* 1); thus e.g. Brandt-Ehlers 'zügelloser Wut'; cf. [Cic.] *Exil.* 21 *omnia perpeti, quae uolet furor libidinosus*.

efferata: see *OLD* s.v. *effero*^{2} 2 for more examples of *efferare* meaning 'to work up into a state of fury', as e.g. Liv. 5,27,10 *efferati odio iraque*; cf. in the *Met.* e.g. 8,29 (200,20 f.) *efferantur* with GCA 1985,258 ad loc; 9,40 (233,22 f.) *nullis precibus mitigari militem magisque ... efferari* with GCA 1995,331 ad loc. On the dichotomy *feritas-mansuetudo* in the *Met.* in general and in book 10 specifically, see Introd. 2.4.3.2; see also on ch. 16 (249,6 f.) *ad explorandam mansuetudinem* and on ch. 22 (254,5) *rabido*.

nudam: Van der Vliet's *nuda<ta>m* is unnecessary; it can be understood from the context that the girl's clothes have been removed for the lashing. The adjective *nudam* suggests – more than *nudatam* does – an absolute defenselessness; cf. *OLD* s.v. *nudus* 4 'open to attack'. It would even be possible to take *flagris* as a dative with *nudus*: 'defenseless against the lashes'; cf. e.g. Luc. 5,720 *nudas Aquilonibus undas*. In the translation, *flagris* has been taken as an instrumental ablative with *uerberat*.

ultime: Valpy: 'ultime verberare Graecum est: ἐσχάτως μαστιγῶσαι'. *Ultime* is attested only here and 1,7 (7,9), both times meaning 'to the limit'; the *ThLL* material offers no other parallels for this. But Priscianus remarks: *antiqui ... et 'saepior' et 'saepissimus' protulisse inueniuntur, sicut 'ultra ulterius ultime'* (GLK 3,80,6).

quod res erat, clamantem: the phrase *quod res erat* is practically identical with 'the truth'. See on ch. 8 (243,16) *ut res est*, with references; see also *GCA* 1995,220 on 9,25 (221,18-23).

quo<d>que ... bulliret: F has *quoque*. The emendation is by Oudendorp. See *GCA* 1985,41 on 8,3 (178,9-15), with references, on the confusion of *quo* and *quod* in late Latin. See above, on 255,28 f. *nuntiaret, quod ... uocaret* for the *quod*-clause instead of the accusative and infinitive.

paelicatus indignatione: cf. 8,22 (194,5 f.) *dolore paelicatus* with *GCA* 1985,189 ad loc. on *paelicatus* 'the fact or condition of being a *paelex*'.

indignatione bulliret: for the metaphorical use of *bullire*, *ThLL* s.v. *bullio* 2243,52 f. gives our passage as the first (cf. also 2,30; 50,14 *risus ebullit*). Then e.g. Hier. *Ep.* 22,7 *sola libidinum incendia bulliebant*; Aug. *serm.* 180,7,8 *uiuit* (sc. *periurus*) ... *et quodam modo scatet et bullit luxuriis*. In its literal meaning the verb is found from Vitruvius onward; it is frequent in Apicius and in medical texts. See Kißel on Pers. 3,116 f. *feruescit sanguis et ira / scintillant oculi* on medical-philosophical theories at the background of metaphorical language in common language as well as poetry.

titione candenti inter media femina detruso ... necauit: a similar torture is experienced by the ass in 7,28 (176,8 f.) *ardentemque titionem ... mediis inguinibus obtrudit*; see *GCA* 1981,271 f. ad loc. on the *titio* (firebrand) in the Althaea-Meleager myth, clearly alluded to in that passage; cf. ibid. 12 f. *ceterum titione delirantis Althaea Meleager asinus interisset* with *GCA* 1981,273 f. ad loc. There we have a comic, scatological scene, where the ass manages to escape death by torture by blinding his tormentor with *liquida fimus*; our passage, however, is not comic and contains no humorous mythological allusion. The girl dies a gruesome death. Although Hildebrand maintains 'Titionem autem muliebris vindictae non infrequens adiumentum fuisse' there is only one example to be found: Ael. *VH* 13,2 σχίζαν ἁρπάσασα ... ἡμίκαυτον, ταύτῃ τὸν παῖδα ἀπέκτεινεν, remarkably enough also in a story about a series of murders in a family. Aelian probably found this story in an anthology unknown to us and developed it (see Wilson 1997,10 ff.). It is possible that Apuleius derived this part of his tale also from this or another anthology; cf. G. Anderson in *ANRW* 2,33,1,107 f. on the technique, common in the Second Sophistic, of incorporating anecdotes familiar from florilegia in the framework of fiction.

The inversion of the *titio-* motif as compared to 7,28 (see above; there Lucius escapes death, here the girl does not) creates gloomy expectations for Lucius' confrontation with this murderous woman when the main story resumes.

femina: see *GCA* 1985,213 on 8,25 (196,19-21) on the occurrences of *femina* in the *Met.*, often as the object of malicious or equivocal acts.

detruso: for *detrudere* i.q. *defigere*, *ThLL* s.v. *detrudo* 844,44 f. (all places are given) gives only Ov. *Met.* 11,73 (sc. *Bacchus*) *pedum digitos ... / traxit et in solidam detrusit acumine terram*; for thrusting a weapon into someone's body, only our passage and Hyg. *Fab.* 88 (82,42-83,1 Marshall) *Pelopia ... gladium ... in pectus sibi detrusit* are given.

necauit: after the series of historical presents in which the story is told from 255,24 *comminiscitur* onward (see note there), this episode is concluded with a perfect; see on ch. 17 (249,22-26) *iubet ... tradidit* with references.

The first victim of the Murderess of Five has died: an innocent girl; the second victim will be the not so innocent physician (ch. 26); the third victim will be the innocent husband (ch. 27); the fourth victim will be the young, innocent daughter of the murderess, and the fifth the wife of the physician, as greedy as her husband (these last two victims will die in ch. 28). For three out of the five victims of this murderess's *multiforme facinus* (ch. 28: 259,18) the reader's pity is evoked. The grotesque death scenes of both the physician and his wife (ch. 26: 258,4 f. and ch. 28: 259,13 f. respectively) rather set the reader off laughing (see notes ad locc.).

CHAPTER XXV

The woman enlists the help of a physician to poison her husband, the brother of her first victim.

256,15-17 Tunc acerbae mortis exciti nuntiis frater et maritus accurrunt uariisque lamentationibus defletam puellam tradunt sepulturae: Then, startled by the messages about her bitter death, her brother and her fiancé came running and, having wept over the girl with various laments, consigned her to burial.

acerbae mortis: see on ch. 5 (240,11) *acerba filii morte*. Many expressions and motifs from the first inner tale recur in this one; see on ch. 24 (255,26-256,1) and App. III.

maritus: the brother's friend, to whom the girl had been promised in marriage (ch. 23: 255,15 f.). Since the marriage had not yet been performed, she was still living at her brother's house. The use of *maritus* for *sponsus* is rather uncommon. Forcellini s.v. gives [Tib.] 3,4,31 (Lygdamus) *ut iuueni primum uirgo deducta marito*. ThLL s.v. 404,70 f. gives a few examples in Verg. A. of its use 'de procis'. Verg. A. 2,344 has *gener* in the sense of 'future son-in-law'; Servius remarks on this passage: *etiam maritus dicitur et qui est et qui esse uult*. In our passage, the designation *maritus* for her future husband emphasizes the tragic nature of the girl's death.

accurrunt: the previous episode having been concluded with a perfect, the story is now resumed with a historical present (see on ch. 24 *comminiscitur*, 255,24 and *necauit*, 256,14). See *GCA* 1995,292 on 9,35 (229,9-11) for the absolute use of *accurro*; ibid. 265 on 9,31 (226,11-13) for the occurrence of *accurrere* in the *Met*. 'in situations implying an emotional upheaval' (which is the case here).

uariis lamentationibus defletam puellam tradunt sepulturae: the many *a*-sounds seem to illustrate the wails.

tradunt sepulturae: Apuleius generally uses the verb *sepelire*. In three passages in the *Met*., however, he opts for the expression *tradere sepulturae*: here; 4,12 (84,11-12) *quem ... sepulturae traditum*; and 9,30 (cited below in this note). In these passages, *tradere sepulturae* seems to mean more than merely 'bury'; rather, it seems to connote the entire religious ceremony surrounding the burial of a beloved person, as mentioned explicitly in 9,30 (226,8-10) *summis plangoribus summisque lamentationibus atque ultimo lauacro procurant peractisque feralibus officiis, frequenti prosequente comitatu, tradunt sepulturae* (on these *feralia officia* see also *DNP* s.v 'Bestattung', 2,590 f. [Kierdorf] with references). An electronic search yielded many passages in Hyginus for this phrase, e.g. Hyg. 72,1,2 (about Antigone) *Creon ... edixit ne quis Polynicen ... sepulturae traderet*; four passages from the *Digesta*, citing imperial ordinances or legal documents from the first, second, and third centuries A.D. about the right to burial (e.g. *Dig*. 11,7,39; 47,12,3,4;); cf. e.g. 28,7,27 (Modestinus) *laudandus est magis quam accusandus heres, qui reliquias testatoris non in mare secundum ipsius uoluntatem abiecit, sed memoria humanae condicionis sepulturae tradidit*. Cf. also the passages cited from Justin by *GCA* 1977,99 on 4,12 (84,11-12): Justin. 9,4,4 and 12,2,15 *corpus eius Thurini publice redemptum sepulturae tradiderunt*. The phrase should not be translated as equivalent to *sepelire*; a better translation, connoting the entire ceremonial surrounding a burial, is 'consigned her to burial' (Walsh 1995).

As shown by Church 1904,427 f., the use of *sepultura* in the concrete meaning (= *sepulcrum*) is first attested with certainty in Christian funeral inscriptions and literature. In the *Met.*, *sepultura* is always found in the abstract meaning of 'burial' (*pace GCA* 1985,136 on 8,14: 187,24-26. Even in that passage there is no longer any cogent reason to assume the concrete meaning when one reads with Lipsius *[m]unita sepultura* or, with *GCA* ad loc., *inunita sepultura*). In this book cf. e.g. ch. 6 (241,1) *pompae funebres et sepultura*; cf. also 2,20 (41,16).

256,17-22 Nec iuuenis sororis suae mortem tam miseram et quae minime par erat inlatam aequo tolerare quiuit animo, sed medullitus dolore commotus acerrimaeque bili<s> noxio furore perfusus exin flagrantissimis febribus ardebat, ut ipsi quoque iam medela uideretur esse necessaria: The young man could not bear the wretched death that had been inflicted on his sister - one that was not at all deserved - with equanimity; shaken to the core with grief and imbued with the injurious venom of the bitterest bile, he began as a result to burn with intensely blazing fevers so that it was now apparent even to him that a remedy was needed.

mortem tam miseram et quae minime par erat inlatam: thus F, followed by practically all editors. If *quae* is retained, *mortem* is the antecedent of *quae minime par erat*, with *ei* (sc. *sorori*) supplied before *minime par erat*; for such ellipsis in the *Met.* see on ch. 4 (239,3) *exasperandum ... leniendum* (for a different case see on ch. 30: 261,16 f. *malum ... gerens <ei> qui Paris uidebatur*). Then the meaning is 'the ... death, which did not befit her in the least'. See *OLD* s.v. *par*[1] 11c for *par* with a dative, meaning '(of actions, objects) adequate ... matching, fitting'. Cf. e.g. *Epiced. Drusi* 211 f. *tu letum optasti ... / par tibi*. Robertson alone adopts Oudendorp's proposal *qua* instead of *quae*. The reason for Oudendorp's objection to *quae* (supported by Hildebrand) is that in their opinion *quae ... par erat*, with *mortem* as the antecedent, is not good Latin. The reading *qua* disposes of any problems in referring the relative to *mortem*, since the subject of *par erat* would then be *soror*: 'the ... death, which she did not deserve in the least' (with *par* in the sense of *digna*). However, the word order argues for *mortem* as the antecedent of *quae*. Less acceptable, therefore, is the proposal of Augello 1977,218, who retains *quae* but refers it to *sororis*: *mortem* (sc. *<in eam>*), *quae minime par erat*.

mortem tam miseram et quae...: *variatio*, in which *mortem* is qualified first by an attribute, then by a relative clause. Cf. 5,22 (120,21 f.) *corpus ... luculentum et quale...*; 6,9 (134,11) *laetissimum cachinnum ... et qualem...* (see Bernhard 1927,150 f.).

medullitus dolore commotus: for the rare adverb *medullitus*, which, after examples in archaic literature, is not attested until Apuleius, see *GCA* 1981,91 on 7,2 (155,17-156,1); add *ThLL* s.v. 602,48 f. Here the figurative meaning (already in Ennius, *Sat.* 3,7) is combined with a concrete, corporeal meaning, as appears from what follows in this pericope. For *medulla* as 'sedes affectuum' *ThLL* s.v. *medulla* 601,32 f. mentions particularly passages referring to the consuming fire of passion (e.g. Catul. 35,15; Verg. *A*. 4,66; in this book cf. ch. 3: 238,23 with the note there). In the context of grief, such as we have here, *medulla* is attested much less frequently; cf. e.g. Hor. *Ep.* 1,10,28 *certius ... damnum propiusue medullis*; Ov. *Met.* 14,431 f. *luctibus extremum tenues liquefacta medullas / tabuit*. Cf.

also Apul. *Met.* 8,7 (182,10) (Charite) *penitus i<n medul>lis luctu ac maerore carpebat animum.*

acerrimaeque bili<s> noxio furore perfusus: the translations differ, depending on how *bilis* is taken here: figuratively: 'anger, ill temper, ... madness...' (*OLD* s.v. 2), or literally: 'bile'. In the latter case we see here a clear clinical picture of an illness recognized in antiquity as melancholy, as Mudry 1992,172 f., with textual and bibliographical references, argues.

Mudry does not discuss the textual problem in this passage: F had *bili*, which in φ a later hand changed to *bilis*, the reading adopted by all modern editors. Hildebrand, however, defended F's reading *bili* (printed by Eyssenhardt and apparently accepted by Oldfather s.v. *bilis*), taking *acerrimae ... bili* as a dativus (in)commodi with *noxio furore*: '(pervaded by) the madness which was damaging to his *bilis*'. Then we would have to translate *acerrimae* proleptically: 'a madness which damagingly caused his bile to become extra bitter'. *Bili<s> ... furore*, adopted here, should be taken as equivalent to *bili furente*; cf. *Apol.* 50,4 *perniciosa illa dulcedo* (sc. a damaging liquid caused by corporeal disequilibrium) *intus cohibita et bili atrae sociata, uenis omnibus furens peruasit.*

The textual problem, indicative of the difficulties which readers confronting this passage have always felt, is reflected by the diverging interpretations of translators wrestling with its precise meaning. There is probably a deliberate vagueness and even ambiguity on the part of the author, which may reflect a controversy between the physicians of that time (signalled by Mudry 173): some held that emotions were the cause of black bile, others that black bile was the cause of mental disease. Our passage clearly suggests that the young man has become ill from extreme grief (the word order encourages us to connect *furore perfusus*). But in *Apol.* 49,3-50,4 Apuleius is apparently of the opinion that *ater bilis*, mixed with other bad corporeal liquids (*perniciosa ... dulcedo*), is responsible for diseases of the brain, especially epilepsy.

acerrimaeque bilis: arguing that *atra bilis* (cf. 'melancholy') is the normal expression, Oudendorp proposed *aterrimae* for *acerrimae*, but there is no need to alter F's reading: cf. Pers. 2,12 f. *Hercule! pupillumue utinam, quem proximus heres / impello, expungam, nam et est scabiosus et acri / bile tumet*; Ps. Hippocr. *Epist. ad Maec.* 3 *nascitur ... bilis acida et amara, quae dicitur mater morborum.* In his notes on Pers. 2,12 f., Kißel compares for *acris bilis* Galen. 15, p. 637 K., where black bile is called ὀξεῖα; Chrys. *Hom. in Matth.* 63,3 (= PG 58,606), where the adjective πικρά is used for bile; see also *ThLL* s.v. *acer* 360,24 f. ('suci corporis'). Mudry 1992,175 adds another argument for retaining F's *acerrimae*: the adjective *acer* is quite often used, not only in medical literature, for irritating foods or juices, and therapeutical action against such irritation is regularly described with the verb *lenire*, which is used in this chapter too (256,28-257,1 *praecordiis leniendis*; see the note there).

perfusus: this strengthens the presumably intentional ambiguity signalled above. *Perfundere*, literally 'to pour (through), overspread (with liquid), suffuse', etc. (*OLD* s.v. *perfundo* 1-3), is frequently used metaphorically for 'to suffuse, imbue (with an emotion)'; see *OLD* s.v. 5.

exin: for the slightly pleonastic adverb in the apodosis after preceding participle constructions, von Geisau 1912,33 compares the use of *sic* (= οὕτως). Cf. 7,23 (171,18) *exinde* with *GCA* 1981,234 ad loc. Here, as there, we have a mixture of temporal and causal connotations, and *exin* marks a progression.

ut ipsi quoque iam medela uideretur necessaria: Hanson: 'that he too now seemed to need medicine'; Vallette: 'qu'il paraissait indispensable de lui donner des soins à son tour'. Up to now there has been no one else who needed *medela* (the sister is already dead); *ipsi quoque* must be taken with *uideretur*: '(the opinion was that the young man needed *medela*), and to him, too, *medela* seemed necessary'. Thus Helm-Krenkel: 'so daß auch ihm schon ein Heilmittel dringend erforderlich schien'. Apparently the woman convinces her husband, the sick *iuuenis*, that he needs treatment. In that case we may speak of irony: the woman will arrange the poisoning of her husband under the guise of the administration of a medicinal draught.

256,22-28 Sed uxor, quae iam pridem nomen uxoris cum fide perdiderat, medicum conuenit quendam notae perfidiae, qui iam multarum palmarum spectatus proeliis magna dexterae suae tropaea numerabat, eique protinus quinquaginta promittit sestertia, ut ille quidem momentarium uenenum uenderet, illa autem emeret mortem mariti sui: But the wife, who had long since lost the name of 'wife' along with her loyalty, approached a physician of notorious bad faith, who was distinguished for his many victories in combat and could count considerable trophies won by his own hand; she at once offered him fifty thousand sesterces so that he would sell a quick-acting poison and she would buy the death of her husband.

At this point the story takes an odd, illogical turn: after she has committed the first murder out of jealousy, thus removing her supposed rival, the woman is now planning to murder her own husband, for whose sake she committed the earlier murder in the first place. The woman, it seems, is setting out on a random murdering spree: she will kill her husband, the physician himself, and her own young daughter. Shumate 1996,102 speaks of a 'domino effect' and explains it as an 'epistemological breakdown'. The text, however, rather suggests a breakdown of *fides* in all its aspects: in her mad jealousy the woman has lost her *fides*, i.e. her loyalty to, as well as her faith in, her husband. As has been mentioned in the previous chapter, this development is the work of *Fortuna*, who has sent *Riualitas* to the once peaceful family.

The unusual transition, which has no 'logical' motivation, can be best explained in terms of treatment of literary sources: from here on Apuleius is working with a different intertext (see App. III). The story started with a typical comic theme (see the notes on ch. 23: 254,23 f. and App. III); comedy drew these themes from folktale elements (see also Thompson, J21,2), which existed in a narrative form. The theme of 'unjust suspicion' is known not only from comedy but also from novels (see Trenkner 1958,92 f. with references). With the grisly murder of the innocent girl, Apuleius has already left the comic intertext behind. Via the theme (found also in some novels) of 'unjust suspicion' leading to the murder of an innocent person, the story is now going more and more in the direction of the 'crime stories' found in the *declamationes*. As the following notes will show, it is remarkable that in this crime story there are several verbal similarities with orations of Cicero, especially the *pro Cluentio*. It is well-known that this oration in particular had an important influence on the teaching of rhetoric (see below on *qui iam multarum palmarum* ...). See also Winterbottom 1984,590 on Quint. *Decl.* 388,11 about Cicero's *pro Cluentio* as a speech very much in the mind of the Master of that *declamatio*.

quae ... nomen uxoris cum fide perdiderat ... medicum conuenit ... notae perfidiae: the play on words *fide - perfidiae* emphasizes the central role of *fides* (or the lack of it) in this part of the story.

medicum ... notae perfidiae: this *medicus* is the counterpart of the good physician in the first story; see comm. on ch. 8 (243,7 f.) *unus e curia senior prae ceteris compertae fidi atque auctoritatis praecipuae medicus*. See also App. III on elements which connect the two inner tales of this book. The two contrasted doctors make us wonder how these stories would have run if the parts of the good and the evil doctor had been reversed (see also on *medicus* ch. 8: 243,8 f., about the *nouerca*'s 'error'). At the end of this book our ass, too, will 'end up in a different story' (see App. III).

qui iam multarum palmarum spectatus proeliis magna dexterae suae tropaea numerabat: the text in F shows no sign of corruption. No modern editor adopts Van der Vliet's *<multisque> spectatus proeliis* or follows Helm 1904 in deleting *spectatus proeliis* as a gloss. Apuleius develops here one of Cicero's 'winged' words: Cic. *S. Rosc.* 6,17 *alter plurimarum palmarum uetus ac nobilis gladiator* (see Landgraf ad loc.). The genitive of quality *multarum palmarum* is a gladiator's expression; cf. *CIL* 2,1739,2 *(opl)omachus palmaru(m) XX*. But already in Cicero this term is used metaphorically for a murderer who has committed many murders (*gladiator* = *sicarius*). Cf. also *Rhet. Her.* 4,39,51 *sanguinolenta palma, crudelissima uictoria potiti*. *Palma* in the metaphorical sense of 'victory, first place' is common in Latin of all periods (*OLD* s.v. 5 and 6).

In Cicero's *pro Cluentio*, too, a doctor appears who is notorious for his 'victories' in poisoning cases: Cic. *Clu.* 14,40 *ad quam cum adduxisset medicum illum suum iam cognitum et saepe uictorem, per quem interfecerat plurimos*. Cicero's *pro Cluentio* was popular reading material for future orators (Fuhrmann 1970,14; see also the numerous *testimonia* in the edition of Rizzo 1991,38 f.): the poisoning case that Cicero conducted there was undoubtedly a source of inspiration for many *declamationes* (Hammer 1923,20 f.).

spectatus proeliis: although the physician still appears as a 'winner' in this introduction, he is no match for the woman in the next chapter, where the qualification *spectatissimus* (ch. 26: 258,6) is ironical.

tropaea: on the one hand, this continues the metaphorical use of *multarum palmarum* (cf. Cic. *Ver.* 2,115 *utrum hoc signum cupiditatis tuae an tropaeum necessitudinis atque hospitii ... esse uoluisti?*; Cic. *Dom.* 100 *in ea urbe in qua tropaea de me et de re publica uideam constituta*), and our passage is, indeed, mentioned by *OLD* s.v. *tropaeum* for a metaphorical use of the word. But *tropaea ... numerabat* undoubtedly also refers to the high fees the physician charges for his poisons. Cf. Annaratone: 'che poteva ... annoverare ricchi trofei'.

quinquaginta promittit sestertia: a fantastic amount; for the prices of poison in the stories of this book, see on ch. 9 (243,19) *centumque aureos solidos* with references. In view of the woman's lack of *fides*, emphasized in this sentence, the verb *promittit* becomes especially significant: neither the *medicus* himself, nor his wife, whom he orders ch. 26 (258,5-6) to claim the *promissa merces*, receives a penny from her.

ut ille ... momentarium uenenum uenderet, illa ... emeret mortem mariti: a chiastic arrangement of object-verb/verb-object, parallellism in alliteration (*uenenum uenderet/emeret mortem mariti*), and anaphora of *ille* illustrate the close alliance of the criminal couple who, as was mentioned above, match each other perfectly in their loss – and lack – of *fides*. That a lack of *fides* is a bad basis for a partnership is shown by the continuation of the story, when the woman forces the physician to poison himself as well.

momentarium uenenum: here, the meaning of *momentarius* has to be 'quick-acting' (see also on ch. 19: 243,18 *uenenum praesentarium*); elsewhere Apuleius uses *momentarius* meaning 'of brief duration, temporary', which is common in legal texts; see *GCA* 1995,39 f. on 9,1 (203,16) with references; Heumann-Seckel s.v. *momentaneus, momentarius*; *ThLL*. s.v. *momentarius* 1391,19 mentions as its first occurrence Papin. *Dig*. 34,1,8, followed by passages in Apuleius.

ille quidem ... illa autem...: the repetition *ille ... illa* enhances the solidarity of the two criminal negotiators (see above). *Ille ... ille*, like *hic ... hic...*, is used in colloquial language (LHSz 2,182; KSt 2,2,70). Our text follows Brandt-Ehlers, Helm-Krenkel, and Hanson in retaining F's reading *illa*. Other editors follow Van der Vliet, who printed *ipsa*, comparing 11,27 (289,9 f.) *nam et illi studiorum gloriam et ipsi grande compendium sua comparare prouidentia*.

emeret mortem: for the sake of the contrast with *uenenum uenderet* (see the note above) Apuleius creates the daring expression *mortem emere*. See on ch. 5 (240,5) *mortem ebibit*.

mariti sui: the possessive is often redundant in the *Met*. (see *GCA* 1995,42 on 9,2: 203,20 *suo* with references), but in this passage *sui* (placed last in the sentence) emphasizes the seriousness of the crime: 'the death of her own husband'.

256,28-257,3 Quo compecto simulatur necessaria praecordiis leniendis bilique subtrahendae illa praenobilis potio, quam sacram doctiores nominant, sed in eius uice\<m\> subditur alia Proserpinae sacra Saluti: According to this agreement, a counterfeit was made of that well-known drug, necessary for easing gastric pains and dissolving bile, which the more educated call 'the sacred' – but in its place another drug was secretly substituted, sacred to Proserpina Salus.

Quo compecto: with Robertson, Brandt-Ehlers, Augello 1977,218, and Hanson, Stewech's conjecture *compecto* is accepted here, which was already defended by Oudendorp. F has *confecto*; in the margin Robertson signaled a rasure, where in his view the first hand had written *conspect..*; φ has, indeed, *conspecto*; a* have *conspectu*. Hildebrand defended *confecto*, because in his opinion the doctor and the woman do not make an agreement, but simply make preparations for the poisoning. Van der Vliet, Helm, and Giarratano-Frassinetti adopt F's reading *confecto*. There are, however, two reasons to prefer *compecto*. The first is that the first hand in the margin of F, group a*, and φ have *conspecto* (unacceptable here); *ThLL* s.v. *compaciscor* 1996,25 f. gives several examples of *compect...* corrupted to *conspect...* (e.g. Pl. *Ps*. 543; Suet. *Aug*. 15). Thus F at *Apol*. 74,2 (see Hunink 1997,190 n. 1 ad loc.). The other reason is that the partners in crime have indeed reached an agreement (contra Hildebrand).

simulatur ... subditur: the passive forms reflect the action as performed by the criminal couple, which by agreement (*quo compecto*) is acting as a collective.

simulatur necessaria ... potio: see *OLD* s.v. *simulo* 5 'to make, produce ... a fraudulent imitation of, counterfeit, simulate'.

praecordiis leniendis bilique subtrahendae: the concise, medical-technical translation of Walsh has been borrowed here. The combination of truly concrete medical terms and metaphorical expressions in this phrase is lost in translation: *praecordiis leniendis* means (in a concrete sense) 'soothing the inner organs' (Hanson) and (metaphorically) 'soothing the emotional distress' (Brandt-Ehlers: 'zur Linderung der Gemütskrankheit'). For *lenire* 'in re medica' see *ThLL* s.v. *lenio* 1142,14 f., with e.g. Cels. 6,6,8^c *latentia acria lenire* (ibid. 36 f. our passage is also noted). *Bili subtrahendae* in a concrete, medical sense means 'draw off bile', but also metaphorically 'dispel the bad mood'. For *bilis* 'anger, ill temper...' see *OLD* s.v. 2; for *subtrahere* 'to take away, remove or withhold (immaterial or abstract things)' see *OLD* s.v. *subtraho* 6a. Brandt-Ehlers translate the first part metaphorically (see above), but the second part concretely: 'zum Entzug von Galle'. Most translations opt for a concrete, strongly medically coloured rendition in both parts; thus e.g. Vallette: 'à calmer les entrailles et évacuer la bile'. The doctor, the murderess's accomplice, shows off his learning in recommending a medical treatment; in this context a concrete translation, as technical as possible, is preferable.

bili ... subtrahendae: for *subtrahere* as a medical term ('to draw off morbid matter') *OLD* s.v. *subtraho* 1d mentions besides our passage only Cels. 3,4,2 *eam materiem, quae laedere uidebatur, ducendo ... aluum subtrahebant*. More usual in this context is *detrahere*. See *ThLL* s.v. *detraho* 833,52 f. ('i.q. humores, sucum, sanguinem, materiam, demere, purgere, extrahere').

illa praenobilis potio: in the first inner tale a (good) physician speaks about a well-known medicine in similar terms; see ch. 11 (245,1 f.) *mandragoram illum ... famosum*. On the use of *ille* see the note there. See App. III on the elements connecting the two inner stories.

For *praenobilis* see *GCA* 1985,32 on 8,1 (177,5-10), which does not mention our passage. *Praenobilis* is not attested before Apuleius (*ThLL* s.v. 730,70 f.); after him, a few passages in Prudentius are noted (Prud. *ham.* 698 ; *c. Symm.* 1,111 and 2,644).

potio, quam sacram doctiores nominant: Beroaldus supposed that hellebore is meant: 'Apud priscos potio hellebori principalis habebatur, et sacra, quae trahit alvum, et bilem pituitasque'. This is derived from Plin. *Nat.* 25,22,54 *nigrum* (sc. *melampodion*) *medetur paralyticis, insanientibus, ... trahit ex aluo bilem, pituitas, aquas* and 25,24,60 *medetur ita morbis comitialibus, ut diximus, uertigini, melancholicis, insanientibus*. Pliny, however, never mentions a *sacra potio* in this connection. Beroaldus also records an anecdote told in Pliny about hellebore, but neither he nor the other early commentators (who borrow much of his note verbatim) can, in spite of all the extra information they give, remedy the problem that nowhere in Latin is hellebore called a *sacra potio*. Beroaldus' assumption keeps recurring in modern commentators (e.g. Vallette, note 1 ad loc.). Van Thiel 1971 (1,148, Anm. 189) also supposes that here 'schwarze Nieswurz' (= hellebore) is meant and adduces Greek parallels like Diosc. 4,162,2 f., who describes its wide range of effects in terms very much like those in our passage: καθαίρει δὲ τὴν κάτω κοιλίαν ἄγων φλέγμα καὶ χολήν. ... ὠφελεῖ δὲ ἐπιληπτικούς, μελαγχολικούς, ἀρθριτικούς, παραλελυμένους, (cf. also the Pliny passages cited above). Van Thiel sees the correspondence with the Dioscourides passage as a support of his opinion that this part of the story also occurred in the Greek Μεταμορφώσεις, whose author obviously had medical knowledge (as appears from the *Onos*). But Van Thiel cannot find a precise Greek parallel for the name *sacra potio* for this medicine; neither is the fact that Dioscourides elsewhere (2,65) speaks of the purifying effect of κολοκυνθίς (= gourd) as ἡ ... διὰ τῆς κολοκυνθίδος ἱερὰ δόσις, of much avail.

Haupt's solution to this problem was to read *potio, quam sacram <Saluti> doctiores nominant*. The problematic *Saluti* at the end of this sentence (see below on *Proserpinae* *sacra Saluti*) was thus moved forward and connected with *sacram*, so that *potio sacra Saluti* could be understood as 'beneficial potion'. Haupt is followed by Brandt-Ehlers ('Lebenselixier'), Hanson ('life's elixir'), and evidently also by Walsh ('The Health-offering').

Mudry 1992,175 f. understood the text of F in its literal sense and found in a passage of Scribonius Largus the explanation of the name of a very famous (*praenobilis*) potion, called *sacra potio* by scholars (*doctiores*), which evidently is highly effective in curing the type of illness the young man is suffering from. This medicine is the *Antidotos hiera Paccii Antiochi ad uniuersa corporis uitia*, described in Larg. 97-107. Scribonius Largus tells in c. 97 how this formula was developed by the Greek physician Paccius Antiochus, who was working in Rome at the time of Tiberius. Paccius guarded the secret of the formula jealously during his lifetime, but Scribonius Largus was able to detect it in a document posthumously dedicated to Tiberius, which had been deposited in a public library. In c. 98 Largus mentions that he always keeps some of this versatile (*ad plura uitia efficaciter*) remedy in stock. In c. 99 Largus reports that this medicine is administered as a potion (*prodest data pondere duum ex aquae mulsae cyathis quattuor*); he also offers some explanations for the name of the remedy, which is called *antidotos hiera* by Paccius but not by everyone else: *dicitur enim a quibusdam picra, quia amara est, a quibusdam diacolocynthidos*. This also explains Apuleius' addition that the *doctiores* (i.e. those who have read medical texts like Largus' *Compositiones*) call this potion *sacra potio* (see further Mudry 1992,177-180, where at the end the precise formula is given). Apuleius himself should be counted among the *doctiores*; certainly he had a broad medical knowledge, and from a citation in Prisc. *GLK* 2,203 it appears that he even wrote a work *De Medicinalibus*. Cf. also his learned discussion of epilepsy in *Apol.* 49-51. It is therefore unnecessary to follow Van Thiel in ascribing to the Greek Vorlage those passages in the *Met.* that give evidence of medical knowledge (see also Schmidt in *GCA* 1995, App. I on 9,11: 211,15 f.).

sacram ... Proserpinae sacra: an Apuleian play on words with the two meanings of *sacer* ('holy' and 'dedicated to'); see Callebat 1968,472 with more examples. This pun would be lost if one were to follow Haupt in adding <*Saluti*> to the first *sacram* (see the previous note). Cf. a similar play on two meanings of *secundus* in 6,13 (138,3-4) *nec tamen ... secundi laboris periculum secundum testimonium meruit*.

in eius uice<m>: F and φ have the ablative. All editors adopt the emendation by Stewech; see *GCA* 1985,276 on 8,31 (202,17) *uicem*. See also on ch. 10 (244,7 f.) *in uicem*.

subditur alia Proserpinae sacra Saluti: the personification was proposed by Leo. According to Kaibel, *Proserpina Salus* is a romanization of Κόρη Σώτειρα; for more examples see Roscher s.v. *Soteira* XIII, e.g. Paus. 8,31,1 τὴν Κόρην δὲ Σώτειραν καλοῦσιν οἱ Ἀρκάδες. There are no parallels in Latin for *Proserpina Salus*; Roscher s.v. *Salus* follows Haupt's proposal to move *Saluti* (see above on *potio, quam sacram doctiores nominant*), which would contrast *Proserpina* to *Salus*. With Robertson, Giarratano-Frassinetti, and Helm-Krenkel the reading of F is retained here, even if the combination *Proserpina Salus* remains problematic. Kaibel's explanation is the most plausible; cf. also Vallette, note 3 ad loc.: 'ce surnom donné ici à Proserpine caractérise la reine des enfers comme étant celle qui délivre et guérit tous les maux'. Carlesi translates *alia Proserpinae sacra Saluti* with 'un'altra sacra alla morte', and explains (note 3 ad loc.) the phrase as a euphemism: 'Questo sincretismo religioso, per cui si viene a riunire in un tutto diciamo così organico la salute e la morte, è secondo noi da intendersi più che altro in senso eufemistico'.

Brakman (followed by Helm and Brandt-Ehlers) proposed to delete *Saluti* as a gloss on *sacra* (see the note on *sacra* above). While his paleographical explanation is unconvincing, his proposal is attractive because the deletion of *saluti* would make the pun on *sacer* (see above, on *sacram* ... *Proserpinae sacra*) more pointed. Another solution is the move proposed by Haupt (see above), which is adopted by Hanson. Plasberg proposed *Proserpinae sacra <non> Saluti*; Van der Vliet *Proserpinae sacra saluti <infesta>*.

257,3-5 Iamque praesente familia et nonnullis amicis et adfinibus aegroto medicus poculum probe temperatum manu sua porrigebat: And now, in the presence of the household and a few friends and relatives, the doctor wanted to hand the patient the cup with the potion, carefully mixed by his own hand.

Iamque ... porrigebat: for '*iam* de préparation' see on ch. 5 (240,7-9) *iamque ... insimulabant*. The continuation of the story will show that *porrigebat* is a conative imperfect.

praesente familia et ... amicis et adfinibus: the singular participle *praesente* (or *absente*) is often combined with plural nouns: this can be explained by the frequent first position of *praesente* (*absente*) with the proper names following in protocol style. For more examples see ThLL s.v. *praesens* 838,55 f. 'numero non congruente'. Cf. Ter. *Eu.* 649 *absente nobis*, with Tromaras 1994,212 ad loc. with references; *Rhet. Her.* 4,11,16 *praesente multis*. According to LHSz 2,445, *praesente* and *absente* have almost become prepositions. Cf. also Donatus ad Ter. *Eu.* 649, who calls the usage an archaism and remarks: *pro praepositione ..., ut si diceret 'coram amicis'*. The copulative link with *familia* renders the incongruence less obvious here.

The detailed mention of witnesses at the administration of the potion contributes to the dramatic irony in the next chapter. See on *carissimo mihi marito* ch. 26 (257,9).

poculum probe temperatum manu sua porrigebat: cf. ch. 4 (239,25 f.) *uenenum ... diligenter dilutum ... praeparat*, and especially ch. 7 (242,19-22) *quod uenenum sua manu temperatum dandum fratri reddiderit, quod ... poculum sua ... manu porrexerit puero*. On the many elements connecting the two inner tales in this book, see above, on 256,15 *acerbae mortis* and 256,23 f. *medicum ... notae perfidiae*; see also App. III.

CHAPTER XXVI

The murderess forces the physician to drink first from the poisoned cup prepared for her husband.

257,5-10 Sed audax illa mulier, ut simul et conscium sceleris amoliretur et quam desponderat pecuniam lucraretur, coram detento calice: 'Non prius', inquit, 'medicorum optime, non prius carissimo mihi marito trades istam potionem quam de ea bonam partem hauseris ipse': But that shameless woman, who intended, at one stroke, both to get rid of her partner in crime and to save the money she had promised, personally stayed the cup and said: 'Not yet, my good doctor, not yet will you give my beloved husband that draught – not until you have drunk a generous part of it yourself.'

The motif of a doctor tasting the medicine before the patient so that the patient can be sure it is not poisonous (cf. Ach.Tat. 4,16,4) is cleverly reversed here: the woman, who knows that the medicine is poisonous, forces the doctor, who knows it too, to taste it first.

A similar incident (without a physician) occurs in Justin's epitome of Pompeius Trogus' *Historiae Philippicae* 39,2,7 f.: Grypos' mother offers him a cup of poison, but he forces her to drink first, ostensibly because of *pietas* but in reality because he knows a murder is being attempted: *sic uicta regina scelere in se uerso ueneno, quod alii parauerat, extinguitur*. This story, which is told in Justin as if it were an episode from a novel (and may have been recounted at even greater length in Trogus), is mentioned in a single sentence in Appian. *Syr.* 69.

There is also reversal of a motif found in the first story of this book, where a 'poisoned' cup (which in reality contained not poison but a sleeping draught) was drained by someone other than its intended recipient, so that two lives were saved. In our passage, poison passing as medicine is taken not only by the person for whom it is intended but also by someone else; this results in two deaths.

This is the only chapter of the story in which direct discourse is found, and twice at that; in both cases the speaker is the murderess. The result is that at this 'moment suprême' the story, which is otherwise narrated at a rather brisk pace, comes briefly to a complete halt (narration time = narrated time), which brings the suspense to a climax. See Introd. **1.6** and **1.6.4**. Moreover, the many insincerities in the woman's direct discourse, which are understood by the well-informed reader but not by the fictional spectators, are a source of dramatic irony (see several notes in this chapter, e.g. below on *medicorum optime*).

audax: in Apuleius' works this adjective occurs only three times: *Apol.* 89,6 *o falsum audax et nimium, o mendacium uiginti annorum exsilio puniendum!*; *Met.* 5,23 (121,13. in the vehement apostrophe to the *lucerna*) *hem audax et temeraria lucerna*; and here. The adjective, which is always accusatory, connotes 'impious self-assertion' (Nisbet-Hubbard ad Hor. *C.* 1,3,25).

conscium ... amoliretur: *amoliri* with a personal object is attested first Curt. 8,5,17: cf. also Petr. 10,7 *iam dudum ... amoliri cupiebam custodem molestum*. See also Koestermann on Tac. *Ann.* 2,42,1. But before Apuleius the verb means 'loco submovere, non tollere aut perdere' (*ThLL* s.v. *amolior* 1965,77 f.). Apuleius goes one step further in using *amoliri* here indeed as 'perdere'.

lucraretur: true parallels for *lucrari* meaning 'to save on' expenses are found mostly in legal literature, e.g. Paul. *Dig.* 40,7,20 pr.; Ulp. *Dig.* 32,3,2. But cf. Plin. *Nat.* 18,68 *marina aqua subigi (triticum), quod plerique in maritimis locis faciunt occasione lucrandi salis.*

quam desponderat pecuniam: for *despondere* in its broader meaning 'promise', *ThLL* s.v. *despondeo* 750,46 f. gives examples from Cicero onward, e.g. *Prov.* 36 *is ut eam* (sc. *prouinciam*) *desponsam, non decretam habere uideatur.*

coram: 'in person' (*OLD* s.v. 1b).

non ... trades: the future indicative in a command or a prohibition occurs frequently in colloquial language and legal documents; in dialogue, as the examples in LHSz 2,311 show, it reflects the speaker's firm expectation as to the other person's future behaviour, thus becoming an order (see Pinkster 1990,226), and is often used for solemn, emphatic denials. This is the case in our passage, as is also shown by the duplicated *non prius* (see the next note). Cf. Pl. *Bacch.* 515 *numquam edepol uiua me inridebit* (see also Callebat 1968,100).

non prius ... non prius: with the anaphora the woman adds weight to her gesture (*detento calice*).

medicorum optime: to the fictional spectators this is a polite phrase; to the reader it is an ironical reference to the introduction of the doctor (ch. 25: 256,23 f.) as the undisputed winner in evil practices. See also the next note and below on *priusquam ... appareat.*

carissimo mihi marito: again (see the previous note) the reader is the only one to recognize the hypocrisy of these words and to enjoy the act of the loving wife the woman is putting on for the fictional audience (*praesente familia et nonnullis amicis* ch. 25: 257,3-4).

257,10-11 'Unde enim scio, an noxium in ea lateat uenenum?': 'For how do I know whether there is noxious poison lurking in it?'

Unde ... scio: Quint. *Decl.* 321 has someone defend himself against a charge of having administered poison to his brother in the presence of witnesses by arguing that that would have been stupid, saying (23): *uenenum do: et unde scio an exhausta potione statim concidat?* Our murderess, on the other hand, wants to be sure that the poison is truly deadly. The reader's question, how the woman would achieve the poisoning of her husband after the doctor has drunk the medicine and died, remains unanswered. On other loose ends in this story, see below on *sed aegre ... abire concessit.*

Callebat 1968,102 sees here and in 1,15 (14,9) *unde ... scio an conuectore illo tuo ... iugulato fugae mandes praesidium?* a case of the deliberative indicative (thus also Molt on 1,15). But the question *unde scio an ...?* is to be regarded as a variant of the usual *haud scio an ..., nescio an ...*: 'I am inclined to think, probably'. See *OLD* s.v. *an* 8; in the examples there we sometimes find a subjunctive, e.g. Cic. *de Orat.* 2,18 *haud sciam an nulla (ineptia) sit maior,* but it is certainly not deliberative (see LHSz 2,335); *scio* should be regarded as a true indicative.

noxium ... lateat uenenum: see on ch. 5 (240,3) *in quo uenenum latebat.*

257,11-14 'Quae res utique te tam prudentem tamque doctum uirum nequaquam offendit, si religiosa uxor circa salutem mariti sollicita necessariam adfero pietatem.': 'Surely this precaution does not offend you, so prudent and so experienced a man, when as a devoted wife, concerned about my husband's well-being, I give due weight to the proper sense of duty.'

utique ... nequaquam: with this emphatic negative the woman makes it clear from the start that she will tolerate no contradiction.

Callebat 1968,97, with references, discusses the increasing frequency of *utique*, often in combination with a negative, from the early Empire onward. In the *Met.* the particle is generally found in direct discourse.

te tam prudentem ... doctum: to the onlookers this sounds like a polite phrase addressed to the physician. The reader, who is better informed, understands the menacing irony: the physician may indeed be called *prudens*, for he knows the potion's properties (*OLD* s.v. *prudens* 1 'well aware of what one does or of the consequences of one's action'): for a negative meaning of *prudens* cf. *Apol.* 52,4 *at tu, miser, prudens et sciens delinquis*. In chapter 25 it was mentioned that the physician has much experience in poisoning, and is therefore *doctus* (*OLD* s.v. *doctus* 2 'taught by practice or experience, expert'). On the irony in the woman's speech see above on *medicorum optime*.

offendit: thus F. Most editors (including Helm) follow Van der Vliet's conjecture *offendet*. This is attractive (the future tense would reinforce the commanding tone of the words; see above on *trades*) but unnecessary. The present lends the remark a sort of universal validity: 'a sensible person does not object to a safety measure like this'. Terzaghi retains the transmitted reading; Augello 1977,218 agrees.

circa salutem ... sollicita: again, the reader hears the irony (see above on *medicorum optime*) in the woman's description of herself. She is indeed concerned about her husband's health: she does not want him to get well!

This is the only passage in the *Met.* where *sollicitus* is construed with *circa* (for the various constructions with *sollicitus*, see GCA 1995,88 on 9,8: 208,16-19, and Callebat 1968,217 f.). Cf. *Apol.* 72,4 *facit omnia circa honorem meum obseruanter, circa salutem sollicite, circa amorem callide*.

LHSz 2,226 discuss the development of the metaphorical use of *circa* ('as to...') in imperial prose (see also ch. V,58 of Furneaux' Introduction to Tac. *Ann.*). Cf. in the *Met.* 6,8 (134,5) *quantos labores circa tuas inquisitiones sustinuerimus*. Cf. the examples in Christian authors in Blaise s.v. *circa* 3.

necessariam adfero pietatem: cf. Cic. *Div. Caec.* 25 *qui nihil se arbitrabantur ad iudicia ... praeter fidem et ingenium afferre oportere*, and further examples in *OLD* s.v. *affero* 2c 'to bring (qualities...) with one into a situation'.

The overtone 'closely connected by family ties', which can be clearly heard in *necessarius*, is lost in translation. See on ch. 3 (238,27 f.) *necessarii facinoris*.

257,15-20 Qua mira desperatione truculentae feminae repente perturbatus medicus excussusque toto consilio et ob angustiam temporis spatio cogitandi priuatus, antequam trepidatione aliqua uel cunctatione ipsa daret malae conscientiae suspicionem, indidem de po[r]tione gustauit ampliter: By the amazing audacity of the heartless woman the doctor was suddenly thrown into confusion and completely driven out of his wits; through lack of time he was deprived of an interval for thought; and sooner than arouse the suspicion of a bad conscience by panicking or even by tarrying, he took a generous taste of that same potion.

As the suspense reaches its climax, a series of participial phrases and a long dependent clause postpone the inevitable ending, which is described in a very short main clause. First, the doctor's confusion and indecision are illustrated by *perturbatus ... excussus ... priuatus* (the latter two participial phrases arranged chiastically); there follows the dependent clause *antequam ... daret ... suspicionem*, which contains the motivation of his eventual reaction. For a similar procedure, in which the author slowly works up to a climax, see on ch. 5 (239,27-240,4), which also deals with a fatal draught from a poisoned cup.

desperatione: the word occurs only here in Apuleius' works and it has the unusual meaning 'audacity, insolent behaviour'. This puzzled earlier scholars, who proposed conjectures like *despectione* (Colvius), *deieratione* (Salmasius), and *protestatione* (Castiglioni). Pricaeus, however, defended *desperatione* as meaning 'audacia perdita ac profligata'. Similarly, the adjective *desperatus* is frequently used as invective (see on *desperatissimum ... latronem* ch. 11: 245,3).

After our passage, *OLD* s.v. *desperatio* 3 notes two inscriptions: *CIL* 5,2781, in which freedmen's indictment of their *domini* or *patroni* is described as *desperatio*, and *CIL* 8,8924, in which an insurrection is called a *desperatio*. Cf. also Vulg. 2 *reg.* 2,26 *desperatio periculosa*; id. *Sirach* 27,24. *ThLL* s.v. *desperatio* 738,11 f. notes the meaning in our passage as 'metonymice i.q. temeritas'. Cf. Arn. *Nat.* 1,25 *quid promere temerariae uocis desperatione temptatis ?* and 6,1; Tert. *Apol.* 50,4 *merito itaque uictis non placemus; merito desperati et perditi existimamur. sed haec "desperatio et perditio" penes nos in causam gloriae et famae uexillum uirtutis extollunt.*

truculentae feminae: cf. *truculenta mulier* below. In both cases the adjective expresses the doctor's dismay at his accomplice's brutality.

excussus ... consilio: cf. Stat. *Theb.* 2,570 *agmen excutitur coeptis.*

toto consilio: here, as often in the *Met.*, *totus* is synonymous with *omnis*; see *GCA* 1995,34 on 9,1 (202,26) *totis pedibus*, with references.

spatio cogitandi: *OLD* s.v. *spatium* 10 gives other examples for 'time available for a purpose', often with the gerund in the genitive, or with *ad*; cf. Cic. *Fin.* 4,1 *spatium sumamus ad cogitandum.*

indidem de potione: the adverb reinforces the prepositional phrase. Cf. *GCA* 1985,138 on 8,14 (188,1-4) *ibidem ad sepulcrum*. When we read the phrase from the doctor's point of view (cf. above on *truculentae feminae*), *indidem* is even more striking: he knows only too well what he is drinking. Cf. 6,13 (138,11 f.), where Venus knows very well how dangerous is the task she is giving Psyche: *indidem mihi de summi fontis penita scaturrigine ... rorem ... defer.*

po[r]tione: in F, the *r* is erased by the first hand.

gustauit ampliter: Callebat 1968,518 points out that the use of *ampliter* as an intensive is Plautine (Bernhard 1927,134 calls *ampliter* 'vulgär' because of the suffix *-iter*). For the word order, cf. below in this chapter (258,4) *peruadit aegerrime*; see comm. on ch. 32 (263,3) *constitit amoene*. In Plautus, too, *ampliter* almost always occurs at the end of the sentence (or verse); e.g. *Bac.* 677; *Cist.* 598. The archaism is revived by Gellius (Marache

1957,209); cf. e.g. Gel. 10,3,4 *ecquid est quod aut ampliter insigniterque ... dixerit ?* Marache translates here 'avec grandeur', and this connotation is also possible here: the doctor sees no other course than to play his part as best he can and so, 'avec grandeur', he gulps down a big mouthful.

257,20-21 Quam fidem secutus adulescens etiam, sumpto calice, quod offerebatur hausit: Relying on this sign of good faith, the young man too, taking the cup, drank what was administered to him.

fidem secutus: *fidem sequi* is a legal term for 'to rely on (a person's) good faith'; see *OLD* s.v. *sequor* 10c, which cites e.g. Gaius *Inst.* 4,70 *qui ita negotium gerit, magis patris dominiue quam filii seruiue fidem sequitur.* The phrase occurs also in a non-legal sense, meaning 'to submit to, place oneself under the protection of...', e.g. Cic. *Ver.* 5,124 *nos semper ... amicitiam fidemque populi Romani secuti sumus*. See Freyburger 1986,70 with references.

offerebatur: for *offerre* 'to administer' (e.g. a remedy), cf. Cels. 4,20,3 *offerre potui mulsum*.

257,21-24 Ad istum modum praesenti transacto negotio medicus quam celerrime domum remeabat, salutifera potione pestem praecedentis ueneni festinans extinguere: When he had thus completed the business at hand, the doctor wanted to go home as quickly as possible, in a hurry to use a salutary potion to quench the pernicious effect of the poison that had gone before.

Ad istum modum: see on ch. 12 (245,11).

praesenti ... negotio: in addition to our passage, Apuleius uses this forensic expression, used in formulas of legal *acta* (Norden 1912,154 with n. 5), also in 2,13 (36,4 f.) and 7,13 (163,27). None of these passages gives us reason to assume that *praesens* is equivalent to *hic* (contra Callebat 1968,291), but rather, in all of them *praesens negotium* stands emphatically for 'the matter which is of interest at that moment' (see *OLD* s.v. *praesens* 11).

remeabat: the following sentence makes it clear that this is a conative imperfect.

salutifera potione: cf. Stat. *Ach.* 1,117 *nosse salutiferas dubiis animantibus herbas.* Before Apuleius, *salutifer* occurs only in poetry. The adjective is first attested in Ovid, who created it, according to the commentators; see Bömer on Ov. *Met.* 2,642; Lyne on *Ciris* 477. Apuleius uses it three times: our passage, *Met.* 4,25 (94,6 *spei salutiferi*), and *Mun.* 27,20 *salutifera opera* (Bajoni 1994,1817 ad loc. refers to Ov. *Ep.* 21,174 *salutiferam opem*). After Apuleius, *salutifer* is attested in the prose of Christian authors, e.g. Lact. *Inst.* 4,12,6 *saluator, quia cunctis gentibus salutifer uenit*; see Blaise s.v. *salutifer* for more examples.

pestem ... ueneni ... extinguere: cf. Plin. *Nat.* 20,178 (sc. *origanum Heraclium*) *uenena opii et gypsi extinguit decoctum*, and see *ThLL* s.v. *exstinguo* 1922,13 f. for other occurrences (Apul. *Met.* 9,3: 204,21-22 is included incorrectly).

pestem ... ueneni: cf. [Quint.] *Decl.* 17,11 (342,6 f. Håkanson) *lentum (uenenum) et quod tarda peste consumat*.

praecedentis ueneni: the poison is already on its way, and must be 'overtaken' by the beneficial potion. Therefore, *praecedens* here means literally 'going ahead, going before' and cannot be equated with *ille* (see also Callebat 1968,292). For the image of a poison 'on its way', cf. [Quint.] *Decl.* 13,6 (271,20 Håkanson) (sc. *uenenum*) *ineuitabilem pestem ... grassantem*.

festinans: no one knows better than the physician that haste is of the utmost importance: the woman instructed him to prepare a fast-working poison (ch. 25: 256,27 *momentarium uenenum*).

257,24-258,1 Nec eum obstinatione sacrilega, qua semel coeperat, truculenta mulier ungue latius a se discedere passa est – 'priusquam', inquit, 'digesta potione medicinae prouentus appareat' –, sed aegre precibus et obtestationibus eius multum ac diu fatigata tandem abire concessit: But holding with unholy stubbornness to her original plan, the cruel woman did not let him to move more than a nail's breadth away from her – 'not until' she said 'the potion has been digested and the treatment proves successful' – and reluctantly, having at last become very weary of his pleas and entreaties, she finally gave him permission to leave.

obstinatione sacrilega, qua semel coeperat: *obstinatio* was one of the key-words in the polemics between Christians and pagans. Christians used the word for the stubbornness with which the pagans held on to their gods. Cf. Tert. *Nat.* 1,4,11 (*ThLL* s.v. *obstinatio* 241,77 f. with more examples); Cypr. *Ep.* 4,4 *sciant se cum hac sua inpudica obstinatione numquam a nobis admitti in ecclesia posse*. The combination with *sacrilegus* is also attested in that context: Cypr. *Ep.* 54,3 *superba est ista obstinatio et sacrilega praesumptio*. Conversely, pagans used the word *obstinatio* for the stubbornness with which Christians refused to worship several gods (emperors); cf. Tert. *Nat.* 1,17,2 *prima obstinatio est ... quod inreligiosi dicamur in Caesares*. See *ThLL* s.v. *obstinatio* 241,66 f. for more examples; see also Schmidt 1997,52 and 60. St. Augustine uses the phrase e.g. *Ep.* 108,3 *superba est ista praesumptio et sacrilega obstinatio, quam sibi furor prauus adsumit, et, dum sibi semper aliquid amplius, quam mitis iustitia deposcit, adsumunt, de ecclesia pereunt et, dum se insolenter extollunt, ipso suo tumore caecati ueritatis lumen amittunt*; also Aug. *Cresc.* 2,34,43; 3,69,80; *Gaud.* 2,3,3; 2,13,14.

In *Met.* 9,14 (213,20) the *pistor*'s wife is said to worship one god *sacrilega praesumptione*; Schmidt 1997 argues that she is a Christian. In our passage Apuleius apparently uses the phrase *obstinatio sacrilega* as a common expression of denigration, also when this is not in the context of religious controversy.

truculenta mulier: cf. above in this chapter, *truculentae feminae*.

ungue latius: the expression is proverbial (see Otto 1890,356 with examples). In the two other passages in the *Met.* where it is found, the context is an erotic (2,18: 39,19-21) or otherwise loving (11,17: 280,5 f.) relationship, where the subject (first Fotis, then Isis) does not allow Lucius to remove himself from her *ungue latius*. In those passages the homodiegetic actorial narrator interprets that as love or thoughtfulness, whereas the reader with an overall view of the *Met.* may see it rather as an exercise of power over the naive Lucius. However that may be, in our passage the murderess certainly has the physician in her power and takes pains to keep him by her side so that he cannot save his own life.

'priusquam', inquit, '...appareat': this is not a genuine parenthesis (pace Bernhard 1927,93; his other examples are not comparable). Rather this is an oratio recta interruption in a passage of oratio obliqua. The interruption has a double effect: first, it makes the

account more lively; second, the narrator can again (see above on *medicorum optime*) use the woman's direct discourse to voice the ambiguities that are perceptible only to the well-informed reader (see also the next note).

prouentus appareat: thus F, after a correction. Originally F had *probentur*; a second hand changed *b* to *u*, erased the compendium for *-ur*, and added the compendium for *-us*, to produce *prouentus*. In the margin of F there is an *e*, written by the first hand but now almost illegible because of erasure (over the compendium for *pro* is a dot); φ has *euentus probentur*; a *d* in the margin indicates that a correction is needed. The a* mss. offer *euentus probatus*. The uncertainty in the transmission is probably due to the fact that the ambiguity of *prouentus* was not appreciated; but that ambiguity fits well in the series of ambiguities in the woman's speeches in this chapter (see above on *carissimo mihi marito*). *Prouentus* means 'favourable result' (see also *GCA* 1977,128 f. on 4,16: 87,6-7). The woman's fictional audience (her sick husband and the relatives) understand this as 'recovery'; to the murderess herself, the doctor, and the readers it means 'successful effect of the deadly poison'.

sed aegre ... tandem abire concessit: some interpreters add this passage to the examples of illogical transitions in this tale, because they regard it as an incomprehensible error on the cunning woman's part that she allows the doctor to go home after all (thus e.g. Van Thiel 1971,147). To the contrary: sly as she is, she keeps a tight rein on the course of events, first by keeping the doctor beside her long enough for the poison's effect to be irreversible, and then by allowing him to leave before he drops dead on the spot, which would arouse the onlookers' suspicion. In addition, she puts on a good act for the audience, by suggesting that she is letting the doctor go home reluctantly (*aegre*), and only because she is weary (*multum ac diu fatigata*) of his pleading.

aegre: F and φ had *aegra*. Everyone adopts Beroaldus' *aegre*.

precibus et obtestationibus: the climactically juxtaposed synonyms (see Bernhard 1927,166 for other examples in the *Met.*) illustrate the doctor's repeated pleas.

multum ... fatigata: see on ch. 23 (255,16) *multum ... dilecto*; cf. below in this chapter *multum ... saucius*.

multum ac diu: cf. Pl. *Mos.* 85 *multum et diu cogitaui*; the combination is frequent in Latin of all periods; cf. Liv. 42,25,9 *postremo multum ac diu uociferatum reuerti postero die iussisse*.

258,1-4 Interdum perniciem caecam totis uisceribus furentem medullae penitus adtraxerant, multum denique saucius et grauedine somnulenta iam demersus domum peruadit aegerrime: Meanwhile, his vitals had already completely absorbed the invisible destruction that raged in all his bowels, and at last, much afflicted and already overwhelmed by a sluggish lethargy, he reached his home with the greatest difficulty.

Interdum: = *interea*; see *GCA* 1981,154 on 7,11 (162,21-24), with references.

perniciem caecam totis uisceribus furentem: cf. [Quint.] *Decl.* 13,6 (271,19 f. Håkanson) (*uenenum*) *ineuitabilem pestem occulta fraude grassantem*.

perniciem caecam: our passage is mentioned in *ThLL* s.v. *pernicies* 1588,9 f. among examples of the metonymic use of *pernicies* 'de morbis, venenis, sim.'. But the heading 'metonymic' disregards the notion of 'death, ruin' that undoubtedly plays a part here; compare e.g. Plin. *Nat.* 25,123 *ociore etiam quam aspidum pernicie*; Tac. *Ann.* 6,26,3 *Agrippinae pernicies ... Plancinam traxit*; cf. also Quint. *Decl.* 246,4 *notiora sunt quaedam* (sc. *uenena*) *pernicie*.

Apuleius uses the combination *pernicies caeca* also in *Apol.* 26,9 for the non-perceptible destruction that can be caused by a *magus*. After Apuleius it is found in Cypr. *De zelo et liuore* 1,1 *et fit caeca et occulta pernicies quae dum minus perspicitur ut caueri a prouidentibus possit, inprouidas mentes latenter adfligit*.

For *caecus* (= *absconditus*) used of poison cf. Lucr. 6,822 (*ales*) *impediatur ... caeco correpta ueneno* (poisonous vapours from the *Averna loca*); cf. Ov. *Met.* 9,174 f. *caecaque medullis / tabe liquefactis* with Bömer ad loc.

medullae ... adtraxerant: for *attrahere* meaning 'soak up, absorb (fluids)' *ThLL* s.v. *attraho* 1160,12 f. gives as the earliest passage Cels. 6,8,1 *attrahaturque spiritu is sucus* (sc. *in nasum*) *donec in ore gustus eius sentiatur*.

multum ... saucius: see on ch. 23 (255,16) *multum ... dilecto*.

saucius: 'afflicted' (from other causes than wounds); see *OLD* s.v. *saucius*. Cf. *Apol.* 69,2 *mulier ... diutino situ uiscerum saucius*; *Met.* 2,15 (37,7-8) *mihi ... fatigationis hesternae ... saucio*; see also *GCA* 1977,169 f. on 4,22 (92,2). *Saucius* can also mean 'drowsy' (*GCA* 1995,68 on 9,5: 206,18-20, with further references; Smith ad Petr. 67,11); the physician is drugged and, as a consequence, dizzy.

It seems over-subtle to detect 'images of love' in this passage, as Finkelpearl 1998,152 f. does.

grauedine somnulenta ... demersus: cf. 2,25 (46,2-3) *me somnus profundus in imum barathrum ... demergit*. See Keulen in *AAGA* 2,1998,174 and n. 29 on *demergere* (and *praecipitare*) in contexts of disaster or death in the *Met*.

Our passage is listed in *ThLL* s.v. *demergo* 482,8 f. under the metaphorical use of the verb (i.q. *deicere, obruere ... opprimere*). Cf. after Apuleius Arn. *Nat.* 5,2 *uictos somno atque altissimi soporis obliuione demersos*. It is possible that Apuleius in *grauedine ... demersus* deliberately chooses medical terminology to describe an ailing doctor, although the parallels in medical authors are later than Apuleius: e.g. Theod. Prisc. *Log.* 2,13 *grauedine et sensus occupatione demersis*. *Demergere* is used frequently in Cael. Aur. as a technical term for *aliquem in soporem compellere, sopire*. *ThLL* s.v. *demergo* 481,68 f. devotes a separate lemma to this: cf. e.g. Cael. Aur. *acut.* 2,10,76 *ex capitis causa, quam Graeci* σκότωσις *uocant, demersi aegri uidentur*; ibid. 2,32,171 *aegrotantes multis diebus marcore quodam demersi moriuntur*. It is tempting to suppose that Apuleius, like Cael. Aurelianus, is using *demersus* to translate a Greek medical term used by Soranus.

Apuleius uses a similar metaphor in an opposite situation: 2,1 (24,18) *somno ... emersus* (see Van Mal - Maeder 1998,64 ad loc.); 9,41 (234,19 f.) *tandem uelut emersus graui crapula* (see *GCA* 1995,339 ad loc.).

grauedine somnulenta: the somewhat over-elaborate phrase helps to illustrate the doctor's long, laborious way home. For *grauedo* see on *grauedinis* ch. 11 (245,2).

somnulenta: this adjective is not attested before Apuleius, who uses it in two other passages: 1,26 (24,10) and 8,12 (186,27 f.) *somnolentis tenebris*; see *GCA* 1985,124 f. ad loc.

domum peruadit: see on ch. 35 (266,1) *Cenchreas peruado*.

258,4-7 Vixque enarratis cunctis ad uxorem mandato, saltem promissum mercedem mortis geminatae deposceret, sic elisus uiolenter spectatissimus medicus effundit spiritum: And having barely told her the whole story, he bade his wife to demand at least the promised fee for the redoubled death; then, in violent death throes, that most illustrious physician breathed his last.

The narrator describes the wicked doctor's demise in such an ironic manner that he prevents his audience from feeling pity for him (see also below on *spectatissimus*). The doctor's last wish, uttered to his wife with his last breath, is an order to collect payment. On the one hand this illustrates the avarice which the narrator has attributed to him from the start (see on *tropaea numerabat* ch. 25: 256,25). On the other hand, this last commission lays the foundation for the continuation of the story.

enarratis cunctis: cf. 8,14 (187,19) *enarratis ... singulis*. See *GCA* 1985,4 f. on how 'the author constructs a careful ... chain of information' in the tale of Charite. In our story information is twice passed on by a dying person; cf. below in ch. 28 (259,13-14) *iamque ab ipso exordio crudelissimae mulieris cunctis atrocitatibus diligenter expositis*; see Hofmann 1993b,138 f. on these and other instances of 'Parodie des Erzählens'; cf. 4,12 (84,7-11), with *GCA* 1977,99 f.

Although the doctor manages to tell his wife everything, she will nevertheless fall into the murderess's trap in the next chapter, driven by her love of lucre.

ad uxorem mandato: for the construction *mandare ad*, *ThLL* s.v. *mando* 267,2 f. gives this passage as the earliest example, followed by *Vulg. Num.* 15,23 *quae ... mandauit (deus) ... ad uos* (cf. ibid. *Hebr.* 9,20 *testamenti, quod mandauit ad uos deus*). As a possible earlier example *ThLL* (265,11) gives Liv. 31,11,8 *haec ad Carthaginienses mandata sunt*; cf. also Tert. *adv. Marc.* 4,17 p. 477,2 *ad illos et legis et prophetarum eloquia mandauerat*.

The verb *mandare* is frequently used of a dying person's last wish (see *ThLL* s.v. *mando* 263,64 f.). Cf. e.g. Verg. *Ecl.* 5,40 f. *spargite humum foliis, inducite fontibus umbras, / pastores - mandat fieri sibi talia Daphnis - / et tumulum facite et tumulo superaddite carmen*. Ov. *Trist.* 1,2,53 f. *est aliquid, fatoue suo ferroue cadentem / in solida moriens ponere corpus humo, / et mandare suis suprema et habere sepulcrum / et non aequoreis piscibus esse cibum*. The trivial last wish of the dying physician is an ironic play on the poetic tradition of the *mandata morituri* (on which see Cairns 1972,90 f.).

mandato ... deposceret: for the ablative absolute in which the noun is replaced by a clause, see the references given on ch. 16 (248,22 f.) *cognito quod res erat* (see also on *addito* ch. 24: 255,29). For the subjunctive without *ut* with *mandato*, c.f. 8,4 (179,1 f.) *mandato ... inuaderent*; see *GCA* 1985,49 with references (the construction 'originates in colloquial language').

mortis geminatae: the doctor remains business-like until his death: his wife is to demand the fee for the poison from which not only the *iuuenis* but also he himself will die.

sic elisus: *sic* (= οὕτως; see Van der Paardt 1971,25 on 3,1: 52,11 with references) summarizes and refers back to what happened earlier.

elisus uiolenter ... effundit spiritum: Robertson and Callebat (1968,479) follow Van der Vliet's proposal to read here *elisum* (with *spiritum*); they point out the expression *elidere spiritum* (8,14: 188,6) or *elidere animam* (9,38: 232,11-12). In our passage, however, this suggestion would lead to the harsh hyperbaton *elisum ... spiritum*. With Helm, Giarratano-Frassinetti, and Terzaghi the manuscript reading is retained here; Augello 1977,219 also defends it: although there are examples of *elidere spiritum / animam*, the verb can also take a personal object, e.g. Suet. *Cal.* 26,4 *omnes fustibus abegit; elisi ... uiginti amplius equites*; Min. 30,2 *filios ... adstrangulatos misero mortis genere elidere*.

With the reading *elisus*, the phrase divides symmetrically into two blocks, separated by their common subject: *elisus uiolenter spectatissimus medicus effundit spiritum*. The main clause *effundit spiritum* is placed with some emphasis at the end of the sentence. For *effundere spiritum* (or *animam*) see *ThLL* s.v. *effundo* 223,31 f. Cf. e.g. Verg. *A.* 1,98 *animam ... effundere*; Tac. *Hist.* 66,4 *id solum referre, nouissimum spiritum per ludibrium et contumelias effundant an per uirtutem*; *Ann.* 2,70,1 *effundendus spiritus*.

spectatissimus medicus: in the previous chapter (256,24) the doctor was described as successful in questionable cases: *multarum palmarum spectatus proeliis*; in this chapter (257,8) the murderess addressed him as *medicorum optime*, a dramatic irony that the reader could already enjoy (see the note there). Now, by means of this final ironic superlative, the narrator stifles any pity that the reader might have felt for the infamous doctor, who was outdone in infamy by his partner in crime.

CHAPTER XXVII

The murderess lures a fourth victim into her trap.

258,8-10 Nec ille tamen iuuenis diutius uitam tenuerat, sed inter fictas mentitasque lacrimas uxoris pari casu mortis fuerat extinctus: The young man for his part had failed to hold on to life any longer and, among the feigned and insincere tears of his wife, had died under the same circumstances of death.

ille: F has *illa*; ς has *ille*, adopted by all editors. As usual in the *Met.* this word refers back, in this case to the *iuuenis*, who had been mentioned before but had faded into the background for some time (Callebat 1968,279). A good alternative would be *illo*, suggested by Helm in his app. crit., as a comparative ablative with *diutius*: 'not longer than he (sc. medico)'; cf. *pari casu mortis*. Robertson mentions Helm's proposal with 'fortasse recte'.

uitam tenuerat: the combination, though it has an exact English equivalent, as shown by the translations of both Hanson and Walsh (the latter's translation has partly been adopted here), is rare in Latin; see *GCA* 1995,62 on 9,5 (205,26-27), with references.

tenuerat ... fuerat extinctus: the pluperfects mark the preparatory material' for the coming story; see Kroon & Rose 1996,75, fig. 1: 'narrative structure and the distribution of Latin tenses'; ibid. 83 f. on the use of the pluperfect for 'the presentation of ... events that took place before the orientation point in the past'. In the next sentence the imperfect *aderat* constitutes that orientation point in the past, against the background of which the 'important main storyline events' take place. These events are described in the perfect and the historical present (see also below on *respondit ... pollicetur*).

fictas mentitasque lacrimas: for the combination *fictus ... mentitus* cf. Ov. *Ep.* 11,69 f. *anus ficta ... sacra facit*; (sc. Aeolus) *mentita ... sacra reuelat*. As often in the *Met.*, two synonyms are combined to indicate a climax; cf. e.g. 9,17 (216,1-7) *adfixus atque conglutinatus* with *GCA* 1995,165; ibid. 168 on 9,18 (216,8-16) *instinctus atque inflammatus*, with references. Kronenberg's proposal *fictas <lamentationes> mentitasque lacrimas* is therefore unnecessary, however attractive paleographically (*lamentationes* could have been overlooked by the scribe in view of the following ***ment**itasque*) and despite the expression *mentitis lamentationibus* in ch. 5 (240,28). For *fictas ... lacrimas* cf. Ter. *An.* 558 *lacrimae confictae dolis*; Sen. *Ep.* 99,20 *(lacrimae) nec cessant nec fluunt umquam tam turpiter quam finguntur; eant sua sponte.*

For the passive use of the perfect participle of the deponent *mentiri* many examples are given by *ThLL* s.v. *mentior* 778,13 f. See also *GCA* 1977,50 f. on 4,5 (77,24-26) *mentita lassitudine*. The combination *mentitae lacrimae* is unparalleled; however, for the idea of feigned tears see 5,17 (116,11: Psyche's sisters) *lacrimis ... pressura palpebrarum coactis* (the model for this is Sinon in Verg. *A.* 2,196); the murderer Thrasyllus does manage to feign grief for his victim, it is true, *sed solae lacrimae procedere noluerunt*: 8,6 (180,23).

258,10-12 Iamque eo sepulto, paucis interiectis diebus, quis feralia mortuis litantur obsequia, uxor medici pretium geminae mortis petens aderat: He had already been buried and, after the interval of a few days during which funeral rites are observed for the dead, the doctor's wife was at the door, demanding the fee for the double murder.

Iamque: on '*iam* d'ouverture' see on ch. 12 (245,21).

paucis ... diebus, quis feralia ... litantur obsequia: this refers to the nine days during which the rites of purification took place; these days ended with the *nouemdiale sacrificium* and the *cena nouemdialis* at the graveside. On funeral rites in the *Met.* in general see *GCA* 1985, App. I; see also *GCA* 1995,268 on 9,31 (226,20-22) *nono die* with references; add *NP* 2,591 s.v. 'Bestattung' [Kierdorf]. During the nine days no business could be conducted. The addition *paucis interiectis diebus* emphasizes the haste with which the doctor's wife comes over to settle her business (cf. also *iamque*).

quis: = *quibus*. This archaic form, which occurs quite often in the *Met.*, is not found in Apuleius' other works; see Van der Paardt 1971,159 f. on 3,21 (68,6) with extensive references.

feralia mortuis litantur obsequia: *litare* is originally intransitive, and is so used in all other passages in the *Met.* (see e.g. Van der Paardt 1971,72 f. on 3,8: 57,28 *litate*). For the transitive use of *litare* ('fere i.q. supplicando peragere, efficere, sim.') *ThLL* s.v. *lito* 1512,55 f. mentions, before our passage, exclusively passages in poetry, usually with the object *sacra*: e.g. Verg. *A.* 4,50 *sacris litatis*, where Servius remarks that Vergilius 'nove dixit'. In connection with funeral sacrifices cf. also Ov. *Met.* 14,156. Cf. Stat. *Silv.* 3,3,213 f. (*Epicedium* for Claudius Etruscus) *hic* (sc. *filius tuus*) *sacra litabit / manibus eque tua tumulum tellure leuabit*.

feralia ... obsequia: the combination is unique. For an *obsequium* paid to the deceased, *ThLL* s.v. *obsequium* 183,53 f. mentions our passage as the first; then Iust. 23,2,8 *ut ... exequiarum officium ... obsequio debitae pietatis impleret*. Almost all the passages noted by *ThLL* have *obsequium* in the singular, meaning 'deference due to the dead', whereas in our passage *feralia obsequia* must mean something like 'funeral rites, funeral sacrifices', as in e.g. Ov. *Tr.* 3.3.81 *feralia munera*; cf. 9,30 (226,9) *feralibus officiis*. More comparable to our passage is Sulp. Sev. *Chron.* 2,51,8 *magnis obsequiis celebrata ... funera*.

pretium geminae mortis petens: the vocabulary shows how exactly the woman carries out the *mandatum* of her dying husband: he instructed her *saltem mercedem mortis geminatae deposceret* (see the previous chapter).

aderat: 'she was already there'; cf. 5,21 (119,17 f.) *maritus aderat*. On the imperfect see above on the pluperfects *tenuerat, ... fuerat extinctus*.

258,12-17 Sed mulier usquequaque sui similis, fidei supprimens faciem, praetendens imaginem, blandicule respondit et omnia prolixe adcumulateque pollicetur et statutum praemium sine mora se redditura constituit, modo pauxillum de ea potione largiri sibi uellet ad incepti negotii persecutione<m>: And the woman, true to her nature in every situation, suppressed the true face of trustworthiness and offered a show of its likeness; she responded pleasantly and promised her everything generously and abundantly; she expressed her intention to pay the agreed price at once, without delay, if she would just be so kind as to give her a tiny bit of that drink in order to complete the unfinished transaction.

usquequaque sui similis: at this point in the story the narrator has 'forgotten' that the woman is what she is only by the actions of *Fortuna* and *Riualitas* (ch. 24: 255,20 f.). For *usquequaque* in the transferred sense of 'in every conceivable situation', see *OLD* s.v. 2 and cf. e.g. Catul. 39,2 (Egnatius) ... *renidet usquequaque*. For Apuleius' use of this colloquial and slightly old-fashioned adverb, see Callebat 1968,539.

sui similis: when *sui similis* describes the person meant by *se* (i.e. the phrase means 'self-consistent'), it is usually complimentary; e.g. Cic. *Tim.* 6,5 *quod semper unum <et> idem et sui simile* (translation of Pl. *Tim.* 28C τὸ κατὰ ταὐτὰ καὶ ὡσαύτως ἔχον); Apul. *Pl.* 1,8, 198 *ut sit nihil indigens, sed operiens omnia coercensque contineat, pulcher et admirabilis, sui similis sibique respondens* (see Beaujeu's note ad loc. for the connection of this passage with the *Timaeus*). In our passage the 'self-consistency' of the woman is, of course, meant ironically. When *sui similis* describes someone other than *se*, it is often uncomplimentary; e.g. Pl. *Trin.* 284 *malus bonum malum esse uolt, ut sit sui similis*; Ter. *Phormio* 501 (GE:) *quam uterquest similis sui!*; frequently in Cicero, e.g. *Ver.* 2,3,22 *nequitia luxuria audacia sui simillimum iudicauit*; cf. Tac. *Hist.* 1,38,1 *quem ... auaritia sui simillimum iudicabat*.

fidei supprimens faciem, praetendens imaginem: the word order, with *fidei* first, results in rhyming phrases *supprimens faciem, praetendens imaginem*, which are parallel in structure but contrasted in content. The opposition between *facies* (the true face) and *imago* (an imitation) also occurs in Tac. *Dial.* 34,5 *qui faciem eloquentiae, non imaginem praestaret*; cf. Quint. *Inst.* 10,2,11 *quidquid alteri simile est, necesse est minus sit eo, quod imitatur, ut umbra corpore et imago facie et actus histrionum ueris adfectibus*. The allusion to acting is obvious: the woman has already shown herself a consummate actress in the previous chapters; cf. also her feigned tears above. Cf. Aug. *Civ.* 6,9 *hanc ipsam faciem* (sc. *theologiae ciuilis*), *cuius illa* (sc. *theatrica*) *imago est*.

fidei ... faciem: for *facies* used with personified abstracts, *ThLL* s.v. *facies* 53,10 f. cites e.g. Cic. *Off.* 1,5,15 *formam quidem, ipsam ... et tamquam faciem honesti uides*; Sen. *Ep.* 102,13 *ueritatis una uis, una facies*. Both *supprimere (fidei) faciem* and *praetendere (fidei) imaginem*, though unparalleled expressions, are easy to understand; for *supprimere* 'to suppress true feelings' cf. *OLD* s.v. *supprimo* 5; e.g. Luc. 6,228 *ille tegens alta suppressum mente furorem*. For *praetendere* 'to offer or show deceptively' cf. *OLD* s.v. *praetendo* 5. Therefore there is no need for alterations to F's text, like the one proposed by a *vir doctus* in Oudendorp: *fidei sub prima facie praetendens imaginem*, or Van der Vliet's *<fraudis> supprimens faciem*. Vulcanius wanted to delete *praetendens imaginem*. See also on ch. 23 (255,12 f.) *plebeiam facie tenus praetendens humanitatem*.

blandicule: hapax legomenon (*ThLL* s.v. 2028,34 f.).

respondit et ... pollicetur et ... constituit: the historic present (*prolixe*) *pollicetur* illustrates the perfect (*blandicule*) *respondit*. Because *se reddituram constituit* is also an illustration of the gracious response, this form is probably to be taken as a historic present, not a perfect.

prolixe ... pollicetur: the same alliterative phrase is used in ch. 4 (239,4-5) for the equally empty promises of the stepson; see the note there.

prolixe adcumulateque: for the adverb of the past passive participle of *accumulo*, *ThLL* s.v. 342,9 f. notes only our passage and *Rhet.Her.* 1,17,27 *ut ... munus hoc accumulatissime tuae largiamur uoluntati*; in Cic. *Flacc.* 89 *id non solum fecit, sed etiam prolixe cumulateque fecit* a varia lectio *accumulateque* has been transmitted. *Cumulate* is more common; cf. Plin. *Pan.* 55,11 *quod ... prolixe tibi cumulateque contingit*.

praemium ... se reddituram constituit, modo ... uellet: *modo* ('if only...') with the subjunctive is often used in direct discourse; see *ThLL* s.v. *modus* (*modo*) 1300,76 f. In a conditional clause in indirect discourse (= *dummodo*), as here, it is found in e.g. Tac. *Agr.* 15,4 *recessuros, ut diuus Iulius recessisset, modo uirtutem maiorum suorum aemularentur.*

pauxillum de ea potione: the use of the diminutive and of the 'innocent' term *potio* instead of *uenenum* (see on ch. 9: 243,25 *potionem*) reflects the veiled words, spoken *blandicule* by the cunning woman. See also below on *ad incepti negotii persecutionem.*

pauxillum de: the neuter singular of *pauxillus* occurs as a noun more than once with a partitive genitive or with *de* + ablative (*ThLL* s.v. *pauxillus* 863,8 f.). In the book of recipes of Marcellus, *De medicamentis* (ca. 400 A.D.) we find 8,89 *de splene asini arefacto ... pauxillum. ThLL* s.v. *pauxillulus* 862,8 f. gives examples of this construction in comedy, e.g. Pl. *Truc.* 940 *dan tu mihi de tuis deliciis ... quicquid pauxillulum?*; Ter. *Phorm.* 36 f. *erat ei de ratiuncula /... relicuom pauxillulum / nummorum.*

ad incepti negotii persecutione<m>: F had originally *ab ... persecutione*; a second hand changed *ab* to *ob*; φ and A (the main representative of Class I; see Introd. **4.1**) have *ab*. Castiglioni and all subsequent editors adopt *ad*, the emendation of ς. To the original *persecutione* (perseverance of the preceding *potione*?) a second hand in F added a Nasalstrich: *persecutionem.*

Here too, the woman is using 'veiled' language (see above on *pauxillum de ea potione*), although the reader who knows the rest of the story understands what is meant by *persecutio incepti negotii*. To the doctor's wife, *negotium* refers to the financial transaction that still has to be concluded. *Persecutio* in the sense of the completion of an unfinished enterprise is attested only here (*ThLL* s.v. *persecutio* 1683,1 f.). This may be legal terminology (*OLD* s.v. *persecutio* 3); cf. e.g. *Rhet.Her.* 2,12,18 *quaeritur in translationibus primum num aliquis eius rei actionem, petitionem, aut persecutionem habeat.* Cf. also Tert. *Idol.* 23,1 (about people who borrow money against collateral) *tempus persecutionis et locus tribunalis et persona praesidis*, where Waszink-van Winden ad loc. (288) cite our passage to illustrate the meaning 'the carrying through or completion (of an enterprise)'. For *persequi* in the sense of 'to complete' cf. e.g. Ov. *Met.* 8,774 *persequitur scelus ille suum*; see Bömer ad loc. for parallels.

258,17-21 Quid pluribus? Laqueis fraudium pessimarum uxor inducta medici facile consentit et, quo se gratiorem locupleti feminae faceret, properiter domo petita<m> totam prorsus ueneni pyxidem mulieri tradidit: Need I say more? The doctor's wife, lured into the snares of the most evil stratagems, readily consented and, to ingratiate herself even more with the wealthy woman, she gave the whole box, which she quickly fetched from home, to the woman.

Quid pluribus?: KSt 2,2,552 f. point out the occurrence of similar ellipses of a verbum dicendi in Cicero's orations and letters, especially in transitional passages. On ellipses of verbs, typical of colloquial language, see Hofmann LU 170, with examples from comedy; cf. also *Apol.* 77,4 *quid multis ?* with Hunink 1997,197 and n. 1 ad loc. Cf. Petr. 70,11 *quid multa ?* (also ibid. 76,2).

laqueis fraudium pessimarum uxor inducta medici: nowhere else are the words *uxor medici* separated (see e.g. above 258,11, and below in 259,6). The remarkable word order illustrates the content: the *uxor medici* is led into the snares of deceit.

laqueis ... inducta: cf. Quint. *Inst.* 5,7,11 *inducuntur (testes) in laqueos.* The hunting metaphor of 'snares of deceit' was twice used in ch. 24 (255,24 and 256,7) in the same connection (the murderess luring her victim into an ambush); see the notes there.

consentit ... tradidit: F's original reading was *consentit* (also read by φ), later changed to *consensit*. I follow Robertson and Giarratano-Frassinetti in adopting *consentit* (as do Brandt-Ehlers and Hanson). Helm prints *consensit*, the reading of F after correction, and of a* (a sub-group of the mss. of Class I; see Introd. **4.1**). The present tense is the lectio difficilior, as it is coordinated with the perfect *tradidit*. But coordination of historical present and perfect (with *et* or *-que*) occurs frequently in the *Met.*; cf. in this book ch. 17 (249,24-26) *iubet ... tradidit*; ch. 24 (256,10-14) *uerberat ... necauit*. See Callebat 1968,429 f. with examples and references; LHSz 2,307 and 815; see also Pinkster in *AAGA* 2,1998,110 on 5,23 (121,1-3) *depromit ... pupugit*.

quo se gratiorem locupleti feminae faceret: *locupleti* is a meaningful addition: the physician's wife is as greedy as her husband, and any possible sympathy from the reader is ruled out in advance; see on ch. 26 (258,6) *spectatissimus medicus*. In what follows, the physician's wife becomes more or less responsible for the further crimes because she assents so readily and, in order to curry favour with the wealthy woman, gives her (a murderess!) *totam prorsus ueneni pyxidem*.

faceret: thus φ. F shows, after correction, *facet*; originally it probably had *facere*, and in the margin something like & seems to have been erased, as Robertson mentions.

properiter ... petitam totam prorsus ... pyxidem: the alliteration of *p* and *t* seems to illustrate the movements of the doctor's wife, as she trots back and forth in her haste and eagerness.

properiter: for this poetic, archaic adverb, revived by Apuleius and *poetae nouelli*, see *GCA* 1981,33 f. on 6,26 (148,5-9), and ibid. 247 on 7,25 (172,22-24). See Mattiacci in *AAGA* 2,1998,127 f., with references, on Apuleius' affinity with the *poetae nouelli*.

petita<m> ... pyxidem: on *petere* with the ablative without preposition, see Van Mal-Maeder 1998,287 on 2,20 (41,12-15), with examples. The emendation of *petita* in F is by Oudendorp.

totam prorsus ... pyxidem: in this phrase one hears the narrator's horror: the doctor's wife gives her – would you believe! (*prorsus*) – the entire box of poison, without even being asked! ('*pauxillum*', the woman had said). The consequences will follow immediately. *Prorsus* enhances *totam*; for *prorsus* with words as *totus, cunctus*, see Callebat 1968,538.

258,21-22 Quae grandem scelerum nancta materiam longe lateque cruentas suas manus porrigit: And now that she had obtained ample material for crimes she stretched forth her blood-stained hands far and wide.

In a sudden stylistic switch after a preceding section full of colloquialisms, the consequences of the doctor's wife's imprudent action are presented in one sentence notable for its long syllables and many *a*-vowels. The seemingly innocent woman of the previous section, who spoke so *blandicule*, now assumes a sinister appearance.

grandem scelerum nancta materiam: cf. ch. 3 (238,16-17) *illa nancta solitudinis ... occasionem*; 8,5 (179,14-19) *Thrasyllus ... nactus fraudium opportunum decipulum*.

grandem: Callebat 1968,406 f. clearly shows that the use of *grandis* rather than *magnus* (which occurs much more frequently in Apuleius' works) is based in each case on a deliberate choice: the adjective presents the item it qualifies not in an objectively measurable size, but in the dimension it possesses for the person in question. In this book see also ch. 7 (242,17-18) *grande silentii praemium* (with *praemium* also in ch. 19: 251,26 and ch. 23: 254,19); ch. 15 (248,11) *grande dedecus*.

scelerum ... materiam: *materia* is used here in a double sense. On the one hand it is concrete: 'material, substance', i.e. the poison (*ThLL* s.v. *materia* 464,14 f. 'i.q. subsidium, principium, fundamentum'); for this meaning cf. e.g. cf. [Quint.] *Decl.* 4,12 (74,9 Håkanson) *aptissimam facinori ... materiam*; cf. also Tert. *Idol.* 4,1 *materiam idololatriae*, 'the material occasion, the means' (thus Waszink-van Winden 113 ad loc., with references). But it is also used here meaning *facultas, occasio* (*ThLL* s.v. *materia* 464,53 f.); for this latter meaning cf. e.g. Sen. *Dial.* 12 (*Cons. Helv.*),6,2 *ostendendae uirtuti nancta materiam*; [Quint.] *Decl.* 8,17 (168,14-15 Håkanson) *contigit tibi magna experimentorum materia, medice: aegri duo et languor idem*.

In a different sense it is found in Petr. 98,9, where Giton calls himself *omnium scelerum materia*, which he explains as *ego causa sum*.

longe lateque: in addition to our passage, this alliterative combination occurs once more in the *Met.*: 5,1 (104,5-6) *partes longe lateque dispositae domus*. *OLD* s.v. *longe* 1b gives examples from poetry and prose from Naev. *trag.* 49 *late longeque transtros ... feruere* onward; cf. Verg. *A.* 6,378 *longe lateque per urbes*; see also the examples given by *OLD* s.v. *late* 1b. In a figurative sense, as here, cf. e.g. Cic. *Orat.* 72 *hunc locum longe et late patentem philosophi solent in officiis tractare*; Cic. *Leg.* 1,34 *hanc beneuolentiam tam late longeque diffusam*. The combination is very frequent also in Christian authors. One passage is cited here in full because its description of a deceitful person (like our murderess) evokes the image of an octopus with dangerous tentacles: Ambr. *Hex.* 21 *Et ideo cauendi sunt qui crines suae fraudis et brachia longe lateque dispergunt uel speciem induunt multiformem. Isti enim polypi sunt nexus plurimos habentes et callidorum ingeniorum uestigia, quibus inretire possunt quidquid in scopulos suae fraudis incidet*. On the octopus as a traditionally cunning animal, especially because of its flexible limbs, reaching out in all directions, see Detienne-Vernant 1974,45 f, with references.

cruentas ... manus: this expression (cf. also 7,27: 175,20-21 *latronis cruentis manibus*) is used in Latin of all periods for 'hands defiled with murder'. Cf. e.g. Sal. *Jug.* 31,12 *homines sceleratissumi, cruentis manibus, immani auaritia, nocentissumi et idem superbissimi, quibus fides decus pietas, postremo honesta atque inhonesta omnia quaestui sunt*; Cic. *Mil.* 7,20; 16,43. Tac. *Hist.* 1,44,2; etc. In Verg. *G.* 4,15 we find the expression in connection with the tale of Procne and Philomela; in *declamationes*, too, it always occurs in the context of murder of one's own family, as it does here. E.g. Sen. *Con.* 1,7,14 *ut exprobarem tibi cruentatas in conspectu patris fraterno sanguine manus*; Quint. *Decl.* 328,13 *demens eram, ... si uiuerem cum eo, quem cruentas manus habere sciebam*; 372,1 *quam merito cruentas perdiderit manus*; [Quint.] *Decl.* 8,20 (171,23 f. Håkanson); 19,6. The combination continues to be quite frequent in Christian authors; cf. e.g. Firm. Mat. *Err.* 11,5 *hic est Cabirus cui Thessalonicenses quondam cruento cruentis manibus supplicabant*; Eus. Gall. *Collectio homiliarum* 15, line 110 *nunc iam in auctorem reus cruentas manus ... extendit*; the same phrase ibid. *Serm.* 8, line 154.

The Furies, too, have bloody hands: *Ibis* 228 *terque cruentatas increpuere manus*; Sen. *Med.* 15 (*sceleris ultrices deae*) *atram cruentis manibus amplexae facem*; 771. For the metonymic use of the Furies in connection with this murderess, see on ch. 24 (256,8-9) *libidinosae furiae stimulis efferata*.

manus porrigit: the gesture of *manus porrigere* can be both friendly ('to hold out one's hand, offering help'; see *OLD* s.v. *porrigo* 5a) and aggressive, as here. For the latter meaning, see *OLD* s.v. *porrigo* 5b; e.g. Ov. *Tr.* 4,9,10 *nostra suas istinc porriget ira manus*; Curt. 7,8,19 *iam etiam ad pecora nostra auaras et insatiabiles manus porrigis*; Sen. *Dial.* 11 (*Cons. P.*),17,1 *debes ... ferre aequo animo fortunam ad te quoque porrigentem manus, quas ne ab eis quidem per quos iuramus abstinet.*

CHAPTER XXVIII

After despatching her fourth and fifth victim, the murderess is exposed and condemned *ad bestias*.

The woman, who was led by jealousy to begin her series of murders, now kills not only the doctor's wife but also her own little daughter, thus recalling Medea (López 1976,373). Mason 1971,163 points out the suitability of Corinth as the setting for this tale, since the story of Medea is specifically Corinthian, and remarks (n. 16) that 'Medea as a type-figure of murderesses is found in Juv. 8,643'.

The three women who play important parts in book 10 correspond with Phaedra, Pasiphaë, and Medea, who are related to each other; see on ch. 19 (251,24-25) *ad instar asinariae Pasiphaae*. Drake 1969,349 sets the three 'abnormal women unable to love' in book 10 of the *Met.* in opposition to Psyche, Plotina and Charite.

258,23-24 Habebat filiam paruulam de marito, quem nuper necauerat: She had a small daughter by the husband whom she had recently killed.

Habebat filiam: the finite verb, placed first in the sentence, connects this sentence closely with the preceding one; see Bernhard 1927,12 for other examples. The imperfect gives background information for the new developments announced in *quae ... manus ... porrigit* (ch. 27: 258,21-22).

The turn of phrase *habebat filiam* recalls the formulaic manner in which *declamationes* often present their themes. See ch. 2 (237,3) *dominus aedium habebat iuuenem filium*; ch. 23 (254,23 f.) *maritum habuit, cuius pater...*, with notes ad locc. The absence of proper names in the two inner tales of book 10 also recalls the *declamationes* (those that are not on historical themes). For this aspect of *declamationes* see Zinsmaier 1993,8. See also the extensive discussion by Finkelpearl 1998,157 f. on the remarkable absence of proper names in the tenth book.

paruulam: cf. in the next sentence *infantulae*, and below 259,5 *paruulae*. The diminutives convey the narrator's pity (Portalupi 1974,118).

258,24-26 Huic infantulae quod leges necessariam patris successionem deferrent, sustinebat aegerrime inhiansque toto filiae patrimonio imminebat et capiti: She was extremely vexed that the laws assigned the father's inalienable inheritance to this little girl, and because she coveted her daughter's whole patrimony she actually threatened her life.

Huic infantulae quod leges necessariam patris successionem deferrent: in case of the absence or invalidity of a will, the inheritance of a deceased father was automatically conferred to the children who lived in the testator's house as next of kin (Norden 1912,150; Kaser 1, ²1971,714 and notes 4 and 5, with references). The children in the house, who were the first to inherit, were called *heredes necessarii*: 'forced' heirs, i. e. heirs on the basis of their relationship (see also *OLD* s.v. *heres* 1b). Cf. Gaius *Inst.* 2,156 *sui ... et necessarii heredes sunt uelut filius filiaue*. The phrase *necessariam patris successionem* is used for 'the succession to the father as a *heres necessarius*'. For *successio* in the context of an inheritance cf. e.g. Sen. *Dial.* 6 *(Cons. M.)*,9,2 *paternae hereditatis successionem*; Gaius *Inst.* 2,157 *unde etiam si quis intestatus mortuus sit, prima causa est in successione liberorum.* For the remarkable word order see the next note.

infantulae: the diminutive is attested first in Apuleius. The masculine form occurs twice in book 8; see *GCA* 1985,143 f. on 8,15 (188,15-17) with references, and ibid. 189 on 8,22 (194,9). Add Facchini Tosi 1986,123 with n. 74. Here, the diminutive underlines the little girl's helplessness (see also on *paruulam* in the previous sentence). *Huic infantulae*, already standing out through its first position in the sentence (even before the conjunction *quod*), receives more emphasis because of the hyperbaton with *deferrent*.

deferrent: 'conferred'; see *OLD* s.v. *defero* 11a. For *deferre* as a legal term see Norden 1912,140; Kaser 1,²1971,716 n.3.

sustinebat aegerrime: an Apuleian variation on expressions like *aegre ferre* etc.; see *GCA* 1985,190 on 8,22 (194,12-18) *aegerrime sustinens*, with references.

inhians ... toto ... patrimonio: the story about Telyphron in 2,21-30 contains all the themes which in the later books of the *Met.* are distributed over several stories (Van Thiel 1971,78 n. 64), including greed for an inheritance (2,27: 47,16-19) *haec ... sororis meae filium ... ob praedam hereditariam extinxit ueneno*.

Inhiare with a dative is found in classical Latin prose. In Plautus and poetry, *inhiare* 'uehementer appetere (cf. ἐπιχαίνω and LSJ s.v. 2) is usually construed with an accusative (KSt 2,1,270). Also in a context of 'panting for an inheritance' e.g. Pl. *St.* 605 *tuam hereditatem inhiat quasi esuriens lupus*. The phrase *quasi lupus* refers to the proverb behind *inhiare*, namely λύκος ἔχαινεν (see Petersmann ad loc. with references). Cf. *Apol.* 97,5 (about Rufinus, who coveted the inheritance to no avail) *quasi caeca bestia in cassum hiauit*, where commentators discuss the wolf metaphor.

toto: according to Callebat 1968,126, this form of the dative (only here and 11,17: 279,21) is not an archaism (thus Leumann-Hofmann, *Lat. Gr.* 1963,291) but a form common in the spoken language. Callebat gives examples from Caesar onward and points out similar forms in Pompeian inscriptions (see Väänänen ²1959,150). Cf. also 11,16 (278,6) *totae*.

258,26-259,4 Ergo certa defunctorum liberorum matres sceleratas hereditates excipere, talem parentem praebuit, qualem exhibuerat uxorem, prandioque commento pro tempore et uxorem medici simul et suam filiam ueneno eodem percutit: And so, assured that mothers condemned to surviving their child receive the inheritances of their deceased children, she proved herself to be the same kind of mother as she had shown herself a wife; she contrived a meal to suit the time of day, and struck both the doctor's wife and simultaneously her own daughter with the same poison.

defunctorum liberorum matres sceleratas heriditates excipere: this is a reference to the *Senatus Consultum Tertullianum* from the reign of Hadrian (Norden 1912,63 f.; Kaser 1,1971,701 f. with notes; Kaser 2,²1975, 503 f. and n. 44). According to this decree, precursors of which go back to the reign of Claudius, the mother received extensive rights of succession. When children died who had no living father or descendants, their inheritance fell to the (free-born) mother rather than to any other relative, provided she had borne three children.

That condition is not met here, but, as Vallette ad loc. (129, n. 1) rightly remarks, the primary function of this sentence is to provide a plausible motive for the murder of the young daughter.

matres sceleratas hereditates excipere: some translators wrongly connect *sceleratas* with *hereditates* (e.g. Helm-Krenkel: 'daß Mütter verstorbener Kinder die unselige Erbschaft derselben antreten'; Hanson: 'crime-tainted legacies'). The combination should be *matres sceleratas*. The expression *mater scelerata/pater sceleratus* is attested in funeral inscriptions, where it is used for parents who survive their children (e.g. *CIL* VI,9961 *Annia Helpis mater scelerata*; X,310 *ego scelerata mater*; *ILCV* (Diehl) 4191 *sceleratus pater*, etc.). The thought behind this is that such a parent is a victim of violation of the natural law that children ought to survive their parents. The expression is also found in literary texts like the Pseudo-Ovidian *Ad Liviam de morte Drusi* 135 *tene ego sustineo positum scelerata uidere?* See the richly documented Appendix F '*Parentes scelerati, impii, crudeles*', in Schoonhoven 1992, especially ibid. 226 f., on *sceleratus* in the context of *mors immatura*; ibid. 229 on our passage: 'here the current epitaphic formula is in such a way exploited as to acquire a very literal application'. Schoonhoven suggests that 'perhaps the best way ... to illustrate her (sc. this murderess's) becoming a *mater scelerata* in the epitaphic sense would be to put *matres sceleratas* between inverted commas'. The ambiguity cannot be rendered in translation. Annaratone translates beautifully: 'una madre che abbia la disgrazia di perdere il figlio'. Here, too, the 'epitaphic' meaning has been opted for: 'mothers condemned to surviving their child'; thus Vallette: 'mères condamnées à survivre à leurs enfants'. Other translators opt for the other side of *sceleratas*, e.g. Brandt-Ehlers: 'Mütter nach einem Verbrechen'; Walsh: 'unscrupulous mothers'. The mother of a deceased son calls herself *scelerata* also in [Quint.] *Decl.* 10,6 and 10,18; for the ambiguity there see Stramaglia 1999,317 f., who proposes the translation 'sciagurata' (= 'vittima di sciagura' as well as 'causa di sciagura').

Some scholars misunderstanding *matres sceleratas*, the reading in F, φ, and a*, sought to emend. Eyssenhardt wished to delete *sceleratas*; Van der Vliet proposed *certa matres <mater> scelerata[s]*, which is based on the fact that in F a second hand has changed *matres sceleratas* to *mater scelerata*. Seyffert suggested *superstites* instead of *sceleratas*. Stewech adopted Pricaeus' proposal to read *celeratas* (then to be connected with *hereditates*); Helm in his app. crit. proposes *matres relictas*. Oudendorp defended the reading of the mss., referring to inscriptions (see above); Armini 1928,321 f. and Castiglioni 1938,560 f. also defend the reading of the mss.

talem parentem praebuit, qualem exhibuerat uxorem: the parallelism is combined with chiasmus. Cf. (also on this woman) ch. 25 (256,22 f.) *uxor, quae iam pridem nomen uxoris cum fide perdiderat*.

Unnatural mothers frequently occur in *declamationes*. Cf. Quint. *Decl.* 388,31 *in multis nihil matris ultra titulum est*; for a prototype of unnatural mothers, ibid. 32 refers to Sassia in Cicero's *Pro Cluentio*; see Winterbottom 1984,594 ad loc.; cf. Cic. *Clu.* 12 *nam Sassia, mater huius Habiti - mater enim a me in omni causa, tametsi in hunc hostili odio et crudelitate est, mater, inquam, appellabitur*. On *declamationes* and Cicero's *Pro Cluentio* see on ch. 25 (256,24 f.) *qui iam ... tropaea numerabat*. See Thome 1993,418 f. for (stepmothers and) mothers as possible murderers of their (step)children as a literary, fictional theme against the background of historical reality ('schaudernd-freimütig behandelte römische Realität'); cf. Juv. 6,627 f.

praebuit ... percutit: on the alternation of perfect and historic present, see on ch. 27 (258,14-15) *respondit ... pollicetur*.

parentem praebuit: the omission of *se* gives the two parallel cola (see note above) some extra pithiness. The usual phrase meaning 'show oneself as' is *se praebere*. However, cf. Ter. *Ph.* 476 *Phormio ... strenuom hominem praebuit* with Dziatzko-Hauler ad loc.; on p. 248 of the Anhang they offer a defense of the mss. reading (without *se*) referring to other passages, and making the plausible explanation: 'In allen diesen Fällen steht ein Personalbegriff prägnant im Sinne des Ideals, der Rolle (*exemplum, partes*) einer solchen Personlichkeit. Bes. die rhetorischen Schriften bieten Beispielen dieses Sprachgebrauchs in Fülle'. Cf. Sen *Con.* 9,6 (29), 13 *et promisit oratorem et praestitit*; Petr. 97,9 *ut ... ostenderet fratrem*; see KSt 2,1,93 with other examples. For *exhibere* 'show oneself' without a reflexive, cf. e.g. Quint. *Inst.* 12,2,7 *qui ... operibus uere ciuilem uirum exhibeat*; see *OLD* s.v. *exhibeo* 5b.

qualem: thus a*; in F and φ a second hand emended the original *quale* to *qualem*.

prandioque commento: from Livy onward, the passive use of the perfect participles of deponent verbs increases, especially in Late Latin (LHSz 2,139); in the case of *comminisci*, Flobert 1975,351 gives as the first occurrence Pl. *Truc.* 450 *commentum male*; cf. also *Apol.* 58,3 *quam ... subtiliter compositum et ueri similiter commentum me ... non domi meae potius facturum fuisse*. For a possible active variant *comminiscere* see 4,11 (82,15-18) *comminiscimus* with *GCA* 1977,86 ad loc.

pro tempore: the phrase is to be connected with *commento* 'contrived in accordance with the time of day' (see the examples in *OLD* s.v. *tempus* 10c). Cf. 9,33 (227,22) *receptusque comiter pro tempore* with *GCA* 1995,280 ad loc.

et uxorem medici simul et ... filiam ueneno eodem percutit: cf. Cic. *Clu.* 30 *qui* (sc. Oppianicus) *uxori suae ... cum ipse poculum dedisset ... eodemque ueneno C. Oppianicum fratrem necauit*; Juv. 6,641 f. *tune duos una, saeuissima uipera, cena? / tune duos? 'septem, si septem forte fuissent'* (see above on *talem parentem...* on murderous mothers in Latin literature).

For the position of *simul* cf. 1,25 (23,20) *et nummis simul priuatus et cena*; see Bernhard 1927,26. See ibid. 172 on *simul* as a reinforcement of *et ...et ....*

259,4-13 Sed paruulae quidem tenuem spiritum et delicata ac tenera praecordia conficit protinus uirus infestum, at uxor medici, dum noxiis ambagibus pulmones eius pererrat tempestas detestabilis potionis, primum suspicata, quod res erat, mox urgente spiritu iam certo certior contendit ad ipsam praesidis domum magnoque fidem eius protestata clamore et populo concitato tumultu, utpote tam immania detectura flagitia, efficit, statim sibi simul et domus et aures praesidis patefierent: And the little girl's breath was weak, her bowels were delicate and tender: the murderous poison destroyed them forthwith. But the doctor's wife, who, when the stormy violence of the abominable potion spread through her lungs in noxious circuits, at first suspected what was the matter and next, when she was gasping for breath, was absolutely certain, ran straight to the governor's house; with great clamour she publicly invoked his protection and caused a disturbance among the people; because she announced she would reveal such dreadful crimes, she brought it off that at the same time the house and the ears of the governor were at once opened to her.

Sed: for non-adversative *sed* in narrative transitions see on ch. 2 (237,9-12) *sed ... adiecit*.

paruulae tenuem spiritum ... delicata ac tenera praecordia conficit ... uirus: the little daughter's vulnerability, emphasized by three adjectives, is brought out by the syntax as well: not she but the *uirus* is the subject of this part of the sentence. The doctor's wife offers resistance; consequently, she is the agent in the continuation of the sentence: *at uxor medici...*

spiritum et ... praecordia conficit ... uirus ... pulmones pererrat tempestas ... potionis: 'The *praecordia* like the φρένες were not only, with the heart, the seat of the conscious mind, but also received drink'; thus Onians 1951,42 f., who quotes e.g. Hor. *Epod*. 3,5 *quid hoc ueneni saeuit in praecordiis?* See Onians on the belief that drink went to the lungs; cf. Juv. 4,138 f. *cum pulmo Falerno / arderet*. In Ov. *Met*. 2,800 f. (where *Inuidia* poisons Aglauros at Minerva's instigation) the poison goes to *praecordia* and *pulmo*.

uirus infestum: for the development of *uirus* as a neutre of the second declination see Perotti 1989,340, with references. For *infestus* meaning 'noxius, periculosus, perniciosus' cf. *ThLL* s.v. 1409,4 f; cf. e.g. Sen. *Oed*. 29 f. *lues / infesta*; Colum. 6,13,2 *est ... infesta pestis bubulo pecori*. Before Apuleius, the combination *uirus infestum* is attested only in Plin. *Nat*. 8,101 (in an enumeration of antidotes used by animals) *coruus occiso chamelone, qui etiam uictori suo nocet, lauro infestum uirus exstinguit*. See Thome 1993,453 f. on the use and development of *uirus* in Latin. While *uenenum* usually means a single poison, *uirus* is often used for a mixture of poisons; thus e.g. Tac. *Ann*. 12,66,2 *eius mulieris* (sc. Locusta, a poisoner) *ingenio paratum uirus*; ibid. 13,15,5 *decoquitur uirus cognitis antea uenenis rapidum*.

tempestas ... potionis: the imagery, though bold, is understandable (see *OLD* s.v. *tempestas* 4 and 5 for *tempestas* in figurative contexts). Cornelissen proposes to follow the *Aldina*: *iam pestis* instead of *tempestas*. Helm in his app. crit. refers to Zen. Veron. 1,9,1 *ebibita ueneni tempestas* (see Weyman 1893,352 f. on Zeno as a reader of Apuleius).

suspicata, quod res erat: cf. 9,25 (221,22-23) *quod res erat tandem suspicatur* with *GCA* 1995,220 ad loc.; cf. also on ch. 24 (256,10) *quod res erat clamantem*.

urgente spiritu: literally: 'when her breath pressed her'. Cf. Cic. *Tusc*. 2,20 (in a translation of Soph. *Tr*. 1046 ff. *urgensque grauiter pulmonum haurit spiritus*: the poison of the cloak affects Hercules' respiratory system; cf. Soph. *Tr*. 1054 f. βέβρωκε σάρκας, πλεύμονες τ'ἀρτηρίας / ῥοφεῖ ξυνοικοῦν).

certo certior: Callebat 1968,524 sees this as a direct borrowing from Plautus Pl. *Capt*. 644, the only passage before Apuleius where the expression is used as an adjective: *nihil, inquam, inuenies magis hoc certo certius*. Otto 1890,81 calls it a proverbial expression. As an adverb it occurs 9,41 (235,6-9); see *GCA* 1995,344 ad loc. with references.

praesidis: see on ch. 23 (254,20) *praesidis*.

fidem eius protestata: examples of *fides* meaning 'protection by a magistrate' are given by *ThLL* s.v. *fides* 667,22 f. The usual meaning of *protestari* is 'to testify publicly' (*OLD* s.v. *protestor*), but here the verb is used meaning 'to appeal to', like *testari* (*OLD* s.v. *testor* 1d). Cf. 4,27 (95,24 f.) *clamore percito formonsae raptum uxoris conquerens populi testatur auxilium*. It is possible that the prefix is used here in the same way as in verbs of utterance (*proclamare, proloqui*); hence the translation 'she publicly invoked his protection'. Cf. Amm. 24,2,19 *fidem Romanam pansis manibus protestantes*.

utpote ... detectura: the phrase indicates the cause of the subsequent *efficit ... patefierent*.

The use of *utpote* with a participle increased from the Augustan period onward (possibly under the influence of Greek ἅτε; cf. also *quippe*); see LHSz 2,385; KSt 2,1,791 f.

efficit ... patefierent: for the subjunctive without *ut* with *efficere*, cf. 1,7 (6,14) *effeci, sequatur*. For other examples and references see Callebat 1968,106 f.

simul et domus et aures praesidis patefierent: for this type of zeugma, where conjunctions (often *et ... et ...*) separate those parts of the sentence to which the zeugmatic word (in this case the shared verb form *patefierent*) applies, LHSz 2,832 f. gives numerous examples; cf. e.g. Verg. *A*. 5,508 *pariter ... oculos telumque tetendit*. Bernhard 1927,162 points out that zeugma is relatively rare in Apuleius. It here certainly has a humoristic effect, and adds to the comic relief in the grotesque death scene of the final victim of the murderess in this otherwise dreadful tale (see the introductory note to the next section).

259,13-17 Iamque ab ipso exordio crudelissimae mulieris cunctis atrocitatibus diligenter expositis, repente mentis nubilo turbine correpta semihiantes adhuc compressit labias et, attritu dentium longo stridore reddito, ante ipsos praesidis pedes exanimis corruit: And now that she had carefully described all the barbarities of the most cruel woman from the very beginning, she was suddenly seized by a fit of dizziness that clouded her mind, she pressed her lips, half-open as yet, close together and, producing a long, grating sound by gnashing her teeth, she fell dead, right at the governor's feet.

Iamque ... expositis, ... corruit: the repetition of the motif of a dying person who has just enough time to reveal a crime, is notable: the doctor himself just managed to tell his wife everything before he died (see on ch. 26: 258,4 *enarratis cunctis*). Van Thiel 1971,147 speaks of a 'stümperhafter Abklatsch des zweiten Teils der Geschichte'. From a literary point of view we have here a kind of parody on the bizarre murder stories in the *declamationes*. In the framing tale the embedded story of the hyperbolically malicious woman has a motivating function: it is she with whom our main character must copulate in the Corinthian theatre. In the reader this embedded tale elicits both suspense and nausea, and at the narrative level it supplies the ass with a motive for fleeing.

Iamque: on *iam* 'd'ouverture' see on ch. 12 (245,21) *iamque*.

atrocitatibus: 'cruelties'. The plural is attested here for the first time and remains very rare; see *ThLL* s.v. *atrocitas* 1105,33 f.; after Apuleius, Tert. *Anim*. 56 *praecipue per atrocitates*; *Nat*. 1,7 *tantarum atrocitatum tolerantia*; Verec. *Cant*. 2,20 *si quis ... uiolentiarum atrocitatibus delectetur* (see Bernhard 1927,102 on plural abstracts in Apuleius). In our passage the legal connotation of *atrocitas* certainly also plays a role: in legal terminology the word is used to indicate a particularly grave offense (Mommsen, *Röm.Strafr.* 789 and n. 2; Heumann-Seckel s.v. *atrocitas* 1; *ThLL* 1106,63 f.), and is therefore important in determining the penalty. This is referred to in the next sentence with *minus quidem quam merebatur*.

repente mentis nubilo turbine correpta: as in *Apol*. 50,6 (about epileptics) *repentino mentis nubilo obtorpescunt*, the phrase clearly refers to loss of consciousness (see Hijmans 1987,458 and n. 261, discussing the use of *mens* in Apuleius). Whereas the *Apology* passage uses the words *mentis nubilum* ('fogginess of the mind', with *nubilum* as a nominalized neuter adjective), we have here *nubilus turbo mentis* ('a foggy fit of dizziness of the mind'). *OLD* s.v. *turbo* 4c sets our passage apart. Apuleius combines the figurative use of *turbo* 'sudden violent disturbance' (see *OLD* s.v. 2b; cf. e.g. Ov. *Am*. 2,9,28 *nescio quo miserae turbine mentis agor*) with the concrete image of a whirlwind (*OLD* 2a); for *turbo nubilus* cf. e.g. *turbo niger* in Catul. 68,63 *in nigro iactatis turbine nautis*; Verg. *G.* 1,320. In a daring image, the 'befogging' effect of the poison is compared with a whirlwind which darkens the atmosphere as it sweeps the woman off: *correpta* (cf. earlier *tempestas ... potionis*). For *corripere* as a common term for disease striking man (or beast), cf. 4,14 (85,10-13) *repentina correpta pestilentia* with *GCA* 1977,112.

turbine: thus a*; F had originally *mirbine*, but a different hand changed *mi* to *tu*; φ has *mirbine*.

nubilo: cf. Pl. *Cist.* 210 (Alcesimarchus describing himself in love) *ita nubilam mentem animi habeo*; Stat. *Theb.* 3,227 f. *hunc* (sc. Mars) *ubi ... / Iuppiter ... tota perfusum pectore belli / tempestate uidet: 'Talis mihi, nate, per Argos, / talis abi, sic ense madens, hac nubilus ira'*.

correpta: this is ς's emendation for F's *correpto* (Helm Praef. *Fl.* XLII). According to Robertson, a second hand in φ had already emended *correpto* to *correpta*.

semihiantes: in F, a second hand changed the original *semantes* to *semjantes*; φ has *semantes*, over which a quite recent hand wrote *hia*. The scribes had a similar problem with *semihianti* in 5,18 (117,16). *Semihians* is first attested in Catullus (61,213); according to the commentators ad loc. it is a Catullan neologism. After that the adjective is not found until Apuleius, who uses it three times: here; *Met.* 5,18; and *Fl.* 15,10 *quod interim canticum uidetur ore tereti semihiantibus in conatu labellis eliquare*. See Callebat 1994,1650 f. for similar poetisms in Apuleius' prose, and ibid. n. 183 for the many adjectives with *semi-*, especially in the *Met.*

adhuc: = *etiam tum*; for this use see LHSz 2,484 f. with examples from Cicero onward. On its frequent use with participles in Apuleius, see *GCA* 1995,193 on 9,22 (219,15-18).

attritu dentium longo stridore reddito: *stridor* means 'a grating sound' (*OLD* s.v. *stridor* 1a), and *dentium stridor* means 'gnashing of teeth', e.g. Cels. 2,7,25; Amm. 16,12,13; 30,6,6. The addition *attritu* therefore is slightly superfluous, but it not only contributes to the length of the description (*longo stridore*) but also adds to its sound effects: note the many *t*'s and the 'grating' combinations *-ttr-* and *-str-*. In *stridore reddito* the *d*'s and *r*'s suggest the death rattle (cf. also the repeated *-re-*).

exanimis corruit: *corruere* is often used of falling in battle. Van Mal-Maeder 1998,262 on 2,17 (39,5-10) cites examples.

259,17-23 Nec ille, uir alioquin exercitus, tam multiforme facinus excetrae uenenatae dilatione languida passus marcescere confestim cubiculariis mulieris adtractis ui tormentorum ueritatem eruit atque illa<m>, minus quidem quam merebatur, sed quod dignus cruciatus alius excogitari non poterat, certe bestiis obiciendam pronuntiauit: He, a worried man in any case, did not let the venomous serpent's multiform crime fade through sluggish inactivity on his part, but at once summoning the woman's slaves used the force of torture to get at the truth; his sentence – less, indeed, than she deserved, but since another appropriate punishment could not be contrived – his unequivocal sentence was that she should be thrown to the beasts.

Following Robertson, the comma is placed after *ille*. Helm: *Nec ille uir, alioquin exercitus*. *Nec ... facinus dilatione ... passus marcescere*: criminals usually benefit from their case being postponed. Cf. Quint. *Decl.* 319, where the speaker repeatedly recurs to the harm caused by delaying the trial of an *adultera uenifica* (his wife). In 319,9 the speaker suggests what might motivate the woman to ask to be tried first for *adulterium*: *sed occurrunt illae cogitationes: 'Quaeretur de adulterio et quaeretur diu, et extrahetur iudicium, sicut adhuc extrahitur, ut sequatur adulterii poenam alia subscriptio, alii iudices et alia sortitionis fortuna. Interim ... multum fata possunt'*.

uir alioquin exercitus: without exception, the translators render *exercitus* by 'experienced', a not uncommon meaning of *exercitus* (and *exercitatus*). But this apposition has to explain the *praeses*'s quick action: not only is the case of grave concern to him, but he is also *alioquin exercitus*: either 'upset anyway' (because of the woman having died at his feet) or 'generally a *uir exercitus*: a man of many worries'. Hence the translation 'worried'. *ThLL* s.v. *exerceo* (*exercitus*) 1378,51 f. gives numerous examples of *exercitus* 'i.q. labore, opere, molestiis sim. agitatus > sollicitus, vexatus sim.'. Cf. e.g. Pl. *Merc.* 228 *in somnis ... fui homo exercitus*; Cato *Or. frg.* 41 M *me sollicitum atque exercitum habitum*; Pl. *Trin.* 1089 f. *nunc hic disperii miser / propter eosdem quorum causa fui hac aetate exercitus*; Cic. *Planc.* 78 *quo quidem etiam magis sum non dicam miser - nam hoc quidem abhorret a uirtute uerbum - sed certe exercitus*; Tac. *Agr.* 39,3 *talibus curis exercitus* (see Ogilvie-Richmond ad loc., who translate 'agitated'). In Plin. *Epist.* 6,13,1 *exercitus* is used as a synonym of *laboriosus*; cf. also Gel. 9,3,2 *Philippus, cum in omni fere tempore negotiis belli uictoriisque adfectus exercitusque esset*. The word *exercitus* occurs once elsewhere in the *Met.*: 6,12 (137,7) *Psyche, tantis aerumnis exercita*; in 11,29 (290,9) the comparative of the adverb, *exercitius*, is used meaning 'more anxiously'.

multiforme facinus: cf. Cypr. *Donat.* 10 *multiformi genere peccandi*. See comm. on ch. 34 (265,9) *multiforme scelus* (also about this woman's crimes).

excetrae: this is the generally accepted emendation of Elmenhorst. In F *excetra* has been crossed out; in the margin one word has been eraded, which according to Robertson ended in *-e*. φ has *exceterum*; a* have *execrate*. *Excetra* as a term of abuse for a woman is attested in Pl. *Cas.* 644 *iam tibi istuc cerebrum dispercutiam, excetra tu*; *Pseud.* 218; Liv. 39,11,2 (Duronia referring to Hispala) *illius excetrae delenimentis et uenenis imbutum* (sc. *Aebutium*).

cubiculariis mulieris adtractis ui tormentorum ueritatem eruit: the taking of evidence from slaves was allowed only under torture; however, slaves were not allowed to give evidence against their own masters or mistresses (Mommsen, *Röm.Strafr.* 412 f. and 432; see *DNP* 4,585 s.v. 'Folter' [Haase]). But this probably did not apply to this woman, who was not a Roman citizen and thus did not enjoy the protection of the *ciuitas Romana* (Schumacher 1982,116 and n. 27).

Cubicularii are naturally well informed about their masters' behaviour. In Quint. *Decl.* 328,8 the father of a murdered son mentions that he has tortured the son's *cubicularii* in order to get evidence: *seruum torsi, cubicularium eius qui occisus est*.

adtractis ui: F had *adtracti sui*; a second hand separated the words correctly.

ueritatem eruit: F had *ueritate meruit*; a different hand placed a Nasalstrich on *ueritate*. In φ a second hand separated the words correctly. Cf. 3,8 (58,7) *tormentis ueritas eruenda*. *Veritatem eruere* is a legal term for bringing evidence to the surface; e.g. Modest. *Dig.* 22,5,7 *serui responso tunc credendum est, cum alia probatio ad eruendam ueritatem non est*; Quint. *Inst.* 12,9,3 *at si iuris anfractus aut eruendae ueritatis latebras adire cogetur,...* But *eruere* is used also in non-legal contexts meaning 'unearth, bring to light (something hidden)'; cf. Sen. *Oed.* 825 f. *siue ista ratio siue fortuna occulit, / latere semper patere quod latuit diu: / saepe eruentis ueritas patuit malo*; cf. ibid. 297 *fata eruantur* with Töchterle 1994 ad loc.

illa<m>: this is ç's emendation for *illa* in F (Helm, Praef. *Fl.* XLVII).

minus quidem quam merebatur, sed quod ... non poterat: *minus ... merebatur* is a parenthesis; the *quod* clause not only explains *pronuntiauit*, but is linked with the parenthesis by *quidem ... sed*. For the development of this kind of hybrid construction, see LHSz 2,429 f. We hear the narrator, in pseudo-oral style, describing the thought-process of the *praeses* as he pronounces the sentence. Callebat 1968 rightly discusses parenthesis in the *Met.* under two aspects: 'réalisme familier' (108 f., where he compares the 'meandering phrases' of Proust), and 'interférences artistes' (462 f.).

minus quidem quam merebatur: this remark recalls the archaic legal concept of *talio*, as Elster 1991,141 notes. Cf. Sen. *Con.* 10,4,9 *exigi a te talio non potest*; see Gellius' discussion (20,1,14) of *illa lex talionis*. It is probable that this reflects the narrator's own opinion about 'an eye for an eye', since he has almost completed this embedded tale and is about to return to the main narrative. It is also possible, of course, that the thoughts of the *praeses* are quoted here (see the previous note); however, cf. the similar remarks by the *anus*-narratrix about Psyche's sisters in 5,11 (111,23) and 5,27 (124,21).

bestiis obiciendam pronuntiauit: cf. the ending of the first inner story, ch. 12 (245,23 f.) *nouercae quidem perpetuum indicitur exilium, seruus uero patibulo suffigitur*. Both stories end according to the rules of poetic justice (see App. III). The sentence of *bestiis obicere* (see on ch. 23: 254,20 *bestiis addicta*) is in accordance with the *lex Cornelia de sicariis et ueneficis*, which includes murder by poisoning. This punishment applied only to *humiliores*; the punishment for *honestiores* was *deportatio* (see on ch. 12: 245,23 f.). Although the woman, referred to as *uilis* in the introduction (ch. 23: 254,19), is rich (*locuples*: ch. 27: 258,19), she apparently does not belong to the *honestiores* in Corinth who had Roman citizenship; see Elster 1991,140 f.

pronuntiauit: for *pronuntiare* with the accusative and infinitive, see on ch. 8 (243,1 f.) *eum ... insui ... pronuntiaret*. After a series of historic presents starting with *percutit* (258,4), the story is concluded with a perfect (see on ch. 16: 249,26 *tradidit*).

CHAPTER XXIX

With disgust and fear Lucius awaits his performance in the theatre, but the arrival of spring and roses gives him some hope. On the day of the *munus* he is escorted to the theatre, where he enjoys watching the preludes to his own performance.

260,1-5 Talis mulieris publicitus matrimonium confarraturus ingentique angore oppido suspensus expectabam diem muneris, saepius quidem mortem mihimet[u] uolens consciscere, priusquam scelerosae mulieris contagio macularer uel infamia publici spectaculi depudescerem: Such was the woman with whom I would have to celebrate a marriage ceremony in public, and, in extreme suspense because of my great choking terror, I awaited the day of the show, often wishing to bring death on myself rather than be polluted by the contagion of that wicked woman or lose my dignity by the disgrace of the public spectacle.

Talis mulieris: *talis* refers to the story about this murderess told in the previous chapters; *talem (...fabulam)* in ch. 23 (254,21 f.) and *talis* here frame the embedded tale of chapters 23-28. The same framing technique occurs in e.g. 9,25 (222,9), where the embedded tale of the fuller's wife is rounded off with *talium ... epularum*; see *GCA* 1995,224 ad loc. *Talis*, moreover, often opens a new pericope; cf. *GCA* 1981,224 on 7,22 (170,19-21).

mulieris ... matrimonium: for the genitive of the partner in *matrimonium*, see *ThLL* s.v. *matrimonium* 479,62 f., with examples from Cicero onward.

publicitus: Apuleius always uses this archaic adverb to mean 'publicly', 'en plein public' (see Scobie 1975,101 on 1,10: 9,11, with references). According to *LS*, the adverb has this meaning as early as Pl. *Per.* and Caecil. *com.* 185; Georges s.v. *publicitus* agrees. However, the lemma in *OLD* s.v. *publicitus* 2 suggests that this use of the adverb is typically Apuleian. Van der Paardt 1971,126 on 3,16 (64,6) assumes that *publicitus* is an archaism when used in the meaning 'publicly'. But even in the other meaning, 'on behalf of the state', 'financed by the state' (*OLD* s.v. *publicitus* 1), the adverb does not occur in Ciceronian Latin and should therefore be regarded as archaic. It is attested in Enn. *Ann.* 6,183, and in comedy. The adverb reappears in Gellius (7,14,4; 16,10,1; see also Marache 1957,208) and Apuleius; after Apul. it is attested in *SHA*, Ausonius and Mart. Capella.

See on *publicitus* and related terms as key-words in this episode the comm. on ch. 34 (265,14) *publice*.

matrimonium confarraturus: with bitter irony the narrator uses a term which indicates the most ceremonious and sacred form of Roman marriage (i.e. *confarreatio*) to allude to the public mating with the murderess that the ass is expected to perform. Cf. the marriage of Cupid and Psyche which, although the term is not mentioned explicitly, has all the characteristics of *confarreatio*. This is, moreover, strongly suggested by the phrase (6,24: 146,25) *sic rite Psyche conuenit in manum Cupidinis* (see Vallette's note 2 ad loc.). *Confarreatio* was probably no longer in use in Apuleius' time; earlier it was presumably celebrated only in the higher circles of society (Kaser ²1971,76 f.). Treggiari 1991,21 f. supports her statement that 'the Romans retained a sentimental respect for this form' with several references, e.g. Plin. *Nat.* 18,3,10.

In ch. 34 (265,10 f.) the irony is continued: there the narrator calls the public mating *praeclaris nuptiis*, and refers to the preparations for the scene as 'the spreading out of the *torus genialis*' (see comm. ad loc.).

confarraturus: thus F, and φ after correction (by a second hand) from *conferraturus*. All editors have accepted Philomathes' *confarr<e>aturus*. Hildebrand, however, defended the reading of the most important manuscripts. He pointed out the form *farratus* ('loaded with *far*') in Juv. 11,108 and Pers. 4,31 (*confarreatio* was named after the sacrificial cake, made of *far*, which played an important role in the ceremony). *ThLL* s.v. *confarr(e)o* 170,51 also accepts *confarraturus* in our passage and cites (53 f.) Hier. *Ep.* 41,4 *praetermitto scelerata mysteria quae dicuntur de lactente puero et de uicturo martyre confarrata*. Thus also Georges s.v. *confarr(e)o*. The passage from Jerome provides an example of the form *confarratus* at the time when Sallustius was preparing the recension of F's ancestor.[1]

ingentique angore: for the hyperbolic use of *ingens* see on *ingens ... trepidatio* in ch. 10 (244,7).

oppido: in Apuleius this adverb regains the frequency it had in the comic poets; see Van der Paardt 1971,77 on 3,9 (58,12) with references.

mortem mihimet uolens consciscere: *mortem (letum, necem) sibi consciscere* is a common expression for committing suicide; see *ThLL* s.v. *conscisco* 369,74 f., with examples from Cicero onward. For this and other Latin terms for committing suicide, see Van Hooff 1990,139 f. The neutral term will become more specific in the next sentence - suicide with a sword - when mention is made of the ass's inability to handle a *gladius*. In the previous books the narrator frequently mentioned Lucius' plans to take his own life; however, these plans were immediately frustrated, as they will be here. Cf. e.g. 7,24 (172,5 f.) with *GCA* 1981,239 f. ad loc. It is possible that these repeated, but never realized, suicidal intentions are a parody of the Greek novel, in which the protagonists are often represented as entertaining a desire to commit suicide in which, of course, they never succeed (it would spoil the happy ending). See Wesseling 1993,31 f., with references in notes, on this motif in the Greek novel; see also Kenney 1990,19 for the motif in the tale of Cupid and Psyche (five narrowly prevented suicide attempts by Psyche). In our passage, however, the parody is aimed not only at the genre of the Greek novel; in view of the explicitly mentioned loss of *pudor*, fun is also made of the many suicides motivated by *pudor* in Latin historiography. The ass's suicidal intentions at this moment are motivated by *priusquam ... depudescerem*; see Van Hooff 1990,107 f. and his index s.v. *pudor* for this common reason for suicide in antiquity. The wretched ass will not be able to follow the example of so many famous Roman generals who, to avoid *pudor*, threw themselves on their swords after losing a battle.

mihimet uolens: this is the generally accepted emendation by Rohde of *mihi metu uolens* in F and φ. In F the *u* of *metu* has been erased; according to Helm en Robertson the *t* of *met.* in F may have been an *a*: *mea* instead of *met*. Another hand wrote *manu* in the margin, which would have yielded *mortem mihi mea uolens manu consciscere*, which is the reading of manuscript δ (Dorvillianus). This latter reading was defended by Hildebrand, who noted that the next sentence emphasizes the fact that the ass regrets his lack of human

---

[1] The scriba of F has copied Sallustius' *subscriptiones* to the individual books of the *Met*. From the *subscriptio* at the end of book 9 we know that this recension took place in the years 395 and 397 (see Reynolds 1983,16).

hands. However, Rohde's emendation is to be preferred because it comes closest to the original situation in F: *metu* with *u* erased.

scelerosae mulieris contagio: *contagium* occurs twice in the *Met.*: here and in ch. 34 (265,15). In his other works, Apuleius always uses the form *contagio, -onis*, which, according to Paul. *Fest.* p. 59 M., is preferable. *ThLL* s.v. *contagium* 626,78 f. states that the neuter noun of the second declension is found almost exclusively in poetry from Lucretius onward, until it appears in the prose of Gellius and Apuleius. In poetry, however, one always finds the plural *contagia*, and its position is practically always immediately before the sixth foot of the hexameter; e.g. Lucr. 3,345 and 740. Cf. Mar.Vict. *G.L.* 6,25,10 *contagio apud omnes ueteres scriptum est ... sed poetarum licentia primo fecit contagia*.

Contagium is used with the genitive, here *mulieris*, in ch. 34 (265,15) *feminae*, in the general sense of 'the action of touching, contact' (*ThLL* s.v. *contagium* 627,1 f.). However, its more specific meaning of *infectio* or *maculatio* ('infection or pollution with an evil of any kind'; cf. *ThLL* ibid. 627,21 f.) is implied as well, as is shown by the subsequent *macularer*. Thome 1993,272 f. discusses the development of the *contagio/-ium* metaphor in Latin literature from Ennius *trag.* 294 onward, with rich documentation.

In the end, the ass will find the means to save his *pudor* and to avoid the *contagium* with the murderess. He will run away. No mention is made here of the possibility of a flight; it would have spoilt the suspense; see comm. on ch. 34 (265,14-15) *pudorem ... contagium*.

macularer: here and 9,26 (222,15 f. *larem ... maculasset*, again with *infamia*) the verb is used in a pejorative sense: 'to disgrace', 'to spoil, taint' (*OLD* s.v. *maculo* 3). In ch. 34 (265,3) the verb occurs in a more positive sense: 'to mark with coloured patches, variegate' (*OLD* ibid. 2).

infamia publici spectaculi: here speaks Lucius the Roman citizen, who is aware that an actor in Rome is marked by *infamia* both morally and legally. See Dupont 1985,95 f.; Zucchelli 1995,318 with notes 112 and 113.

depudescerem: the lexica give a confused account of the meaning and occurrences of this verb. *ThLL* s.v. *depudesco* 617,53 f. rightly gives our passage as the first occurrence of *depudesco* (also Bernhard 1927,120). *OLD* incorrectly quotes Ov. *Ep.* 4,155 s.v. *depudesco*, but *ThLL* correctly quotes it s.v. *depudet*: i.q. *pudere desinit* (so also Georges and *LS*).

One may take *depudescerem* with the ablative *infamia*, to mean 'be shamed by' (thus e.g. Hanson), but we may suspect that Apuleius has coined a characteristically etymologizing verb (compare ch. 15: 248,14 f. *per ... cauernam rimantur* with comm.): *de-* + *pudesco* in this context must mean 'lose one's *pudor*' (through the *infamia publici spectaculi*). Compare also, e.g., Apuleius' original and literal use of *detestatio* ('castration') in 7,23 (171,18) and *GCA* 1981,233 ad loc.

Pudor here is 'one's honour or self-respect' (see *OLD* s.v. *pudor* 3). It is the imminent loss of this *pudor* which provokes the ass's thoughts of suicide; cf. our note above on *mortem mihimet uolens consciscere*. After Apuleius this use of *depudesco* is, according to Blaise s.v., found in Hier. *Ep.* 22,7 *non depudesco infelicitatis meae* (but J. Divjak reads *erubesco* there). *ThLL* mentions Aug. *Conf.* 8,2,4 *depuduit uanitati et erubuit ueritati*, in which, however, *depuduit* is impersonal.

260,5-7 Sed priuatus humana manu, priuatus digitis, ungula rutunda atque mutila gladium stringere nequaquam poteram: But I was deprived of a human hand, deprived of fingers, and with my round and worn-out hoof I could not by any means draw a sword.

With the approach of the anamorphosis (but only the re-reader of the *Met.* is aware of that), the protagonist's complaints about his animal shape are increasing; cf. the fears of the ass, just before his amorous adventure with the Corinthian *matrona* in ch. 22 (253,12 f.; see comm. ad loc.). Throughout his existence as an ass Lucius never until now expressed regrets that he could not grasp something with his hoof. His present complaints about the inconveniences of his ass's body are undoubtedly related to the very 'human' treatment which he has been enjoying since his adoption into Thiasus' household. See Introd. **2.4.3.2** on the ass's 'humanity' in this book.

priuatus humana manu, priuatus digitis, ungula rutunda: cf. the description of the metamorphosis 3,24 (70,11 f.) *in extimis palmulis perdito numero toti digiti coguntur in singulas ungulas*; in 3,25 (70,20 f.) Lucius cannot remonstrate with Fotis about her unfortunate mistake: *iam humano gestu simul et uoce priuatus*. At the anamorphosis the hooves are changed back into hands: (11,13: 276,6 f.) *pedum plantae per ungulas in digitos exeunt, manus non iam pedes sunt, sed in erecta porriguntur officia*.

priuatus humana manu, priuatus...: the anaphora heightens the pathos of the complaint; note the many *a*-sounds and the repetition of *-man- -man-* in *humana manu*.

et mutila: even with his hoof not *mutila*, the ass could not draw a sword; but the adjective makes him seem more pitiable and also recalls the many laborious journeys the ass had to make, often burdened with heavy loads. Cf. e.g. 4,4 (77,11 f.) *etiam ungulis extritis iam claudus et titubans*; 7,17 (167,9 f.) *nec saxeas tantum sudes incursando contribam ungulas* with *GCA* 1981,194 ad loc.; in 8,23 (195,15 f.) the *praeco* points contemptuously at the ass's *extritis ungulis* (see *GCA* 1985,201 ad loc.). When the ass is in service to the *pistor* and works daily in the treadmill, he points out, in his description of his *iumentarium contubernium* (9,13: 212,11 f.), their *ungulas multiuia circumcursione in enorme uestigium porrecti* (212,18 f.) and fears he will suffer the same fate (212,20 f.).

260,7-12 Plane tenui specula solabar clades ultimas, quod uer in ipso ortu iam gemmulis floridis cuncta depingeret et iam purpureo nitore prata uestiret et commodum dirrupto spineo tegmine spirantes cinnameos odores promicarent rosae, quae me priori meo Lucio redderent: From a tiny little ray of hope I still derived some comfort in this ultimate disaster, namely that spring, which was just beginning, already coloured everything with buds like little jewels and already clad the meadows with a radiant glow, and that, newly broken from their prickly cover and breathing scents of cinnamon, there were springing forth in all their brilliance roses, which could turn me back into my own former Lucius.

The mention of spring's arrival moves the author behind the narrator to create a fine literary miniature (descriptions of the seasons belonged to the rhetorical exercises offered by schools of rhetoric; see Theon *Progymn.* 118,20 Spengel), rich in evocative allusions and intertextual references, some of which are noted below.

This elaborate description of spring, which is in marked contrast with the preceding references to pollution and Lucius' ugly worn-down hoof, provides a prelude to the charming scene which will soon unfold before the ass's eyes, and is thus a first allusion to the *locus amoenus* of the stage set of the Paris pantomime (see on ch. 30: 261,3 f.; see for another reference to spring's loveliness below, on *laetissimi graminis, quod in ipso germinabat aditu*). But it is possible that the announcement of spring points even farther ahead. In our passage we encounter various motifs familiar from other poetic descriptions of spring; indeed, our description fits in so closely with the spring poems of the Greek Anthology (*Anth. Pal.* 10,1-16) that it immediately becomes obvious that two traditional elements are absent here: there is no mention either of birds (the *Anth.Pal.* usually mentions swallows) or of the beginning of the sailing season (which in the *Anth.Pal.* is always connected with the beginning of spring; cf. also e.g. Hor. *Carm.* 1,4; Catul. 46; Ov. *Fast.* 4,131). The sea has become calm now that Zephyrus is blowing again, and Priapus, as the god of sailors, calls them to set out to sea. These elements of spring, which are absent in our passage, are found in 11,7, both birds (271,21 f. *canorae ... auiculae*) and a calm sea (271,26 f.), which presages the imminent Ploiaphesia. Thus, the beginning of spring is split at the end of the *Met.*: the description begun here but never 'finished' is the prelude to the fully completed spring scene described in 11,7. There, a description of the festive *pompa* for Isis follows; here we also have a *pompa*, which introduces the games in the theatre of Corinth. Here, in spite of the enjoyment of the sensual spectacle, we detect an undertone of mortal fear (ch. 34: 265,15 f.). There, where the *pompa* for Isis precedes Lucius' release from his ass's skin, the elation and festivity of the *spectaculum* is permeated with the promise of deliverance (announced 11,6: 270,12 f.).

Nowhere explicitly mentioned in our passage, but implicitly present because of the many verbal allusions to spring poetry, is the connection of Spring with Venus (cf. e.g. Lucr. 1,1 f. and Ov. *Fast.* 4,125 f.). But the description of spring will soon be followed by the pantomime, in which a dancer impersonates 'Aphrodite Pandemos' (see ch. 31 with comm.). In the perfect spring of Book 11, Lucius encounters Isis, who will be repeatedly equated with *caelestis Venus* (cf. 11,2: 267,7 f.; 11,5: 269,21 f.).

Plane tenui specula: the faintness of the gleam of hope is indicated in three ways: by the diminutive, by *tenui*, and by the adverb *plane*. *Plane* reinforces *tenui* (see Bernhard 1927,108 on this type of reinforcement of adjectives by means of adverbs) but can also be taken with the entire phrase *tenui specula solabar*; see on ch. 15 (248,1) and e.g. GCA 1981,259 on 7,26 (174,18-22).

tenui specula solabar clades ultimas: for this use of *solari* cf. Verg. G. 1,293 *longum cantu solata laborem*; A. 10,829 f. *hoc tamen infelix miseram solabere mortem: / Aeneae magni dextra cadis*. Cf. (with *consolari*) Cic. *Vat.* 28: *hac una re miseriam suam consolatur*; Cic. *Att.* 4,18,2: *dicendi laborem delectatione oratoria consolor*.

specula: this diminutive of *spes* can be regarded as a 'diminutif familier' (E-M. s.v. *specula*). GCA 1995,315 on 9,38 (231,27) mention the examples in the *ThLL* material. Apuleius uses the word in three passages, all in the *Met.*, with a definite diminutive force ('a tiny ray of hope'): here; 6,5 (132,8 f., Psyche to herself) *quin igitur ... cassae speculae renuntias*; and 9,38 (231,26 f.) *non nullam tamen sagacissimo iuueni prouentus humanior uindictae speculam subministrauit*. Evidently, the diminutive indicates in all three passages that it is but a 'gleam of hope', which is depicted by the speaker as unlikely to be realized.

uer: the emendation of ς for *uel* in F and φ. In φ a *manus recentissima* wrote the correction *uer* in the margin. See Helm, Praef. *Fl.* XLV on the confusion of *l* and *r*, which is frequent in F.

iam ... iam: this anaphora may be a signal to the reader that this is a reference to traditional spring poetry. When Latin poets imitate and paraphrase the Greek spring poems, they use the repeated *iam* in order to translate the characteristic series of ἤδη (see the first sixteen poems in *Anth.Pal.* 10). Cf. Catul. 46,1 *iam uer egelidos refert tepores* (*iam* ibid. 2, 7 and 8), with Syndikus 1984,240 and n. 3; Hor. *Carm.* 1,4,3 and 5 (*soluitur acris hiems*); ibid. 4,12 (*iam ueris comites*) with *iam* twice in the first strophe (see also Col. 10,256 f., cited in the next note).

gemmulis floridis cuncta depingeret: because of the strong resemblance to *Peruigilium Veneris* 13 *ipsa gemmis purpurantem pingit annum floridis*, Apuleius is sometimes put forward as the author of that poem (see Clementi 1936,89 and 137 with a reference to Heidtmann 1842, but cf. Brakman 1928,254 f.; on the date and authorship of the *PV* see Catlow 1980,18 f.; Bernardi Perini 1995,139 f.). The image is found also in Lucr. 5,1395 f. *anni / tempora pingebant uiridantes floribus herbas*; cf. *Culex* 70 f. *florida cum tellus, gemmantes picta per herbas / uere notat dulci distincta coloribus arua*; *A.L.* 569,1 (Vomanius, p. 63 Riese I) *uer pingit uario gemmantia prata colore*; Col. 10,256 f.: *iam uer purpureum, iam uersicoloribus anni / foetibus alma parens pingi sua tempora gaudet*.

gemmulis: the diminutive is used here meaning both *paruum germen (floris)* and *lapillus pretiosus* (the metaphorical use). *ThLL* s.v. *gemmula* 1759,71 f. gives our passage as the first for *gemmula* 'i.q. parvum germen (floris)', and then Arn. *Nat.* 3,23 *gemmulas et pubescentes herbas adurit ... frigus*. But meaning *lapillus pretiosus* (*ThLL* 1759,73 f.) the diminutive is already attested in Fron. *ad M. Caes.* 4,3,6 (58,24 f. VdH) *uerba ... alii caelo et marculo, ut gemmulas, exculpunt*. In *gemmulis floridis*, Apuleius clearly activates both meanings of *gemma* (*OLD* s.v. *gemma* 1 and 2). Naturally, in descriptions of spring we often find *gemma* (or the verb *gemmare*) meaning 'bud' and 'to come into bud' respectively; cf. e.g. Verg. *G.* 2,335 (*pampinus*) *trudit gemmas et frondes explicat omnis*; Ov. *Fast.* 4,128 *nunc tumido gemmas cortice palmes agit*; see also the quotation from *Culex*, Columella and *A.L.* 569,1 in the previous note. Cf. Tiberianus *Carm.* 1,8 (in a description of a river in springtime) *inter ista dona ueris gemmeasque gratias* (see Mattiacci 1990,97 f. ad loc.).

Metaphorically used for eyes like jewels, *gemmula* occurs in l. 10 of a poem ascribed to Apuleius (*PLM.* 4,104 f. Baehrens = *A.L.* 712 Riese, *Apulei ex Menandro*) *et pupularum nitidas geminas gemmulas*. On the attribution of this poem to Apuleius, see Mattiacci 1988,194 f.; Harrison 1992,83 f.

floridis: here, of course, the adjective refers literally to the flowers, but also, as elsewhere, to the bright colours of spring. See *GCA* 1977,107 on 4,13 (84,22-25) for these two meanings of *floridus*.

purpureo: Hildebrand rightly remarks: 'purpureae enim omnes res cuiusque coloris dicuntur, quae pulchrae sunt atque in aspectu suo splendent'. Cf. Verg. *Ecl.* 9,40 *hic uer purpureum*, with Coleman's remark that one must not think of a special colour here, but that the epithet must mean 'glowing, richly coloured'; cf. also Coleman on Verg. *Ecl.* 5,38. In Col. 10,257 f., describing spring, *purpureus* again means 'of many colours': *iam uer purpureum, iam uersicoloribus anni / fetibus alma parens pingi sua tempora gaudet*. See on ch. 22 (253,16 f.) *purpurantes*.

nitore: cf. Ov. *Fast.* 4,126: *uere nitent terrae*; 5,207 *uere fruor semper: semper nitidissimus annus*.

prata: the flowering meadows are a recurrent element in the spring poems of *Anth.Pal.* 10,1-16; cf. e.g. 10,5,3 f. ἤδη καὶ λειμῶνες ὑπὲρ πετάλων ἐχέαντο / ἄνθεα ... Hor. *Carm.* 1,4,4 varies with *nec prata canis albicant pruinis*, as in *Carm.* 4,12,3 *iam nec prata rigent*.

et ... promicarent rosae: after the general reflection on spring's arrival, we find the point of the *tenuis specula* late in this long sentence. The position of *rosae* at the end of the main clause is effective. The theme of roses is not uncommon in spring poetry (e.g. *Anth.Pal.* 10,16,1 f.; of course also in Columella's garden poem: 10,260 f. *et ingenuo confusa rubore / uirgineas adaperta genas rosa praebet honores*; cf. Florus in *PLM* 4,279,1 f. *uenerunt aliquando rosae per ueris amoeni / ingenium*). For roses as a favourite theme of the *poetae nouelli* from the 2nd century A.D. onwards, see Mattiacci 1990,96 f. on Tiberianus *Carm.* 1,8-10, with many examples. Because spring is the season of Venus (see above in the introductory note to this pericope), roses, as the flowers of Venus (for the mythology on this topic see *GCA* 1977,31 on 4,2: 75,12-15 with references), often play a special part in spring poetry, e.g. *Peruigilium Veneris*, Stanza 3; see the richly documented commentary of Catlow 1980,62 f. But in the *Met.* the roses are naturally an important motif as the antidote for the metamorphosis; see the extensive commentary of *GCA* 1977,29 f. on 4,2 (75,10 f.); cf. also 7,15 (165,9-12) with *GCA* 1981,177 (see below, on *quae me priori meo Lucio redderent*). See also the detailed note, with further references, by Van Mal-Maeder 1998,240 f. on 2,16 (37,19-20) *rosa ... tuberante*.

commodum: see on *commodum* ch. 12 (245,16).

dirrupto: see on *dirrupta* ch. 22 (253,20).

spineo: 'prickly'; first attested Ov. *Met.* 2,789; see Bömer ad loc. The adjective draws the attention of the reader to the fact that roses are never easy to pick: in Ov. *Met.* 2,789 *spineus* is used for the *baculum* of Invidia.

cinnameos odores: 'scents of cinnamon', an odd characterization of the scent of roses. In the *Met.*, a scent of cinnamon is regularly ascribed to divine or 'deified' beings. 2,8 (32,5: Venus) *cinnama flagrans*; see Van Mal-Maeder 1998,171 f. ad loc.; 2,10 (33,14 f.; see Van Mal-Maeder 1998,191), where Lucius speaks excitedly of Fotis' *iam patentis oris inhalatu cinnameo* (in 2,17 the narrator compares her explicitly with Venus); 5,13 (113,21: Psyche to Amor) *per istos cinnameos ... crines tuos*; 8,9 (184,15 f.: Charite on the deceased Tlepolemus, whom she reveres like a god) *adhuc odor cinnameus ambrosei corporis per nares meas percurrit* (see *GCA* 1985,101 ad loc., with references about 'Wohlgeruch und Heiligkeit'; cf. 11,4: 269,10, where Isis is described as *spirans Arabiae felicia germina*, with Harrauer ad loc.). To the re-reader, the description of the roses as *spirantes cinnameos odores* points ahead to the divine intervention to which Lucius will eventually owe his anamorphosis. The roses, which have been mentioned at intervals in the *Met.* as the antidote, are now for the first time shrouded in divinity. It is, indeed, a deity to whom the main character prays 11,2 (267,23) *redde me meo Lucio*; cf. here *rosae, quae me ... meo Lucio redderent*.

The adjective *cinnameus* is first attested in Apuleius' *Met.* (see *GCA* 1985,101; Facchini Tosi 1986,138).

promicarent: Apuleius uses this verb (also found in Naevius) in a new meaning. See Van der Paardt 1971,85 on 3,10 (59,19) and 161 on 3,21 (68,10 f.), with references. In

3,10 the verb refers to gushing tears; in 3,21 to the feathers suddenly sprouting from Pamphile as she changes into an owl. In our passage not only does the verb give a vivid image of the roses rapidly swelling out of their buds, but its literal meaning (*micare* 'gleam, glitter') also plays a part.

rosae, quae me priori meo Lucio redderent: because *rosae* ends the main clause, the subsequent relative clause *quae ... redderent* comes as the final climax of the sentence. The remarkable phrasing 'roses, which were to give me back to my former Lucius' suggests that Lucius is in quest of his former self. One cannot help comparing this with the two cruelly separated lovers in the Greek novel, who throughout the story hope to find each other again and in the end, with divine help, indeed get each other back. In the *Met.* Lucius the ass hopes for a happy reunion with his 'former Lucius': cf. the prayer of the ass in 11,2, which (267,23 f.) concludes with *redde me meo Lucio, ac si quod offensum numen inexorabili me saeuitia premit, mori saltem liceat, si non licet uiuere*. That expression, too, is close to the idea of a wrathful deity who cruelly separates the lovers from each other in e.g. Chariton's novel and in Xen. *Eph*. See also the following note.

priori meo Lucio: ever since the metamorphosis the narrator has repeatedly used the name Lucius as the name 'not of the I whose thinking persisted, but as the name of the visible human body the ego has lost'; thus Winkler 1985,151, who 150 f. discusses all the relevant passages in the *Met*. The necessary conclusion from this phrase, i.e. that the ass was Lucius no more, causes the re-reader of the *Met*. to question whether the main character, who was 'reborn' in book 11, should still be identified with the Lucius of the first books. In this connection, Gianotti 1986,43 and n. 29 points out the absence of *priori* in 11,2 (cited above). After the initiation (11,23 f.) the name Lucius no longer occurs in the *Met*.; in 11,27 (289,7 f.) we suddenly read *Madaurensem*; see Van der Paardt 1981,106 f. on that passage. See also ch. 19, where the narrator conspicuously fails to mention that when Lucius the ass arrives in Corinth, he has in fact returned to his home town; see the commentary ad loc.

260,13-14 Dies ecce muneri destinatus aderat: ad conseptum caueae prosequente populo pompatico fauore deducor: And see, the day appointed for the games was here: I was taken to the enclosure of the theatre in procession amid the cheers of the crowd accompanying me.

The *Onos* has neither the inner tale of our chapters 23-28, nor the partly gloomy, partly hopeful reflections of the main character in the beginning of this chapter (see above), nor the description of the pantomime in chapters 29-34; instead, the transition from Menekles' decision to exhibit the ass and the lady to the day of the performance in the theatre is made in one sentence (53,1): εἶτα τὸ τελευταῖον τῆς ἡμέρας ἐκείνης ἐνστάσης, ἐν ᾗ τὰς φιλοτιμίας ἦγεν ὁ ἐμὸς δεσπότης, εἰσάγειν ἔγνωσάν με εἰς τὸ θέατρον. But even here the *Met*. is not strictly parallel to the *Onos* because our text, through *ecce*, invites the reader to be a spectator, and evokes the image of the ass as a pantomime star, the favourite of the public. See for the next and final reflections of the *Onos* in book 10 comm. on ch. 34 (265,11-13) *et iam torus...*; see also Introd. **2.3** on the relation between *Onos* and *Met*.

Dies ecce ... aderat: ad conseptum ... deducor: paratactically and asyndetically, the

357

second sentence follows the first as its logical consequence (Bernhard 1927,48 f.). Callebat 1968,440 f. discusses this stylistic usage and points out its dual effect: on the one hand it is intended to suggest the spontaneity of unorganized spoken language, but on the other hand it is used deliberately to isolate the latter clause from the former, thus making it more emphatic.

Dies ecce: this new opening interrupts the reader's (and the narrator's) reflections and warns her/him to prepare her/himself visually for what is about to happen (soon an extensive *ecphrasis* will follow; see below on *prospectu gratissimo*). See also *GCA* 1985,72 on 8,6 (181,8 f.) with references.

ad conseptum caueae: 'as far as the theatre complex'. As the next sentence will show, the ass is left to wait outside the wall; *conseptum* ('enclosure') suggests a complex of buildings enclosed by a wall (*GCA* 1985,270 on 8,30: 201,19-25). Cf. 3,2 (53,15 f.) *caueae conseptum* with Van der Paardt 1971,35 ad loc. Also 11,19 (281,1) *intra conseptum templi* with Gwyn Griffiths ad loc.

caueae: in ch. 23 also, the theatre is called *(populi) caueam*. There Vallette in n. 1 concludes that, because the spectacle is called *munus*, the Corinthian amphitheatre is meant, and that the dance performances also take place there. But Fick 1990,223 f. points out that the Roman amphitheatre, the ruins of which can be seen in Corinth, is later in date, and that we should assume that the Greek theatre of Corinth, reconstructed after the earthquake of 79 A.D., could accommodate not only theatre performances but also gladiatorial games and *uenationes*. It is debatable, however, whether a discussion of this kind is relevant to the world of fantasy evoked in the *Met*. Despite the attempts of many scholars, the events related in the *Met*. cannot be tied to a historical time; see *GCA* 1995,348 on 9,42 (235,21) *fidem Caesaris*, with references. The fact that the geographical references in this fictional world, indeterminate until now, become rather explicit from 10,18 onward, serves a literary purpose especially: the real city of Corinth mentioned here evokes the image of a prosperous provincial town, which in addition had a (primarily literary) reputation as a 'cesspool of vice', appropriate to this episode. See Introd. **2.3**.

Here, in ch. 23, and again in ch. 34 (265,5), the theatre is referred to by the term *cauea* (pars pro toto), mainly because of the prospect, so terrifying to the ass, of having to copulate with the murderess 'en plein public'. In 3,2 (53,15 f.) *caueae conseptum* explicitly refers to the spectators' seats in the theatre; otherwise, only *theatrum* is used (ibid. 53,14 and passim in that episode; see Oldfather s.v. *theatrum* for the other passages in Apuleius' works). *OLD* s.v. *cauea* 4b cites only two passages for *cauea* in the wider sense of 'theatre': Pl. *Truc.* 931 and Cic. *Leg.* 2,38.

prosequente populo pompatico fauore deducor: the comparison of the ass with a celebrated *histrio*, begun in ch. 17 (250,1) with *saltare* (see the note there) and taken up repeatedly since then, culminates here in the description of his journey to the theatre for a performance that fills him with horror.

Note the *o*-assonance and the alliteration of *p*.

pompatico fauore: a romanizing feature, since in Rome theatrical games were always preceded by a ceremonial *pompa* (Dupont 1985,46 f.). The official who presided over the games - in our case Thiasus - rode in a carriage at the head of the procession. Actors, musicians, and the audience accompanied the cortege. The egocentric narrator, however, describes the scene as if all *pompaticus fauor* is meant for himself.

The adjective *pompaticus* is first attested in literary works of the second century A.D.;

Fron. *ad Marc. Caes.* 3,17,3 (50,1 VdH.; see also Marache 1957,56 f.) uses it meaning 'pompous, ceremonious'. Here, with *fauor*, it has the literal meaning 'associated with ceremonial processions'. Callebat 1968,134 assumes that the adjective belonged to colloquial language but was given a special, literal meaning by Apuleius (cf. above on *depudescerem* on this typically Apuleian etymologizing treatment of vocabulary). After Apuleius, *pompaticus* is attested in this literal meaning in e.g. Tert. *Val.* 16 *ibi demum, aduentu pompatico eius concussa, Achamoth protinus uelamentum sibi obduxit*; [Cypr.] Append.A (ed. Hartel) c. 22 *pompatico gressu*. But the adjective continues to be used, also meaning 'pompous', by Christian authors (Blaise s.v. *pompaticus*). See also Billotta 1975,60, who correctly points out that *pompaticus* is used here not only for the sake of semantic refinement, but also because of the alliteration. It is doubtful whether the adjective, which had probably become part of colloquial language, should be considered as a conscious graecism (contra Eicke 1956,28 f.).

deducor: the verb may have been chosen for its special use of the escorting of a bride to her new home (*OLD* s.v. *deduco* 10b). The ass is escorted to the place where his 'marriage' will be consummated (for the many allusions to marriage in this episode see on ch. 32: 263,6-7 *uelut nuptialis epulas obiturae dominae*; see also below in this chapter, on connections between the *pyrrica* and marriage).

260,15-19 Ac dum ludicris scaenicorum choreis primitiae spectaculi dedicantur, tantisper ante portam constitutus pabulum laetissimi graminis, quod in ipso germinabat aditu, libens adfectabam, subinde curiosos oculos patente porta spectaculi prospectu gratissimo reficiens: And while the opening of the show was dedicated to a performance of stage-dancing by the actors, I meanwhile stood before a door and gladly tried to reach some forage of wonderfully lush grass which sprouted right there at the entrance, and repeatedly feasted my curious eyes, through the open door, on a most charming view of the show.

primitiae spectaculi: cf. 4,16 (86,22) *uenationis sui primitias*; 11,5 (270,10) *primitias commeatus* (there indicating the opening of the celebration of the sailing season, the so-called Ploiaphesia). *Primitiae* means literally 'first fruits (of agricultural produce offered to a deity), first offering'. The transferred use of *primitiae* meaning 'beginnings' is first found in epic poetry: Verg. *A.* 11,156 *primitiae iuuenis miserae bellique propinqui / dura rudimenta!* (cf. also e.g. V.Fl. 3,516; Stat. *Theb.* 6,146). Apuleius is not the first to apply this use in prose: we find it in Quint. *Decl.* 315,23 and Gel. *pr.* 13 *primitias quasdam et libamenta ingenuarum artium dedimus*, where *quasdam* and the addition *et libamenta* (referring to the literal meaning of the word) show that Gellius still regards it as a bold metaphor in prose.

spectaculi... spectaculi...: the repetition emphasizes the visual character of the image which will be evoked in the forthcoming *ecphrasis*.

constitutus: for *constitutus* as a substitute for the non-existent participle of *esse*, see *GCA* 1977,86 on 4,11 (82,15-18).

pabulum laetissimi graminis: the genitivus inhaerentiae with *pabulum* is not abundant (contra Eicke 1965,39[2]) or pleonastic. Ever since Lucius' metamorphosis, the narrator has stressed his distaste for animal fodder (see Introd. **2.4.3.1**). The addition of *laetissimi graminis* to *pabulum*, the general term for animal feed (see *GCA* 1985,181 on 8,21: 193,5), has therefore a strong surprise effect, further enhanced by *libens adfectabam*. Just when the complicated blurring of the borderline between man and animal (see Introd. **2.4.3.2**) is about to culminate in the ass's mating with the *uilis aliqua*, Lucius the ass deliberately chooses his animal side: for the first time he not only admits to eating typical animal food – he even finds it delicious.

pabulum: in F and φ *pauulum* has been changed to *pabulum* by a different hand. Cf. on *pabulum* ch. 17 (250,11).

graminis, quod ... germinabat: the expression recalls the joyful description of springtime (lines 8-12), which concluded in the *actor*'s hope of returning to his human form. The sweet young grass in the meadows is a topos in descriptions of spring. Cf. Hor. *Carm*. 4,7,1 *redeunt iam gramina campis*; cf. also the *molle gramen* of Lucr. 2,29, where the *amoenitas* of the passage is connected with spring. See also Mattiacci 1990,93 on Tiberianus, *Carm*. 1,5 *subter autem molle gramen...*

adfectabam: before Apuleius, *adfectare* meaning 'appetere', 'attingere', is attested only in Verg. *A*. 3,670; in the *Met*. it is found 1,2 (2,18); 1,19 (18,3); and 3,29 (74,1: the ass tries to eat roses). The use of the verb, which when it means 'strive after' usually has an abstract object (see *OLD* s.v. *affecto*), remains rare after Apuleius (*ThLL* s.v. *affecto* 1184,32 f.).

subinde: only in the *Met*. does Apuleius use *subinde* as a synonym for *saepe*. This is a development of the spoken language: in Romance languages *subinde* wins out over *saepe*, as in French 'souvent' (Callebat 1968,149 with references).

curiosos oculos ... prospectu ... reficiens: cf. Plin. *Ep*. 5,6,13, where the author introduces an *ecphrasis* of the manor and his *uilla* as follows: *magnam capies uoluptatem, si hunc regionis situm ex monte prospexeris ..., quocumque inciderint oculi, reficientur*.

As in 2,1 (24,24) *curiose singula considerabam*, the connotations 'attentive' and 'curious' overlap here (see Van Mal-Maeder 1998,69). On curiosity in the *Met*. see Hijmans in *GCA* 1995,362 f. (with all relevant literature), especially 373 f. on the combination curiosity - tale/description - delight.

Although the ass enjoys the *pabulum ... graminis*, he finds watching the dance a greater source of refreshment than food. After continually being an object of curiosity in this book himself (see Introd. **2.4.2**), he can finally feed his customary *curiositas* again, and thus feast his eyes. This leads to the subsequent *ecphrasis*. Cf. 9,12 (211,27-212,1), where the ass – tired and hungry though he is, and in miserable circumstances – finds it more important to observe than to eat (*postposito cibo ... inoptabilis officinae disciplinam cum delectatione*

---

[2] In chapters 29-34 the stylistic investigations of Eicke 1965,24-61 have been of great value for this commentary; to avoid repetition, this footnote makes general acknowledgement of this. It must be noted, however, that Eicke's interpretation of Apuleius' stylistic devices in this *ecphrasis* differs from my own. Eicke, although alert in detecting stylistic nuances, is not sufficiently sensitive to the deeper relation between form and content to be detected so often in Apuleius' text. He has accordingly a low esteem of Apuleius' 'äußerst affektierte und gekünstelte Redeweise', which he calls 'ungeheuer aufgebläht und schwülstig' (Eicke 1965,46, and similarly passim).

quadam arbitrabar) and, as here, presents what he sees in an *ecphrasis*. In our passage too, the ass's situation is far from pleasant.

His intense delight in the splendid spectacle which the narrator now describes to his readers argues against interpreting Lucius' escape from the theatre as a flight to Isis from a world which has become repulsive to him (see Zimmerman-de Graaf 1993,154 f.). Rather his flight (ch. 35) is inspired by shame and fear for his life.

260,20-25 Nam puelli puellaeque uirenti florentes aetatula, forma conspicui, ueste nitidi, incessu gestuosi, Graecanica<m> saltaturi pyrricam dispositis ordinationibus decoros ambitus inerrabant nunc in orbe<m> rotatum flexuosi, nunc in obliquam seriem conexi et in quadratum patorem cuneati et in cateruae discidium separati: For young boys and girls in the bloom of fresh youth, conspicuous in their beauty, splendidly dressed, moving gracefully, were about to perform a Pyrrhus dance in Greek fashion; drawn up in lines, they weaved about in graceful patterns; now, wheeling around, they arranged themselves into a turning circle, now they combined into a slanting line; and they fanned out into a hollow square, and split into two separate groups.

The description of the dance forms a 'dance of words' itself. A long, carefully constructed sentence describes the beauty of the young dancers in three short, syntactically uniform, asyndetic cola with final rhyme; these cola combined have the same number of syllables as the introductory phrase:

Nam puelli puellaeque uirenti florentes aetatula (18)
forma conspicui (6)
ueste nitidi (5)   (6 + 5 + 7 = 18)
incessu gestuosi (7)

Next, the dance is announced:

Graecanicam saltaturi pyrricam
dispositis ordinationibus decoros ambitus inerrabant

Finally, the choreographical figures (*decoros ambitus*) are imitated in language. These four cola continue the final rhyme of the description of the dancers' beauty (see above), again showing syntactical parallelism. They can be divided into two bicola: the first bicolon is asyndetic with anaphora of *nunc*; the second bicolon is syndetic (*et ...et ...*). The first two cola show chiasmus: *orbem rotatum / obliquam seriem*; the second couple has variation: *in quadratum patorem / in cateruae discidium*.

nunc in orbem rotatum flexuosi (11)
nunc in obliquam seriem conexi (11)
et in quadratum patorem cuneati (12)
et in cateruae discidium separati (12)

The sentence contains only one finite verb, *inerrabant*, placed almost in the middle of the sentence.

puelli puellaeque: a phonetic *callida iunctura* (this is the term used by Facchini Tosi 1986,160 f., who discusses all occurrences in Apuleius). As in 9,27 (223,22-27) *pulchellum puellum* (see *GCA* 1995,239 ad loc.), the diminutive *puellus* (an archaism, according to Suet. *Cal.* 8,3) enhances the juncture's rhythm and assonance. It also gives *puellae* its original force as a diminutive. Moreover, *puelli* lends a slightly erotic tone to the description right at the beginning. Cf. line 2 of a poem now generally ascribed to Apuleius and quoted by Gellius (19,11), *meum puellum sauior*, with Dahlmann 1979,12 f., with references, on the erotic connotation of *puellus*.

uirenti florentes aetatula: Apuleius transforms stock expressions referring to *flos aetatis* (see Brown on Lucr. 4,1105) into a sonorous and delicate phrase, with assonance in *uirenti florentes*. For *florere aetate* and similar phrases, see *OLD* s.v. *floreo* 5b; cf. e.g. Verg. *Ecl.* 7,4 *ambo florentes aetatibus*. *Florens* itself can also indicate youth, as e.g. Lucr. 3,1008 *aeuo florente puellas*. For *uirenti ... aetatula* cf. e.g. Sil. 5,414 *uirentes ... annos*. The diminutive *aetatula* has a hypocoristic function. Abate 1982,68 f. discusses several passages in the *Met.* where the use of diminutives in erotic contexts is noteworthy. The phrase in its entirety recalls the usual warning in love poetry to enjoy love while one is still young. Cf. Hor. *Carm.* 1,9,15 f. *nec dulcis amores / sperne puer .../ donec uirenti canities abest*, with Nisbet-Hubbard ad loc.; Var. *Men.* 87 *properate uiuere, puerae, qua sinit aetatula / <uestra> ludere*, with Cèbe ad loc.

forma conspicui, ueste nitidi, incessu gestuosi: on the colometry see the introduction to this pericope. The first two cola describe only the young dancers' looks; the third and longest colon makes the transition to their dancing, which is then described.

ueste nitidi: cf. Var. *Men.* 1271,43 (462 Astbury; Non. 368 M.) *ubi nitidi ephebi ueste pulla candidi / modeste amicti <cultus> pascunt pectore*. Used of clothing, *nitidus* often suggests not only 'brightly coloured' but also 'elegant, well-groomed (as a sign of affluence), spruce' (*OLD* s.v. *nitidus* 6). Cf. Gel. 1,5,1 *cultu corporis nitido uenustoque nimisque accurato fuisse*; *SHA Clod. Alb.* 11,7,1 *in uestitu nitidissimus fuit, in conuiuio sordidissimus*; ibid. *Gord.* 6,6,1 *uini parcus, cibi parcissimus, uestitu nitidus*. That connotation fits here: Thiasus has spared no effort or expense for his show.

incessu gestuosi: the repetition of *-es* and *-u* and the two spondees at the beginning lend this colon a rhythm that seems to illustrate the introductory dancing steps. The adjective *gestuosus* is attested only three times, once in Gel. 1,5,2 and twice in the *Met.*: here and 11,11 (274,25) *gressu gestuosus* (with the same sound effects as in our passage and alliteration as well). Ernout 1949,75 compares it with *uultuosus* (attested from Cic. *Or.* 18,60) and regards both adjectives as creations of rhetorical literature.

Graecanica<m> ... pyrricam: the emendation *Graecanica<m>* for *Graecanica* in F is by ς. The *pyrrica* was originally a Greek war-dance, part of the ephebes' military training. By the classical period the military element of the *pyrrica* had been virtually forgotten, and young girls participated in the dance as well as boys; see Dar.-Sagl. s.v. *saltatio* 1033 f. with references; *RE* s.v. 'Tanzkunst' 2240 f. [Warnecke]; and esp. the exhaustive study of Ceccarelli 1998. Athen. 14,631 b-c says that in his time the *pyrrica* has become a Dionysiac dance (see Ceccarelli 1998,67 f. and 211 f.). See Steinmetz 1982,352 on the *pyrrica* as a typical phenomenon of the theatre in the second century A.D. That a *pyrrica* could also tell a mimetically expressed story appears from e.g. Suet. *Nero* 12,2,1 *inter pyrricharum argumenta taurus Pasiphaam ligneo iuuencae simulacro abditam iniit* (see Ceccarelli 1998,156 f.). Cf. the Pasiphaë mime in which the ass is to perform, planned after this ballet and the Paris pantomime (see comm. on ch. 23: 254,17-21). On the *pyrrica* as a prelude to *uenationes* see Ceccarelli 1998,158, with references.

Particularly relevant to our passage is the connection between the *pyrrica* and initiatory ceremonies, and especially marriage ceremonies; see Ceccarelli 1998,61 f. and 208 f. (iconographic evidence); further discussion, with references, of this aspect of the *pyrrica* can be found via Ceccarelli's index s.v. *Matrimonio*; see on the theme of marriage as a connecting element in all three parts of the *munus* described in this episode the comm. on ch. 32 (263,6-7) *uelut nuptialis epulas obiturae dominae*.

On the *pyrrica* as a 'duello amoroso' see Ceccarelli 1998,158, who in n. 81 quotes our passage, and *Anth. Lat.* 104 Shackleton Bailey (= 115 R.), 1-4: *De pyrrhica. In spatio Veneris simulantur proelia Martis, / cum sese aduersum sexus uterque uenit. / femineam maribus nam confert pyrrhica classem / et uelut in morem militis arma mouet.* Cooper 1980,465 f. discusses our *pyrrica* as a symbol of the theme of sexual reversal in the *Met.*

The addition *Graecanicam* seems to be intended for Roman readers: in imperial Rome, this originally Greek dance was a favourite festive dance; see Ceccarelli 1998,147 f.; on its often wanton character cf. e.g. Plin. *Nat.* 8,5 *lasciuienti pyrriche conludere*. On *Graecanicus* meaning 'adapted from Greek', see Mason in *AAGA* 1978,1 with references (= Mason in Harrison 1999,218); Fick-Michel 1991,19.

saltaturi pyrricam: F has *saltatur ipyrrica*. Hildebrand divided the words correctly. Blümner objected to the future participle *saltaturi* because, according to him, the dance is already in progress. He proposed to read *Graecanicae saltaturae pyrricae*, genitive with *dispositis ordinationibus*: 'after taking their positions for the Greek dance, the pyrrica'. That *saltatura* is unexampled he does not find objectionable in an author like Apuleius. Brakman shared Blümner's objection to the future participle, and assumed that *saltat* was a scribe's error for *saltat;* (= *saltatus*), to be deleted as a gloss on *Graecanicae pyrricae*.

The manuscript reading (with Hildebrand's word division) is retained by all editors. *Graecanicam saltaturi pyrricam* can be connected with the preceding *forma ... gestuosi*: 'who, beautiful in appearance, brilliantly dressed, with graceful steps started to dance a Greek pyrrica'. The dance is described in a single long sentence, which describes the dancers' entrance and the dancing figures they perform. In the next sentence the dance is already over.

decoros ambitus inerrabant: *inerrare* 'to wander or roam in' is usually construed with a dative. From *ThLL* s.v. *inerro* 1308,31 f. it appears that the construction with an accusative is found only in Apuleius. In 11,2 (267,15; sc. Proserpina) *lucos diuersos inerrans* the verb is used transitively, 'i.q. pererrare'. In our passage we have a proleptic cognate accusative indicating the result of the action (*ambitus inerrabant = ambitus inerrando efficiebant*). See KSt 2,1,281 f.; LHSz 2,39 f.; Müller 1908,22 f. Cf. e.g. Lucan. 4,74 f. *densos / inuoluere globos*; Stat. *Theb.* 3,116 f. *miserabile currunt / certamen*. The examples in Müller 1908 show that this usage is mainly poetical.

nunc ... flexuosi, nunc ... conexi, et ... separati: cf. the dance of boys and girls in the description of the shield in Hom. *Il.* 18,593 f., especially the variations in formation described in 599 f.: οἵ δ' ὁτὲ μὲν θρέξασκον ἐπισταμένοισι πόδεσσι, / ῥεῖα μάλ', ὡς ὅτε τις τροχὸν ἄρμενον ἐν παλάμῃσιν / ἑζόμενος κεραμεὺς πειρήσεται, αἴ κε θέῃσιν·

/ ἄλλοτε δ' αὖ θρέξασκον ἐπὶ στίχας ἀλλήλοισι.

On the colometry see the introductory note to this pericope.

in orbem ... flexuosi ... in ... seriem conexi ... in patorem cuneati ... in ... discidium separati: the fourfold repetition of *in* + accusative (see Callebat 1968,227 f. on Apuleius' frequent use of this construction) illustrates the symmetry in the dancing formations described here.

in orbe<m> rotatum flexuosi: *orbem* is Oudendorp's emendation, accepted by all editors, for *orbe* in F. *Flexuosus* ('winding') is said of rivers or roads; cf. 9,11 (211,6 f. *propellor ad incurua spatia flexuosi canalis*; see GCA 1995,110 on *flexuosi*. Here its unusual use to describe the dancers who are turning around in varying circles, produces the effect that it rhymes with *gestuosi* (see above).

For a similar, somewhat pleonastic, precision cf. 2,7 (30,20 f.) (*Photis*) *uasculum ... rotabat in circulum ... in orbis flexibus crebra succutiens*.

in patorem cuneati: cf. Liv. 44,4,4 *iugum montis in angustum dorsum cuneatum*; see Numminen 1938,128 f.

260,25-261,2 At ubi discursus reciproci multinod*as* ambages tubae terminalis cantus explicuit, au*l*aeo subducto et complicitis siparis scaena disponitur: But when the final trumpet signal had unravelled the tangled twists and turns of the alternating dancing pattern, the curtain was opened, the backcloths were folded, and the stage was set.

discursus reciproci multinodas ambages: the chiasmus underscores the complexity of the choreography.

multinodas ambages: thus φ, and F in the margin. In the text F has *multinodes*, which is also the reading in a* (see Introd. **4.1** on this group of mss.). Armini 1932,91 argues for *multinodes*, on the ground that it is not uncommon for such compound adjectives to vary in declension. But Apuleius uses *multinodus* as an adjective of the second declension in two other passages (see GCA 1985,248 on 8,28: 199,14-18). In our passage, the error may have been caused by the proximity of *ambages*. Oudendorp and Hildebrand adopted Scaliger's proposal *multimodas*. This would spoil the image of unravelling knots in *multinodas ambages ... explicuit*. See GCA 1995,274 on 9,32 (227,4-9) on the various meanings of *ambages* in the *Met.*; the use here is comparable to that in 7,15 (165,25), where the ass goes round and round in the mill.

tubae terminalis cantus: the trumpet signal is imitated in sound: *terminalis* in its unusual meaning 'announcing the end' was probably chosen because of the alliteration. Apuleius' clarion call is less exaggerated than Ennius' famous verse (*Ann.* 140) *at tuba terribili sonitu taratantara dixit*. The adjective *terminalis* meaning 'marking a boundary' is attested in Hyg. *agrim.* 75,20 *cippus ... monumentalis ..., non terminalis*. On adjectives in *-alis* in Apuleius, see GCA 1985,145 on 8,15 (188,19) *gaudiali* with references.

explicuit ... complicitis: paronomasia accompanies the transition of one scene to the next.

aulaeo subducto et complicitis siparis: chiasmus (see Bernhard 1927,32 for other examples in the *Met.*).

The Pyrrhus-dance was apparently performed in front of the stage, in the *orchestra*. Now the *scaena* is revealed: the *aulaeum* was the large curtain that was pulled down at the beginning of a performance and raised at the end; remains of Roman theatres show a slot under the stage-floor, near the front of the stage, into which the curtain was dropped (Austin ad Cic. *Cael.* 65,27 *aulaeum tollitur*: this is the first mention of the *aulaeum*. Cf. Verg. *G.* 3,25, where the *Britanni*, woven into the *aulaeum*, seem to lift the curtain; see Thomas ad loc.). The smaller *siparia* covered parts of the stage, and were apparently used to cover or uncover various pieces of scenery. See Beacham 1995,171 f. on *aulaeum* and *siparia*, with references; Dar.-Sagl. s.v. *siparium* 1347.

In 1,8 (8,13-14) Aristomenes uses the same terms metaphorically, when he asks Socrates to come to the point and tell his story: *aulaeum ... dimoueto et siparium scaenicum complicato*.

aulaeo: Beroaldus' emendation, adopted by all editors, of *albeo* in F (where a second hand changed *b* to *u*).

siparis: thus F and φ; *sipariis* ς. See on ch. 5 (240,22) *mendacis*.

CHAPTER XXX

The decor of the pantomime 'The Judgement of Paris'. Paris receives instructions from Mercury; enter Juno and Minerva.

261,3-7: Erat mons ligneus, ad instar incliti montis illius, quem uates Homerus Idaeum cecinit, sublimi[s] instructus fabrica, consitus uirectis et uiuis arboribus, summo cacumine, de manibus fabri fonte manante, fluuialis aquas eliquans: There was a wooden mountain, in the style of that famous mountain of which the poet Homer sang as Ida, constructed with superior craftmanship; it was densely planted with greenery and live trees and, at the very top, from a fountain rising by the maker's hands, it made clear water trickle down in a stream.

Here begins the description of the Pantomime of the Judgment of Paris. For the origins and later developments of this form of theatre, see Rotolo 1957, with testimonia; Opelt 1978,452 f.; Steinmetz 1982,348 f., with rich documentation; Beacham [2]1995,140 f.; Zucchelli 1995,317 f. An important ancient source of information about the pantomime is Lucian's *De saltatione* (see the bilingual edition of Beta-Nordera 1992, with an extensive introduction, notes, and bibliographical references). A more accurate term for the performance presented here is probably 'mimo saltatorio' (the term used by Cicu 1988,181 f. and 189 f.), because the pantomime in its strict sense was performed by only one actor, without a mask, while a chorus recited – beforehand or simultaneously – the words describing the actor's mimic gestures (cf. Lucian. *Salt.* 29). But in the Roman theatre from Augustus onward, pantomime and 'mimo saltatorio' seem to have grown gradually towards each other. See Rotolo 1957,239 f.; Beta-Nordera 1992,18 f.; Gianotti 1996,279 and n. 69.

The pantomime as it flourished from the time of Augustus onward has its origin in a change in the presentation of tragedy: the verbal expression became separated from the mimic representation (Opelt 1978, 452 f.). The themes of pantomime, as of tragedy, were found in mythology. *RE* s.v. 'Pantomimus',847 f. [Wüst] gives a list of themes and titles; a supplementary list is found in Kokolakis 1959,53 f., which includes the Judgement of Paris (see also Steinmetz 1982,350 and n. 148, with references). Luc. *Salt.* 45 mentions τὴν ἐπὶ τῷ μήλῳ κρίσιν as the subject of pantomimes (see Beta-Nordera 128 f., n. 94 ad loc., with references). Aug. *Civ.* 18,10, often cited as evidence for the popularity of the Judgement of Paris as a theme of pantomime appears to refer directly to our passage when he writes that the Judgement of Paris is one of the themes that *inter theatricos plausus cantantur atque saltantur*.

The performance described here clearly shows the eroticism which often characterized pantomimes of this kind and gave rise to violent criticism from Christians (Weismann 1972), and also from moralizing pagans (Finkelpearl 1991,227 f. discusses moralizing criticism of mime and pantomime in general; see also Zimmerman-de Graaf 1993,149 f., with references). Gianotti 1996,277 is probably right in suggesting that the criticism from Christians had a double motivation: on the one hand the Christians disapproved of the lasciviousness of these performances, while on the other hand they feared the dissemination and revitalization of pagan mythology, which provided the themes of the widely popular pantomimes.

For another allusion to the Judgement of Paris in the *Met.* see Introd. **2.5.3**.

Erat mons ligneus: 'there was a ... mountain' or 'it (i.e. the *scaena* mentioned in the previous sentence) was a ... mountain'. For the first position of the verb, see on *fuit*, ch. 19 (251,20).

Ambitious structures like this were not uncommon in Roman theatres; cf. Sen. *Ep.* 88,22 (cited in ch. 34: 264,29-265,6). Strabo 6,2,6 describes the execution of a Sicilian robber, which was carried out in a theatre, in front of a set depicting Mount Aetna, the robber's sphere of activity, built especially for the occasion. See also below on *summo cacumine ... fonte manante*.

This mountain is represented as a 'locus amoenus' (see below on *uirectis*), and contrasts with the 'locus horridus' of the mountain where the robbers lived (4,6: 78,22 f.; see Schiesaro 1985). It is the first mountain in the *Met.* that is not presented as precipitous, difficult to climb, or menacing to the person confronted with it. See De Biasi 1990,8 f. on the many mountains in the *Met.* that function as poetical 'topoi'.

mons ligneus: all through the description of this pantomime, different elements emphasize the artificiality of the performance (see below in this chapter on *de manibus fabri*; *fluuialis aquas eliquans*; *pecuarium simulabat magisterium*; *malum ... bracteis inauratum*; *in deae Iunonis speciem similis*; *quam putares Mineruam*). In 2,4 f. the artificiality of the Diana-Actaeon sculpture is also continuously emphasized, but in addition its naturalness is praised. In our passage the illusionary element prevails (see the notes below; Zimmerman 1993,148; Laird 1995,62 f.). On the mirroring function of this *ecphrasis* devoted to the pantomime, see Introd. **2.5.3**.

ad instar ... montis ..., quem ... Homerus Ideaum cecinit: the illusion is carried to extremes: this *scaena* is a depiction not of the real Mount Ida but of the Ida described in Homer's poem. This artifical mountain, complete with trees, fountain, and running river water, indeed illustrates the common Homeric epithets 'wooded' (*Il.* 21,449; cf. *consitum arboribus*) and 'many-fountained' (e.g. *Il.* 8,47; 11,183; 14,283 and passim; cf. *fonte manante*; in *Il.* 12,18 f. an enumeration of the rivers running from Mount Ida to sea; cf. *fluuialis aquas eliquans*). But since Homer's cursory reference to the Judgement in *Il.* 24,28-30 does not mention Mount Ida, the reference to Homer here is not enough to suggest that the Judgement of Paris is about to be performed. See below on *in modum Paridis*.

ad instar: see on ch. 1 (236,21).

incliti montis illius: *illius* reinforces the laudatory quality of *incliti*. Callebat 1968,276, who gives further examples, regards it as an element in Apuleius' typically abundant style, rather than a weakening of the demonstrative force of *ille*.

Idaeum: sc. *montem*. Cf. Lucr. 5,663 *Idaeis ... e montibus*; Ov. *Fast.* 4,264 *in Idaeo ... iugo*.

sublimi: F has *sublimis*; the emendation is by φ. The expression *sublimi ... fabrica* is also found elsewhere in the *Met.*: 5,2 (104,16 *horrea sublimi fabrica perfecta*); cf. 6,3 (130,27 *sollerti fabrica*); 6,6 (132,17 *subtili fabrica*). The error *sublimis* is easily understandable: the scribe referred the adjective back to *mons*, which was still in his mind.

consitus: 'densely planted'; see *GCA* 1977,132 on 4,17 (87,14-16).

uirectis et uiuis arboribus: alliteration and assonance of *i*.

uirectis: *uirecta* is a key term, as it were, in the description of a 'locus amoenus' (Mattiacci

1990,92, with references); cf. Hor. *Ars* 17; Serv. ad Verg. *A*. 5,734. Cf. *laetissima uirecta* in 4,2 (75,10-12) and *pratentibus uirectis* in 8,18 (191,20), both passages where a 'locus amoenus' is evoked (see the notes in *GCA* 1977,28 f. and 1985,167 ad locc.). An important aspect of the 'locus amoenus' is its hedonistic, sensual, non-utilitarian quality (Schönbeck 1962,16). Cf. Serv. ad Verg. *A*. 5,734: *amoena sunt loca solius uoluptatis plena, quasi amunia, unde nullus fructus exsoluitur*.

summo cacumine: cf. Verg. *A*. 6,678 *dehinc summa cacumina linquunt*, where Austin remarks that the slightly pleonastic expression is 'rather grandiose; but it helps to suggest contour'. Here one might say that it helps to underline the very loftiness of the structure. Cf. also Lucr. 6,464, where the transparent beginnings of clouds are taken upwards by the wind *ad summa cacumina montis*. Cf. in the *Met*. 1,10 (10,3-4) *ciuitatem summo uertice montis ... sitam*; 2,10 (33,4-5) *qua fine summum cacumen capillus ascendit*, where Van Mal-Maeder 1998,185 ad loc. points out the 'homophonie de la tournure', which Apuleius evidently appreciated.

de manibus fabri: the instrumental use of *de* + ablative is frequent in the *Met*.; see the discussion in Van Mal-Maeder 1998,113 on 2,4 (27,20-21), with references.

This phrase is one of the many references in this passage to the artificial and illusory (see above on *mons ligneus*).

manibus fabri ... manante fluuialis aquas eliquans: assonance of *a*.

fabri ... fonte ... fluuialis: alliteration.

fluuialis aquas eliquans: the usual meaning of *eliquare* is 'to purify (... by straining)'; thus e.g. 1,2 (2,16). In *Fl*. 15,10 Apuleius writes *canticum ... semihiantibus ... labellis eliquare*; cf. Pers. 1,34 f. *Phyllidas, Hypsipylas uatum et plorabile siquid / eliquat*, where Kißel ad loc. discusses the metaphorical use of *eliquare*, also in the Apuleius passages; he argues that the literal meaning of 'straining (juice)' plays a part, since the words (or the singing) 'trickle' through a small opening, so that *eliquare* is not identical with *effundere* (thus *ThLL* s.v. *eliquo* 392,37 f.). In our passage, *eliquans* suggests that the artifical fountain sends forth a clear, thin trickle, which reinforces the aspect of artificiality in this passage (see above on *mons ligneus*). After Apuleius, Tertullian (*Pall*. 3) uses *eliquare* for the spinning of a fine thread: (*Mercurium autumant ...*) *tractu prosequente filum eliquasse*.

261,7-10 Capellae pauculae tondebant herbulas et in modum Paridis Frygii pastoris, barbaricis amiculis umeris def<l>uentibus, pulchre indusiatus adulescens, aurea tiara contecto capite, pecuarium simulabat magisterium: A few goats were browsing blades of grass, and a young man, beautifully arrayed as Paris, the Phrygian shepherd, with an Oriental mantle flowing from his shoulders and a gold-coloured tiara covering his head, posed as a cattle herder.

Capellae ... tondebant herbulas: the pastoral atmosphere is enhanced by an appropriate allusion to Verg. *Ecl*. 10,7 *dum tenera attondent simae uirgulta capellae*. In that passage the 'pose' of a shepherd is assumed by the poet; here an actor poses as Paris, who himself had assumed the part of shepherd only temporarily. Cf. also 5,25 (122,24-25) *proxime ripam uago pastu lasciuiunt comam fluuii tondentes capellae*. For *tondere* as an agrarian term for 'pruning', 'mowing', but also 'grazing', see the extensive article in *EV* s.v. *tondeo* [Facchini Tosi].

capellae pauculae ... herbulas: Abate 1982,82 f. rightly points out the 'sonic effect and hypocoristic colouring' of this and other clusters of diminutives in the description of the spectacle (see also on ch. 29: 260,20 f., and on ch. 31: 262,1-4). For the occurrences in the *Met.* of the diminutive *pauculus*, see *GCA* 1995,83 on 9,8 (208,4-7).

in modum Paridis Frygii pastoris: the reading of F has been retained. Hildebrand defended it, and Robertson, Terzaghi, and Giarratano-Frassinetti also retain F's reading, as does Augello 1977,219. Scriverius deleted *Frygii pastoris* as a gloss. Oudendorp deleted *Paridis* as a gloss, and Helm followed him. It is true that *pastor ille* is sufficient as a reference to Paris, e.g. in 4,30 (98,13); cf. also Hor. *Carm.* 1,15,1 *pastor cum traheret* with Nisbet-Hubbard ad loc. But in our passage it has only just become clear that the setting is the background for a performance of the 'Judgement of Paris'. The athetesis of *Paridis* was cancelled by Helm 1956 (= Helm-Krenkel [6]1970).

From the somewhat laboured description it appears that we are about to see a performance of that part of the myth in which Paris, as a shepherd boy on Mount Ida, judges the beauty contest. The judgement of Paris is treated very briefly in Homer (*Il.* 24,28 f.); Proclus' *Chrestomathia* shows that it was narrated more fully in the *Cypria*. Euripides in particular evokes it in various tragedies (see the richly documented discussion by Stinton 1965 = Stinton 1990). Hellenistic poets often give the story a romantic cast; so also Ov. *Ep.* 16,53 f. The *Anth. Lat.*, in the *Carmina Vergiliana* (Vol. 4,198 f. Baehrens), includes a poem called *Iudicium Paridis*. In *Dares Phrygius* 7 the judgement of Paris is presented in the form of a dream (see Beschorner 1992,93 f.).

In his description of the actors' costumes and attire, Apuleius refers to illustrations of the Judgement of Paris, a favourite subject on early Greek vases and Etruscan mirrors, and at the time of the *Met.*'s composition still frequent in wall paintings, sarcophagi, and other reliefs, mosaics, and coins (Clairmont 1951; *LIMC* 7,176-188 s.v. 'Paridis Iudicium' [Kossatz-Deissmann]). Of particular interest is a mosaic from the so-called Atrium House in Antioch (dated 130/150 A.D., now in the Louvre museum in Paris), where the Judgement is represented together with the two figures of Eros and Psyche (*LIMC* 7,2 nr. 77; Clairmont 1951: K 272; Campbell 1988,19 f. and pl. 70).

See Slater 1998,19 f. on Apuleius' counting on, and exploitation of the 'visual repertoire' of his (contemporary) readers.

def<l>uentibus: F and φ have *defuentibus*; a second hand in φ has added the *l*.

pulchre indusiatus adulescens: the archaic *indusiatus* (see *GCA* 1985,235 f. on 8,27: 198,11) always has a connotation of effeminacy in the *Met.*; see Van Mal-Maeder 1998,279 on 2,19 (40,20-21). In Hom. *Il.* 3,39 f. Hector rebukes Paris for his vanity and effeminacy; cf. also *Il.* 6,326 f.; ibid. 13,769 f. For *pulcher*, used not only for natural beauty but also for 'beauté acquise', Monteil 1964,97 f. cites Ter. *Phormio* 105 before our passage and 2,19; cf. Tib. 2,5,7 f. *nitidus pulcherque ueni: nunc indue uestem / sepositum, longas nunc bene pecte comas.* Cf. in the *Met.* also 11,8 (272,5) (*anteludia*) ... *exornata pulcherrime*.

aurea tiara: in most representations of the Judgement (see above), Paris is seen with the typical Phrygian *tiara*: a turban-like hat with flaps over the ears. Its qualification *aurea* is remarkable because the *tiara* is never made of metal. We may think of gold thread, or of *aureus* meaning 'shining like gold; bright yellow' (*OLD* s.v. *aureus* 4) or 'of great excellence, beauty; splendid' (*OLD* s.v. 5). Possibly, *aurea* is used to suggest that the most usual version of the myth is being followed here, in which Paris is recognized as a prince even before the judgement. This version is also followed in e.g. Ov. *Ep.* 16,52 f. (see Kenney 1996, Introd. 6 f.).

pecuarium simulabat magisterium: as the first example of *magisterium* meaning 'officium ... moderatoris (regentium, custodientum bestias)' *ThLL* s.v. 89,59 f. mentions 7,20 (169,23) and our passage. After Apuleius, cf. Valer. Cem. *hom.* 1,5 *pastorale magisterium*.

This phrase is one of many that underline the artificial and illusory aspect of what is being described (see above on *mons ligneus*).

261,10-15 Adest luculentus puer nudus, nisi quod ephebica chlamida sinistrum tegebat umerum, flauis crinibus usquequaque conspicuus, et inter comas eius aureae pinnulae cognatione simili sociatae prominebant; quem caduceum et uirgula Mercurium indicabant: There appeared a radiantly beautiful boy, naked but for an ephebic mantle that covered his left shoulder; he was conspicuous far and wide because of his blond hair, and between his locks small golden wings protruded which, because they were exactly alike, became one whole; the herald's staff, a tree branch, identified him as Mercury.

Adest: the initial position of this verb, and of *insequitur* and *inrupit* below, illustrates the rapidity with which the different actors succeed each other on the stage.

luculentus puer nudus: assonance of *u*. For *luculentus* used of physical beauty see *GCA* 1977,185 on 4,25 (93,22-94,3), with references. Krabbe 1989,132 tries to establish a meaningful connection between the seven occurrences of the adjective in the *Met.* but fails to convince.

nudus, nisi quod ... tegebat: see LHSz 2,587 f. for the restrictive turn of phrase *nisi quod*, common from Plautus onward. The description of the figure of Mercury will immediately have reminded contemporary readers of the statues of Hermes that were common during the early empire (see above, on *in modum Paridis Frygii pastoris*, on Apuleius' exploitation of his readers' 'visual repertoire', with reference to Slater 1998): Hermes as an ephebe, naked, with a mantle over one shoulder; thus e.g. *LIMC* s.v 'Hermes' 943 (Hermes of Naucydes); 946a, the Richelieu Hermes (an Antonine copy of a fourth century B.C. original). In the context of representations of the Judgement of Paris Hermes is also often depicted seminude with an ephebic mantle over his shoulder; examples in *LIMC* 7,2 s.v. 'Paridis iudicium'. Ibid. nr. 83 is a stucco funeral relief from Rome of ca. 160/170 A.D; its representation of the Judgement of Paris comes quite close to Apuleius' description in all respects: a nude Mercury with a short mantle thrown over his left shoulder. Cicu 1988,190 n. 21 points out the strong resemblance between this description and the wall painting in the *Casa dei Gladiatori* in Pompeii (Bieber 1961,232, fig. 775).

Relevant to the description of Mercury here is Apuleius' description of his Mercury statuette in *Apol.* 63,7 f.: *quam facies eius decora et suci palaestrici plena sit, quam hilaris dei uultus, ut decenter utrimque lanugo malis deserpat, ut in capite crispatus capillus sub imo pillei umbraculo appareat, quam lepide super tempora pares pinnulae emineant, quam autem festiue circa humeros uestis substricta sit*.

ephebica chlamida sinistrum ... umerum: as a first declension noun *chlamida* is attested only in Apuleius (here and 11,24: 285,28); elsewhere it is always *chlamys* (or *chlamis*), *-idis*. The effect here is parallellism in the two rhyming adjective-noun combinations *ephebica chlamida* and *sinistrum umerum* (Facchini Tosi 1986,105).

F had *ephoebica*; the emendation is by φ. The Greek noun *ephebus* is common in Latin from Plautus onward; the adjective is attested only here.

cognatione: thus F and φ, here retained with Giarratano-Frassinetti and Terzaghi. See Augello 1977,219 f. and n. 27; he follows Armini 1928,323, who defended F and argued that *cognatio* here means 'correspondence' or 'cohesion', with a reference to passages where *cognatus* means 'grown together'. It is not clear what *simili* must mean in that case. It is simpler to follow *ThLL* s.v. *cognatio* 1478,66 f., and understand *cognatio* here as 'i.q. *similitudo*' (for our passage see ibid. 1479,8 f.). The combination *cognatio similis* is then comparable to such combinations as *opem salutarem* (5,5: 107,5; other examples in Bernhard 1927,175). Cf. Tac. *Dial.* 25,4 *esse quandam iudicii ac uoluntatis similitudinem et cognationem*; Plin. *Nat.* 17,104 *quae ... pariter florentia eiusdem horae cognationem sucorumque societatem habent* (note the similarity to our combination *cognatione sociatae*). Earlier scholars had no difficulties with F's reading. Van der Vliet was the first to remark (without changing F's text): '*cognatio* vix sincerum; num fuit *concatenatio* vel *copulatio*?'; Wiman reads *coronatione*; Helm *conglutinatione*. Robertson follows Helm's earlier suggestion *colligatione*.

In this somewhat laborious phrase Apuleius is probably referring to representations of Hermes in which two small, symmetrical and identical wings protrude from his head as if they are part of his hair; see e.g. *LIMC* s.v. 'Hermes' 946 (e.g. the Richelieu Hermes; see above) and 953.

quem caduceum et uirgula Mercurium indicabant: thus F, retained by Helm, Giarratano-Frassinetti, and Terzaghi, and defended by Augello 1977,220, who regards the position of the synonyms as typically Apuleian and compares 5,25 (122,28) *rusticanus et opilio* (also in 10,33: 264,6); 7,23 (171,10-11) *propter luxuriam lasciuiamque amatoriam*; *Pl.* 1,18 (218) *artus ac membra*. Bernhard in *Gnomon* 6,1930,307 supported Wiman's defense of F; Koziol 33 f. on 'synonyme Substantiva koordiniert' also retains F and explains *caducaeum et uirgula* = *caducea uirgula*. Robertson deleted *caduceum*; so also Mazzarino; Soping (a *vir doctus* mentioned by Oudendorp) wished to delete *et uirgula*; he also changed *indicabant* to *indicabat*, which was adopted by Robertson. Oudendorp defended F by explaining *caduceum et uirgula* as a hendiadys: *caducei uirgula*. Hildebrand also defended F but explained *et* as *id est*.

Helm et alii adduce 11,11 (274,21-22) as a parallel: *Anubis, laeua caduceum gerens, dextera palmam uirentem quatiens*. This parallel is rightly rejected by Robertson, for in our passage Mercury holds the golden apple in his right hand. Nevertheless, F can be retained, because of the arguments advanced above.

caduceum: the spelling of φ; F has *caducaeum*. Augello 1977,220 thinks that *caducaeum* can be retained; however, we may assume that Apuleius wrote the prosodically correct form *caduceum* (= κηρύκειον). In 11,10 (274,10) F also has *caduceum*.

261,15-19 Is saltatorie procurrens malumque bracteis inauratum dextra gerens <ei>, qui Paris uidebatur, porrigit, quid mandaret Iuppiter, nutu significans et protinus gradum scitule referens e conspectu facessit: He came forward with dancing steps and, carrying an apple gilded with gold leaf in his right hand, he handed it to the actor who represented Paris, indicating with motions of his head what Jupiter commanded; immediately afterwards he gracefully retraced his steps and disappeared from view.

saltatorie: the adverb is attested only here. The adjective is attested only twice, in Scip. min. *orat.* 20 and Cic. *Pis.* 22, in both passages with denigrating associations of effeminacy and depravity.

malum ... bracteis inauratum: again, the artificial and illusory aspect is emphasized (see above on *mons ligneus*). Gold leaf is used especially for stage properties; thus, *brattea* often has a connotation of 'illusion', 'glamour'. Cf. Ov. *Ars* 3,231 f. *aurea quae splendent ornatu signa theatro, / inspice: contemnes, brattea ligna tegit.* Mart. 8,33,3 f. (on a thin gold bowl he received from one Paulus) *hac fuerat nuper nebula tibi pegma perunctum, / pallida quam rubri diluit unda croci; / an magis astuti derasa est ungue ministri / brattea, de fulcro quam reor esse tuo ?.* Cf. Hil. *Syn.* 89 *timeo aurum bracteae, quia me fallere possit interius ... haec est ... secundum essentiam similitudo, si massa massae consimilis non fallat in bractea*; Sol. *Praef.* 2 (sc. *libro*) *si animum propius intenderis, uelut fermentum cognitionis magis ei inesse quam bratteas eloquentiae deprehendes.*

ei, qui...: the demonstrative pronoun is absent in F; in ς *ei* has been supplied. All modern editors adopt the reading of ς, or follow Castiglioni's <*adulescenti*> (thus Robertson and Giarratano-Frassinetti). Without <*ei*> it is unclear who is the indirect object of *porrigit* and the antecedent of *qui*. See Helm, Praef. *Fl.* 56 f.; LHSz 2,555 f. for examples of specific situations (not comparable to our passage) in which similar ellipses of the demonstrative pronoun do occur in archaic and colloquial Latin.

Baehrens 1912,327 f. finds <*ei*> in our passage unnecessary and gives examples of similar ellipses, such as Quint. *Decl.* 296,9 *illud certe in casum non cadit, quod gladius in triclinio fuerit, quod conuiciari incipiat, cuius occidendi ius habuerit*; Winterbottom 1984,112 follows Schenkl (*conuiciari* <*ei*> *incipiat*; see Winterbottom 1984,416 ad loc., with references). Cf. in Apuleius *Mun.* 7 (302) *sed in altera parte orbis iacent insularum aggeres maximarum, Brittanniae duae, et Albion et Hibernia, quas supra diximus esse, maiores* (Moreschini and Beaujeu supply <*iis*>); *Pl.* 1,12 (206) *instabile enim quiddam et incurrens intercedere solere, quae consilio fuerint et meditatione suscepta, quae non patiatur meditata ad finem uenire* (here the editors do not supply *iis* before *quae*).

quid mandaret Iuppiter, nutu significans: the first specific reference to the mimic skill of pantomime actors upon which Luc. *Salt.* 62 f. elaborates with some anecdotes (cf. ibid. 64 διανεύων οὗτος ἕκαστα μοι ἑρμηνεύσει). See also on ch. 31 (262,11-12) *procedens quieta et inadfectata gesticulatione nutibus honestis ... pollicetur.*

scitule: the adverb indicates, of course, that this dancer is well versed in his art (he is *scitus*); but the diminutive gives it a hypocoristic nuance as well, which transmits to the reader the describer's delight in the spectacle (cf. Van Mal-Maeder 1998,278 on 2,19: 40,20); see above on *capellae pauculae ... herbulas.*

e conspectu facessit: see on ch. 21 (252,13) *facessunt.*

261,19-21 Insequitur puella uultu honesta in deae Iunonis speciem similis: nam et caput stringebat diadema candida, ferebat et sceptrum: Next entered a girl with a respectable face, resembling the goddess Juno in appearance: for a shining diadem encircled her head, and she also carried a sceptre.

Insequitur puella: the initial position of the finite verb (cf. above on *adest* and below on *inrupit alia*) suggests the rapidity with which the actors succeed each other on the stage.

See Rotolo 1957,240 f. on female pantomime actors, whose appearance on the stage is attested early and becomes increasingly common during the empire.

puella uultu honesta: the role of Juno requires a respectable and dignified appearance.

Accordingly, the mask of the dancer representing Juno shows a *uultus honesta* (see on the question of the mask also on ch. 32: 263,19 *saltare solis oculis*). The actor in a pantomime wore a small mask with the mouth closed, in contrast to the masks in tragedy and comedy (Steinmetz 1982,349 f.); Lucian. *Salt*. 29 τὸ δὲ πρόσωπον αὐτὸ ὡς κάλλιστον καὶ τῷ ὑποκειμένῳ δράματι ἐοικός, οὐ κεχηνὸς δὲ ὡς ἐκεῖνα ἀλλὰ συμμεμυκός). It seems therefore incorrect to take *honesta* to mean 'handsome' (*GCA* 1981,221 on 7,21: 170,10-14 and *OLD* s.v. *honestus* 4 cite our passage for that meaning). Cf. below, ch. 31 (262,12) 'Juno''s *nutibus honestis*.

in deae Iunonis speciem similis: in the *Met.*, women are quite often compared with Roman goddesses (Van Mal-Maeder 1998,255 on 2,17: 38,17); most notably Fotis and Psyche are both likened to Venus.

The expression is somewhat tautological, a contamination of *similis in* + accusative and *in speciem* + genitive. Again, this underlines the illusionary aspect of the scene (see above on *mons ligneus*): the dancer looks like (*similis*) an image (*species*) of Juno; thus, she portrays not the goddess herself but a *species* of the goddess.

For the rare turn of phrase *similis in* + accusative see Furneaux and Goodyear on Tac. *Ann*. 2,39,2 *forma haud dissimili in dominum erat*. Phrases with *in* + accusative are frequent in the *Met*. and have been discussed in detail. See Van Mal - Maeder 1998,75 on 2,2 (25,10 f.) with full references.

diadema candida: in classical Latin *diadema* is neuter, as in Greek. For its use as a first declension feminine, *ThLL* 944,68 f. gives before Apuleius only Pompon. *com*. 164. See also Neue-Wagener 1,501 f., who give mainly pre-classical examples of Greek nouns in *-ma* treated as first declension feminines; cf. the ablative plural *schemis* in 4,20 (89,17-19) and *GCA* 1977,151 f. ad loc. with references. Apuleius usually adheres to classical genders (see *GCA* 1981,272 on 7,28: 176,7-11 *liquida fimo ... egesta* with references). In our passage, the morphological variation may have been motivated by the homoioteleuton, as so often in Apuleius. Facchini Tosi 1986,104 f. does not discuss our passage but gives other examples of variations motivated by euphony in the forms of Greek nouns in *-ma*. See also above on *ephebica chlamida*.

261,21-24 Inrupit alia, quam putares Mineruam, caput contecta fulgenti galea, et oleaginea corona tegebatur ipsa galea, clypeum attollens et hastam quatiens et qualis illa, cum pugnat: Another dancer rushed in, whom you could take for Minerva, her head covered with a glittering helmet, and the helmet itself was covered with a wreath of olive branches; she raised her shield high and shook her lance, just like the well-known 'Minerva in combat'.

Inrupit alia...: the finite verb in the first position (see above on *insequitur puella*) makes a direct link with the preceding text, especially when, as here, the sentence is joined asyndetically to the previous one. See Bernhard 1927,11 f. with other examples; cf. e.g. 4,31 (99,17) *adsunt Nerei filiae*; 7,13 (163,22) *procurrunt parentes*. Cf. in book 10 ch. 7 (241,23) *placuit salubre consilium*.

Inrupit suggests the impetuous movement of the dancer who portrays Minerva as Athena Promachos (see below on *qualis illa, cum pugnat*). For the difference between the goddesses' entrances, cf. above on Juno: *insequitur*; below on Venus: *introcessit*.

quam putares Mineruam: the second person singular draws the reader in as a spectator.

This phrase once more points out the illusory character of the performance: precisely by emphasizing that Minerva looks like the real thing, it stresses that she is make-believe. See the acute remarks by Van Mal - Maeder 1998,105 on 2,4 (27,7) *creduntur*, with references.

oleaginea corona tegebatur ipsa galea: the helmet crowned with an olive wreath (a reference to the gift by which Athena won the contest with Poseidon) points to the two aspects of Minerva/Athene: goddess of war, but also bringer of culture. Cf. Tert. *Cor.* 12,2 *cum et olea militia coronatur, ad Mineruam est idolatria, armorum aeque deam, sed et pace cum Neptuno inita ex hac arbore coronatam*. On the olive as a symbol of peace, see also Van der Paardt 1981,71 on 3,8 (57,20-21) *ramos oleagineos ... quatientes*; cf. Verg. *G.* 2,425 *placitam Paci ... oliuam*.

On many ancient coins, Athena is represented with an olive wreath around her helmet (see on the Perseus Website in the 'coin index' e.g. Dewing 89; 412; 415; 1597; BCMA 1914.6.6; 1919.58.95). Minerva is going to promise Paris military triumphs (see ch. 31: 262,21-23); for the olive wreath in Roman military triumphs see e.g. Plin. *Nat.* 15,19; Gel. 5,6,3 f.

For the thematic function of garlands in the *Met.* see Fick-Michel 1991,303 f.; Hijmans in *GCA* 1995,383.

clypeum attollens: there is only one other passage where *attollere* is used in connection with a shield: Verg. *A.* 8,731, where Aeneas takes the shield on his shoulders (*attollens umero*), symbolically taking on the heavy burden of *famamque et fata nepotum*, which are represented on the shield. By using *attollens* in a concrete sense for the lifting of a shield, Apuleius banalizes the heavily symbolical line in Vergil.

The spelling *clypeus*, besides *clipeus* and *clupeus*, is not uncommon (see ThLL s.v. *clipeus* 1351,32 f.).

qualis illa, cum pugnat: *illa* refers to the representations of Athena Promachos in visual art, with which the public was familiar.

CHAPTER XXXI

Entrance of the dancer representing Venus. Dance of Juno and her attendants. Dance of Minerva and her attendants.

261,24-262,1 Super has introcessit alia, uisendo decore praepollens, gratia coloris ambrosei designans Venerem, qualis fuit Venus, cum fuit uirgo, nudo et intecto corpore perfectam formonsitatem professa, nisi quod tenui pallio bombycino inumbrabat spectabilem pubem: Immediately after these yet another girl entered, whose appearance was by far the greatest feast for the eye; with the charm of her ambrosial complexion she portrayed Venus as Venus was when still a maiden; her body nude and unclad, she openly showed her perfect beauty, except that with a gossamer silk gown she veiled her admirable loins.

For Juno's introduction scarcely three Teubner lines sufficed, for Minerva's scarcely four. Venus, on the other hand, is introduced in ten lines. Moreover, the dances of Juno and Minerva and their attendants, in which they make their promises to Paris (in this chapter, eight and ten lines respectively), are described more briefly than the dance of Venus (ch. 32: 263,1-24). It is clear that the narrator regards Venus as the main character of the Pantomime.

Venus is a prominent character throughout the *Met.*, and each appearance of the goddess (or that of pseudo-Venuses like Fotis, Psyche, and our dancer) is an opportunity for a flowery description in which certain aspects recur, such as the birth of Venus: here in 262,4-6; for the first time in 2,8 (32,2 f.); see Van Mal-Maeder 1998,169 ad loc. on the possible references to sculpture and painting; 4,28 (97,5-6). In the next chapter we will find another recurrent element in Venus' retinue; see the introductory note to ch. 32.

In this passage, there are some verbal references back to Fotis and Psyche as impersonations of Venus, and to Venus herself in the Amor and Psyche episode; see the individual notes. It is significant that this last Venus figure, who kaleidoscopically combines all earlier Venus figures in the *Met.*, disappears in ch. 34 into a chasm at the bottom of the theatre, together with the illusionary mountain (Zimmerman-de Graaf 1993,159 f.).

Super has introcessit alia: 'in close succession to them yet another girl made her entrance'. The narrator gives a vivid image of the rapid entrances of the dancers succeeding each other. This dancer's importance is emphasized by describing her entrance in four words, in comparison to two each for her predecessors (ch. 30: 261,19 *insequitur puella*; 261,21 *inrupit alia*. On the word order see the notes there).

introcessit: *introcedere* is attested only here and 5,3 (105,12) (an invisible musician entertains Psyche in Cupid's palace) *quidam introcessit et cantauit inuisus*. It may be an Apuleian coinage: in both cases a remarkable verb indicates a remarkable entrance. In 5,3 the entrance is only heard, not seen; in our passage on the contrary the visual aspect ist emphasized: a pantomime actress is only to be seen, not heard.

uisendo decore praepollens: cf. *Fl.* 15,7 (on a statue of Bathyllus) *adulescens est uisenda pulchritudine*. See comm. on ch. 2 (237,9-10) *forma magis quam moribus in domo mariti praepollens* on the two sides of *praepollens*, which apply here as well: this actress who impersonates Venus surpasses the others in beauty, but also 'is powerful by her beauty'; this points ahead to the victory of Venus in ch. 32. Cf. also ch. 33 (264,9-10) *eruditione doctrinaque praepollens Palamedes*.

gratia coloris ambrosei: cf. 2,9 (32,7) *color gratus*. There it refers to hair, here to complexion (see Van Mal-Maeder 1998,175 ad loc., with examples of *color gratus* referring to complexion).

designans Venerem: see on ch. 30 (261,19-20) *in deae Iunonis speciem similis*.

qualis fuit Venus, cum fuit uirgo: relative clauses often have the finite verb in first position (Bernhard 1927,15 f. gives examples). Here the parallel position of *fuit ... fuit* emphasizes the perfect tense: the goddess Venus was a *uirgo* once (but no longer). Cf. 4,28 (97,9), where the people see Psyche as *Venerem aliam, uirginali flore praeditam*.

nudo ... nisi quod ... inumbrabat spectabilem pubem: this description recalls the description of 'Vice' in Xenophon's retelling of Prodikos' allegory of Heracles at the crossroads; cf. Xen. *Mem.* 2,1,22 ...ἐσθῆτα δέ, ἐξ ἧς ἂν μάλιστα ὥρα διαλάμποι. On instances in literature of the Judgement of Paris as an allegorical choice of lives see Stinton 1990,23 f. (= Stinton 1965,9 f.), with references. In Athen. 510c the Judgement of Paris is expressly compared with 'Heracles at the crossroads'.

nudo et intecto corpore: the second, negative adjective repeats the meaning of the first, positive adjective (Bernhard 1927,167 collects examples). Here the redundancy lends extra sensuality to the depiction, as in 3,20 (67,14-15) *intecti atque nudati bacchamur in Venerem*. In 9,30 (225,19) the expression *nudis et intectis pedibus* occurs in a context of mourning (see *GCA* 1995,261 ad loc.).

formonsitatem professa: cf. Ov. *Ars* 3,433 *sed uitate uiros cultum formamque professos*.

formonsitatem: for the spelling see comm. on ch. 21 (253,9) *formonsae*. *Formo(n)sitas* is before Apuleius attested only in Cic. *Off.* 1,126 meaning 'bodily health'. Apuleius uses the word twelve times in the *Met.*, always for the physical beauty of women and goddesses. See Monteil 1964,46 f. on the development of the meaning of *formo(n)sus* and *formo(n)sitas*.

nisi quod: on this restrictive phrase see on ch. 30 (261,11). Unlike Juno and Minerva, Venus carries no attributes. In representations of the Judgement of Paris from the earliest time onward, Aphrodite/Venus always has the fewest attributes (Clairmont 1951,108 f.). Increasingly she is depicted almost nude or, as here, wearing a revealing chiton (Clairmont 1951,109 and n. 144).

pallio bombycino: *bombyx* is the silk-moth or silk-worm (in *GCA* 1985,237 on 8,27: 198,11-16 incorrectly called a 'purple-snail'). For the adjective cf. Plin. *Nat.* 11,76; Juv. 6,260 *panniculus bombycinus* with Ferguson's extensive note ad loc., with references, on the origin of Roman silk. As in the Juvenal passage, the adjective here suggests luxury, in this case the sumptuousness of the pantomime organized by the wealthy Thiasus.

inumbrabat spectabilem pubem: an evocative phrase. *Spectabilis* can mean both 'worth looking at' (*OLD* s.v. 2) and 'able to be seen', as in Ov. *Tr.* 3,8,35 f. *ante oculos ueluti spectabile corpus / adstat fortunae forma tegenda meae* (*OLD* 1). Translators have to choose. E.g. Brandt-Ehlers '... die Scham beschattete, die aber sichtbar blieb'; Annaratone: 'le segrete grazie pur degne d'esser viste'.

Cf. 2,17 (38,19 f.) *glabellum feminal ... potius obumbrans ... quam tegens*. See *GCA* 1995,122 on 9,12 (212,4) *magis inumbrati quam obtecti* with references. For the motif of 'la nudité dévoilée' in the *Met.*, see Van Mal-Maeder 1998,253 f. on 2,17 (38,15-39,1), with references.

262,1-4 Quam quidem laciniam curiosulus uentus satis amanter nunc lasciuiens reflabat, ut dimota pateret flos aetatulae, nunc luxurians aspirabat, ut adhaerens pressule membrorum uoluptatem grafice <de>li[ci]niaret: And moreover, an inquisitive breeze, full of mischief, now very fondly wafted this shift up so that it moved aside and the blossom of her youthfulness was revealed, now, in high spirits, blew against it so that the garment clung tightly and traced the exquisite outlines of her delectable body.

The curiosity of the personified wind, which mischievously blows the dancer's dress aside, titillates the curiosity of the Corinthian audience in the theatre, of the the ass outside the entrance, of the narrator as he recalls the scene, and thence of the reader. See Teuber 1993,216 f. on the *Met.* as a 'Genußvolle Inszenierung der verbotenen Neugier'; see also Introd. **2.4.2**.

The dress fluttering in the breeze, which enhances rather than covers Venus' nudity, is a favourite detail in Pompeian wall paintings of the Judgement (Clairmont 1951,109). The image of the wind, blowing up the thin garment of a beautiful girl, has enjoyed a considerable fortune in literature since Moschos' *Europa* (129-130). Graverini 1999,243 f. follows its traces in Greek literature, and in Latin literature especially from Ovid (*Met.* 2,833 and *Fast.* 5,603 f.) onward; he discusses our passage 244 f., and points to the original use Apuleius makes of this traditional motif in 4,35, where Psyche is carried away by Zephyrus.

lacinia: Apuleius is the first to use this noun in the sense of 'clothing'. See Van Mal-Maeder 1998,167 on 2,8 (31,21), with references.

curiosulus ... aetatulae ... pressule: the diminutive *curiosulus* is hapax legomenon. Combined with the two other diminutives in this sentence, it emphasizes the erotic atmosphere (Abate 1978,82 f.). The diminutives contribute to the musicality of the syllables *la-, -lu, -li, -lae, -le* (see Facchini Tosi 1986,118 f. with references and examples).

satis amanter: for *satis* in the sense of *ualde* see the references in ch. 14 (246,26); for *satis amanter* cf. 2,6 (30,8) (sc. Fotis) *te ... satis amanter cooperuit*.

nunc lasciuiens reflabat, ... nunc luxurians aspirabat, ...: the two cola (eight and nine syllables respectively), are linked by anaphora, rhyme, and parallel form. In sound, they illustrate the rhythmic effect of the breeze blowing to and fro. The *ut-* clauses dependent on them have different constructions.

reflabat: cf. 2,4 (27,9) *ueste reflatum* (the sculpture of Diana), with Van Mal-Maeder 1998,107 ad loc.

ut ... pateret flos aetatulae: for *patere* referring to 'partes corporis quae conspici possunt quia non teguntur vestibus' *ThLL* s.v. *pateo* 662,5 f. gives as first passage *Priapea* 29,4 *ostendas mihi coleos patentes*, and then many passages in Ovid and other poets. Cf. Mart. 11,70,5 f. *ah facinus! tunica patet inguen utrimque leuata, / inspiciturque tua mentula facta manu*.

Flos aetatulae has the connotation 'fere i.q. pulchritudo' (*ThLL* s.v. *flos* 935,49 f.) combined with that of 'integritas, pudicitia' (*ThLL* 935,56 f.). Cf. e.g. Catul. 62,46 (*uirgo*) *cum castum amisit polluto corpore florem*; Ov. *Met.* 10,85 *aetatis breue uer et primos carpere flores*. The previous sentence emphasized that this girl resembles a virginal Venus. Cf. 4,28 (97,9) on Psyche, *uirginale flore praeditam*. See also on ch. 29 (260,20) *uirenti*

florentes aetatula.
Is Apuleius playing here on the image of a real flower opening and the metaphorical 'flower of virginity' being unveiled? Although the idea is attractive, few parallels have been found for *patere* in connection with flowers. But cf. Mart. 11,18,15 f., on a very small manor where *non boletus hiare, non mariscae / ridere aut uiolae patere possunt*; see Kay ad loc. on Martial's play with *patere*.

luxurians: 'elated, playful, frisky'. *Luxuriare* is used for the frolicking or gamboling of animals (*OLD* s.v. *luxurio* 2), but also frequently in a moralistic context meaning 'to revel immoderately' (*OLD* s.v. 3), so that our passage also suggests the 'sauciness' of the breeze. Apuleius uses the verb only here (in *Soc.* 23,173, *luxuriat* occurs in a citation from Verg. A. 11,497).

adhaerens pressule: sc. *lacinia*. On the diminutive adverb see on ch. 21 (252,20) *pressule*.

membrorum uoluptatem: 'the delight of her body' = 'her delectable body'; for a similar genitive with *uoluptas* cf. e.g. Lucr. 1,140 f. *sperata uoluptas / suauis amicitiae*. In addition to 'body', *membra* can also mean 'private parts' in this context (cf. above *flos aetatulae*); see Van Mal-Maeder 1998,156 on 2,7 (30,24-31,1) *steterunt ... membra* with references (*OLD* s.v. *membrum* 1b).

grafice: see *GCA* 1985,236 on 8,27 (198,13) about the spelling and meaning of *grafice*. In our passage, the notion of 'eleganter' is relevant besides that of 'quasi in pictura'.

deliniaret: this reading is proposed by Vulcanius for *liciniaret* in F. Helm prints *liciniaret*. However, a verb *liciniare* is nowhere attested; Robertson supposes that the scribe's error is caused by the preceding *laciniam*. Salmasius' proposal *liniaret* or *linearet* has been adopted by many editors (Robertson, Frassinetti, Brandt-Ehlers, Hanson; see also Augello 1977,220). Here *deliniaret* has been selected because the (rare) *lineare* is only attested meaning 'to make or keep straight' (*OLD* s.v. *lineo*), which does not apply here. Apuleius uses *delineare* in the sense required here in *Fl.* 7,6 (*Alexandri effigiem*) *solus Apelles coloribus delinearet*; cf. also Plin. *Nat.* 35,89.

For the notion that a tight-fitting garment reveals the contours of the body cf. Ach. Tat. 1,1,11 καὶ ἐγίνετο τοῦ σώματος κάτοπτρον ὁ χιτών.

262,4-6 Ipse autem color deae diuersus in speciem, corpus candidum, quod caelo demeat, amictus caerulus, quod mari remeat: And also the goddess's colours offered a contrast to the eye: her body radiantly white because she descends from heaven; her clothing deep blue because she emerges from the sea.

Ipse autem color deae: the words *ipse autem* indicate that, just as the wind has a contrasting effect, so do the colours of the goddess. Thus Annaratone: 'Anche l'aspetto della dea offriva allo sguardo un contrasto di colori'.

corpus candidum, quod caelo demeat, amictus caerulus, quod mari remeat: four cola (5, 6, 6, 6 syllables), syntactically parallel in form, and with rhyming verbs (Bernhard 1927,89 f. gives other examples; see ibid. 224 f. on Gliederreim; Callebat in *AAGA* 1978,181).

Venus' both being born from the sea and coming from heaven apparently was a favourite theme in visual art as well as in rhetoric. Cf. Philostr. *Imag.* 2,1,4 (subject are the Ὑμνήτριαι of the painting described) τὴν Ἀφροδίτην ἐκφῦναι τῆς Θαλάττης λέγουσιν ἀπορροῇ τοῦ Οὐρανοῦ ... τὴν γένεσιν δὲ ἱκανῶς ᾄδουσιν· ἀναβλέπουσαι μὲν γὰρ ἐμφαίνουσιν, ὅτι ἀπ' οὐρανοῦ, τὰς δὲ χεῖρας ὑπτίας ὑποκινοῦσαι δηλοῦσιν, ὅτι ἐκ θαλάττης.

In the tale of Cupid and Psyche Venus' birth from the sea is elaborated upon in 4,28 (97,5-6); in 4,31 she returns to the sea and remains there until 5,29 (126,11) *emergit e mari*. In 6,6 she ascends to heaven (132,26 f. *Caelum filiae panditur et summus aether cum gaudio suscipit deam*); see further below, on *mari remeat*.

demeat ... remeat: *demeare* in the meaning of 'descend' is not attested before Fronto (*ad M. Caes.* 4,3: 59,20 vdH.) and remains rare (see *GCA* 1985,80 on 8,7: 181,25-182,1; Harrauer on 11,6: 271,2). The combination of *demeare* and *remeare* is also found 1,19 (17,13) *neque deorsum demeare neque sursum remeare*; cf. also 6,2 (130,11-12) *demeacula ... remeacula* with Facchini Tosi 1986,125 and n. 80.

mari remeat: the sea as the birthplace and element of Venus is frequently emphasized in the *Met*. Cf. 2,17 (38,15-18: Fotis compared with 'Aphrodite anadyomene') with Van Mal-Maeder 1998,255 ad loc.; see Keulen in *AAGA* 2,1998,177 and n. 36.

262,6-10 Iam singulas uirgines, quae deae putabantur, <sui comitabantur> comites, Iunonem quidem Castor et Pollux, qu*o*rum capit*a* cassides o*u*atae stellarum apicibus insignes contegebant, sed et isti Castores erant scaenici pueri: Now the girls who represented goddesses were flanked each by her own companions: Juno by Castor and Pollux, whose heads were covered by oval helmets distinguished by crowns of stars, and these *Castors*, too, were boys of the theatre group.

uirgines, quae deae putabantur, <sui comitabantur> comites: our text follows a proposal by Oudendorp, with Giarratano-Frassinetti, Terzaghi, and Hanson (see also Augello 1977,221). Everyone agrees that F lacks a verb with *singulas uirgines* as its object. The scribe's eye must have skipped from *putabantur* to *comites*, so that an intermediate verb, also ending in *-bantur*, was omitted. Not only is Oudendorp's conjecture paleographically attractive (one of the words beginning with *comit-* was skipped), it also results in an etymological play (*comitabantur comites*). Paleographically attractive is also Petschenig's *<sui tutabantur>*, followed by Robertson and Brandt-Ehlers; however, *sequebantur* (Helm's conjecture, followed by Brandt-Ehlers) or *comitabantur* fits better into the context. Van der Vliet suggests *<sui quamque stipabant>*.

Castor et Pollux: for the Dioscuri as Juno's special *comites* no parallels can be found (see *LIMC* s.v. 'Dioskouroi' 592 f. [Hermary]: 'Les Dioscures "au service d'une déesse" ', with references). During the Roman empire, especially in the second century A.D., they are, as astral deities, often associated with the Trias Capitolina on sarcophagi; see *LIMC* 3,1 631 f. [Gury] and the description ibid. of nos. 38, 78-79, 101. Notable is a marble relief from the Roman sanctuary of Juppiter Dolichenus on the Aventine, where the busts of Sarapis and Isis are represented centrally over an altar, with Juppiter Dolichenus and Juno Regina on either side. The two upper corners hold busts of the *Castores* (*LIMC* 3,1 cat. no. 115, p. 623). See Beard-North-Price 1998,281, with references, on the usurpation of the Roman state cult by Dolichene deities.

The appearance of the Dioscuri in a performance of 'The Judgement of Paris' (which resulted in the abduction of Helen) may also refer to the role of the twins as rescuers, e.g. of their sister Helen after she had been abducted by Theseus. See *RE* s.v. 'Dioskuren' 1116 f. [Bethe] on the connection between the Dioscuri and Helen; *DNP* s.v. 'Dioskuroi' 674 [Scheer].

quorum capita: emendation by ς of *quarum capite* in F.

cassides ouatae stellarum apicibus insignes: the twins' egg-shaped helmets refer to the version of the myth in which they, together with Helena (and Clytaemnestra), are born from Leda's egg; cf. Hor. *S.* 2,1,26 f. *Castor gaudet equis; ouo prognatus eodem / pugnis.* The stars on their headgear are known from iconography (*LIMC* 3,1,592 f. [Hermary]; ibid. 611 f. [Gury], and ibid. cat. nos. 134-141 for Roman illustrations), and are also frequently found on coins of both the Republican and the Imperial periods (*LIMC* 3,1,618 [Gury]; cat. nos. 68-71).

ouatae: this is Salmasius' generally accepted emendation for *obatae* in F.

isti... scaenici pueri: the reader's attention is repeatedly called to the illusory character of the performance (see on ch. 30: 261,19 f. *in deae Iunonis speciem similis*).

Castores: this expression for Castor and Pollux together is frequent in Latin (*OLD* s.v. *Castor* 2).

262,10-14 Haec puella uarios modulos Iastia concinente tibia procedens quieta et inadfectata gesticulatione nutibus honestis pastori pollicetur, si sibi praemium decoris addixisset, et sese regnum totius Asiae tributuram: To the tones of an Ionian pipe playing varied melodies this girl stepped forward with calm and unaffected gestures, and with dignified movements of her head promised the shepherd that, if he awarded her the prize for beauty, she for her part would endow him with power over the whole of Asia.

uarios modulos Iastia concinente tibia: as in *Fl.* 4,1, Apuleius characterizes the Ionian (*Iastium*) melody as varied (*Tibicen ... Antigenidas), ... omnimodis peritus modificator, seu tu uelles Aeolion simplex siue Iastium uarium seu Ludium querulum seu Phrygium religiosum seu Dorium bellicosum.* See West 1992,182 f. on the 'several faces' of the Ionian mode, with references.

Iastia: Oudendorp's emendation of *Iastia* in F, where a second hand wrote ᵘ over -*ia*. ς have *lasciua*. In *Fl.* 4,1, cited in the previous note, *Iastium* is an emendation of *asii* in F. *Iastius* is the technical term for 'Ionian' in works on musical theory. Cf. Max. Tyr. 7,1 (1,1 Konaris) Ἰάστιος; Pl. *Laches* 188d uses the adverb ἰαστί in contrast with δωριστί; in *Rep.* 398e Glauco answers Socrates' question 'Which are the ἁρμονίαι expressing softness and the ones used at drinking parties?' with ' Ἰαστί, ... καὶ λυδιστί '; they then conclude that these modes are not appropriate for inculcating courage. See Comotti 1989,128 f.; West 1992,179 f. about Greek theories on the properties of the various scales and modes; Wille 1967,434 f. on the science of musical ethics in the Roman world. Apuleius is said to have written a *De musica* (Cassiod. *Art.* 5, *mus.* 10,1212).

tibia: this is the *aulos*, a double, reed-blown pipe. It is not comparable to our flute. See Landels 1998,24 f. on the *tibia*, discussing the misleading practice of Classical translators of using the word 'flute'; he proposes as alternative translations either the technically accurate term 'reed-blown double pipe', or, less exact, 'pipes', but decides to use 'aulos' in his book.

inadfectata gesticulatione: *inadfectatus* is first attested in Quint. *Inst.* 8,3,87 as a positive qualification of ἀφέλεια; cf. ibid. 9,4,17 *gratiam ... simplicis atque inadfectati coloris.* See further Van Mal-Maeder 1998,86 on 2,2 (26,7) *inadfectatum capillitium.*

gesticulatione: this noun is not attested until the first century A.D. and remains rare.

It occurs the first time in a context comparable to ours, in V.Max. 2,4,4 (*poeta Livius*) ... *sui operis actor, cum saepius a populo reuocatus uocem obtudisset, adhibito pueri ac tibicinis concentu gesticulationem tacitus peregit*; Quint. *Inst.* 11,3,183 uses the word in a comparison between the performance of an actor and that of an orator. Apuleius uses it only in this chapter, twice, to refer to the technique of χειρονομία of mime artists. See Rotolo 1957,230 f. with rich documentation. Cf. e.g. Tac. *Dial.* 26,3 on the 'eloquence' of *histriones*: *ut oratores nostri tenere dicere, histriones diserte saltare dicantur*; Aristaen. *Ep.* 1,26 ἀντὶ χρωμάτων καὶ γλώττης χειρὶ πολυσήμῳ ... κεχρημένη. Lucian. *Salt.* 63-64 tells two anecdotes about the mimetic art of the *pantomimus*. See also on ch. 32 (263,20-21 *nisu brachiorum polliceri uidebatur*.

nutibus honestis: see on ch. 30 (261,19) *uultu honesta*.

si sibi praemia decoris addixisset: note the parallellism with Minerva's condition below *si sibi formae uictoriae tradidisset*, and chiasmus of *praemium decoris / formae uictoriam*.

addixisset, et sese ... tributuram: in his reaction to a 'vir doctus' who proposed *ei* here, Oudendorp defended F's *et* in the sense of 'vicissim'. Castiglioni 1938,561 f. abandons his earlier proposal to delete *et* (as a dittography after *addixisset*); that proposal was followed by Giarratano-Frassinetti, Robertson, Brandt-Ehlers, and Hanson.

There is no need to wonder how the dancer is to convey *Asia* by means of gestures: the audience knows the story. Cf. Lucian. *Dearum Iudicium* (*Dial. Deorum* 20) 11 ἦν γάρ με, ὦ Πάρι, δικάσῃς εἶναι καλήν, ἁπάσης ἔσῃ τῆς Ἀσίας δεσπότης.

262,14-17 At illam, quam cultus armorum Mineruam fecerat, duo pueri muniebant, proeliaris deae comites armigeri, Terror et Metus, nudis insultantes gladiis: But the girl whom her military outfit had turned into Minerva was flanked by two boys, the armour-bearing companions of the goddess of battle, Terror and Fear, who leapt forward with bare swords.

illam, quam .... fecerat: the reader is again reminded that everything described here is an illusion; see on ch. 30 (261,19 f.) *in deae Iunonis speciem similis*.

proeliaris deae comites armigeri: chiasmus. In Stat. *Theb.* 3,425 *Pauor* is called the *armiger* of Mars.

After Plautus, the adjective *proeliaris* is not attested until Apuleius, who uses it three times in the *Met*. In all three passages *proeliaris* is used in the context of mock combat: 3,6 (56,9) in Lucius' exaggerated account of his fight with the 'robbers'; 8,16 (190,4) in the comical description of the shepherds arming themselves like soldiers before a battle (*in speciem proelii*); and here in the description of the dancer portraying a *proeliaris dea*. Cf. Pl. *Curc.* 573 *pugnae proeliares*: the soldier Therapontigonus is bragging.

Terror et Metus: in Hom. *Il.* 4,440 f. Δειμός and Φόβος, along with Ἔρις, the brothers and comrades-in-arms not of Athena but of Ares (as in e.g. 15,119); however, in these lines they follow immediately after Athena so that a superficial reader may regard them as 'companions' of Athena: (4,439) ὦρσε δὲ τοὺς μὲν Ἄρης, τοὺς δὲ γλαυκῶπις Ἀθήνη / Δειμός τ' ἠδὲ Φόβος ... . On Homer as the starting point for investigation of the development of allegory see Whitman 1987,14 f.: 'Homer's work is both a revealing point of departure and a recurrent point of reference for the early allegoric tradition'. Latin poets, too, are fond of allegorizing personifications. Cf. the many personified abstractions at the entrance to the underworld in Verg. *A.* 6,273 f. (see Austin ad loc.), including (276) *Metus. Terror* as a personification is first attested in Ov. *Met.* 4,485; see Bömer ad loc. See also the extensive note of Smolenaars on Stat. *Theb.* 7,47-54 (personified aspects of war) with references. For personifications in Apuleius see on ch. 24 (255,20) *saeua Riualitas*.

insultantes: the generally accepted emendation by ς of *insaltantes* in F, φ, and a*. According to Robertson, the first *a* in F is not in a Beneventan hand; in that case, F may originally have had *insultantes*.

262,17-19 At pone tergum tibicen <D>orium canebat bellicosum et permiscens bombis grauibus *tinn*itus acutos in modum tubae salt*ationis* agilis uigorem suscitabat: And behind her a piper played a warlike Dorian tune; through the deep bass tones he played shrill descants and like a war trumpet he roused the vigour of her energetic dance.

tibicen Dorium: F has *tibicenorium*; the emendation is by Philomathes. *Dorium* is also used as a noun in *Fl.* 4,1 *seu tu uelles Aeolion simplex siue Iastium uarium seu Ludium querulum seu Phrygium religiosum seu Dorium bellicosum*; cf. Cael. Aurel. *Chron.* 1,5,175 *ut in bello quam* (sc. *modulationem*) *Dorion appellant*.

Dorium ... bellicosum: see the *Florida* citation in the previous note; West 1992,179 f. discusses the Dorian mode, with references to ancient sources like Plato *Rep.* 398e-399c.

permiscens bombis grauibus tinnitus acutos: this refers to playing the double aulos: see *Fl.* 3,5: *primus Hyagnis in canendo manus discapedinauit, primus duas tibias uno spiritu animauit, primus laeuis et dexteris foraminibus, acuto tinnitu et graui bombo, concentum musicum miscuit*. See West 1992,103 f., with references, on the ancient practice of playing auloi in pairs, and 105 on onomatopaeic Greek and Latin words describing the different registers. The lowest notes are likened to the buzzing of wasps (*bombus*). The higher registers were commonly characterized as screeching (*tinnitus*). Cf. Catul. 64,262-264 *aut tereti tenuis tinnitus aere ciebant; / multis raucisonos efflabant cornua bombos / barbaraque horribili stridebat tibia cantu* with Quinn ad loc.

tinnitus: F has *innutus*; the emendation is by ς.

saltationis: F has *saltitionis*; the emendation is by ς.

262,19-23 Haec inquieto capite et oculis in aspectu[m] minacibus citato et intorto genere gesticulationis alacer demonstrabat Paridi, si sibi formae uictoriam tradidisset, fortem tropaeisque bellorum inclitum suis adminiculis futurum: With restless movements of the head and eyes that looked at him menacingly she made it clear to Paris, in a tempestuous and whirling kind of mime, that if he awarded her the victory in the beauty contest he would be brave and famous for war trophies through her help.

inquieto capite: cf. Juno's *quieta gesticulatio* above.

oculis in aspectu[m] minacibus: Schoppe's emendation of *aspectum* in F is generally accepted (ς: *inspectu*); see Helm, Praef. *Fl.* 47, with examples in F of dittography of *m*. Cf. 2,2 (26,8-9) *oculi ... in aspectu micantes* with Van Mal-Maeder 1998,87 ad loc. For the use of *in* meaning 'with respect to', cf. 9,14 (213,17-18) *in rapinis ... auara, in sumptibus ... profusa* with *GCA* 1995,138 ad loc.

oculis ... minacibus: a probable reference to the 'regard fascinant' of Athena Glaukopis, symbolized by the Gorgo on her shield (see Detienne-Vernant 1974,175 f. and n. 35); *RE* s.v. 'Glaukopis' 1406 f. [Jessen]. Cf. Hom. *Il.* 1,200 δεινὼ δέ οἱ ὄσσε φάανθεν; Lucian. *Deor. Dial.* 19,1 φοβερὰ γάρ ἐστι καὶ χαροπὴ καὶ δεινῶς ἀνδρική. In Lucian. *Dear. Iud.* (= *Deor. Dial.* 20),10 Aphrodite summons Athena to take of her helmet and stop frightening Paris: ' ... ἢ δέδιας μή σοι ἐλέγχηται τὸ γλαυκὸν τῶν ὀμμάτων ἄνευ τοῦ φοβεροῦ βλεπόμενον;'

citato et intorto genere gesticulationis: *intortus*, 'crooked, twisted', can qualify diverse things (see e.g. Kißel on Pers. 5,38 *intortos ... mores*). Here the *citato et intorto ... gesticulatione* of 'Minerva' is contrasted with the *quieta et inadfectata gesticulatio* of 'Juno' (above). *Intortus* suggests both a whirling motion and convoluted gestures. For the first connotation Sen. *Nat.* 7,4,1 is comparable: (on the origin of comets) *turbine quodam aeris concitati et intorti*; for 'complicated' cf. Pl. *Cist.* 729 f. *inuoluolum, quae in pampini folio intorta implicat se: / itidem haec exorditur sibi intortam orationem*; cf. Physiogn. 59 *manus tenues et intortae loquacem demonstrant.* Apuleius uses the adjective once more in *Fl.* 13,2 for the sound of the night owl.

alacer demonstrabat: for the predicative use of *alacer* see *GCA* 1985,180 on 8,21 (193,2) *exurgit alacer*; cf. Verg. *A.* 10,729 *sic ruit in densos alacer Mezentius hostis.*

This is the only passage where *-er* is attested as the feminine ending; it may be an archaism. Cf. Serv. on *A.* 6,685 *sciendum antiquos et 'alacris' et 'alacer' et 'acris' et 'acer' tam de masculino quam de feminino genere dixisse: nunc masculino utrumque damus, de femineo 'alacer' et 'acer' numquam dicimus.* See on *alacer* as a feminine form Neue-Wagener 2,16 f.

si sibi ... futurum: cf. Lucian. *Dear. Iud.* (= *Dial. Deor.* 10),12 (Athena) Παρέστηκά σοι (cf. here *suis adminiculis*), καὶ ἤν με, ὦ Πάρι, δικάσῃς καλήν, οὔποτε ἥττων ἄπει ἐκ μάχης, ἀλλ' ἀεὶ κρατῶν· πολεμιστὴν γάρ σε καὶ νικηφόρον ἀπεργάσομαι.

si sibi formae uictoriam tradidisset: see above, on *si sibi praemium decoris addixisset*.

formae uictoriam: brachylogy for 'the victory in the beauty contest'. Cf. the phrase (dating back to Ennius) *uictoria regni* in Ov. *Met.* 9,49, with Börner ad loc. (on his correspondence with Szantyr about the unclassifiable genitive). Cf. also Tac. *Ann.* 16,4,1 *senatus ... offert imperatori uictoriam cantus adicitque facundiae coronam.*

As the direct object of *traderet, formae uictoriam* refers also to the tangible apple, the symbol of victory in the beauty contest; cf. below, ch. 32 (263,23-24) *iuuenis malum ... uelut uictoriae calculum puellae tradidit.*

tropaeis inclitum: cf. V. Max. 2,2,3 *C. Mari, quia gemina lauru coronatam senectutem tuam, Numidicis et Germanicis inlustrem tropaeis.*

suis adminiculis: *adminiculum* is originally, in a concrete sense, a support for plants and vines; later it is used to mean a metaphorical support or help, with the concrete meaning often still present, as e.g. Sen. *Ep.* 41,5 *non potest res tanta sine adminiculo numinis stare.* This is the only example in the *Met.*, but cf. Apul. *Apol.* 15,14 *sine ullo foris amminiculo; Pl.* 2,5 (227) *uirtutem, quod bonum suapte natura adminiculo non indiget*; ibid. 2,23,253; *Ascl.* 11 *cum dei opera sit mundus, eius pulchritudinem qui diligentia seruat atque auget, operam suam cum dei uoluntate coniungit, cum speciem, quam ille diuina intentione formauit, adminiculo sui corporis diurno opere curaque componit*; de pluralis ibid. 22 *diis ... nullis indigentibus rationis disciplinaeque adminiculis.* Cf. Hier. *Ep.* 133,6 *cum dei contemnas adminiculum, hominum quaeris auxilia?*; Arn. (Iunior) *Psal.* 123,12 *habes unde uincere, parata sunt adminicula, incipe proeliari, dominus te cum.*

CHAPTER XXXII

The dance of Venus.

263,1-8 Venus ecce cum magno fauore caueae in ipso meditullio scaenae, circumfuso populo laetissimorum paruulorum, dulce subridens constitit amoene: illos teretes et lacteos puellos diceres tu Cupidines ueros de caelo uel mari commodum inuolasse; nam et pinnulis et sagittulis et habitu cetero formae praeclare congruebant et uelut nuptialis epulas obiturae dominae coruscis praelucebant facibus: See, amid loud applause from the audience Venus, smiling sweetly, stood gracefully at the very centre of the stage, surrounded by a crowd of the most charming little children: those smooth, milky-white little boys, you would say that they were real Cupids who had just flown in from the sky or sea; for by both their tiny wings and little arrows and the rest of their outfit they splendidly matched the image, and as if she was on her way to a wedding feast they lit the road in front of their mistress with flaming torches.

Venus ... fauore caueae ... scaenae: the illusory element is again emphasized here (see on ch. 30: 261,19-20 *in deae Iunonis speciem similis*).

Venus ecce: one can imagine that, during the dances of Juno and Minerva, Venus continued her dance in the background. Now, with *Venus ecce*, she is in the spotlight again. See the next note and Van Mal-Maeder 1998,106 on 2,4 (27,7) *ecce lapis ...* .

ecce ... illos ... diceres tu: these ecphrastic elements work together to involve the reader as a spectator of the scene described.

cum magno fauore caueae: this dancer is the audience's favourite even before she has 'danced' her promise to Paris in the 'Iudicium Paridis'. During the dances of Juno and Minerva, the spectators' reaction was not mentioned. *Cauea* is used here metonymically for 'audience, spectators'; cf. V.Fl. 4,228 *nec sonat Oebalius caueae fauor*; Stat. *Theb.* 1,423 *caueae dissensus*.

in ipso meditullio scaenae: the original meaning of *meditullium* is 'the interior (of a country)'; see Van der Paardt 1971,191 on 3,27 (72,3-4) *in ipso ... meditullio ... aediculae*. For the somewhat wider meaning 'the centre (of other places)' *ThLL* s.v. *meditullium* 581,35 f. notes first Apuleius *Met.*; then Amm. 18,9,2; 22,8,6; Tert. *Anim.* 15,5 *in superciliorum meditullio*. For the metaphorical use too (e.g. Apul. *Pl.* 2,5,228) Apuleius is the first mentioned (*ThLL* 581,51 f.). The thematic connection seen by Krabbe 1989,129 f. between the passages with *meditullio* in the *Met.* and in *Pl.* is unconvincing.

circumfuso populo ... paruulorum: Venus' retinue is a recurring element in the passages describing her in the *Met.* Like our passage, 2,8 (32,3-5) mentions *Cupidinum populus* and *Gratiarum chorus* (see *Gratiae gratissimae* below); see Van Mal-Maeder 1998,169 ad loc. In 4,31 (99,16 f.) the marine retinue of Venus is described; in 5,28 (126,2-3) Venus herself mentions the Nymphs, the Hours, and the Graces; in 6,6 (132,20 f.) a flock of birds accompanies her to heaven.

laetissimorum paruulorum: of course *laetissimus* can mean 'very cheerful' (cf. e.g. Hanson 'happy'; Vallette 'joyeux'), but it probably refers in the first place to the delightful looks of the plump little Cupids. See *OLD* s.v. *laetus* 1; cf. above ch. 29 (260,18) *laetissimi graminis*; 4,2 (75,11) *laetissima uirecta*.

dulce subridens constitit amoene: chiasmus.

dulce subridens: cf. Catul. 51,5 *dulce ridentem* (based on Sappho 31,4 γελαίσας ἱμέροεν); Hor. *C.* 1,22,23 f. *dulce ridentem Lalagen amabo, / dulce loquentem*; Pers. 3,110 *subrisit molle puella*; see Kißel ad loc., with references, on this cognate accusative with *subridere*. In 6,13 (138,4) we see a different Venus, *subridens amarum*.

constitit amoene: F has *constituta mone* (an *e caudata* has been erased over the *o* of *mone*, according to Robertson); φ has *cōstituta moene*. The words are correctly divided in ς, yielding a word order frequent in the *Met.*: the finite verb in the penultimate position, followed by an adverb (Möbitz 1924,124 f.). Cf. e.g. 1,11 (10,17) *stertebat altius*; in this book ch. 16 (248,24) *delectatur eximie*; ch. 26 (257,19-20) *gustauit ampliter*; ibid. 258,3-4 *domum peruadit aegerrime*.

illos teretes et lacteos puellos ... Cupidines ueros: *teretes et lacteos puellos* seems to describe sculptures of putti or the white skin conventionally given to children in frescoes; see below on *formae ... congruebant*. From the Hellenistic period onward, Cupids are represented as putti, e.g. on the frieze of the temple of Venus Genetrix in Rome, rebuilt 113 A.D. See Fliedner 1971,70 f.; Fliedner examines 98 f. the occurrences of swarms of Erotes from Greek poetry onward; in his view, their marked increase in number in Latin poetry of the first century A.D. derives from visual art. See also Van Mal-Maeder 1998,171 on 2,8 (32,4) *toto Cupidinum populo*. Philostr. *Imag.* 1,6 describes a painting with Ἔρωτες; see comm. Schönberger 291 f. ad loc.

Red-figure Greek vases with illustrations of the Judgement of Paris often show winged Erotes around Aphrodite. Very different is the god Eros who is often depicted with Paris as a counsellor, persuading him to award the prize to Aphrodite. The special tie between Paris and Aphrodite is sometimes expressed by the fact that both are accompanied by Erotes (Clairmont 1951,112 f.). In Sil. 7,441 f. (Proteus tells about the Judgement) Venus is accompanied to Paris by several Cupids.

In late Classical literature a swarm of winged Erotes is often found in the context of a wedding (cf. below, *nuptiales cenas* and *coruscis facibus*). See Fliedner 1974,105 and n. 45, with references.

teretes ... puellos: 'smooth', 'flawless'; cf. Hor. *Epod.* 11,27 f. *sed alius ardor aut puellae candidae / aut teretis pueri*; Nisbet-Hubbard on Hor. *C.* 2,4,21 *teretes ... suras*.

lacteos: 'milky white'; cf. 5,22 (120,15) *ceruices lacteas* (of the sleeping Amor).

diceres tu: thus F. Castiglioni wanted to delete *tu*, 'fortasse recte' according to the app. crit. of Giarratano-Frassinetti (*tu* could be due to dittography before *Cu-*). The pronoun is not strictly necessary (cf. e.g. ch. 30: 261,21-22 *quam putares Mineruam*), but cf. 4,6 (79,8 f.) *ea tu ... dixeris atria*. Both in 4,6 and here we have a case of ecphrasis: the reader is addressed somewhat emphatically and urged to visualize the scene depicted here (see also *GCA* 1977,61 ad loc.).

et pinnulis et sagittulis: polysyndeton and homoeoteleuton; the hapax legomenon *sagittula* may have been created to achieve sound effect (see Facchini Tosi 1986,123 f. with references and other examples in Apuleius).

formae ... congruebant: *forma* means here 'likeness, image (of artistic representations)' (*OLD* s.v. *forma* 14b); cf. e.g. Ov. *Pont.* 2,8,57 f. *felices illi, qui non simulacra, sed ipsos, / quique deum coram corpora uera uident. / quod quoniam nobis inuidit inutile fatum,*

/ *quos dedit ars, uultus effigiemque colo.* / *sic homines nouere deos, quos arduus aether* / *occulit, et colitur pro Ioue forma Iouis.* Currie 1996,155 remarks: 'In an inversion of an aesthetic of mimesis Lucius praises real children for their successful transformation into *objets d'art*'.

uelut cenas nuptiales obiturae dominae: the allusion to a wedding is evocative. It recalls the tale of Amor and Psyche, where Venus is associated with marriage more than once: in 5,28 (125,18 *non nuptiae coniugales*) the absence of marriages is attributed to Venus' absence from the earth; in 6,6 (132,18) her own marriage is called to mind (*nuptiale munus* is the chariot on which she is carried to heaven); in 6,11 (136,5-7) Venus returns from a *conuiuium nuptiale*; finally 6,24: at the *cena nuptialis* (146,13) in honour of the wedding of Amor and Psyche, she dances (146,19-22): *Horae rosis ... purpurabant omnia, Gratiae spargebant balsama, ... Venus suaui musicae superingressa formonsa saltauit.* But each allusion to a wedding during the games here in the Corinthian theatre (see also in ch. 29 on 260,22 *pyrricam*) also ominously foreshadows the spectacle that is intended to be the culmination of this festival: the 'marriage' of the ass and the condemned murderess (cf. ch. 29: 260,1 *matrimonium confarraturus*; ch. 34: 265,10-11 *praeclaris nuptiis ... torus genialis*). At the level of the performance of the Judgement of Paris, the reference to a wedding is here ironical: the story will result in Venus assisting Paris in one of the most famous cases of adultery in mythology, the abduction of Helen.

coruscis ... facibus: burning torches were an indispensable element at the *deductio* of the bride to the house of the bridegroom; this took place after the *cena*, at nightfall (see *DNP* 5,655 s.v. 'Hochzeitsbräuche und Ritual' [Haase]).

Except here, the combination *coruscae faces* is found only in epic poetry, e.g. Lucan. 3,498 f. (the besieged Massilians make a sortie to set fire to the Roman camp) *ultro acies inferre parant armisque coruscas / nocturni texere faces*. In V.Fl. 1,621 f. during a storm at sea the Argonauts are surprised by the *coruscae ... faces* of lightning; in Sil. 8,649 f. *coruscae ... faces* also refers to lightning (one of the bad portents for the battle of Cannae). In the light of these passages it seems somewhat comical that the pretty little putti are carrying epic *coruscae faces*.

263,8-12 Et influunt innuptarum puellarum decorae suboles, hinc Gratiae gratissimae, inde Horae pulcherrimae, quae iaculis floris serti et soluti deam suam propitiantes scitissimum construxerant chorum, dominae uoluptatum ueris coma blandientes: Charming youthful groups of unwed girls also streamed in, on this side as supremely graceful Graces, on that as exquisitely beautiful Hours; worshipping their goddess by scattering loose flowers and garlands, they had lined up in a most skillful formation, charming the mistress of pleasure with the adornment of spring.

Et influunt ... suboles: the position of the verb at the beginning of the sentence, immediately after the initial *et*, illustrates the rapid sequence of the actors coming on stage; see on ch. 30 (261,10) *adest ... puer*; ibid. 261,19 *insequitur puella*; 261,21 *inrupit alia*; ch. 31 (261,24 f.) *introcessit alia*. The reader gets the impression of a superbly organized production.

innuptarum puellarum decorae suboles: four long words (4, 4, 3, and 3 syllables) suggest a long stream (*influunt*) of girls. The appositions *hinc Gratiae ..., inde Horae ...* suggest dancers on either side of Venus, in groups of three. There is no agreement on the precise number of Graces and Hours, but they are most often represented as three; see *DNP* 2,1102 f. s.v. 'Charites' [Schachter] and ibid. 5,716 f. s.v. 'Horai' [Heinze].

The plural of *suboles* is rare since the word by itself indicates a collective: 'offspring', 'generation'. But cf. Cic. *Tusc.* 2,10,23 *Titanum suboles, ... aspicite religatum asperis ... saxis* (sc. *Prometheum*). Translating a line of Aeschylus Cicero finds *suboles* suitable; in *De orat.* 3,153 he regards the word as too archaic for prose, but suitable for an elevated style.

The genitive with *suboles* usually indicates whose offspring is meant; here, however, *innuptarum puellarum* is a genitivus definitivus.

Gratiae ... Horae: cf. 6,24 (146,19-22), cited above in the note on *uelut nuptiales cenas*. On sarcophagi, the Graces primarily embody harmony and conjugal happiness, and are sometimes represented together with the Hours (Sichterman in Andreae-Koch *Antiken Sarkophagreliefs* 12,2: *Die Mythologische Sarkophage*, 83 f. with references). On the sculptures in the theatre of Sabratha, Graces are represented next to the relief illustrating the Judgement of Paris (Caputo 1959,21 and fig. 80).

In 5,28 (126,1-3) Venus calls the Graces her *ministerium*. In the same sentence the Hours are mentioned, as well as the Nymphs and the Muses. In 6,24 (146,19-20) the Hours and Graces add lustre to the wedding of Amor and Psyche. In Greek poetry the Graces are often associated with the Hours; cf. *h.Ap.* 194 Χάριτες καὶ ἐΰφρονες Ὧραι. They occur together in Aphrodite's retinue in e.g. Hes. *Erg.* 73-76. Cf. also Arist. *Pax* 456 (Trygaeus brings a toast) Ἑρμῇ, Χάρισιν, Ὥραισιν, Ἀφροδίτῃ, Πόθῳ: a series of deities 'representing all the brightness of life and love' (Merry ad loc.). More than once the Graces and Hours are mentioned as companions of peace (cf. Arist. *Av.* 1321: together with the personified abstraction 'Hesychia' as the deities ruling the utopian city; *Thesm.* 300). Thus, as *comites* of Venus but at the same time companions of peace, the Hours and Graces are contrasted in our passage with Minerva's *comites* Terror and Metus (ch. 31: 262,16).

gratissimae: the first of three superlatives in this sentence (*pulcherrimae, scitissimum*), which together help to convey the describer's enthusiasm.

Horae pulcherrimae: when qualifying deities, *pulcher* has besides 'beautiful' always the association of benevolence toward humans. See Monteil 1964,77 with examples. Cf. Ov. *Met.* 8,780 f. (Ceres) *adnuit his capitisque sui pulcherrima motu / concussit ... agros*.

iaculis floris ... soluti: the wider use of *iaculum* ('throwing-spear') for 'fere i.q. res quae iacitur' is noted by *ThLL* s.v. *iaculum* 77,37 f. first here in Apuleius; cf. also Apul. *Mun.* 3 (295) (*aër inferior*) *telis fulminum et missilium caelestium iaculis ignescit*; Min. 3,6 *ut illud iaculum* (sc. *testa iacta*) *... dorsum maris raderet*; Tert. *Res.* 20 (*Christus*) *faciem non auertens a sputaminum iaculis*.

floris serti et soluti: cf. Stat. *Theb.* 10,788 f. *hi sertis, hi ueris honore solutos / accumulant artus*.

In 2,16 (37,19-20) Fotis adorns herself with *rosa serta et rosa soluta* (see Van Mal-Maeder 1998,241 f. ad loc.); in 4,29 (98,2-3) people worship Psyche, who is regarded as Venus, with *floribus sertis et solutis*. Our dancer (representing Venus) is honoured *iaculis floris serti et soluti*. Thus the expression is used in the *Met.* for a flowery tribute to three pseudo-Venuses. In 11,9 (272,26-27) women in the Isis procession strew the ground with *flosculis*.

Cf. Chariton 3,2,17 (the wedding of Callirhoe and Dionysius) πάντες οὖν ἀνεβόησαν "ἡ Ἀφροδίτη γαμεῖ". πορφυρίδας ὑπεστρώννυον καὶ ῥόδα καὶ ἴα; 8,1,12 ἄνθη καὶ στεφάνους ἐπέβαλλον αὐτοῖς (at the wedding of Chaereas and Callirhoe upon their return).

propitiantes: usually, *propitiare* ('win over, propitiate') is a religious term (see the examples in *OLD* s.v. *propitio*). In the *Met.*, this term forms another (see also above on *floris serti et soluti*) connection between the three pseudo-goddesses and Isis. Cf. 2,10 (33,17) (Lucius to Fotis) *nisi tu propitiaris* with Van Mal-Maeder 1998,192 ad loc. In 4,29 (98,1) in the person of Psyche *Veneris absentis nomen propitiatur*; in book 11 the verb is used three times in connection with Isis (11,2: 267,15; 11,9: 273,8 in a context comparable to ours; 11,26: 287,29). As early as Plautus *propitiare* is used 'irreverently' of placating a lover; cf. Pl. *Cur.* 124 *tibi amantes propitiantes uinum potantes dant omnes*.

scitissimum construxerant chorum: F originally had *scites scitissimum*, but *scites* has been crossed out; in order to retain F's original reading, Philomathes proposed *scite scitissimum*; Robertson in his app. crit. wonders 'an *scitae*?'. But *scites* is crossed out in F, possibly by the first hand; moreover, φ and a* have only *scitissimum*.

For *scitus* meaning 'having practical knowledge' (of artistic performance), see *OLD* s.v. 2b; see also on ch. 30 (261,18) *scitule*.

dominae uoluptatum: in 5,28 (125,16 f.) the *gauia* mentions *non uoluptas ulla* as the first of the consequences of Venus' absence. As *domina uoluptatum*, mistress of sensual pleasures, the Venus mentioned here stands in sharp contrast with Isis as *elementorum omnium domina* (11,5: 269,13); cf. also 11,7 (271,23-24) *orbis ... totius dominam*.

Cf. Porph. ad Hor. *C.* 1,30,7 *scire autem debemus Venerem non tantum concubituum uerum etiam dominam esse omnium elegantiarum*. Zeno Ver. *Tract.* 2,4,16 uses Apuleius' phrase in a passage about transitoriness: *Nonne statim illa, quae erat domina uoluptatum, fit praeda morborum?*.

ueris coma: for the instrumental ablative with *blandientes* cf. Ov. *Met.* 10,555 *opportuna sua blanditur populus umbra*. For *ueris coma*, flowers as 'spring's tresses', no parallel can be found, which induces Wower to propose *ueris dono*. But the image can be taken as an Apuleian variation on the image of flowers or foliage as the 'tresses' of the earth, as in e.g. Tib. 2,1,48 *deponit flauas annua terra comas* (see Svennung 1945,102 f.); cf. Apul. *Mun.* 23 (340) *uiridantibus comis caesariatam ... terram* (the counterpart of ps.Ar. Περὶ κόσμου 397a24 "Η τε γῆ φυτοῖς κομῶσα). Cf. *Met.* 5,25 (122,24: the grass on a riverbank) *comam fluuii*.

263,12-13 Iam tibiae multiforabiles cantus Lydios dulciter consonant: Now the pipes with their many finger holes played Lydian songs in sweet harmony.

tibiae multiforabiles: *multiforabilis* is attested only here; like *multiforatilis* in *Fl.* 3,1 (see below) it is probably an Apuleian neologism for Greek πολύτρητος; cf. *Anth.Pal.* 9,266 "Ιμερον αὐλήσαντι πολυτρήτων διὰ λωτῶν; 505.5 Εὐτέρπη δονάκεσσι πολυτρήτοισι λιγαίνει; cf. Poll. 4,80 καὶ τέως μὲν τέτταρα τρυπήματα εἶχεν ὁ αὐλός· πολύτρητον δ' αὐτὸν ἐποίησε Διόδωρος ὁ Θηβαῖος. *ThLL* s.v. *multiforatilis* 1585,42 f. reads, with Leumann 1917,66, *multiforatilis* also in our passage and so does not list *multiforabilis*.

The *tibia* (see on ch. 31: 262,11 *tibia*) with many finger holes is a late development. Cf. Hor. *A.P.* 202 f. *tibia non, ut nunc, orichalco uincta, tubaeque / aemula: sed tenuis, simplexque foramine pauco*, with Brink ad loc. Cf. Apul. *Fl.* 3,1 (Hyagnis) *rudibus adhuc musicae saeculis solus ante alios cantus canere, nondum quidem tam flexanimo sono nec tam pluriformi modo nec tam multiforatili tibia.* See West 1992,86 f. on the number of holes that *auloi* could have, and on the archeological evidence of *auloi* with up to 24 holes, with a valve system. The musician could choose which set of openings he wanted to use for a certain scale; see also Landels 1998,34-38. In our passage, after the *Iastia* and the *Doricum* (see the previous chapter), the Lydian scale can now be selected: the *tibiae* with many holes produce richly varied melodies. The same notion is expressed by *crebro flectendo* in Var. *Men.* 365 (Cèbe 359,XII) *saepe totius theatri tibiis crebro flectendo commutari mentes, erigi animos eorum.* See Cèbe 1990,1518 f. ad loc. In our passage, too, the beguiling effect on the audience is mentioned (see the next pericope).

cantus ... consonant: ThLL s.v. *consono* 482,59 f. notes only our passage and Boeth. *mus.* 4,8; 4,17 and 4,18 as examples of the verb used transitively.

cantus Lydios: Plato calls the Lydian mode 'slack' and therefore bars it from his state (*Rep.* 398e, cited above on ch. 31: 262,11 *Iastia*); see West 1992,181 f. In 4,33 (101,11-12) the *modus Ludius* is called *querulus* (thus also *Fl.* 4,1). There were, however, several Lydian modes of which only two (the Mixolydian and the Syntonolydian) were regarded as lamentatory; thus Plato *Rep.* 398e Τίνες οὖν θρηνώδεις ἁρμονίαι; ... Μιξολυδιστί, ... καὶ συντονολυδιστί. Cassiod. *Var.* 2,40,4, who discusses the effect of different modes, says of the *modus Lydius*: *Lydius contra nimias curas animae taediaque repertus remissione reparat et oblectatione corroborat*; see Wille 1967,701 n. 1125 with further references.

cantus: both 'song' and 'magic incantation'; see below on *mulcentibus*.

263,13-19 Quibus spectatorum pectora suaue mulcentibus, longe suauior Venus placide commoueri cunctantique lente uestigio et leniter fluctuante spi[n]nula[s] et sensim adnutante capite coepit incedere mollique tibiarum sono delicatis respondere gestibus et nunc mite coniuentibus, nunc acre comminantibus gestire pupulis et nonnumquam saltare solis oculis: And while these melodies sweetly beguiled the spectators' hearts, Venus, far more sweetly, started to move gently; and with a languid and restrained step, and gently undulating spine, and gradually beckoning head, she started to dance and to respond to the soft song of the pipes with delicate movements and to gesticulate with eyes now languidly closed, now sharply threatening, and, indeed, sometimes to perform a ballet with her eyes alone.

In three passages in the *Met.*, Venus or someone identified with Venus performs a dance: in 2,7 (30,21-23) Fotis stands in front of her cooking-pots, swaying her hips: ... *membra sua leniter inlubricans, lumbis sensim uibrantibus, spinam mobilem quatiens placide decenter undabat*; see Van Mal-Maeder 1998,154 ad loc. (for Fotis as Venus see e.g. 2,17). In 6,24 (146,19-22) Venus, accompanied by the Hours and Graces, dances at the wedding of Amor and Psyche: *Horae rosis et ceteris floribus purpurabant omnia, Gratiae spargebant balsama ... Venus suaui musicae superingressa formonsa saltauit*. In the description of Venus' dance here, those earlier dances are recalled through verbal reminiscences; the reader is supposed to remember the previous dancing Venuses as he reads about this final dance (see Zimmerman-de Graaf 1993,151 f.; Gianotti 1996,280 f.). Especially in the dance of Fotis and in that of the present Venus there is an emphasis on seductive body movements, and in both cases the effect on the spectator is described immediately afterwards (Lucius in 2,7: 30,23-31,1; Paris below, 263,23-24). See also Introd. **2.5.3**.

Quibus spectatorum ... suaue ... suauior Venus: note the many *s* sounds and the assonance of *u*.

spectatorum pectora ... mulcentibus: see West 1992,31 f. on music's potency; ibid. 33: *auloi* (= *tibiae*) were considered especially powerful; Wille 1967,437 f.; ibid. 38 f. on the close connection between music and magic. Cf. in the *Met.* 8,30 (201,21) *cantus ... Frygii mulcentibus modulis. Mulcere* ('beguile') is frequently used of the effect of music (examples in *OLD* s.v. *mulceo* 4).

suaue mulcentibus ... longe suauior Venus: if the music casts a sweet spell over the audience, the comparative *suauior* describing *Venus* implies an even sweeter spell cast by her dance. Cf. the frequent use of θέλγειν in connection with dancers; e.g. *Anth.Pal.* 7,563,4 f. τεῇ δ' ὄλβιστε, σιωπῇ νῦν στυγερῇ τελέθει, τῇ πρίν ἐθελγόμεθα; ibid. 9,505,9,1 Σιγῶ, φθεγγομένη παλάμης θελψίφρονα παλμόν.

placide ... lente ... leniter ... sensim: all these adverbs, except *lente*, are found in the description of Fotis' dance (see the introductory note to this pericope).

commoueri ... coepit: the dancer had come to a halt (above: *constitit*) in the centre of the *scaena*; now a skillfully composed sentence with many long syllables describes how she slowly starts to move again. *Coepit* with the infinitives *commoueri, incedere, respondere, gestire,* and *saltare* has here its own full meaning; it is therefore impossible to see this as the beginning of the later development of *coepi(t)* with infinitive as a periphrastic perfect (see also *GCA* 1981,146 on 7,10: 161,25-162,1, with references).

cunctantique lente uestigio (10) *et leniter fluctuante spinula* (11) *et sensim adnutante capite* (10): a polysyndetic tricolon. The participles, one in each colon, have an assonantal effect; each participle is qualified by an adverb.

cunctantique lente uestigio: the redundancy of *lente* with *cunctanti uestigio* is functional (see above on *commoueri ... coepit*); that applies to most of the examples given by Bernhard 1927,177 for adverbs that 'überflüssig zum Verbum treten'. Cf. on ch. 20 (252,9-12) *desuper ... superstruunt*; see also *GCA* 1995,219 f. on 9,25 (221,21 f.) *et iterato rursum et frequentato saepius*.

leniter fluctuante spinula: F had *fluctuantes pinnulas*; the clever emendation, adopted by everyone, is by a 'vir doctus' in Oudendorp.

Fotis, too, dances with provocatively swaying hips as she cooks (see the quotation in the introductory note to this pericope). See Lawler 1964,133 f. on courtesans rotating the hips while dancing.

molli ... sono delicatis respondere gestibus: cf. 6,24 (146,21-22) *Venus suaui musicae superingressa formonsa saltauit* (see the introductory note to this pericope). *Mollis* describing the Lydian melodies played by the *tibiae* recalls the qualification μαλακός used by Plato (*Rep.* 398e) for this type of tonality. *Mollis* is frequent as a qualification of measure, rhythm, or sound (*ThLL* s.v. *mollis* 1377,29 f.), but often has the additional connotation of 'sensuous, erotic'; it is also used by elegiac poets as a catchword for their poetry; e.g. Prop. 2,1,2 *mollis ... liber*; ibid. 2,34,42 *ad molles membra resolue choros. Delicatus* has, besides the meaning 'elegant, luxurious', often the further connotation 'wanton, frivolous'. *Mollis* and *delicatus* are frequently found in combination; e.g. Cic. *Fin.* 1,11,37 *ea, quae uoluptaria, delicata, mollis habeatur disciplina*; *Off.* 1,30,106 *quam sit turpe diffluere luxuria et delicate ac molliter uiuere*; Sen. *Ep.* 51,6 *nihil delicate, nihil molliter esse faciendum*; Mart. 9,11,8 f. *quodsi Parrhasia sones in aula / respondent Veneres Cupidinesque, / nomen nobile, molle, delicatum*.

adnutante capite: *adnutare* is archaic. *ThLL* s.v. *adnuto* 792,61 f. gives before our passage only Naev. *com.* 76 *alii adnutat, alii adnictat, alium amat, alium tenet*; ibid. 111; and Pl. *Merc.* 436 f. *ibidem mihi / etiam nunc adnutat: addam sex minas*.

nunc mite coniuentibus, nunc acre comminantibus: an asyndetic parallel dicolon, with anaphora and homoeoteleuton; see Facchini Tosi 1986,141 with references on *mite*, which, unattested before Apuleius and selected here for its rhyme, is isosyllabic with *acre*, attested only here in Apuleius.

mite coniuentibus ... pupulis: *coniuere* commonly means 'close the eyes' (*OLD* s.v. *coniueo* 1), but also 'turn a blind eye, overlook' (*OLD* ibid. 3); cf. Ulp. *Dig.* 40,1,4,1 *uerum coniuentibus oculis credendum est suis nummis eum redemptum*.

saltare solis oculis: even if the description of the fictional artist cannot be regarded in itself as a reliable source, this phrase, supported by other evidence, suggests that in some cases mimes wore no masks (see also on ch. 30: 261,19 *uultu honesta*). Rotolo 1957,229 n. 3 cites examples of this, all of which are later than Apuleius, and concludes cautiously that from the second or third century A.D. onward the mask for mime artists may gradually have fallen into disuse. Cf. e.g. Aug. *De doctr. crist.* 2,3,4 (*histriones*) *cum oculis ... quasi fabulantur*; *Anth.Pal.* 16,283,3 f. (on the statue of a dancer) ὄμμα δέ οἱ καὶ ταρσὰ ποδήνεμα, καὶ σοφὰ χειρῶν / δάκτυλα καὶ Μουσῶν κρέσσονα καὶ Χαρίτων; see Rotolo l.c. for other references.

263,19-22 Haec ut primum ante iudicis conspectum facta est, nisu brachiorum polliceri uidebatur, si fuisset deabus ceteris antelata, daturam se nuptam Paridi forma praecipuam suique consimilem: As soon as she stood in front of the judge, with a gesture of her arms she seemed to promise that, if she were preferred to the other goddesses, she would give Paris a bride of exceptional beauty and very like herself.

ante iudicis conspectum: *ante conspectum* is rare; it is attested in Fest. 224,10 L. (205 M.) (*aues praepetes*) *ante conspectum uolent nostrum*. *ThLL* s.v. *conspectus* 490,63 f. cites *Gloss.* 2,297,28 ἐναντίον, τὸ ἀντικρύ. In Apuleius it occurs also 11,24 (286,17) *prouolutus ... ante conspectum deae* (Fredouille ad loc. rightly: 'peut-être même "devant la déesse"'), after Apuleius in Amm. 20,8,9 and in passages in the Vulgate and in Christian authors.

facta est: cf. 5,2 (104,14) *intra limen sese facit*. *Facere* or *se facere* in the sense of *ire, uenire* is probably colloquial, but becomes more frequent especially in late Latin prose; see Callebat 1968,173 with references; cf. also an expression like *obuius factus* (9,39: 232,29-233,2; see *GCA* 1995,324 ad loc.).

nisu brachiorum pollicere uidebatur: on the complex gestural language of the mime artist, see on ch. 31 (262,12) *gesticulatione*; cf. *Anth.Pal.* 7,563,3 (Paulus Silentiarus) on the artistic skill of the mime Chryseomallos: νεύμασιν ἀφθόγγοισι; *Anth.Pal.* 9,505,9 Σιγῶ, φθεγγομένη παλάμης θελξίφρονα παλμόν, / νεύματι φωνήεσσαν ἀπαγγέλλουσα σιωπήν; *Anth. Lat.* 1,111 (= *PLM* 4,287b), 7 f. *pugnat ludit amat bacchatur uertitur adstat, / inlustrat uerum, cuncta decore replet. / tot linguae quot membra uiro, mirabilis ars est, / quae facit articulos ore silenti loqui*; see also Gianotti 1996,285 and n. 101.

si fuisset ... antelata: in dependent clauses, Apuleius usually keeps to the final position of the verb customary in classical Latin. An initial position aims at a rhetorical effect ('Belebung der Rede'), according to Bernhard 1927,15 f., who collects the examples. Bernhard ibid. 10 f. shows by means of percentages that the initial position of the finite verb in dependent clauses is frequent in rhetorical Latin (e.g. Cicero). Cf. e.g. also 10,2 (238,3) *cum uideas* ... ; 10,7 (242,17) *quod promisisset* ...; 10,18 (251,9-10) *quod haberet* ..., in all of which a speaker makes an emphatic statement. So the dancer is here described as expressing herself in emphatic rhetorical language - without saying a word.

Whereas the conditions made by Juno (ch. 31: 262,13) and Minerva (ibid. 262,22) are parallel in form (see the note there), here Venus herself is the subject of the conditional clause, and only here are the other two contestants mentioned: *deabus ceteris*.

263,23-24 Tunc animo uolenti Frygius iuuenis malum, quod tenebat, aureum uelut uictoriae calculum puellae tradidit: Then wholeheartedly the Phrygian youth gave the apple he held in his hand, the golden apple, as if it were his vote for victory, to the girl.

A short, sober sentence gives the 'ending' (familiar to everyone, of course) of the Judgement of Paris. All the greater will be the reader's surprise in the next chapter when he hears the narrator's outraged reaction, which is entirely unforeseen here.

animo uolenti: cf. Sal. *Jug.* 73,3 *et Romae plebes litteris, qua de Metello ac Mario missae erant, cognitis uolenti animo de ambobus acceperant*. In addition to 'willingly, wholeheartedly', the phrase also has some connotation of 'deliberately'; cf. Verg. *A.* 7,216 f. *consilio hanc omnes animisque uolentibus urbem / adferimur*.

Frygius iuuenis: ring composition; cf. ch. 30 where Paris, *Frygii pastoris*, is introduced.

uictoriae calculum: strictly speaking the *calculus* is the voting-pebble with which jury members cast their votes for acquittal or conviction (see on ch. 8: 243,5). In the phrase here the meaning of *calculus* is between the concrete meaning 'voting-pebble' (the concrete, golden apple as *calculus*) and the figurative 'opinion, judgement' (*uictoriae calculum*). For the latter, cf. 7,9 (160,16) *calculis omnibus ducatum latrones unanimes ei deferunt*; see also *GCA* 1981,70 on 6,31 (152,24-153,1).

CHAPTER XXXIII

The narrator moralizes about the corruptness of judges.

264,1-7 Quid ergo miramini, uilissima capita, immo forensia pecora, immo uero togati uulturii, si toti nunc iudices sententias suas pretio nundinantur, cum rerum exordio inter deos et homines agitatum iudicium corruperit gratia et originalem sententiam magni Iouis consiliis electus iudex rusticanus et opilio lucro libidinis uendiderit cum totius etiam sui stirpis exitio?: So why are you surprised, you inferior individuals, or rather forum cattle, or better still vultures in togas, if all judges today sell their verdicts for money like market goods, when already at the beginning of history a case involving gods and humans was corrupted by favouritism, and the peasant judge, a cattle-herder, chosen on the advice of the great Jupiter, sold the primal verdict for the profit of lust, resulting in the ruin of his whole tribe?

The description of Venus bribing Paris leads the narrator to burst into a diatribe against corrupt jurisdiction. 'Complaining about the dishonesty of contemporary judges is a conventional sentiment' (thus Smith 1968,53, who gives examples in Latin literature; Sandy 1968,116 n.90 points out the denunciation of lawyers in Fielding, *Joseph Andrews* 2,1, also in a digression); cf. e.g. the elegiac verses spoken by Ascyltus in Petr. 14,2 *quid faciant leges, ubi sola pecunia regnat ...* and Panayotakis 1995,24, with references, on the possible background of these lines.

While the judgement of Paris is here regarded as the prototype of corrupt judgements, this element of the judgement is wisely ignored by Venus in 4,30 (98,13-14), where she refers to her selection by Paris (*ob eximiam speciem*); instead, she emphasizes Paris' *iustitia* and *fides* (see Van Mal-Maeder, Zimmerman in *AAGA* 2,1998,98 f.). See Zimmerman-de Graaf 1993,154 f. on this diatribe as a retrospective statement of the narrator (see Van Mal-Maeder 1998,20 on similar 'développements dissertatifs' in *Met.* 2,2; 2,8 and 9; 2,19). Others regard this outburst of rage as a reaction of Lucius the ass as observer of the scene (e.g Gianotti 1986,42 f. and n. 27; see Zimmerman-de Graaf 1993,154 n. 30 for further references). Eicke 1956,53 points out the remarkable difference in style between the well-wrought periodic composition of the rhetorical *indignatio* in this chapter and the predominantly paratactic style of the preceding description. This difference in style, as well as in tone, indicates that the narrator has suddenly adopted a different voice. The similarity of this tirade to Cynic diatribes has often been pointed out (e.g. by Mason 1971,163). The narrator steps forward out of the story and like a Cynic philosopher delivers a sermon occasioned by the theater performance. A similar situation may be suggested in Var. *Men.* 218-219 (*Inglorius*); see Cèbe 1983,1023 f. ('le Cynique *inglorius* ... Posté à un endroit que devaient hanter, pour des raisons faciles à diviner, les prêcheurs de son espèce, il interpelle la foule rassemblée pour la représentation ...'). Herodianus (the historian) 1,9,3-5 describes how a (Cynic) philosopher suddenly appears on the stage immediately before a theater performance and lectures the emperor Commodus (see Hahn 1989,33 f. and 173 f. with further references). See also Moles 1996,114, with references, on the missionary zeal of Cynic philosophers.

The angry tone of this passage is also in keeping with the image of a Cynic philosopher. Cf. Var. *Men.* 75 (*Caue canem*) with Cèbe 1975,313 f. and n. 2 ad loc.; see Dudley 1937,43. For additional Cynic signals see the individual notes on this chapter.

All the elements of *indignatio* mentioned by Quintilian (see Zundel 1989 s.v. *indignatio, indignari*) are used in this tirade. At its end, the speaker himself actually refers to this discourse as *indignationis meae*. Quint. *Inst.* 4,3,15 discusses *indignatio* as a form of *egressio*; cf. below, where the narrator calls himself back: *rursus unde decessi reuertar ad fabulam*.

Quid ergo miramini: this rhetorical question is quite appropriate in an *indignatio* (Quint. *Inst.* 9,2,10); cf. also below, *quale autem ...*; *nonne ...* .

The present tense *miramini* refers to the 'now' of the auctorial narrator (see Introd. **3.5**); cf. also *nunc* and *nundinantur*. See also *GCA* 1995,132 on 9,13 (213,4-6) *gratas gratias ... memini*.

uilissima capita ... forensia pecora ... togati uulturii: although in these three cola the combinations of attributive and noun are isosyllabic and parallel in form, the climactic effect of 'wachsende Glieder' is achieved by *immo* with the second colon, and *immo uero* with the third. There is also a climax in content, from the patronizing address of *uilissima capita* (helpless victims of injustice; see the next note), via the contemptuous reference to *forensia pecora* (blockheads in the forum), to the caustic invective aimed at the real culprits, the money-grabbing, corrupt judges (*togati uulturii*).

uilissima capita: for *caput* 'person, individual' see *GCA* 1985,148 on 8,15 (189,3) *humanis capitibus*; cf. also 9,10 (210,1) *impuratissima illa capita*. *Vilissima capita* is more pitying than accusatory. The combination *capita uiliora* or *uilissima* is first attested in Livy (*ThLL* s.v. *caput* 405,10 f.), who often uses the expression in a context of 'inferior' victims, e.g. 9,9,19 *nos interim, ... uilia haec capita luendae sponsioni feramus et nostro supplicio liberemus Romana arma*; cf. also ibid. 9,26,22; 24,5,13; 25,6,9; Sen. *Oed.* 521 (Oedipus to Creon) *mitteris Erebo uile pro cunctis caput, arcana sacri uoce ni retegis tua* (see Töchterle ad loc.); Quint. *Decl.* 338,13 *uilissimum istud caput*.

immo ... Immo uero. cf. 1,12 (11,21-12,1) *sero, immo statim, immo uero iam nunc ...*; for the rhetorical coloration of *immo uero* in a climax, see *GCA* 1981,93 on 7,2 (155,17-156,1), with references.

forensia pecora: appropriate companions for Paris, who in the same sentence is called *iudex rusticanus et opilio*. As a term of invective, *pecus* occurs in Cicero's orations (see Thome 1993,47 and n.87, with references). For this use see *ThLL* s.v. *pecus* 953,52 f. with passages from Pl. *Truc.* 269 onward. When human beings are compared with *pecora*, the intent is usually to illustrate their stupidity; cf. Sal. *Cat.* 1,1; ibid. 58,21. Hor. *S.* 1,3,100 refers to the first human beings as *mutum et turpe pecus*. Cf. Hor. *Ep.* 1,19,19 *o imitatores, seruum pecus* (see also Svennung 1945,97). Cf. the stock type 'Pecorone' in Commedia dell' arte.

In our passage the expression also recalls *Met.* 1,9 (9,3-5), where the witch Meroe *alium de foro, quod aduersus eam locutus esset, in arietem deformauit et nunc aries ille causas agit*. Elsom 1985,153 sees in our passage a connection with Sophocles' Ajax, where 'his madness ... involves his mistaking animals for men, specifically sheep for Odysseus and Agamemnon' (cf. the next sentence of the text, where the case of Ajax against Odysseus is mentioned). Scobie in *AAGA* 1978,218 f. cites *Mam.* 40 in Francisco Delicado's *Retrato de la Lozana Andaluza* (1528), where Aldonza says about two lawyers: 'como dixo Apuleyo, bestias letadros'.

togati uulturii: an original variant on *uulturii paludati*, as Cicero calls his arch-enemies Gabinius and Piso in *Sest.* 71,12. Thome 1993,35, n. 61 gives earlier references for *uulturius* as an invective in orations. See also MacKendrick 1995, index s.v. 'Animals, metaphors from' for examples of Cicero comparing his enemies to animals. For *uulturius* as a symbol of greed cf. also Catul. 68,124; see Svennung 1945,100 on *uultur* in Catul., with Greek examples.

sententias ... nundinantur: *nundinari* is hapax legomenon in Apuleius' works. The verb is well-chosen because of the meaning which the noun *nundinae* can have: 'a market (in pejorative sense, of traffic in things which should not be made the subject of trade)'; thus *OLD* s.v. *nundinae* 2b. For the intransitive verb *nundinari* in a pejorative sense, cf. Liv. 22,56,3 *Poenum sedere ad Cannas in captiuorum pretiis praedaque alia nec uictoris animo nec magni ducis more nundinantem*.

sententias suas: the possessive is used emphatically: 'they barter their own verdicts!' It results in a strong *s*-alliteration.

rerum exordio: 'at the beginning of world history', said somewhat hyperbolically of the event that caused the Trojan war. For the expression cf. Gel. 14,1,20 *primo caeli atque mundi exordio*. Lucretius used the combination (*cunctarum*) *rerum exordia* six times (e.g. 2,333 and 1062) for the atoms; for *rerum exordium* 'world's beginning' this passage in Apuleius is the first. After Apuleius, the combination becomes frequent in Christian authors (in the sense 'the beginning of creation'), e.g. Tert. *Apol.* 48,11 ... *ut prima haec pars* (sc. *aeui*) *ab exordio rerum quam incolimus, temporali aetate ad finem defluat*; Cassian. *Incarn.* 7,2 *ab exordio rerum*.

gratia: ambiguously used, meaning not only 'beauty, charm' (cf. above, ch. 31: 261,25-26 *gratia coloris ambrosei designans Venerem*) but also 'partiality, favouritism' (*OLD* s.v. *gratia* 3).

originalem sententiam: the 'proto'-judgement. Apuleius is the first to use the adjective in this sense (*ThLL* s.v. *originalis* 978,50 f.). Although our evidence is inconclusive, it is possible that the adjective was used in this meaning in technical works; cf. e.g. Paul. *Dig.* 50,1,22,4 *ad originalem patriam ... non restituitur*. As a technical grammatical term it occurs meaning 'prototypical' in e.g. Fortun. *Gramm.* 6,283,14 *originalia metra sunt* ...; ibid. 291,3. After Apuleius it is frequent in Christian authors, e.g. Hier. *adv. Iovin.* 1,27 *originale exemplum*; Aug. *Civ.* 16,27 *paruulum propter originale peccatum, quo primum dei dissipatum est testamentum, generatio disperderet, nisi regeneratio liberet*.

Apuleius is also the first to use *originalis* as a qualification of human beings and gods (*ThLL* ibid. 979,51 f.); cf. 11,2 (267,4-5) *Ceres alma frugum parens originalis*.

magni Iouis consiliis electus iudex rusticanus et opilio: there is an obvious irony in great Jupiter's having chosen a 'rustic judge'. This event is represented quite differently by Venus in 4,30 (98,13-14) *pastor ille, cuius iustitiam fidemque magnus comprobauit Iuppiter*. On this contrast see the introductory note to this section. The disdainful *iudex rusticanus* (almost an oxymoron) fits in well with *forensia pecora* (see the note above). In the *Apol.* Apuleius frequently uses *rusticanus* disdainfully to describe his accusers, e.g. *Apol.* 10,6 (also combined with *opilio*) *Aemilianus, uir ultra Vergilianos opiliones ... rusticanus*; cf. *Met.* 5,25 (122,28), where Pan refers to himself somewhat disparagingly as *rusticanus et opilio*.

opilio: for the frequency and etymology of *u/opilio*, see *GCA* 1985,29 on 8,1 (176,21), with references.

264,7-12 Sic hercules et aliud sequens iudicium inter inclitos Achiuorum duces celebratum, uel cum falsis insimulationibus eruditione doctrinaque praepollens Palamedes proditionis damnatur, uirtute Martia praepotenti praefertur *Ulixes* modicus Aiaci maximo: So, by Hercules, has also another, later, judgement become famous among the renowned leaders of the Achaeans, for example when on the ground of false allegations Palamedes, most influential through his knowledge and learning, is condemned for treason, and the mediocre Ulysses is preferred to the formidable Ajax, unsurpassed in warlike valour.

In his *indignatio* the speaker now cites examples of injustice that are unrelated to bribery. These examples are, however, much in keeping with a motif that prevails throughout the *Met.*, namely the fear of being condemned while innocent, a motif that possibly also refers to the concrete author behind the narrator(s), Apuleius Madaurensis, the author of the *Apologia* (see also below, on *eruditione doctrinaque praepollens*); see Zimmerman-de Graaf 1993,157 and n. 41; Shumate 1996,92 f. Cf. e.g. the staged trial against Lucius during the Risus festival in book 3; in 7,3 (156,7-8) and 7,22 (170,19-21) the ass cannot defend himself against false accusations. In the first inner story of this tenth book the stepson is about to be convicted while innocent (chs. 5-10); in the second inner story an innocent young girl is murdered by her brother's wife merely because this wife suspects her of *paelicatus* (ch. 24).

The lack of confidence in a fair trial, which is present below the surface in the first inner tale of book 10, is very obvious in this tirade. See on ch. 6 (241,12-13) *accusationis manifestis probationibus ... ambagibus*.

Various suggestions have been made to add or shift conjunctions in this sentence: Robertson reads *sequens<que>* and follows Leo in deleting *uel* after *celebratum*; Leky defends the manuscript reading with the argument that *uel* means here 'exempli causa'; see also LHSz 2,501 f. with examples for *uel* = *uelut* (frequent in Plautus and in Cicero's letters, in later authors to be considered an archaism). Helm, Giarratano-Frassinetti, and Terzaghi retain *uel* (Augello 1977,221 agrees). The second problem: in ς <*uel*> was added before *uirtute*, 'fortasse recte' according to Robertson. Van der Vliet reads <*uel heres Achilli*>; Helm 1907 supplied <*uel cum*>, but in Helm's more recent edition (1931; ²1955) F's reading is retained. It is indeed possible to retain the manuscript reading: in this outraged tirade, the second example of an unfair *iudicium* (*uirtute ... maximo*) is asyndetically connected with the first. Castiglioni 1938,562 f. mentions this as an argument for retaining F, but still proposes to supply <*uel uiro*>.

The only emendation of F adopted here is accepted by all editors, namely *Ulixes* for *auxies* in F, where the same hand had already written *.d.* in the margin to indicate that emendation was needed.

hercules: see on ch. 11 (244,24).

cum ... Palamedes ... damnatur: Palamedes plays no part in the *Iliad*; the false accusation of treason occurs in the *Cypria* (*EGF* p. 20 K) and was the subject of Greek tragedies. The false accusation is made by Odysseus, who was exposed by the shrewd Palamedes when he attempted to shirk the Trojan expedition by feigning madness (cf. also Ov. *Met.* 13,55 f.; 308). Austin on Verg. *A.* 2,82 remarks: 'Palamedes' condemnation and death was a byword for an unjust judgement' and 'it is clear from *ad Herenn.* 2,28 that *mors indigna Palamedi* was a stock theme in Roman rhetoric schools'. See the extensive references in Austin l.c. and in the article 'Palamede' by Corbato in *EV*.

The mention of Palamedes here, and of Ajax later in the sentence, is undoubtedly a reference to Plato's *Apol.* 41b, where Socrates says he is looking forward after his death to meeting Palamedes or Ajax, 'or any other man of old who lost their lives through an unjust judgement'; Cic. *Tusc.* 1,41,98 translates Socrates' words: *quanta delectatione autem adficerer, cum Palamedem, cum Aiacem, cum alios iudicio iniquo circumuentos conuenirem.* But Palamedes' unjust fate was apparently also a favourite subject with authors of the Second Sophistic. His prominent position in the Greek army and the envy it caused is mentioned in Philostr. *Heroic.* 10,5 f. Cf. also Philostr. *VA* 6,21, where Apollonius, similarly in a tirade about justice and injustice, brackets Palamedes and Socrates together; ibid. 3,22 Apollonius meets among the Brahmans a reincarnation of Palamedes, who is embittered: 'he found his bitterest enemies in Odysseus and Homer; for the one laid an ambush against him of people by whom he was stoned to death, while the other denied him any place in his Epic; and because neither the wisdom with which he was endowed was of any use to him, ... and because he was outwitted by Odysseus in spite of his innocence, he has conceived an aversion to philosophy and deplores his ill-luck' (transl. Conybeare).

eruditione doctrinaque praepollens: see on ch. 31 (261,25) *uisendo decore praepollens*. Palamedes' influence because of his keen insight is often emphasized. Cf. Lucian. *Calumn.* 28 ὁ συνετώτατος τῶν Ἀχαιῶν κἂν τοῖς ἄλλοις ἄριστος; cf. also Philostr. *VA* 6,21, cited in the previous note. Palamedes is portrayed in glowing terms in Dictys (see Merkle 1989,166 f.), 2,15 *ita uir optimus acceptusque in exercitu, cuius neque consilium umquam neque uirtus frustra fuit, circumuentus a quibus minime decuerat indigno modo interiit.*

Eruditio and *doctrina* are practically synonymous here; *eruditio* is 'knowledge acquired through instruction' (*OLD* s.v. *eruditio* 2); *doctrina*, 'skill acquired by teaching, training' (*OLD* s.v. *doctrina* 4b). Both nouns suggest a thorough schooling. The same combination is found in Cic. *Tusc.* 2,11,27 *haec* (sc. the works of poets) *a pueritia legimus ediscimus, hanc eruditionem liberalem et doctrinam putamus*; it is remarkable that Apuleius in *Apol.* 91,2 uses the same combination again to suggest that the crimes imputed to him are his *eruditio* and *doctrina*. Immediately afterwards, in the following sentence, he uses the same nouns to emphasize that his very *eruditio* and *doctrina* are the qualities that link him with the judge, Claudius Maximus, against his *stulti* and *impoliti* accusers. The concrete author, Apuleius, is very much present at the background of this tirade (see the introductory note to this section).

praepollens Palamedes proditionis ... praepotenti praefertur: alliteration of *p-* and *pr-*.

uirtute ... Aiaci maximo: another example of injustice is linked asyndetically with the previous one. The dispute between Ajax and Odysseus over Achilles' armour probably formed the opening of the *Ilias parva* (see *DNP* 5,934, 'Ilias mikra' [Latacz], with references) and is the theme of Sophocles' *Ajax*. Ov. *Met.* 12,620-13,390 consists largely of the ingenious speech with which Odysseus convinces the Greeks that he is entitled to the armour, and ends with Ajax' madness and suicide.

Observe the ingenious word order: the phrase begins and ends with laudatory qualifications of Ajax, with *praefertur Ulixes modicus* interposed. This results in contrasting *Ulixes modicus* and *Aiaci maximo*. While *Aiax maximus* echoes the Homeric μέγας Τελαμώνιος Αἴας (e.g. *Il.* 5,610; 14,409; cf. 16,358 Αἴας δ', ὁ μέγας; 9,169), a new epithet, *modicus*, has been applied to Odysseus to enhance the contrast.

264,12-13 Quale autem et illud iudicium apud legiferos Athenienses catos illos et omni<s> scientiae magistros?: And what sort of trial was the one before the clever lawgiving Athenians, those masters of every science?

Quale ... illud iudicium: the second rhetorical question in this *indignatio* (see above on *Quid ... miramini*). In questions or emotional exclamations, ellipsis of a form of *esse* is common; cf. e.g. 9,16 (215,1-4) *quanto melior Philesitherus ...*; see *GCA* 1995,154 ad loc. with references.

legiferos Athenienses: derisively, the speaker uses an elevated and rare epithet that, like the Greek θεσμοφόρος, is used especially for gods, notably Ceres/Demeter. Cf. Verg. *A.* 4,58 *legiferae Cereri*. The epithet is hapax legomenon in Apuleius' works; besides the Vergil passage cited above, it is attested only in Ov. *Am.* 3,10,41 *Minos ... legifer*. See the next note on the less elevated register of the immediately following qualification *catos*.

Athenienses catos illos: as often, *ille* (here 'those famous ...') highlights the ironical use of the adjective; cf. e.g. 5,24 (122,10 Amor on Psyche's sisters) *illae ... consiliatrices egregiae*. In *Apol.* 24,6, where *Athenienses catos* stands without *illos*, there is no question of irony. *Catus* 'means "sharp", both literally and metaphorically' (Nisbet-Hubbard on Hor. *C.* 1,10,3); it is clearly defined by Varro *L.* 7,3,46: *cata acuta. hoc enim uerbo dicunt Sabini; quare 'catus Aelius Sextus* (sc. in Enn. *Ann.* 331)' *non, ut aiunt, sapiens, sed acutus*. Differently from *OLD*, *LS* distinguish the use of *catus* 'in a good sense' (s.v. 2A) and 'in a bad sense, sly, crafty, cunning ...' (2B), for which examples are given especially from comedy; e.g. Pl. *Poen.* 1107 f. *eu, hercle mortalem catum,/ malum crudumque et callidum / et subdolum*. The wording suggests a contrast between the self-interested craftiness of the Athenians and the divine wisdom of Socrates (see the notes in the next section).

omni<s> scientiae: this emendation by a second hand in F has been adopted by all editors; see Helm Praef. *Fl.* XLVII for further examples of haplography of *s* in F.

264,14-21 Nonne diuinae prudentiae senex, quem sapientia praetulit cunctis mortalibus deus Delphicus, fraude et inuidia nequissimae factionis circumuentus uelut corruptor adulescentiae, quam frenis cohercebat, herbae pestilentis suco noxio peremptus est relinquens ciuibus ignominiae perpetuae maculam, cum nunc etiam egregii philosophi sectam ei<u>s sanctissimam praeoptent et summo beatitudinis studio iurent in ipsius nomen!: Is it not true that that divinely wise old man, whom the god of Delphi exalted above all mortals, was persecuted, through the fraud and envy of a malicious mob, as a corrupter of the young men, whom he actually curbed and restrained, and was killed by the deadly juice of a poisonous herb, thus leaving to his fellow-citizens the taint of perpetual disgrace, because even now outstanding philosophers prefer his noble teachings, and in their highest pursuit of happiness swear allegiance precisely to his name?

This account of the unjust execution of Socrates includes a eulogy of Socrates. Many scholars have pointed out the contrast between the historical Socrates, who is praised here, and his wretched namesake of the Aristomenes story in the first book (see e.g. Van der Paardt in *AAGA* 1978,82 f.; Tatum 1979,42; Schlam 1992,16). This 'Socrates', who was thought by his family to be dead, sought refuge with a witch in Thessaly; the real Socrates refused to go to Thessaly to escape conviction (Plato, *Crito* 53d). Yet the 'Socrates' of Book 1 dies in Thessaly after being a 'walking dead' for some time; our passage emphasizes that although the real Socrates was put to death his teachings are still (*nunc etiam*) alive.

In connection with the Cynical elements in this diatribe it is relevant to remember that Socrates was a hero of the Cynics (D.L. 6,103; Dudley 1937,86; Long 1988,151 f. and 164) and that Antisthenes, regarded in antiquity as the founder of Cynicism, was a close follower of Socrates and was present at his death (Plato, *Phaedo* 59b).

Nonne: the third rhetorical question in this *indignatio* (see above on *quale ... illud iudicium*).

diuinae prudentiae senex, quem ... deus Delphicus: Socrates is described by two connected periphrases. Cf. the periphrasis for the hemlock, *herbae ... noxio*, below. Cf. 3,23 (69,7-8) *supremi Iouis certus nuntius uel laetus armiger*; see Van der Paardt 1971,171 ad loc., with references. With all these periphrases in this *nonne* sentence the speaker addresses an educated audience that recognizes whom he is talking about. Maurach [2]1989,30 f. pleads for a distinction between different forms of poetic periphrasis (see ibid. 54-59) and gives references; 54 on the 'Raffinierungsperiphrase' he cites Lausberg par. 598 'Die Verhüllung gibt dem Leser ein Rätsel auf, dessen Lösung ... ihm intellektuelle Genugtuung verschafft'. See Maurach 55 f. on periphrases of 'Bekannte Namen'.

diuinae prudentiae: Socrates' prudence is exalted to a divine wisdom, and thus forms an even greater contrast with the cunning of the Athenians in the previous sentence (see above on *catos illos*). The combination *diuina prudentia* is rare, and used always of gods; first in Cic. *ND* 2,80 *efficitur omnia regi diuina mente atque prudentia*; then, in a mocking sense, of the wisdom of Priapus in Petr. 18,3 *adiuuaturos nos diuinam prudentiam uel periculo nostro*. In the *Asclepius*, which is to be attributed to Apuleius (see Hijmans 1987,411 f.; Hunink 1996,288 f.), an (exceptional) human being is endowed with *diuina prudentia*: *Ascl.* 16 *is homo* (sc. the human being who, through the rationality given him by the gods, avoids *malitiae fraudes, dolos uitiaque*) *est diuina intellegentia prudentiaque munitus; fundamentum est enim disciplinae in summa bonitate consistens*. Cf. Gel. 19,2,8 *Hippocrates, ... diuina uir scientia*. I found only one attestation of the phrase *diuina prouidentia* in Christian Latin: Chrys. *Serm.* 73 *ut non humanam solum, sed etiam diuinam prudentiam percipiant*.

quem ... praetulit ... deus Delphicus: a reference to the famous story that Socrates' friend Chaerephon, having asked the oracle of Delphi whether anyone existed wiser than Socrates, received the answer: 'No one is wiser than Socrates' (Plato *Apol.* 21a); cf. *Soc.* 17 (157) *Socrates, uir adprime perfectus et Apollinis ... testimonio sapiens*.

fraude et inuidia ... circumuentus: the passive of *circumuenire* is apparently a fixed expression in this context; cf. e.g. Cic. *Tusc.* 1,98 (cited above on *cum Palamedes ... damnatur*; Dictys 2,15 (cited above on *eruditione doctrinaque praepollens*); further examples in *OLD* s.v. *circumuenio* 6, 'to prosecute or convict unjustly'.

suco noxio: see on ch. 5 (239,27 f.) *noxii ... homines*.

relinquens ... maculam: a reference to Pl. *Apol.* 38c Οὐ πολλοῦ γ' ἕνεκα χρόνου, ὦ ἄνδρες Ἀθηναῖοι, ὄνομα ἕξετε καὶ αἰτίαν ὑπὸ τῶν βουλομένων τὴν πόλιν λοιδορεῖν, ὡς Σωκράτη ἀπεκτόνατε, ἄνδρα σοφόν.

cum nunc etiam egregii philosophi ... iurent: nunc ... praeoptent ... iurent also refers to the 'now' of the auctorial narrator (see above on *Quid ... miramini*). The speaker means the *philosophi Platonici*, among whom Apuleius explicitly numbers himself in the *Apology* (Hijmans 1987,416 with references). This reference to the real author of the *Met.* is, however, immediately fused with the self-irony of *asinum philosophantem* in the next sentence; see the note there. It is impossible to build a serious Platonic interpretation of the *Met.* on this kind of passage. See Gr. Anderson 1982,78 f. on Apuleius' 'whimsical alternation of comic and serious' and the various explanations proposed for it. Anderson suggests (ibid. 79, with examples) that second-century sophists found such σπουδογέλοιον in the most urbane and literary works of Plato (cf. also Trapp 1990 on Plato's influence on the literature of the Second Sophistic).

sectam ... sanctissimam: cf. Sen. *Ep.* 83,9 *Zenon, uir maximus, huius sectae fortissimae ac sanctissimae conditor*.

beatitudinis: Apuleius is the first to use this noun frequently; see *GCA* 1981,55 on 6,29 (150,17-151,1).

iurent in ipsius nomen: 'swear allegiance to'; see *OLD* s.v. *iuro* 5b for this use of *iurare* with *in* + accusative.

264,21-24 Sed nequis indignationis meae reprehendat impetum secum sic reputans: 'Ecce nunc patiemur philosophantem nobis asinum?', rursus, unde decessi, reuertar ad fabulam: But lest someone find fault with the vehemence of my *indignatio* and thinks to himself, 'Look here, are we going to put up with an ass lecturing us on philosophy?', I will return to the story from where I digressed.

In 7,10 (162,1-2), too, the narrator ironizes *asini ... iudicio* after an outburst of moral indignation; see *GCA* 1981,147 f. ad loc. There it is a direct reaction to Charite's behaviour, misunderstood by the actorial narrator (7,10. 161,26-28 *coepit risu laetissimo gestire, ut mihi merito subiret uituperatio totius sexus*). Another example is found in ch. 13 (246,23), where *nec ... eram ... uere asinus* refers to the *actor* Lucius, an ass in his outward appearance only.

indignationis meae ... impetus: 'my attack of indignation' (thus e.g. Hanson; Vallette; see *OLD* s.v. *impetus* 7); or 'the violence of my *indignatio*' (Annaratone: 'il calore della mia indignazione'); see the introductory note to this chapter on this tirade as a rhetorical *indignatio*. See *OLD* s.v. *impetus* 4b for 'vigour, ardour (of a speaker ...)'.

secum ... reputans: '*Ecce ... asinum*': see Bernhard 1927,53 on the preference in the *Met.* for lively *oratio recta* as opposed to *oratio obliqua*. In this book the only examples of extended *oratio obliqua* are ch. 6 (241,18-23), ch. 7 (242,15-22), and ch. 15 (247,27-248,6).

Ecce nunc patiemur: for the first position of the verb immediately after an interjection (here *ecce nunc*), cf. 7,11 (162,27) *hem oblita es ...*. See Bernhard 1927,17 for further examples.

patiemur philosophantem ... asinum: a possible reference to an anecdote about the Cynic philosopher Diogenes (D.L. 6,64): when someone reproachfully said to him: 'οὐδὲν εἰδὼς φιλοσοφεῖς', he answered: 'Even if I am but a pretender to wisdom, that in itself is philosophy (φιλοσοφεῖν)'. See Bracht Branham 1996,91 f. on the implications of this passage.

The narrator puts this objection into the mouth of one of his imagined readers, who holds to the fiction that an ass is telling the story, and objects to the incongruity of an *asinus philosophans* (see also 9,30: 225,10-13, and *GCA* 1995,258 ad loc.). This leads the interpreting reader to reflect on the question who is actually speaking here. The narrator in the *Met.* has practically constantly kept to the homodiegetic-actorial narrative style, i.e. he has presented the story as 'experiencing I'; sometimes, however, he forgets this role for a moment, as he does here. In other passages he plays with the fiction of a narrating ass, e.g. 6,25 (147,4-6), at the end of the tale of Amor and Psyche overheard by the ass: *sed astans ego non procul dolebam mehercules, quod pugillares et stilum non habebam, qui tam bellam fabellam praenotarem*.

The construction of an accusative noun and partic. praes. with *pati* is before Apuleius only attested in poetry (see *ThLL* s.v. *patior* 724,57 f.), e.g. Verg. *A.* 1,385 f. *nec plura querentem / passa Venus*; cf. in the *Met.* 5,31 (128,16 f.) *quis ... te deum, quis hominum patietur passim cupidines populis disseminantem?*

philosophantem ... asinum: Winkler 1985,150 points out the ambiguity of this expression: ' "Philosophizing" refers in the first place to the sermonette just ... uttered by the narrator *in the present time*, not by the actor in the past; since he is not supposed to be an ass any longer, *asinus* inconspicuously acquires a transferred sense as "fool" '. Smith 1996,310 f. discusses many instances in the *Met.*, where the narrator bursts out in indignation and then undercuts his own indignation; Smith interestingly places these elements of the *Met.* in the context of the Roman satiric tradition and asks: 'To what extent is the satiric narrator stereotyped as a "thinking ass"?'.

The rooster in Lucian's *Gallus* moralizes at length about the theme 'wealth alone does not make for happiness' (Lucian. *Gall.* 20 f.); ibid. 4 when the rooster says that he is really Pythagoras, Micyllus exclaims: Τοῦτ' αὖ μακρῷ ἐκείνου τερατωδέστερον, ἀλεκτρυὼν φιλόσοφος.

In the meaning 'to ... utter sententious reflections, moralize' (*OLD* s.v. b), *philosophari* is known not only from comedy but also from an apparently much-quoted line of Ennius (*Scaen.* 28 Jocelyn) *philosophari est mihi necesse, paucis; nam omnino haud placet*. This line is cited by Apuleius in *Apol.* 13,1 (see Hunink 1997 ad loc.); Cicero refers to it three times (*Rep.* 1,30; *Tusc.* 2,1,1; *de Orat.* 2,37,156); cf. also Gel. 5,15,9. On the use and meaning of *philosophari* in colloquial Latin and especially in Plautus, see Grilli 1996,74 f. with references. Cf. Pl. *Ps.* 687 (after a general discussion on Fortuna's power and people's stupidity) *sed iam satis est philosophatum: nimis diu et longum loquor*.

nobis: in view of its position between *philosophantem* and *asinum* it is preferable to construe this dative with *philosophantem* (thus e.g. Vallette; Hanson: 'lecturing us on philosophy') instead of taking it as a 'dativus ethicus'.

unde decessi ... reuertar: cf. Sen. *Dial.* 10 (*Breu.*),13,8 *ut illo reuertar, unde decessi*. The *asinus philosophans* concludes his *egressio* with a reference to Seneca philosophus.

CHAPTER XXXIV

Conclusion of the *Iudicium Paridis* pantomime. Preparations for the performance of Lucius and the condemned murderess.

264,25-29 Postquam finitum est illud Paridis iudicium, Iuno quidem cum Minerua tristes et iratis similes e scaena redeunt, indignationem repulsae gestibus professae, Venus uero gaudens et hilaris laetitiam suam saltando toto cum choro professa est: When the Judgement of Paris was completed, Juno and Minerva went back off stage, gloomy and acting angry, with gestures making a show of their indignation at their rejection; Venus, however, gloating and happy, made a show of joy in a dance performed with the entire chorus.

After his indignant interruption, the narrator resumes the description of the performance as promised (ch. 33: 264,24 *reuertar ad fabulam*).

Iuno ... cum Minerua ... redeunt: when a singular subject is linked to another subject by *cum*, the predicate is sometimes plural. KSt 2,1,27 f. give examples especially in pre- and postclassical Latin. See Callebat 1968,335 f. Cf. 3,26 (71,22 f.) *uector meus cum asino capita conferunt*, with Van der Paardt 1971,189 ad loc.

redeunt ... professa est: the *fabula* is resumed with a historical present; in the same sentence the last part of the actual ballet ends with a perfect; then a new event starts with *tunc ... prorumpit*. As the description of the pantomime concludes, the events on the *scaena* happen in rapid succession; there is no more time for detailed descriptions with imperfects, which predominate in chapters 29-32 from *inerrabant* onward (ch. 29: 260,23).

iratis similes: after the diatribe of the previous chapter, which interrupts the *ecphrasis*, the reader is reminded, by a Vergilian ecphrastic signal, that this is the description of a ballet, in which Juno and Minerva are represented by dancers. Cf. Verg. *A.* 5,254 *anhelanti similis* (sc. Ganymedes, pictured on the *chlamys*); 8,649 *indignanti similem similemque minanti* (sc. Porsenna on the shield); cf. in the *Met.* 7,1 (154,15), where a robber reports how he played a role *dolentique atque indignanti similis*; 8,25 (196,23) about a hypocritical priest *similis indignanti* (see *GCA* 1985,215 ad loc.).

professae ... professa: see Bernhard 1927,154 for further examples of repetition of the same word in one sentence, a rare phenomenon in the *Met*. To some of these repetitions Bernhard attributes a rhetorical motivation; e.g. 1,9 (9,1-4) *deformauit ... deformauit*, where the repetition underlines the witch's magical practices. Cf. also 9,15 (214,1-3) *iubebat ... iubebat* with *GCA* 1995,144 ad loc. In our passage, the parallelism underlines the contrast between the demeanour of Juno and Minerva on the one hand and Venus on the other: *tristes et iratis similes* versus *gaudens et hilaris*; *indignationem ... gestibus professae* versus *laetitiam ... saltando professa est*. The parallelism recalls the image of the symmetrical choreography of the ballet; cf. ch. 29 (260,20-25) describing the Pyrrhus dance; ch. 32 (263,11; sc. *Gratiae* and *Horae*) *scitissimum construxerant chorum*.

264,29-265,4 Tunc de summo montis cacumine per quandam latentem fistulam in excelsum prorumpit *uino crocus diluta sparsimque defluens pascentis circa capellas odoro perpluit imbre, donec in meliorem maculatae speciem canitiem propriam luteo colore mutarent*: Then, from the highest mountain top, through an invisible pipe, saffron dissolved in wine spouted into the air and, flowing down in droplets, rained in a fragrant shower over the goats grazing all around, until, dyed to a greater beauty, they changed their natural grey to a bright yellow colour.

de ... cacumine per ... fistulam ... prorumpit ... crocus: this may refer to Sen. *Ep.* 90,15 (Seneca contrasts the true *sapiens* with someone who invents ingenious but useless things) *qui inuenit quemadmodum in immensam altitudinem crocum latentibus fistulis exprimat*. Finkelpearl 1991,231 f. believes that 'the *auctor* Apuleius has made the *auctor* Lucius blindly introduce the moral (i.e. Senecan) view of the spectacle as a way of ironically exposing the lack of the moral judgment that he (Lucius/*auctor*) elsewhere attributes to himself then' (but see below on *montem ... terrae uorago recepit* for another possible interpretation of this and other allusions in this passage).

prorumpit ... crocus: does this suggest an ejaculation? Finkelpearl 1991,224 f. thinks it does, and in her extensive discussion puts forward a few parallels for the erotic connotations of saffron; she also refers to the Priapus, made of pastry, spouting saffron in Petr. 60,6, where no one can fail to notice the obscene meaning. See however the following note for the widespread use of saffron in theatres and for other possible connotations. That theatres had ingenious systems for spouting saffron perfume in the air appears from the Seneca passage (cited above), which has no obscene connotation whatsoever. Mart. 11,8,1 f. also refers to saffron being spouted into the air: *lassa quod hesterni spirant opobalsama dracti, / ultima quod curuo quae cadit aura croco*; see Kay ad loc.

uino crocus diluta: *crocus* is feminine only here; it is usually masculine, or neuter *crocum*. Against Oudendorp, who proposed emendations, Hildebrand defended the feminine, referring to 1,1 (1,7-8) *Hymettos Attica et Isthmos Ephyrea et Taenaros Spartiaca*, 'de cuius correctione frustra interpretes desudarunt'. Greek usually has the masculine κρόκος, but the feminine occurs e.g. Strabo 361; 370 (see also Callebat 1968,62). See Neue-Wagener 1,931 f. on the variable gender of plant names in Latin, e.g. *cytisus*, which is both feminine and masculine but is also found as the neuter *cytisum*; cf. also *lotos* (*-us*) feminine, but masculine in Mart. 8,51,14.

The remarkable word order (Bernhard 1927,26) illustrates the idea that the saffron has been dissolved in wine. On this process cf. Plin. *Nat.* 21,33 *crocum uino mire congruit, praecipue dulci, tritum ad theatra implenda*.

Sprinkling saffron in theatres as a perfume was such common practice that Horace can use *crocus* metonymically for 'the stage': *Ep.* 2,1,79 f. *recte necne crocum floresque perambulet Attae / fabula*; see Brink ad loc. The first passage referring to this practice is Lucr. 2,416 *et cum scena croco Cilici perfusa recens est*; Ov. *Ars* 1,103 mentions it as an example of decadence.

sparsim: 'in drops; in a scattered manner'. Except here, the adverb is attested only in Gel. 11,2,5, in an abstract sense: *praeterea ex eodem libro Catonis haec etiam sparsim et intercise comminemus*. In this last meaning it occurs frequently in Christian authors, e.g. Lact. *Inst.* 1,2,6 *sparsim dicere nos necesse est*. For a more concrete use, as in our passage, cf. Prud. *Peri.* 5,225 f. *subter crepante aspergine / scintillat excussus salis / punctisque feruens stridulis / sparsim per artus figitur*.

capellas ... perpluit imbre: the verb is hapax legomenon in the works of Apuleius, who gives it an original, transitive meaning: 'sprinkle'. Otherwise, *perpluere* is common as an intransitive verb: 'come through, leak through' (of rain). *ThLL* s.v. *perpluo* 1653,56 f. gives our passage as the first for 'pluendo perfundere, madefacere aliquid'; then only Pallad. 12,15,1 *abies (Gallica), ..., nisi perpluatur, (est) leuis, rigida et in operibus siccis perenne durabilis*.

odoro ... imbre: before Apuleius, *odorus* is attested exclusively in poetry (*ThLL* s.v. *odorus* 476,10); Apuleius uses it also 4,2 (75,25) *in modum floris odori* (correction by ς of *inodori* in F; see *GCA* 1977,35 ad loc.). For the notion of a 'downpour' of saffron in the theatre cf. Mart. 5,25,7 f. *rubro pulpita nimbo / spargere*; 9,38,5 *lubrica Corycio quamuis sint pulpita nimbo*. On the scent of saffron see below on *suaue fraglante cauea*.

donec ... mutarent: for a discussion and examples of *donec* with a subjunctive in the *Met.*, see *GCA* 1981,273 on 7,28 (176,9-11 *donec ... confoedassem* with references. For a subjunctive in the dependent clause with a historical present in the main clause, see on ch. 3 (238,13-14) *unde ... caperet ... decunctatur*.

luteo colore: the goats are dyed the colour appropriate to a wedding. Cf. Catul. 61,8 f. *flammeum cape laetus, huc / huc ueni, niueo gerens / luteum pede soccum*, with Quinn ad loc.; 68,134 (Cupid as an attendant to the bride) *fulgebat crocina candidus in tunica*. For the wedding symbolism in this pantomime, see also on ch. 32 (263,6-7) *uelut nuptialis epulas obiturae*. Cf. also *torus genialis* below.

The allusion to Verg. *Ecl.* 4,42 f. is obvious and noted by many: (in the forthcoming Golden Age) *nec uarios discet mentiri lana colores, / ipse sed in pratis aries iam suaue rubenti / murice, iam croceo mutabit uellera luto, / sponte sua sandyx pascentis uestiet agnos*. Finkelpearl 1991,232 calls it 'an inappropriate introduction of the elevated and literary amid the base and popular'. But it is possible that the allusion is there for the sake of effect and contrast: whereas Vergil emphasizes the fact that the colouring of the wool happens naturally and spontaneously and is not caused by human hands, our passage stresses the artificiality of the spectacle, whose effect is caused by ingenious techniques. This Vergilian allusion is surrounded by two Senecan allusions (see above on *de summo montis cacumine per quandam latentem fistulam ... prorumpit ... crocus* and below on *montem ... terrae uorago decepit*), both of which describe theatrical illusion.

265,4-6 I a m q u e t o t a s u a u e f r a g l a n t e c a u e a m o n t e m i l l u m l i g n e u m t e r r a e u o r a g o d e c e p i t: And now that the whole theatre was smelling sweet, a chasm in the earth swallowed the wooden mountain.

suaue fraglante cauea: for the adverbial use of the neuter adjective, see on ch. 32 (263,14) *suaue*. Though we translate *cauea* as 'theatre' ('pars pro toto'; see on *caueae* ch. 29: 260,14), we must also think of it as the auditorium, where the audience are seated, being refreshed by the saffron perfume to prepare them for the 'wedding' of the *uilis aliqua* and the ass. The sprinkling of saffron in theatres originally had a ceremonial function, as appears from e.g. Prop. 4,1,16 *sollemnes ... crocos*; Ov. *Fast.* 1,75 f.; cf. also Sallustius ap. Macr. *Sat.* 3,13,8 *simul croco sparsa humus et alia in modum templi celeberrimi*. See Miller 1989,195 f. on the ritual *ludorum commissio* (and its travesty in Petr. 60). A welcome and sought-after effect of sprinkling saffron was its scent, which overcame the odours of a close-packed crowd.

fraglante: for the development (by dissimilation) of *fragrare* into *fraglare*, see the references in *GCA* 1977,210 f., in a discussion of the variants *flagrare/fraglare* in F in the meaning of both *ardere* and *olere*; see also Van Mal-Maeder 1998,172 on 2,8 (32,5) *fraglans*.

montem ... terrae uorago decepit: cf. Sen. *Ep*. 88,22 *ludicrae sunt, quae ad uoluptatem oculorum atque aurium tendunt. His adnumeres licet machinatores, qui pegmata per se surgentia excogitant et tabulata tacite in sublime crescentia et alias ex inopinato uarietates aut dehiscentibus, quae cohaerebant, aut his, quae eminebant, paulatim in se residentibus. His imperitorum feriuntur oculi omnia subita, quia causas non nouere, mirantium*. The 'I' in Calp. *Ecl*. 7,69 f. is an example of Seneca's naive admirer of uncomprehended miracles of technology: *A! trepidi quotiens se discindentis harenae / uidimus in partes, ruptaque uoragine terrae / emersisse feras; et in isdem saepe cauernis / aurea cum subito creuerunt arbuta nimbo*.

montem illum ligneum: the reference to ch. 30 (261,3) *erat mons ligneus* places a frame around the description of the *Iudicium Paridis*, which started there.

In this last sentence of the description of the brilliant pantomime, the illusion of Mount Ida and its events is shattered; literary reminiscences enhance the suggestion that everything was but an illusion (see Zimmerman-de Graaf 1995,159 f.). Once again, Lucius is faced with the harsh reality: *Ecce quidam miles ...* .

decepit: thus F, retained by practically all editors, and defended also by Oudendorp and Hildebrand. Thus also Kronenberg 1928,44 f. (*decepit* = καθεῖλε); see also Augello 1977,221. The manuscript reading offers the 'lectio difficilior', for *decepit* must have an unusual meaning, 'to take down, swallow down'. However, this literal, etymologizing use of *de-cipere* is typically Apuleian; see the note on *adserere* in ch. 7 (242,15), with references. Helm alone borrows *recepit* from ς, a reading preferred by Finkelpearl 1991,224 n. 7 because of the sexual connotations she brings out in this passage (226 f., where she points out many double-entendres).

265,7-11 Ecce quidam miles per mediam plateam dirigit cursum petiturus iam populo postulante illam de publico carcere mulierem, quam dixi propter multiforme scelus bestis esse damnatam meisque praeclaris nuptiis destinatam: And now a soldier set off down the middle of the street, on his way, as the people were now demanding, to fetch the woman from the city prison who, as I mentioned before, was condemned to the beasts because of her multiform crimes, and destined for a splendid wedding with me.

Ecce quidam miles: Van Mal-Maeder 1994,221 (with examples in n. 36 and 37) discusses the use of *quidam* in the *Met*. when a new actor is introduced; since this often implies a new element in the action, it adds to the suspense. Also combined with *ecce* it is found in e.g. 2,32 (51,14) *ecce tres quidam uegetes*. With *ecce* the narrator draws the reader's attention to the new situation, and to the change of focus which this often entails. Cf. e.g. 3,11 (60,1-3) *ecce ... ipsi magistratus ... ingressi ... gestiunt*, with Van der Paardt 1971,87 ad loc.; 6,25 (147,6 f.) *ecce ... latrones adueniunt*, with *GCA* 1981,27 ad loc. See also above on ch. 12 (245,15).

per mediam plateam dirigit cursum: the description of soldier's entry recalls the manner in which one actor in comedy often describes the entry of another. Cf. Pl. *Trin*. 1006 *quis hic est qui huc in plateam cursuram incipit?* Cist. 534 *quis hic est qui recta platea cursum huc contendit suum?*

dirigit cursum: 'set course'. It appears from *ThLL* s.v. *dirigo* 1240,41 f. that *dirigere cursum* is a nautical term. Cf. Cic. *ND* 2,131 *ab (uentis Etesiis) maritimi cursus celeres et certi diriguntur*; Vell. 1,4,1 *classis cursum esse directum ... columbae antecedentis uolatu*; Sen. *Ep.* 16,3 *(philosophia) sedet ad gubernaculum et per ancipitia fluctuantium dirigit cursum.*

petiturus iam populo postulante illam de publico carcere mulierem: note the alliteration of *p. Illam ... mulierem* is the object of *petiturus*, but possibly also of *postulante*: the people are calling for 'the woman from the city prison'. The word order presents *illam de publico carcere mulierem* as one phrase, a 'quotation' of what the people are demanding. For this use of *de* cf. e.g. Cic. *Or.* 47 *non enim declamatorem aliquem de ludo aut rabulam de foro quaerimus*; Clu. 163 *coponem de uia Latina*; Mil. 65 *popa ... de circo maximo*. Cf. in the *Met.* e.g. 1,9 (9,3) *alium de foro*. See Löfstedt Synt. I,361.

petiturus: see on ch. 13 (246,21) *refecturi*.

multiforme scelus: the woman has beaten one person to death (ch. 24) and poisoned several others (ch. 25, 26 en 28); cf. *multiforme facinus* in ch. 28 (259,18) about the same woman: the narrator quotes himself (*ut iam dixi*). For the singular cf. e.g. Plin. *Nat.* 2,116 *radiorum ... multiformi iactu flagellatus aer*; the adjective in itself connotes plurality. But cf. ch. 19 (251,22) *multiformibus ludicris*.

bestis ... damnatam: *bestis* is probably an ablative (the dative with *damnare* is rare and poetic; cf. e.g. Bailey on Lucr. 6,1232 *morti damnatus*). Apuleius uses the ablative in 1,9 (9,7-8); elsewhere the verb is construed with a genitive, e.g. 4,13 (85,2) *damnatorum capitum funera*; 4,31 (99,8-10). For the many constructions with *damnare* see KSt 2,1,466 f., with examples.

bestis: thus F (φ has *bestiis*); see on *mendacis* ch. 5 (240,22).

meis ... praeclaris nuptiis: 'the ... wedding with me'. The possessive replaces the objective genitive with *nuptiae*; cf. e.g. Liv. 29,23,8 *se ... nuptiis ciuis Carthaginiensis ... cum populo Carthaginiensi iunctum*; Apul. *Apol.* 22,5 *mihi ... nuptias Pudentillae inuidisses*. As *praeclaris* indicates, *nuptiis* is used here ironically, as in 7,21, where the *puer* accuses the ass of erotic intentions toward passers-by: (170,4-7) *et ... temptat libidines et ... inuitat ad nuptias*. See *GCA* 1981,220 ad loc. with references; add Adams 1982,159 f. The ironic use of *praeclarus* (which is not restricted to Apuleius: *ThLL* s.v. *praeclarus* 488,25 f. devotes a separate lemma to the ironic use of the adjective) cf. e.g. 4,34 (102,4-5, in Psyche's bitter-ironical speech) *haec erunt ... egregiae formonsitatis meae praeclara praemia*).

265,11-13 Et iam torus genialis scilicet noster futurus accuratissime disternebatur lectus Indica testudine perlucidus, plumea congerie tumidus, ueste serica floridus: And what was obviously going to be our nuptial bed was already being made up with utter precision, shining with Indian tortoise-shell, puffy with a mass of down, and brightly coloured with silk cloths.

Ch. 29 contains only one sentence with a parallel in the *Onos* (see on 260,12-13 *dies ecce muneri ... deducor / Onos* 53,1); it is followed by the long *ecphrasis*, for which the *Onos* has no parallel. The description of the bed here seems to run somewhat parallel with the first part of *Onos* 53,2: κλίνη ἦν μεγάλη, ἀπὸ χελώνης Ἰνδικῆς πεποιημένη, χρυσῷ ἐσφηνωμένη. In our present chapter, the *Met.* finally moves away from the *Onos*, but at the same time the *Onos* leaves a fragmentary echo two more times: here and *praeter pudorem ... metu etiam* below; see the note there, and Introd. **2.3**.

torus ... scilicet noster futurus: for this predicative use of the future active participle to indicate an outsider's intention or what is destined by fate (rather than to express the noun's own purpose, as e.g. a few lines above, *miles ... petiturus ... mulierem*), cf. e.g. 9,42 (236,4-5) *hortulanum poenas scilicet capite pensurum*; cf. also 7,2 (155,8-10) *equum ... suum ... uectorem futurum*. Further examples in Von Geisau 1916,279.

torus genialis: this exalted designation of the bed in which the copulation of ass and *uilis aliqua* is to be exhibited is strongly ironic. See Van Mal-Maeder 1998,143 on 2,6 (30,3) *genialem torum*. In 9,26 (222,14 f.) the *pistor*'s hypocritical wife uses the phrase metonymically for 'virtuous marriage'.

disternebatur lectus: the first time the ass has a real bed at his disposal is 9,2 (204,15-16) *super constratum lectum ... somnum humanum quieui*; there he sleeps the sleep of the innocent in a bed not intended for him (see also *GCA* 1995,47 ad loc.). The second time is 10,20 (252,6-8) *eunuchi ... terrestrem nobis cubitum praestruunt* (see the notes there); there a luxurious bed, described in detail, is prepared purposely on the floor for the ass and the *matrona*, who indeed use it. The bed prepared for the ass and the *uilis aliqua* is also described in detail, but the ass will not use it (he will eventually sleep *in quodam mollissimo harenae gremio*: ch. 35: 266,6). *Disternere* is attested only here (*ThLL* s.v. *disterno* 1519,1 f.); as a conjecture of Beroaldus it is generally accepted in 2,15 (37,12) *distratum fuerat*; see Van Mal-Maeder 1998,237 ad loc.

Indica ... floridus: asyndetic isocolic tricolon, with rhyme (Bernhard 1927,67). Within this tricolon chiasmus can be observed: *Indica testudine* (adjective - noun) / *plumea congerie* (adjective - noun) / *ueste serica* (noun - adjective).

Indica testudine perlucidus: in *Onos* 53,2 (cited above in the introductory note to this section) the entire bed is made from tortoise-shell and set with gold. The shell of the Indian turtle (which was found in the river Ganges) was as big as a barrel (Aelian. *HA* 12,41; 16,14). Apuleius romanizes: the use of tortoise-shell as a veneer for beds, among other things, was especially in vogue with Romans (see *RE* s.v. 'Schildkröte' 430,46 f. [Gossen-Steiner]). Plin. *Nat.* 9,13,39 *testudinum putamina secare in laminas lectosque et repositoria his uestire Caruilius Pollio instituit*. Cf. Ov. *Met.* 2,737 f. *pars secreta domus ebore et testudine cultos / tris habuit thalamos* with Bömer ad loc. The use of *testudo* as a veneer for beds connotes extravagant luxury; thus e.g. Juv. 11,93 f. (during the time of Cato and the Fabii) *nemo inter curas et seria duxit habendum / qualis in Oceani fluctu testudo nataret*; Mart. 12,66,4 f. *et casa diuitiis ambitiosa latet / gemmantes prima fulgent testudine lecti*. For 'Indian tortoise-shell' cf. Luc. 10,120 f. *ebur atria uestit, / et suffecta manu foribus testudinis Indae / terga sedent*.

perlucidus: 'brilliant, shining' (cf. Martialis' *fulgent testudine lecti* in the previous note). For this use of *perlucidus* = *ualde lucidus*, *ThLL* s.v. *perlucidus* 1520,43 f. cites as the first occurrence Cic. *ND* 2,30 *mundi ille feruor purior, perlucidior*; cf. Apul. *Mun.* 22 (338) *mundus ... splendore perlucidus*. For another meaning of *perlucidus* 'de rebus, quae lucem transmittunt' (*ThLL* s.v. 1519,57 f.), cf. e.g. 9,4 (205,9) *aquae perlucidae*. In 11,3 (268,2) *perlucidum simulacrum* (of Isis), interpretations of *perlucidum* are divided between 'shining' (thus Harrauer; Hanson 'radiant'; and Helm-Krenkel: 'leuchtendes Bild') and 'transparent' (thus e.g. Brandt-Ehlers 'ein schemenhaftes Wesen'). Krabbe 1989,134 f. collects five instances of the use of *perlucidus* in the *Met.* and tries (in vain) to detect a connection between them.

plumea congerie tumidus: cf. ch. 20 (252,6-7) *puluillis ... uentose tumentibus pluma delicata* (about the bed made on the floor for the *matrona* and the ass). In the combination *plumea congeries* the adjective replaces the genitive of a noun: 'an accumulation of feathers'; cf. e.g. 3,27 (72,1) *auxilio rosario*; 6,31 (153,11) *uirginalis fugae*; see Bernhard 1927,111 for further examples. But *plumea*, although used here in an original manner, recalls passages like Var. *Men.* 448 *in testudineo lecto culcita plumea in die dormire* (cf. Cic. *Tusc.* 3,19,46 *eripiamus huic aegritudinem. quo modo? conlocemus in culcita plumea*); Ov. *Met.* 11,610 f. *in medio torus est ebeno sublimis in atra, / plumeus, unicolor, pullo uelamine tectus* (sc. *Somnus*' bed).

ueste serica floridus: here the reader may remember the warning by Sen. *Ben.* 7,9,5 *sericas uestes ... in quibus nihil est quo defendi ... pudor possit*. Cf. the following sentence, which opens with *at ego, praeter pudorem ...*

Here, *floridus* has the meaning of 'gaily coloured, bright'; see Van Mal-Maeder 1998,166 on 2,8 (31,19) *floridae uestis hilaris color* about the connotations of *floridus*, with references.

265,13-21 At ego praeter pudorem obeundi publice concubitus, praeter contagium scelestae pollutaeque feminae, metu etiam mortis maxime cruciabar sic ipse mecum reputans, quod in amplexu Venerio scilicet nobis cohaerentibus, quaecumque ad exitium mulieris bestia fuisset immissa, non adeo uel prudentia sollers uel artificio docta uel abstinentia frugi posset prouenire, ut adiacentem lateri meo laceraret mulierem, mihi uero quasi indemnato et innoxio parceret: But I for my part, beside my shame at having sexual intercourse in public, beside the contamination of a criminal, tainted woman, was especially tormented by the fear of death; for I thought to myself that, since we would of course be entwined in love's embrace, whatever animal was let in to kill the woman could not possibly turn out to be so cleverly discerning, or so skilfully trained, or so decently restrained, that it would maul the woman lying by my side but spare me as unconvicted and innocent.

The narrator gives a clear list of motives for the ass's flight from the theatre: shame of copulating in public, aversion from copulating with a criminal, and fear of death, *metu ... mortis*, which is enlarged upon in the rest of the sentence. The narrator's text contains no suggestion that the flight of the main character of the *Met.* is an attempt to turn his back on a depraved world, as the secundary literature often claims. See Zimmerman-de Graaf 1993,143 f. with references; see also on ch. 35 (265,22-23) *non de pudore iam, sed de salute ipsa sollicitus*.

In this sentence we see for the last time in the *Met.* a (partial) parallel with the text of the *Onos* (53,5) ἐγὼ δὲ ἅμα μὲν ἡδούμην ἐν τῷ θεάτρῳ κατακείμενος, ἅμα δὲ ἐδεδίειν μή που ἄρκτος ἢ λέων ἀναπηδήσεται. See above on *et iam torus ...* (265,11-13).

At ego: see on ch. 13 (246,1) *At ego*.

praeter pudorem ... publice ... praeter ... pollutae...: the *p-* alliteration dominates here; it is followed by *m-* alliteration in *metu ... mortis maxime*.

pudorem ... contagium: cf. ch. 29 (260,3-5) *mortem mihi uolens consciscere, priusquam scelerosae mulieris contagio macularer uel infamia publici spectaculi depudescerem*. There Lucius was still claiming that he would rather commit suicide than submit to this disgrace, and regretted that as an ass he was not physically capable of doing that (see the notes there). At that point he did not mention the possibility of escape, so that his flight in ch. 35, at a moment of high suspense, comes as a complete surprise.

obeundi ... concubitus: see on ch. 21 (253,9-10) *amplexus obiturus*.

publice: here 'in public, publicly' (*OLD* s.v. *publice* 5); contrasting with *domi* in 2,8 (31,14-15) *caput capillumque ... puplice prius intueri et domi postea perfrui*. In ch. 23 (254,20-21) this same event is described with *incoram publicam*; in ch. 29 (260,1) with *publicitus* and 260,5 with *infamia publici spectaculi*; see the notes there. For a more positive use of *publice*, cf. ch. 17 (250,11) *rumor publice crebruerat* (see the note there).

concubitus: after his previous ironic references to the planned theatre performance as a 'wedding' (see above on *nuptiis* and *torus genialis*; also on ch. 29: 260,1 *matrimonium confarraturus*), the narrator now calls a spade a spade: 'sexual intercourse'. See *GCA* 1985,109 on 8,10 (185,13-16) *concubitus*; cf. also 5,18 (117,8), where Psyche's sisters suggest that she is sleeping with a snake: *faetidi periculosique concubitus*.

contagium scelestae pollutaeque feminae: for this use of *polluere* cf. Juv. 8,218 f. *(nec) Electrae iugulo se polluit aut Spartani / sanguine coniugii*; Stat. *Theb.* 2,113 *pollutus ... fraterno sanguine Tydeus*. In most examples the notion of 'make dirty, soil, stain' is present (e.g. through an ablative *sanguine*); here there is no ablative that indicates the means by which the woman has become *polluta*; cf. 9,37 (231,11) *pollutissimo diuite*, where *GCA* 1995,311 ad loc. interprets 'morally corrupt'. But both here and there it is clear that the meaning must be 'stained with blood through murder', and in our passage the notion of 'being sullied' is enhanced by the preceding *contagium*. See on ch. 29 (260,4) *scelerosae mulieris contagio*.

scelestae ... feminae: Adams 1972,234 f. discusses the gradual development of the use of *femina*, which was generally a respectful term in Latin. But Plautus already sometimes uses pejorative adjectives with *femina*; cf. Pl. *Pers.* 208 *feminam scelestam*; *Truc.* 131 *mala tu femina es*. 'In the hands of Apuleius *femina* has degenerated to such an extent that it can be constantly used with uncomplementary adjectives ...' (Adams l.c., 238 with references).

metu etiam mortis maxime: the four words include five *m-* sounds. It is tempting to hear indignant sputtering in the *p*'s of the preceding phrase (see above), and fearfully trembling lips in the *m*'s here.

in amplexu Venerio nobis cohaerentibus: *cohaerere* is usual for 'cling together, embrace' (*OLD* s.v. 1c) without erotic connotations; cf. e.g. Quint. *Inst.* 8,3,68 *alii extremo complexu suorum cohaerentes*. But the addition *in amplexu Venerio* gives the verb the erotic connotation frequently attested for the simple verb (*ThLL* s.v. *haereo* 2495,45 f.; see also Pichon s.v.). Adams 1982,181 f. gives further examples, some of which have compounds of *haereo*. Our phrase recalls Lucr. 4,1113 *usque adeo cupide in Veneris compagibus haerent*; that line recurs in 4,1201 f., with the addition of *in triuiis* (4,1203; Lucretius is describing copulating dogs). See the extensive note ad loc. by Brown, who points out the Greek συνέχονται, which is used in e.g. Arist. *HA* 540a 24 f.: συνέχονται ἐν τῇ ὀχείᾳ πολὺν χρόνον, ὥσπερ καὶ αἱ κύνες; cf. Theophr. *Char.* 28,3 οὐ γὰρ οἷον λῆρος ἐστι τὸ λεγόμενον, ἀλλ' ὥσπερ αἱ κύνες ἐν ταῖς ὁδοῖς συνέχονται. In our passage, which deals with a bestial spectacle and emphasizes the public aspect of this lovemaking (see above on *publice*), *cohaerentibus* is undoubtedly meaningful. Cf. also Plin. *Nat.* 10,173 *auertuntur et canes, phocae, lupi in medioque coitu inuitique etiam cohaerent* (Lucius, too, is *inuitus*).

uel prudentia sollers uel artificio docta uel abstinentia frugi: three cola of 7, 8, and 8 syllables, with anaphora of *uel* and syntactic parallelism. The elaborate structure emphasizes the irony of expecting these qualities in *quaecumque ... bestia*. It is possible to detect here a pagan's disbelief of the stories (which may already have been spreading at the time when Apuleius wrote the *Met.*) about Christian martyrs who were thrown to the beasts but miraculously rescued. Elliott 1987,146 f. quotes many examples. Cf. e.g. the story of St. Euphemia: various *bestiae* refused to hurt her, and four lions and two bears approached her *caute simul et reuerenter* and kissed her feet *humane*.

prudentia sollers: 'clever in understanding'; the ablative *prudentia* represents the sphere of cleverness. Cf. Plin. *Nat.* 28,94 *sollers ambagibus uanitas Magorum*.

artificio docta: 'trained with skill (that is, by a skillful trainer), see on ch. 14 (246,25-26) *furatrinae ... artificium*.

abstinentia frugi: the symmetry of the three cola has been taken to extremes. Here the ablative either is an 'ablativus modi' with *frugi* (Hanson: 'temperately moderate'), or indicates in what respect the animal is *frugi* (Brandt-Ehlers: 'bieder enthaltsam').

adiacentem lateri meo: *adiacere* is commonly used in a topographical sense. From the point of view of the *bestia* the woman will be no more than an accidental adjunct to the ass; cf. 1,23 (21,12-13) *erit tibi adiacens et ecce illud cubiculum honestum receptaculum* (this is the only passage, apart from ours, where the verb occurs in Apuleius). Two passages only are attested for a sexual connotation: V. Flacc. 2,191 f. ... *sua cuique furens infestaque coniunx / adiacet*, and Col. 12,1,2 *uilicum ... complexibus adiacentem feminae*. The line of Valerius Flaccus may account for the use of this rare verb here because it occurs in a passage full of imminent doom, immediately before the women of Lemnos murder their husbands.

laceraret mulierem, mihi uero ... parceret: the chiastic order of verb-object vs. (indirect) object-verb supports the contrast in content.

CHAPTER XXXV

The ass flees from the theatre to the beach at Cenchreae.

265,22-266,3 Ergo igitur non de pudore iam, sed de salute ipsa sollicitus, dum magister meus lectulo probe coaptando destrictus inseruit et, tota familia partim ministerio uenationis occupata, partim uoluptario spectaculo adtonita, meis cogitationibus liberum tribuebatur arbitrium nec magnopere quisquam custodiendum tam mansuetum putabat asinum, paulatim furtiuum pedem proferens po<r>tam, quae proxima est, potitus iam cursu me celerrimo proripio sexque totis passuum milibus perniciter confectis Cenchreas peruado, quod oppidum audit quidem nobilissimae coloniae Corinthiensium, adluitur autem Aegaeo et Saronico mari: And so I was no longer concerned about my disgrace but about my very survival. While my impresario attended busily to the proper arrangement of the bed and I - the whole staff being partly occupied in assisting with the *uenatio*, partly spellbound by the sensual spectacle - was given a free hand in my deliberations and nobody thought that such a tame ass had to be watched much, I gradually took stealthy steps toward the nearest gate, and when I reached it I set off at a fast gallop; covering a full six miles at top speed, I arrived at Cenchreae, a town that counts as part of the illustrious colony of the Corinthians, and is moreover washed by the Aegean Sea and the Saronic Gulf.

Ergo igitur: see on ch. 3 (238,4) *ergo igitur*. The phrase, here at the beginning of a long sentence, both sums up the fear expressed in the previous sentence and points ahead to the action inspired by that fear: *pedem proferens portam ... potitus ... me ... proripio*.

non de pudore: on Lucius' *pudor* see the introductory note to ch. 34 (265,13-21) *At ego ... cruciabar ... parceret*.

de salute ipsa sollicitus: note the sound-play in *sal-, -sa, soll-* . The linear reader understands *salus* as 'survival', especially in view of the fear (expressed in the previous sentence) of being mauled by wild animals. Only the re-reader of the *Met.* suspects a deeper meaning because of the *salus* brought by Isis in the eleventh book; cf. e.g. 11,21 (283,6-8, in the explanation of Isis' priest) *nam et inferum claustra et salutis tutelam in deae manu posita ipsamque traditionem ad instar uoluntariae mortis et precariae salutis celebrari*; cf. also 11,25 (286,25 f.) *salutarem porrigas dexteram* (in a prayer to Isis). In 11,1 (266,20 f.) we can already see a transition from *salus* = 'survival' to *salus* = 'salvation': *fato scilicet iam meis ... cladibus satiato et spem salutis ... subministrante augustum specimen deae praesentis statui deprecari*. On the 'thematic pressure' of *salus* in the tenth book see Introd. **2.4.6**.

dum ... inseruit ... tribuebatur .... nec... putabat: for the use of present and imperfect indicative with *dum*, see LHSz 2,613. The shift from present to imperfect in this sentence is obscured by the long intervening ablative absolute *tota familia ... occupata ... adtonita*; see also Callebat 1968,345 f. *Dum* may have a causal function here (LHSz 2,614); cf. 9,13 (212,24 f.) *recreabar, dum ... libere ... omnes et agunt et loquuntur*, where *GCA* translate 'I was cheered up ... seeing that everybody ...'.

magister meus: the *libertus* to whom Thiasus delegated the care of the ass has been variously described from ch. 17 (249,25-26) onward: in ch. 19 (251,16) he is referred to as *praeposito illi meo*, and later in the same chapter (251,26) somewhat ironically as *altore meo* (see the note there); when in ch. 23 he alerts his master to the *nouum spectaculum* that the ass could provide, he is called, as here, *magister meus* (254,12). Numerous passages suggested that the ass could be regarded as a celebrated *histrio* (see on ch. 17: 250,1 *saltare*); so for this passage, in the context of the preparation of Lucius' performance as a 'star', the translation 'impresario' has been chosen, a connotation which was also present in ch. 23. See *ThLL* s.v. *magister* 78,44 f.; cf. Mart. 1,41,12 *de Gadibus improbus magister*, where Friedländer ad loc. explains: 'Tanzmeister oder Impresario der durch die Unzüchtigkeit ihrer Tänze verrufenen Gaditanischen Tänzerinnen'; Amm. 14,6,19 *tria milia saltatricum ... cum choris totidemque ... magistris*.

lectulo ... coaptando: *coaptare* is first attested in Apuleius: here and 9,8 (208,12) *matrimonium ... coaptantes* (see *GCA* 1995,86 f. ad loc.). For the preparation of this unique bed, which has already been described in ch. 34 (265,12-13) in a remarkable tricolon, a unique compound is used.

destrictus: thus F. The reading of ς is *districtus*, adopted by Robertson. But *destrictus*, too, can have the meaning *attentus, acer, expeditus* which is required here. See *GCA* 1995,165 on 9,17 (216,3) (*lanificio*) *destrictam* (sc. *dominam*), with references.

partim ... occupata, partim ... adtonita: two cola (of 16 and 15 syllables respectively) illustrate how the entire *familia* is completely engaged in the preparation for the performance in which a *uenatio* will be incorporated into the story of Pasiphaë as a *uoluptarium spectaculum* (on this kind of *spectaculum* see the introductory note to 254,17-21 in ch. 23).

uoluptario spectaculo adtonita: cf. 2,2 (25,8) *sic attonitus ... cruciabili desiderio stupidus*, where Van Mal-Maeder 1998,73, with references, lists the frequent cases in the *Met.* of people who are reduced to a state of shock by an unusual spectacle. See also *GCA* 1995,117 on 9,12 (211,29) *familiari curiositate attonitus et satis anxius*.

meis cogitationibus liberum tribuebatur arbitrium: for a discerning analysis of this remarkable phrase, see Hofmann 1993a,134 f. He points out that the passive verb lacks a nomen agentis, which cannot be supplied from the context. The agent is rather the abstract author himself (see Introd. **3.2**) who, at a decisive moment in the ass's story (where the *Met.* leaves the *Onos*; see the introductory note to ch. 34: 265,11-13 above), takes control and '...Wohl und Wehe, Gedanken und Handlungen des *narrateur* und der *acteurs* bestimmt, die letztlich alle seine Kreationen sind.' See Introd. **2.4.8**.

Gianotti 1986,43 and n. 28 interprets Lucius' choice as proof that he has learned from his ordeals and finally makes a moral choice, thus re-crossing the borderline between animal and human. This interpretation, however, is not confirmed by the text of the *Met.*; it is inspired by Gianotti's view of the *Met.* as a 'moral fable presented for a didactic purpose' (for a recent assessment see Harrison 1996,510-516). This is not the only choice Lucius makes during his existence as an ass; elsewhere, too, he shows himself capable of making his own choices. Cf. e.g. 3,29 (74,1 f.: his common sense tells him not to eat roses at that moment); 4,5 (78,8 f.: he decides not to feign lameness and to resign himself to the inevitable); 9,4 (205,10 f.: he deliberately shows himself as a very gentle ass); 9,26 and 27 (he is determined to punish the *adulter*).

liberum ... arbitrium: this combination is frequent in e.g. Livy, and also in legal documents, e.g. Ulp. *Dig.* 42,5,8,3 *liberum arbitrium creditoribus datum uidetur, quanto tempore locent*;

see *OLD* s.v. *arbitrium* 4d.

tam mansuetum ... asinum: the 'tame ass' has a position almost in the middle of this long sentence, concealed by the hustle and bustle described in the first part of the sentence. Now he starts to act on his own.

mansuetum: see on ch. 16 (249,7) *mansuetudinem*.

paulatim ... pedem proferens portam ... proxima ... potitus ... proripio ... passuum ... perniciter ... peruado: alliteration.

paulatim furtiuum pedem proferens portam, quae proxima est: the many long syllables illustrate the deliberate but slow preparation for flight.

furtiuum pedem proferens: although *pedem proferre* is a common expression (*OLD* s.v. *profero* 1b), the combination *furtiuum pedem* is unique.

cursu me celerrimo proripio ... perniciter: Lucius rushes equally hurriedly into the adventure of magic in 2.6 (29,19-22). Van Mal-Maeder 1998,137 ad loc. sees our passage reflected there: 'Lucius montrera la même impatience à s'initier aux mystères d'Isis qu'aux mystères des arts magiques'. But in our passage Lucius runs away because he is afraid. As yet he knows nothing of the initiation, and in 11,12 (275,22 f.) he shows remarkable calm and self-control as he approaches the priest who holds the wreath of roses that will set him free: *placido ac prorsus humano gradu cunctabundus paulatim obliquati corpore ... sensim inrepo*.

portam ... potitus: the accusative with *potiri* is archaic and seldom found in Classical Latin except *Rhet. Her.* (e.g. 4,39,51; 4,44,57), Lucr. e.g. 3,1038. Callebat 1968,181 f. assumes that this use continued to exist in the spoken language; see LHSz 2,122.

portam, quae proxima est: because the ass was tethered outside the theatre (ch. 29: 260,13 f. *ad conseptum caueae ... deducor ... ante portam constitutus*), this must refer to one of the city gates of Corinth. The remains of the Corinthian theatre are on the North side of Acrocorinth, from where the road ran downhill to Cenchreae.

po<r>tam: this is the emendation for *potam* by a second hand in F, and by φ.

sexque totis passuum milibus ... confectis Cenchreas peruado: the distance mentioned here agrees with the actual distance between the Cenchrean Gate of ancient Corinth and the remains of Cenchreae (see Gwynn Griffiths in the introduction of his commentary on book 11, 14 f., with references in notes). This exact specification of the distance is noteworthy in the otherwise vague geography (see Introd. **1.5**): on the one hand it emphasizes that the ass covers this long distance (cf. *totis*) at a full gallop; on the other hand, the mention of this accurate distance marks this flight from the Corinthian theatre as the narrator's flight from one fictional world to another, towards a new 'reality' (see above on *meis cogitationibus liberum tribuebatur arbitrium*). For a good survey of the historical Cenchreae, with extensive references and supported by archeological, iconographical, and numismatic findings, see Hohlfelder 1976.

cursu me: F had *cursū &*; another hand changed that to *cursu me*; φ has *cursū &*. The a* group of manuscripts (part of Class I; see Introd. **4.1**) has *cursu me*, followed by Helm. Robertson has *cursu me<m>et*, followed by Hanson.

Cenchreas peruado: for the accusative of direction with *peruadere* 'to make one's way, penetrate to a point' (*OLD* s.v. *peruado* 3), cf. Liv. 26,7,6 *ut ... clam Capuam peruadat*. Both here and in ch. 26 (258,3-4) *domum peruadit*, the destination is reached with difficulty: here a long distance is covered at a gallop, there the drugged doctor barely manages to drag himself home.

quod oppidum audit ... nobilissimae coloniae Corinthiensium: for *audire* used as Greek ἀκούω, κλύω, 'to hear oneself called, be called', cf. e.g. Hor. *S.* 2,7,101 *subtilis ueterum iudex et callidus audis*; cf. the expression *bene (male) audire* for 'have a good, bad name'. See KSt 2,1,15 and 100. Cf. in the *Met.* e.g. 2,9 (32,19 f.) *mulier ... nisi capillum distinxerit, ornata non possit audire*; see Van Mal-Maeder 1998,181 ad loc.

Helm proposed *quod oppidum audit quidem <emporium> nobilissimae coloniae Corinthiensium* (cf. Liv. 32,17,3 *Cenchreas, Corinthiorum emporium*). None of the editors has adopted this proposal, nor has Helm himself included it in the text.

quidem ... autem: here, *autem* means 'moreover'. It emphasizes one of Cenchreae's aspects that plays an important role from now on, namely its situation by the sea. For this use of *quidem ... autem* see *OLD* s.v. *autem* 3c.

adluitur ... mari: the explicit mention that Lucius has arrived at the beach reminds one of Doody's observation (Doody 1996,321), that in many novels 'the place between water and land functions most obviously and overtly as a threshold. Its presence signifies the necessity of passing from one state to another. It is liminality made visible and palpable.'

nobilissimae coloniae Corinthiensium: on Corinth's fame in Roman times, see on ch. 18 (250,19) *Corintho*. But the superlative *nobilissimae* acquires an ironical connotation here because of the 'Vanity Fair' associations of this city, which have been emphasized from ch. 19 on (see Introd. **2.3**); cf. Cic. *Ver.* 5,79 *Nico, ille nobilissimus pirata*; in the *Met.* e.g. 2,18 (39,22-40,1) *uesana factio nobilissimorum iuuenum pacem publicam infestat*.

266,3-4 I n i b i p o r t u s e t i a m t u t i s s i m u m n a u i u m r e c e p t a c u l u m m a g n o f r e q u e n t a t u r p o p u l o : There is also a harbour, a safe refuge for ships, which is visited by many people.

portus ... tutissimum ... receptaculum: like *de salute ipsa sollicitus* above (265,22-23; see the note there), the re-reader of the *Met.* will regard this as a reference to the 'safe haven' of the Isis cult mentioned by the priest in 11,15 (277,5-7) *multis ... exanclatis laboribus magnisque Fortunae tempestatibus ... actus ...ad portum Quietis et aram Misericordiae tandem, Luci, uenisti*.

tutissimum ... receptaculum: cf. Curt. 5,9,8 *proinde si Bactra, quod tutissimum receptaculum est, petimus*; Amm. 29,5,25 *exin profectus fundum ... muro circumdatum ualido receptaculum Maurorum tutissimum ... euertit*.

266,4-7 V i t a t i s e r g o t u r b u l i s e t e l e c t o s e c r e t o l i t o r e p r o p e i p s a s f l u c t u u m a s p e r g i n e s i n q u o d a m m o l l i s s i m o h a r e n a e g r e m i o l a s s u m c o r p u s p o r r e c t u s r e f o u e o : Therefore I avoided the masses and sought out a secluded part of the coast and, close to the spray of the waves, stretched out in a wonderfully soft hollow of the beach, I refreshed my weary body.

turbulis: attested only here, 11,6 (270,14) and 11,7 (271,16). Like *turbela*, it is an Apuleian neologism; see *GCA* 1977,154 f. on 4,20 (90,3-6) *populi circumfluentis turbelis* and *OLD* s.v. *turbula*: 'a small company of people'; however, neither here nor in 11,6 and 7 is *turbula* to be regarded as a diminutive. Cf. e.g. *turbulentare* 'to affect with unrest', also an Apuleian neologism; see Van Mal-Maeder 1998,208 on 2,12 (35,3). Then, *turbula* could mean 'a confused, disorderly irregular mass' (cf. the adverb *turbulente* 'with violent disorderliness'). See Zucchelli 1970,31 and 35 f. on the non-diminutive suffix *-ulo/a-*, productive in Latin of all periods; Facchini Tosi 1986,124 f. discusses other non-diminutive Apuleian neologisms in *-lo-*.

in ... mollissimo harenae gremio: after being carried away by Zephyrus, Psyche is gently laid down *cespitis gremio* (4,35: 103,4) and, like Lucius, enjoys a refreshing sleep (cf. *dulcis somnus* below). See Dowden in *AAGA* 2,12 f. on the resemblance of this sleep of Lucius and Psyche's first sleep: (13) 'these instances of sleep are the transition to another world'. Dowden compares Odysseus' sleep after his home-coming in Ithaca: (14) 'When Odysseus wakes, he meets the goddess Athene herself'. See below on the epic sunset concluding book 10.

harenae gremio: for the largely poetic use of *gremium* as 'a place to rest', *ThLL* s.v. *gremium* 2324,6 f. cites Cl. Don. ad Verg. *A*. 8,406, *significatio gremii diuersitatem tenet. gremium enim intellegitur non solum sedentis sinus uerum etiam quicquid homini ad requiem praestiterit locum*; cf. (also about an arrival at dusk) Verg. *A*. 3,508 f. *sol ruit interea et montes umbrantur opaci. / sternimur optatae gremio telluris ad undam / sortiti remos passimque in litore sicco / corpora curamus; fessos sopor inrigat artus*.

lassum corpus ... refoueo: cf. Ov. *Met*. 8,537 *corpus refouentque fouentque*; *Culex* 213 *tu lentus refoues iucunda membra quiete*. Cf. also the last line of the Vergil passage cited in the previous note.

lassum: cf. *lassa genua* ch. 2 (237,22); see references there for *lassus* = *fessus*.

266,7-9 Nam et ultimam diei metam curriculum solis deflexerat et uespernae me quieti traditum dulcis somnus oppresserat: For the sun chariot, too, had already rounded the last turning-post of the day, and when I had given myself up to the quiet of the evening a sweet sleep had overcome me.

ultimam diei metam curriculum solis deflexerat: cf. Verg. *A*. 5,835 f. *mediam caeli Nox umida metam / contigerat* and (in a description of the afternoon) Ov. *Met*. 3,145 *sol ex aequo meta distabat utraque*.

For the poetic *curriculum solis* cf. Cic. *Arat*. 15 f. *at dextra laeuaque ciet rota fulgida Solis / mobile curriculum* (imitated in Aus. *Ecl*. 25,15 f.); see also *GCA* 1981,81 on 7,1 (154,6) *solis curriculum* (in a description of dawn).

metam ... deflexerat: according to *GCA* 1995,274 f. on 9,32 (227,5-7) *annus ... ad hibernas Capricorni pruinas deflexerat*, the verb means '(the year,) on its curved course, had arrived at ... But here the text has *metam ... deflexerat* without *ad*, and *OLD* s.v. *deflecto* 3 suggests (only for our passage) 'to alter one's course round (a point), round'. Cf. Vallette: 'avait ... doublé la borne extrême du jour'; Hanson: 'had raced round the last turning-post of the day'. The images suggest indeed a chariot rounding the *meta* in a race, though the expression *metam deflexerat* is not attested in a context of chariot races; *metam* and *curriculum* support this imagery. *ThLL* s.v. *deflecto* 359,24 f. includes our passage with examples of *deflectere* 'i.q. *uitare*' and explains *deflexerat* here as '*praeteruectum erat*'.

After the dramatic flight with which it started, this chapter (and thus book 10) ends in an atmosphere of peace and quiet. Similarly, Vergil in book 11 ends a day of fighting and bloodshed with a poetic description of nightfall: Verg. *A*. 11,913 f. *ni roseus fessos iam gurgite Phoebus Hibero / tingat equos noctemque die labente reducat*. Cf. also V.Fl. 5,177, where the arrival in Colchis (as a deviation from Apoll. Rh.) coincides with nightfall: *sol propius flammabat aquas extremaque fessis / coeperat optatos iam lux ostendere Colchos*;

see Gärtner 1998,213 f. and ibid. 219 on the symbolism of morning, night, and evening in V.Fl.: 'Der Abend symbolisiert Ankunft oder Ende'. That applies also to Verg. *A.* 3,508 f., cited above on *harenae gremio*, and to our passage. Junghanns 1932,126 remarks that 'nach altem epischen Brauch' several books in the *Met.* end with sleep; this is explicitly the case only at the end of books 1 and 2. That the books 3, 4, 6, 7, and 9 end with sleep or at any rate with night, can only be concluded from the beginning of a new day, or the awakening of the protagonist in the subsequent books, 4, 5, 7, 8, and 10 respectively. Nowhere in the *Met.* except here do we find at the end of a book a poetic description of nightfall. Extensive poetic descriptions of dawn, however, occur in 3,1 (see Van der Paardt 1971,23 f. ad loc.) and 7,1 (see *GCA* 1981,80 f. ad loc.). In book 9, a phase in the adultery tale is marked with a parodistic epic description of nightfall (9,22: 220,3-5) and a similar epic description of dawn (9,28: 224,9). Therefore, the poetic description of nightfall here at the end of book 10 is unusual (see Introd. **1.3**). In 11,7 (271,14 f.) the new day breaks with *noctis atrae fugato nubilo sol exurgit aureus*, immediately followed by an extensive poetic description of spring.

In epic arrivals at nightfall, the people involved usually arrive at the shore from the sea. Apuleius makes a variation on this theme: Lucius arrives safely at the beach after his flight from the interior. Still, the priest in 11,15 (cited above on *portus ... tutissimum ... receptaculum*) compares him to someone who has reached a safe harbour after many perils at sea; see also the note on ch. 13 (246,1-2) *at ego tunc temporis fatorum fluctibus uolutabar*.

uespernae: thus F; in φ an original *uespernae* has been changed to *uesper<ti>nae*. A has *uespertinae*, and so have ς, followed by Helm and most editors. Pecere 1987,101, with notes, prefers to read *uespertinae* here, as one of the instances where only Class I (of which A is the most important representative; see Introd. **4.1**) has preserved the original, correct reading. F has forms of *uespertinus* in *Fl.* 13,1; *Met.* 3,9 (59,8); 9,17 (216,4); 11,10 (274,4). With Terzaghi and Giarratano-Frassinetti *uespernae* is retained here. Terzaghi in his introduction (xxix f.) eloquently defends the forms of *uespernus* in F, pointing to formations like *hodiernus, hesternus, ueternus*, and to the expression *uesperna* (meaning *uesperna cena*) in Plautus *fr. inc.* 82 (41), p. 152,91 Goetz-Scholl. In 3,1 (52,8-9) Van der Paardt 1971,25 also defends F's *uesperni*.

dulcis somnus: cf. the γλυκὺς ὕπνος that comes to Zeus in Hom. *Il.* 1,610, and the sleep with which *Il.* 7, 8, 9 and *Od.* 1, 5, and 7 end; see the previous note, and above on *mollissimo harenae gremio*.

somnus oppresserat: the expression, attested in Latin of all periods, always connotes a very deep sleep, and often occurs in a context where people, who are in such deep sleep, do not notice what happens around them, or where a sudden event surprises people, who are *oppressi somno*. Cf. e.g. Caes. *BC* 2,38,4 *hos* (sc. *Numidas*) *oppressos somno dispersos adorti magnum eorum numero interficiunt*; Amm. 29,5,54 (*Firmus*) *oppressis altiore somno custodibus peruigil ipse ... relicto cubili manibus repens et pedibus longius sese discreuit*. In our passage, the pluperfect *oppresserat* suggests that this final sentence of book 10 forms the setting for surprising events to come.

APPENDIX I

APULEIUS' *'PHAEDRA'*

Tout texte se situe à la jonction de plusieurs textes dont il est à la fois la relecture, l'accentuation, la condensation, le déplacement et la profondeur. D'une certaine manière, un texte vaut ce que vaut son action intégratrice et destructrice d'autres textes.
(Philippe Sollers, in: *Tel Quel. Théorie d'ensemble*, Paris 1969,75)

Met. 10,2-12

First, the narrator introduces the dramatis personae of the story that he has announced as *scelestum ac nefarium facinus* (ch. 2: 237,1 f.), and mentions the passion conceived by the *nouerca* for her stepson. Then he turns to his audience with the following words: *iam ergo, lector optime, scito te tragoediam, non fabulam legere et a socco ad coturnum ascendere* (ch. 2: 237,12 f.). Before long, even a casual linear reader of the story that follows cannot but conclude that the narrative has initially many points in common with the tragedy of Phaedra and Hippolytus, but soon widely diverges from it. Many concrete readers have allowed the 'misleading' introduction to play an important role in their appreciation of the story as a whole. The condemnation by Walsh 1970,171 has often been quoted: 'Our author seems hardly to have known how his story was going to end when he launched it, and this gives us the clearest picture of the rapidity with which he assembles different stories into an uneasy unity'. Smith 1972,522 f. in his reaction to Walsh (and to Perry 1967,254) ties this introduction in with other 'misleading clues' given by the narrator of the *Met.* He rightly calls our attention to the constant appeal to the reader's intellectual activity: 'Metamorphosis is truly the reigning god in this novel, and its effect on us is enhanced by the narrator's seeming inability (or the author's puckish refusal) to provide the reader in advance with precise road signs'. Mason in *AAGA* 1978,1 (= Mason 1999,217) remarks that the allusion to a Greek tragedy, quoted above, and similar phrases in the *Met.* 'are clearly meant to make the reader think about the work's relationship to various literary forms'.[1] In the commentary ad loc. the expression *lector optime* is explained as an exhortation to the reader to apply himself to a *lectio optima* of the story presented.[2] A *lector optimus* will, for example, mark the references to various earlier literary works, and read the story not only for the sake of its plot (which does not always run smoothly)[3]

---

1 Cf. also Erbse 1950,111 f. Like Mason, he reads the promise made in the prologue (1,1: 2,3-4: *lector intende, laetaberis*) as an assurance that the reader's enjoyment will consist in becoming aware, as he reads, of the surprising new forms in which familiar motifs are treated in the *Met.*

2 See also on *ad librum profero* ch. 2: 237,2 f. about the emphasis on the written, literary character of this tale.

3 See 5.4 of this Appendix on the inconsistent plot as a phenomenon that can also be explained in intertextual terms.

but for the many surprising turns, which are often caused by the ever-changing literary background against which this new story is projected.[4]

The following discussion is an effort to account for the notion that 'our author seems hardly to have known how his story was going to end when he launched it' (see above) in a more positive way by applying Nimis' 'prosaics' reading to this tale, 'by attending to the way one thing leads to another - on the assumption that the actual linear unfolding of each story will reflect in some way its actual composition. This means that the narrative is not necessarily an "act of implicit structurating towards the ending", but rather a more tentative, experimental movement, feeling its way towards an end that is not yet fully realized ...'.[5] As Nimis has argued elsewhere, in such a 'prosaics' approach to the ancient novels allusions to traditional genres like epic, drama and other poetic genres may be considered to 'hint at the kind of story we are to hear. They provoke in the reader what Umberto Eco calls "inferential walks", preliminary hypotheses about what will happen next and how things will turn out'.[6] It will be shown that in this densely allusive tale the activity of the reader is enlisted precisely in this way.

The commentary signals and discusses references (occurring in miscellaneous forms) to other texts. However, some notes threatened to become 'top-heavy' with information. Therefore a brief survey is given here of the various motifs in this story, with their places in the history of literature, and with references to the relevant secondary literature.[7] Finally a survey will be given of the similarities and differences between the dramatis personae and their literary predecessors in their characterization and actions. This will lead to some conclusions about Apuleius' originality in his treatment of a widespread and popular motif.[8]

1. The 'Potiphars wife' motif before Attic tragedy.

The basic theme of the (older, married) woman who falls in love with a young man, and who, when he does not reciprocate her love, accuses him falsely of an assault on her virtue, can be found in the narrative repertory of almost all peoples (Thompson K 2111). It is usually called the 'Potiphar's wife motif' or 'Potiphar motif', after the story of Joseph's attempted seduction by Potiphar's wife in Genesis 39 (see 5.1 below).

Whether the Greeks had a native version of this motif in their own tales or borrowed it from the Orient is irrelevant here; in either case, several variants of the motif can be recognized in Greek mythology long before Attic tragedy.[9] This can be concluded from

---

4   See Appendix III on the generic shifts in both inner tales of book 10.

5   Nimis 1999,217 f.; see Introd. **2.2** on the application of Nimis' 'Prosaics of the Novel' to the vexed question of the unity of the *Met.* as a whole.

6   Nimis 1994,403, discussing the allusions in the beginning of Chariton's *Chaereas and Callirhoe*, and quoting Eco 1979,31-33.

7   Only those literary backgrounds that are truly motivating forces in the story will be discussed in this Appendix. For more superficial allusions and references to Greek and Latin literature, such as found throughout the *Met.*, the commentary should be consulted.

8   Yohannan 1968,23 mentions Apuleius and Heliodorus only in passing. Hadas 1959,156 f. offers a slightly more detailed discussion of Apuleius' version and the occurrence of the motif in Greek romances; Scarcella 1993,385 f. (= Scarcella 1985,213 f.) concentrates mainly on Heliodorus' version of the story, but gives many references to relevant secondary literature in his notes.

9   See Scarcella 1993,385 f., n. 1 and 2, with literature; see also Heubeck 1955.

the occurrence of related plots in the epic,[10] in historiography,[11] and in Hesiod[12] and Pindar.[13] These mythological tales have frequently provided material for the Attic tragedians.[14] Likewise, the figures of Hippolytus, Phaedra, and Theseus must quite early have become the main characters in a story closely connected with the Potiphar motif.[15] Euripides took this legend and moulded the old motif into the tragic conflict that in one way or another inspired, or served as an example for, practically all subsequent treatments. At the same time other narrative schemes based on the Potiphar motif continue to make themselves felt,[16] like those in which the woman tempting the young man is not his stepmother but, for example, the wife of his host (the type of Bellerophon). The extreme misogyny and the oath of chastity sworn to Artemis that characterize Hippolytus are absent in other treatments of the Potiphar motif; in them the young man has different motivations for his refusal, such as his pledge to his beloved (the Greek novel), or respect for the temptress's husband (Joseph, Antheus, Bellerophon), whether or not combined with religious scruples (Joseph; Hippolytus, too, is motivated by his devotion to Artemis). All these variants will be discussed in 5 of this Appendix.

2. Euripides' two Hippolytus tragedies of Euripides and their influence.

There is no need here to enter deeply into the problems concerning the relationship between Euripides' first *Hippolytus*, lost but for a few fragments, and the second *Hippolytus*,[17] which is extant. Important is the following information, which is, at least, beyond doubt.

The studies dealing with the two Hippolytus tragedies of Euripides always refer to the second play as *Hippolytus Stephanephoros* or *Hippolytus Stephanias*.[18] This epithet is based on a characteristic scene from this tragedy (73 f.), in which Hippolytus is wearing a wreath in front of Artemis' image. The epithet is old: Aristophanes of Byzantium uses it as a standard name.[19] The first Hippolytus tragedy written by Euripides is referred to as the *Hippolytus Kaluptomenos*,[20] presumably after a scene (no longer extant) in which

---

10 Hom. *Il.* 6,155 f.: Bellerophon and Anteia (in another tradition her name is Stheneboia); ibid. 9,447 f. Phoinix and Phthia.
11 The story of Peleus and Astydameia in Apollod. 3,13,3 is probably based on Pherekydes.
12 The story of Peleus is also found in Hesiod. frg. 208 (Merkelbach-West).
13 *Nem.* 4,54 f. and 5,27 f. with the story of Peleus (here Akastos' wife is called Hippolyte).
14 See Trenkner 1958,64 f. and n. 2, with extensive references; Tschiedel 1969,16 f.
15 Cf. Aristophanes *Ran.* 1052, where Euripides, when criticized for his depraved female characters, asks Aeschylus in response: 'But wasn't the story true I composed about Phaedra?' Aeschylus answers the question with: 'Indeed it is true'. See further Barrett 1992,6 f.: 'The legend before Attic Tragedy'; cf. also Herter 1940 and Fauth 1958.
16 Parthenius, in his outlines for elegiac topics dedicated to Gallus, mentions the stories about Cleoboia (14) and Neaira (18).
17 The literature about this play is vast. A thorough discussion, which cites the most important literature, is the introduction to the commentary of Euripides' *Hippolytus* by Barrett 1964 (page numbers throughout this appendix refer to the paperback edition Barrett 1992); see also Roisman 1999,253 f.
18 Henceforth referred to as '*Hipp.Steph.*'.
19 This also applies to the epithet *Kaluptomenos* for the first Hippolytus tragedy (henceforth referred to as '*Hipp.Kal.*'). See Barrett 1992, with n. 1; 37 with n. 1.
20 Frg. 428-447 N.

Hippolytus veils his head in shame as a reaction to Phaedra's proposition.[21] The Athenian audience disapproved of this first tragedy: the depiction of Phaedra as the shameless woman who makes her indecent propositions to Hippolytus in person (that is, the woman as she is always depicted in the traditonal stories based on the Potiphar motif) was regarded as offensive.[22]

In 428 B.C. Euripides won the prize in tragedy with his second *Hippolytus* (*Hipp.Steph.*). Here the figure of Phaedra has been freed of the offensive traits of her predecessor in the *Hipp.Kal.* Aphrodite says in a prologue that she wants to revenge herself on Hippolytus, who refuses to pay her respect, having devoted himself entirely to Artemis. He abhors women and wants nothing to do with love. Aphrodite announces that she has made Phaedra burn with passion for Hippolytus. As the action begins, Hippolytus comes on stage, and in his first scene his purity and intolerance become apparent right away. At first, Phaedra desperately tries to suppress her love; when she does not succeed she pines away from grief, determined not to confide her feelings to anyone. The nurse, however (who obviously assumes many of the actions that were so damaging to the first Phaedra),[23] manages to worm Phaedra's secret out of her and, in order to save Phaedra from death, reveals her passion to Hippolytus, trying to persuade him to reciprocate his stepmother's feelings. Shocked, Hippolytus reacts violently, accusing Phaedra herself of shamelessness, the very thing she is totally innocent of. The nurse has made Hippolytus swear an oath of silence, but Phaedra is not convinced that he will keep his promise. To save her family from disgrace and to punish Hippolytus for his brusque and unfair behaviour, she writes, before she hangs herself, a message to Theseus in which she accuses Hippolytus of having assaulted her virtue. Theseus believes her message, seeing it confirmed by her suicide, and lays a curse on his son. Hippolytus tries to convince his father of his innocence but cannot reveal the truth, bound as he is by his oath of silence. Having been banished by Theseus, Hippolytus is driving his chariot along the seashore when Poseidon, responding to Theseus' curse, sends a monstrous bull from the sea. The horses bolt and Hippolytus is fatally injured in the crash. Dying, he is carried on to the stage, where Artemis has just revealed the truth to Theseus. Artemis promises Hippolytus ritual honours and a cult in Troizen, and father and son become reconciled before Hippolytus dies.

In addition to the fact that Phaedra, in the general opinion, has acquired a much nobler and truly tragic character in this second tragedy, the reverse side of Hippolytus' chastity, namely his narrow-minded intolerance, is shown here to better effect.[24]

3. Sophocles' *Phaedra*.

Sophocles' tragedy on this theme, of which only a few fragments are extant, is generally assumed to have been written after the *Hipp.Kal.* and before the *Hipp.Steph*. The few conclusions about this tragedy that can be drawn from the fragments have been formulated with justified

---

21 See, however, for different ideas on the origin of this title, Roisman 1999.
22 Cf. *Arg. Hipp.Steph.* 25 f. ἔστι δὲ οὗτος Ἱππόλυτος δεύτερος, ὁ καὶ στεφανίας προσαγορευόμενος, ἐμφαίνεται δὲ ὕστερος γεγραμμένος· τὸ γὰρ ἀπρεπὲς καὶ κατηγορίας ἄξιον ἐν τούτῳ διώρθωται τῷ δράματι. See also Roisman 1999.
23 On the role of the nurse see 6C of this Appendix, the discussion of the *nouerca*.
24 For further changes supposedly made by Euripides, see Barrett 1992,13 f.

reservation by Barrett.[25] The possibility of influences from Sophocles' *Phaedra* will be raised occasionally in the following section; it is important to keep in mind that such suggestions are highly hypothetical.

4. The Phaedra-Hippolytus theme in Greek and Roman literature after Attic tragedy, and in Seneca's *Phaedra*.

As we know, Euripides' tragedies exercised a great influence on literature from the fourth century B.C. onward. For a long time the assumption was that any treatment of the Phaedra-Hippolytus theme after Euripides, if it diverged from the well-known *Hipp.Steph.*, must go back to the *Hipp.Kal*. Today, however, it is recognized that not only Sophocles' *Phaedra*, but also other literary treatments (some known to us by title only) may have had an influence on later literature. For example, a tragedy named *Hippolytos* is mentioned by Suda s.v. Λυκόφρων. Of another *Hippolytos*, a work of the early Hellenistic poet Sopatros of Paphos, two verses have been handed down in Athenaios (3,101a); it is unknown whether this was a poem or a tragedy.

The first treatment of the theme in Roman literature is known to us not from drama but from the epic:[26] Verg. *A*. 7,761 f.[27] names Hippolytus as the father of a Latin king, Virbius, and also mentions Hippolytus having a wife, Aricia:[28] (765 f.) *namque ferunt fama Hippolytum, postquam arte nouercae / occiderit patriasque expleret sanguine poenas / turbatis distractus equis, ad sidera rursus / aetheria et superas caeli uenisse sub auras, / Paeoniis reuocatum herbis et amore Dianae*. In this, Vergil follows an earlier identification of the Italic deity Virbius with the local demi-god of Troizen, Hippolytus. This identification was possible because of a very ancient variant[29] of one of the tales connected with Asklepios: the god was said to have brought Hippolytus back to life at the request of Artemis. The Romans identified the resurrected Hippolytus with the deity Virbius, who was worshipped in the shrine of Diana at Aricia; they possibly based themselves on Callimachus, *Ait*. Frg. 190 (Pfeiffer). Ovid, too, treats the Hippolytus theme in connection with the Virbius legend: *Met*. 15,498-546 and *Fast*. 6,733-62.[30] This shows that other treatments of the Phaedra-Hippolytus theme, in addition to Euripides' tragedies, have influenced Roman literature. In his *Heroides* Ovid includes a letter from Phaedra to Hippolytus (*Ep*. 4). The Phaedra emerging from this letter is far removed from the tragic, noble Phaedra of the *Hipp.Steph.*; it is usually assumed that in this letter Ovid has based himself especially on the *Hipp.Kal*. Prudence

---

25 Barrett 1992,12 f.; the fragments are cited in full and discussed 22 f.; see also the discussion by Radt *TrGrF*. 4,475 f.
26 Tschiedel 1969,39 f. notes that, though the early Roman tragedians made extensive use of the materials they found in the Attic tragedians, especially Euripides, Seneca's is the first Roman tragedy based on the *Hippolytus* tragedies of Euripides.
27 There are elements of Euripides' Phaedra story in the Dido episode: see the detailed discussion in Petriconi 1962,163 f.
28 Cf. Racine, in whose *Phèdre* Hippolyte is betrothed to Aricie.
29 According to Apollod. (3,10,3 f.) this variant was already found in the epic Ναυπάκτια (ascribed to Carcinus of Naupactus, probably 7th or 6th century B.C.). Hyg. *Fab*. 251. See Barrett 1992,8 with n. 1.
30 The connection with the Phaedra story in Apuleius calls for this brief discussion of Hippolytus' 'resurrection', which was obviously supposed to be generally known in Roman literature. See 6B of this Appendix.

is called for, however, because of the reasons mentioned above (at the beginning of 4). It is generally accepted that in the *Hipp.Kal.* Phaedra declares her love to Hippolytus herself,[31] and that the intermediation of the nurse was one of the chief modifications that Euripides made in his second *Hippolytus* (see above). But since the personal declaration of love is one of the basic elements of the Potiphar motif, one should not assume that all post-Euripidean versions in which the woman herself declares her love are directly derived from the *Hipp.Kal.*[32] This much is certain: that, as far as shamelessness is concerned, the Phaedra in *Hipp.Kal.* is still quite close to her sisters in the traditional stories based on the Potiphar motif. It is also certain that this is the type of woman that we encounter repeatedly in the treatments of the motif in the ancient novel (see 5 of this Appendix). In view of Euripides' great influence on later literature, one may assume that many of the novels were influenced by the *Hipp.Kal.* However, because we know so little about the *Hipp.Kal.*, we cannot be certain whether any particular detail in the many novellas based on the Potiphar motif is traceable to the *Hipp.Kal.*, or reflects traditional narrative material. Cf. e.g. the influence of the Antiochus story (5.3 of this Appendix).

After Euripides, by far the most famous treatment of the tragic conflict between Phaedra and Hippolytus is Seneca's *Phaedra*.[33] For a long time, Seneca too was believed to have based himself entirely on the now lost *Hipp.Kal.* Nowadays, however, the emphasis on establishing sources has given way to an emphasis on demonstrating Seneca's originality and autonomy in adapting older material from tragedy.[34] The references to Seneca's *Phaedra* in Apuleius' stepmother-story have been studied more than once, and will be discussed below (see 7 of this Appendix).

5. The Potiphar motif in ancient literature after Attic tragedy, up to Apuleius.

5.1 The motif in the Jewish tradition.

The story to which the motif owes its name is found in Genesis 39,7-20 (9th century B.C.), which goes back to a 13th-century Egyptian story of Anpu, his wife, and his brother Bata.[35] Braun 1938,44-93 shows that the version of the story of Joseph and Potiphar's wife in chapters 3-9 of the pseudo-epigraphical 'Testaments of the Twelve Patriarchs' was influenced by Euripides' *Hippolytus*.[36]

Philo of Alexandria retells the Potiphar story in 'Περὶ Ἰωσήφ' (40-53): Potiphar's

---

31 Roisman 1999,183 however, considers this unlikely.
32 Zintzen 1960 is quite optimistic in this respect: on the basis of Seneca's *Phaedra*, he wants to reconstruct Euripides' lost *Hipp.Kal.* from all passages where Seneca's tragedy differs from the *Hipp.Steph.* and where those differences correspond with comparable passages in Josephus and the Greek novels (see 5 of this Appendix).
33 Tschiedel 1969,57 f. discusses the influence of this tragedy on later Western European literature. Van der Paardt 1982,78 f. discusses an interesting treatment of Seneca's *Phaedra* by Hugo Claus.
34 A survey of this discussion can be found in Grimal 1963,297-314 and in the Introduction to his edition and commentary on the *Phaedra*, Paris 1965; Herter 1971,44-77 with extensive references. See also Fiorencis-Gianotti 1990,77 with notes 15 and 16.
35 See the first chapter in Yohannan 1968; Tschiedel 1969,5-15 with references; Gunkel [7]1966,422; Redford 1970,91-93.
36 See Hadas 1959,153 f.; Yohannan 1968,16 f.

wife falls in love with Joseph (40) and tries by physical force to bring him to her bed (41); Joseph protests in a long speech (42-48); his seducer denounces him to her husband (49-51); and Potiphar has Joseph imprisoned. Finally (52-53) Philo criticizes Potiphar's rashness and injustice in condemning Joseph unheard and in misreading the evidence, but points out that allowances should be made for Potiphar, who leads the thankless life of a chef.

Josephus, *AJ* 2,39-59, give a longer, more complex version of the story. A careful examination of how Josephus' version expands on that of Philo is given by Braun 1934,23-117, who, however, shows that Josephus, following the rhetorically coloured tradition of historiography in his time, uses the story mainly as a moralistic *exemplum*. Braun also points out the similarities between Josephus' version and comparable embedded tales in Greek novels, tracing them back to the schools of rhetoric, and notes the influence of Euripides' two Hippolytus tragedies: 'von ihnen ist die spätere Produktion ... abhängig oder wenigstens nachhaltig beeinflußt'.

5.2. The Greek novel

In several Greek novels, embedded tales or side-episodes to the main story line are built around the Potiphar motif.[37] As episodes in the main narrative they serve as additions to the series of assaults on the chastity and plighted troth of one or other of the sorely tried main characters. Thus they illustrate the young man's steadfastness and loyalty to his beloved, able as he is to resist an older woman's attempts at seduction. Because of the novel's traditional 'happy ending' for the two main characters, everything always turns out well for the young man in these stories; the woman who attempted to lead him astray is punished. Since, apart from the Knemon story in Heliod. 1,9 f., these side-episodes usually take place during the wanderings of the separated lovers, a domestic situation is unlikely: in these circumstances it is not a stepmother who wants to seduce the young man, but for instance the wife of a host, or a temporary foster mother.[38] In Xenophon *Ephes*. 2,5-11 Manto, the daughter of the brigand chief falls in love with Habrokomes. When he rejects her advances, she tells her father that Habrokomes has assaulted her virtue. But in Heliodorus' story of Knemon,[39] which is very cunningly woven into the framing tale, we encounter a stepmother again (here the main character of the inner story is not the main character of the novel itself): Knemon tells this story to the two main characters of the novel as something that happened to him at home in Athens, and drove him away from Athens. Thus, by including a version of the favourite Potiphar motif as an inner story in his *Metamorphoses*, Apuleius also closely follows the tradition of these embedded tales in the Greek novel.[40]

---

37 Xenophon, *Ephesiaka* 2,3-11 and 3,12; Achilles Tatius, *Leukippe and Kleitophon* 5,11 f.; Flav. Philostratus, *Vita Apollonii*, 6,3 f. and 7,42 f.; Heliodorus, *Aethiopika* 1,9 f. and 7,9 f. See Huber-Rebenich 1999,193 f. for an instance of the Potiphar motif in the *Peudo-Clementines*.
38 See on early instances of these variants 1 of this Appendix.
39 See Morgan 1989,99-113.
40 See Wehrli 1965,133-154.

5.3. Antiochus and Stratonice.

The story of Antiochus and Stratonice is, in more than one way, a 'mirroring' of the Hippolytus story. This tale, a favourite in late antiquity, goes back to very old novellistic material, according to Mesk 1913,366 f. The physical symptoms of lovesickness are always at the center of this tale: they lead a perceptive physician to the cause of the illness from which Antiochus is wasting away.[41] Antiochus, who has fallen in love with his stepmother Stratonice, refuses to yield to this passion, which he perceives as shameful and impossible, and becomes ill with grief. A wise physician not only acutely makes the right diagnosis, but also uses his diplomatic skills so that eventually everything works out for the best: in order to save his son from death, Antiochus' father agrees to a marriage between his wife, Stratonice, and his son. In romantic historiography this tale was connected with the Seleucid dynasty, and that is the form in which it first reaches us: Plut. *Dem.* 38; Appian *Syr.* 59-61; in Valerius Maximus as an *exemplum* of paternal love (5,7. ext.1); Lucian *Syr.D.* 17 f. The story was often linked with the biographies of famous physicians, such as Erasistratos.[42] Galen, too, knows the story and recognizes the psychosomatic basis of 'lovesickness' (14,630 K; 16,309 K; 18/2,40 K). According to Lucian, *Salt.* 59, it is also found in the repertory of pantomime.[43] Disconnected from its historical names, the story was also a source of inspiration for rhetorical exercises; cf. Sen. *Con.* 6,7. A later version (with different names) can be found in Aristaenetus, *Ep.* 1,13. Cf. also Quint. *Decl.* 291, with Winterbottom 1984, who gives references to other declamations built around this tale of Antiochus and Stratonice.

In Heliod. 4,8 the wise physician Akesinos recognizes Charikleia's illness as lovesickness by the familiar symptoms. In his 'Phaedra', Apuleius takes up the Antiochus story in a highly original manner (see 7 of this Appendix).

5.4. The mime.[44]

The Potiphar motif also figures in several variants in mime. This appears from a 'scenario' (transmitted almost complete) of the 'Mime of the Poisoner' (*Ox.Pap.* 413).[45] a slave (who has a sweetheart) does not respond to the advances of a married woman. She wants to revenge herself on him, but after many complications it is she who is punished in the end. It has often been noted that Apuleius, when describing certain incidents and scenes in the *Met.*, frequently refers to the mimes which were so popular in his day.[46] In this he does not differ from other ancient novelists. Sudhaus 1906,267 n. 2 already stated: 'Das Verhältnis des Romans zur mimischen Bühne erfordert eine eigene Darstellung',

---

41 The story is associated with Antiochus I Soter, son of Seleucus I; see Brodersen 1985,459-469; idem 1989,169 f.; *DNP* 1,767 f. s.v. 'Antiochos I' [Ameling].
42 See Amundsen 1974,333 and n. 62; Suda s.v. 'Eristratos'.
43 See also Swain 1992,76 f.
44 Steinmetz 1982,361-367 gives a lucid summary of the different types of mimes (preliterary, subliterary, and literary), which developed from the earliest times onward, and of the situation in the second century A.D., with references to all relevant literature in notes.
45 For an edition and discussion, see Wiemken 1972,81 f.
46 See e.g. *GCA* 1985,214 on 8,25 (196,19-21); Winkler 1985,160-65 and 287-91; Fick-Michel 1991,115 f. collects many examples from the *Met*; also Andreassi 1997.

adding many reminiscences of the mime in Chariton, Achilles Tatius, and Heliodorus.[47] Reich 1903,589 f. was the first to assume that the entire tale of *Met.* 10,2-12 is a mime retold by Apuleius; Sudhaus 1906,262 agreed. Subsequently, Wiemken 1972,139 f. reconstructed Apul. *Met.* 10,2-12 as a mime, complete with division into acts and scenes. His reconstruction shows, however, that Apuleius' story does not quite tally with the mimic staging that was supposed to be behind it. Steinmetz 1982,368 f., who goes even farther in reconstructing a mime on the basis of our story, tries to eliminate those elements that Wiemken still acknowledged as examples of an 'epische Zutat' or a 'gelegentliche Stagnation'. But to see Apuleius' version as merely a mime rewritten in narrative form is a negation of the rich and varied literary tradition which, as will be shown below, is incorporated in Apuleius' 'Phaedra'. Nevertheless, the reconstructions by Wiemken and Steinmetz show that the story contains a number of elements which contemporaneous readers would immediately associate with the popular mime. What Sullivan says of Petronius' *Satyricon*, '...that mime subjects and situations provide part of the grist for Petronius' sophisticated and literary mill'.[48] It is conceivable that Apuleius interspersed his 'Phaedra' with obvious mime-reminiscences for the very purpose of showing his contemporaneous audience how a tragic Phaedra could degenerate into a common, evil poisoner.

Even some patent absurdities in the plot of Apuleius' tale (see e.g. on *finitum est iudicium* ch. 7: 242,24) may be explained as a feature of the mime: according to Wiemken 1972,65, the preference for dramatic effect over consistency of plot is characteristic of the mime.

Related to the mime in *Ox.Pap.* 413 mentioned above is the coarse parody of the Potiphar motif found in ch. 75 of the Aesopus novel, where the slave Aesopus sleeps with Xanthos' wife.[49]

A fragment of Dec. Laberius' mime *Belonistria*[50] suggests that its plot was related to the Potiphar motif. The extant line reads: *domina nostra priuignum suum / amat efflictim*.[51]

In the commentary, possible references to a mime situation have been pointed out in the following notes: ch. 3 (238,7-10); 238,21 f. *isti enim tui oculi* ...; *diutina deliberatione* ch. 4 (239,11); *forte fortuna puer ... continuo perduxit haustu* ch. 5 (239,28 f.); *iamque ... insimulabant* ch. 5 (240,7 f.). The courtroom scene, too, described in ch. 7 f., can be compared with similar scenes in the mime.[52] The interchange of sleeping-potion and deadly poison, which we find in our story, is found in more than one mime (see on *dedi uenenum, sed somniferum* ch. 11: 245,1).

---

47 See also Cataudella 1966,3 f.; Wiemken 1972,167 with n. 24 and 25; Mignogna 1996 and 1997.
48 Thus Sullivan 1968,223, in an enlightening section, 'Mime and Comedy Situations' (219-225), which is in part applicable to Apuleius' *Met.* as well. From the earliest time there is a constant, lively exchange of themes and motives between the mime — subliterary and literary, and continually evolving — on the one side, and the 'higher' forms of literature on the other side. For a thorough and richly documented study of the theatrical elements in Petronius' *Satyrica* see C. Panayotakis 1995.
49 On this episode see Holzberg (ed.) 1992,58 with n. 90.
50 Transmitted Non. 124,21; see Bonaria 1965,41.
51 The writer of mimes, Laberius (first century A.D.), was assiduously read (e.g. because of his language) during the time of the archaists: a large number of his fragments have reached us through Gellius (cf. Bonaria 1965,7 f. and 38 f.). Laberius' younger contemporary, Publilius Syrus, was also often quoted because of his pithy *sententiae*.
52 See C. Panayotakis 1995,153 with n. 3, and see the commentary on *patres in curiam conuenirent* ch. 7 (241,24).

5.5 *Declamationes*.

It has already been noted (5.3 above), that Sen. *Con.* 6,7 deals with a situation similar to the intrigue found in the Antiochus story. Such situations were common in the *declamationes*:[53] Quintilian criticizes their subject matter, including *saeuiores tragicis nouercae* (Quint. *Inst.* 2,10,5). The criticism could be made even more strongly about the later *Declamationes Maiores*.[54] These nineteen highly polished *controuersiae* are clearly not meant as school exercises: they are the model speeches, recited in public and published afterwards, of a number of rhetors, all presumably of the 2nd century A.D.[55] Steinmetz 1982,188 f., who discusses some examples, remarks that these elaborate fictive *controuersiae* were at the time of their origin enjoyed by the public for more than one reason: not only were they appreciated as examples of rhetorical skill, but their bizarre and gruesome themes evidently responded to the public's sensationalism. Another reason for their popularity may be that, like the mystery novels of our time, they gave the readers (or audience) an opportunity to participate in sorting out contradictory evidence and pointing out the true culprit. For the references to *declamationes* in our story, see e.g. on *ueneni* ch. 9 (244,5).

6. The dramatis personae of Apuleius' Phaedra story and their literary predecessors.

The narrator draws his reader's attention explicitly to the tragic intertext of the tale that he is introducing (see the opening section of this appendix). Besides, it has emerged above that the Potiphar motif (of which the Phaedra-Hippolytus motif is a special variant), is present in many different literary traditions. Now we can examine the relation between Apuleius' Phaedra story and the entire intertext discussed in the previous paragraphs.[56] This will enable us to make a pronouncement on Apuleius' originality in his treatment of the intertext, and on the function of his own transformations.[57] Those transformations can be illustrated by the 'doings and dealings' of the dramatis personae, which do or do not agree with those of their brothers and sisters in the intertext. The commentary has consistently paid attention to this aspect of the story in various notes, so that here a survey will suffice, with references to the relevant notes at the end of each section.

6A The *dominus aedium*.

---

53 See the commentary on *nouerca* ch. 2 (237,9). Stepmothers, poison, and disturbances of the family occur e.g. Sen. *Con.* 4,5 and 6; 7,1 and 5; 9,5 and 6. On the *declamationes*, see Steinmetz 1982,167 f.

54 It is generally agreed that the *Declamationes Maiores* are not by Quintilian; see Sussman (in the introduction to his translation of the *Declamationes Maiores*) 1987,VII f., with references.

55 See Steinmetz 1982,189. Sussman 1987,XI and n. 48 is even convinced of a point in time close to Apuleius. He finds the dating proposed by Hammer, Weyman, and Deratani persuasive and continues (245): 'Indeed, during the process of translation, this feeling became more entrenched when determining subsidiary meanings for words in the *MD* and searching for appropriate parallel usages: these quite often closely matched those in Apuleius'.

56 An intertextual relation exists when different texts have at least one element in common. This element is called an 'intertexteme'. A group of texts connected by one or more intertextemes is called an 'intertext'. In our case, the Potiphar motif is the intertexteme of the intertext described in 1 through 5 of this Appendix. For this terminology see Claes 1988,50 f.

57 See on 'transformations' Introd. **2.3**.

The most important difference between the *dominus aedium* and Theseus is that the *dominus aedium* is not a mythical monarch but a prosperous, bourgeois inhabitant of a small Greek provincial town. He is never characterized directly. His wife is in charge: she can send him away or call him back as she wishes.[58] In this context, not even the one feature that connects him with Theseus, i.e. his credulity, acquires the tragic quality of Theseus' unconditional acceptance of Phaedra's message, and rash condemnation of Hippolytus. At the end of ch. 5 and in ch. 6 he is depicted as a shattered man. Torn between what he feels as the necessity to punish his son and his parental love, he reminds us momentarily of Seneca's Theseus, who is equally torn. In ch. 6 the possibility of his ever becoming a Theseus is disposed of once and for all: for the punishment of his son he depends on the local administrators. All this shows that this *dominus aedium* has more in common with the husbands in the novellistic treatments of the Potiphar motif, who display all the gullibility of the original tale, than with the Theseus of the tragedies. But we have also seen that, nevertheless, the reader is repeatedly urged to compare this father with the tragic Theseus, and to realize what can happen to a story which is transposed from a mythical past to a bourgeois 'present'.[59] When, at the end of the story, the father gets his two sons back, this is explicitly ascribed to his *fortuna*. Fortuna is comparable here with Τύχη in the New Comedy, but with an additional dimension of fickleness and unfairness. It is left to the reader himself to judge whether, in the case of the father's character, the promise has been fulfilled or reversed that there would be a rise from *soccus* to *cothurnus* (ch. 2: 237,12 f.).

See the notes in ch. 2 on *ibidem* (237,1); *pietate* (237,4); *forma magis quam moribus* (237,9 f.); in ch. 4 on *uillulas* (239,15); in ch. 5 on *infelix ... aestuat* (240,23 f.); *ad hoc ... odium* (240,27 f.); in ch. 6 on *uixdum ... et statim ... immittit* (241,1 f.); *nescius fraudium ... mulieris* (241,6); *barbaricae feritatis uel ... impotentiae* (241,20 f.); in ch. 12 on *bono medico* (245,25; 245,26-29).

6B The *iuuenis*.

The *iuuenis*, the stepson in the story, is unmistakably characterized as an antithesis of the tragic Hippolytus.[60] This emerges in his reaction to his stepmother's declaration of love. His refusal does not follow, like that of Euripides' Hippolytus, from a promise of chastity to Artemis and an aversion to the female sex. Nor does he decline his stepmother's proposition because he is faithful to his beloved, as in the Greek novel. His reason for refusal is comparable with Joseph's: his virtue. The fact, however, that he does not refuse at once but keeps stalling with halfhearted excuses makes him unique within the intertext discussed above. Similar delaying tactics are, however, in the Greek novels, employed by e.g. Charicleia in Heliod. 1,22 (explained by her to Theagenes in 1,26) and by Clitophon in Achilles Tatius 5,12-16; 21 and 23. Our stepson never makes the famous gesture (which

---

58 Nowhere it is suggested that this husband is unfaithful to his wife; cf. the allusions in Seneca's *Phaedra* 92 f.; Ov. *Ep.* 4,111 f.
59 Cf. Fiorencis-Gianotti 1990,85: 'sappiamo bene che le peregrinazioni degli eroi attraverso i generi comportano metamorfosi più o meno marcate e che l'ingresso nel romanzo procede generalmente nel senso della degradazione di personaggi e modelli collaudati', with examples.
60 This is effected at once, through his introduction as a *iuuenis probe litteratus atque ob id consequenter pietate, modestia praecipuus* (ch. 2: 237,3 f.). See comm. on *iam ergo ... ascendere* ch. 2 (237,12-14).

was evidently felt to be most impressive) of veiling his head, as in the *Hippolytus Kaluptomenos*.[61]

This *iuuenis* plays no active part in the second part of the story. From the moment the poison meant for this 'anti-Hippolytus' is drunk by his younger brother, it is he who assumes an aspect of the legendary Hippolytus: taken for dead, he is buried, but 'arises from death' (ch. 12). This may be a reference to the Virbius-legend (see 4; see also Tappi 1986,184 f.). The association with Virbius, however, is skillfully linked with the 'deathlike sleep' motif, popular in the novel and the mime.[62]

See on ch. 2 *iam ergo ... ascendere* (237,12-14); ch. 3 *senili tristie ... frontem* (238,8); ch. 4 *non tamen ... exasperandum, sed ... leniendum* (239,2 f.); *domus cladem* (239,8 f.); *ad quendam educatorem senem refert* (239,9 f.); *diutina deliberatione* (239,11); *insontis* (239,26); ch. 5 *puer ille iunior* (239,28); ch. 11 *remeabit ad diem lucidam* (245,8).

6C The *nouerca*.

In the first chapters of the tale (2 and 3) we can perceive a certain dichotomy in the characterization of this woman. Her struggle with her awakening and ultimately indomitable love is drawn with some sympathy.[63] As the abundance of cliches shows, she is in many respects indistinguishable from all the other women in literature who are tormented by an unattainable (or forbidden) love. But from the beginning there is also a 'Potiphar's wife' aspect to her personality; the reader is confronted with the troubling inconsistencies already found in the characterizations of Phaedra by Euripides and Seneca.[64] But when, in ch. 3, she herself declares her love to her stepson, it is clear that the Phaedra of the *Hipp.Steph.* has left the scene for ever.[65] Her declaration of love and attempt to seduce her stepson remind the reader of Seneca's Phaedra and Ovid's in *Ep.* 4. It has already been pointed out that our *nouerca* combines the irrepressible passion of Seneca's Phaedra and the sly, specious arguments of the nurse in Euripides' *Hipp.Steph.*[66] The same could be said of Ovid's Phaedra in *Ep.* 4, where, however, the possibility of a co-actor is eliminated by the epistolary form.

After her stepson's reaction, any suggestion of tragic nobility in this *nouerca* disappears: from now on she is to be equated entirely with the stock character of the evil *nouerca* in the *declamationes* and the merciless schemer in the novellistic treatments of the Potiphar-motif

---

61   On the epithets (already known in Apuleius' time) for the two tragedies, see 2 above. There may be a reference to *Kaluptomenos* in our ch. 3, when not the stepson but the stepmother covers her head (see on *laciniaque contegens faciem* ch. 3: 238,18).

62   See Wesseling 1993,73 f. on this. Merkelbach 1962,79-90 sees in the apparent death of the younger brother an allusion to the mysteries, and in the two brothers an allusion to the Egyptian Bata story. According to him the wise doctor plays the part of Toth-Hermes. The objection against this vision is that it lifts only a few parts out of the story that fit this interpretation, but ignores other parts that would seriously conflict with it. See also Gwyn Griffiths in *AAGA* 1978,154 f.

63   It is therefore incorrect to speak of 'una figura femminile descritta senza simpatia' (Fiorencis-Gianotti 1990,85).

64   For a good summary of this problem see Herter 1971,44 f., with references; Zwierlein 1987. It is not implausible that Apuleius uses this unmistakable dichotomy in his *nouerca* to point out this problem of literary criticism to this readers. See also the last part of the note on *seu naturaliter impudica seu fato ... impulsa ...* ch. 2 (237,10 f.); see also 7 of this Appendix.

65   See on *tunc illa ... adfatur* ch. 3 (238,16 f.).

66   Erbse 1950,112.

and in the mime.[67] Unlike the Phaedra figures in the various tragedies, she reacts with sheer murderousness to her stepson's refusal to comply with her desires. In Apuleius' story the *nouerca* turns to the calumny of her stepson only after her attempt to have him murdered has failed (ch. 5: 240,9-23). The wish to take her own life, so strong (and in all cases carried out) in the Phaedra figures of tragedy, does not exist in this woman.[68]

In the first part of the story this 'Phaedra' plays her role with no nurse as support and confidante.[69] In the second part of the story she uses a devoted slave as her henchman. This character, belonging to both comedy and mime, even becomes the representative of the *nouerca*, who then (from ch. 7 onward) plays no further part in the story.

Through numerous verbal allusions, and also through the characterization of the *nouerca*, the reader is repeatedly invited to consider this story in the light of tragedy.

See on ch. 2 *nouerca* (237,9); *forma magis quam moribus ... praepollens* (237,9 f.); *seu naturaliter impudica seu fato ad extremum impulsa flagitium* (237,10 f.); *oculos ad priuignum adiecit* (237,11 f.); *mulier illa* (237,14); *silentio resistebat* (237,16); *et languore simulato ... ualetudine* (237,19 f.); ch. 4 *nefarium amorem ad longe deterius transtulisset odium* (239,20 f.); *uita miserum priuare iuuenem* (239,24); *uenenum praesentarium* (239,25); *insontis priuigni* (239,26); ch. 5 *pessimae feminae* (239,28 f.); *sed dira illa femina ... unicum* (240,9 f.); *non ... non ... commota* (240,10 f.); *personata nimia temeritate* (240,15 f.).

Once the story leaves the context of tragedy, further characters who appear on the scene have no counterparts in the Hippolytus tragedies:[70] they include the above-mentioned slave, who is the *nouerca*'s accomplice, and the principal actor named on the other side, the wise physician who rescues the innocent *iuuenis*.

6D The *medicus*.

The remarkable parody on Vergil in ch. 2 (237,25 f.) effectively prevents any expectation that a sensible doctor will come to the *nouerca*'s sickbed and make the right diagnosis, and therefore that there can be a dénouement in the style of the Antiochus story (see 5.3), despite the catalogue of symptoms (ch. 2: 237,25-238,4; see the commentary ad loc. on similar enumerations in the Antiochus stories). Hence the sudden appearance of the *medicus* in ch. 8 is all the more surprising. He gives the story a decisive turn, but still the narrator makes it perfectly clear that the happy outcome is owed to *fortuna* (ch. 12: 245,26 f.). The wise physician is therefore only a pawn in *fortuna*'s fickle game. When he appears on stage, the narrative has already evolved quite far from the context of tragedy. If one still wishes (with Tappi 1986,186 and 192; Münstermann 1995,118 f.) to equate him with the dea ex machina Artemis in Euripides' *Hipp.Steph.*, one should be aware of an important difference: shortly before Hippolytus' death, Artemis brings about a reconciliation between Theseus and his son. In our story, the stepson never reappears on the scene at the happy

---

67 Any continuing verbal reminiscences of e.g. Seneca's *Phaedra* serve mainly to enhance the contrast between the tragic Phaedra and this *nouerca*.
68 See on *morituram* ch. 3 (238,25).
69 It is generally assumed that in the *Hipp.Steph.* Euripides introduced the nurse to 'relieve' Phaedra of amoral acts (cf., however, Roisman 1999). In Seneca's *Phaedra*, on the other hand, the nurse articulates the moral side. See also Fiorencis-Gianotti 1990,79 with n. 19; 88 with n. 44.
70 Cf. the disappearance of the *paedagogus*; see comm. on *finitum est iudicium* ch. 7 (242,24).

ending, and a reconciliation is entirely missing.[71] See also below (7 end) on the role of the *medicus*.

7. Apuleius' originality in his Phaedra story.

The preceding observations make it clear that an opinion like Zintzen's, that Apuleius in this story 'von Seneca abhängt',[72] is an incomplete characterization of Apuleius' clever dialogue with the total intertext described above. That this story has more to offer than Zintzen and others would have us believe appears also from the publications briefly discussed below, each of which treats an aspect of the intertextuality in this story.

Wiemken 1972 and Steinmetz 1982 reconstruct the story as a mime (see 5.4).

Tappi 1986 sees the story as an allegory for the insufficiency of political and legal institutions in a society that has lost its sacral foundations, and for which the old myths (such as that of Phaedra and Hippolytus) no longer have any meaning. He also explains the story in psychoanalytical terms, saying that it partly reflects the embitterment of the concrete author Apuleius (cf. the trial in which he had to defend himself against the false accusation by Pudentilla's relatives). But he also instructively examines the specific intertextuality between Apuleius' story and e.g. Euripides' *Hipp.Steph.*

Finkelpearl 1986 devotes a small portion (162-184) of her thesis, 'Metamorphosis of Language in Apuleius' "Metamorphoses"', to this story and examines the verbal reminiscences of Seneca's *Phaedra*, collected earlier by Hammer 1923 and Erbse 1950. By showing that through these allusions Apuleius is practising literary criticism, she points out the literary character of this story (this will be treated below). In chapter 7 of Finkelpearl 1998, the author first puts Apuleius' use of allusion[73] into an immediate context that takes account of the structure and content of book 10; she then (Finkelpearl 1998,176 f.) connects the weight on family relationships in this tale as well as in the other inner tales of book 9 and 10 with the many literary allusions that Apuleius knots up with one another: 'This literary play is another aspect of family relationships, an image that is used by Apuleius as well as other Latin authors to portray literary indebtedness.'

Zwierlein 1987 thinks that Apuleius' *nouerca* may owe something to the Phaedra of Sophocles' lost play, but he rightly calls these (p. 68) 'Spekulationen'. Nevertheless, in his careful reading of Apuleius' story he offers some valuable observations, which support the notion that the story has its own place as a new variant within the intertext described above.

Fiorencis-Gianotti 1990,71-114, who trace the figure of Phaedra through ancient literature, repeatedly point out the anti-traditional treatment of the Phaedra motif in Apuleius' story. They conclude their extensive article with a chapter 'I figli di Teseo', in which they interpret Apuleius' Phaedra story within the framework of the *Met.* as a story about the re-establishment of order through the expulsion of destabilizing forces; in their opinion this is a motivating force throughout the *Met.* They see a connection between the rebirth of Lucius in book

---

71 It is not clear on what Donnini 1981,148 and 158 bases the reconciliation he postulates as the conclusion of this story.
72 Zintzen 1960,5, n.7; cf. also Tschiedel 1969,35, who lumps together all occurrences of the Potiphar motif in the ancient novels, and speaks of an 'ermüdende Gleichformigkeit'.
73 Finkelpearl restricts herself to study of Apuleius' allusions to Latin literature; see Finkelpearl 1998,14 f.

11 and the rebirth of the younger brother in our story, and point out the importance of the seemingly gratuitous reference in 1,23 (21,15) to the *cognomen* of Lucius' father, 'Theseus': Lucius, as Theseus' new son, tells again the ancient tale about an illicit passion that once ended in disaster; but now the tale is rewritten with a happy ending and is therefore interwoven with the 'spirito pedagogico del racconto'.

Thus far the publications, each of which contributes in a stimulating way to a serious approach to Apuleius' story.

The notion that the author himself wanted to draw his readers' attention to this story as his own literary creation, is discussed in the commentary on *ad librum profero* ch. 2 (237,2 f.) and *unicum* ch. 5 (240,10). In addition to the points made there, and Finkelpearl's demonstration of the author's activities in literary criticism, this appendix will try to show further how the author uses intertextual references to stimulate his readers to exercise their own literary criticism.

In his introduction(s) to the story, the narrator repeatedly appeals to the *docti* among his readers, and sometimes creates a conspiratorial feeling of superiority with them.[74] Such readers undoubtedly take extra pleasure in noting and interpreting the literary references. Comparing the behaviour and remarks of these 'common people' to those of their cothurnus-shod counterparts produces, in some passages, a humorous effect. Actors behave inconsistently with the reader's expectations created by the reference(s) to the Hippolytus tragedies; again and again, this leads to reversals in the story, in which the actors move farther and farther from their 'models'.

The physician is introduced in an original and ingenious way. First it is made clear (through literary allusion) that a solution in the style of the wise doctor in the Antiochus story is not to be expected. Later, however, a wise doctor brings the solution. This is not because he is the only one to make a correct diagnosis (the narrator and the *docti* among his audience are quite capable of that, unlike the doctors in ch. 2: 237,25 f.), but because he causes the circumstances to take a turn for the better by revealing things that the narrator and his readers could not possibly know. The physician in his function of sub-narrator undermines the feeling of superior knowledge that the narrator initially inspired in the *lector optimus*. This, too, is a peripeteia (for other peripeties see above): the moment when the narrator no longer tells his story from his position of omniscience, but listens and observes as a bystander (ch. 5: 239,27 f.; see on *exanimis terrae procumbit* ch. 5: 240,5). This, however, becomes clear only during rereading.[75]

8 Conclusions.

- When the author Apuleius began his story, he may not have known how it would end (see the opening section of this Appendix). However, he self-consciously undertook the retelling of an old story in a new context, engaging his audience in the process by giving 'false' or 'half' clues. Confidently, he sets the story as a personal, unique literary creation

---

74 See the commentary on ch. 2 (238,1-4).
75 Not thus Winkler 1985,76 f., who compares this story with the modern 'mystery'. He sees the story neatly divided in two parts: the first a 'crime story', the second a 'detective story'. The reversal from tragedy to comedy is caused, he says, by the shrewd doctor, who reports (ch. 8) that he has caught the slave telling lies. See also Raffaelli 1995,57 f. for this tale as an ancient detective story.

against the background of the supposedly familiar intertext.
- The dialogue with the intertext contains an element of playfulness, and challenges the reader to recognize and interpret allusions, including those that are meant to be parodic and humorous.
- Through this play with literature, the author both actively engages in literary criticism himself and also invites his readers to join in.
- Reading the eleventh book, the reader wonders, 'How could I have known that the narrator is an Isis-priest?', and feels the need to reread the first ten books to answer her/his question, by finding the ambiguities that s/he did not notice earlier. The surprising disclosures of the *medicus* in our story create a similar need to reread - and this is one of the means by which the story is anchored within the *Met.* as a whole.

For the connection between the Phaedra story and the other inner story in book 10, the 'Murderess of Five' (chs. 23-28), see Appendix III.

APPENDIX II

The *spurcum additamentum* to *Met.* 10,21.

A fragment, generally known as the *spurcum additamentum* is added in the margin of some manuscripts of the *Met.*, and contains an extension of the description of the foreplay between the *matrona* and the ass. My commentary on *Met.* 10 is based on F (Laur. 68,2), in which the *spurcum additamentum* does not occur;[1] therefore this fragment is not discussed in the body of the commentary. Still, no commentary on *Met.* 10 should ignore this enigmatic piece of text. This Appendix gives a summary of scholarly discussions of the *spurcum additamentum*. A survey of the manuscript situation (1) is followed by the text of the fragment with a translation (2). Then a brief summary (3) is given of the divergent opinions about the origin and date of the fragment. This is followed by a conclusion (4).

1. The manuscript situation.

A curious fragment, an addition to *Met.* 10,21,[2] can be found in the margin of φ (Laur. 29,2), at the foot of f. 66^r. It was written in φ by Zanobi da Strada, as Billanovich (1953,30 f.; 40) has demonstrated. Billanovich has established that Boccaccio added the fragment in the margin of his autograph of the *Met.*, L1 (Laur. 54,32), at a later date; the fragment may have been brought to his attention by Zanobi da Strada. The presence of a number of disjunctive errors in the *additamentum* in φ and that in L1 excludes L1's dependence on φ in this respect (Mariotti 1956,231): Zanobi and Boccaccio must each independently have copied the fragment from a manuscript they had found in the library of Monte Cassino.[3] The fact that both Zanobi and Boccaccio wrote the fragment in the margin of their respective copies indicates that they also found it in the margin of the manuscript from which they copied it (Pecere 1987,105). In addition to φ and L1, this fragment occurs also in the margin of L2 (Laur. 54,12) and in that of L4 (Laur. 54,24). It is included not in the margin but in the text itself of V5 (Urb.Vat. 199).[4] For the constitution of the text of the fragment, only φ and L1 are important: the *additamentum* in the margin of L2 was copied from φ, and that in L4 from L1. The version in the text of V5 was copied from L4.[5]

The rather corrupt condition of the *spurcum additamentum* in φ and L1[6] suggests

---

1   The *spurcum additamentum* is absent also from A and other manuscripts of Robertson's Class I (see Introd. **4.1**).
2   The fragment is apparently intended to follow ... *nares perfundit meas* (ch. 21: 252,20).
3   Pecere 1987,121 suggests that this manuscript could have been C, of which only the 'Assisi fragments' (see Pecere 1987,101 with references) are extant; it could also have been the ancestor of Class I.
4   Robertson *CQ* 18 (1924),31 (who assumes L1's dependence on φ); see also his app. crit. for this passage.
5   Mariotti 1956,229, n. 2; 230 f.
6   But not as corrupt as it seemed before Mariotti 1956 in his meticulous commentary defended a number of readings which had until then been regarded as corrupt; e.g. 1 *orcium pigam*; *Hyaci*.

on the one hand that the manuscript copied by Zanobi and Boccaccio was difficult to read, and on the other that the *additamentum* was not recently written when Zanobi and Boccaccio copied it.

2. Text[7] and translation.

1   *Et ercle orcium pigam perteretem Hyaci fragrantis et Chie rosacee lotionibus expiauit.*
2   *Ac dein digitis, hypate licanos mese paramese et nete, hastam mei inguinis niuei spurci<ti>ei pluscule excoria<n>s emundauit.*
3   *Et cum ad inguinis cephalum formosa mulier concitim ueniebat ab orcibus, ganniens ego et dentes ad Iouem eleuans Priapo<n> frequenti frictura porrixabam ipsoque pando et repando uentrem sepiuscule tactabam.*
4   *Ipsa quoque, inspiciens quod genius inter antheras excreuerat, modicum illud morule, qua lustrum sterni mandauerat, anni sibi reuolutionem autumabat.*

1   And, by Hercules, she cleansed my round scrotum, my balls, with perfumed wine and rosewater of Chios.
2   And then with her fingers, thumb, forefinger, middle finger, ring finger and little finger, she withdrew the foreskin, and cleared the shaft of my penis of the plentiful whitish dirt.
3   And when the beautiful woman arrived very soon at the top of my penis from my testicles, braying and lifting my teeth toward the sky, I got, through the regular friction, an erection of the penis, and while it moved up and down I often touched her belly with it.
4   She as well, when she saw what came out of my penis among her perfumes, declared that that small delay, during which she had ordered our love-nest to be prepared, had been to her the orbit of a year.

The translation follows the commentary of Mariotti 1956,232-246.

3. Origin and date of the *spurcum additamentum*

Various theories have been advanced, and agreement has not yet been reached.

3.1 The *additamentum* is Apuleian, and was originally an integral part of book 10 of the *Met.*

Elmenhorst thought that Apuleius himself had written the *additamentum* as part of book 10 but in a second edition rejected it as being too obscene. In his edition of 1621 Elmenhorst did not adopt the fragment, which he clearly regarded as an author's variant. Floridus, too, considered the *additamentum* authentic, but in his edition *in usum Delphini* of 1688 he placed the fragment at the end of a list of *obscoena ex apuleiano textu resecta et ad*

---

7   The text printed here follows Mariotti 1956,231 f.; for a concise but lucid critical apparatus, see Mariotti 1956,232. The division into paragraphs is borrowed from Merkelbach 1952.

calcem reiecta (p. 833 f.). Oudendorp, in his commentary on Ruhnken's edition (1786), was convinced that Apuleius could very well have written this fragment; however, he expressed some doubt about its authenticity because it has no parallel in the *Onos*: in other respects the text of this episode in the *Onos* parallels Apuleius' version completely.

In more recent times, Herrmann 1951, in a reaction to Mazzarino 1950 (see below, 3.3), argued that the fragment is an integral part of book 10 and should be placed at the end of chapter 21, after the words of endearment spoken by the *matrona* to the ass.[8] He argues that the fragment is no more pornographic than 8,29 (200,16-22).

The most elaborate recent defense of the authenticity is by Pennisi 1970. According to him, its obscenity is part and parcel of the strategy of the author, who thus intensifies the contrast between base vulgarity in a world without (or before) Isis and the purity and light of a life with Isis (Pennisi 1970,235). Pennisi supports his thesis by a careful comparison of the *Onos* and the Latin *Metamorphoses*, and an extensive commentary, which, although it offers many acute observations on Apuleius' use of his Vorlage, and on his style and vocabulary in general, fails to offer a convincing refutation of Mariotti's detailed investigation of this text (see below, 3.3).

3.2 The *additamentum* is not by Apuleius, but its origin and date cannot be determined.

The fact that both Zanobi and Boccaccio wrote the *additamentum* in the margin of their manuscripts is an indication that it was already an *additamentum* in the margin of the manuscript from which they copied it. It certainly does not indicate that they considered it authentic.[9] Its status as a marginal addition, moreover, makes it impossible to compare it with the famous 'Winstedt fragment', a part of Juvenal's sixth satire found only in one Beneventan manuscript, where, however, it is an integral part of the text, not an addition in the margin.[10]

A succinct discussion of the different arguments advanced against its being written by Apuleius may suffice; counter-arguments which have been - or could be - brought forward will be noted as well. The arguments may broadly be divided into those on a) content and b) style and vocabulary.

a) Content. Hildebrand was the first to point out the difference between the straightforward pornography in this addition and Apuleius' much more subtle descriptions of the lovemaking of Lucius and Fotis in e.g. 2,16-17 and 3,20 'festiviter et lepide, libidines lectoris placide magis titillans, quam violenter perturbans'. This argument of Hildebrand is adopted by e.g. Journoud 1965. It will be clear, however, that arguments based on personal taste rather than on factual evidence may easily be reversed. Hildebrand, however, based his rejection of the *additamentum* on other arguments as well (see below on b) Vocabulary).

The unreliability of arguments based on the 'obscenity' of the fragment, that is to say, on how explicit we think Apuleius is likely to be in passages about sex, is obvious; it is neatly exposed e.g. by Winkler 1985,193: 'Readers who recoil from this episode ...

---

8   Van den Broeck 1988 is the only translator who includes the fragment, following Herrmann in inserting it at the end of 21.

9   Cf. Pecere 1987,105: '... la loro iniziativa sembra piuttosto rispecchiare un atteggiamento tipicamente umanistico verso i vettori dei classici, il quale se esplica nel recupero completo del loro contenuto, in un' ottica filologica "moderna" che non trascura, in quanto parte integrante di una tradizione testuale, nessun particolare o elemento accessorio presente nelle fonti.'

10 A comparison made by Mazzarino 1950,15 f.; Pennisi 1970,41; Pizzica 1981,764.

castrate the text at its most graphic moment. The sentence describing the ass's erection, omitted in F but recovered in the margin of φ, has not only been banished by most scholars as non-Apuleian for inadequate reasons, it has even been assigned the insulting name of *spurcum additamentum*, "the dirty addition" '.[11] However, as Oudendorp already observed, it is remarkable that, while Apuleius' text in this part of book 10 runs completely parallel to the text of the *Onos*, there is nothing in the *Onos* comparable to the text of the *spurcum additamentum*; this is contrary to what may be observed in other parts of the *Met.*: in passages which give rise to obscene descriptions, the *Onos* tends to be more extensive and explicit than the *Met.*; if the *spurcum additamentum* were to be accepted as authentic, it would run counter to the pattern observable in such passages everywhere else.

Another argument, also based on content, against the authenticity of the fragment is that in par. 4 the woman experiences the preparation of the bed (*lustrum sterni*) as an unbearable delay, whereas the eunuchs have already prepared the bed and left the room in ch. 20.[12] I would add that the choice of the term *lustrum* in itself provides an argument against Apuleian authorship. *Lustrum* means either a muddy place, or, mostly in the plural, the haunts of wild beasts, and then also (often, from Plautus onward), a place of debauchery (see Brown on Lucr. 4,1136). Apuleius once uses the noun *lustrum* as derived from *lustrare* (*Apol.* 89,4), which does not apply here (see *OLD* s.v. *lustrum²*). The other noun *lustrum*, connected with *lutum* (*OLD* s.v. *lustrum¹*) occurs in Apuleius only here and in *Apol.* 74,6, where it means 'place of debauchery, den of vice': *libidinum ganearumque locus, lustrum, lupanar ... cunctis probris palam notus*. In our episode, Apuleius has the narrator make a special effort to stress the very human treatment of the ass by the woman, and the purity and sincerity of her love: in his *cubiculum* she has had a real bed spread on the ground (*terrestrem cubitum*), with Tyrian purple, cushions, etc. The author would have spoilt his own strategy by having the woman now suddenly call this bed a *lustrum*.

b) Vocabulary. Hildebrand argued against the authenticity of the fragment on the grounds of, first, the great number of grecisms, which is inconsistent with Apuleius' restraint in using grecisms except for those in daily use in Latin long before him, and, secondly, the complete ignorance of Greek betrayed by the would-be Greek names for the fingers in par. 2. Both these points play an important role in the discussions about the origin and

---

11 Winkler (like Hermann) does not give sufficient weight to the fact that this fragment is transmitted in the margin, and that F does not have it at all. Pennisi thinks that Sallustius Crispus, who at the end of the 4th cent. A.D. revised the late antique codex from which F's ancestor stems, was responsible for athetizing this part of the text (Pennisi 1970,241 f. and 249-252). However, as Pecere 1987 rightly remarks, this means attributing to Crispus Sallustius' edition the characteristics of a modern philological edition, and this is not how the *emendatores* of late antiquity proceeded (see Pecere 1987,104, with references in n. 38).

12 This circumstance is one of the main arguments adduced by those who maintain that the *spurcum additamentum* is a fragment of a parallel narrative about the lovemaking of a woman and an ass, which at one point of the tradition was added as a *locus similis* in the margin of a manuscript of Apuleius' *Metamorphoses* (see below, 3.2.2). Mariotti 1956,242 f., on the other hand, argues that the medieval interpolator (see below, 3.3) cleverly placed the remark of the woman at the end of the *additamentum*; her reference to the unbearable delay caused by the spreading of the bed is to be connected with the other terms of endearment which follow in Apuleius' text right after the point where the *additamentum* would be interpolated.

date of the *spurcum additamentum*, as will be shown below.[13]

In addition to Hildebrand, both Butler and Robertson have, likewise on grounds of content and style, argued against Apuleius as author of the fragment, without hazarding any opinion about its real origin and date. Both think that its corrupt state suggests a date earlier than the Middle Age or early Renaissance.[14] Mariotti 1965, however, has shown that it is not as corrupt as his predecessors supposed.

3.2.1 The *additamentum* is an authentic fragment of a now lost African *recensio plenior* of the *Met.*

As has been shown above, Elmenhorst supposed that the *additamentum* was once part of an earlier recension of the *Met.*, rejected by Apuleius himself in a second edition. The fragment could have been added in the margin of a manuscript of the shorter version by someone who still had access to manuscripts representing the African *recensio plenior*. The corrupt state of the fragment could be due to medieval interpolation. This idea has been adopted and extended by Lavagnini 1950,203 f., who argued that Apuleius first wrote a purely amusing Milesian story of an ass in the style of Sisenna, but after an inner conversion rewrote his story, adding e.g. the Tale of Cupid and Psyche and the Isis book, and deleting among other things our fragment. Lavagnini's idea is a partial adoption of the thesis of Mazzarino 1950 (see 3.2.2).

Recently, Pizzica 1981 has revived the theory that the fragment is authentic, but to uphold it he has had to resort to considerable alterations in the text.[15]

3.2.2 The *additamentum* is originally a fragment from an ass story written by Sisenna.

In 1950 Mazzarino advanced the thesis that with the *spurcum additamentum* we may have recovered an authentic fragment of Sisenna, once added as a *locus similis* in the margin of the African *recensio plenior* of the *Met.* His idea is based on the assumption that there was a *recensio plenior* of the *Met.*, which from the 4th to 6th century A.D. was in use in scholarly circles in North Africa, where a genuine interest in the works of Apuleius, the famous fellow-countryman, went hand in hand with the grammarians' interest in the peculiar Latin of the republican translator of Aristides' *Milesiaka*, Sisenna.[16] Mazzarino's thesis was enthusiastically received by Merkelbach 1952, who welcomed the discovery of a new page to be added to our scarce fragments of Sisenna. He disagreed, however, with Mazzarino's suggestion that Fulgentius' quotations from Apuleius' *Cupid and Psyche*, which show considerable divergence from the received text, indicate that Fulgentius was

---

13 As for the first of these two points, the presence of many grecisms in this fragment is in itself not a decisive argument against its authenticity; Pennisi 1970,209 f. collects all Greek words in the *Met.*, many of which, indeed, were in use in Latin long before Apuleius, but some of which are *hapax legomena* or attested for the first time in the *Met.* Pennisi 1970,213, moreover, shows that Apuleius has a tendency to use grecisms in clusters.

14 Butler 1914, Introd. XXIX; Robertson, in Robertson - Vallette 1940-1945, tome I, Introd. XLII.

15 I have not been able to trace Pizzica's more extensive treatment of the *additamentum* which he announces in a note on p. 763 of his 1981 article.

16 On the attested didactic use of examples taken from Sisenna's translation of the *Milesiaka* by grammarians, see Stramaglia 1996,145 f., with references in notes.

using the supposed *recensio plenior*. Merkelbach proposed a new stemma, in which the tale of the ass and the woman in Aristides' *Milesiaka* was the source of both a Latin version by Sisenna and a tale in the Greek ass story of which the *Onos* is an epitome (see Introd. **2.3**). Both Apuleius' *Met.* and the pseudo-Lucianic *Onos* stem from this Greek ass story. The *spurcum additamentum* might then have been written as a parallel passage from Sisenna's work in the margin of a manuscript of the Latin *Met.* used in the scholarly circles mentioned above. With such a stemma, however, one cannot but wonder why a parallel to the *spurcum additamentum* is absent from the *Onos*.

3.3 The *additamentum* is a clever *lusus* by an erudite medieval interpolator.

On the basis of evidence from the Thesaurus Linguae Latinae, Fraenkel 1953 showed that words like *excorians* and *(anni) reuolutionem*, used by 'Spurcus', as he called the author of the fragment, cannot possibly have come from the pen of a republican author like Sisenna. Moreover, he provided convincing proof that for the curious enumeration of the fingers in par. 2, which has nothing to do with the Greek names for fingers (except *licanos*), 'Spurcus' was inspired by a passage from Boethius' *De institutione musica*. Fraenkel 1953,153: 'There he (Spurcus) read (1, 20, p. 206,18 Friedlein) that the third string was called 'lichanos', *quoniam lichanos digitus dicitur, quem nos indicem vocamus...* As he went on he read this: *Quarta dicitur mese ... quinta est paramese ... septima autem dicitur nete ...* (of *hypate* something had been said earlier, l. 12 f.)'. Fraenkel suggests that 'Spurcus' himself probably knew that of these terms only *lichanos* had something to do with the fingers of the hand, but was '... quite content with seizing a purple patch to dazzle his contemporaries, whom he could confidently expect to be as ignorant of Greek as he was himself'. Fraenkel concluded that 'Spurcus' must have lived after the end of the ancient world, and expressed the hope that, after further investigation of the fragment other scholars would be able to indentify more accurately the period in which it was written.

In 1956 Mariotti published the results of such an investigation: he gives a careful analysis of the text of the *additamentum* by means of an extensive commentary (Mariotti 1956,230-246), summarizing his conclusions at 246 f. Further, he shows convincingly that in several places the text is less corrupt than scholars had hitherto supposed.

That this is a medieval text was already suggested by Fraenkel 1953, and his assumption is proved correct and refined by Mariotti's detailed linguistic discussion of several words and phrases. As to the misleading list of Greek terms for the five fingers, Mariotti agrees with Fraenkel that it must come from a deliberate mystification of Boethius' discussion of the strings, but considers it not as an attempt to 'dazzle his contemporaries', but as 'una di quelle leggerezze dei dotti medievali che spesso a noi sembrano inconcepibili' (Mariotti 1956,236 n. 2).

The author shows an acute awareness of Apuleian stylistics. This appears from several clever Apuleian coinages and phrases (which have fooled some scholars into considering the *additamentum* as authentic Apuleius; see Mariotti 1956,249, with notes), as pointed out in several of Mariotti's notes in the commentary.[17] It is well known that the eleventh century was a period in which Apuleius' works, especially the *Met.*, profited from the

---

17 But in his zeal to imitate his model the falsarius sometimes betrays himself, as Mariotti 1956,241 shows, e.g. in his note on *porrixabam* (par. 3).

climate of cultural renaissance at Monte Cassino. From that time onward, rediscovered and read with renewed stylistic awareness, they became a model to be imitated.[18]

The author of the *additamentum* shows a remarkable knowledge of anatomy and medical technical terms, as appears from several of Mariotti's notes. This may suggest that he was one of the *eruditi* who shared in the heyday of renewed medical studies (especially of anatomy and physiology) that spread from the School of Salerno throughout Southern Italy, and flourished at Monte Cassino in the eleventh century.[19] The frankness and gusto with which the author treats his subject makes it impossible, according to Mariotti (247 f.), to date him before the twelfth century.

4 Conclusion.

Mariotti 1956 shows that there can be no doubt about the medieval origin of the *spurcum additamentum*.[20] Thus it has no place in the text of the *Met.* Its proper place is the apparatus criticus, since it will continue to be significant to investigators of the *Met.*, and especially of the circulation of copies produced at Monte Cassino from the eleventh century onward, some of which had already left the monastery before Zanobi's discovery (Pecere 1987,105).

---

18 See Pecere 1987,103 f., with references, on the direct and indirect evidence of the use of Apuleius as a model.
19 See Pecere 1987,105 with n. 41.
20 Its date may be a bit earlier than Mariotti assumes (Pecere 1987,121).

APPENDIX III

Generic shifts in the two inner tales of this book, and the function of these tales.

Summary of the two tales:

Chs. 2-12: A woman falls in love with her stepson. Having become ill with love, she finally reveals her love to him and attempts to seduce him. When, because of his repeated excuses, the woman understands that the young man has no intention of complying with her wishes, her love turns to hatred. She charges a trusted slave with the task of murdering her stepson. However, the poisoned cup is mistakenly drained by the woman's own son. She now accuses her stepson of both the murder of his younger brother and attempts at seduction and violence toward her. Her husband believes her and publicly demands that the young man be punished. The matter is taken to court. The slave's false evidence convinces everyone of the young man's guilt. At the last moment, a wise physician turns the tide by revealing that the slave, who had come to him to buy poison, had aroused his suspicion: therefore, as a precaution, the doctor had given him a strong sleeping potion instead. All go to the newly-dug grave and find the younger brother, who has just awakened. Now the entire truth comes to light and the guilty are punished.

Chs. 23-28: A woman, who already had a son and was pregnant again, had been ordered by her husband to kill the baby if it were a girl. While the husband is away on a trip, the woman gives birth to a girl. Instead of killing the baby, she gives it to neighbours. When the girl has reached marriageable age, the mother tells the secret about the girl to her son. He does not betray the secret, but he takes the girl into his family and gives her in marriage to a good friend. His wife, however — the very woman with whom Lucius, the ass will have to perform in the theatre — becomes mad with jealousy and kills the girl in a gruesome manner. The brother becomes ill with grief, and his wife decides to dispose of him as well. With the help of a criminal physician she has him poisoned; moreover, she forces the physician to take poison himself. Just before he dies, he tells his wife what has happened, urging her to claim the fee for the poison he has supplied. When, to this end, the doctor's widow goes to see the murderess, the evil woman poisons her too, along with her own young daughter. Before she dies, however, the doctor's widow manages to reveal everything to the *praeses*, who condemns the murderess *ad bestias*.

The survey studies devoted to the entire *Metamorphoses* usually pay much attention to the function of the inner tales of the early books within the framing story. The literature on the function of the story of Amor and Psyche (*Met.* 4,28-6,24) is also quite extensive. Less attention is paid to the function of the inner tales in books 7, 8, and 9; however, this has been corrected by the *GCA* commentaries, which discuss this issue at length. The tenth book is usually treated quite cursorily in the survey studies: they treat the first books with their intriguing inner stories in great detail and discuss Amor and Psyche at length; but before entering into an extensive discussion of the eleventh book (the 'Isis book') they confine themselves to remarking that the world of books 8, 9, and 10 becomes increasingly gloomy and oppressive. As to the tenth book, they often still cite or paraphrase the remark by Dornseiff 1938,226 f.: 'Buch 8, 9 und 10 wachsen sich in sichtlichen Steigerung von Greueln und Peripetien zu einem Inferno aus, das auf das Purgatorio des 11. Buches vorbereitet'.[1]

Tatum 1969 modifies Dornseiff's statement by pointing out that the 'inferno'-like atmosphere of the tenth book is not found in the main story. Indeed, up to his planned performance in the theatre, the narrator presents a rather sunny outlook on his existence again, the first for a long time; he even succeeds in imparting to the reader his intense enjoyment of the spectacles in the theatre preceding his own performance.[2] Consequently, Tatum concludes that the increasingly pessimistic image of society is found only in the two inner tales, and that through his initiation into the cult of Isis Lucius turns his back on this depraved society. However, there are a few objections to this opinion.

The image of society in these stories is less gloomy than Tatum suggests: opposite the evil, ruthless women and their accomplices (the slave in the first story, the unscrupulous doctor in the second) we see characters of integrity and honour (the innocent young man and the wise physician in the first story, the mother and the brother in the second). Moreover, both tales are characterized by a high degree of poetic justice: the evil pay the penalty for their crimes. Even in the most gruesome murder story there are unmistakably moments of comic relief: in his dying hour, the avaricious physician urges his wife to claim the money for the poison he has supplied. This woman in her turn renders the equivalent of an operatic 'dying aria' when she gives the *praeses* a full and detailed account of the murderess's crimes.[3]

In addition, it is not quite correct to regard initiation into an ancient mystery-cult as a 'turning away from society'. Burkert [2]1991,23 f. emphasizes that someone who had been initiated into an ancient mystery-cult by no means turned his back on society; on the contrary, he remained an active participant. Lucius, too, continues to participate fully in Roman society after his initiation; as Burkert ibid. 24 says, he even 'wird nun endlich in die respektable, bürgerliche Gesellschaft integriert'.[4] Indeed, the entire idea of these inner tales reflecting an image of society becomes invalid when it is shown that these stories are playing with literary conventions.[5]

The two stories are meant to be read in combination with each other;[6] they are connected by several elements. Each is a family drama. The main character of each story is an evil and ultimately also murderous woman. The first story expresses hesitation whether she is 'naturally impudent or driven by *fatum* to the ultimate outrage'.[7] As to the woman in the second story, we are told that *Fortuna* is jealous of the harmonious atmosphere in

---

1   Cf. also Heath 1983,63 with n. 24.
2   See Zimmerman - de Graaf 1993,145 f.
3   See comm. on ch. 26 (258,4) *enarratis cunctis*; ch. 28 (259,14) *cunctis ... expositis*.
4   See also Habinek 1990.
5   Schmidt 1989,63 f. reveals a similar play with literary conventions in Apul. *Met.* 9,23 and 27.
6   For the connection of these two stories with the story of *Met.* 9,33-38 ('three murder stories'), see Hammer 1923,24-26 and Junghanns 1932,176 f.; Kautzky 1989 discusses the three tales in their connection as three 'family tragedies'.
7   Ch. 2 (237,10 f.) *seu naturaliter impudica seu fato ad extremum impulsa flagitium.*

the household to which the woman belongs, and therefore sends *Riualitas*.[8] Whereas in the first story *Fortuna* is responsible for a surprisingly happy ending, in the second story she is the instigator of a turn for the worse. Thus the tales are also connected by *Fortuna*'s opposite actions.[9] Further, in both stories a physician plays an important part. In the first story he is a paragon of uprightness and common sense and saves the innocent young man from the death sentence. In the second story he is an avaricious, unscrupulous physician, reminiscent of the doctors found in satire, epigram, and anecdote.[10] In both tales the wicked woman is assisted by a devoted slave; in both tales poison, acquired for a high prize, plays a role. Both end with a victory of justice.

The first story is based on a motif from tragedy. The narrator emphasizes this by mentioning that the reader will rise from *soccus* to *cothurnus*, thus inviting the reader to direct her/his attention to the generic backgrounds of this story.[11] Before long, the reader's expectations as to the continuation and outcome of the story, which were awakened by the reference to tragedy, are countered: the *nouerca*, who at first showed many characteristics of the tragic Phaedra, changes in ch. 4 to the type of the wicked stepmother of the novel, mime,[12] and *declamationes*.[13] This development in her characterization is brought about by her stepson's 'wrong' (i.e. 'not corresponding with the convention of tragedy') reaction to her declaration of love. To the perceptive reader it was obvious from the beginning that this stepson was no Hippolytus.[14] This actor in the story 'resists' that Hippolytus-role; he deliberately acts differently from Hippolytus.[15] The same applies to the 'Theseus' of our story: true, he shows Theseus' credulity (a trait for which Theseus is regularly criticized in ancient literature),[16] but as a bourgeois paterfamilias in a provincial town he lacks his tragic predecessor's heroic stature.[17] This, too, has consequences for the further development of the story. By the time the *nouerca* has definitively left the 'Phaedra' model (see above) and buys poison through her slave — himself a conventional accomplice from comedy, mime, and novel[18] — the reader has adjusted his expectations about the development of the story. But her/his expectations are countered again, and this time most surprisingly,[19] in ch. 8 with the appearance of the *medicus*. He, too, resists the conventional role expected of him in the generic context toward which the tale has evolved: that of the avaricious,

---

8 Ch. 24 (255,17 f.) *Sed haec bene atque optime plenaque cum sanctimonia disposita feralem Fortunae nutum latere non potuerunt, cuius instinctu domum iuuenis protinus se direxit saeua Riualitas. Et ilico haec ... uxor eius ... coepit puellam ... primum suspicari, dehinc detestari, dehinc crudelissimis laqueis mortis insidiari.*

9 See also Introd. **2.4.1**.

10 See comm. on *medicus* ch. 8 (243,8 f.); *centumque aureos solidos* ch. 25 (243,19).

11 See the introduction to Appendix I.

12 See Appendix I,5.4.

13 See Appendix I,5.5.

14 See Appendix I,6B, which also refers to the relevant notes in the commentary.

15 See comm. on ch. 4 (239,2 f.) *... non tamen negationis intempestiua seueritate putauit exasperandum, sed cautae promissionis dilatione leniendum.*

16 See comm. on ch. 5 (240,23 f.); also Appendix I,6A.

17 See comm. on ch. 4 (239,15) *uillulas*, and on ch. 6 (241,1 f.).

18 See Appendix I,6C.

19 Most surprisingly, because the *medicus* does not reveal his real part in the story until the very end, so that both the reader and the actors in the story find that they have misinterpreted the 'facts' up to that point. See comm. on *exanimis terrae procumbit* ch. 4 (240,5).

unscrupulous provider of poison.[20]

Thus, one of the ways to read this story and note its peripeties is to observe the incapacity, sometimes even refusal, of the actors to stay within the limits of their parts, which are defined by generic conventions.[21]

Even though the second story has no formal introduction, the *litterati* among the readers will realize at once that it begins with a motif from comedy.[22] This is a typical example of an open space, a 'Leerstelle', which the reader is supposed to fill in on the basis of the other lines of connection between the stories, which are outlined above.[23] The theme of the abandoned child - who grows up among strangers but, as an adult, is eventually recognized and acknowledged by its family after many complications, which are thus brought to a happy conclusion - is an intertexteme[24] held in common by a large group of comedies. A fixed element in the comedies connected by this theme is the recognition-token.[25] Thus, on the basis of the beginning of this story the reader can form a pattern of expectations about its intrigue and happy ending; however, the story turns into an accumulation of atrocious murders. Here, too, the new turn in the story is brought about by actors stepping out of roles determined by the convention of the genre. First the mother, in order to prevent the girl's brother from falling in love with his own sister (a frequent situation in comedy), of her own accord informs her son of the situation.[26] The brother arranges everything most honourably, but this is not to *Fortuna*'s liking.[27] In other words, *Fortuna* is going to take action not as the benevolent Τύχη, who according to the convention of comedy brings everything to a happy conclusion, but as the cruel, fickle power whose unfathomable actions have been frequently discussed by the narrator in the course of the *Met*.[28] From this point *Riualitas* exerts her destructive influence, turning the brother's wife into a murderess. A signet ring, the recognition token par excellence which 'puts the seal' on the happy ending in so many comedies, becomes a lethal weapon in the hands of this murderess.[29]

Reading the two tales in this way, one can observe how these stories have a foreshadowing

---

20 See comm. on *non patiar ... hercules, non patiar* ch. 11 (244,24 f.).
21 Frangoulidis, in a forthcoming article in *Scholia*, investigates a case of role-changing in the Tale of the Miller's Wife (*Met*. 9,14-14).
22 And from the ancient novel; see Kudlien 1989,25 f.
23 One of the functions of the 'Leerstelle', as defined by Iser 1976, is to mark the connection between different parts of the text by deliberately refraining from making connections that are necessary for a proper understanding. It is up to the reader to reconstruct these 'missing links', in keeping with the structure of the text. (Formulation after Segers ²1984,39.)
24 For this term see Appendix I,6 with note.
25 Cf. Satyrus, *Vita Euripidis* 39 VII,8-22 Arrighetti (= *P.Oxy* 1176,VII) βιασμοὺς παρθένων, ὑποβολὰς παιδίων, ἀναγνωρισμοὺς διά τε δακτυλίων καὶ διὰ δεραίων, ταῦτα γάρ ἐστι δήπου τὰ συνέχοντα τὴν νεωτέραν κωμῳδίαν.
26 Ch. 23 (255,7 f.): *filio suo tacitum secretum aperuit. nam et oppido uerebatur, ne quo casu, caloris iuuenalis impetu lapsus, nescius nesciam sororem incurreret.*
27 See the quotation from ch. 24 (255,17 f.) in note 8 of this Appendix.
28 See Introd. **2.4.1**.
29 Ch. 24 (255,26 f.) *Anulo mariti surrepto ... mittit quendam seruulum ..., qui puellae nuntiaret, quod eam iuuenis profectus ad uillulam uocaret ad sese, addito, ut sola et sine ullo comite quam maturissime perueniret. Et ne qua forte nasceretur ueniendi cunctatio, tradit anulum marito subtractum, qui monstratus fidem uerbis adstipularetur. At illa ... respecto etiam signo eius, quod offerebatur, nauiter ... incomitata festinat.*

function for the framing tale.[30] At the end of book 10, Lucius, the ass refuses to play the part expected from him, that of an actor in a pantomime of Pasiphaë.[31] But earlier in the book he aroused all kinds of expectations in his master that he truly would be such a willing actor: by his overzealous performance in the company of parasites around Thiasus,[32] by his ready assent to being coached and, like a celebrated *histrio*,[33] being pampered, and by his compliance to the desires of the *matrona*. By refusing to keep up that part, which by now he finds too dangerous, he changes the course of the story. As the good doctor in the first story took the place of the evil doctor intended by the *nouerca*, so Isis, with her healing power and *diuina prouidentia*, steps forward as 'dea ex machina' in the framing story, driving away *saeua Fortuna*. From a burlesque story about a human being in an ass's body (as the *Onos* is to the end) the narrative of the *Met.* turns into an aretalogy of Isis (see Introd. **2.3**).

Not only does the narrator as *actor* abandon his part. The narrator as *auctor*, too, appears increasingly reluctant to confine himself to the narration of entertaining and amusing stories.[34]

The two inner stories with their parallelism and antithesis (the first story changing from impending doom to happy ending, the second showing the reverse, changing from expected happy dénouement to horror story) illustrate together how the actors, by stepping out of their parts as defined by a generic context or by deliberately refusing to play those parts, can drastically influence the course and the generic context of a story. Similarly, when the ass flees from the theatre, no longer prepared to play the part expected of him, he takes his own story to a new intertextual environment. Although recent studies, on the basis of sound arguments, question the seriousness of the religious tone of book 11,[35] it cannot be denied that at the end of book 10 the *Metamorphoses* severs the intertextual relationship with the *Onos*, and 'though the contrast in relation to the first ten books does seem less pronounced than is generally stated, the "book of Isis" nevertheless remains a curious appendix, whose overall tonality differs from the one dominating the Milesian books'.[36]

---

30 The foreshadowing function of the inner stories in the first book has been demonstrated by many. See e.g. Tatum 1969,487 f.; Sandy 1972,232 f.
31 See Frangoulidis 1999,131 n. 35 on the contrast between Lucius' refusal to re-enact the Pasiphaë tale, and Thrasyleons willing assumption and performance to the bitter end of the bear's role in *Met.* 4,13-21.
32 See Introd. **2.5.1**.
33 See comm. on *saltare* ch. 17 (250,1).
34 Cf. also Hofmann 1993a. On the narrator as *actor* and as *auctor*, see Introd. **3.5**. For the narrator 'stepping out of his part' see also Zimmerman - de Graaf 1993,153 f.; Zimmerman 1999.
35 See Harrison 1996,513 f.; Van Mal - Maeder 1997b, with references.
36 Van Mal - Maeder 1997b,110.

BIBLIOGRAPHY

I. Abbreviations

AAGA: B.L. Hijmans jr. - R.Th. van der Paardt, edd., *Aspects of Apuleius' Golden Ass, a collection of original papers*, Groningen 1978.
AAGA 2: M. Zimmerman, S. Panayotakis et alii, edd., *Aspects of Apuleius' Golden Ass. Vol. II. Cupid and Psyche*, Groningen 1998.
ALL: *Archiv für lateinische Lexikographie und Grammatik*, ed. E. Wölfflin, Leipzig 1884-1909.
ANRW: H. Temporini, W. Haase, Hrsg., *Aufstieg und Niedergang der Römischen Welt*, 1972 - ...
Blaise: A. Blaise, *Dictionnaire Latin-Français des Auteurs Chrétiens*, Turnhout 1954.
CIL: *Corpus Inscriptionum Latinarum*, Berlin, 1863-.
Dar.-Sagl.: C.R. Daremberg - E. Saglio, *Dictionnaire des Antiquités grecques et romaines*, 5 vols., Paris 1877-1919.
DNP: H. Cancik, H. Schneider, *Der Neue Pauly. Enzyklopädie der Antike*, Stuttgart 1996 - ...
E-M: A. Ernout - A. Meillet, *Dictionnaire étymologique de la langue latine*, Paris ^{4}1979 (3rd ed. of E-M 1959-1960, with add. and corr.)
EV: F. Della Corte, ed., *Enciclopedia Virgiliana*, 6 vols., Roma 1984-91.
Ernout-
Thomas: A. Ernout - F. Thomas, *Syntaxe latine*, Paris ^{2}1959.
GCA: *Groningen Commentaries on Apuleius* (see Bibliography Part II).
GCN: *Groningen Colloquia on the Novel*, ed. H. Hofmann, Groningen, 1988 - 1995; edd. H. Hofmann and M. Zimmerman, Groningen 1996 - 1998.
Georges: K.E. Georges, *Ausführliches lateinisch-deutsches Handwörterbuch*, 8e Aufl. von H. Georges, 2 Bde., Hannover etc. 1913-18.
Heumann-
Seckel: H. Heumann- E. Seckel, *Handlexikon zu den Quellen des römischen Rechts*, Graz ^{11}1971.
Hofmann,
LU: J.B. Hofmann, *Lateinische Umgangssprache*, Heidelberg ^{4}1978.
KlP: K.Ziegler, W.Sontheimer, H.Gärtner (Hrsg.): *Der kleine Pauly. Lexikon der Antike. Auf der Grundlage von Pauly's Realencyclopädie der classischen Altertumswissenschaft bearb. unter Mitwirkung zahlr. Fachgelehrter.*
Krebs-
Schmalz: J.Ph. Krebs, *Antibarbarus der Lateinischen Sprache*, 7th ed. by J.H. Schmalz, I-II, Basel 1905-1907.
KSt: R. Kühner - C. Stegmann, *Ausführliche Grammatik der lateinischen Sprache*, Hannover 1912-14.
LHSz 2: M. Leumann - J.B. Hofmann - A. Szantyr, *Lateinische Grammatik II (Syntax und Stilistik)*, München 1965.
LIMC: *Lexicon Iconographicum Mythologiae Classicae*, Zürich - München 1981-.
LS: Ch.T. Lewis - Ch. Short, *A Latin Dictionary*, Oxford 1879.
LSJ: H.G. Liddell - R. Scott - H. Stuart Jones - R. McKenzie, *A Greek-English Lexicon*, Oxford 1958 (repr.).
Neue-
Wagener: F. Neue - C. Wagener, *Formenlehre der lateinischen Sprache*, Leipzig ^{3}1892-1905.
OLD: *Oxford Latin Dictionary*, Oxford 1968-82.
Oldfather: W.A. Oldfather - H.V. Canter - B.E. Perry, *Index Apuleianus*, Middletown 1934.
RAC: *Reallexicon für Antike und Christentum*, Stuttgart, 1950-
RE: *Realencyclopädie der classischen Altertumswissenschaft*, Stuttgart 1894- ...
SAG: B.L. Hijmans Jr., V. Schmidt, edd., Collected papers of the 'Symposium Apuleianum Groninganum', 23-24 Oct. 1980.

ThLL: *Thesaurus Linguae Latinae*, Leipzig-Stuttgart 1900-...
Walde-
Hofmann: A. Walde - J.B. Hofmann, *Lateinisches etymologisches Wörterbuch*, Heidelberg ²1938 (repr. 1966).

II. Editions, commentaries and translations of Apuleius' *Metamorphoses*.

(Only those quoted in this commentary have been listed here. Full bibliographies of Apuleian studies are to be found in *GCA* 1977-1995)

Editions

F. Eyssenhardt, *Apulei Met. Libri XI*, Berlin 1868.

J. Van der Vliet, *Lucii Apulei Met. Libri XI*, Leipzig 1897.

R. Helm, *Apulei Opera quae supersunt I: Met. Libri XI*, Leipzig ³1931 (reprint with addenda 1955).

C. Giarratano, *Apulei Met. Libri XI*, Torino 1929 (²1960 by P. Frassinetti).

D.S. Robertson - P. Vallette (Coll. Budé), 3 vols., Paris 1940-1945 (²1956).

F. Carlesi - N. Terzaghi, *Apuleio, Gli XI Libri delle Metamorfosi. Traduzione di F. Carlesi. Testo critico riveduto da N. Terzaghi*, Firenze 1954.

R. Helm, *Apuleius, Metamorphosen oder Der goldene Esel. Lateinisch und Deutsch*, Berlin 1956 (⁶1970 by W. Krenkel).

E. Brandt - W. Ehlers, *Apuleius, Der goldene Esel. Lateinisch und Deutsch*, München 1958 (³1980); repr. 1989 with a new Introduction and Bibliography by N. Holzberg (549 f.).

P. Scazzoso, *Apuleio, Metamorfosi. Edizione critica con traduzione e note*, Milano 1971.

J.A. Hanson, *Apuleius, Metamorphoses*, edition with an English translation, 2 vols. (Loeb Class. Libr.), London 1989.

Complete commentaries on the *Metamorphoses*

Beroaldus, F. *Commentarii a Philippo Beroaldo conditi in Asinum Aureum Lucii Apulei*, Bononiae 1500.

Oudendorp, F., *Appulei Opera Omnia, I: Met.* ed. D. Ruhnken, Lugduni Batavorum 1786 (Vol. III ed. J. Bosscha, Lugd. Bat. 1823 contains the commentaries by Beroaldus and Pricaeus).

Hildebrand, G.F., *Apulei Opera Omnia, I: Met.*, Leipzig 1842 (repr. Hildesheim 1968).

Valpy, A.I., *L. Apulei opera Ex editione Oudendorpiana cum notis et interpretationibus in usum delphini*, London 1825.

Commentaries on individual books or parts of the Metamorphoses

I   M. Molt, *Ad Apulei Madaurensis Met. Librum Primum Commentarius Exegeticus*, Diss. Groningen 1938.
        A. Scobie, *Apuleius Met. (Asinus Aureus) I*, Meisenheim am Glan 1975.
II   B.J. De Jonge, *Ad Apulei Madaurensis Met. Librum Secundum Commentarius Exegeticus*, Diss. Groningen 1941.
        D.K. Van Mal - Maeder, *Apulée. Les Métamorphoses. Livre II, 1-20. Introduction, texte, traduction et commentaire*, Diss. Groningen 1998.
        Van Mal - Maeder's commentary on the whole of Book II as another volume of *GCA* is forthcoming.
III   R.Th. van der Paardt, *L. Apuleius Madaurensis, The Met.: A commentary on book III with text and introduction*, Diss. Groningen, Amsterdam 1971.
IV   B.L. Hijmans Jr. - R.Th. van der Paardt - E.R. Smits - R.E.H. Westendorp Boerma - A.G. Westerbrink, *Apuleius Madaurensis, Metamorphoses, Book IV 1-27. Text, Introduction and Commentary*, Groningen 1977 (= *GCA* 1977).
IV-VI   P. Grimal, *Apulei Metamorphoseis IV,28-VI,24*, Paris 1963; ²1976.
        E.J. Kenney, *Apuleius, Cupid and Psyche*, Cambridge 1990.
        C. Moreschini, *Il Mito di Amore e Psiche in Apuleio. Saggio, Testo di Apuleio, Traduzione e Commento*, Naples 1994.

V   J.M.H. Fernhout, *Ad Apulei Madaurensis Met. Librum Quintum Commentarius Exegeticus*, Diss. Groningen, Middelburg 1949.
VI-VII B.L. Hijmans Jr. - R. Th van der Paardt - V. Schmidt - R.E.H. Westendorp Boerma - A.G. Westerbrink, *Apuleius Madaurensis Metamorphoses, Books VI 25-32 and VII, Text, Introduction and Commentary*, Groningen 1981 (= GCA 1981).
VIII   B.L. Hijmans Jr. - R.Th. van der Paardt - V. Schmidt - C.B.J. Settels - B. Wesseling - R.E.H. Westendorp Boerma, *Apuleius Madaurensis, Metamorphoses Book VIII, Text, Introduction and Commentary*, Groningen 1985 (= GCA 1985).
        C.R. Wohlers, *A Commentary on Apuleius' Metamorphoses, Book VIII*, Diss. State Univ. of New Jersey, 1986.
IX   B.L. Hijmans Jr. - R.Th. van der Paardt - V. Schmidt - B. Wesseling - M. Zimmerman, *Apuleius Madaurensis, Metamorphoses Book IX, Text, Introduction and Commentary*, Groningen 1995 (= GCA 1995).
        S. Mattiacci, *Apuleio, le novelle dell'adulterio (Metamorfosi IX). Traduzione con testo a fronte*, Firenze 1996.
XI   A. Marsili, *Apuleio, Metamorfosi L. XI (il libro dell'esoterismo)*, Pisa 1964.
        Chr. Harrauer, *Kommentar zum Isisbuch des Apuleius*, Diss. Wien 1973.
        J.C. Fredouille, *Apulée, Met. Livre XI* (Coll. Érasme), Paris 1975.
        J. Gwyn Griffiths, *Apuleius of Madauros. The Isis-Book (Met. Book XI), edited with an introduction, translation and commentary*, Leiden 1975.

Translations (see also above, under Editions and Commentaries)

C. Annaratone, *Apuleio. Le metamorfosi o l'asino d'oro, testo latino a fronte*, Milano 1977; [14]1996
G. D'Anna, *Lucio Apuleio. L'asino d'oro*, Roma 1995.
R. Graves, *The Transformations of Lucius, otherwise known as the Golden Ass*, Harmondsworth 1950.
H.J. Boeken, *Herscheppinge of de Gouden Ezel van L. Apuleius*, Amsterdam 1901.
M.A. Schwartz, *De Gouden Ezel, Metamorphosen, Roman van Apuleius*, Haarlem 1970.
S. Van den Broeck, *Apuleius Metamorphosen*, Antwerpen-Baarn 1988.
J.A. Hanson, *Apuleius, Metamorphoses*, edition with an English translation, 2 vols. (Loeb Class. Libr.), London 1989.
P.G. Walsh, *Apuleius. The Golden Ass. Translated with introduction and explanatory notes*, Oxford 1994.
M. Manara, *L'asino d'oro*, Milano 1999.

III. General Bibliography of studies referred to in this commentary
(Standard commentaries on ancient texts have not been included in this bibliography; they are referred to in the commentary as, e.g. 'Pease ad Verg. A. ...', 'Börner ad Ov....')

Aalto, P.A. 1949, *Untersuchungen über das lateinische Gerundium und Gerundivum*, Helsinki.
Abate, F.R. 1978. *Diminutives in Apuleian Latinity*, Diss. Ohio State University.
Abbott, F.F., Johnson, A.C. 1926. *Municipal Administration in the Roman Empire*, Princeton.
Adams, J.N. 1972. 'Latin Words for "Woman" and "Wife"', *Glotta* 50, 234-255.
    1982 ([2]1987). *The Latin Sexual Vocabulary*, London.
    1995. *Pelagonius and Latin veterinary terminology in the Roman Empire*, Leiden - New York - Köln.
Albrecht, M. von. [2]1983. *Meister römischer Prosa. Von Cato bis Apuleius*, Darmstadt: Lizenzausgabe 1984 of Heidelberg 1983.
Alperowitz, M. 1992. *Das Wirken und Walten der Götter im griechischen Roman*, Heidelberg.
Alpers, K. 1996. 'Zwischen Athen, Abdera und Samos. Fragmente eines unbekannten Romans aus der Zeit der Zweiten Sophistik', in: M. Billerbeck, J. Schamp (edd.), *Kainotomia. Die Erneuerung der griechischen Tradition*, Freiburg (Swiss), 19-55.
Amarelli, F. 1990. 'Apuleio: la testimonianza di un laico del diritto', *Index* 18, 93-100.
Amundsen, D.W. 1974. 'Romanticizing the ancient medical profession', *BHM* 68, 320-337.

Anderson, G. 1976. *Studies in Lucian's Comic Fiction*, Leiden.
    1982. *Eros Sophistes. Ancient Novelists at Play*, American Classical Studies 9, Chico, Ca.
    1989. 'The Pepaideumenos in Action: Sophists and their Outlook in the Early Empire', in: *ANRW* 2,33,1, 79-108.
André, J. 1961. *L'alimentation et la cuisine à Rome*, Paris.
Armini, H. 1928. 'Studia Apuleiana', *Eranos* 26, 273-339.
Arnaldi, F. 1959. 'L'episodio di Ifi nelle "Metamorfosi" di Ovidio (IX, 666 sgg.) e l' XI libro di Apuleio', *Atti del Convegno internationale Ovidiano, Sulmona, maggio 1958*, Roma, 371-375.
Augello, G. 1977. *Studi Apuleiani. Problemi di testo e loci vexati delle Metamorfosi*, Palermo.
Axelson, B. 1945. *Unpoetische Wörter. Ein Beitrag zur Kenntnis der lateinischen Dichtersprache*, Lund.
Baehrens, W.A. 1912. *Beiträge zur lateinischen Syntax, Philologus*, Supplementband 12.
Bal, M. ³1985. *De theorie van vertellen en verhalen. Inleiding in de narratologie*, Muiderberg.
Baldwin, B. 1983. *The Philogelos or Laughter-lover*, Amsterdam.
Barrett, W.S. 1992. *Euripides Hippolytos*, Oxford (= paperback edition of Barrett 1964).
Bartsch, S. 1989. *Decoding the Ancient Novel*, Princeton.
    1994. *Actors in the Audience. Theatricality and Doublespeak from Nero to Hadrian*, Cambridge, Mass. - London.
Beacham, R.C. 1995. *The Roman Theatre and its Audience*, London 1991 (paperback 1995).
Beard, M., North, J., Price, S. 1998. *Religions of Rome. Volume 1. A History; Volume 2. A Sourcebook*, Cambridge.
Berger, A. 1953. *Encyclopedic Dictionary of Roman Law*, Transactions of the American Philosophical Society 43, 335-808.
Bernardi Perini, G. 1995. 'Per la datazione del *Pervigilium Veneris*', in *Storia letteratura e arte a Roma nel secondo secolo dopo Cristo. Atti del Convegno Mantova, 8-9-10 ottobre 1992*, Firenze, 139-158.
Bernhard, M. 1927. *Der Stil des Apuleius von Madaura*, Stuttgart (repr. Amsterdam 1965).
Beschorner, A. 1992. *Untersuchungen zu Dares Phrygius*, Tübingen.
Beta, S., Nordera, M. 1992. *Luciano. La Danza*, Venezia.
Biasi, L. De. 1990. *Le descrizioni del paesaggio naturale nelle opere di Apuleio: aspetti letterari*, MAT 14.
Bieber, M. 1961. *The History of the Greek and Roman Theatre*, Princeton, NJ.
Bigorra, M. 1983. 'Hispanische Latinität und sprachliche Kontakte im römischen Hispanien', in: *ANRW* 2,29,2, 819-852.
Billanovich, G. 1953. *I primi umanisti e le tradizioni dei classici latini*, Freiburg.
Billotta, C. 1975. 'Note sulle Metamorfosi di Apuleio', in: Bonanno, E., Milazzo, V., Billotta, C., *Note linguistiche su Catone, Catullo ed Apuleio*, Catania, 41-68.
Binder, G., Merkelbach, R. 1968. edd., *Amor und Psyche*, Wege der Forschung 126, Darmstadt.
Blümner, H. 1912. *Technologie und Terminologie der Gewerbe und Künste bei Griechen und Römern*, Leipzig.
Bocciolini, P.L. 1986. 'Suggestioni Apuleiane nella Mandragola di Niccolò Macchiavelli', *A&R* 31, 159-170.
Boldrini, S. 1989. 'Il pasto della vedova: cibo, vino, sesso, da Petronio a J. Amado', in: *GCN* 2, 121-131.
Bompaire, J. 1958. *Lucien écrivain, imitation et création*, Paris.
Bonaria, M. 1965. *I Mimi Romani*, Roma.
Boswell, J. 1988. *The Kindness of Strangers. The Abandonment of Children in Western Europe from Late Antiquity to the Renaissance*, New York.
Bowersock, G.W. 1969. *Greek Sophists in the Roman Empire*, Oxford.
    1994. *Fiction as History. Nero to Julian*, Berkeley - Los Angeles - London.
Bowie, E.L. 1970. 'Greeks and their past in the Second Sophistic', *Past & Present* 46, 1-41.
Bracht Branham, R. 1996. 'Defacing the Currency: Diogenes' Rhetoric and the Invention of Cynicism', in: Bracht Branham, R. and Goulet-Cazé, M-O., edd., *The Cynics. The Cynic Movement in Antiquity and Its Legacy*, Berkeley - Los Angeles - London, 81-104.
Braun, M. 1934. *Griechischer Roman und hellenistische Geschichtschreibung*, Frankfurter Studien zur Religion und Kultur der Antike, Frankfurt am Main.
Brecht, F.J. 1930. *Motiv- und Typengeschichte des griechischen Spott-Epigramms*, Philologus Suppl. Band 22,2, Leipzig.
Bremmer, J.N. 1997. 'Jokes, Jokers and Jokebooks in Ancient Greek Culture', in: Bremmer, J.N. and Roodenburg, H., edd., *A Cultural History of Humour. From Antiquity to the Present Day*, Cambridge, 11-28.

Brodersen, K. 1985. 'Der liebeskranke Königssohn und die seleukidische Herrschaftsauffassung', *Athenaeum* N.S. 63, 459-469.

 1989. *Appians Abriss der Seleukidengeschichte (Syriake 45,232-70,369). Text und Kommentar*, München.
Bruneau, Ph. 1965. 'Illustrations antiques du Coq et de l'Âne de Lucien', *BCH* 89, 349-357.
Buckland, W.W. 1908. *The Roman Law of Slavery*, Cambridge.
Burkert, W. 1991. *Antike Mysteriën. Funktionen und Gehalt*, München.
Cairns, F.1972. *Generic Composition in Greek and Roman Poetry*, Edinburgh.
Callebat, L. 1964. 'L'archaïsme dans les Métamorphoses d'Apulée', *REL* 42, 346-361 (= Callebat 1998, 182-194).
 1968. *Sermo Cotidianus dans les Métamorphoses d'Apulée*, Caen.
 1978. 'La prose des *Métamorphoses*: Génèse et spécifité', in: *AAGA*, Groningen, 167-187 (= Callebat 1998, 95-122).
 1994. 'Formes et modes d'expression dans les *Métamorphoses* d'Apulée, in: *ANRW* 2,34,2, 1616-1664 (= Callebat 1998, 123-179).
Caputo, G. 1959. *Il teatro di Sabratha e l'architettura teatrale Africana*, Roma.
Carilli, M. 1980. '*Proluvium*. Studi Noniani VI', *Publ. Ist. di Fil. Class. e Medioev.* LXIII Univ. di Genova, Fac. di Lett., 55-61.
Carrière, J.C. 1984. *Plutarque, Oeuvres Morales, T. XI^2 Préceptes politiques*, Paris.
Cataudella, Q. 1966. 'Mimo e Romanzo', *RCCM* 8, 3-11.
Catlow, L. 1980. *Pervigilium Veneris, edited with a translation and a commentary*, Bruxelles (Coll. Latomus vol. 172).
Cavallini, E. 1978. 'Motivi Saffici in Apuleio', *GFF* 1, 91-93.
Ceccarelli, P. 1998. *La pirrica nell' antichità greco-romana*, Pisa - Roma.
Chausserie-Laprée, J.P. 1969. *L'expression narrative chez les historiens latins. Histoire d'un style*, Paris.
Church, J.E. 1904. 'Sepultura = sepulcrum', *ALL* 13, 427-428.
Cicu, L. 1988. *Problemi e strutture del mimo a Roma*, Sassari, Gallizzi.
Claes, P. 1988. *Echo's echo's. De kunst van de allusie*, Amsterdam.
Clairmont, C. 1951. *Das Parisurteil in der antiken Kunst*, Zürich.
Coleman, K.M. 1990. 'Fatal Charades: Roman Executions Staged as Mythological Enactments', *JRS* 80, 44-73.
Colin, J. 1965. 'Apulée en Thessalie: fiction ou vérité?', *Latomus* 24, 330-345.
Comotti, G. 1989. *Music in Greek and Roman Culture*, Baltimore - London (Transl. by R.V. Munson of Comotti 1979).
Cooper, G. 1980. 'Sexual and Ethical Reversal in Apuleius: the Metamorphoses as Anti-Epic', in: C. Deroux, ed., *Studies in Latin Literature and Roman History II*, 436-466.
Courcelle, P. 1976. 'Des sources antiques à l'iconographie médiévale', in: G. Lazzati, ed., *Ambrosius Episcopus. Atti del Congresso internazionale di studi Ambrosiani nel XVI centenario della devozione di sant' Ambrogio alla cattedrale episcopale, Milano 2-7 dec. 1974*, Milano, 171-199.
Crawly, E. [4]1932. *The mystic Rose. A study of primitive marriage and of primitive thought in its bearing on marriage*, London.
Crismani, D. 1993. 'Filtri, veleni, diagnosi mediche nel romanzo greco', in: S, Sconocchia, L. Toneatto, edd., *Lingue technique del greco e del latino. Atti del I. Seminario internazionale sulla letteratura scientifica e tecnica greca e latina (25-27 marzo 1992)*, Trieste.
 1997. *Il teatro nel romanzo Ellenistico d'amore e di avventure*, Torino.
Crook, J.A. 1986. 'Women in Roman Succession', in: B. Rawson, ed., *The Family in Ancient Rome. New Perspectives*, Ithaca, N.Y.
Cupaiuolo, F. 1967. *La formazione degli avverbi in latino*, Napoli.
Currie, S. 1996. 'The empire of adults: the representation of children on Trajan's arch at Beneventum', in: J. Elsner, ed., *Art and Text in Roman Culture*, Cambridge, 153-181 (notes pp. 308-312).
Dahlmann, H. 1979. *Ein Gedicht des Apuleius? (Gellius 19,11)*, Wiesbaden.
Damon, C. 1997. *The Mask of the Parasite. A Pathology of Roman Patronage*, Ann Arbor.
Danesi Marioni, G. 1996. 'Oltre il genere: L'*Octavia* e l'Elegia', *Prometheus* 22, 145-156.
Deichgräber, K. 1950. *Professio medici. Zum Vorwort des Scribonius Largus*, Wiesbaden (Abh. d. Akad. d. Wissenschaften u. d. Literatur Mainz, nr. 9).
Detienne, M., Vernant, J.-P. 1974. *Les ruses d'intelligence: La Mètis des Grecs*, Paris.
Dewar, M. 1991. *Statius Thebaid IX. Edited with an English translation and commentary*, Oxford.

Donnini, M. 1981. 'Apuleius *Met.* X,2-12: Analogi e Varianti di un racconto', *MCSN* 3, 145-160.

1981a. 'Il "racconto" sull' amore incestuoso in Pietro Pittore', *MCSN* 3, 237-246.

Doodey, M.A. 1996. *The True Story of the Novel*, New Brunswick.

Dornseiff, F. 1938. 'Lukios und Apuleius' *Metamorphosen*', *Hermes* 73, 222-233.

Dowden, K. 1982. 'Apuleius and the Art of Narration', *CQ* 32, 419-435.

1993. 'The Unity of Apuleius' Eighth Book & the Danger of Beasts', in: *GCN* 5, 91-109.

1994. 'The Roman Audience of the Golden Ass', in: J. Tatum, ed., *The Search for the Ancient Novel*, Baltimore London, 419-434.

Drake, G.C. 1969. 'Lucius' Business in the Metamorphoses', *Papers on Language and Literature* 5 (4), 339-361.

Dudley, D.R. 1937. *A History of Cynicism from Diogenes to the Sixth Century A.D.*, London (repr. Hildesheim 1967).

Duncan-Jones, R. [2]1982. *The Economy of the Roman Empire*, Cambridge.

Dupont, F. 1985. *L'acteur-roi ou le théâtre dans la Rome antique*, Paris.

Ebel, H. 1970. 'Apuleius and the present time', *Arethusa* 3, 155-176.

Eco, U. 1979. *The Role of the Reader*, Bloomington - London.

Edgeworth, R.J. 1979. 'Does "purpureus" mean bright?', *Glotta* 57, 281-291.

Effe, B. 1975. 'Entstehung und Funktion personaler Erzählsweisen in der Erzählliteratur der Antike', Poetica 7, 135-157.

Eicke, W. 1956. *Stilunterschiede in den Metamorphosen des Apuleius*, Diss. Göttingen.

Eichenbeer, C. 1986. 'Tintinnabulum', *Vox Latina* 22, 158-159.

Elliott, A.G. 1987. *Roads to Paradise. Reading the Lives of the Early Saints*, Hanover - London.

Elsom, H. 1985. *Apuleius and the Writing of Fiction and Philosophy in the Second Century AD*, Diss. Cambridge Univ.

1989. 'Apuleius and the Movies', in: *GCN* 2, 145-150.

Elster, M. 1991. 'Römisches Strafrecht in den Metamorphosen des Apuleius', in: *GCN* 4, 135-154.

Erbse, H. 1950. 'Griechisches und Apuleianisches bei Apuleius', *Eranos* 48, 107-126.

Ernout, A. 1949. *Les Adjectifs Latins en -osus et en -ulentus*, Paris.

Evans, E.C. 1969. *Physiognomics in the Ancient World*, Transactions of the American Philosophical Society 59,5, Philadelphia.

Facchini Tosi, C. 1986. 'Forma e suono in Apuleio', *Vichiana* 15, 98-168.

Fantham, E. 1975. 'Virgil's Dido and Seneca's tragic heroines', *G&R* 22, 1-10.

1989. 'Mime: the missing link in Roman Literary History', *CW* 82/3, 153-163.

Farnell, L.R. 1921. *Greek Hero Cults and ideas of immortality*, The Gifford Lectures, Oxford.

Fauth, W. 1958/9. *Hippolytos und Phaidra. Bemerkungen zum religiösen Hintergrund eines tragischen Konflikts*, Abh. d. Akad. d. Wiss. u.d. Lit. Mainz. Geistes- und sozialwissensch. Kl., Jhrg. 1958,9; Jhrg. 1959,8, Wiesbaden.

Fehling, D. 1974. *Ethologische Überlegungen auf dem Gebiet der Altertumskunde. Phallische Demonstration - Fernsicht - Steinigung*. München (Zetemata 61).

Felice, E. De. 1957. 'Problemi di aspetto nei più antichi testi francesi', *Vox Romanica* 16, 1-51.

Ferrari, M.G. 1968. 'Aspetti di letterarietà nel *Florida* di Apuleio', *SIFC* 40, 85-147.

Fick, N. 1990. 'Die Pantomime des Apuleius (*Met.* X,30-34,3), in: J. Blänsdorf, ed., *Theater und Gesellschaft im Imperium Romanum*, Tübingen, 223-232.

Fick - Michel, N. 1991. *Art et Mystique dans les Métamorphoses d'Apulée* (Centre de recherches d'histoire ancienne, vol. 109; Institut Félix Gaffiot, vol. 10), Paris.

Finkelpearl, E. 1986. *Metamorphosis of Language in Apuleius' "Metamorphoses"*, Diss. Harvard.

1991. 'The Judgment of Lucius: Apuleius, *Metamorphoses* 10,29-34', *ClAnt.* 10, 221-236.

Fiorencis, G., Gianotti, G.F. 1990. 'Fedra e Ippolito in provincia', *MD* 25, 71-114.

Fliedner, H. 1974. *Amor und Cupido. Untersuchungen über den römischen Liebesgott*, Meisenheim am Glan.

Flobert, P. 1975. *Les verbes déponents Latins des origines à Charlemagne*, Paris.

Forbes, R.J. 1964. *Studies in ancient technology* Vol. IX, Leiden.

Fraenkel, E. 1922. *Plautinisches in Plautus*, Berlin.

1953. 'A sham Sisenna', *Eranos* 51, 151-154 (= Kleine Beiträge zur klassischen Philologie 2, 391 f., Rome 1965).

Franz, M.L. Von. 1970. *A Psychological Interpretation of the Golden Ass of Apuleius*, Zürich; revised and enlarged edition: *The Golden Ass of Apuleius. The Liberation of the Feminine in Man*, Boston - London 1992.
Frassinetti, P. 1960. 'Cruces Apuleianae (Metamorfosi)', *Athenaeum* 38, 118-131.
Freyburger, G. 1986. *Fides. Étude sémantique et religieuse depuis les origines jusqu' à l'époque augustéenne*, Paris.
Fry, G. 1984. 'Philosophie et mystique du thème de la Fortune dans les Métamorphoses d'Apulée', *QUCC* 18, 137-170.
Fuhrmann, M. 1970. *Marcus Tullius Cicero. Sämtliche Reden*, Band 11, Zürich - Stuttgart.
Fusillo, M. 1988. 'Textual Patterns and Narrative Situations in the Greek Novel', in: *GCN* 1, 17-31.
Gärtner, U. 1998. '*Quae magis aspera curis nox*. Zur Bedeutung der Tageszeiten bei Valerius Flaccus', *Hermes* 126, 202-220.
Geisau, J. Von. 1912. 'De Apulei syntaxi poetica et graecanica', Diss. Münster.
1916. 'Syntaktische Graecismen bei Apuleius', *IF* 36, 70-98; 242-287.
Geisler, H.J. 1969. *P. Ovidius Naso, Remedia Amoris, mit Kommentar zu vers 1-396*, Diss. Berlin.
Gianotti, G.F. 1986. *"Romanzo" e ideologia. Studi sulle* Metamorfosi *di Apuleio*, Napoli.
Grasmück, E.L. 1978. *Untersuchungen zur Verbannung in der Antike*, Rechts- und Staatswissenschaftliche Veröffentlichungen der Görres-Gesellschaft N.F. Heft 30, Paderborn - München - Wien - Zürich.
Gray-Fow, M.J.G. 1988. 'The Wicked Stepmother in Roman Literature and History: an Evaluation', *Latomus* 47, 742-757.
Grilli, A. 1996. 'Divagazioni sulla commedia latina', in: Consonni, C., ed., *Menandro fra tradizione e innovazione. Atti del Convegno Nazionale di Studi Monza 6-7 maggio 1995*, Milano, 71-89.
Grimal, P. 1963. 'L'originalité de Sénèque dans la Tragédie de Phèdre', *REL* 41, 297-314.
Guastella, G. 1985. 'La rete del sangue', *MD* 15, 49-123.
Gülich, E. 1976. 'Ansätze zu einer kommunikations-orientierten Erzähltextanalyse', in: W. Haubrichs, ed., *Erzählforschung* 1, Göttingen, 224-255.
Gunkel, S.H. [7]1966. *Genesis übersetzt und erklärt*, Göttingen.
Gwyn Griffiths, J. 1978. 'Isis in the *Metamorphoses* of Apuleius', in: *AAGA*, Groningen, 141-166.
Habinek, T.N. 1990. 'Lucius' Rite of Passage', *MD* 25, 49-69.
Hadas, M. 1959. *Hellenistic Culture. Fusion and Diffusion*, New York.
Hägg, T. 1971. *Narrative Technique in Ancient Romances. Studies of Chariton, Xenophon Ephesius, and Achilles Tatius*, Stockholm.
Hahn, J. 1989. *Der Philosoph und die Gesellschaft. Selbstverständnis, öffentliches Auftreten und populäre Erwartungen in der hohen Kaiserzeit*, Stuttgart.
Hammer, S. 1923. 'De Narrationum Apul. Metam. Libro X Insertarum compositione et exemplaribus', *Eos* 26, 6-26.
1925. 'De Apulei arte narrandi novae observationes', *Eos* 28, 51-77.
Harrauer, C., Römer, F. 1985. 'Beobachtungen zum Metamorphosen-Prolog des Apuleius', *Mnemosyne* 38, 353-372.
Harrison, S.J. 1992. 'Apuleius eroticus: *Anth.Lat.* 712 Riese, *Hermes* 120, 83-89.
Hauri-Karrer, A. 1972. *Lateinische Gebäcksbezeichnungen*, Diss. Zürich.
Heath, J.R. 1982. 'Narration and Nutrition in Apuleius' *Metamorphoses*', *Ramus* 9, 57-77.
Heine, R. 1962. *Untersuchungen zur Romanform des Apuleius von Madaura*, Diss. Göttingen.
1978. 'Picaresque Novel versus Allegory', in: *AAGA*, Groningen, 25-42.
Heinze, R. [3]1915. *Virgils epische Technik*, Leipzig - Berlin ([5]Stuttgart 1965).
Herrmann, L. 1951. 'Le fragment obscène de l'Âne d'or (X,21)', *Latomus* 10, 329-332.
Herter, H. 1940. 'Theseus und Hippolytos', *RhM* 89, 273-292.
1971. 'Phaidra in griechischer und römischer Gestalt', *RhM* 114, 44-77.
Heubeck, A. 1955. 'Mythologische Vorstellungen des Alten Orients im archaischen Griechentum', *Gymnasium* 62, 508-525.
Hijmans, B.L. 1978. 'Significant names and their function in Apuleius' *Metamorphoses*', in: *AAGA*, Groningen, 107-117.
1986. 'Charite worships Tlepolemus-Liber', *Mnemosyne* 39, 350-364.

1987. 'Apuleius, Philosophus Platonicus', in: *ANRW* 2,36,1, 395-475.
Hiltbrunner, O. 1954. 'Vir Gravis', in: *Sprachgeschichte und Wortbedeutung. Festschrift Albert Debrunner*, Berlin, 195-207.
1958. *Latina Graeca. Semasiologische Studien über lateinische Wörter im Hinblick auf ihr Verhältnis zu griechischen Vorbildern*, Bern.
Hofmann, H. 1993a. 'Die Flucht des Erzählers', in: *GCN* 5, 111-141.
1993b. 'Parodie des Erzählens - Erzählen als Parodie. Der Goldene Esel des Apuleius', in: W. Ax, R. Glei, edd., *Literaturparodie in Antike und Mittelalter*, Trier, 119-151.
Hohlfelder, R.L. 1976. 'Kenchreae on the Saronic Gulf: Aspects of its Imperial History', *CJ* 71, 217-226.
Holzberg, N. 1984. 'Apuleius und der Verfasser des griechischen Eselsromans', *WJA* 10, 161-177.
1992. ed., *Der Äsop-Roman. Motivgeschichte und Erzählstruktur*, Tübingen.
1995. *The Ancient Novel: an Introduction*, London.
1998. *De roman in de oudheid*, Amsterdam.
Hooff, A.J.L. Van. 1990. *From Autothanasia to Suicide. Self-killing in Classical Antiquity*, London - New York.
Hoppe, H. 1903. *Syntax und Stil des Tertullian*, Leipzig.
Horstmanshoff, H.F.J. 1992. 'Gemeen goed, over de rol van het vergif tijdens Nero's principaat', *Lampas* 25, 32-56.
Huber - Rebenich, G. 1999. 'Hagiographic Fiction as Entertainment', in: H. Hofmann, ed., 187-212.
Hunter, R. 1985. *The New Comedy of Greece and Rome*, Cambridge.
Iser, W. 1976. *Der Akt des Lesens: Theorie ästhetischer Wirkung*, München.
Jacquinod, B. 1992. 'Le double accusatif dans les *Métamorphoses* d'Apulée', *RPh* 66, 81-92.
Jackson, R. 1988. *Doctors and Diseases in the Roman Empire*, London, British Museum Publications.
James, P. 1987. *Unity in Diversity. A Study of Apuleius' Metamorphoses*, Olms - Weidmann: Altertumswissenschaftliche Texte und Studien Band 16, Hildesheim - Zürich - New York.
1988. 'Cupid at Work and at Play', in: *GCN* 1, 113-121.
Jones, A.H.M. [4]1971. *The Greek City from Alexander to Justinian*, Oxford.
Jones, F. 1991. 'Subject, topic, given and salient: sentence beginnings in Latin', *PCPS* 37, 81-105.
Jones, C.P. 1986. *Culture and Society in Lucian*, Cambridge, Mass. - London.
Jong, I.J.F. de 1989. *Narrators and Focalizers. The Presentation of the Story in the Iliad*, Amsterdam.
Journoud, S. 1965. 'Apulée conteur: Quelques réflections sur l'épisode de l'Âne et la Corinthienne (Métam. X.19.3-22.5)', *Acta Classica Univ. Scient. Debrecen*, 33-37.
Junghanns, P. 1932. *Die Erzählungstechnik von Apuleius' Metamorphosen und ihrer Vorlage*, *Philologus*, Suppl. 24.
Kajanto, I. 1981. 'Fortuna', in: *ANRW* 2,17,1, 502-558.
Kaser, M. [2]1971. *Das römische Privatrecht. Vol. I: Das altrömische, das vorklassische und klassische Recht*, München.
[2]1975. *Das römische Privatrecht. Vol. II: Die nachklassischen Entwicklungen*, München.
Kautzky, W. 1989. *Drei 'Familientragödien' in den Metamorphosen des Apuleius (Met. 9,33-38; 10,2-12; 10,23-28)*, Diss. Wien.
Kenney, E.J. 1990a. 'Psyche and her Mysterious Husband', in: D.A. Russell, ed., *Antonine Literature*, Oxford, 175-198.
Kirchhoff, A. 1903. *De Apulei clausularum compositione et arte*, Fleckeisen Jahrb. f. cl. Phil., Suppl. 28.
Kißel, W. 1990. *Aules Persius Flaccus, Satiren, Herausgegeben, übersetzt und kommentiert*, Heidelberg.
Klaerr, R. 1974. *Plutarque, Oeuvres Morales, T. VII[2] De l'amour des richesses... (etc.). Texte établi et traduit par R. Klaerr/Y.Vernière*, Paris.
Kleberg, T. 1934. *Värdshus och värdshusliv i den Romerka antiken*, Diss. Göteborg.
Klibansky, R., Regen, F. 1993. edd., *Die Handschriften der philosophischen Werke des Apuleius*, Göttingen.
Koch, G., Sichtermann, H. 1982. *Römische Sarkophage*, München.
Kokolakis, M. 1959. 'Pantomimus and the treatise Περὶ ὀρχήσεως (De saltatione)', *Platon* 11, 3-56.
Konstan, D. 1983. *Roman Comedy*, Ithaca - London.
1994. *Sexual Symmetry. Love in the Ancient Novel and Related Genres*, Princeton.

Krabbe, J.K. 1989. *The Metamorphoses of Apuleius*: American University Studies, Series XVII Classical Language and Literature, Vol. 9, New York.

Krautter, H. 1971. *Philologische Methode und humanistische Existenz. Filippo Beroaldo und sein Kommentar zum goldenen Esel des Apuleius*, München.

Kristeva, J. 1969. *Semeiotikè*, Paris.

Kroon, C.H.M. 1989. 'Causal connectors in Latin: the Discourse function of *Nam, Enim, Igitur* and *Ergo*', in: M. Lavency, D. Longrée, edd., *Actes du Vme colloque de Linguistique Latine, Publications Linguistiques de Louvain*, 231-243.

— 1995. *Discourse Particles in Latin. A Study of Nam, Enim, Autem, Vero and At*, Diss. Amsterdam.

— 1998. 'Discourse particles, tense, and the structure of Latin narrative texts', in R. Risselada, ed., *Latin in Use. Amsterdam Studies in the Pragmatics of Latin*, Amsterdam, 37-61.

Kroon, C.H.M., Rose, P. 1996. '*Atrociter corruptus?* The study of "narrative" tenses in Amminaus Marcellinus' *Res Gestae*', in: R. Risselada, J.R. de Jong, A.M. Bolkestein, edd., *On Latin. Studies in honour of Harm Pinkster*, Amsterdam, 71-89.

Kudlien, F. 1970. 'Medical Ethics and Popular Ethics in Greece and Rome', *Clio Medica* 5, 91-121.

— 1989. 'Kindesaussetzung im antiken Roman: Ein Thema zwischen Fiktionalität und Lebenswirklichkeit', in: *GCN* 2, 25-44.

Kussl, R. 1990. 'Die Metamorphosen des 'Lucios von Patrai': Untersuchungen zu Phot. Bibl. 129', RhM 133, 379-388.

Lacey, W.K. 1986. *Patria Potestas* in: B. Rawson, ed., *The Family in Ancient Rome: New Perspectives*, Ithaca, NY 1986, 121-144.

Lämmert, E. [8]1983. *Bauformen des Erzählens*, Stuttgart.

Landels, J.G. 1998. *Music in Ancient Greece and Rome*, London - New York.

Lassen, E.M. 1992. 'The Ultimate Crime. *Parricidium* and the Concept of Family in the Late Roman Republic and Early Empire', *C&M* 43, 147-161.

Lateiner, D. 1998. 'Blushes and Pallor in Ancient Fiction', *Helios* 25, 163-189.

Lavagnini, B. 1950. *Studi sul romanzo greco*, Messina - Firenze.

Lawler, L.B. 1964. *The Dance in Ancient Greece*, Seattle - London.

Lazzarini, C. 1985. 'Il modello Virgiliano nel lessico delle *Metamorfosi* di Apuleio', *SCO* 35, 131-160.

Leeman, A.D. 1963. *Orationis Ratio, the Stylistic Theories and Practice of the Roman Orators, Historians and Philosophers*, Amsterdam (repr. Amsterdam 1986).

Leeman, A.D, Pinkster, H. 1981. edd., *M.Tullius Cicero* De Oratore Libri III, *Kommentar. 1.Band, Buch I,1-165*, Heidelberg.

— 1985. edd., *M.Tullius Cicero* De Oratore Libri III, *Kommentar. 2.Band, Buch I,166-265; Buch II,1-98*, Heidelberg.

Lefèvre, E. 1978. *Das römische Drama*, Darmstadt.

Lelièvre, F.J. 1954. 'The Basis of Ancient Parody', *G&R* N.S. 1, 66-81.

Lesky, A. 1941. 'Apuleius von Madaura und Lukios von Patrae', *Hermes* 76, 43-74 (= *Gesammelte Schriften*, 1966, 549-578).

Leumann, M. 1917. *Die lateinische Adjectiva auf* -lis, Strassburg.

Lévi-Strauss, C. 1964. *Le cru et le cuit*, Paris.

Lieberg, G. 1962. *Puella divina*, Amsterdam.

Lintvelt, J. 1981 ([2]1989). *Essai de Typologie Narrative. Le "Point de Vue", Théorie et Analyse*, Paris.

Löfstedt, E. 1908. *Spätlateinische Studien*, Uppsala.

— 1911. *Philologischer Kommentar zur Peregrinatio Aetheriae*, Uppsala (repr. Darmstadt 1966).

— 1917. *Arnobiana*, Lund - Leipzig.

— 1918. *Kritische Bemerkungen zu Tertullians Apologeticum*, Lund.

— 1936. *Vermischte Studien zur lateinischen Sprachkunde und Syntax*, Lund.

— [2]1942. *Syntactica I*, Lund (repr. 1956).

— 1933. *Syntactica II*, Lund (repr. 1956).

Long, A.A. 1988. 'Socrates in Hellenistic Philosophy', *CQ* 38, 150-171.

López, V.C. 1976. 'Tratiamento del mito en las novelle de las Metamorfosis de Apuleyo', *CFC* 10, 309-373.

Lyne, R.O.A.M. 1978. *Ciris. A poem attributed to Vergil*, Cambridge.

— 1980. *The Latin Love Poets from Catullus to Horace*, Oxford.

— 1989. *Words and the Poet. Characteristic Techniques of Style in Vergil's Aeneid*, Oxford.

MacKendrick, P. 1995. *The Speeches of Cicero. Context, Law, Rhetoric*, London.
MacKibben, W.T. 1951. 'In bovem mugire', *CPh* 46, 165-172.
Maeder, D. 1991. *Au Seuil des Romans Grecs: Effets de réel et effets de création*, in: *GCN* 4, 1-33.
Maehler, H. 1990. 'Symptome der Liebe im Roman und in der griechischen Anthologie', in: *GCN* 3, 1-12.
Mal - Maeder, D. Van. 1994. 'Sens et fonction du pronom/adjectif *quidam* dans les *Métamorphoses* d'Apulée', *MH* 51, 214-225.
Marache, R. 1957. *Mots nouveaux et mots archaïques chez Fronton et Aulu-Gelle*, Paris.
Marchetta, A. 1991. *L'autenticità Apuleiana del De Mundo*, Roma.
Mariotti, S. 1956. *Lo spurcum additamentum ad Apul. Met. 10,21*, *SIFC* 27 (8), 229-250.
Marrou, H.-I. [4]1958. *Histoire de l'éducation dans l'Antiquité*, Paris.
Mason, H.J. 1971. 'Lucius at Corinth', *Phoenix* 25, 160-165.
    1978. '*Fabula Graecanica*: Apuleius and his Greek Source', in: *AAGA*, Groningen, 1-15 (= H.J. Mason in S.J. Harrison, ed., 1999, 217-236, with an afterword added).
    1983. 'The distinction of Lucius in Apuleius' *Metamorphoses*', *Phoenix* 37, 135-143.
    1984. 'Physiognomy in Apuleius' *Metamorphoses* 2,2', *CPh* 79, 307-309.
    1994. 'Greek and Latin Versions of the Ass-story', in: *ANRW* 2,34,2, 1665-1707.
Mattiacci, S. 1988. 'L'*odarium* dell'amico di Gellio e la poesia novella', in: V. Tandoi, ed., *Disiecti membra poetae*, III, Foggia, 194-208.
    1990. *I carmi e i frammenti di Tiberiano*, Firenze.
Maurach, G. 1975. *Plauti Poenulus*, Heidelberg.
    1988. *Der Poenulus des Plautus*. Heidelberg.
    [2]1989. *Enchiridion Poeticum. Zur lateinischen Dichtersprache*, Darmstadt.
Mazzarino, H. 1950. *La Milesia e Apuleio*, Torino.
Melin, B. 1946. *Studia in Corpus Cyprianeum*, Uppsala.
Mellet, S. 1985. 'Présent de Narration et Parfait dans le Conte de Psyché', *REL* 63, 148-160.
Menge, H. [14]1965, *Repetitorium der lateinischen Syntax und Stilistik*. München.
Merkelbach, R. 1952. *La nuova pagina di Sisenna e Apuleio*, *Maia* 5, 234-241.
    1962. *Roman und Mysterium in der Antike*, München.
Merkle, S. 1989. *Die Ephemeris belli Troiani des Diktys von Kreta*, Studien zur klassischen Philologie 44, Frankfurt am Main - Bern - New York - Paris.
Mesk, J. 1913. *Antiochos und Stratonike*, *RhM* 68, 366-399.
Méthy, N. 1983. 'Fronton et Apulée: Romains ou Africains?', *RCCM* 15, 37-47.
Mette-Dittmann, A. 1991. *Die Ehegesetze des Augustus*, Stuttgart.
Mignogna, E. 1996. 'Narrativa greca e mimo. Il romanzo di Achille Tazio' *SIFC* 14, 232-242.
    1997. 'Leucippe in Tauride (Ach. Tat. 3,15-22): mimo e "pantomimo" tra tragedia e romanzo', *MD* 38, 225-236.
Millar, F. 1981. 'The World of the Golden Ass, *JRS* 71, 63-75 (= F. Millar in: S.J. Harrison, ed. 1999, 247-268).
Miller, J.F. 1989. 'A Travesty of Ritual in Petronius ("Satyricon" 60)', *Hermes* 117, 192-204.
Minyard, J.D. 1985. *Lucretius and the late republic: an essay in Roman intellectual history*, Leiden.
Möbitz, O. 1922. 'Die Stellung des Verbums in den Schriften des Apuleius', *Glotta* 13, 116-126.
Moles, J.L. 1996. 'Cynic Cosmopolitanism', in Bracht Branham, R., and Goulet-Cazé, M-O., edd., *The Cynics. The Cynic Movement in Antiquity and Its Legacy*, Berkeley - Los Angeles - London, 105-120.
Monteil, P. 1964. *Beau et Laid. Contribution à une étude historique du vocabulaire esthétique en Latin*, Paris.
Montero Cartella, E. 1973. *Aspectos Lexicos y Literarios del Latin Erotico*, Diss. Santiago.
Morgan, J.R. 1989. 'The Story of Knemon in Heliodoros' *Aethiopika*, *JHS* 109, 99-113.
Mudry, P. 1992. 'Le médecin félon et l'énigme de la potion sacrée (Apulée, *Métamorphoses* 10,25), in: *Maladie et maladies. Histoire et conceptualisation. Mélanges Grmek*, EPHE, Genève, 171-180.
Müller, C.F.W. 1908. *Syntax des Nominativs und Akkusativs im Lateinischen*, Leipzig - Berlin.
Murgatroyd, P. 1982. *Ovid with Love. Selections from Ars Amatoria I and II*, Chicago.
Neesen, L. 1981. 'Die Entwicklung der Leistungen und Ämter (*munera et honores*) im römischen Kaiserreich des zweiten bis vierten Jahrhundert', *Historia* 30, 203-235.
Nethercut, W.R. 1968. 'Apuleius' Literary Art. Resonance and Depth in the *Metamorphoses*', *CJ* 64, 110-119.
    1969. 'Apuleius' *Metamorphoses*. The Journey', *Agon* 3, 97-134.
Neuenschwander, P. 1913. *Der bildliche Ausdrück des Apuleius von Madaura*, Diss. Zürich.

Nimis, S. 1994. 'The Prosaics of the Ancient Novels', *Arethusa* 27, 387-411.

— 1998. 'Memory and Description in the Ancient Novel', *Arethusa* 31, 99-122.

— 1999. 'The Sense of Open-endedness in the Ancient Novel', *Arethusa* 32, 215-238.

Nordeblad, J.B. 1932. *Gaiusstudien*, Lund.

Norden, E. ³1915. *Die antike Kunstprosa vom VI. Jahrhundert v. Chr. bis in die Zeit der Renaissance*, Berlin (repr. 1958).

Norden, F. 1912. *Apuleius von Madaura und das römische Privatrecht*, Leipzig - Berlin.

Noy, D. 1991. 'Wicked Stepmothers in Roman Society and Imagination', *Journal of Family History* 16, 345-361.

Numminen, P. 1938. *Das lateinische* in *mit Akkusativ bis zu Augustus' Tod*, Helsinki.

Ogilvie, R.M. 1971. 'Monastic Corruption', *G&R* 18, 32-34.

Onians, R.B. 1951. *The Origins of European Thought about the Body, the Mind, the Soul, the World, Time and Fate*, Cambridge.

Önnerfors, A. 1956. *Pliniana. In Plinii maioris nat.hist. studia gramm. semantica critica*, Diss. Uppsala.

Opeku, F. 1979. 'Physiognomy in Apuleius', *Latomus* 164, 467-474.

Opelt, I. 1965. *Die lateinischen Schimpfwörter und verwandte sprachliche Erscheinungen. Eine Typologie*, Heidelberg.

— 1978. 'Das Drama in der Kaiserzeit', in: E. Lefèvre, ed., *Das römische Drama*, Darmstadt, 427-460.

Orders, J.D. 1971. *Isiac elements in the Metamorphoses of Apuleius*, Diss. Vanderbilt Univ. Nashville.

Otto, A. 1890. *Die Sprichwörter und sprichwörtlichen Redensarten der Römer*, Leipzig. "Nachträge Otto" = R. Häussler (Hrsg.), *Nachträge zu A. Otto, Sprichwörter...*, Hildesheim 1968.

Paardt, R.Th. Van der. 1978. 'Various aspects of narrative technique in Apuleius' Metamorphoses', in: *AAGA*, Groningen, 75-94.

— 1981. 'The Unmasked "I", Apuleius, Metamorphoses XI,27', *Mnemosyne* 34, 96-106 (= R. Th. Van der Paardt in S.J. Harrison, ed., 1999, 237-246).

— 1982. 'Een bevlogen Nederlandse herdichting': Seneca's Phaedra in de bewerking van Hugo Claus, in: R. Th Van der Paardt, *Antieke motieven in de moderne Nederlandse letterkunde. Een eigentijdse Odyssee*, Amsterdam, 78-98.

Panayotakis, C. 1995. *Theatrum Arbitri. Theatrical Elements in the* Satyrica *of Petronius*, Leiden - New York - Köln.

— 1997. 'Baptism and Crucifixion on the Mimic Stage', *Mnem.* 50, 302-319.

Panhuis, D.G.J. 1982. *The communicative perspective in the sentence. A study of Latin word order*, SLCS (= Studies in Language Companion Series) Vol. II, Amsterdam - Philadelphia.

Pease, A.S. 1907. 'Notes on Stoning among the Greeks and Romans', *TAPhA* 38, 5-18.

Pecere, O. 1987. 'Qualche riflessione sulla tradizione di Apuleio a Montecassino', in: Cavallo, G., ed., *Le strade del Testo*, Bari, 97-124.

Pennisi, G. 1970. *Apuleio e l'"Additamentum" a "Metamorphoses" X,21*, Messina.

Penwill, J.L. 1975. 'Slavish Pleasures and Profitless Curiosity: Fall and Redemption in Apuleius' Metamorphoses', *Ramus* 4, 49-82.

— 1990. '*Ambages Reciprocae*: Reviewing Apuleius' Metamorphoses', *Ramus* 19, 1-25.

Perkins, J. 1995. *The Suffering Self. Pain and Narrative Representation in the Early Christian Era*, London - New York.

Perrot, J. 1961. *Les dérivés Latins en* -men *et* -mentum, Paris.

Perotti, P.A. 1989. 'Quattro strani nomi neutri: *pelagus, uirus, uulgus, caput*', *Latomus* 48, 339-343.

Perry, B.E. 1926. 'An interpretation of Apuleius' Metamorphoses, *TAPA* 57, 238-260.

— 1967. *The Ancient Romances. A Literary-historical account of their origins*, Berkeley - Los Angeles.

Petriconi, H. 1962. 'Die verschmähte Astarte', *Romanistisches Jahrbuch* 13, 149-185.

Pichon, R. 1966. *Index Verborum Amatorium*, Hildesheim (reprint of Pichon 1902, *De sermone amatorio apud Latinos elegiarum scriptores*, Paris).

Pinkster, H. 1983. 'Tempus, Aspect and Aktionsart in Latin', in: *ANRW* 2,29,2, 270-319.

— 1986. '*Ego, tu, nos*. Opmerkingen over het gebruik van subjektpronomina, in het bijzonder in Cic. *de Oratore* II', *Lampas* 19, 309-322.

— 1990. *Latin Syntax and Semantics*, London - New York.

— 1992. 'The Latin Impersonal Passive', *Mnemosyne* 45, 159-177.

Pizzica, M. 1981. 'Ancora sull' *additamentum* ad Apul. *Met.* X 21', in: AA.VV., *Letterature Comparate. Studi in onore di Ettore Paratore vol. 2ndo*, Bologna, 763-772.

Poeschl, V. 1964. ed., *Bibliographie zur antiken Bildersprache* (bearbeitet von H. Gaertner und W. Heyke). Heidelberger Akad. der Wiss., Bibliothek der Klassischen Altertumswissenschaften N.F. 1 Reihe, Heidelberg.

Pomeroy, S.B. 1975. *Goddesses, Whores, Wives, and Slaves. Women in Classical Antiquity*, New York.

Portalupi, F. 1974. *Frontone, Gellio, Apuleio. Ricerca stilistica. Parte I*, Torino.

Powell, J.G.F. 1988. *Cicero, Cato Maior de Senectute, edited with introduction and commentary*, Cambridge.

Preston, K. 1916. *Studies in the diction of the Sermo Amatorius in Roman Comedy*, Chicago (repr. New York - London 1978).

Prince, G. 1973. 'Introduction à l'étude du narrataire', *Poétique* 14, 178-196.

Rabinowitz, P. 1977. 'Truth in Fiction: A Reexamination of Audiences', *Critical Inquiry* 4, 121-141.

Rayment, Ch.S. 1959. 'Rhetorical connotations of *uenenum*, *CB* 35, 49-53.

Reardon, B.P. 1989. ed., *Collected Ancient Greek Novels*, Berkeley - Los Angeles - London.

1991. *The Form of Greek Romance*, Princeton.

Redford, D.B. 1970. *A study of the biblical story of Joseph*, Leiden.

Reich, H. 1903. *Der Mimus. Ein litterar- und entwicklungsgeschichtlicher Versuch*, Berlin (repr. Olms 1974).

Reitzenstein, R. 1912. *Das Märchen von Amor und Psyche bei Apuleius*, Leipzig (= Binder - Merkelbach 1968, 87-158).

Reynolds, L.D. 1983. ed., *Texts and transmission. A survey of the Latin classics*, Oxford.

Reynolds, L.D., Wilson, N.G. [3]1991. *Scribes and Scholars. A Guide to the Transmission of Greek and Latin Literature*, Oxford.

Riefstahl, H. 1938. *Der Roman des Apuleius*, Frankfurt am Main.

Risselada, R. 1997. 'Bacchanalia & pragmatiek: textuele samenhang in Livius 39.9-14.3', *Lampas* 30, 101-121.

Rizzo, S. 1991. *M. Tulli Ciceronis Pro A. Cluentio habita oratio*, Roma.

Robert, L. 1940. *Les gladiateurs dans l'Orient Grec*, Paris.

Robertson, D.S. 1924. 'The Manuscripts of the *Metamorphoses* of Apuleius', *CQ* 18, 27-42; 85-99.

Robinson, O.F. 1995. *The Criminal Law of Ancient Rome*, London.

Rohde, E. [3]1914. (ed. W. Schmid) *Der griechische Roman und seine Vorläufer*, Leipzig 1876; 4th ed., reprint of 3rd ed., with a Preface by K. Kerényi, Hildesheim 1960; 5th ed. (reprint of 4th): Hildesheim 1974.

Roisman, H.M. 1999. 'The Veiled Hippolytus and Phaedra', *Hermes* 127, 397-409.

Rosén, H. 1995. 'The Latin Infinitivus Historicus Revisited', *Mnem.* 48 (5), 536-564.

Rosenmeyer, P.A. 1999. 'Tracing *Medulla* as a *Locus Eroticus*', *Arethusa* 32, 19-47.

Rotolo, V. 1957. *Il Pantomimo. Studi e testi*, Palermo.

Rousselle, A. 1983. *Porneia: de la maitrise du corps à la privation sensorielle IIe-IVe siècles de l'ère chrétienne*, Paris.

Ruiz de Elvira, A. 1954. 'Syntactica Apuleiana', *Emerita* 22, 99-136.

Russell, D.A. 1990. ed., *Antonine Literature*, Oxford.

Sallmann, K. 1988. 'Irritation als produktionsästhetisches Prinzip in den *Metamorphosen* des Apuleius', in: *GCN* 1, 81-102.

Sandy, G.N. 1968. *Comparative Study of Apuleius' Metamorphoses and other Prose Fiction of Antiquity*, Diss. Ohio State Univ. Columbus.

1973. 'Foreshadowing and Suspense in Apuleius' *Metamorphoses*', *CJ* 68, 232-235.

1974. '*Serviles voluptates* in Apuleius' *Metamorphoses*', *Phoenix* 28, 234-244.

1978. 'Book 11: Ballast or Anchor?', in: *AAGA*, Groningen, 123-140.

1993. 'West Meets East: Western Students in Athens in the Mid-Second Century A.D.', in: *GCN* 5, 163-174.

1994. 'Apuleius' "Metamorphoses" and the Ancient Novel', in: *ANRW* 2,34,2, 1511-1573.

Scarcella, A. 1993, 'Gli amori di Fedra fra tragedia e romanzo', in: P. Liviabelli Furiani, L. Rosetti, edd., *Romanzo e romanzieri. Note di narratologia greca*, Perugia, 385-408 (repr. of the same article in: *Atti delle giornate di studio su Fedra*, Torino 1985, 213-239).

Schlam, C.C. 1968. *The Structure of the Metamorphoses of Apuleius*, Diss. Columbia Univ., New York.
    1970. 'Platonica in the *Met.* of Apuleius', *TAPhA* 101, 477-487.
    1971. 'The Scholarship on Apuleius since 1938', *CW* 64, 285-309.
    1978. 'Sex and Sanctity: the relationship of male and female in the *Metamorphoses*, in: *AAGA*, Groningen, 95-105.
    1981. 'Man and Animal in the *Metamorphoses* of Apuleius, in: *SAG*, Groningen, 115-142.
    1992. *The Metamorphoses of Apuleius. On making an ass of oneself*, Chapel Hill - London.
    1993. 'Cupid and Psyche: Folktale and Literary Narrative', in: *GCN* 5, 63-73.
Schlicher, J.J. 1933. 'Non-assertive elements in the language of Historians', *CPh* 28, 289-300.
Schmeling, G. 1996. ed., *The Novel in the Ancient World*, Leiden - New York - Köln.
Schmidt, V. 1979. 'Der *viator* in Apuleius' *Metamorphosen* (Apuleiana Groningana VI)', *Mnemosyne* 32, 173-176.
    1989. 'Ein Trio im Bett: "Thema con variazioni" bei Catull, Martial, Babrius und Apuleius', in: *GCN* 2, 63-73.
    1990. 'Moralische Metaphorik bei Apuleius und im christlichen Latein am Beispiel *morum squalore*, *WS* 103, 139-143.
Schoonhoven, H. 1992. *The Pseudo-Ovidian Ad Liviam de morte Drusi. A critical text with introduction and commentary*, Groningen.
Schrijnen, J. 1939. *Collectanea Schrijnen*: Chr. Mohrmann, ed., *Verspreide opstellen van Dr. Jos Schrijnen*, Nijmegen - Utrecht.
Schuerewegen, F. 1987. 'Réflexions sur le narrataire', *Poétique* 70, 247-254.
Schumacher, L. 1982. *Servus Index. Sklavenverhör und Sklavenanzeige im republikanischen und kaiserzeitlichen Rom*, Wiesbaden.
Scobie, A. 1969. *Aspects of the Ancient Romance and its Heritage*, Meisenheim am Glan.
    1978. 'The Structure of Apuleius' *Metamorphoses*, in: *AAGA*, Groningen, 43-61.
    1978. 'The Influence of Apuleius' Metamorphoses in Renaissance Italy and Spain', in: *AAGA*, Groningen, 211-230.
Seelinger, R.A. 1986. 'Spatial Control: A reflection of Lucius' progress in the *Metamorphoses*', *TAPhA* 116, 361-368.
Segers, R.T. ²1984. *Het lezen van literatuur. Een inleiding tot een nieuwe literatuurbenadering*, Groningen. (¹Baarn 1980).
Shackleton Bailey, D.R. 1988. 'On Apuleius' *Metamorphoses*, *RhM* 131, 167-177.
Shumate, N. 1988. 'The Augustinian Pursuit of False Values as a Conversion Motif in Apuleius' *Metamorphoses*', *Phoenix* 42, 35-60.
Siewierska, A. 1988. *Word Order Rules*, London.
Sittl, K. 1890. *Die Gebärden der Griechen und Römer*. (repr. 1970, Hildesheim - New York).
Skulsky, H. 1981. *Metamorphosis, the Mind in Exile*, Harvard.
Skutsch, F. 1914. *Kleine Schriften*, Hrsg. W. Kroll, Leipzig - Berlin.
Slater, N. 1985. *Plautus in Performance. The Theatre of the Mind*, Princeton.
Smet, R. De 1987. 'La notion de lumière et ses fonctions dans les *Métamorphoses* d'Apulée', Studia Varia Bruxellensia, Leuven, 29-41.
Smith, W.S. 1968. *Lucius of Corinth and Apuleius of Madaura. A Study of the Narrative Technique of the Met. of Apuleius*, Diss. Yale University, New Haven.
    1972. 'The Narrative Voice in Apuleius' *Metamorphoses*, *TAPhA* 103, 513-534.
    1995. 'Interlocking of Theme and Meaning in the *Golden Ass*', in: *GCN* 5, 75-89.
Smolak, K. 1973. *Das Gedicht des Bischofs Agrestius (Einleitung, Text, Übersetzung u. Kommentar)*, Wien.
Sobrino, E.O. 1977-... *Léxico de Valerio Máximo*, Madrid.
Solin, H. 1971. *Beiträge zur Kenntnis der griechischen Personennamen in Rom*, Helsinki (Societas Scientiarum Fennica. Commentationes Humanarum Litterarum 48).
    1982. *Die griechische Personennamen in Rom*, Berlin - New York.
Solodow, J.B. 1978. *The Latin particle* quidem. *American Classical Studies* 4, The American Philological Association.
Sommer, F. 1914. *Handbuch der lateinischen Laut- und Formenlehre*, Heidelberg.
Stadter, P. 1965. *Plutarch's Historical Methods. An Analysis of the* Mulierum Virtutes, Cambridge, Mass.

Stanzel, F.K. [5]1976. *Typische Formen des Romans*, Göttingen.
Stark, R. 1957. 'Sapphoreminiszenzen', *Hermes* 85, 325-336.
Steinmetz, P. 1982. *Untersuchungen zur römischen Literatur des zweiten Jahrhunderts nach Christi Geburt*, Wiesbaden.
Stinton, T.C.W. 1965. 'Euripides and the Judgement of Paris', *JHS* Suppl. 11, 1-77 (= T.C.W. Stinton 1990, *Collected Papers on Greek Tragedy*, Oxford, 17-75).
Stramaglia, A. 1999. *Res inauditae, incredulae. Storie di fantasmi nel mondo greco-latino*, Bari.
Sudhaus, S. 1906. 'Der Mimus von Oxyrrhynchos', *Hermes* 41, 247-277.
Sullivan, J.P. 1968. *The Satyricon of Petronius: A Literary Study*, London.
Summers, R.G. 1967. *A Legal Commentary on the Metamorphoses of Apuleius*, Diss. Princeton Univ.
Sussmann, L.A. 1987. *The Major Declamations ascribed to Quintilian. A Translation*, Frankfurt am Main - Bern - New York.
Svennung, J. 1935. *Untersuchungen zu Palladius und zur lateinischen Fach- und Volkssprache*, Lund.
— 1945. *Catulls Bildersprache*, Uppsala Universitets Årsskrift 3.
Swain, S. 1992. 'Novel and Pantomime in Plutarch's "Antony"', *Hermes* 120, 83-89.
Tappi, O. 1986. 'Interdiscorsività e intertestualità in una 'novella' di Apuleio (*Metamorfosi* 10,2-12) Fenomenologia del tabù dell'incesto', in: *Semiotica della novella latina: Atti del seminario interdisciplinare 'La novella latina'*, Roma, 179-197.
Tatum, J.H. 1969. *Thematic Aspects of the Tales in Apuleus' Metamorphoses*, Diss. Princeton Univ.
— 1994. ed., *The Search for the Ancient Novel*, Baltimore - London.
Teuber, B. 1993. 'Zur Schreibkunst eines Zirkusreiters: Karnevaleskes Erzählen im "Goldenen Esel" des Apuleius und die Sorge um sich in der antiken Ethik', in: S. Döpp, ed., *Karnevaleske Phänomene in antiken und nachantiken Kulturen und Literaturen. Stätten und Formen der Kommunikation im Altertum I*, Trier, 179-238.
Thiel, H. Van. 1971-72. *Der Eselsroman*, Zetemata 54, München, I: Untersuchungen; II: Synoptische Ausgabe.
Thome, G. 1993. *Vorstellungen vom Bösen in der lateinischen Literatur. Begriffe, Motive, Gestalten*, Stuttgart.
Töchterle, K. 1994. *Lucius Annaeus Seneca. Oedipus. Kommentar mit Einleitung, Text und Übersetzung*, Heidelberg.
Traina, A. 1977. *Forma e Suono*, Roma.
— 1982. 'Epilegomeni a Forma e Suono', *MD* 9, 9-29.
Traina, G. 1981. 'Su una accezione del termine "balteus"', *SRIL* 4, 135-137.
Trapp, M.B. 1990. 'Plato's Phaedrus in Second-Century Greek Literature', in: D.A. Russell, ed., *Antonine Literature*, Oxford, 141-173.
Treggiari, S. 1991. *Roman Marriage*, Oxford.
Trenkner, S. 1958. *The Greek Novella in the Classical Period*, Cambridge.
Tromaras, L. 1994. *P. Terentius Afer. Eunuchus. Einführung, kritischer Text und Kommentar*, Hildesheim (transl. of Tromaras 1991, Thessaloniki, by M. Petersen und L. Tromaras).
Tschiedel, H.J. 1969. *Phaedra und Hippolytus. Variationen einen tragischen Konfliktes*, Diss. Erlangen-Nürnberg.
Turner, P. 1960. 'Pater and Apuleius', *Victorian Studies*, 290-296.
Väänänen, V. [3]1966. *Le Latin vulgaire des inscriptions pompéiennes*, Berlin.
— [3]1981, *Introduction au latin vulgaire*, Paris.
Veyne, P. 1965. 'Apulée à Cenchrées', *RPh* 39, 241-251.
— 1976. *Le Pain et le Cirque. Sociologie Historique d'un pluralisme politique*, Paris.
Vietmeier, K. 1937. *Beobachtungen über Caelius Aurelianus als Übersetzer medizinischer Fachausdrücke*, Diss. Münster.
Vogel, M. 1973. *Onos Lyras. Der Esel mit der Leier* (Orpheus Schriftenreihe zu Grundfragen der Musik XIII), Düsseldorf.
Walsh, P.G. 1970. *The Roman Novel. The Satyricon of Petronius and the Metamorphoses of Apuleius*, Cambridge.
— 1981. 'Apuleius and Plutarch, in: H. Blumenthal, R. Markus, edd., *Neoplatonism and Early Christian Thought. Essays in honour of A.H. Armstrong*, London, 20-32.
— 1988. 'The rights and wrongs of curiosity (Plutarch to Augustine)', *G&R* 35, 73-85.
Watson, P.A. 1995. *Ancient Stepmothers: Myths, Misogyny and Reality*, Leiden - New York - Köln.
Wehrli, F. 1965. 'Einheit und Vorgeschichte der griechisch-römischen Romanliteratur', *MH* 22, 133-154.
Weinrich, H. [2]1971. *Tempus. Besprochene und erzählte Welt*, Stuttgart - Berlin - Köln - Mainz.

Weinreich, O. 1930. Review of F. Dornseiff: *Das Alphabet in Mystik und Magie*, Leipzig - Berlin ²1925, *Gnomon* 6, 361-368.
Weismann, W. 1972. *Kirche und Schauspiele*, Würzburg.
Wesseling, B. 1988. 'The Audience of the Ancient Novel', in: *GCN* 1, 67-79.
1993. *Leven, Liefde en Dood: motieven in antieke romans*, Diss. Groningen.
West, M.L. 1992. *Ancient Greek Music*, Oxford.
Westerbrink, A.G. 1978. 'Some Parodies in Apuleius' *Metamorphoses*', in: *AAGA*, Groningen, 63-73.
Westermann, J.F. 1939. *Archaïsche en archaïstische woordkunst*, Diss. Amsterdam.
Weyman, C. 1893. 'Studien zu Apuleius und seinen Nachamern', *SBAW* II, München, 321-392.
Whitman, J. 1987. *Allegory. The Dynamics of an Ancient and Medieval Technique*. Oxford.
Wiedemann, T. 1989. *Adults and Children in the Roman Empire*, London.
Wiemken, H. 1972. *Der griechische Mimus. Dokumente zur Geschichte des antiken Volkstheater*, Bremen.
Wille, G. 1967. *Musica Romana. Die Bedeutung der Musik im Leben der Römer*, Amsterdam.
Wilson, N.G. 1997. *Aelian. Historical Miscellany*, Cambridge, Mass. - London.
Winkler, J.J. 1985. *Auctor and Actor. A Narratological Reading of Apuleius's The Golden Ass*, Berkeley - Los Angeles - London.
Wiseman, J. 1979. 'Corinth and Rome 228 BC-AD 267', in: *ANRW* 2,7,1, 438-548.
Wlosok, A. 1975. 'Amor and Cupid', *HSCP* 79, 165-179.
Wolterstorff, G. 1917. 'Artikelbedeutung von *ille* bei Apuleius', *Glotta* 8, 197-226.
Yohannan, J.D. 1968. *Joseph and Potiphar's Wife in World Literature. An Anthology of the Story of the Chaste Youth and the Lustful Stepmother*, New York.
Zimmerman - de Graaf, M. 1993. 'Narrative Judgment and Reader Response in Apuleius' *Metamorphoses* 10,29-34. The Pantomime of the Judgment of Paris', in: *GCN* 5, 143-161.
Zinsmaier, T. 1993. *Der von Bord geworfene Leichnam. Die sechste der neunzehn größeren pseudoquintilianischen Deklamationen. Einleitung, Übersetzung, Kommentar*, Studien zur klassischen Philologie Band 83, Frankfurt am Main - Bern - New York - Paris.
Zintzen, C. 1960. *Analytisches Hypomnema zu Seneca's Phaedra*, Beiträge zur klassischen Philologie Heft 1, Maisenheim am Glan.
Zucchelli, B. 1970. *Studi sulle formazioni latini in -lo- non diminutive e sui lori rapporti con i diminutive*, Firenze.
1995. 'Mimus halucinatur ... Il teatro-spettacolo del II. secolo', in: *Storia letteratura e arte a Roma nel secondo secolo dopo Cristo. Atti del Convegno Mantova, 8-9-10 ottobre 1992*, Firenze, 295-319.
Zundel, E. 1989. *Clavis Quintilianea. Quintilians 'Institutio oratoria' aufgeschlüsselt nach rhetorischen Begriffen*, Darmstadt.
Zurli, L. 1981.'Il Modello attanziale di una novella Apuleiana', *MCSN* 3, 411-424.
1987. 'Un arcaismo in Apuleio', *GIF* 39, 217-221.
Zwierlein, O. 1987. *Seneca's Phaedra und ihre Vorbilder*, Stuttgart.

IV. Apuleian Studies since 1995 (including some items of before 1995, not listed in *GCA* 1995). Continuation of the bibliographies in *GCA* 1977-1995.

Albrecht, M. Von. 1997. 'Novel. Apuleius', in M. von Albrecht, *A History of Roman Literature*, Vol. 2, Leiden - New York - Köln, 1449-1467.
Andreassi, M. 1997. 'Osmosis and contiguity between "low" and "high" Literature: *Moicheutria* (*POxy* 413 verso) and Apuleius', in: *GCN* 8, 1-21.
Annequin, J. 1996. 'Rêve, roman, initiation dans les "Métamorphoses" d'Apulée', *DHA* 22, 133-201.
Babo, M. 1997. 'Zu Apul. *Met.* 8,26'. *Mnem.* 50, 81-85.
Bajoni, M.G. 1994. 'la novella del *dolium* in Apuleio "Metamorfosi" IX,5-7 e in Boccaccio "Decameron" VII,2', *Giorn. Stor. Letter. Ital.* 171, 217-225.
1998. '*Lucius utricida*. Per un' interpretazione di Apul. *Met.* 2,32 pp. 51-52 Helm', *RhM* 141, 197-203.
Bechtle, G. 1995. 'The Adultery Tales in the Ninth Book of Apuleius' *Metamorphoses*', *Hermes* 123, 106-116.
Bohec, Y. Le 1996. 'Apulée et les sciences dites exactes', in: M. Khanoussi, P. Ruggeri, C. Vismara, edd., *L' Africa romana. Atti dell' XI convegno di studio Cartagine, 15-18 dic. 1994*, Ozieri, 59-69.
Bradley, K.R. 1997. 'Law, magic, and culture in the *Apologia* of Apuleius', *Phoenix* 51, 203-223.

1998. 'Contending with Conversion: Reflections on the Reformation of Lucius the Ass', *Phoenix* 52, 315-334.
Brancaleone, F. 1994. 'Considerazioni sulle citazioni apuleiane e pseudo-apuleiane nel *Cornu Copiae* di Perotti', *Stud. Umanist. Piceni* 14, 49-45.
— 1995. 'Il senex/draco in Apuleio *Met.* VIII,19-21: referenti folclorico-letterari e tecnica narrativa apuleiana', *Aufidus* 9 (27), 45-72.
Brandão, J.L.L. 1996. 'O romance de Cárite: una tragedia en quatro actos', *Humanitas* 48, 183-195.
Brodersen, S. 1998. 'Cupid's Palace - A Roman Villa (Apul. *Met.* 5,1)', in: *AAGA 2*, Groningen, 113-126.
Byrd, K. 1995. 'The Myth of Psyche and Cupid as an Allegory for Survivors of Child Sexual Abuse', *The Arts in Psychotherapy: an International Journal* 22 (5), 403-412.
Callebat, L. 1998. *Langages du roman latin*, (Spudasmata Band 71), Hildesheim – Zürich – New York.
Campangne, H. 1996. 'Les *Amours de Psyché et de Cupidon*: La Fontaine commentateur d'Apulée, *Société d'Étude du XVIIe Siècle* 48, 911-922.
Cardauns, B. 1996. 'Ländliche Szenerie und bukolische Motive in den *Metamorphosen* des Apuleius', in: S. Horlacher, M. Islinger, edd., *Expeition nach der Wahrheit. Festschrift zum 60. Geburtstag von Theo Stemmler*, Heidelberg, 491-502.
Carver, R.H.F. 1999. 'The rediscovery of the Latin novels', in: H. Hofmann, ed., 253-268.
Clarke, B. 1995. *Allegories of Writing. The Subject of Metamorphosis*, Albany.
Crismani, D. 1996. '*Heu medicorum ignarae mentes* ... Medici e malanni nel romanzo latino: tra scienza, superstizione e magia', *Sileno* 22, 43-56.
Cueva, E. 1999. 'The Art and Myth of *Cupid and Psyche*', in: S. Byrne, E. Cueva, edd., *Veritatis Amicitiaeque Causa*, Waucondu, 53-69.
Debidour, M. 1994. 'Lucien et les Trois Romans de l'Âne', in: A. Billault, ed., *Lucien de Samosate. Actes du Colloque International de Lyon, 30 sept. - 1 oct. 1993*, Paris, 55-63.
De Filippo, J. 1999. '*Curiositas* and the Platonism of Apuleius' *Golden Ass*', in S.J Harrison, ed., 1999, 269-289.
D'Elia, S. 1996. 'Su Apuleio e l'età degli Antonini', in: G. Germano, ed., *Classicità, medioevo e umanesimo. Studi in onore di Salvatore Monti*, Napoli, 243-257.
Di Piro, A. 1995. 'Le Metamorfosi di Apuleio nella tradizione indiretta. I testi', *Invigilata lucernis* 17, 55-76.
Domingues, J. 1994. 'A anuência de un predestinado (Apuleio, *As. aur.* XI)', *Humanitas* 46, 199-216.
Dowden, K. 1998. 'Cupid and Psyche: A Question of the Vision of Apuleius', in: *AAGA 2*, Groningen, 1-22.
Drake, G. 2000. 'Apuleius' Tales within Tales in *The Golden Ass*', in: C.S. Wright, J.B. Holloway, edd., 3-27.
Ellsworth, O.B. 2000. 'Musical Representations of the Ass', in: C.S. Wright, J.B. Holloway, edd., 93-96.
Fantham, E. 1995. 'Aemilia Pudentilla: or the wealthy widow's choice', in: R. Hawley, B.M. Levick, edd., *Women in Antiquity: New Assessments*, London, 221-232.
Fauth, W. 1998. 'Magie und Mysterium in den Metamorphosen des Apuleius', in: E. Dassmann et alii, edd., *Chartulae. Festschrift für Wolfgang Speyer*, Munster (Westfalen), 131-144.
Fernández Contreras, M.A. 1997. 'El tema de la hospitalidad en Apuleyo (*Met.* 1,21-26), *Habis* 28, 107-125.
Finkelpearl, E.D. 1998. *Metamorphosis of Language in Apuleius. A Study of Allusion in the Novel*, Ann Arbor.
— 1999. 'Psyche, Aeneas and an Ass: Apuleius, *Metamorphoses* 6,10-6,21', in: S.J. Harrison, ed., 290-306.
Fleury, P., Zuinghedau, M., Mary, G. 1997. edd., *Apulée, Apologie-Florides. Concordance. Documentation lexicale et grammaticale. Tome 1: A-M; Tome 2: N-Z*, Hildesheim - Zürich - New York.
Fornés Pallicer, N. 1995. 'El relato con transpoción en la fábula de Cupido y Psique (Apul. *met.* 4,28-6,24)', *AFB* 18 (6), 75-80.
Frangoulidis, S.A. 1994. 'Venus and Psyche's Sisters in Apuleius's Tale of Cupid and Psyche', *CB* 70, 67-72.
— 1995. 'Contextuality in the sisters' death in Apuleius' tale of Cupid and Psyche', *PP* 281, 140-144.
— 1996. 'Wedding Imagery in Apuleius' Tale of Tlepolemus/Haemus, *A&R* 41, 196-202.
— 1997a. 'New Comedy in Apuleius' Tale of *Cupid and Psyche*', in: S.A. Frangoulidis, *Handlung und Nebenhandlung: Theater, Metatheater und Gattungsbewußstsein in der römischen Komödie. Drama. Beiträge zum antiken Drama und seiner Rezeption, Beiheft* 6, Stuttgart, 145-177.
— 1997b. 'Intratextuality in Apuleius' *Metamorphoses*', *AC* 66, 293-299.
— 1999a. 'Theatre and spectacle in Apuleius' tale of the robber Thrasyleon (*Met.* 4.13-21)', in: B. Zimmermann, ed., *Griechisch-römische Komödie und Tragödie III*, Stuttgart, 113-135.
— 1999b. '*Cui videbor veri similia dicere proferens vera?* Aristomenes and the Witches in Apuleius' Tale of Aristomenes', *CJ* 94, 375-391.

1999c. '*Scaena feralium nuptiarum*: Wedding Imagery in Apuleius' tale of Charite (*Met.* 8.1-14), *AJP* 120, 601-619.

.... (forthcoming) 'Role-changing in Apuleius' Tale of the Miller's Wife (*Met.* 9.14-31)', in: *Scholia*.

Franz, M-L. Von. 1997. *Die Erlösung des Weiblichen im Manne: der Goldene Esel des Apuleius in tiefenpsychologischen Sicht/ übers. aus dem Engl. von G. Henney. Aktualisierte, überarb. Neuaufl.* Zürich - Düsseldorf.

Fusillo, M. 1996. 'How Novels End: Some Patterns of Closure in Ancient Narrative', in: D. Roberts, R. Dunn, D. Fowler, edd., *Classical Closure. Reading the End in Greek and Latin Literature*, Princeton, 209-227.

Gianotti, G.F. 1995. 'In viaggio con l'asino', in: F. Rosa, F. Zumbon, edd., *Pothos: il viaggio, la nostalgia*, Trento, 107-132.

1996. 'Forme di consumo teatrale: mimo e spettacoli affini', in: O. Pecere, A. Stramaglia, edd., *La letteratura di consumo nel mondo greco-latino. Atti del convegno internazionale (Cassino, 14-17 settembre 1994)*, Cassino, 267-292.

Graevenitz, G. Von. 1996. 'Das Ich am Ende: Strukturen der Ich-Erzählung in Apuleius' Goldenem Esel und Grimmelshausens Simplicissimus', in: K. Stierle, R. Warning, edd., *Das Ende: Figuren und Denkform (Poetik und Hermeneutik* 16), 123-154.

Graverini, L. 1996. 'Apuleio, Virgilio e la "Peste di Atene" Note ad Apul. met. IV 14, *Maia* 48, 171-188.

1997. '*In historiae specimen* (Apul. *Met.* 8.1.4). Elementi della litteratura storiografica nelle *Metamorfosi* di Apuleio', *Prometheus* 23, 247-278.

1998. 'Memorie Virgiliane nelle *Metamorfosi* di Apuleio: Il racconto di Telifrone (II 19-30) e l'assalto dei coloni ai servi fuggitivi (VIII 16-18), *Maia* 50, 123-145.

1999. 'Sulle ali del vento: Evoluzione di un' immagine, tra Ovidio ed Apuleio', *Prometheus* 25, 243-246.

Grilli, A. 1997. 'Le streghe e il romanzo d'Apuleio', in: *Accademia nazionale virgiliana di scienze lettere ed arti. Atti e memorie* n.s. 65, Mantova, 19-27.

Habermehl, P. 1996. '*Quaedam divinae mediae potestates*. Demonology in Apuleius' *De deo Socratis*', in: *GCN* 7, 117-142.

Harrison, S.J. 1996. 'Apuleius' *Metamorphoses*', in: G. Schmeling, ed., *The Novel in the Ancient World*, Leiden - New York - Köln, 491-516.

1997. 'From Epic to Novel: Apuleius *Metamorphoses* and Vergil's *Aeneid*', *MD* 39, 53-73.

1998a. 'The Milesian Tales and the Roman Novel', in: *GCN* 9, 61-73.

1998b. 'Some Epic Structures in *Cupid and Psyche*', in: *AAGA* 2, Groningen, 51-68.

1999. ed., *Oxford Readings in The Roman Novel*, Oxford.

2000. *Apuleius. A Latin Sophist*, Oxford.

Hidalgo de la Vega, M.J. 1996. 'La religiosidad en Apuleyo de Madaura', in: J. Mangas, J. Alvar, edd., *Homenaje a José María Blázquez III. Historia de Roma*, Madrid, 87-105.

Hoag, J.D. 2000. 'The Virgin Prefigured', in: C.S. Wright, J.B. Holloway, edd., 49-54.

Hoevels, F.E. 1996. 'Zur Psychoanalyse des Psychemärchens und des Apuleius', in: F.E. Hoevels, *Psychoanalyse und Literaturwissenschaft. Grundlagen und Beispiele*, Freiburg, 39-84.

Hofmann, H. 1997. 'Sprachhandlung und Kommunikationspotential: Diskursstrategien im "Goldenen Esel", in M. Picone, B. Zimmermann, edd., 137-169.

1999. ed., *Latin Fiction. The Latin Novel in Context*, London - New York.

Holloway, J.B. 2000. 'The Asse to the Harpe: Boethian Music in Chaucer', in: C.S. Wright, J.B. Holloway, edd., 73-91.

2000a. 'Apuleius and *Midsummer Night's Dream*: Bottom's Metamorphoses', in: C.S. Wright, J.B. Holloway, edd., 123-137.

Horsfall, N. 1995. 'Apuleius, Apollonius of Tyana, Bibliomancy. Some neglected dating criteria', in: G. Bonamente, G. Paci, edd., *Historiae Augustae Maceratense*, Bari, 169-177.

Hunink, V.J.C. 1995a. 'Apuleius, *Florida* IX,34 f.', *Hermes* 123, 382.

1995b. 'The prologue of Apuleius' *De deo Socratis*', *Mnem.* 48, 292-312.

1996a. 'Apuleius and the "Asclepius"', *VChr* 50, 288-308.

1996b. 'Notes on Apuleius' *Apology*', *Mnem.* 49, 159-167.

1997a. *Apuleius of Madauros. Pro se de Magia (Apologia)*, vol. 1: Text; vol. 2: commentary, Amsterdam.

1997b. 'A sea-monster in court (Apul. *Apol.* 32)', *MH* 54, 62-64.

1998a. 'Two Erotic Poems in Apuleius' *Apology*', in: C. Deroux, ed., *Studies in Latin Literature and Roman History IX*, Bruxelles, 448-461.

1998b. 'Comedy in Apuleius', in: *GCN* 8, 97-113.

1998c. 'The enigmatic Lady Pudentilla', *AJP* 119, 275-291.

1999. 'Wie dichten kan is nog niet dom genoeg. Gerrit Komrij en Apuleius', *Lampas* 32, 60-69.

2000. 'Apuleius, Pudentilla, and Christianity', *VChr* 54, 80-94.

Iljuschechkin, V. 1995. '*Cara mea Photis*', in: *Women in the Ancient World*, Moscow, 131-141.

1997. 'Legal and Illegal Marriage in Apuleius', in: *Power, Men, Society and the Ancient World. Papers of the Conference of the Ancient Association*, Moscow, 392-396.

James, P. 1998. 'The Unbearable Lightness of Being: *Levis Amor* in the *Metamorphoses* of Apuleius', in: *AAGA 2*, Groningen, 35-50.

Jones, F. 1995. 'Punishment and the Dual Plan of the World in the Metamorphoses of Apuleius', *LCM* 20, 13-19.

Jong, J.L. de 1998. '"Il pittore a le volte è pure poeta": *Cupid and Psyche* in Italian Renaissance Painting', in: *AAGA 2*, Groningen, 189-215.

Kahane, A. 1996. 'The Prologue to Apuleius' *Metamorphoses*. A Speech Act Analysis', in: *GCN* 7, 75-102.

Kahane, A., Laird, A. 2000. edd., *A Companion to the Prologue to Apuleius Metamorphoses*, (forthcoming) Oxford.

Keulen, W.H. 1997. 'Some Legal Themes in Apuleian Context', in M. Picone, B. Zimmermann, edd., 203-229.

1998. 'A Bird's Chatter: Form and Meaning in Apuleius' *Met.* 5,28', in: *AAGA 2*, Groningen, 165-188.

2000. 'Significant Names in Apuleius: A "Good Contriver" and his Rival in the Cheese Trade (*Met.* 1,5)', 'Apuleiana Groningana X', *Mnem.* 53, 310-321.

Korenjak, M. 1997. 'Eine Bemerkung zum Metamorphosenprolog des Apuleius', *RhM* 140, 328-332.

Korpanty, J. 1997. 'Syllabische Homophonie in lateinischer Dichtung und Prosa', *Hermes* 125, 330-346.

Laird, A. 1997. 'Description and Divinity in Apuleius' *Metamorphoses*', in: *GCN* 8, 59-85.

Lausberg, M. 1995. 'Apuleius. Der goldene Esel', in: H.V. Geppert, ed., *Grosse Werke der Literatur IV. Eine Ringvorlesung an der Universität Augsburg 1994/5*, Tübingen-Basel, 67-79.

Lee Too, Y. 1996. 'Statues, mirrors, gods: controlling images in Apuleius', in: J. Elsner, ed., *Art and Text in Roman Culture*, Cambridge, 133-152; 304-308.

Lefèvre, E. 1997. *Studien zur Struktur der Milesischen Novelle bei Petron und Apuleius*. Akademie der Wissenschaften und der Literatur Mainz: Abhandlungen der geistes- und sozialwissenschaftlichen Klasse 5, Stuttgart.

Lev Kenaan, V. 2000. '*Fabula anilis*: the Literal as a Feminine Sense', in: C. Deroux, ed., *Studies in Latin Literature and Roman History X*, Bruxelles, 370-391.

Lucarini, C.M. 1999. 'Su alcune imitazioni di Lucrezio in un capitolo dei Florida apuleiani', *MD* 42, 223-224.

Maggiulli, G., Giolito, M.F.B. 1996. *L'altro Apuleio: problemi aperti per una nuova edizione dell' herbarius* (Studi Latini, 17), Napoli.

Magnaldi, G. 1996. 'La compresenza della lectio falsa e della lectio emendata nel cod. laurenziano 68.2 (F) delle Metamorfosi di Apuleio, *Sileno* 22, 199-228.

Mal - Maeder, D. Van. 1995. '*L'Ane d'Or* ou les métamorphoses d'un récit: illustration de la subjectivité humaine', in: *GCN* 6, 103-125.

1997a. 'Descriptions et descripteurs: mais qui décrit dans les "Metamorphoses" d'Apulée?', in M. Picone, B. Zimmermann, edd., 171-201.

1997b. '*Lector intende: laetaberis*. The enigma of the last book of Apuleius' *Metamorphoses*', in: *GCN* 8, 87-118.

forthcoming: 'Déclamations et romans. La double vie des personnages romanesques (le père, le fils et la belle-mère assassine', in: *Actes du colloque sur le roman grec, Tours 18-20 novembre 1999*, ...

Mal - Maeder, D. Van, Zimmerman, M. 1998. 'The Many Voices in *Cupid and Psyche*', in: *AAGA 2*, Groningen, 83-102.

Martinez, D. 2000. 'Magic in Apuleius' *Metamorphoses*', in: C.S. Wright, J.B. Holloway, edd., 29-35.

Mason, H.J. 1999a. 'The *Metamorphoses* of Apuleius and its Greek Sources', in: H. Hofmann, ed., 103-112.

1999b. '*Fabula graecanica*: Apuleius and his Greek Sources', in: S.J. Harrison, ed., 217-236.

Mattiacci, S. 1998. 'Neoteric and Elegiac Echoes in the Tale of Cupid and Psyche by Apuleius', in: *AAGA 2*, Groningen, 127-150.

May, R. 1998. 'Köche und Parasit. Elemente der Komödie in den *Metamorphosen* des Apuleius', in: *GCN* 9, 131-155.

Mazzoli, G. 1995. 'Apuleio: metamorfosi, conversione e loro logiche, in: *Storia, letteratura e arte a Roma nel II sec. dopo Cristo. Atti del Convegno Mantova 8-9-10 ottobre 1992*, Firenze, 193-211.

McCreight, Th.D. 1998. '*Apuleius, Lector Sallustii*: Lexicographical, Textual and Intertextual Observations on Sallust and Apuleius', *Mnem.* 51, 41-63.

Merkelbach, R. 1995. Isis Regina - Zeus Sarapis. *Die griechisch-ägyptische Religion nach den Quellen dargestellt*, Stuttgart-Leipzig.

Methy, N. 1996. 'La divinité suprème dans l'oeuvre d'Apulée, *REL* 74, 247-269.

—— 1997. 'Deus Exsuperantissimus: une divinité nouvelle? A propos de quelques passages d'Apulée', *AntCl* 68, 99-117.

Mignogna, E. 1996. 'Carite ed Ilia: Sogni di sogni', in: *GCN* 7, 95-102.

Millar, F. 1999. 'The World of the *Golden Ass*', in: S.J. Harrison, ed., 247-268.

Moreschini, C. 1995. '"Una piacevole storia": la novella di Amore e Psiche nelle *Metamorfosi* di Apuleio', *Humanitas* 50, 277-296.

—— 1999. 'Towards a History of the Exegesis of Apuleius: the Case of the "Tale of Cupid and Psyche"', in: H. Hofmann, ed., 215-228.

Morton Braund, S. 1999. 'Moments of Love: Lucretius, Apuleius, Monteverdi, Strauss', in: S. Morton Braund, R. Mayer, edd., *Amor: Roma. Love & Latin Literature. Eleven essays (and one poem) by former reearch students presented to E.J. Kenney on his seventy-fifth birthday*, Cambridge, 174-198.

Müller, H. 1998. *Liebesbeziehungen in Ovids Metamorphosen und ihr Einfluß auf den Roman des Apuleius*, Göttingen - Braunschweig.

—— 2000. '*Apuleius reversus* - Wielands fragmentarisches Gedicht "Psyche" ', in: M. Baumbach, ed., *Tradita et Inventa. Beiträge zur Rezeption der Antike*, Heidelberg, 271-280.

Münstermann, H. 1995. *Apuleius. Metamorphosen literarischen Vorlagen*, Stuttgart - Leipzig.

Murgatroyd, P. 1997a. 'Three Apuleian Openings', *Latomus* 56, 126-133.

—— 1997b. 'Apuleian Ecphrasis: Cupid's Palace at *Met.* 5,2,2', *Hermes* 125, 357-366.

Nicolai, R. 1999. 'Quis ille? Il proemio delle Metamorfosi di Apuleio e il problema del lettore ideale', *MD* 42, 143-164.

Nolan, E.P. 2000. 'Narrative Enta[i]led: Metamorphic Reflexivity in Ovid and Apuleius', in: C.S. Wright, J.B. Holloway, edd., 37-48.

O'Brien, M. 1998. '"For every tatter in its mortal dress": Love, the Soul and her Sisters', in: *AAGA 2*, Groningen, 23-34.

Paardt, R.Th. Van der. 1996. 'Hoe ge(s)laagd is het slot van Apuleius' *Metamorphosen*?', *Lampas* 29, 67-79.

—— 1999. 'The Unmasked "I": Apuleius, *Met.* 11,27', in: S.J. Harrison, ed., 237-246.

Panayotakis, S. 1996. *Thesaurus Fraudis. Forms and Functions of Deception in Apuleius' Metamorphoses (Met. 4,24-6,30)*, Diss. Rethymno 1996.

—— 1997a. '"The Master of the Grave": A Note on Apuleius, *Met.* 9,2 (203,26 H): Apuleiana Groningana IX', *Mnem.* 50, 295-301.

—— 1997b. '*Insidiae Veneris*: Lameness, Old Age and Deception in the Underworld (Apul. *Met.* 6,18-19)', in: *GCN* 8, 23-39.

—— 1998a. 'On Wine and Nightmares: Apuleius *Met.* 1,18', in: *GCN* 9, 115-129.

—— 1998b. 'Slander and War Imagery in Apuleius' Tale of Cupid and Psyche (Apul. *Met.* 5,5-5,21)' in: *AAGA 2*, Groningen, 151-164.

Papaioannou, S. 1998. 'Charite's rape, Psyche on the Rock and the Parallel Function of Marriage in Apuleius' *Metamorphoses*', *Mnem.* 51, 302-324.

Paratore, E. 1995. 'La favola di Amore e Psiche in Apuleio, in: *Storia, letteratura e arte a Roma nel II sec. dopo Cristo. Atti del Convegno Mantova 8-9-10 ottobre 1992*, Firenze, 175-192.

Pasetti, L. 1999. 'La morfologia della preghiera nelle *Metamorfosi* di Apuleio', *Eikasmos* 10, 247-271.

Penwill, J.L. 1998. 'Reflections on a "happy ending": the case of Cupid and Psyche', *Ramus* 27, 160-182.Picone M., Zimmermann, B. 1997. edd., *Der antike Roman und seine mittelalterliche Rezeption*, Basel - Boston - Berlin.

Pinkster, H. 1998. 'The use of narrative tenses in Apuleius' *Amor and Psyche*', in: *AAGA 2*, Groningen, 103-111.

Pittaluga, S. 1997. 'Narrativa e oralità nella commedia mediolatina (e il fantasma di Apuleio), in M. Picone, B. Zimmermann, edd., 307-320.

Puccini, G. 1998. 'La folie amoureuse dans les *Métamorphoses* d'Apulée', *BAGB* 4 (Febr. 1999), 318-336.
Raffaelli, R. 1995. 'Prova d'innocenza. la passione, il delitto, il colpo di scena in un racconto di Apuleio', in: R. Raffaelli, ed., *Il mistero nel racconto classico. Convegno del XIII Mystfest. Cattolica 29 giugno 1992*, Urbino (Quattro-Venti), 53-66.
Revard, S.P. 2000. 'Isis in Spenser and Apuleius', in: C.S. Wright, J.B. Holloway, edd., 107-121.
Rosati, G. 1997. 'Racconto e interpretazione: forme e funzioni dell'ironia drammatica nelle "Metamorfosi" di Apuleio', in: M. Picone, B. Zimmermann, edd., 107-127.
Sallmann, K. 1995. 'Erzählendes in der *Apologia* des Apuleius, oder: Argumentation als Unterhaltung', in: *GCN* 6, 137-157.
— 1996. 'Lucius bei den Lästrygonen. Zu Apuleius, *Metamorphosen* 8,19-21, in: R. Faber, B. Seidensticker, edd., *Worte, Bilder, Töne. Studien zur Antike und Antikenrezeption, Bernhard Kytzler zu ehren*, Würzburg, 179-185.
Sallmann, K., P.L. Schmidt 1997. 'L. Apuleius (Marcellus?)', in: R. Herzog, P.L. Schmidt, edd., *Handbuch der lateinischen Literatur der Antike, Band IV*, München 1997, 292-318.
Sandy, G.N. 1997. *The Greek World of Apuleius. Apuleius and the Second Sophistic*, Leiden.
— 1999. 'Apuleius' *Golden Ass*: from Miletus to Egypt, in: H. Hofmann, ed., 81-102.
— 1999a. 'The Tale of Cupid and Psyche', in: H. Hofmann, ed., 126-138.
Santini, C., Zurli, L. 1996. *Ars narrandi. Scritti di narrativa antica in memoria di L. Pepe*, Napoli.
Schindel, U. 1996. 'Die Verteidigungsrede des Apuleius', in: Mölk, U., ed., *Études Literatur und Recht: literarische Rechtsfälle von der Antike bis in die Gegenwart*, Göttingen, 13-24.
Schmidt, V. 1995. '*Revelare* und *Curiositas* bei Apuleius und Tertullian', in: *GCN* 6, 127-135.
— 1997. 'Reaktionen auf das Christentum in den *Metamorphosen* des Apuleius', *VChr* 51, 51-71.
Schoeck, R.J. 2000. 'Chaucer and Huizinga: The Spirit of *Homo Ludens*', in: C.S. wright, J.B. Holloway, edd., 97-106.
Shanzer, D. 1996. '*Piscatum opiparem...praestinaui*: Apuleius, *Met.* 1,24-25', *RFIC* 124, 445-454.
Shumate, N. 1996. *Crisis and Conversion in Apuleius' Metamorphoses*, Ann Arbor.
— 1996b. '"Darkness Visible": Apuleius reads Virgil', in: *GCN* 7, 103-116.
— 1999. 'Apuleius' *Metamorphoses*: the inserted tales, in: H. Hofmann, ed., 113-125.
Slater, N.W. 1997. 'Vision, Perception, and Phantasia in the Roman Novel', in M. Picone, B. Zimmermann, edd., 89-105.
— 1998. 'Pasion and Petrifaction: The Gaze in Apuleius', *CPh* 93, 18-48.
Smith, W.S. 1996. 'The satiric voice in the Roman novelistic tradition', in J. Knuf (ed.), *Unity and Diversity. Proceedings of the Fourth International Conference on Narrative*, Univ. of Kentucky, 309-317.
— 1998. 'Cupid and Psyche Tale: Mirror of the Novel', in: *AAGA* 2, Groningen, 69-82.
— 1999. 'The Narrative Voice in Apuleius' *Metamorphoses*', in: S.J. Harrison, ed., 195-216.
Stramaglia, A. 1996. 'Fra "consumo" e "impegno": usi didattici della narrativa nel mondo antico', in: O. Pecere, A. Stramaglia, edd., *La letteratura di consumo nel mondo Greco-Latino. Atti del Convegno Internazionale Cassino, 14-17 settembre 1994*, Bari, 97-166.
— 1996a. 'Prisciano e l'Epitoma historiarum di Apuleio', *RevFil* 124, 192-198.
— 1996b. 'Apuleio come auctor: premesse tardoantiche di un uso umanistico' *Stud. Umanist. Piceni* 16, 137-161.
Tappi, O. 1995. 'Il mito di Ippolito in Euripide, Seneca ed Apuleio', in: M. Rossi Cittadini, ed., *Presenze classiche nelle letterature occidentali. Il mito dall'età antica all'età moderna e contemporanea. Atti del Convegno internazionale di didattica Perugia, 7-10 nov. 1990*, Perugia, 483-491.
Tasinato, M. 1994. *Sulla curiosita: Apuleio e Agostino*, Parma.
— 1997. 'La métamorphose du curieux: à propos de "L'Âne d'or"', in: Cassin, B. et Labarrière, J-L., edd., *Études L'animal dans l'antiquité; sous la dir. de Gilbert Romeyer Dherbey*, Paris, 483-490.
Tatum, J. 1999. 'The Tales in Apuleius' *Metamorphoses*', in: S.J. Harrison, ed., 157-194.
Töchterle, K. 1998. 'Apuleius als Isisjünger im Rahmen der Erzählstruktur seines Romans', in: *Religion - Literatur - Künste. Aspekte eines Vergleichs. Hrsg. von Peter Tschuggnall (Im Kontext. Beiträge zu Religion, Philosophie und Kultur* 4), Innsbruck, 179-190.
Weingarten, S. 1997. 'Jerome and the *Golden Ass*', *Studia patristica* (Deutsche Akademie der Wissenschaften zu Berlin) 33, 383-392.
Witte, A.E. 1997. 'Calendar and Calendar Motifs in Apuleius' *Metamorphoses*', in: *GCN* 8, 41-58.
Wlosok, A. 1999. 'On the Unity of Apuleius' *Metamorphoses*', in: S.J. Harrison, ed., 142-156.

Wolff, C. 1999. 'L'enlèvement de Charité (Apulée, *Métamorphoses*) et les témoignages épigraphiques', *REG* 112, 253-258.

Wright, C.S. 2000. 'The Metamorphoses of Cupid and Psyche in Plato, Apuleius, Origen, and Chaucer', in: C.S. Wright, J.B. Holloway, edd., 55-72.

Wright, C.S., J.B. Holloway, edd., 2000. *Tales within Tales. Apuleius through Time. Essays in honor of professor emeritus Richard J. Schoeck*, New York.

Zimmerman, M. 1996. 'Apuleius von Madaura', in: *DNP* 1, 910-914.

— 1999. 'When Phaedra Left the Tragic Stage". Generic Switches in Apuleius' *Metamorphoses*', in: B. Roest, H. Vanstiphout, edd., *Aspects of Genre and Type in Pre-modern Literary Cultures*, Groningen, 101-127.

— 2000. '*Quis ille ... lector*: Addressee(s) in the Prologue and throughout the Met.', in: A. Kahane, A. Laird, edd. (forthcoming), ...

Zimmerman, M., Panayotakis, S. et alii 1998. edd., *Aspects of Apuleius' Golden Ass Vol. II: Cupid and Psyche* (= *AAGA* 2), Groningen.

INDEX RERUM

ablative absolute
  marks transition 57
ablative of gerund
  modal - 290
abstractum pro concreto 126, 172
adjective(s)
  adverbial use of neuter - 404
  predicative use of - 126
  replaces genitive of a noun 408
  replaces possessive genitive 128
  with synonymous prepositional phrase 309
  in *-lis* 301
adverbs
  in *-ter* 291
  in *-tim* 88
allegory 376, 381
alliteration 87, 93, 100, 108, 110, 114, 128, 130, 137, 144, 161, 177, 193, 244, 279, 288, 296, 299, 338, 358, 364, 367, 368, 395, 397, 406, 408, 409, 413
alliterative enumeration 206
ambiguity 79, 93, 98, 103, 128, 162, 277, 330
anacoluthon 298
anaphora 77, 93, 116, 145, 219, 247, 325, 353, 355, 377
Antheus 104
anticipation 223
anticlimax 99
Antiochus and Stratonice 77, 424
  see also App. I
ἀπροσδόκητον 52
Apuleius
  author of *De re publica* 133
  concrete author 61
  interest in *ostenta* 245
  linguistic creativity 276
  philosophus platonicus 62
archaism 175, 186, 189, 201, 219, 229, 235, 244, 250, 253, 271, 299, 327, 338, 350, 362, 369, 391, 413
Areopagus 138
ass
  associated with Dionysus 254
  beast of burden 54
  prices of - 53, 240
assonance 102
asyndeton 63, 187, 215, 217
Athena
  'regard fascinant' 382
audience of novel 51

aulaeum 364
Bellerophon 104
Beroaldus 257, 285, 321
black bile 317
book
  beginning 51
  epic closure 415
brachylogy 265, 383
burial customs 190
characterization
  by direct discourse 154
  cooks of Thiasus 212, 213
  Lucius 62
  of father in Phaedra tale 64, 67
  of narrator 101
  physician in Phaedra tale 161, 174
  rich master (Thiasus) 200, 203, 227, 231, 241, 252
  soldier 52, 56, 58, 198
  stepson in Phaedra tale 99
  stepmother in Phaedra tale 428
chiasmus 54, 73, 75, 100, 110, 127, 139, 141, 152, 187, 192, 242, 271, 282, 343, 364, 385, 407, 410
class jurisdiction 191
colloquialism 337
colometry 77, 127, 182, 198, 221, 256, 301, 361, 377
  an-isocolic tricolon 144
  anaphoric tricolon 410
  asyndetic isocolic tricolon 407
  asyndetic parallel dicolon 391
  asyndetic tetracolon 116
  asyndetic tricolon 233
  polysyndetic tricolon 390
  rhyming tetracolon 247, 378
  tricolon 304, 307
  tricolon with crescendo 187, 394
  'Wachsende Glieder' 126
comedy 52, 194, 301, 303, 309, 405
  cluster of reminiscences of - 218
  cooks 215, 218, 221
  miles gloriosus 199
  seruus currens 164
comic relief 346
comparative
  juxtaposition with positive 232
concinnitas 141
cookery 201, 234
Corinth 250
  'Vanity Fair' 263, 292

Cupido 70
Cupids
  in art and poetry 385
Cynic philosophers 393
declamationes 165, 295, 318, 339, 341, 346, 426
deponent
  deierari 219
  ludificare/ludificari 175
deus ex machina 185
diatribe 393
Dido 69, 71, 77, 80, 92
diminutive(s)
  cluster of - 206, 276, 369, 377
  hypocoristic value 261
  in erotic context 362
Dionysian associations 222, 236, 238, 249, 254
Dioscuri 379
divinity
  scent of cinnamon 356
doors
  symbolism of open and closed - 228
education
  and virtue 61
elegy 76
ellipsis 77, 96
  of *esse* 398
epanalepsis 161, 174
etymology 59, 145, 187, 225, 352, 359, 405
eunuchs 269
euphemism 161
Euripides
  Hipp. Kal. 83, 86, 88, 104
  see also App. I
exile
  perpetuum exilium 192
Exordialtopik 60
father in Phaedra tale
  comparison with Theseus 124
fatum and *fortuna* 196
fiction
  'Beglaubigungsformel' 139
  - and reality 132
figura etymologica 238
'fisiologia della paura' 167
foreshadowing 143
Fortuna
  horn of plenty 204
  saevissima 101
  sudden reversal 195
  see also personification
funeral rites 335
Furies 116, 312, 339
future indicative
  in a command 325
gaze 98

genitive
  in *-i* of nouns in *-es* 152
geography 57, 413
gesture 244
  caput scalpere 168
  genua contingere 126
  suggested by deictic pronouns 175
gladiator shows
  prisoners bought for - 293
Gratiae 387
grauitas 99
grecism(s) 181, 436
Greek novel 351, 357
Greek provincial towns
  duties of the rich in - 251
  local justice in - 137
  power relations in - 133
hapax legomenon 257, 336, 371, 377, 385, 388
hendiadys 97
Heracles
  - at the crossroads 376
Hercules 175, 288
Hermes
  iconography 370
Hippocratic Oath 177
Hippolytus 61, 95
  'kaluptomenos' 420
historical infinitive 132, 133, 167
homoeoteleuton 54, 373, 385
Horae 387
hyperbaton 166
hyperbole 166, 216, 224, 238, 282, 283
imperatives
  present - and future - combined 236
imperfect
  in *-ibam* 202, 212
incest 127
inconsistency 125
indignatio 394
infanticide 296
inheritance
  laws on - 341
intertextuality 74, 76, 144, 165, 202, 272, 276, 284, 312
  contrastive allusion 404
  parody 77
  terminology 426
  transformations 426
invective
  excetra 348
  furcifer 107
  pecus 394
  uulturius 395
Iphis 297

467

irony 52, 63, 74, 96, 100, 130, 135, 150, 194, 217, 231, 242, 266, 277, 292, 326, 332, 333, 350, 406, 407, 410, 414
   dramatic - 82, 83, 87, 128, 203, 214, 220, 284, 311, 324
   uxor egregia 312
Joseph
   and Potiphar's wife 83
Judgement of Paris
   - in art 369
   - in literature 369
laughter 234, 240
Leda 265
legal archaisms 137
legal terminology 84, 103, 135, 165, 177, 187, 189, 215, 220, 303, 310, 325, 328, 337, 342, 346, 348
light
   candle- 272
litotes 212, 261, 282, 290
locus amoenus 367
Lollianus 273
love
   as illness 73
   enters through the eyes 91
   ignis 71
   insanity 80, 264
   lovesickness 424
   pallor amantium 74
   symptoms 70, 75, 76
   the sea of - 85
   uulnus 73
Lucius
   and women 278, 285
   loss of name 357
Lucius ass
   asinus philosophans 401
   butt of laughter 228
   pantomimus 244, 247, 358
   parasitus 237
   spectaculum 228
   naive actorial narrator 278
   object of curiosity 225
   various burdens of - 255
Machiavelli
   novella 'Mandragola' 180, 195
mandragora 180
mansuetudo/mansuetus 233
martyrs 410
Medea 116, 341
medical terminology 181, 183, 331
metaphor
   bullire 313
   calcare religionem 155
   domus expugnatio 119
   fluctus 197

metaphor (cont.)
   hunting - 338
   lacerare 171
   legal - 187, 189
   nautical - 76
   palma 319
   procella Fortunae 100
   tropaeum 319
   uadum 85
   ueris coma 388
Milesiaka 168, 437
Mime 66, 82, 87, 91, 96, 104, 114, 136, 158, 168, 424
   - 'of the Poisoner' (Ox. Pap. 413) 179
   - and Greek novel 179
   Charition 112
Minerva
   iconography 374
mirroring 225, 230, 268, 278
   with contrast 228
motif(s)
   apparent death 113
   contrasting - in the two inner tales 163
   '*crimen uersum*' 120
   fear of being innocently condemned 396
   haste 95
   hope 102
   '*monosis*' - 87
   poison taken by wrong person 109, 324
   Potiphar - 418
   Potiphar - in Greek novel 423
   Potiphar - in Jewish tradition 422
   roses 356
   shared - by the two inner tales 308
   sleeping draught instead of poison 179
   soothing by making promises 96
   theft 210
mourning 125
mules
   breeding of - 255
music
   - and magic 390
   auloi 389
   Dorian mode 382
   Iastium (Ionian mode) 380
   Lydian modes 389
mythological comparisons 221, 264
mythological tales
   staged as gladiatorial shows 292
narrative
   actorial 268
   auctorial 394
   'brièveté narrative' 291
   change of - situation 113, 140, 153
   change of - voice 393

narrative (cont.)
  complication 65
  - economy 52, 114
  free indirect discourse 129, 199
  information passed on by dying person 332
  'loose ends' 330
  metanarrative phrase 59, 248
  polyscopical presentation 156
  strategy 185, 200, 248
  tempo 212, 235, 324
narrator
  auctorial - 82, 86
  egocentric - 358
  'fonction evaluative' 123
  homodiegetic actorial - 228
  limited perspective 54
  poses as a historian 141
  self-irony 400
  subjectivity of - 246
neologism 414
  diminutives 286
  for sound effect 243
  in Plautine style 276
  nouns in *-tor* 244
old age
  auctoritas of - 154
onomatopoeia 169, 257, 382
Onos
  relation *Onos/Met.* 197, 204, 213, 229, 240, 242, 248, 256, 259, 277, 278, 357, 406, 408
oxymoron 75, 211, 222
Palamedes 396
pantomime 366, 424
  masks 372
  χειρονομία 381
parataxis 124, 136, 186, 357
parenthesis 54, 310, 349
paronomasia 263, 364
participle
  - construction following main verb 204
  future -, final use 252
  present -, with final nuance 145
Pasiphaë 264, 288
passive
  impersonal - 186
pathos 126, 164, 353
Pax Romana 135
Penelope 97
perfume 274
periphrasis 399
personification 191, 205, 229, 288, 305, 309
  Fortuna 101
  Metus and *Terror* 381
  Veritas/Aletheia 191
Peruigilium Veneris 355

Phaedra 80, 104
Philemon 232
physician(s)
  good - and bad - 319
  avaricious - in literature 158
  prestige of - 152
physiognomy 66
Plutarch in the Met. 62
poena cullei 149
poetae novelli 338, 356
poetic justice 192, 349
poison
  fast-working - 157
polyptoton 91, 131, 300
polysyndeton 182, 256, 279, 385
possessive pronoun 217
  replaces objective genitive 260
Proserpina Salus 322
proverb 93, 264, 342
Pyrrica 362
  connected with initiation 363
Racine, *Phèdre* 93
reader
  address to the learned - 78
  apostrophized 63, 68
  as spectator 373
  'inferental walks' 418
  must fill in 'Leerstelle' 193
  need to re-read 179
  'rezeptionssteuernde Signale' 60, 67, 68
  role of - in the Met. 160, 164
  visual repertoire of - 369
recognition token 308
redundancy 64, 270, 299
register
  alternation of - 168
  comedy 54, 161, 206, 208, 221, 232, 235
  epic 125, 126, 168
  formal 165
  poetic 416
rhetorical question 394, 398
rhyme 279, 307, 336, 364, 377, 407
rhythm 362
  cretics 110, 303
  heroic clausula 302
  trochaic 94
Risus festival 230
Roman satire 401
Roman soldiers
  in the provinces 56, 199
Roman theatres 367
Rome
  and the Greek provincial towns 132
  in the *Met.* 199

saffron
    in theatre 403, 404
scholasticus 100
Seneca, *Phaedra* 422
sermo cotidianus 196, 248, 274
sermo familiaris 78
signet rings
    importance of - in Rom. society 163
    iron - for slaves 172
significant name
    Thiasus 249
Silenus 254
Sinon
    paradigm of trickery 147
siparia 365
Sisenna 88, 286, 437
slaves
    may acquire property 200
sleep
    transition to another world 415
Socrates 399
Sophocles, *Phaedra* 420
sound effects 347
sound-play 188, 232, 280, 302, 411
spelling
    ex(h)ibere 164
    exumie 228
    passar/passer 286
    quandiu 70
    quanquam 212
    quanque 269
σπουδογέλοιον 400
spring
    - poetry 355
    - poetry: roses 356
    description of - 353, 360
stepmother 105, 115
    in *declamationes* 65, 106
    in Greek and Latin literature 64
    uses poison 107
    wicked - in world literature 65
stoning 131
subject pronoun
    pragmatical function 196
suicide 351
    vocabulary of - 160
suspense 113, 148, 149, 177, 185, 324, 327, 409
synecdoche 150
tense
    'authorial' perfect 223, 296
    conative imperfect 213, 328
    functional variation 188
    futurum exactum in subordinate clause 165
    historical present 52
    historical present - imperfect 167, 258

tense (cont.)
    historical present - perfect 240, 338
    imperfect 120, 201
    introductory *fuit* 262
    perfect - historical present 81, 118, 136, 186, 344
    perfect as episode marker 81, 96, 112, 171, 262
    pluperfect indicates 'setting' 148, 334, 416
    present - refers to time of narration 60
    variation 72, 145
    'verschobenes Plusquamperfectum' 125
theatrical illusion 367, 372, 380, 381, 405
theme(s)
    appearance and reality 256, 257, 263
    curious crowds 259
    death and resurrection 183
    disaster 99
    false accusation 142
    fortuna 64, 67, 204
    fraus 211
    laughter 225
    loss of home 259
    man and beast 233, 235, 287
    marriage 363
    mira 173, 225
    mistaken beliefs 121, 307
    parricidium 117
    Phaedra-Hippolytus 421
    pursuit of spectacula 188
    salus 178, 411
    thirst for novelty 230
    true/false identity 311
    tutela 302
    wild animals 246
    see also Introd. **2.4**
Theseus 98
    credulity 121
tin 274
topos
    deathlike sleep 181
    mandata morituri 332
    '*puella diuina*' 283
    speechless lover 86
    spurned love > hatred 104
torture 172
    of slaves 348
trial
    in Greek novels and in mime 136
Τύχη 304
variatio 126, 167, 316
Venus 375
    dancing - 389
Virbius
    and Hippolytus 421
wedding imagery 386, 404
wine and sex 279

470

women in the Met.
  compared to goddesses 373
word order 103, 131
  numeral follows noun 195
  subject at end of sentence 190
  verb in first position 79, 136, 176, 204, 215-217, 262, 281, 367, 370
  verb in first pos. in subord. clause 258
word-play 145, 188, 322
zeugma 346

INDEX VERBORUM

acceptare 261
accersere 170
acerba mors 117
ad instar 56
adaeque 64
adfatus 277
adfectare 360
adfici 220
adicere oculos ad 67
adluctari 243
adminiculum 383
adnutare 391
adorare 186
adstipulari 310
adulter 162
aerumna 117
afannae 169
agitare 80
alacer (fem.) 383
allegatio 134
altercari 219
altercatio 141
alternatio 168
altius 80
altor 265
ambroseus 283
amoliri 324
ampliter 327
animo uolenti 392
apparare (with final dative) 173
arbitrari 229
artifex 79
artificium 210
atque ob id 62
atrocitas 346
audire (be called) 414
aureus 157
bacchari 72
balbutire 169
balsamum 274

basiolum 275
bellule 232
bene quod 217
bilis 317
blaterare 160
calculus 151
cantharus 236
capax 93
capistrum 278
capulus 189
catus 398
cauea 294
  = audience 384
causificari 161
certo certior 345
cetera (adverbial use) 215
chlamida (1rst decl.) 370
cinnameus 356
ciuiliter 134
ciuitatula 57
clanculo 217
coaptare 412
cohaerere 409
commodum 189
commorsicare 285
compellare 214
compescere 134
competere 182
comprimere (uiolare) 120
concinnare 201
conclamare (with accus. and infin.) 130
concubitus 266
condignus 194
coniectura 142
conscientia 144
constantia 170, 217
contagium 352
contemperare 237
contrectare 172
contubernalis 204

471

conuenticulum 262
conuiuium 234
coperculum 188
corradere 261
crocus (fem.) 403
cruciarius 143
cruciatus uitae 160
crustula 206
curia 129
curiose 188
curriculo 164
curriculum solis 415
cursor 118
de proprio 303
decipulum 312
decunctari 86
decurio 58
deformis 75
delabi 91
deliciae 225
demeare 379
denique (transitional) 129
depacisci 266
deponere 187
depudescere 352
desolare 302
desperatio 327
desperatus 182
detrimentum 74
deuertere 58
diadema (1rst decl.) 373
diducere 54
dies (fem.) 184
dii boni 78
diligere 277
di(r)rumpere 284
discedere a(b) 216
disciplina 56
dissignare 59, 60
dissitus 101
disternere 407
diuina prudentia 399
domuitio 253
dotalis seruus 105
ducatus 58
ducere (compounds) 53
dum (causal function) 411
  with imperfect indicative 411
ecce 188, 405
eculeus 172
educator 99
edulia 201
efferare 312
efficax (with gen.) 181
effundere spiritum 333

effutire 169
electilis 221
elementum 70
eliquare 368
emancipatus 105
en ecce 164
enim 146, 176, 296
ephippium 257
equidem 53
ergo 155
ergo igitur 80
eruere ueritatem 348
esca (bait) 233
esitare 230
esurienter 233
examussim 74
exanimis 113
exasperare 96
exemplar 116
exemplum (precedent) 135
exercitus (agitatus) 348
exhorrescere 95
eximius 52
exinde 166
  - ut 164
exoticus 234
expectare 265
exsecrabilis 103
extremus 115
fabula 69, 295
fabulosus 193
(se) facere (ire, uenire) 391
facessere 271
factitare 219
famigerabilis 247
familia 114
famosus (with gen.) 180
feralia obsequia 335
feralis 305
fercula 231
fidem sequi 328
fides 171
flos aetatulae 377
formo(n)sitas 376
forte fortuna 110
fraus 111
  = furtum 211
frequentare 294
frons striata 83
frustrari 103
fucatus 257
funerare 122
furatrina 210
furor 80
gannitus 285

gemmula 355
generosus 255
genialiter 238
genitale 284
gerere 83
gesticulatio 380
gestuosus 362
gloria 252
grandis 338
grauedo 181
gremium 415
haerere 85
hamus 207
hercules 175, 288
hic idem 306
humanitas 302
iaculum 387
iam
   'd'ouverture' 191, 346
   'de preparation' 114
idem ille 121
ille 367, 398
   with poss. pronoun 253
immittere (se -, with dative) 126
impendio 97
impense 275
impotentia 52
in consecutive/final 88
in immensum 216
in summa 285
inalbare 272
incomitatus 311
inconcinne 161
incoram (with gen.) 122
indignari 145
inducere 164
indusiatus 369
inerrare 363
inextricabilis 159
infantula 342
ingens 166
inhiare 342
inscendere (sexual sense) 282
insimulare 115
instringere 190
intortus 383
intrimentum 202
introcedere 375
inuadere 226
iste 141
lacertulus 207
laser(picium) 234
lassus 75
latro (with gen. criminis) 220
latus (risus latissimus) 228

legifer 398
lenire 321
liberalis 222, 226
liberum arbitrium 412
libido 291
litare 335
litteratus 62
lubricus 104
lucrari 325
luculentus 253
lucunculus/lucuntulus 207
lustrum 436
luxuriare 378
madefacere (inebriare) 279
magister 412
magisterium 370
mandatu (dative) 310
marcentes oculi 75
mater scelerata 343
materia 339
matrona 263
maturare 102
medela 90
meditullium 384
medulla 91
medullitus 316
mellitus 201
mentiri 73
merito 93
meta diei 415
militariter 54
modestia 63
mollis 390
momentarium uenenum 320
mors (mortem ebibere) 112
mos maiorum 134
mulsum 236
multinodus 364
multum (intensifying adverb) 302
nam 165
nequam 162
nisi quod 77
nitidus 362
non olim 159
nouissime 283
noxa 148
noxius 109
nubilus 347
nummularius 163
nundinari 395
nuntiare quod 309
nutare 86
nutus (Fortunae -) 305
obire (amplexus) 279
oboedire (with intern. accus.) 245

473

obstinatio 329
operari in, with accus. 127
opimus quisque 212
opiparus/opiparis 206
orificium 153
originalis 395
origo 89
paedagogus 114
pallor infernus 167
pastus 220
pax placida 135
peculiare 241
perargutus 257
peregre proficisci 296
peremptorius 177
perhaurire 238
perire (amore) 92
perlucidus 407
pernicies 330
perperam pronuntiare 155
perpluere 404
persuadere (with infin.) 101
peruadere (with accus.) 413
peruigil 288
phalera 256
philosophari 401
pinguities 222
pistor dulciarius 201
plane 220, 354
plebeius 301
plusculus 59
polluere 409
pompaticus 358
populares 133
porrigere 251
 - manus 340
postliminio mortis 189
potio 161
praebibere 237
praecauere 162
praeco 137
praedestinare 203
praelucere 55
praemicare 56
praenobilis 321
praenotare 163
praepollere 66
praepositus 58
praesentarius 157
praestruere 270
praesumptio 173
praetendere 302, 336
pressule 275
primitiae 359
prius est, ut 248

procedere (with adverb) 210
proeliaris 381
proferre ad 61
prolixe polliceri 97
prolubium 280
promicare 356
pronuntiare (with infin.) 148
propter (with accus. gerund.) 56
prorsum 54
prorsus 141, 273
prorumpere in audaciam 88
prosapia 250
protestari (fidem -) 345
prouidentia 194
publicitus 350
puellus 362
pulcher 279
punctum temporis 195
purpurare 283
purpureus 283, 355
querela (with gen.) 216
quidam 159
quoad 104
religio 92
  iudicii - 170
renidere 230
reparare matrimonium 64
rerum exordium 395
reualescere 169
rimari 224
rogus (grave) 125
rubor 70
rumpere (silentium) 81
sacculus 163
sacra potio 322
saginare 208
salutifer 328
sanctimonia 304
sapidus 202
sarcina (pregnancy) 296
saucius 331
saxeus ('Terminus der Metamorphosensprache') 283
scilicet 82, 245
scitamentum 207
scitule 372
scurrula 235
secta 178
sed
  affirmative function 287
  transitional function 65, 69, 345
sedulo 56
semiclausus 169
semihians 347
sententiae pares 150
sequior (- sexus) 297

sequius 87
seruulus 58, 154, 309
simul (conjunction) 142
sincerus 277
sistere (obsequium -) 84
solidus 231
  aureus - 158
sollicitus
  circa 326
  with infin. 157
somnulentus 331
sparsim 403
spatium 98
specula 354
stabulum 57
stilus 150
subinde ('souvent') 360
subreptio 219
subtrahere 310
succuba 307
suculentus 223
sui similis 336
supergredi 65
suspiritus 76
taberna 164
taenia (strophium) 273
talio 349
tam magnus 282
tamen 52
tantillum 143
tarditas 76
tenere (in erotic context) 285
terminalis 364
thalamus 128
tibia 380, 388

tintinnabulum 257
totus = omnis 327
tradere sepulturae 315
trepidus 89
triduanus 251
tristitia 83
tunc temporis 196
turbula 414
uadimonium 103
ualde 236
uapor 76
uapulare 53
ubertim 88
ubi (with indic. imperf.) 71
uel certe 144
uenenum (vox media) 179
uentose 269
uespera 205
ueternus 159
uilissima capita 394
uillula 102
uirecta 367
uirus 345
uixdum 124
ultime 312
ululabilis 114
ungue latius 329
unicus 116, 203
uocula 285
usquequaque 336
utcumque 84
utique 326
utpote (with partic.) 346
utrimquesecus 217

INDEX LOCORUM

Accius
  trag. 403 Dangel 197
Achilles Tatius
  1,1,11 378
  1,4,4 91
  3,10 277
  4,2,1 68
  4,4,8 158
  4,16,4 324
  5,12-16 427
  6,7,4 88
Ad Liviam de morte Drusi
  135 343
Aelianus
  VH 13,2 313

Aetna
  421 238
Afranius
  com. 259 201
Alexis
  fr. 12 206
Ambrosius
  Abr.
  2,8,52 181
  Hex.
  3,2,7 310
  21 339
  Psalm.
  118 75

Ammianus
  14,1,1 100
  14,6,19 412
  15,3,7 280
  15,5,30 262
  16,12,66 159
  18,6,11 169
  18,9,2 384
  20,8,9 391
  20,9,1 119
  22,8,1 199
  22,9,10 230
  24,2,19 345
  26,6,7 97
  27,3,13 262
  28,4,29 262
  29,5,25 414
  29,5,54 416
  31,14,6 97
Anacreon
  26,4 f. 91
Anthologia Latina
  1,111 391
  115 363
  279,3 f. 88
  712 355
  712,15 285
Anthologia Palatina
  7,563,3 391
  9,266 388
  10,1-16 354
  10,5,3 f. 356
Apollonius Rhodius
  3,652 f. 85
  3,962 f. 75
  3,964 f. 75
Apuleius
  Apol.
  3,6 169
  3,9 97
  4,9 66
  10,6 182, 395
  12,5 277
  15,5 97
  15,14 383
  16,7 83
  24,6 398
  26,9 331
  28,7 f. 62
  50,4 317
  50,6 346
  51,4 90
  63,4 164
  63,7 f. 370
  64,7 89

Apuleius
  Apol. (cont.)
  69,2 331
  69,6 165
  72,4 326
  75,7 266
  81,2 264
  91,2 397
  97,5 342
  As.
  11 383
  12 194
  16 399
  41 296
  Fl.
  2,6 102
  3,1 388
  3,5 382
  3,8 169
  4,1 380, 382
  7,6 378
  13,2 383
  15,10 347, 368
  15,27 192
  16,7 69, 182
  17,4 61
  17,6 181
  17,8 159
  17,15 302
  18,21 312
  18,33 97
  19 183
  19,3 187
  21,1 164
  Met.
  1,1 205, 234
  1,2 230, 360
  1,6 88
  1,7 76, 312
  1,8 365
  1,9 267, 296, 394, 402
  1,10 131, 239, 368
  1,11 124
  1,12 394
  1,15 325
  1,18 91, 152
  1,19 230, 271, 360, 379
  1,20 67, 194, 196
  1,22 259
  1,23 410
  1,25 189, 344
  1,26 331
  2,1 225, 239, 331
  2,2 412
  2,3 100, 216, 219

476

Apuleius
 Met. (cont.)
 2,4 367
 2,5 68
 2,6 66, 377, 413
 2,8 409
 2,10 52, 76, 92, 98, 388
 2,11 272
 2,12 259
 2,13 230
 2,15 214, 271, 285, 331
 2,16 91, 92, 279, 387
 2,17 104, 276
 2,18 97, 329, 414
 2,20 234, 316
 2,21 93
 2,21-30 342
 2,22 248
 2,24 186
 2,25 157, 302, 331
 2,27 131
 2,28 127, 189
 2,29 126, 312
 2,30 176, 305, 313
 3,1 88, 124
 3,2 239
 3,5 277
 3,6 381
 3,7 302
 3,9 85
 3,10 228
 3,12 228, 230
 3,13 89
 3,16 161
 3,17 62
 3,18 298
 3,19 171, 285
 3,24 222, 281, 286
 3,25 189
 3,29 360
 4,3 114
 4,6 367
 4,16 359
 4,25 328
 4,27 345
 4,28 376, 379
 4,29 216, 259, 387, 388
 4,30 89, 369, 393
 4,31 273, 275, 379
 4,33 72, 131, 277
 4,34 239, 406
 4,35 186, 253, 377, 415
 5,1 339
 5,2 237, 391
 5,3 375

Apuleius
 Met. (cont.)
 5,4 268, 277
 5,5 88
 5,7 114, 126, 167, 189
 5,9 172
 5,11 136, 349
 5,13 285, 300
 5,15 263
 5,16 219
 5,17 205, 245
 5,18 296, 347
 5,20 56
 5,21 81, 277
 5,22 272, 316
 5,23 76, 126
 5,24 254
 5,25 75, 368, 388, 395
 5,26 288
 5,27 81, 349
 5,28 307, 388
 5,31 193, 295, 401
 6,1 205
 6,2 125, 299, 379
 6,5 354
 6,6 74, 286, 379
 6,7 60
 6,8 215, 326
 6,9 98, 228, 316
 6,11 274
 6,12 312, 348
 6,13 210, 237, 274, 327, 385
 6,15 244
 6,16 230, 305
 6,17 88, 304
 6,19 265
 6,20 111
 6,21 167, 183, 188
 6,22 67, 299
 6,23 300
 6,24 165, 233, 244, 283, 387, 389
 6,25 401
 6,28 256
 6,31 63, 233
 7,1 51
 7,11 222
 7,15 242
 7,21 282
 7,27 125
 8,1 311
 8,8 169
 8,11 87
 8,14 316
 8,19 88
 8,22 59

477

Apuleius
 Met. (cont.)
 8,24 233
 8,28 56
 8,31 194
 9,3 225, 233
 9,4 56
 9,9 220
 9,12 62
 9,13 411
 9,14 59, 329
 9,17-21 309
 9,18 158
 9,24 88
 9,27 194
 9,32 57, 204
 9,34 166
 9,35 250
 9,37 409
 9,38 354
 9,39 233
 11,1 56, 74, 197
 11,2 388
 11,3 407
 11,4 356
 11,5 359
 11,7 354, 416
 11,9 387
 11,10 56, 276
 11,11 362
 11,12 413
 11,13 165, 239, 281, 283
 11,14 85
 11,15 100, 164
 11,17 329
 11,19 204
 11,20 295
 11,22 183
 11,23 259, 301
 11,25 100, 305
 11,27 259
 11,29 348
 11,30 256
 Mun.
 3 387
 19 74
 23 388
 27 328
 Pl.
 1,12 67
 1,15 277
 2,5 383
 2,6 63
 2,9 200

Apuleius
 Pl. (cont.)
 2,15 172
 2,18 182
 Soc.
 3 233
 11 56
 17 134, 399
 20 97
 23 250, 256
Aristaenetus
 Ep.
 1,13 73, 78
 1,26 381
Arnobius
 1,12 248
 1,25 327
 2,45 100
 2,76 100
 3,23 355
 4,36 263
 5,2 331
 6,21 235
 7,28 168
Arnobius
 Psal.
 123,12 383
Augustinus
 C. Iul.
 5,13,49 269
 Ciu.
 6,9 336
 12,18 168
 16,27 395
 18,10 366
 Conf.
 2,3-9 226
 6,15 101
 Doct.Chr.
 2,16,26 161
 Ep.
 108,3 329
 242,5 191
 in epist. Ioh.
 5,2 190
 Man.
 2,6,41 201
 Quaest. euang.
 1,38 263
 Serm.
 20 239
 180,7,8 313
 Trin.
 11,2,3 237

Aurelius Victor
  Orig.
  13,1 54
Ausonius
  11,15,4 (Green) 90
  26,21 (Green) 181
Boethius
  Cons.
  5,2,12 181
Caesar
  BC
  2,38,4 416
Calpurnius
  Ecl. 7,69 f. 405
Cassianus
  Incarn.
  7,2 395
Cassiodorus
  Hist. eccl.
  2,1,9 56
  Var.
  2,40,4 389
Cato
  Or. frg.
  41 M 348
  R.
  106,2 201
Catullus
  46,1 355
  51,5 385
  61,213 347
  68,124 395
  78a,1 f. 276
  100,7 71
Celsus
  5,25 180
  6,8,1 331
Chariton
  1,2,5 305
  1,5,1 119
  2,4,1 61
  2,8,3-4 304
  3,2,17 387
  6,4,2 257
Cicero
  Amic.
  95 257
  Arat. Frg.
  2,2 272
  Caec.
  51 171
  Cael.
  65,27 365
  Clu.
  2,5 134

Cicero
  Clu. (cont.)
  6,15 80
  11,31 128
  12 343
  14,40 319
  19,54 168
  30 344
  54,148 162
  63,178 164
  176 309
  Div.
  1,20 133
  ND
  2,80 399
  Orat.
  72 339
  Quinct.
  93 305
  S. Rosc.
  6,17 319
  Sest.
  73 197
  Tusc.
  1,36,87 296
  1,41,98 397
  2,11,27 397
  4,26,56 305
  Vat.
  34 134
Ciris
  477 328
Clemens Alex.
  Paed.
  3,3 300
Columella
  5,3,9 216
  6,13,2 345
  10,101 283
  10,257 f. 355
  10,309 280
  12,1,2 410
Curtius
  5,9,8 414
  8,5,17 324
Cyprianus
  Ad Quir.
  1,24 272
  De zelo et liuore
  1,1 331
  Donat.
  10 348
  Ep.
  4,4 329
  54,3 329

Cyprianus
  Ep. (cont.)
  55,17 170
  67,6,2 187
Dictys Cretensis
  1,20 253
  2,15 397
Ennius
  Ann.
  10,352 282
  scen.
  48 160
  Epiced. Drusi
  298 311
Euripides
  Cycl.
  417 f. 112
  Hipp.Steph.
  79 f. 68
  243 f. 89
  253 f. 91
  393 f. 70
  413 f. 94
  Ion
  1512 f. 304
Firmicus Maternus
  Err.
  11,5 339
  Math.
  1,3,7 134
  8,11,3 201
Fronto
  Ad Ant. Imp.
  1,2,1 277
  Ad M. Caes.
  3,17,3 359
  4,3 379
  4,3,6 355
Fulgentius
  Aet.
  13 90
  Myth.
  1, pr. 75
  3,9 269
Gaius
  Inst.
  2,100 248
Galenus
  18,2 78
Gellius
  praef. 13 359
  3,5 225
  4,11,10 280
  7,4,1 157

Gellius (cont.)
  7,14,4 350
  9,3,2 348
  9,6,3 220
  10,3,4 328
  10,17,2 161
  11,2,5 403
  13,17,1 302
  14,1,20 395
  17,8,8 164
  18,8,1 207
  19,2,8 399
  19,9,9 88
  19,14,8 170
Heliodorus
  1,9 f. 126
  1,10 105
  1,10,2 93
  1,13,1 125
  1,13,4 131
  1,14,1 192
  1,22 427
  1,26,2 97
  4,8 424
  5,24 277
  7,2,2 68
  7,9,3 78
  7,20,4 104
  7,21,4 96
  7,26,17 97
  8,6 105
  8,7,7 109
Herodas
  1,9,3-5 393
Hieronymus
  adv. Iov.
  1,27 395
  comm. Is.
  16,57,17 239
  Dan.Prol.
  32 116
  Ep.
  2,7 313
  41,4 351
  52,11,4 223
  54,15 65
  119,11,2 163
  133,6 383
Hilarius
  Syn. 89 372
  Historia Apollonii
  1,1 262
  18 75, 76
  27 169

480

Homerus
Il.
18,593 f. 363
Horatius
Ars
129 f. 61
231 169
Carm.
1,4,3 355
1,22,7 193
1,24,6 191
2,7,26 72
4,7,1 360
Epod.
7,17 f. 128
S.
2,2,95 223
2,2,126 101
2,5,16 128
Ibis
228 339
Iamblichus
Babyl.
4 179
Josephus
AJ.
2,39 68
2,39-59 423
2,54 105
2,58 123
Justine Martyr
Apol.
1,27 297
1,27,3 300
Justinus
3,6,6 196
39,2,7 324
Juvenalis
2,8 83
6,332-334 265
6,441 257
6,634 f. 69
6,641 f. 344
7,174 f. 261
9,92 146
10,297 f. 66
10,328 105
10,360 f. 269
Lactantius
Inst.
4,12,6 328
4,27,3 83
Laevius
frg. 9 97

Livius
8,39,14 160
9,9,19 394
22,56,3 395
23,12,8 137
39,11,2 348
45,40,8 203
Ps. Longinus
De subl.
10,2 74
Longus
2,39.1 277
Lucanus
1,95 128
2,380 f. 178
4,74 f. 363
5,720 312
9,616 f. 112
Lucianus
Cal.
5 191
26 121
28 397
Deor. Dial.
19,1 383
Gall.
20 f. 401
Macrob.
25 232
Salt.
62 f. 372
63-64 381
Syr. D.
17 75, 77
Lucilius
252 269
1155 163
Lucretius
2,29 360
2,416 403
2,1032 272
3,152 f. 166
3,226 f. 202
4,1113 409
4,1155-1169 286
5,11 f. 197
5,1102 202
5,1395 f. 355
6,822 331
6,1127 220
Macrobius
2,2,11 289
7,14,1 207
Marius Victorinus
G.L. 6,32,29 169

Martianus Capella
  8,809 226
Martialis
  1,41,12 412
  3,22,4 112
  3,93,4 83
  5,25,7 f. 404
  8,33,3 f. 372
  8,54 66
  11,6,16 286
  11,40,1 285
  11,60,7 f. 288
  11,70,5 f. 377
  11,104,11 277
  12,15,4 f. 225
  14,220 202
  14,222 201
Menander
  Sent.
  33,13 191
Minucius Felix
  3,6 387
  5,9 56
  9,7 288
  25,11 289
Naevius
  com.
  113 222
Onos
  4,6 68
  45,8 53
  46,1 51
Ovidius
  Am.
  2,6,25 f. 135
  Ars
  1,541 f. 254
  3,231 f. 372
  3,501 f. 287
  3,643 163
  3,765 280
  3,795 f. 277
  Ep.
  4,7 85
  4,9 86
  4,15 91
  4,53 67
  4,63 f. 93
  4,129 f. 81
  4,161 f. 92
  4,175 f. 88
  16,290 66
  21,174 328
  Fast.
  4,513 f. 311

Ovidius (cont.)
  Met.
  2,642 328
  4,485 382
  6,224 296
  7,696 66
  9,49 383
  9,523 f. 86
  9,528 f. 81
  9,530 f. 92
  9,666 f. 297
  10,95 238
  10,346 f. 84
  10,420 88
  15,47 f. 150
  15,500 104
  Pont.
  2,3,87 85
  2,9,47 61
  Rem.
  44 89
  Tr.
  1,3,25 119
Pacuvius
  fr. inc.
  20 83
Papinius
  Dig.
  34,1,8 320
Paulinus Nolanus
  Carm.
  18,257 90
  24,865 266
  31,408 162
  Ep.
  32,12 163
Paulus
  Dig.
  11,7,40 187
Pausanias
  8,31,1 322
Persius
  1,34 f. 368
  2,12 f. 317
  3,116 313
  6,68 f. 275
Peruigilium Veneris
  13 355
  23 f. 356
Petronius
  10,7 324
  14,2 393
  18,3 399
  27,3 269
  29,7 118

Petronius (cont.)
  47,8 257
  67,11 331
  85,6 275
  98,9 339
  102,13 284
  111,1 262
  127,4 277
Phaedrus
  2,7,1 f. 257
  3,7,2 f. 223
Philo
  Jos.
  41 104
Philogelos
  3 100
  139 158
Philostratus
  Her.
  10,5 f. 397
  Imag.
  1,6 385
  1,27,3 191
  2,1,4 378
  VA
  6,21 397
Plato
  Apol.
  21a 399
  38c 399
  41b 397
  Gorgias
  464b 200
  Phaedr.
  237a 88
  251b 91
Plautus
  Amph.
  118 61
  As.
  865 f. 206
  Aul.
  755 f. 161
  Bac.
  92 105
  Cas.
  138 286
  644 348
  872 f. 226
  Cist.
  559 f. 253
  644 90
  729 f. 383
  Cur.
  124 388

Plautus
  Cur. (cont.)
  431 207
  Men.
  17 262
  32 262
  209 207
  891 159
  1063 93
  Merc.
  228 348
  Mil.
  1 f. 56
  581 233
  Mos.
  730 f. 221
  756 80
  848 80
  Poen.
  152 73
  366 90
  Ps.
  631 171
  687 401
  816 234
  Rud.
  1320 253
  1321 296
  St.
  605 342
  760 f. 283
  Trin.
  284 336
  Truc.
  42 207
Plinius Maior
  Nat.
  8,101 345
  10,173 410
  18,68 325
  20,232 160
  25,123 330
  29,2-22 158
Plinius
  Ep.
  2,11,9 160
  2,20,8 160
  3,1,9 220
  5,6,13 360
  Pan.
  43,5 207
Plutarchus
  Dem.
  38,4 74

Plutarchus (cont.)
Mor.
798a-825f.(*Praec.r. g.*) 132
814c-815a (*Praec.r. g.*) 132
Pomponius Mela
1,65 146
Porphyrio
Hor. *Ep.*
1,19,3 164
Hor. *S.*
1,1,78 160
2,3,187 219
Priapea
29,4 377
52,6 241
Priscianus
G.L. 3,111,14 f. 161
Propertius
4,8,55 f. 119
Prudentius
Apoth.
411 269
Ham.
57 *praef.* 223
Peri.
1,84 56
2,125 f. 261
5,225 f. 403
10,192 307
Psych.
702 f. 167
Symm.
2,772 f. 119
Publilius Syrus
6-7 305
31 89
Quintilianus
Decl.
244,2 192
246,4 331
263,12 150
291 424
306 296
315,23 359
319,9 348
321 158, 161
321,23 325
327,3 116
328,8 348
328,13 339
331,10 171
338,13 394
371,5 144
372,1 339
388,11 318

Quintilianus
Decl. (cont.)
388,31 343
Inst.
7,4,39 160
10,1,75 64
10,2,11 336
11,3,183 381
Ps. Quintilianus
Decl.
1,1 108
2,7 116
4,12 339
5 296
5,16 190
5,19 124
6,1 123
7,6 144
8,17 339
8,20 339
10,6 343
11,6 93
11,9 164
13,5 112
13,6 329, 330
15,9 277
16 296
17,5 168
17,11 165, 328
Rhetorica ad Her.
2,5,8 168
4,33 305
4,39,51 319
Sallustius
Cat.
1,1 394
7,6 166
10,1 100
14,4 169
15,5 141
Hist. Frg.
3,14 265
Jug.
31,12 339
32,1 170
73,3 392
85,10 250
104,4 311
Sappho
fr.
2D (31 L-P),11 75
Seneca
Con.
1,1,10 197
2,2,4 123

Seneca
  Con. (cont.)
  4,6 64, 116
  7,3,8 112
  8,4 122
Seneca phil.
  Ag.
  183 f. 64
  Apoc.
  9,4 57
  Ben.
  5,3,2 101
  7,9,5 408
  7,17,1 301
  Dial.
  1 (*Prou.*),3,9 269
  6 (*Cons. M.*),17,5 133
  6 (*Cons. M.*),26,2 160
  10 (*Breu.*),18,1 197
  11 (*Cons. P.*),6,4 252
  Ep.
  41,5 383
  77,8 261
  83,9 400
  88,22 405
  90,15 403
  101,10 203
  Her.O.
  877 178
  Med.
  15 339
  Oed.
  29 f. 345
  521 394
  825 f. 349
  1004 164
  Phaed.
  134 70
  159 f. 94
  184 f. 71
  277 f. 230
  282 91
  361 71
  364 75
  366 78
  367 75
  379-80 75
  431 f. 83
  453 82
  483 f. 68
  559 f. 116
  583 101
  592 f. 86
  602 86
  609 f. 81

Seneca phil.
  Phaed. (cont.)
  623 92
  646 f. 93
  798 f. 82
  826 f. 119
  915 f. 82
  946 183
  Phoen.
  42 164
Servius
  Verg. A.
  4,152 188
SHA
  Clod. Alb. 11,7,1 362
  Spart. Ael. 5,1 66
Sidonius Apollinaris
  Ep.
  1,2,3 223
Silius Italicus
  1,219 111
  5,198 f. 239
  6,146 167
  6,570 85
  7,441 f. 385
  12,18 280
Sophocles
  frg.
  301 Radt 191
  680 Radt 67
  O.C.
  431 f. 131
Statius
  Silv.
  1,6,33 183
  3,3,213 f. 335
  Theb.
  1,423 384
  3,116 f. 363
  4,480 f. 183
  6,137 242
  7,47-54 382
Strabo
  3,5,11 274
  6,2,6 367
  8,6,20 263
Suetonius
  Aug.
  91,2 257
  Cl.
  35,2 172
  Dom.
  18,2 66
  Tit.
  3,1 66

Sulpicius Severus
 Chron.
 2,51,8 335
Tabula Cebetis
 33,3 61
Tacitus
 Ann.
 1,33,5 116
 4,60,3 230
 6,26,3 330
 6,32,7 116
 12,2,1 116
 12,5,2 131
 14,15,2 263
 15,50,7 87
 16,34,2 271
 Dial.
 26,3 381
 34,5 336
 Ger.
 5,2-3 220
 Hist.
 2,54,1 170
Terentius
 Eu.
 193 f. 265
 Hau.
 626 f. 298
 634 f. 299
 Ph.
 54 146
 501 336
 745 f. 169
Terentius Maurus
 G.L.
 6,340 168
 6,328 169
Tertullianus
 An.
 15,5 384
 17,14 176
 25,5 177
 35,6 190
 56 346
 Apol.
 33,2 127
 48,11 395
 50,4 327
 Cor.
 12,2 374
 Idol.
 1,3 211
 4,1 339
 23,1 337

Tertullianus (cont.)
 Ieiun.
 2 163
 Mart.
 4,5 159
 Mon.
 9,10 162
 Nat.
 1,4,11 329
 1,7 346
 1,17,2 329
 2,7 134
 Pall.
 3 368
 Pud.
 7,8 145
 17 252
 Res.
 7 189
 20 387
 32 189
 Spect.
 2,10 211
 Val.
 16 359
Theophrastus
 Char. 28,3 409
Tiberianus
 Carm.
 1,5 360
 1,8 355
Tibullus
 2,6,52 285
Valerius Flaccus
 2,191 410
 2,659 217
 4,228 384
 5,177 415
 8,88 86
Valerius Maximus
 2,7,8 273
 5,7, ext. 1 77
 8,2,2 102
 9,12, ext. 6 232
Varro
 L. 7,5,93 169
 Men.
 75 394
 85 225
 87 362
 97 257
 218-219 393
 365 389
 448 408
 1271,43 362

Varro (cont.)
R.
1,21,1 255
Venantius Fortunatus
Carm.
3,6,16 90
Verecundus
Cant.
2,20 346
Vergilius
A.
1,208 166
3,212 f. 221
3,508 f. 415
4,50 335
4,65 77
4,84 93
4,261 f. 270
4,300 72
4,466 f. 311
6,177 186
6,523 312
6,678 368
7,594 100
8,390 300
8,731 374
10,628 88
11,913 f. 415
Ecl.
4,42 f. 404
6,49 f. 266
10,7 368

Vetus Latina
Deut.
11,17 312
Prov.
1,27 119
Vitruvius
4,1,7 83
Vulgata
Eccl.
9,13 219
Ep. Iudae
9 219
Reg.
2,26 327
Sirach
27,24 327
Xenophon
Cyr.
8,8,19 257
Mem.
2,1,22 376
Xenophon Ephesius
1,11,3-6 277
2,5,5 105
2,5,6 119
2,13 97
3,5,5 f. 158
3,5,11 179
Zeno Veronensis
1,1,2 88
1,1,5 190
1,24 202, 233
1,47 94
2,4,16 388

Printed in the United States
By Bookmasters